PHYSICS-BASED VISION

Computer Science Publishing Program

Advisory Board
Christopher Brown, University of Rochester
Eugene Fiume, University of Toronto
Brad Myers, Carnegie Mellon University
Daniel Siewiorek, Carnegie Mellon University

This is one volume of a three-volume series on Physics-Based Vision. The collection is an important reference source for researchers in the field as well as an educational tool. These volumes are sold as a set and separately. Set of all three volumes: ISBN 0-86720-452-4.

PHYSICS-BASED VISION: Principles and Practice

RADIOMETRY, edited by Lawrence B. Wolff, Steven A. Shafer,
 and Glenn E. Healey
ISBN 0-86720-294-7

COLOR, edited by Glenn E. Healey, Steven A. Shafer,
and Lawrence B. Wolff
ISBN 0-86720-295-5

SHAPE RECOVERY, edited by Lawrence B. Wolff, Steven A. Shafer,
and Glenn E. Healey
ISBN 0-86720-296-3

PHYSICS-BASED VISION

Principles and Practice

SHAPE RECOVERY

edited by

Lawrence B. Wolff
Computer Science Department
The Johns Hopkins University
Baltimore, Maryland

Steven A. Shafer
School of Computer Science
Carnegie Mellon University
Pittsburgh, Pennsylvania

Glenn E. Healey
Department of Electrical Engineering
University of California
Irvine, California

Jones and Bartlett Publishers
Boston   *London*

Editorial, Sales, and Customer Service Offices
Jones and Bartlett Publishers
One Exeter Plaza
Boston, MA 02116

Jones and Bartlett Publishers International
P.O. Box 1498
London W6 7RS
England

Library of Congress Cataloging-in-Publication Data

Shape recovery / edited by Lawrence B. Wolff, Steven A. Shafer,
    Glenn E. Healey.
                        p.   cm. -- (Physics-based vision)
        Includes bibliographical references and index.
        ISBN 0-86720-296-3
        1. Computer vision. 2. Optical pattern recognition. I. Wolff,
Lawrence B. II. Shafer, Steven A. III. Healey, Glenn E.
IV. Series.
TA1632.S533   1992
612.39'9--dc20   92-13369
                                                           CIP

Printed in the United States of America

96 95 94 93 92   10 9 8 7 6 5 4 3 2 1

Acknowledgments

B.K.P. Horn. "Height and Gradient from Shading." Proceedings of DARPA Image Understanding Workshop, 1989, pp. 584-595. Reprinted with permission of the author.

J. Oliensis and P. Dupuis. "Direct Method for Reconstructing Shape From Shading." University of Massachusetts Technical Report COINS 92-32, 1992. © 1992, J. Oliensis, P. Dupuis. All rights reserved. Reprinted with permission of the publisher and author.

A.P. Pentland. "Linear Shape from Shading." International Journal of Computer Vision, Vol. 4, No. 2, 1990, pp. 153-162. © 1990, Kluwer Academic Publishers. All rights reserved. Reprinted with permission of the publisher and author.

Q. Zheng and R. Chellappa. "Estimation of Illuminant Direction, Albedo, and Shape from Shading." IEEE Transactions on Pattern Analysis and Machine Intelligence, Vol. 13, No. 7, 1991, pp. 680-702. © 1991, IEEE. All rights reserved. Reprinted with permission of the publisher and author.

R.T. Frankot and R. Chellapa. "Estimation of Surface Topography from SAR Imagery Using Shape from Shading Techniques." Artificial Intelligence, Vol. 43, 1990, pp. 271-310. © 1991, Elsevier Science Publishers. All rights reserved. Reprinted with permission of the publisher and author.

F.P. Ferrie and M.D. Levine. "Where and Why Local Shading Analysis Works." IEEE Transactions on Pattern Analysis and Machine Intelligence, Vol. 11, No. 2, 1989, pp. 198-206. © 1989, IEEE. All rights reserved. Reprinted with permission of the publisher and author.

R.J. Woodham. "Photometric method for determining surface orientation from multiple images." Optical Engineering, Vol. 19, No. 1, 1980, pp. 139-144. © 1980, Society of Photo Optical Instrumentation Engineers. All rights reserved. Reprinted with permission of the publisher and author.

R.J. Woodham. "Surface Curvature from Photometric Stereo." University of British Columbia,

Computer Science Technical Report 90-29, October 1990. © 1990, R. J. Woodham. Reprinted with the permission of the author.

R. Ray, J. Birk, and R.B. Kelley. "Error Analysis of Surface Normals Determined by Radiometry." IEEE Transactions on Pattern Analysis and Machine Intelligence, Vol. 5, No. 6, 1983, pp. 631-645. © 1983. IEEE. All rights reserved. Reprinted with permission of the publisher and author.

R. Onn and A. Bruckstein. "Integrability Disambiguates Surface Recovery in Two-Image Photometric Stereo." International Journal of Computer Vision, Vol. 5, No. 1, 1990, pp. 105-113. © 1990, Kluwer Academic Publishers. All rights reserved. Reprinted with permission of the publisher and author.

E.N. Coleman and R. Jain. "Obtaining 3-Dimensional Shape of Textured and Specular Surfaces Using Four-Source Photometry." CGIP, Vol. 18, No. 4, 1982, pp. 309-328. © 1982, Academic Press. All rights reserved. Reprinted with permission of the publisher and author.

S.K. Nayar, K. Ikeuchi, and T. Kanade. "Determining Shape and Reflectance of Hybrid Surfaces by Photometric Sampling." IEEE Transactions on Robotics and Automation, Vol. 6, No. 4, 1990, pp. 418-431. © 1990, IEEE. All rights reserved. Reprinted with permission of the publisher and author.

H.D. Tagare and R.J.P. de Figueiredo. "A Theory of Photometric Stereo for a Class of Diffuse Non-Lambertian Surfaces." IEEE Transactions on Pattern Analysis and Machine Intelligence, Vol. 13, No. 2, 1991, pp. 133-152. © 1991, IEEE. All rights reserved. Reprinted with permission of the publisher and author.

L.B. Wolff. "Spectral and Polarization Stereo Methods Using a Single Light Source." Proceedings, ICCV 1987, pp. 708-715. © 1987, IEEE. All rights reserved. Reprinted with permission of the publisher and author.

G. Healey and T. Binford. "Local Shape from Specularity." CVGIP, Vol. 42, 1988, pp. 62-86. ©

1988, Academic Press. All rights reserved. Reprinted with permission of the publisher and author.

K. Ikeuchi. "Determining Surface Orientations of Specular Surfaces by Using the Photometric Stereo Method." IEEE Transactions on Pattern Analysis and Machine Intelligence, Vol. 3, No. 6, 1981, pp. 661-669. © 1981, IEEE. All rights reserved. Reprinted with permission of the publisher and author.

A. Blake and G. Brelstaff. "Geometry from Specularities." Proceedings, ICCV 1988, pp. 394-403 © 1988, IEEE. All rights reserved. Reprinted with permission of the publisher and author.

A. Zisserman, P. Giblin, and A. Blake. "The information available to a moving observer from specularities." Image and Vision Computing, Vol. 7, No. 1, 1989, pp. 38-42. © 1989, Butterworth-Heinemann. All rights reserved. Reprinted with permission of the publisher and author.

P. Thrift and C-H. Lee. "Using Highlights to Constrain Object Size and Location." IEEE Transactions on Systems, Man and Cybernetics Vol. 13, No. 3, 1983, pp. 426-431. © 1983, IEEE. All rights reserved. Reprinted with permission of the publisher and author.

J.S. Park and J.T. Tou. "Highlight Separation and Surface Orientations for 3-D Specular Objects." Proceedings ICPR 1990, pp. 331-335 © 1990, IEEE. All rights reserved. Reprinted with permission of the publisher and author.

J.J. Koenderink and A.J. van Doorn. "Geometrical modes as a general method to treat diffuse interreflections in radiometry "J. Opt. Soc. Am., Vol. 73, No. 6, 1983, pp. 843-850. © 1983, Optical Society of America. All rights reserved. Reprinted with permission of the publisher and author.

D. Forsyth and A. Zisserman. "Reflections on Shading." IEEE Transactions on Pattern Analysis and Machine Intelligence, Vol. 13, No. 7, pp. 671-679 © 1991, IEEE. All rights reserved. Reprinted with permission of the publisher and author.

S. Nayar, K. Ikeuchi, and T. Kanade. "Shape from Interreflections." International Journal of Computer Vision, Vol. 6, No. 3, 1991, pp. 173-

195. © 1991, Kluwer Academic Publishers. All rights reserved. Reprinted with permission of the publisher and author.

S.A. Shafer and T. Kanade. "Using Shadows in Finding Surface Orientations." CVGIP Vol. 22, No. 1, 1983, pp. 145-176. © 1983, Academic Press. All rights reserved. Reprinted with permission of the publisher and author.

J.R. Kender and E. M.Smith. "Shape from Darkness: Deriving Surface Information from Dynamic Shadows." Proceedings, ICCV 1987, pp. 539-546. © 1987, IEEE. All rights reserved. Reprinted with permission of the publisher and author.

B.K.P. Horn and B.G. Schunck. "Determining Optical Flow." Artificial Intelligence, Vol. 17, 1981, pp. 185-203. © 1981, North Holland. All rights reserved. Reprinted with permission of the publisher and author.

A. Verri and T. Poggio. "Motion Field and Optical Flow: Qualitative Properties." IEEE Transactions on Pattern Analysis and Machine Intelligence, Vol. 11, No. 9, 1989, pp. 490-495. © 1989, IEEE. All rights reserved. Reprinted with permission of the publisher and author.

R.J. Woodham. "Multiple Light Source Optical Flow." Proceedings, ICCV 1990, pp. 42-46 © 1990, IEEE. All rights reserved. Reprinted with permission of the publisher and author.

A.P. Pentland. "Photometric Motion." IEEE Transactions on Pattern Analysis and Machine Intelligence, Vol. 13, No. 9, 1991, pp. 879-890. © 1991, IEEE. All rights reserved. Reprinted with permission of the publisher and author.

W.E.L. Grimson. "Binocular Shading and Visual Surface Reconstruction." CVGIP , Vol. 28, No. 1, 1984, pp. 19-43. © 1984, Academic Press. All rights reserved. Reprinted with permission of the publisher and author.

G.B. Smith. "Stereo Integral Equation." Proceedings AAAI, 1986, pp. 689-694. © 1986, AAAI. All rights reserved. Reprinted with permission of the publisher and author.

K. Ikeuchi. "Determining a Depth Map Using a Dual Photometric Stereo." International Journal of Robotics Research, Vol. 6, No. 1, 1987, pp. 15-

Contents

Introduction to the Series

Physics-Based Vision

When machine vision first became an area of study distinct from pattern classification, in the late 1960s, researchers discovered the power of perspective geometry for recovering 3D shape information from 2D image data. Thus began what continues to be the major trend in machine vision research and application, in which 2D edges and regions are analyzed geometrically. These edges and regions are found by treating the image data as an arbitrary function $I(x,y)$ and differentiating it or modeling it statistically.

However, such traditional analysis fails on real images, because the function $I(x,y)$ is not arbitrary at all. Instead, it is determined by the laws of optics through the processes of illumination, reflection, and image formation. Since the real world is highly structured, so is the intensity or color data in the image. Traditional methods such as stereo or motion analysis routinely fail because they do not account for the systematic nature of the world, such as the movement of specular highlights across a surface as the camera moves.

In the early 1970s, Berthold Horn at MIT made a further striking observation – these optical laws could actually be used as a source of information to aid in the process of visual interpretation, to supplement or even replace traditional geometric analysis. Horn introduced optical models of reflection and imaging to the vision community, and demonstrated over many years that there was power in this approach.

However, few researchers adopted a similar approach to machine vision through the 1970s and early 1980s, largely because Horn's work raised more questions than it answered:

- How to deal with the inherent ambiguity that remains when optical laws are applied to an image;

- How to segment the image, that is, determine the regions with uniform optical properties, so that each can be analyzed and characterized;

- How to obtain reflection models for real materials, or whether there is perhaps some "universal" reflection model;

- How much calibration of cameras is required, and how to do it;

- How much knowledge about the scene is required, and how to get it in realistic scenarios.

Throughout this period of time, there was no sizable "community" of researchers or practitioners in this area, because of skepticism about whether there could be any satisfactory resolution to these issues. What little research was done in this area was typically tested only on relatively simple, synthetic images generated under highly idealized assumptions. The whole approach of modeling optics for machine vision was not widely adopted. Yet, there was an unmistakable promise in the concept, and an apparent potential for great contributions to the fundamental science of computational vision.

In the mid-1980s, an explosion of research in this area began, leading to the adoption of the term "physics-based vision" to distinguish this area from more traditional approaches based entirely on geometry with trivialized models of image data and imaging optics. Several factors contributed to this onslaught of activity in physics-based vision:

- The introduction of differential geometry into the machine vision community, which allowed optical properties to be cleanly related to geometry;

- The spread of photometric stereo, which was for a long time the only technique from physics-based vision that could be easily reproduced in new laboratories and would consistently give good results;

- The development of simple models of reflection and color theory for machine vision, based on work in the computer graphics community;

- The sudden availability of inexpensive, reliable cameras, automated lenses, and digitizers in the mid-1980s;

- The influx of young researchers into machine vision, many of whom have more faith in optics than in the traditions of machine vision research.

Thus, in the late 1980s, physics-based vision became accessible to many research sites, and the various sub-problems in the field began to be widely recognized and studied. Since that time, there has been an active community of researchers in physics-based vision.

Current Issues in Physics-Based Vision

Not surprisingly, the current issues in physics-based vision can ultimately be reduced to the issues listed previously, which were raised by Horn's early work. Yet, many specific sub-problems are now recognized and have a distinct literature of their own:

- How to model illumination, particularly shadows and interreflection;

- How to model reflection from smooth and rough surfaces;

- How to model color in illumination and reflection (particularly how to normalize images for illumination color, called "color constancy");

- How to model polarization, refraction, and transparency;

- How to segment an image into regions that correspond to individual surfaces of uniform properties in the scene;

- How to model and control lens optics and camera parameters (particularly the method of "depth from focus");

- How to blend optical analysis with surface smoothness assumptions ("shape from shading");

- How to blend geometric stereo and motion image analysis with optical analysis;

- How to use multiple light sources to gain additional constraint ("photometric stereo");

- How to obtain high-quality image data

for research in all these topics.

The State of Research in Physics-Based Vision

As these issues have been raised and addressed in the literature, some questions have been answered with reasonable certainty. For example, the fundamental optics of focusing has been clearly identified and verified experimentally, and several paradigms have been established for exploiting it. Continued research in focusing consists mainly of finding faster and more precise algorithms and hardware, rather than introducing fundamental new concepts.

Unfortunately, the literature of physics-based vision has become scattered throughout many different publications and conferences. Physics-based vision touches on so many areas of optics, geometry, imaging, vision, and robotics that papers tend to appear in conferences in those areas rather than specifically in one journal or conference. Much of the literature is obscure, published in places that are not likely to be within the awareness of the typical reader or researcher in the area. So, while some problems have been "solved," many researchers may not be aware of the true state of the art.

At the same time, while some simple problems have been analyzed fairly well, there are great problems and efforts yet to be addressed. Since they do not appear very clearly in the literature, researchers may not even be aware that these frontiers are waiting to be crossed someday. Two of the most prominent are:

- Physics-Based Image Sensing – The development of new imaging sensors, in the tradition of photometric stereo or "polarization cameras," that exploit strong optical relationships and specially engineered hardware to yield direct measurement of interesting surface properties without the need for symbolic reasoning in software.

- Physics-Based Image Segmentation – Real scenes contain many objects and surfaces. Where specialized sensors cannot be used, a generic color or intensity image must be broken into regions that correspond to each surface, without prior knowledge about the specific objects in the scene.

Physics-based vision is thus at a time of change, as the traditional problems of optical modeling come closer and closer to solution, and the issues of applying these models to vision tasks move to the forefront of research.

This Publication

At this time of rapid progress and change in the field, there is a need to bring together in one place the collected literature of the field of physics-based machine vision. This will give the student or scientist an overview of the state of the art as of mid-1991, in all areas of the field.

This collection was produced because the editors, who are active researchers in the area, felt it was the form of publication most needed to capture the collective wisdom of the community. A textbook might be more concise and clear, but the field is not yet mature enough to support a textbook with a long lifetime. A conference proceedings, or edited collection of newly prepared papers, would be another possible form of publication, but such a collection would of necessity be limited to the few authors and topics for which a new manuscript is available at this moment. It would also fail to provide some papers of great historical interest, such as the NBS and ASTM documents that define standard terminology of radiometry. So, the editors preferred to present the community with a collection of selected papers that were previously published.

Such a collection as this has the great strength that all of the papers here have passed some test of time, and all were selected by the editors through a process of critical comparison with other papers in the literature. However, this kind of collection also suffers from inherent limitations. The editors therefore wish to apologize in advance for omissions of some valuable papers due to limits of space, publication permission, or simply the editors' limited scope of awareness. We hope the collection will be useful nevertheless, and believe it will be so. It cannot present the "final word" in the area, however, since new papers are being produced so rapidly in physics-based vision in 1991 and 1992, even as these volumes are going to press. We therefore present these volumes as a "snapshot" of the current state of the art in the field.

Because of the large number of important papers, we have divided this collection into three volumes: Color, Radiometry, and Shape Recovery. Together, this set of papers should enable researchers in machine vision to gain a current, detailed understanding of what is known in all the exciting areas of research in physics-based vision.

– S.A.S.

Acknowledgments

A publication such as this collection is only made possible by the diligent efforts of many people.

For technical assistance and advice, we thank Shree Nayar, Takeo Kanade, John Krumm, and Reg Willson. They have pointed out important papers and contributed to the overall intellectual structure and scope of the collection.

Our sincere thanks to Alice Peters, of Jones and Bartlett Publishers, for taking on the monumental task of bringing this collection to print, and for coordinating the mountain of paperwork needed to collect these pages and obtain permission to republish them all. We are especially indebted to her for keeping things moving, even when the editors were a bit on the lethargic side!

We also gratefully acknowledge the support of our universities, Carnegie Mellon University, the Johns Hopkins University, and the University of California at Irvine.

Special thanks also to Patty Mackiewicz for handling large amounts of paper, and to Tensie Wenderoth for assistance in the arduous task of preparing permission letters.

– S.A.S., G.E.H., and L.B.W.

Introduction to the Shape Recovery Volume

What is the purpose of physics-based vision? It is to present techniques for determining important object properties by analysis of image sensor data. The other volumes in this series, Radiometry and Color, primarily present the physical laws that govern the creation and measurement of image data. In this volume, we emphasize how those laws can be used for effective measurement of object properties. Some properties, for which the literature is tied closely to basic optics, are also described in the other volumes. In this volume, we discuss particularly the measurement of 3D object and surface shape, which is so important a topic that it posesses a substantial specialized literature in its own right (also see the sections on "Polarization and Refraction" and "Depth from Optics" in the Radiometry volume).

As in this series as a whole, discussions about pure geometry, such as sequences of images from stereo vision systems or moving cameras, are not included in this collection. We likewise omit texture and texture gradients, and geometric analysis of polyhedra and curved surfaces *per se*. Still, there remain many approaches to measuring object shape that are based on direct application of physics-based perception, and are thus within the scope of this series and this volume.

This volume begins with a discussion of shape from shading, the approach developed by Horn that introduced the concept of physics-based machine vision. In the shape-from-shading technique, a model of the geometric dependence of reflection is used to determine surface shape. The reflected intensity can be cast into a representation such as the reflectance map, parameterized by surface orientation coordinates for a given relative position of the light source and camera. This yields reflected intensity as a function of the two degrees of freedom of the surface orientation (vertical and horizontal tilt with respect to the viewer). When the intensity at a pixel is measured, the surface orientation at the corresponding surface point must then lie along the level contour of the reflectance map for that reflected intensity value. This constrains the surface orientation to a one-dimensional family of possible orientations at that point in the scene. Thus, it is not possible to obtain a unique surface orientation at every point by reflection modeling. Additional constraint is needed to solve for unique interpretations of surface shape.

Where can the extra constraint come from? The first two sections of this volume give two possible answers.

The first section, "Shape from Shading," follows Horn's original idea of assuming similarity of the surface orientation at nearby points, i.e., assuming smoothness of the inferred surface. Many variations on the solution of this problem have been proposed, giving rise to a steady stream of papers even now.

The key weaknesses of this method lie in its assumption of surface smoothness and its requirement for a complete characterization of the reflectance properties of the material being studied. These assumptions make the method necessarily imprecise. If one were to take the liberty of controlling the environment, presumably one could obtain more precise results. This is precisely the approach of "Photometric Stereo," the subject of the second section of this volume. In this approach, several different reflectance map functions are obtained, one for each of several light sources at different positions in the scene. The light sources are illuminated, one at a time, and an image is taken for each. The resulting set of images yields one degree of constraint for each light source at each point, and, thus, with two light sources, the result is reduced to a finite number of points (the intersections of the contours in the reflectance maps), and with three or more light sources, all ambiguity can be removed. Further, if a sphere is available as a calibration object, it can be inserted into the scene and used to measure all the reflectance maps empirically, thus avoiding the need for an elaborate closed-form reflectance model or an exhaustive optical measurement of the object. By using an additional light source, additional constraint is obtained, which can be used to solve for surface properties as well, such as roughness. Thus, while shape-from-shading techniques must simplify the modeling of reflection, photometric stereo can deal with more realistic and complex reflection properties. Photometric stereo is one of the most easily reproducible and valuable techniques for physics-based low-level machine vision today.

Photometric stereo still assumes that objects have fairly diffuse reflection, because the contraints will degenerate for mirror-like surfaces.

In this case, however, more direct analysis of this well-behaved and familiar reflection property can be used. That is the subject of the third section, "Shape Recovery from Specular Reflection." There are many formalisms for such analysis, and thus a diversity of sub-topics are addressed within this section. These include roughness measurement for slightly-rough surfaces (such as many metal surfaces); adaptation of photometric stereo for specular surfaces; and analysis of the movement of specular highlights when the camera or light source is moved. This analysis is more theoretical and less mature than photometric stereo in general.

One of the most difficult problems in all methods for reflectance interpretation is the analysis of a system in which two or more surface elements reflect light onto each other. The fundamental assumption in most physics-based vision is that illumination is provided entirely by a well-defined light source. But, if objects reflect onto each other, then the whole concept of "illumination" has to be generalized to include the effects of such mutual reflection ("interreflection"). This very young area of study is the subject of the fourth section of this volume, "Shape Recovery from Interreflection." The papers in this section address primarily the description of the basic phenomenon, with the exception of the paper by Nayar *et al.*, which analyzes the case of photometric stereo applied to a concave surface that reflects onto itself. Additional material on the topic of interreflection is found in the section on "Color Interreflection" of the Color volume. In nearly all of this work, as in the basic shape-from-shading literature, it is assumed that the surfaces being viewed present only diffuse reflection, with little or no specular component.

There is one pure-geometry technique that is nevertheless related to optical phenomena – shape recovery from shadows. The fifth section in this volume addresses this topic. In the papers collected here, shadows are assumed to be cast by well-defined point light sources. Of course, in the real world, illumination also comes by interreflection from other objects, and when there are well-defined light sources, they are finite in extent. There has been occasional reference to such models in the literature, but none that proposes how to analyze the resulting "fuzzy" shadows. This area therefore demands additional study.

The final two sections of this volume address issues in the integration of physics-based vision into larger vision systems.

It is well known that stereo and motion sequence image analysis are prone to make errors due to radiometric factors usually ignored. The sixth section, "Radiometric Analysis of Stereo and Motion," addresses this topic. This analysis, such as optical flow, usually makes some assumption about the reflectance properties of the surface being viewed. Much of the literature assumes perfectly diffuse (Lambertian) reflection; some of the works are more general, allowing for rough surfaces that reflect according to some other model. In general, these approaches to low-level vision involve simultaneously applying geometric constraints from stereo or motion analysis with radiometric constraints similar to those of shape-from-shading. In particular, it is usually assumed that a given point on the surface being viewed will reflect a constant intensity into the camera, even as the camera moves. Thus, highly specular surfaces do not lend themselves well to analysis by these techniques.

The final section is a small but important literature that so far emanates from a single group, Ikeuchi *et al.* We generalize from their methods to call this section "Physics-Based Sensor Fusion." In this work, Ikeuchi explicitly models various types of low-level vision method, including particularly photometric stereo, to show how knowledge about the task can be used to select a sensor and to determine automatically a strategy for using that sensor in a given task. His uniform model of many sensors is particularly interesting and relevant to researchers in physics-based vision. It helps clarify the particular assumptions under which some techniques, such as photometric stereo, might or might not be expected to work.

Taken as a whole, the papers in this volume give an overview of how physics-based vision insight can be applied to the task of measuring important properties in the scene. As time goes on, more and more effort is being devoted to the development of such applications of physics-based vision.

– S.A.S.

Shape from Shading

Historically, shape from shading is the oldest area in physics-based vision. As a problem in computer vision, it is one of the most fundamental, one of the easiest to state, and one of the most complicated to solve: Given a single intensity image of a smooth curved object, how can the shape of the object be recovered? This assumes that each pixel value accurately represents the light reflected from a corresponding point. Before the machine vision community became interested in this problem, shape from shading was already being studied in celestial astronomy, particularly for recovering the shape of lunar topography from images of the moon [1]. The doctoral dissertation of Berthold Horn in 1970 [2] generalized this earlier work and introduced shape from shading to the vision community. For the first time, the vision community became aware of the relationship between vision and the physical modeling of the world. Recently, *Shape from Shading*, by Horn and Brooks [3], was published, containing a comprehensive collection of papers on the subject through 1988. That book also reviews shape from shading and contains an extensive bibliography. This section contains recent papers on shape from shading that have appeared since the publication of the Horn and Brooks book.

Shape from shading is an ill-posed problem. For a single intensity image of an object there can be a number of different surfaces that are consistent with this intensity information given the known reflectance properties. The conditions for a shape-from-shading problem are typically idealistic. They usually assume orthographic imaging, a distant point light source relative to the size of the object, and Lambertian reflectance with uniform albedo across the object. Many shape-from-shading algorithms initially assume the light source incident orientation is known. More recently, estimating the illuminant direction is becoming an integral part of shape-from-shading algorithms. Even under such idealistic conditions, shape-from-shading algorithms are still so underconstrained that they need the incorporation of additional information. Oliensis and Dupuis [12] need the existence of singular points caused by local intensity maxima. Pentland [13] needs to assume that the reflectance function must be approximately linear over a certain orientation range. Zheng and Chellappa [14] assume local spherical surface structure or equal distribution of surface orientations for some of their

methods. Ferrie and Levine [16] assume local surface conditions of their own.

It is appropriate to start with a recent paper by Horn [11] on an iterative scheme for shape from shading that fuses gradient and height information within a variational principle. This technique has a number of features:

1. It enforces a fundamental mathematical constraint on smooth surfaces called *integrability*.

2. It uses a departure-from-smoothness penalty term to bring initial estimates of height and gradient to close vicinity of the correct solution, weighting this term less and less upon successive iterations as the solution gets closer.

3. For better accuracy, it linearizes the reflectance function within a local neighborhood of the current gradient estimate.

4. It decides when to stop iterating.

The first method based upon a variational principle for shape from shading was by Ikeuchi and Horn [4]. That method attempted to minimize the sum of the squared brightness error and departure-from-smoothness over the image region corresponding to the object. Iterations were based upon discretization of the corresponding Euler-Lagrange equations. A number of other shape-from-shading schemes from variational principles are summarized in Horn and Brooks [5]. Later, Frankot and Chellappa [6] modified the Ikeuchi-Horn method to incorporate surface integrability. Integrability means that the derivative of the p surface gradient with respect to image coordinate y must equal the derivative of the q surface gradient with respect to image coordinate x. For a definition of gradients p and q see the paper by Horn [7] in the "Intensity Reflection Models" section of the Radiometry volume. A gradient map that does not obey this integrability constraint everywhere will not represent a real surface. This means that no smooth height map above the image plane will ever be consistent with a surface gradient map that is not integrable. In this most recent paper by Horn on shape from shading, integrability is enforced by forcing the first derivatives of the height information to be consistent with the surface gradients. An integrability term is quantified as the sum of squared differences between the first derivatives of height and the estimates for p and q. This is different from the way previous shape-from-shading methods enforce integrability using only surface gradients. Horn also has found that testing for small values of this new integrability term serves as a good indicator for when to stop iterating. For the initial iterations, Horn also utilizes the departure-from-smoothness term used in the Ikeuchi-Horn algorithm. This term is good for initially guiding the method toward a correct solution, but makes the method "walk away" from correct solutions when it is very close. Therefore the departure from smoothness term fades out as the solution becomes more correct. For a complete description of this method including implementation details see [8].

The next paper, by Oliensis and Dupuis [12], presents a promising new approach to the shape from shading problem. This paper also shows some direct comparison with Horn's shape from shading method presented in the previous paper. Oliensis and Dupuis formulate shape from shading in terms of an optimal control problem involving the minimization of a cost function. The central method that is proposed robustly recovers shape in an image region containing a pixel that is a local maximum in image intensity (i.e., a singular point), and object points within this region are either all concave or all convex (i.e., unimodal). Even more, the iterative method that is presented is relatively fast and provably convergent. The central method is then extended to image regions containing concave, convex, and saddle points, as well as multiple singular points.

The next paper, by Pentland [13], shows that under some conditions, the shape-from-shading problem actually has a closed-form solution. If the reflectance map over a range of surface orientations contained in an image region can be approximated by a known linear function in surface gradients p and q, then the Fourier coefficients for the height function can be directly computed for the object surface over this region. Pentland illustrates how a wider range of surface orientations can best be approximated as a linear combination of p and q for Lambertian reflectance when light is incident very obliquely

relative to viewing. If the incident orientation of light is known and the reflectance is Lambertian, then these linear coefficients can be derived. When incident orientation is unknown, Pentland uses a maximum likelihood method originally proposed in [9] to estimate what he calls the "general illuminant direction" for that image region. Pentland's original method for estimating the illuminant direction looks at the distribution of the derivatives of image intensity with respect to different directions, making the strong assumption that surface orientations are uniformly distributed. In this paper, Pentland extends estimation of the illuminant direction to the Fourier domain utilizing the magnitudes of the Fourier components of image intensity within a selected freqency band in a given direction. The newer method works under assumptions about the uniformity of the distribution for the magnitudes of a given spatial frequency band in different orientations. With only estimation of the azimuth angle for incident light orientation, the Fourier coefficients for the object height function can be computed up to a multiplicative ambiguity.

Zheng and Chellappa [14] explore additional robust methods for the estimation of the illuminant direction, incorporating this estimate into a new shape-from-shading method based on the calculus of variations. Previous methods for estimating illuminant direction, by Pentland and by Lee and Rosenfeld, are discussed. The methods for estimating illuminant direction presented in this paper also estimate Lambertian albedo, even in the presence of a bias such as that produced by an ambient component of incident light (e.g., skylight). Two methods are presented for estimating the azimuth of the illuminant direction. The first method makes the assumption that the surface is locally spherical and looks at expectation values of estimates obtained from first derivatives of image intensity in different directions. The second method utilizes shading at contour boundaries. A method is then presented that simultaneously estimates the slant of the illuminant direction and the Lambertian albedo. This method assumes that surface orientations are uniformly distributed in 3D space and accounts for the image statistics of self-occlusion and foreshortening. Once the illumination direction and albedo have been determined, Zheng and Chellappa propose a variational shape-from-shading method that, like the method in Horn [11], simultaneously computes height and gradient. While they incorporate the same brightness error and integrability terms as Horn, Zheng and Chellappa do not use a regularization term for departure from smoothness. Instead, they use a term that insures consistency with the image gradient intensity. To make this method more efficient, they use a hierarchical structure implementation. A number of experimental results are presented. Performance of the estimation for the illuminant direction presented in this paper is compared with the performance of a number of existing methods. The shape from shading method is performed on a number of synthetic and real examples.

The next paper, by Frankot and Chellappa [15], is interesting because it adapts a standard shape-from-shading method, used in computer vision, to the specific physical characteristics of synthetic aperture radar (SAR) imagery. This paper is quite different from others appearing in the collection of papers on shape recovery in that it discusses shape recovery using the principles of image formation for another type of imaging sensor. Because of the fundamental differences between the physics of SAR image formation and that of video cameras, existing shape recovery algorithms developed for computer vision are not directly applicable to SAR imagery. The coordinate system used for SAR strip maps with respect to the geometry of the slant plane is different from that for video camera images. Also, the reflectance characteristics of materials at longer radar wavelengths can be very different from those of visible wavelengths. An additional pixel area factor must be introduced into the reflectance model by SAR image coordinates. Frankot and Chellappa discuss these issues and modify an existing shape-from-shading algorithm [6] that they previously developed, incorporating integrability constraints. Experimentation is performed on SAR imagery of aerial views and from the Venus Radar Mapper.

The last paper in this section, by Ferrie and Levine [16], is an extension of work on shape-from-local shading analysis initiated by Pentland [9]. This paper proves a general local surface condition under which local surface orientation can be computed from Lambertian reflectance. The surface condition is expressed in terms of the light source coordinate system origi-

nally used by Lee and Rosenfeld [10]. Consider the transformation from image-centered world coordinates (i.e., x-y-z) to mutually orthogonal light source coordinates (i.e., u-v-w, where w is parallel to the known incident orientation of the light source). A theorem is proven stating that the image intensity gradient with respect to coordinates u and v is parallel to the tilt (i.e., azimuth) of the surface normal when a specific relation holds (equation 5), involving the first and second derivatives of the surface as a height function in light source coordinates. The slant of the normal in light source coordinates can be obtained from the pixel intensity. A sphere is a particular instance of a surface that obeys the necessary and sufficient local condition of the theorem, so this is a generalization of previous work on obtaining shape from local shading conditions assuming local surface conditions. Error analysis is performed for shape recovery of ellipsoidal surfaces and other types of surfaces violating the local condition. Reasonable accuracy is seen to be attainable as long as surface curvature and foreshortening is not too high.

– L.B.W.

References

[1]   Rindfleisch, T. "Photometric Method for Lunar Topography." *Photogrammetric Engineering* **32** (2): 262-277. March 1966.

[2]   Horn, B.K.P. "Shape from Shading: A Method for Obtaining the Shape of a Smooth Opaque Object from One View." PhD Thesis, Department of Electrical Engineering, MIT. 1970.

[3]   Horn, B.K.P., and Brooks, M. "Shape from Shading." 1989. MIT Press, Cambridge, MA.

[4]   Ikeuchi, K., and Horn, B.K.P. "Numerical Shape from Shading and Occluding Boundaries." *Artificial Intelligence* **17** (1-3): 141-184, August 1981. Reprinted in [3].

[5]   Horn, B.K.P., and Brooks, M.J. "The Variational Approach to Shape from Shading". *Computer Vision, Graphics, and Image Processing* **33** (2): 174-208, February, 1986. Reprinted in [3].

[6] Frankot, R.T. and Chellappa, R. "A Method for Enforcing Integrability in Shape from Shading Algorithms." *IEEE Trans. on Pattern Analysis and Machine Intelligence* **PAMI-10** (4): 439-451, 1988. Reprinted in [3].

[7] Horn, B.K.P. "Understanding image intensities." *Artificial Intelligence* **8**: 1-31, 1977. Reprinted in "Intensity Reflection Models" section of the *Radiometry* volume in this series.

[8] Horn, B.K.P. "Height and Gradient from Shading." *International Journal of Computer Vision* **5**(1), August 1990.

[9] Pentland, A.P. "Local Shading Analysis." *IEEE Trans. on Pattern Analysis and Machine Intelligence* **PAMI-6**(2): 170-187, March 1984. Reprinted in [3].

[10] Lee, C.-H., and Rosenfeld, A. "Improved Methods of Estimating Shape from Shading using the Light Source Coordinate System." *Artificial Intelligence* **26** (2): 125-143. Reprinted in [3].

Papers Included in This Collection

[11] Horn, B.K.P. "Height and Gradient from Shading." In *Proc. Image Understanding Workshop*. DARPA, May, 1989. Pages 584-595.

[12] Oliensis, J., and Dupuis, P. "Direct Method for Reconstructing Shape from Shading." University of Massachusetts Technical Report COINS 92-32, 1992.

[13] Pentland, A.P. "Linear Shape From Shading." *International Journal of Computer Vision* **4**(2): 153-162, 1990.

[14] Zheng, Q., and Chellappa, R. "Estimation of Illuminant Direction, Albedo, and Shape from Shading." *IEEE Trans. on Pattern Analysis and Machine Intelligence* **PAMI-13**(7): 680-702, June 1991.

[15] Frankot, R.T., and Chellappa, R. "Estimation of Surface Topography from SAR Imagery Using Shape from Shading Techniques." *Artificial Intelligence* **43**: 271-310, 1990.

[16] Ferrie, F.P., and Levine, M.D. "Where and Why Local Shading Analysis Works." *IEEE Trans. on Pattern Analysis and Machine Intelligence* **PAMI-11** (2): 198-206, 1989.

Height and Gradient from Shading

Berthold K.P. Horn

Artificial Intelligence Laboratory

Massachusetts Institute of Technology

Abstract:

The shape-from-shading method described here enforces integrability and can deal with complex wrinkled surfaces. It allows fusion of shading information with height and gradient information obtained using other vision modalities such as binocular stereo or direct motion vision. The new method uses a regularizer to prevent divergence initially, but obtains the exact solution despite this, because it can drop the "departure from smoothness" penalty term once it gets near the solution. Two main features distinguish the new method from existing iterative schemes: simultaneous representation of both height and gradient and local linear expansion of the reflectance map about the present estimate of the gradient. If a number of implementation details are dealt with carefully, then the algorithm actually converges to the exact algebraic solution when presented with exact numerical data. Straightforward implementation leads to a scheme that, like other iterative schemes involving diffusion-like effects, takes time proportional to the square of the number of pixels in the image. This suggests that proper multi-grid implementation is called for.

The algorithm has been applied to synthetic images of smooth objects, as well as surfaces with discontinuities in gradient, such as crater-like shapes and polyhedra. The surface is recovered correctly given appropriate boundary conditions, without the need to first segment the image at the edges. Application to digital terrain models permits comparison of the recovered shape with the "ground truth."

1. Background

A special case of the shape-from-shading problem, applicable to surfaces with unusual reflecting properties, was solved by [Rindfleisch 66]. For the special reflectance properties he considered, a profile of the solution surface can be obtained by integrating along predetermined straight lines in the image plane. The general problem was formulated and solved in [Horn 70, 75]. There the method of characteristic strip expansion is used to solve the nonlinear first-order partial differential *image irradiance equation*. The *reflectance map* makes the analysis of shape-from-shading algorithm much easier, provided that both light sources and viewer are far away from the scene being viewed [Horn 77] [Horn & Sjoberg 79]. Several iterative schemes, mostly based on minimization of some functional containing an integral of the brightness error, arose later [Woodham 77] [Strat 79] [Ikeuchi & Horn 81] [Kirk 84] [Brooks & Horn 85] [Horn & Brooks 86] [Kirk 87] [Frankot & Chellappa 88]. For a collection of papers on shape from shading, as well as a review of the subject and an extensive bibliography, see *Shape from Shading* [Horn & Brooks 89].

The new method presented here was developed in part as a response to recent attention to the problem of integrability [Horn & Brooks 86] [Frankot & Chellappa 88], and exploits the idea of a coupled system of equations for depth and slope [Harris 86, 87] [Horn 88]. It borrows from well-known variational approaches to the problem [Ikeuchi & Horn 81] [Brooks & Horn 85], as well as an existing least-squares method for estimating surface shape given a needle map (see [Ikeuchi 84], chapter 11 in [Horn 86], and [Horn & Brooks 86]). For one choice of parameters, the new method becomes similar to one of the first iterative methods ever developed for shape from shading on a regular grid [Strat 79], while it degenerates into another well-known method [Ikeuchi & Horn 81] for a different choice of parameters. If, on the other hand, the brightness error term is dropped, then it degenerates into a well-known interpolation method [Harris 86, 87]. The computational effort grows rapidly with image size, so the new method can benefit from proper multigrid implementation [Brandt 77] [Brandt & Dinar 79] [Brandt 80, 84], as can existing iterative shape-from-shading schemes [Terzopolous 83, 84] [Kirk 84, 87].

It was found that a linear expansion of the reflectance map about the current estimate of the surface gradient leads to more rapid convergence. More importantly, this modification allows the scheme to converge in many cases where the simpler schemes diverge, or get stuck in local minima of the functional. Most existing iterative shape-from-shading methods handle only relatively simple surfaces. Such schemes can benefit from a retrofit of this idea.

The new scheme was tested on a number of synthetic images of increasing complexity, including some generated from digital terrain models of wrinkled surfaces, such as a glacial cirque with a number of gulleys. It recovered surface orientation at all points to within a degree or two in direction of the normal vector after a few hundred iterations. To attain this accuracy, several details of the implementation had to be carefully thought through [Horn 89]. Simpler surfaces are easier to process—with good results even when several of the implementation choices were not made in an optimal way. Similarly, these details may be less important for real images, were other error sources may dominate.

To conserve space, no detailed review of shape-from-shading work or photoclinometry is given here. For this the reader is referred to the collection of papers in [Horn & Brooks 89]. Similarly, there is not enough space to discuss several important implementation details—for these, see [Horn 89].

2. New Coupled Height and Gradient Scheme

The new shape-from-shading scheme will be presented through a series of increasingly more robust variational methods. We start with the simplest.

2.1 Fusing Height and Gradient Recovery

One way of fusing the recovery of gradient from shading with the recovery of height from gradient, is to represent both gradient (p, q) and height z in one variational scheme and to minimize something like

$$\iint \left(\big(E(x, y) - R(p, q)\big)^2 + \mu\big((z_x - p)^2 + (z_y - q)^2\big) \right) dx\, dy. \tag{1}$$

Note that, as far as $p(x, y)$ and $q(x, y)$, are concerned, this is an ordinary calculus problem (since no partial derivatives of p and q appear in the integrand). Differentiating the integrand with respect to $p(x, y)$ and $q(x, y)$ and setting the result equal to zero leads to

$$p = z_x + \frac{1}{\mu}(E - R)R_p \qquad \text{and} \qquad q = z_y + \frac{1}{\mu}(E - R)R_q. \tag{2}$$

Now $z(x, y)$ does not occur directly in $\big(E(x, y) - R(p, q)\big)$ so as far as height is concerned, we actually just need to minimize

$$\iint \big((z_x - p)^2 + (z_y - q)^2\big)\, dx\, dy. \tag{3}$$

The Euler equation for this variational problem [Horn 86] is just

$$\Delta z = p_x + q_y. \tag{4}$$

Altogether then we have one equation for each of the unknowns p, q and z.

These three equations are clearly satisfied when $p = z_x$, $q = z_y$ and $E = R$. That is, if a solution of the original shape-from-shading problem exists, then it satisfies this system of equations exactly (which is more than can be said for most other systems of equations for this problem obtained using a variational approach). It is instructive to substitute the expressions obtained for p and q (equation (2)) in $p_x + q_y$:

$$p_x + q_y = z_{xx} + z_{yy} + \frac{1}{\mu}\Big((E - R)\big(R_{pp}p_x + R_{pq}(p_y + q_x) + R_{qq}q_y\big) \tag{5}$$

$$- \big(R_p^2 p_x + R_p R_q(p_y + q_x) + R_q^2 q_y\big) + (E_x R_p + E_y R_q)Bigr).$$

Since $\Delta z = (p_x + q_y)$ (equation (4)), we note that the three equations above for p, q and z are satisfied when

$$\big(R_p^2 p_x + R_p R_q(p_y + q_x) + R_q^2 q_y\big) - (E_x R_p + E_y R_q) = (E - R)\big(R_{pp}p_x + R_{pq}(p_y + q_x) + R_{qq}q_y\big). \tag{6}$$

This is exactly the equation obtained at the end of section 4.2 in [Horn & Brooks 86], where an attempt was made to directly impose integrability using the constraint $p_y = q_x$ (where it was stated that no convergent iterative scheme had been found for solving this complicated nonlinear partial differential equation directly).

Note that the natural boundary conditions for z are

$$c\,z_x + s\,z_y = c\,p + s\,q, \tag{7}$$

where (c, s) is a normal to the boundary.

The coupled system of equations above for p, q and z immediately suggests an iterative scheme

$$p_{kl}^{(n+1)} = \{z_x\}_{kl}^{(n)} + \frac{1}{\mu}(E - R)R_p,$$

$$q_{kl}^{(n+1)} = \{z_y\}_{kl}^{(n)} + \frac{1}{\mu}(E - R)R_q, \tag{8}$$

$$z_{kl}^{(n+1)} = \overline{z}_{kl}^{(n)} + \frac{\epsilon^2}{\kappa}\left(\{p_x\}_{kl}^{(n+1)} + \{q_y\}_{kl}^{(n+1)}\right),$$

where we have used the discrete approximation of the Laplacian for z:

$$\{\Delta z\} \approx \frac{\kappa}{\epsilon^2}(\overline{z}_{kl} - z_{kl}). \tag{9}$$

This new iterative scheme works well when the initial values given for p, q and z are close to the solution. In fact, it will converge to the exact solution if it exists, that is, if there exist a discrete set of values $\{z_{kl}\}$ such that $\{p_{kl}\}$ and $\{q_{kl}\}$ are the discrete estimate of the first partial derivatives of z with respect to x and y respectively and

$$E_{kl} = R(p_{kl}, q_{kl}) \tag{10}$$

In this case the functional we wished to minimize can actually be reduced to zero. It should be apparent that for this to happen, the estimator used for the Laplacian must match the sum of the convolution of the discrete estimator of the x derivative with itself and the convolution of the discrete estimator of the y derivative with itself[1].

The algorithm can easily be tested using synthetic height data z_{kl}. One merely estimates the partial derivatives using suitable discrete difference formulae and then uses the resulting values p_{kl} and q_{kl} to compute the synthetic image E_{kl}. This construction guarantees that there will be an exact solution. If a real image is used, there is no guarantee that there is an exact solution and the algorithm can at best find a good discrete approximation of the solution of the underlying continuous problem. In this case the functional will in fact not be reduced exactly to zero. In some cases the residue may be quite large. This may be the result of aliasing introduced when sampling the image, as discussed in [Horn 89], or because in fact the image given could not have arising from shading on a homogeneous surface with the reflectance properties and lighting as embodied in the reflectance map.

It turns out that the iterative algorithm developed in this section, while simple, is not very stable unless one is close to the exact solution, particularly when the surface is complex and the reflectance map not close to linear in the gradient. It can be improved greatly by linearizing the reflectance map. It can also be stabilized by adding a penalty term for departure from smoothness. This allows one to come close to the correct solution, at which point the penalty term is removed in order to prevent it from distorting the solution. Consider first the introduction of a penalty term for departure from smoothness.

2.2 Incorporating Departure from Smoothness Term

We now combine the iterative method of [Ikeuchi & Horn 81] for recovering p and q from $E(x, y)$ and $R(p, q)$ with the scheme for recovering z given p and q. We look directly for a minimum of

$$\iint \left((E(x, y) - R(p, q))^2 + \lambda(p_x^2 + p_y^2 + q_x^2 + q_y^2) + \mu((z_x - p)^2 + (z_y - q)^2) \right)\,dx\,dy. \tag{11}$$

The Euler equations of this calculus of variations problem lead to the following coupled system of second-order partial differential equations:

$$\lambda\Delta p = -(E - R)R_p - \mu(z_x - p),$$

$$\lambda\Delta q = -(E - R)R_q - \mu(z_y - q), \tag{12}$$

$$\Delta z = p_x + q_y.$$

---

[1]This and related matters are taken up in the implementation section of [Horn 89].

A discrete approximation of these equations can be obtained by using the discrete approximation of the Laplacian operator introduced above (equation (9)):

$$\{\Delta f\}_{kl} \approx \frac{\kappa}{\epsilon^2}(\overline{f}_{kl} - f_{kl}),\tag{13}$$

where $\overline{f}_{kl}$ is a local average of f_{kl}. Using the discrete approximation of the Laplacian we obtain:

$$\frac{\kappa\lambda}{\epsilon^2}(\overline{p}_{kl} - p_{kl}) = -(E - R)R_p - \mu(z_x - p_{kl}),$$
$$\frac{\kappa\lambda}{\epsilon^2}(\overline{q}_{kl} - q_{kl}) = -(E - R)R_q - \mu(z_y - q_{kl}),\tag{14}$$
$$\frac{\kappa}{\epsilon^2}(\overline{z}_{kl} - z_{kl}) = p_x + q_y.$$

where E, R, R_p, and R_q are the corresponding values at the point (k, l), while z_x, z_y, p_x and q_y are discrete estimates of the partial derivative of z, p and q there. We can collect all of the terms in p_{kl}, q_{kl} and z_{kl} on one side to obtain

$$(\kappa\lambda' + \mu)p_{kl} = (\kappa\lambda'\,\overline{p}_{kl} + \mu z_x) + (E - R)R_p,$$
$$(\kappa\lambda' + \mu)q_{kl} = (\kappa\lambda'\,\overline{q}_{kl} + \mu z_y) + (E - R)R_q,\tag{15}$$
$$\frac{\kappa}{\epsilon^2}z_{kl} = \frac{\kappa}{\epsilon^2}\overline{z}_{kl} - (p_x + q_y),$$

where $\lambda' = \lambda/\epsilon^2$. These equations immediately suggest an iterative scheme, where the right hand sides are computed using the current values of the z_{kl}, p_{kl}, and q_{kl}, with the results then used to supply new values for the unknowns appearing on the left hand sides[2].

From the above it may appear that $R(p, q)$, $R_p(p, q)$, and $R_q(p, q)$ should be evaluated using the "old" values of p and q. One might, on the other hand, argue that the local average values $\overline{p}$ and $\overline{q}$, or perhaps even the gradient estimates z_x and z_y, are more appropriate. Experimentation suggests that the scheme is most stable when the local averages $\overline{p}$ and $\overline{q}$ are used.

The above scheme contains a penalty term for departure from smoothness, that is, it has been regularized. Consequently it may appear that it cannot possibly converge to the exact solution, instead producing some smooth distorted surface. Indeed, it appears that the iterative scheme will "walk away" from the correct solution when it is presented with the solution as initial conditions, much as some earlier iterative schemes do. It turns out, however, that the penalty term is needed only to assure convergence when far from the solution. When we come closer to the solution, λ' can be reduced to zero and so the penalty term drops out. It is tempting to leave the penalty term out right from the start, since this simplifies the equations a great deal. The contribution from the penalty term does, however, help damp out instabilities when far from the solution and so is needed to avoid divergence in that situation.

2.3 Relationship to Existing Techniques

- Recently a new method has been developed that combines an existing iterative scheme for recovering surface orientation from shading with a projection onto the subspace of integrable gradients [Frankot & Chellappa 88]. Their approach is to alternately take one step of the iterative scheme [Ikeuchi & Horn 81] and then to find the integrable solution "nearest" to the result. The integrable gradient is then provided as initial conditions for the next step of the iterative scheme, thus ensuring that the gradient field never departs too far from integrability. The integrable gradient closest to a given gradient field is found using orthonormal series expansion and by exploiting the fact that differentiation in the spatial domain corresponds to multiplication by frequency in the transform domain.

- Similar results can be achieved by using instead the method described in [Ikeuchi 84] [Horn 86] [Horn & Brooks 86] for recovering the height $z(x, y)$ that best matches a given gradient. The resulting surface can

---

[2]These equations need to be solved iteratively both because the system of equations is so large and because of the fact that the reflectance map $R(p, q)$ is typically nonlinear.

then be differentiated to obtain initial values for $p(x, y)$ and $q(x, y)$ for the next step of the iterative scheme. This works, but not as well as the new scheme described in the previous section.

- Next, note that we obtain the scheme of [Ikeuchi & Horn 81] (who ignore the integrability problem) if we drop the departure from integrability term in the integrand—that is, when $\mu = 0$. If we instead remove the departure from smoothness term in the integrand—that is, when $\lambda = 0$—we obtain something reminiscent of the iterative scheme of [Strat 79], although Strat dealt with the integrability issue in a slightly different way.

- Finally, if we drop the brightness error term in the integrand, we obtain the scheme of [Harris 86, 87] for interpolating from depth and slope. He minimizes

$$\iint \left(\lambda(p_x^2 + p_y^2 + q_x^2 + q_y^2) + \left((z_x - p)^2 + (z_y - q)^2\right) \right) dx\, dy.$$

and arrives at the Euler equations

$$\lambda \Delta p = -(z_x - p), \quad \lambda \Delta q = -(z_y - q), \quad \text{and} \quad \Delta z = p_x + q_y. \tag{16}$$

Now consider that

$$\Delta(\Delta z) = \Delta(p_x + q_y). \tag{17}$$

Since application of the Laplacian operator and differentiation commute we have

$$\Delta(\Delta z) = (\Delta p)_x + (\Delta q)_y, \tag{18}$$

or

$$\lambda \Delta(\Delta z) = -(z_{xx} - p_x) - (z_{yy} - q_y), \tag{19}$$

and so

$$\lambda \Delta(\Delta z) = -\Delta z + (p_x + q_y) = 0. \tag{20}$$

So this method actually solves the bi-harmonic equation for z by solving a coupled set of Poisson's equations in an elegant, stable way that permits introduction of constraints on both height z and gradient (p, q). This is a good method for interpolating from sparse depth and surface orientation data.

The biharmonic equation has been employed to interpolate digital terrain models (DTMs) from contour maps. Such DTMs were used, for example, in [Horn & Bachman 78] [Horn 79] [Sjoberg & Horn 83]. The obvious implementations of finite difference approximations of the biharmonic operator, however, tend to be unstable because some of the weights are negative, and because the corresponding coefficient matrix lacks diagonal dominance. Also, the treatment of boundary conditions is complicated by the fact that the support of the biharmonic operator is so large. The scheme described above circumvents both of these difficulties.

2.4 Boundary Conditions & Nonlinearity of Reflectance Map

So far we have assumed that suitable boundary conditions are available, that is, the gradient is known on the boundary of the image region to which the computation is to be applied. If this is not the case, the solution is likely not to be unique. We may nevertheless find a solution by imposing so-called *natural* boundary conditions [Courant & Hilbert 62]. The natural boundary conditions for the variational problem described here can be shown to be

$$c\, p_x + s\, p_y = 0 \quad \text{and} \quad c\, q_x + s\, q_y = 0 \tag{21}$$

and

$$c\, z_x + s\, z_y = c\, p + s\, q \tag{22}$$

where (c, s) is a normal to the boundary. That is, the normal derivative of the gradient is zero and the normal derivative of the height has to match the slope in the normal direction computed from the gradient.

In the above we have approximated the original partial differential equations by a set of discrete equations, three for every picture cell (one each for p, q and z). If these equations were linear, we could directly apply all of the existing theory relating to convergence of various iterative schemes and how one solves such equations efficiently, given that the corresponding coefficient matrices are sparse[3]. Unfortunately, the equations are in

---

[3]See [Lee 88] for a discussion of the convergence of a particular iterative shape-from-shading scheme.

general not linear, because of the nonlinear dependence of the reflectance map $R(p, q)$ on the gradient components p and q. In fact, in deriving the above simple iterative scheme, we have essentially treated $R(p, q)$, and its derivatives, as constant (independent of p and q) during any particular iterative step.

2.5 Local Linear Approximation of Reflectance Map

We can do a lot better, while preserving the apparent linearity of the equations, by approximating the reflectance map $R(p, q)$ locally by a linear function of p and q. There are several options for choice of reference gradient for the series expansion, so let us keep it general for now at (p_0, q_0)[4]. We have

$$R(p, q) \approx R(p_0, q_0) + (p - p_0)\, R_p(p_0, q_0) + (q - q_0)\, R_q(p_0, q_0) + \cdots \tag{23}$$

Again, gathering all of the term in p_{kl} and q_{kl} on the left hand sides of the equations, we now obtain

$$
\begin{aligned}
(\lambda'' + R_p^2)\, p_{kl} + R_p R_q\, q_{kl} &= (\kappa\lambda' \overline{p}_{kl} + \mu z_x) + (E - R - p_0 R_p - q_0 R_q) R_p, \\
R_q R_p\, p_{kl} + (\lambda'' + R_q^2)\, q_{kl} &= (\kappa\lambda' \overline{q}_{kl} + \mu z_y) + (E - R - p_0 R_p - q_0 R_q) R_q,
\end{aligned}
\tag{24}
$$

while the equation for z remains unchanged. Here we have abbreviated

$$\lambda'' = \kappa\lambda' + \mu. \tag{25}$$

It is convenient to rewrite these equations in terms of quantities relative to the reference gradient:

$$
\begin{aligned}
\delta p_{kl} &= p_{kl} - p_0 & \text{and} && \delta q_{kl} &= q_{kl} - q_0 \\
\delta \overline{p}_{kl} &= \overline{p}_{kl} - p_0 & \text{and} && \delta \overline{q}_{kl} &= \overline{q}_{kl} - q_0 \\
\delta z_x &= z_x - p_0 & \text{and} && \delta z_y &= z_y - q_0
\end{aligned}
\tag{26}
$$

This yields

$$
\begin{aligned}
(\lambda'' + R_p^2)\, \delta p_{kl} + R_p R_q\, \delta q_{kl} &= \kappa\lambda'\, \delta \overline{p}_{kl} + \mu\, \delta z_x + (E - R) R_p, \\
R_p R_q\, \delta q_{kl} + (\lambda'' + R_q^2)\, \delta q_{kl} &= \kappa\lambda'\, \delta \overline{q}_{kl} + \mu\, \delta z_y + (E - R) R_q.
\end{aligned}
\tag{27}
$$

(The equations clearly simplify somewhat if we choose either $\overline{p}$ and $\overline{q}$ or z_x and z_y for the reference gradient p_0 and q_0.) We can view the above as a pair of linear equations for δp_{kl} and δq_{kl}. The determinant of the 2×2 coefficient matrix

$$D = \lambda''(\lambda'' + R_p^2 + R_q^2) \tag{28}$$

is always positive, so there is no problem with singularities. The solution is given by

$$
\begin{aligned}
D\, \delta p_{kl} &= (\lambda'' + R_q^2)\, A - R_p R_q\, B, \\
D\, \delta q_{kl} &= (\lambda'' + R_p^2)\, B - R_q R_p\, A,
\end{aligned}
\tag{29}
$$

where

$$
\begin{aligned}
A &= \kappa\lambda'\, \delta \overline{p}_{kl} + \mu\, \delta z_x + (E - R) R_p, \\
B &= \kappa\lambda'\, \delta \overline{q}_{kl} + \mu\, \delta z_y + (E - R) R_q.
\end{aligned}
\tag{30}
$$

(There are various interesting ways of rewriting these formulae). This leads to a convenient iterative scheme where the new values are given by

$$p_{kl}^{(n+1)} = p_0^{(n)} + \delta p_{kl}^{(n)} \quad \text{and} \quad q_{kl}^{(n+1)} = q_0^{(n)} + \delta q_{kl}^{(n)}, \tag{31}$$

in terms of the old reference gradient and the increments computed above. This new version of the iterative scheme does not require a great deal more computation, since the partial derivatives R_p and R_q are required in any case. It has been determined empirically that this scheme converges under a much wider set of circumstances than the one presented earlier.

Experimentation with different reference gradients, including the old values of p and q, the local average $\overline{p}$ and $\overline{q}$, as well as z_x and z_y showed that the accuracy of the solution as well as the convergence is affected by this choice. It became apparent that if we do not want the scheme to "walk away" from the correct solution, then we should use the old value of p and q for the reference p_0 and q_0.

---

[4]The reference gradient will, of course, be different at every picture cell, but to avoid having subscripts on the subscripts, we will simple denote the reference gradient at a particular picture cell by (p_0, q_0).

2.6 When to Stop Iterating

It is often difficult to decide when to stop an iteration. If we knew what the underlying surface was, we could just wait for the gradient of the solution to approach that of the surface. But, other than when we test the algorithm on synthetic images, we do not know what the surface is, otherwise we would probably not be using a shape-from-shading method in the first place! Some other tests include:

- The brightness error

$$\iint \big(E(x,y) - R(p,q)\big)^2 \, dx\, dy \tag{32}$$

should be small. Unfortunately this error becomes small after just a few iterations, so it does not yield a useful stopping criterion.

- The departure from smoothness

$$\iint (p_x^2 + p_y^2 + q_x^2 + q_y^2)\, dx\, dy \tag{33}$$

also drops as the solution is approached, but it does not constitute a particularly good indicator of approach to the solution. In particular, when one comes close to the solution, one may wish to reduce the parameters λ, perhaps even to zero, in which case further iterations may infact reduce smoothness in order to better satisfy the remaining criteria.

- One of the measures of lack of integrability

$$\iint \big((z_x - p)^2 + (z_y - q)^2\big)\, dx\, dy \tag{34}$$

appears to be useful, since it drops slowly and often keeps on changing until the solution has converged.

- Another measure of lack of integrability

$$\iint (p_y - q_x)^2 \, dx\, dy \tag{35}$$

is not quite as useful, since it can at times become quite small, or stop changing significantly, even when z is still inconsistent with p and q.

- One can also keep track of the rate of change of the solution with iterations

$$\iint \left(\frac{dp}{dt}\right)^2 + \left(\frac{dq}{dt}\right)^2 \, dx\, dy. \tag{36}$$

One should not stop until this has become quite small. In most cases it helps to continue for a while after the above measures stop changing rapidly; since the solution often continues to adjust.

3. Some Experimental Results

Shown in Figure 1 are synthetic images of a crater and of the shape recovered by the new algorithm. The image in Figure 1(a), corresponding to lighting from the Northwest, is the input provided to the algorithm, while Figure 1(c) is a synthetic image of the computed shape viewed under the same lighting conditions. Comparison of these two images, however, does not provide a useful test of the algorithm, since the brightness error, that is, the difference between these two images, becomes very small after just a few iterations, even though the surface shape at that stage of the computation is likely to still be quite inaccurate. To get an idea of how well such an algorithm really works, one needs to compare images of the original surface and that recovered by the algorithm under *different* lighting conditions. Shown in Figure 1(b) and 1(d) are images of the original surface and that recovered by the algorithm when the light source is placed in the Northeast. In this case the two images are identical, since the algorithm recovered the original shape with high accuracy after a few hundred iterations, under the assumption that the gradient is zero on the boundary of the image.

Many iterative schemes for shape from shading use the gradient to represent shape, and some of these schemes do not enforce integrability. In this situation showing an image of the recovered "surface" under the same lighting conditions as those used to obtain the input image is next to useless as a test of performance. In fact it is possible in this case to obtain a suitable gradient field in one step! That is, if neither integrability nor smoothness is enforced, the problem is so underconstrained that one can arrange for the "surface" to yield an arbitrary second image under different specified lighting conditions. Shown in Figure 3(a) and 3(b) are synthetic images of a digital terrain model for two different lighting conditions. In Figure 3(c) and 3(d) we see synthetic images of the computed gradient field "solution" under the same specified lighting conditions. The gradient field is computed by application of the photometric stereo method [Woodham 78, 80] at each point in the image[5]. This points out the importance of synthetic images of the recovered surface obtained with assumed lighting *different* from the lighting of the original scene.

To test the algorithm on more complex surfaces, a digital terrain model was interpolated from a portion of a contour map using methods developed earlier for work with digital terrain models [Horn & Bachman 78] [Horn 79] [Sjoberg & Horn 83]. Bradford Washburn of the Boston Museum of Science kindly supplied a new detailed contour map of the Mt. Washington region of the Presidential Range in the White Mountains of New Hampshire. The area chosen for this work is Huntington's ravine, a glacial cirque with several major gullies[6], a contour map of which is shown in Figure 2. Heights on a 113×85 grid were interpolated from the digitized contour map. Synthetic images of this surface illuminated from the Northwest and the Northeast are shown in Figure 4(a) and 4(b). The image shown in Figure 4(a) is provided as input to the algorithm. Given the surface gradient on the boundary, the algorithm converges to the exact solution (to machine precision) after several thousand iterations. Synthetic images of the computed surface after just a few hundred iterations are shown in Figure 4(c) and 4(d), under the same lighting conditions used for the images of the original surface.

4. Conclusion

A new iterative scheme for recovering shape from shading has been developed and implemented. The new scheme recovers height and gradient at the same time. Linearization of the reflectance map about the local average surface orientation greatly improves the performance of the new algorithm and could be used to improve the performance of existing iterative shape-from-shading algorithms. The new algorithm has been successfully applied to complex wrinkled surfaces.

5. Acknowledgements

Michael Caplinger kindly provided pointers to relevant publications on photoclinometry, in particular the Ph.D. thesis of R.L. Kirk [Kirk 87] at the California Institute of Technology. Michael Brooks drew my attention to the fact that existing iterative schemes "walk away" from the correct solution and that regularization does not "pick one of the infinite number of solutions" of an ill-posed problem, as sometimes mistakenly stated [Brooks 85]. Bradford Washburn supplied a detailed topographic map of the Mt. Washington area of the White Mountains in New Hampshire from which one of the digital terrain model used in the experiments here was interpolated. Joel Moses found a way for the Electrical Engineering and Computer Science Department to help cover the cost of the author's travel to the photoclinometry workshop held at Arizona State University, February 12–13, 1989, which provided much of the impetus for this paper.

6. References

Blake, A., A. Zisserman & G. Knowles (1985) "Surface Descriptions from Stereo and Shading," *Image & Vision Computing*, Vol. 3, No. 4, pp. 183–191. Also in (1989) *Shape from Shading*, Horn, B.K.P. & M.J. Brooks (eds.), MIT Press, Cambridge, MA.

Brandt, A. (1977) "Multi-level Adaptive Solutions to Boundary-Value Problems," *Mathematics of Computation*, Vol. 31, No. 138, April, pp. 333-390.

---

[5]This bizarre gradient field is, of course, not integrable and so does not correspond to any actual three-dimensional surface.

[6]The gullies are steep enough to be of interest to ice-climbers.

Brandt, A. (1980) "Stages in Developing Multigrid Solutions," in *Numerical Methods for Engineering*, Absi, E., R. Glowinski, P. Lascaux, H. Veysseyre (eds.), Dunod, Paris, pp. 23–44.

Brandt, A. (1984) *Multigrid Techniques: 1984 Guide with Applications to Fluid Dynamics*, Monograph available as GMD-Studie No. 85, from GMD-F1T, Postfach 1240, D-2505, St. Augustin 1, West Germany.

Brandt, A. & N. Dinar (1979) "Multigrid solutions of elliptic flow problems," in Parter, S.V. (ed.) *Numerical Methods for PDE*, Academic Press, New York, NY.

Brooks, M.J. (1985) Personal communication.

Brooks, M.J. & B.K.P. Horn (1985) "Shape and Source from Shading," *Proceedings of the International Joint Conference on Artificial Intelligence*, Los Angeles, CA, August 18–23, pp. 932–936. Also in (1989) *Shape from Shading*, Horn, B.K.P. & M.J. Brooks (eds.), MIT Press, Cambridge, MA.

Bruss, A.R. (1982) "The Eikonal Equation: Some Results Applicable to Computer Vision," *Journal of Mathematical Physics*, Vol. 23, No. 5, pp. 890–896, May. Also in (1989) *Shape from Shading*, Horn, B.K.P. & M.J. Brooks (eds.), MIT Press, Cambridge, MA.

Courant, R. & D. Hilbert (1962) *Methods of Mathematical Physics*, Volume I, Wiley, New York, NY.

Frankot, R.T. & R. Chellappa (1988) "A Method for Enforcing Integrability in Shape from Shading Algorithms," *IEEE Transactions on Pattern Analysis and Machine Intelligence*, Vol. 10, No. 4, pp. 439–451, July. Also in (1989) *Shape from Shading*, Horn, B.K.P. & M.J. Brooks (eds.), MIT Press, Cambridge, MA.

Harris, J.J. (1986) "The Coupled Depth/Slope Approach to Surface Reconstruction," S.M. Thesis, Department of Electrical Engineering and Computer Science, MIT. Also Technical Report 908, Artificial Intelligence Laboratory, MIT, Cambridge, MA.

Harris, J.J. (1987) "A New Approach to Surface Reconstruction: The Coupled Depth/Slope Model," *Proceedings of the International Conference on Computer Vision*, London, England, June 8–11, pp. 277–283.

Horn, B.K.P. (1970) "Shape from Shading: a Method for Obtaining the Shape of a Smooth Opaque Object from One View," Ph.D. Thesis, Department of Electrical Engineering, MIT. Also Technical Report TR-79, Project MAC, MIT, Cambridge, MA. Also Technical Report TR-232, Artificial Intelligence Laboratory, MIT, Cambridge, MA.

Horn, B.K.P. (1975) "Obtaining Shape from Shading Information," Chapter 4 in *The Psychology of Computer Vision*, P.H. Winston (ed.), McGraw Hill, New York, NY, pp. 115–155. Also in (1989) *Shape from Shading*, Horn, B.K.P. & M.J. Brooks (eds.), MIT Press, Cambridge, MA.

Horn, B.K.P. (1977) "Understanding Image Intensities (sic)," *Artificial Intelligence*, Vol. 8, No. 2, pp. 201–231, April. Also in (1987) *Readings in Computer Vision*, Fischler, M.A. & O. Firschein (eds.), Kaufmann, pp. 45–60.

Horn, B.K.P. (1979) "Automatic Hill-Shading and the Reflectance Map," *Image Understanding Workshop*, Palo Alto, CA, April 24–25, pp. 79–120. Also, *Proceedings of the IEEE*, Vol. 69, No. 1, pp. 14–47, January. Also (1982) *Geo-Processing*, Vol. 2, No. 1, pp. 65–146, October.

Horn, B.K.P. (1986) *Robot Vision*, MIT Press, Cambridge, MA & McGraw-Hill, New York, NY.

Horn, B.K.P. (1988) "Some Ideas on Parallel Analog Networks for Machine Vision," Memo 1071, Artificial Intelligence Laboratory, MIT, Cambridge, MA, December.

Horn, B.K.P. (1989) "Height and Gradient from Shading," Memo 1105, Artificial Intelligence Laboratory, MIT, Cambridge, MA, March.

Horn, B.K.P. & B.L. Bachman (1978) "Using Synthetic Images to Register Real Images with Surface Models," *Communications of the ACM*, Vol. 21, No. 11, pp. 914–924, November. Also "Registering Real Images Using Synthetic Images," in *Artificial Intelligence: An MIT Perspective* (Volume II), Winston, P.H. & R.H. Brown (eds.), MIT Press, Cambridge, MA, pp. 129–160.

Horn, B.K.P. & M.J. Brooks (1986) "The Variational Approach to Shape from Shading," *Computer Vision, Graphics and Image Processing*, Vol. 33, No. 2, pp. 174–208, February. Also in (1989) *Shape from Shading*, Horn, B.K.P. & M.J. Brooks (eds.), MIT Press, Cambridge, MA.

Horn, B.K.P. & M.J. Brooks (eds.) (1989) *Shape from Shading*, MIT Press, Cambridge, MA, May.

Horn, B.K.P. & R.W. Sjoberg (1979) "Calculating the Reflectance Map," *Applied Optics*, Vol. 18, No. 11, pp. 1770–1779, June. Also in (1989) *Shape from Shading*, Horn, B.K.P. & M.J. Brooks (eds.), MIT Press, Cambridge, MA.

Ikeuchi, K. (1984) "Reconstructing a Depth Map from Intensity Maps," *International Conference on Pattern Recognition*, Montreal, Canada, July 30–August 2, pp. 736–738. Also (1983) "Constructing a Depth Map from Images," Memo 744, Artificial Intelligence Laboratory, MIT, Cambridge, MA, August.

Ikeuchi, K. & B.K.P. Horn (1981) "Numerical Shape from Shading and Occluding Boundaries," *Artificial Intelligence*, Vol. 17, No. 1–3, pp. 141–184, August. Also in (1989) *Shape from Shading*, Horn, B.K.P. & M.J. Brooks (eds.), MIT Press, Cambridge, MA.

Kirk, R.L. (1984) "A Finite-Element Approach to Two-Dimensional Photoclinometry," brief abstract in *Bulletin of the American Astronomical Society*, Vol. 16, No. 3, pg. 709.

Kirk, R.L. (1987) "A Fast Finite-Element Algorithm for Two-Dimensional Photoclinometry," Part III of Ph.D. Thesis, Division of Geological and Planetary Sciences, California Institute of Technology, Pasadena, CA.

Lee, C.-H. & A. Rosenfeld (1985) "Improved Methods of Estimating Shape from Shading using the Light Source Coordinate System," *Artificial Intelligence*, Vol. 26, No. 2, pp. 125–143. Also in (1989) *Shape from Shading*, Horn, B.K.P. & M.J. Brooks (eds.), MIT Press, Cambridge, MA.

Lee, D. (1988) "Algorithms for Shape from Shading and Occluding Boundaries," *Proceedings of the IEEE Conference on Computer Vision and Pattern Recognition*, June 5–9, Ann Arbor, MI, pp. 478–485. Also in (1989) *Shape from Shading*, Horn, B.K.P. & M.J. Brooks (eds.), MIT Press, Cambridge, MA.

Malik, J. & D. Maydan (1989) "Recovering Three Dimensional Shape from a Single Image of Curved Objects," *IEEE Transactions on Pattern Analysis and Machine Intelligence*, Vol. 11, No. 4. Also in (1989) *Shape from Shading*, Horn, B.K.P. & M.J. Brooks (eds.), MIT Press, Cambridge, MA.

Pentland, A.P. (1984) "Local Shading Analysis," *IEEE Transactions on Pattern Analysis and Machine Intelligence*, Vol. 6, No. 2, pp. 170–187, March. Also in (1989) *Shape from Shading*, Horn, B.K.P. & M.J. Brooks (eds.), MIT Press, Cambridge, MA.

Pentland, A.P. (1988) "Shape Information from Shading: A Theory about Human Perception," Technical Report 103, Vision Sciences, MIT Media Laboratory, MIT, Cambridge, MA, May.

Rindfleisch, T. (1966) "Photometric Method for Lunar Topography," *Photogrammetric Engineering*, Vol. 32, No. 2, pp. 262–277, March. Also (1965) "A Photometric Method for Deriving Lunar Topographic Information," Technical Report 32-786, Jet Propulsion Laboratory, California Institute of Technology, Pasadena, CA, September.

Saxberg, B.V.H. (1988) "A Modern Differential Geometric Approach to Shape from Shading," Ph.D. Thesis, Department of Electrical Engineering and Computer Science, MIT, Cambridge, MA.

Sjoberg, R.W. & B.K.P. Horn (1983) "Atmospheric Effects in Satellite Imaging of Mountainous Terrain," *Applied Optics*, Vol. 22, No. 11, pp. 1702–1716, June.

Strat, T. (1979) "A Numerical Method for Shape from Shading for a Single Image," S.M. Thesis, Department of Electrical Engineering and Computer Science, MIT, Cambridge, MA.

Terzopoulos, D. (1983) "Multilevel Computational Processes for Visual Surface Reconstruction," *Computer Vision, Graphics and Image Processing*, Vol. 24, pp. 52–96. Also (1982) "Multi-level Reconstruction of Visual Surfaces: Variational Principles and Finite Element Representation, Memo 671, Artificial Intelligence Laboratory, MIT, Cambridge, MA, April.

Terzopoulos, D. (1984) "Multigrid Relaxation Methods and the Analysis of Lightness, Shading, and Flow," Memo 803, Artificial Intelligence Laboratory, MIT, Cambridge, MA, October. Also chapter 10 in *Image Understanding 84*, Ullman, S. & W. Richards (eds.), Ablex Publishing Corporation, Norwood, NJ, pp. 225–262.

Woodham, R.J. (1977) "A Cooperative Algorithm for Determining Surface Orientation from a Single View," *International Joint Conference on Artificial Intelligence*, Cambridge, MA, August 22–25, pp. 635–641.

Woodham, R.J. (1978) "Photometric Stereo: A Reflectance Map Technique for Determining Surface Orientation from a Single View," *Image Understanding Systems & Industrial Applications, Proceedings of the Society of Photo-Optical Instrumentation Engineers*, Vol. 155, pp. 136–143.

Woodham, R.J. (1980) "Photometric Method for Determining Surface Orientation from Multiple Images," *Optical Engineering*, Vol. 19, No. 1, January-February, pp. 139–144. Also in (1989) *Shape from Shading*, Horn, B.K.P. & M.J. Brooks (eds.), MIT Press, Cambridge, MA.

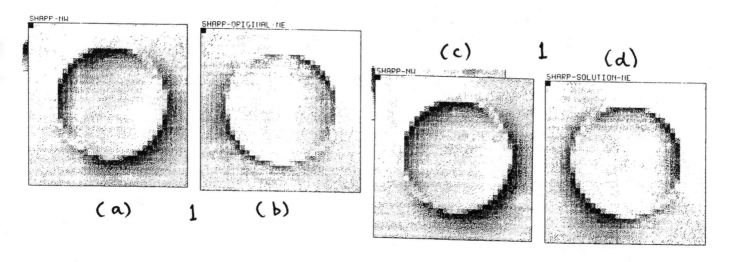

1

(a)   1   (b)

(c)   1   (d)

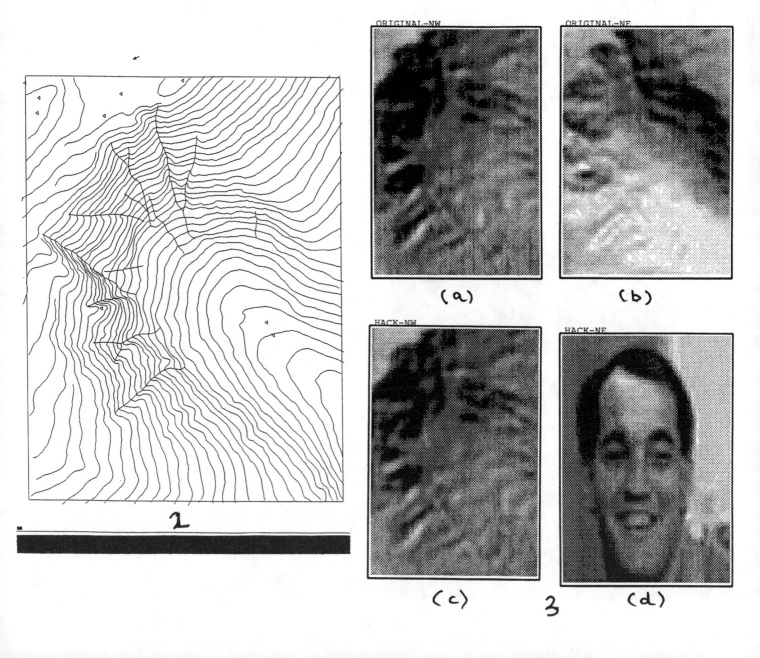

2

3

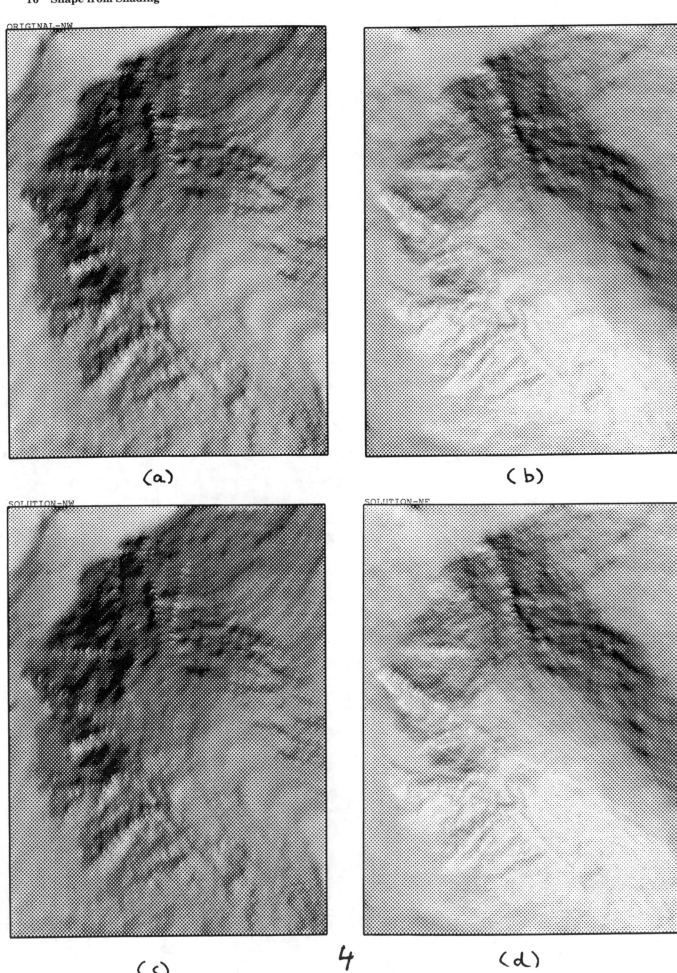

(a)

(b)

(c)

4

(d)

Direct Method For Reconstructing Shape From Shading

John Oliensis†
Department of Computer Science
University of Massachusetts at Amherst
Amherst, Massachusetts 01003

Paul Dupuis‡
Box F, Division of Applied Mathematics
Brown University
Providence, Rhode Island 02912 *

Abstract

A new approach to shape from shading is described, based on a connection with a calculus of variations/optimal control problem. An explicit representation is given for the surface corresponding to a shaded image; uniqueness of the surface (under suitable conditions) is an immediate consequence. The approach leads naturally to an algorithm for shape reconstruction that is simple, fast, provably convergent, and, in many cases, provably convergent to the correct solution. In contrast with standard variational algorithms, it does not require regularization. Given a continuous image, the algorithm can be proven to converge to the continuous surface solution as the image sampling frequency is taken to infinity. Experimental results are presented for synthetic and real images, for general lighting direction.

1   Introduction

Shape from shading has traditionally been considered an ill–posed problem, with potentially infinitely many different surfaces corresponding to a shaded image. Therefore, most algorithms for reconstructing shape have incorporated *regularization* techniques to guarantee recovery of a unique, 'physically reasonable' surface solution.

More recently, it was suggested that shape from shading need not be ill–posed when the image contains singular points, i.e., maximally bright image points [1,5,18,19,16,15]. This was shown for the case of illumination from—or symmetric around—the camera direction in [16]. In addition, a general shaded image was shown to *uniquely* determine shape under the assumed lighting conditions [16]. Singular points provided the essential constraints.

Singular points continue to give strong constraints on the surface solutions for illumination from a general direction [15]. Thus, shape from shading should not be assumed ill–posed in general, and regularization should be used with caution. Also, the image of the occluding boundary gives no useful constraint on surface reconstruction [15]. Singular points, therefore, provide the primary constraints.

Nevertheless, shape–from–shading algorithms in the past have not taken full advantage of the strong constraints due to singular points. Algorithms based on the method of characteristic strips [4] have used these constraints explicitly, but in an approximate way. These algorithms have usually been applied to rather simple images, and are nonrobust in the presence of noise.

Most recent algorithms for recovering shape from shading have been based on the variational approach (e.g., [7,6,5]). These algorithms have had significant successes on complex images, but do not explicitly use the singular point constraints. This is seen experimentally in the fact that these algorithms do better on images with many singular points than on images with just one (see below and also [11]); yet for such simple images, the sole singular point is known to directly and uniquely constrain the surface reconstruction [1,19].

In this paper, an algorithm is presented that takes full advantage of the singular point constraints. It is simple, fast, provably convergent, and, in many cases, provably convergent to the correct solution. In particular, if the surface is known to be *unimodal* at a singular point in the image (i.e., locally concave or convex at this point), then the algorithm provably reconstructs the correct surface in a region around the singular point. The algorithm is robust against noise and, unlike previous algorithms, does not employ regularization. There is no problem with false minima, in contrast to the standard variational approach. Finally, this approach is capable of dealing with some orientation discontinuities—images for which the intensity function is only piecewise continuous.

The algorithm is based on establishing the equivalence of shape from shading to a calculus of variations/optimal control problem. For the general case with illumination from an arbitrary direction, the optimal control problem can be extended to a differential game. In general, a variety of optimal control/differential game formulations is possible [20,2].

This equivalence facilitates the theoretical analysis of shape from shading, and makes the algorithm highly adaptable. It also gives intuition about the convergence performance of the algorithm. Below, we present a simple uniqueness proof for shape from shading which generalizes from the local uniqueness results of Bruss [1] and Saxberg [19]. This is possible because, in the optimal control representation, an expression for the surface

*This work was supported by the National Science Foundation under grants IRI-9113690, CDA-8922572†and NSF-DMS-9115762‡, and by a grant from DARPA, via TACOM, contract number DAAE07-91-C-R035†.

corresponding to a shaded image can be exhibited explicitly. Some of the results presented in this paper have also been derived by E. Rouy and A. Tourin [20].

2   Shape from Shading as a Problem of Optimal Control: Heuristic Derivation

The imaged surface is assumed to be Lambertian, and viewed from above along the $-\hat{z}$ direction. It is represented in the explicit form $z(x,y)$, where $z : \mathbf{R}^2 \to \mathbf{R}$ is the *height function* to be reconstructed. We consider first the simpler case of illumination along the viewing direction $-\hat{z}$ (vertical light). The case of illumination from a general direction is discussed later.

Under these conditions, the image irradiance equation is:

$$I(x,y) = \frac{1}{(1 + |\nabla z(x,y)|^2)^{1/2}}. \qquad (2.1)$$

It is convenient to rewrite this in the eikonal form:

$$|\nabla z(x,y)|^2 = \frac{1}{(I(x,y))^2} - 1 \equiv V(x,y), \qquad (2.2)$$

where $I(x,y) \in (0,1]$, $V(x,y) \in [0,\infty)$. This type of equation arises frequently in the dynamical programming approach to problems of optimal control. In this section, the connection of shape–from–shading to an optimal control problem is derived heuristically using dynamic programming, in the simplified situation where the image contains a single singular point. Note that this derivation does not generalize directly to the multiple singular point case. A rigorous argument which does apply to this more general situation is presented below in Section 5.

We show that the height function z has a representation as the solution to a calculus of variations/optimal control problem, and that this representation gives a solution of eq. 2.2. The optimal control representation is more specific than the partial differential eq. 2.2, which in general has additional (even classical) solutions. Other possible representations for the height function z could also be considered [20, 2]; the one described below is chosen for its algebraic simplicity. In Section 4, we discuss a modification of this calculus of variations problem by the inclusion of a terminal cost, as is necessary for the multiple singular point case.

Consider the following control problem: a 'particle' initially located at (x_0, y_0) moves in the image plane in response to control parameters u, v, according to:

$$\dot{x} = u, \quad \dot{y} = v, \quad x(0) = x_0, \quad y(0) = y_0. \quad (2.3)$$

The control parameters are to be chosen to minimize a cost function for the particle's trajectory $(x(s), y(s))$:

$$U(x_0, y_0, T) = \inf\{$$
$$\tfrac{1}{2} \int_0^T ds\, \left(u(s)^2 + v(s)^2 + V(x(s), y(s))\right)\}. \qquad (2.4)$$

In this equation, the minimal cost has been defined as a function of the trajectory's starting point (x_0, y_0).

The infimization is over all piecewise continuous functions $u(\cdot)$, $v(\cdot)$ on $[0, T]$. Let

$$U(x,y) = \lim_{T\to\infty} U(x,y,T).$$

$U(\cdot)$ will turn out, in the unimodal case, to be the surface $z(x,y)$ up to a translation. A *unimodal* surface is one with a single local maximum or local minimum. To show this formally, we assume that $U(\cdot)$ is a differentiable function of the starting point, and formally demonstrate using a dynamical programming argument that it satisfies eq. 2.2.

Let δT be a small time increment. Then the principle of optimality implies

$$U(x_0, y_0, T) = \inf_{(u,v)}\{$$
$$U(x(\delta T), y(\delta T), T - \delta T) \qquad (2.5)$$
$$+ \tfrac{1}{2} \int_0^{\delta T} ds\, \left(u(s)^2 + v(s)^2 + V(x(s), y(s))\right)\}.$$

The explicit infimization is now over the part of the trajectory with $s \in [0, \delta T]$; the infimization over the rest of the trajectory is included in the cost function $U(\cdot, T - \delta T)$. Since δT is small, U can be expanded to first order in this quantity, which gives (for $\delta T \to 0$):

$$\frac{\partial U}{\partial T}(x,y,T) = \inf_{(u(0),v(0))}\{$$
$$\tfrac{1}{2}\left(u^2(0) + v^2(0) + V(x,y)\right) \qquad (2.6)$$
$$+ \frac{\partial U}{\partial x}(x,y,T)u(0) + \frac{\partial U}{\partial y}(x,y,T)v(0)\}.$$

Performing the minimization over $u(0)$ and $v(0)$ yields:

$$u(0) = -\frac{\partial U}{\partial x}(x,y,T), \quad v(0) = -\frac{\partial U}{\partial y}(x,y,T), \quad (2.7)$$

and

$$\frac{\partial U}{\partial T}(x,y,T) =$$
$$\tfrac{1}{2}\left[V(x,y) - \left(\frac{\partial U}{\partial x}(x,y,T)\right)^2 - \left(\frac{\partial U}{\partial y}(x,y,T)\right)^2\right]. \qquad (2.8)$$

Suppose that the image region under consideration is a small neighborhood of a singular point, at which $I = 1$ and $V = 0$. A minimal cost trajectory clearly moves toward regions of smaller V, and will converge to the singular point at which the incremental cost is zero. As the trajectory converges to this point, the total cost along the trajectory converges to a *finite* value. Therefore, the integration limit T in eq. 2.4 can be taken to infinity, and $U(x,y)$ is well defined. Since the time derivative vanishes, $U(x,y)$ satisfies:

$$\left(\frac{\partial U(x,y)}{\partial x}\right)^2 + \left(\frac{\partial U(x,y)}{\partial y}\right)^2 = V(x,y). \qquad (2.9)$$

Since eq. 2.9 is just the image irradiance equation, eq. 2.2, it suggests that $U(\cdot)$ *can be identified with* $z(x,y)$. Also, u and v can be identified with $-p$ and $-q$, respectively, from eq. 2.7, where $(p, q) \equiv \nabla z$. Thus the minimal cost trajectories are curves of steepest descent, and are just the *characteristic strips* [4,15].

Note also that $U \geq 0$, and that $U = 0$ only at the singular point. Thus, the solution to the image irradiance equation that is locally concave at the singular point has been automatically selected by this formulation; the solution that is locally convex at the singular point is just its negative. The function U is unique, since it is equal to the infimum of the cost in the optimal control problem, which must be unique. Since an infimum of the cost always exists, the function U always exists. It must be continuous, but need not be differentiable.

This formulation also gives a way of computing U. Clearly, $U(x, y, 0) = 0$ for all (x, y), while $U(x, y, T)$ is monotonically increasing in time: extending a trajectory cannot result in a reduced cost. Therefore, by solving eq. 2.8 iteratively in time, with initial condition $U(\cdot, T) = 0$ at $T = 0$, a sequence of functions $U(x, y, T)$ is obtained which at every point converges monotonically upward to $z(x, y)$ as $T \to \infty$. Because this convergence is pointwise monotonic, it is clearly stable.

For the actual implementation, an iterative procedure is used that is justified by its exact relation to a discretized control problem [8]. The continuous image plane is replaced by an image discretized into pixels, and the trajectory described by eq. 2.3 is approximated by a Markov process. This is described in detail in the next section. It can be shown that this gives a discrete approximation U^h to U, which converges to the continuous U as the spatial grid size h approaches zero [9,13]. However, a naive discretization of eq. 2.8 does *not* necessarily give a stably convergent algorithm.

3   Algorithm Description

A more detailed description of the algorithm and its derivation is now presented. We consider a control problem defined on the discrete grid of pixels and chosen to approximate the continuous calculus of variations problem described above. h is the pixel spacing. For the discrete case, a 'particle' trajectory is a sequence of discrete jumps between grid sites—a poor approximation to a continuous trajectory. In order to better approximate a continuous trajectory on a discrete grid, an element of randomness is introduced.

The control problem is as follows: a 'particle', with initial image plane location $\phi_0 \equiv (i_0, j_0)h$, jumps between neighboring pixel sites in response to control parameters $\mathbf{C} \equiv (u(k), v(k))$, where k indicates the time step. (A 4–neighborhood is assumed.) The jumps are probabilistic, but it is required that on average

$$\langle \phi(k + 1) - \phi(k) \rangle = \Delta t \mathbf{C}(k), \qquad (3.10)$$

in analogy with eq. 2.3. Here Δt is the time increment from time step k to step $k+1$, and $<>$ denotes the noise average. Let $\eta(k)$ be the random vector representing the jump at time k: $\eta(k) \equiv \phi(k + 1) - \phi(k)$. The jump probabilities are assigned as follows. When $u = v = 0$, $\mathbf{P}(\eta = 0) = 1$, with all other probabilities zero. In this case, Δt is arbitrarily chosen to be 1. Otherwise,

$$\mathbf{P}\left(\eta(k) = h(\mathrm{sgn}(u), 0) \mid C(k) = (u, v), (C(i), \eta(i)), i < k\right)$$

$$= \Delta t |u|/h = |u|/(|u| + |v|)$$

$$\mathbf{P}\left(\eta(k) = h(0, \mathrm{sgn}(v)) \mid C(k) = (u, v), (C(i), \eta(i)), i < k\right)$$

$$= \Delta t |v|/h = |v|/(|u| + |v|), \qquad (3.11)$$

again with all other probabilities zero. Eq. 3.11 implies that the particle jumps by one lattice site at each iteration (for a nonzero control), and therefore moves on the lattice with maximum speed, causing the algorithm to converge quickly. This has been achieved by taking Δt to depend explicitly on the controls as $\Delta t = h/(|u| + |v|)$. It is clear that eq. 3.11 implies eq. 3.10.

The analog to the calculus of variations problem is as follows: choose the control parameters to minimize the *expected* cost for the discrete trajectories:

$$U^h(\phi_0, K) = \inf\{$$

$$\left\langle \tfrac{1}{2} \sum_{k=0}^{K} \Delta t\, (u(k), v(k))\, (u(k)^2 + v(k)^2 + V(\phi(k))) \right\rangle\}, \qquad (3.12)$$

where the infimization is over all nonanticapative control sequences $\{(u(k), v(k)), k = 0, \ldots K\}$ (i.e., controls which do not depend on the future history of the particle) [8]. It can be shown the value function U^h for this discrete control problem converges to the continuous value function as the grid spacing is taken to zero [9, 13].

A dynamical programming equation can be derived for this control problem as in the previous section:

$$U^h(\phi_0, K) = \inf_{(u(0), v(0))}\{$$

$$\tfrac{1}{2}\Delta t(u(0), v(0))\, (u(0)^2 + v(0)^2 + V(\phi_0)) \qquad (3.13)$$

$$+ \langle U^h(\phi_0 + \eta, K - 1) \rangle\}.$$

The expectation in this equation is easily calculated from eq. 3.11; for nonzero controls it is

$$\frac{|u| U^h(\phi_0 + h(\mathrm{sgn}(u), 0)) + |v| U^h(\phi_0 + h(0, \mathrm{sgn}(v)))}{|u| + |v|}.$$

Performing the minimization in eq. 3.13 is slightly complicated since the cases with $\mathbf{C}$ in different quadrants must be treated separately. Eventually, the following simple algorithm is obtained. Define

$$U^h_{N1} = \mathrm{Min}(U^h(\phi \pm (1, 0)h),$$

$$U^h_{N2} = \mathrm{Min}(U^h(\phi \pm (0, 1)h),$$

and let $D_N \equiv U^h_{N2} - U^h_{N1}$. The update equation is

$$\hat{U}^h(\phi, K + 1) = \begin{cases} \tfrac{1}{2}\left((2h^2 V - D_N^2)^{1/2} + U^h_{N2} + U^h_{N1}\right) \\ \qquad \text{if } h^2 V(\phi) > D_N^2 \\ \\ h|V|^{1/2}(\phi) + \mathrm{Min}_i(U^h_{Ni}) \\ \qquad \text{otherwise.} \end{cases}$$

$$(3.14)$$

The lower case corresponds to the minimum in eq. 3.13 being realized on one of the axes in the u–v plane (with the origin excluded); the upper corresponds to an off-axis minimum. As in the previous section, the initial value for $U^h(\phi, \cdot)$ can be taken as 0. Since the expected cost for an optimal trajectory cannot decrease with time, an iterative solution $U^h(\phi, K)$ to the above equation increases monotonically at every point. This algorithm is more efficient than the one previously reported in [14] because the time increment Δt is adjusted optimally as a function of the controls. In fact, one can show in the case of a single singular point that the iterative scheme described above is a contraction, and thus any initial condition can be used. We note, however, that in general it is better to use a large initial condition. Such an initial condition is necessary in the setup of the next section, which deals with the case of multiple singular points.

To avoid indeterminacy, it is necessary to impose the boundary condition that no trajectory exits the image, as is easily done [14]; the significance of this is discussed below. Then, assuming that there are singular points in the image where $V = 0$, as $k \to \infty$ all optimal trajectories must converge to the singular points. Thus $U^h(\phi, K)$ converges monotonically as $K \to \infty$ to a solution $z = U^h(\phi)$; in fact, convergence occurs in a finite number of iterations [13]. This solution satisfies a discretized version of the shape–from–shading equation [14], and is always nonnegative, since the summand in eq. 3.12 is. Also, $z = 0$ at a singular point: a trajectory beginning at a singular point achieves minimal cost by remaining there, since $V = 0$ at the point. Thus, z attains a local minimum at a singular point. Also, as in eq. 2.7, the expected optimal trajectories are approximate curves of steepest descent [14].

The algorithm described in this section is appropriate for *unimodal* images—images containing just one singular point where the height has either a local minimum or maximum. For these images, the iterative solution of eq. 3.14 will correctly reconstruct the original surface at all points where this surface is theoretically determined [15]—that is, at all points connected by a steepest descent curve on the original surface to the singular point. Such points "learn" their height from the singular point. In contrast, at other image points the surface reconstruction can be ambiguous [15]. These ambiguous points lie on steepest descent curves that exit the image rather than terminating at the singular point. Imposing the boundary condition as above that no trajectory exits the image only affects the surface reconstruction at these ambiguous points. Our algorithm does not necessarily reproduce the original surface at ambiguous points. A modified algorithm appropriate for the multimodal case (many singular points, or even singular sets) is described in the next section.

4 Modifications of the Algorithm

An important modification introduces a *terminal cost* term into the cost function. This gives an algorithm capable of dealing with multimodal images. Including this term, the minimal cost is (compare eq. 3.12):

$$U^h(\phi_0, K) = \inf_{(u,v)} \ \Big\langle g(\phi(K)) + \tfrac{1}{2} \times$$

$$\sum_{k=0}^{K-1} \Delta t\, (u(k), v(k))\, \big(u(k)^2 + v(k)^2 + V(\phi(k))\big)\Big\rangle. \tag{4.15}$$

The terminal cost, $g(\phi(K))$, introduces a penalty term for a trajectory stopping at the position $\phi(K)$. It causes an optimal trajectory to not remain in regions of high terminal cost, and converge instead to points of low terminal cost. This can dramatically improve the convergence speed of the algorithm even in the case of a single singular point. A high terminal cost is necessary for the multimodal setup with many singular points, where it can be used to distinguish between singular points of different type (concave, convex, saddle). In the final surface solution, only a concave–type singular point should be the terminus for optimal trajectories, since these are descending curves. By placing a high terminal cost at other singular points, trajectories can be prohibited from terminating at these points. Then the surface solution will only be "learned" from the concave singular points. Also, if the heights of the concave singular points are known, e.g., using stereo, then this can be specified in the algorithm by setting the terminal costs at these points equal to their heights. Since the singular points are distinctive, it is likely that their heights, and the local nature of the surface, can be determined easily from stereo.

The algorithm can also be adapted easily to the case in which the heights are known at the maximum singular points. We are investigating the possibility of using preliminary, incorrect reconstructions as the basis for determining the correct relative heights of two local minima whose "domains of attraction" touch.

The dynamical programming equation corresponding to the cost in eq. 4.15 is exactly the same as eq. 3.14, as is easily seen. The algorithm differs only in the initial condition for U^h: clearly, U^h should be set initially to $g(\phi)$, not 0 as before. Thus, from the optimal control viewpoint, the choice of initial values for U^h in the algorithm has a concrete and intuitive interpretation.

In another modification, the minimizing controller is allowed to terminate the motion of the particle at any time, and pay the terminal cost corresponding to its stopping point. Since the controller prefers to halt the motion rather that permit an increased cost, the cost cannot increase over time. Thus, this results in an algorithm that converges monotonically. The dynamical programming equation is similar to the previous one: the updated value for $U^h(\phi)$ should now be taken as

$$\text{Min}\left(\hat{U}^h(\phi), g(\phi)\right),$$

where $g(\phi)$ is the terminal cost, and $\hat{U}^h(\phi)$ is as in eq. 3.14. The extra minimization in this updating equation accounts for the possibility that the particle stops after zero iterations, with the entire cost given by the terminal cost.

The algorithm described above is of the Jacobi type, with the surface updated everywhere in parallel at each iteration. It can be shown that the algorithm also converges if implemented via Gauss–Seidel, with updated surface estimates used as soon as they are available [13]. Our experiments show that this produces a significant speedup.

5 Proof of Equivalence

In this section we will assume the situation of *vertical light*, as described in Section 2. For this case (and under suitable assumptions) the height function has a representation in terms of an associated calculus of variations problem. For the general case of *oblique light* there is a representation in terms of a differential game [13].

The data available for the determination of the function $z(\cdot)$ is encoded in the intensity function $I(x, y)$ determined by eq. 2.1. I is well defined at all points (x, y) where $z(\cdot)$ is differentiable. We will always assume that the function $I(\cdot)$ is defined on a bounded open set of the form $G = \cap_{i=1}^{N} G_i$, $N < \infty$, where each G_i has a C^1 boundary ∂G_i. Let $\hat{n}_i(x, y)$ denote the inward normal to G_i at $(x, y) \in \partial G_i$. First consider the following situation.

Assumption 5.1 1. $z(\cdot)$ is C^1 on $\overline{G}$.
  2. There is exactly one point $(\tilde{x}, \tilde{y})$ such that $\nabla z(\tilde{x}, \tilde{y}) = 0$.
  3. $(\tilde{x}, \tilde{y})$ is a local minimum.
  4. $\nabla z(x, y) \cdot \hat{n}_i(x, y) < 0$ whenever $(x, y) \in \partial G \cap \partial G_i$.

(4) implies that the steepest descent direction is always inward on the boundary. We next define a calculus of variations problem. Fix $(x, y) \in \overline{G}$, and set

$$U(x, y) = \inf \int_0^\tau L(\phi(s), \dot{\phi}(s)) ds. \qquad (5.16)$$

Here $\tau = \inf\{t : \phi(t) = (\tilde{x}, \tilde{y})\}$, and the infimum is over all piecewise continuously differentiable paths $\phi : [0, \infty) \to \overline{G}$ that satisfy $\phi(0) = (x, y)$. The variational integrand $L(\cdot)$ is given by

$$
\begin{aligned}
L((x, y), (u, v)) &= \frac{1}{2}(u^2 + v^2) + \frac{1}{2}\left(\frac{1}{I(x, y)^2} - 1\right) \\
&= \frac{1}{2}(u^2 + v^2) + \frac{1}{2}|\nabla z(x, y)|^2.
\end{aligned}
$$

We follow the usual convention of defining $\inf \emptyset = +\infty$. Thus if $\phi(t) \neq (\tilde{x}, \tilde{y})$ for all t, then $\tau = +\infty$.

Theorem 5.2 *Under the conditions of Assumption 5.1 we have*

$$z(x, y) - z(\tilde{x}, \tilde{y}) = U(x, y).$$

Proof. Let $\phi(\cdot)$ be any piecewise continuously differentiable path that starts as (x, y). For all $\varepsilon \geq 0$ define

$$\tau^\varepsilon = \inf\{t : |\phi(t) - (\tilde{x}, \tilde{y})| \leq \varepsilon\}.$$

Fix $\delta > 0$ and choose $\varepsilon > 0$ such that

$$z(x, y) \leq z(\tilde{x}, \tilde{y}) + \delta$$

for $|(x, y) - (\tilde{x}, \tilde{y})| \leq \varepsilon$.

To prove $z(x, y) - z(\tilde{x}, \tilde{y}) \leq U(x, y)$, we consider two cases. First assume $\tau^\varepsilon = +\infty$. By Assumption 5.1 there exists $c > 0$ such that

$$L((x, y), (u, v)) \geq c$$

for all (x, y) satisfying $|(x, y) - (\tilde{x}, \tilde{y})| \geq \varepsilon$ and all $(u, v) \in \mathbf{R}^2$. Thus, in such a case

$$\int_0^\tau L(\phi(s), \dot{\phi}(s)) ds = \int_0^{\tau^\varepsilon} L(\phi(s), \dot{\phi}(s)) ds = +\infty.$$

Next assume $\tau^\varepsilon < \infty$. By the chain rule,

$$\frac{d}{dt}[-z(\phi(t))] = -\nabla z(\phi(t)) \cdot \dot{\phi}(t) \leq \frac{1}{2}|\dot{\phi}(t)|^2 + \frac{1}{2}|\nabla z(\phi(t))|^2$$

almost surely in t. Therefore

$$
\begin{aligned}
z(x, y) - z(\tilde{x}, \tilde{y}) &\leq z(x, y) - z(\phi(\tau^\varepsilon)) + \delta \\
&= -[z(\phi(\tau^\varepsilon)) - z(\phi(0))] + \delta \\
&= \int_0^{\tau^\varepsilon} -\nabla z(\phi(t)) \cdot \dot{\phi}(t) dt + \delta \\
&\leq \int_0^{\tau^\varepsilon} L(\phi(t), \dot{\phi}(t)) dt + \delta \\
&\leq \int_0^{\tau} L(\phi(t), \dot{\phi}(t)) dt + \delta.
\end{aligned}
$$

Sending $\delta \to 0$ we obtain $z(x, y) - z(\tilde{x}, \tilde{y}) \leq U(x, y)$.

To prove $z(x, y) - z(\tilde{x}, \tilde{y}) \geq U(x, y)$, let $\phi(\cdot)$ be a solution (note that there may not be uniqueness since z is only assumed C^1) to the equation

$$\dot{\phi}(t) = -\nabla z(\phi(t)), \quad \phi(0) = (x, y).$$

By Assumption 5.1 $\phi(\cdot)$ never touches ∂G for $t > 0$, and therefore the solution is well defined for all $t > 0$. Let $\tau = \inf\{t : \phi(t) = (\tilde{x}, \tilde{y})\}$ and let $a \wedge b$ denote the smaller of a and b. For any $t < \infty$, we have

$$
\begin{aligned}
z(x, y) - z(\tilde{x}, \tilde{y}) &\geq z(\phi(0)) - z(\phi(t \wedge \tau)) \\
&= -[z(\phi(t \wedge \tau)) - z(\phi(0))] \\
&= \int_0^{t \wedge \tau} -\nabla z(\phi(s)) \cdot \dot{\phi}(s) ds \\
&= \int_0^{t \wedge \tau} |\nabla z(\phi(s))|^2 ds \\
&= \int_0^{t \wedge \tau} L(\phi(s), \dot{\phi}(s)) ds.
\end{aligned}
$$

Sending $t \to \infty$ we conclude that

$$z(x, y) - z(\tilde{x}, \tilde{y}) \geq \int_0^\tau L(\phi(s), \dot{\phi}(s)) ds \geq U(x, y).$$

∎

The solution to the calculus of variations problem uniquely identifies the height function up to an overall translation in z. This ambiguity can be removed by specifying $z(\tilde{x}, \tilde{y})$.

We next consider a more general situation involving more than one stationary point. Let M be the set of local minima of $z(\cdot)$.

Assumption 5.3 1. $z(\cdot)$ is C^1 on $\overline{G}$.
  2. The value of $z(\cdot)$ is known on M.
  3. $\nabla z(x, y) \cdot \hat{n}_i(x, y) < 0$ whenever $(x, y) \in \partial G \cap \partial G_i$.

Define the terminal cost function

$$g(x, y) = \begin{cases} z(x, y) & \text{if } (x, y) \in M, \\ +\infty & \text{otherwise.} \end{cases}$$

Consider the calculus of variations problem

$$U(x,y) = \inf \left[\int_0^\tau L(\phi(s), \dot{\phi}(s))ds + g(\phi(\tau)) \right]. \quad (5.17)$$

Here the infimum is over all $\tau < \infty$ and absolutely continuous paths $\phi : [0, \tau] \to \overline{G}$ that satisfy $\phi(0) = (x, y)$. Unlike the case of a single stationary point, it is necessary that a terminal cost be included in order to guarantee that trajectories do not get "stuck" at stationary points that are not local minima.

We have the following result for this case.

Theorem 5.4 *Under the conditions of Assumption 5.3 we have*

$$z(x, y) = U(x, y).$$

Remarks on the proof. The proof is very similar to that of Theorem 5.2 and will only be sketched. Consider any path $\phi(\cdot)$ which starts at (x, y) and for which the cost

$$\int_0^\tau L(\phi(s), \dot{\phi}(s))ds + g(\phi(\tau)) \quad (5.18)$$

is finite. Boundedness of the cost implies $\phi(\tau) \in M$. Suppose $\phi(\tau) = (\tilde{x}, \tilde{y})$. The proof of Theorem 5.2 then shows that $z(x, y) - z(\tilde{x}, \tilde{y}) \leq \int_0^\tau L(\phi(s), \dot{\phi}(s))ds$. Together with the definition of $g(\cdot)$ this implies $z(x, y) \leq U(x, y)$.

Next consider the reverse inequality. As in the proof of Theorem 5.2, we would like to construct a particular path $\phi(\cdot)$ that starts at (x, y) so that the cost (5.18) is arbitrarily close to $z(x, y)$. We first note that by a perturbation argument [15,12,17] we can assume that there are at most finitely many points such that $\nabla z(x, y) = 0$. It can be shown that there exists a dense subset D of $\overline{G}$ with the property that whenever the path $\phi(\cdot)$ satisfies

$$\dot{\phi}(t) = -\nabla z(\phi(t)), \phi(0) \in D,$$

then $\phi(t)$ converges to a local minimum $(\tilde{x}, \tilde{y})$ of $z(\cdot)$ as $t \to \infty$. Using the argument of Theorem 5.2 and the fact that $z(\phi(t))$ is nondecreasing we conclude $z(x, y) \geq U(x, y)$ for $(x, y) \in D$. By continuity of both $z(\cdot)$ and $U(\cdot)$ (which is easy to prove) we have $z(x, y) \geq U(x, y)$ for $(x, y) \in \overline{G}$. ∎

Previous uniqueness proofs [1,19,16] assumed that $z(x, y)$ was at least C^2; here z is only assumed C^1. A fortiori, no conditions are placed on the second derivatives of the intensity; in particular, the singular points are not required to be "good" or "nondegenerate" [19,16].

6   Illumination from a General Direction

For a Lambertian surface, the image irradiance equation for the intensity is:

$$I(x, y) = \hat{L} \cdot \frac{(-z_x, -z_y, 1)}{(1 + z_x^2 + z_y^2)^{1/2}},$$

where $\hat{L}$ is a unit vector giving the light source direction, and z_x, z_y are partial derivatives of the height. For simplicity and w.l.o.g., we take the x-component of $\hat{L}$

to be zero. After some algebra, this equation may be rewritten as:

$$I^2 z_x^2 + J z_y^2 + 2 L_z L_y z_y + (I^2 - L_z^2) = 0,$$

with $J(x, y) \equiv I^2(x, y) - L_y^2$.

Define a new variable $\xi \equiv (x, y, z) \cdot \hat{L}$ measuring the "height" along the light direction rather than the viewer direction $\hat{z}$. This is done so that the local cost at singular points will be zero, like V previously, causing optimal trajectories to terminate at these points. Then

$$\xi_x = L_z z_x, \qquad \xi_y = L_y + L_z z_y.$$

Substituting in the previous equation yields

$$I^2 \xi_x^2 + J \xi_y^2 + 2(1 - I^2) L_y \xi_y - (1 - I^2) = 0.$$

J, the coefficient of ξ_y^2, is positive in an image region B that includes the singular points. When $I^2 = L_y^2$, the angle between the surface normal and $\hat{L}$ is large enough that it may correspond to a point on the occluding boundary.

In the image region B, we consider a control problem analogous to that of Section 2: a 'particle' initially located at (x, y) is controlled using the parameters u, v:

$$\dot{x} = I^2(x, y)u, \qquad \dot{y} = J(x, y)v - (1 - I^2(x, y))L_y.$$

u, v are chosen to infimize a cost function for the particle's trajectory

$$U(x, y, T) = \inf_{(u,v)}$$

$$\tfrac{1}{2} \int_0^T ds(I^2(x, y)u^2 + J(x, y)v^2 + (1 - I^2(x, y))). \quad (6.19)$$

As before the integrand is nonnegative throughout the region B, and the local cost $1 - I^2$ vanishes at singular points. Eq. 2.4 for the vertical–light case $L_y = 0$ can be recovered by dividing eq. 6.19 by I^2.

This control problem is essentially equivalent to the one previously considered, and results similar to those of the previous sections are easily obtainable. In particular, by a Schwarz inequality argument as in Section 5,

$$\begin{aligned}
\frac{d}{dt}[-\xi(\phi(t))] &= -\nabla\xi(\phi(t)) \cdot \dot{\phi}(t) \\
&= -\xi_x I^2 u - \xi_y \left(Jv - (1 - I^2)L_y \right) \\
&\leq \tfrac{1}{2}(I^2 u^2 + Jv^2 + \\
&\quad I^2 \xi_x^2 + J \xi_y^2 + 2\xi_y(1 - I^2)L_y) \\
&= \tfrac{1}{2} \left(I^2 u^2 + Jv^2 + 1 - I^2 \right),
\end{aligned}$$

which is just the integrand of eq. 6.19. This gives the necessary generalization for the rigorous proof of equivalence. Similarly, an algorithm can be defined in the same way as before, and will recover the correct solution near concave (or convex) singular points.

In the image region where $I^2 - L_y^2 < 0$, the optimal control representation of the problem no longer suffices. Instead, there is a representation in terms of a *differential game* (see e.g. [3]). However, it is a particularly simple one, in which the opposing controllers effectively direct the 'particle' motion in orthogonal directions, and where the cost also splits into a sum of terms depending on the different control parameters. Thus, the Isaacs condition and the existence of a "value" follow.

The 'particle' dynamics for the differential game are:

$$\dot{x} = I^2 u, \qquad \dot{y} = J\left(\theta(J)v_1 + \theta(-J)v_2\right) - (1 - I^2)L_y,$$

where

$$\theta(x) = \begin{cases} 1 & \text{if } x \geq 0, \\ 0 & \text{if } x < 0. \end{cases}$$

When $I^2 - L_y^2 < 0$, a restriction on the control direction can be imposed:

$$L_y \hat{C}_y \leq -\operatorname{sgn}(L_y)\sqrt{L_y^2 - I^2},$$

where $\hat{C}$ is the unit vector in the $(\dot{x}, \dot{y})$ direction. This follows from the requirement that the surface is visible, i.e. that the height function $z(x, y)$ is a graph.

The player associated with u and v_1 seeks to minimize the value function of the game, while the v_2 player seeks to maximize it. The value that opposing players attempt to control is

$$U(\phi, t) \equiv \tfrac{1}{2} \times$$

$$\int_0^T ds(I^2 u^2 + J(\theta(J)v_1^2 + \theta(-J)v_2^2) + (1 - I^2)).$$

A precise description of the differential game is somewhat technical (see e.g. [3]). Here we simply note that the properly defined value gives the height function (under suitable conditions), and that an algorithm on a discrete grid for approximating this value function can be derived that is similar to the vertical–light algorithm.

The algorithm is as follows: define $V \equiv (1 - I^2)/J$, generalizing from the vertical light case. Also, define

$$\xi_{N2}^h \equiv \begin{cases} \operatorname{Min}(h^{-1}\xi(\phi \pm h(0,1)) \pm VL_y) & \text{if } J > 0 \\ h^{-1}\xi(\phi - \operatorname{sgn}(L_y)h(0,1)) - V|L_y| & \text{if } J < 0, \end{cases}$$

and

$$\xi_{N1}^h = \operatorname{Min}(h^{-1}\xi(\phi \pm h(1,0)), \qquad D_N \equiv \xi_{N2}^h - \xi_{N1}^h,$$

where D_N is again the natural generalization from the vertical light case. Finally, define

$$S = \frac{I|J|^{1/2}}{I^2 + J} \left| VL_z^2(I^2 + J)/J - D_N^2 \right|^{1/2}.$$

For $J > 0$, the update equation is:

$$\hat{\xi}(\phi) = h \begin{cases} \xi_{N1}^h + |V|^{1/2}L_z \\ \quad \text{if } D_N > |V|^{1/2}L_z \\[2mm] S + \frac{I^2\xi_{N1}^h + J\xi_{N2}^h}{I^2 + J} \\ \quad \text{if } -|V|^{1/2}L_z(I/J^{1/2}) \leq D_N \leq |V|^{1/2}L_z \\[2mm] \xi_{N2}^h + |V|^{1/2}L_z(I/J^{1/2}) \\ \quad \text{if } D_N < -|V|^{1/2}L_z(I/J^{1/2}). \end{cases}$$

For $J < 0$, the update equation is:

$$\hat{\xi}(\phi) = h \begin{cases} \xi_{N2}^h - |V|^{1/2}L_z(I/|J|^{1/2}) \\ \quad \text{if } D_N < |V|^{1/2}L_z(I/|J|^{1/2}) \\[2mm] S + \frac{I^2\xi_{N1}^h + J\xi_{N2}^h}{I^2 + J} \\ \quad \text{otherwise.} \end{cases}$$

This algorithm clearly reduces to the previous one for vertical light when $L_y = 0$, $J = I^2$, $L_z = 1$. Although it is apparently singular at $J = 0$ or $I^2 + J = 0$, the correct update can be shown to depend continuously on these quantities. If necessary, to avoid artificial numerical instabilities while maintaining the algorithm's speed, the original image intensity can be perturbed slightly to avoid such zeros. For greater speed per iteration, most of the intensity–dependent terms in the above algorithm can be precomputed. Then, at each lattice site, the algorithm requires in each iteration at most a single square root operation, and five multiplications.

This algorithm, as in the vertical light case, can be modified to give monotonic convergence. Instead of $\hat{\xi}(\phi)$, take the updated value for ξ as

$$\operatorname{Min}\left(\hat{\xi}(\phi), g(\phi)\right),$$

where g is the terminal cost, i.e. the (large) initial value for $\xi(\phi)$. As before, this extra minimization corresponds in the differential game to allowing the minimizing player to halt the particle trajectory at any time. The minimizer will stop the motion rather than pay an increased cost for a longer trajectory, and therefore additional iterations cannot increase the value of $\xi(\phi)$. This algorithm also converges if implemented via Gauss–Seidel [13].

7   Experiments

Figure 1 displays a 32 by 32 surface parabolic surface which is assumed to be imaged from above. The image has one singular point. Assuming vertical light, the image intensity was first computed using the discretization of the derivative implicit in eq. 3.14 [14]. With this choice, the original surface is a fixed point of the algorithm and should be reconstructed exactly. Using Jacobi updates, the algorithm converged to the correct solution to within, on average, one part in 10^7 after 63 iterations. In general, the convergence time is expected to be on the order of the maximum length of an optimal trajectory. Since from eq. 3.11 an optimal trajectory jumps one lattice site per iteration, when the number of iterations becomes greater than the maximum trajectory length, then all image points are able to "learn" their heights from the singular points. For the given surface, the maximal trajectory length is on the order of 32, since trajectories starting at the image corners must zigzag to the singular point at the center of the image.

Convergence using Gauss–Seidel updating was faster: it was obtained after just 4 iterations. Gauss–Seidel was performed by changing the direction of the pass over the image after each iteration [2].

For an image obtained by analytically differentiating the displayed surface, the average and maximal errors were .8 and 1.6 (the latter obtained at the image boundary), compared with a range for the surface height of 25. The algorithm has also been applied to a noisy image of this surface; the result is a noisy approximation of the surface. The surface was also reconstructed assuming oblique lighting.

For comparison, Figs. 2, 3 display the result of applying our implementation of Horn's algorithm [5] to a similar surface. The intensity is computed differently than before, using the discrete forward derivatives appropriate for this algorithm. Even after 3072 iterations, the algorithm has not converged to the correct solution. We have also implemented the variational algorithms of [10] and [21], and applied them to this surface with similar results. As also noted by [11], standard variational algorithms often give a wrong, saddle–shaped surface for such simple images containing one singular point.

Figure 4 shows a more complicated 128 by 128 surface. As for Figure 1, the intensity was first computed assuming the discretization of eq. 3.14. The algorithm this time incorporated a terminal cost—an initial value for U—which was large everywhere but at the concave singular points. At these points, U was initialized to the known height values. For vertical light, the algorithm converged to a perfect reconstruction of the original surface in 100 iterations. As expected, the convergence time is on the order of the longest optimal trajectory. Using Gauss–Seidel, convergence was achieved in 10 iterations. When the intensity was derived analytically, the algorithm again converged in 10 iterations using Gauss–Seidel, with an average error of 1.7 compared to a surface range of 51 (Figure 5). Because the surface does not obey the boundary condition that it is decreasing in from the boundary (Section 3), the reconstruction is incorrect in places at the boundary, though it is good in the interior. This is clear in Figure 6, which displays the difference between the reconstruction and the original surface. This surface was also reconstructed assuming oblique light at an angle of 17.5° to the vertical. For an intensity derived as for eq. 3.14, convergence to within one part in 10^{-7} was obtained within 120 iterations. Using Gauss–Seidel, convergence was obtained in 11 iterations. Reconstruction for the analytically–derived intensity function was obtained in 14 iterations, with an average error of 2.2. As previously, the reconstruction was good in the interior but incorrect along one boundary (Figure 7).

Figure 8 shows the result for vertical light of applying the algorithm without the terminal cost. The algorithm reconstructs a surface that is locally concave at all singular points; it is correct in the neighborhood of those singular points where the surface is in fact locally concave. Note the sharp orientation discontinuities at the boundaries between the regions associated with different singular points.

Finally, our algorithm has been applied to the real 200×200 image shown in Figure 9, which was provided to us by Yvan Leclerc of SRI. The light is from above at $(0, .488, .873)$. For the reconstruction, just one singular point was used, located on the tip of the nose, although the image actually contains several. This has the effect of planing down the surface bumps associated with the other singular points. Figure 10 shows the reconstruction obtained using Gauss–Seidel after 6 iterations, illuminated from the same direction as the original. Figure 11 shows this reconstruction illuminated from below. Convergence has essentially been achieved over the face. This reconstruction took about 9 seconds of CPU time on a DEC 5000 workstation. Standard variational algorithms typically require thousands of iterations [5]. Finally, Figure 12 shows the surface reconstruction.

For comparison, Figures 13, 14 display the reconstruction obtained by the authors of [10] using a more standard variational method, developed for the purpose of including stereo information. Stereo information was used as an initial condition for this reconstruction.

Acknowledgments

We thank Yvan Leclerc for providing the image and reconstruction displayed in Figures 9, 13, 14, and for enjoyable conversations. We also thank Martin Bichsel for sending us [2].

References

1. A. R. Bruss, "The Eikonal Equation: Some Results Applicable to Computer Vision," *Journal of Math. Phys.* 23(5): 890-896, May 1982.

2. M. Bichsel, "A Simple Algorithm for Shape from Shading," MIT Media Lab Technical Report No. 172, October 1991.

3. R. J. Elliott, *Viscosity Solutions and Optimal Control*, Longman Scientific and Technical, New York, NY: 1987.

4. B.K.P. Horn, "Obtaining Shape from Shading Information," in *The Psychology of Computer Vision*, P. H. Winston (ed.), McGraw Hill: New York, 1975, pp. 115-155.

5. B.K.P. Horn, "Height and Gradient From Shading," *International Journal of Computer Vision* Vol. 5 No. 1, pp. 37–75, 1990.

6. B. K. P. Horn and M. J. Brooks, "The Variational Approach to Shape from Shading," *Computer Vision, Graphics, and Image Processing*, Vol. 33, pp. 174–208, 1986.

7. K. Ikeuchi and B. K. P. Horn, "Numerical Shape from Shading and Occluding Boundaries," *Artificial Intelligence*, Vol. 17, Nos. 1–3, pp. 141–184, August 1981.

8. H. J. Kushner, "Numerical methods for stochastic control problems in continuous time,", *SIAM J. Control and Optimization*, Vol. 28, pp. 999–1048, 1990.

9. H. J. Kushner and P. Dupuis, *Numerical Methods for Stochastic Control Problems in Continuous Time*, Springer–Verlag: New York, 1992.

10. Y. G. Leclerc and A. F. Bobick, "The Direct Computation of Height from Shading," *Proc. IEEE Conference on Computer Vision and Pattern Recognition*, Lahaina, Maui, Hawaii, 1991, pp. 552-558.

11. Y. G. Leclerc and A. F. Bobick, *personal communication*.

12. J. Milnor, *Morse Theory*, Annals of Mathematics Studies 51. Princeton University: New Jersey, 1970.

13. Paul Dupuis and J. Oliensis, "Direct method for reconstructing shape from shading," in preparation.

14. J. Oliensis and Paul Dupuis, "Direct method for reconstructing shape from shading," *Proc. SPIE Conf. 1570 on Geometric Methods in Computer Vision*, San Diego, California, July 1991, pp. 116-128.

15. J. Oliensis, "Shape from Shading as a Partially Well–Constrained Problem," *Computer Vision, Graphics, and Image Processing: Image Understanding*, Vol. 54, No. 2, pp. 163-183, 1991.

16. J. Oliensis, "Uniqueness in Shape From Shading," *The International Journal of Computer Vision*, Vol 6, No. 2, pp. 75-104, 1991.

17. J. Palis and W. de Melo, *Geometric Theory of Dynamical Systems*. Springer-Verlag: NY, 1982.

18. B. V. H. Saxberg, "An Application of Dynamical Systems Theory to Shape From Shading," in *Proc. DARPA Image Understanding Workshop*, Palo Alto, CA, May 1989, pp. 1089-1104.

19. B. V. H. Saxberg, "A Modern Differential Geometric Approach to Shape from Shading," MIT Artificial Intelligence Laboratory, TR 1117, 1989.

20. E. Rouy, A. Tourin, "A Viscosity Solutions Approach To Shape–From–Shading," June 1991, to appear in *SIAM J. on Numerical Analysis*.

21. R. Szeliski, "Fast Shape from Shading," *Computer Vision, Graphics, and Image Processing: Image Understanding*, Vol. 53, pp. 129-153, 1991.

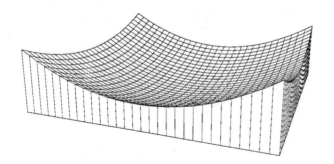

Fig. 1 Parabolic surface.

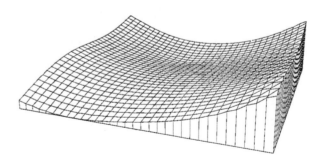

Fig. 2 Horn's algorithm: 128 iterations.

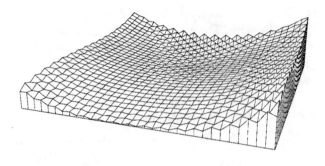

Fig. 3 Horn's algorithm: 3072 iterations.

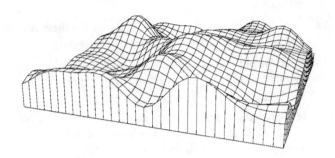

Fig. 4 Complex surface.

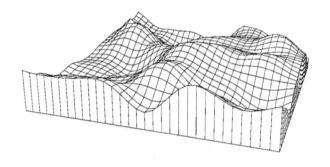

Fig. 5 Reconstruction.

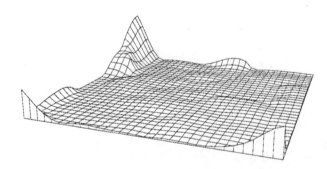

Fig. 6 Difference Surface.

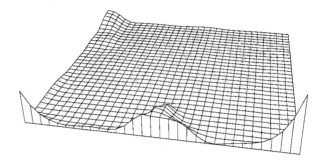

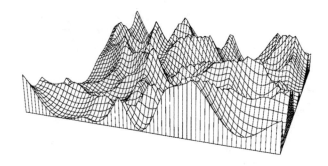

Fig. 7 Difference Surface.

Fig. 8 Result with no terminal cost.

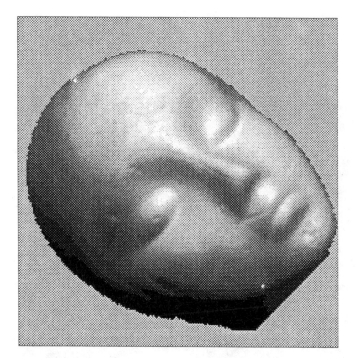

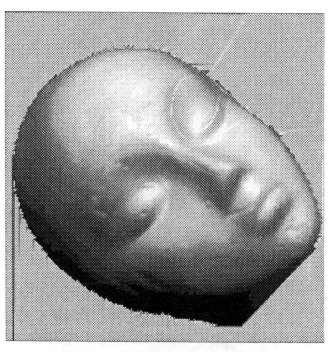

Fig. 9 Mannequin image.

Fig. 10 Reconstruction lighted from above.

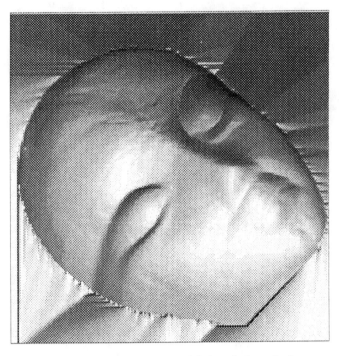

Fig. 11 Reconstruction lighted from below.

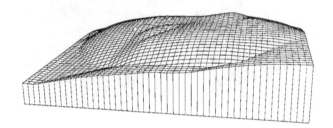

Fig. 12 Surface Reconstruction.

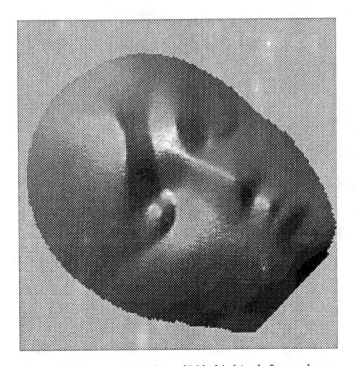

Fig. 13 Reconstruction [10] lighted from above.

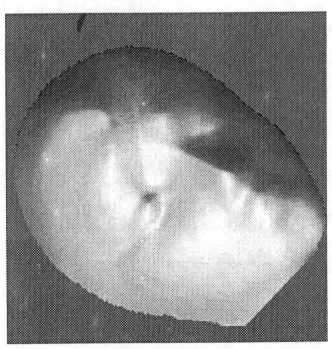

Fig. 14 Reconstruction [10] lighted from below.

Linear Shape From Shading

ALEX P. PENTLAND

Vision and Modeling Group, The Media Lab, Massachusetts Institute of Technology, Room E15–387, 20 Ames St., Cambridge, MA 02138

Abstract

In many situations the reflectance function of a surface is approximately linear, and there is an efficient closed-form solution to the shape-from-shading problem. When boundary conditions (e.g., edges, singular points) are not available, good estimates of shape may still be extracted by using the assumption of general viewing position. An improved method for estimating the illuminant direction is also presented.

1 Introduction

The extraction of shape from shading has a relatively long history within the field of computer vision. There have been two general classes of algorithm developed: global algorithms, which propagate information across a shaded surface starting from points with known surface orientation, and local algorithms, which attempt to estimate shape from local variations in image intensity.

Global algorithms, primarily due to Horn and his students [5, 6, 7], use assumptions about surface shape—primarily that the surface is smooth in some sense—in order to extract estimates of surface orientation. The smoothness assumption is used to relate adjoining points, enabling spatially isolated information about absolute surface orientation (which must be derived using some other technique) to be iteratively propagated across the surface. The use of a smoothness assumption, however, implies that the algorithms will not produce exact solutions except under certain conditions [8]. A subsequent integration step is normally required to convert estimated surface orientation into an estimate of surface shape.

Local algorithms, originally suggested by Pentland [1], also use assumptions about surface shape in order to extract estimates of surface orientation from the shading information within a small image neighborhood. As with the global estimation algorithms, integration is normally required to obtain the surface shape. These local methods of estimating surface orientation have been shown capable of producing good estimates of shape [1, 2, 3], however, they do not produce exact estimates except in quite limited situations [2, 4].

In this article I develop a new type of shape-from-shading algorithm, one that uses assumptions about the reflectance function, rather than using assumptions about the surface shape. The basic idea of this algorithm is to construct a linear approximation to the true reflectance function, thus permitting an extremely efficient closed-form solution for the surface shape. One important characteristic of the solution is that good estimates of shape can be obtained even when boundary conditions are not available, by use of the assumption of general viewing position.

2 The Imaging of Surfaces: Linear Reflectance Functions

The first step is to review the physics of how image shading is related to surface shape. As an example, let us start by considering a distantly illuminated surface whose shape is defined by the function $z = z(x, y)$, and with reflectance function $I(x, y) = R(p, q, \mathbf{L})$ where p and q are the slope of the surface along the x and y image directions respectively, for example,

$$p = \frac{\partial}{\partial x} z(x, y) \qquad q = \frac{\partial}{\partial y} z(x, y) \qquad (1)$$

and $\mathbf{L} = (x_L, y_L, z_L)$ is a unit vector in the mean illuminant direction. For mathematical simplicity, I will also assume orthographic projection onto the x, y plane, that the surface is not self-shadowing, and that $z < 0$ within the region of interest.

Given an image region with mean surface orientation (p_0, q_0), we can form a linear approximation to the reflectance function by taking a Taylor expansion of R around $(p, q) = (p_0, q_0)$ [9, 12],

$$I(x, y) \approx R(p_0, q_0, \mathbf{L})$$
$$+ (p - p_0) \frac{\partial R(p, q, \mathbf{L})}{\partial p}\bigg|_{p=p_0, q=q_0}$$
$$+ (q - q_0) \frac{\partial R(p, q, \mathbf{L})}{\partial q}\bigg|_{p=p_0, q=q_0} \quad (2)$$

Given a point on a smooth surface it is always possible to choose a neighborhood over which this approximation is quite accurate, because one can always find a neighborhood that contains a small range of (p, q) values, as is illustrated in figure 1a. Over a sufficiently small range of (p, q) values the true reflectance function $R(p, q, \mathbf{L})$ can always be accurately approximated by equation (2), as is illustrated by figure 1b.

Further, when the illuminant is at a large angle to the viewer (as in figure 1b) equation (2) provides a good approximation to the true reflectance function over *most* of the range of p and q. In general the range of (p, q) that can be accurately modeled by a single linear approximation becomes larger as the illuminant becomes more oblique, and smaller as the illuminant moves closer to the viewer.

As an example, for a Lambertian reflectance function and $(p_0, q_0) = (0, 0)$, the linear approximation to image intensity $I(x, y)$ will be

$$I(x, y) \approx \rho\lambda[\cos \sigma + p \cos \tau \sin \sigma$$
$$+ q \sin \tau \sin \sigma] \quad (3)$$

where ρ is the albedo of the surface, λ is the strength (flux density) of the illuminant at the surface, τ is the tilt of the illuminant (the angle the image plane component of the illuminant vector makes with the x-axis), and σ is its slant (the angle the illuminant vector makes with the z-axis), so that $\mathbf{L} = (x_L, y_L, z_L) = (\cos \tau \sin \sigma, \sin \tau \sin \sigma, \cos \sigma)$. When $\sigma > 45°$ (i.e., the illuminant is more than 45 degrees from the viewer) this approximation to the Lambertian reflectance function is accurate to within 10% for $-0.2 < p, q < 0.2$, a range typical of mountainous terrain in aerial imagery. It is accurate over the range $-1 < p, q < 1$ when $\sigma > 75°$.

Thus, within a constrained region it is often the case that the true surface reflectance function can be accurately approximated by a linear reflectance function. This can allow us to use specialized algorithms for solving the shape-from-shading problem that are much more efficient than techniques that solve the problem in complete generality. It can also free us from the need to know the surface's reflectance function, as we merely need to have a sufficiently restricted range of (p, q) or sufficiently oblique illumination for the linear approximation to be a good one.

3 Shape Recovery

Given a linear reflectance function, we have that

$$I(x, y) = k_1 + pk_2 + qk_3 \quad (4)$$

for some constants k_1, k_2 and k_3. I will refer to the vector (k_2, k_3, k_1) as the "generalized illuminant direction,"

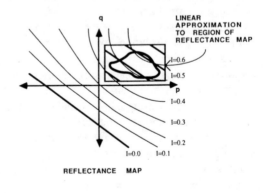

(A)   **(B)**

Fig. 1. (a) For smooth surfaces, a small image patch corresponds to a small range of (p, q) values. (b) Over a small range of (p, q) values, there is always a good linear approximation to the true reflectance function.

by analogy to the case of a Lambertian surface with mean normal $(p_0, q_0) = (0, 0)$ where we have that

$$k_1 = \cos \sigma$$

$$k_2 = \cos \tau \sin \sigma$$

$$k_3 = \sin \tau \sin \sigma \qquad (5)$$

and so $\mathbf{L} = (k_2, k_3, k_1)$.

Equation (4) may be transformed into the Fourier domain in order to obtain a convenient and efficient solution. Let $F_z(f, \theta)$ be the complex Fourier spectrum of $z(x, y)$ (where f is radial frequency and θ is orientation), then, because p and q are the partial derivatives of $z(x, y)$, their Fourier transforms $F_p(f, \theta)$ and $F_q(f, \theta)$ are simply

$$F_p(f, \theta) = 2\pi \cos (\theta) f e^{i\pi/2} F_z(f, \theta) \qquad (6)$$

$$F_q(f, \theta) = 2\pi \sin (\theta) f e^{i\pi/2} F_z(f, \theta) \qquad (7)$$

Equation (4) can now be rewritten in the Fourier domain as

$$F_I(f, \theta) = H(f, \theta) F_z(f, \theta) \qquad (8)$$

where $F_I(f, \theta)$ is the Fourier spectrum of the image and $H(f, \theta)$ is a linear transfer function which relates the Fourier transform of the image to that of the surface. Ignoring the singular DC term, $H(f, \theta)$ is simply

$$H(f, \theta) = 2\pi f e^{i\pi/2}[k_2 \cos \theta + k_3 \sin \theta] \quad (9)$$

Thus given a linear reflectance function, the surface shape can be estimated in closed form by use of the inverse transfer function, $H^{-1}(f, \theta)$,

$$F_z(f, \theta) = H^{-1}(f, \theta) F_I(f, \theta)$$

$$= (2\pi f e^{i\pi/2}[k_2 \cos \theta + k_3 \sin \theta])^{-1} F_I(f, \theta) \quad (10)$$

Assuming that the generalized illuminant direction is known, equation (10) may be used to recover the Fourier components of the surface shape. If only the ratio k_2/k_3 is known (i.e., the tilt component of the generalized illuminant direction), the surface's Fourier components may be recovered up to a multiplicative constant. Estimation of the generalized illuminant direction is discussed in section 3.1.

3.0.1 Boundary Conditions.

The Fourier components of the surface that are exactly perpendicular to the illuminant cannot be seen in the image data, and must either be obtained from other information sources or simply set to some default value. When boundary conditions—information about surface shape from con-

tours, singular points, or other sources—are available, they can be used to determine the Fourier components perpendicular to the illuminant; in this manner an exact recovery of surface shape can be achieved.

When boundary conditions are not available (as is often the case), the assumption of general viewing position may be invoked to argue that these unseen Fourier components should be assumed to be zero, because if they were large then small variations in viewing geometry would produce large changes in the estimated surface shape. I have found that in practice these default boundary conditions produce good estimates of shape whenever the surface is complex and irregular, however for regular geometric forms the estimated surface shape can be substantially in error.

3.0.2 Noise Sensitivity.

The recovery process can be improved by use of Weiner filtering to remove noise and nonlinear components of the image intensity pattern [10]. If the contaminating noise $N(f, \theta)$ is modeled as being proportional to $\|(k_2 \cos \theta + k_3 \sin \theta)\|$ (for example, as a fixed fraction of the spectral power along each image orientation), and the surface $S(f, \theta)$ is modeled as a fractal Brownian function [11, 12] whose power spectrum is proportional to f^{-4} (or, equivalently, as a second-order Markov random field or as a "thin-plate" model) then the optimal RMSE estimate of surface shape is

$$F_z(f, \theta) = H^{-1}(f, \theta) \|H(f, \theta)\|^2 \, [\|H(f, \theta)\|^2$$

$$+ \frac{\|N(f, \theta)\|}{\|S(f, \theta)\|}]^{-1} F_I(f, \theta)$$

$$= \{2\pi \sin (\sigma) f e^{i\pi/2}[sd + (k_2 \cos \theta$$

$$+ k_3 \sin \theta)]\}^{-1} F_I(f, \theta) \qquad (11)$$

where $s = \text{Sign}[\cos (\tau - \theta)]$ and $0.5 < d < 0.75$. In actual practice equation (11) has been found to perform much better than equation (10).

3.1 Estimating the Illuminant Direction

Pentland [13] introduced a method of estimating illuminant direction from the distribution of image derivatives as a function of image direction. The method works by assuming a statistically uniform distribution of surface orientations, and then performing a maximum-likelihood analysis to estimate the cosine variation in image gradient magnitude induced by the directionality of the illuminant. In summary, the result is that

$$(x_L^*, y_L^*) = (\beta^T\beta)^{-1}\beta^T(dI_1, dI_2, \ldots, dI_n) \quad (12)$$

where (x_L^*, y_L^*) are the unnormalized x and y components of the illuminant direction, β is a $2 \times n$ matrix of directions (dx_i, dy_i) and dI_i is the mean magnitude of $dI(x, y)/dx_i + dI(x, y)/dy_i$.

Given (x_L^*, y_L^*), the complete illuminant direction is simply

$$x_L = x_L^*/k, \quad y_L = y_L^*/k, \quad z_L = \sqrt{1 - x_L^2 - y_L^2}, \quad (13)$$

where

$$k = \sqrt{E(dI^2) - E(dI)^2} \quad (14)$$

and $E(dI)$ is the expected value of $dI/dx_i + dI/dy_i$ over all directions i.

This method has proven to be quite robust [2, 3, 13, 14], however the assumption of uniformly distributed surface orientations is disagreeably strong. This method can be substantially improved by observing that the illuminant produces a similar effect *in each frequency band*. Thus, if I make the much weaker assumption that the power in a particular spatial frequency band is uniformly distributed over orientation—or, more precisely, is not distributed in a way that is correlated with the illuminant effects—then I can use a similar method to estimate the illuminant direction, substituting the magnitude of the Fourier components for magnitude of the first derivatives. In particular, equation (12) becomes

$$(x_L^*, y_L^*) = (\beta^T\beta)^{-1}\beta^T(m_1, m_2, \ldots, m_n) \quad (15)$$

where the m_i are the magnitude of the Fourier components within the selected frequency band in direction (dx, dy).

When applied to an image region, this technique produces an estimate of what I have called the *generalized illuminant direction*, that is, an estimate of the orientation and magnitude of illumination effects within the region. For the purposes of shape recovery one can use equation (15) to determine (x_L^*, y_L^*), and then set $k_2 = x_L^*$, $k_3 = y_L^*$. The surface shape can then be estimated up to an overall multiplicative ambiguity.

3.2 A Biological Mechanism

The ability to recover surface shape by use of equation (11) suggests a parallel filtering mechanism for recovering shape from shading. Such a mechanism may be relevant to biological vision, as it is widely accepted that early stages of the human visual system can be regarded as being composed of filters tuned to orientation, spatial frequency, and phase [15, 16, 17]. Figure 2

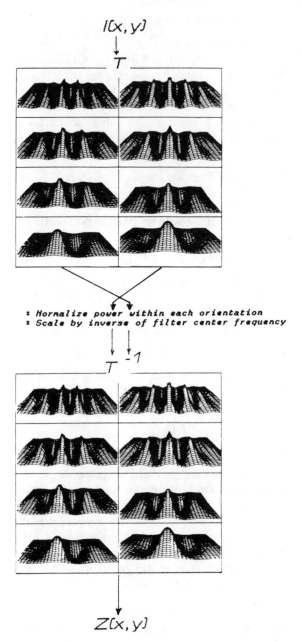

Fig. 2. A shape-from-shading mechanism: A transformation **T** produces localized measurements of sine and cosine phase frequency content; and then the inverse transformation is applied, switching sine and cosine phase amplitudes and scaling the filter amplitude in proportion to the central frequency. The output of this process is the recovered surface shape.

illustrates a mechanism based on filters with similar characteristics. The transformation **T** is a decomposition of the image using filters that form an orthonormal basis set and which are localized in both space and spatial frequency.

In order to recover surface shape from this filter set, the transformations indicated in equation (11) must be performed, as indicated in figure 2. These transformations are: (1) phase-shift the filter responses by $\pi/2$, accomplished by switching the outputs of the sine and cosine phase filters; (2) scale the filter amplitude by $1/f$, where f is the filter's central spatial frequency; (3) normalize average filter responses within each orientation to remove the illumination's directional bias; and (4) reconstruct an elevation surface from the scaled amplitudes of the filter set. The final step, reconstruction, can be accomplished by passing the signal through a second, identical set of filters. This produces the estimated surface shape within the windowed area of the image (the "receptive field" of the filters). For more detail see reference [14].

4 Surface Recovery Results

I have applied equation (11) to both synthetic images of complex surfaces, such as is shown in figure 3a (this is a fractal Brownian surface with $D = 2.3$; max (p, q) ≈ 5.0), as well as to complex natural images such as shown in figures 4 through 7. In these examples no knowledge of boundary conditions was employed; instead, the assumption of general viewing position was used to obtain default boundary conditions as described above.

4.1 Synthetic Imagery

The use of synthetic imagery is necessary to answer the two important questions concerning this method: One, is the Taylor series approximation a good one; and two, is the recovery stable and accurate? Figure 3b shows the distribution of intensity values obtained when the surface of figure 3a is illuminated from **L** $= (1, 1, 1)/\sqrt{3}$. Figure 3c shows the distribution of errors

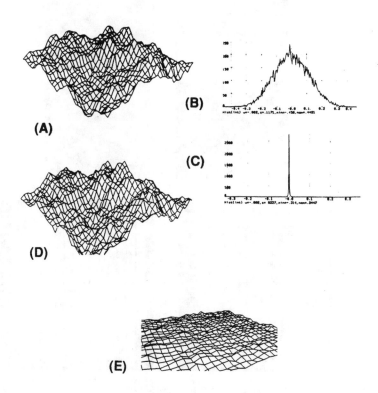

Fig. 3. A fractal Brownian surface. (b) The distribution of intensities within the image of the surface in (a). (c) The distribution of differences between the image and our linear-term-only Taylor series approximation. (d) The surface recovered from shading (compare to (a)). (e) The errors in the recovery process.

between the full imaging model and the Taylor series approximation using only the linear terms. As can be seen, the approximation is a good one, even though this surface is often steeply sloped (for example, max (p, q) ≈ 5.0).

Figure 3d shows the surface recovered by use of equation (11). Figure 3e shows the differences between the original surface and the recovered surface. As can be seen, the recovery errors are uniformly distributed across the surface. These errors have a standard deviation that is approximately 5% of the standard deviation of the original surface. It appears that these errors can be attributed to the linear approximation breaking down for steeply sloped regions of the surface.

4.2 Natural Imagery

The first example using natural imagery is one where the true reflectance function is already nearly linear,

so that we can expect accurate surface recovery. Figure 4a shows an image of a plaster cast of a nickel, together with a range image showing the surface shape extracted from this image by the shape-from-shading mechanism. As part of the recovery process, the illuminant direction was estimated from the Fourier transform of the image, as described above.

Because most people find it difficult to interpret range images I have also illustrated the recovered surface shape in another manner, as shown in figure 4c. This image is generated by using standard computer graphics techniques to first render a shaded, perspective view of the recovered surface shape, and then to project straight lines onto the surface. These straight lines are seen as bending surface contours in the resulting image. This image gives most viewers an accurate impression of the actual recovered surface shape.

By comparing figure 4c to a real nickel the reader can determine that the surface recovery is in fact quite

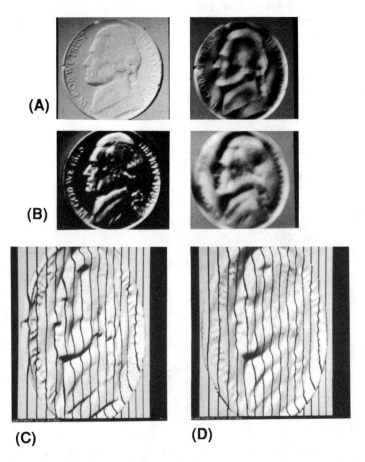

(A)

(B)

(C)   **(D)**

Fig. 4. (a) Image of a plaster cast of a nickel and the extreced range image. (b) Image of a·shiny new nickel and the extracted range image. (c) A shaded perspective view of the surface extracted from the plaster cast image. (d) A shaded perspective view of the surface extracted from the shiny nickel image.

accurate. The main defect is that the areas surrounding the head are not sufficiently flat.

Figure 4b shows a second example of recovering surface shape, this time using an image of the very shiny metal surface of a new nickel. In this case we can expect surface recovery to be somewhat less accurate, as the surface's reflectance function is quite nonlinear. Figure 4d shows the surface recovered from figure 4b. As expected the surface recovery is somewhat less accurate than when a diffusely reflecting plaster nickel was used, however, the differences between the two examples are surprisingly small. This example shows the ability of this linear shape-from-shading mechanism to deal with a wide range of reflectance functions, given only that the range of (p, q) is small or that the illumination is sufficiently oblique.

A third example of shape recovery is shown in figure 5. Figure 5a shows a bas-relief sculpture from the New York Metropolitan Museum of Art. This example was chosen to illustrate the effect of variable surface albedo (average reflectance) on the recovery process, as there is significant darkening of the surface in the lower left and upper right corners due to surface dirt. Because the shape-from-shading mechanism does not have input from color or other reflectance mechanisms, it will misinterpret these changes in surface reflectance as changes in shape. Figures 5b and 5c show two shaded perspective views of the recovered surface. It can be seen that although the surface shape recovery is generally accurate, in the lower left and upper right corners there are bulges that are due solely to changes in surface albedo.

The fourth example, shown in figure 6a, also has variable surface albedo. It is of a mountainous region outside of Phoenix, Arizona, that has been the subject of intensive study so that it is possible to compare our shape-from-shading algorithm to results obtained using stereopsis. In particular, the Defense Mapping Agency

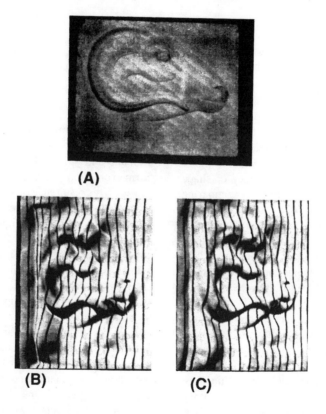

(A)

(B)   (C)

Fig. 5. (a) An image of a bas-relief sculpture of a ram's head, from the New York Metropolitan Museum of Art. (b), (c) Shaded perspective views of the recovered surface.

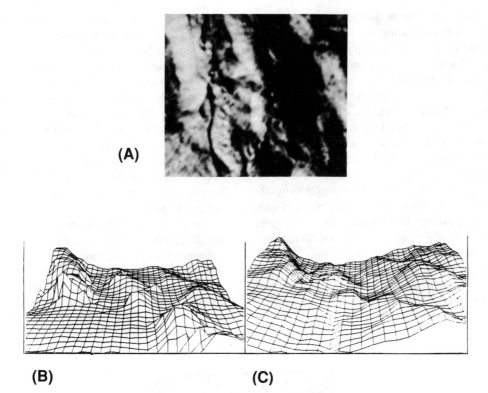

(A)

(B)   **(C)**

Fig. 6. (a) An image of a mountainous region outside of Phoenix, Arizona. (b) A perspective view of a digital elevation map of this region, obtained from a stereo pair by the Defense Mapping Agency. (c) A perspective view of the elevation map recovered from shading information alone, by use of equation [11].

has created a digital elevation map of this region using their interactive stereo system. A perspective view of this stereo elevation map is shown in figure 6b.

Figure 6c shows a perspective view of the elevation map recovered from the shading information in figure 6a, by use of equation (11). The accuracy of shape recovery for this image can be assessed by comparing the perspective view of the stereo-derived surface (figure 6b) with that of the shading-derived surface (figure 6c). It can be seen that although the shading-derived elevation surface displays a pronounced low-frequency distortion (presumably due to variations in the surface albedo), the details of the recovered surface are still fairly accurate.

A final example of shape recovery is shown in figure 7. Figure 7a is a complex image widely used in image compression research. Figures 7b and c show two shaded perspective views of the recovered surface in the neighborhood of the face. The eyes, cheek, chin, lips, nose, and nostrils can all be clearly seen in the recovered surface, and are generally correct. The wavy, dark area in the lower right is a small portion of the woman's hair.

5 Summary

Often the true reflectance function within an image region can be accurately approximated by a linear function of p and q. In such cases there is a simple closed-form expression that relates surface shape to image intensity. This result may be especially useful in applications where near-real-time performance is required. Further, because the technique can be implemented by use of linear filters similar to those thought to exist in biological visual systems, it may serve as a model for human perception. Experimental results indicate that the recovery process is stable and can be quite accurate.

Special aspects of this approach are that it makes no assumption about surface smoothness or shape, and that it does not require (but can make use of) boundary conditions to obtain an estimate of shape. To avoid requiring known boundary conditions I have used the assumption of general viewing position to fill in missing boundary conditions with default values. The use of these default boundary conditions seems to produce the most accurate shape estimates for complex, highly textured surfaces. When boundary conditions are

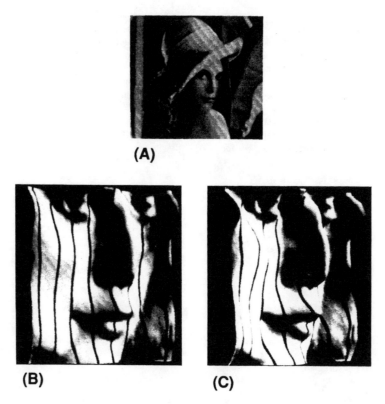

(A)

(B)   **(C)**

Fig. 7 (a) An image widely used in image compression research. (b), (c) Two shaded perspective views of the recovered surface.

available, of course, they can be directly incorporated into the shape estimate as described above.

I believe that this approach to shape-from-shading is ideally suited to the recovery of detailed surface shape within relatively small image regions, a task that is difficult to perform using other cues such as stereo or motion. Because there is no smoothness assumption, the technique can be directly applied to complex (but still continuous) natural surfaces such as hair, cloth, or mountains. One natural method of integrating coarse stereo (or motion) information with this shape-from-shading technique would be to combine their shape estimates in the frequency domain, weighting the stereo information most heavily in the low frequencies and the shading information most heavily in the higher frequencies.

Acknowledgments

This research was made possible by National Science Foundation, Grant No. IRI-87-19920. I wish to thank Berthold Horn, Ted Adelson, and David Heeger for their comments and insights.

References

1. A.P. Pentland, "Local analysis of the image," *IEEE Trans. Pattern Anal. Mach. Recog.* 6(2):170–187, 1984.
2. F.P. Ferrie, and M.D. Levine, "Where and why local shading works," *IEEE Trans. Pattern Anal. Mach. Recog.* 17(1), 1989.
3. D. Knill, and D. Kersten, "Learning a near-optimal estimator for surface shape from shading, *Comput. Vision, Graph., Image Process.* to appear, 1989.
4. G.B. Smith, "Shape from shading: An assessment," *SRI AI Center Tech. Note 287*, SRI International, Menlo Park, CA, 1983.
5. B.K.P. Horn, "Understanding image intensities," *Artificial Intelligence* 8(2): 210–231, 1977.
6. K. Ikeuchi and B.K.P. Horn, "Numerical shape from shading and occluding boundaries," *Artificial Intelligence* 17:141–185, 1981.
7. B.K.P. Horn, and M.J. Brooks, "The variational approach to shape from shading," *Comput. Vision, Graph., Image Process.* 33:174–208, 1986.

8. G.B. Smith, Personal communication.

9. T. Simchony and R. Chellappa, "Direct analytical methods for solving Poisson equations in computer vision problems," *IEEE Comput. Vision Workshop*, Miami Beach, FL, December 1987.

10. E. Adelson and A. Pentland, "Weiner filtering to improve shape from shading," In preparation, 1989.

11. A. Pentland, "Fractal-based description of natural scenes," *IEEE Trans. Pattern Anal. Mach. Recog.* 6(6):661–674, 1984.

12. P. Kube and A. Pentland, "On the imaging of fractal surfaces," *IEEE Trans. Pattern Anal. Mach. Vision* 10(5):704–707, 1988.

13. A.P. Pentland, "Finding the illuminant direction," *J. Opt. Soc. Amer.* 72(4):448–455, 1982.

14. A.P. Pentland, "Shape information from shading: A theory of human perception," *Proc. 2nd Intern. Conf. Comput. Vision*, pp. 404–413, 448–455, Tampa, FL, December 5–8, 1988.

15. J. Daugman, "Two-dimensional analysis of cortical receptive field profiles," *Vision Research* 20:846–856, 1980.

16. E. Adelson and J. Bergen, "Spatiotemporal energy models for the perception of motion," *J. Opt. Soc. Amer. A* 2(2):284–299, 1985.

17. A. Watson and A. Ahumada, "Model of human visual-motion sensing," *J. Opt. Soc. Amer. A* 2(2):322–342, 1985.

Estimation of Illuminant Direction, Albedo, and Shape from Shading

Qinfen Zheng and Rama Chellappa, *Senior Member, IEEE*

Abstract—A robust approach to recovery of shape from shading information is presented. Assuming uniform albedo and Lambertian surface for the imaging model, we first present methods for the estimation of illuminant direction and surface albedo. Two methods for estimating the azimuth of the illuminant are presented. One is based on local estimates on smooth patches. The other method uses shading information along image contours. The elevation of the illuminant and surface albedo are estimated from image statistics, taking into consideration the effect of self-shadowing. With the estimated reflectance map parameters, we then compute the surface shape using a new procedure that implements the smoothness constraint by requiring the gradients of reconstructed intensity to be close to the gradients of the input image. The new algorithm is data driven, stable, updates the surface slope and height maps simultaneously, and significantly reduces the residual errors in irradiance and integrability terms. A hierarchical implementation of the SFS algorithm is presented. Typical results on synthetic and real images are given to illustrate the usefulness of our approach.

Index Terms— Early vision, illuminant direction estimation, regularization, shape from shading.

I. Introduction

SHAPE from shading (SFS) [1], [2] refers to the process of reconstructing the 3-D shape of an object from its 2-D intensity image. In computer vision, SFS is implemented by first modeling image brightness as a function of surface geometry and then reconstructing a surface that, under the given imaging model, generates an image close to the input image. This problem was formally introduced by Horn over 20 years ago [3], [4]. Since then there have been many significant improvements in both theoretical and practical aspects of this problem [1], [5]. The success of SFS depends on two factors: 1) a suitable imaging model that specifies the relationship between surface shape and image brightness, and 2) a good numerical algorithm for the reconstruction of shape from the given image.

As far as the imaging model is concerned, there are two issues to be considered: 1) how to model the relationship between surface shape and image brightness, and 2) how to estimate the image model parameters. These are related problems, as a good model should be accurate in predicting the image intensities for most surfaces under normal illumination

Manuscript received August 3, 1990; revised January 9, 1991. This work was supported by the National Science Foundation under Grant MIP-84-51010.

The authors are with the Department of Electrical Engineering, Institute for Advanced Computer Studies and Center for Automated Research, University of Maryland, College Park, MD 20702.

IEEE Log Number 9100895.

conditions and simple enough for estimation and implementation. In SFS research, the imaging model is specified through a reflectance map [3]–[7]

$$I = \mathcal{R}(p, q)$$

where I is the scene radiance and $\mathcal{R}$ is the reflectance map function, with $p = \frac{\partial z}{\partial x}$ and $q = \frac{\partial z}{\partial y}$ being the partial derivatives of height z with respect to image coordinates. In this paper, we consider only the Lambertian model of image formation [3]–[5]. Assuming orthographic projection with the z axis parallel to the optical axis of camera and the positive z direction pointing to the camera, the Lambertian model can be written as

$$
\begin{aligned}
\mathcal{R}(p, q) &= \eta \cos \theta_i + \sigma_0 \\
&= \eta \left(\vec{N} \cdot \vec{L} \right) + \sigma_0 \\
&= \eta \frac{\cos \gamma - p \cos \tau \sin \gamma - q \sin \tau \sin \gamma}{\sqrt{1 + p^2 + q^2}} + \sigma_0 \quad (1)
\end{aligned}
$$

where η is the composite albedo, which includes factors such as strength of illumination and the reflectivity of the surface. For uniform illumination, η is constant if the surface is optically uniform. θ_i, the incidence angle, is the angle between the surface normal and the direction toward the light source. $\vec{N} = (-p, -q, 1)/\sqrt{1 + p^2 + q^2}$ is the surface normal at position $(x, y, z(x, y))$ [7]. $\vec{L} = (\cos \tau \sin \gamma, \sin \tau \sin \gamma, \cos \gamma)$ is the unit vector for the illuminant direction, where τ, the tilt angle of the illuminant (also called the azimuth of the illuminant), is the angle between $\vec{L}$ and the x–z plane, γ, the slant angle, is the angle between $\vec{L}$ and the positive z axis ($\frac{\pi}{2} - \gamma$ is the elevation of the illuminant). $\vec{L}$ is constant for parallel illumination. σ_0 is the bias brightness depending on background illumination, digitizer calibration, and so on.

Under the assumptions of a Lambertian surface, point light source, and uniform albedo, the reflectance map is determined by the parameters τ, γ, η, and σ_0. Pentland [8] estimated the illuminant direction from the distribution of image derivatives. By assuming an umbilical surface and that the change in surface normal is distributed isotropically, a maximum-likelihood analysis was performed to estimate τ and γ. This approach was later extended to the Fourier domain [9], [10]. The assumption that the change in surface normal is isotropically distributed may not always be valid. In fact, even for a perfect sphere image, due to self-shadowing, the change in surface normal of the illuminated part may not be isotropically distributed. Hence, the $d\bar{z}$ term in [1, p. 455] may not be zero. Later, Brooks and Horn [11] introduced an iterative algorithm that alternatively estimates the surface normals and light source direction. To avoid being stuck in a local minimum, an initial state close to the true surface shape may often be required. Assuming the surface patches to be locally spherical and using a Gaussian sphere model for the distribution of surface normals, Lee and Rosenfeld [12] presented a method for the estimation of illuminant direction. They estimated the elevation of illuminant and albedo from the statistics of image intensities. The effects of projection and sampling on the surface normal distribution were also considered. In Lee and Rosenfeld's derivation for the azimuth estimator, it was assumed that the estimation is implemented in a region that can be approximated by local spherical patches and that, for each fixed radius R, the azimuth of the surface normal is symmetric [1, p. 335, Theorem 4]. Recently, Horn [5] estimated the slant angle (the polar angle) by solving $E\{I\} = \eta \cos \gamma$ and the azimuth of the illuminant by computing the axis of least inertia through the origin of a scattergram of the brightness gradient (I_x, I_y).

In this paper, we introduce two methods for estimating the azimuth of the illuminant. In one of the methods, the azimuth of the illuminant is obtained by averaging the local estimates, while the other method uses a maximum-likelihood analysis of the image intensity along object boundaries. For estimation of γ and η, instead of the Gaussian sphere assumption [12], we assume the tilt and slant angles of the surface normals to be uniformly distributed in 3-D space. The issue of variations in image statistics due to changes in the elevation of the illuminant direction is also addressed. Experiments on various synthetic and real images show that our illuminant direction estimators compare favorably to existing estimators and that the estimated reflectance map parameters are useful for solving the SFS problem.

With the reflectance map determined, the SFS problem becomes one of finding the best way to reconstruct a surface $z(x, y)$ satisfying the image irradiance equation

$$I(x, y) = \mathcal{R}(p, q) \qquad (2)$$

where $I(x, y)$ is the image intensity at position (x, y). Algorithms for solving (2) can be roughly grouped into two categories. One approach is to find a closed-form solution [9], [13], [14]. This is faster but limited to simple reflectance maps and the availability of boundary conditions. The other approach treats the SFS problem as a constrained optimization problem [5], [15]–[18]. The optimization approach is generally more flexible for including additional constraints and is more robust to image noise and modeling errors.

In this paper, we follow the constrained optimization approach for the SFS problem. A typical cost function is [1], [5], [16], [18]

$$\iint \{[I(x, y) - \mathcal{R}(p, q)]^2 + \lambda(p_x^2 + p_y^2 + q_x^2 + q_y^2)$$
$$+ \mu[(z_x - p)^2 + (z_y - q)^2]\} \, dx \, dy \qquad (3)$$

where the first term corresponds to the requirement that the image synthesized from the reconstructed shape be close to the input image. The third term comes from the requirement of integrability [16], [17], i.e., the SFS result should correspond to a physical surface. The second term is the regularization term often used to ensure the convergence of the iteration process. This term pushes the reconstruction toward a smooth surface. Although it helps to stabilize the minimization process, it has several drawbacks. First of all, it causes the solution "to walk away" from the ground truth, even if the ground truth is used as an initial condition [5]. Second, it flattens the SFS reconstruction, causing distortions along image discontinuities. And finally, the SFS results will depend on the value of λ used. The choice of λ is critical, as it should be large enough to avoid instability and small enough to produce a meaningful solution. A solution to this problem is to use an adaptive Lagrangian multiplier to reduce oversmoothing along image boundaries [19]. Another solution is to let λ gradually decrease as the iterations proceed [5]. In this paper, we introduce a new cost function that does not use the quadratic regularization term. Instead, we require the gradients of the reconstructed image to be close to the gradients of the input image. Using calculus of variations [16] and a linear approximation of the reflectance map [5], a new iterative scheme is developed. In this scheme, the slope and height maps are updated simultaneously. Experiments with both synthetic and real images show that the resulting algorithm is stable and results in lower residual errors in irradiance and integrability terms.

By combining reflectance map parameter estimation and the new iterative scheme for optimization, we obtain a robust SFS algorithm. We call it robust because the reflectance map parameters estimated from different bands of color images, subimages of the same scene, images with different resolutions, and stereo image pairs are all consistent, and the SFS algorithm produces good results on a number of real images.

The organization of the paper is as follows: Section II presents the illuminant direction and albedo estimators, in which we first briefly review some well known illuminant direction estimators and then introduce our methods. Section III presents the SFS algorithm and its hierarchical implementation. In Section IV, we present typical results for illuminant direction, albedo estimation, and recovery of shape. A summary is given in Section V.

II. Estimation of Illuminant Direction and Albedo

A. Image Model

In the Lambertian reflectance model (1), let the surface normal $\vec{N}$ be

$$\vec{N} = (N_x, N_y, N_z) = (\cos \alpha \sin \beta, \sin \alpha \sin \beta, \cos \beta) \qquad (4)$$

where $\alpha = \alpha(x, y)$ and $\beta = \beta(x, y)$ are the tilt and slant angles of the surface normal at $(x, y, z(x, y))$. After substitution of (4) into (1), the reflectance map can be rewritten as

$$\mathcal{R}(p, q) = \eta(\cos \tau \sin \gamma \cos \alpha \sin \beta + \sin \tau \sin \gamma \sin \alpha \sin \beta$$
$$+ \cos \gamma \cos \beta) + \sigma_0$$
$$= \eta(\cos(\alpha - \tau) \sin \beta \sin \gamma + \cos \beta \cos \gamma) + \sigma_0.$$

$$(5)$$

B. Review of Earlier Works

1) *Pentland's Method:* Pentland's method [8] can be summarized as follows. Let dI_i be the derivative of image intensity along a particular direction (dx_i, dy_i) and $d\bar{I}_i$ be the average of dI along (dx_i, dy_i). The regression model relating $d\bar{I}_i$'s and (dx_i, dy_i)'s is

$$
\begin{pmatrix} d\bar{I}_1 \\ d\bar{I}_2 \\ \vdots \\ d\bar{I}_N \end{pmatrix} = \begin{pmatrix} dx_1 & dy_1 \\ dx_2 & dy_2 \\ \vdots & \vdots \\ dx_N & dy_N \end{pmatrix} \begin{pmatrix} \hat{x}_L \\ \hat{y}_L \end{pmatrix} \qquad (6)
$$

where $(\hat{x}_L, \hat{y}_L)$ are the unnormalized x and y components of the τ estimate, and N is the total number of directions considered. Solving for $(\hat{x}_L, \hat{y}_L)$ one obtains

$$
\begin{pmatrix} \hat{x}_L \\ \hat{y}_L \end{pmatrix} = (B^t B)^{-1} B^t \begin{pmatrix} d\bar{I}_1 \\ d\bar{I}_2 \\ \vdots \\ d\bar{I}_N \end{pmatrix}
$$

where B is the matrix of direction vector (dx_i, dy_i) $i \in (1, \cdots, N)$ as shown in (6). The azimuth of the illuminant is computed as

$$
\tau = \arctan \left(\frac{\hat{y}_L}{\hat{x}_L} \right).
$$

Further, the variances of dI_i are independent of direction i and can be expressed as

$$
E\{dI^2\} = E\left\{ (dI_i)^2 \right\} = \eta^2 \, dr^2 + (E\{dI\})^2 \qquad \forall \, i
$$

where η is the albedo of the surface and dr is the expected magnitude of $d\vec{N}$. The slant angle of the illuminant can be computed as

$$
\gamma = \begin{cases} \arccos \left(\sqrt{1 - (\hat{x}_L^2 + \hat{y}_L^2)/k^2} \right), & \text{if } \hat{x}_L^2 + \hat{y}_L^2 \leq k^2 \\ 0, & \text{otherwise} \end{cases}
$$

where

$$
k = \eta \, dr = \sqrt{E\{dI^2\} - (E\{dI\})^2}. \qquad (7)
$$

In our experiments with Pentland's method reported in Section IV-A, we let $N = 8$ and let the direction matrix be

$$
B = \begin{pmatrix} 1 & \frac{\sqrt{2}}{2} & 0 & -\frac{\sqrt{2}}{2} & -1 & -\frac{\sqrt{2}}{2} & 0 & \frac{\sqrt{2}}{2} \\ 0 & \frac{\sqrt{2}}{2} & 1 & \frac{\sqrt{2}}{2} & 0 & -\frac{\sqrt{2}}{2} & -1 & -\frac{\sqrt{2}}{2} \end{pmatrix}^t
$$

and k in (7) is computed as

$$
k = \sqrt{\overline{E\{dI^2\}} - (E\{dI\})^2}
$$

where $\overline{E\{dI^2\}}$ is the average of $E\{(dI_i)^2\}$ for $i = 1, \cdots, 8$, and $E\{dI\}$ is the expected value of $dI/dx_i + dI/dy_i$ over the whole region and all i's.

2) *Lee and Rosenfeld's Method:* Lee and Rosenfeld [12] assumed the surface patches to be locally spherical and derived the probability density function for a Gaussian sphere as

$$
f_{\alpha\beta} = \frac{1}{2\pi} \sin 2\beta. \qquad (8)
$$

Using (8), they derived the illuminant direction estimator summarized below:

1) The azimuth of the illuminant is estimated as

$$
\tau = \arctan \frac{E\{I_y\}}{E\{I_x\}}
$$

where I_x, I_y are the first-order partial derivatives of image intensity with respect to the local spherical coordinates, and the expectations are taken over the whole region. Since it is not clear how to evaluate the derivatives of image intensity with respect to local spherical coordinates, in our implementation of this method (for comparison purposes), we computed I_x and I_y as the partial derivatives of image intensity with respect to image coordinates.

2) The slant angle of the illuminant direction γ satisfies

$$
E\{I\} = 4\eta \frac{(\pi - \gamma) \cos \gamma + \sin \gamma}{3\pi (1 + \cos \gamma)} \qquad (9)
$$

$$
E\{I^2\} = \frac{\eta^2}{4} (1 + \cos \gamma) \qquad (10)
$$

where the expectations are taken over the whole image. To compute γ and η from (9) and (10), one first solves for γ from

$$
\frac{E\{I\}}{\sqrt{E\{I^2\}}} = 8 \frac{(\pi - \gamma) \cos \gamma + \sin \gamma}{3\pi (1 + \cos \gamma)^{3/2}}. \qquad (11)
$$

The right-hand side of (11) is a monotonically decreasing function of γ. Therefore, there exists a unique solution for γ as long as $\xi = \frac{E\{I\}}{\sqrt{E\{I^2\}}}$ is no greater than $\frac{2\sqrt{2}}{3}$. In our implementation of Lee and Rosenfeld's algorithm reported in Section IV-A, we let $\gamma = 0$ for ξ greater than $\frac{2\sqrt{2}}{3}$. Since for $\gamma = \pi$ the right-hand side of (11) is undetermined and our tests are limited to $\gamma \leq \frac{\pi}{2}$, in our implementation of the above estimator, we thresholded[1] γ to $\frac{5}{6}\pi$ whenever ξ is smaller than 0.80576. After γ is estimated, the albedo of the surface can be determined by

$$
\eta = \frac{1}{a^2 + b} \left(a E\{I\} + \sqrt{b E\{I^2\}} \right) \qquad (12)
$$

where

$$
a = \frac{4[(\pi - \gamma) \cos \gamma + \sin \gamma]}{3\pi (1 + \cos \gamma)}
$$

$$
b = \frac{1 + \cos \gamma}{4}.
$$

In deriving (9) and (10), Lee and Rosenfeld normalized the integrals by the area of the illuminated portion of the sphere. We feel this is inappropriate. The integrals should be divided by the projection area of the sphere on the image plane, i.e., the average should be done on both the illuminated part and the portion in the shadow. The modified formulas after taking this into consideration are

$$
E\{I\} = \frac{2}{3\pi} \eta ((\pi - \gamma) \cos \gamma + \sin \gamma) \qquad (13)
$$

$$
E\{I^2\} = \frac{\eta^2}{8} (1 + \cos \gamma)^2. \qquad (14)
$$

---

[1] This thresholding always improves the performance of the algorithm.

Both the original and modified forms of Lee and Rosenfeld's γ and η estimator are evaluated in the experiments reported in Section IV-A.

C. Estimation of the Azimuth of the Illuminant

1) Solution 1: Local Voting Method: Let us assume that, for any point $(x_o, y_o, z(x_o, y_o))$, its neighbors can be locally approximated by a spherical patch:

$$
\begin{aligned}
x &= a(x_o, y_o) + r(x_o, y_o)\sin\beta\cos\alpha \\
y &= b(x_o, y_o) + r(x_o, y_o)\sin\beta\sin\alpha \qquad (15) \\
z &= c(x_o, y_o) + r(x_o, y_o)\cos\beta
\end{aligned}
$$

where $(a(x_o, y_o), b(x_o, y_o), c(x_o, y_o))$ is the center of the sphere and $r(x_o, y_o)$ is the radius of the sphere,[2] and α and β are the tilt and slant angles of the surface normal. From (15), we obtain the following relations:

$$
\begin{aligned}
\frac{x - a}{r} &= \sin\beta\cos\alpha \\
\frac{y - b}{r} &= \sin\beta\sin\alpha \\
\cos\beta = \frac{z - c}{r} &= \sqrt{1 - \left(\frac{x-a}{r}\right)^2 - \left(\frac{y-b}{r}\right)^2}
\end{aligned}
$$

For a small increment along the direction $\vec{s} = (\delta x, \delta y)$, the corresponding increments in (α, β) is $(\delta\alpha_s, \delta\beta_s)$ and the following relations hold

$$
\delta x = -r\sin\beta\sin\alpha\,\delta\alpha_s + r\cos\beta\cos\alpha\,\delta\beta_s \qquad (16)
$$

$$
\delta y = r\sin\beta\cos\alpha\,\delta\alpha_s + r\cos\beta\sin\alpha\,\delta\beta_s \qquad (17)
$$

$$
\sin\beta\,\delta\beta_s = \frac{-\frac{x-a}{r}\cdot\frac{\delta x}{r} - \frac{y-b}{r}\cdot\frac{\delta y}{r}}{\sqrt{1 - \left(\frac{x-a}{r}\right)^2 - \left(\frac{y-b}{r}\right)^2}}
$$

$$
= \frac{-\sin\beta\cos\alpha\,\delta x - \sin\beta\sin\alpha\,\delta y}{r\cos\beta}. \qquad (18)
$$

On the other hand, from the image model (5), an increment in intensity due to $(\delta\alpha_s, \delta\beta_s)$ is

$$
\delta I_s = \eta[-\sin(\alpha - \tau)\sin\beta\sin\gamma\,\delta\alpha_s \\
+ \cos(\alpha - \tau)\cos\beta\sin\gamma\,\delta\beta_s - \sin\beta\cos\gamma\,\delta\beta_s]. \qquad (19)
$$

Substitution of (16)–(18) into (19) leads to

$$
\begin{aligned}
\delta I_s = \eta\Big[&(\cos\alpha\sin\beta\sin\gamma\,\delta\alpha_s + \sin\alpha\cos\beta\sin\gamma\,\delta\beta_s)\sin\tau \\
&+ (-\sin\alpha\sin\beta\sin\gamma\,\delta\alpha_s \\
&\quad + \cos\alpha\cos\beta\sin\gamma\,\delta\beta_s)\cos\tau \\
&- \frac{\sin\beta\cos\alpha\,\delta x + \sin\beta\sin\alpha\,\delta y}{r\cos\beta}\cos\gamma\Big] \\
= \frac{\eta}{r}\,&(\delta x, \delta y)\begin{pmatrix}\sin\gamma\cos\tau - \cos\gamma\tan\beta\cos\alpha \\ \sin\gamma\sin\tau - \cos\gamma\tan\beta\sin\alpha\end{pmatrix}.
\end{aligned}
$$

---

[2] Here the sphere is a local approximation, the radius and center of the sphere depend on the local surface shape.

Let $\vec{s}$ take different directions yielding

$$
d\vec{I} = B\vec{X}
$$

where

$$
d\vec{I} = \begin{pmatrix}\delta I_1 \\ \delta I_2 \\ \vdots \\ \delta I_N\end{pmatrix}
$$

$$
B = \begin{pmatrix}\delta x_1 & \delta y_1 \\ \delta x_2 & \delta y_2 \\ \vdots & \vdots \\ \delta x_N & \delta y_N\end{pmatrix}
$$

$$
\vec{X} = \begin{pmatrix}\tilde{x}_L \\ \tilde{y}_L\end{pmatrix} = \frac{\eta}{r}\begin{pmatrix}\sin\gamma\cos\tau - \cos\gamma\tan\beta\cos\alpha \\ \sin\gamma\sin\tau - \cos\gamma\tan\beta\sin\alpha\end{pmatrix}.
$$

N is the number of measured directions for $\vec{s}$, and $\tilde{x}_L$ and $\tilde{y}_L$ are the x and y components of the local estimate of the tilt of the illuminant, respectively. $\vec{X}$ can be solved using

$$
\vec{X} = (B^t B)^{-1} B^t\, d\vec{I}.
$$

It is shown in the Appendix that

$$
E_{x,y}\left\{\frac{\tilde{x}_L}{\sqrt{\tilde{x}_L^2 + \tilde{y}_L^2}}\right\} = \cos\tau \cdot F(\gamma) \qquad (20)
$$

and

$$
E_{x,y}\left\{\frac{\tilde{y}_L}{\sqrt{\tilde{x}_L^2 + \tilde{y}_L^2}}\right\} = \sin\tau \cdot F(\gamma) \qquad (21)
$$

where

$$
\begin{aligned}
F(\gamma) &= \int_{\Omega_\beta} p(\beta)\,d\beta\,\frac{1}{2\pi}\int_{-\pi}^{\pi} \\
&\cdot \frac{\sin\gamma\cos\beta - \cos\gamma\sin\beta\cos\alpha}{\sqrt{\sin^2\gamma\cos^2\beta + \cos^2\gamma\sin^2\beta - \frac{1}{2}\sin 2\gamma\sin 2\beta\cos\alpha}} \\
&\cdot d\alpha. \qquad (22)
\end{aligned}
$$

From (20) and (21), the estimate of illuminant azimuth can be computed as

$$
\tau = \arctan\left(\frac{E_{x,y}\left\{\frac{\tilde{y}_L}{\sqrt{\tilde{x}_L^2 + \tilde{y}_L^2}}\right\}}{E_{x,y}\left\{\frac{\tilde{x}_L}{\sqrt{\tilde{x}_L^2 + \tilde{y}_L^2}}\right\}}\right). \qquad (23)
$$

Derivations of (20)–(22) are given in the Appendix.

It should be pointed out that when doing local estimation, we ignore points where $d\vec{I} = \vec{0}$. Physically, these points correspond to a planar patch, where no estimation of the azimuth of the illuminant can be made based on local intensity information. Theoretically, there might exist errors in our method due to the local spherical approximation. An extreme example is the case of a cylindrical surface, which cannot be approximated by spherical patches. For a cylindrical surface, the gradient of the image intensity, and hence, the estimated azimuth of the illuminant is always toward the direction perpendicular to the axis of the cylinder. However, as the local estimates on symmetric parts of a cylinder will cancel each other, the net error caused by a cylindrical patch is usually negligible.

2) Solution 2: Contour-Based Method: It is well known that information such as the shape of an object boundary and shading along the object boundary are important for human vision [2]. Here, we introduce an estimation method based on shading analysis around object boundaries.

Assume that for each closed image boundary, (say) obtained by a zero-crossing edge detector, the slant angles of the surface normals along the boundary are constant.[3] Therefore, the tilt angle of a boundary pixel α is just the tilt angle of the boundary contour in the image plane, and the summations of $\cos \alpha$ and $\sin \alpha$ over the closed boundary are zero. Consider a boundary curve with pixels $\{ I_j \mid j = 1, 2, \cdots, N \}$, where N is the number of pixels on the curve. We write the irradiance equation for the jth pixel as[4]

$$I_j = \eta(\cos \tau \sin \gamma \cos \alpha_j \sin \beta + \sin \tau \sin \gamma \sin \alpha_j \sin \beta$$
$$+ \cos \gamma \cos \beta)$$
$$= (\cos \alpha_j, \sin \alpha_j) \begin{pmatrix} \eta \sin \gamma \sin \beta \cos \tau \\ \eta \sin \gamma \sin \beta \sin \tau \end{pmatrix} + \eta \cos \gamma \cos \beta.$$

For the entire curve, the irradiance equations can be written in matrix form as

$$\vec{I} = E\vec{X} + \vec{F} \tag{24}$$

where

$$\vec{I} = \begin{pmatrix} I_1 \\ I_2 \\ \vdots \\ I_N \end{pmatrix}$$

$$E = \begin{pmatrix} \cos \alpha_1 & \sin \alpha_1 \\ \cos \alpha_2 & \sin \alpha_2 \\ \vdots & \vdots \\ \cos \alpha_N & \sin \alpha_N \end{pmatrix}$$

$$\vec{X} = \begin{pmatrix} x_1 \\ x_2 \end{pmatrix} = \eta \sin \gamma \sin \beta \begin{pmatrix} \cos \tau \\ \sin \tau \end{pmatrix}$$

$$\vec{F} = \eta \cos \gamma \cos \beta \vec{I}_N$$

$$\vec{I}_N = \underbrace{(1, 1, \cdots, 1)}_{N}{}^t.$$

Solving for $\vec{X}$ in (24) we get

$$\vec{X} = (E^t E)^{-1} E^t \vec{I} - (E^t E)^{-1} E^t \vec{F}.$$

Since the boundary is assumed to be closed, we have $E^t \vec{F} = \vec{0}$, and therefore

$$\vec{X} = (E^t E)^{-1} E^t \vec{I}.$$

[3] An occluding boundary is a special case of this assumption.

[4] Here, for simplicity of presentation, we assume that the bias σ_0 has been removed from the input intensity.

The azimuth of the illuminant is computed from $\vec{X}$ by

$$\tau = \arctan \frac{x_2}{x_1}.$$

In practice, due to sampling effects, there may be small variations in the slant angles of boundary pixels and the column sums of the E matrix may not be zero. We first subtract the means from both sides of (24) and compute $\vec{X}$ by

$$\vec{X} = (E'^t E')^{-1} E'^t \vec{I}' \tag{25}$$

where

$$\vec{I}' = \vec{I} - \left(\frac{1}{N} \sum_{j=1}^{N} I_j \right) \vec{I}_N$$

$$E' = E - \vec{I}_N \left(\frac{1}{N} \sum_{j=1}^{N} \cos \alpha_j, \frac{1}{N} \sum_{j=1}^{N} \sin \alpha_j \right).$$

One may notice that to form the E matrix we need the tilt angle α for each boundary pixel. Under the assumption that the slant angles of the surface normals along the boundary are approximately constant, the tilt angles of the surface normals along the boundary are just the tilt angles of the curve normals in the image plane. One only needs to detect the normals of the boundary pixels in the image plane. The positive direction of normal can be determined by comparing the intensity variations on both sides of the boundary and using knowledge of the intensity variations between the background and the object. In our algorithm, we just detect zero-crossings as boundaries, estimate the tangent of the curve by smoothing the zero-crossing edge, and compute the intensity variances on both sides of the edge along directions perpendicular to the tangent of the curve. If the difference between these two variances is above a threshold, the side with smaller variance is chosen as the background. For boundary pixels where the intensity variances on both sides of the boundary are almost the same, the positive direction of the boundary normal can be determined by the continuity of boundary normals or those pixels can be simply ignored. Since $\vec{X}$ only contains two variables, (25) is highly over-determined, and the omission of less reliable pixels will not affect the solution.[5] It is obvious that estimation of the normal directions can be improved if we segment the image first.

Another factor to be clarified is the handling of the intensity values of the boundary pixels. In a digital image, the pixels along the boundary could belong to either side of the boundary or their values could be composite results from the slopes of both sides. In our implementation, the intensities of the boundary pixels are determined by a local prediction using the values of their interior neighbors. To be more specific, the intensity of each boundary pixel is computed as

$$I_b = 2I_{b-1} - I_{b-2} \tag{26}$$

where subscripts $b - 1$ and $b - 2$ indicate 1 and 2 units away from the boundary (inside the object and along the normal to

[5] Note that we have forced the column sums of E' to be zero by subtracting out the mean values.

the boundary). I_{b-1} and I_{b-2} are linearly interpolated from the values at the four nearest image grid points. In (26), it is assumed that the second derivative of the image intensity along the normal direction is zero.

D. Estimation of γ and η

For estimating γ and η, we need the distribution properties of α and β. For a general scene, the range of α could be $[0, 2\pi)$. Since there is no preference for the tilt angle, an acceptable assumption regarding the distribution of α is

$$f_\alpha = \frac{1}{2\pi}.$$

On the other hand, for the distribution of β, the effects of self-occlusion and foreshortening of the imaging process should be considered. In 3-D space, it is equally possible for a surface patch to have a slant angle between 0 and π; but due to self occlusion, only patches facing the camera can be seen, so the range of β is $[0, \pi/2]$. Since for natural scenes the percentage of "flat" surface patches is much higher than that predicted by the Gaussian sphere model, the assumption that β is uniformly distributed in 3-D space results in a β distribution that is closer to the histogram of surface normals measured in an image plane. It is difficult to say which assumption about the distribution of β is better. It depends on the class of scenes under investigation.[6] The projection area of a unit patch with slant angle β into image plane is $\cos\beta$. Therefore, the distribution of β in the image plane is

$$f_\beta = k\cos\beta$$

such that

$$\int_0^{\pi/2} k\cos\beta\, d\beta = k\sin\beta\big|_0^{\pi/2} = k = 1$$

yielding

$$f_\beta = \cos\beta.$$

For general images, we can assume that α and β are independent. The statistical model for the distribution of surface normals is

$$f_{\alpha\beta} = f_\alpha \cdot f_\beta = \frac{\cos\beta}{2\pi}. \tag{27}$$

Using (27) we can evaluate the statistical moments of image intensity. Special care should be taken for shadow area. Here we only consider the case of self-shadowing. For a pixel, if the incidence angle is greater than $\pi/2$ the pixel will not be illuminated, and its brightness is zero. So the actual image intensity is[7]

$$I(\alpha, \beta) = \max\{\eta[\cos(\alpha - \tau)\sin\beta\sin\gamma + \cos\beta\cos\gamma], 0\}.$$

[6] Our method is valid for any kind of β distribution. For other surface normal distributions, it is easy to obtain the corresponding $f_1(\gamma)$ and $f_2(\gamma)$ by substitution of $\frac{\cos\beta}{2\pi}$ in (30) and (31) with the given or assumed distribution function and followed by numerical integration.

[7] Here for simplicity of presentation we assume that σ_0 in (1) is zero.

The first two moments of image intensities are

$$\bar{I} = \int_{\Omega_I} I p(I)\, dI$$

$$= \int_{\Omega_{\alpha\beta}} I(\alpha, \beta) p(\alpha, \beta)\, d\alpha\, d\beta$$

$$= \frac{1}{2\pi} \int_0^{2\pi} \int_0^{\pi/2} I(\alpha, \beta)\cos\beta\, d\alpha\, d\beta \tag{28}$$

$$\overline{I^2} = \int_{\Omega_I} I^2 p(I)\, dI$$

$$= \int_{\Omega_{\alpha\beta}} I^2(\alpha, \beta) p(\alpha, \beta)\, d\alpha\, d\beta$$

$$= \frac{1}{2\pi} \int_0^{2\pi} \int_0^{\pi/2} I^2(\alpha, \beta)\cos\beta\, d\alpha\, d\beta. \tag{29}$$

The curve

$$\cos(\alpha - \tau)\sin\beta\sin\gamma + \cos\beta\cos\gamma = 0$$

is an ellipse. Due to symmetry, we know that $\bar{I}$ and $\overline{I^2}$ are functions of η and γ only and can be written as

$$\bar{I} = \eta f_1(\gamma) \quad \text{and} \quad \overline{I^2} = \eta^2 f_2(\gamma)$$

where

$$f_1(\gamma) = \frac{1}{2\pi\eta} \int_0^{2\pi} \int_0^{\pi/2} I(\alpha, \beta)\cos\beta\, d\alpha\, d\beta \tag{30}$$

$$f_2(\gamma) = \frac{1}{2\pi\eta^2} \int_0^{2\pi} \int_0^{\pi/2} I^2(\alpha, \beta)\cos\beta\, d\alpha\, d\beta. \tag{31}$$

We compute $f_1(\gamma)$, $f_2(\gamma)$, and $f_3(\gamma) = f_1(\gamma)/\sqrt{f_2(\gamma)}$ by a numerical method and approximate the results by seventh-order polynomials in $\cos\gamma$. The results are

$$f_1(\gamma) \approx \sum_{i=0}^{7} a_i \cos^i \gamma$$

$$f_2(\gamma) \approx \sum_{i=0}^{7} b_i \cos^i \gamma$$

$$f_3(\gamma) \approx \sum_{i=0}^{7} c_i \cos^i \gamma$$

where the coefficients are

$a_o = 0.1615$	$b_o = 0.0834$	$c_o = 0.5577$
$a_1 = 0.3959$	$b_1 = 0.2169$	$c_1 = 0.6240$
$a_2 = 0.3757$	$b_2 = 0.2487$	$c_2 = 0.1882$
$a_3 = -0.0392$	$b_3 = 0.1836$	$c_3 = -0.6514$
$a_4 = -0.3077$	$b_4 = 0.0048$	$c_4 = -0.5350$
$a_5 = 0.1174$	$b_5 = -0.1086$	$c_5 = 0.9282$

$$a_6 = \quad 0.1803 \quad b_6 = -0.0043 \quad c_6 = \quad 0.3476$$
$$a_7 = -0.0984 \quad b_7 = \quad 0.0424 \quad c_7 = -0.4984.$$

since $f_3(\gamma)$ is a monotonically decreasing function of γ, γ can be uniquely found from

$$\frac{E_{x,y}\{I\}}{E_{x,y}\{I^2\}} = f_3(\gamma)$$

where $E_{x,y}\{I\}$ and $E_{x,y}\{I^2\}$ are the ensemble averages of the image intensities and the square of the image intensities, respectively. Subsequently, η can be computed by solving

$$\begin{cases} \eta f_1(\gamma) = E_{x,y}\{I\} \\ \eta \sqrt{f_2(\gamma)} = \sqrt{E_{x,y}\{I^2\}}. \end{cases} \tag{32}$$

The minimum mean-square error solution for (32) is

$$\eta = \frac{1}{f_1^2(\gamma) + f_2(\gamma)}$$
$$\cdot \left(E_{x,y}\{I\} \cdot f_1(\gamma) + \sqrt{E_{x,y}\{I^2\}} \cdot f_2(\gamma) \right).$$

In our implementation of this method, if $\dfrac{E_{x,y}\{I\}}{\sqrt{E_{x,y}\{I^2\}}} > f_3(0) = 0.96191$, we let $\gamma = 0$.

III. SFS Algorithm

A. Formulation

The estimated illuminant parameters and surface albedo can be used to solve the SFS problem. Traditional methods enforce the requirement that the reconstructed image be close to the input image using the irradiance equation

$$\mathcal{R}(p, q) = I(x, y). \tag{33}$$

It seems that (33) has used all the information contained in the input image, but in iterative SFS algorithms, the surface reconstruction is updated at each pixel separately. For each pixel, the right side of (33) is the value of the driven function while (p, q) on the left side of (33) are treated as free variables. No relationship among the neighboring pixels is enforced in (33). The quadratic smoothness term is used in (3) to enforce the condition that the reconstructed surface should be smoothly connected. Unfortunately, the quadratic smoothness term uniformly suppresses changes in surface shape, irrespective of changes in intensities. It is natural that variations in image intensity are related to the changes in surface shape. In areas where image intensity changes rapidly, the corresponding surface segment may not be smooth, and smoothing over this region should be reduced. One way to overcome the drawbacks of the quadratic smoothness constraint is to let the value of λ adapt to the smoothness of the local intensity variations [19]. Since SFS is an intensity-driven process, this adaptive smoothing can be implemented more efficiently by requiring the gradients of the reconstructed intensity to be equal to the gradients of the input image, as in (34):

$$\mathcal{R}_x(p, q) = I_x(x, y)$$
$$\mathcal{R}_y(p, q) = I_y(x, y). \tag{34}$$

Since $\mathcal{R}(p, q)$ is an implicit function of x and y, the derivatives on the left-hand side of (34) are defined. By incorporating (33) and (34), computation of shape from shading can be formulated as a constrained optimization problem minimizing

$$\iint F(p, q, Z) \, dx \, dy \tag{35}$$

where

$$F = [\mathcal{R}(p, q) - I(x, y)]^2$$
$$+ [\mathcal{R}_p(p, q)p_x + \mathcal{R}_q(p, q)q_x - I_x(x, y)]^2$$
$$+ [\mathcal{R}_p(p, q)p_y + \mathcal{R}_q(p, q)q_y - I_y(x, y)]^2$$
$$+ \mu\left[(p - Z_x)^2 + (q - Z_y)^2\right]. \tag{36}$$

The last term in (36) comes from the integrability constraint [16], [17], where μ is a weighting factor. Note that the quadratic smoothness terms present in almost all published work have been dropped. Using calculus of variations, minimization of (35) is equivalent to solving the following Euler equations:

$$F_p - \frac{\partial}{\partial x} F_{p_x} - \frac{\partial}{\partial y} F_{p_y} = 0$$

$$F_q - \frac{\partial}{\partial x} F_{q_x} - \frac{\partial}{\partial y} F_{q_y} = 0 \tag{37}$$

$$F_Z - \frac{\partial}{\partial x} F_{Z_x} - \frac{\partial}{\partial y} F_{Z_y} = 0.$$

In (36), by approximating the reflectance map around (p, q) by Taylor series expansion of up to first-order terms, F_p in (37) can be written as

$$\frac{1}{2} F_p = [\mathcal{R} - I(x, y)]\mathcal{R}_p + \mu(p - Z_x). \tag{38}$$

Let variables with primes $(')$ represent the values after updating and the variables without primes stand for the values before updating. Then

$$p' = p + \delta p, \quad q' = q + \delta q \quad \text{and} \quad Z' = Z + \delta Z. \tag{39}$$

The corresponding increments in the partial derivatives of (p, q, Z) after updating are

$$\begin{array}{lll} p_x' = p_x - \delta p & q_x' = q_x - \delta q & Z_x' = Z_x - \delta Z \\ p_y' = p_y - \delta p & q_y' = q_y - \delta q & Z_y' = Z_y - \delta Z \\ p_{xx}' = p_{xx} - 2\delta p & q_{xx}' = q_{xx} - 2\delta q & Z_{xx}' = Z_{xx} - 2\delta Z \\ p_{yy}' = p_{yy} - 2\delta p & q_{yy}' = q_{yy} - 2\delta q & Z_{yy}' = Z_{yy} - 2\delta Z. \end{array} \tag{40}$$

After substituting (39) and (40) into (38) and expanding the reflectance map $\mathcal{R}$ up to linear terms we obtain[8]

$$\frac{1}{2} F_p = [\mathcal{R} + \mathcal{R}_p \, \delta p + \mathcal{R}_q \, \delta q - I(x, y)]\mathcal{R}_p$$
$$+ \mu(p - Z_x + \delta p + \delta Z). \tag{41}$$

---

[8] The higher order derivatives $\mathcal{R}_{pp}$, $\mathcal{R}_{pq}$, and $\mathcal{R}_{qq}$ are zero due to the linear approximation of $\mathcal{R}$ around (p, q).

The other terms in (37) can be derived similarly, and the results are listed as follows:

$$\frac{1}{2}\frac{\partial}{\partial x}F_{p_x} = (\mathcal{R}_p p_{xx} + \mathcal{R}_q q_{xx} - I_{xx})\mathcal{R}_p \\ - 2\mathcal{R}_p^2 \delta p - 2\mathcal{R}_p \mathcal{R}_q \delta q \tag{42}$$

$$\frac{1}{2}\frac{\partial}{\partial y}F_{p_y} = (\mathcal{R}_p p_{yy} + \mathcal{R}_q q_{yy} - I_{yy})\mathcal{R}_p \\ - 2\mathcal{R}_p^2 \delta p - 2\mathcal{R}_p \mathcal{R}_q \delta q \tag{43}$$

$$\frac{1}{2}F_q = [\mathcal{R} + \mathcal{R}_p \delta p + \mathcal{R}_q \delta q - I(x,y)]\mathcal{R}_q \\ + \mu(q - Z_y + \delta q + \delta Z) \tag{44}$$

$$\frac{1}{2}\frac{\partial}{\partial x}F_{q_x} = (\mathcal{R}_p p_{xx} + \mathcal{R}_q q_{xx} - I_{xx})\mathcal{R}_q \\ - 2\mathcal{R}_p \mathcal{R}_q \delta p - 2\mathcal{R}_q^2 \delta q \tag{45}$$

$$\frac{1}{2}\frac{\partial}{\partial y}F_{q_y} = (\mathcal{R}_p p_{yy} + \mathcal{R}_q q_{yy} - I_{yy})\mathcal{R}_q \\ - 2\mathcal{R}_p \mathcal{R}_q \delta p - 2\mathcal{R}_q^2 \delta q \tag{46}$$

$$F_Z = 0 \tag{47}$$

$$\frac{1}{2}\frac{\delta}{\delta_x}F_{Z_x} = -\mu(p_x - Z_{xx} - \delta p + 2\delta Z) \tag{48}$$

$$\frac{1}{2}\frac{\delta}{\delta_y}F_{Z_y} = -\mu(q_y - Z_{yy} - \delta q + 2\delta Z). \tag{49}$$

After substituting (41)–(49) into (37) and writing it in a matrix form, we obtain

$$\begin{pmatrix} 5\mathcal{R}_p^2 + \mu & 5\mathcal{R}_p\mathcal{R}_q & \mu \\ 5\mathcal{R}_p\mathcal{R}_q & 5\mathcal{R}_q^2 + \mu & \mu \\ -1 & -1 & 4 \end{pmatrix}\begin{pmatrix} \delta p \\ \delta q \\ \delta Z \end{pmatrix} = \begin{pmatrix} C_1 \\ C_2 \\ C_3 \end{pmatrix}$$

or equivalently

$$\begin{pmatrix} 5\mathcal{R}_p^2 + \frac{5}{4}\mu & 5\mathcal{R}_p\mathcal{R}_q + \frac{1}{4}\mu & 0 \\ 5\mathcal{R}_p\mathcal{R}_q + \frac{1}{4}\mu & 5\mathcal{R}_q^2 + \frac{5}{4}\mu & 0 \\ -1 & -1 & 4 \end{pmatrix}\begin{pmatrix} \delta p \\ \delta q \\ \delta Z \end{pmatrix} \\ = \begin{pmatrix} C_1 - \frac{1}{4}\mu C_3 \\ C_2 - \frac{1}{4}\mu C_3 \\ C_3 \end{pmatrix} \tag{50}$$

where

$$C_1 = (-\mathcal{R} + I + \mathcal{R}_p p_{xx} + \mathcal{R}_q q_{xx} - I_{xx} + \mathcal{R}_p p_{yy} \\ + \mathcal{R}_q q_{yy} - I_{yy})\mathcal{R}_p - \mu(p - Z_x)$$

$$C_2 = (-\mathcal{R} + I + \mathcal{R}_p p_{xx} + \mathcal{R}_q q_{xx} - I_{xx} + \mathcal{R}_p p_{yy} \\ + \mathcal{R}_q q_{yy} - I_{yy})\mathcal{R}_q - \mu(q - Z_y)$$

$$C_3 = -p_x + Z_{xx} - q_y + Z_{yy}.$$

Solving (50) we obtain the updating scheme

$$\begin{cases} \delta_p = \frac{4}{\Delta}\left[\left(C_1 - \frac{1}{4}\mu C_3\right)\left(5\mathcal{R}_q^2 + \frac{5}{4}\mu\right) \right. \\ \qquad \left. -\left(C_2 - \frac{1}{4}\mu C_3\right)\left(5\mathcal{R}_p\mathcal{R}_q + \frac{1}{4}\mu\right)\right] \\ \delta_q = \frac{4}{\Delta}\left[\left(C_2 - \frac{1}{4}\mu C_3\right)\left(5\mathcal{R}_q^2 + \frac{5}{4}\mu\right) \right. \\ \qquad \left. -\left(C_1 - \frac{1}{4}\mu C_3\right)\left(5\mathcal{R}_p\mathcal{R}_q + \frac{1}{4}\mu\right)\right] \\ \delta Z = \frac{1}{4}(C_3 + \delta p + \delta q) \end{cases}$$

where Δ is the determinant of the coefficient matrix, which is always positive since

$$\Delta = 4\left[\left(5\mathcal{R}_q^2 + \frac{5}{4}\mu\right)\left(5\mathcal{R}_q^2 + \frac{5}{4}\mu\right) \right. \\ \left. -\left(5\mathcal{R}_p\mathcal{R}_q + \frac{1}{4}\mu\right)^2\right] \\ = 4\left\{5\mu\left[\mathcal{R}_p^2 + \mathcal{R}_q^2 + \frac{1}{4}(\mathcal{R}_p - \mathcal{R}_q)^2\right] + 1.5\mu^2\right\} \\ > 0.$$

Therefore, the iterative scheme is stable.

B. Implementation of the Algorithm

1) Hierarchical Structure: Hierarchical implementation is an efficient way of reducing the computations arising in complex image-related tasks [20]. Currently known iterative solutions to SFS are typically globally constrained but involve local updating. To implement a hierarchical SFS algorithm, we first need to specify the structure to be used. In our implementation, the image resolution is reduced by a factor of 2 between adjacent resolution layers. The image size for the lowest resolution layer is between 32 and 64. The input images for various resolution layers are derived from the given highest resolution image by averaging the pixels that belong to the same cell in the low-resolution layer. An important issue in hierarchical implementation is the communication of the results from one layer to another. The surface shape descriptions should be consistent between different resolution layers. Let the variables with a tilde (~) stand for the shape descriptors of the higher resolution layer while the variables without a tilde denote those of the lower resolution layer. The transition rules are as follows:

Rule 1: The illuminant direction and albedo are the same

$$(\tilde{\tau}, \tilde{\gamma}, \tilde{\eta}, \tilde{\sigma}_0) = (\tau, \gamma, \eta, \sigma_0).$$

This assumption is made based on our experiments reported in [19] where we found that the estimated illuminant direction and surface albedo are almost insensitive to changes in resolution.[9]

Rule 2: The surface descriptions of a higher resolution layer are interpolated from the descriptions of the adjacent lower resolution layer. Let $\tilde{M}$ be the image size of the

---

[9]The illuminant direction and albedo can also be estimated for each layer independently.

higher resolution layer.[10] For $i, j \in \left\{2, \cdots, \tilde{M}\right\}$, the shape descriptions for the higher resolution layer are

$$
\left(\tilde{p}, \tilde{q}, \tilde{Z}\right)_{i,j} =
$$

$$
\begin{cases}
(p, q, 2Z)_{\frac{i}{2}, \frac{j}{2}}, & \text{if } i \text{ and } j \text{ are evens} \\[4pt]
\frac{1}{2}\left[(p, q, 2Z)_{\frac{i+1}{2}, \frac{j}{2}} \right. \\
\left. \quad + (p, q, 2Z)_{\frac{i-1}{2}, \frac{j}{2}}\right], & \text{if } i \text{ is odd and } j \text{ is even} \\[4pt]
\frac{1}{2}\left[(p, q, 2Z)_{\frac{i}{2}, \frac{j+1}{2}} \right. \\
\left. \quad + (p, q, 2Z)_{\frac{i}{2}, \frac{j-1}{2}}\right], & \text{if } i \text{ is even and } j \text{ is odd} \\[4pt]
\frac{1}{4}\left[(p, q, 2Z)_{\frac{i+1}{2}, \frac{j+1}{2}} \right. \\
\quad + (p, q, 2Z)_{\frac{i+1}{2}, \frac{j-1}{2}} \\
\quad + (p, q, 2Z)_{\frac{i-1}{2}, \frac{j+1}{2}} \\
\left. \quad + (p, q, 2Z)_{\frac{i-1}{2}, \frac{j-1}{2}}\right] & \text{if } i \text{ and } j \text{ are odds.}
\end{cases}
$$

$$(51)$$

Rule 3: The natural boundary condition is used for the interpolation of boundary pixels. For example, for the boundaries of $i = 1$ and $j = 1$,

$$
\begin{cases}
(\tilde{p}, \tilde{q})_{1,j} = 2(\tilde{p}, \tilde{q})_{2,j} & \tilde{Z}_{1,j} = \tilde{Z}_{2,j} - \tilde{p}_{1,j}, \\
\qquad - (\tilde{p}, \tilde{q})_{3,j} & \text{for } j \geq 2 \\
(\tilde{p}, \tilde{q})_{i,1} = 2(\tilde{p}, \tilde{q})_{i,2} & \tilde{Z}_{i,1} = \tilde{Z}_{i,2} - \tilde{q}_{i,1}, \\
\qquad - (\tilde{p}, \tilde{q})_{i,3} & \text{for } i \geq 2 \\
(\tilde{p}, \tilde{q})_{1,1} = 2(\tilde{p}, \tilde{q})_{2,2} & \tilde{Z}_{1,1} = \tilde{Z}_{2,2} - \tilde{p}_{1,1} \\
\qquad - (\tilde{p}, \tilde{q})_{3,3} & \qquad + \tilde{q}_{1,1}
\end{cases}
$$

$$(52)$$

In our work, we just use the simplest pyramid method for image sampling and interpolation. A more sophisticated method of hierarchical implementation can be found in [20]. Also, as pointed out by Ron and Peleg [21], due to the nonlinearity of the reflectance map, it is better to use knowledge of surface reflectance when reducing the resolution.

2) Iterative Scheme: Combining the issues of reflectance map parameter estimation, hierarchical implementation, and our new SFS formula, we obtain the robust SFS algorithm outlined below:

Step 1: Estimation of the reflectance map parameters $(\tau, \gamma, \eta, \sigma_0)$.

Step 2: Normalization of the input image:

$$\hat{I} = (I - \sigma_0)/\eta.$$

Reduce the input image size to that of the lowest resolution layer and set the values of p^o, q^o, and z^o to zero.

---

[10] Here, for simplicity of presentation, we assume the image frame is square and $\tilde{M}$ is even. The extension to the rectangular image case is obvious. If $\tilde{M}$ is odd we can enforce the natural boundary conditions along $i = \tilde{M}$ and $j = \tilde{M}$ using Rule 3.

Step 3: Update the current shape reconstruction. For each pixel, the partial derivatives are approximated by

$$
\begin{aligned}
p_x &= p^k_{(x+1,y)} - p^k_{(x,y)} \\
p_{xx} &= p^k_{(x+1,y)} + p^k_{(x-1,y)} - 2p^k_{(x,y)} \\
p_{yy} &= p^k_{(x,y+1)} + p^k_{(x,y-1)} - 2p^k_{(x,y)} \\
q_y &= q^k_{(x,y+1)} - q^k_{(x,y)} \\
q_{xx} &= q^k_{(x+1,y)} + q^k_{(x-1,y)} - 2q^k_{(x,y)} \\
q_{yy} &= q^k_{(x,y+1)} + q^k_{(x,y-1)} - 2q^k_{(x,y)} \\
Z_x &= Z^k_{(x+1,y)} - Z^k_{(x,y)} \\
Z_{xx} &= Z^k_{(x+1,y)} + Z^k_{(x-1,y)} - 2Z^k_{(x,y)} \\
Z_y &= Z^k_{x,y+1} - Z^k_{(x,y)} \\
Z_{yy} &= Z^k_{(x,y+1)} + Z^k_{(x,y-1)} - 2Z^k_{(x,y)} \\
\hat{I}_{xx} &= \hat{I}_{(x+1,y)} + \hat{I}_{(x-1,y)} - 2\hat{I}_{(x,y)} \\
\hat{I}_{yy} &= \hat{I}_{(x,y+1)} + \hat{I}_{(x,y-1)} - 2\hat{I}_{(x,y)}
\end{aligned}
$$

where for values outside the image frame, we use natural boundary conditions similar to Rule 3 of Section III-B-1. The shape reconstruction is updated by:

$$
\begin{aligned}
\delta p &= (C_1 A_{22} - C_2 A_{12})/\Delta & p^{k+1} &= p^k + \delta p \\
\delta q &= (C_2 A_{11} - C_1 A_{12})/\Delta \quad \text{and} & q^{k+1} &= q^k + \delta q \\
\delta Z &= (C_3 + \delta p + \delta q)/4 & Z^{k+1} &= Z^k + \delta Z
\end{aligned}
$$

where

$$
\begin{aligned}
A_{11} &= 5\mathcal{R}_p^2 + 1.25\mu \\
A_{12} &= 5\mathcal{R}_p\mathcal{R}_q + 0.25\mu \\
A_{22} &= 5\mathcal{R}_q^2 + 1.25\mu \\
\mathcal{R} &= \mathcal{R}\left(p^k_{(x,y)}, q^k_{(x,y)}\right) \\
\mathcal{R}_p &= \mathcal{R}_p\left(p^k_{(x,y)}, q^k_{(x,y)}\right) \\
\mathcal{R}_q &= \mathcal{R}_q\left(p^k_{(x,y)}, q^k_{(x,y)}\right) \\
C_3 &= -p_x - q_y + Z_{xx} + Z_{yy} \\
C_1 &= (\varepsilon - \epsilon)\mathcal{R}_p - \mu\left(p^k - Z_x\right) - 0.25\mu C_3 \\
C_2 &= (\varepsilon - \epsilon)\mathcal{R}_q - \mu\left(q^k - Z_y\right) - 0.25\mu C_3 \\
\epsilon &= \mathcal{R} - \hat{I}_{(x,y)} \\
\varepsilon &= \mathcal{R}_p(p_{xx} + p_{yy}) + \mathcal{R}_q(q_{xx} + q_{yy}) - \hat{I}_{xx} - \hat{I}_{yy} \\
\Delta &= A_{11}A_{22} - A_{12}^2.
\end{aligned}
$$

If {(Solution is stable) OR (Iteration has reached $N_{\max}$ of current layer)} continue to Step 4, otherwise repeat Step 3.

Step 4: If {Current image is in the highest resolution} stop; Otherwise {

- Increase the image size and expand the shape reconstruction to the adjacent higher resolution layer by (51)–(52);
- Reduce the normalized input image to the current resolution;
- Go to Step 3. }.

TABLE I
SUMMARY OF FORMULAS FOR ILLUMINANT DIRECTION AND ALBEDO ESTIMATION

Pentland's Method τ: $\tau = \arctan \frac{\hat{y}_L}{\hat{x}_L}$; $\begin{bmatrix} \hat{x}_L \\ \hat{y}_L \end{bmatrix} = (B^t B)^{-1} B^t \begin{bmatrix} d\bar{I}_1 \\ d\bar{I}_2 \\ \vdots \\ d\bar{I}_N \end{bmatrix}$

γ: $\gamma = \arccos \left(1 - (\hat{x}_L^2 + \hat{y}_L^2)/k^2\right)^{1/2}$; $k = \left(\boldsymbol{E}\{dI^2\} - (\boldsymbol{E}\{dI\})^2\right)^{1/2}$

Lee & Rosenfeld's Method τ: $\tau = \arctan\left(\boldsymbol{E}\{I_y\}/\boldsymbol{E}\{I_x\}\right)$

γ: Original Form: $\dfrac{\boldsymbol{E}\{I\}}{\sqrt{\boldsymbol{E}\{I^2\}}} = 8 \dfrac{(\pi-\gamma)\cos\gamma + \sin\gamma}{3\pi(1+\cos\gamma)^{3/2}}$

Modified Form: $\dfrac{\boldsymbol{E}\{I\}}{\sqrt{\boldsymbol{E}\{I^2\}}} = \dfrac{4\sqrt{2}}{3\pi} \cdot \dfrac{(\pi-\gamma)\cos\gamma + \sin\gamma}{1+\cos\gamma}$

η: $\eta = \dfrac{1}{a^2+b}\left(a\boldsymbol{E}\{I\} + \sqrt{b\boldsymbol{E}\{I^2\}}\right)$

For Original Form: $a = \dfrac{4}{3\pi}\dfrac{(\pi-\gamma)\cos\gamma + \sin\gamma}{1+\cos\gamma}$; $b = \dfrac{1+\cos\gamma}{4}$.

For Modified Form: $a = \dfrac{2}{3\pi}\left[(\pi-\gamma)\cos\gamma + \sin\gamma\right]$; $b = \dfrac{(1+\cos\gamma)^2}{8}$.

Our Approach τ: Local: $\tau = \arctan\left(\dfrac{\boldsymbol{E}\left\{\hat{x}_L/\sqrt{\hat{x}_L^2+\hat{y}_L^2}\right\}}{\boldsymbol{E}\left\{\hat{y}_L/\sqrt{\hat{x}_L^2+\hat{y}_L^2}\right\}}\right)$; $\begin{bmatrix} \hat{x}_L \\ \hat{y}_L \end{bmatrix} = (B^t B)^{-1} B^t \begin{bmatrix} \delta I_1 \\ \delta I_2 \\ \vdots \\ \delta I_N \end{bmatrix}$

Contour: $\tau = \arctan \dfrac{x_2}{x_1}$; $\vec{X} = (E^t E)^{-1} E^t \begin{bmatrix} I_1 \\ I_2 \\ \vdots \\ I_N \end{bmatrix}$; $E = \begin{bmatrix} \cos\alpha_1 & \sin\alpha_1 \\ \cos\alpha_2 & \sin\alpha_2 \\ \vdots & \vdots \\ \cos\alpha_N & \sin\alpha_N \end{bmatrix}$

γ: $\dfrac{\boldsymbol{E}\{I\}}{\sqrt{\boldsymbol{E}\{I^2\}}} = 0.5577 + 0.6240\cos\gamma + 0.1882\cos^2\gamma - 0.6514\cos^3\gamma$

$- 0.5350\cos^4\gamma + 0.9282\cos^5\gamma + 0.3476\cos^6\gamma - 0.4984\cos^7\gamma$

η: $\eta = \left[\boldsymbol{E}\{I\} \cdot f_1(\gamma) + (\boldsymbol{E}\{I^2\} \cdot f_2(\gamma))^{1/2}\right] \div \left(f_1^2(\gamma) + f_2(\gamma)\right)$.

IV. EXPERIMENTAL RESULTS

A. Illuminant Direction and Albedo Estimates

To illustrate the usefulness of our illuminant direction and albedo estimators, we first tested the algorithms on a number of synthetic images. The tested images include 1) spheres, 2) ellipses with the ratio of major axis (parallel to the x axis) to minor axis equal to 2, 3) spheres with additive Gaussian noise, and 4) Mozart statue images synthesized from laser range data. For each case, the test images were generated using $\eta = 200$, $\sigma_0 = 0$ and various combinations of τ and γ. Fig. 1 shows typical test images synthesized using $\tau = 45°$, $\gamma = 45°$, $\eta = 200$, and $\sigma_0 = 0$. In our testing of the contour-based method, we used a zero-crossing edge detector to get the boundaries. For comparison purposes, both Pentland's [8] and Lee and Rosenfeld's [12] methods were implemented and tested on the same images. The formulas for various approaches are summarized in Table I. From Table I, we can see that for the estimation of τ, when I_x and I_y are approximated by the derivatives with respect to image coordinates, Lee and Rosenfeld's method is just a special case of Pentland's approach with

$$B = \begin{pmatrix} 1 & 0 \\ 0 & 1 \end{pmatrix}.$$

For estimation of γ and η, our method is similar to Lee and Rosenfeld's approach in that both solve for γ from a monotonically decreasing function. However, the functions are different. Fig. 2 shows plots of the functions used to derive

Fig. 1.   Typical synthetic images used in testing illuminant direction and surface albedo estimators. The images shown are synthesized using the Lambertian reflectance map model with parameters $\tau = 45°$, $\sigma = 45°$, $\eta = 200$, and $\sigma_0 = 0$. The noise is additive Gaussian with zero mean and standard deviation 10.

γ and η. It can be seen that γ is a monotonic function of $\boldsymbol{E}\{I\}/\sqrt{\boldsymbol{E}\{I^2\}}$. Note that the dynamic range for the modified Lee and Rosenfeld formula has been increased.

Figs. 3 and 4 show the estimates for the sphere and Mozart images with the background and boundary pixels removed first. Here, due to space limitations, only two profiles corresponding to $\gamma = 45°$ and $\tau = 45°$ are shown for each case. The plots in Figs. 3 and 4 are presented in the following order:

(a) Estimation of τ for images generated with $\gamma = 45°$, $\eta = 200$, $\sigma_0 = 0$, and $\tau = 0, 15°, 30°, \dots, 345°$.

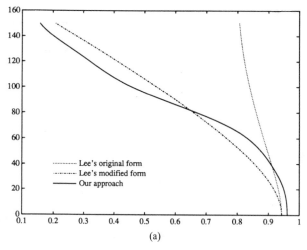

(a)

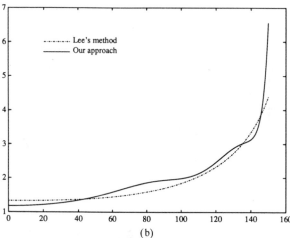

(b)

Fig. 2. In both Lee and Rosenfeld's and our methods, γ and η are obtained from image statistics. (a) γ is a monotonic function of $E\{I\}/\sqrt{E\{I^2\}}$. (b) $\eta \cdot (E\{I\}/E\{I^2\})$ is a function of γ. Note the increase in dynamic range in our estimator.

(b) Estimation of γ for images generated with $\gamma = 45°$, $\eta = 200$, $\sigma_0 = 0$, and $\tau = 0, 15°, 30°, \ldots, 345°$.

(c) Estimation of η for images generated with $\gamma = 45°$, $\eta = 200$, $\sigma_0 = 0$, and $\tau = 0, 15°, 30°, \ldots, 345°$.

(d) Estimation of τ for images generated with $\tau = 45°$, $\eta = 200$, $\sigma_0 = 0$, and $\gamma = 0, 15°, 30°, \ldots, 90°$.

(e) Estimation of γ for images generated with $\tau = 45°$, $\eta = 200$, $\sigma_0 = 0$, and $\gamma = 0, 15°, 30°, \ldots, 90°$.

(f) Estimation of η for images generated with $\gamma = 45°$, $\eta = 200$, $\sigma_0 = 0$, and $\gamma = 15°, 30°, \ldots, 90°$.

The labels used in Figs. 3 and 4 are defined as:

Ideal: The true values.

Pentland: Implementation of Pentland's method.

Lee: Implementation of Lee and Rosenfeld's τ estimator.

Lee-1: Implementation of the original form of Lee and Rosenfeld's γ and η estimator.

Lee-2: Implementation of the shadow compensated form of Lee and Rosenfeld's γ and η estimator.

Local: Estimation of τ by our local voting method.

Contour: Estimation of τ by our image contour based method.

Uniform: Implementation of our γ and η estimator.

The conclusions we reached based on the simulations can be summarized as follows.

1) For estimation of τ, when the image is a perfect sphere (background and boundary pixels are excluded), all four methods work quite well. The estimates from Pentland's, Lee and Rosenfeld's, and our local voting method are all nearly perfect. The estimate obtained by the contour-based method may be sensitive to changes in illuminant elevation. This may due to the fact that the contours detected by using the zero crossing method vary with changes in illuminant elevation. Even a uniform background degrades the performances of both Pentland's and Lee and Rosenfeld's methods.

2) For estimation of τ for sphere images contaminated by Gaussian noise, the local and contour methods are more robust to noise, while both Pentland's and Lee and Rosenfeld's methods degrade when the background pixels are not excluded from the estimation.

3) For estimation of τ, the local and contour methods are more robust when the images change from spheres to ellipses. For ellipse images, the local voting method gives accurate results, independent of the relative orientations of the illuminant azimuth and the axes of the ellipse. For other methods, the errors increase when the illuminant azimuth is away from the axes of the ellipse. Maximum error occurs when the illuminant is from a direction midway between the axes of the ellipse.

4) For estimation of τ from relatively complex images such as Mozart, the results obtained by both the local and contour methods are still quite accurate except for the case of $\gamma = 15°$ where the error in τ estimated by the local method is $-63.65°$. For all the cases considered, the results obtained by the local and contour methods are better than the results obtained by other methods.

5) For estimation of γ from ideal sphere images, the modified Lee and Rosenfeld method works better than our method since the distribution of surface normals fits the Gaussian sphere model. The performances of Pentland's method and the original form of Lee and Rosenfeld's method are poor when γ is relatively large, due to the self-shadowing effect, which is not taken into account by these methods.

6) For all four methods, inclusion of a uniform background decreases the values of the estimated γ. Pentland's method is particularly sensitive to this and results in the estimated values of γ being always less than 0.6° although the true values of γ varied from 15° to 90°.

7) For estimation of γ from sphere images contaminated by Gaussian noise, Pentland's method is severely affected by noise. For sphere images with background excluded, the values of γ estimated by Pentland's method changed from 2.70° to 9.16° while the true values of γ varied from 15° to 90°. The γ values estimated by both Lee and Rosenfeld's and our methods are robust to Gaussian noise.

8) For estimation of γ from ellipse images, the estimate obtained by Pentland's method is dependent on the orientation of the major axis of the ellipse. In contrast to this,

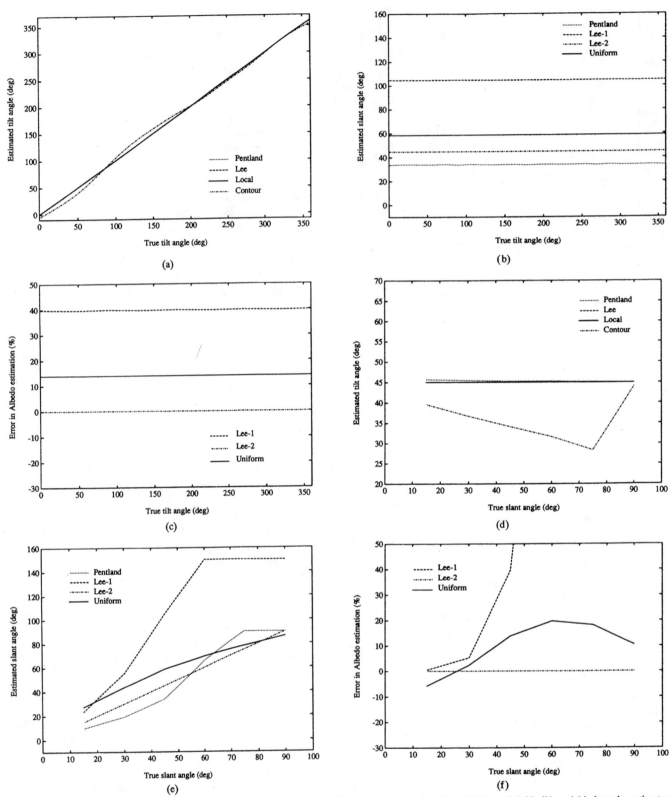

Fig. 3.   Estimation of illuminant direction and albedo from images of a sphere. (See text for an explanation of the legends.) (a), (b), and (c) show the estimates of τ, γ, and η from images of a sphere generated with parameters $\gamma = 45°$, $\eta = 200$, $\sigma_0 = 0$, and $\tau = 15° \times k$ for $k = 0, \ldots, 23$. (d), (e), and (f) show the estimates of τ, γ, and η from images of sphere generated with parameters $\gamma = 45°$, $\eta = 200$, $\sigma_0 = 0$, and $\tau = 15° \times k$ for $k = 1, \ldots, 6$.

the values of γ estimated by both Lee and Rosenfeld's and our methods are robust to the change from sphere to ellipse.

9) For estimation of γ from Mozart images, our method is the best in terms of robustness against changes in

illuminant azimuth and linearity when the true γ changes from 15° to 90°. The performance of Pentland's method is poor. The estimates obtained by both the original and modified forms of Lee and Rosenfeld's method level off for small γ (less than 30°). The estimates obtained by

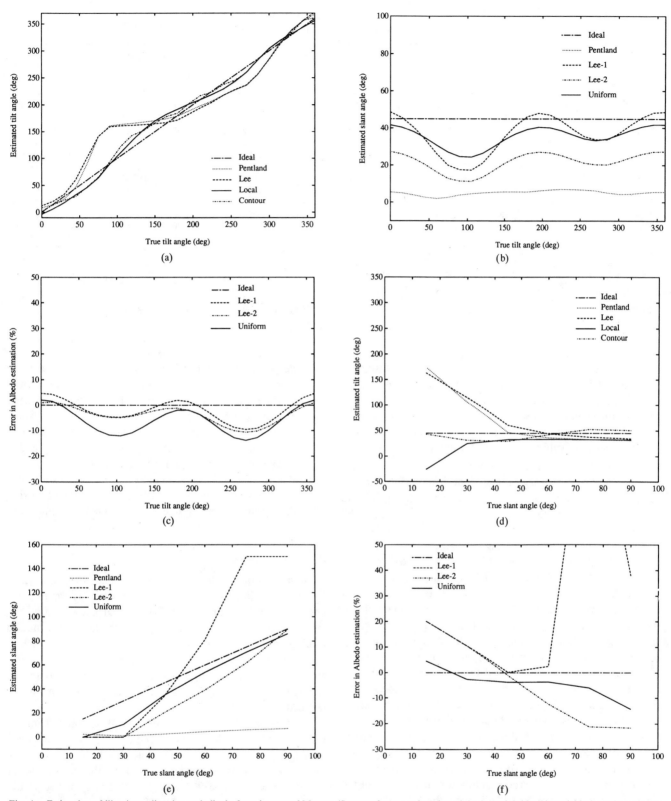

Fig. 4. Estimation of illuminant direction and albedo from images of Mozart. (See text for an explanation of the legends.) (a), (b), and (c) show the estimates of τ, γ, and η from images of Mozart generated with parameters $\gamma = 45°$, $\eta = 200$, $\sigma_0 = 0$, and $\tau = 15° \times k$ for $k = 0, \ldots, 23$. (d), (e), and (f) show the estimates of τ, γ, and η from images of Mozart generated with parameters $\gamma = 45°$, $\eta = 200$, $\sigma_0 = 0$, and $\tau = 15° \times k$ for $k = 1, \ldots, 6$.

our method also level off when the true γ is less than 15°. The original form of Lee and Rosenfeld's method performs poorly when the true γ is relatively large.

10) The performance of η estimation is strongly dependent on the accuracy of γ estimation. Estimated values of η

using the original form of Lee and Rosenfeld's method tend to be too high due to the self-shadowing effect not being accounted for. For ellipse images, η estimates tend to be related to the relative orientations of the illuminant azimuth and the ellipse. For the sphere and ellipse images,

TABLE II
ILLUMINANT DIRECTION AND ALBEDO ESTIMATION FOR REAL IMAGES

Image	Our Method				Pentland's Method		Lee & Rosenfeld's Method				
	τ	γ	η	σ_0	τ	γ	τ	γ_o	η_o	γ_m	η_m
Lenna-1.b	10.79	54.08	127.73	41.00	48.96	0.71	49.64	79.01	134.14	38.36	116.02
Lenna-1.g	7.74	59.52	192.01	3.00	37.98	0.96	36.86	103.36	231.25	44.68	167.62
Lenna-1.r	9.29	42.89	190.47	54.00	39.62	0.94	39.30	48.05	193.78	27.01	187.20
Lenna-1.w	11.73	52.46	162.27	37.00	41.04	0.95	40.64	73.40	167.60	36.59	149.07
Pepper-1.b	26.09	52.77	137.46	0.00	122.19	0.43	119.09	77.02	144.03	37.74	125.87
Pepper-1.g	32.74	45.25	221.72	0.00	151.21	0.91	151.24	56.38	226.76	30.47	214.68
Pepper-1.r	45.16	7.65	146.72	6.00	122.05	1.39	120.20	0.00	169.89	0.00	169.89
Pepper-1.w	32.04	32.27	154.23	2.00	132.39	1.05	130.71	26.83	161.68	16.69	160.65
Pepper-2.b	21.34	56.19	172.88	0.00	76.05	2.92	79.22	87.80	188.74	40.88	154.89
Pepper-2.g	13.00	46.95	243.97	0.00	299.79	3.34	292.05	59.77	248.87	31.78	233.27
Pepper-2.r	22.56	6.50	201.31	0.00	206.88	2.66	215.91	0.00	232.87	0.00	232.87
Pepper-2.w	20.40	24.06	173.24	0.00	282.54	0.79	277.52	0.00	186.66	0.00	186.66
Pepper-3.b	23.25	59.06	149.29	0.00	39.06	1.63	47.02	101.77	178.47	44.33	131.28
Pepper-3.g	15.92	58.20	255.96	0.00	312.61	2.05	303.75	97.25	294.16	43.29	225.05
Pepper-3.r	22.00	17.85	185.45	11.00	304.46	0.74	297.63	0.00	207.31	0.00	207.31
Pepper-3.w	18.56	34.55	163.15	4.00	335.30	1.37	327.56	29.97	169.62	18.36	168.13
Renault-2	157.05	46.08	132.09	14.00	105.05	2.27	104.19	55.17	133.51	29.98	126.82
Renault-3	168.41	44.75	130.58	14.00	110.06	1.87	109.76	51.98	132.02	28.68	126.43

η estimated by using the modified Lee and Rosenfeld method is the most accurate, whereas for the Mozart images, our method works the best.

11) For the synthetic images tested, our method gives reasonably good results for all the situations considered. The estimates are sufficiently good for applications to SFS.

We further tested the above estimators on some real images, including color images, images of different resolutions, subimages of a larger scene, and a stereo image pair. The results are listed in Table II, in which ".r", ".g", and ".b" represent the red, green, and blue bands, respectively, and ".w" represents black/white image generated by a weighted sum of the three color bands. It should be noted that, for real images, there exists a bias in image intensity depending on the film exposure and processing. In the results given in Table II, we detect this bias by finding the minimum of the image intensity array and adjust the image intensities by subtracting this bias. Since for most images there are shadow pixels that have the value of the bias, this simple method works quite well. In these tests, we used the local voting method to estimate the illuminant azimuth. According to our experiments, the local voting method works quite well as long as the scene is not dominated by cylindrical objects. Since the local voting method is much simpler and the performance of the contour-based estimate is dependent on the accuracy of the boundary detection method used, we recommend the local voting method for real images. For Lee and Rosenfeld's method we tested both the original and the modified forms. In Table II, γ_o and η_o represent the estimates obtained by using the original form of Lee and Rosenfeld's method, while γ_m and η_m represent the results obtained by using the shadow-compensated formulas.

The following observations can be made based on the results of our experiments on real images:

1) τ and γ estimated by our method are the best in terms of consistency between different color bands of the same image.

2) Pepper-1 and Pepper-2 are two subimages of a large scene: hence, the τ and γ estimated from them should be the same. As shown in Table II, the results obtained by our method are consistent.

3) Pepper-2 and Pepper-3 are two images of the same scene at different resolutions. As shown in Table II, τ and γ estimated by our method are consistent.

4) For estimation of γ, Pentland's method is hardly useful for practical purposes, and the results obtained by using the original form of Lee and Rosenfeld's method are unstable.

B. SFS Experiments

We tested our SFS algorithm on more than ten real images. Due to space limitations, we only present six examples here, one for a synthetic image and five for real images. In all the experiments we let $\mu = 1$ and N_{max} for the highest resolution layer be 500. The iterations start from $(p, q, Z) = (0, 0, 0)$ and the partial derivatives of the reflectance map, $\mathcal{R}_p$ and $\mathcal{R}_q$, are computed numerically. All the images presented in our examples are 256×256. The 3-D plots of height maps are reduced to 64×64.

Fig. 5 shows the SFS results on a synthetic Mozart image. Fig. 5(a) is the true height map used to generate the synthetic image. Fig. 5(b) gives a 3-D plot of (a). Fig. 5(c) is the input image that is synthesized from (a) with the parameters $\tau = 45°$, $\gamma = 45°$, $\eta = 250$, and $\sigma_0 = 0$. The estimated values of these parameters are $\tau = 31.03°$, $\gamma = 34.88°$, $\eta = 240.84$, and $\sigma_0 = 0$. Fig. 5(d) is the height map reconstructed by the SFS algorithm. A 3-D plot of (d) is shown in Fig. 5(e). Fig. 5(f) shows the image generated from the SFS result using the same reflectance map parameters as the input image. Figs. 5(g) and (h) compare the p maps of ground truth and that obtained by SFS. Figs. 5(i) and (j) compare the q map of ground truth and that obtained by SFS. A comparison of the reconstructed (Z, p, q) with the ground truth shows that there

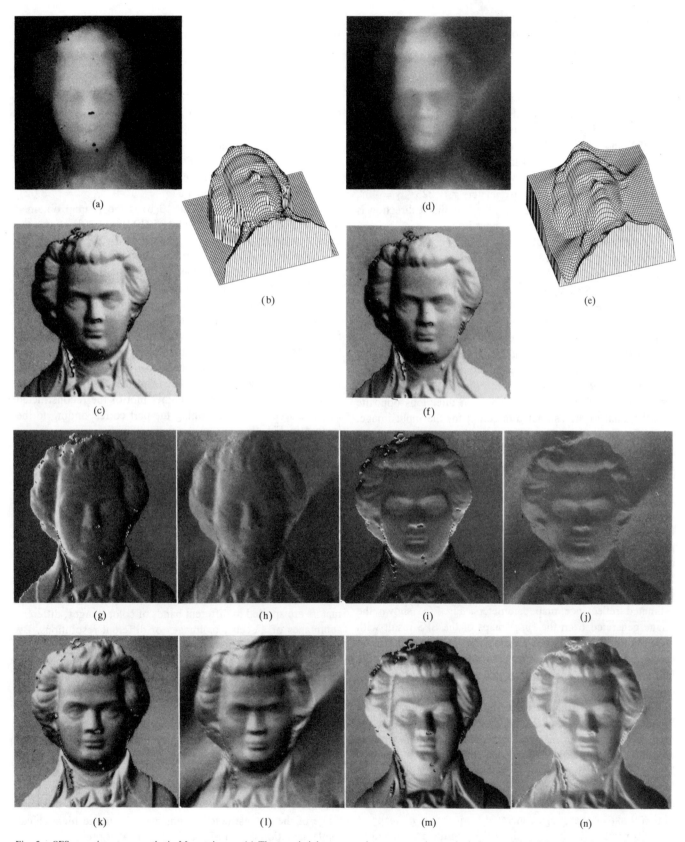

Fig. 5.   SFS experiment on synthetic Mozart image. (a) The true height map used to generate the synthetic image. (b) A 3-D plot of the true height map. (c) The input image, which is synthesized from (a) with parameter $\tau = 45°$, $\gamma = 45°$, $\eta = 250$, $\sigma_0 = 0$. (d) The height map reconstructed by the SFS algorithm. (e) A 3-D plot of the reconstructed height map. (f) The image generated from the SFS result using the same reflectance map parameters as the input image. (g) True Z_x map. (h) The SFS reconstructed p map. (i) True Z_y map. (j) The SFS reconstructed q map. (k) The image synthesized from the true height with $\tau = 135°$. (l) The image synthesized from the SFS result with $\tau = 135°$. (m) The image synthesized from the true height with $\tau = 225°$. (n) The image synthesized from the SFS result with $\tau = 225°$.

are errors in the background region and a rotation distortion in the SFS result, which is probably due to a lack of proper boundary conditions. Apart from that, the reconstruction is successful. This conclusion is supported by the similarities between the images generated from the ground truth and the SFS result using different illuminant directions. Figs. 5(k) and (l) compare images synthesized from the ground truth and the SFS result, both using the parameters $\tau = 135°$, $\gamma = 45°$, $\eta = 250$, and $\sigma_0 = 0$. The illuminant direction is orthogonal to the illuminant in the input image. Figs. 5(m) and (n) give another image pair, the images synthesized from the ground truth and the SFS result using parameters $\tau = 225°$, $\gamma = 45°$, $\eta = 250$, and $\sigma_0 = 0$. In this case, the illuminant direction is opposite to the illuminant in the input image.

Fig. 6(a) shows the input Lenna-1.g image. The reflectance map parameters estimated by our algorithm are $\tau = 7.74°$, $59.52°$, $\eta = 192.01$, and $\sigma_0 = 3$. Fig. 6(b) is the height map obtained by the SFS algorithm. Fig. 6(c) shows a 3-D plot of (b). Figs. 6(d) and (e) are the p, q maps of the SFS results. Fig. 6(f) shows the image synthesized from the reconstructed (p, q) maps using the estimated reflectance map parameters. Figs. 6(g)–(i) show images synthesized from the reconstructed (p, q) maps using parameters $\gamma = 59.52°$, $\eta = 192.01$, $\sigma_0 = 3$, and τ equals to 97.74°, 187.74°, and 277.26° respectively, corresponding to whether illumination from directions opposite or orthogonal to the estimated direction for the input image. It can be seen from Figs. 6(b)–(e) that the shapes of the face and shoulder are recovered correctly and that features such as the nose, lips, cheeks, chin, etc. are easily identified. The images synthesized from the SFS result using different illuminant directions are consistent.

Fig. 7 gives another example of SFS on a human face image. Fig. 7(a) is the input image. The estimated reflectance map parameters are $\tau = 163.11°$, $\gamma = 65.20°$, $\eta = 294.17$, and $\sigma_0 = 9.0$. Fig. 7(b) is the Z map obtained by SFS. Fig. 7(c) is the 3-D plot of (b). Fig. 7(d) shows the image generated from the (p, q) maps of the SFS result using the estimated reflectance map parameters. Fig. 7(e) shows the image generated from the (p, q) maps of the SFS result with the azimuth of illuminant changed to $\tau = 73.11°$. It can be seen that there are errors due to albedo variations near the hair and eyebrows, apart from which the shape of the face is correctly reconstructed.

Fig. 8 shows SFS on the Lenna-2 image, a black and white low-resolution version of the Lenna-1 image. Fig. 8(a) is the input image. The estimated reflectance map parameters are $\tau = 23.84°$, $\gamma = 54.08°$, $\eta = 181.55$, and $\sigma_0 = 3.0$. Fig. 8(b) is the Z map obtained by SFS. Fig. 8(c) is a 3-D plot of (b). Fig. 8(d) shows the image generated from the (p, q) maps of the SFS result using the estimated reflectance map parameters. Fig. 8(e) shows the image generated from the (p, q) maps of the SFS result with the azimuth of the illuminant changed to $\tau = 113.84°$. This example shows the performance of the SFS algorithm on images of different resolutions. Fig. 8(f) shows another plot of the reconstructed height map but only containing the part corresponding to the images in Fig. 6. As can be seen, the plots in Figs. 8(f) and 6(c) are comparable.

Fig. 9 gives an example of SFS on an image of a single pepper. Fig. 9(a) is the input image Pepper-1.g. The estimated reflectance map parameters are $\tau = 32.74°$, $\gamma = 45.25°$, $\eta = 221.85$, and $\sigma_0 = 0$. Fig. 9(b) is the Z map obtained by SFS. Fig. 9(c) is a 3-D plot of (b). Fig. 9(d) shows the image generated from the (p, q) maps of the SFS result using the estimated reflectance map parameters. Fig. 9(e) shows the image generated from the (p, q) maps of the SFS result with the azimuth of the illuminant changed to $\tau = 122.74°$.

Fig. 10 shows the SFS results on a multipepper image. Fig. 10(a) is the input image Pepper-3.g. The estimated reflectance map parameters are $\tau = 15.92°$, $\gamma = 58.02°$, $\eta = 225.78$, and $\sigma_0 = 0$. Fig. 10(b) is the Z map obtained by SFS. Figs. 10(c) is a 3-D plot of (b). Fig. 10(d) shows the image generated from the (p, q) maps of the SFS result using the estimated reflectance map parameters. Fig. 10(e) shows the image generated from the (p, q) maps of the SFS result with the azimuth of the illuminant changed to $\tau = 105.92°$. This is another example of images of different resolutions. Whereas Fig. 9(a) is an image of a single pepper, Fig. 10(a) is more complicated with many small peppers and albedo variations. There are noticeable errors due to shadows and albedo variations, but locally the shapes for most of the objects are visible and correct, irrespective of the changes in image resolution. Fig. 10(f) shows another plot of the reconstructed height map but only containing the part corresponding to the images in Fig. 9.

V. Summary

A practical solution to shape from shading (SFS) should include estimation of illuminant direction, surface albedo, and reconstruction of shape using the estimated reflectance map parameters. In this paper, we have presented methods for estimating reflectance map parameters in a Lambertian imaging model. Tests on synthetic images show that our estimators are more robust and accurate than existing methods. The results of testing on several real images are consistent when the estimators are applied to different bands of color images, different subimages of a scene, or images of different resolutions. By incorporating estimates of illuminant direction and surface albedo into our SFS algorithm, we have obtained encouraging results for a number of real images. In our new SFS algorithm, the smoothness assumption is implemented by requiring the gradients of the reconstructed intensity to be close to the gradients of the input image. Under this formulation, as more constraints are derived from the input image and the slope and height maps are updated simultaneously, the algorithm is more stable. In addition, removal of the quadratic smoothness term from the cost function dramatically decreases the errors in the irradiance and integrability terms and increases the dynamic range of the reconstructed height map. A simple hierarchical implementation of the SFS algorithm is also presented.

We have noticed reconstruction errors due to the surface albedo variation and the lack of proper boundary information. It seems that the use of color information to extract the highlights [22] and segmentation of the image into uniform albedo regions [23] may improve the performance of the SFS

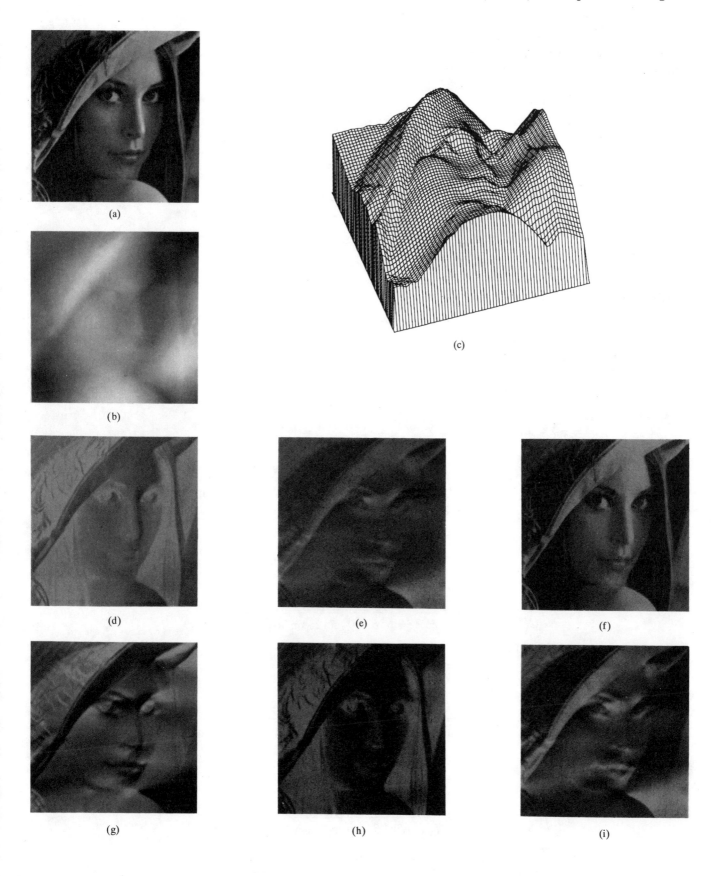

Fig. 6.   SFS on Lenna-1.g. (a) The input image. (b) The height map Z obtained by the SFS algorithm. (c) A 3-D plot of (b). (d) and (e) are the p, q maps of the SFS results. (f) The image synthesized from the reconstructed (p, q) maps using the estimated reflectance map. (g), (h), and (i) are images synthesized from the reconstructed (p, q) maps using τ equal to $97.74°$, $187.74°$, and $277.26°$, respectively, corresponding to illumination from directions opposite or orthogonal to the estimated direction for the input image.

algorithm. Currently, we are also working on integrating our SFS approach with a boundary-based method [24] and on extensions to SAR imagery [25] and multiple images [18].

From Section II-C-1, we have

$$\tilde{x}_L = \sin\gamma\cos\tau - \cos\gamma\tan\beta\cos\alpha$$

$$\tilde{y}_L = \sin\gamma\sin\tau - \cos\gamma\tan\beta\sin\alpha$$

so that

$$\frac{\tilde{x}_L}{\sqrt{\tilde{x}_L^2 + \tilde{y}_L^2}} = \frac{\sin\gamma\cos\tau - \cos\gamma\tan\beta\cos\alpha}{\sqrt{\sin^2\gamma + \cos^2\gamma\tan^2\beta - 2\sin\gamma\cos\gamma\tan\beta\cos(\tau-\alpha)}}$$

$$= \frac{\sin\gamma\cos\tau\cos\beta - \cos\gamma\sin\beta\cos\alpha}{\sqrt{\sin^2\gamma\cos^2\beta + \cos^2\gamma\sin^2\beta - \frac{1}{2}\sin 2\gamma\sin 2\beta\cos(\tau-\alpha)}}.$$

Assume that α is uniformly distributed:

$$p(\alpha) = \frac{1}{2\pi}.$$

The ensemble average of local estimate can then be computed as

$$E_{x,y}\left\{\frac{\tilde{x}_L}{\sqrt{\tilde{x}_L^2 + \tilde{y}_L^2}}\right\} = E_{\alpha,\beta}\left\{\frac{\tilde{x}_L}{\sqrt{\tilde{x}_L^2 + \tilde{y}_L^2}}\right\}$$

$$= \int_{\Omega_\beta} p(\beta)\,d\beta\,\frac{1}{2\pi}\int_{-\pi}^{\pi}\frac{\sin\gamma\cos\tau\cos\beta - \cos\gamma\sin\beta\cos\alpha}{\sqrt{\sin^2\gamma\cos^2\beta + \cos^2\gamma\sin^2\beta - \frac{1}{2}\sin 2\gamma\sin 2\beta\cos(\tau-\alpha)}}\,d\alpha. \tag{53}$$

Notice that

$$\int_{-\pi}^{\pi}\frac{\sin\gamma\cos\tau\cos\beta}{\sqrt{\sin^2\gamma\cos^2\beta + \cos^2\gamma\sin^2\beta - \frac{1}{2}\sin 2\gamma\sin 2\beta\cos(\tau-\alpha)}}\,d\alpha$$

$$= \int_{\tau-\pi}^{\tau+\pi}\frac{\sin\gamma\cos\tau\cos\beta}{\sqrt{\sin^2\gamma\cos^2\beta + \cos^2\gamma\sin^2\beta - \frac{1}{2}\sin 2\gamma\sin 2\beta\cos\alpha}}\,d\alpha$$

$$= \cos\tau\int_{-\pi}^{\pi}\frac{\sin\gamma\cos\beta}{\sqrt{\sin^2\gamma\cos^2\beta + \cos^2\gamma\sin^2\beta - \frac{1}{2}\sin 2\gamma\sin 2\beta\cos\alpha}}\,d\alpha \tag{54}$$

$$\int_{-\pi}^{\pi}\frac{\cos\gamma\sin\beta\cos\alpha}{\sqrt{\sin^2\gamma\cos^2\beta + \cos^2\gamma\sin^2\beta - \frac{1}{2}\sin 2\gamma\sin 2\beta\cos(\tau-\alpha)}}\,d\alpha$$

$$= \int_{\tau-\pi}^{\tau+\pi}\frac{\cos\gamma\sin\beta\cos(\tau-\alpha)}{\sqrt{\sin^2\gamma\cos^2\beta + \cos^2\gamma\sin^2\beta - \frac{1}{2}\sin 2\gamma\sin 2\beta\cos\alpha}}\,d\alpha$$

$$= \int_{-\pi}^{\pi}\frac{\cos\gamma\sin\beta(\cos\tau\cos\alpha + \sin\tau\sin\alpha)}{\sqrt{\sin^2\gamma\cos^2\beta + \cos^2\gamma\sin^2\beta - \frac{1}{2}\sin 2\gamma\sin 2\beta\cos\alpha}}\,d\alpha$$

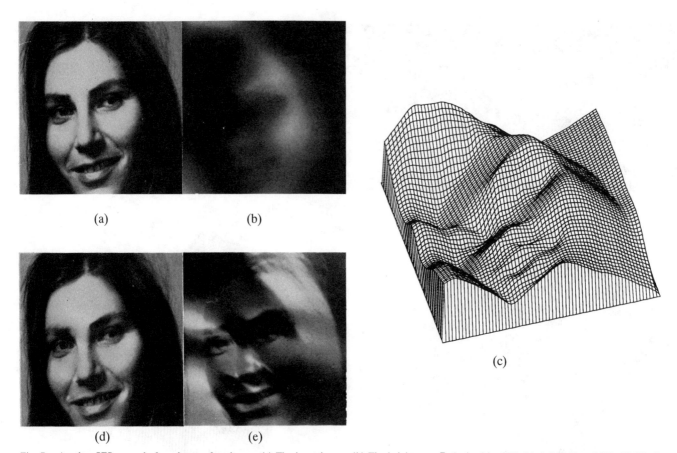

Fig. 7.   Another SFS example for a human face image. (a) The input image. (b) The height map Z obtained by SFS. (c) A 3-D plot of (b). (d) The image generated from the (p, q) maps of the SFS result using the estimated reflectance map parameters. (e) The image generated from the (p, q) maps of the SFS result with the illuminant azimuth changed to the orthogonal direction, i.e., $\tau = 73.11°$.

$$= \int_{-\pi}^{\pi} \frac{\cos \gamma \sin \beta \cos \tau \cos \alpha}{\sqrt{\sin^2 \gamma \cos^2 \beta + \cos^2 \gamma \sin^2 \beta - \frac{1}{2} \sin 2\gamma \sin 2\beta \cos \alpha}} \, d\alpha$$

$$= \cos \tau \int_{-\pi}^{\pi} \frac{\cos \gamma \sin \beta \cos \alpha}{\sqrt{\sin^2 \gamma \cos^2 \beta + \cos^2 \gamma \sin^2 \beta - \frac{1}{2} \sin 2\gamma \sin 2\beta \cos \alpha}} \, d\alpha. \tag{55}$$

Substitution of (54) and (55) into (53) gives

$$E_{x,y} \left\{ \frac{\tilde{x}_L}{\sqrt{\tilde{x}_L^2 + \tilde{y}_L^2}} \right\} = \cos \tau \cdot F(\gamma) \tag{56}$$

where

$$F(\gamma) = \int_{\Omega_\beta} p(\beta) \, d\beta \, \frac{1}{2\pi} \int_{-\pi}^{\pi} \frac{\sin \gamma \cos \beta - \cos \gamma \sin \beta \cos \alpha}{\sqrt{\sin^2 \gamma \cos^2 \beta + \cos^2 \gamma \sin^2 \beta - \frac{1}{2} \sin 2\gamma \sin 2\beta \cos \alpha}} \, d\alpha. \tag{57}$$

Similarly, for the y component of τ estimation, we have

$$\frac{\tilde{y}_L}{\sqrt{\tilde{x}_L^2 + \tilde{y}_L^2}} = \frac{\sin \gamma \sin \tau \cos \beta - \cos \gamma \sin \beta \sin \alpha}{\sqrt{\sin^2 \gamma \cos^2 \beta + \cos^2 \gamma \sin^2 \beta - \frac{1}{2} \sin 2\gamma \sin 2\beta \cos(\tau - \alpha)}}$$

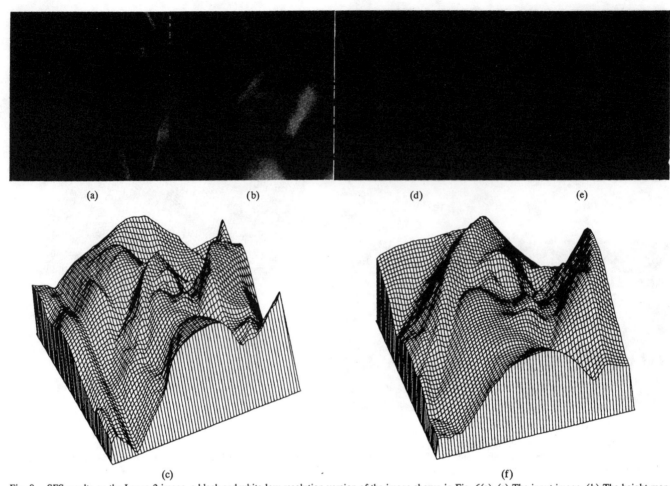

(a)   (b)   (d)   (e)

(c)   (f)

Fig. 8.   SFS results on the Lenna-2 image, a black and white low resolution version of the image shown in Fig. 6(a). (a) The input image. (b) The height map Z obtained by the SFS algorithm. (c) A 3-D plot of (b). (d) The image generated from the (p,q) maps of the SFS result using the estimated reflectance map parameters. (e) The image generated from the (p,q) maps of the SFS result with the illuminant azimuth changed to the orthogonal direction, i.e., $\tau = 113.84°$. (f) A 3-D plot of the part of the reconstructed height map corresponding to the images in Fig. 6. It can be seen that the plots in (f) and Fig. 6(c) are comparable.

$$E_{x,y}\left\{\frac{\tilde{y}_L}{\sqrt{\tilde{x}_L^2 + \tilde{y}_L^2}}\right\} = E_{\alpha,\beta}\left\{\frac{\tilde{y}_L}{\sqrt{\tilde{x}_L^2 + \tilde{y}_L^2}}\right\}$$

$$= \int_{\Omega_\beta} p(\beta)\, d(\beta)\, \frac{1}{2\pi} \int_{-\pi}^{\pi} \frac{\sin\gamma \sin\tau \cos\beta - \cos\gamma \sin\beta \sin\alpha}{\sqrt{\sin^2\gamma \cos^2\beta + \cos^2\gamma \sin^2\beta - \frac{1}{2}\sin 2\gamma \sin 2\beta \cos(\tau-\alpha)}}\, d\alpha. \tag{58}$$

Consider the first term in the integrand

$$\int_{-\pi}^{\pi} \frac{\sin\gamma \sin\tau \cos\beta}{\sqrt{\sin^2\gamma \cos^2\beta + \cos^2\gamma \sin^2\beta - \frac{1}{2}\sin 2\gamma \sin 2\beta \cos(\tau-\alpha)}}\, d\alpha$$

$$= \sin\tau \int_{-\pi}^{\pi} \frac{\sin\gamma \cos\beta}{\sqrt{\sin^2\gamma \cos^2\beta + \cos^2\gamma \sin^2\beta - \frac{1}{2}\sin 2\gamma \sin 2\beta \cos\alpha}}\, d\alpha \tag{59}$$

and the second term in the integrand is

$$\int_{-\pi}^{\pi} \frac{\cos\gamma \sin\beta \sin\alpha}{\sqrt{\sin^2\gamma \cos^2\beta + \cos^2\gamma \sin^2\beta - \frac{1}{2}\sin 2\gamma \sin 2\beta \cos(\tau-\alpha)}}\, d\alpha$$

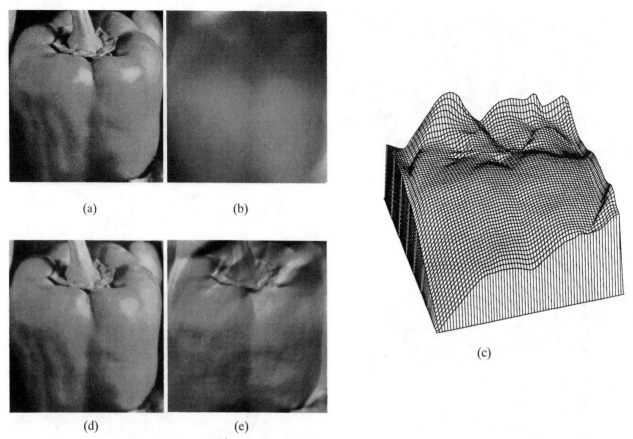

Fig. 9.   SFS results on a single pepper image. (a) The input image Pepper-1.g. (b) The height map Z obtained by the SFS algorithm. (c) A 3-D plot of (b). (d) The image generated from the (p, q) maps of the SFS result using the estimated reflectance map parameters. (e) The image generated from the (p, q) maps of the SFS result with the illuminant azimuth changed to the orthogonal direction, i.e., $\tau = 122.74°$.

$$= \int_{\tau-\pi}^{\tau+\pi} \frac{\cos\gamma \sin\beta \sin(\tau - \alpha)}{\sqrt{\sin^2\gamma \cos^2\beta + \cos^2\gamma \sin^2\beta - \frac{1}{2}\sin 2\gamma \sin 2\beta \cos\alpha}}\, d\alpha$$

$$= \int_{-\pi}^{\pi} \frac{\cos\gamma \sin\beta(\sin\tau \cos\alpha - \cos\tau \sin\alpha)}{\sqrt{\sin^2\gamma \cos^2\beta + \cos^2\gamma \sin^2\beta - \frac{1}{2}\sin 2\gamma \sin 2\beta \cos\alpha}}\, d\alpha$$

$$= \int_{-\pi}^{\pi} \frac{\cos\gamma \sin\beta \sin\tau \cos\alpha}{\sqrt{\sin^2\gamma \cos^2\beta + \cos^2\gamma \sin^2\beta - \frac{1}{2}\sin 2\gamma \sin 2\beta \cos\alpha}}\, d\alpha$$

$$= \sin\tau \int_{-\pi}^{\pi} \frac{\cos\gamma \sin\beta \cos\alpha}{\sqrt{\sin^2\gamma \cos^2\beta + \cos^2\gamma \sin^2\beta - \frac{1}{2}\sin 2\gamma \sin 2\beta \cos\alpha}}\, d\alpha. \tag{60}$$

Substitution of (59) and (60) into (58) gives

$$E_{x,y}\left\{ \frac{\tilde{y}_L}{\sqrt{\tilde{x}_L^2 + \tilde{y}_L^2}} \right\} = \sin\tau \cdot F(\gamma). \tag{61}$$

Combining (56) and (61), we obtain

$$\frac{E_{x,y}\left\{ \dfrac{\tilde{y}_L}{\sqrt{\tilde{x}_L^2 + \tilde{y}_L^2}} \right\}}{E_{x,y}\left\{ \dfrac{\tilde{x}_L}{\sqrt{\tilde{x}_L^2 + \tilde{y}_L^2}} \right\}} = \frac{\sin\tau}{\cos\tau} \tag{62}$$

which leads to (23).

One practical problem associated with the assumption of a uniform distribution for α is that, although α of the true surface normal is uniformly distributed, the distribution of α's for illuminated surface parts is generally not uniform due to self-shadowing. An interesting observation regarding the derivation of (23) is that the requirement of a uniform distribution for α can be replaced by the condition that the distribution of α is symmetric about $\alpha = \tau$, which happens to be the case when self-shadowing is present. So our local method is robust to effects due to self-shadows.

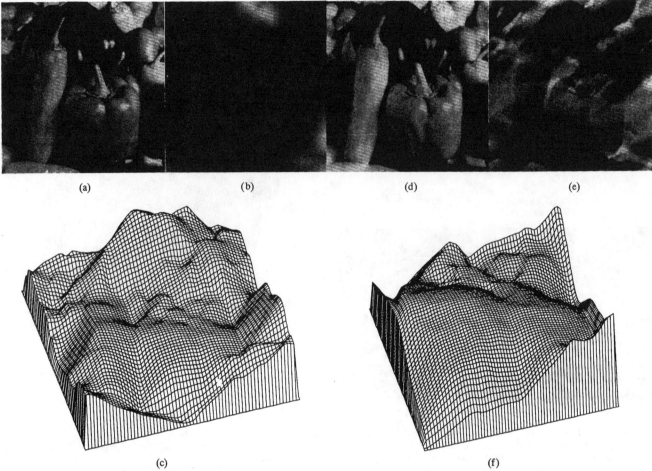

Fig. 10.   SFS results on a multipepper image. (a) The input image Pepper-3.g. (b) The height map Z obtained by SFS. (c) A 3-D plot of (b). (d) The image generated from the (p, q) maps of the SFS result using the estimated reflectance map parameters. (e) The image generated from the (p, q) maps of the SFS result in the illuminant azimuth changed to the orthogonal direction, i.e., $\tau = 105.92°$. (f) A 3-D plot of the part of the reconstructed height map corresponding to the images in Fig. 9.

In the above derivation, for simplicity of presentation, we have implicitly assumed α and β to be independently distributed. The derivation of (23) is valid for all distributions of $p(\alpha, \beta)$ as long as the marginal distribution of α is symmetric about $\alpha = \tau$, i.e., the following condition is satisfied

$$p(\tau - \alpha | \beta) = p(\tau + \alpha | \beta) \qquad \forall \, \alpha \in (0, \pi).$$

ACKNOWLEDGMENT

The authors are thankful to Dr. R. T. Frankot, Prof. B. K. P. Horn, Prof. A. Pentland, and anonymous referees for several useful comments. We are also thankful to S. Chandrashekhar and B. S. Manjunath for making critical comments on preliminary versions of this paper. The laser range data of Mozart used in this experiment was provided by A. Huertas of the Institute for Robotics and Intelligent Systems, University of Southern California.

REFERENCES

[1] B. K. P. Horn and M. J. Brooks, *Shape From Shading*. Cambridge, MA: MIT Press, 1989.
[2] V. S. Ramachandran, "Perception of shape and shading," *Nature*, vol. 331, no. 14, pp. 163–166, Jan. 1988.
[3] B. K. P. Horn, "Shape from shading: A method for obtaining the shape of a smooth opaque object from one view," Ph.D. dissertation, Dept. of Electrical Eng., MIT, Cambridge, MA, 1970.
[4] ——, "Obtaining Shape from Shading Information," in P. H. Winston, Ed., *The Psychology of Machine Vision*. New York: McGraw-Hill, 1975, pp. 115–155.
[5] ——, "Height and gradient from shading," *Int. J. Comput. Vision*, vol. 5, no. 1, pp. 584–595, Aug. 1990.
[6] ——, "Hill shading and the reflectance map," *Proc. IEEE*, vol. 69, no. 1, pp. 14–47, Jan. 1981.
[7] ——, *Robot Vision*. Cambridge, MA: MIT Press, 1986.
[8] A. P. Pentland, "Finding the illuminant direction," *J. Opt. Soc. Amer. A*, vol. 72, no. 4, pp. 448–455, Apr. 1982.
[9] ——, "Local shading analysis," *IEEE Trans. Pattern Anal. Machine Intell.*, vol. PAMI-16, no. 2, pp. 170–187, Mar. 1984.
[10] ——, "Shape information from shading: A theory about human perception," in *Proc. Int. Conf. Comput. Vision*, 1988, pp. 404–413.
[11] M. J. Brooks and B. K. P. Horn, "Shape and source from shading," in *Proc. Int. Joint Conf. Artificial Intell.*, (Los Angeles), Aug. 1985, pp. 932–936.
[12] C. H. Lee and A. Rosenfeld, "Improved methods of estimating shape from shading using the light source coordinate system," in B. K. P. Horn and M. J. Brooks, Eds., *Shape from Shading*. Cambridge, MA: MIT Press, 1989, pp. 323–569.
[13] A. P. Pentland, "Linear shape from shading," *Int. J. Comput. Vision*, vol. 4, pp. 153–162, 1990.
[14] T. Simchony, R. Chellappa, and M. Shao, "Direct analytic methods for solving Poisson equations in computer vision problems," *IEEE Trans. Pattern Anal. Machine Intell.*, vol. PAMI-12, no. 5, pp. 435–446, May 1990.

[15] K. Ikeuchi and B. K. P. Horn, "Numerical shape from shading and occluding boundaries," *Artificial Intell.*, vol. 17, pp. 141–184, Aug. 1981.

[16] B. K. P. Horn and M. J. Brooks, "The variational approach to shape from shading," *Comput. Vision, Graphics, Image Processing,* vol. 33, pp. 174–208, Nov. 1986.

[17] R. T. Frankot and R. Chellappa, "A method for enforcing integrability in shape from shading algorithms," *IEEE Trans. Pattern Anal. Machine Intell.,* vol. PAMI-10, no. 4, pp. 439–451, July 1988.

[18] M. Shao, T. Simchony, and R. Chellappa, "New algorithms for reconstruction of a 3-D depth map from one or more images," in *Proc. Comput. Vision Pattern Recognition* (Ann Arbor, MI), June 1988, pp. 530–535.

[19] Q. Zheng and R. Chellappa, "A robust algorithm for inferring shape from shading," Tech. Rep. USC-SIPI Rep. 159, Univ. of Southern California, Los Angeles, 1990.

[20] R. Szeliski, "Fast surface interpolation using hierarchical basis functions," *IEEE Trans. Pattern Anal. Machine Intell.,* vol. 12, no. 6, pp. 513–528, June 1990.

[21] S. Peleg and G. Ron, "Nonlinear multiresolution: A shape-from-shading example," *IEEE Trans. Pattern Anal. Machine Intell.,* vol. 12, no. 12, pp. 1206–1210, 1990.

[22] G. J. Klinker, S. A. Shafer, and T. Kanade, "The measurement of highlights in color images," *Int. J. Comput. Vision,* vol. 2, pp. 7–32, 1988.

[23] A. C. Hurlbert, "The computation of color," Tech. Rep. 1154, MIT AI Lab., Cambridge, MA, 1989.

[24] J. Malik and D. Maydan, "Recovering three-dimensional shape from a single image of curved objects," *IEEE Trans. Pattern Anal. Machine Intell.,* vol. 11, no. 6, pp. 555–566, June 1989.

[25] R. T. Frankot and R. Chellappa, "Estimation of surface height in synthetic aperture radar images using shape from shading techniques," *Artificial Intell.,* vol. 43, June 1990.

Qinfen Zheng received the B.S. and M.S. degrees in electrical engineering from the University of Science and Technology of China in 1981 and 1984, respectively. He is currently working toward the Ph.D. degree in electrical engineering at the University of Southern California, Los Angeles.

During 1984–1986, he was a Lecturer in the Department of Electronics, University of Science and Technology of China. His current research interests include image processing, computer vision, and remote sensing.

Mr. Zheng received the 1984 Guo Mo-Ruo Gold Medal from the University of Science and Technology of China.

Rama Chellappa (S'79–M'81–SM'83) was born in Madras, India. He received the B.S. degree (honors) in electronics and communications engineering from the University of Madras in 1975, the M.S. degree (with distinction) in electrical communication engineering from the Indian Institute of Science in 1977, and the M.S. and Ph.D. degrees in electrical engineering from Purdue University, West Lafayette, IN, in 1978 and 1981, respectively.

During 1979–1981, he was a Faculty Research Assistant at the Computer Vision Laboratory, University of Maryland, College Park. Since 1986, he has been an Associate Professor in the Department of Electrical Engineering Systems, and in September 1988, he became the Director of the Signal and Image Institute at the University of Southern California, Los Angeles. In June 1991, he joined the Department of Electrical Engineering at University of Maryland, College Park, as a Professor. He also is affiliated with the University of Maryland Institute for Advanced Computer Studies (UMIACS) and the Center for Automation Research. His current research interests are in signal and image processing, computer vision, and pattern recognition.

Dr. Chellappa is a member of Tau Beta Pi and Eta Kappa Nu. He coedited two volumes of selected papers on image analysis and processing, published in 1985. He served as an Associate Editor for IEEE TRANSACTIONS ON ACOUSTICS, SPEECH, AND SIGNAL PROCESSING and is currently a co-editor of *Computer Vision, Graphics, and Image Processing: Graphic Models and Image Processing.* He was a recipient of a National Scholarship from the Government of India during 1969–1975. He received the 1975 Jawaharlal Nehru Memorial Award from the Department of Education, Government of India, the 1985 Presidential Young Investigator Award, and the 1985 IBM Faculty Development Award. He also received the 1990 Excellence in Teaching Award from the School of Engineering at the University of Southern California. He was the General Chairman of the 1989 IEEE Computer Society Conference on Computer Vision and Pattern Recognition, and the IEEE Computer Society Workshop on Artificial Intelligence for Computer Vision, and he was Program Co-Chairman of the NSF-sponsored Workshop on Markov Random Fields for Image Processing, Analysis, and Computer Vision.

Estimation of Surface Topography from SAR Imagery Using Shape from Shading Techniques

Robert T. Frankot*

Hughes Aircraft Company, Radar Systems Group, El Segundo, CA, USA

Rama Chellappa**

Signal and Image Processing Institute, University of Southern California, Department of EE-Systems, Los Angeles, CA 90089-0272, USA

ABSTRACT

In this paper a practical method is demonstrated for estimating topography of natural terrain from the radiometric, or shading, information in a synthetic aperture radar (SAR) image. While this problem has been considered before for radar, methods available in the computer vision literature have not previously been utilized in its solution. We treat this as a computer vision problem, viz. shape from shading (SFS).

A review of the relevant characteristics of SAR imagery is presented followed by a formulation of the SFS problem for SAR. Because of the noise inherent in SAR imagery a cost minimization approach is used which allows for noise and incorporates a regularization term in the cost function. Previously developed numerical methods are adapted to SAR imagery by incorporating radar reflectance models and by solving for surface slopes in a rotated system of coordinates—one which represents surface height relative to a plane parallel to the line-of-sight.

Two difficulties are recognized. First, unknown reflectance model parameters must be estimated from the image data. Second, shading provides reliable information about the high frequency components of the surface but not the low frequency components. Both difficulties are reduced if auxiliary low resolution surface height information is available. This is demonstrated by combining Shuttle Imaging Radar-B (SIR-B) SAR images with much lower resolution terrain elevation data to construct high resolution terrain elevation estimates.

The estimation of Venusian surface topography from Magellan SAR imagery is discussed and methods are suggested for combining shading information with geometric stereo.

*Supported in part by the Hughes Doctoral Fellowship Program.

**Supported in part by the NSF Grant No. MIP 84–51010, matching funds from Hughes Aircraft Company, IBM and AT&T and the Joint Services Electronics Program at the University of Southern California through the Air Force Office of Scientific Research under contract F49620–88-C-0067.

1. Introduction

In this paper we address the problem of estimating surface topography given a single synthetic aperture radar (SAR) image of natural terrain. The basic approach is to model the observed image intensity in terms of the surface orientation through a so-called computational vision model. Then that relationship is used to solve for the surface slopes from which a surface height estimate is constructed.

The use of radar backscatter power to extract terrain surface orientation, sometimes referred to as radarclinometry [46], has been considered before. Cosgriff, Peake and Taylor [11], while concentrating on clutter modeling for system design purposes, discussed the possibility of radarclinometry and suggested a solution method using multiple radar images. This is a concept similar to photometric (or radiometric) stereo [48] which utilizes multiple images obtained with illumination sources at different orientations but with the camera fixed relative to the surface. Application of radiometric stereo requires a precise registration between multiple images made with different illumination angles. For radar imagery, the changes in illumination geometry affect the image coordinate system such that precise registration requires knowledge of surface topography, the unknown that we seek. Because of this complication radiometric stereo is not considered further in this paper, although it should be examined in the future for SAR in combination with geometric stereo.

Wildey [46, 47] developed algorithms for reconstructing surface topography from the shading in a single SAR image by directly inverting the differential equation relating surface height to image intensity, subject to the assumption that the surface is locally cylindrical (i.e., the surface curvature is zero in some direction). The solution method relies on the ability to estimate the direction in which the surface curvature vanishes which, in turn, requires estimation of image intensity derivatives. This approach to radarclinometry does not utilize the numerical methods or the regularization theory available in the computer vision literature. The local cylindricity assumption is restrictive and reliable estimation of intensity derivatives is difficult for coherent imagery, such as SAR. Further, the direct inversion solution is unstable in the presence of noise and vulnerable to error accumulation.

We treat radarclinometry as a computer vision problem, recognizing that it is simply shape from shading (SFS) for SAR imagery. Several SFS algorithms already exist for visual imagery [18, 23, 25, 27, 40] that provide more general solutions, more effective methods for applying additional constraints, and more efficient numerical computation than previously considered for radarclinometry. For an excellent coverage of past research in SFS the reader is referred to [24, 25].

Because of fundamental differences between the physics of SAR image formation and that of conventional images at visible wavelengths, existing SFS algorithms are not directly applicable to SAR imagery. The slant-range/cross-range coordinate system of SAR strip maps is very different from the azimuth/elevation coordinates of conventional photographs. The reflectance characteristics are also different, partly because radar wavelengths are much longer than optical wavelengths and partly due to an additional pixel area factor introduced into the reflectance model by SAR image coordinates. The noise inherent to synthetic aperture imaging also poses additional problems. Based on these modeling issues, we have adapted the SFS method from [17] to SAR imagery.

To explain the rationale behind our SAR SFS algorithm, consider the following SFS problem formulation: Let $I(r, y)$ be the observed image intensity and $u(r, y)$ be the unknown surface height above (r, y). For convenience, (r, y) is chosen to be a plane parallel to the line-of-sight, the "slant plane" inherent in SAR image formation. The relationship between image intensity and surface slopes can be expressed by the approximation [17],

$$I(r, y) \approx \mathcal{R}(u_r, u_y, \boldsymbol{\beta}, \eta) , \tag{1}$$

where $u_r = \partial u / \partial r$ and $u_y = \partial u / \partial y$ are the surface slopes, $\boldsymbol{\beta}$ is the illumination direction vector, from the surface to the radar, and η is the albedo or intrinsic reflectivity of the materials composing the surface. $\mathcal{R}$, referred to as the reflectance map, is the radiometric relationship between the surface orientation and image intensity. In addition to the parameters $\boldsymbol{\beta}$ and η, a shape parameter and additive bias term will be introduced in Section 2. Assume that multiple reflections are insignificant, that η and $\boldsymbol{\beta}$ are known over the entire image, and $\mathcal{R}$ is spatially invariant. The problem of reconstructing u given I through (1) can be expressed as one of solving a nonlinear partial differential equation in r and y [23], an inverse problem.

An image is a projection of a three-dimensional (3D) world into a 2D signal, and vision is, in some sense, the inverse of that projection. Hence, vision is a highly under-constrained, or ill-posed, problem requiring additional knowledge or simplifying assumptions. Although formulated in a more restricted domain, SFS poses similar problems. The primary difficulty with estimating surface topography from radiometric, i.e., shading, information alone is that the representation in (1) is never exact. This is because of noise in the observed image intensity and imperfect modeling. Even in the absence of noise and modeling errors, the solution to (1) may be underconstrained. Consequently, additional constraints are required.

We have combined five essential features in developing a constrained minimization solution to the SFS problem for SAR imagery. First, an imperfect fit between the observed image intensity and the estimated surface is explicitly accounted for through a mean squared-error term. Instead of trying to exactly solve (1), the sum of squared-errors between the observed image and its prediction (given the surface derivative estimates and a reflectance model) is minimized. Second, a regularization penalty constraint encourages smoothness in the estimated surface. We have applied the sum-of-squared values of the second partial derivatives of the surface. Ikeuchi and Horn [27], and Brooks and Horn [7] developed iterative SFS algorithms that minimized the sum of the above two criteria using the methods of variational calculus. Third, self-consistency of the estimated surface should be enforced. We enforce integrability of the surface slopes (u_r, u_y), one form of self-consistency, as a projection constraint: Given nonintegrable surface slope estimates an integrable set of estimates is constructed. An additional condition not addressed in this paper is that any shadows in the observed image should also be predicted by the estimated surface. Fourth, we have utilized the low resolution surface height data often available from radar altimetry or other sources. The low resolution data is used both to replace low frequency surface height information not available from shading alone and to obtain estimates of the reflectance model parameters. Finally, we incorporate the SAR image coordinates and reflectance models from Section 2.

Given a SAR image and a companion digital terrain elevation model (DTM) at much lower resolution, the surface estimation procedure is as follows: The DTM is registered to the SAR imagery. Reflectance model parameters are estimated such that the mean squared-error between the SAR image and its prediction from the low resolution DTM is minimized. The function $\mathscr{R}$ is represented by a model with unknown parameters, dependent on both scene characteristics and sensor characteristics. Given suitable estimates of those parameters, the SFS algorithm iteratively estimates the terrain surface slopes (u_r, u_y). At each iteration, integrability of those surface slopes is enforced and, by the same process, a surface height estimate is constructed. This is accomplished using a fast least-squares procedure that involves a weighted sum of the Fourier transforms of the estimates for u_r and u_y [18]. The Fourier transform of the DTM is substituted for the low frequency portion of the surface estimate, which is not adequately represented by shading information. This difficulty is fundamental because image intensity is a noisy function of surface height derivatives. It is exacerbated for SAR imagery because of the often highly directional nature of $\mathscr{R}$ and the presence of speckle noise.

The above approach was tested using real SAR imagery produced by the Shuttle Imaging Radar-B (SIR-B) and independently derived DTMs. The resulting surface reconstructions compared favorably with the high resolution DTM. This may be applicable to the Magellan project's Venus Radar Mapper which will provide high resolution SAR imagery of the surface of Venus along with orders of magnitude lower resolution radar altimetry data [31] as did Pioneer Venus [33]. Using the techniques presented in Sections 3 and 4, one could combine the altimetry data and the SAR imagery to construct high resolution topographic maps of Venus.

Very recently, Simchony and Chellappa [40] have applied orthogonal transforms to directly solve for the surface slopes in the SFS problem and to enforce integrability in that solution. For linear reflectance maps the solution is obtained noniteratively. For nonlinear reflectance maps a few iterations of the direct algorithm using the Jacobi–Picard method are sufficient. They have shown how to efficiently utilize very general boundary conditions, and how to combine sparse stereo depth maps with photometric stereo and monocular shading. This algorithm is currently being considered for SAR imagery.

The research presented in this paper is a first step towards developing model-based machine perception techniques for SAR image understanding. Much more has to be done to incorporate other sources of information in the context of our work. The use of basic image analysis and scene analysis techniques, as well as the utilization of frequency diversity, polarization diversity, and multiple images, needs further investigation for SAR imagery.

The organization of this paper is as follows. In Section 2, we formulate computational vision models needed for applying SFS to SAR imagery. In Section 3, the SFS problem is formulated for SAR imagery, an algorithm is presented that solves for the terrain surface relative to slant plane coordinates and then applies a rotation of coordinates to transform the surface into ground coordinates. Practical application of SFS to topographic mapping of Venus is also discussed. Section 4 presents the experimental methods used in testing the SFS algorithm on SIR-B SAR imagery and compares the resulting surface reconstructions with a stereoscopically derived DTM. Conclusions and possible extensions of this research are discussed in Section 5.

2. Computational Vision Models for SAR Imagery

By following a common modeling approach for both radar and visual images it is possible to gain better insight into the *similarities* between, say, SAR images and aerial photographs. By comparing specific models for radar and visual images derived by the same approach it is also possible to gain insight into the *differences* between SAR images and aerial photographs. This knowledge is useful for applying computer vision research originally considered for visual imagery to SAR imagery.

We will discuss the following modeling issues for SAR imagery of natural terrain:

(1) the spatial deformations introduced in projecting from a 3D scene to 2D image;
(2) reflectivity characteristics, expressed in terms of both the reflectance map and albedo;
(3) observation noise characteristics.

Each category is discussed below.

2.1. SAR image coordinate system

An image can be thought of as the projection of a 3D scene into a 2D representation. For an image created using conventional optics the spatial tranformation from 3D to 2D is given by the perspective projection.

The coordinate system for a SAR strip map is very different, as depicted in Fig. 1. For simplicity, consider the case of a straight flight path with the antenna main beam orthogonal to the flight path. Assume that the x-axis is lined up with the r-axis. Then x may be referred to as ground range and is related to slant range r by

$$r^2 = x^2 + (h - z)^2 \,, \tag{2}$$

where h is the radar altitude and the origin is located on the ground directly

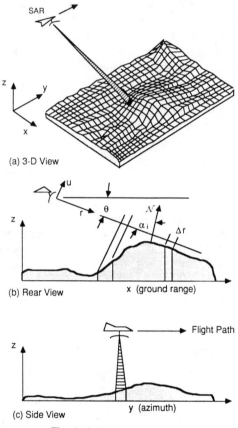

(a) 3-D View

(b) Rear View x (ground range)

(c) Side View y (azimuth)

Fig. 1. SAR imaging geometry.

below the radar. The second SAR strip map axis, by design, represents the along track distance y. It is referred to as cross-range or azimuth. Thus, SAR image coordinates are a projection of the physical scene $(x, y, z(x, y))$ into (r, y) coordinates.

For conventional photographs the image coordinates are often approximated by an orthographic projection of the surface coordinates relative to a plane *orthogonal* to the line-of-sight. For example, the coordinate system for high altitude aerial photographs taken from Nadir could be represented closely by an orthographic projection of the surface coordinates if the field of view is small compared to altitude. For SAR strip maps, the image coordinates can be approximated by an orthographic projection of the surface coordinates relative to a plane *parallel* to the line-of-sight.

To formalize this approximation, suppose that r is large relative to the image size so that arcs of constant range are approximately straight lines. Equivalently, the angle between the line-of-sight and the (x, y) plane, the depression angle θ, varies only slightly across the image. Then the cylindrical coordinates (r, y, θ) can be represented by a locally cartesian coordinate system (r, y, u), where $u \approx r(\theta_0 - \theta)$ and θ_0 is the mean, or reference, depression angle. The "slant plane" then refers to the plane defined by $u = 0$ in the (r, y, u) system. The surface height $u(r, y)$ relative to the slant plane is given by the following rotation of $z(x, y)$:

$$\begin{pmatrix} r \\ y \\ u \end{pmatrix} = \begin{pmatrix} \cos\theta_0 & 0 & -\sin\theta_0 \\ 0 & 1 & 0 \\ \sin\theta_0 & 0 & \cos\theta_0 \end{pmatrix} \begin{pmatrix} x \\ y \\ z \end{pmatrix} + \begin{pmatrix} r_0 \\ y_0 \\ u_0 \end{pmatrix}, \tag{3}$$

where (r_0, y_0, u_0) is an arbitrary reference point. Here the transformation from slant plane surface coordinates to SAR image coordinates is indeed an orthographic projection.

One property of SAR imagery is foreshortening of the mountain sides that slope upward as r increases. In extreme cases, an increase in ground range x will decrease the slant range so that features in SAR imagery may appear in reversed order. This condition, referred to as layover, does not occur provided that the surface slope z_x satisifies

$$z_x \leq \frac{1}{\tan\theta}, \tag{4}$$

or, in slant plane coordinates

$$|u_r| < \infty. \tag{5}$$

In the absence of layover, $z(x, y)$ being single-valued implies that $u(r, y)$ is single-valued. If both $z(x, y)$ and $u(r, y)$ are single-valued functions then the data structure needed for representing the terrain and the methods used for synthesizing an image are very simple. Mulitple values of u due to layover can be accommodated by extending the data structure and the reflectance model.

Note that the surface height u relative to the slant plane will have a ramp component—a term that increases approximately linearly with increasing range. For computation and storage purposes, the dynamic range of u can be reduced significantly by removing this ramp trend, giving

$$u_1(r, y) = u(r, y) - (r - r_0) \tan \theta_0 .$$
(6)

This transformation is utilized in the SFS algorithm of Section 3.

To evaluate the reflectance map for surface reconstruction or image synthesis it is necessary to evaluate the angle of incidence α_i. The cosine of the angle of incidence is simply the normalized dot-product between the surface normal and the illumination vector,

$$\cos \alpha_i = \frac{\boldsymbol{\beta} \cdot \mathcal{N}}{\|\boldsymbol{\beta}\| \|\mathcal{N}\|} .$$
(7)

This has a particularly simple form when expressed in (r, y, u) coordinates. Here $\boldsymbol{\beta} = (-1, 0, 0)$ and $\mathcal{N} = (-u_r, -u_y, 1)$ so that

$$\cos \alpha_i = \frac{u_r}{\sqrt{u_r^2 + u_y^2 + 1}} ,$$
(8)

where

$$u_r = \frac{\partial u}{\partial r} = \frac{\partial u_1}{\partial r} + \tan \theta_0$$

and

$$u_y = \frac{\partial u}{\partial y} = \frac{\partial u_1}{\partial y} .$$

Note that a point at which u_r passes through zero while decreasing is a shadow entry point and that $|u_r| \to \infty$ when transitioning to or from an area in layover.

For computer implementation, $u(r, y)$ is represented in a 2D array with constant sample spacing in r and y as in a SAR strip map. Standard finite central difference approximations to the partial derivatives yield

$$u_y(k, l) = \frac{u(k, l + 1) - u(k, l - 1)}{2\Delta y}$$
(9)

and

$$u_r(k, l) = \frac{u(k + 1, l) - u(k - 1, l)}{2\Delta r}$$

or, in terms of the de-ramped version,

$$u_r(k, l) = \frac{u_1(k+1, l) - u_1(k-1, l) + 2\Delta r \tan \theta_0}{2\Delta r}$$

$$= u_{1_r}(k, l) + \tan \theta_0 , \tag{10}$$

where u_{1_r} is the central difference approximation to $\partial u_1 / \partial r$.

This representation requires a method for resampling a DTM from ground coordinates to slant plane coordinates and vice versa. Such a method was developed which is similar to the summed area table method used in computer graphics [21] and is amenable to high speed implementation.

2.2. SAR reflectance maps

This section summarizes relevant prior research in radiometry and develops a modeling approach for SAR reflectance maps. The following five parameters are known to affect the characteristics of terrain backscatter for radar [11]: incidence angle, surface roughness, transmitter frequency, surface dielectric constant, and polarization. We are mainly interested in understanding the effects of incidence angle on backscattered power, although that functional relationship depends on the other four parameters. The reflectance map also depends on the geometric properties of the illumination source and the geometric properties of image formation and is parameterized to separate factors unique to SAR image formation from factors due to electromagnetic scattering properties of the surface.

The component of the reflectance map that depends on surface orientation can be expressed as the product of three factors: albedo η, an area factor A, and the apparent radar cross-section (RCS) σ^0 per unit area

$$\mathcal{R}(u_r, u_y, \boldsymbol{\beta}) = \eta \sigma^0(u_r, u_y, \boldsymbol{\beta}) A(u_r, u_y) . \tag{11}$$

Albedo denotes the total proportion of incident power that is reradiated by the surface in all directions [11], and σ^0 is specified relative to an isotropic scatterer with albedo given by η. The resulting reflectance map is normally much more directional than if the same surface was viewed by a passive imaging system at visible wavelengths. There are two physical reasons for this. First, the area factor is different for SAR imagery than for conventional photographs in that the SAR pixel is formed in slant-range/cross-range coordinates instead of azimuth/elevation. By itself, A is more directional than the reflectance map for conventional photographs of a Lambertian surface used in much of computer vision research. Second, any given surface tends to be much smoother relative to radar wavelengths than for visible wavelengths. Hence, σ^0, by itself, also tends to be more directional than the reflectance map for a visible image of the same surface.

A typical SAR reflectance map is plotted in Fig. 2 along with a reflectance

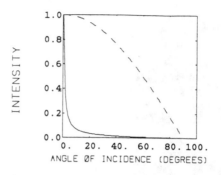 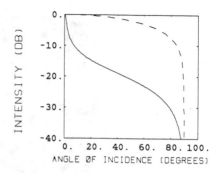

Fig. 2. A typical SAR image reflectance map and Lambertian reflectance map plotted on the same scale. The left-hand plot uses a linear scale and the right-hand plot uses a logarithmic scale. ——— : SAR reflectance map; – – – – : cosine law.

map for a visual image of an ideal Lambertian surface illuminated by a point source. This helps to illustrate the drastic difference between the characteristics of radar imagery and aerial photographs. A visual comparison of SAR imagery with aerial photographs is shown in Fig. 3. Figure 3(a) shows a simulated aerial photograph with illumination from the left 60 degrees above the horizon. The Lambertian reflectance model from Fig. 2 was used with the camera at Nadir. Figure 3(b) shows a simulated SAR image of the same area with the same illumination geometry, i.e., a 60-degree depression angle, and the SAR reflectance model from Fig. 2. The effect of the directional reflectance is clearly visible in the higher contrast of the SAR image. A closer examination also reveals the foreshortening of mountain slopes facing the radar.

2.2.1. *Area factor*

Two different parameterizations for area/RCS have been used in the radar literature. One parameterization uses the area of a pixel projected onto the surface times the normalized radar cross-section. A second parameterization uses the area projected into a plane normal to the illumination. The former area factor is referred to as "surface area" and the latter is "illumination area" or "apparent area."

Suppose that the pixels can be described by an ideal rectangular point spread function (PSF) as shown in Fig. 4. The resulting surface area for a pixel is given by

$$A_s = \frac{\Delta r \Delta y}{\cos \alpha_i} \, . \tag{12}$$

The illumination area for the same pixel is given by

$$A_I = \Delta r \Delta y |u_r| \tag{13}$$

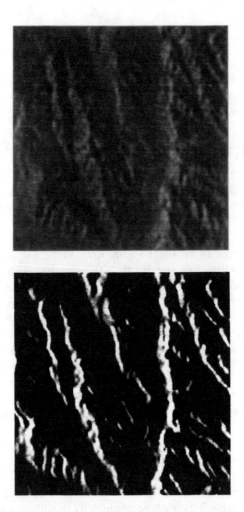

Fig. 3. (a) Simulated aerial photograph. (b) Simulated SAR image. The highly directional
reflectivity and the foreshortening of mountain upslopes is apparent in the SAR image.

providing a very simple expression in terms of the differential geometry of the
surface. Figure 4 depicts the surface and illumination area in slant plane
coordinates for a locally planar surface.

Both forms of area factor have their advantages. The approximation from
(12) gives surface area as a function of α_i only. If RCS is expressed as a
function of α_i and implemented in a lookup table, then the area factor can be
absorbed into the same table, saving computation. Illumination area is more
physically meaningful than surface area [5]. Experimental results comparing

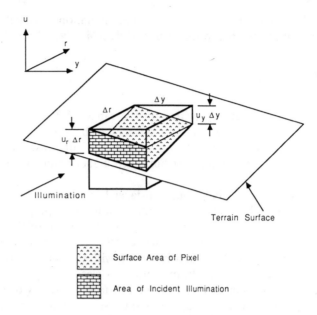

Fig. 4. Surface and illumination area of a SAR image pixel represented in slant plane coordinates.

simulated images with real SAR images described in Section 4 show the illumination area parameterization to provide a more accurate model.

2.2.2. RCS models

Many models for the variation of σ^0 as a function of incidence angle are presented in the literature [3, 4, 30] based on empirical studies and by modeling the various scattering mechanisms that may occur. Some of the models developed by the radar community are similar to those developed for quasi-specular reflection in optics and computer graphics [36, 43]. Clapp considered Lambert's work in photometry as a starting point in developing RCS models [10]. Clapp's first model [30] is given by $\sigma^0 = \cos \alpha_i$ if it is used in conjunction with the illumination area parameterization. The relation $\sigma^0 = $ constant, Clapp's third model, results in the familiar reflectance map

$$A_I \sigma^0(\alpha_i) \propto \cot(\alpha_i) ,$$

when combined with A_I for a flat surface. This was derived by modeling the surface as being composed of many layers of spheres, each absorbing some fraction of the incident power and reradiating the remainder isotropically [30].

Radar clutter is often more directional than indicated by the above models. The generalized Lambert model, $\sigma^0(\alpha_i) = \cos^k \alpha_i$, is an empirical remedy for this and has also been considered for computer animation of visual scenes [36]. A further generalization, based on empirical data, is given by [28]

$$\sigma^0(\alpha_i) = \frac{\cos^k\alpha_i}{\sin^l\alpha_i} . \tag{14}$$

It has been suggested that (14) with k in the range of 3 to 4 may provide a reasonable model for relatively smooth surfaces such as asphalt [30], and that $l = 0$, with $k \in [1, 2]$ is appropriate for very rough surfaces. In experiments from Section 4, $l = 0$ was appropriate but much higher values were needed for k.

Scattering models for partially rough surfaces based on stochastic models of surface microstructure have also been considered in radar [42] and optics [43]. Most radar clutter is neither perfectly specular nor perfectly diffuse but somewhere in between. Accordingly, early clutter modeling research attempted to combine the physics of specular reflection with that of reflection by rough surfaces. In a geometrical optics framework, this was accomplished by modeling the surface as a collection of many smooth facets, each with well-defined reflectivity properties but oriented at random. Since each facet is a specular reflector the expression for σ_0 is related to the average number of facets oriented towards the radar.

Similar models have been developed where the surface is modeled as a continuous random process and the methods of physical optics are used to develop the expression for RCS. In this case, RCS depends on the proportion of surface points oriented towards the radar and the average Gaussian curvature at those points, which in turn depends on the root-mean-square (RMS) surface roughness and correlation length. The model reported by Barrick [3], assuming Gaussian distributed surface height, expresses RCS by

$$\sigma^0(\alpha_i) = \frac{K}{s^2\cos^4\alpha_i} \exp\left\{-\frac{\tan^2\alpha_i}{s^2}\right\}, \tag{15}$$

where s is the RMS surface slope, and K is not a function of α_i. A different expression is obtained for the case of exponentially distributed surface slopes [3]. It was found in Section 4 that, for the available imagery, Barrick's model with Gaussian height provided a better fit than Barrick's exponential slope model or the empirical model in (14).

The reflectance models used for intermediate angles of incidence may not be valid at the extremes near grazing and near vertical incidence. For example, as $\alpha_i \rightarrow \frac{1}{2}\pi$ specular reflection takes over because the Rayleigh criterion for a rough surface is inversely proportional to $\cos \alpha_i$ [5]. Thus, for finite surface roughness, the surface becomes optically smooth near grazing, an effect that has been observed in radar clutter [30]. A second problem is that surface undulations from multiple physical sources can take on a wide range of scales. This effect has been investigated by modeling surface height as the sum of independent random fields each with different slope statistics [5, 49] resulting in better predictions for backscatter when α_i is small. The continuing advances in the application of electromagnetic scattering theory to image prediction, e.g. [1], may provide improved reflectance models needed for computer vision problems like SFS.

Albedo depends on the electrical properties of the surface materials and any ground cover. For example, water might either increase *or* decrease albedo substantially depending on whether the moisture is on vegetation, in vegetation, on asphalt, or in the form of deep snow or shallow snow [11]. The functional form of σ^0 depends on surface microstructure relative to the wavelength, and can vary locally in ways that are difficult, if not impossible, to distinguish from albedo variation. Frequency diversity [6, 12] and polarization diversity provide some information on variations in the electrical properties of the surface being imaged. That, in turn, could help estimate albedo variations. Random field models [16] may be appropriate models for use in albedo estimation or for treating unknown modeling errors, such as albedo variation, as a source of noise. Noise sources that are intrinsic to the SAR image formation process, rather than scene characteristics, are discussed below.

2.3. Observation noise

The dominant source of noise for SAR imagery is speckle, which arises from interference between the returns from multiple scatterers within a resolution element. For complicated surfaces and resolution much larger than a wavelength the complex amplitude of the speckle can be modeled approximately as complex Gaussian noise multiplied by the signal. The correlation length of the speckle is then determined by the width of the PSF of the imaging system. Thermal noise from the radar electronics introduces a second noise source with complex amplitude modeled as white complex Gaussan noise added to the image. A third source of noise arises from the image amplitude accumulated in the pixel sidelobes. Because SAR image amplitude is formed essentially by calculating a weighted Fourier transform of a finite aperture, sidelobes in the PSF are inherent. This noise amplitude accumulated in the sidelobes of any given pixel is the coherent summation of many different weighted signal amplitudes, each dependent on the radar backscatter in some area. For natural terrain images, the resulting noise is approximately independent of the signal in any particular pixel, approximately white and Gaussian with variance dependent on the level of the overall backscatter in a large neighborhood.

Speckle, thermal noise, and sidelobe noise have very similar statistical properties, except that speckle is a multiplicative noise source. A dual additive–multiplicative noise source is equivalent to a single multiplicative noise source with additive bias [50], giving the following model for image intensity

$$I(r, y) = [G_s \eta \sigma^0(u_r, u_y, \boldsymbol{\beta}) A_I(u_r, u_y) + \sigma^2_{\text{bias}}] \, n(r, y) , \qquad (16)$$

where σ^2_{bias} is the combined power of the thermal and sidelobe noise, $n(r, y)$ is unit power random field distributed as chi-squared with two degrees of freedom, and G_s is the radar system gain.

For our purposes G_s includes all of the terms of the radar equation not appearing in $\eta \sigma^0 A_I$, such as wavelength, range attenuation, transmitter power, duty factor, etc., but also includes compensation for range dependence, antenna beam-shape, and calibration factors. One goal in the design and calibration of high quality SAR systems is for G_s to be a known constant throughout the image. We will assume that

$$G_s = 1 . \qquad (17)$$

For radars without absolute calibration, G_s is assumed to be an unknown constant. Then we lump it with η so that our albedo estimates in Section 4 are only relative values.

The noise variance can be reduced at a cost of spatial resolution by averaging neighbouring pixels.

However, if the thermal noise and sidelobe noise levels are significant, then the bias term will remain and must be accounted for regardless of the amount of spatial averaging. For example. SEASAT SAR imagery, among the highest quality publicly available at this time, has an integrated sidelobe ratio (ISLR) of only 6 to 20 dB, depending on the processing method used [37]. Because ISLR measures the ratio of mainlobe energy to total sidelobe energy, this means that σ^2_{bias} can be as high as 6 dB below the average value of $\eta \mathcal{R}$ in a region—surely a significant bias level. For the SAR imagery used in Section 4, σ^2_{bias} was actually larger than the average value of $\eta \sigma^0 A_I$.

3. Shape from Shading Approach for SAR Imagery

Suppose that the reflectance map is known and that sufficient noncoherent averaging has been performed so that the SFS problem reduces to one of reconstructing $u(r, y)$ given $I(r, y)$ through the relationship

$$I(r, y) \approx \mathcal{R}(u_r, u_y, \boldsymbol{\beta}) , \qquad (18)$$

where

$$\mathcal{R} = \eta \sigma^0(u_r, u_y, \boldsymbol{\beta}) A_I(u_r, u_y) + \sigma^2_{\text{bias}} . \qquad (19)$$

We have represented the surface topography relative to the slant plane as formulated in (3). The resulting algorithm reconstructs $u(r, y)$, an orthographic projection of (r, y, u), given I. The algorithms reported by Ikeuchi and Horn [27], Brooks and Horn [7], and Frankot and Chellappa [15, 18] solve for surface slopes by minimizing mean-squared intensity error criterion balanced against a surface smoothness criterion. For SAR imagery we solve for $u(r, y)$, instead of $z(x, y)$, by minimizing the following cost function

$$\varepsilon = \int \int [I - \mathscr{R}(\hat{u}_r, \hat{u}_y)]^2 + \lambda \cdot (\hat{u}_{rr}^2 + 2\hat{u}_{ry}^2 + \hat{u}_{yy}^2) \, dr \, dy \ . \qquad (20)$$

Along with the cost function in (20) an integrability criterion is enforced. The algorithm constrains the surface slopes (u_r, u_y) to satisfy

$$\frac{\partial}{\partial y} u_r = \frac{\partial}{\partial r} u_y \ , \qquad (21)$$

or $u_{ry} = u_{yr}$. Suppose that we are presented with a possibly nonintegrable pair of slope functions $[\hat{u}_r(r, y), \hat{u}_y(r, y)]$ such that any number of surface reconstructions $\hat{u}$ could be obtained depending upon the path of integration. The least-squares integrability projection algorithm finds the pair of slope functions $[\tilde{u}_r(r, y), \tilde{u}_y(r, y)]$ that satisfy (21) simultaneously with minimizing the distance

$$d\{(\hat{u}_r, \hat{u}_y), (\tilde{u}_r, \tilde{u}_y)\} = \int \int (\hat{u}_r - \tilde{u}_r)^2 \, K_r + (\hat{u}_y - \tilde{u}_r)^2 \, K_y \, dr \, dy \ , \qquad (22)$$

where $K_r + K_y = 1$. The constants K_r and K_y are relative weights assigned to u_r and u_y, respectively. It is helpful to set $K_r > K_y$ because the error in u_r is normally smaller than the error in u_y. Iterative and noniterative algorithms have been reported for enforcing this constraint [18, 26]. We use a noniterative approach.

The constrained minimization problem defined by (20), (21), and (22) can be solved by extending the iterative algorithm presented in [18]. The resulting algorithm is now summarized. Denote the surface slope estimates after the kth iteration as $[\tilde{u}_r, \tilde{u}_y]_k$. The surface slope estimates for the next iteration are obtained by the following five steps:

Step 1. Obtain a smoothed version, $[\breve{u}_r, \breve{u}_y]_k$, of the previous iterate using

$$\breve{u}_y(l, m) = \tfrac{1}{5}[\tilde{u}_y(l, m + 1) + \tilde{u}_y(l, m - 1) + \tilde{u}_y(l + 1, m)\tilde{u}_y(l - 1, m)]$$
$$+ \tfrac{1}{20}[\tilde{u}_y(l - 1, m - 1) + \tilde{u}_y(l - 1, m + 1)$$
$$+ \tilde{u}_y(l + 1, m + 1) + \tilde{u}_y(l + 1, m - 1)] \qquad (23)$$

and similarly for $\breve{u}_r$.

Step 2. Simulate the SAR image by evaluating the reflectance map with the smoothed slope estimates, giving $\mathcal{R}(\breve{u}_r, \breve{u}_y)$ for every range-azimuth sample location (l, m).

Step 3. Calculate the partial derivatives of the reflectance map with respect to u_r and u_y. The derivatives are evaluated using the smoothed surface slopes from Step 1,

$$\mathcal{R}_r(\breve{u}_r, \breve{u}_y) = \frac{\partial}{\partial a} \mathcal{R}(a, b)\Big|_{a=\breve{u}_r, b=\breve{u}_y} \tag{24}$$

and

$$\mathcal{R}_y(\breve{u}_r, \breve{u}_y) = \frac{\partial}{\partial b} \mathcal{R}(a, b)\Big|_{a=\breve{u}_r, b=\breve{y}}.$$

Numerical derivatives are used to provide greater flexibility, allowing the use of a reflectance map lookup table and, if necessary, an empirical reflectance map. Normally $\mathcal{R}_r \gg \mathcal{R}_y$, suggesting that $\hat{u}_r$ has less error than $\hat{u}_y$. This is what Wildey referred to as "poor photometric leverage for the cross-slopes" [46].

Step 4. Update the slope estimates using the recursion [7],

$$\begin{bmatrix} \hat{u}_r \\ \hat{u}_y \end{bmatrix}_{k+1} = \begin{bmatrix} \breve{u}_r \\ \breve{u}_y \end{bmatrix}_k + \lambda_1 (I - \mathcal{R}(\breve{u}_r, \breve{u}_y)) \begin{bmatrix} \mathcal{R}_r(\breve{u}_r, \breve{u}_y) \\ \mathcal{R}_y(\breve{u}_r, \breve{u}_y) \end{bmatrix}, \tag{25}$$

where λ_1 is inversely proportional to λ in (20). The new slope iterate obtained from (25) is virtually guaranteed to be nonintegrable.

Step 5. Enforce integrability using the following projection constraint [18] on the Fourier series of $[\hat{u}_r, \hat{u}_y]_{k+1}$

$$\tilde{U}(\omega) = \frac{K_r a_r^*(\omega)\hat{U}_r(\omega) + K_y a_y^*(\omega)\hat{U}_y(\omega)}{K_r|a_r(\omega)|^2 + K_y|a_y(\omega)|^2}, \tag{26}$$

where $\hat{U}_r(\omega)$ and $\hat{U}_y(\omega)$ represent the discrete Fourier transforms (DFT) of $[\hat{u}_r, \hat{u}_y]_{k+1}$ respectively, $\tilde{U}(\omega)$ represents the DFT of the new estimate of surface height $\tilde{u}(r, y)$. The vector $\omega = (\omega_r, \omega_y) \in (2\pi n/N, 2\pi m/N)$, with $n, m \in \{0, 1, \ldots, N-1\}$ for images of size $N \times N$. The coefficients a_r and a_y are given by the frequency response of the partial differentiation operators in r and y, respectively. For example, if we approximate the surface slopes using first-order central differencing then the frequency response is $a_y(\omega) = j \sin \omega_y$ and similarly for a_r. The Fourier transform of the new surface slope iterates are given by

$$\tilde{U}_r(\omega) = a_r(\omega)\tilde{U}(\omega) \quad \text{and} \quad \tilde{U}_y(\omega) = a_y(\omega)\tilde{U}(\omega) \tag{27}$$

with the final step in the iteration that of performing the inverse DFT of (27) to get $[\tilde{u}_r, \tilde{u}_y]_{k+1}$. The integrability projection constraint from (26) doubles as an efficient 2D integrator for constructing a surface from noisy slope estimates utilizing all of the available data.

The same process is repeated until the intensity mean-squared error is sufficiently small or until a predetermined number of iterations have been completed. The overall procedure follows the structure shown in Fig. 5.

The integrability projection used in the SFS algorithm has some distinct advantages. The main advantage is that it is noniterative—it constructs a surface from noisy slope estimates in one pass utilizing all of the available data, unlike simple spatial integration. A second advantage is computational efficiency. It utilizes fast Fourier transform (FFT) algorithms routinely used for SAR image formation. Hence the method is efficient in terms of the number of computations required, the ability to utilize high speed FFT processors, and synergy with SAR image formation hardware and software. A third advantage is modularity.

Figure 6 shows the improvement of the above fast least-squares integration method over simple spatial integration for reconstructing a surface from noisy slope estimates. The top plot, Fig. 6(A), shows the noise-free surface. Forward difference approximations to the surface slopes (z_x, z_y) were calculated and then each sample corrupted by additive white Gaussian noise. The noise standard deviation was 0.25 for each slope component, and the maximum value for the true surface slopes was about 0.8. Figure 6(B) shows the reconstruction obtained by simple spatial integration of those noisy derivatives along a single

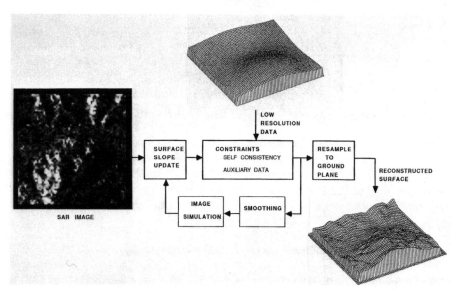

Fig. 5. Block diagram of the SAR SFS approach.

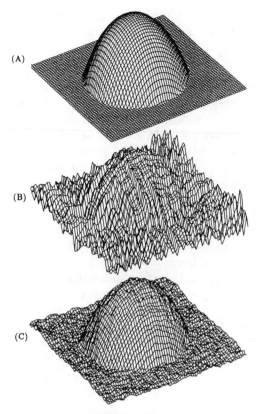

(A)

(B)

(C)

Fig. 6. Superiority of the fast least-squares integration method over simple spatial integration for reconstructing a surface from noisy slopes. (A) Noise-free surface. (B) Reconstruction from noisy slopes obtained by simple spatial integration along a single path. (C) Reconstruction using least-squares integration.

set of paths covering the entire image. The spatial integration procedure is as follows:

Step 1. For an image of size $N \times N$ let the height $\hat{u}(\frac{1}{2}N, \frac{1}{2}N)$ at the image center be an arbitrary constant. Then integrate out from the center using the following recursion:

$$
\hat{u}(\tfrac{1}{2}N, i) = \begin{cases} \hat{u}(\tfrac{1}{2}N, i-1) + \hat{u}_y(\tfrac{1}{2}N, i-1)\,\Delta y \\ \quad \text{for } i \in \{\tfrac{1}{2}N+1, \ldots, N-1\}, \\ \hat{u}(\tfrac{1}{2}N, i+1) - \hat{u}_y(\tfrac{1}{2}N, i)\,\Delta y \\ \quad \text{for } i \in \{\tfrac{1}{2}N-1, \ldots, 1\}. \end{cases} \tag{28}
$$

This gives the height along a line through the center of the image.

Step 2. Integrate in both directions from this centerline using the following recursion:

$$\hat{u}(j,i) = \begin{cases} \hat{u}(j-1,i) + \hat{u}_r(j-1,i)\,\Delta r \\ \qquad \text{for } j \in \{\tfrac{1}{2}N+1, \ldots, N-1\}\,, \\ \hat{u}(j+1,i) - \hat{u}_r(j,i)\,\Delta r \\ \qquad \text{for } j \in \{\tfrac{1}{2}N-1, \ldots, 1\}\,, \end{cases} \qquad (29)$$

$$i \in \{1, \ldots, N\}\,.$$

Error propagation is apparent from the ridge lines that appear on the reconstructed surface. Figure 6(C) shows the surface reconstruction obtained using the fast least-squares integration described above. Error propagation is greatly reduced and a much better reconstruction results.

It is possible to apply other constraints in a similar manner. This is represented in the block diagram of Fig. 5. The integrability constraint is a form of self-consistency. Another form of self-consistency is that shadows appearing in the image should correspond to shadows predicted by surface reconstruction. The second class of constraints comes from auxiliary data sources. This might come from altimetry data, stereopsis, and higher level scene analysis. If auxiliary information is local in nature it can be applied as a constraint directly to the surface. If it is global in nature it may be more conveniently applied in the frequency domain. Altimetry data and stereo data tend to be of lower resolution than SAR imagery obtained by the same radar system and, accordingly, may be useful as global low frequency constraints for surface reconstruction. This is discussed below.

3.1. Low frequency information

Note that (26) is valid only for $\boldsymbol{\omega} \neq (0,0)$. Low frequency surface height information is lost in the image formation process, since image intensity is a function of the derivatives of surface height. A surface reconstructed based on SFS techniques inevitably suffers from low frequency errors, the severity depending upon observation noise characteristics.

One advantage of the Fourier-based integrability constraint is that low frequency information from other sources can easily be included during or after iteration of the SFS algorithm. This can be accomplished by performing the DFT of the low resolution surface height information, denoted by $U_L(\boldsymbol{\omega})$. This can be precomputed with modest computational cost. The appropriate low frequency terms of U_L are used to replace the low frequency DFT coefficients $\tilde{U}(\boldsymbol{\omega})$, in effect treating U_L as a projection constraint. The algorithms of Brooks and Horn [7] and Ikeuchi and Horn [27], which our algorithm is based upon, require knowledge of boundary conditions. While boundary conditions are generally not available, low frequency information sometimes is. Further, availability of low resolution surface height data can, for all practical purposes, eliminate the need for boundary conditions in addition to replacing lost low frequency information [14, 18].

The significance of this issue for SAR imagery is now illustrated by an example. Figure 7 demonstrates the results of SFS with and without auxiliary low frequency information. The surface estimates were obtained from a SIR-B SAR image window of 64×64 pixels with 75-meter pixel spacing after noncoherent averaging. In Fig. 7(A) a section from a DTM of the same area is shown. The surface reconstruction given only the shading information in a SAR image shown in Fig. 7(B). Notice that the slopes in the range direction are fairly accurate while the slope estimates in the azimuth direction are not. This is partly a consequence of unknown boundary conditions and partly due to the fact that image intensity is a very weak function of the azimuth slopes. A low resolution surface is shown in Fig. 7(C). This was obtained from the five lowest frequency Fourier coefficients of Fig. 7(A). The results of using SFS to

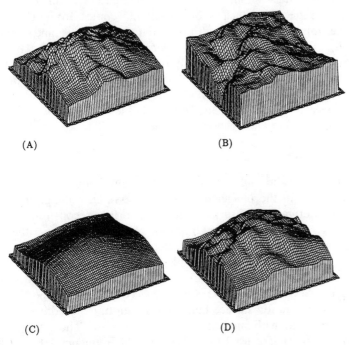

(A)   (B)

(C)   (D)

Fig. 7. Comparison of SFS with and without low resolution DTM. (A) Section from DTM co-registered with SAR image. (B) Surface reconstruction given only the shading information in a SAR image. (C) Low resolution surface obtained from the five lowest frequency Fourier coefficients of the DTM. (D) Surface reconstruction obtained using SFS algorithm to combine the low resolution surface with high resolution image intensity information.

combine the low resolution surface with high resolution image intensity information is shown in Fig. 7(D). Interestingly, the distorted surface of Fig. 7(B) gives a lower value for the cost function in (20) than does the true surface. In this particular instance, both the intensity prediction error and the surface smoothness criterion were lower for the distorted surface. Tests on simulated imagery seem to indicate that this is not due solely to modeling error: Similar results were obtained for simulated speckled imagery, but not for simulated noise-free imagery. The general trend is as expected: as the noise level increases so does the corruption of low frequency surface information in the image.

3.2. Venus Radar Mapper

The Magellan project's Venus Radar Mapper will provide high resolution (nominally 150 meter) SAR imagery of the surface of Venus along with much lower resolution (5 to 50 kilometers depending on operating altitude) radar altimetry data [31]. It is believed that the Magellan SAR imagery will provide new information about the geology of Venus, which in turn will create more insight into the evolution of the solar system. For example, certain significant geological features, such as folds and faults, appear as banded terrain in SAR imagery. Bands from 10 to 20 kilometers wide have been observed in previously obtained radar images of Venus and scientists would like to resolve bands as small as 5 kilometers [8]. The altimetry data might not be able to resolve the bands, but the Magellan SAR imagery certainly will.

Using the techniques presented above, the altimetry data and the SAR imagery could be combined to construct high resolution topographic maps of Venus. The Magellan scenario, where SAR imagery is combined with orders of magnitude lower resolution altimetry data for surface reconstruction, is tested in Section 4 using SIR-B SAR imagery. The depression angle for the Magellan SAR imagery will be anywhere from 40 to 80 degrees, depending on orbital position. Imagery near 45 degrees depression should provide the best compromise between shadowing and layover. The higher depression angle imagery is still useful but the likelihood of encountering layover is much greater. Noncoherent integration of anywhere from 4 to 30 looks, depending on orbital position and the demands placed upon the communication link, will be performed to reduce speckle. If 30-look imagery is indeed available, then the SFS algorithm can probably be applied without any additional noncoherent integration at the full resolution specified for the SAR imagery.

Earlier scientific observations point out potential difficulties in applying SFS to SAR imagery of Venus. It has been observed that surface roughness is often higher at high elevation on the surfaces of both Earth and Venus, apparently due to erosion at mountains and sedimentation in valleys [35]. Because the reflectance map is a function of surface roughness, this may introduce distortion into the surface topography estimates obtained by SFS. There also appears to be correlation between high albedo and high elevation [35]. Thus, while albedo variations on the surface of Venus appear to be much lower than those typical of Earth, they are significant, and their effect on SFS may be correlated with surface structure.

Prior scientific work also provides possible solutions to the above difficulties. Scattering laws have been derived which provide families of reflectance maps parameterized by RMS surface roughness and albedo [3, 35]. Such reflectance models have been used to estimate surface roughness and albedo from Pioneer Venus altimetry and reflectivity data [35] at resolutions comparable to that of the altimetry data. A similar method practical for applying SFS is illustrated in Section 4. The likely absence of cultural features and vegetation may practically eliminate the need for any higher resolution estimates of albedo.

4. Experimental Results

The SFS algorithm presented in Section 3 was tested on simulated and real SAR imagery. Simulation results are presented in [14, 17]. The results for real SAR imagery are presented below.

4.1. Experimental approach for SIR-B SAR imagery

A set of three SIR-B SAR images, an aerial photograph, and a DTM derived stereoscopically from aerial photographs (all for the same location) were used as test cases. These were provided by Dr. Gitta Domik of the Vexcel Corporation. The area coverage was near the town of José de San Martin in Argentina. Figure 8 shows a SAR image simulated from the DTM with and without speckle noise, one of the SIR-B SAR images, and a registered aerial photograph. Proceeding diagonally across the aerial photograph a riverbed and a roadway are clearly visible, and a great deal of other albedo variations are evident. A small airport can be seen in the upper left hand corner of the aerial photograph. The town of José de San Martin is just to the right of the airport but is not discernable at this resolution.

Comparison of the images with registered terrain elevation data revealed some important characteristics of this data set. The empirical reflectance map for the aerial photograph was very close to the often assumed Lambertian characteristic. Albedo variations present in the aerial photograph prevented successful application of any current SFS technique. As expected, the reflectance map was much more directional and the albedo variation much less severe for the SAR imagery. The SAR albedo variation appeared to be significant but did not cause catastrophic failure.

For each of the three SAR images we used the following experimental procedure:

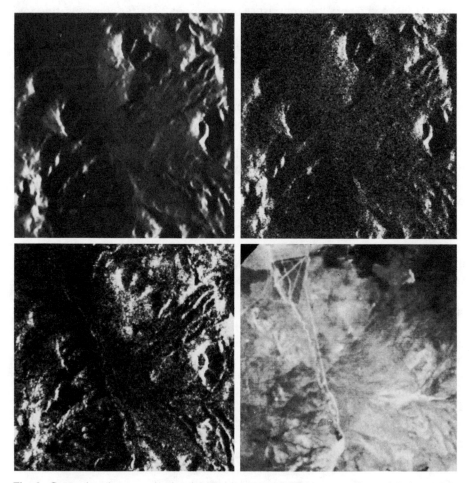

Fig. 8. Comparison between simulated SAR image, real SAR image, and an aerial photograph. Top-left: Simulated noise-free SAR image given a DTM (includes additive noise bias term). Top-right: Simulated SAR image including 28-look speckle pattern. Bottom-left: Real SIR-B SAR image. Bottom-right: Aerial photograph.

Step 1. *Reduce SAR image pixel spacing to match the DTM pixel spacing.* The original SIR-B pixel spacing is about 12.5 meters while the DTM sample spacing is 37.5 meters, a reduction factor of 3. Resolution reduction was performed by averaging 3×3 blocks of pixels. The original SAR image is obtained as a noncoherent average of four looks. The equivalent number of looks for a 37.5 meter pixel is then 36, assuming independent speckle samples. However, SAR imagery is normally slightly oversampled. The equivalent number of looks estimated using the ratio of the square of image mean to image variance in a very low contrast region is about 28 (after compensating for intensity variations due to topography).

Step 2. *Precisely register DTM to SAR image.* This allows us to compare the reflectance parameters for the different images, evaluate signal to noise ratio, and compare the SAR image-based surface reconstruction with the DTM. To estimate the transformation we simulated a SAR image given the DTM and approximate knowledge of imaging geometry. Next we performed an exhaustive search over translation, rotation, and scale, selecting those parameter values which maximized the normalized cross-correlation. This is discussed in detail in [14]. The orthographic projection representation in the slant plane provided an excellent model for the SAR coordinates: Sub-pixel registration accuracy between simulated and observed images was achievable after compensating only for translation, rotation, and scaling of the ground coordinates relative to SAR image coordinates.

Step 3. *Generate low resolution DTM.* In each case, the Fourier transform of the registered high resolution DTM was obtained, all but the lowest frequency 0.1% of the coefficients were set to zero, and then the inverse Fourier transform of the resulting spectrum was performed. This represents an additional resolution reduction factor of about 23 in range and azimuth, roughly simulating the Magellan scenario.

Step 4. *Estimate reflectance map parameters using low resolution DTM.* This ensures that the SFS test results represent the useful case where the high resolution surface structure is unknown.

Step 5. *Execute SFS algorithm given a SAR image and low resolution DTM.* Ten iterations of the algorithm from Section 3 where performed in each case. The total execution time for a 256×256 image.was 45 minutes on an unloaded Micro VAX, including resampling into ground plane coordinates. Most of the operations needed for this algorithm are suitable for pipeline and parallel architectures, so that the execution time could be greatly reduced.

Details of these results are presented below.

4.2. Reflectance parameter estimation

Reflectance models from Section 2 were fit to the SAR imagery using both the low resolution and high resolution DTMs. Three types of parameters need to be estimated: Additive noise bias, albedo, and shape parameters. (k, l in (14) and s in (15) are examples of shape parameters.) An exhaustive search over the parameter space was used in each case to select those values which minimize the following mean-squared prediction error

$$\varepsilon_\mathrm{p} = \frac{1}{M_\Omega} \sum_{(l,m)\in\Omega} \left[I(l, m) - \mathcal{R}(u_r(l, m), u_y(l, m)) \right]^2 , \qquad (30)$$

where M_Ω denotes the number of pixels in the domain Ω under consideration. Equation (30) is just the sample second moment of the error between the observed image intensity and predicted image intensity. We compared the results using the generalized Lambert model and Barrick's rough surface model with Guassian and exponential surface slope probability density functions (PDF). This was done for various images, DTM resolutions, and image resolutions. Barrick's model with Gaussian height PDF nearly always resulted in lower mean-squared prediction error than the exponential model and the generalized Lambert model, although the visual realism of the image simulation was about the same in each case. Reflectance parameters were fairly stable as a function of image resolution. Each parameter varied slightly as a function of DTM resolution. The error in the parameter estimate obtained using a low resolution DTM appears to be somewhat predictable but no attempt was made to compensate for it in our experiments.

The two different area factor parameterizations, illumination area and surface area, were compared when used in conjunction with Barrick's (Gaussian) RCS model. Use of illumination area resulted in consistently lower mean-squared prediction error. Visually, the quality of image simulation did not vary significantly between the two area factor parameterizations.

Figure 9 shows a scatter plot of observed SAR image intensity versus $\cos \alpha_i$ for the SAR image of Fig. 8 (bottom-left), providing an empirical reflectance map. The nominal depression angle is 32.9 degrees so that the value of $\cos \alpha_i$ is approximately 0.84 for flat ground and the surface orientation data centers itself around this value. Notice from Fig. 9 that the reflectance is a strong function of $\cos \alpha_i$ at high angles of incidence but only a very weak function at low angles of incidence. Accordingly, the up-slopes (areas increasing in height as slant range increases) have much more contrast and higher intensity than the down-slopes. Small-signal suppression due to additive noise and intensity quantization therefore destroys shading information on the down-slopes.

Tables 1–3 show the reflectance map parameter estimates obtained from the three SIR-B SAR images given high and low resolution DTMs. In each case we used Barrick's RCS model for Gaussian surface slopes with the illumination area parameterization. RMS surface roughness (at scales comparable to the radar wavelength) determines the shape of the RCS curve with the resulting reflectance map being more directional the lower the roughness. The surface roughness parameter was estimated to be between $\tan^{-1}s = 17.5$ and $\tan^{-1}s = 24$ degrees in each case.

RMS prediction error between real and simulated image intensity is also given in Tables 1–3. The prediction error was calculated in each case using the high resolution DTM to predict image intensity through the reflectance model. In the first column, an indication of prediction error with no modeling error was obtained by simulating a 28-look speckled image with the same reflectance map parameters as the real SAR image. The mean-squared error between the

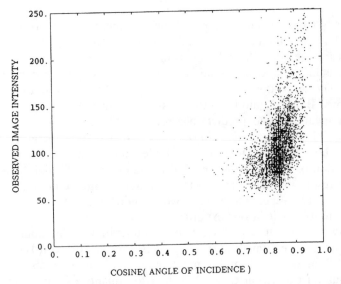

Fig. 9. Scatter plot of observed SAR image intensity versus $\cos \alpha_i$, where α_i is the angle of incidence, SIR-B image with pixel spacing reduced to 37.5 meters. The nominal depression angle is 32.9 degrees giving a mean $\cos \alpha_i \approx 0.84$.

simulated speckled image and the simulated image without speckle was then computed. The second prediction error column in Tables 1–3 uses the same reflectance map parameters (estimated using the high resolution DTM) and compares predicted image intensity to the observed SAR image intensity. The third prediction error column uses reflectance map parameter estimates obtained given the low resolution DTM. This is the situation that would be encountered in practice.

4.3. Signal to noise ratio

A measure of signal to noise ratio (SNR) specially defined for SFS is presented in Tables 1–3. This measure is given by

$$\frac{\sigma_I^2 - \varepsilon_p}{\varepsilon_p}, \tag{31}$$

where

$$\sigma_I^2 = \frac{1}{M_\Omega} \sum_{(l,m)\in\Omega} I^2(l, m) - \left(\frac{1}{M_\Omega} \sum_{(l,m)\in\Omega} I(l, m) \right)^2 \tag{32}$$

is the sample variance of the observed image and ε_p is the intensity prediction error defined in equation (30). Several points are evident from Tables 1–3. First, comparison of SNR for simulated speckle images with that of real images

Table 1
Reflectance map parameter estimates, resulting prediction error statistics, and shape from shading SNR measure for SIR-B SAR image in the upper left-hand corner of Fig. 11

	Simulated image with speckle. No modeling errors	Parameters estimated using high resolution DTM	Parameters estimated using low resolution DTM
Surface roughness $\tan^{-1} s$ (degrees RMS)	–	19.1	17.5
η	–	12.2	11.6
σ^2_{bias}	–	77.7	84.9
Intensity prediction RMS error	19.46	28.55	28.72
SNR (dB)	1.5	-1.04	-1.16

Table 2
Reflectance map parameter estimates, resulting prediction error statistics, and shape from shading SNR measure for SIR-B SAR image in the top row, center column of Fig. 11.

	Simulated image with speckle. No modeling errors	Parameters estimated using high resolution DTM	Parameters estimated using low resolution DTM
Surface roughness $\tan^{-1} s$ (degrees RMS)	–	23.5	23.0
η	–	13.6	15.5
σ^2_{bias}	–	38.0	38.8
Intensity prediction RMS error	8.56	10.49	10.57
SNR (dB)	.13	-2.85	-3.0

Table 3
Reflectance map parameter estimates, resulting prediction error statistics, and shape from shading SNR measure for SIR-B SAR image in the top row, right-hand column of Fig. 11

	Simulated image with speckle. No modeling errors	Parameters estimated using high resolution DTM	Parameters estimated using low resolution DTM
Surface roughness $\tan^{-1} s$ (degrees RMS)	–	24.1	20.5
η	–	10.6	9.2
σ^2_{bias}	–	78.1	88.1
Intensity prediction RMS error	19.74	25.27	25.50
SNR (dB)	.01	-1.68	-1.88

indicates a 2 to 3 dB loss due to modeling errors, variations in G_s, and all other sources for these particular cases. This, together with the inter-pass stability of the reflectance parameter estimates, seems to indicate good relative calibration of SIR-B imagery. We also conjecture that spatial variations of reflectance parameters, i.e., albedo, noise bias, and surface roughness account for most of the modeling error. Second, comparison of SNR using high resolution versus low resolution reflectance parameter estimates indicate only an additional 0.2 dB loss for using the low resolution estimates. This demonstrates successful reflectance map estimation from low resolution topography. Third, the SNR is very low (even without modeling error), suggesting that future improvements might be obtained through optimal filtering of speckle noise.

4.4. Low frequency information

The advantage of including low frequency information was demonstrated in Fig. 7. The same kind of approach was applied to the 256×256 pixel SAR images corresponding to Tables 1–3. The procedure described in the beginning of Section 4.1 was followed. Figure 10 shows an image simulated from the low resolution DTM. This illustrates how little low frequency surface information is available in image intensity and also a possible difficulty in estimating reflectance map parameters from low resolution surface data. The higher slope values are not well represented so that the reflectance map is fit mostly to data with

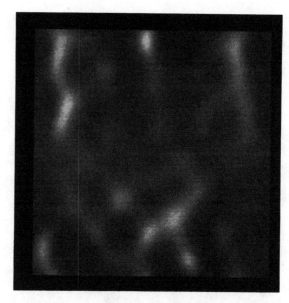

Fig. 10. SAR image simulated from the same low resolution DTM used to aid surface reconstruction. This illustrates how little low frequency surface information is available in image intensity.

angle of incidence near the radar depression angle. This indicates that some degree of extrapolation is required and, therefore, care must be taken in selecting an appropriate reflectance model class.

4.5. Surface reconstructions

4.5.1. *Images predicted from surface reconstructions*

Figure 11 shows three original SAR images and intensity predictions given SFS results. The top row shows the three observed SAR images corresponding to Tables 1–3, respectively. In each case the range direction and the illumination is along the horizontal axis. The first two images are taken from about 12 degrees difference in depression angle and about 1.3 degrees difference in orientation or aspect. The third image has about 81 degrees aspect and illumination difference from the first two images. Surface reconstructions from each of the SAR images were obtained and then each surface reconstruction was used to predict each of the original SAR images. The second row shows the three predicted SAR images given the SFS results of the top-left SAR image. The third row shows predicted images given the SFS results of the top-center SAR image, and the fourth row does the same given the top-right SAR image.

Comparison of the observed images with predicted images show excellent

Fig. 11. Three original SAR images and their intensity predictions given SFS results. The top row shows the three observed SAR images corresponding to Tables 1–3, respectively. In each case the range direction and the illumination is along the horizontal axis. The second row shows the three predicted SAR images given the SFS results of the top-left SAR image. The third row shows predicted images given the SFS results of the top-center SAR image, and the fourth row does the same given the top-right SAR image.

intensity predictions for similar imaging geometries, as expected. Prediction of the first two SAR images given the third (and vice versa) provides a worst-case example because of the near orthogonal aspect difference. This means we are using mostly the estimates of azimuth slope for one image to predict the intensity of the other image. The left and center images in the bottom row show very good predictions of the first and second SAR images, respectively. The predictions of the third SAR image given in the rightmost column, second and third rows, are of fair quality. They show some loss of the structures that were in the downslopes of the observed image and some distortions due to albedo variations, yet most of the structure is still recognizable.

The large illumination differences also present some difficulty in deriving stereo correspondences. The predictive ability of SFS results might support stereo matching in this case [29].

4.5.2. *Comparison with the DTM*

Actual surface reconstructions are now compared with the "true DTMs." Figures 12–14 show 64×64 overviews of the SFS results showing a favorable

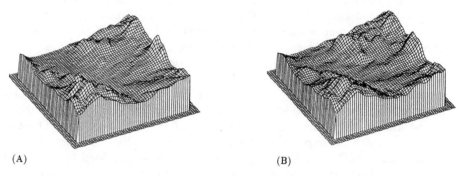

(A)   (B)

Fig. 12. 64×64 sample overviews of the SFS results for the first SAR image in Fig. 11. (A) DTM. (B) Surface reconstruction from SAR image and low resolution data.

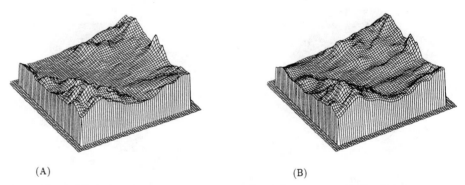

(A)   (B)

Fig. 13. 64×64 sample overviews of the SFS results for the second SAR image in Fig. 11. (A) DTM. (B) Surface reconstruction from SAR image and low resolution data.

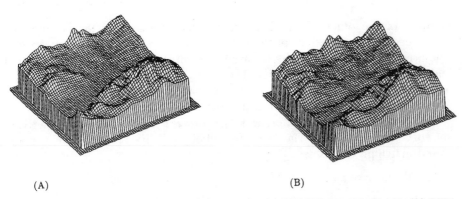

(A)   (B)

Fig. 14. 64 × 64 sample overviews of the SFS results for the third SAR image in Fig. 11. (A) DTM.
(B) Surface reconstruction from SAR image and low resolution data.

comparison between the DTM and the surface reconstruction. The reconstructions correspond to the three SAR images in Fig. 11. Some apparent differences can be observed along drainage patterns in the surface, perhaps due to albedo variations or surface roughness variations.

Figure 15 shows a full resolution window of one of the mountains from the DTM and its reconstruction from the third SAR image. Finally, Fig. 16 provides 1D cuts diagonally across the DTM and surface reconstruction obtained from the first SAR image. Table 4 provides RMS error for the surface reconstructions. First the standard deviation of the high resolution DTM is given for reference. Second, the standard deviation of the error between the low resolution DTM and the high resolution DTM is provided as a basis of comparison. Third, the standard deviation of the surface reconstruction error is given for all three images.

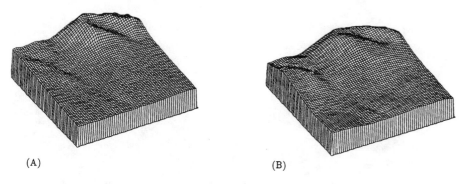

(A)   (B)

Fig. 15. Full resolution subarea view of the SFS results for the third SAR image in Fig. 11. (A) DTM. (B) Surface reconstruction from SAR image and low resolution data.

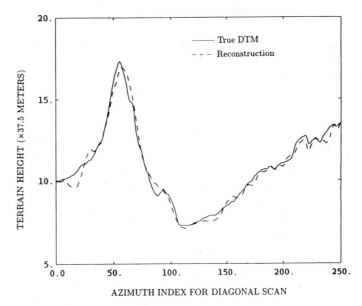

Fig. 16. 1D diagonal cuts across the DTM and surface reconstruction obtained from the first SAR image.

Table 4 shows that, in the experiments presented above, SFS provided a modest improvement over the RMS error of the low resolution surface data. Comparison of Fig. 11 with Fig. 7 and the comparison provided by Fig. 7 show that SFS provided intensity prediction capability and structural detail not available from the low resolution data.

Table 4
Surface height reconstruction accuracy

	SAR image		
	1	2	3
Standard deviation of high resolution DTM (meters)	84.3	84.0	80.0
Standard deviation of high resolution DTM minus low resolution DTM (meters)	16.8	21.2	17.5
Standard deviation of surface reconstruction error (meters)	14.4	17.6	14.1

5. Conclusions and Extensions

A SAR image-based SFS algorithm was developed for surface topography estimation. The slant plane parameterization of surface height and the use of Fourier basis functions in the SFS formulation provide a conceptually simple formulation and allow a computationally efficient implementation. Use of auxiliary low resolution surface data as a constraint in SFS was introduced and successfully applied to SAR imagery. The low resolution data was also used for estimating reflectance map parameters. For the purposes of radarclinometry, the availability of low resolution surface height information eliminates the need for, and is more useful than, absolute radar calibration. Application of SFS to Magellan SAR imagery was discussed and is expected to be similar to the SIR-B application tested in Section 4. Several possible extensions to this work have become apparent—additional practical issues for Magellan, the fusion of shading information with geometric stereo, and the estimation of reflectance parameter variations. These are discussed below.

To apply the techniques presented in this paper to Magellan, some practical issues must be addressed. The altimetry data must be registered with the SAR imagery. It is necessary to achieve registration accuracy comparable to the SAR image resolution, which is much finer than the altimetry resolution. While this is possible, it requires a much larger integration area than considered in this paper, perhaps extending thousands of SAR image pixels in range and azimuth. For reflectance map estimation from altimetry data a radar cross-section model suitable for the conditions on Venus should be carefully selected, as discussed in Section 4. Low resolution estimates of albedo and terrain surface roughness will result as a byproduct of SFS.

Additional research is needed for handling layover and shadows. The possibility of layover introduces both a spatial ambiguity and a radiometric ambiguity not considered in this paper. The radiometric ambiguity is essentially the same as that which occurs in visual imagery at points of the surface that are normal to the incident illumination ($\alpha_i = 0$). For example, consider the partial sphere surfaces in [18]. If the illumination was from directly overhead, it would be impossible to tell from image intensity alone whether the partial sphere extended above the plane or below the plane. In visual imagery, this type of ambiguity is in the depth direction only—it is not observable in the image. For SAR imagery, however, a zero crossing of α_i means a change of the slant range ordering of features as ground range increases. It may be possible to detect layover conditions by detecting likely zero crossings of α_i from inconsistencies between observed image intensity and that predicted by SFS results. Similarly, shadows are difficult to detect even in images with constant albedo because of the uncertainty introduced by additive thermal and sidelobe noise. A predictive approach to shadow detection may reduce this difficulty, as suggested in [18].

Earlier, Ikeuchi and Horn [27] developed a similar algorithm that, instead of using gradient space (z_x, z_y) was parameterized in stereographic coordinates. Stereographic coordinates eliminated the difficulty of handling points where z_x, z_y, or both are very large. A similar problem exists for SAR imagery when layover occurs. It may be useful to represent the surface in a more general coordinate system where singularities do not occur for any admissable surface orientation.

Because vision is a highly underdetermined problem, the fusion of information from different images and from different cues within a single image is important. For example, it has been suggested that SFS complements stereogrammetry [29]. By utilizing radiometric information it should be possible to improve the reliability, accuracy, and resolution of topography estimates available from radar-stereogrammetry. For SAR imagery, a tradeoff exists between two competing effects: The larger the difference in look angles for the stereo image pair the less sensitive the surface reconstruction is to errors in stereo correspondence and, on the other hand, the errors in stereo correspondence grow as the disparity between the look angles increases [29]. In many cases the human eye is not even able to recognize that two SAR images are of the same terrain if they are made from drastically different look angles because the change in illumination geometry causes changes in shading. Hence, the radiometric and geometric information contained in the images are synergistic.

It is difficult to obtain reliable stereo matches, especially in the presence of speckle noise. In order to obtain reliable matches, the resolution of stereo matches are necessarily low for SAR imagery: Feature-based matches require extended features and matching by correlation requires large integration subareas [13, 38] for reliability. The resolution of the matches can be improved without compromising reliability by using smaller subareas and then resolving ambiguities with shading information. The image shading predicted by the stereoscopically derived surface reconstruction should approximately fit the shading in the observed image. A second-order requirement is that the variance of the observed image intensity exceeds the variance of the stereo-predicted shading component by at least some threshold, predicted by speckle characteristics.

Similarly, the precision of stereo matches can be improved by accounting for shading differences that occur between SAR stereo image pairs. Two correction approaches, *intensity prediction* and *intensity compensation*, are discussed below. The intensity prediction method extracts high frequency surface information using SFS techniques and then forms a predicted image, as in Section 4. Stereo matching of, say, the first SAR image with its prediction given the second SAR image allows the computation of a residual parallax error, used for estimating a residual surface. The intensity compensation method starts with a stereoscopically derived surface reconstruction and then predicts a local shading ratio between the two images. Given the surface reconstruction, the aspect difference between the two images, knowledge of the parallax errors, and the reflectance map it is possible to compute the shading compensation. If additive noise terms are low, the correction is insensitive to albedo variations. After shading compensation the stereo matching procedure is repeated with greater achievable accuracy.

Radiometric stereo can also be extended to SAR imagery and applied simultaneously with traditional geometric stereo. In applying radiometric stereo and in the above intensity prediction and correction methods to SAR imagery the problem of surface-height-dependent registration errors arises. The local registrations provided by the initial stereo correspondences may be sufficiently accurate to allow radiometric stereo, geometric stereo, and monocular shading cues to bootstrap each other. New methods for extracting stereo depth-maps from visual images [2], if re-evaluated for SAR imagery, may provide better methods for utilizing both radiometric and geometric information.

This paper has considered the estimation of surface height when the reflectance properties of the surface are constant. The estimation of surface topography simultaneously with variations in albedo and other surfaces properties, such as roughness, is a much more difficult problem. Multi-spectral Landsat imagery has been used to segment albedo variations independent of surface topography [12, 20]. In a similar manner, it may be possible to detect variations in albedo using multi-frequency radar imagery [6]. The recent analysis of multi-polarization radar imagery [44] may provide insight into the utilization of phase data and polarization diversity for inferring surface structure. For example, it is possible to distinguish between surface and volume scattering mechanisms, and therefore reflectance map classes, using the phase differences between images sensed with different polarizations.

More research is needed in order to make use of these additional information sources. Models are needed which are general enough to account for the effects of surface roughness, the dielectric properties of the surface, polarization diversity, and frequency diversity yet are tractable enough to be useful for image analysis. The stochastic approaches to vision problems considered by Marroquin, Mitter and Paggio [32], and Chellappa [9] may help to provide a framework for algorithm development given a suitable model.

The full power of numerical methods for solving differential equations has not been fully utilized in SFS and other image analysis applications. The direct approach of Simchony and Chellappa [40] is potentially useful for SAR imagery. With the direct approach, it is possible to approximate the surface slopes consistent with a given intensity function, apply smoothness constraints, enforce fairly general boundary conditions, enforce integrability, and fuse shading information with stereo information in a unified algorithm. This is currently being considered for SAR imagery.

ACKNOWLEDGEMENT

Alan Weber's technical support as the SIPI computer laboratory manager and Ray Schmidt's photographic processing are gratefully acknowledged. Gitta Domik and Franz Leberl of the Vexcel Corporation have provided the imagery and DTMs needed for testing the SAR shape from shading algorithm, and participated in some enlightening technical discussions. The anonymous reviewers provided some very helpful suggestions. We would also like to thank Ralph Hudson, Dan Evans, and Rich Wojslaw of Hughes Aircraft Company for numerous technical discussions.

The first author would like to acknowledge the financial support of the Hughes fellowship program and to thank Sue Baumgarten and Tim Jentes for their continuing support as department managers.

REFERENCES

1. E. Bahar and S. Chakrabarti, Full-wave theory applied to computer aided graphics for objects, *IEEE Comput. Graph. Appl.* **7** (1987) 46–60.
2. S.T. Barnard, A stochastic approach to stereo vision, in: *Proceedings AAAI-86*, Philadelphia, PA (1986) 676–680.
3. D.E. Barrick, Rough surface scattering based on the specular point theory, *IEEE Trans. Antennas Propagat.* (1968) 838–850.
4. D.K. Barton, ed., *Radars, Vol. V: Radar Clutter* (Artech House, Norwood, MA, 1975).
5. P. Beckmann and A. Spizzichino, *The Scattering of Electromagnetic Waves from Rough Surfaces* (Pergamon, Oxford, 1963).
6. A.R. Benton and R.W. Newton, The utility of multi-frequency radar in the coastal zone environment, *IEEE Geosci. Remote Sens. Soc. Newslett.* **9** (1985) 4–8.
7. M.J. Brooks and B.K.P. Horn, Shape and source from shading, in: *Proceedings IJCAI-85*, Los Angeles, CA (1985) 932–936.
8. D.B. Campbell, J.W. Head, J.K. Harmon and A.A. Hine, Venus: Identification of banded terrain in the mountains of Ishtar Terra, *Science* **221** (1983) 644–647.
9. R. Chellappa, Model based approaches for some image understanding problems, *Proc. SPIE* **758** (1987) 39–49.
10. R.E. Clapp, A theoretical and experimental study of radar ground return, Tech. Rept. 1024, MIT Radiation Laboratory, Cambridge, MA (1946).
11. R.L. Cosgriff, W.H. Peake and R.C. Taylor, Terrain scattering properties for sensor system design, Tech. Rept., Engineering Experiment Station, Ohio State University, Columbus, OH (1960).
12. P.T. Eliason, L.A. Soderblom and P.S. Chavez Jr, Extraction of topographic and spectral albedo information from multispectral images, *Photogrammetric Eng. Remote Sens.* **47** (1981) 1571–1579.
13. R.T. Frankot, SAR Image Registration by Multi- Resolution Correlation, *Proc. SPIE* **432** (1983) 195–203.
14. R.T. Frankot, Computational vision algorithms for synthetic aperture radar imagery, Ph.D. Dissertation, Department of Electrical Engineering, Signal and Image Processing Institute, University of Southern California, Los Angeles, CA (1987).
15. R.T. Frankot and R. Chellappa, An improved algorithm for the shape from shading problem, in: *Proceedings Conference on Systems and Signal Processing*, Bangalore, India (1986).
16. R.T. Frankot and R. Chellappa, Lognormal random field models and their applications to radar image synthesis, *IEEE Trans. Geosci. Remote Sens.* (1987) 195–207.
17. R.T. Frankot and R. Chellappa, Application of a shape from shading technique to synthetic aperture radar imagery, in: *Proceedings International Geoscience and Remote Sensing Symposium*, Ann Arbor, MI (1987) 1323–1329.

18. R.T. Frankot and R. Chellappa, A method for enforcing integrability in shape from shading algorithms, *IEEE Trans. Pattern Anal. Machine Intell.* **10** (1988) 439–451.

19. L.C. Graham, Synthetic interferometer radar for topographic mapping, *Proc. IEEE* **64** (1974) 763–768.

20. R.M. Haralick, J.B. Campbell and S. Wang, Automatic inference of elevation and drainage models from a satellite image, *Proc. IEEE* **73** (1985) 1040–1053.

21. P.S. Heckbert, Survey of texture mapping, *IEEE Comput. Graph. Appl.* **6** (1986) 56–67.

22. J.C. Holtzman, V.S. Frost, J.L. Abbott and V.H. Kaupp, Radar image simulation, *IEEE Trans. Geosci. Remote Sens.* **16** (1978) 296–303.

23. B.K.P. Horn, Obtaining shape from shading information, in: P.H. Winston, ed., *The Psychology of Machine Vision* (McGraw-Hill, New York, 1975) 115–155.

24. B.K.P. Horn, *Robot Vision* (McGraw-Hill, New York, 1986).

25. B.K.P. Horn and M.J. Brooks, The variational approach to shape from shading, *Comput. Vision Graph. Image Process.* **33** (1986) 174–208.

26. K. Ikeuchi, Constructing a depth map from images, AI Memo No. 744, MIT, Cambridge, MA (1983).

27. K. Ikeuchi and B.K.P. Horn, Numerical shape from shading and occluding boundaries, *Artificial Intelligence* **17** (1981) 141–184.

28. W. Keydel, Application and experimental verification of an empirical backscattering cross section model for the earth's surface, *IEEE Trans. Geosci. Remote Sens.* **20** (1982) 67–71.

29. F. Leberl, G. Domik, J. Raggam, J. Cimino and M. Kobrick, Multiple incident angle SIR-B experiment over Argentina: Stereo radargrammetric analysis, *IEEE Trans. Geosci. Remote Sens.* **24** (1986) 482–491.

30. M.W. Long, *Radar Reflectivity of Land and Sea* (Artech House, Norwood, MA, 1983).

31. Magellan project radar system analysis methods and performance estimates, Hughes Aircraft Company, DRD No. SE011, El Segundo, CA (1986).

32. J. Marroquin, S. Mitter and T. Poggio, Probabilistic solution of ill-posed problems in computational vision, *J. Am. Stat. Assoc.* **82** (1987) 76–89.

33. H. Masursky, E. Eliason, P.G. Ford, G.E. McGill, G.H. Pettengill, G.G. Schaber and G. Schubert, Pioneer Venus results: Geology from images and altimetry, *J. Geophys. Res.* **85** (1980) 8232–8260.

34. A.P. Pentland, The visual inference of shape: Computation from local features, Ph.D. Dissertation, Department of Psychology, MIT, Cambridge, MA (1982).

35. G.H. Pettengill, E. Eliason, P.G. Ford, G.B. Loriot, H. Masursky and G.E. McGill, Pioneer Venus results: Altimetry and surface properties, *J. Geophys. Res.* **85** (1980) 8261–8270.

36. B.T. Phong, Illumination for computer generated pictures, *Commun ACM* **18** (1975) 311–317.

37. S.H. Pravdo, B. Huneycutt, B.M. Holtand and D.M. Lheld, SEASAT synthetic aperture radar users manual, JPL Publication 82–90 (1983).

38. H.K. Ramapriyan, J.P. Strong, Y. Hung and C.W. Murray Jr., Automated matching of pairs of SIR-B images for elevation mapping, *IEEE Trans. Geosci. Remote Sens.* **24** (1986) 462–472.

39. T. Reindfleisch, Photometric method for lunar topography, *Photogrammetric Eng.* (1966) 262–276.

40. T. Simchony and R. Chellappa, Direct analytic methods for solving Poisson equations in computer vision problems, in: *Proceedings IEEE Computer Society Workshop on Computer Vision*, Miami Beach, FL (1987).

41. M.I. Skolnik, ed., *Radar Handbook* (McGraw-Hill, New York, 1970).

42. L.M. Spetner and I. Katz, Two statistical models for radar terrain return, *IEEE Trans. Antennas Propagat.* **8** (1960) 242–246.

43. K.E. Torrance and E.M. Sparrow, Theory for off-specular reflection from roughened surfaces, *J. Opt. Soc. Am.* **57** (1967) 1105–1114.

44. F.T. Ulaby, D. Held, M.C. Dobson, K.C. McDonald and T.B.A Senior, Relating polarization

phase difference of SAR signals to scene properties, *IEEE Trans. Geosci. Remote Sens.* **25** (1987) 83–92.

45. J. van Diggelen, A photometric investigation of the slopes and heights of the ranges of hills in the maria of the moon, *Bull. Astronom. Inst. Netherlands* **11** (1951).

46. R.L. Wildey, Topography from single radar images, *Science* **224** (1984) 153–156.

47. R.L. Wildey, Radarclinometry, *Earth Moon Planets* **36** (1986) 217–247.

48. R.J. Woodham, Photometric method for determining surface orientation from multiple images, *Opt. Eng.* **19** (1980) 139–144.

49. S.T. Wu and A.K. Fung, A noncoherent model for microwave emissions and backscattering from the sea surface, *J. Geophys. Res.* **77** (1972) 5917–5929.

50. C. Wu, B. Barkan, B. Huneycutt, C. Leang and S. Pang, An introduction to the interim digital SAR processor and the characteristics of the associated Seasat SAR imagery, JPL Publication 81-26 (1981).

Received May 1988; revised version received March 1989

Where and Why Local Shading Analysis Works

FRANK P. FERRIE AND MARTIN D. LEVINE

Manuscript received December 10, 1986; revised July 7, 1988. Recommended for acceptance by W. Grimson. This work was supported in part by the Natural Sciences and Engineering Research Council of Canada under Grant A4156, by an FCAR Grant awarded by the Department of Education, Province of Québec, under Grant EQ-633, and by the Medical Research Council of Canada under Grant MRC-3236. The work of M. D. Levine was supported by the Canadian Institute for Advanced Research.

The authors are with the Computer Vision and Robotics Laboratory, McGill Research Centre for Intelligent Machines, McGill University, Montreal, P.Q., Canada H3A 2A7.

IEEE Log Number 8825642.

Abstract—Can shape be recovered from a local analysis of shading? Although much has been written against the exact recovery of shape in general, this would seem to contradict the practical experience that shape from shading often works, at least qualitatively. We therefore look at the problem from a different point of view, and show that the analysis can be sufficiently constrained to permit unambiguous recovery at the expense of some distortion in the recovered shape, provided that certain constraints are met. We derive a precise criterion for exact surface recovery and show that, as a result of surface geometry, elliptic and hyperbolic surfaces can be recovered to reasonable accuracy provided that surface curvature and/or foreshortening is limited. The application of local analysis of shading to complex surfaces is described, and results on artificial and real data are also presented.

Index Terms—Image analysis, image understanding, local computation, shape for shading.

I. INTRODUCTION

There is an apparent contradiction in the shape-from-shading literature. Although practical experience indicates that shape can be inferred from the local analysis of shading [12], [13], mathematical analyses support the opposite. Much has been written to support the contention that shape cannot be recovered exactly, e.g., Bruss [1], Ikeuchi and Horn [8], Smith [15]. But what if one were willing to accept some distortion of the estimated surfaces, say for the purpose of obtaining a *qualitative* description of shape. Could this still provide a valid and useful description? We contend that it can, and

have argued elsewhere in detail for the role of such qualitative descriptions [3]. For different reasons, Pentland [13], [14] showed that the inherent ambiguity of local analysis could be reduced by making strong assumptions about the nature of the surface being estimated, specifically that it be locally spherical. But he did not address the consequences of this assumption from a quantitative point of view nor did he apply his local analysis to the recovery of complex surfaces.

To reemphasize our general motivation, we seek an initial description of objects that is coarse enough to avoid the details of image noise and object particulars, but fine enough to be adequate for tasks such as identifying, manipulating, and avoiding collisions with objects [3], [18]. Our motivation can best be summarized by Fig. 1(a)–(c) which show the image of a stone owl statuette, the surfaces recovered from this image using local shading analysis, and a rendition composed of volumetric primitives estimated from these surfaces. In order to use local analysis of shading to compute such descriptions, we have to answer the following questions.

• What are the requirements for unique and exact surface recovery?

• What is the effect on the shape of a surface if these requirements are relaxed?

• How can the local estimates be integrated to yield an estimate of a surface; what additional boundary conditions are required?

The purpose of this paper is to answer the first two of these questions and provide some insight into the third. By doing so, we show that, where appropriate constraints are met, local analysis of shading can provide the basis for qualitative descriptions of shape.

The principal contributions of this paper are as follows.

• A precise criterion for exact surface recovery that is somewhat less restrictive than Pentland's sphericity assumption.

• An analysis which shows that, as a result of surface geometry, elliptic, hyperbolic, and doubly curved surfaces can be recovered to reasonable accuracy provided that surface curvature and/or foreshortening is limited.

• A demonstration that local analysis of shading can be applied to the recovery of complex surfaces.

Our approach is to apply local constraints about surface geometry and scale to restrict the estimation of local surface orientation to a unique interpretation, i.e., with the ambiguity of a reversal of the surface in depth. For example, there is an infinite number of

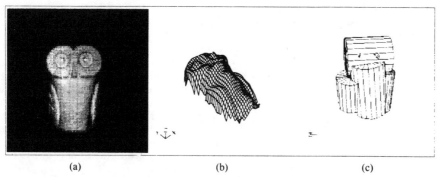

Fig. 1. (a) CCD television image of a stone owl sculpture. (b) Surfaces reconstructed from local analysis of shading. (c) Ellipsoid–cylinder model computed from reconstructed surfaces.

surfaces at successively higher order that can produce the same intensity distribution. By locally constraining surface geometry, e.g., Pentland's [13] sphericity assumption, one also limits the class of surfaces that can produce a given intensity distribution. The latter constraint clearly implies an *a priori* knowledge of scale since it assumes that the image is sampled so as to constrain the structure of local surface patches.[1]

In contrast, methods such as proposed by Ikeuchi and Horn [8] deal with ambiguity through global minimization and the application of appropriate boundary conditions. These methods can avoid the ambiguity inherent in local approaches and are differentially constrained by assumptions about surface shape and scale. However, the determination of boundary conditions such as the localization of discontinuities and occluding contours is in itself a nontrivial task [10], [9]. Errors in this process can have far-reaching effects because they are propagated over the entire surface. Thus, one can see where local surface estimation would be useful.

We begin by considering the process of image formation using a simplified model [5], [6], [13], and then the conditions under which reasonable estimates of local surface orientation can be derived with this model. From here, we show that simple surfaces such as ellipsoids and hyperboloids can be recovered to high degrees of accuracy, provided that certain constraints are met. By decomposing the surfaces of more complex objects into piecewise-continuous segments, we can apply our shape-from-shading procedure to more generalized surfaces.

II. Estimating Local Surface Orientation

In the following sections, we consider a simplified model of image formation in order to determine *what* can be recovered from measurements of image intensity. By examining the errors incurred in this process, as we deviate from ideal conditions, we gain an important insight as to why the local approach to shape from shading works as well as it does.

A. A Simplified Model of Image Formation

The actual process by which images are created is indeed a complex one. For example, consider how images are formed in a camera. Direct illumination from light sources within the scene and secondary illumination from nearby objects are reflected off the surfaces of an object and directed onto a photosensitive film by an optical lens. The relative positions of object, light sources, and camera affect the intensity distribution recorded on film and thus the composition of the image. By considering only a single light source and ignoring the effects of secondary illumination, a simplified model can be obtained (Fig. 2) [4]–[6]. Let N be the unit

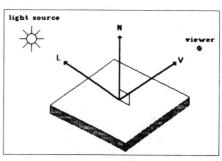

Fig. 2. Simplified model of image formation.

normal vector to a planar surface path. V the direction of view of a camera or observer,[2] and L the direction of a light source infinitely distant from the surface. To simplify further, we will assume that the surface has a Lambertian reflectance function [13].

Given these assumptions, the intensity recorded at each point in the image will be

$$I = \rho\lambda N \cdot L \qquad (1)$$

where ρ is the surface albedo and λ is the incident light flux. This simplified irradiance equation is a function of six unknowns, ρ, λ, and two parameters each defining the unit vectors N and L. Pentland's approach to solving (1) was to employ constraints from differential geometry in the local neighborhood of N in relation to derivatives of I to reduce the number of unknowns. We have taken a different approach, similar to that of Lee and Rosenfeld [11] by assuming that the position of the light source L is either known or can be estimated.

B. Change of Coordinates and Local Analysis

From (1), it can be seen that for a Lambertian surface, I is dependent only on surface geometry (L is a constant). Thus, I and functions of I can be computed in any convenient coordinate system and related to one another by a change of coordinates. For convenience, we choose a coordinate system $\langle u, v, w \rangle$ where the w axis is parallel to the light source direction L, i.e., $L = \langle 0, 0, 1 \rangle$ [11]. Since the position of the light source is assumed known, we can determine the parameters of the transformation T_l such that $\langle u, v, w \rangle = T_l \langle x, y, z \rangle$.[3] Consequently, (1) simplifies to

$$I = \rho\lambda N_w \qquad (2)$$

where N_w is the w component of the surface vector N_l.

---

[1] For example, a surface can be approximated by local planar patches if sampled densely enough. Pentland [13] assumed that surfaces were approximated by local second-order sections. The information required is the scale at which to sample the image so that local approximations to the surface meet constraints.

[2] Orthographic projection is assumed with the V direction corresponding to the Z axis of an $\langle x, y, z \rangle$ coordinate system.

[3] We will use the l subscript to refer to quantities relative to $\langle u, v, w \rangle$ coordinates when this is not clear from context. T_l depends on three rotation parameters, two of which are determined by rotating $\vec{z}$ into L. The remaining parameter can be chosen arbitrarily (i.e., zero).

Using the convention of [16], [17], [13], we define N through the use of two angles, tilt τ and slant σ that define N in relation to the plane of the viewer as follows:[4]

$$\sigma = \cos^{-1}(N_z) \qquad \tau = \tan^{-1}(N_y, N_x). \qquad (3)$$

We can similarly define τ_l and σ_l with respect to the uv plane by substituting the u, v, and w components of N_l into the above expressions. Because the relationship between the xy and uv planes is known through T_l,[5] there is no loss of generality in solving for τ_l and σ_l. From (2) and (3), we observe that the slant angle σ_l is given by

$$\sigma_l = \cos^{-1}\left(\frac{I}{\rho\lambda}\right). \qquad (4)$$

This assumes that the proportionality constant $\rho\lambda$ can either be measured or determined.

The idea behind shape-from-shading algorithms is to systematically relate variations in image intensities to variations in surface geometry. Pentland [13] did this under the assumption that the surface was locally spherical; here we prove a more general result.

Theorem: Let $\bar{\tau}_l$ be defined as the tilt vector, that is, the unit vector in the uv plane originating from point p at an angle τ_l with respect to the u axis. The intensity gradient with respect to the uv plane will have the same direction as $\bar{\tau}_l$ if and only if

$$\frac{f_u^2 - f_v^2}{f_u f_v} = \frac{f_{uu} - f_{vv}}{f_{uv}}. \qquad (5)$$

Clearly, this theorem provides an aid to estimating the tilt τ_l,[6] and extends previous results by providing a necessary and sufficient condition.

Proof: We proceed by examining the relationship between dN_w, which is known from dI_l, and the surface tilt τ_l for a surface $w = f(u, v)$ in orthographic projection to the uv plane. The unit normal N_l at a point p, $w = f(u_p, v_p)$ is given by

$$N_l = \frac{\langle -f_u, -f_v, 1 \rangle}{\sqrt{1 + f_u^2 + f_v^2}}. \qquad (6)$$

From (6), it follows that

$$\tau_l = \tan^{-1}(f_v, f_u) \quad \text{and} \quad N_w = \frac{1}{\sqrt{1 + f_u^2 + f_v^2}}. \qquad (7)$$

Applying the chain rule to the expression for N_w results in the following:

$$dN_w = \frac{\partial N_w}{\partial u} du + \frac{\partial N_w}{\partial u} dv$$

$$dN_w = -\left\{ \frac{f_u f_{uu} + f_v f_{vu}}{(f_u^2 + f_v^2 + 1)^{3/2}} du \right.$$
$$\left. + \frac{f_u f_{uv} + f_v f_{vv}}{(f_u^2 + f_v^2 + 1)^{3/2}} dv \right\}. \qquad (8)$$

If $\bar{\tau}_l$ is the tilt vector, then from (8) and (7), we can see that the gradient of N_w will have the same direction as $\bar{\tau}_l$ if and only if

$$\frac{f_v}{f_u} = \frac{f_u f_{uv} + f_v f_{vv}}{f_u f_{uu} + f_v f_{vu}} \qquad (9)$$

or, equivalently,

$$\frac{f_u^2 - f_v^2}{f_u f_v} = \frac{f_{uu} - f_{vv}}{f_{uv}}, \qquad (10)$$

provided that $f_{uv} = f_{vu}$. Notice, however, that dN_w is related to dI_l by differentiating (2), i.e.,

$$dI_l = \rho\lambda dN_w. \qquad (11)$$

Thus, (5) provides the necessary and sufficient conditions under which the intensity gradient direction has the same direction as the surface tilt vector $\bar{\tau}_l$ in light source coordinates. But (11) assumes that the intensity gradient direction is specified with respect to the uv plane. This poses no problem as the gradient direction can be computed with respect to the image plane and transformed into uv coordinates through T_l. One can readily see that (5) is satisfied for a spherical surface of the form $f(u, v) = \sqrt{R^2 - u^2 - v^2}$ since

$$\frac{f_v}{f_u} = \frac{f_u f_{uv} + f_v f_{vv}}{f_u f_{uu} + f_v f_{vu}} = \frac{v}{u}, \qquad (12)$$

but this is by no means the only surface that does so.

Observation: It follows from (12) that in order to obtain a unique interpretation,[7] we must also ensure that the surface is locally second order. That is, the surface must be sampled such that the resulting local neighborhood corresponds to a second-order surface.

Thus, from measurements of I and its gradient direction relative to $\langle u, v, w \rangle$ coordinates, we may estimate τ_l and σ_l subject to the above constraints. The same can be expressed in more familiar $\langle x, y, z \rangle$ coordinates by application of T_l^{-1}; hence, we will use $\langle x, y, z \rangle$ in further discussion unless stated otherwise.

III. Error Components in Local Shading Analysis

In order to reconstruct the shape of an object, it is important to understand how each of the component processes affects the *overall* recovery of shape. Errors in estimating local surface orientation using the simple model outlined in the previous section arise from three sources.

• Uncertainty in parameter estimation: the light source direction vector L and the albedo term $\rho\lambda$.
• The shape of the local neighborhood does not fulfill the conditions required by (5).
• Error in determining the direction of the intensity gradient of the local neighborhood.

We treat each in turn.

A. Estimating L and $\rho\lambda$

The first step in estimating local surface orientation is the determination of the illuminant direction L for the surface and constants $\rho\lambda$ for a particular estimation neighborhood. Pentland [12], in the spirit of Witkin [17], suggested the assumption of an isotropic distribution of surface normals within a scene. Since $dI = \rho\lambda dN \cdot L$, then $d\bar{I} = \rho\lambda d\bar{N} \cdot L$ where $d\bar{I}$ and $d\bar{N}$ are the means of dI and dN, respectively. Assuming that the distribution of $d\bar{N}$ is known and that dI is measurable for different directions within the image, Pentland suggested using a maximum likelihood procedure for estimating L. He obtained the following result:

$$(\hat{L}_x \quad \hat{L}_y) = (\beta' \beta)^{-1} \beta'(d\bar{I}_1 \quad d\bar{I}_2 \cdots d\bar{I}_n) \qquad (13)$$

where $\hat{L}_x$ and $\hat{L}_y$ are the nonnormalized x and y components of the light source direction vector L, β is a $2 \times n$ matrix of directions (dx_i, dy_i), and $d\bar{I}_i$ is the means of dI over the estimation region along each of n image directions (dx_i, dy_i). The full illuminant direction is given by

$$L_x = \frac{\hat{L}_x}{k} \quad L_y = \frac{\hat{L}_y}{k} \quad L_z = \sqrt{1 - L_x^2 - L_y^2}$$

where

$$k = \sqrt{E(dI^2) - E(dI)^2} \qquad (14)$$

and $E(dI)$ is the expected value of dI. The $\rho\lambda$ term in (11) is accounted for by the parameter k above. Pentland addressed the

---

[4]In this paper, the notation $\tan^{-1}(y, x)$ is used to specify the four-quadrant inverse tangent function.

[5]Subject to the restriction that the range of T_l is limited such that surface points under consideration are visible from both the xy and uv planes.

[6]The surface tilt τ_l is the angle associated with $\bar{\tau}_l$.

[7]With a 180° ambiguity. See Pentland [13] for details regarding how this can be resolved using the illuminant direction.

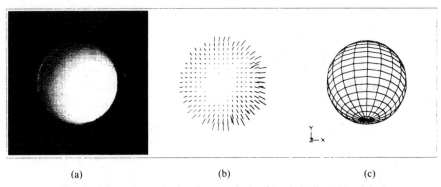

(a)   (b)   (c)

Fig. 3. Sphere reconstruction from analysis of local shading: (a) original image, (b) estimated surface normals, (c) best ellipsoidal fit to the reconstructed surface.

problem of estimating $\rho\lambda$ by introducing a further assumption, that the estimation region for L was spherical. From this, he was able to show that an estimator for $\rho\lambda$ was the standard deviation of dI along any particular image direction (dx_i, dy_i) [12]. An alternate approach to estimating these parameters is presented in Lee and Rosenfeld [11].

We applied Pentland's estimator for the light source direction L to the image of the sphere shown in Fig. 3(a). This image was artificially generated with the light source positioned in the lower right quadrant.[8] Using a sphere eliminates any concern over the surface not satisfying (5). The $\rho\lambda$ constant was estimated by simply taking the min/max of the intensity distribution over the surface and scaling slant such that minimum and maximum intensities corresponded to slant angles of 90° and 0°, respectively. Fig. 3(b) shows the resulting distribution of surface normals estimated using our algorithm, and Fig. 3(c) the best ellipsoidal fit to the reconstructed surface. To recover the generating parameters for the sphere, we fit an ellipsoid to the reconstructed surface and observed the ratios of the major axes. One would expect identical axis lengths for a perfect sphere, and deviations from unity to indicate a measure of "roundness." Results are summarized in Table I (Appendix).

The above experiment was repeated for different light source positions and confirmed the findings of Lee and Rosenfeld [11] with regard to the accuracy of Pentland's L position estimator. The emphasis of our experiments, however, was on obtaining upper bounds on reconstruction error for a given uncertainty in light source position L. We assumed that L was known to within 15° to 20° of true position, and found that quite precise recovery of scene generation parameters was indeed possible. In fact, as can be verified by Table I, L position errors of up to 20 percent have little effect on parameter recovery for a sphere. Three light source positions were used in the reconstruction process: the exact position used to generate the image, the estimated position computed with Pentland's procedure, and a "forced" position selected such that L was at maximum tolerance. Notice that the ratios of axis lengths, which must be unity for a sphere, are within 5 percent for all L positions.

B. Effects of Nonspherical Surfaces

A more interesting question with regard to Pentland's sphericity assumption is what happens when the algorithm is applied to nonspherical surfaces. Given (5), we can determine errors in tilt estimation analytically. A good strategy to pursue in studying this effect is to consider how tilt estimates are distorted as a spherical surface is deformed into either an elliptic or hyperbolic surface. As

before, it is convenient to work in $\langle u, v, w \rangle$ coordinates, but this does not affect the generality of our results for the reasons stated earlier. We begin by considering functions of the form

$$f(u, v) = c\sqrt{\pm\left(1 - \frac{v^2}{b^2} - \frac{u^2}{a^2}\right)} \qquad (15)$$

where the discriminant is positive for an elliptic surface and negative for a hyperbolic surface, both of which are centered at the origin with principal axes a, b, and c parallel to the coordinate axes.

If we apply (5) to the above, we find that the estimated tilt angle $\hat\tau$ is given by

$$\hat\tau_l = \tan^{-1}\left(a^2 v\left(\left(\frac{b^2}{a^2} - 1\right)u^2 + a^2\right),\right.$$
$$\left. b^2 u\left(\left(\frac{a^2}{b^2} - 1\right)v^2 + b^2\right)\right) \qquad (16)$$

for *both* elliptic and hyperbolic surfaces. The actual tilt angle τ, again for both surfaces, is

$$\tau_l = \tan^{-1}(a^2 v^2, b^2 u). \qquad (17)$$

Fig. 4 shows a plot of tilt estimation error, i.e., $|\hat\tau_l - \tau_l|$, as a function of eccentricity ratio a/b, obtained from (16) and (17). A ratio of 1 corresponds to a purely spherical surface, with large ratios tending towards cylindrical surfaces. Notice that for even small ratios, the error is quite substantial. To gauge the effects of this error, we applied our reconstruction algorithm to the canonical examples of an ellipsoid and a torus. In the first example [Fig. 5(a)], an image of an ellipsoid with axis ratios 100 : 70 : 35 was generated with its principal axes parallel to the coordinate axes. The tilt error distribution for this surface is shown in Fig. 6 as a surface map with the highest point corresponding to a tilt error of approximately 20 percent. In Fig. 5(b), the resulting distribution of surface normals is shown, and in Fig. 5(c) a view of the best ellipsoidal fit to the reconstructed surface. The results of this experiment are summarized in Table II (Appendix).

This experiment shows that relatively precise recovery of ellipsoidal surfaces is possible, despite the pessimistic predictions from the above analysis. On comparing the effects of different light source positions, it would appear that the L vector uncertainty, within the range specified earlier, results in a parameter variation of about 5 percent, similar to that for a sphere. Note also that this variation includes a component due to the reconstruction procedure, as the surfaces are randomly sampled to provide data for parameterization. All parameter values are within 5 percent of their actual values as recovered from an original image.[9] What, then,

---

[8]The image was 128 × 128 pixels in dimension. A uniform noise distribution was added to the image with a mean of 3.12 percent of the maximum intensity and standard deviation of 5.78 percent. Hardware problems with our frame buffer also tended to contribute shot noise on the order of 20 percent.

[9]The image has added to it a uniform noise distribution with mean and standard deviation both equal to 10 percent of maximum intensity. Image dimensions are 128 × 128 pixels.

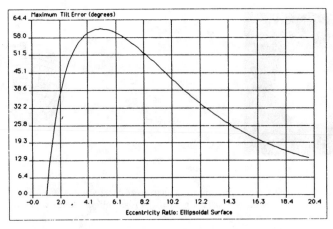

Fig. 4. Tilt estimation error as a function of eccentricity.

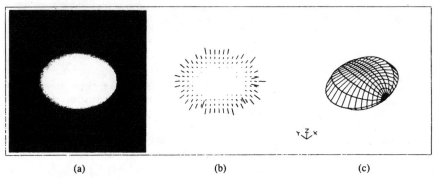

(a)   (b)   (c)

Fig. 5. Ellipsoid reconstruction: (a) original image, (b) estimated surface
normals, (c) best ellipsoidal fit to the reconstructed surface.

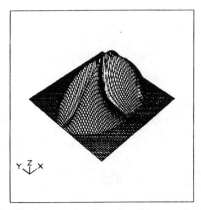

Fig. 6. Tilt error as a function of position on an ellipsoid.

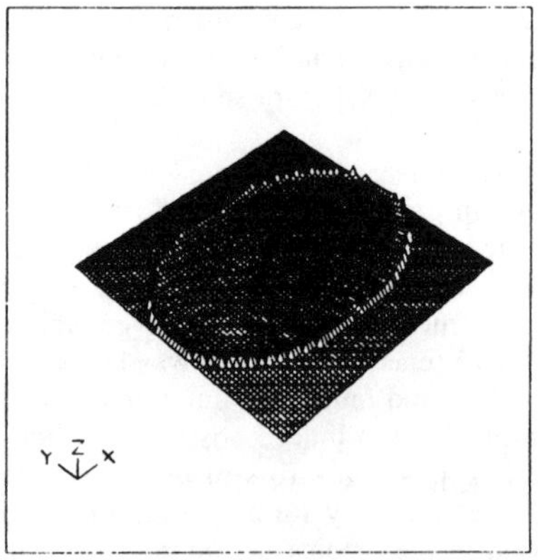

Fig. 7. Height differential error as a function of position on an ellipsoid.

accounts for these results? To answer this question, we must consider the effect of tilt uncertainty when interpolating along the surface.

C. The Effect of Interpolation

Reverting back to $\langle x, y, z \rangle$ coordinates, if we consider the simplest form of interpolation, i.e., along a plane T_p tangent to a point p lying on a surface S at position (x_p, y_p), the height differential is given by [2]

$$\Delta z(\Delta x, \Delta y) = \frac{\Delta x \sin \sigma \cos \tau + \Delta y \sin \sigma \sin \tau}{-\cos \sigma} \quad (18)$$

where σ and τ are the slant and tilt angles, respectively, at position (x_p, y_p) on surface S.

Now consider the distribution of tilt error (shown in Fig. 6) in relation to the interpolation function described by (18). In particular, notice that tilt errors tend to fall off with increasing slant. Consequently, the $\sin \sigma$ term in (18) serves to attenuate tilt error. This is demonstrated in Fig. 7 which shows the distribution of error in Δz as a function of position on the surface shown earlier in Fig. 6. As it turns out, the most significant errors occur on the periphery of the surface, in contrast to the tilt error. In addition, the magnitude of this error appears to be sufficiently bounded so as not to introduce undue distortion into the surface reconstruction. In a sense, then, foreshortening saves the day by attenuating the previously calculated tilt errors.

Thus far, our examples have not dealt with surfaces of high curvature (resulting from either geometry or foreshortening). A sur-

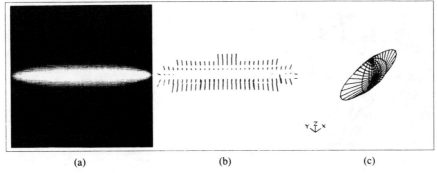

| (a) | (b) | (c) |

Fig. 8. Ellipsoid reconstruction (high eccentricity): (a) original image, (b) estimated surface normals, (c) best ellipsoidal fit to the reconstructed surface.

face with high eccentricity is used in the next experiment as an approximation. Our model [Fig. 8(a)] is an ellipsoidal surface centered at the origin with axes ratios of $100:20:50$. The resulting surface normal field is shown in Fig. 8(b) and a view of the best ellipsoidal fit to the reconstructed surface is shown in Fig. 8(c). The latter is displayed along the z axis which accentuates the deformation caused by high eccentricity. Results are summarized in Table III (Appendix).

As in the previous examples, light source position errors within the specified range of 20 percent do not greatly affect the variation of recovered parameters. In general, rotation angles are more precise due to the elongation of the ellipsoid, which improves the estimation of axis directions. Axis ratios, however, are considerably more distorted, but still within 20 percent of their actual values. The observation here is that regions of high curvature on a surface, due either to foreshortening or actual structure, will be ''stretched'' out of shape. Although shading information alone in these cases is insufficient for accurate surface recovery, it can still be sufficient for qualitative estimates of shape. To get an idea of the error component due to tilt estimation errors in this case, errors in the height differential Δz are plotted as a function of position on the ellipsoidal surface of Fig. 8(a) and shown in Fig. 9 to the same scale as in Fig. 7. As might be expected, there is a significant increase in the magnitude of the differential error along the periphery of the surface where slant angles are large.

As a final example, we consider the reconstruction of the half torus shown in Fig. 10(a). The criterion for evaluation used was the mean circularity of the circular cross section,[10] computed by radially sampling the torus and fitting an ellipse to each sample. Fig. 10(b) shows the resulting surface normal field, and Fig. 10(c) the reconstructed surface obtained from a single view. The results of this experiment are summarized in Table IV (Appendix). For an ideal torus, the major axes of an ellipse fit to a cross section should be equal for all radial samples. Thus, the mean value of cross-sectional axis ratios would seem to be a reasonable measure of shape fidelity for a torus. The results of the experiment indicate an acceptable reconstruction error.

D. Localizing the Intensity Gradient

Up to now, we have confirmed local surface estimation to smooth, convex surfaces. But what happens, for example, when we apply our estimation procedure to a nonconvex surface such as one formed by the intersection of several convex surface components? An example is shown in Fig. 11(a), the resulting surface normal field in Fig. 11(b), and the reconstructed surface in Fig. 11(c). Note that the resulting normal field in the vicinity of the intersections is incorrect, resulting (in this particular case) in an

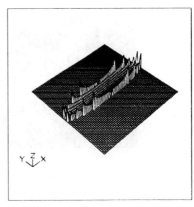

Fig. 9. Height differential error as a function of position on an ellipsoid with high eccentricity.

inversion of what are supposed to be protrusions out of the surface [Fig. 11(c)]. It is assumed that dI is estimated within a continuous neighborhood of each point in the image. However, such is not the case in the vicinity of discontinuities arising from shadows, changes in reflectance, or the geometry of the surface. Since surface orientation estimates must rely on support from continuous local neighborhoods, the accurate location of these discontinuities is a prerequisite to surface recovery [10].

In the above example, the neighborhood used for estimating the gradient was allowed to span discontinuities arising from the intersection of two surfaces, leading to the results shown. As a first approximation to locating discontinuities and correctly placing operator support, we repeated the experiment using the output of a Sobel operator as a guide. Estimation regions for I and dI were placed[11] so as to lie to one side of edge discontinuities found by the operator, much in the same way that floor tiles line up against a wall. The resulting surface normal field is shown in Fig. 12(a) and the reconstructed surface in Fig. 12(b). Notice that the surface is now reconstructed correctly.[12]

E. Recovering Piecewise-Continuous Surfaces

Finally, a short comment is in order regarding the application of local shading analysis to the recovery of piecewise-continuous surfaces. The examples of Figs. 11 and 12 show that one cannot correctly estimate local surface orientation from shading without accounting for discontinuities in the intensity function. The same

---

[10]Image dimensions are 128×128. The circular cross section is 24 pixels across.

[11]This is done automatically by the algorithm.

[12]As a point of interest, the surface projections are Gaussian cones formed by rotating a Gaussian profile about the axis of symmetry. It happens that this surface satisfies (5) exactly.

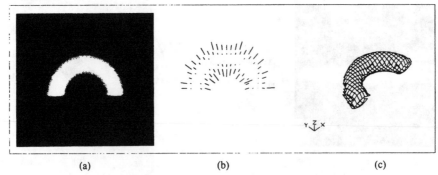

(a)   (b)   (c)

Fig. 10. Torus reconstruction: (a) original image, (b) estimated surface normals, (c) reconstructed surface.

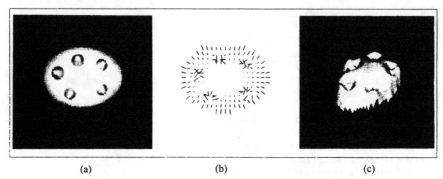

(a)   (b)   (c)

Fig. 11. Reconstruction of a nonconvex object (synthetic data) with incorrect estimation regions: (a) original image, (b) estimated surface normals, (c) reconstructed surface.

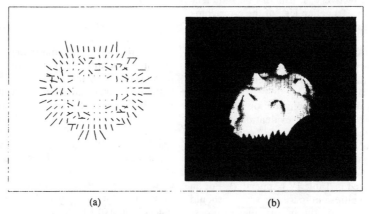

(a)   (b)

Fig. 12. Reconstruction of a nonconvex object (synthetic data) with correct estimation regions: (a) estimated surface normals, (b) reconstructed surface.

holds for the process of surface recovery in which depth is estimated from orientation. Since these processes involve the propagation of information over the whole surface [2], [7], one must determine how information is propagated across discontinuities. In recovering the surface shown earlier in Fig. 1(a), it was assumed that discontinuities correspond to creases on the surface everywhere except at occluding contours (i.e., depth is continuous everywhere except at an occluding contour). Points on the surface where $|N_z|$ falls off towards zero were subsequently marked as occluding contours, providing constraints for the surface recovery algorithm.

IV. CONCLUSIONS

In this paper, we examined an apparent contradiction in the shape-from-shading literature. Although practical experience suggests that shape can be inferred from the local analysis of shading, mathematical analyses support the opposite. We derived a criterion for exact surface recovery and showed that, as a result of surface geometry, elliptic and hyperbolic surfaces could be recovered to reasonable accuracy provided that surface curvature and/or foreshortening were limited. In other words, by relaxing the requirement that surfaces be recovered *exactly*, we found that local analysis of shading can provide useful descriptions of shape as evidenced by the results presented in this paper.

APPENDIX

TABLE I
SPHERE GENERATION PARAMETERS

Exact L:	< 0.4160, −0.2774, 0.8660 >		
Estimated L:	< 0.4849, −0.3332, 0.8086 >	ΔL: 6.05°	
Forced L:	< 0.4849, −0.3332, 0.7500 >	ΔL: 19.35°	

A. Using actual L

	Estimated	Actual	$\Delta^\dagger$
Centroid X	0.0	1.5900	1.24%
Centroid Y	0.0	1.7100	1.34%
Centroid Z	0.0	2.0500	1.60%
Axis A	0.9881	1.0	1.19%
Axis B	1.0170	1.0	1.70%
Axis C	0.9587	1.0	4.13%

B. Using estimated L

	Estimated	Actual	Δ
Centroid X	0.0	1.3700	1.07%
Centroid Y	0.0	1.3500	1.05%
Centroid Z	0.0	0.3840	0.30%
Axis A	0.9849	1.0	1.51%
Axis B	1.0064	1.0	0.64%
Axis C	1.0259	1.0	2.59%

C. Using forced L

	Estimated	Actual	Δ
Centroid X	0.0	−0.5000	0.39%
Centroid Y	0.0	1.7300	1.35%
Centroid Z	0.0	0.0300	0.02%
Axis A	1.0484	1.0	4.84%
Axis B	1.0367	1.0	3.67%
Axis C	0.9843	1.0	1.57%

TABLE II
ELLIPSOID GENERATION PARAMETERS

Exact L:	< 0.1504, −0.0868, 0.9848 >		
Estimated L:	< 0.1555, −0.1432, 0.9774 >	ΔL: 3.27°	
Forced L:	< 0.1555, −0.1432, 0.9000 >	ΔL: 22.76°	

A. Using actual L

	Estimated	Actual	$\Delta^\dagger$
Centroid X	−0.5400	0.0	0.42%
Centroid Y	0.5740	0.0	0.45%
Centroid Z	0.8925	0.0	0.70%
Rotation X	−4.0354	0.0	4.48%
Rotation Y	2.4400	0.0	2.71%
Rotation Z	0.2225	0.0	0.25%
Axis A	0.9836	1.0000	1.64%
Axis B	0.7176	0.7000	2.51%
Axis C	0.3554	0.3500	1.54%

B. Using estimated L

	Estimated	Actual	Δ
Centroid X	2.2278	0.0	1.74%
Centroid Y	1.3689	0.0	1.07%
Centroid Z	1.0101	0.0	0.79%
Rotation X	2.9441	0.0	3.27%
Rotation Y	2.1095	0.0	2.34%
Rotation Z	1.8816	0.0	2.09%
Axis A	0.9597	1.0000	4.03%
Axis B	0.7265	0.7000	3.79%
Axis C	0.3613	0.3500	3.23%

C. Using forced L

	Estimated	Actual	Δ
Centroid X	−1.1633	0.0	0.91%
Centroid Y	1.6122	0.0	1.26%
Centroid Z	1.0082	0.0	0.79%
Rotation X	2.9224	0.0	3.25%
Rotation Y	2.2325	0.0	2.48%
Rotation Z	0.9676	0.0	1.08%
Axis A	0.9719	1.0000	2.81%
Axis B	0.7052	0.7000	0.52%
Axis C	0.3618	0.3500	3.37%

TABLE III
ELONGATED ELLIPSOID GENERATION PARAMETERS

Exact L:	< 0.0000, 0.0000, 1.0000 >		
Estimated L:	< 0.0000, −0.1741, 0.9847 >	ΔL: 10.04°	
Forced L:	< 0.1555, −0.1432, 0.9000 >	ΔL: 22.76°	

A. Using actual L

	Estimated	Actual	$\Delta^\dagger$
Centroid X	0.8004	0.0	0.63%
Centroid Y	0.5382	0.0	0.42%
Centroid Z	1.3488	0.0	1.05%
Rotation X	−0.0616	0.0	0.07%
Rotation Y	1.6553	0.0	1.84%
Rotation Z	0.1134	0.0	0.13%
Axis A	1.1863	1.0000	18.63%
Axis B	0.1920	0.2000	4.00%
Axis C	0.5274	0.5000	5.48%

B. Using estimated L

	Estimated	Actual	Δ
Centroid X	0.9642	0.0	0.75%
Centroid Y	1.0568	0.0	0.83%
Centroid Z	1.0968	0.0	0.86%
Rotation X	0.3112	0.0	0.35%
Rotation Y	0.4500	0.0	0.50%
Rotation Z	−0.0315	0.0	0.04%
Axis A	1.1281	1.0000	12.81%
Axis B	0.1851	0.2000	7.45%
Axis C	0.5404	0.5000	8.08%

C. Using forced L

	Estimated	Actual	Δ
Centroid X	0.4768	0.0	0.37%
Centroid Y	1.0253	0.0	0.80%
Centroid Z	1.4662	0.0	1.15%
Rotation X	−0.2102	0.0	0.23%
Rotation Y	6.1904	0.0	6.88%
Rotation Z	−0.3948	0.0	0.44%
Axis A	0.9533	1.0000	4.67%
Axis B	0.1870	0.2000	6.50%
Axis C	0.5773	0.5000	15.46%

TABLE IV
TORUS GENERATION PARAMETERS

Exact L:	< 0.0000, 0.0000, 1.0000 >		
Estimated L:	< 0.0163, −0.0716, 0.9974 >	ΔL: 4.13°	
Forced L:	< 0.0163, −0.0716, 0.9000 >	ΔL: 20.00°	

A. Using estimated L

	Estimated	Actual	$\Delta^\dagger$
X Section Ratio:	1.1015	1.0	10.15%

B. Using forced L

	Estimated	Actual	Δ
X Section Ratio:	1.1174	1.0	11.17%

$\dagger \Delta$ is computed as the difference between estimated and actual parameter values normalized by the maximum value of each parameter.

ACKNOWLEDGMENT

The authors wish to thank S. W. Zucker, B. Kimia, and P. T. Sander for their helpful discussions throughout the course of this work.

REFERENCES

[1] A. Bruss, "The image irradiance equation: Its solution and application," M.I.T. AI Memo 623, Cambridge, MA, June 1981.
[2] F. P. Ferrie, "Reconstructing and interpreting the 3D shape of moving objects," Ph.D. dissertation, Dep. Elec. Eng., McGill Univ. Montréal, P.Q., Canada, Mar. 1986.
[3] F. P. Ferrie and M. D. Levine, "Deriving coarse 3D models of objects," in *Proc. IEEE Comput. Soc. Conf. Comput. Vision Pattern Recognition*, Univ. Michigan, Ann Arbor, June 1988.
[4] B. K. P. Horn, "Shape from shading: A method for obtaining the

shape of a smooth opaque object from one view," M.I.T. MAC TR-79, Cambridge, MA, 1970.

[5] ——, "Obtaining shape from shading information," in *The Psychology of Computer Vision*, P. H. Winston, Ed.   New York: McGraw-Hill, 1975, pp. 115-155.

[6] ——, "Understanding image intensities," *Art. Intell.*, no. 8, pp. 201-231, 1977.

[7] K. Ikeuchi, "Constructing a depth map from images," M.I.T. AI Memo 744, Cambridge, MA, 1983.

[8] K. Ikeuchi and B. K. P. Horn, "Numerical shape for shading and occluding boundaries," *Art. Intell.*, vol. 17, no. 1-3, pp. 141-184, Aug. 1981.

[9] Y. G. Leclerc, "Capturing the local structure of image discontinuities in two dimensions," in *Proc. IEEE Conf. Comput. Vision Pattern Recognition*, San Francisco, CA, June 1985, pp. 34-39.

[10] Y. G. Leclerc and S. W. Zucker, "The local structure of image discontinuities in one dimension," *IEEE Trans. Pattern Anal. Machine Intell.*, vol. PAMI-9, pp. 341-355, May 1987.

[11] C. Lee and A. Rosenfeld, "Improved methods of estimating shape from shading using the light source coordinate system," Univ. Maryland, College Park, Tech. Rep. TR-1277, 1983.

[12] A. P. Pentland, "Finding the illuminant direction," *J. Opt. Soc. Amer.*, vol. 72, pp. 448-455, Apr. 1982.

[13] ——, "Local shading analysis," *IEEE Trans. Pattern Anal. Machine Intell.*, vol. PAMI-6, pp. 170-187, Mar. 1984.

[14] ——, "Shading into texture," *Art. Intell. J.*, vol. 29, pp. 147-170, June 1986.

[15] G. B. Smith, "Shape from shading: An assessment," SRI Tech. Note 287, Menlo Park, CA, 1983.

[16] K. A. Stevens, "Surface perception from local analysis of texture and contour," Ph.D. dissertation, Dep. Elec. Eng. Comput. Sci., M.I.T., Cambridge, 1979.

[17] A. P. Witkin, "Recovering surface shape and orientation from texture," *Art. Intell.*, vol. 17, no. 1-3, pp. 17-45, Aug. 1981.

[18] S. W. Zucker, "Early vision," in S. Shapiro, Ed., *The Encyclopedia of Artificial Intelligence*.   New York: Wiley, 1987.

Photometric Stereo

Shape recovery from reflectance and shading information contained in a single image is highly underconstrained. Photometric stereo is a methodology that uses multiple images of a fixed object scene under different illumination conditions to provide additional constraints on surface shape from reflectance. Typically, multiple images of a scene are taken from a fixed view respective to a light source at different incident orientations. Constraints on surface shape are applied locally from reflectance at each pixel with respect to each illumination condition.

It is interesting to compare photometric stereo with traditional stereo used to determine the position of points in space. In the first place there is no correspondence problem to solve with photometric stereo, as the image plane is fixed relative to the scene. Constraints from reflectance are directly applied at each pixel for multiple images. While traditional stereo can be completely passive with two or more cameras, photometric stereo requires an active illumination environment either manipulated mechanically in the laboratory or naturally occuring (e.g., motion of the sun). Photometric stereo and traditional stereo have a useful duality in that they perform shape recovery under complementary scene conditions. While photometric stereo can recover local surface orientation over smooth regions where reflectance properties are known, traditional stereo can recover depth from correspondence of scene discontiniuties producing image edges, corners and texture. The duality of these two stereo methods is discussed in [1], which is reprinted in the "Physics-Based Sensor Fusion" section in this volume.

For the most part, the first four articles discuss the theory of photometric stereo for Lambertian reflecting surfaces with some consideration of non-Lambertian reflectance. The last four articles discuss photometric stereo for primarily non-Lambertian reflecting surfaces emphasizing the role of a strong specular component. Important issues discussed are (i) How many different light sources does it take to constrain the orientation of a surface normal to a unique value? (ii) What specifications on the geometric configuration for light sources are necessary for unique normal recovery, as well as for sufficient mutual illumination coverage over a wide range of surface orientations? and (iii) What are the errors involved in surface recovery from multiple light sources? The last article considers photometric stereo in a more general sense whereby illumination conditions are altered not necessarily by geometry but by incident wavelength and/or polarization. These are in turn instances of "generalized stereo."

The first two papers in this section are by Robert Woodham, who pioneered photometric stereo. These papers are augmentations and extensions of parts of his 1978 doctoral thesis [2]. Much of Woodham's thesis discusses constraints on surface curvature from reflectance values in a monocular view, with constraints on surface orientation from multiple images respective to different illumination conditions discussed in later portions. The first paper describes recovery of surface orientation from multiple illumination, while the second paper extends photometric stereo to constraining surface curvature that is underconstrained from a monocular view.

In the first paper [7], photometric stereo is introduced as a technique for recovering surface orientation from the combination of constraints provided by reflectance maps respective to different incident orientations of a point light source. Woodham uses equal reflectance loci constraints for a surface normal in gradient space according to the reflectance map as described originally by Horn [3]. As was shown by Horn, surface orientation can be constrained by the value recorded at each pixel, from a single reflectance map, to be on an equal reflectance locus in gradient space. Almost always this is a curve with an infinite number of points. Woodham shows that reflectance values at a pixel respective to two point light sources at distinct incident orientations constrains surface orientation to be on the intersection of two equal reflectance loci in gradient space. For realistic reflectance maps, this intersection consists of a finite number of points in gradient space. Woodham gives a more detailed analysis for Lambertian reflectance where equal reflectance loci are conic section curves, with the rare exception of a single point for the maximum reflectance value. From two point light sources surface orientation can be constrained at a pixel to within no worse than two points in gradient space. For surface normals lying in the same plane formed by the incident orientations of the two light sources, point tangency of conic sections in gradient space will occur and the solution will be unique. In general, Woodham gives a short but rigorous proof that for Lambertian reflectance three noncoplanar incident orientations of point light sources are necessary and sufficient to recover surface orientation uniquely for any surface normal that is mutually illuminated. Additional incident orientations of light sources coplanar with any two incident light sources do not provide additional information. Furthermore, Woodham shows that the local albedo for Lambertian reflectance corresponding to a pixel need not be known to derive orientation using three noncoplanar light sources, and that the albedo itself can be simultaneously determined as well. Finally, Woodham discusses the tradeoff between accuracy of surface normal determination in the presence of reflectance errors, and the total range of surface orientations mutually illuminated with respect to a given multiple light source configuration.

The second paper by Woodham [8] shows that using the same set of multiple images for determining surface orientation from photometric stereo, surface curvature can be determined from the intensity gradients at a pixel. Surface curvature here means *viewer-centered curvature* in terms of the derivatives of gradient coordinates p and q with respect to both image coordinates x and y. Because of surface integrability constraints, this represents a set of three independent derivatives. From these quantities and knowledge of local surface orientation, viewpoint invariant curvature quantities such as Gaussian curvature can be derived. Constraints on surface curvature from reflectance are obtained by differentiating the equation between image irradiance and reflected radiance. The result is a set of two equations in the three viewer-centered curvature variables, knowing the local surface orientation. These equations involve the intensity gradient. With two or more images under different illumination conditions, local surface curvature becomes overconstrained. Therefore, if local surface orientation is initially unknown at a pixel, it can be determined from photometric stereo taking a sufficient number of images, after which the intensity gradients from these images can be used to overconstrain local surface curvature. Woodham actually initially considers all four derivatives in p and q with respect to image

coordinates x and y to be independent, solves for these four variables using six equations derived from three images, and applies integrability constraints afterward.

The paper by Ray, Birk, and Kelley [9] gives a detailed error analysis of surface normal recovery from photometric stereo on Lambertian materials. Experiments on some non-Lambertian and textured surfaces are also performed. Many possible causes of radiometric errors are discussed, and the main results of practical significance are summarized very well in the abstract.

While Woodham formally proved that a configuration of three noncoplanar point light sources is necessary and sufficient to recover local surface orientation uniquely from Lambertian reflectance, the paper by Onn and Bruckstein [10] considers additional information provided by surface integrability. This paper suggests a technique for disambiguating two point surface orientation solutions provided by two-light-source photometric stereo on a Lambertian reflecting object. Such ambiguous surface orientation solutions lie on opposite sides of the plane formed by the incident orientations of the two light sources. For a large class of smooth surfaces, Onn and Bruckstein show that the integrability constraint is satisfied only for the true surface orientation solutions, disambiguating which side of the plane formed by the two light sources the true surface orientation is contained.

The paper by Coleman and Jain [11] considers the shape recovery problem from photometric stereo for surfaces that can have in addition to a diffuse Lambertian component a significant specular component. Sometimes, using three-light-source photometric stereo, a specularity will arise at an object point respective to one of the light sources, and this generates a large computed error in surface orientation. Coleman and Jain suggest a technique for detecting when such specularities arise, and use a fourth light source to insure that a correct surface orientation can always be computed. The idea is to compute albedo and surface orientation from the four sets of three light sources that are possible. If there is a specularity at a point for one of these light sources, then there will be a large deviation between the computed albedos. In particular, one of the four computed albedos will be significantly lower than the rest, and this one corresponds to the three light sources for which no specularity occurs.

While specularities have usually been regarded to be an annoyance to earlier photometric stereo methods, some researchers have taken the opposite tack of using the specular component of reflection as a primary source of information for shape recovery. Katsushi Ikeuchi was the first to develop shape from photometric stereo on purely specular reflecting surfaces, and this is described in [4], reprinted in the section "Shape Recovery from Specular Reflection" in this volume. The next paper in this section, by Nayar, Ikeuchi, and Kanade [12], considers a photometric stereo technique for recovering shape from surfaces exhibiting both a Lambertian diffuse component and a specular spike component. (i.e., a *hybrid* surface). These reflection components can vary in relative strength, even being purely Lambertian or purely specular. The technique described determines 2D surface orientation and the relative albedo strength of the diffuse and specular reflection components. Reflectance at an object point is sampled from a number of light sources at different incident orientations within a 2D plane. The key is to use extended rather than point light sources so that a non-zero specular component is detected from more than just one light source. In fact the extended nature of the light sources and their spacing are made so that for a hybrid surface, a non-zero specular component results from two consecutive light sources, with the rest of the observed reflectances being from a pure Lambertian component. A least squares fit of the combined Lambertian and specular reflectance functions is made to the sampled reflectance data over all the individual light sources, with respect to the albedo coefficients and an orientation parameter. Some additional processing is discussed for better accuracy.

The paper by Tagare and deFigueiredo [13] extends the theory of photometric stereo to non-Lambertian reflecting surfaces with respect to the number of point light sources required for a unique determination of surface orientation. Tagare and deFigueiredo propose a general reflectance framework involving a normal lobe (diffuse lobe), a forescatter lobe, and a backscatter lobe, in context with a number of reflectance models including the Torrance-Sparrow and the Beckmann-Spizzichino models. They then abstract a general m-lobed reflectance model that is a linear combination of m reflectance functions; each function has the imposed condition that it is monotonic increasing (i.e., never decreasing) with respect to the cosine of the angle between the surface normal and the incident direction of light. Associated with each of the m lobes is a multiplicative coefficient representing the albedo (i.e., relative strength) of that lobe. Tagare and deFigueiredo prove the interesting result that it still takes only three light sources to derive surface orientation uniquely, even assuming such a general m-lobed reflectance framework. Furthermore, the multiplicative factor in front of the linear combination of m reflectance functions can also be derived, and specifications are given for the configuration of three light sources that will produce unique surface orientation recovery. This paper also addresses the issue of how many light sources it takes to mutually illuminate any surface normal within the entire visible hemisphere with three or more light sources, to insure complete shape reconstruction.

The papers in this section so far have considered varying illumination conditions for photometric stereo by altering incident geometry of light sources. The final paper in this section by Wolff [14] extends the notion of photometric stereo to more general varying illumination conditions, particularly varying incident wavelength (i.e., color) and/or polarization. Assuming the Torrance-Sparrow reflectance model, "spectral stereo" recovers shape constraints on rough colored metals such as copper or gold for which reflected color is dependent upon surface orientation. As an illustration, the paper by Cook and Torrance [5], contained in the "Intensity Reflection Models" section of the Radiometry volume, shows how copper becomes more blue going from smaller to higher angles of incidence. The dependency of specularly reflected light from these types of metals on the color of incident illumination allows resolution of the specular component and the diffuse component from rough interreflections (assumed to be Lambertian). Surface orientation is then derived from the intersection of the reflection component equal reflectance loci. Similarly, "polarization stereo" which is variable incident linear polarization on dielectric surfaces, resolves these specular and diffuse reflection components to recover surface orientation. These types of techniques can lead further to a formulation of "generalized stereo," whereby any physical parameter within an imaging system can be varied between successive images, possibly providing additional constraints on surface orientation or other physical features [6].

– L.B.W.

References

[1] Ikeuchi, K. and Kanade, T. "Modeling Sensors: Toward Automatic Generation of Object Recognition Programs." *Computer Vision, Graphics, and Image Processing* **48**: 50-79, 1989. Reprinted in "Physics-Based Sensor Fusion" section in this volume.

[2] Woodham, R.J. "Reflectance Map Techniques for Analyzing Surface Defects in Metal Castings." MIT AI Lab Tech Report AI-TR-457, June 1978.

[3] Horn, B.K.P. "Understanding Image Intensities." *Artificial Intelligence* 8: 1-31, 1977. Reprinted in "Intensity Reflection Models" section of the *Radiometry* volume of this series.

[4] Ikeuchi, K. "Determining Surface Orientations of Specular Surfaces by Using the Photometric Stereo Method." *IEEE Trans. on Pattern Analysis and Machine Intelligence* **PAMI-3** (6): 661-669, 1981. Reprinted in "Shape Recovery from Specular Reflection" section in this volume.

[5] Cook, R.L., and Torrance, K.E. "A Reflectance Model for Computer Graphics." *Computer Graphics* **15** (3): 307-316, 1981. Reprinted in "Intensity Reflection Models" section of the *Radiometry* volume of this series.

[6] Wolff, L.B. "An Introduction to Generalized Stereo Techniques." In *Proc. of DARPA Image Understanding Workshop*. DARPA, April 1988. Pages 756-768.

Papers Included in This Collection

[7] Woodham, R.J. "Photometric Method for Determining Surface Orientation from Multiple Images." *Optical Engineering* **19** (1): 139-144, 1980.

[8] Woodham, R.J. "Surface Curvature from Photometric Stereo." University of British Columbia, Computer Science Technical Report 90-29, October 1990.

[9] Ray, R., Birk, J., and Kelley, R.B. "Error Analysis Of Surface Normals Determined By Radiometry." *IEEE Trans. on Pattern Analysis and Machine Intelligence* **PAMI-5** (6): 631-645, November 1983.

[10] Onn, R., and Bruckstein, A. "Integrability Disambiguates Surface Recovery in Two-Image Photometric Stereo." *International Journal of Computer Vision* **5** (1): 105-113, 1990.

[11] Coleman, E.N., and Jain, R. "Obtaining 3D Shape of Textured and Specular Surfaces Using Four-Source Photometry." *Computer Vision, Graphics, and Image Processing* **18** (4): 309-328, April 1982.

[12] Nayar, S.K., Ikeuchi, K., and Kanade, T. "Determining Shape and Reflectance of Hybrid Surfaces by Photometric Sampling." *IEEE Trans. on Robotics and Automation* **6** (4): 418-431, August 1990.

[13] Tagare, H.D., and deFigueiredo, R.J.P. "A Theory of Photometric Stereo for a Class of Diffuse Non-Lambertian Surfaces." *IEEE Trans. on Pattern Analysis and Machine Intelligence* **PAMI-13** (2): 133-152, February 1991.

[14] Wolff, L.B. "Spectral and Polarization Stereo Methods Using a Single Light Source." In *Proc. International Conference on Computer Vision (ICCV)*. London, England. IEEE, 1987. Pages 708-715.

Photometric method for determining surface orientation from multiple images

Robert J. Woodham

Department of Computer Science
University of British Columbia
2075 Wesbrook Mall
Vancouver, B.C., Canada
V6T 1W5

Abstract. A novel technique called photometric stereo is introduced. The idea of photometric stereo is to vary the direction of incident illumination between successive images, while holding the viewing direction constant. It is shown that this provides sufficient information to determine surface orientation at each image point. Since the imaging geometry is not changed, the correspondence between image points is known *a priori*. The technique is photometric because it uses the radiance values recorded at a single image location, in successive views, rather than the relative positions of displaced features.

Photometric stereo is used in computer-based image understanding. It can be applied in two ways. First, it is a general technique for determining surface orientation at each image point. Second, it is a technique for determining object points that have a particular surface orientation. These applications are illustrated using synthesized examples.

Key Words: bidirectional reflectance distribution function (BRDF), image processing, imaging geometry, incident illumination, photometric stereo, reflectance map, surface orientation.
Optical Engineering 19:1:139–144 (January/February 1980).

I. INTRODUCTION

Work on computer-based image understanding has led to a need to model the imaging process. One aspect of this concerns the geometry of image projection. Less well understood is the radiometry of image formation. Relating the radiance values recorded in an image to object shape requires a model of the way surfaces reflect light.

A reflectance map is a convenient way to incorporate a fixed scene illumination, surface reflectance and imaging geometry into a single model that allows image intensity to be written as a function of surface orientation. This function is not invertible since surface orientation has two degrees of freedom and image intensity provides only one measurement. Local surface shape cannot, in general, be determined from the intensity value recorded at a single image point. In order to determine object shape, additional information must be provided.

This observation has led to a novel technique called photometric stereo in which surface orientation is determined from two or more images. Traditional stereo techniques determine range by relating two images of an object viewed from different directions. If the correspondence between picture elements is known, then distance to the object can be calculated by triangulation. Unfortunately, it is difficult to determine this correspondence. The idea of photometric stereo is to vary the direction of the incident illumination between successive images, while holding the viewing direction constant. It is shown that this provides sufficient information to determine surface orientation at each image point. Since the imaging geometry is not changed, the correspondence between image points is known *a priori*. The technique is photometric because it uses the radiance values recorded at a single image location, in successive views, rather than the relative positions of displaced features.

Original manuscript 5015 received Feb. 20, 1979.
Revised manuscript received March 12, 1979.
Accepted for publication July 18, 1979.
This paper is a revision of a paper presented at the SPIE seminar on Image Understanding Systems & Industrial Applications, Aug. 30-31, 1978, San Diego, which appears in SPIE Proceedings Vol. 155.

II. THE REFLECTANCE MAP

The fraction of light reflected by an object surface in a given direction depends upon the optical properties of the surface material, the surface microstructure and the spatial and spectral distribution and state of polarization of the incident illumination. For many surfaces, the fraction of the incident illumination reflected in a particular direction depends only on the surface orientation. The reflectance characteristics of such a surface can be represented as a function $\phi(i,e,g)$ of the three angles i, e and g defined in Figure 1. These are called, respectively, the *incident*, *emergent* and *phase* angles. The angles i and e are defined relative to a local surface normal. $\phi(i,e,g)$ determines the ratio of surface radiance to irradiance measured per unit surface area, per unit solid angle, in the direction of the viewer. The reflectance function $\phi(i,e,g)$ defined here is related to the bidirectional reflectance distribution function (BRDF) defined by the National Bureau of Standards.[1]

Image forming systems perform a perspective transformation, as illustrated in Figure 2(a). If the size of the objects in view is small compared to the viewing distance, then the perspective projection can be approximated as an orthographic projection, as illustrated in Figure 2(b). Consider an image forming system that performs an orthographic projection. To standardize the imaging geometry, it is convenient to choose a coordinate system such that the viewing direction is aligned with the negative z-axis. Also, assume appropriate scaling of the image plane such that object point (x,y,z) maps onto image point (u,v) where u = x and v = y. With these assumptions, image coordinates (x,y) and object coordinates (x,y) can be referred to interchangeably.

If the equation of an object surface is given explicitly as:

$$z = f(x,y)$$

then a surface normal is given by the vector:

$$\left[\frac{\partial f(x,y)}{\partial x}, \frac{\partial f(x,y)}{\partial y}, -1 \right]$$

If parameters p and q are defined by:

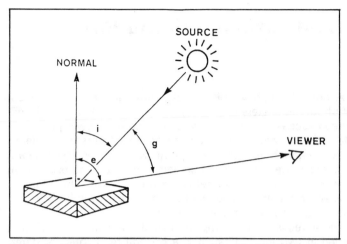

Figure 1.   Defining the three angles i, e and g. The incident angle i is the angle between the incident ray and the surface normal. The emergent angle e is the angle between the emergent ray and the surface normal. The phase angle g is the angle between the incident and emergent rays.

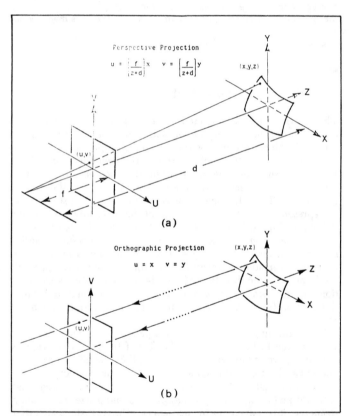

Figure 2.   Characterizing image projections. (a) illustrates the well-known perspective projection. [Note: to avoid image inversion, it is convenient to assume that the image plane lies in front of the lens rather than behind it.] For objects that are small relative to the viewing distance, the image projection can be modeled as the orthographic projection illustrated in (b). In an orthographic projection, the focal length f is infinite so that all rays from object to image are parallel.

$$p = \frac{\partial f(x,y)}{\partial x} \text{ and } q = \frac{\partial f(x,y)}{\partial y}$$

then the surface normal can be written as [p,q,–1]. The quantity (p,q) is called the *gradient* of f(x,y) and *gradient space* is the two-dimensional space of all such points (p,q). Gradient space is a con-

venient way to represent surface orientation. It has been used in scene analysis.[2] In image analysis, it is used to relate the geometry of image projection to the radiometry of image formation.[3] This relation is established by showing that image intensity can be written explicitly as a function of gradient coordinates p and q.

An ideal imaging device produces image irradiances proportional to scene radiances. In an orthographic projection, the viewing direction, and hence the phase angle g, is constant for all object points. Thus, for a fixed light source and viewer geometry, the ratio of scene radiance to irradiance depends only on gradient coordinates p and q. Further, suppose each object surface element receives the same incident radiance. Then, the scene radiance, and hence image intensity, depends only on gradient coordinates p and q.

The *reflectance map* R(p,q) determines image intensity as a function of p and q. A reflectance map captures the surface reflectance of an object material for a particular light source, object surface and viewer geometry. Reflectance maps can be determined empirically, derived from phenomenological models of surface reflectivity or derived from analytic models of surface microstructure.

In this paper, it will be assumed that image projection is orthographic and that incident illumination is given by a single distant point source. Extended sources can be modeled as the superposition of single sources. The reflectance map can be extended to incorporate spatially varying irradiance and perspective. A formal analysis of the relation between the reflectance map and the bidirectional reflectance distribution function (BRDF) has been given.[4]

Expressions for cos(i), cos(e) and cos(g) can be derived using normalized dot products of the surface normal vector [p,q,–1], the vector $[p_s,q_s,-1]$ which points in the direction of the light source and the vector [0,0,–1] which points in the direction of the viewer. One obtains:

$$\cos(i) = \frac{1 + pp_s + qq_s}{\sqrt{1 + p^2 + q^2}\ \sqrt{1 + p_s^2 + q_s^2}}$$

$$\cos(e) = \frac{1}{\sqrt{1 + p^2 + q^2}}$$

$$\cos(g) = \frac{1}{\sqrt{1 + p_s^2 + q_s^2}}.$$

These expressions can be used to transform an arbitrary surface reflectance function φ(i,e,g) into a reflectance map R(p,q).

One simple idealized model of surface reflectance is given by:

$$\phi_a(i,e,g) = \varrho \cos(i).$$

This reflectance function corresponds to the phenomenological model of a perfectly diffuse (lambertian) surface which appears equally bright from all viewing directions. Here, ϱ is a reflectance factor and the cosine of the incident angle accounts for the foreshortening of the surface as seen from the source. The corresponding reflectance map is given by:

$$R_a(p,q) = \frac{\varrho (1 + pp_s + qq_s)}{\sqrt{1 + p^2 + q^2}\ \sqrt{1 + p_s^2 + q_s^2}}.$$

A second reflectance function, similar to that of materials in the maria of the moon and rocky planets, is given by:

$$\phi_b(i,e,g) = \frac{\varrho \cos(i)}{\cos(e)}.$$

This reflectance function corresponds to the phenomenological model of a surface which reflects equal amounts of light in all directions. The cosine of the emergent angle accounts for the foreshortening of the surface as seen from the viewer. The corresponding reflectance map is given by:

$$R_b(p,q) = \frac{\varrho\,(1 + pp_s + qq_s)}{\sqrt{1 + p_s^2 + q_s^2}}.$$

It is convenient to represent R(p,q) as a series of iso-brightness contours in gradient space. Figure 3 and Figure 4 illustrate the two simple reflectance maps $R_a(p,q)$ and $R_b(p,q)$, defined above, for the case $p_s = 0.7$, $q_s = 0.3$ and $\varrho = 1$.

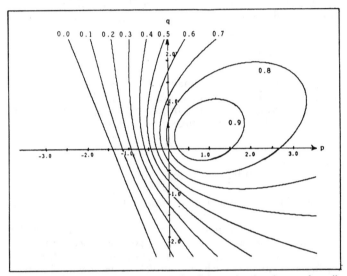

Figure 3. The reflectance map $R_a(p,q)$ for a lambertian surface illuminated from gradient point $p_s = 0.7$ and $q_s = 0.3$ (with $\varrho = 1.0$). The reflectance map is plotted as a series of contours spaced 0.1 units apart.

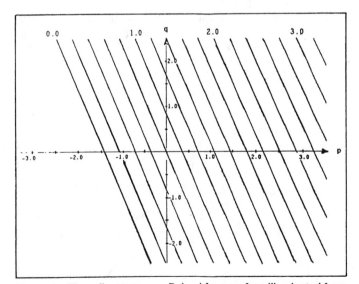

Figure 4. The reflectance map $R_b(p,q)$ for a surface illuminated from gradient point $p_s = 0.7$ and $q_s = 0.3$ (with $\varrho = 1.0$). The reflectance map is plotted as a series of contours spaced 0.2 units apart.

Reflectance map techniques

Using the reflectance map, the basic equation describing the image-forming process can be written as:

$$I(x,y) = R(p,q). \tag{1}$$

One idea is to use Eq. (1) directly to generate shaded images of surfaces. This has obvious utility in computer graphics applications including hill-shading for automated cartography[5] and video input for a flight simulator.[6] Synthesized imagery can be registered to real imagery to align images with surface models. This technique has been used to achieve precise alignment of Landsat imagery with digital terrain models.[7]

Equation (1) can also be used in image analysis to determine object shape from image intensity. Equation (1) is a nonlinear first-order partial differential equation. Direct solution is tedious.[8] More generally, one can think of Eq. (1) as one equation in the two unknowns p and q. Determining object shape from image intensity is difficult because Eq. (1) is underdetermined. In order to calculate object shape, additional assumptions must be invoked.

Recent work has helped to make these assumptions explicit. For certain materials, such as the material of the maria of the moon, special properties of surface reflectance simplify the solution.[3,8,9] Other methods for determining object shape from image intensity embody assumptions about surface curvature.[3,10] Simple surfaces have been proposed for use in computer aided design.[11] When properties of surface curvature are known *a priori*, they can be exploited in image analysis.[12] This is useful, for example, in industrial inspection since there are often constraints on surface curvature imposed by the drafting techniques available for part design and by the fabrication processes available for part manufacture.[13]

Reflectance map techniques deepen our understanding of what can and cannot be computed directly from image intensity. Photometric stereo is a novel reflectance map technique that uses two or more images to solve Eq. (1) directly.

III. PHOTOMETRIC STEREO

The idea of photometric stereo is to vary the direction of incident illumination between successive views, while holding the viewing direction constant. Suppose two images $I_1(x,y)$ and $I_2(x,y)$ are obtained by varying the direction of incident illumination. Since there has been no change in the imaging geometry, each picture element (x,y) in the two images corresponds to the same object point and hence to the same gradient (p,q). The effect of varying the direction of incident illumination is to change the reflectance map R(p,q) that characterizes the imaging situation.

Let the reflectance maps corresponding to $I_1(x,y)$ and $I_2(x,y)$ be $R_1(p,q)$ and $R_2(p,q)$ respectively. The two views are characterized by two independent equations:

$$I_1(x,y) = R_1(p,q). \tag{2}$$

$$I_2(x,y) = R_2(p,q). \tag{3}$$

Two reflectance maps $R_1(p,q)$ and $R_2(p,q)$ are required. But, if the phase angle g is the same in both views (i.e., the direction of illumination is rotated about the viewing direction), then the two reflectance maps are rotations of each other.

For reflectance characterized by $R_b(p,q)$ above, Eqs. (2) and (3) are linear equations in p and q. If the reflectance factor ϱ is known, then two views are sufficient to determine surface orientation at each image point, provided the directions of incident illumination are not collinear in azimuth.

In general, Eqs. (2) and (3) are nonlinear so that more than one solution is possible. One idea would be to obtain a third image:

$$I_3(x,y) = R_3(p,q) \tag{4}$$

to overdetermine the solution.

For reflectance characterized by $R_a(p,q)$ above, three views are sufficient to uniquely determine both the surface orientation and the reflectance factor ϱ at each image point, as will now be shown.[14] Let $\underline{I} = [I_1, I_2, I_3]'$ be the column vector of intensity values recorded at a point (x,y) in each of three views (' denotes vector transpose). Further, let

$$\underline{n_J} = [n_{11}, n_{12}, n_{13}]'$$

$$n_2 = [n_{21}, n_{22}, n_{23}]'$$
$$n_3 = [n_{31}, n_{32}, n_{33}]'$$

be unit column vectors defining the three directions of incident illumination. Construct the matrix N where

$$N = \begin{bmatrix} n_{11} & n_{12} & n_{13} \\ n_{21} & n_{22} & n_{23} \\ n_{31} & n_{32} & n_{33} \end{bmatrix}$$

Let $n = [n_1, n_2, n_3]'$ be the column vector corresponding to a unit surface normal at (x,y). Then,

$$I = \varrho N n$$

so that,

$$\varrho n = N^{-1} I$$

provided the inverse N^{-1} exists. This inverse exists if and only if the three vectors n_1, n_2 and n_3 do not lie in a plane. In this case, the reflectance factor and unit surface normal at (x,y) are given by:

$$\varrho = |N^{-1} I|$$

and

$$n = (1/\varrho) N^{-1} I . \qquad (5)$$

Unfortunately, since the sun's path across the sky is very nearly planar, this simple solution does not apply to outdoor images taken at different times during the same day.

Even when the simplifications implied by $R_a(p,q)$ and $R_b(p,q)$ above do not hold, photometric stereo is easily implemented. Initial computation is required to determine the reflectance map for each experimental situation. Once calibrated, however, photometric stereo can be reduced to simple table lookup and/or search operations. Photometric stereo is a practical scheme for environments, such as industrial inspection, in which the nature and position of the incident illumination is known or can be controlled.

The multiple images required for photometric stereo can be obtained by explicitly moving a single light source, by using multiple light sources calibrated with respect to each other or by rotating the object surface and imaging hardware together to simulate the effect of moving a single light source. The equivalent of photometric stereo can also be achieved in a single view by using multiple illuminations which can be separated by color.

Applications of photometric stereo

Photometric stereo can be used in two ways. First, photometric stereo is a general technique for determining surface orientation at each image point. For a given image point (x,y), the equations characterizing each image can be combined to determine the corresponding gradient (p,q).

Second, photometric stereo is a general technique for determining object points that have a particular surface orientation. This use of photometric stereo corresponds to interpreting the basic image-forming Eq. (1) as one equation in the unknowns x and y. For a given gradient (p,q), the equations characterizing each image can be combined to determine corresponding object points (x,y). This second use of photometric stereo is appropriate for the so-called industrial "bin-of-parts" problem. The location in an image of key object points is often sufficient to determine the position and orientation of a known object on a table or conveyor belt so that the object may be grasped by an automatic manipulator.

A particularly useful special case concerns object points whose surface normal directly faces the viewer (i.e., object points with p = 0 and q = 0). Such points form a unique class of image points whose intensity value is invariant under rotation of the illumination direction about the viewing direction. Object points with surface normal directly facing the viewer can be located without explicitly determining the reflectance map R(p,q). The value of R(0,0) is not changed by varying the direction of illumination, provided only that the phase angle g is held constant.

These applications of photometric stereo will now be illustrated using a simple, synthesized example. Consider a sphere of radius r centered at the object space origin. The explicit representation of this object surface, corresponding to the viewing geometry of Figure 2(b), is given by:

$$z = f(x,y) = -\sqrt{r^2 - x^2 - y^2} . \qquad (6)$$

The gradient coordinates p and q are determined by differentiating Eq. (6) with respect to x and y. One finds:

$$p = \frac{-x}{z} \text{ and } q = \frac{-y}{z}$$

Suppose that the sphere is made of a perfectly diffusing object material and is illuminated by a single distant point source at gradient point (p_s, q_s). Then, the reflectance map is given by $R_a(p,q)$ above so that the corresponding synthesized image is:

$$I(x,y) = \begin{cases} 0 & \text{if } x^2 + y^2 > r^2 \\ \max(0, R_a(-x/z, -y/z)) & \text{otherwise} \end{cases} \qquad (7)$$

Equation (7) generates image intensities in the range 0 to ϱ. In the example below, r = 60 and $\varrho = 1$.

Multiple images are obtained by varying the position of the light source. Consider three different positions. Let the first be $p_s = 0.7$ and $q_s = 0.3$ as in Figure 3. Let the second and third correspond to rotations of the light source about the viewing direction of $-120°$ and $+120°$ respectively (i.e., $p_s = -0.610$, $q_s = 0.456$ and $p_s = -0.090$, $q_s = -0.756$). Let the three reflectance maps be $R_1(p,q)$, $R_2(p,q)$ and $R_3(p,q)$. The phase angle g is constant in each case. Let the corresponding images generated by Eq. (6) be $I_1(x,y)$, $I_2(x,y)$ and $I_3(x,y)$.

First, consider image point x = 15, y = 20. Here, $I_1(x,y) = 0.942$, $I_2(x,y) = 0.723$ and $I_3(x,y) = 0.505$. Figure 5 illustrates the reflectance map contours $R_1(p,q) = 0.942$, $R_2(p,q) = 0.723$ and $R_3(p,q) = 0.505$. The point p = 0.275, q = 0.367 at which these three contours intersect determines the gradient corresponding to

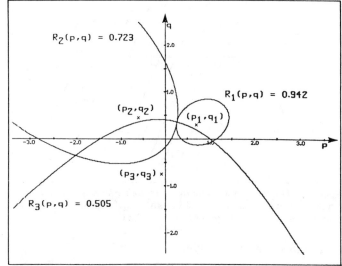

Figure 5. Determining the surface orientation (p,q) at a given image point (x,y). Three reflectance map contours are intersected where each contour corresponds to the intensity value at (x,y) obtained from three separate images. $I_1(x,y) = 0.942$, $I_2(x,y) = 0.723$ and $I_3(x,y) = 0.505$.

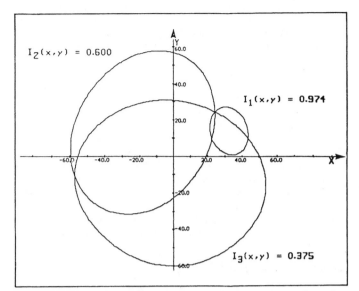

Figure 6. Determining image points (x,y) whose surface orientation is a given (p,q). Three image intensity contours are intersected where each contour corresponds to the value at (p,q) obtained from three separate reflectance maps. $R_1(p,q) = 0.974$, $R_2(p,q) = 0.600$ and $R_3(p,q) = 0.375$.

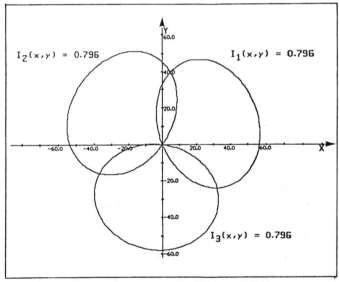

Figure 7. Determining image points (x,y) whose surface normal directly faces the viewer. Three image intensity contours are intersected where each contour corresponds to the value at (0,0) obtained from three separate reflectance maps. Note that the reflectance map value at (0,0) does not change with light source position, provided the phase angle g is held constant.

image point x = 15, y = 20.

Second, consider gradient point p = 0.5, q = 0.5. Here, $R_1(p,q) = 0.974$, $R_2(p,q) = 0.600$ and $R_3(p,q) = 0.375$. Figure 6 illustrates the image intensity contours $I_1(x,y) = 0.974$, $I_2(x,y) = 0.600$ and $I_3(x,y) = 0.375$. The point x = 24.5, y = 24.5 at which these three contours intersect determines an object point whose gradient is p = 0.5, q = 0.5.

Finally, Figure 7 repeats the example given in Figure 6 but for the case p = 0, q = 0. Here, $R_1(p,q) = R_2(p,q) = R_3(p,q) = 0.796$. Object points with surface normal directly facing the viewer form a unique class of points whose image intensity is invariant for rotations of the light source about the viewing direction. The point x = 0, y = 0 at which these three contours intersect determines an object point with surface normal directly

facing the viewer. This result would hold even if the form of R(p,q) is unknown.

Accuracy considerations

Photometric stereo is most accurate in regions of gradient space where the density of reflectance map contours is great and where the contours to be intersected are nearly perpendicular. Several factors influence the density and direction of reflectance map contours. The reflectance properties of the surface material play a role. Figures 3 and 4 illustrate the difference between two idealized materials viewed under identical conditions of illumination. In general, increasing the specular component of reflection will increase the density of contours in one region of gradient space at the expense of other regions. Using extended light sources rather than point sources will alter the shape and distribution of reflectance map contours. Imaging systems can be configured to exploit these facts.[15]

For a given surface material, the main determiner of accuracy is the choice of phase angle g. In photometric stereo, there is a trade-off to acknowledge. A large phase angle increases the density of reflectance map contours in illuminated portions of gradient space. At the same time, a large phase angle results in more of gradient space lying in shadow. A practical compromise must be arrived at for each application.

The relative positions of the light sources must also be considered. Figures 8 and 9 give some indication of the trade-off associated with light source position. In each case, reflectance is

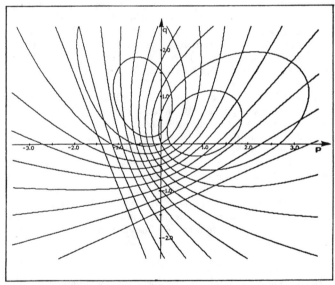

Figure 8. Superimposed reflectance maps $R_1(p,q)$ and $R_2(p,q)$ where $R_1(p,q)$ is $R_a(p,q)$ with $p_s = 0.7$, $q_s = 0.3$, $\varrho = 1$ and $R_2(p,q)$ is $R_a(p,q)$ with $p_s = -0.3$, $q_s = 0.7$, $\varrho = 1$. Each region indicates how an error in intensity measurement determines a corresponding error in the estimation of surface gradient (p,q).

assumed to be characterized by $R_a(p,q)$ above. Figure 8 considers a two-source configuration in which the light source directions are separated by 90° in azimuth with respect to the viewer. Figure 8 superimposes reflectance map contours, spaced 0.1 units apart, for $R_1(p,q)$ and $R_2(p,q)$ where $R_1(p,q)$ is $R_a(p,q)$ with $p_s = 0.7$ $q_s = 0.3$ $\varrho = 1$ and $R_2(p,q)$ is $R_a(p,q)$ with $p_s = -0.3$ $q_s = 0.7$ $\varrho = 1$. Each region of Figure 8 corresponds to a region of equal measurement error. For example, if $I_1(x,y)$ is determined to lie between 0.4 and 0.5 and $I_2(x,y)$ is determined to lie between 0.5 and 0.6 then surface orientation can be determined to ± 6.8° of its true value. This corresponds to an area of gradient space in the third quadrant where the error regions are small. Here, a measurement error of 1 gray level in 10 in each of $I_1(x,y)$ and

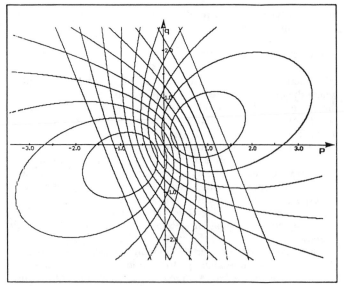

Figure 9. Superimposed reflectance maps $R_1(p,q)$ and $R_2(p,q)$ where $R_1(p,q)$ is $R_a(p,q)$ with $p_s = 0.7$, $q_s = 0.3$, $\varrho = 1$ and $R_2(p,q)$ is $R_a(p,q)$ with $p_s = -0.7$, $q_s = -0.3$, $\varrho = 1$. Each region indicates how an error in intensity measurement determines a corresponding error in the estimation of surface gradient (p,q).

$I_2(x,y)$ constrains surface orientation to within $\pm 6.8°$. On the other hand, if $I_1(x,y)$ is determined to lie between 0.9 and 1.0 and $I_2(x,y)$ is determined to lie between 0.5 and 0.6 then surface orientation can be determined to $\pm 25.8°$ of its true value. This corresponds to an area of gradient space in the first quadrant where the error regions are large. Here, a measurement error of 1 gray level in 10 in each of $I_1(x,y)$ and $I_2(x,y)$ only constrains surface orientation to within $\pm 25.8°$.

Figure 9 repeats the example of Figure 8 but with the second light source separated by $180°$ in azimuth from the first. In this configuration, error regions are smallest in the second and fourth quadrants of gradient space. Combinations using more than two light sources can be arranged to achieve a desired overall accuracy. One idea is to choose four directions of illumination, spaced evenly in azimuth with respect to the viewer and having a relatively large phase angle g.[13] In such a configuration, most points of interest are illuminated by at least three independent sources and contours can be selected to intersect which are nearly perpendicular and where error regions are small.

CONCLUSIONS

Surface orientation can be determined from the image intensities obtained under a fixed imaging geometry but with varying lighting conditions. Photometric methods for determining surface orientation can be considered complementary to methods based on the identification of corresponding points in two images taken from different viewpoints:
1. Traditional stereo allows the accurate determination of distances to objects. Photometric stereo is best when the surface gradient is to be found.
2. Traditional stereo works well on rough surfaces with discontinuities in surface orientation. Photometric stereo works best on smooth surfaces with few discontinuities.
3. Traditional stereo works well on textured surfaces with varying surface reflectance. Photometric stereo is best when applied to surfaces with uniform surface properties.

Photometric stereo does have some unique advantages:
1. Since the images are obtained from the same point of view, there is no difficulty identifying corresponding points in the two images. This is the major computational task in traditional stereo.
2. Under appropriate circumstances, the surface reflectance factor can be found because the effect of surface orientation on image intensity can be removed. Traditional stereo provides no such capability.
3. Describing object shape in terms of surface orientation is preferable in a number of situations to description in terms of range or altitude above a reference plane.

Photometric stereo depends on a detailed understanding of the imaging process. In addition, the imaging instrument must be of high caliber so that the gray levels produced can be dependably related to scene radiance. Fortunately, our understanding of image formation and the physics of light reflection has advanced sufficiently, and the quality of imaging devices is now high enough, to make this endeavor feasible.

ACKNOWLEDGMENTS

The author would like to thank Berthold K. P. Horn for his help and guidance. Mike Brady, Anni Bruss, Mark Lavin, Tomas Lozano-Perez, Alan Mackworth, David Marr and Patrick Winston provided useful comments and criticisms.

Work reported herein was conducted while the author was at the Artificial Intelligence Laboratory of the Massachusetts Institute of Technology. Support for the laboratory's artificial intelligence research is provided in part by the Advanced Research Projects Agency of the Department of Defence under Office of Naval Research Contract number N00014-75C-0643.

REFERENCES

1. Nicodemus, F. E., Richmond, J. C. and Hisa, J. J., "Geometrical considerations and nomenclature for reflectance," NBS Monograph 160, National Bureau of Standards, Washington, D. C., 1977.
2. Mackworth, A. K., "Interpreting pictures of polyhedral scenes," *Artificial Intelligence*, Vol. 4, pp. 121-137, 1973.
3. Horn, B. K. P., "Understanding image intensities," *Artificial Intelligence*, Vol. 8, pp. 201-231, 1977.
4. Horn, B. K. P. and Sjoberg, R. W., "Calculating the reflectance map," *Applied Optics*, Vol. 18, No. 11, pp. 1770-1779, 1979.
5. Horn, B. K. P., "Automatic hill-shading using the reflectance map," *Proc. Image Understanding Workshop*, Palo Alto, California, April 1979.
6. Strat, T. M., "Shaded perspective images of terrain," TR-463, M.I.T. A.I. Laboratory, Cambridge, Mass., 1978.
7. Horn, B. K. P. and Bachman, B. L., "Using synthetic images to register real images with surface models," *Comm. ACM*, Vol. 21, No. 11, pp. 914-924, 1978.
8. Horn, B. K. P., "Obtaining shape from shading information," *The Psychology of Computer Vision*, P. H. Winston (ed.), McGraw-Hill, pp. 115-155, 1975.
9. Rindfleisch, T., "Photometric method for lunar topography," *Photogrammetric Engineering*, Vol. 32, pp. 262-276, 1966.
10. Woodham, R. J., "A cooperative algorithm for determining surface orientation from a single view," *Proc. IJCAI-77*, pp. 635-641, Cambridge, Mass., 1977.
11. Huffman, D. A., "Curvature and creases: a primer on paper," *Proc. Conf. Computer Graphics, Pattern Recognition and Data Structures*, IEEE Pub. 75CH0981-1C, pp. 360-370, 1975.
12. Woodham, R. J., "Relating properties of surface curvature to image intensity," *Proc. IJCAI-79*, pp. 971-977, Tokyo, Japan, 1979.
13. Woodham, R. J., "Reflectance map techniques for analyzing surface defects in metal castings," TR-457, M.I.T. A.I. Laboratory, Cambridge, Mass., 1978.
14. Horn, B. K. P., "Three source photometry," (personal communication), 1978.
15. Ikeuchi, K. and Horn, B. K. P., "An application of the photometric stereo method," *Proc. IJCAI-79*, pp. 413-415, Tokyo, Japan, 1979.

Surface Curvature from Photometric Stereo

by

R.J. Woodham[1]

Technical Report 90-29

October 1990

Laboratory for Computational Vision
Department of Computer Science
University of British Columbia
Vancouver, B.C., CANADA

email: woodham@cs.ubc.ca

Abstract

A method is described to compute the curvature at each point on a visible surface. The idea is to use the intensity values recorded from multiple images obtained from the same viewpoint but under different conditions of illumination. This is the idea of photometric stereo. Previously, photometric stereo has been used to obtain local estimates of surface orientation. Here, an extension to photometric stereo is described in which the spatial derivatives of the intensity values are used to determine the principal curvatures, and associated directions, at each point on a visible surface. The result shows that it is possible to obtain reliable local estimates of both surface orientation and surface curvature without making global smoothness assumptions or requiring prior image segmentation.

The method is demonstrated using images of several pottery vases. No prior assumption is made about the reflectance characteristics of the objects to be analyzed. Instead, one object of known shape, a solid of revolution, is used for calibration purposes.

1. Fellow of the Canadian Institute for Advanced Research.

1   Introduction

The purpose of computational vision is to produce descriptions of a 3D world from 2D images of that world, sufficient to carry out a specified task. Computer vision systems are required to perform at least three generic tasks: 1) recognition 2) localization and 3) inspection. Research emphasis typically is placed on recognition tasks. But, increasingly applications require careful attention to localization and to inspection. Localization is the determination of the 3D position and attitude of a known object or surface. Inspection is the detailed monitoring of known surfaces for defects or changes. Robustness on any task is improved when computer vision systems make use of all the information available in an image, not just that obtained from a sparse set of features.

This paper demonstrates that reliable local estimates of the curvature at each point on a visible surface can be determined using photometric stereo. These estimates are obtained prior to image segmentation and are not based on any global measure of surface smoothness. Photometric stereo itself is not new. It was first described by Woodham in his thesis [1] and in subsequent journal articles [2, 3]. Photometric stereo determines a dense representation of the orientation at each visible point on a surface. First implemented by Silver [4], photometric stereo has since been used by Horn, Ikeuchi and colleagues both for recognition tasks [5] and for localization tasks [6, 7, 8, 9, 10].

The overall approach is based on principles of physical optics. An image irradiance equation is developed to determine image irradiance as a function of surface orientation. This equation cannot be inverted locally since image brightness provides only one measurement while surface orientation has two degrees of freedom. Photometric stereo allows for the local determination of surface orientation by using multiple images, obtained with the identical geometry but under different conditions of illumination. Three (or more) images overconstrain the solution. Computations of local surface orientation can be fast, accurate and robust. Once surface orientation is known, surface curvature also is determined locally from the partial derivatives of image irradiance. Local curvature estimates also are robust since, once again, the solution is overconstrained.

Physical optics determines that an image irradiance equation exists but says very little about the particular form that image irradiance equation must take. Of course, one can exploit situations where the reflectance properties of a material are known to be of a particular functional form. Formal analysis of these situations helps to establish the existence, uniqueness and robustness of solution methods under varying degrees of uncertainty and approximation. Implementation also is facilitated because the resulting computations typically involve equations of known form with unknown coefficients that can be determined as a problem of parameter estimation.

Here, no prior assumption is made about the reflectance characteristics of the objects to be analyzed. Instead, reflectance properties are measured using a calibration object of known shape, in this case a solid of revolution. Measurements from a calibration object of known shape are directly applicable to the analysis of other objects of unknown shape but made of the same material and illuminated and viewed under the same conditions. In principle, materials with any reflectance properties can be handled.

Section 2 provides the background and theory. Section 3 discusses a particular implementation and reports on the experiments performed. Finally, Section 4 provides a brief discussion and summary of the conclusions following from the work reported.

2 Background and Theory

A given spatial arrangement of objects, made of a given set of materials, illuminated in a given way, and viewed from a given vantage point, determine an image according to the laws of physical optics. Geometric equations determine where each point on a visible surface appears in the image and corresponding radiometric equations determine its brightness and color.

The standard geometry of shape from shading is assumed. That is, let the object surface be given explicitly by $z = f(x,y)$ in a left-handed Euclidean coordinate system, where the viewer is looking in the positive Z direction, image projection is orthographic, and the image XY axes coincide with the object XY axes. The *gradient*, (p,q), is defined by

$$p = \frac{\partial f(x,y)}{\partial x} \quad \text{and} \quad q = \frac{\partial f(x,y)}{\partial y} \tag{1}$$

so that a surface normal vector is $[p, q, -1]$. An image irradiance equation can be written as

$$E(x,y) = R(p,q) \tag{2}$$

where $E(x,y)$ is the image irradiance and $R(p,q)$ is called the *reflectance map*. A reflectance map combines information about surface material, scene illumination and viewing geometry into a single representation that determines image brightness as a function of surface orientation.

Given an image, $E(x,y)$, and the corresponding reflectance map, $R(p,q)$, the problem of shape from shading is to determine a smooth surface, $z = f(x,y)$, that satisfies the image irradiance equation over some domain Ω, including any initial conditions that may be specified on the boundary $\partial\Omega$ or elsewhere. There is a substantial, but scattered, literature on shape from shading. Two essential references are Horn's text [11] and the collection of papers edited by Horn and Brooks [12]. With a single image, shape from shading problems typically are solved by exploiting *a priori* constraints on the reflectance map, $R(p,q)$, *a priori* constraints on surface curvature, or global smoothness constraints. Photometric stereo, on the other hand, makes use of additional images.

2.1 Photometric Stereo

Photometric stereo uses multiple images obtained under the identical geometry but under different conditions of illumination. For example, two image irradiance equations

$$\begin{aligned} E_1(x,y) &= R_1(p,q) \\ E_2(x,y) &= R_2(p,q) \end{aligned} \tag{3}$$

provide two equations in the two unknowns, p and q. But, these equations are, in general, nonlinear so that the solution typically is not unique. Three image irradiance equations

$$
\begin{aligned}
E_1(x,y) &= R_1(p,q) \\
E_2(x,y) &= R_2(p,q) \\
E_3(x,y) &= R_3(p,q)
\end{aligned}
\tag{4}
$$

in general overconstrain the solution at each point, (x,y), because three intensity measurements, $E_1(x,y)$, $E_2(x,y)$, and $E_3(x,y)$, are used to estimate two unknowns, p and q.

Conceptually, the idea of photometric stereo is straightforward. Using a calibration object of known shape, one can build a lookup table mapping triples of measured brightness values, $[E_1, E_2, E_3]$, to the corresponding gradient, (p,q). If each image is accurate to $2^8 = 256$ gray values then the full table would have $2^8 \times 2^8 \times 2^8 = 2^{24}$ entries. Literally building a table of this size may be prohibitive, in terms of memory. Various table compression techniques are possible. Indeed, one would expect the resulting table to be sparse since Equation (4) defines the parametric equations, in parameters p and q, of a surface in E_1, E_2, E_3 space.

In any event, computation of the solution can be fast, accurate and robust, as various implementations have demonstrated. But, even though the computation of surface orientation can be accurate and robust, there can still be problems in locally differentiating surface orientation to obtain surface curvature. This would certainly be the case, for example, if the gradients represented were quantized into too small a set of possibilities.

Therefore, it is useful to examine what more information about surface curvature can be extracted from the image irradiance equation. Before doing this, it first is necessary to define a representation for surface curvature.

2.2   Surface Curvature

There are three degrees of freedom to the curvature at a point on a smooth surface. Consequently, three parameters are required to specify curvature. One representation is in terms of the 2×2 matrix of second partial derivatives of the surface $z = f(x,y)$. Let $\mathbf{H}$ be the matrix,

$$
\mathbf{H} = \begin{bmatrix} \frac{\partial^2 f(x,y)}{\partial x^2} & \frac{\partial^2 f(x,y)}{\partial x \partial y} \\ \frac{\partial^2 f(x,y)}{\partial y \partial x} & \frac{\partial^2 f(x,y)}{\partial^2 y} \end{bmatrix}
\tag{5}
$$

$\mathbf{H}$ is called the *Hessian matrix* of $z = f(x,y)$. For notational convenience, let

$$
p_x = \frac{\partial^2 f(x,y)}{\partial x^2}, \quad p_y = \frac{\partial^2 f(x,y)}{\partial x \partial y}, \quad q_x = \frac{\partial^2 f(x,y)}{\partial y \partial x} \quad \text{and} \quad q_y = \frac{\partial^2 f(x,y)}{\partial y^2}
\tag{6}
$$

It may appear that four parameters are required to specify $\mathbf{H}$. But, for smooth surfaces, $\mathbf{H}$ is symmetric. That is, $p_y = q_x$. Therefore, only three parameters are required after all. $\mathbf{H}$ is a viewer-centered representation of surface curvature because its definition depends on the explicit form of the surface function, $z = f(x, y)$, and on the fact that the viewer is looking in the positive Z direction.

From the Hessian, $\mathbf{H}$, and the gradient, (p, q), one can determine a viewpoint invariant representation of surface curvature. Let $\mathbf{C}$ be the matrix,

$$\mathbf{C} = (1 + p^2 + q^2)^{-\frac{3}{2}} \begin{bmatrix} q^2 + 1 & -pq \\ -pq & p^2 + 1 \end{bmatrix} \mathbf{H} \tag{7}$$

Further, let k_1 and k_2 be the two eigenvalues of $\mathbf{C}$, with associated eigenvectors ω_1 and ω_2. Then, k_1 and k_2 are the principal curvatures, with directions ω_1 and ω_2, at $z = f(x, y)$. The principal curvatures, k_1 and k_2, are viewpoint invariant surface properties since they do not depend on the viewer-centered XYZ coordinate system. In differential geometry, there are a variety of surface representations from which viewpoint invariant principal curvatures can, in principle, be determined. Equation (7) determines principal curvatures from the Hessian matrix, $\mathbf{H}$, and the gradient, (p, q). The terms in Equation (7) involving the gradient, (p, q), can be interpreted as the corrections required to account for the geometric foreshortening associated with viewing a surface element obliquely.

The directions ω_1 and ω_2 are viewpoint dependent. Although the directions of principal curvature are orthogonal in the object-centered coordinate system defined by the local surface normal and tangent plane, they are not, in general, orthogonal when projected onto the image plane. Thus, k_1, k_2, ω_1 and ω_2 together constitute four independent parameters that can be exploited. (Because they are viewpoint dependent, the directions ω_1 and ω_2 are not often used in surface representations proposed for object recognition. Note, however, that Brady et. al. [13] argue that, in many cases, the lines of curvature form a natural parameterization of a surface).

The *Gaussian curvature*, K, also called the *total curvature*, is the product, $K = k_1 k_2$, of the principal curvatures. The *mean curvature*, H, is the average, $H = (k_1 + k_2)/2$, of the principal curvatures. It follows from elementary matrix theory that

$$K = \det(\mathbf{C}) \quad \text{and} \quad H = \frac{1}{2} \operatorname{trace}(\mathbf{C}) \tag{8}$$

The expression for K further simplifies to

$$K = \frac{1}{(1 + p^2 + q^2)^2} \det(\mathbf{H}) \tag{9}$$

Thus, the sign of det (**H**) is the sign of the Gaussian curvature. Besl and Jain [14, 15] classify sections of surface into one of eight basic types based on the sign and zeros of Gaussian and mean curvature.

Clearly, if one could locally determine the Hessian, **H**, then one could locally compute the curvature matrix, **C**, using the gradient, (p, q), obtained from photometric stereo and Equation (7). Given **C**, one could examine its eigenvalue/eigenvector structure to determine any local curvature representation involving the principal curvatures, k_1 and k_2, and their associated directions, ω_1 and ω_2, including both the Gaussian curvature, K, and the mean curvature, H.

2.3   Determining the Hessian

By taking partial derivatives of the image irradiance Equation (2) with respect to x and y, two equations are obtained which can be written as the single matrix equation

$$\begin{bmatrix} E_x \\ E_y \end{bmatrix} = \mathbf{H} \begin{bmatrix} R_p \\ R_q \end{bmatrix} \tag{10}$$

(Here, and in what follows, subscripts x, y, p and q denote partial differentiation and the dependence of E on (x, y) and of R on (p, q) often is omitted for clarity). The vector $[E_x, E_y]$ is normal to the contour of constant brightness in the image, $E(x, y)$, at the given point (x, y). The vector $[R_p, R_q]$ is normal to the contour of constant brightness in the reflectance map, $R(p, q)$, at the given gradient (p, q). Equation (10) alone is not enough to determine the Hessian, **H**. But, with photometric stereo, one such equation is obtained for each image. With two light source photometric stereo

$$\mathbf{H} = \begin{bmatrix} E_{1x} & E_{2x} \\ E_{1y} & E_{2y} \end{bmatrix} \begin{bmatrix} R_{1p} & R_{2p} \\ R_{1q} & R_{2q} \end{bmatrix}^{-1} \tag{11}$$

With three light source photometric stereo

$$\mathbf{H} = \begin{bmatrix} E_{1x} & E_{2x} & E_{3x} \\ E_{1y} & E_{2y} & E_{3y} \end{bmatrix} \mathbf{M} \left((\mathbf{M}^T \mathbf{M})^{-1} \right)^T \tag{12}$$

where

$$\mathbf{M} = \begin{bmatrix} R_{1p} & R_{1q} \\ R_{2p} & R_{2q} \\ R_{3p} & R_{3q} \end{bmatrix} \tag{13}$$

(^{T} denotes matrix transpose). Equation (12) is the standard least squares estimate of the solution to an overdetermined set of linear equations. It can be extended, in the obvious way, to situations in which more than three light sources are used.

It is useful to consider whether the matrix inverses required in Equations (11) and (12) can be guaranteed to exist. The essential observation is that the matrices whose inverses are required are defined entirely in terms of the reflectance maps, $R_i(p,q)$, independent of the particular images, $E_i(x,y)$. Thus, for a particular surface material, the key factor to control the existence and robustness of the computation is the nature and the distribution of the light sources. No useful local information is obtained when $[R_p, R_q]$ is zero. This occurs at local extrema of $R(p,q)$ and at gradients, (p,q), shadowed from the light source. There also may be gradients, (p,q), where two of the $[R_p, R_q]$ vectors are nearly parallel. Local degeneracies can be eliminated and the effects of shadows minimized when three, rather than two, light source photometric stereo is used.

It also is important to note that in Equation (12) the magnitude of $[R_p, R_q]$ plays the role of a "weight" that pulls the three source solution towards an image irradiance equation for which the magnitude of $[R_p, R_q]$ is large (and consequently away from an image irradiance equation for which the magnitude of $[R_p, R_q]$ is small). This has a desirable effect because locations in an image at which the magnitude of $[R_p, R_q]$ is small will contribute minimal information, and thus it is good that they are discounted. Because of this, points that are shadowed with respect to one of the light sources need not be considered as a special case. Indeed, when one of the $[R_p, R_q]$ vectors is zero, the three light source solution, given by Equation (12), reduces to the two light source solution, given by Equation (11).

2.4   Integrability

As we saw above, if a surface is locally smooth then the Hessian, **H**, is symmetric. Given two images, $E_i(x,y)$ and $E_j(x,y)$, $i \neq j$, with corresponding reflectance maps, $R_i(p,q)$ and $R_j(p,q)$, the Hessian, **H**, is given by Equation (11). When one expands Equation (11) and checks the resulting matrix for symmetry, one finds that **H** is symmetric iff

$$[E_{ix}, E_{iy}] \cdot [R_{jp}, R_{jq}] = [E_{jx}, E_{jy}] \cdot [R_{ip}, R_{iq}] \tag{14}$$

($\cdot$ denotes vector inner product). Therefore, in a three light source configuration, one obtains three equations, as in Equation (14) above, involving the vectors $[E_{ix}, E_{iy}]$ and $[R_{jp}, R_{jq}]$, $i = 1, 2, 3$ $j = 1, 2, 3$ $i \neq j$. These equations can be used to check the consistency of the local estimates of the Hessian matrix, **H**. Alternatively, it is possible that lack of consistency could be used to detect discontinuities in surface orientation.

In any event, when one estimates the Hessian, $\mathbf{H}$, using either Equation (11) or (12), it is unlikely that the estimated Hessian, $\hat{\mathbf{H}}$, will be exactly symmetric, owing to numerical error. Symmetry can be forced by projecting $\hat{\mathbf{H}}$ onto the closest symmetric matrix. An obvious candidate for the closest symmetric matrix is the so-called symmetric part of $\hat{\mathbf{H}}$, given by

$$\frac{\hat{\mathbf{H}} + \hat{\mathbf{H}}^T}{2} \tag{15}$$

Frankot and Chellappa [16] observed that their projection of a non-integrable set of gradients, (p, q), onto a (closest) integrable set caused additional smoothing, leading to more rapid convergence in their shape from shading algorithm. Using Equation (15), one can project the estimated Hessian, $\hat{\mathbf{H}}$, onto a (closest) symmetric matrix. This can be done after estimating the Hessian, $\mathbf{H}$, with Equation (11) or (12) and prior to estimating the curvature matrix, $\mathbf{C}$, with Equation (7).

2.5   Validating the Estimate of the Hessian

One would like to exploit the redundancy inherent in an overdetermined problem in order evaluate the validity of the estimated solution. The validity of estimate of the Hessian, $\hat{\mathbf{H}}$, can be expressed quantitatively using an extension of Equation (10). Define a matrix of residuals, $\mathbf{R} = [r_{ij}]$, by

$$\mathbf{R} = \begin{bmatrix} E_{1x} & E_{2x} & E_{3x} \\ E_{1y} & E_{2y} & E_{3y} \end{bmatrix} - \hat{\mathbf{H}} \begin{bmatrix} R_{1p} & R_{2p} & R_{3p} \\ R_{1q} & R_{2q} & R_{3q} \end{bmatrix} \tag{16}$$

Using the Frobenius matrix norm, a relative error term is given by the ratio

$$\left(\frac{\sum r_{ij}^2}{E_{1x}^2 + E_{1y}^2 + E_{2x}^2 + E_{2y}^2 + E_{3x}^2 + E_{3y}^2} \right)^{\frac{1}{2}} \tag{17}$$

This error term combines components due to measurement uncertainty in $[E_{ix}, E_{iy}]$ and to systematic modeling error either in the image irradiance equations (4) or in the determination of $[R_{ip}, R_{iq}]$, $i = 1, 2, 3$.

3   Implementation and Experimental Results

3.1   Experimental Setup

The objects used in this study were pottery vases. Pottery, in bisque form, is a reasonably diffuse reflector although no particular assumption is made (or required) concerning the underlying surface reflectance function. The vases were imaged from a distance of about 3m using a CCD camera equipped with a C-mount 50mm telephoto lens. In this configuration, the variation in surface relief is small compared to the distance to the camera so that image projection is well modeled as orthographic. Each vase was imaged three times from the identical viewpoint but under different conditions of illumination. The different illuminations were achieved using three different light sources, each of which was a standard 35mm slide projector. Each projector was focussed, to the extent possible with standard lenses, to produce a collimated beam. The light sources were sufficiently distant that any variation in surface relief was negligible compared to the distance to the light source. Therefore, it is reasonable to assume that scene irradiance was independent of depth. The CCD camera was operated with its automatic gain control (AGC) suppressed. This is required so that the brightness values obtained for images of different scenes, but under identical conditions of illumination, can be directly compared. The effect of inter-reflection was minimized by housing the vases in a custom "studio" with matte black walls and ceiling. All other lights in the room were turned off prior to each image acquisition.

3.2   Calibration

One way to obtain a reflectance map is to measure it using a calibration object of known shape. Measurements from a calibration object support the analysis of other objects provided the other objects are made of the same material and are illuminated and viewed under the same imaging conditions. Calibration by measurement has the added benefit of automatically compensating for the transfer characteristics of the sensor. Ideally, the calibration object would have visible surface points spanning the full range of gradients, (p, q). A sphere, for example, is a good choice. Solids of revolution are another choice. For a solid of revolution, it is possible to determine the gradient, (p, q), and the Hessian matrix, $\mathbf{H}$, at each visible surface point by geometric analysis of the object's bounding contour.

To simplify calibration, we make the axis of the solid of revolution parallel to the image plane. Without loss of generality, we can assume a coordinate system in which this axis is aligned with the image Y-axis. Under these assumptions, a solid of revolution is the volume swept out by moving a circular cross section along the image Y-axis while magnifying or contracting it in a smoothly varying way. Let $r = h(y)$ be the radius of the circular cross section and let $h'(y)$ and $h''(y)$ be its first and second derivatives with respect to y.

If (x, y) is any visible surface point, the corresponding gradient, (p, q), is given by

$$p = \frac{x}{\sqrt{r^2 - x^2}} \quad \text{and} \quad q = \frac{-r\, h'(y)}{\sqrt{r^2 - x^2}} \tag{18}$$

and the elements of the corresponding Hessian matrix, $\mathbf{H}$, are given by

$$
\begin{aligned}
p_x &= \frac{r^2}{(r^2 - x^2)^{\frac{3}{2}}} \\[2mm]
q_y &= \frac{x^2\, h'(y)^2 - r\, (r^2 - x^2)\, h''(y)}{(r^2 - x^2)^{\frac{3}{2}}} \\[2mm]
p_y &= q_x = \frac{-r\, x\, h'(y)}{(r^2 - x^2)^{\frac{3}{2}}}
\end{aligned}
\tag{19}
$$

Figure 1 shows the three images of the calibration vase obtained from the three different light source positions. The object's bounding contour is easily determined. The particular method used consists of three steps. First, the three images are summed together. Second, the intensity histogram of the sum is computed. Third, a single threshold is selected to separate object points from background points. Simple thresholding of the summed image is sufficient because, by design, the histogram always is distinctly bimodal. Once the object silhouette is determined, values for $h'(y)$ and $h''(y)$ can be estimated. Of course, some smoothing of the bounding contour is required to overcome local quantization effects. Here, smoothing and derivative estimation is combined by filtering the boundary curve with the first and second derivatives of the Gaussian using the particular method described by Lowe [17].

Thus, a solid of revolution is a useful calibration object because it is possible, by geometric analysis alone, to determine the gradient, (p, q), the Hessian matrix, $\mathbf{H}$, and, using Equation (7), the principal curvatures and associated directions at each visible surface point. At each (x, y), the five parameters required, p, q, p_x, q_y and $p_y = q_x$, depend only on r, $h'(y)$ and $h''(y)$. In practice, the measurement of r, $h'(y)$ and $h''(y)$ can be made both accurate and robust.

3.3   Lookup Tables for Photometric Stereo

Photometric stereo does not, in fact, require that reflectance maps be determined explicitly. It is sufficient that the required information be represented implicitly in the lookup tables used to determine the gradient, (p,q), as a function of the measured triple of brightness values, $[E_1, E_2, E_3]$.

Here, the lookup table constructed was of dimension $2^5 \times 2^5 \times 2^5 = 2^{15}$. For the given table size, the goal is to use the available entries to provide the best resolution possible in the estimate of the gradient, (p,q). The technique of histogram equalization was used to achieve table compression. Table entries are disproportionately allocated to brightness values that occur frequently on the calibration object. This provides good discrimination between nearby brightness values that occur frequently at the expense of poorer discrimination in ranges of brightness values that occur less frequently or not at all.

Each image point on the calibration object was sampled. The brightness triple, $[E_1, E_2, E_3]$, determined the table location. The corresponding gradient was calculated using Equation (18). The gradient was then converted into a unit surface normal and entered into the table. Multiple triples, $[E_1, E_2, E_3]$, can map to the same table location. The resulting surface normals were averaged and converted back to gradients as a post-processing step. Some table interpolation is done, at the user's discretion, also as a post-processing step to fill in missing table entries.

By construction, this lookup table achieves good discrimination between brightness triples, $[E_1, E_2, E_3]$, that correspond to possible measurements from points on the calibration object. Space in the table is not effectively utilized for this purpose when entries are allocated to impossible brightness triples, $[E_1, E_2, E_3]$. Thus, the particular lookup table design is not best for segmentation, defined in this context to be the separation of object points from non-objects points.

Once the lookup table is established, images from the other objects are quickly analyzed. For each additional object, the input is the triple of images, $E_1(x,y)$, $E_2(x,y)$, and $E_3(x,y)$, and the output is a file giving the gradient, (p,q), at each point. A bitmap file also is produced to indicate those points at which the gradient, (p,q), was estimated.

3.4   Determining the Reflectance Maps

The reflectance maps, $R_1(p,q)$, $R_2(p,q)$, and $R_3(p,q)$, are required for curvature estimation since their partial derivatives, with respect to p and q, are needed in Equations (11) and (12). To determine the reflectance map, it is convenient to solve the inverse of Equation (18). That is, given a gradient, (p,q), we want to determine a visible surface point, (x,y), at which to measure brightness. This can be done in a two step process. First, given (p,q), we find a value of y such that

$$h'(y) = \frac{-q}{\sqrt{1+p^2}} \tag{20}$$

In general, this value of y will not be unique. In practice, it is convenient to choose a range for y over which the function $h'(y)$ is monotonic. This guarantees that a unique value of y can be obtained. Given y, we also know the radius, $r = h(y)$, and we obtain the required x as

$$x = \frac{r\,p}{\sqrt{1+p^2}} \tag{21}$$

Figure 2(a) shows the analysis of the occluding boundary of the calibration object of Figure 1. Superimposed upon the boundary, as a thicker curve, is the portion chosen over which $h'(y)$ is monotonic. Normals to the boundary curve also are plotted at selected intervals. Unfortunately, not all values of the gradient, (p, q), occur in Figure 2(a). One way to obtain additional coverage is to repeat the analysis using three additional images (not shown) of the calibration object simply placed upside down. This analysis is shown in Figure 2(b). Figure 3 shows the three reflectance maps obtained by combining the results of Figures 2(a) and 2(b). In Figure 3, the axis tick marks are one unit apart so that the range covered is $-2.5 \leq p \leq 2.5$ and $-2.5 \leq q \leq 2.5$. Some areas still are missing (i.e., black) in all three reflectance maps, $R_1(p, q)$, $R_2(p, q)$ and $R_3(p, q)$, because the results of Figures 2(a) and 2(b) do not yet span the full range of possible gradients. One remedy would be to combine the above results with measurements from three additional images of the same calibration vase re-positioned so that the axis of revolution was aligned with the image X-axis. This was not done here.

3.5   Determining Surface Curvature

To determine surface curvature at each surface point, we need to know the gradient, (p, q), and the twelve partial derivatives, E_{ix}, E_{iy}, R_{ip}, R_{iq}, $i = 1, 2, 3$. The gradient, (p, q), is obtained as the output from photometric stereo, as described in Section 3.3. The reflectance maps, $R_i(p, q)$, $i = 1, 2, 3$, are obtained as described in Section 3.4. The images, $E_i(x, y)$, and reflectance maps are further processed to estimate partial derivatives. One could compute the twelve partial derivatives explicitly by combining the appropriate directional derivative with some degree of local Gaussian smoothing. In the current implementation, there was insufficient memory available to store all twelve partial derivative results. Therefore, each image and reflectance map was smoothed with a 2D Gaussian and the required partial derivatives were estimated using simple local differencing, as required. This reduced the on-line storage requirement to the six files, $E_i(x, y)$, $R_i(p, q)$, $i = 1, 2, 3$, and the gradients, (p, q).

For each object point for which the gradient is known and for which $R_i(p, q)$ is defined, Equation (12) is used to estimate the Hessian matrix, $\mathbf{H}$. The resulting Hessian is made symmetric using Equation (15). The curvature matrix, **C**, is determined using Equation (7). From the matrix **C**, the principal curvatures, k_1 and k_2, their associated directions, ω_1 and ω_2, the Gaussian curvature, K, and the mean curvature, H, are derived, as described in Section 2.2. The relative error of the estimate of **H** also is determined using Equation (17).

3.6   Results

This paper is not about surface reconstruction directly. Nevertheless, it is convenient to perform some surface reconstruction in order to examine the results of photometric stereo.

Reconstructing a surface, $z = f(x,y)$, given the gradient, (p,q), is a problem of integration. Given a point, (x,y), and the corresponding gradient, (p,q), the change in height, dz, corresponding to a small movement $[dx, dy]$ is given by

$$dz = p\,dx + q\,dy \qquad (22)$$

This suggests a very simple surface reconstruction scheme. Given an initial point, $z_0 = f(x_0, y_0)$, one can use Equation (22) to trace a path along which depth is reconstructed. Figure 4 shows a plot of a surface reconstructed from the results of photometric stereo applied to the calibration object of Figure 1. Given an initial value, $z_0 = f(x_0, y_0)$, Equation (22) was used to reconstruct a single depth profile in the vertical (i.e., column) direction. Using the values so obtained as initial conditions, Equation (22) was then used to reconstruct depth profiles in the horizontal direction, one profile for each image row.

The images shown in Figure 1 are 256×256. To avoid clutter, Figure 4 plots every fourth row and column. No smoothing has been performed. The quality of the reconstruction is due to the local accuracy achieved with photometric stereo. Of course, one would expect this example to be accurate since, after all, it is the example of the calibration object itself.

Figure 5 shows curvature results for the calibration object. In this and in the examples to follow, the figure consists of three parts, (a), (b) and (c). The mean curvature, H, is shown in Figure 5(a). The Gaussian curvature, K, is shown in Figure 5(b). The results are scaled to $2^8 = 256$ values and offset so that middle gray represents zero, lighter points represent positive values and darker points represent negative values. The relative error of the estimate of the Hessian, computed using Equation (17), is shown in Figure 5(c). Darker points represent larger relative error. As one would expect, curvature remains relatively constant over the body of the calibration vase. At the base and at the neck; negative curvatures are seen.

Figure 6 shows three images of the calibration vase now with its top in place. Each image is 320×256. These images were obtained with the identical conditions of illumination as in

Figure 1. Figure 7 shows a plot of a surface reconstructed from the results of photometric stereo. The surface reconstruction and subsequent plotting were performed exactly as described above for Figure 4. Again, no smoothing has been performed. The quality of the reconstruction is due to the local accuracy achieved with photometric stereo. Detail at the neck and at the top is well maintained.

Figure 8 shows curvature results for the topped vase. As expected, the results for the body of the vase are very close to those obtained in Figure 5. Interesting local detail emerges at the top. High positive mean and Gaussian curvature is seen at the top tip and at the lip where the top sits on the base. Negative mean and Gaussian curvature separates the lip of the top from the main body of the top.

Figure 9 shows the three images obtained for the most complex object analyzed, a long necked vase with a handle. Each image is 320×192. Again, these images were obtained with the identical conditions of illumination as in Figure 1. Figure 10(a) shows a plot of a surface reconstructed from the results of photometric stereo. The surface reconstruction and subsequent plotting were performed exactly as described above for Figure 4. In this case, while the simple surface reconstruction algorithm is sufficient to give some idea of the local accuracy achieved with photometric stereo, it is not sufficient to obtain a reconstruction over the entire surface. Any scheme based on Equation (22) will be suspect since it will be difficult to make errors that propagate along the neck compatible with errors that propagate along the handle.

Figure 10(b) shows a plot of a surface reconstructed from the results of photometric stereo using an implementation of Harris' method of surface reconstruction [18, 19]. This method finds the surface, $z = f(x, y)$, that minimizes

$$\int \int \left(\left((z_x - p)^2 + (z_y - q)^2 \right) + \lambda \left(p_x^2 + p_y^2 + q_x^2 + q_y^2 \right) \right) \mathrm{dx}\ \mathrm{dy} \qquad (23)$$

Imposing a global smoothness term, $\left(p_x^2 + p_y^2 + q_x^2 + q_y^2 \right)$, helps to combine the handle and the neck in the reconstruction. At the same time, in the absence of prior boundary conditions, the global smoothness term causes the depth discontinuities at the top and at the bottom of the vase to be lost. The result in Figure 10(a) preserves local detail but is incomplete. The result in Figure 10(b) is complete but fails to preserve local detail.

Figure 11 shows curvature results for the long necked vase with a handle. This example provides the greatest variety of curvature values of any of the examples considered. The long neck has moderately high positive mean curvature and negative Gaussian curvature, except for its middle section where it is essentially cylindrical and the Gaussian curvature is effectively zero. The handle has very high positive mean curvature throughout. Its Gaussian curvature is highly positive at the top where the handle curves sharply. Elsewhere along the handle, the Gaussian curvature is nearly zero since the handle is nearly cylindrical. Where the handle joins the main body of the vase, both the mean curvature and the Gaussian curvature become sharply negative. The relative error measure is quite low on the neck, on the handle and especially where the handle joins the main body of the vase. This indicates that the local curvature estimates are reliable.

Finally, it is important to point out that all the curvature results shown in Figures 5, 8 and 11 are dense, local estimates. Any apparent global coherence of the result is a consequence of the computation, not a consequence of any global smoothness assumption embedded therein. In particular, the object boundary plays no role in the computation. The local results would be identical even if the object boundary was obscured.

4 Discussion and Conclusions

Multiple images acquired under the identical viewing geometry but different conditions of illumination provide additional local constraint to determine shape from shading. One way to exploit this fact is to obtain better estimates of local surface orientation. Photometric stereo does this accurately and robustly with minimal computational requirements compared to the iterative schemes typically required for shape from shading from a single image.

Here, it has been demonstrated that one can obtain, in addition, estimates of local second-order surface curvature. This represents a new capability for local shading analysis. The computational requirements remain quite modest. The method described does require knowledge of $[R_p, R_q]$ for each image. But, this also is the case for methods for determining shape from shading from a single image. The method also requires estimates of $[E_x, E_y]$ for each image. Interestingly, Horn's original method for shape from shading, based on characteristic strip expansion, also required estimates of $[E_x, E_y]$. Modern variational formulations of shape from shading, however, typically do not require $[E_x, E_y]$. Of course, estimates of $[E_x, E_y]$ are required for several other vision problems, including edge detection and optical flow. Thus, multiple light source curvature estimation does not place undue demands on what is to be measured, compared to alternatives. The resulting computation is direct without requiring any iteration steps.

The particular formulation for curvature, given in Equation (7), was proposed in [1, 3]. As argued above, this expression nicely decouples a viewer-centered representation for curvature, given by the Hessian, $\mathbf{H}$, from viewpoint dependent foreshortening, given in terms of the gradient, (p, q). The Hessian matrix is key because it relates the intensity gradient, $[E_x, E_y]$, and the reflectance map gradient, $[R_p, R_q]$. The notion that intensity gradients can be used to estimate the Hessian, $\mathbf{H}$, was noted in [1] and further developed, in the context of multiple light sources, by Wolff [20, 21]. Penna and Chen [22] also considered shape from shading with multiple light sources. They derived analytic expressions for surface curvature based on the assumption of Lambertian reflectance and single distant point light sources.

The current work, including an earlier conference paper [23], represents the first experimental demonstration that surface curvatures can, in fact, be estimated locally in shape from shading. The approach makes no prior assumption about the reflectance properties of the objects in view. In particular, it does not assume Lambertian (or any other) reflectance function. The robustness of the approach does depend on the accuracy with which the reflectance maps, $R(p, q)$, and their gradients, $[R_p, R_q]$, are known. Careful calibration can lead to accuracy in measurement. Careful choice and positioning of the light sources can be used to make the computation of the Hessian, $\mathbf{H}$, well-conditioned.

As shapes analyzed become more complex, segmentation based on surface curvature becomes more important. To specify the local properties of a surface up to curvature requires six parameters since there is one degree of freedom for range, two for surface orientation and three for curvature. If only a single measurement, say range, is available locally, then the problem is underconstrained. The usual approach is to interpolate a high-order surface with desired properties using measurements otained over extended regions. But, this begins to beg the question since one no longer has reliable local estimates of curvature upon which segmentation can be based. The approach demonstrated here is to seek additional local information. Multiple images acquired from the same viewpoint but under different conditions of illumination provide useful additional information. In principle, each image provides three independent pieces of local information, one for brightness and two for the two partial spatial derivatives of brightness. (To be truly independent, one would need an image sensor that measured partial derivatives directly). With three images one obtains nine local measurements which is sufficient to overconstrain the local solution. Thus, accuracy in local curvature estimation relates directly to the quality of imaging. Robustness can be achieved by overdetermining the computation locally, rather than by imposing global smoothness constraints.

Segmentation has always been a "chicken-and-egg" problem in computational vision. The contribution of this work is to demonstrate that surface curvature can be computed locally and reliably prior to segmentation. This, in turn, should allow future segmentation schemes to be more robust.

Acknowledgement

The work described in this paper benefited from discussions with A.K. Mackworth, D.G. Lowe, J.J. Little and J.M. Varah. L.B. Wolff pointed out the connection to his work. D.G. Lowe supplied software for curve smoothing. Y. Li implemented a version of Harris' surface reconstruction method and produced the surface shown in Figure 10(b). Y. Li and S. Kingdon assisted with image acquisition in the laboratory. Pottery used in the experiments was obtained with the help of the staff at Steveston Ceramics, Steveston, BC. Support for the work described was provided, in part, by the Natural Science and Engineering Research Council of Canada (NSERC) and, in part, by the Canadian Institute for Advanced Research (CIAR).

References

[1] R. J. Woodham, "Reflectance map techniques for analyzing surface defects in metal castings," AI-TR-457, MIT AI Laboratory, Cambridge, MA, 1978.

[2] R. J. Woodham, "Photometric method for determining surface orientation from multiple images," *Optical Engineering*, vol. 19, pp. 139–144, 1980. Reprinted in [12].

[3] R. J. Woodham, "Analysing images of curved surfaces," *Artificial Intelligence*, vol. 17, pp. 117–140, 1981.

[4] W. M. Silver, "Determining shape and reflectance using multiple images," SM thesis, MIT Dept. Electrical Engineering and Computer Science, Cambridge, MA, 1980.

[5] K. Ikeuchi, "Recognition of 3-D objects using the extended Gaussian image," in *Proc. 7th Int. Joint Conf. on Artificial Intelligence*, pp. 595–600, 1981.

[6] P. Brou, "Using the Gaussian image to find the orientation of objects," *Int. J. Robotics Research*, vol. 3, no. 4, pp. 89–125, 1984.

[7] B. K. P. Horn and K. Ikeuchi, "The mechanical manipulation of randomly oriented parts," *Scientific American*, vol. 251, pp. 100–111, August 1984.

[8] K. Ikeuchi, "Determining attitude of object from needle map using extended Gaussian image," AI-Memo-714, MIT AI Laboratory, Cambridge, MA, 1983.

[9] K. Ikeuchi, B. K. P. Horn, S. Nagata, T. Callahan, and O. Feingold, "Picking up an object from a pile of objects," in *Robotics Research: The First International Symposium* (M. Brady and R. Paul, eds.), pp. 139–162, Cambridge, MA: MIT Press, 1984.

[10] K. Ikeuchi, H. K. Nishihara, B. K. P. Horn, P. Sobalvarro, and S. Nagata, "Determining grasp configurations using photometric stereo and the prism binocular stereo system," *Int. J. Robotics Research*, vol. 5, no. 1, pp. 46–65, 1986.

[11] B. K. P. Horn, *Robot Vision*. Cambridge, MA: MIT Press, 1986.

[12] B. K. P. Horn and M. J. Brooks, eds., *Shape from Shading*. Cambridge, MA: MIT Press, 1989.

[13] M. Brady, J. Ponce, A. Yuille, and H. Asada, "Describing surfaces," *Computer Vision Graphics and Image Processing*, vol. 32, pp. 1–28, 1985.

[14] P. J. Besl and R. C. Jain, "Three-dimensional object recognition," *ACM Computing Surveys*, vol. 17, pp. 75–145, 1985.

[15] P. J. Besl and R. C. Jain, "Invariant surface characteristics for 3D object recognition in range images," *Computer Vision Graphics and Image Processing*, vol. 33, pp. 33–80, 1986.

[16] R. T. Frankot and R. Chellappa, "A method for enforcing integrability in shape from shading algorithms," *IEEE Trans. Pattern Analysis and Machine Intelligence*, vol. 10, pp. 439–451, 1988. Reprinted in [12].

[17] D. G. Lowe, "Organization of smooth image curves at multiple scales," *Int. J. Computer Vision*, vol. 3, pp. 119–130, 1989.

[18] J. G. Harris, "The coupled depth/slope approach to surface reconstruction," AI-TR-908, MIT AI Laboratory, Cambridge, MA, 1986.

[19] J. G. Harris, "A new approach to surface reconstruction: the coupled depth/slope model," in *Proc. 1st Int. Conf. on Computer Vision*, pp. 277–283, 1987.

[20] L. B. Wolff, "Surface curvature and contour from photometric stereo," in *Proc. DARPA Image Understanding Workshop, 1987*, pp. 821–824, 1987.

[21] L. B. Wolff, "Accurate measurement of second order variations of a smooth object surface using reflectance maps," in *Proc. SPIE Vol. 1003 Sensory Fusion: Spatial Reasoning and Scene Interpretation (1988)*, pp. 59–62, 1988.

[22] M. A. Penna and S. S. Chen, "Shape-from-shading using multiple light sources," *Int. J. Intelligent Systems*, vol. 1, pp. 263–291, 1986.

[23] R. J. Woodham, "Determining surface curvature with photometric stereo," in *Proc. IEEE Conf. Robotics and Automation, 1989*, pp. 36–42, 1989.

Figure Captions

Figure 1 Three images of the vase used as the calibration object. Light source 1 comes from a direction to the left and slightly above the viewing direction. Light source 2 comes from a direction to the right and slightly above the viewing direction. Light source 3 comes almost exactly from the viewing direction. $E_1(x,y)$, $E_2(x,y)$ and $E_3(x,y)$ are shown respectively as (a), (b), and (c).

Figure 2 Geometric analysis of the boundary of the calibration object is used to determine the gradient, (p,q), at each image point, (x,y). Superimposed upon the boundary, as the thicker curve, is the portion chosen over which $h'(y)$ is monotonic. Selected normals to the boundary curve also are shown. The analysis of the images of Figure 1 is shown in (a). In order to obtain additional coverage in the gradient space, the analysis was repeated using three additional images (not shown) of the calibration object placed upside down. This analysis is shown in (b).

Figure 3 The three reflectance maps determined by measurements from the calibration object. $R_1(p,q)$, $R_2(p,q)$ and $R_3(p,q)$ are shown respectively as (a), (b), and (c). The axis tick marks are one unit apart so that the range covered is $-2.5 \leq p \leq 2.5$ and $-2.5 \leq q \leq 2.5$. The black areas in (c) correspond to gradients not obtained from the calibration object, either from Figure 2(a) or from Figure 2(b). Additional dark areas in (a) and (b) correspond to points shadowed from the light source.

Figure 4 Plot of the surface of the calibration vase reconstructed from the gradients, (p,q), obtained from photometric stereo.

Figure 5 Curvature results for the calibration vase. The mean curvature, H, is shown in (a). The Gaussian curvature, K, is shown in (b). In each case the result has been scaled so that middle gray is zero, lighter points represent positive values and darker points represent negative values. The relative error of the estimate of the Hessian is shown in (c). Darker points represent larger relative error.

Figure 6 Three images of the calibration vase with its top in place. The three images were obtained with the identical conditions of illumination as in Figure 1. $E_1(x,y)$, $E_2(x,y)$ and $E_3(x,y)$ are shown respectively as (a), (b), and (c).

Figure 7 Plot of the surface of the calibration vase with its top in place reconstructed from the gradients, (p,q), obtained from photometric stereo.

Figure 8 Curvature results for the calibration vase with its top in place. The mean curvature, H, is shown in (a). The Gaussian curvature, K, is shown in (b). The relative error of the estimate of the Hessian is shown in (c).

Figure 9 Three images of the most complex object analyzed, a long necked vase with a handle. Again, the three images were obtained with the identical conditions of illumination as in Figure 1. $E_1(x,y)$, $E_2(x,y)$ and $E_3(x,y)$ are shown respectively as (a), (b), and (c).

Figure 10 Plots of the surface of the long necked vase with a handle. The result with the algorithm used for Figures 4 and 7 is shown in (a). The result using an implementation of Harris' method of surface reconstruction is shown in (b).

Figure 11 Curvature results for the long necked vase with a handle. The mean curvature, H, is shown in (a). The Gaussian curvature, K, is shown in (b). The relative error of the estimate of the Hessian is shown in (c).

Figure 1

(a)

(b)

(c)

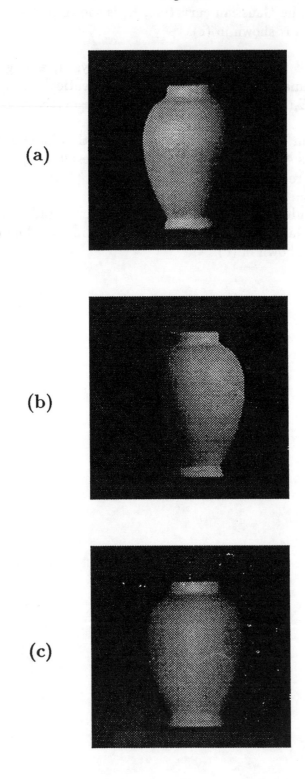

Figure 2

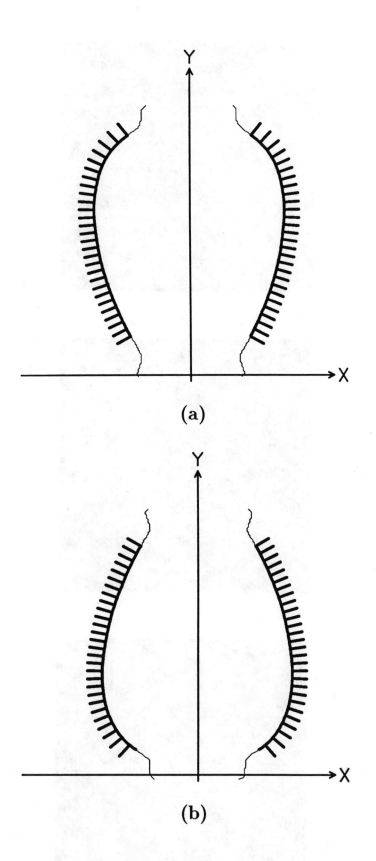

(a)

(b)

Figure 3

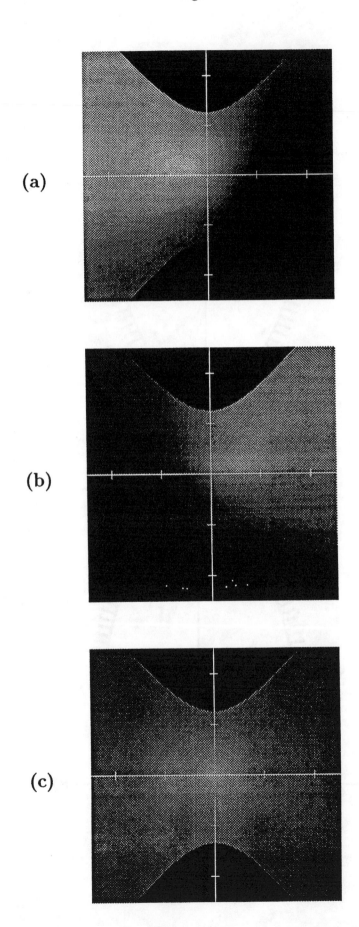

(a)

(b)

(c)

Figure 4

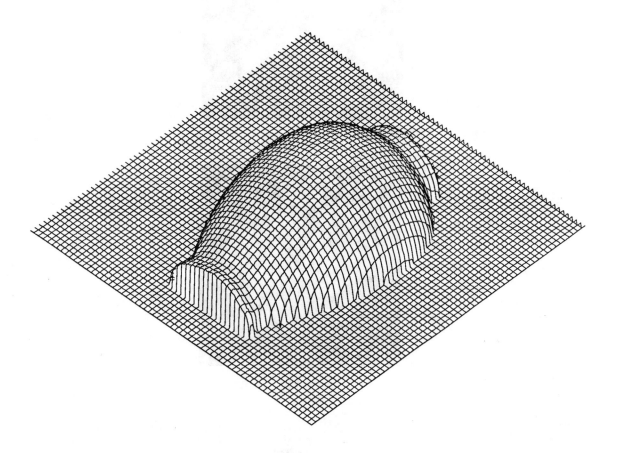

Surface plot of calibration vase

Figure 5

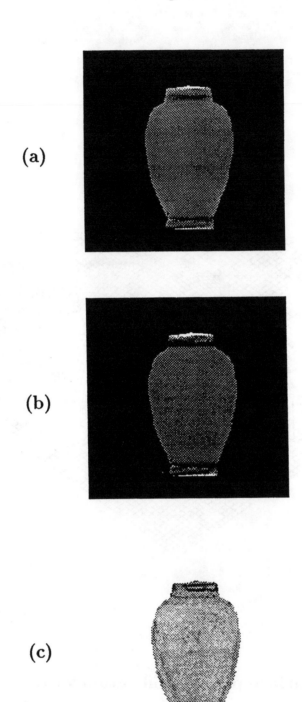

(a)

(b)

(c)

Figure 6

(a)

(b)

(c)

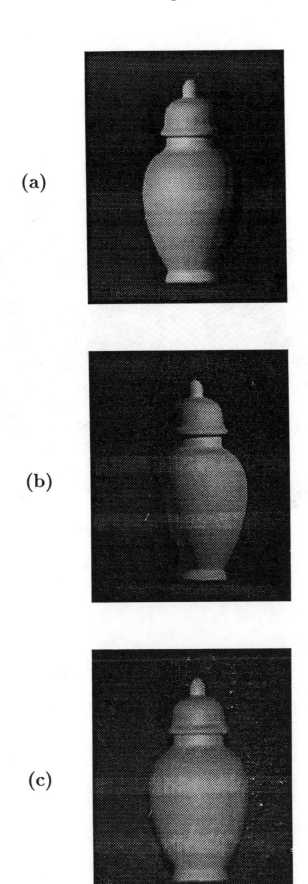

Figure 7

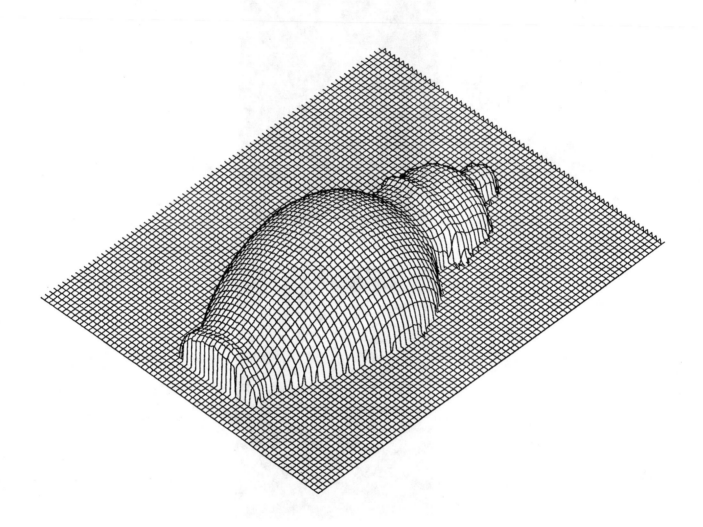

Surface plot of topped vase

Figure 8

(a)

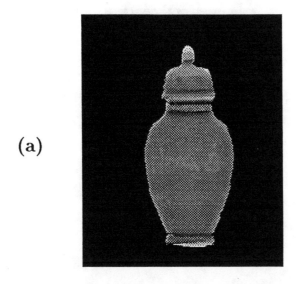

(b)

(c)

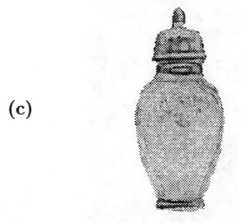

Figure 9

(a)

(b)

(c)

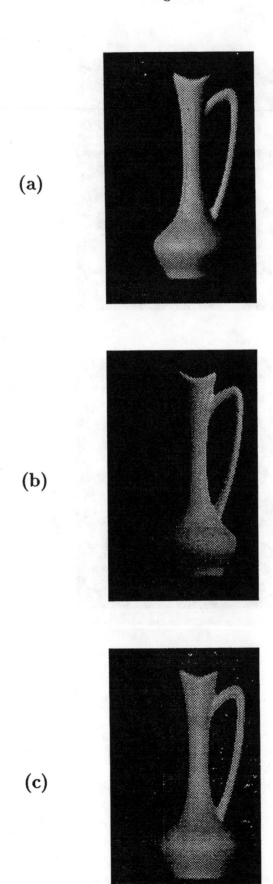

Figure 10

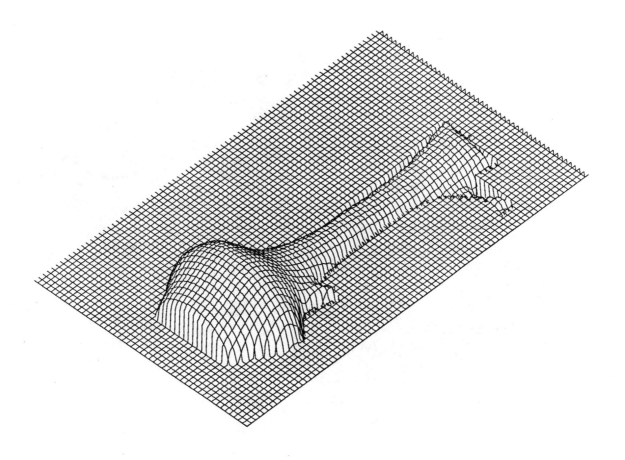

(a)

Surface plot of handled vase

Figure 10

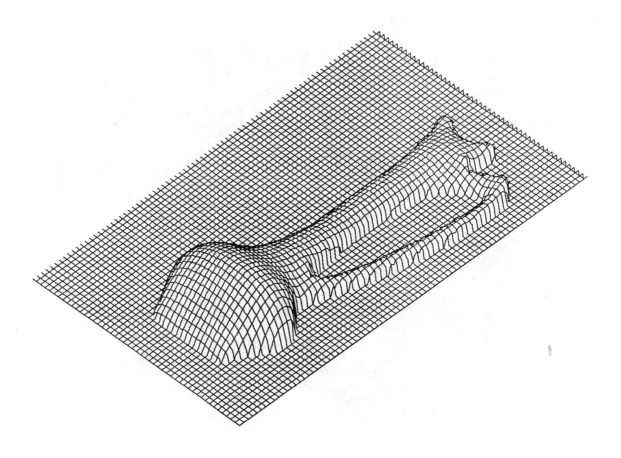

(b)

Surface plot of handled vase (Harris reconstruction)

Figure 11

(a)

(b)

(c)

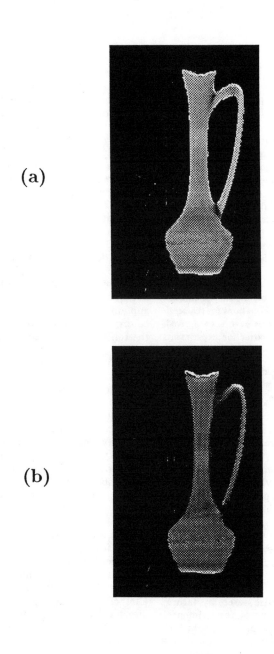

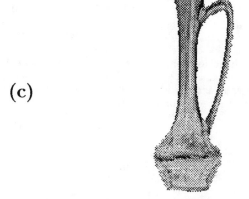

Error Analysis of Surface Normals Determined by Radiometry

RAJARSHI RAY, JOHN BIRK, AND ROBERT B. KELLEY

Abstract—Surface normals can be computed from three images of a workpiece taken under three distinct lighting conditions without requiring surface continuity. Radiometric methods are susceptible to systematic errors such as: errors in the measurement of light source orientations; mismatched light source irradiance; detector nonlinearity; the presence of specular reflection or shadows; the spatial and spectral distribution of incident light; surface size, material, and microstructure; and the length and properties of the light source to target path. Typically, a 1° error in surface orientation of a Lambertian workpiece is caused by a 1 percent change in image intensity due to variations in incident light intensity or a 1° change in orientation of a collimated light source. Tests on a white nylon sphere indicate that by using modest error prevention and calibration schemes, surface angles off the camera axis can be computed within 5°, except at edge pixels. Equations for the sensitivity of surface normals to major error sources have been derived. Results of surface normal estimation and edge extraction experiments on various non-Lambertian and textured workpieces are also presented.

Index Terms—Computer vision, edge extraction, Lambertian reflectance, needle diagram, photometric stereo, radiometric stereo, reflectance mapping, sensitivity analysis, surface orientation.

I. INTRODUCTION

The technique of photometric stereo uses a reflectance mapping procedure [1]–[4] to compute an estimate of the orientation of a surface point. Three different images of a workpiece are taken by a stationary camera by varying the direction of illumination [5], [6]. Since every object point corresponds to one pixel in each of the images and the images correspond to different light sources, the orientation can be obtained from the point of intersection of reflectance curves of those light sources. The limitations of this technique are the assumptions of Lambertian reflection and point source illumination. Hence there are accuracy problems in using this technique for engineering practice.

Woodham [7] stated that since photometric stereo, by nature, is an overdetermined problem subject to numerous experimental errors, one cannot expect to find an exact practical solution. Investigations have been made to modify the theory of photometric stereo for non-Lambertian reflections and distributed light sources [7], [8]. Ikeuchi and Horn proposed an experimental scheme using extended light sources to illuminate an overhead Lambertian plane and also illuminate a partially hidden object by the reflected light [9]. This scheme used a complex experimental setup with three linear lamps, a hidden TV camera, precomputed reflectance maps, and lookup tables. The on-line output lacked accuracy at certain regions on the object surface. It is claimed that the performance can be improved by the off-line application of iterative relaxation heuristics. Recently, Ikeuchi [10] used the idea of propagation of

Manuscript received October 29, 1981; revised January 7, 1983.
R. Ray is with Object Recognition Systems, Inc., Princeton, NJ 08540.
J. Birk is with the Hewlett-Packard Company, Palo Alto, CA 93303.
R. B. Kelley is with the Robotics Research Center, University of Rhode Island, Kingston, RI 02881.

constraints, as previously used by Marr and Poggio [11], Horn [12], and Zucker [13] to obtain local surface normals from the distortions of surface texture in an image [14].

This correspondence addresses the problem of implementing the technique of photometric stereo on non-Lambertian workpieces by identifying various systematic errors and some means to rectify these errors. The effects of specular reflection and shadows can be minimized to a great extent by choosing appropriate light source locations. Different locations of light sources may be chosen for different orientations of the workpiece. The distance between the light source and the object should also be kept large compared to the object size in order to produce nearly collimated incident light on the object surface. Other sources of error can also be controlled by using various thresholding and calibration schemes. The magnitude of experimental errors in output surface angles can be estimated by the input light source angles and intensities, camera noise, etc. by means of an error analysis. The problem of applying photometric techniques on workpieces with several colors is also investigated. In this case, in spite of the fact that the reflected light spectra may vary considerably from the incident spectra, surface normals can be determined using reflectance equations.

The technique does not necessarily require that the incident and reflected radiations be optically visible. Hence throughout this work, the method will be referred to as a radiometric technique.

The major contributions of present work are in 1) the identification of major sources of error, 2) the derivation of mathematical equations for sensitivity and an investigation into the extent of various errors, and 3) a presentation of output data from laboratory experiments performed on non-Lambertian workpieces with or without multiple colors.

II. REFLECTANCE THEORY

When a ray of light strikes the surface of an object, specular and diffuse reflections take place. These reflection characteristics depend on the surface material, surface microstructure, incident wavelength, and the direction of incidence [4]. However, it is possible to visualize some ideal surfaces called Lambertian surfaces which scatter incident light equally in all directions and appear equally bright from all directions

According to Lambert's cosine law [15], the image intensity corresponding to a Lambertian reflecting surface is given by the relationship

$$I(x, y) = \rho(x, y) \cos i \qquad (1)$$

where I = image irradiance at the image point (x, y), $\rho(x, y)$ = a constant named the "albedo" factor, and i = angle of incidence. When the size of the object is small compared with the viewing distance, a perspective transformation is unnecessary and image coordinates can be directly related to the object coordinates. This assumption is made throughout this presentation (see basic assumptions below).

If the viewing direction is aligned with the z-axis of the object coordinate system the normal vector to a surface $z = f_0(x, y)$ is $(-p_n, -q_n, 1)$ [32] (Appendix A) where

$$p_n = \partial z/\partial x \quad \text{and} \quad q_n = \partial z/\partial y \qquad (2)$$

and the corresponding light source vector is $(-p_l, -q_l, 1)$. We also obtain [16]

$$I(x, y) = p(x, y) \frac{1 + p_n p_l + q_n q_l}{\sqrt{1 + p_n^2 + q_n^2} \sqrt{1 + p_l^2 + q_l^2}} \qquad (3)$$

by taking the normalized dot product of the two vectors using (1). Hence, the values of p_n and q_n can be determined uniquely by solving the following set of three nonlinear equations:

$$I_1(x, y) = p(x, y) \frac{1 + p_n p_{1l} + q_n q_{1l}}{\sqrt{1 + p_n^2 + q_n^2} \sqrt{1 + p_{1l}^2 + q_{1l}^2}} \qquad (4)$$

$$I_2(x, y) = p(x, y) \frac{1 + p_n p_{2l} + q_n q_{2l}}{\sqrt{1 + p_n^2 + q_n^2} \sqrt{1 + p_{2l}^2 + q_{2l}^2}} \qquad (5)$$

$$I_3(x, y) = p(x, y) \frac{1 + p_n p_{3l} + q_n q_{3l}}{\sqrt{1 + p_n^2 + q_n^2} \sqrt{1 + p_{3l}^2 + q_{3l}^2}} \qquad (6)$$

given the measured values of image intensities I_1, I_2, I_3 and the measured values of the three gradient space light source coordinates (p_{1l}, q_{1l}), (p_{2l}, q_{2l}), and (p_{3l}, q_{3l}), respectively.

The basic assumptions in this theory are as follows:

1) the light source is assumed to be a uniform point source at infinity;

2) the object surface is assumed to be a Lambertian reflector;

3) the object size is much smaller than the viewing distance; and

4) the surface point is directly illuminated by the light sources, i.e., there is no occlusion with respect to light sources or mutual reflection by other object parts.

In terms of azimuth angle ϕ_n (measured counterclockwise from the x-axis) and the zenith angle θ_n (measured between the surface normal and the z-axis), the surface normal gradients can be written as

$$p_n = -\cos \phi_n \tan \theta_n \qquad (7)$$

and

$$q_n = -\sin \phi_n \tan \theta_n. \qquad (8)$$

Similarly, for the light source angles ϕ_l and θ_l, we can get the corresponding gradients p_l and q_l as

$$p_l = -\cos \phi_l \tan \theta_l \qquad (9)$$

and

$$q_l = -\sin \phi_l \tan \theta_l. \qquad (10)$$

The surface normal vector involving the two unknowns p_n and q_n in (4), (5), and (6) can be uniquely determined by a method of algebraic solution of three nonlinear equations (Appendix B). For

$$A_1 = \sqrt{1 + p_{1l}^2 + q_{1l}^2}, \quad A_2 = \sqrt{1 + p_{2l}^2 + q_{2l}^2}, \quad \text{and}$$
$$A_3 = \sqrt{1 + p_{3l}^2 + q_{3l}^2},$$

$$
\begin{aligned}
k = & \frac{(I_1 A_1 - I_2 A_2)(I_3 A_3 p_{2l} - I_2 A_2 p_{3l}) - (I_2 A_2 - I_3 A_3)(I_2 A_2 p_{1l} - I_1 A_1 p_{2l})}{(I_2 A_2 p_{1l} - I_1 A_1 p_{2l})(I_2 A_2 q_{3l} - I_3 A_3 q_{2l}) - (I_3 A_3 p_{2l} - I_2 A_2 p_{3l})(I_1 A_1 q_{2l} - I_2 A_2 q_{1l})} \\[2mm]
& + \frac{(I_2 A_2 - I_3 A_3)(I_1 A_1 p_{3l} - I_3 A_3 p_{1l}) - (I_3 A_3 - I_1 A_1)(I_3 A_3 p_{2l} - I_2 A_2 p_{3l})}{(I_3 A_3 p_{2l} - I_2 A_2 p_{3l})(I_3 A_3 q_{1l} - I_1 A_1 q_{3l}) - (I_1 A_1 p_{3l} - I_3 A_3 p_{1l})(I_2 A_2 q_{3l} - I_3 A_3 p_{2l})} \\[2mm]
& + \frac{(I_3 A_3 - I_1 A_1)(I_2 A_2 p_{1l} - I_1 A_1 p_{2l}) - (I_1 A_1 - I_2 A_2)(I_1 A_1 p_{3l} - I_3 A_3 p_{1l})}{(I_1 A_1 p_{3l} - I_3 A_3 p_{1l})(I_1 A_1 q_{2l} - I_2 A_2 q_{1l}) - (I_2 A_2 p_{1l} - I_1 A_1 p_{2l})(I_3 A_3 p_{1l} - I_1 A_1 q_{3l})}
\end{aligned} \qquad (11)
$$

and

$$
\begin{aligned}
m = & \frac{(I_3 A_3 - I_1 A_1) + q_n(I_3 A_3 q_{1l} - I_1 A_1 q_{3l})}{(I_1 A_1 p_{3l} - I_3 A_3 p_{1l})} \\[2mm]
& + \frac{(I_1 A_1 - I_2 A_2) + q_n(I_1 A_1 q_{2l} - I_2 A_2 q_{1l})}{(I_2 A_2 p_{1l} - I_1 A_1 p_{2l})} \\[2mm]
& + \frac{(I_2 A_2 - I_3 A_3) + q_n(I_2 A_2 q_{3l} - I_3 A_3 q_{2l})}{(I_3 A_3 p_{2l} - I_2 A_2 p_{3l})}
\end{aligned} \qquad (12)
$$

where $p_n = (\frac{1}{3})m$ and $q_n = (\frac{1}{3})k$ and also

$$p_{1l} = -\cos \phi_{1l} \tan \theta_{1l}; q_{1l} = -\sin \phi_{1l} \tan \theta_{1l};$$
$$p_{2l} = -\cos \phi_{2l} \tan \theta_{2l}; q_{2l} = -\sin \phi_{2l} \tan \theta_{2l};$$
$$p_{3l} = -\cos \phi_{3l} \tan \theta_{3l}; q_{3l} = -\sin \phi_{3l} \tan \theta_{3l}; \qquad (13)$$

barring degeneracy (a typical case of degeneracy is when the three lights are on the same straight line).

Therefore, by measuring the angles $\theta_{1l}, \theta_{2l}, \theta_{3l}, \phi_{1l}, \phi_{2l},$ and ϕ_{3l} the light source gradients can be obtained and then using the intensity values $I_1, I_2,$ and I_3 the magnitudes of p_n and q_n can be determined. Since (11) and (12) do not involve any terms containing $\rho(x, y)$ an albedo factor which varies over the surface can be accommodated. The workpiece need not have uniform reflectivity.

III. Sources of Error

An experimental scheme using reflectance equations and radiometric techniques is susceptible to various errors. These errors are due to theoretical assumptions, image processing problems and limitations of the system architecture [17]-[19]. It is possible to decrease errors by consideration of the error sources and by implementation of preventive measures.

A. Specular Reflection and Highlights

The industrial workpieces in this study were assumed to behave as Lambertian reflectors. However, most industrial workpieces do not have Lambertian reflection characteristics. These objects give specular reflection for various orientations and also from various edges, corners and curvatures [20], [21]. For all objects, in the practical sense, both specular and diffuse reflections occur together. However, specular reflections can be avoided by using extra images and by changing the location and orientation of the light sources [22].

During experiments, the occurrence of specular reflection causes a drastic change in intensity. The intensity of some pixels exceeds the dynamic range of the camera and blooming takes place, thereby degrading the pixels in the neighborhood. For highly polished surfaces, the specular component of reflected light gives an impression of a virtual light source to an observer. Even for less polished surfaces, the image of a bright light source may be produced, in spite of significant attenuation of the specular component, and a "smearing out" may occur [20].

B. Measurement of Light Source Orientations

The accuracy of the computed values of p_n and q_n are dependent on the accuracy of measurement of the angles θ_{1l}, $\theta_{2l}, \theta_{3l}, \phi_{1l}, \phi_{2l},$ and ϕ_{3l}. Accurate measurements of these angles can be obtained by two calibration techniques, as follows.

1) From (4), (5), and (6), we find $\theta_l = \theta_{1l} = \theta_{2l} = \theta_{3l}$, $\cos \theta_l = 1/(\sqrt{1 + p_l^2 + q_l^2})$ and $A_1 = A_2 = A_3 = 1/\cos \theta_l$ if the light sources are placed symmetrically about the optical axis.

Now if we set $p_n = q_n = 0$, in these equations, we obtain, $I_1(x, y) = I_2(x, y) = I_3(x, y) = \rho(x, y) \cos \theta_l$.

In other words, the image intensities obtained from each of the three light sources are the same for an object surface directly

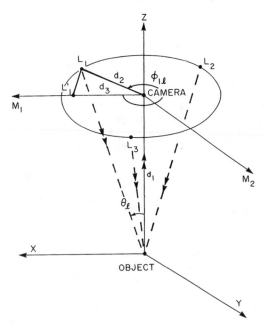

Fig. 1. Calibration distances; C = camera, O = object, L_1, L_2, L_3 = light sources, L'_1 = projection of light source L_1 on the xz-plane. θ_1 = zenith angle of light sources, ϕ_1 = azimuth angle of L_1. The plane containing the points M_1, M_2, C, L_1, L_2, and L_3 is parallel to the xy plane.

facing the camera. Therefore, the first step in the calibration procedure is to place a planar calibration surface normal to the camera axis. Then the light source magnitude and location are adjusted so that $I_1 = I_2 \pm 0.02 = I_3 \pm 0.02$ and the light sources are on the same plane as the camera, where 0.02 is the order of the camera and scanner noise in gray scale.

A value for θ_l can be obtained by measuring the distance d_1 between the camera and the object and the normal distance d_2 from the optical axis of the camera to the three light sources (Fig. 1). Hence,

$$\tan \theta_l = d_2/d_1 \qquad (14)$$

and

$$\theta_l = \tan^{-1} d_2/d_1; \qquad (15)$$

where

$$0 \leqslant \theta_l \leqslant 90°.$$

The values of ϕ_l can also be determined by measurement. Assuming that the light sources and the camera are on a plane parallel to the xy-plane and d_3 is the distance between the camera and the projection of the light source on the xz-plane containing the optical axis

$$\cos \phi_l = \cos (360° - \phi_l) = d_3/d_2 \qquad (16)$$

and

$$\phi_l = \cos^{-1} d_3/d_2; \qquad (17)$$

where

$$0 \leqslant \phi_l \leqslant 360°$$

and the included angle between the above distance and the radius of the circle of light sources is a right angle.

2) The next step in the calibration procedure is to position a rectangular parallelepiped such that three distinct surfaces are clearly visible from the viewing position. The directions of the three surface are known a priori. Now using one light source a picture is taken to determine the intensities of light reflected from these three surfaces. Hence, assuming diffuse reflections and point invariant albedo factor, we find

$$I_1 = \rho \cdot \frac{1 + p_l p_{1n} + q_l q_{1n}}{\sqrt{1 + p_l^2 + q_l^2} \sqrt{1 + p_{1n}^2 + q_{1n}^2}} \qquad (18)$$

$$I_2 = \rho \cdot \frac{1 + p_l p_{2n} + q_l q_{2n}}{\sqrt{1 + p_l^2 + q_l^2} \sqrt{1 + p_{2n}^2 + q_{2n}^2}} \qquad (19)$$

$$I_3 = \rho \cdot \frac{1 + p_l p_{3n} + q_l q_{3n}}{\sqrt{1 + p_l^2 + q_l^2} \sqrt{1 + p_{3n}^2 + q_{3n}^2}} \qquad (20)$$

for a point on one planar surface with gradient (p_{1n}, q_{1n}), a point on the second planar surface with gradient (p_{2n}, q_{2n}) and a point on the third planar surface with gradient (p_{3n}, q_{3n}). The light source orientation (p_l, q_l) can be computed from these equations in a manner analogous to solving (4) to (6), due to symmetry in these equations.

Similarly, two more experiments can be performed using the other two light sources. Finally the values of $\theta_l, \phi_{1l}, \phi_{2l}$, and ϕ_{3l} determined by this method can be cross-checked with the measured values of the same angles using (15) and (17) in calibration method 1).

C. Nonlinearity of Camera Response

The solid-state GE TN 2200 camera used for experiments had a nonlinear transfer characteristic:

$$V \propto I^{1.075} \qquad (21)$$

where I = input illumination and V = scanning voltage output as obtained by calibration.

The response of this camera is quite different at very high intensities. For our experiments, which were limited to the medium intensity region of camera response, (21) was used to compute input illumination of the camera from camera output data.

Precautions are needed to avoid dark current and saturation effects. Two thresholds were chosen for filtering out degraded data in the image due to these effects.

The lower threshold was also used to eliminate shadows and the image background from the rest of the image. Image intensity data whose magnitude was in between the two thresholds was used for further analysis and surface normal computations.

D. Imaging Geometry

1) Orthographic Projection: In order to achieve orthographic projection, the distance between the workpiece and the camera should be much larger than any single dimension of the workpiece. For example, for a metallic cylinder of diameter 0.6 in and length 2.4 in, the camera is positioned approximately 6 ft away from the center of the cylinder. Moreover, an optical lens of high focal length can be used so that all light rays from object to image plane are approximately parallel.

2) Collimation of Incident Light: The light sources and the camera are mounted on the same plane, which is perpendicular to the z axis of the coordinate system. Hence, the distance between the workpiece and any light source is larger than the distance between the workpiece and the camera (Fig. 1). Therefore, the light rays reaching the surface of the workpiece are almost parallel.

E. Matching of Light Sources

The three light sources should be perfectly matched in their spatial and spectral output ratings. The wavelength of reflected light is dependent on the wavelength of incident light and the color of the object. Therefore, for a colored object, if three light sources of three different wavelengths are used, the color spectra of reflected lights, if any, will widely vary from one another.   Under these circumstances, the radiometric stereo technique can not be applied because the surface has a different albedo factor for every light source.

Light sources with different shapes give rise to different brightness distributions [15], [23].   For radiometric stereo, light sources with uniform brightness distribution over a small solid angle are required.   Moreover, since irradiance decreases as distance increases, according to inverse square law [21], a circular arrangement of lights was used.   The lights were mounted around the camera in a plane perpendicular to the optical axis.   Hence, $\theta_{1l} = \theta_{2l} = \theta_{3l} = \theta_l$, which gave equal intensity of incident illumination on the object surface from all three sources.

F. Presence of Shadows and Mutual Reflection

Shadows cast on an object surface and mutual reflection of light from various points of the same or other object can also result in considerable error [5], [6].

G. Spectral Distribution of Light

It is found by reflectance studies that scattering of light by surfaces is closely related to the incident wavelength.   According to modern rough surface scatter theories, scattering is more predominant when the wavelength in the spectral region is comparable to the surface irregularities.   Diffuse scattering generally takes place at relatively slight roughness and also at low angles of incidence [22].

H. Surface Material

Surface material influences the scattering and polarization of light.   With very low incidence angles, frosted opal glass, matte paint, and certain powders behave as perfect diffusers [4].   The albedo factor and surface gloss are also dependent on the properties of the surface material.   In this connection, it should be pointed out that the radiometric technique of determining surface gradients does not work for any optically transparent or translucent substances.

I. Miscellaneous

Although not as significant as the previous errors, there are other sources of possible error, viz. 1) spurious noise in detector or scanner, 2) defocusing, 3) limited resolution of camera, 4) thermal instability of detector and light sources, 5) motion blur, 6) nonuniform spatial response of the detector, 7) optical system aberrations, 8) diffraction effects, 9) stray light, and 10) optical properties of the medium [19].

IV. SENSITIVITY ANALYSIS

Since the principle of radiometric stereo can be implemented using multiple digitized images, the nature and extent of image degradations can be a key factor in estimating the source of inaccuracy in output data.   The sensitivity of the stereo algorithm to changes in various input parameters can be analyzed using (13) to (16). These equations can be algebraically solved. The surface gradients can be written as

$$q_n = f(I_1, I_2, I_3, \theta_l, \phi_{1l}, \phi_{2l}, \phi_{3l}) \qquad (22)$$

and

$$p_n = g(I_1, I_2, I_3, \theta_l, \phi_{1l}, \phi_{2l}, \phi_{3l}) \qquad (23)$$

for two different functions f and g.

Now if small changes are made in $I_1, I_2, I_3, \theta_l, \phi_{1l}, \phi_{2l}$, and ϕ_{3l} we can estimate deviations in the values of q and p as well. The deviation in q_n and p_n can be written as

$$dq_n = \sum_{i=1}^{3} \frac{\partial f}{\partial I_i} \, dI_i + \frac{\partial f}{\partial \theta_l} \, d\theta_l + \sum_{i=1}^{3} \frac{\partial f}{\partial \phi_{il}} \, d\phi_{il} \qquad (24)$$

TABLE I
ERRORS IN SURFACE ORIENTATION (IN DEGREES) VERSUS INTENSITY
ERROR (IN NORMALIZED GRAY SCALE VALUES)

Conditions: $\theta_l = 30°$, $\phi_{1l} = 30°$, $\phi_{2l} = 150°$, $\phi_{3l} = 270°$, $\theta_n = 30°$, $\phi_n = 120°$, $I_1 = 0.7500$, $I_2 = 0.9665$, $I_3 = 0.5335$, $p_n = 0.2889$, $q_n = -0.5$

Image i	Errors in		
	Intensity $\lvert dI_i \rvert$	Zenith Angle $\lvert d\theta_n \rvert$	Azimuth Angle $\lvert d\phi_n \rvert$
1	0.01	0.11°	1.52°
2	0.01	0.46°	0.76°
3	0.01	0.68°	0.76°

and

$$dp_n = \sum_{i=1}^{3} \frac{\partial g}{\partial I_i} \, dI_i + \frac{\partial g}{\partial \theta_l} \, d\theta_l + \sum_{i=1}^{3} \frac{\partial dg}{\partial \phi_{il}} \, d\phi_{il} \qquad (25)$$

if the partial derivatives exist for the data values used in the calculations.   Using (4)–(6) all partial derivatives in (24) and (25) may be derived (Appendix C).   Hence, we can find reasonable estimates of errors in dp_n and dq_n. Since the surface gradient is related to the surface normal angles θ_n and ϕ_n, we also obtain from (7) and (8)

$$\theta_n = \tan^{-1} \sqrt{p_n^2 + q_n^2} = f_\theta(p_n, q_n) \qquad (26)$$

$$\phi_n = \tan^{-1}(q_n/p_n) = f_\phi(p_n, q_n) \qquad (27)$$

for two different functions f_θ and f_ϕ.   Hence, the errors in the values of θ_n and ϕ_n can be written in terms of dp_n and dq_n as follows:

$$d\theta_n = \frac{\partial f_\theta}{\partial p_n} \, dp_n + \frac{\partial f_\theta}{\partial q_n} \, dq_n \qquad (28)$$

and

$$d\phi_n = \frac{\partial f_\phi}{\partial p_n} \, dp_n + \frac{\partial f_\phi}{\partial q_n} \, dq_n. \qquad (29)$$

Therefore, using these equations, it is possible to estimate the magnitude of errors in θ_n and ϕ_n due to small changes in various parameters as described below.

A. Intensity Error

Table I presents the sample errors in θ_n and ϕ_n due to errors in intensity measurements only.   This kind of error may be due to detector nonlinearity, detector noise or mismatched light sources.   If in (29) $dI_1 = dI_2 = dI_3$, the value of $d\phi_n$ is equal to zero (in absence of other errors).   The light intensity in this table signifies the grey scale intensity of magnitude 0 to 255 normalized to a range of 0 to 1.

B. Light Source Error

1) Error in Zenith Angle Measurement: Table II shows the errors in surface orientation due only to small errors in the measurement of the zenith angle of the light sources. ϕ_n is unaffected if deviations in θ_l are the same for all three light sources.   However, deviations in θ_n are proportional to errors in θ_l.

2) Errors in Azimuth Angle Measurement: Errors in surface normal orientations for an inaccurate measurement of the azimuth angle of light sources is also indicated in Table II.

TABLE II
ERRORS IN SURFACE ORIENTATION (IN DEGREES) VERSUS ERRORS IN
MEASUREMENT OF INPUT ANGLES (IN DEGREES)

Conditions: $\theta_l = 30°$, $\phi_{1l} = 30°$, $\phi_{2l} = 150°$, $\phi_{3l} = 270°$, $\theta_n = 30°$, $\phi_n = 60°$, $I_1 = 0.9665$, $I_2 = 0.7500$, $I_3 = 0.5335$, $p_n = -0.2887$, $q_n = -0.5$

Light Angle	Light Angle Deviation	Surface Angles	
		$\lvert d\theta_n \rvert$	$\lvert d\phi_n \rvert$
θ_l	1°	1.00°	0.00°
ϕ_{1l}	1°	0.10°	0.17°
ϕ_{2l}	1°	0.05°	0.67°
ϕ_{3l}	1°	0.15°	0.17°

TABLE III
ERRORS IN SURFACE ORIENTATION (IN DEGREES) VERSUS LIGHT
SOURCE ZENITH ANGLE MAGNITUDE (IN DEGREES)

Conditions: $\phi_{1l} = 30°$, $\phi_{2l} = 150°$, $\phi_{3l} = 270°$, $\theta_n = 30°$, $\phi_n = 60°$, $\theta_n = -0.2887$, $q_n = -0.5$, $dI_1 = 0.01$, $dI_2 = 0.01$, $dI_3 = 0.01$, $d\theta_l = 1.0°$, $d\phi_{1l} = 1.0°$, $d\phi_{2l} = 1.0°$, $d\phi_{3l} = 1.0°$

Light Angles	Light Intensities			Surface Angles	
θ_l	I_2	I_2	I_3	$\lvert d\theta_n \rvert$	$\lvert d\phi_n \rvert$
5°	0.9005	0.8627	0.8250	5.27°	1.0
10°	0.9281	0.8529	0.7777	2.82°	1.0
20°	0.9619	0.8138	0.6657	1.65°	1.0
30°	0.9665	0.7500	0.5335	1.33°	1.0
40°	0.9418	0.6634	0.3851	1.25°	1.0
50°	0.8884	0.5567	0.2250	1.33°	1.0
60°	0.8080	0.4330	0.0580	1.57°	1.0

3) Errors as a Function of Zenith Angle Magnitude: Table III shows the errors in surface orientation due to the magnitude of the zenith angle settings of the light source in the presence of errors in image intensity and input zenith angle. Table III is made for the case with $\theta_n = 30°$ and $\phi_n = 60°$. The angular error $\lvert d\theta_n \rvert$ is quite large at small values of θ_l.

From (11) and (13) we find that the numerator and the denominator on the right side of (11) are both proportional to $\tan \theta_l$. As θ_l tends to zero, both numerator and denominator tend to zero. This explains the large magnitude of $d\theta_n$ at small values of θ_l. Moreover, when the three sources are very close to one another ($\theta_l = 5°$), the differences among I_1, I_2, I_3 are quite small. On the other hand, if θ_l is sufficiently large ($\theta_l = 60°$), the surface may not receive sufficient light from one of the three sources, as evident from Table III.

4) Noncollimation of Light Sources: If the incident light is noncollimated, there will be spatial variations in θ_l and ϕ_l for the same light source. These effects will appear in the computations as errors in angular measurements of θ_l and ϕ_l, as shown in Table II.

C. Perspective Distortion

By perspective transformations, the coordinates of the image point are $[x_i, y_i]$ for an object point $[x, y, z]$, where $x_i = fx/(f + d - z)$ and $y_i = fy/(f + d - z)$. Here, d is the distance along z-axis between the origin of the object coordinate system and the origin of the image coordinate system and f is the focal length of the lens. Hence, the image intensities at pixel location $[x_i, y_i]$ should be used to calculate the surface gradients at the object point $[x, y, z]$. The present system assumes an orthographic projection system and uses image intensities at $[x_i, y_i]$ to compute gradient at $[x_i, y_i, z]$. In this case, the output surface profile may appear distorted, only if the object is large as compared to viewing distance.

For zenith angles of surface normals below 7.5° in magnitude ($\tan \theta_n = \theta_n$ in radians to two decimal places when $\theta_n < 7.5°$), difficulties exist for a meaningful interpretation of ϕ_n. Under these circumstances, the value of ϕ_n can be anywhere in the range of 0–360°. It is also difficult to estimate the surface normal orientations when θ_n exceeds about 40°, since usually the surface point enters the occlusion region of one light source or the other or may be partially occluded by other parts of the object. This problem may be addressed by using more than three light sources, more than one camera, and by a selective choice of three sources depending on the surface point location and apparent orientation [7].

V. EXPERIMENTAL RESULTS

Experiments to estimate surface normals were performed using various industrial objects. Calibration techniques and optical arrangements were emphasized. For noise reduction purposes, each of the three different 64 × 64 image arrays I_{ijk} where: $i = 1, 2, \cdots, 64$, $j = 1, 2, \cdots, 64$, and $k = 1, 2, 3$ was obtained by averaging 25 picture frames taken under identical conditions, such that

$$I_{ijk} = (1/25) \sum_{l=1}^{25} I_{ijkl}.$$

After obtaining the gray scale data for the three image arrays, each of the image arrays is also convolved with a noise reduction mask,

$$H = \frac{1}{9} \begin{bmatrix} 1 & 1 & 1 \\ 1 & 1 & 1 \\ 1 & 1 & 1 \end{bmatrix}$$

to reduce the effect of noise in the TV camera. Needle diagrams and histograms of computed surface angles were made for the test objects. The objects included 1) a white planar bookcover, 2) a metal cylinder, 3) a conduit junction box, 4) a nylon sphere, 5) a connecting rod, and 6) a soup can with different colors. These were tested at various orientations.

The empty patches in the needle diagrams correspond to regions having cast shadows or highlights. These diagrams represent a viewer centered description of the object surface (Figs. 2–6).

In the histograms, the range of θ_n is from 0–90° whereas the range for ϕ_n is from 0–360°. The histogram bin width is 5°. The histograms for the planar objects show that the computed normal directions over the entire image are consistently within an error range of ±5°. For better verification, the planar bookcover was mounted at various fixed orientations. The results were found to conform with the set orientations. Fig. 2(b) shows a unique surface normal at $20° \leqslant \theta_n \leqslant 25°$ and $185° \leqslant \phi_n \leqslant 190°$. Fig. 3(c).(i) shows the zenith angles from 0–40°. Fig. 3(c).(ii) indicates that most of the azimuth angles are at $170° \leqslant \phi_n \leqslant 180°$ and at $340° \leqslant \phi_n 350°$. At high values of θ_n, many surface points enter the occlusion regions of at least one light source which explains the gradual decay of the histogram plot in Fig. 3(c).(i) after $\theta_n = 30°$; it also caused the lack of symmetry in the heights of the two peaks in the histogram plot in Fig. 3(c).(ii). The sharp drop between 20 and 25° in the θ_n histogram is due to experimental errors. The magnitudes of such errors in θ_n and ϕ_n histograms are approximately ±5 and ±10°, respectively.

The software for picture taking and storing image data were written in Fortran and run on a Computer Automation LSI 2/20 computer which was linked to an ITEL AS/5 computer and to a Grinnel GMR-26 raster graphics display generator. Programs for surface angle computations, sensitivity analysis, and needle diagrams were run on the ITEL AS/5 computer

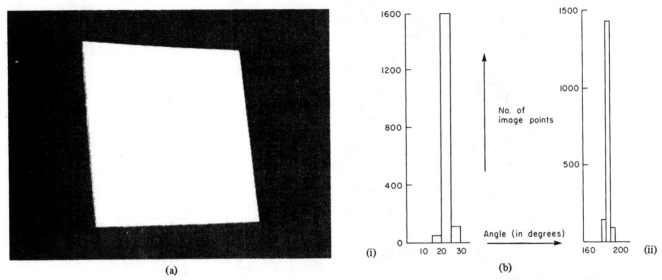

Fig. 2. An inclined planar bookcover. (a) Picture of the bookcover. (b) Histograms for surface point orientations: (i) θ_n histogram, (ii) ϕ_n histogram.

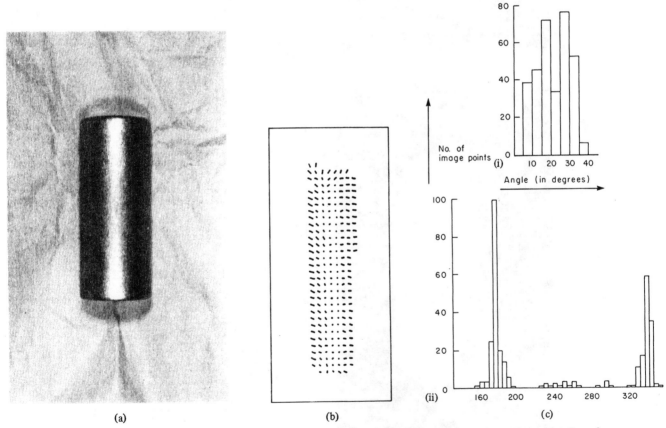

Fig. 3. A metallic upright cylinder. (a) Picture of the cylinder. (b) Needle diagram of surface point orientation of a metallic upright cylinder. (c) Histograms for surface point orientations: (i) θ_n histogram, (ii) ϕ_n histogram.

using interactive IBM CALL-MVS Fortran and on batch IBM OS Fortran IV (H EXTENDED) compilers. A Tektronis 4006 graphic terminal was used for graphic purposes.

The final verification of experimental results was done by using the experimentally computed surface normals of a solid sphere 1.5 in in diameter. Theoretical values of surface normals were also computed for every pixel in the needle diagram, as follows.

The center of the needle diagram (collinear with the center of the sphere and along the optical axis) can be estimated at location (27, 28) where row = 27 and column = 28 from the experimental data for surface normals. The radius for the sphere in terms of number of pixels was computed by using the relationship $r = s/\xi$, where ξ = angle in radians subtended by an arc on the surface of the sphere joining the center of the needle diagram and an extreme end point in a row at the center of the sphere, r = the radius of the sphere in pixels, and s = the length of the arc in pixels. Using (27, 28) as an initial

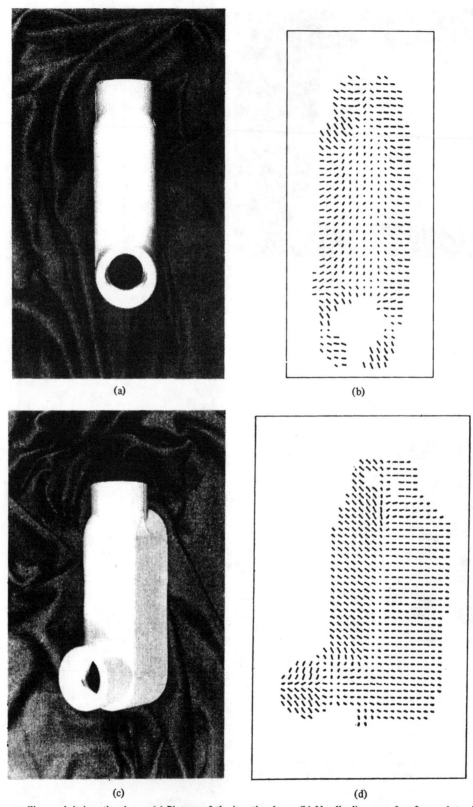

Fig. 4. A metallic conduit junction box. (a) Picture of the junction box. (b) Needle diagram of surface point orientation of a metallic conduit junction box. (c) Picture of the metallic conduit junction box from another view. (d) Needle diagram of surface point orientation of a metallic conduit junction box from another view.

guess for the center and r as the initial guess for radius, a hill-climbing algorithm [24] was used for better estimates.

The deviation between the theoretical and experimental values of surface normals is shown in Fig. 7 [the asymmetry with respect to the center is because of many pixels falling into the occlusion regions; a more symmetric pattern could be obtained by reducing the magnitude of the lower threshold used on the camera intensity data; the same asymmetry can be seen in Fig. 8(a)–(d)]. The deviation was computed at each pixel location, as shown in Fig. 8. The probable causes

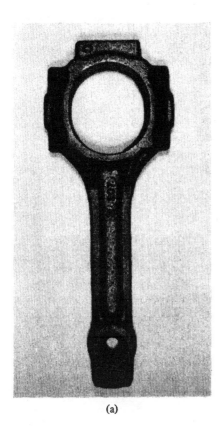

(a)

(b)

Fig. 5. A cast iron connecting rod. (a) Picture of the connecting rod. (b) Needle diagram of surface point orientation of a cast iron connecting rod.

(a)

(b)

Fig. 6. A textured soup can. (a) Picture of the soup can. (b) Needle diagram of surface point orientation of a textured soup can. (The absence of computed normals occurred due to specular reflection.)

of these deviations were sought using the sensitivity equations. For every theoretically computed surface normal corresponding to every pixel in the needle diagram, a perturbation scheme was used based on the sensitivity analysis, to find a good correlation with experimental values. It is evident from the results of this perturbation involving 204 pixels that a match between experi-

mental and theoretical values was obtained at many pixel locations for intensity errors within 2 percent and errors in the measurement of angles of the order of $4°$. The seven parameters for each pixel were $d\theta_l$, $d\phi_{1l}$, $d\phi_{2l}$, $d\phi_{3l}$, dI_{1l}, dI_{2l}, dI_{3l}. Next, an analysis was made to determine the magnitude of errors attributable to the three light sources, using the same seven pixel parameters just listed. The magnitude of error may differ from one light source to another, but will be consistent over the entire image for each light source. From sensitivity analysis, it is shown that two major sources of light source errors were 1) improper measurement of light source orientation, 2) intensity mismatches among the light sources. Using a least mean square error analysis, it was found that the following magnitudes of these errors, when substituted in sensitivity analysis equations, generally accounted for the differences, if any, between the experimental and theoretical values of the surface normals of the sphere:

$$d\theta_l = 0°, \quad d\phi_{1l} = -14°, \quad d\phi_{2l} = 8°, \quad d\phi_{3l} = -5°,$$

$$dI_{1l} = -0.02, \quad dI_{2l} = 0.05, \quad dI_{3l} = 0.05$$

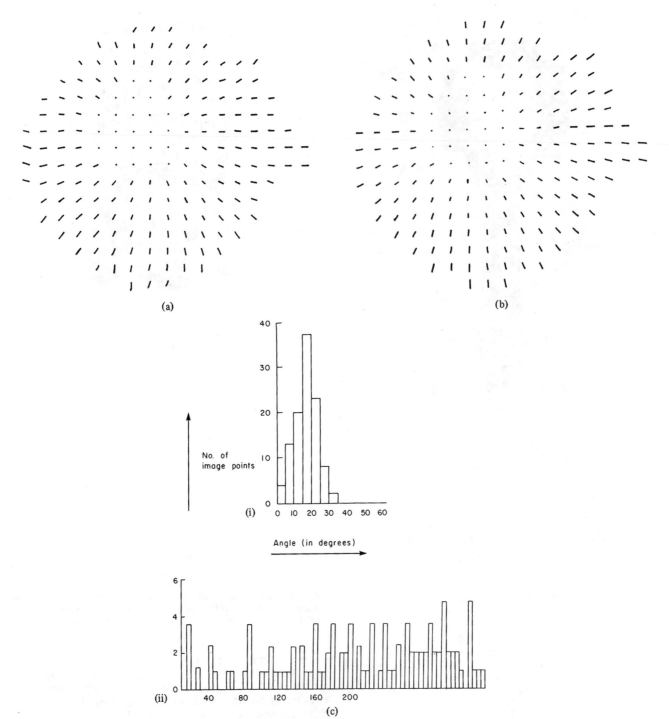

Fig. 7. (a) Experimentally determined surface normals of a sphere. (b) Theoretically determined surface normals of the sphere. (c) Histograms for surface point orientations: (i) θ_n histogram, (ii) ϕ_n histogram.

where dI_{1l}, dI_{2l}, and dI_{3l} are the errors in image intensities due to errors in intensity of the three light sources. The magnitude of error in θ_n and ϕ_n, as output from the sensitivity analysis based on the light source and intensity errors mentioned above, will be called $|d\theta_n(\text{SENS})|$ and $|d\phi_n(\text{SENS})|$.

The magnitudes of $|d\theta_n| = |\theta_n(\text{EXPERIMENTAL}) - \theta_n(\text{THEORETICAL})|$ and $|d\phi_n| = |\phi_n(\text{EXPERIMENTAL}) - \phi_n(\text{THEORETICAL})|$ were shown in Fig. 8(a) and (b). The values of $|d(d\theta_n)| = |d\theta_n - d\theta_n(\text{SENS})|$ and $|d(d\phi_n)| = |d\phi_n - d\phi_n(\text{SENS})|$ are shown in Fig. 8(c) and (d). Low values of $|d(d\theta_n)|$ and $|d(d\phi_n)|$ over the entire image demonstrate that the light source errors were the major contributors to the magnitudes of $|d\theta_n|$ and $|d\phi_n|$ for the experimental data collected. Therefore, it is possible

to get more accurate results by careful measurements of light source angles.

Next, the nature of the TV camera noise associated with each pixel was investigated. A pixel correction scheme was applied such that it is consistent in the three images but it varies in magnitude from one pixel to another. As Fig. 8(e) indicates, a correction of pixel intensity of the order of 0.04 made all the values of $|d(d\theta_n)|$ equal to or less than $5°$. However, pixel correction cannot be applied to $|d(d\phi_n)|$, because an equal change in intensity in corresponding pixels in the three images does not change the value of $d\phi_n$ (as shown in Table I).

It can be noticed that $|d(d\theta_n)|$ still has some high values at

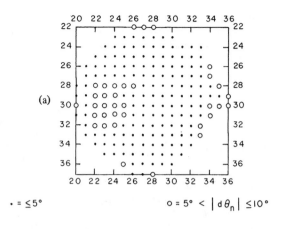

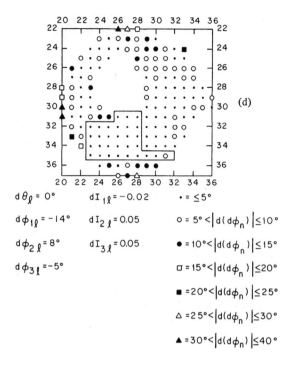

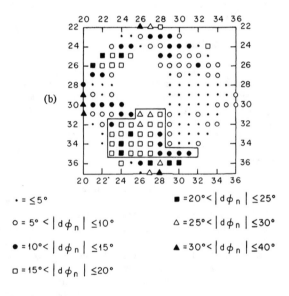

$\cdot = \leq 5°$

$o = 5° < |d\theta_n| \leq 10°$

$d\theta_\ell = 0°$ $dI_{1\ell} = -0.02$ $\cdot = \leq 5°$

$d\phi_{1\ell} = -14°$ $dI_{2\ell} = 0.05$ $o = 5° < |d(d\phi_n)| \leq 10°$

$d\phi_{2\ell} = 8°$ $dI_{3\ell} = 0.05$ $\bullet = 10° < |d(d\phi_n)| \leq 15°$

$d\phi_{3\ell} = -5°$ $\square = 15° < |d(d\phi_n)| \leq 20°$

$\blacksquare = 20° < |d(d\phi_n)| \leq 25°$

$\triangle = 25° < |d(d\phi_n)| \leq 30°$

$\blacktriangle = 30° < |d(d\phi_n)| \leq 40°$

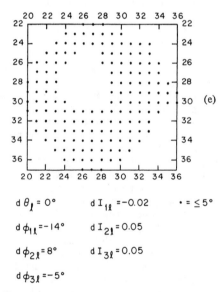

$\cdot = \leq 5°$

$o = 5° < |d\phi_n| \leq 10°$ $\triangle = 25° < |d\phi_n| \leq 30°$

$\bullet = 10° < |d\phi_n| \leq 15°$ $\blacktriangle = 30° < |d\phi_n| \leq 40°$

$\square = 15° < |d\phi_n| \leq 20°$

$\blacksquare = 20° < |d\phi_n| \leq 25°$

$d\theta_\ell = 0°$ $dI_{1\ell} = -0.02$ $\cdot = \leq 5°$

$d\phi_{1\ell} = -14°$ $dI_{2\ell} = 0.05$

$d\phi_{2\ell} = 8°$ $dI_{3\ell} = 0.05$

$d\phi_{3\ell} = -5°$

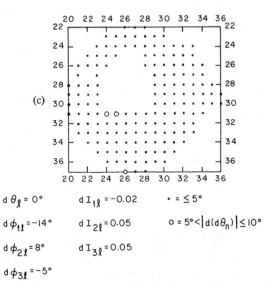

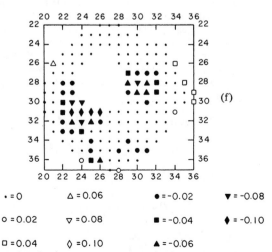

$d\theta_\ell = 0°$ $dI_{1\ell} = -0.02$ $\cdot = \leq 5°$

$d\phi_{1\ell} = -14°$ $dI_{2\ell} = 0.05$ $o = 5° < |d(d\theta_n)| \leq 10°$

$d\phi_{2\ell} = 8°$ $dI_{3\ell} = 0.05$

$d\phi_{3\ell} = -5°$

$\cdot = 0$	$\triangle = 0.06$	$\bullet = -0.02$	$\blacktriangledown = -0.08$
$o = 0.02$	$\triangledown = 0.08$	$\blacksquare = -0.04$	$\blacklozenge = -0.10$
$\square = 0.04$	$\lozenge = 0.10$	$\blacktriangle = -0.06$	

FIG. 8. (a) Deviation in $|d\theta_n| = |\theta_n(\text{EXP}) - \theta_n(\text{THEORY})|$. (b) Deviation in $|d\phi_n| = |\phi_n(\text{EXP}) - \phi_n(\text{THEORY})|$. (c) Magnitude of $|d(d\theta_n)| = |d\theta_n - d\theta_n(\text{SENS})|$. (d) Magnitude of $|d(d\phi_n)| = |d\phi_n - d\phi_n(\text{SENS})|$. (e) Magnitude of $|d(d\theta_n)|$ after light source and pixel correction. (f) Nature of pixel correction required to make $|d(d\theta_n)| \leq 3°$.

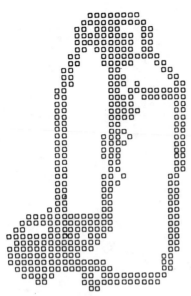

Fig. 9. Edge extraction from surface orientations of a conduit junction box.

the edge pixels which may be attributed to the fact that the intensities at edge pixels are obtained by averaging the intensity over a window partially covered by the surface and partially covered by the background and the nonexistence of various differentials.

Furthermore, another pixel correction scheme was used in order to obtain $|d(d\theta_n)|$ values equal to or less than $3°$. This required correction of pixel intensities ranging from 0.00–0.10 [Fig. 8(f)]. The estimated magnitude of detector noise is less than or equal to 0.04 in normalized gray scale intensity. The pixels requiring a correction value of more than 0.04 in intensity may have errors due to 1) geometric irregularities in the surface of the sphere, 2) transfer characteristics of the camera, since the pixels with high intensities requiring high correction magnitudes are located near the center of the sphere, and 3) noncollimation of light sources.

This analysis proves that even in the absence of continuity information or under a time constraint not permitting iterative computations, it is possible to estimate surface normal orientations quite accurately. It also validates the reflectance equations and sensitivity formulations presented in this paper.

The surface orientations given in the needle diagrams can be used to extract geometric edges. Edge extraction from orientation information is often more useful than intensity edge extraction because it is based on the three-dimensional properties of an object instead of its surface reflectivity variations. In the latter case, there may be errors due to camera noise, shadows, blooming, transfer characteristic and intensity thresholding. Thus, false intensity edges may appear. The following gradient magnitude operator was used to extract edges from the orientation data of the conduit junction box (Fig. 9):

$$\theta_n'(i, j) = [\theta_n(i, j + 1) - \theta_n(i, j - 1)]^2$$

$$+ [\theta_n(i + 1, j) - \theta_n(i - 1, j)]^2;$$

$$\phi_n'(i, j) = [\phi_n(i, j + 1) - \phi_n(i, j - 1)]^2$$

$$+ [\phi_n(i + 1, j) - \phi_n(i - 1, j)]^2;$$

$$G(i, j) = [\theta_n'(i, j) + \phi_n'(i, j)]^{0.5};$$

$$H(i, j) = \begin{cases} 4 & \text{if } G(i, j) \geqslant 0.5 \text{ radians} \\ 0 & \text{if } G(i, j) < 0.5 \text{ radians} \end{cases} \tag{30}$$

where $\theta_n(i, j)$ and $\phi_n(i, j)$ denote the zenith and azimuth angles of the surface normal corresponding to location (i, j) in the 64×64 initial images. $H(i, j)$ represents a binary edge detection operator.

VI. CONCLUSIONS

A study has been conducted which provides insight into the practical application of the principle of radiometric stereo. Difficulties, remedies, and accuracy are addressed. The sensitivity analysis and the experimental setup used for the investigations show that it is possible to apply the theory of radiometric stereo in practice. It can be implemented using normal light sources and non-Lambertian objects in an industrial world, in absence of strong specular reflection and shadows. It also lays a foundation for further work involving cast shadows, mutual reflection, highlights, changes in light source geometry and wavelength, and the detection of light sources [25]. This technique may also be integrated to industrial robot systems for the inspection of industrial products or for acquiring a workpiece [26]. The success of this method lies on the identification of the major errors and their contribution in terms of sensitivity analysis.

The results of experiments on a broad range of workpieces, including metallic, nonmetallic, planar, curved and textured objects indicate the generality of the technique. Various feature based methods have been suggested in the past for estimating the pose of a workpiece [27]. But no general technique for extracting local features on many workpieces at arbitrary viewing angles has been proposed, as yet. The radiometric technique does not suffer from this shortcoming. For unique applications radiometric stereo can be improved using the characteristics of combined reflectance or various approximations to Lambertian reflection [3], [28], [29].

The sensitivity equations were derived to investigate into the error performance of this technique. The relative impact of the deviations in magnitudes of various variables was studied [30]. By using a geometric model of a sphere and experimental data, it was found that the sensitivity equations can be used successfully to explain the differences between theory and practice. However, this sensitivity analysis is valid only for small errors. Hence, errors due to specular or mutual reflection and shadows cannot be explained by this analysis.

The present work uses direct computations as opposed to time consuming iterative procedures. The roots of direct computations are very often more prone to roundoff [31] and systematic errors compared to iterative solutions. Our calculations show that it is possible to achieve as good an accuracy as $5°$ for zenith angles and $10°$ for azimuth angles (except at edge pixels and pixels with very high or very low intensities). The results can be improved by a better calibration of camera transfer characteristics. The speed of execution of the software can be also improved by using assembly language, hardware modules for floating-point arithmetic, and lookup tables for surface normal computations from intensity data. It is possible to obtain information about orientation discontinuities and curvatures of optically opaque objects using these techniques in the absence of strong specular reflection or shadows. The object size should be kept quite small with respect to the viewing distance.

APPENDIX A
GRADIENT REPRESENTATIONS

Surface gradients can be represented by using an object coordinate system with axes x, y, and z. For $p_n = \partial z/\partial x$ and $q_n = \partial z/\partial y$, two vectors on the surface of an object can be defined as $(1, 0, p_n)$ and $(0, 1, q_n)$. The surface normal vector $\tilde{n}$ can be obtained by taking the cross-product of these two surface vectors. Hence, $\tilde{n} = (1, 0, p_n) \times (0, 1, q_n) = (-p_n, -q_n, 1)$. Similarly, the light source vector $\tilde{l}$ can also be written as [3] (Fig. 10) $\tilde{l} = (-p_1, -q_1, 1)$.

$$p_n(I_1 A_1 p_{3l} - I_3 A_3 p_{1l}) = (1 + q_n q_{1l})I_3 A_3 - (1 + q_n q_{3l})I_1 A_1.$$
(39)

Therefore, from (37), (38), and (39) we get (11) by elimination of p_n and (12) by substitution.

APPENDIX C
SENSITIVITY ANALYSIS OF ERRORS

From Appendix B, we get

$$q_n = f[I_1, I_2, I_3, \theta_l, \phi_{1l}, \phi_{2l}, \phi_{3l}]$$
(40)

and

$$p_n = g[I_1, I_2, I_3, \theta_l, \phi_{1l}, \phi_{2l}, \phi_{3l}]$$
$$= F[q_n, I_1, I_2, I_3, \theta_l, \phi_{1l}, \phi_{2l}, \phi_{3l}].$$
(41)

Hence, using error analysis [33], we obtain

$$dq_n = \sum_{i=1}^{3} \frac{\partial f}{\partial I_i} dI_i + \frac{\partial f}{\partial \theta_l} d\theta_l + \sum_{i=1}^{3} \frac{\partial f}{\partial \phi_{il}} d\phi_{il}$$
(42)

and

$$dp_n = \sum_{i=1}^{3} \frac{\partial F}{\partial I_i} dI_i + \frac{\partial F}{\partial q_n} dq_n + \frac{\partial F}{\partial \theta_l} d\theta_l$$

$$+ \sum_{i=1}^{3} \frac{\partial F}{\partial \phi_{il}} d\phi_{il}.$$
(43)

Equation (11) can be modified as

$$q_n = \frac{1}{3} n = \frac{1}{3}\left[\frac{n_1}{d_1} + \frac{n_2}{d_2} + \frac{n_3}{d_3}\right]$$
(44)

and (12) can be modified as

$$p_n = \frac{1}{3} m = \frac{1}{3}\left[\frac{m_1}{D_1} + \frac{m_2}{D_2} + \frac{m_3}{D_3}\right]$$
(45)

where

$$n_1 = I_1 I_2 \cos\phi_{3l} - I_2^2 \cos\phi_{3l} + I_2 I_3 \cos\phi_{2l} - I_1 I_2 \cos\phi_{2l}$$
$$+ I_2^2 \cos\phi_{1l} - I_2 I_3 \cos\phi_{1l},$$
(46)

$$n_2 = I_2 I_3 \cos\phi_{1l} - I_3^2 \cos\phi_{1l} + I_3 I_1 \cos\phi_{3l} - I_2 I_3 \cos\phi_{3l}$$
$$+ I_3^2 \cos\phi_{2l} - I_3 I_1 \cos\phi_{2l},$$
(47)

$$n_3 = I_3 I_1 \cos\phi_{2l} - I_1^2 \cos\phi_{2l} + I_1 I_2 \cos\phi_{1l} - I_3 I_1 \cos\phi_{1l}$$
$$+ I_1^2 \cos\phi_{3l} - I_1 I_2 \cos\phi_{3l},$$
(48)

$$d_1 = \tan\theta_l(-I_2 I_3 \cos\phi_{1l} \sin\phi_{2l} - I_1 I_2 \cos\phi_{2l} \sin\phi_{3l}$$
$$+ I_2^2 \sin\phi_{3l} \cos\phi_{1l} - I_2^2 \cos\phi_{3l} \sin\phi_{1l}$$
$$+ I_2 I_3 \sin\phi_{1l} \cos\phi_{2l} + I_1 I_2 \cos\phi_{3l} \sin\phi_{2l}),$$
(49)

$$d_2 = \tan\theta_l(-I_3 I_1 \cos\phi_{2l} \sin\phi_{3l} - I_2 I_3 \cos\phi_{3l} \sin\phi_{1l}$$
$$+ I_3^2 \sin\phi_{1l} \cos\phi_{2l} - I_3^2 \cos\phi_{1l} \sin\phi_{2l}$$
$$+ I_3 I_1 \sin\phi_{2l} \cos\phi_{3l} + I_2 I_3 \cos\phi_{1l} \sin\phi_{3l}),$$
(50)

$$d_3 = \tan\theta_l(-I_1 I_2 \cos\phi_{3l} \sin\phi_{1l} - I_3 I_1 \cos\phi_{1l} \sin\phi_{2l}$$
$$+ I_1^2 \sin\phi_{2l} \cos\phi_{3l} - I_1^2 \cos\phi_{2l} \sin\phi_{3l}$$
$$+ I_1 I_2 \sin\phi_{3l} \cos\phi_{1l} + I_3 I_1 \cos\phi_{2l} \sin\phi_{1l}),$$
(51)

$$m_1 = (I_3 - I_1) + (I_1 \sin\phi_{3l} - I_3 \sin\phi_{1l})q_n \tan\theta_l,$$
(52)

$$m_2 = (I_1 - I_2) + (I_2 \sin\phi_{1l} - I_1 \sin\phi_{2l})q_n \tan\theta_l,$$
(53)

$$m_3 = (I_2 - I_3) + (I_3 \sin\phi_{2l} - I_2 \sin\phi_{3l})q_n \tan\theta_l,$$
(54)

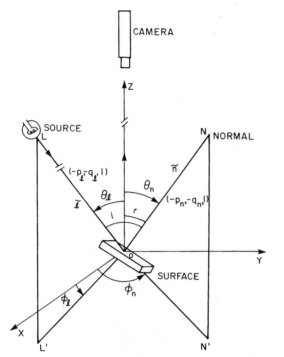

Fig. 10. Experimental imaging geometry. i = angle of incidence, r = angle of reflection, n = surface normal vector, l = light source vector.

APPENDIX B
SOLUTION OF REFLECTANCE EQUATIONS

The basic equations for reflectance calculations using a stationary camera are

$$I_1(x, y) = p(x, y) \frac{1 + p_n p_{1l} + q_n q_{1l}}{\sqrt{1 + p_n^2 + q_n^2} \sqrt{1 + p_{1l}^2 + q_{1l}^2}}$$
(31)

$$I_2(x, y) = p(x, y) \frac{1 + p_n p_{2l} + q_n q_{2l}}{\sqrt{1 + p_n^2 + q_n^2} \sqrt{1 + p_{2l}^2 + q_{2l}^2}}$$
(32)

$$I_3(x, y) = p(x, y) \frac{1 + p_n p_{3l} + q_n q_{3l}}{\sqrt{1 + p_n^2 + q_n^2} \sqrt{1 + p_{3l}^2 + q_{3l}^2}}$$
(33)

where, I_1, I_2, I_3 are the intensities, (p_{1l}, q_{1l}), (p_{2l}, q_{2l}) and (p_{3l}, q_{3l}) are the three light source gradients and (p_n, q_n) is the surface gradient.

Assuming $A_1 = \sqrt{1 + p_{1l}^2 + q_{1l}^2}$, $A_2 = \sqrt{1 + p_{2l}^2 + q_{2l}^2}$ and $A_3 = \sqrt{1 + p_{3l}^2 + q_{3l}^2}$, we get by substitution of A_1, A_2 and A_3 and elimination of $p(x, y)$ from (4), (5), and (6),

$$\frac{I_1 A_1}{I_2 A_2} = \frac{1 + p_n p_{1l} + q_n q_{1l}}{1 + p_n p_{2l} + q_n q_{2l}}$$
(34)

$$\frac{I_2 A_2}{I_3 A_3} = \frac{1 + p_n p_{2l} + q_n q_{2l}}{1 + p_n p_{3l} + q_n q_{3l}}$$
(35)

and

$$\frac{I_3 A_3}{I_1 A_1} = \frac{1 + p_n p_{3l} + q_n q_{3l}}{1 + p_n p_{1l} + q_n q_{1l}}.$$
(36)

From the above equations, we get by cross multiplications and transpositions,

$$p_n(I_2 A_2 p_{1l} - I_1 A_1 p_{2l}) = (1 + q_n q_{2l})I_1 A_1 - (1 + q_n q_{1l})I_2 A_2$$
(37)

$$p_n(I_3 A_3 p_{2l} - I_2 A_2 p_{3l}) = (1 + q_n q_{3l})I_2 A_2 - (1 + q_n q_{2l})I_3 A_3$$
(38)

$$D_1 = \tan \theta_l (I_3 \cos \phi_{1l} - I_1 \cos \phi_{3l}), \tag{55}$$

$$D_2 = \tan \theta_l (I_1 \cos \phi_{2l} - I_2 \cos \phi_{1l}), \tag{56}$$

$$D_3 = \tan \theta_l (I_2 \cos \phi_{3l} - I_3 \cos \phi_{2l}). \tag{57}$$

Therefore, we can determine

$$
\begin{aligned}
\frac{\partial f}{\partial \phi_{1l}} = \frac{1}{3} \big[& \{ d_1(I_2 I_3 - I_2^2) \sin \phi_{1l} - n_1 \tan \theta_l (I_2 I_3 \sin \phi_{1l} \\
& \cdot \sin \phi_{2l} - I_2^2 \sin \phi_{3l} \sin \phi_{1l} - I_2^2 \cos \phi_{3l} \cos \phi_{1l} \\
& + I_2 I_3 \cos \phi_{1l} \cos \phi_{2l}) \}/d_1^2 \\
& + \{ d_2(I_3^2 - I_2 I_3) \sin \phi_{1l} - n_2 \tan \theta_l (-I_2 I_3 \cos \phi_{3l} \\
& \cdot \cos \phi_{1l} + I_3^2 \cos \phi_{1l} \cos \phi_{2l} + I_3^2 \sin \phi_{1l} \sin \phi_{2l} \\
& - I_2 I_3 \sin \phi_{1l} \sin \phi_{3l}) \}/d_2^2 \\
& + \{ d_3(I_3 I_1 - I_1 I_2) \sin \phi_{1l} - n_3 \tan \theta_l (-I_1 I_2 \cos \phi_{3l} \\
& \cdot \cos \phi_{1l} + I_3 I_1 \sin \phi_{1l} \sin \phi_{2l} - I_1 I_2 \sin \phi_{3l} \sin \phi_{1l} \\
& + I_3 I_1 \cos \phi_{2l} \cos \phi_{1l}) \}/d_3^2 \big],
\end{aligned}
\tag{58}
$$

$$
\begin{aligned}
\frac{\partial f}{\partial \phi_{2l}} = \frac{1}{3} \big[& \{ d_1(I_1 I_2 - I_2 I_3) \sin \phi_{2l} - n_1 \tan \theta_l (-I_2 I_3 \\
& \cdot \cos \phi_{1l} \cos \phi_{2l} + I_1 I_2 \sin \phi_{2l} \sin \phi_{3l} - I_2 I_3 \sin \phi_{1l} \\
& \cdot \sin \phi_{2l} + I_1 I_2 \cos \phi_{3l} \cos \phi_{2l}) \}/d_1^2 \\
& + \{ d_2(I_3 I_1 - I_3^2) \sin \phi_{2l} - n_2 \tan \theta_l (I_3 I_1 \sin \phi_{2l} \\
& \cdot \sin \phi_{3l} - I_3^2 \sin \phi_{1l} \sin \phi_{2l} - I_3^2 \cos \phi_{1l} \cos \phi_{2l} \\
& + I_3 I_1 \cos \phi_{2l} \cos \phi_{3l}) \}/d_2^2 \\
& + \{ d_3(I_1^2 - I_3 I_1) \sin \phi_{2l} - n_3 \tan \theta_l (-I_3 I_1 \cos \phi_{1l} \\
& \cdot \cos \phi_{2l} + I_1^2 \cos \phi_{2l} \cos \phi_{3l} + I_1^2 \sin \phi_{2l} \sin \phi_{3l} \\
& - I_3 I_1 \sin \phi_{2l} \sin \phi_{1l}) \}/d_3^2 \big],
\end{aligned}
\tag{59}
$$

$$
\begin{aligned}
\frac{\partial f}{\partial \phi_{3l}} = \frac{1}{3} \big[& \{ d_1(I_2^2 - I_1 I_2) \sin \phi_{3l} - n_1 \tan \theta_l (-I_1 I_2 \cos \phi_{2l} \\
& \cdot \cos \phi_{3l} + I_2^2 \cos \phi_{3l} \cos \phi_{1l} + I_2^2 \sin \phi_{3l} \sin \phi_{1l} \\
& - I_1 I_2 \sin \phi_{3l} \sin \phi_{2l}) \}/d_1^2 \\
& + \{ d_2(I_2 I_3 - I_3 I_1) \sin \phi_{3l} - n_2 \tan \theta_l (-I_3 I_1 \cos \phi_{2l} \\
& \cdot \cos \phi_{3l} + I_2 I_3 \sin \phi_{3l} \sin \phi_{1l} - I_3 I_1 \sin \phi_{2l} \sin \phi_{3l} \\
& + I_2 I_3 \cos \phi_{1l} \cos \phi_{3l}) \}/d_2^2 \\
& + \{ d_3(I_1 I_2 - I_1^2) \sin \phi_{3l} - n_3 \tan \theta_l (I_1 I_2 \sin \phi_{3l} \\
& \cdot \sin \phi_{1l} - I_1^2 \sin \phi_{2l} \sin \phi_{3l} - I_1^2 \cos \phi_{2l} \cos \phi_{3l} \\
& + I_1 I_2 \cos \phi_{3l} \cos \phi_{1l}) \}/d_3^2 \big],
\end{aligned}
\tag{60}
$$

$$
\begin{aligned}
\frac{\partial f}{\partial I_1} = \frac{1}{3} \big[& \{ I_2(d_1(\cos \phi_{3l} - \cos \phi_{2l}) - n_1 \\
& \cdot \tan \theta_l (\sin (\phi_{2l} - \phi_{3l}))) /d_1^2 \} \\
& + \{ I_3(d_2(\cos \phi_{3l} - \cos \phi_{2l}) - n_2 \\
& \cdot \tan \theta_l (\sin (\phi_{2l} + \phi_{3l}))) /d_2^2 \} \\
& + \{ d_3(I_3 \cos \phi_{2l} - 2I_1 \cos \phi_{2l} + I_2 \cos \phi_{1l} - I_3 \\
& \cdot \cos \phi_{1l} + 2I_1 \cos \phi_{3l} - I_2 \cos \phi_{3l}) - n_3 \\
& \cdot \tan \theta_l (2I_1 \cos \phi_{3l} \sin \phi_{2l} - I_3 \cos \phi_{1l} \sin \phi_{2l} - I_2 \\
& \cdot \cos \phi_{3l} \sin \phi_{1l} + I_3 \sin \phi_{1l} \cos \phi_{2l} + I_2 \cos \phi_{1l} \\
& \cdot \sin \phi_{3l} - 2I_1 \cos \phi_{2l} \sin \phi_{3l}) \}/d_3^2 \big],
\end{aligned}
\tag{61}
$$

$$
\begin{aligned}
\frac{\partial f}{\partial I_2} = \frac{1}{3} \big[& \{ d_1(I_1 \cos \phi_{3l} - 2I_2 \cos \phi_{3l} + I_3 \cos \phi_{2l} - I_1 \\
& \cdot \cos \phi_{2l} + 2I_2 \cos \phi_{1l} - I_3 \cos \phi_{1l}) - n_1 \\
& \cdot \tan \theta_l (2I_2 \cos \phi_{1l} \sin \phi_{3l} - I_1 \cos \phi_{2l} \sin \phi_{3l} - I_3 \\
& \cdot \cos \phi_{1l} \sin \phi_{2l} + I_1 \sin \phi_{2l} \cos \phi_{3l} + I_3 \cos \phi_{2l} \\
& \cdot \sin \phi_{1l} - 2I_2 \cos \phi_{3l} \sin \phi_{1l}) \}/d_1^2 \\
& + \{ I_3(d_2(\cos \phi_{1l} - \cos \phi_{3l}) - n_2 \\
& \cdot \tan \theta_l (\sin (\phi_{3l} - \phi_{1l}))) /d_2^2 \} \\
& + \{ I_1(d_3(\cos \phi_{1l} - \cos \phi_{3l}) - n_3 \\
& \cdot \tan \theta_l (\sin (\phi_{3l} + \phi_{1l}))) /d_3^2 \big],
\end{aligned}
\tag{62}
$$

$$
\begin{aligned}
\frac{\partial f}{\partial I_3} = \frac{1}{3} \big[& \{ I_2(d_1 (\cos \phi_{2l} - \cos \phi_{1l}) - n_1 \\
& \cdot \tan \theta_l (\sin (\phi_{1l} + \phi_{2l}))) /d_1^2 \} \\
& + \{ d_2(I_2 \cos \phi_{1l} - 2I_3 \cos \phi_{1l} + I_1 \cos \phi_{3l} - I_2 \\
& \cdot \cos \phi_{3l} + 2I_3 \cos \phi_{2l} - I_1 \cos \phi_{2l}) - n_2 \tan \theta_l (2I_3 \\
& \cdot \cos \phi_{2l} \sin \phi_{1l} - I_2 \cos \phi_{3l} \sin \phi_{1l} - I_1 \cos \phi_{2l} \\
& \cdot \sin \phi_{3l} + I_2 \sin \phi_{3l} \cos \phi_{1l} + I_1 \cos \phi_{3l} \\
& \cdot \sin \phi_{2l} - 2I_3 \cos \phi_{1l} \sin \phi_{2l}) \}/d_2^2 \} \\
& + \{ I_1(d_3(\cos \phi_{2l} - \cos \phi_{1l}) - n_3 \\
& \cdot \tan \theta_l (\sin (\phi_{1l} - \phi_{2l}))) /d_3^2 \big],
\end{aligned}
\tag{63}
$$

$$
\begin{aligned}
\frac{\partial f}{\partial \theta_l} = \frac{1}{3} \big[& \{ -n_1 d_1 /(\cos^2 \theta_l \tan \theta_l) \}/d_1^2 \\
& + \{ -n_2 d_2 /(\cos^2 \theta_l \tan \theta_l) \}/d_2^2 \\
& + \{ -n_3 d_3 /(\cos^2 \theta_l \tan \theta_l) \}/d_3^2 \big],
\end{aligned}
\tag{64}
$$

$$
\begin{aligned}
\frac{\partial F}{\partial \phi_{1l}} = \frac{1}{3} \big[& \{ D_1(-q_n \tan \theta_l I_3 \cos \phi_{1l}) - m_1(- \tan \theta_l I_3 \\
& \cdot \sin \phi_{1l}) \}/D_1^2 + \{ D_2(q_n \tan \theta_l I_2 \cos \phi_{1l}) \\
& - m_2(\tan \theta_l I_2 \sin \phi_{1l}) \}/D_2^2 \big],
\end{aligned}
\tag{65}
$$

$$
\begin{aligned}
\frac{\partial F}{\partial \phi_{2l}} = \frac{1}{3} \big[& \{ D_2(-q_n \tan \theta_l I_1 \cos \phi_{2l}) - m_2(- \tan \theta_l I_1 \\
& \cdot \sin \phi_{2l}) \}/D_2^2 + \{ D_3(q_n \tan \theta_l I_3 \cos \phi_{2l}) \\
& - m_3(\tan \theta_l I_3 \sin \phi_{2l}) \}/D_3^2 \big],
\end{aligned}
\tag{66}
$$

$$
\begin{aligned}
\frac{\partial F}{\partial \phi_{3l}} = \frac{1}{3} \big[& \{ D_1(q_n \tan \theta_l I_1 \cos \phi_{3l}) \\
& - m_1(\tan \theta_l I_1 \sin \phi_{3l}) \}/D_1^2 \\
& + \{ D_3(-q_n \tan \theta_l I_2 \cos \phi_{3l}) \\
& - m_3(- \tan \theta_l I_2 \sin \phi_{3l}) \}/D_3^2 \big],
\end{aligned}
\tag{67}
$$

$$
\begin{aligned}
\frac{\partial F}{\partial q_n} = \frac{1}{3} \big[& \{ D_1 \tan \theta_l (I_1 \sin \phi_{3l} - I_3 \sin \phi_{1l}) \}/D_1^2 \\
& + \{ D_2 \tan \theta_l (I_2 \sin \phi_{1l} - I_1 \sin \phi_{2l}) \}/D_2^2 \\
& + \{ D_3 \tan \theta_l (I_3 \sin \phi_{2l} - I_2 \sin \phi_{3l}) \}/D_3^2,
\end{aligned}
\tag{68}
$$

$$\frac{\partial F}{\partial \theta_l} = \frac{1}{3} \left[\left\{ D_1 q_n \frac{1}{\cos^2 \theta_l} (I_1 \sin \phi_{3l} - I_3 \sin \phi_{1l}) - \frac{m_1}{\cos^2 \theta_l} \right. \right.$$
$$\left. \cdot (I_3 \cos \phi_{1l} - I_1 \cos \phi_{3l}) \right\} / D_1^2$$
$$+ \left\{ D_2 \frac{q_n}{\cos^2 \theta_l} (I_2 \sin \phi_{1l} - I_1 \sin \phi_{2l}) - \frac{m_2}{\cos^2 \theta_l} \right.$$
$$\left. \cdot (I_1 \cos \phi_{2l} - I_2 \cos \phi_{1l}) \right\} / D_2^2$$
$$+ \left\{ D_3 \frac{q_n}{\cos^2 \theta_l} (I_3 \sin \phi_{2l} - I_2 \sin \phi_{3l}) - \frac{m_3}{\cos^2 \theta_l} \right.$$
$$\left. \left. \cdot (I_2 \cos \phi_{3l} - I_3 \cos \phi_{2l}) \right\} / D_3^2 \right], \tag{69}$$

$$\frac{\partial F}{\partial I_1} = \frac{1}{3} \left[\left\{ D_1 (-1 + q_n \tan \theta_l \sin \phi_{3l}) \right. \right.$$
$$\left. - m_1 (- \tan \theta_l \cos \phi_{3l}) \right\} / D_1^2$$
$$+ \left\{ D_2 (1 - q_n \tan \theta_l \sin \phi_{2l}) \right.$$
$$\left. \left. - m_2 (\tan \theta_l \cos \phi_{2l}) \right\} / D_2^2 \right], \tag{70}$$

$$\frac{\partial F}{\partial I_2} = \frac{1}{3} \left[\left\{ D_2 (-1 + q_n \tan \theta_l \sin \phi_{1l}) \right. \right.$$
$$\left. - m_2 (- \tan \theta_l \cos \phi_{1l}) \right\} / D_2^2$$
$$+ \left\{ D_3 (1 - q_n \tan \theta_l \sin \phi_{3l}) \right.$$
$$\left. \left. - m_3 (\tan \theta_l \cos \phi_{3l}) \right\} / D_3^2 \right], \tag{71}$$

$$\frac{\partial F}{\partial I_3} = \frac{1}{3} \left[\left\{ D_1 (1 - q_n \tan \theta_l \sin \phi_{1l}) \right. \right.$$
$$\left. - m_1 (\tan \theta_l \cos \phi_{1l}) \right\} / D_1^2$$
$$+ \left\{ D_3 (-1 + q_n \tan \theta_l \sin \phi_{2l}) \right.$$
$$\left. \left. - m_3 (- \tan \theta_l \cos \phi_{2l}) \right\} / D_3^2 \right]. \tag{72}$$

Using the values of the above partial derivatives it is possible to estimate the magnitude of dp_n and dq_n for various nominal values of dI_1, dI_2, dI_3, $d\theta_l$, $d\phi_{1l}$, $d\phi_{2l}$, and $d\phi_{3l}$.

Again, since

$$\theta_n = \nu(p_n, q_n) = \tan^{-1} \sqrt{p_n^2 + q_n^2} \tag{73}$$

and

$$\phi_n = k(p_n, q_n) = \tan^{-1} \left(\frac{q_n}{p_n} \right), \tag{74}$$

we can write

$$d\theta_n = \frac{\partial \nu}{\partial p_n} dp_n + \frac{\partial \nu}{\partial q_n} dq_n$$
$$= \frac{p_n dp_n + q_n dq_n}{(1 + p_n^2 + q_n^2) \sqrt{p_n^2 + q_n^2}} \tag{75}$$

and

$$d\phi_n = \frac{\partial k}{\partial p_n} dp_n + \frac{\partial k}{\partial q_n} dq_n$$
$$= \frac{p_n dp_n - q_n dq_n}{p_n^2 + q_n^2} \tag{76}$$

which denote the sensitivity of the surface normal.

ACKNOWLEDGMENT

The authors would like to thank the members of the University of Rhode Island Robotics Research Center for their help and advice.

REFERENCES

[1] B. Horn, "Shape from shading: A method for obtaining the shape of a smooth opaque object from one view," Ph.D. dissertation, Dep. Elec. Eng., M.I.T., MAC TR-79, 1970.

[2] B. Horn, "Image intensity understanding," Artificial Intell. Lab., M.I.T., AIM-335, 1975.

[3] B. Horn, "Hill-shading and the reflectance map," in Proc. Image Understanding Workshop, Palo Alto, CA, SAI-80-895-WA, Apr. 1979, pp. 79–120.

[4] B. Horn and R. Sjoberg, "Calculating the reflectance map," Artificial Intell. Lab., M.I.T., AIM-498, 1978.

[5] B. Horn, R. Woodham, and W. Silver, "Determining shape and reflectance using multiple images," Artificial Intell. Lab., M.I.T., AIM-490, 1978.

[6] R. Woodham, "Photometric stereo: A reflectance map technique for determining surface orientation from image intensity," SPIE Image Understanding Syst. & Industrial Applications, vol. 155, 1978.

[7] R. Woodham, "Reflectance map techniques for analyzing surface defects in metal castings," Artificial Intell. Lab., M.I.T., AI-TR-457, 1978.

[8] K. Forbus, "Light source effects," SPIE Image Understanding Syst. & Industrial Applications, vol. 55, pp. 50–53, 1978.

[9] K. Ikeuchi and B. Horn, "An application of the photometric stereo method," Artificial Intell. Lab., M.I.T., AIM-539, 1979.

[10] K. Ikeuchi, "Shape from regular patterns," in Proc. 5th Int. Conf. Pattern Recognition, vol. 2 of 2, FL, 1980.

[11] D. Marr and T. Poggio, "Cooperative computation of stereo disparity," Artificial Intell. Lab., M.I.T., AIM-364, 1976.

[12] B. Horn, "Determining lightness from an image," Comput. Graphics Image Processing, vol. 3, no. 4, pp. 277–299, 1974.

[13] S. Zucker, "Relaxation labelling and the reduction of local ambiguities," in Proc. IJCPR, 1976, pp. 852–861.

[14] J. Kender, "Shape from texture: 2884–An aggregation transform that maps a class of textures into surface orientation," in Proc. IJCAI, 1980, pp. 475–480.

[15] R. Kingslake, Ed., Applied Optics and Optical Engineering, vols. I and II. New York: Academic, 1965.

[16] F. Nicodemus, J. Richmond, J. Hsia, I. Ginsberg, and T. Limperis, "Geometrical considerations and nomenclature for reflectance," NBS Monograph 160, Nat. Bureau Standards, U.S. Dep. Commerce, Washington, DC, 1977.

[17] R. Haralick, "Automatic remote sensor image processing," in Digital Picture Analysis, A. Rosenfield, Ed. New York: Springer-Verlag, 1976.

[18] D. Marr, "Representing visual information," in Computer Vision Systems, A. Hanson and E. Riseman, Eds. New York: Academic, 1979.

[19] H. Andrews and B. Hunt, Digital Image Restoration. Englewood Cliffs, NJ: Prentice-Hall, 1977.

[20] L. Krakauer, "Computer analysis of visual properties of curved objects," Ph.D. dissertation, Dep. Elec. Eng., M.I.T., MAC TR-82, 1971.

[21] A. Chappell, Ed., Optoelectronics: Theory and Practice (Texas Instruments Electronics Series). New York: McGraw-Hill, 1978.

[22] E. Lavin, Specular Reflection, Monographs on Applied Optics, no. 2, Imperial College of Sci. Technol. New York: American-Elsevier, 1971.

[23] H. Keitz, Light Calculations and Measurements, PHILIPS Technical Library, Eindhoven, Holland, 1971.

[24] B. Horn and B. Bachman, "Using synthetic images to register real images with surface models," Commun. Ass. Comput. Mach., ACM, vol. 21, pp. 914–924, Nov. 1978.

[25] S. Ullman, "Visual detection of light sources," in Artificial Intelligence, vol. 2, P. H. Winston and R. H. Brown, Eds. Cambridge, MA: M.I.T. Press, 1979.

[26] J. Birk et al., "General methods to enable robots with vision to acquire, orient and transport workpieces," Univ. Rhode Island, Grant APR74-13935, 5th Rep., 1979.

[27] N. Chen, "Visually estimating workpiece pose in a robot hand using the feature points method," Ph.D. dissertation, Dep. Elec. Eng., Univ. Rhode Island, 1979.

[28] B.-T. Phong, "Illumination for computer generated images," Commun. Ass. Comput. Mach., vol. 18, no. 6, 1975.

[29] H. Gouraud, "Continuous shading of curved surfaces," IEEE Trans. Comput., vol. C-20, pp. 623–629, June 1971.

[30] G. Dahlquist, A. Bjorck, and N. Anderson, *Numerical Methods*. Englewood Cliffs, NJ: Prentice-Hall, 1974.

[31] G. Forsythe, "Pitfalls in computation, or why a math book isn't enough," Stanford Univ., Tech. Rep. CS147, Jan. 1970.

[32] G. Thomas, Jr., *Calculus and Analytic Geometry*. Reading, MA: Addison-Wesley, 1972.

[33] F. Hildebrand, *Advanced Calculus for Applications*. Englewood Cliffs, NJ: Prentice-Hall, 1976.

Integrability Disambiguates Surface Recovery in Two-Image Photometric Stereo

RUTH ONN
Department of Electrical Engineering, Cornell University, Ithaca, NY 14853, U.S.A.

ALFRED BRUCKSTEIN
Department of Computer Science, Technion, IIT, Haifa, Israel

Abstract

Two images of a Lambertian surface obtained under different illumination conditions, determine the local surface normals up to two possible orientations. We show that for smooth surfaces, the local integrability constraints usually resolve the problem of deciding between the two possibilities. We also provide a complete characterization of the surfaces that remain ambiguous under given illumination conditions.

1 Introduction

Several investigators proposed algorithms for inferring the shape of an object from a shaded image, see for example, (Horn 1975; Horn and Brooks 1986; Ikeuchi and Horn 1981; Pong et al. 1984; Bruckstein 1988). The problem of shape-from-shading is not well posed, and there might exist a large number of surfaces that could have given rise to a particular image, even under the same conditions of lighting and the same surface reflectance properties. This ambiguity inherent in a single image was circumvented, in the work mentioned above by using more or less stringent constraints on the imaged object, or by assuming various types of prior information about it.

Photometric stereo procedures, (see Woodham 1980; Marr 1982), use multiple images of an object, taken under different illumination conditions, to remove the ambiguity inherent in a single image. Many of the tools developed for the single-image, classical, shape-from-shading process, such as reflectance-map description of surface reflectivity properties (Horn 1977, 1981) procedures for depth recovery from normals are naturally used in conjunction with photometric stereo.

This work reexamines the photometric stereo problem and presents a new method that recovers the surface normals of a height/depth profile from two shaded images of it. It becomes apparent from our analysis that under Lambertian reflectivity assumptions, given two different shaded images of a smooth object its shape can be, in most cases, uniquely determined at all points where self-shadows do not occur.

This article is organized as follows. In section 2 the imaging model and some basic theoretical results are presented. Then, section 3 shows how continuity and integrability can be exploited to obtain unambiguous surface normal recovery at points illuminated by both light sources. We conclude with a numerical example and a short discussion of the limitations and generalizations of the method.

2 Photometric Stereo with Two Views

2.1 Formulation of the Problem

The two-view photometric stereo problem is the following. We are provided two images of the same surface, produced with the same camera position relative to the surface but under different illumination directions. It is required to reconstruct from this data the height profile of the surface.

The height reconstruction is shown to be possible under the following assumptions:

a. The height profile is twice differentiable.
b. The surface reflectance is Lambertian (Horn 1975, 1977, 1981)

c. Both images are produced from the same position, with a single distant point light source and a distant view point.

d. The direction and brightness of the illumination sources are given.

The problem is to determine the surface orientation (i.e., surface normals) at each point in the image plane. Reconstruction of the height profile compatible with these orientations is a relatively straightforward process (Horn and Brooks 1986).

2.2 The Imaging Model

Imaging systems perform the perspective projection, but here a distant view point is assumed, and the orthographic projection therefore constitutes a good approximation. This is so because the imaged surface comprises only a small solid angle for the viewer. The viewing direction can then be aligned with the z axis so the point (x, y) on the imaged surface is portrayed by point (x, y) on the image, see figure 1.

The model for the generation of image intensities is the following. If the height profile is represented by the equation $z = H(x, y)$ and if the function $H(x, y)$ is differentiable, then (see Do Carmo 1976) at each point the normal vector to the surface $N(x, y)$ is given by

$$N(x, y) = [-p(x, y), -q(x, y), 1] \quad (1)$$

where

$$p(x, y) = \left(\frac{\partial H}{\partial x}\right) \qquad q(x, y) = \left(\frac{\partial H}{\partial y}\right)$$

The intensity at a point in an image of a Lambertian surface, depends only on the angle between the illumination vector and the normal vector at the point. Let A denote the illumination vector, that is, the unit vector pointing in the direction of the light source. The components of A are a_x, a_y, a_z. Let $<A, B>$ denote the scalar product of vectors A and B, and $|B|$ denote the length of a vector B. Then the image intensity I_A at point (x, y) is given by:

$$I_A(x, y) = \frac{<N(x, y), A>}{|N(x, y)|}$$

$$= \frac{1}{(1 + p^2 + q^2)^{1/2}} \cdot$$

$$[(-p(x, y)a_x - q(x, y)a_y + a_z] \quad (2)$$

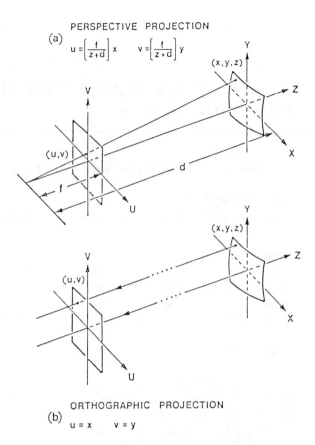

PERSPECTIVE PROJECTION

(a) $\quad u = \left[\frac{f}{z+d}\right] x \qquad v = \left[\frac{f}{z+d}\right] y$

ORTHOGRAPHIC PROJECTION

(b) $\quad u = x \qquad v = y$

Fig. 1. Characterizing the image projections. (a) The perspective projection. For a viewing distance that is large in comparison to the object size, image projection can be modeled by the orthographic projection illustrated in (b). In orthographic projection all rays from object surface to image are parallel. (from Woodham [1980]).

The second image will be $I_B(x, y)$ described by an expression similar to (2), with the components b_x, b_y, b_z of the second illumination vector B, substituted for a_x, a_y, a_z. In order to find the surface orientations, these two images will be used.

2.3 The Ambiguity in Recovering the Normals

Let us ask the following question: at the point (x_0, y_0) what can locally be inferred about the surface normal given the two intensities $I_A(x_0, y_0)$ and $I_B(x_0, y_0)$? Since the dependence of these intensities on the surface orientations at point (x_0, y_0), $p(x_0, y_0)$, and $q(x_0, y_0)$ is given, the partial derivatives must obey the following set of equations:

$$I_A = (-pa_x - qa_y + a_z)(1 + p^2 + q^2)^{-1/2} \qquad (3)$$

$$I_B = (-pb_x - qb_y + b_z)(1 + p^2 + q^2)^{-1/2}$$

Let

$$T \overset{\Delta}{=} (1 + p^2 + q^2)^{1/2} \qquad (4)$$

Rearranging (3) yields

$$pa_x + qa_y = a_z - I_A T \qquad (5)$$

$$pb_x + qb_y = b_z - I_B T$$

Regarded as two linear equations in two unknowns, these equations can be solved for p and q in terms of T, providing solutions of the form

$$p = c_p T + d_p \qquad (6)$$

$$q = c_q T + d_q$$

Recalling the definition of T in equation (4), that is, $T^2 - p^2 - q^2 = 1$, the solutions for p and q may be inserted providing a quadratic equation for T of the form:

$$K_2 T^2 + K_1 T + K_0 = 0 \qquad (7)$$

where K_i are functions of I_A, I_B, a_x, a_y, a_z, b_x, b_y and b_z.

Solving (7) produces two solutions for T, they can be called T_1 and T_2. If the two solutions for T are inserted in (6), we obtain two pairs of partial derivatives (p_1, q_1) and (p_2, q_2), corresponding to two normals, N_1 and N_2. This is all that can be obtained using the local constraints provided by two images at the point (x_0, y_0). So far, the only assumption made on the height profile was that it has first derivatives.

At this point we recall the classical geometric interpretation of the above algebraic manipulations. The intensity at each point in an image of a Lambertian surface gives the angle between the normal at that point and the illumination direction. Thus the locus of all normals that could have produced the intensity I_A at point (x_0, y_0) is a (Monge) cone, with apex at (x_0, y_0) and axis in the illumination direction and having an opening angle determined by arc cos (I_A). If the brightness at the same point when illuminated from two different directions (photometric stereo) is known, the normal at (x_0, y_0) must belong to two such cones. Therefore it belongs to their intersection. Two cones with the same apex either intersect along two or one half-lines or do not intersect at all (except for the common apex). The case of no intersection can not occur for genuine photometric stereo images and will not be considered

here. The case of one intersection produces an unambiguous solution, which corresponds to one solution for T in equation (7), and is of some significance as will become apparent. The general case is that of two solutions out of which only one is the "true" normal and this can be seen to agree with the algebra above.

Note that, given two images of photometric stereo, the above described method can be used only on the parts of the surface that are illuminated in both images. Therefore the *image plane* will be redefined as all points that are out of the self shadow in both images.

In order to correctly recover the height profile the "true" normals have to be chosen. An immediate way to choose the true normals would be by taking yet another image under a different lighting condition. This was indeed proposed by Woodham (1980). However we can also exploit the lateral constraints on the normals due to the assumed continuity and smoothness of the surface. It seems that this was understood by the proponents of the method, however no theoretical analysis of this issue was ever carried out.

The late David Marr, in his discussion of photometric stereo states that, given the data, at all points in the image plane "the surface orientation is narrowed down to just two possibilities. This essentially solves the problem since the choice can usually be made by using continuity information or by taking a third picture with yet another lighting position" (Marr 1982). The main theoretical contribution of this article is to analyze the way in which continuity and surface smoothness constraints disambiguate the recovery of the normals and thus pave the way for surface recovery.

3 Using the Continuity and Integrability Information

3.1 Using the Continuity Constraint

Assume that the normals to the height profile are continuous, and consider the function $T(x, y)$, where T was defined above, that is, $T = (1 + p^2 + q^2)^{-1/2}$. T is clearly continuous, being the continuous function of the (continuous) variables p and q. Denote the two solutions of the quadratic equation (7), T_1 and T_2 and let the T_1 solution be defined as corresponding to the normal with a positive projection on the direction of the vector $A \times B$, T_2 being the other solution. By the discussion at the end of the previous section it is obvious that the two possible solutions will be symmetric with respect to the plane defined by the two illumination vectors A and B, unless they both collapse to a single solution situated in this plane.

Let us further define the following three sets of image points:

$$V_0 \overset{\Delta}{=} \{\text{points where } T = T_1 = T_2\}$$
$$V_1 \overset{\Delta}{=} \{\text{points where } T = T_1 \neq T_2\}$$
$$V_2 \overset{\Delta}{=} \{\text{points where } T = T_2 \neq T_1\}$$

Obviously every point on the image plane belongs to one and only one of the three sets. We shall now show that the V_0 regions and the self-shadow regions divide the image plane into connected regions in each of which the normals continuously vary on the same side of the illumination-vectors-defined plane. This result follows from the following.

LEMMA: *Let (x_1, y_1) be a point on the image belonging to V_1, (x_2, y_2) a point belonging to V_2, and P any path from (x_1, y_1) to (x_2, y_2) where P is wholly contained in the above defined image plane. Then P must contain a point belonging to V_0.*

Proof. $T(x, y)$ is continuous on a closed set, that means that for any $\delta > 0$ there can be found an ϵ such that for any $(\hat{x}, \hat{y})$ and $(\tilde{x}, \tilde{y})$, if $|(\hat{x}, \hat{y}) - (\tilde{x}, \tilde{y})| < \epsilon$ then $|T(\hat{x}, \hat{y}) - T(\tilde{x}, \tilde{y})| < \delta$. Consider any path P defined as above. Further consider $T_d = |T_1(x, y) - T_2(x, y)|$, along the path P. T_d is a continuous function in continuous variables and therefore continuous. The path P is a closed set and therefore T_d has a minimum value on P, call it T_m. Suppose P doesn't contain any point from V_0, i.e., $T_m > 0$. Then ϵ_{m1} can be found such that for any $(\hat{x}, \hat{y})$ and $(\tilde{x}, \tilde{y})$, if $|(\hat{x}, \hat{y}) - (\tilde{x}, \tilde{y})| < \epsilon_{m1}$ then $|T(\hat{x}, \hat{y}) - T(\tilde{x}, \tilde{y})| < T_m/2$, from the same considerations T_1 too is continuous so ϵ_{m2} can be found such that for any $(\hat{x}, \hat{y})$ and $(\tilde{x}, \tilde{y})$, if $|(\hat{x}, \hat{y}) - (\tilde{x}, \tilde{y})| < \epsilon_{m2}$ then $|T_1(\hat{x}, \hat{y}) - T_1(\tilde{x}, \tilde{y})| < T_m/4$. Let $\epsilon_m = \min(\epsilon_{m1}, \epsilon_{m2})$. Any point $(\hat{x}, \hat{y})$ close enough to (x_1, y_1) — (i.e., $|(\hat{x}, \hat{y}) - (x_1, y_1)| < \epsilon_m$) — must also belong to V_1. That is so because while $|T(\hat{x}, \hat{y}) - T(x_1, y_1)| < T_m/2$,

$$|T_1(x_1, y_1) - T_2(\hat{x}, \hat{y})| \geq |T_1(\hat{x}, \hat{y}) - T_2(\hat{x}, \hat{y})|$$
$$- |T_1(x_1, y_1) - T_1(\hat{x}, \hat{y})|$$
$$\geq T_m - \frac{T_m}{4} > \frac{T_m}{2}$$

This argument can be progressed all the way along P till (x_2, y_2), thus finding that (x_2, y_2) too belongs to V_1. This is in contradiction to the assumption that it belongs

to V_2, therefore T_m must be zero and T_d must be zero somewhere. (Of course T_d cannot be less than zero because of the way it is defined.)   Q.E.D.

It follows from this result that the image plane is divided into distinct connected regions each wholly contained in one of the three sets V_0, V_1, V_2, and if we could label each region we would know the true normals everywhere on the image plane. Moreover any two regions contained in V_1 and V_2 respectively, must be separated by a region (possibly a curve) contained in V_0. The points belonging to V_0 coincide with the points where the quadratic equation (7) will have only one solution and its discriminant will be zero.

In the next section we shall show how the assumption that the function $H(x, y)$ is twice differentiable can be used to identify to which of the sets the points of each region belong.

3.2 Using the Integrability Constraint

The two functions $p(x, y)$ and $q(x, y)$ are not independent. They are connected by the fact that for a function $H(x, y)$, for which the second derivatives exist, they obey the following equation

$$\left[\frac{\partial^2 H}{\partial x \partial y} \right] = \left[\frac{\partial^2 H}{\partial y \partial x} \right] \tag{8}$$

which means for p and q that

$$\left[\frac{\partial p}{\partial y} \right] = \left[\frac{\partial q}{\partial x} \right] \tag{9}$$

In general only one of the two pairs of functions (p_1, q_1) and (p_2, q_2) provided by solving (7) will satisfy (9). "In general" here has the following meaning: (9) does not hold for both (p_1, q_1) and (p_2, q_2) unless the height profile satisfies some very specific constraints. These constraints are discussed below.

Suppose that a surface generates the partials p and q. Given the illumination directions A and B, and the photometric stereo data, we shall be able to determine (at each point on the surface illuminated from both directions) a pair of normals, N_t, the true normal $[-p, -q, 1]$ and a reflected normal N_r. Let us consider for simplicity that the two directions A and B are both in the plane $x - z$ being symmetric with respect to the z axis, i.e., $A = [-\sin\theta, 0, -\cos\theta]$ and $B = [\sin\theta, 0, -\cos\theta]$ for some θ. In this case the true and reflected normals will simply be

$$N_t = [-p, -q, 1] \quad \text{and} \quad N_r = [-p, q, 1] \quad (10)$$

This means that we must have

$$\frac{\partial}{\partial y} p = \frac{\partial}{\partial x} q = -\frac{\partial}{\partial x} q \quad (11)$$

implying that

$$\frac{\partial^2}{\partial x \, \partial y} H(x, y) = 0 \quad (12)$$

Therefore, both choices for the surface normal, provided by the photometric stereo information, will obey the integrability condition only if the surface obeys, within some region, equation (12). The general solution of this equation is easily seen to be a function of the form

$$H(x, y) = F(x) + G(y) \quad (13)$$

with arbitrary smooth functions $F(\cdot)$ and $G(\cdot)$.

The above discussion might seem to be restricted to the case of illumination directions A and B as specified above, however, note that we can always choose a coordinate transformation that brings us to this case, and the illuminated surface, in these new coordinates would have to satisfy (12) in order to have an ambiguous solution, even when integrability is tested on both choices of normals. Note that the coordinate transformation does not affect the shading data, which, in the Lambertian case, is independent of the position of the viewer. In the appendix, we worked out the partial differential equation that would have to be satisfied by ambiguous surfaces in the original, general coordinate system case, however we note that this is just the image of the simple equation (12), under some coordinate transformations.

In conclusion, we shall not be able to choose between the two normals by checking integrability, in the cases when the surface can be expressed as (13), in the suitably defined coordinate system (induced by the illumination directions!). An obvious example of a surface that has the form (13) is the case of planar surfaces. Such surfaces will remain ambiguous for all illumination directions. In general, the condition that the surface has to satisfy to remain ambiguous is seen to be very stringent, and dependent on the illumination directions. A surface of the form will not remain such, if a general coordinate transformation is performed.

We can conclude from the above discussion that, since arbitrary curved surfaces will usually not satisfy (13), with respect to the given directions of illumination, it can be expected that for all of the connected regions R, separated by V_0 points and/or self-shadows, only one of the following expressions will be (close to) zero

$$\int_{(x, y) \in R} \left[\frac{\partial p_1}{\partial y} - \frac{\partial q_1}{\partial x} \right]^2 dxdy \quad (14a)$$

$$\int_{(x, y) \in R} \left[\frac{\partial p_2}{\partial y} - \frac{\partial q_2}{\partial x} \right]^2 dxdy \quad (14b)$$

From the knowledge which of the two expressions is null, a labeling of the regions follows. If (14a) is close to zero, the pairs (p_1, q_1) are the true surface normals over region R, and the points of R belong to V_1, If (14b) is almost zero, the pairs (p_2, q_2) describe the correct surface over region R, and the points of R belong to V_2. As all the points belonging to V_0 have already been found, the pair (p, q) is determined for each point in the image plane, and we may proceed to the second part of the reconstruction. In the unfortunate but nongeneric, and rare case when some region remains ambiguous, that is, both expressions (14a and b) are zero, we shall have to check both solutions and decide which one best fits the boundary conditions provided by the neighboring regions.

If the surface normals at each point in the image plane have been determined, the complete surface recovery requires a height from normals procedure. Height reconstruction from normals is a standard problem, and several methods have been proposed in the literature. We used in our implementation a well-known method, based on the suggestions of Horn and Brooks [1986].

4. Simulation Results and Discussion

The procedure theoretically discussed in the previous section was implemented and tested on several synthetically produced photometric stereo images. The scenes were composed of two to three Gaussians of different heights and breadth, one of the test profile being depicted in figure 2.

The synthetic shading images were produced by first calculating the analytic normal to the surface at each point. Two illumination directions were chosen and described by unit vectors pointing in the direction of the "light sources." Surface portions hidden from the illumination direction were found by a simple raytracing algorithm. At all other points, the image intensity was computed according to (2) and discretized to 8 bits. The two different images, $I_A(i, j)$ and $I_B(i, j)$ generated for a given height profile, were the input of the photometric stereo procedure. An example of pairs

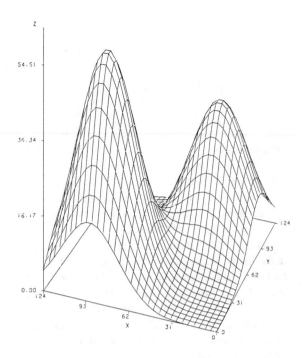

Fig. 2. Example of a two-gaussian height profile used in the simulations.

of such images is shown in figure 3, corresponding to the profile of figure 2. The surface reconstruction procedure first determines points that belong to V_0 (as defined in section 3), that is, points where there is no ambiguity as to the normal direction, were determined by checking for identical pairs (p_1, q_1) and (p_2, q_2). Practically, this is accomplished by defining a set of points in the image plane larger then V_0: those points for which the discriminant of the quadratic equation (7) which was derived in section 2 from the set of equations (4) and (5), is small. These points were found by thresholding the discriminant and they defined, together with the points in the image plane that were in the self-shadow in either of the images I_A or I_B, a mask we called the boundary mask. Such a mask for the height profile of figure 2 can be seen in figure 4. Then, a standard connected-components algorithm, as for example the one described by Rosenfeld and Kak (1982), was used to separate the connected regions in the image plane separated by the boundary mask. For each of the resulting connected regions in the image plane the discrete analogs of the two integrals in (14) were calculated, and were used to unambiguously

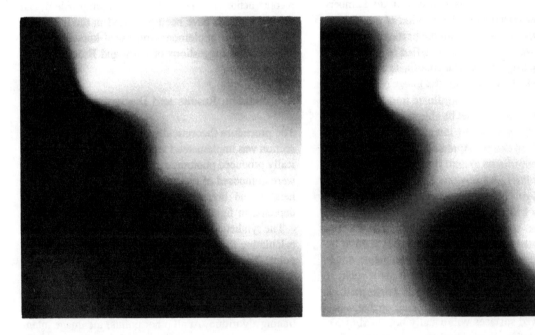

Fig. 3. The two images used in the simulation: synthetic images of the profile depicted in figure 2, nonnormalized illumination directions are (1, 1, 1) and (.33, .67, 1) respectively.

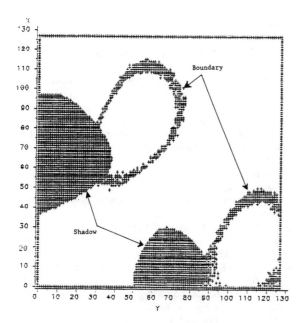

Fig 4. The boundary mask obtained for the two gaussians height profile, depicted in figure 2. The filled patches are the shadows and are not part of the image plane. The thickness of the boundaries (V_0 regions) is caused by the method by which they were practically obtained, via thresholding.

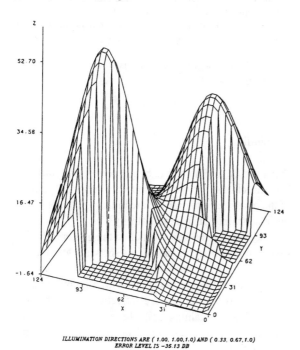

Fig. 5. Reconstruction of the height profile depicted in figure 2. The illumination directions are (1, 1, 1) and (.33, .67, 1) the rms error level achieved is −35.13 dB.

recover the surface normals. The local normals, $p(i, j)$ and $q(i, j)$, together with the shadow mask were used in an implementation of a standard height from normals algorithm. The profile recovery results were then compared to the original height profile. The result of the height recovery procedure, for the example discussed above is shown in figure 5.

In summary, we have presented a new method for reconstructing a height profile from only two shaded images of it. Previous discussions of photometric stereo (Ikeuchi and Horn 1981; Ikeuchi 1987; Marr 1982) suggested that a third image be taken to remove the ambiguity in determining the local surface normals, and thereby obtaining the shape of the imaged object. This is a very simple and good idea, since it removes the ambiguity locally, without any need to use lateral information based on surface smoothness assumptions. However, from studies of monocular shape-from-shading, it becomes clear that for smooth surfaces, a lot of information on the height profile is available even in a single shaded image of it, therefore the question of conditions under which complete surface recovery is possible from only two shaded images provided by photometric stereo arises naturally.

We discussed the issue of exploiting continuity and smoothness of the imaged surfaces in the photometric stereo framework. We showed that, in general, under Lambertian reflectance properties, surface smoothness enables a complete resolution of the local ambiguity in recovering the surface normal. In the first part of the reconstruction process for every point that is illuminated in both images two different normals are found. Incorporating continuity considerations reduces the ambiguity first by defining regions in the image where the knowledge of the solution at any one point determines the true solution for the whole region, and then using local integrability to differentiate between the two solutions, pointing out the more probable one.

We believe that this method could be extended to images of surfaces with reflection functions different from the Lambertian rule. By using the reflectance map technique, (Horn 1981; Woodham 1981), it may happen for many reflectance properties that only two different normals are compatible with the shading data at most points in the image. As the arguments of section 2.2 can be generalized for any reflectance function that is continuous in the surface normals, a process of defining regions within which the solutions are interdependent and determining the more probable solution for each region could possibly be followed much along the lines of the method proposed above.

Shape-from-shading methods are usually applied on images of smooth, continuous surfaces. The method described here requires continuity of the first derivatives as well, but it can be extended to surfaces with discontinuities in the first derivatives if the assumption of a uniform reflectance function is retained. Under this assumption discontinuities in the surface would appear as discontinuities in the image brightness, that is as edges. An edge detector can be used and smooth regions thus defined. The algorithm then treats each smooth region as a separate image and the resulting height profiles must then be integrated perhaps by using methods developed for interpreting line drawings—see, for instance (Ballard and Brown 1982; Marr 1982; Rosenfeld and Kak 1982). This is also the approach by Ikeuchi (1987) where photometric stereo (using three images) is used together with binocular stereo.

As noted in the text and can also be seen by the "holes" in the reconstructed height profiles, the photometric stereo method provides the height only at points that are not in self-shadow in both images. A natural way to fill in the gaps is to use methods of classical shape from shading at points where shading information is available from one illumination direction, and perhaps topological constraints where no information is available at all. Because the height profile and the surface normals are known on the boundary of the shadow, shape-from-shading methods that require boundary information on a closed curve, such as those proposed by Horn and Brooks (1986), Ikeuchi and Horn (1981), and Bruckstein (1988), can be applied. Further work is needed in integrating monocular shape from shading in the photometric stereo, so that the whole surface may be recovered.

5 Acknowledgement

The comments of Prof. Takeo Kanade on the possiblity of simplifying equation (A.5) by a rotation of the optical axis that sets a to zero, eventually led to the explicit analysis of the ambiguity. We thank him for his patience and help, both technical and editorial. Interesting discussions on the subject of this paper with Mr. Dror Maydan and Dr. Ofer Zeitouni are also gratefully acknowledged. Finally, we thank our reviewers for their constructive comments that contributed a lot to improving the presentation of this paper.

References

D.H. Ballard and C.M. Brown, *Computer Vision*. Prentice Hall: Englewood Cliffs, NH, 1982.

A.M. Bruckstein, "On shape from shading methods," *Comp. Vision, Graphics Image Process.* 44:139–154, 1988.

M.P. Do Carmo, *Differential Geometry of Curves and Surfaces*, Prentice Hall: Englewood Cliffs, NJ 1976.

B.K.P. Horn "Obtaining shape from shading information." In P.H. Winston (ed), *The Psychology of Computer Vision*, pp. 115–155, McGraw-Hill: New York, 1975.

B.K.P. Horn, "Understanding image intensities," *Artificial Intelligence*, 8:201–231, 1977.

B.K.P. Horn, "Hill shading and the reflectance map," *Proc IEEE*, (1):1981.

B.K.P. Horn and M.J. Brooks, "The variational approach to shape from shading," *Comp. Vision, Graphics Image Processing.* 33:174–203, 1986.

K. Ikeuchi and B.K. P. Horn, "Numerical shape from shading and occluding boundaries," *Artificial Intelligence* 17:141–184, 1981.

K. Ikeuchi, "Determining a depth map using dual photometric stereo," *Intern. Robotics Res.* (1), 1987.

D. Marr *Vision*. Freeman: San Francisco, 1982.

T.C. Pong, R.M. Haralick, and L.G. Shapiro, "The facet approach to shape from shading," *Proc 2nd Workshop Comp. Vision: Representation and Control*, Annapolis, Maryland, April 30–May 2, 1984.

A. Rosenfeld and A. Kak, *Digital Picture Processing*, vols. 1 and 2 Academic Press: San Diego, CA, 1982.

R.J. Woodham, "Photometric method for determining surface orientation from multiple images," *Optical Engineering*, (1) 139–144, 1980.

R.J. Woodham, "Analysing images of curved surfaces," *Artificial Intelligence* 17:117–140, 1981.

Appendix

What can be said about the height profile and illumination directions, for which the two solutions T_1 and T_2 of the quadratic equation (7) are indistinguishable using the constraints of differentiability?

In addressing the above problem the geometric interpretation is best reconsidered. As shown before the two solutions for the normal at a particular point are formed as the intersection of two cones with a common apex. Hence the two solutions are reflections of each other in the plane containing both their axes. Let **f** be the unit vector in the direction of the cross product of the illumination directions:

$$f \stackrel{\Delta}{=} \frac{A \times B}{|A \times B|}$$

Each cone's axis is an illumination direction, therefore the two solutions are reflections of each other with respect to the plane perpendicular to **f**. Let the true normal be designated by N_t and the other solution by N_r (for reflected), then the relation between them will be given by

$$N_r = N_t - 2 \langle N_t, f \rangle f \tag{A1}$$

More explicitly consider two illumination directions which produce $f = [a, b, c]$, and recall that $N_t = [-p, -q, 1]$, then N_r is described by

$$N_r = [-p, -q, 1] - 2(-ap - bq + c)[a, b, c]$$
$$= [(2a^2 - 1) \cdot p + 2abq - 2ac,$$
$$2abp + (2b^2 - 1) \cdot q - 2bc,$$
$$2acp + 2bcq - 2c^2 + 1)] \tag{A2}$$

Assuming N_r too describes a smooth surface (just like N_t does), the following equations should give the partial derivatives of that surface:

$$p_r = -\frac{(2a^2 - 1) \cdot p + 2abq - 2ac}{2acp + 2bcq - 2c^2 + 1} \tag{A3a}$$

$$q_r = -\frac{2abp + (2b^2 - 1) \cdot q - 2bc}{2acp + 2bcq - 2c^2 + 1} \tag{A3b}$$

Further assuming that the surface is twice differentiable we must have that $\partial p_r/\partial y = \partial q_r/\partial x$, and thereby the following partial differential equation must be satisfied by the surface $H(x, y)$, that provided N_t,

$$\left(2(a^2 + c^2) - 1\right) \frac{\partial^2 H}{\partial x\, \partial y} + 2ab \frac{\partial^2 H}{\partial^2 y}$$
$$-2bc \left[\frac{\partial H}{\partial y} \cdot \frac{\partial^2 H}{\partial x\, \partial y} - \frac{\partial H}{\partial x} \cdot \frac{\partial^2 H}{\partial^2 y} \right]$$
$$= \left(2(b^2 + c^2) - 1\right) \cdot \frac{\partial^2 H}{\partial x\, \partial y} + 2ab \frac{\partial^2 H}{\partial^2 x}$$
$$- 2ac \left[\frac{\partial H}{\partial x} \cdot \frac{\partial^2 H}{\partial^2 x} - \frac{\partial H}{\partial y} \cdot \frac{\partial^2 H}{\partial y\, \partial x} \right] \tag{A4}$$

This yields, by rearrangement,

$$2(a^2 - b^2) \frac{\partial^2 H}{\partial x\, \partial y} - 2ab \left[\frac{\partial^2 H}{\partial^2 x} - \frac{\partial^2 H}{\partial^2 y} \right]$$
$$- 2c \cdot \left[\frac{\partial H}{\partial y} \cdot \frac{\partial^2 H}{\partial^2 x} - a \frac{\partial H}{\partial x} \cdot \frac{\partial^2 H}{\partial y\, \partial x} \right.$$
$$\left. + b \frac{\partial H}{\partial y} \cdot \frac{\partial^2 H}{\partial x\, \partial y} - b \frac{\partial H}{\partial x} \cdot \frac{\partial^2 H}{\partial^2 y} \right] = 0 \tag{A5}$$

This rather complicated-looking equation is simply the general image of the very simple equation (12), for arbitrary illumination directions. If A and B are chosen so as to yield $c = 0$ and either a or b equal to 0, we clearly recover (2.12). If only $c = 0$, we get the simpler equation

$$2(a^2 - b^2) \frac{\partial^2 H}{\partial x\, \partial y} - 2ab \left[\frac{\partial^2 H}{\partial^2 x} - \frac{\partial^2 H}{\partial^2 y} \right] = 0 \tag{A6}$$

Suppose, for example that the image surface looks like

$$H(x, y) = mx^2 + ny^2 \tag{A7}$$

with both m and n negative, that is, we have a quadratic mountain. Inserting (A7) into (A6), we can get conditions on the parameters a and b that ensure unambiguous recovery of the surface from photometric stereo. We have ambiguity if

$$4ab(m - n) = 0 \tag{A8}$$

and therefore, if $m \neq n$, we must have both a and b different from zero for complete surface recovery. This would indeed be the case for two arbitrarily chosen illumination directions. Clearly the case $m = n$ is rotationally symmetric and the ambiguity cannot be removed keeping $c = 0$, as is intuitively clear.

Obtaining 3-Dimensional Shape of Textured and Specular Surfaces Using Four-Source Photometry[1]

E. North Coleman, Jr., and Ramesh Jain

Department of Computer Science, Wayne State University, Detroit, Michigan 48202

Received April 27, 1981; revised July 1, 1981

The *photometric stereo method* is extended to four-source photometry for obtaining 3-dimensional shapes of visually textured and specular surfaces from intensity values. The table look-up approach (based on reflectance maps) for determining surface normals is shown to be of limited value in this context and a more direct method of computing these normals is used. Our method also eliminates the requirement of a preliminary system calibration procedure. The method is applied to real images as a test of its applicability.

1. INTRODUCTION

Most research in scene understanding and image processing has relied heavily on the information obtained from an image. The dependence on one image has limited the success of such systems to toy worlds or severely constrained domains. Clearly, information about the 3-dimensional shapes of the surfaces in an image will dramatically enhance the efficacy of a scene understanding system.

Several methods are available for obtaining depth information about surfaces. These methods are divided into what Woodham [17] refers to as direct methods and indirect methods. Direct methods are those which try to measure range (distance) directly [1, 9]. In this category are time-of-flight techniques such as pulsed laser and phase shift based systems. Depth information is the only information available from such systems.

Indirect methods are those which attempt to determine distance by measuring parameters calculated from images of the illuminated object. As an indirect method, stereo vision utilizes triangulation to compute distance [2, 3, 10, 11, 15, 19]. Using optical flow one can compute the relative distance to points on the surface of an object [13]. Surface vectors can be constructed based on how image points *flow* from one frame to the next. Stereo vision and some optical flow [14] techniques require a relationship between surface points in one frame and the same points in another frame. This correspondence problem can only be solved if the surface of the object being viewed is textured or has nonuniform gray levels.

A third indirect method for obtaining surface shape is by analysis of the radiometry of image formation [4–8, 16–18]. Commonly known as *shape from shading*, this method can be applied wherever the direction of incident illumination is known and/or can be controlled. It is this technique which is the subject of this paper.

Horn [4] showed how shape could be determined by solving nonlinear, first-order partial differential equations to find components of the surface gradient. While the gradient could not be determined locally, numerical integration of the equations

[1]This research was partially supported by the National Science Foundation under the Grant MCS 8100148.

permitted characteristic curves to be traced out on the object surface.

In conjunction with Horn, Woodham [17] developed a method for determining surface shape without requiring solution of a system of equations. Using a single light source (one image), limitation of possible surface orientations to iso-brightness contours in gradient space is first achieved. The actual gradient at each point is then determined by using relaxation-type algorithms. Woodham [17, 18] also details a method for locally determining surface gradients, called *photometric stereo*, which uses multiple sources of illumination.

Multiple-source photometry is usually implemented using look-up tables indexed by *n*-tuples of intensity values (one from each image). The look-up table serves as an inverse reflectance map for transforming image intensity values to surface normals. To obtain a reflectance map, the system is calibrated using a sphere having a constant surface reflectance factor. Shape can be determined for only those objects having reflectance properties identical to the calibration sphere. Silver [16] has shown this method to be very effective in solving for shapes with uniform matte surfaces.

Specular reflections, or highlights, appear on a surface when the angle between the viewer and source of illumination is bisected by the surface normal. By producing a mirror-like reflection off an object's surface, specularity causes measured intensity values to be higher by the magnitude of the specular component. The degree of specularity can be informally defined as the glossiness of a surface.

By elevating intensity values, specular reflection produces incorrect surface gradients, which are not accounted for in shape from shading algorithms. Although attempts have been made to quantify the specular component in reflectance functions and reflectance maps, these functions are contrived for certain cases and fail to solve the general problem [8, 16].

Visual texture can be thought of as a pattern or variance of intensity appearing on an object's surface. In this paper the visual texture will be considered as resulting from nonuniform surface albedo. To derive surface normals for textured surfaces the intensity values and reflectance factors must be known at each point. The use of table look-up techniques and associated calibration for different surface properties is very cumbersome for determining the shape of visually textured objects.

The motivation behind this paper is to adapt multiple-source photometry to surfaces varying in both specularity and visual texture. Toward this end it will be shown how surface normals can be computed by solving sets of simultaneous linear equations. Detailed by Woodham [17], this method can be used on textured surfaces. Furthermore, it will be shown how using a fourth source of illumination, specular reflections can be detected. Once discovered, the specular component can be removed from the computation of a local normal vector.

2. SURFACE SHAPE FROM INTENSITY

Suppose a surface is defined explicitly by an equation of the form

$$z = F(x, y). \tag{2.1}$$

There are several methods for expressing the surface orientation at each point (x, y, z) on this surface. If we choose to represent surface orientation with normal

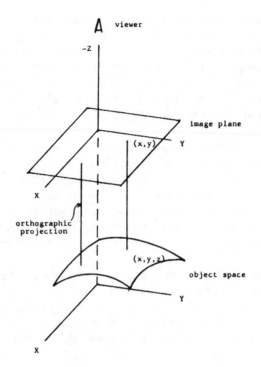

FIG. 1. Surface–viewer geometry. Objects lie on the x–y plane in object space. Image projection is orthographic onto the image plane. Viewer is along the negative Z axis.

vectors, the orientation of any point on the surface can be written as

$$N = (Fx, Fy, -1), \qquad (2.2)$$

where Fx and Fy are the first partial derivatives of F with respect to x and y, respectively. The vector N is an outward surface normal at (x, y). The term outward refers to the direction of the normal with respect to the viewer. In all cases, the viewer will be along the negative Z axis in relation to the surface being viewed (see Fig. 1). The surface normal $(0, 0, -1)$ points directly at the viewer and is orthogonal to the image plane.

To simplify the geometry we assume that the distance between the viewer and the object being viewed is large in relation to the object's size. This allows us to approximate the perspective projection of the imaging device by an orthographic projection.

Using two variables p and q, we define

$$p = Fx \quad \text{and} \quad q = Fy.$$

From this, the surface normal of $F(x, y)$ at any point (x, y) can be written as $(p, q, -1)$.

The quantity (p, q) is defined as the gradient of F. Gradient space is the two dimensional vector space spanned by the set of all such gradients (p, q). Hence, each noncollinear surface normal maps into a unique gradient (p, q) in gradient space.

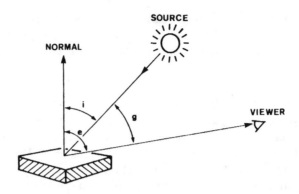

FIG. 2. Definition of incident, emittance, and phase angles. The source–viewer geometry above shows the incident angle i between the source vector and surface normal; emittance angle e between the view vector and surface normal; and the phase angle g between the source vector and view vector.

2.1 Shape from Shading

The fundamental fact upon which the photometric method is based is that isotropic surfaces have a unique value of image intensity for a particular surface orientation and reflectance factor. In other words, given a reflectance factor which accounts for the optical properties of surface microstructure, measured intensity depends solely upon surface orientation and illumination.

A surface photometric function $Q(i, e, g)$ for a single source can be defined in terms of the angles i, e and g. These angles are called the incident angle (i), emittance angle (e) and phase angle (g). These angles quantify the relationships between the source vector, view vector and surface normal vector as shown in Fig. 2. Each of these vectors can be written in gradient space coordinates as

$$V = (0, 0, -1) \qquad \text{(view vector)}, \qquad (2.3)$$

$$S = (ps, qs, -1) \qquad \text{(source vector)}, \qquad (2.4)$$

$$N = (p, q, -1) \qquad \text{(normal vector)}. \qquad (2.5)$$

Given the conditions for a single source of illumination, a mapping can be constructed between intensity and gradient space coordinates. This mapping, denoted by $G(p, q)$, is called the reflectance map. From the reflectance map, Woodham [17] illustrates how a single intensity value restricts the p and q values of the surface normal to a particular iso-brightness contour. The goal of shape from shading is to isolate which (p, q) value on the contour is the correct surface gradient.

One method of generating the reflectance map is through calibration. A sphere can be scanned, relating measured intensity values to known surface normals at each (x, y) point on the surface. The data are then structured to be indexed by intensity value forming a kind of inverse reflectance map.

2.2. Single-Source Photometry

Once a reflectance map is established, the process of determining the shape of sample objects can begin. When a single source of illumination is used, a single-image intensity value maps into many possible surface orientations. To resolve these ambiguities, algorithms developed to solve for surface shape, using a single source, assume certain surface constraints. Woodham [17] assumes surfaces to be uniform, matte, convex and smooth with continous first and second partial derivatives. From this assumption, his iterative algorithm propagates these constraints until converging on a solution for the entire surface.

2.3 Multiple Source Photometry

Photometric stereo, in essence, is multiple-source photometry where two or more images of an object are obtained from the same viewpoint. In each image the object is illuminated from a different direction by a single source. This gives rise to a n-tuple of intensity values for each (x, y) point on the surface.

The first step in multiple-source photometry is to establish a reflectance map for each source of illumination. Then by tracing iso-brightness contours for each source/intensity the intersection point for all contours can be found. This intersection point satisfies the intensity value requirements for each source and is thus the surface gradient at the corresponding image point (x, y).

It has been shown [18] that a minimum of three distinct iso-brightness contours is needed to locally determine the surface gradient for a Lambertian surface. This implies that a minimum of three sources is needed. For the contours to intersect at a single point the source vectors cannot be collinear.

When using table look-up techniques, shape can be determined for surfaces having photometric properties identical to the surface used in calibration of reflectance maps, implying that the specular component of all sample surfaces must be identical to that cast in the reflectance map. Additionally, specularity cannot be detected, as there is no indicator to show if an intensity value is elevated due to specular reflection. Furthermore, when establishing a reflectance map the surface reflectance factor R is made constant for all points on the surface [5]. This forces a uniformity of intensity on the surface and thus complicates the application of table look-up techniques to visually textured surfaces.

2.4. A Direct Solution for the Lambertian Surface

Assuming a Lambertian surface, limitations of table look-up techniques can be overcome by solving for surface normal and reflectance factor when three images, obtained using three different positions of a light source, are available [7, 18]. This is accomplished by beginning with the imaging equation

$$I(x, y) = R^*\cos(i) = R^*(S.N)/|S||N|. \tag{2.6}$$

If it is assumed that the source and normal vectors, S and N, are unit vectors, the denominator for Eq. (2.6) becomes 1. Equation (2.6) can now be written as

$$I(x, y) = R^*(S.N) = R^*(Sx, Sy, Sz).(Nx, Ny, Nz), \tag{2.7}$$

where (Sx, Sy, Sz) are the known components of the source vector and (Nx, Ny, Nz) are the unknown components of the surface normal.

Since (2.7) is an equation with three unknowns, a minimum of three sources and associated intensity values is needed to compute the surface normal at each point. Given the sources $S1$, $S2$, and $S3$ along with intensity values $I1$, $I2$, and $I3$ at (x, y)

a set of simultaneous equations can be formed to solve for N [18]:

$$\begin{bmatrix} I1 \\ I2 \\ I3 \end{bmatrix} = \begin{bmatrix} S1x & S1y & S1z \\ S2x & S2y & S2z \\ S3x & S3y & S3z \end{bmatrix} \begin{bmatrix} Nx \\ Ny \\ Nz \end{bmatrix}. \tag{2.8}$$

If we use Ms to symbolize the source matrix, I the intensity feature vector at (x, y) and N the normal vector, Eq. (2.8) becomes

$$\bar{I}(x, y) = R*[Ms]\bar{N}. \tag{2.9}$$

To solve for the reflectance factor, R, and unit normal, N, Eq. (2.9) can be written as

$$R*\bar{N} = [Ms]^{-1}\bar{I}. \tag{2.10}$$

Using Eq. (2.10) the surface normal can be computed directly from a triplet of intensity values I and the inverse of the source matrix Ms. For Ms to have an inverse the source vectors $S1$, $S2$, and $S3$ must not be collinear.

The reflectance factor, R, can be found simply by taking the magnitude of the right side of Eq. (2.10). This is because the surface normal, N, is of unit length.

$$R = |[Ms]^{-1}\bar{I}| \tag{2.11}$$

Once the reflectance factor is found the unit normal can be computed as

$$N = (1/R)*[Ms]^{-1}\bar{I}. \tag{2.12}$$

Using Eq. (2.12), all three components of the unit surface normal can be found. It is necessary to compute all three components as the unit surface normal will not necessarily have $Nz = -1$.

2.5. Handling Visual Texture

By solving for the unit normal vector in the previous section, it has also been shown that the surface reflectance factor R can be determined locally at each (x, y) point on a surface. This implies that R need not be constant over the surface. Regardless of how R varies, it can still be computed at each point using Eq. (2.11).

Visual texture can be thought of as a pattern caused by a change in the surface reflectance factor from point to point on a given surface. Indeed, shading models have been developed in computer graphics utilizing a variable reflectance factor to effect surface intensity [12]. Thus, it can readily be seen that applying Eq. (2.10) allows surface normals to be computed when the object is visually textured, as R is computed locally at each point. In fact a surface relative formulation of texture can be expressed as

$$T(x, y) = R(x, y)/R\text{max}, \tag{2.13}$$

where Rmax is the maximum value of R computed over the entire surface. $T(x, y)$ thus ranges from 0 to 1.

2.6. Overcoming Specular Distortion

One method of overcoming specularity problems in a shading model is by incorporating terms into the reflectance function to account for the specular component [16]. Building such terms into the reflectance function, however, ties the model to a single expression of specularity. A more flexible method is needed which enables the specular component to vary from one surface to another or even across the same surface. The approach taken here is to develop a shape from shading method based on four sources of illumination and four images for each surface.

As was shown in Section 2.4, three sources are all that are needed to uniquely determine surface normals for a Lambertian surface. If, however, a point on the surface is subject to specular reflection from one of the three sources, the computed normal vector will be incorrect due to an elevated intensity value. By adding a fourth source, it becomes possible to compute a set of four surface normal vectors for each point; i.e., one normal for each permutation of three intensity values. It is this redundancy which allows tagging and removal of the specular source.

To see how this is accomplished first assume we are given four measured intensity values at a point (x, y) on a surface; one intensity from each source/image. If none of the intensities has a specular component, the resulting four surface normals ($R^*\overline{N}$ from Eq. (2.10)) will appear as in Fig. 3a. On the other hand, suppose the intensity value from an arbitrary source/image (source four in this case) contains a specular component elevating its value. The resulting four normals computed will be similar to the case illustrated in Fig. 3b.

It can readily be seen that there is a greater deviation in both direction and magnitude of the vectors in Fig. 3b than for those in Fig. 3a. Three of the normal vectors in Fig. 3b (the three computed using the fourth source) are affected by a specular component. Because of this reason, their magnitudes, R, are greater and they are skewed more in the direction of the specular source.

A method can now be developed to eliminate specular effects using a thresholding procedure. The first step is to compute a relative deviation in the surface reflectance factor R at each point on the surface. This can be done using the formula

$$R\text{dev} = \left[\sum_{i=1}^{4} (Ri\text{-}R\text{mean}) \right] / (4^*R\text{min}), \qquad (2.14)$$

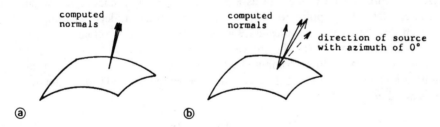

ⓐ   ⓑ

FIG. 3.(a) Computed normals at a single point on the surface when no specular component is present. Mean deviation among normals is small. (b) Computed normals at a single point with source at 0° exhibiting specularity. Intensity value from this source is elevated causing a high deviation among these normals.

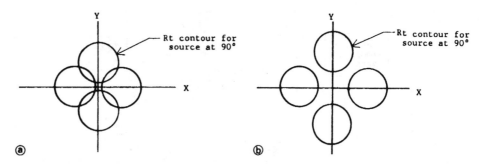

FIG. 4. Threshold specularity contours, Rt, in the image plane for a sphere. (a) Overlapping specularity contours indicate specularity too great for source placement. (b) Sources adjusted to accommodate specularity; contours not overlapping.

where Ri is each reflectance factor computed at (x, y) and $R\min$ is the smallest of these. A reflectivity deviation map can be displayed for the entire surface showing the reflectance deviation Rdev at each point (see Fig. 9). In the reflectivity deviation map, the range of deviation is divided into 36 intervals, each assigned a character from 0 through Z.

On a reflectivity deviation map, specular regions will be characterized by high reflectance deviation. Before finding the surface normal at each point, a threshold value Rt is chosen representing the largest amount of reflectance deviation allowed before specularity occurs.

When computing surface normals, Rdev at each point is checked against the threshold value Rt. If Rdev at a point is less than or equal to Rt, a specular component is not considered to be present. The surface normal is computed as the average of all four normals calculated at this point. Rdev greater than Rt indicates a specular contribution at this point from one of the sources. To eliminate this specular component, the surface normal is chosen from the permutation of the three intensity values which have the smallest reflectance factor.

In practice, the use of a threshold value will allow many surfaces to be analyzed successfully. A limiting factor is that the specular component cannot be so great as to cause specular regions from two or more sources to overlap. This can be overcome to some degree by adjusting the angle of incidence for each source to prevent overlap, as in Fig. 4.

Finally, the phase angles between all source vectors and the view vector must not be so large as to prevent all four sources from contributing measurable intensity values throughout the arc of specular reflection. For most cases a phase angle of up to 60 degrees can be used (30 degrees above the image plane) but under special circumstances the optimum source angles may have to be determined experimentally.

3. A WORKING SYSTEM

A system consisting of specialized imaging hardware and a series of computer programs was developed to verify the approach proposed above. A high-level layout of this system is shown in Fig. 5.

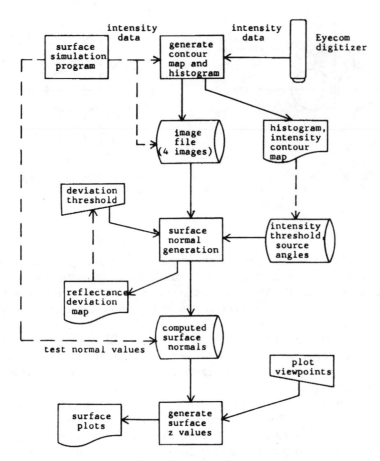

FIG. 5. System flowchart.

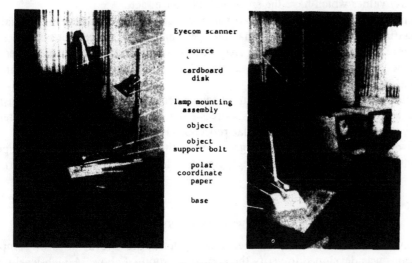

FIG. 6. Lamp support and setup showing Eyecom digitizer with jig, constructed to control source angles and object registration.

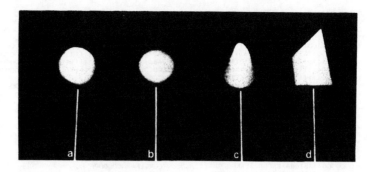

FIG. 7. Sample objects for experiment: (a) sphere; (b) oblate spheroid; (c) truncated cone; (d) square pyramid.

3.1. The Setup

Before actual digitization of the images could begin, a jig had to be made to control the source distance, source angles, and object viewpoint. The device shown in Fig. 6 was used for this purpose. A lamp assembly was mounted on a $\frac{1}{2}$-inch dowel by an adjustable clamp. This allowed control over the altitude of the angle of incidence relative to the image plane. To avoid calibration, a single lamp was used for all four images.

The lamp mounting assembly was made to swivel on a plywood base. An altitude of approximately 55 degrees above the image plane was chosen for the source. An exact measure of the source angle was achieved by measuring the shadow length cast by the object support bolt (see Fig. 6).

Four azimuth angles of 356, 86, 176, and 266 degrees were chosen; one for each source of illumination. A piece of polar coordinate paper was placed on the base to indicate these angles and to mark shadow lengths. Moving the lamp to a particular source location simply required rotating the lamp mounting assembly on the object support bolt. When the shadow cast by the support bolt was in line with the desired azimuth angle, the source was then in position.

The sample objects in Fig. 7 were glued to a small stage which could be screwed onto the object support bolt. The support bolt itself was secured to the plywood base. Neither the bolt nor the stage would move when the light source was rotated. This ensured perfect registration between the four digitized images of each surface.

The distance between the lamp and each surface was about 2 feet; between the scanner's lens and each surface about 18 inches. A 75-watt soft white light bulb was used to provide a relatively uniform source of illumination. The light from this source passed through a one-inch hole in a cardboard disk covering the end of the lamp. The disk was used to increase uniformity of source direction and intensity.

3.2. Picture Digitization

All images were digitized directly using an Eyecom high resolution digitizer. The resulting output was a 480 by 480 array of pixels, each containing an 8-bit gray level code (0–255). The Eyecom was operated in the linear mode.

A flat black background was used to simplify object isolation within the image. Black felt squares made up this background. In addition a black box was placed over the object stage area allowing only light from the source onto the object's surface.

```
0100100010010010011000010100111011111111111110011000010100111111111111101110110110111010100000000000000000
10000000111001110111111101111101111101111110111100011111111111111011111010000010100000000000000000
10111000100100111111110100101111111111111011111111110111111111110111110000011100000000000000000
1101001011001011111110001110111111111111111111111111121111111011111111011100011001000000000000000
000010100001100111101011111111111111110110111111111111110111111101011111110101010000000000000000
010110110100110001100110111111111111111111111122233555556645432211111111111111010100100000000001000000000
1001101001111011111111101110111111011111234567899AAABBABAA98753221110111111110101001000000000000
00001111000011011011011111111111110013456889AABCCDDDEEDDEDDEDDCA8642101111111101010000000000000
00001111101111111111111111111111111000124577899AABBCDDDEFFFGGGGGGGHGGFFFDB85311111101000100000000000000
00001110001111011111111111111000013567899ABBBCDDEEEFFGHHHIIIIIIIIIJHHHGFD941110001000000000000000
000000010101011111101011111000012355779AABBCDDEEFFFGGGGHIIHJIJJJKJJJJIKJIIHFD84111000000000000000000
0000000001111111101111100001356779AABBCCDDEFFFFGGHHHIJJJJKKLKKKKKKKJJIHGE7311111010000000000000000
0000000000000000001111111100013456789ABBBBCDDFFEFFGHGHIJJJJKKLKLLMMLLLLLMLLKKJJGDB21110000000000000000
00000000010001001111100001345779AABCCDDDDEFFFGGGHHIIIKJJKLLLLLLMMMMMMLMMLLKKIGB410000000000000000
0000000000000000001000001345678919ABCCDDEEEFFGGGHHHIIJIJKKKKLLMMMMMNNNMMMMMMLLJIID520000000000000000
0000000000000000000100001235689AABCDDDEEEFFFFGFGHIIIIJJJJKLLLLMMNMNNNNNNNNNMMMLKJF82110000000000000000
0000000000000000000000002456898ABBCDDDDEEFFFGHGGHHHJJKJJJKLLKMLLMMMNNNONNOOONNONMMKGA40000000000000000
0000000000000000000000000234579AABBCDDEDEFFGGGGGHHIIIIJKKJJKKLLLLMMMMNNOONNNNOONNOONNMKHB30100000000000000
00000000000000000000000001245789ABBCCCDEEEFFGGHHHHIIJJJJJJKKKKMMMLMNNNNODODOOOOPPODOPOODMKHA2010000000000000
00000000000000000000000001135788AABBCBDEEEFFGGFGHIIIJJJJJJJKKLLKLLMMMNOODOOOPPOPOPPPPPPOPPONLH6110000000000000
0000000000000000000000011346789AABBBCDEFFFFGGGHHHIJJJJJKKKKJLLLLKLNNNNODDPOPPQQPPPQQPOQPPOOMKD3010000000000
000000000000000000000245789AABBBDDDEEFGGGFGHIIIJJJJJJKLKKKLMLMNOODOPOPPPQQQQQQQQQQPPPODMH810000000000000
00000000000000000000124679AAAABCCDEEEFFGHHHHHIIIHIJKKKLLLLLLLNMMNOOOOPPPQPQRQQQQPOPPPONKE5000100000000000
0000000000000000000135779AAABBCDEEEEFFHGGHIIIIJJJKKLLLMMMMMNNNNOPPODPOPPQQQQQQPQQPPONLIA1100000000000
00000000000000000011246789AABBBCDDEFFGGGGHHIIJJIIJJJKKMMLLMMNNNOONOOPPOPPQQPQQQQQQPPPONMJE2000000000000
000000000000000000011346789999ABCDDDEEGGHHHHIHHHIJJJIKKKKLMNNNOOPPPPPPPPPPPOOQPPQRQQPPPONMLH40010000000
000000000000000000011346789999ABACCDEEFFFGHHHGHGGHHIKIJKKLLMNNNOPRRRRRQPPPPQQQQQQQPQQQOOPPOMLJ600100000000
00000000000000000000124567899AABCCDDEFGFFFGGHHIIHHHHJLLLMLMMOPPRSTUTSRQPPPPPOPPQQPPPQQPPOONMK900100000
0000000000000000000235778999ABCDDDEEFFFGGGHHIIIIHJMMMNMMNNOOQSSUVVTSRRRQPPQPPPQPQPQPQPOONNNML J H901000000000
000000000000000000012346789999ABCDCDDEEEGGGGHIIJJJJJKNLOONNOPPQSUWWTTTSRRQQPPPPPQPPQPPNMMJ8100000000
000000000000000000011246789AABBCCCDEEFFGHHIIJJJKKLLMLMMNNPPPPRSTWXWTTSSRRQQPODPPPPPPPPPOML J8100000000
000000000000000000002356789ABBCBDEDEEFGHHIIJJKJKLMMMNMMNOPQQQSTUWUTRRSSQQQQPPOOOPQPPODOONKH71110010000
00000000000000000001356899AAABCDDDDEFFFHIIIJKKKLKMMNNNOPOOPQQRSSSRTSRQQRQQPPPODOOOOPOONNJG500100000
000000000000000000012346689999AABBDDEEEEFGGHHJJJKLLMMMMNOOONPPPQRSRRRORRSRQQQQPPPNODDOOONMMJF3010000000
000000000000000000012467799AABBCCEDFEFFGGIIJJKKKMMMNNOOPOPQQQRRQQQQQRRRPPQQPPPPPONNNDOONMKJD200010000
000000000000000000012456789AABCCDDEFFGGHHIIJKKKKLMMMNMNPOPPPPQQQRQQQQQRQQQPPQPPOPOPONNNNMML J H91010001000000
0000000000000000000010134678999ABCCDDDEFGGHHHIJJJKKKMNMNMNOOOPPPPPPQPPPQQQQQQPPQPQ00DOONNNNLKIE50000000000
000000000000000000012456899AAABCCDEEEFGIHHIIKKJKKLLMNNNNNOODPOOPPPQQPPPPQQQQPOONNDOONMMLJG8201000000010
00000000000000000001356789AABBBCCDDEEFGIHIIIJIKKLKLMNNMNNPOOPPPOPPODPPPQPODONNNMMMKKIC311000000000
000000000000000000012446889AAABBCDDEFFFFHIIHIJKKKKKLMNNNNNOOOPPODDPOPPPPPQPNOONNMLKJGG6101000000000
00000000000000000001245678AAABBCCDDEFFFGHIIIJJKKKKKKLNNNNNPOOPONOODOOOPPPONNNMKKJGA11110000000000
000000000000000000011346678ABBBCCDDEFFFGGHIJJJKJKKKLLLMNNMNONNOONODONONNONNNMLKJHC4111011010000000
00000000000000000000124567779AABCCDDEFFFFGGHIIJJJKJKKKLLLMMMMMMNNOONMNNNNNNNNNNNMMMLIIHC4110000001000000
000000000000000000012356789AACCCDDDEEEFFGGGHIIIJJKKKKLLLMML MMNNNNNMNMNMMMMMML KJGA3101110100000000
0000000000000000000012356789AABBCDEEEEFFEGGGHHIIIKKJKLLLLMMMMMMMMMLLMLLLLKKR JHF721110000000000
00000000000000000001000000112446789AABCDEDEEFEGGGGHHIHIJKKKKKLLLMLLLMMLLMMLKLKJIIGE81111010010100100000
00000000000000000001000000133567789ABBDDDEEFFGGGGHIIIJJJJJKKKLLLKLLLLLKKKKJIGFB52111110000000000000
00000000000000000111221110000002345678A9ABCCDDEFFFGGGHHIHIJJJJKKJJJJJJJKJKJIHGFB6211111011110000000100
0000000000000000001011111111110000023456789ABBCDDDEFFFGHHIIIIIIIJIJJJIJIJJIHHGFC921121111110111101100100
000000000000000000011111112110000123567789ABBCDDDEFEFGGGHHHHHHHHHHHGGFEC83211111211111111100000010
00000000100111112111111111121100001234567899AABBBCDDDEEEEFFEFFFFGFFEFEECCB974211112121111111111110000000
0000000001111111111111111111111110000123556799AAAAABCDBCDDDDDDDDDDCCBBA853211211111111111111100000100000
000000001110111111111111111111121111010123466789899AAAAAABBBAABA986432111111111111110111110000001000000
0000110110111111111111111111111111111100112345566777788776543211111111111111111111101111000010000
0000111111111111121111111111111111111111111111111122233222221111111121111111101111100001000010000000
0111110110011111111111111111111111111111101111211111111111110111111111101111111011110110011001000000000
110110111111111111111111111111111111111111111111111101111111111111010101110010000000000000
```

FIG. 8. Sample intensity contour map for a single image of the sphere, illuminated by light source at 356° azimuth. Intensity value at each point must exceed the threshold level of '2' for the point to be considered as lying on the surface.

Once the images were digitized, they were then processed by a program to generate intensity histograms and intensity contour maps (Fig. 8). The contour maps and histograms were used to determine intensity threshold values for object boundaries.

3.3. Surface Normal Generation

Surface normal generation was accomplished by the method detailed in Section 2.4. As can be seen from Eq. (2.12) a triplet of intensity values must be multiplied by the inverse of the source matrix, Ms. Before this inverse is computed, source vectors must be derived. The input used to generate these source vectors consisted of the cast shadow length, support bolt height and azimuth angle in degrees for each source.

Four source matrices were created, one for each permutation of three source vectors. Each matrix contained source vectors as follows:

$$M1 = (S1, S2, S3), \quad M2 = (S2, S3, S4),$$
$$M3 = (S3, S4, S1), \quad M4 = (S4, S1, S2),$$

where Si is the source vector for source i. The inverse for each matrix was computed using Gaussian elimination with partial pivotal condensation. It can be seen from Eq. (2.13) that the inverse does not change for a given source geometry, hence each inverse need be computed only once.

Computation of the surface normal vectors was very straightforward. Each triplet of intensity values $(I1, I2, I3)$ at a point (x, y) was multiplied by the appropriate inverse ($M1$ in this case) to give the normal. The normal was reduced to a unit

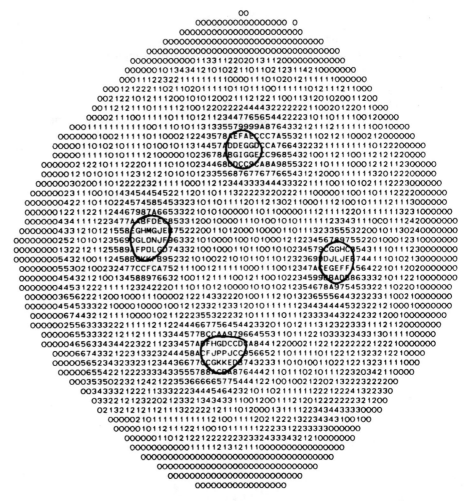

FIG. 9. Sample reflectivity deviation map. Specularity is indicated by contours outlining regions where the mean deviation among surface normals exceeds the threshold level of 'C'.

normal and the reflectance factor extracted. Prior to computing the normal, all intensity values had to exceed predetermined threshold levels to ensure that the point is on the surface.

As is described in Section 2.6, the program determined reflectance deviation at each point on the surface where four normals could be computed. This deviation was then translated into a reflectivity deviation map as shown in Fig. 9. From this map we are able to select the maximum deviation allowed between a set of normals at each point. Note how specular conditions give rise to high deviation as indicated by circled regions.

After the selected deviation threshold is entered, the final normal values are computed. These values represent an average of four vectors if the deviation threshold is not exceeded. Otherwise, the vector corresponding to the lowest reflectance factor is used. All output vectors are unit surface normals to insure correct operation of the depth conversion procedure.

3.4. Depth Conversion

The final step in generating the actual surface is the conversion from surface normals to depth information. That is, for every (x, y) point and normal vector N at (x, y) a z value with respect to the image plane must be computed.

First, assume a surface patch as shown in Fig. 10. Also assume each of the surface normals $N0, N1, N2, N3$ is known at the points $(0,0), (1,0), (0,1), (1,1)$, respectively. Finally, a starting z value at $(0,0)$ is either chosen or known. To compute z values at the remaining three points a function must be chosen to specify how the normal varies along the edges of the patch.

If the points $(0,0)$ and $(1,0)$ are very close relative to surface size, the curve between these points can be approximated by its average tangent line. When considering the distance between pixels, this condition holds.

Given the following normal vectors:

$$N0 = (n0x, n0y, n0z) \text{ at } (0,0),$$
$$N1 = (n1x, n1y, n1z) \text{ at } (1,0),$$
$$N2 = (n2x, n2y, n2z) \text{ at } (0,1),$$
$$N3 = (n3x, n3y, n3z) \text{ at } (0,1),$$

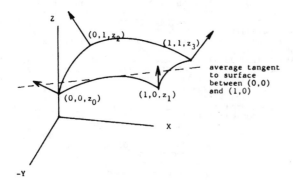

FIG. 10. Surface patch and normal vectors. Approximation to surface between (x, y) points $(0,0)$ and $(1,0)$ can be made by using the average tangent line if points are sufficiently close.

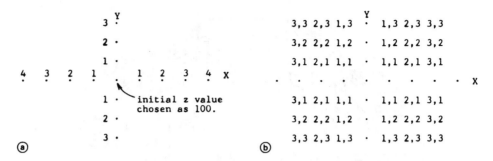

FIG. 11. Illustration of depth conversion order for points on the object's surface. (a) Initially, z values are calculated along the x and y axes through the center point of the image. The order in which z values are calculated is illustrated numerically. (b) After z values are established along the axes, z values are computed for points in each quadrant in column major order as illustrated.

we wish to compute z at $(1, 0)$ which is along the x axis from $(0, 0)$. The tangent line desired passes through the point $(0, 0, z)$ and is perpendicular to the average normal between these points. This line can be expressed as

$$ax + b(z(1,0) - z(0,0)) = 0, \tag{3.1}$$

where

$$a = (n0x + n1x)/2, \tag{3.2}$$

$$b = (n0z + n1z)/2. \tag{3.3}$$

This gives

$$z(1,0) = z(0,0) - x(a/b) \text{ with } x = 1. \tag{3.4}$$

Similarly, approximation along the y axis to find z at $(0, 1)$ gives

$$z(0,1) = z(0,0) - y(a/b) \text{ with } y = 1. \tag{3.5}$$

Here

$$a = (n0y + n2y)/2, \tag{3.6}$$

$$b = (n0z + n2z)/2. \tag{3.7}$$

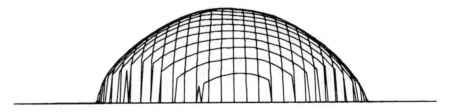

FIG. 12. Sphere plotted results. Surface generated from measured intensity values. Profile view; viewpoint $(5, -15, 0)$.

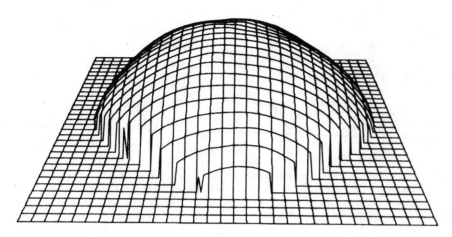

FIG. 13. Sphere plotted results. Surface generated from measured intensity values. Viewpoint coordinates: (5, −15, 15).

To arrive at $z(1, 1)$, two values are computed. One value, $z1(1, 1)$, is arrived at by going from $(1, 0)$ to $(1, 1)$ in the y direction. The second value, $z2(1, 1)$, is obtained by going from $(0, 1)$ to $(1, 1)$ along the x direction. The two values are averaged to give $z(1, 1)$:

$$z(1, 1) = (z1(1, 1) + z2(1, 1))/2.$$

z values can also be computed going along the negative x and y directions if $a - 1$ is substituted for x and y in Eq. (3.4) and (3.5), respectively. This is useful if the value of z at $(1, 1)$ is known and the z values at the other three points are to be computed.

The algorithm for depth conversion begins by choosing an arbitrary z value for the point in the center of the image. Next, z values are determined at all points along the x and y axes passing through this center point (see Fig. 11a). Finally, z values are computed for the remaining points in each quadrant in the order shown in Figure 11b. The final z values are offset as necessary to make Zmin = 0 (minimum z value).

3.5. Results

Two types of input data were used to determine the operational characteristics of the system. The first type was data generated by the simulation program; the second, digitized images from the Eyecom scanner. Here we discuss the results of our

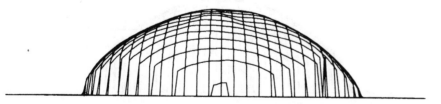

FIG. 14. Oblate spheroid plotted results. Surface generated from measured intensity values. Profile view; viewpoint (5, −15, 0).

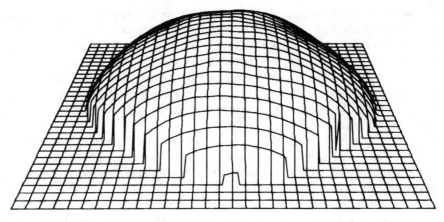

FIG. 15. Oblate spheroid plotted results. Surface generated from measured intensity values. Viewpoint coordinates: $(5, -15, 15)$.

experiments with the real data. The results from the simulation data are available in [20].

Four objects were chosen to determine the system's capabilities with actual images. These objects were a sphere, oblate spheroid, truncated cone and square pyramid as shown in Fig. 7. All four objects were made of wood, finished naturally with varnish. The surfaces were thus visually textured (wood grain) with varying degrees of specularity.

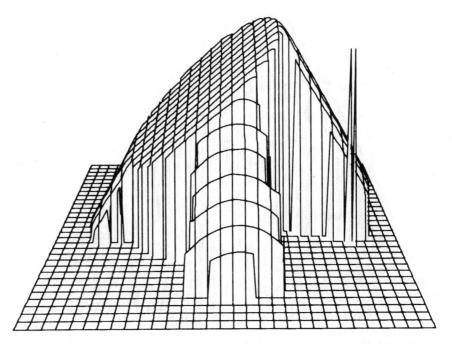

FIG. 16. Truncated cone plotted results. Surface generated from measured intensity values. Viewpoint coordinates: $(5, -15, 15)$.

Before normals were computed, a reflectivity deviation map was printed for each object. These maps were examined and a threshold deviation code of "*C*" was chosen as the maximum deviation allowable for all cases. From these maps, four high deviation areas were identified on the sphere and spheroid surfaces. These areas result from specular reflections from each of the sources. On the other hand, the truncated cone and pyramid show specularity only along the edge points. This is as was expected, for the surfaces of these objects were not inclined at the proper angle for specular reflection.

The plotted results for each object can be seen in Figs. 12 through 19. For each surface two views are given. These plots show how the essential characteristics of each surface were preserved; each object can be readily identified. This achieved the fundamental objective of this experiment.

On the plotted surfaces of the sphere and spheroid, valleys or dips are visible. These dips are due mainly to the nonuniformity of the light source. That is, a flat white disk placed under the scanner did not register a constant intensity at all points. These surface irregularities are not sufficient to cause the surfaces to be unrecognizable.

The sphere and spheroid surfaces do show profile differences when overlayed, the spheroid being more squat. There was not enough intensity information near the horizon, however, to generate the portions of these surfaces where they differ the most.

The cone and pyramid gave excellent results. Of particular interest is edge definition and uniformity on the faces. All planar surfaces have distinct edges and

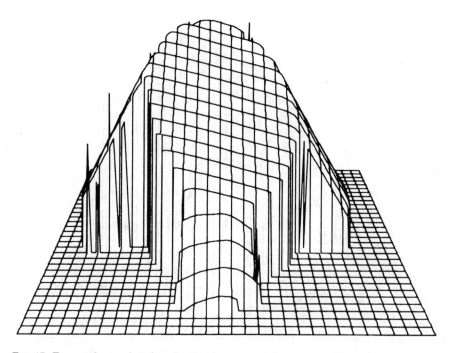

FIG. 17. Truncated cone plotted results. Surface generated from measured intensity values. Viewpoint coordinates: ($-15, 5, 15$).

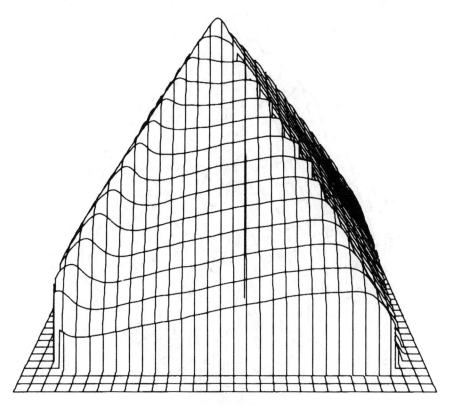

FIG. 18. Square pyramid plotted results. Surface generated from measured intensity values. Viewpoint coordinates: (5, −15, 15).

constant surface orientations. Algorithms using interpolation or iteration tend to round these edges and hence are best suited to smoothly curved surfaces.

Profile comparisons between actual objects and the generated surfaces indicated the plotted surfaces were somewhat flatter. One reason for this appears to be the shortness of the camera distance with respect to object size, making the perspective projection of the imaging device too pronounced to be effectively approximated by an orthographic projection. This flatness can also be attributed to the difference between the actual reflectance function and the Lambertian model. Better results may be obtained by using accurate reflectance maps for the objects. In all cases, however, the results were very promising and demonstrated the method's ability to handle visually textured, specular objects.

4. CONCLUSION

This paper extends the scope of *photometric stereo* to textured surfaces having specularity. It is shown that to obtain 3-dimensional shapes of surfaces with texture and specularity, four light sources may be used. An approach is presented to obtaining the 3-dimensional shape of such surfaces. The experimental setup in our laboratory for studying our approach used a common 75-watt soft white light bulb without any sophisticated method of controlling illumination. A simple algorithm was developed for depth-conversion to obtain relative depths of points on the

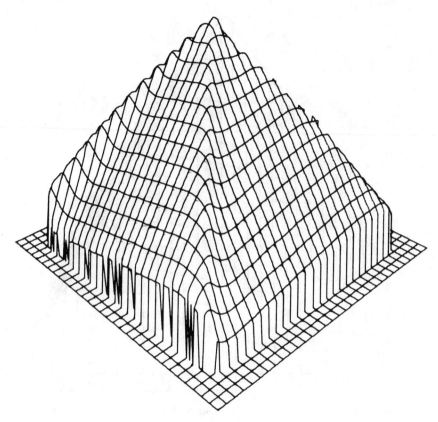

FIG. 19. Square pyramid plotted results. Surface generated from measured intensity values. Viewpoint coordinates: $(-15, -15, 15)$.

surface starting with the depth of a single point. The results of our experiments are very encouraging. There are very few points for which the computed Z information was wrong. Such noise points can be easily corrected by using a smoothness constraint or by using a more sophisticated setup.

ACKNOWLEDGMENTS

We are thankful to the referee for his constructive criticism, which resulted in a significant improvement in the quality of this paper. It is a pleasure to acknowledge the assistance of Susan Haynes in the preparation of this paper.

REFERENCES

1. R. O. Duda, D. Nitzan, and P. Barrett, Use of range and reflectance data to find planar regions, *IEEE Trans. Pattern Anal. Mach. Intell.* **PAMI-1**, 1979, 259.
2. D. B. Gennery, A Stereo Vision System for an Autonomous Vehicle, Proc. 5th IJCAI, 1977, p. 576.
3. D. B. Gennery, Object Detection and Measurement Using Stereo Vision, Proc. 6th IJCAI, 1979, p. 320.
4. B. K. P. Horn, Obtaining shape from shading information, in *The Pyschology of Computer Vision* (P.H. Winston, Ed.), McGraw–Hill, New York, 1975.
5. B. K. P. Horn, Understanding Image Intensities, *Artificial Intell.* **8**, 1977, 201.
6. B. K. P. Horn, R. J. Woodham, and W. M. Silver, Determining Shape and Reflectance using Multiple Images, A. I. Memo 490, MIT A.I. Laboratory, August 1978.

7. B. K. P. Horn and R. W. Sjoberg, Calculating the reflectance map, Appl. Opt. **18**, 1979, 1790.

8. K. Ikeuchi and B. K. P. Horn, An Application of the Photometric Stereo Method, A. I. Memo 539, MIT A. I. Laboratory, August 1979.

9. R. A. Lewis and A. R. Johnston, A Scanning Laser Rangefinder for a Robotic Vehicle, Proc. 5th IJCAI, 1977, p. 762.

10. H. P. Moravec, Visual Mapping by a Robot Rover, Proc. 6th IJCAI, 1979, p. 598.

11. R. Nevatia, Depth measurement by motion stereo, *Computer Graphics and Image Processing*, **1**, 1976, p. 203.

12. W. M. Newman and R. F. Sproull, *Principles of Interactive Computer Graphics*, McGraw–Hill, New York, 1979.

13. K. Prazdny, The Information in Optical Flow, TR-915, Computer Science Center, University of Maryland, College Park, July 1980.

14. J. M. Prager, Segmentation of Static and Dynamic Scenes, COINS Technical Report 79-7, Dept. of Computer and Information Science, University of Massachusetts at Amherst, May 1979.

15. T. Sato, Automotive Stereo Vision Using Deconvolution Techniques, Proc. 6th IJCAI, 1979, p. 763.

16. W. M. Silver, "Determining Shape and Reflectance Using Multiple Images," M.S. Thesis, M.I.T. A.I. Laboratory, May 1980.

17. R. J. Woodham, "Reflectance Map Techniques for Analyzing Surface Defects in Metal Castings," AI-TR-457, MIT A.I. Laboratory, June 1978.

18. R. J. Woodham, Photometric method for determining surface orientation from multiple images, *Opt. Eng.* **19**, 1980, p. 139.

19. Y. Yakimovsky and R. Cunningham, A system for extracting three-dimensional measurements from a stereo pair of TV cameras, *Computer Graphics and Image Processing*, **7**, 1978, p. 195.

20. E. N. Coleman, "Shape from Intensity with Visually Textured, Specular Surfaces," M.S. Thesis, Department of Computer Science, Wayne State University, Detroit, March 1981.

Determining Shape and Reflectance of Hybrid Surfaces by Photometric Sampling

SHREE K. NAYAR, MEMBER, IEEE, KATSUSHI IKEUCHI, MEMBER, IEEE, AND TAKEO KANADE, SENIOR MEMBER, IEEE

Abstract—Machine vision can benefit greatly from the development and utilization of accurate reflectance models. Our hybrid reflectance model is a linear combination of Lambertian and specular components and is obtained from the primary reflection components by making surface assumptions. Hence, Lambertian and specular surfaces are special instances of hybrid surfaces. We present a method for determining the shapes of hybrid surfaces without prior knowledge of the relative strengths of the Lambertian and specular components of reflection. The object surface is illuminated using extended light sources and is viewed from a single direction. Surface illumination using extended sources makes it possible to ensure the detection of both Lambertian and specular reflections. Uniformly distributed source directions are used to obtain an image sequence of the object. This method of obtaining photometric measurements is called photometric sampling. An extraction algorithm uses the set of image intensity values measured at each surface point to compute orientation as well as relative strengths of the Lambertian and specular reflection components. The simultaneous recovery of shape and reflectance parameters enables the method to adapt to variations in reflectance properties from one scene point to another. Experiments were conducted on Lambertian surfaces, specular surfaces, and hybrid surfaces. The measured surface orientations are found to be highly accurate, and the estimated reflectance parameters are consistent with the reflectance characteristics of the surfaces.

I. INTRODUCTION

MOST MACHINE vision problems involve the analysis of images resulting from the reflection of light. The apparent brightness of a point depends on its ability to reflect incident light in the direction of the sensor; this is commonly known as its reflectance properties. Therefore, the prediction or interpretation of image intensities requires a sound understanding of the various mechanisms involved in the reflection process. Although shape extraction methods are being developed and refined, it is also essential for the vision community to research and utilize more sophisticated reflectance models. Once a "general" reflectance model is made available, we are free to make reflectance assumptions that are appropriate for the vision application at hand. The result, a more specific model, may then be used to develop efficient shape extraction techniques.

Shape from shading [4], [6], [13], photometric stereo [2], [7], [18], and local shape from specularity [3] are examples of techniques that extract three-dimensional shape information from image intensities. All of these techniques rely on prior knowledge of surface reflectance properties. The reflectance properties are either assumed or measured using a calibration object of known shape. In many real-world applications, such as those involving surfaces of different reflectance characteristics, the calibration approach is not a practical one. Therefore, existing shape extraction methods are often used by assuming surface reflectance to be either Lambertian or specular. Many surfaces encountered in practice are hybrid in reflectance, that is, their reflectance models are linear combinations of Lambertian and specular models. Therefore, Lambertian and specular models are only limiting instances of the hybrid model. It is desirable to have a method that is capable of extracting the shape of hybrid surfaces including, as special cases, those that are purely Lambertian or specular.

In many industrial applications, surface polish and roughness are found to be important inspection criteria. In such cases, surface reflectance properties may be interpreted as measures of these criteria. Furthermore, reflectance properties may be used to segment an image into different regions; each region may then be regarded as a different surface to aid the process of inspection. For these reasons, it would be of great value to have a technique that could, in addition to determining shape, also estimate the reflectance properties of each surface point.

We begin this paper with a summary of the various mechanisms involved in the reflection process. By considering both physical optics and geometrical optics approaches, the primary components of reflection are identified. By making assumptions related to the microscopic shape of surfaces, the primary reflection components are simplified to obtain the hybrid reflectance model. The object of interest is illuminated using multiple extended light sources and is viewed from a single direction. The sources are uniformly distributed around the object and are sequentially scanned, one by one, to obtain an image sequence of the object. We refer to this method of obtaining photometric measurements as *photometric sampling*. An extraction algorithm uses the image sequence and the hybrid reflectance model to determine object shape. Shape information is extracted *without* prior knowledge of the relative strengths of the Lambertian and specular reflection components. In addition, the extraction algorithm also estimates reflectance parameters at surface points. The *simultaneous* recovery of shape and reflectance enables the method to adapt to variations in hybrid reflectance from one surface point to the next.

Manuscript received November 1, 1988; revised March 14, 1990. This work was supported by Westinghouse Electric Corporation and by DARPA under Contract F33615-87-C-1499.

S. K. Nayar is with the Department of Electrical and Computer Engineering and the Robotics Institute, Carnegie Mellon University, Pittsburgh, PA 15213.

K. Ikeuchi and T. Kanade are with the Department of Computer Science and the Robotics Institute, Carnegie Mellon University, Pittsburgh, PA 15213.

IEEE Log Number 9037734.

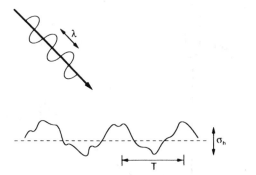

Fig. 1. Surface reflection is closely related to the microscopic surface profile and the wavelength of incident light.

II. SURFACE REFLECTION

A. A Unified Perspective

When light is incident on a boundary interface between two different media, it is reflected according to well-known laws. There are two different approaches to optics and, consequently, two different approaches to the study of reflection. Physical or wave optics is based directly on electromagnetic wave theory and uses Maxwell's equations to study the propagation of light. Geometrical or ray optics on the other hand, uses the short wavelength of light to simplify many of the light propagation problems. Although geometrical reflectance models may be construed as mere approximations to physical reflectance models, they possess simpler mathematical forms that often render them more usable than physical models. However, geometrical models are applicable only when the wavelength of incident light is small when compared to the dimensions of the *microscopic* surface imperfections. Therefore, it is incorrect to use these models to interpret or predict reflections from smooth surfaces; only physical models are capable of describing the underlying reflection mechanism.

In [11], we have unified physical and geometrical approaches to describe reflection from surfaces that may vary from smooth to rough. More specifically, we have focused on the Beckmann–Spizzichino (physical optics) model and the Torrance–Sparrow (geometrical optics) model. The surface height is modeled as a continuous stationary random process with standard deviation σ_h representing the physical *roughness* of the surface (Fig. 1). The spatial variation of the surface is described in terms of a correlation function that represents the dependence between the heights of different points on the surface. The spatial frequency of the surface is determined by the correlation distance T. The incident light is assumed to be a plane electromagnetic wave with wavelength λ. The reflectance curves predicted by the physical and geometrical models are obtained by varying the three parameters σ_h, T, and λ. From studying the behaviors of the physical and geometrical optics models, it is seen that surface radiance may be decomposed into three primary reflection components, namely, the *diffuse lobe*, the *specular lobe*, and the *specular spike*.

The diffuse component results from two main mechanisms. In one case, light rays that impinge on the surface are reflected many times between surface undulations before they are scattered into space. If these *multiple reflections* occur in a random manner, the incident energy is distributed in all directions, resulting in diffuse reflection. Another mechanism leading to diffuse reflection is the *internal scattering*[1] of light rays. In this case, the light rays penetrate the surface and encounter microscopic inhomogeneities in the surface medium. The light rays are repeatedly reflected and refracted at boundaries between regions of differing refractive indices. Some of the scattered rays find their way back to the surface in a variety of directions, resulting in diffuse reflection.

Specular reflection is composed of two primary components: the specular lobe and the specular spike. The lobe component spreads around the specular direction, and the spike component is zero in all directions except for a very narrow range around the specular direction. The relative strengths of the two components are dependent on the microscopic roughness of the surface. A detailed analysis of the characteristics of the three reflection components is given in [11]. We summarize our findings with the following remarks:

- The diffuse component may be represented by the Lambertian model [9]. This model has been used extensively to test shape-from-shading and photometric stereo techniques, and the results have indicated that it performs reasonably well. More accurate models [8], [14] may be used at the cost of functional complexity.
- The Beckmann–Spizzichino physical optics model predicts both the specular lobe and spike components. For a very smooth surface ($\sigma_h \ll \lambda$), the spike component dominates, and the surface behaves like a mirror. As the roughness increases, however, the spike component shrinks rapidly, and the lobe component begins to dominate. The two components are simultaneously significant for only a small range of roughness values.
- A "sharp" specular component may result from the specular spike component when the surface is smooth ($\sigma_h/\lambda < 1.5$) *and/or* the specular lobe component when the surface is gently undulating ($\sigma_h/T < 0.02$).
- The Torrance–Sparrow geometrical optics model provides a good approximation of the specular lobe component of the Beckmann–Spizzichino model. Both models are successful in predicting *off-specular* peaks in the specular lobe component. Due to its simpler mathematical form, the Torrance–Sparrow model may be used to represent the specular lobe component.
- The Torrance–Sparrow model is not capable of describing the mirror-like behavior of smooth surfaces, and it should not be used to represent the specular spike component because it would produce erroneous results.
- The specular lobes of both Torrance–Sparrow and Beckmann–Spizzichino models tend to have *specular peaks*, rather than off-specular peaks, when the viewing direction is fixed and the source direction is varied.

In shape extraction techniques such as photometric stereo and structured highlight, images of the observed object are obtained by varying the source direction while keeping the viewing direction constant. The shape extraction method de-

---

[1] This mechanism is often referred to as "body" reflection.

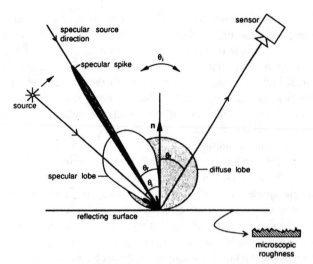

Fig. 2. Polar plots of the primary reflection components as functions of the source angle for a given viewing direction.

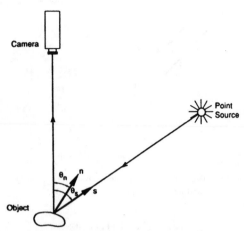

Fig. 3. Two-dimensional illumination and imaging geometry. A surface element with orientation θ_n reflects light from the point source direction θ_s into the camera.

scribed in this paper is based on the same approach. The shapes and functional forms of individual reflection components are different for the case in which the viewing direction is varied and the case in which the source direction is varied. We emphasize this difference by introducing a new representation of the reflection components. Fig. 2 shows polar plots of the diffuse lobe, specular lobe, and specular spike. The magnitudes of the three components of surface radiance in the sensor direction are determined by intersections made by the lobes with the line joining the source and the origin. The diffuse component is represented by the Lambertian model, the specular lobe component by the Torrance–Sparrow model, and the specular spike component by the spike component of the Beckmann–Spizzichino model.

B. Hybrid Reflectance Model

In this paper, we assume that the surfaces of interest are smooth, i.e., either the surface roughness is comparable to the wavelength of incident light ($\sigma_h/\lambda < 1.5$), or the surface is gently undulating ($\sigma_h/T < 0.02$), or both. From the previous discussion we see that under these conditions, both the spike and lobe components can be significant only in a narrow region around the specular direction. Therefore, we will combine the spike and lobe components into a single component, namely, the *specular component*. We also assume that the surfaces under consideration are nonhomogeneous. Therefore, a diffuse component of reflection may result from the internal scattering mechanism. We use the Lambertian model to represent the diffuse component. The combination of the above-mentioned two components is referred to as the *hybrid reflectance model*.

Consider the illumination of an object by a point source of light, as is shown in Fig. 3. Light energy reflected by the surface in the direction of the camera causes an image of the surface to be formed. The intensity at any point in the image of the surface may be expressed as

$$I = IL + IS \qquad (1)$$

where IL is the Lambertian intensity component, and IS is the specular intensity component.

We will express the two components of image intensity in terms of the parameters that describe the two-dimensional imaging and illumination geometry shown in Fig. 3. In two dimensions, the source direction vector s, surface normal vector n, and viewing direction vector v lie in the same plane. Therefore, directions are represented by a single parameter, namely, the zenith angle θ.

1) Lambertian Component: The brightness of a Lambertian surface is proportional to the energy of incident light. As can be seen in Fig. 3, the amount of light energy falling on a surface element is proportional to the area of the surface element as seen from the source position, which is often referred to as the foreshortened area. The foreshortened area is a cosine function of the angle between the surface orientation direction θ_n and the source direction θ_s. Therefore, the Lambertian intensity component IL may be written as

$$IL = A \cos(\theta_s - \theta_n) \qquad (2)$$

where the constant A determines the fraction of incident energy that is diffusely reflected. We have assumed that the angle of incidence ($\theta_s - \theta_n$) is greater than $-\pi/2$ and less than $\pi/2$, i.e., IL is always greater than zero.

2) Specular Component: Since the specular intensity component IS is a very sharp function of the source direction, it may be approximated by the delta function [11]

$$IS = B\delta(\theta_s - 2\theta_n). \qquad (3)$$

The basic *photometric function*[2] relates image intensity to surface orientation, surface reflectance, and point source direction and may be written by substituting (2) and (3) into (1) to obtain

$$I = A \cos(\theta_s - \theta_n) + B\delta(\theta_s - 2\theta_n). \qquad (4)$$

The constants A and B in (4) represent the relative strengths of the Lambertian and specular components of reflection, respectively. We call A and B the reflectance parameters. We

[2] The photometric function is similar to the image irradiance [5] equation since image intensity is assumed to be proportional to image irradiance.

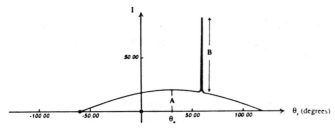

Fig. 4. Basic photometric function $I(\theta_s)$ for a hybrid surface.

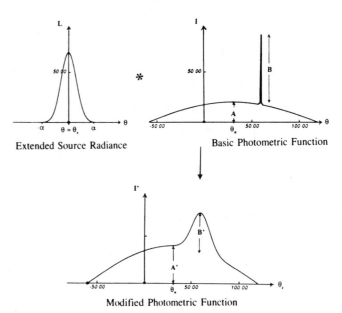

Extended Source Radiance   Basic Photometric Function

Modified Photometric Function

Fig. 5. Photometric function for extended source illumination is obtained by convolving the basic photometric function with the extended source radiance function.

see that $A > 0$ and $B = 0$ for a purely Lambertian surface, $A = 0$ and $B > 0$ for a purely specular surface, and $A > 0$ and $B > 0$ in general.

Our objective is to determine orientation and reflectance at each surface point from a set of image intensities that result from changing the source direction θ_s. Therefore, we will often refer to the basic photometric function as $I(\theta_s)$, which is a relation between image intensity and source direction. Fig. 4 shows a plot of the basic photometric function for a hybrid surface of given orientation.

III. PHOTOMETRIC SAMPLING USING EXTENDED SOURCES

A. Why Extended Sources?

We propose to illuminate the object surface by using extended sources, rather than point sources, for the following reasons:

- In the case of point source illumination, specular reflection is not detected unless $\theta_s = 2\theta_n$ exactly. In order to determine shape and reflectance parameters of specular and hybrid surfaces, specular reflections must be captured in the measured intensities. To detect specular reflections from surface points of all orientations, an infinite number of point sources need to be positioned around the surface. Such an approach is unrealistic from the perspective of practical implementation. Unlike a point source, an extended source emits light from an area of points rather than a single point. Therefore, a small number of extended sources may be used to ensure the detection of specular reflections.
- In the case of point source illumination, image intensities due to specular reflections are often observed to be much greater than intensities resulting from Lambertian reflections [15]. Therefore, it is difficult to measure both components in the same image. Extended source illumination tends to make the image intensities due to Lambertian and specular reflections comparable to one another. A specular surface element of a given orientation will reflect light from a small area on the extended source into the camera. On the other hand, a Lambertian surface element of the same orientation reflects light from all points on the extended source into the camera. This feature of the proposed illumination scheme makes it possible to measure both Lambertian and specular reflections in the same image.

In Appendix A, we have shown how extended sources are generated. The extended source radiance function $L(\theta, \theta_s)$ is derived, and the parameters that determine the direction and

limits of an extended source are defined. These results will be extensively used in the following discussions.

B. Photometric Function for Extended Sources

The photometric function for point source illumination (see (4)) needs to be modified for extended source illumination. An extended source may be thought of as a collection of point sources in which each point source has a radiant intensity that is dependent on its position on the extended source. The intensity of light reflected by a surface may be determined by computing the integral of the light energies reflected from all points on the extended source. Therefore, the modified photometric function $I'(\theta_s)$ is determined by convolving the basic photometric function $I(\theta)$ with the extended source radiance function $L(\theta, \theta_s)$. This operation is illustrated in Fig. 5. For a surface point of orientation θ_n, the Lambertian component IL' of the modified photometric function is determined to be

$$IL' = A \int_{\theta_s - \alpha}^{\theta_s + \alpha} L(\theta, \theta_s) \cos(\theta - \theta_n)\, d\theta. \qquad (5)$$

The limits of the integral are determined by the width of the extended source (Appendix A). It can be shown [10] that IL' is a cosine function of the angle between the surface orientation and the direction corresponding to the "center of mass" of the extended source radiance distribution $L(\theta, \theta_s)$. In our case, since the extended source is symmetric with respect to the source direction θ_s, the center of mass of the radiance function is in the direction θ_s. Therefore, we obtain

$$IL' = A' \cos(\theta_s - \theta_n) \qquad (6)$$

where the constant A' is proportional to A [10] and, hence, also represents the strength of the Lambertian component.

Similarly, the specular intensity component IS' resulting

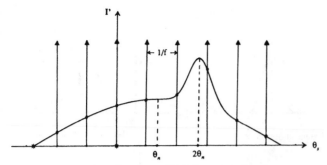

Fig. 6.   Sampling the modified photometric function.

from the extended source $L(\theta, \theta_s)$ is determined to be

$$IS' = B \int_{\theta_s - \alpha}^{\theta_s + \alpha} L(\theta, \theta_s)\delta(\theta - 2\theta_n)\, d\theta \qquad (7)$$

or

$$IS' = BL(2\theta_n, \theta_s). \qquad (8)$$

Strictly speaking, the result of the above integral is dependent on the exact shape of the specular spike and lobe. However, since both components are significant only in the specular direction $2\theta_n$, it is reasonable to assume that the specular intensity IS' is proportional to $L(2\theta_n, \theta_s)$, whereas the constant of proportionality is dependent on the exact shape of the two components. In light of this, we will use the constant B', rather than B, to represent the strength of the specular component of the photometric function.

The *modified photometric function* relates image intensity I' to extended source direction θ_s and is expressed as the sum of the components IL' and IS':

$$I' = A' \cos(\theta_s - \theta_n) + B'L(2\theta_n, \theta_s). \qquad (9)$$

Since the parameters A' and B' are proportional to the parameters A and B, respectively, they may be used to represent the reflectance properties of the surface point.

C. Sampling

The process of measuring image intensities corresponding to different source directions is equivalent to sampling the modified photometric function $I'(\theta_s)$, as is shown in Fig. 6. Samples of the photometric function may be obtained by moving an extended source around the object and obtaining images of the object for different source positions. An alternative approach would be to distribute an array of extended sources around the object such that each source illuminates the object from a different direction. The entire array of extended sources may be sequentially scanned such that for each scan, a single source is active, and an image of the object surface is obtained. We have chosen to use this alternative approach in our experiments. We will confine the sampling process to two dimensions: the surface normal vector, viewing direction vector, and source direction vectors for all extended sources, are coplanar. The sequential scanning of extended sources positioned in the directions $\{\theta_i: i = 1, 2, \cdots M\}$ results in a set of image intensities $\{I_i': i = 1, 2, \cdots M\}$ measured at each point on the object surface.

The number of samples measured at each surface point is determined by the frequency f at which $I'(\theta_s)$ is sampled. In order to extract the shape and the reflectance parameters of hybrid surfaces, both Lambertian and specular components of image intensity must be detected. Since we have used a delta function for the specular reflection model, the period of the modified photometric function that contains specular intensities is equal to the width 2α of the extended source radiance function. In the following section, we will show that in general, at least two photometric samples must have nonzero specular intensities for the extraction technique to work. Hence, the photometric function must be sampled at a frequency greater than or equal to the *minimum sampling frequency*[3] $f_{\min}$, where

$$f_{\min} = \frac{1}{\alpha}. \qquad (10)$$

Note that at this minimum frequency, the radiance distributions of adjacent extended sources overlap each other for an interval of α.

IV. Extracting Shape and Reflectance

Given the set of image intensities $\{I_i'\}$ measured at a surface point, we want to determine the orientation θ_n and reflectance parameters A' and B' of the point. We will first develop techniques to compute orientations of purely Lambertian and purely specular surfaces. Later, these techniques will be used to extract orientations and reflectance parameters of *general* hybrid surfaces.

A. Lambertian Surfaces

Consider the case where the surface of an object is known to be purely Lambertian. The task is to determine the shape of the object. The photometric samples for a Lambertian surface point may be written as

$$I_i' = A' \cos(\theta_i - \theta_n). \qquad (11)$$

We would like to compute the orientation θ_n and the strength of the Lambertian reflection component A'.

Toward this end, an error E is formulated to be the sum of the errors in measured samples over the entire set of samples:

$$E = \sum_{i=1}^{M} [I_i' - A' \cos(\theta_i - \theta_n)]^2. \qquad (12)$$

By using the conditions

$$\frac{\partial E}{\partial \theta_n} = 0 \quad \text{and} \quad \frac{\partial E}{\partial A'} = 0 \qquad (13)$$

we can determine values of θ_n and A' that minimize the error E. The above minimization is simplified by expressing $\cos(\theta_i - \theta_n)$ as a dot product of the source and normal vectors.

---

[3] It is assumed that the interval of the modified photometric function that contains specular intensities is small compared with the total width of the photometric function. Therefore, sampling frequencies that ensure the detection of specular intensities will provide a sufficient number of Lambertian intensity samples.

B. Specular Surfaces

Now consider the case where the object surface is known to be purely specular, and the shape of the object is to be determined. The photometric samples for a specular point may be written as

$$I_i' = B'L(2\theta_n, \theta_i). \tag{14}$$

We wish to determine the orientation θ_n and the specular strength B' from the intensity set $\{I_i'\}$. Let us assume that the specular direction $2\theta_n$ lies between the directions θ_k and θ_{k+1} of two adjacent extended sources. Further, let us assume that the photometric function is sampled using the minimum frequency f_{min}, i.e., $\theta_{k+1} = \theta_k + \alpha$. Then, since the surface is specular, only the samples I_k' and I_{k+1}' will have nonzero values. We see that when θ_n increases, $2\theta_n$ approaches θ_{k+1}, I_k' decreases, and I_{k+1}' increases. Similarly, when θ_n decreases, $2\theta_n$ approaches θ_k, I_k' increases, and I_{k+1}' decreases. In fact, from (14), we see that the intensity ratio I_k'/I_{k+1}' is equal to the ratio $L(2\theta_n, \theta_k)/L(2\theta_n, \theta_{k+1})$. Since the extended sources have decaying radiance functions (Appendix A), this ratio is a monotonic function of the angle $2\theta_n$. Since the radiance functions of the extended sources are known *a priori*, we can precompute and store in memory the correspondence between I_k'/I_{k+1}' and θ_n.

Given the image intensity set $\{I_i'\}$ at a specular surface point, the nonzero image intensities in the set are first identified. If only a single intensity value, for instance I_k', is greater than zero, then we know that $2\theta_n = \theta_k$. If two image intensities, say I_k' and I_{k+1}', are greater than zero, the ratio I_k'/I_{k+1}' is used to determine θ_n. Once θ_n is found, B' is obtained by using (14):

$$B' = \frac{I_k'}{L(2\theta_n, \theta_k)}. \tag{15}$$

C. Hybrid Surfaces

The modified photometric function for hybrid surfaces is given by (9). At each surface point, we want to determine A', B', and orientation θ_n from the measured samples $\{I_i': i = 1, 2, \cdots M\}$ of the photometric function. Toward this end, we will develop an algorithm that attempts to separate the Lambertian and specular components of each measured image intensity and then computes surface orientations using the methods given above for Lambertian and specular surfaces.

The extraction algorithm is based on two constraints, namely, the *sampling frequency constraint* and the *unique orientation constraint*. By sampling the modified photometric function at the minimum sampling frequency f_{min}, we can ensure that only two consecutive image intensities in the intensity set $\{I_i'\}$ contain nonzero specular components. For each k in the interval $0 < k < M$, I_k' and I_{k+1}' are hypothesized as being the two intensities that have specular components. All remaining intensities in the set $\{I_i': i = 1, 2, \cdots M\}$ must represent only Lambertian components of reflection. These intensities are used to compute the surface orientation θ_{nl} and the Lambertian strength A' (Section IV-A). The Lambertian components IL_k' and IL_{k+1}' are determined and used to sep-

arate the specular components IS_k' and IS_{k+1}' from I_k' and I_{k+1}', respectively. The surface orientation θ_{ns} and specular strength B' are computed from IS_k' and IS_{k+1}' (Section IV-B).

Next, the physical constraint that each surface point has a unique orientation is exploited. An estimate θ_{nk} of the orientation is found as a weighted average of the orientations θ_{nl} and θ_{ns}. The weights are proportional to the strengths of the two components of reflection. We support this method of weight selection because the surface orientation that is computed from intensities resulting from the stronger of the two reflection components is less sensitive to image noise and is, therefore, more reliable. An orientation error e_k is found by comparing θ_{nk} with θ_{nl} and θ_{ns}. Using the above approach, orientation errors are computed for all k, where $0 < k < M$. The orientation and reflectance parameters computed for the value of k that minimizes the orientation error are assigned to the surface point under consideration. This process is repeated for all points on the object surface.

It is important to note that the extraction algorithm is also capable of determining shape and reflectance of purely Lambertian and purely specular surfaces.

1) Extraction Algorithm:

Step 1: If all intensities I_i' measured at the image point (x, y) are less than the minimum intensity threshold T, assign the point (x, y) to "background" and **stop**.

Step 2: Let $k = 1$ and e_0 equal a large positive number.

Step 3: Assume that image intensities I_k' and I_{k+1}' consist of nonzero specular components of reflection. All remaining intensities I_i' (where $i \neq k$ and $i \neq k + 1$) are used with the Lambertian model to compute the surface orientation θ_{nl} and Lambertian strength A_k' (Section IV-A).

Step 4: The specular components IS_k' and IS_{k+1}' are separated from the image intensities I_k' and I_{k+1}':

$$IS_k' = I_k' - A_k' \cos(\theta_k - \theta_{nl})$$

$$IS_{k+1}' = I_{k+1}' - A_k' \cos(\theta_{k+1} - \theta_{nl}). \tag{16}$$

If $IS_k' < 0$ or $IS_{k+1}' < 0$, set $k = k + 1$ and go to **Step 2**.

Step 5: If $IS_k' = 0$ and $IS_{k+1}' = 0$, let $B_k' = 0$. Otherwise, determine the surface orientation θ_{ns} and the specular strength B_k' by using specular intensities IS_k' and IS_{k+1}' and the specular model (Section IV-B).

Step 6: The best estimate of surface orientation, for the kth iteration, is determined to be

$$\theta_{nk} = \frac{A_k' \theta_{nl} + B_k' \theta_{ns}}{A_k' + B_k'}. \tag{17}$$

The orientation error e_k is determined to be

$$e_k = \frac{A_k' |\theta_{nl} - \theta_{nk}| + B_k' |\theta_{ns} - \theta_{nk}|}{A_k' + B_k'}. \tag{18}$$

Step 7: If $e_k < e_{k-1}$, then

$$\theta_n = \theta_{nk}, \quad A' = A_k', \quad B' = B_k'. \tag{19}$$

If $k < M - 1$, set $k = k + 1$ and go to **Step 2**. Otherwise, **stop**.

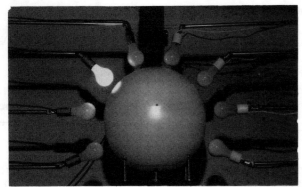

Fig. 7.   Photograph of the experimental setup used to demonstrate the photometric sampling concept.

In order to account for errors in image intensities due to the presence of noise, the implemented version of the above algorithm uses upper and lower bounds while testing inequalities, such as $IS'_k < 0$ and $IS'_{k+1} < 0$.

V. EXPERIMENTS

A. Experimental Setup

We have conducted experiments to demonstrate the practical feasibility of the photometric sampling concept. A photograph of the experimental setup used to implement photometric sampling is shown in Fig. 7. A 14-in diameter lamp shade is used as the spherical diffuser, and extended light sources are generated on the diffuser's surface by illuminating it using incandescent light bulbs. All light bulbs are assumed to have the same radiant intensity and are equidistant from the center of the diffuser. In our experiments, a source termination angle of $\alpha = 32°$ is used, and sampling is performed at the minimum frequency determined by (10). The object is placed at the center of the diffuser and is viewed by a camera through a 1-in diameter hole at the top of the diffuser. The current setup uses a WV-22 model Panasonic CCD camera that has a 512×480 pixel resolution. The complete imaging system, which is comprised of lenses and camera, has a physical resolution of 0.002 in per pixel width. In the current implementation, the light bulbs, camera, and object are all placed in the same plane. This two-dimensional setup is capable of measuring only orientations of surface normal vectors that lie on a single plane in orientation space. For each extended source, an image of the object is digitized and stored in memory. The sequence of object images, which are generated by scanning the array of extended sources, is processed on a 3/60 SUN workstation.

B. Results

Fig. 8 shows photometric samples measured at a point on the surface of a plastic object using the above experimental setup. The measured intensity values are represented by black dots. The reflectance model of the plastic surface includes both Lambertian and specular components. The orientation of the surface point was known *a priori*. Using the orientation value, the two measured samples that were expected to consist of both Lambertian and specular intensities were identified and are marked in the figure as "$L+S$". All remaining image intensities result from Lambertian reflection and are marked

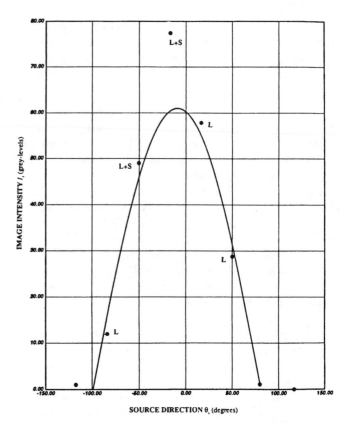

Fig. 8.   Samples of the photometric function measured at a hybrid surface point. By using the known orientation of the surface point, the two intensities that have specular reflections are identified and marked "$L+S$." The remaining points result solely from Lambertian reflection, and the cosine function that best fits these points is shown as a solid curve.

in the figure as "L." The cosine function that best fits the Lambertian intensities is represented by the solid curve. The specular components were extracted from the two intensities that are marked as "$L+S$." Two estimates of surface orientation were computed using the Lambertian and the specular components of the image intensities. Both computed orientations were found to be within $2.5°$ of the actual orientation value. Similar experiments were conducted on Lambertian and specular surfaces [10]. The results indicated that the hybrid model used in this paper does quite well in describing reflectance of light by smooth surfaces.

The experimental setup and the extraction algorithm were used to extract surface properties of a number of objects. Figs. 9, 10, 11, and 12 show the results of the extraction method applied to objects with different surface reflectance properties. For each object, a photograph of the object is followed by two reflectance images (Lambertian and specular), a needle map produced by the extraction algorithm, and a depth map that is constructed from the needle map. The intensity at each pixel in the reflectance images is proportional to the strength of the reflectance model component the image represents. The needle map is a representation of surface orientations. At each point on a needle map, the length of the needle is proportional to the tilt of the surface away from the viewing direction of the camera. All needles originate from the dots that constitute the resolution grid of the needle map. To help evaluate the performance of the extraction algorithm, we have included a

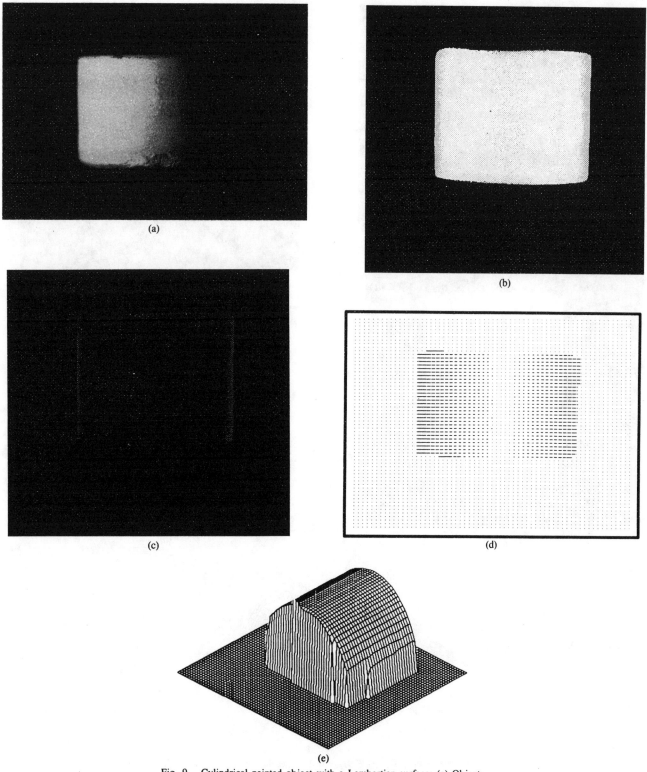

Fig. 9.   Cylindrical painted object with a Lambertian surface: (a) Object;
(b) Lambertian strength; (c) specular strength; (d) needle map; (e) depth
map.

depth map of each object that is obtained by integrating the orientations in the needle map. Note that the reconstructed surfaces are displayed at some arbitrary offset level in all the depth maps.

The object shown in Fig. 9 is cylindrical and its surface is Lambertian. Fig. 10 is the photo of a prism-shaped object

that has a highly specular surface. An interesting application for the proposed method is seen in Fig. 11. The object is a metal bolt that has a hexagonal-shaped head. The painted surface of the head is Lambertian in reflection, whereas the threaded section of the bolt is specular. Surface orientations are measured only along the thin edges of the threads since

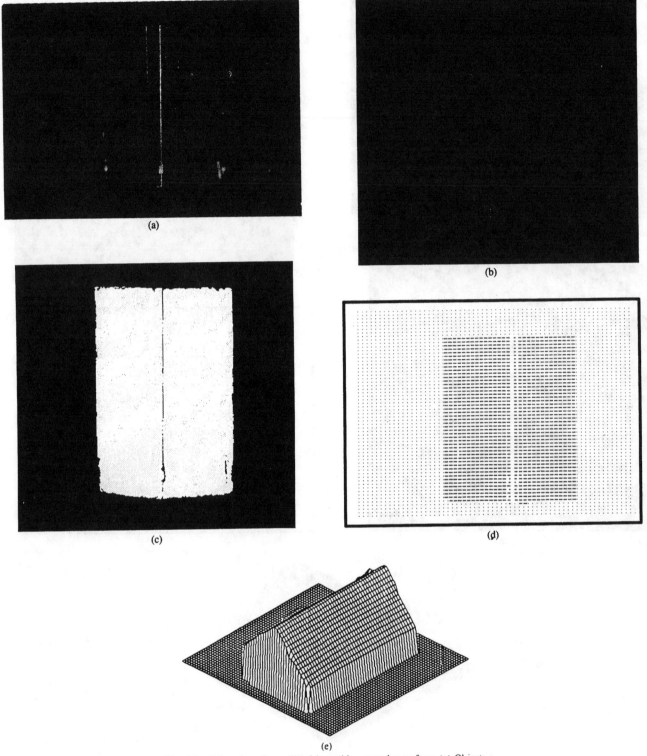

Fig. 10.   Prism-shaped metallic object with a specular surface: (a) Object;
(b) Lambertian strength; (c) specular strength; (d) needle map; (e) depth
map.

surface orientations in the grooves between threads lie outside the range of orientations that the current two-dimensional system is capable of measuring. While generating needle maps, surface orientations are sampled to make room for the display of needles. In the process of sampling, a considerable number of orientations measured on the threads of the bolt are lost. Hence, the orientations measured on a few threads are displayed at a higher resolution. We have not included a depth map of the bolt because its needle map has many disjoint regions and is difficult to integrate.

All the above experiments were conducted on surface points that are either Lambertian or specular. A major advantage of the photometric sampling method, over other shape extraction techniques, lies in its ability to determine the shape and

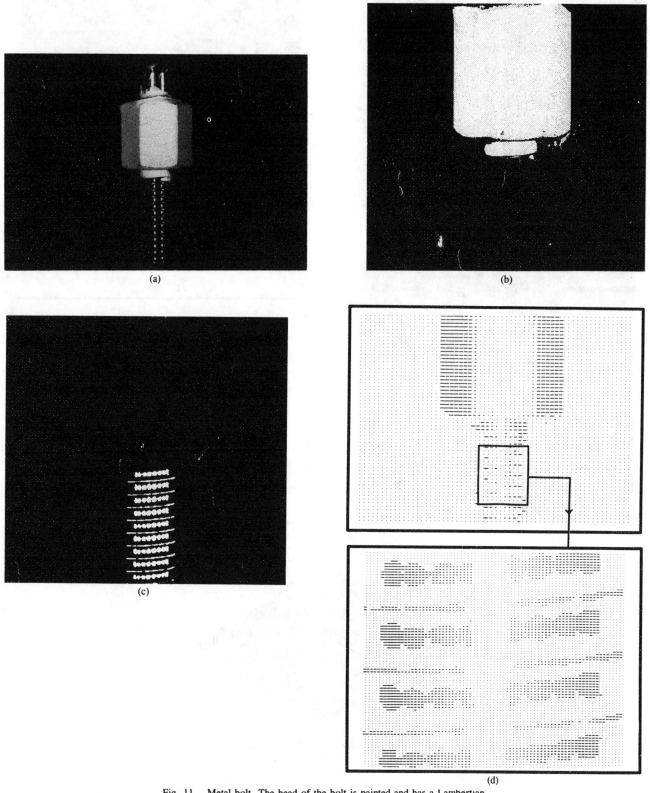

Fig. 11.   Metal bolt. The head of the bolt is painted and has a Lambertian
surface, whereas the threaded section has a specular surface: (a) Object;
(b) Lambertian strength; (c) specular strength; (d) needle map.

reflectance of hybrid surfaces. The surfaces of many manu-
factured plastic objects seem to fall into this category. The
Lambertian component is produced by the internal scattering mechanism, whereas the sharp specular component results
from the smoothness of the surface. Fig. 12 shows the photo

of a plastic object that is cylindrical in shape. As expected,
nonzero Lambertian and specular strengths are seen in the
reflection images.

An important feature of all the above results is that the
surface properties at a pixel are computed solely from the

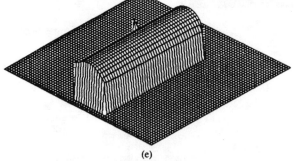

Fig. 12. Cylindrical plastic object with a hybrid surface: (a) Object; (b) Lambertian strength; (c) specular strength; (d) needle map; (e) depth map.

intensities recorded at that pixel. The needle maps and re-flectance images have not been subjected to any filtering or regularization operations. An error analysis was conducted to estimate the measurement accuracy of the current setup. Fig. 13 shows the surface orientations measured along a horizontal section of the hybrid cylindrical sample shown in Fig. 12. The actual orientation values along the section are computed using the known radius of the cylinder. The errors in the measured orientations θ_{error} are plotted in Fig. 14. From these errors, the following quantities were computed: *mean orientation error* $= 1.022°$, *mean absolute orientation error* $= 1.656°$, *standard deviation in orientation error* $= 0.189°$, and *maximum orientation error* $= 5.596°$. The estimated reflectance parameters were found to be consistent with the appearance

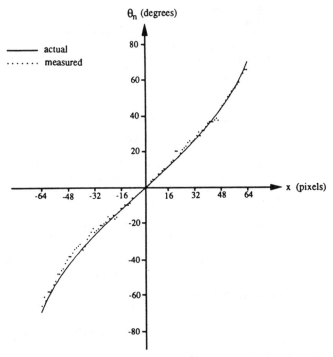

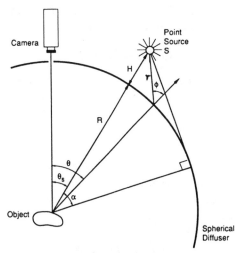

Fig. 15. Extended source.

Fig. 13. Measured and actual surface orientations along a horizontal section of the hybrid cylindrical object shown in Fig. 12.

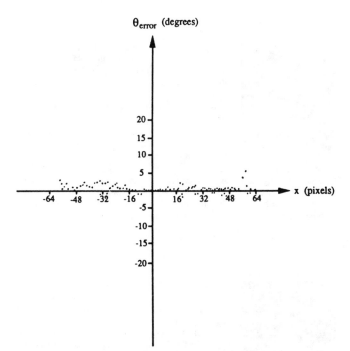

Fig. 14. Errors in measured orientations computed from the measured and actual orientation values plotted in Fig. 13.

of the surface samples used to conduct the above experiments. A more formal evaluation of the reflectance measurement accuracy of the proposed method is in progress.

VI. Conclusions

We conclude this paper with the following remarks:

- The hybrid reflection model is obtained by studying various reflection mechanisms and by making assumptions related to the microscopic structure of the surface.

- The photometric sampling method uses uniformly distributed source directions to obtain a set of image intensity values at each surface point.
- Surface illumination using extended light sources makes it possible to capture both Lambertian and specular reflections in the image intensities.
- The extraction algorithm uses the image intensities to simultaneously recover shape and reflectance parameters of hybrid surfaces, including Lambertian and specular surfaces. Objects comprised of combinations of the aforementioned surface classes can also be handled by the algorithm.
- The extraction algorithm is local in that the orientation and reflectance of a surface point are computed solely from image intensities recorded at that point.
- Accurate orientation estimates are obtained by using both Lambertian and specular components of the image intensities.

We are currently in the process of extending the theory and experimental setup to three dimensions. We are also interested in using the most general form of the reflectance model described in Section II in order to increase the range of surfaces that can be handled by the photometric sampling method.

Appendix A

Generating Extended Sources

There are numerous ways of generating extended light sources. In this Appendix, we present the approach that we have chosen to use. An extended source can be generated by illuminating a sheet of light-diffusing material with a point light source. Fig. 15 illustrates the illumination of a section of a circular diffuser of radius R. The point source is placed at a distance H from the diffuser's surface, and the viewed object is placed at the center of the circle. Let us assume that the diffuser is "ideal," i.e., incident energy is scattered equally in all directions. Then, the radiance[4] $L(\theta, \theta_s)$ of the

---

[4] Radiance is defined as the flux emitted per unit of foreshortened surface area per unit solid angle. Radiance is measured in watts per square meter per steradian ($W \cdot m^{-2} \cdot sr^{-1}$).

inner surface of the diffuser is proportional to the irradiance[5] $E(\theta, \theta_s)$ of the outer surface of the diffuser

$$L(\theta, \theta_s) = CE(\theta, \theta_s) \qquad (20)$$

where C is a constant of proportionality. The analytic expression for the surface irradiance $E(\theta, \theta_s)$ may be derived from the basics of radiometry as

$$E(\theta, \theta_s) = \frac{I \cos \phi}{r^2} \qquad (21)$$

where I is the radiant intensity[6] of the point source S. The radiance of the extended source may be determined by expressing the variables r and ϕ in (21) in terms of the parameters R, H, and θ_s of the illumination geometry:

$$L(\theta, \theta_s) = \frac{CI[(R + H) \cos(\theta - \theta_s) - R]}{[(R + H - R \cos(\theta - \theta_s))^2 + (R \sin(\theta - \theta_s))^2]^{3/2}}. \qquad (22)$$

Throughout this paper, the position of an extended source is denoted by the angle θ_s of the point source used to generate the extended source. The radiance function $L(\theta, \theta_s)$ is symmetric or even, with respect to the source direction $(\theta = \theta_s)$, and its magnitude decreases as θ deviates from θ_s. Points on the diffuser that lie in the interval $\theta_s - \alpha < \theta < \theta_s + \alpha$ receive light from the point source S. Points that lie outside this interval are occluded from the point source by points that lie in the interval. Thus, $L(\theta, \theta_s) = 0$ for $\theta < \theta_s - \alpha$ and $\theta > \theta_s + \alpha$. The *source termination angle* α is determined from Fig. 15 to be

$$\alpha = \cos^{-1} \frac{R}{R + H}. \qquad (23)$$

ACKNOWLEDGMENT

The authors are grateful to B. K. P. Horn, G. Klinker, and J. Krumm for their valuable comments. The members of the VASC center at Carnegie Mellon University provided many useful suggestions.

REFERENCES

[1] P. Beckmann and A. Spizzichino, *The Scattering of Electromagnetic Waves from Rough Surfaces.* New York: Macmillan, 1963.
[2] E. N. Coleman and R. Jain, "Obtaining 3-dimensional shape of textured and specular surface using four-source photometry," *Comput. Graphics Image Processing,* vol. 18, no. 4, pp. 309–328, Apr. 1982.
[3] G. Healey and T. O. Binford, "Local shape from specularity," in *Proc. Image Understanding Workshop,* Feb. 1987, vol. 2, pp. 874–887.
[4] B. K. P. Horn, "Shape from shading: A method for obtaining the shape of a smooth opaque object from one view," MIT Project MAC Internal Rep. TR-79 and MIT AI Lab. Tech. Rep. 232, Nov. 1970.
[5] B. K. P. Horn, "Image intensity understanding," *Artificial Intell.,* vol. 8, no. 2, 1977.
[6] K. Ikeuchi and B. K. P. Horn, "Numerical shape from shading and occluding boundaries," *Artificial Intell.,* vol. 17, nos. 1–3, pp. 141–184, Aug. 1981.
[7] K. Ikeuchi, "Determining surface orientations of specular surfaces by using the photometric stereo method," *IEEE Trans. Patt. Anal. Mach. Intell.,* vol. PAMI-3, no. 6, pp. 661–669, Nov. 1981.
[8] P. Kubelka and F. Munk, "Ein Beitrag sur Optik der Farbanstriche," *Z. tech. Physik,* vol. 12, p. 593, 1931.
[9] J. H. Lambert, *Photometria Sive de Mensura de Gratibus Luminis, Colorum et Umbrae.* Augsburg: Eberhard Klett, 1760.
[10] S. K. Nayar, K. Ikeuchi, and T. Kanade, "Extracting shape and reflectance of Lambertian, specular, and hybrid surfaces," CMU-RI-TR-88-14, Aug. 1988.
[11] S. K. Nayar, K. Ikeuchi, and T. Kanade, "Surface reflection: Physical and geometrical perspectives," CMU-RI-TR-89-7, Mar. 1989.
[12] F. E. Nicodemus, J. C. Richmond, J. J. Hsia, I. W. Ginsberg, and T. Limperis, "Geometrical considerations and nomenclature for reflectance, NBS Monograph 160, Nat. Bureau Standards, Boulder, CO, Oct. 1977.
[13] A. P. Pentland, "Local shading analysis," *IEEE Trans. Patt. Anal. Mach. Intell.,* vol. PAMI-6, no. 2, pp. 170–187, Mar. 1984.
[14] J. Reichman, "Determination of absorption and scattering coefficients for nonhomogeneous media 1: Theory," *Appl. Optics,* vol. 12, no. 8, pp. 1811–1815, Aug. 1973.
[15] A. C. Sanderson, L. E. Weiss, and S. K. Nayar, "Structured highlight inspection of specular surfaces, *IEEE Trans. Patt. Anal. Mach. Intell.,* vol. 10, no. 1, pp. 44–55, Jan. 1988.
[16] W. M. Silver, "Determining shape and reflectance using multiple images," S. M. thesis, Dept. Elect. Eng. Comput. Sci., MIT, Cambridge, MA, June 1980.
[17] K. Torrance and E. Sparrow, "Theory for off-specular reflection from roughened surfaces," *J. Optical Soc. Amer.,* no. 57, pp. 1105–1114, 1967.
[18] R. J. Woodham, "Photometric stereo: A reflectance map technique for determining surface orientation from image intensity," *Proc. SPIE,* vol. 155, pp. 136–143, 1978.

Shree K. Nayar (M'90) received the B.S. degree in electrical engineering from the Birla Institute of Technology, Ranchi, India, in 1984 and the M.S. degree in electrical and computer engineering from the North Carolina State University, Raleigh, in 1986.

He is currently a Research Assistant at the Robotics Institute, Carnegie Mellon University, Pittsburgh, PA, and is working towards the Ph.D. degree in electrical and computer engineering. Since 1988, he has been supported for his dissertation work by a Westinghouse research fellowship. In the summer of 1989, he was a Visiting Research Scientist at the Production Engineering Research Laboratory, Hitachi Ltd., Yokohama, Japan. He has been awarded several patents for his inventions related to machine vision. His research interests include machine vision, robotics, and artificial intelligence.

Katsushi Ikeuchi (M'89) is a senior research scientist (associate professor level) of computer science and robotics at Carnegie Mellon University, Pittsburgh, PA. He received B. Eng. degree in mechanical engineering from Kyoto University, Kyoto, Japan, in 1973, and the M. Eng. and Ph.D. degrees in information engineering from the University of Tokyo, Tokyo, Japan, in 1975 and 1978, respectively.

Since then, he has held several research positions at the Artificial Intelligence Laboratory, Massachusetts Institute of Technology, Cambridge, Electrotechnical Laboratory, Ministry of International Trade and Industry (Japanese government), and the School of Computer Science, Carnegie Mellon University. His research accomplishments in image understanding include the development of "smoothness constraints" wherein the neighboring points have the similar surface orientations, by which he recovered shape from shading and shape from texture, iteratively. He has also pioneered the use of specular reflections to recover surface orientations. Instead of discarding specular reflections, he actively used them for recovering shape and reflectance. Currently, he has been developing a vision algorithm compiler, which converts an object and sensor model into a vision program automatically.

---

[5] Irradiance is defined as the incident flux density and is measured in watts per square meter $(\text{W} \cdot \text{m}^{-2})$.

[6] Radiant intensity of a source is defined as the flux exiting per unit solid angle and is measured in watts per steradian $(\text{W} \cdot \text{sr}^{-1})$.

A Theory of Photometric Stereo for a Class of Diffuse Non-Lambertian Surfaces

Hemant D. Tagare, *Student Member, IEEE,* and Rui J. P. deFigueiredo, *Fellow, IEEE*

Abstract—Photometric stereo is a method of reconstructing a surface from the amount of light reflected by it. This is done by using prior knowledge of the surface reflectance to estimate the surface normal at all visible points. The theory of photometric stereo has been extensively developed for surfaces and illumination geometries that give rise to a Lambertian reflectance map. For non-Lambertian reflectance maps, the theory has been developed for specific cases, but a general theory has not been presented in the literature.

In this paper, we propose a theory of photometric stereo for a large class of non-Lambertian reflectance maps. First, we review the different reflectance maps proposed in the literature for modeling reflection from real-world surfaces. From this, we obtain a mathematical class of reflectance maps to which the maps belong. Next, we show that three lights can be sufficient for a unique inversion of the photometric stereo equation for the entire class of reflectance maps. We also obtain a constraint on the positions of light sources for obtaining this solution.

Next, we investigate the sufficiency of three light sources to estimate the surface normal and the illuminant strength. Finally, we address the issue of completeness of reconstruction. We show that if *k* lights are sufficient for a unique inversion, 2*k* lights are necessary for a complete inversion.

Index Terms—Machine vision, non-Lambertian reflection, photometric stereo, reflectance maps, shape from shading.

I. Introduction

PHOTOMETRIC stereo is a fast and reliable $2\frac{1}{2}$-dimensional surface reconstruction algorithm. Multiple images of a surface are obtained from a camera by illuminating the surface from different directions. The intensities in these images are used to mathematically invert the image formation process, and the surface normal and other characteristics of the surface are obtained at different pixels. Photometric stereo uses prior knowledge about the illumination geometry of the scene and the nature of surface reflection. This knowledge is specified as the *reflectance map* of the surface.

Photometric stereo was developed by Woodham [34], who also developed the theory of photometric stereo for the Lambertian reflectance map in detail. Coleman and Jain [11] proposed the use of four light sources to separate out the specular and Lambertian components in photometric stereo. Ray *et al.* [23] conducted an error analysis of Lambertian photometric stereo. Ikeuchi [15] used distributed light sources for photometric stereo of specular surfaces and Nayar *et al.* [18] extended this and used distributed light sources for photometric stereo of surfaces whose reflection is a sum of specular and Lambertian components. Silver [26] showed how photometric stereo could be conducted using experimentally measured reflectance maps.

Manuscript received April 5, 1989; revised August 24, 1990. Recommended for acceptance by R. Woodham. This work was supported by NASA under Contract NAS 9-17896 and under Grant NAG-9-208, by the State of Texas under Grant TATP 2982, and by a grant from the Computer Science Center of Texas Instruments, Dallas, TX.

H. D. Tagare is with the Departments of Diagnostic Radiology and Electrical Engineering, Yale University, New Haven, CT 06510.

R. J. P. deFigueiredo is with the Department of Mathematics, University of California, Irvine, CA 92717.

IEEE Log Number 9040357.

In this paper, we develop a theory of photometric stereo for a class of surfaces whose diffuse reflection under point light source illumination is non-Lambertian.[1] Such surfaces occur quite readily in real-world imaging situations. For example, it is quite well documented that when a point light source illuminates a rough surface, a significant part of the diffusely reflected light is non-Lambertian [29], [37], [32], [5], [3]. The resulting non-Lambertian reflectance maps can give rise to image formation equations that are significantly nonlinear. A lack of theoretical understanding of these equations can hamper their use in practical applications. Thus, for example, for a given non-Lambertian reflectance map, we may not know how many light sources are sufficient to invert the image formation process. Using an insufficient number of light sources could lead to multiple solutions, causing a loss of confidence in the experimental results. Clearly, a theoretical analysis of non-Lambertian photometric stereo is important, and in this paper we present such an analysis for a large class of non-Lambertian reflectance maps.

In choosing the class of reflectance maps, we have tried to satisfy several conflicting demands—that the class of maps be realistic, that it represent a large number of real-world reflectance maps, and yet that it have enough structure to permit theoretical analysis. Fortunately, as we will see in Section III, it is possible to meet these demands. A survey of reflectance maps proposed in the literature to model real-world reflection reveals that the maps do have common characteristics. Most of the proposed maps have "lobes" and these lobes have a common mathematical structure. We have formalized these properties and propose a class of reflectance maps called "*m*-lobed reflectance maps." Our theory of photometric stereo is developed for these maps. This class of reflectance maps contains all the proposed reflectance maps and most of their simple extensions.

We believe that the most important issue facing a *theory* of non-Lambertian photometric stereo is that of the number of light sources needed to invert the image formation process for obtaining a unique reconstruction. This issue is also central to Woodham's theory of photometric stereo [34]. For the Lambertian reflectance map, Woodham established that three light sources are sufficient for uniquely inverting the image formation process. In Section V, we show that three light sources are also sufficient to yield a unique surface normal for the entire class of *m*-lobed reflectance maps.

We would like to emphasize that only the knowledge about the class of reflectance maps is used to establish this result. It is possible that, by adding other constraints to the problem, the number of light sources can be reduced. For the Lambertian reflectance map, such an approach has been investigated by Onn and Bruckstein [7]. They showed that, for a Lambertian reflectance map, if the height function $z(x, y)$ of the surface has continuous second derivatives and cannot be written as

---

[1] By non-Lambertian we mean "not necessarily Lambertian" in the same way that nonlinear means "not necessarily linear."

$z(x,y) = f(x) + g(y)$, then, using the integrability constraint, the number of light sources can be reduced to two. In this paper, we do not investigate the effect of such additional constraints.

Some knowledge of the illuminant strength is usually required to invert the image formation process and most photometric stereo and shape from shading techniques obtain this knowledge from the image itself. The simplest technique [12] assumes that the reflectance map achieves its maximum value at the location of the maximum intensity in the image. Therefore, the maximum intensity is proportional to the illuminant strength and dividing all the image intensities by the maximum intensity removes the dependence on the illuminant strength. Other techniques of estimating the illuminant strength [10], [21] assume that the imaged object has a uniform distribution of surface normals. It is very easy to encounter situations where these assumptions do not hold, and in those cases the illuminant strength cannot be estimated independent of the surface normal. Both the quantities have to be obtained simultaneously.

In Section VI, we address the issue of whether the illuminant strength can be obtained simultaneously with the surface normal using three light sources. To solve this, we show that the image intensities due to three light sources are constrained to have a manifold structure and that the problem of sufficiency of light sources can be posed as a problem of the geometry of this manifold. Silver [26] also noted this constraint on the image intensities. Using a geometric technique, we obtain a condition for the sufficiency of three light sources to obtain the illuminant strength.

In Section VII, we address the problem of completeness of reconstruction. This problem is illustrated as follows. Let us assume that, for a given reflectance map, we have determined that k light sources are sufficient to obtain a unique inversion of the image formation process. We then set up the k light sources and illuminate the object. Assume that the object is a sphere and we are interested only in reconstructing its visible part. As long as all the k light sources are not positioned along the viewing direction, there will always be visible surface normals on the sphere that will lie in self-shadow with respect to any given light source. Thus, we will not have the k intensity values that we need for inverting the image formation process to estimate the surface normal and other surface parameters. The surface is therefore not completely reconstructible. One solution to this problem is to use more than k lights, say k^* lights, and place them such that at least k of these illuminate every visible surface normal. The problem of complete reconstruction is that of finding (or obtaining bounds on) k^*. In general, this cannot be done without knowing the geometry of the surface. However, for convex surfaces, a relation between k and k^* can be obtained without explicit knowledge of the shape. In Section VII, we show that for convex surfaces $k^* = 2k$.

II. Imaging Geometry and Notation

We assume the imaging geometry of Fig. 1. The object is placed far enough from the imaging plane so that orthogonal projections can be used. The light source is also assumed to be distant. The surface normal at any point on the object surface is represented by n, the optical axis of the camera is along the unit vector r, and the light source is located along the unit vector i. By our assumptions, the vectors r and i are constant over the entire object surface. When multiple light sources are used to illuminate the scene, i_l will denote the unit vector pointing toward the lth light source.

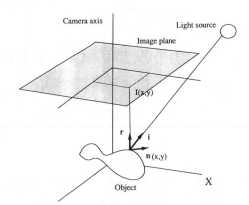

Fig. 1.   The imaging geometry.

The "viewer-centered coordinate system" is assumed to be positioned such that the positive z-axis lies along r and the x–y plane is parallel to the image plane. For vectors in this frame, the first component is the x component, the second the y component, and the third the z component. The inner product between any two vectors u and v is denoted as $u^T v$ and the cross product as $u * v$. Thus, the fact that n is a unit vector is denoted as $n^T n = 1$.

At times, we will use the zenith and azimuth angles θ and ϕ to represent unit vectors, and the convention we adopt with respect to these is as follows. The zenith angle of any unit vector is measured positively down from the z axis while the azimuth angle is measured positively counterclockwise from the x axis. The angles θ and ϕ will usually be subscripted to indicate which vectors they belong to. Thus, θ_n and ϕ_n are the zenith and azimuth angles, respectively, of the vector n while θ_i and ϕ_i are the angles of i.

In the geometry of Fig. 1 note that the set of all visible surface normals is given by $r^T n > 0$. Since the coordinate frame is aligned to have its z axis along r, this condition can also be written as $\pi/2 > \theta_n \geq 0$.

We call the angle between the vectors i and r the "phase angle" and the plane containing i and r the "principal plane." We call the direction along the unit vector n_s the "specular direction," where

$$n_s = \frac{i + r}{\|i + r\|}. \tag{1}$$

Since the mapping from unit vectors to zenith and azimuth angles is one to one, any function $h(x)$ of a unit vector x can also be written as $h(\theta_x, \phi_x)$. Of course, the converse is also true.

If we let $d\omega$ denote the infinitesimal solid angle about the ray along θ, ϕ, then

$$d\omega = \sin \theta \, d\theta \, d\phi.$$

In Section III, we have to evaluate integrals of functions of zenith and azimuth angles θ, ϕ (such as $h(\theta, \phi)$) over all the solid angles, and we will denote this integral as $\int_\omega h(\theta, \phi) \, d\omega$, where

$$\int_\omega h(\theta, \phi) \, d\omega = \int_{-\pi}^{\pi} \int_0^{\pi} h(\theta, \phi) \, \sin \theta \, d\theta \, d\phi.$$

In the unit vector notation, we write the above integral as $\int_\omega h(x) \, d\omega$, where we have implicitly assumed that the vector x varies so as to point toward the center of the solid angle $d\omega$.

We also need a solid angle delta function to use with integrals. This we denote as $\delta_\omega(\theta - \theta_o, \phi - \phi_o)$, and its definition in terms of zenith and azimuth angles is

$$\delta_\omega(\theta - \theta_o, \phi - \phi_o) = \frac{\delta(\theta - \theta_o)\,\delta(\phi - \phi_o)}{\sin\theta_o}$$

where $\delta(\ )$ is the standard Dirac delta function. Note that

$$\int_\omega h(\theta, \phi)\,\delta_\omega(\theta - \theta_o, \phi - \phi_o)\,d\omega = h(\theta_o, \phi_o). \quad (2)$$

Using unit vectors, we write the solid angle delta function as $\delta_\omega(x - x_o)$, and the above equation as

$$\int_\omega h(x)\,\delta_\omega(x - x_o)\,\delta\omega = h(x_o).$$

III. The Reflectance Map

In this section, our main aim is to construct m-lobed reflectance maps. To do this, we briefly present the definition of the reflectance map, then we review the different theories and reflectance maps proposed to model real-world reflection. Finally, we introduce the m-lobed maps.

A reflectance map relates the orientation of the surface normal to the image intensity caused by that orientation [12], [13]. The reflectance map depends on the radiance of the light source and the bidirectional reflectance distribution function (BRDF) of the surface.

The radiance (in watts per square meter per steradian) of a distant point light source that is placed along i is given by

$$L_i(\theta, \phi) = E_o\,\delta_\omega(\theta - \theta_i, \phi - \phi_i)$$
$$= E_o\,\frac{\delta(\theta - \theta_i)\,\delta(\phi - \phi_i)}{\sin\theta_i},$$

where θ_i and ϕ_i are the zenith and azimuth angles, respectively, of i, and E_o is the irradiance of the light source measured perpendicular to i. In the vector notation,

$$L_i(x) = E_o\,\delta_\omega(x - i).$$

The BRDF is a function of the incident and receiving directions (when viewed relative to the surface normal) and is defined as the ratio of the radiance of reflected light in the receiving direction to the irradiance of incident light [19]. Consider a small surface patch and orient a coordinate frame such that the positive z axis aligns with the surface normal. In this frame, let θ_i, ϕ_i be the zenith and azimuth angles of the direction of incident light and θ_r, ϕ_r be the zenith and azimuth angles of reflected light. The BRDF of the surface is written as $f_r(\theta_i, \phi_i, \theta_r, \phi_r)$ and has the units of reciprocal steradians. If the surface is an isotropic reflector, the BRDF has the simpler form $f_r(\theta_i, \theta_r, \phi_r - \phi_i)$ [12]. In terms of the unit normal vectors, we can write the BRDF as $f_r(i, n, r)$.

Given a surface patch oriented along n with a BRDF $f_r(i, n, r)$, and a light source with a radiance $L_i(x)$, the radiance of reflected light along r is

$$L_r(i, n, r) = \int_\omega f_r(x, n, r)L_i(x) \max(0, x^T n)\,d\omega.$$

Alternately, this may be written as

$$L_r(\theta_i, \phi_i; \theta_n, \phi_n; \theta_r, \phi_r) = \int_{-\pi}^{\pi}\int_0^{\pi} f_r(\theta_i', \phi_i', \theta_r', \phi_r')$$
$$\times L_i(\theta, \phi) \max(0, \cos\theta_i')\sin\theta\,d\theta\,d\phi$$

where, θ_i', ϕ_i' are the zenith and azimuth angles of the direction θ, ϕ with respect to the surface normal, and θ_r', ϕ_r' are the zenith and azimuth angles of the direction θ_r, ϕ_r with respect to the surface normal.

Horn and Sjoberg [13] showed that the intensity (gray level) I recorded at any pixel by the imaging apparatus is proportional to $L_r(\ )$. Thus, we have $I = \zeta L_r(\ )$, where ζ is the constant of proportionality of appropriate dimensions so that I is a dimensionless quantity. As the orientation of the surface varies, the intensity I varies. Let I_{max} be the maximum intensity that is recorded over all possible surface normal orientations. Assuming that I_{max} is finite, the reflectance map $R(i, n, r)$ is defined as

$$R(i, n, r) = \frac{\zeta L_r(i, n, r)}{I_{max}}$$
$$= \frac{\zeta}{I_{max}}\int_\omega f_r(x, n, r)L_i(x)\max(0, x^T n)\,d\omega. \quad (3)$$

In terms of zenith and azimuth angles, we have

$$R(\theta_i, \phi_i; \theta_n, \phi_n; \theta_r, \phi_r) = \frac{\zeta}{I_{max}}L_r(\theta_i, \phi_i; \theta_n, \phi_n; \theta_r, \phi_r)$$
$$= \frac{\zeta}{I_{max}}\int_{-\pi}^{\pi}\int_0^{\pi} f_r(\theta_i', \phi_i'; \theta_r', \phi_r')$$
$$\times L_i(\theta, \phi)\max(0, \cos\theta_i')\sin\theta\,d\theta\,d\phi.$$

Note that we have explicitly denoted the dependence of the reflectance map on the incident, normal, and receiving directions. We have also followed the convention [12, p. 219] that the reflectance map is normalized so that its maximum value is 1.

Given the reflectance map, the intensity I is obtained as $I = I_{max}R(i, n, r)$.

Having defined the reflectance map, we will now review some of the BRDF proposed in the literature to model reflection from rough real-world surfaces so that we can substitute the proposed BRDF's in (3) and obtain reflectance maps.

A perfect solid with a planar boundary reflects only in a specular manner [28]. All of the incident radiation from the direction θ_i, ϕ_i is reflected along the direction $\theta_r = \theta_i$, $\phi_r = \phi_i + \pi$. The BRDF for specular reflection is [13]

$$f_r(\theta_i, \phi_i; \theta_r, \phi_r) = \frac{\delta(\theta_i - \theta_r)\,\delta(\phi_i - \phi_r + \pi)}{\cos\theta_i\sin\theta_i}.$$

Alternately,

$$f_r(i, n, r) = \frac{\delta_w(n - n_s)}{2i^T n}. \quad (4)$$

Most solids are not perfectly regular. They have surface and bulk inhomogeneities, and these inhomogeneities cause diffuse reflection. We proposed in [29] that diffuse reflection from the inhomogeneities of a large class of engineering materials is contained in three lobes (as shown in Fig. 2) called the *forescatter lobe*, the *normal lobe*, and the *backscatter lobe*. Fig. 3 shows an example of a measured BRDF [5] that displays all the three lobes.

The forescatter lobe is spread around the specular direction and is purely a surface phenomenon [4]. This lobe has been studied in detail, and a wide variety of theories have been proposed to explain it [3], [32]. A simple explanation of the forescatter lobe is as follows: A rough surface can be modeled as being made up of facets, each facet being a small perfectly plane reflector. All the facets are inclined randomly about the mean surface.

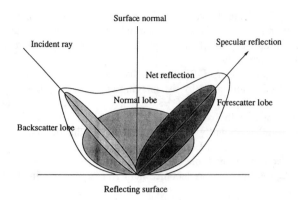

Fig. 2.   The morphology of reflection from rough surfaces.

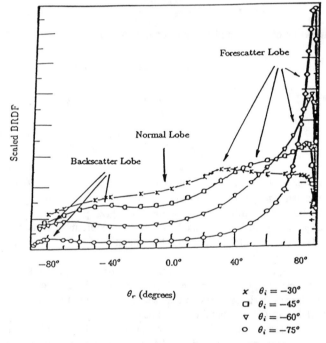

Fig. 3.   BRDF showing three lobes. Adapted from [32].

When light is incident on them, each facet reflects specularly. The distribution of the facets about the mean causes the reflected flux to distribute around the specular direction. Simple, but accurate, mathematical descriptions of the shape of the forescatter lobe can be made from such a facet model [3], [32]. The theory can be made more sophisticated by taking bistatic shadowing [2], [6], [27] into account.

Facet reflection theories usually assume that the surface is isotropic and that the facet inclinations are distributed in such a way that the density of facets whose normals are inclined at zenith and azimuth angle θ, ϕ to the mean surface normal is given by $\Phi^*(\theta)$, where $\Phi^*()$ is a monotonically decreasing function of its argument. Some of the common distributions associated with various facet reflection theories are

Distribution for the Phong Model [22]:

$$\Phi^*(\theta) = \beta_1 \cos^{c_1}(\theta). \qquad (5)$$

Distribution for the Torrance–Sparrow Model [32]:

$$\Phi^*(\theta) = \beta_2 \exp\left(-c_2^2\theta^2\right) \qquad (6)$$

Distribution for the Trowbridge–Reitz Model [33]:

$$\Phi^*(\theta) = \beta_3 \left[\frac{c_3^2}{\cos^2\theta(c_3^2 - 1) + 1}\right]^2. \qquad (7)$$

In (5)–(7) the constants c_1, c_2, and c_3 determine the spread of the distribution and the constants β_1, β_2, and β_3 normalize the distribution so that $\int \Phi^*(\theta) = 1$.

With the facet inclinations distributed according to $\Phi^*(\theta)$, the forescatter lobe can be shown to have the BRDF [29]

$$f_{fsc}(i, n, r) = \alpha_{fsc}S(i, n, r)F(i^T, n, \eta)\frac{\Phi(n_s^T n)}{(i^T n)(r^T n)} \qquad (8)$$

where $S()$ is the bistatic shadowing function, $F()$ is the Fresnel reflectivity [25] (we do not reproduce the formulas for $S()$ and $F()$ since they will not appear in the final formula), the function $\Phi()$ is given by

$$\Phi(x) = \Phi^*\left(\cos^{-1}x\right)$$

and α_{fsc} is a constant of the right dimensions so that the right-hand side of (8) is a valid BRDF. Note that, since $\Phi^*()$ is a monotonically decreasing function of its argument, $\Phi()$ is a monotonically increasing function of its argument.

Before we proceed, we point out that facet models are a ray geometric approximation to rough surface reflection. Physical optics models have also been proposed for modeling rough surface reflection, but we will not discuss these here. We note that

1) the lobe structure of forescatter is apparent in these models too (see, for example [3, Figs. 5.3–5.5]), and
2) for visible light, facet models give a very good approximation to the physical optics models. The Torrance–Sparrow model, for example, is known to give a good approximation to the Beckmann–Spizzichino model [17].

The normal lobe is spread around the mean surface normal. It is not yet clear whether the normal lobe is a surface or a bulk phenomenon, and we refer the reader to [29] for a discussion. Explanations of the origin of the normal lobe as bulk scattering have been the most complete so far, and we will pursue these. Theories of bulk scattering model the bulk as being optically uniform, but filled with point scatterers. The scattering from such a collection can be analyzed using radiative transfer theory [9].

The exact results of radiative transfer theory are reported in [9], and a discussion of some of them can be found in [29]. For now, we will use the result of radiative transfer theory that the normal lobe is approximately Lambertian [29]. Hence,

$$f_{\mathrm{norm}}(i, n, r) = \frac{1}{\pi}. \qquad (9)$$

The backscatter lobe is spread around the incident direction. Most materials display very little (but perceptible) backscatter; paints are one of the substances reported to backscatter strongly [5]. We have not yet been able to locate any substantial theories of the backscatter lobe in the literature and our analysis of the situation is based on the result of radiative transfer theory that scatterers close to the surface cause a backscatter lobe in the net reflected light.

A simple theory of backscatter can be built by assuming that backscatter is caused by scatterers located in a plane parallel to the mean surface [29]. The expression for the BRDF of the backscatter lobe is

$$f_{bsc}(i, n, r) = \alpha_{bsc}S(i, n, r)\frac{p(i^T r)}{(i^T n)(r^T n)}. \qquad (10)$$

where $S(\ )$ is the bistatic shadowing function, $p(\ )$ is the phase function of the scatterers [9], and α_{bsc} is a constant of the right dimensions to make the right-hand side a BRDF.

A real world surface reflects light in all of the above modes, and its BRDF can be written as

$$f_r(i,n,r) = \mu_{\text{spec}} f_{\text{spec}}(i,n,r) + \mu_{fsc} f_{fsc}(i,n,r)$$
$$+ \mu_{\text{norm}} f_{\text{norm}}(i,n,r) + \mu_{bsc} f_{bsc}(i,n,r)$$

where μ's are dimensionless constants and are determined by the proportion of light reflected in each lobe.

Next, consider the reflectance maps that arise from this BRDF and a point light source. Starting with (3), we have

$$L_r(i,n,r) = \int_\omega f_r(x,n,r) L_i(x) \max(0, x^T n)\, d\omega$$

$$= E_o \int_\omega f_r(x,n,r)\, \delta_\omega(x-i) \max(0, x^T n)\, d\omega$$

$$= E_0 \left\{ \frac{\mu_{\text{spec}} \delta_\omega(n-n_s)}{2 i^T n} \right.$$
$$+ \mu_{fsc} \alpha_{fsc} S(i,n,r) \frac{\Phi(n_s^T n)}{(i^T n)(r^T n)}$$
$$+ \mu_{\text{norm}} \alpha_{\text{norm}} \frac{\max(0, i^T r)}{\pi}$$
$$\left. + \mu_{bsc} \alpha_{bsc} S(i,n,r) \frac{p(i^T r)}{(i^T n)(r^T n)} \right\}$$
$$\times \max(0, i^T n).$$

The radiance due to specular reflection is unbounded, and the reflectance map cannot be normalized to 1. However, our main interest is in surfaces that reflect diffusely; hence, we will assume that $\mu_{\text{spec}} = 0$. Then, the reflectance map is

$$R(i,n,r) = \frac{\zeta E_o}{I_{\max}} \left\{ \mu_{fsc} \alpha_{fsc} S(i,n,r) \frac{\Phi(n_s^T n)}{(i^T n)(r^T n)} \right.$$
$$+ \mu_{\text{norm}} \frac{\alpha_{\text{norm}}}{\pi}$$
$$\left. + \mu_{bsc} \alpha_{bsc} S(i,n,r) \frac{p(i^T r)}{(i^T n)(r^T n)} \right\}$$
$$\times \max(0, i^T n).$$

This is a complicated expression, and it is shown in [29] that, for most photometric stereo geometries and for most surfaces, the expression can be simplified to

$$R(i,n,r) = \rho_{fsc} \Phi(n_s^T n) + \rho_{\text{norm}}(i^T n) + \rho_{bsc},$$
$$\text{if } i^T n > 0$$
$$= 0, \quad \text{otherwise}$$

where ρ's are constants of the right dimension that makes $R(\ )$ a valid reflectance map. ρ's are the "albedos."

If we had multiple light sources i_l $l = 1, \cdots, k$, the reflectance map associated with the light source i_l is

$$R(i_l, n, r) = \rho_{fsc} \Phi(n_{sl}^T n) + \rho_{\text{norm}}(i^T n) + \rho_{bsc},$$
$$\text{if } i_l^T n > 0$$
$$= 0, \quad \text{otherwise}, \qquad (11)$$

where $n_{sl} = (i_l^T r)/\|i+r\|$.

Before we proceed further, we demonstrate the utility of this reflectance map. Fig. 4 shows two spherical objects. The sphere at the right was imaged in a photometric stereo apparatus with a single point light source at a phase angle of $25°$. Fig. 5 shows the intensity in the resulting image. The x axis of the figure is the line joining the center of the image of the object with the brightest point of the surface of the object. The y axis is the intensity in the image along this line. Fig. 5 also shows the intensity that would have been present in the data if the reflectance map were Lambertian. Clearly, it is not. Fig. 5 also shows a fit of the reflectance map of (11) to the data. The Torrance–Sparrow model is used in the fit so that the exact expression for the reflectance map is

$$R(i,n,r) = \rho_{fsc} \exp \left\{ -c_2^2 \left(\cos^{-1} n_s^T n \right)^2 \right\}$$
$$+ \rho_{\text{norm}}(i^T n) + \rho_{bsc}, \quad \text{if } i^T n > 0$$
$$= 0, \quad \text{otherwise.} \qquad (12)$$

The parameters used in (12) had values of $\rho_{fsc} = 1.0$, $\rho_{\text{norm}} = 0.5$, $\rho_{bsc} = 0.0$, and $c_2 = 2.578$. These values were obtained interactively so that the intensities due to (12) had a good fit with the data. Clearly, the reflectance map of (12) models the data quite accurately.

Now that we have a form of the reflectance map of (11) from physical considerations, we will generalize it to obtain the m-lobed map. The generalization depends on the following observations about (11):

1) There are three terms in the reflectance map of (11), each term originating from a lobe of reflection. The first two terms display variation with n; the third does not.

2) The first two terms can be written as

$$\rho_1 \Phi_1\left(p_{l1}^T n\right) + \rho_2 \Phi_2\left(p_{l2}^T n\right)$$

where

$$\rho_1 = \rho_{fsc}$$
$$\Phi_1(\ ) = \Phi(\ )$$
$$p_{l1} = n_{sl}$$

and

$$\rho_2 = \rho_{\text{norm}}$$
$$\Phi_2(\ ) = I(\ ), \quad \text{the identity function}$$
$$p_{l2} = i_l.$$

3) The functions $\Phi_1(\ )$ and $\Phi_2(\ )$ above are positive and monotonically increasing functions of their arguments.

4) The vectors p_{l1} and p_{l2} are independent of n and depend only on i_l and r. In fact, p_{l1} and p_{l2} lie in the principal plane. Thus if the azimuth angle of i_l is ϕ_l, then the azimuth angles of p_{l1} and p_{l2} are ϕ_l too. Further, if the zenith angle of i_l is θ_{i_l}, $\pi/2 > \theta_{i_l} > 0$, then the zenith angles of p_{l1} and p_{l2} are

$$\theta_{p_{l1}} = \theta_{i_l}/2$$
$$\theta_{p_{l2}} = \theta_{i_l}.$$

Hence, $\pi/2 > \theta_{p_{l2}} > \theta_{p_{l1}} > 0$.

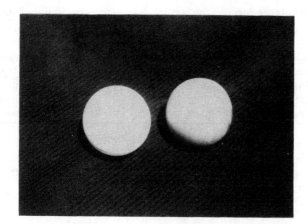

Fig. 4. Two spherical objects. Left: Lambertian. Right: Non-Lambertian.

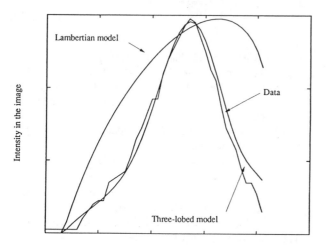

Fig. 5. Intensity in the principal plane.

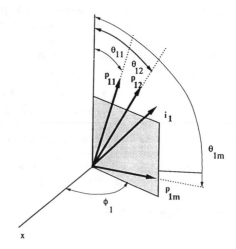

Fig. 6. Principal directions for the m-lobed reflectance map.

An m-lobed map is an extension of the mathematical form of (11). It has m terms, one of which is constant and the $m-1$ remaining of the form $\rho_k \Phi_k(\boldsymbol{p}_{lk}^T \boldsymbol{n})$. The function $\Phi_k(\ )$ and the vector $\boldsymbol{p}_{lk}$ are restricted to have the properties listed above, namely, that $\Phi_k(\ )$ is positive and monotonically increasing while $\boldsymbol{p}_{lk}$ always lies in the principal plane. Formally, the m-lobed map is defined as follows: With each incident direction $\boldsymbol{i}_l$ we associate a set of *principal directions* $\boldsymbol{p}_{lj}$, $j = 1, \cdots, m-1$ in the principal plane, i.e., if

$$\boldsymbol{i}_l = [\sin(\theta_l)\cos(\phi_l) \ \sin(\theta_l)\sin(\phi_l) \ \cos(\theta_l)]^T$$

then

$$\boldsymbol{p}_{lj} = [\sin(\theta_{lj})\cos(\phi_l) \ \sin(\theta_{lj})\sin(\phi_l) \ \cos(\theta_{lj})]^T \quad (13)$$

where $0 < \theta_{l1} < \theta_{l2} < \cdots < \theta_{lm-1} < \frac{\pi}{2}$. Fig. 6 illustrates this.

With each direction $\boldsymbol{p}_{lj}$ we associate $\Phi_j(\ )$, a monotonically increasing function and ρ_j, $(\rho_j > 0)$ an albedo. Then

$$R(\boldsymbol{i}_l, \boldsymbol{n}, \boldsymbol{r}) = \sum_{j=1}^{m-1} \rho_j \Phi_j(\boldsymbol{p}_{lj}^T \boldsymbol{n}) + b, \quad \text{if } \boldsymbol{i}^T \boldsymbol{n} > 0$$

$$= 0, \quad \text{otherwise} \quad (14)$$

where $b \geq 0$ is a constant.

We assume that the term $\sum_{j=1}^{m-1} \rho_j \Phi_j(\boldsymbol{p}_{lj}^T \boldsymbol{n})$ goes to zero as $\boldsymbol{i}_l^T \boldsymbol{n}$ does. Physically, this assumption means that the only lobe

that contributes to the observed intensity as we get closer to the self-shadow region $(\boldsymbol{i}_l^T \boldsymbol{n} \leq 0)$ is the backscatter lobe. This assumption is true for most surfaces.

Note that, in the definition of the m-lobed maps, we have constrained the azimuth angle of the principle directions to be the same as the azimuth angle of the light source. On the other hand, there are no constraints on the zenith angles of the principal directions. For any particular map, we are free to specify the zenith angles. Thus, for example, we may find that for some map, the zenith angles of the principal directions are a function of θ_{i_l} as well as ϕ_{i_l}. Such a map would be nonisotropic. If the zenith angles of the principal directions were a function only of the zenith angle θ_{i_l}, then the map is isotropic (such as the map of (11)). Therefore, the class of m-lobed maps contains isotropic as well as nonisotropic maps.

Finally, since all the principal directions associated with the light source $\boldsymbol{i}_l$ have the same azimuth angle, the vectors $\boldsymbol{p}_{lj}$ for $j = 2, 3, \cdots, m-2$ are contained within the convex cone formed by $\boldsymbol{p}_{l1}$ and $\boldsymbol{p}_{l,m-1}$, i.e., $\boldsymbol{p}_{lj}$ for $j = 2, 3, \cdots, m-2$ can be written as

$$\boldsymbol{p}_{lj} = \beta_{l,1,j}\boldsymbol{p}_{l1} + \beta_{l,m-1,j}\boldsymbol{p}_{l,m-1} \quad (15)$$

with $\beta_{l,1,j} > 0$ and $\beta_{l,m-1,j} > 0$.

IV. THE PHOTOMETRIC STEREO EQUATIONS

In this section, we state the photometric stereo equations. We assume that we have k distinct and identical light sources $\boldsymbol{i}_l$, $l = 1, \cdots, k$ illuminating the scene one at a time. As we mentioned before, the light sources are usually placed in a ring around the camera axis and hence the zenith angles of all the vectors $\boldsymbol{i}_l$ are the same. This is shown in Fig. 7.

If the scene is illuminated by one light source at a time, the resulting k intensities at any pixel are given by

$$\begin{pmatrix} I_1(\boldsymbol{n}) \\ \cdots \\ I_k(\boldsymbol{n}) \end{pmatrix} = I_{\max} \begin{pmatrix} R(\boldsymbol{i}_1, \boldsymbol{n}, \boldsymbol{r}) \\ \cdots \\ R(\boldsymbol{i}_k, \boldsymbol{n}, \boldsymbol{r}) \end{pmatrix}. \quad (16)$$

We call this equation the "unnormalized photometric stereo equation" and would like to solve it for $I_{\max}$ and $\boldsymbol{n}$. We are particularly interested in knowing the value of k and the position of light sources for which there is always a unique solution to the equation.

If $I_{\max}$ can be measured from the images, then the above equation can be written as

$$\begin{pmatrix} I_1^{rel}(\boldsymbol{n}) \\ \vdots \\ I_k^{rel}(\boldsymbol{n}) \end{pmatrix} = \begin{pmatrix} R(\boldsymbol{i}_1, \boldsymbol{n}, \boldsymbol{r}) \\ \vdots \\ R(\boldsymbol{i}_k, \boldsymbol{n}, \boldsymbol{r}) \end{pmatrix}. \qquad (17)$$

where $I_l^{rel}(\boldsymbol{n}) = I_l(\boldsymbol{n})/I_{\max}$. We call this equation the "normalized photometric stereo equation" and would like to solve it for $\boldsymbol{n}$. Here too, our main interest is in the value of k and the positions of the light sources for which the equation has unique solutions.

We are interested in establishing conditions for which the solutions are unique in a "global" sense rather than in the "local" sense of the inverse function theorem. A globally unique solution exists if

1) for (16) we cannot find two distinct sets $(I_{\max_1}, \boldsymbol{n}_1)$ and $(I_{\max_2}, \boldsymbol{n}_2)$ that will yield the same left-hand side, and
2) for (17) we cannot find two distinct surface normals $\boldsymbol{n}_1$ and $\boldsymbol{n}_2$ which will yield the same left-hand side.

We restrict ourselves to investigation of the uniqueness of solution for surface normals that do not lie in the self-shadow of any of the light sources.

V. Inversion of the Normalized Photometric Stereo Equation

In this section, we investigate the solution of the normalized photometric stereo equation (17) when the reflectance map of (14) is substituted in it. The main result of this section is expressed in theorems 5.1, 5.2a, 5.2b, and 5.3. Informally, the result is that the normalized photometric stereo equation does have a unique solution with an m-lobed map and three light sources placed according to Fig. 7.

The uniqueness of solution depends on a property of the principal directions and we begin by establishing that property.

A. The Principal Directions

Consider the light sources of Fig. 7 placed such that light sources 2 and 3 are symmetrical about light source 1. Further, assume that the azimuth angle of light source 1 is zero, i.e.,

$$\phi_{i_1} = 0$$
$$\pi > \phi_{i_2} = -\phi_{i_3} > 0. \qquad (18)$$

Also recall that, for the geometry of Fig. 7, the zenith angles of all light sources are equal, i.e.,

$$\pi/2 > \theta_{i_1} = \theta_{i_2} = \theta_{i_3} > 0. \qquad (19)$$

For the notational convenience, we will denote ϕ_{i_2} (and $-\phi_{i_3}$) by ϕ_i, ϕ_{i_1} by zero, and θ_{i_1}, θ_{i_2}, θ_{i_3} by θ_i.

Given this geometry, the principal directions associated with the first light source always have an azimuth angle of zero, the principal directions associated with the second light source an azimuth angle of ϕ_i, and the principal directions associated with the third light source an azimuth angle of $-\phi_i$. Also, since $\theta_i > 0$, the zenith angles of all principal directions are strictly greater than zero. The azimuth and zenith angles of the principal directions for the general m-lobed map are listed in Table I. Table II shows the principal directions for an isotropic m-lobed map. Since the map is isotropic and the zenith angle of all light sources is the same, the zenith angles of the first principal directions associated with each light source is the same. This also holds for the zenith angles of all the second, third, $\cdots$, $m-1$

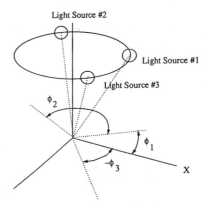

Fig. 7.   Light source positions for a traditional photometric stereo apparatus.

principal directions. In Table II, the equality of zenith angles is made explicit by denoting the value of the zenith angles of all the first principal directions by θ_1, all the second principal directions by $\theta_2, \cdots$, all the $m-1$ principal directions by θ_{m-1}.

Next, consider triplets of principal directions formed in the following manner: the first triplet formed by taking the first principal direction of each of the light source, the second triplet formed by taking the second principal direction of each of the light source, the third triplet formed by taking the third, and so on. There are $m-1$ such triplets, each corresponding to one principal direction.

It is now fairly straightforward to establish that for the general m-lobed map

Lemma 5.1: If three light sources are placed according to (18) and (19) and $\pi > \phi_i > \pi/2$, then any triplet of principal directions such as $\boldsymbol{p}_{1j}, \boldsymbol{p}_{2j}, \boldsymbol{p}_{3j}$ for $1 \le j \le m-1$, is linearly independent. $\square$

If the m-lobed map is isotropic, the result can be sharpened to

Lemma 5.2: If three light sources are placed according to (18) and (19) and $\pi > \phi_i > 0$, then any triplet of principal directions such as $\boldsymbol{p}_{1j}, \boldsymbol{p}_{2j}$, and $\boldsymbol{p}_{3j}$, $1 \le j \le m-1$ is linearly independent. $\square$

Thus, under the conditions of Lemmas 5.1 and 5.2 the matrices

$$H_j = \begin{pmatrix} \boldsymbol{p}_{1j}^T \\ \boldsymbol{p}_{2j}^T \\ \boldsymbol{p}_{3j}^T \end{pmatrix} \qquad (20)$$

are invertible. We will use the invertibility of H_j in our proofs. Note that the condition of invertibility of H_j is common even to Lambertian photometric stereo. For the Lambertian reflectance map, we have only one principal direction which is the direction $\boldsymbol{i}_l$. Hence,

$$H_1 = \begin{pmatrix} \boldsymbol{i}_1^T \\ \boldsymbol{i}_2^T \\ \boldsymbol{i}_3^T \end{pmatrix}.$$

Thus, the invertibility of H_1 means that $\boldsymbol{i}_1$, $\boldsymbol{i}_2$, and $\boldsymbol{i}_3$ are linearly independent. This is a common assumption for establishing the sufficiency of three light sources for normalized Lambertian photometric stereo [34].

TABLE I

ZENITH AND AZIMUTH ANGLES FOR THE PRINCIPAL DIRECTIONS OF THE GENERAL m-LOBED REFLECTANCE MAP

Light Source	Number	Principal Direction Zenith Angle Symbol	Value	Azimuth Angle Symbol	Value
1	1	θ_{11}	$\pi/2 > \theta_{11} > 0$	ϕ_{11}	0
	2	θ_{12}	$\pi/2 > \theta_{12} > \theta_{11} > 0$	ϕ_{12}	0
	...	...	...	...	...
	$m-1$	$\theta_{1,m-1}$	$\pi/2 > \theta_{1,m-1} > \theta_{1,m-2} > \cdots > \theta_{12} > \theta_{11} > 0$	$\phi_{1,m-1}$	0
2	1	θ_{21}	$\pi/2 > \theta_{21} > 0$	ϕ_{21}	$\phi_{21} = \phi$
	2	θ_{22}	$\pi/2 > \theta_{22} > \theta_{21} > 0$	ϕ_{22}	$\phi_{22} = \phi_i$
	...	...	...	...	...
	$m-1$	$\theta_{2,m-1}$	$\pi/2 > \theta_{2,m-1} < \theta_{1,m-2} > \cdots > \theta_{12} > \theta_{11} > 0$	$\phi_{2,m-1}$	$\phi_{2,m-1} = \phi_i$
3	3	θ_{31}	$\pi/2 > \theta_{31} > 0$	ϕ_{31}	$\phi_{31} = -\phi_i$
	2	θ_{32}	$\pi/2 > \theta_{32} > \theta_{31} > 0$	ϕ_{31}	$\phi_{32} = -\phi_i$
	...	...	...	...	...
	$m-1$	$\theta_{3,m-1}$	$\pi/2 > \theta_{3,m-1} > \theta_{3,m-2} > \cdots > \theta_{32} > \theta_{31} > 0$	$\phi_{3,m-1}$	$\phi_{3,m-1} = -\phi_i$

TABLE II

ZENITH AND AZIMUTH ANGLES FOR THE PRINCIPAL DIRECTIONS OF THE ISOTROPIC m-LOBED REFLECTANCE MAP

Light Source	Number	Principal Direction (Isotropic) Zenith Angle Symbol	Value	Azimuth Angle Symbol	Value
1	1	θ_{11}	$\pi/2 > \theta_{11} > 0, \theta_{11} = \theta_1$	ϕ_{11}	0
	2	θ_{12}	$\pi/2 > \theta_{12} > \theta_{11} > 0, \theta_{12} = \theta_2$	ϕ_{12}	0
	...	...	...	...	...
	$m-1$	$\theta_{1,m-1}$	$\pi/2 > \theta_{1,m-1} > \cdots > \theta_{12} > \theta_{11} > 0, \theta_{1,m-1} = \theta_{m-1}$	$\phi_{1,m-1}$	0
2	1	θ_{21}	$\pi/2 > \theta_{21} > 0, \theta_{21} = \theta_1$	ϕ_{21}	$\phi_{21} = \phi$
	2	θ_{22}	$\pi/2 > \theta_{22} > \theta_{21} > 0, \theta_{22} = \theta_2$	ϕ_{22}	$\phi_{22} = \phi_i$
	...	...	...	...	...
	$m-1$	$\theta_{2,m-1}$	$\pi/2 > \theta_{2,m-1} > \cdots \theta_{12} > \theta_{11} > 0, \theta_{2,m-1} = \theta_{m-1}$	$\phi_{2,m-1}$	$\phi_{2,m-1} = \phi_i$
3	3	θ_{31}	$\pi/2 > \theta_{31} > 0, \theta_{31} = \theta_1$	ϕ_{31}	$\phi_{31} = -\phi_i$
	2	θ_{32}	$\pi/2 > \theta_{32} > \theta_{31} > 0, \theta_{32} = \theta_2$	ϕ_{31}	$\phi_{32} = -\phi_i$
	...	...	...	...	...
	$m-1$	$\theta_{3,m-1}$	$\pi/2 > \theta_{3,m-1} > \cdots > \theta_{32} > \theta_{31} > 0, \theta_{3,m-1} = \theta_{m-1}$	$\phi_{3,m-1}$	$\phi_{3,m-1} = -\phi_i$

B. The Normalized Equation

If we assume $k = 3$, we can substitute (14) into (17) and write the resulting equation as

$$\begin{pmatrix} I_1^{\text{rel}}(\boldsymbol{n}) \\ I_2^{\text{rel}}(\boldsymbol{n}) \\ I_3^{\text{rel}}(\boldsymbol{n}) \end{pmatrix} = \sum_{j=1}^{m-1} \rho_j \begin{pmatrix} \Phi_j(\boldsymbol{p}_{1j}^T \boldsymbol{n}) \\ \Phi_j(\boldsymbol{p}_{2j}^T \boldsymbol{n}) \\ \Phi_j(\boldsymbol{p}_{3j}^T \boldsymbol{n}) \end{pmatrix} + \begin{pmatrix} b \\ b \\ b \end{pmatrix}.$$

We are interested in establishing conditions under which this equation has a unique solution. We do this by investigating the conditions under which it has multiple solutions and then positioning the light sources such that those conditions are not met.

If the above equation has multiple solutions, then for some distinct $\boldsymbol{n}_1$ and $\boldsymbol{n}_2$

$$\begin{pmatrix} I_1^{\text{rel}}(\boldsymbol{n}_1) \\ I_2^{\text{rel}}(\boldsymbol{n}_1) \\ I_3^{\text{rel}}(\boldsymbol{n}_1) \end{pmatrix} = \begin{pmatrix} I_1^{\text{rel}}(\boldsymbol{n}_2) \\ I_2^{\text{rel}}(\boldsymbol{n}_2) \\ I_3^{\text{rel}}(\boldsymbol{n}_2) \end{pmatrix}$$

from which we obtain

$$\begin{pmatrix} \sum_{j=1}^{m-1} \rho_j \Phi_j(\boldsymbol{p}_{1j}^T \boldsymbol{n}_1) - \rho_j \Phi_j(\boldsymbol{p}_{1j}^T \boldsymbol{n}_2) \\ \sum_{j=1}^{m-1} \rho_j \Phi_j(\boldsymbol{p}_{2j}^T \boldsymbol{n}_1) - \rho_j \Phi_j(\boldsymbol{p}_{2j}^T \boldsymbol{n}_2) \\ \sum_{j=1}^{m-1} \rho_j \Phi_j(\boldsymbol{p}_{3j}^T \boldsymbol{n}_1) - \rho_j \Phi_j(\boldsymbol{p}_{3j}^T \boldsymbol{n}_2) \end{pmatrix} = 0. \quad (21)$$

We will analyze the existence of (21) for three different conditions: $m = 2$, $m = 3$, and $m > 3$.

C. Case $m = 2$

Equation (21) reduces to

$$\begin{pmatrix} \rho_1 \Phi_1(\boldsymbol{p}_{11}^T \boldsymbol{n}_1) - \rho_1 \Phi_1(\boldsymbol{p}_{11}^T \boldsymbol{n}_2) \\ \rho_1 \Phi_1(\boldsymbol{p}_{21}^T \boldsymbol{n}_1) - \rho_1 \Phi_1(\boldsymbol{p}_{21}^T \boldsymbol{n}_2) \\ \rho_1 \Phi_1(\boldsymbol{p}_{31}^T \boldsymbol{n}_1) - \rho_1 \Phi_1(\boldsymbol{p}_{31}^T \boldsymbol{n}_2) \end{pmatrix} = 0. \quad (22)$$

Since $\Phi_1()$ is a monotonically increasing function and $\rho_1 > 0$, this can be written as

$$\begin{pmatrix} \boldsymbol{p}_{11}^T \\ \boldsymbol{p}_{21}^T \\ \boldsymbol{p}_{31}^T \end{pmatrix} (\boldsymbol{n}_1 - \boldsymbol{n}_2) = 0.$$

Note that $\text{col}(\boldsymbol{p}_{11}^T \boldsymbol{p}_{21}^T \boldsymbol{p}_{31}^T)$ can be identified with H_1 and the above equation written as $H_1(\boldsymbol{n}_1 - \boldsymbol{n}_2) = 0$. If we satisfy the conditions of Lemma 5.1 (or Lemma 5.2), H_1 becomes invertible, and from the above equation we obtain $n_1 - n_2 = 0$, which contradicts our assumption that n_1 and n_2 are distinct. Hence, we have

Theorem 5.1: The normalized photometric stereo equation has a unique solution for two-lobed maps with only three light sources placed according to (18) and (19) with the value of ϕ_i being $\pi > \phi_i > \pi/2$ for the general m-lobed map and $\pi > \phi_i > 0$ for the isotropic m-lobed map. $\qquad\square$

D. Case m = 3

In this case, (21) is

$$\begin{pmatrix} \sum_{j=1}^{2} \rho_j \Phi_j \left(p_{1j}^T n_1 \right) - \rho_j \Phi_j \left(p_{1j}^T n_2 \right) \\ \sum_{j=1}^{2} \rho_j \Phi_j \left(p_{2j}^T n_1 \right) - \rho_j \Phi_j \left(p_{2j}^T n_2 \right) \\ \sum_{j=1}^{2} \rho_j \Phi_j \left(p_{3j}^T n_1 \right) - \rho_j \Phi_j \left(p_{3j}^T n_2 \right) \end{pmatrix} = 0. \qquad (23)$$

Consider the first row of (23). This is

$$\rho_1 \{ \Phi_1 \left(p_{11}^T n_1 \right) - \Phi_1 \left(p_{11}^T n_2 \right) \}$$
$$+ \rho_2 \{ \Phi_2 \left(p_{12}^T n_1 \right) - \Phi_2 \left(p_{12}^T n_{12} \right) \} = 0.$$

Since $\rho_1, \rho_2 > 0$, this equality holds if

$$\{ \Phi_1 \left(p_{11}^T n_1 \right) - \Phi_1 \left(p_{11}^T n_2 \right) \} \geq 0,$$
$$\{ \Phi_2 \left(p_{12}^T n_1 \right) - \Phi_2 \left(p_{12}^T n_2 \right) \} \leq 0 \qquad (24)$$

or

$$\{ \Phi_1 \left(p_{11}^T n_1 \right) - \Phi_1 \left(p_{11}^T n_2 \right) \} < 0,$$
$$\{ \Phi_2 \left(p_{12}^T n_1 \right) - \Phi_2 \left(p_{12}^T n_2 \right) \} > 0. \qquad (25)$$

Since $\Phi_1( )$ and $\Phi_2( )$ are monotonically increasing functions, the conditions of (24) and (25) are equivalent to

$$p_{11}^T n_1 - p_{11}^T n_2 \geq 0, \qquad p_{12}^T n_1 - p_{12}^T n_2 \leq 0 \qquad (26)$$

and

$$p_{11}^T n_1 - p_{11}^T n_2 < 0, \qquad p_{12}^T n_1 - p_{12}^T n_2 > 0. \qquad (27)$$

Further simplifying, we get

$$p_{11}^T (n_1 - n_2) \geq 0, \qquad p_{12}^T (n_1 - n_2) \leq 0 \qquad (28)$$

and

$$p_{11}^T (n_1 - n_2) < 0, \qquad p_{12}^T (n_1 - n_2) > 0. \qquad (29)$$

Now, consider the sets c_1 and c_1^* defined by

$$c_1 = \{ n : p_{11}^T n \geq 0, \ p_{12}^T n \leq 0 \} - \{0\}$$
$$c_1^* = \{ n : p_{11}^T n < 0, \ p_{12}^T n > 0 \}.$$

We can restate the conditions of (28) and (29) in terms of the sets c_1 and c_2 by saying that the first row of (23) holds if $(n_1 - n_2) \in c_1$ or $(n_1 - n_2) \in c_1^*$. We can also define sets c_2, c_2^*, c_3, and c_3^* as

$$c_2 = \{ n : p_{21}^T n \geq 0, \ p_{22}^T n \leq 0 \} - \{0\}$$
$$c_2^* = \{ n : p_{21}^T n < 0, \ p_{22}^T n > 0 \}$$
$$c_3 = \{ n : p_{31}^T n \geq 0, \ p_{32}^T n \leq 0 \} - \{0\}$$
$$c_3^* = \{ n : p_{31}^T n < 0, \ p_{32}^T n > 0 \}.$$

By the same argument as above, it is possible to see that the second row of (23) holds if $(n_1 - n_2) \in c_2$ or $(n_1 - n_2) \in c_2^*$, and the third row holds if $(n_1 - n_2) \in c_3$ or $(n_1 - n_2) \in c_3^*$.

Thus, the sets c_1, c_1^*, c_2, c_2^*, c_3, and c_3^* represent conditions under which at least one row of (23) holds.

The intersection of these sets represents the conditions where at least two rows of (23) hold. The intersections are defined as[2]

$$C_1 = c_1 \cap c_2 \qquad C_1^* = c_1^* \cap c_2^*,$$
$$C_2 = c_2 \cap c_3 \qquad C_2^* = c_2^* \cap c_3^*,$$
$$C_3 = c_3 \cap c_1 \qquad C_3^* = c_3^* \cap c_1^*$$

If any two rows of (23) hold, then $(n_1 - n_2)$ belongs to one of these sets.

Finally, define $\mathcal{C}$ and $\mathcal{C}^*$ to be $\mathcal{C} = C_1 \cap C_2 \cap C_3$ and $\mathcal{C}^* = C_1^* \cap C_2^* \cap C_3^*$. If (23) holds, then $(n_1 - n_2)$ belongs to $\mathcal{C}$ or $\mathcal{C}^*$. Hence,

Lemma 5.3: If the sets $\mathcal{C}$ and $\mathcal{C}^*$ are empty, (23) will not hold for any distinct n_1 and n_2 and the normalized photometric stereo equation will have a unique solution. $\qquad\square$

We will now find explicit expressions for the above sets and convert the condition that $\mathcal{C}$ and $\mathcal{C}^*$ be empty into a constraint on light source positions. The sets c_l, c_l^*, C_l, C_l^*, $\mathcal{C}$, and $\mathcal{C}^*$ possess properties that allow us to simplify the condition of emptiness of $\mathcal{C}$ and $\mathcal{C}^*$. We state the properties of these sets below but postpone their proofs to the Appendix. The Appendix also contains a geometric depiction of the sets that the reader might use. The properties of interest to us are

Property 1: When the point O (the origin of E^3) is added to the sets c_l, c_l^*, C_l, C_l^*, $\mathcal{C}$, and $\mathcal{C}^*$ the resulting sets are convex cones with O (the origin of the space) as the apex.

Property 2: The sets c_l, c_l^*, and C_l, C_l^*, and $\mathcal{C}$, $\mathcal{C}^*$ are complementary in the sense that

$$x \in c_l^* \quad \text{iff} \quad -x \in c_l$$
$$x \in C_l^* \quad \text{iff} \quad -x \in C_l$$
$$x \in \mathcal{C}^* \quad \text{iff} \quad -x \in \mathcal{C}.$$

If $x \neq 0$

$$x \in c_l \quad \text{iff} \quad -x \in c_l^*$$
$$x \in C_l \quad \text{iff} \quad -x \in C_l^*$$
$$x \in \mathcal{C} \quad \text{iff} \quad -x \in \mathcal{C}^*.$$

It follows that $c_l \cap c_l^* = \emptyset \ C_l \cap C_l^* = \emptyset \ \mathcal{C} \cap \mathcal{C}^* = \emptyset$.

From Property 2 it follows that if $\mathcal{C}$ is empty, then so is $\mathcal{C}^*$. Thus, it is sufficient to check for the emptiness of $\mathcal{C}$ only. But, $\mathcal{C}$ is defined in terms of the unstarred sets, and from this it follows that we need to identify the unstarred sets only and evaluate the condition that their intersection is empty.

Note that if any two of the unstarred sets C_1, C_2, and C_3 are empty, then $\mathcal{C}$ will always be empty. Since adding the origin to these sets makes them convex cones, the disjointedness of any two of these sets can be shown by finding a plane in E^3 containing the origin that separates them. This plane is easy to find once we have an explicit presentation for C_1, C_2, and C_3. As we show in the Appendix, if the matrices H_1, H_2, and H_3 are invertible, the sets C_1, C_2, and C_3 are given by

$$C_1 = \{ x : x = \alpha v_1 + \beta v_2 + \gamma v_3 + \delta v_4; \alpha, \beta, \gamma, \delta \geq 0 \} - \{0\},$$
$$C_2 = \{ x : x = \alpha u_1 + \beta u_2 + \gamma u_3 + \delta u_4; \alpha, \beta, \gamma, \delta \geq 0 \} - \{0\},$$
$$C_3 = \{ x : x = \alpha w_1 + \beta w_2 + \gamma w_3 + \delta w_4; \alpha, \beta, \gamma, \delta \geq 0 \}$$
$$- \{0\},$$

---

[2] In general, we would have to consider intersections such as $c_l \cap c_m^*$. But, as we show in the Appendix, these intersections are empty.

where,

$$v_1 = \pm p_{11} * p_{21},$$
$$v_2 = \pm p_{11} * p_{22},$$
$$v_3 = \pm p_{12} * p_{22},$$
$$v_4 = \pm p_{12} * p_{21},$$

$$w_1 = \pm p_{11} * p_{31},$$
$$w_2 = \pm p_{11} * p_{32},$$
$$w_3 = \pm p_{12} * p_{32},$$
$$w_4 = \pm p_{12} * p_{31}.$$

The sign is chosen in these formulas so that the z component of all these vectors is positive.

Using the azimuth and zenith angles for the principal directions from Table I, for the m-lobed map we get the vectors w_j and v_j as

$$w_1 = \pm \begin{pmatrix} \cos\theta_{11}\sin\theta_{31}\sin\phi_i \\ -\sin\theta_{11}\cos\theta_{31}\left(1 - \frac{\tan\theta_{31}}{\tan\theta_{11}}\cos\phi_i\right) \\ -\sin\theta_{11}\sin\theta_{21}\sin\phi_i \end{pmatrix},$$

$$w_2 = \pm \begin{pmatrix} \cos\theta_{11}\sin\theta_{32}\sin\phi_i \\ -\sin\theta_{11}\cos\theta_{32}\left(1 - \frac{\tan\theta_{32}}{\tan\theta_{11}}\cos\phi_i\right) \\ -\sin\theta_{11}\sin\theta_{32}\sin\phi_i \end{pmatrix},$$

$$w_3 = \pm \begin{pmatrix} \cos\theta_{12}\sin\theta_{32}\sin\phi_i \\ -\sin\theta_{12}\cos\theta_{32}\left(1 - \frac{\tan\theta_{32}}{\tan\theta_{12}}\cos\phi_i\right) \\ -\sin\theta_{12}\sin\theta_{32}\sin\phi_i \end{pmatrix},$$

$$w_4 = \pm \begin{pmatrix} \cos\theta_{12}\sin\theta_{31}\sin\phi_i \\ -\sin\theta_{12}\cos\theta_{31}\left(1 - \frac{\tan\theta_{31}}{\tan\theta_{12}}\cos\phi_i\right) \\ -\sin\theta_{12}\sin\theta_{31}\sin\phi_i \end{pmatrix},$$

$$v_1 = \pm \begin{pmatrix} -\cos\theta_{11}\sin\theta_{21}\sin\phi_i \\ -\sin\theta_{11}\cos\theta_{21}\left(1 - \frac{\tan\theta_{21}}{\tan\theta_{11}}\cos\phi_i\right) \\ \sin\theta_{11}\sin\theta_{21}\sin\phi_i \end{pmatrix},$$

$$v_2 = \pm \begin{pmatrix} -\cos\theta_{11}\sin\theta_{22}\sin\phi_i \\ -\sin\theta_{11}\cos\theta_{22}\left(1 - \frac{\tan\theta_{22}}{\tan\theta_{11}}\cos\phi_i\right) \\ \sin\theta_{11}\sin\theta_{22}\sin\phi_i \end{pmatrix},$$

$$v_3 = \pm \begin{pmatrix} -\cos\theta_{12}\sin\theta_{22}\sin\phi_i \\ -\sin\theta_{12}\cos\theta_{22}\left(1 - \frac{\tan\theta_{22}}{\tan\theta_{12}}\cos\phi_i\right) \\ \sin\theta_{12}\sin\theta_{22}\sin\phi_i \end{pmatrix},$$

$$v_4 = \pm \begin{pmatrix} -\cos\theta_{12}\sin\theta_{21}\sin\phi_i \\ -\sin\theta_{12}\cos\theta_{21}\left(1 - \frac{\tan\theta_{21}}{\tan\theta_{12}}\cos\phi_i\right) \\ \sin\theta_{12}\sin\theta_{21}\sin\phi_i \end{pmatrix}.$$

Now consider the z component of the vectors w_j and v_j for ϕ_i in the range $\pi > \phi_i > \pi/2$. Since $\sin\phi_i$ is positive in this range, we will have to consider the formulas for v_j with the positive sign and the formulas for w_j with the negative sign. With these signs, note that the y components of v_j are strictly negative while the y components of w_j are strictly positive. From the definitions of C_1 and C_3 it follows that the y components of all members of C_1 are strictly negative and the y components of all members of C_3 are strictly positive. Therefore, for $\pi > \phi_i > \pi/2$, the x–z plane can separate C_1 and C_3 and we have $C = C_1 \cap C_2 \cap C_3 = \emptyset$. (As a check, we note that, according to Lemma 5.1, the assumption that H_j are invertible holds for the range $\pi > \phi_i > \pi/2$.) This leads to

Theorem 5.2a: The normalized photometric stereo equation has a unique solution with the general three-lobed map if three

light sources are placed according to (18) and (19) with $\pi > \phi_i > \pi/2$. $\square$

If we restrict our attention to isotropic three-lobed maps, we can relax the constraint that $\pi > \phi_i > \pi/2$. For the isotropic three-lobed map the zenith and azimuth angles of the principal directions are shown in Table II. With these, we have

$$w_1 = \pm \begin{pmatrix} \cos\theta_1\sin\theta_1\sin\phi_i \\ -\sin\theta_1\cos\theta_1(1 - \cos\phi_i) \\ -\sin\theta_1\sin\theta_1\sin\phi_i \end{pmatrix}$$

$$w_2 = \pm \begin{pmatrix} \cos\theta_1\sin\theta_2\sin\phi_i \\ -\sin\theta_1\cos\theta_2\left(1 - \frac{\tan\theta_2}{\tan\theta_1}\cos\phi_i\right) \\ -\sin\theta_1\sin\theta_2\sin\phi_i \end{pmatrix}$$

$$w_3 = \pm \begin{pmatrix} \cos\theta_2\sin\theta_2\sin\phi_i \\ -\sin\theta_2\cos\theta_2(1 - \cos\phi_i) \\ -\sin\theta_2\sin\theta_2\sin\phi_i \end{pmatrix}$$

$$w_4 = \pm \begin{pmatrix} \cos\theta_2\sin\theta_1\sin\phi_i \\ -\sin\theta_2\cos\theta_1\left(1 - \frac{\tan\theta_1}{\tan\theta_2}\cos\phi_i\right) \\ -\sin\theta_2\sin\theta_1\sin\phi_i \end{pmatrix}$$

$$v_1 = \pm \begin{pmatrix} -\cos\theta_1\sin\theta_1\sin\phi_i \\ -\sin\theta_1\cos\theta_1(1 - \cos\phi_i) \\ \sin\theta_1\sin\theta_1\sin\phi_i \end{pmatrix}$$

$$v_2 = \pm \begin{pmatrix} -\cos\theta_1\sin\theta_2\sin\phi_i \\ -\sin\theta_1\cos\theta_2\left(1 - \frac{\tan\theta_2}{\tan\theta_1}\cos\phi_i\right) \\ \sin\theta_1\sin\theta_2\sin\phi_i \end{pmatrix}$$

$$v_3 = \pm \begin{pmatrix} -\cos\theta_2\sin\theta_2\sin\phi_i \\ -\sin\theta_2\cos\theta_2(1 - \cos\phi_i) \\ \sin\theta_2\sin\theta_2\sin\phi_i \end{pmatrix}$$

$$v_4 = \pm \begin{pmatrix} -\cos\theta_2\sin\theta_1\sin\phi_i \\ -\sin\theta_2\cos\theta_1\left(1 - \frac{\tan\theta_1}{\tan\theta_2}\cos\phi_i\right) \\ \sin\theta_2\sin\theta_1\sin\phi_i \end{pmatrix}.$$

Now consider the range of ϕ_i for which $(\tan\theta_1/\tan)\theta_2 > \cos\phi_i$ and $\pi > \phi_i$. As before, to get positive z components for w_j, we have to use the negative sign; to get positive z components for v_j, we use the positive sign in the above formulas. Further, for this range of ϕ_i note that $1 - (\tan\theta_2/\tan\theta_1)\cos\phi_i > 0$ and $1 - (\tan\theta_1/\tan\theta_2)\cos\phi_i > 0$. Thus, the y components of all v_j are strictly negative while the y components of all w_j are strictly positive. Hence, as before, the x–z plane can separate C_1 and C_3 giving us $C = \emptyset$.

Theorem 5.2b: The normalized photometric stereo equation has a unique solution with an isotropic three-lobed map if three light sources are placed according to (18) and (19) with

$$\pi > \phi_i > \cos^{-1}\left(\frac{\tan\theta_1}{\tan\theta_2}\right). \tag{30}$$

$\square$

Two comments about the inequality of (30) are in order:

1) For the class of reflectance maps described by (11), we have $\theta_1 = \theta_2/2$. In general, if we consider $\theta_1 = \theta_2/\beta$, where $\beta > 0$, then we have

$$1/\beta = \frac{\theta_1}{\theta_2} > \frac{\tan\theta_1}{\tan\theta_2}.$$

Thus, we can set $\phi_i \geq \cos^{-1}\frac{1}{\beta}$ and always satisfy the inequality of (30). For $\beta = 2$ we get $\phi \geq 60°$. Hence, *for the reflectance map obtained due to the three lobes described in Section III, three light sources placed according to (18) and (19) with the azimuth angle ϕ_i given by $180° > \phi_i \geq 60°$ will yield a globally unique solution to the* *normalized photometric stereo equation.* Silver [26] used this configuration with $\phi_i = 120°$ between any two lights. That is why he was able to reconstruct surfaces using only three light sources.

2) Note that, even as $\beta \to \infty$, if we keep $\phi_i > 90°$, the inequality of (30) is always satisfied.

As a final comment, consider what happens when three light sources are placed according to Theorem 5.2a or 5.2b. The theorems assure us that $\mathcal{C}$ is empty, i.e., given distinct n_1 and n_2, the vector $(n_1 - n_2)$ belongs to at most any two pairs of sets (c_1, c_1^*), (c_2, c_2^*), and (c_3, c_3^*). If the vector does not belong to the pair (c_k, c_k^*) for some k, then it follows from the definition of the sets c_k and c_k^* that one of the following inequalities holds:

$$p_{k1}^T(n_1 - n_2) \geq 0 \qquad p_{k2}^T(n_1 - n_2) > 0 \tag{31}$$

$$p_{k1}^T(n_1 - n_2) > 0 \qquad p_{k2}^T(n_1 - n_2) \geq 0 \tag{32}$$

$$p_{k1}^T(n_1 - n_2) \leq 0 \qquad p_{k2}^T(n_1 - n_2) < 0 \tag{33}$$

$$p_{k1}^T(n_1 - n_2) < 0 \qquad p_{k2}^T(n_1 - n_2) \leq 0. \tag{34}$$

E. Case m > 3

In this case, we will consider (21) in its full generality. As we see below, this case is no more complex than the three-lobed map case, and in fact the analysis for the three-lobed map can be easily extended to the present situation. The technique we adopt for doing this is to form a three-lobed map from the m-lobed map in such a way that establishing the uniqueness of solution for the three-lobed map would establish uniqueness of solution for the m-lobed map.

We construct the three-lobed map out of the m-lobed map by choosing the first lobe, the $m - 1$th lobe and the backscatter lobe of the m-lobed map as the lobes for the three-lobed map, i.e., given the m-lobed reflectance map of (14), we form the reflectance map

$$
\begin{aligned}
R^*(i_l, n, r) &= \rho_1 \Phi_1\left(p_{l1}^T n\right) + \rho_{m-1} \Phi_{m-1} \\
&\quad \times \left(p_{l,m-1}^T n\right) + b, \quad \text{if } i_l^T n \geq 0 \\
&= 0, \qquad\qquad\qquad\qquad \text{otherwise.}
\end{aligned} \tag{35}
$$

Consider the normalized photometric stereo equation with the reflectance map $R^*(\,)$. Since $R^*(\,)$ is a three-lobed map, we know from Theorem 5.2a that three light sources placed according to (18) and (19) with $\pi > \phi_i \geq \pi/2$ will always give a unique solution to the normalized equation. Further, it follows from the discussion at the end of the three-lobed map case that, for some k $(1 \leq k \leq 3)$, one of the conditions in (31), (32), (33), or (34) holds. Since the second lobe of $R^*(\,)$ has the principal direction $p_{k,m-1}$, the conditions in (31), (32), (33), and (34) translate to

$$p_{k1}^T(n_1 - n_2) \geq 0 \qquad p_{k,m-1}^T(n_1 - n_2) > 0 \tag{36}$$

$$p_{k1}^T(n_1 - n_2) > 0 \qquad p_{k,m-1}^T(n_1 - n_2) \geq 0 \tag{37}$$

$$p_{k1}^T(n_1 - n_2) \leq 0 \qquad p_{k,m-1}^T(n_1 - n_2) < 0 \tag{38}$$

$$p_{k1}^T(n_1 - n_2) < 0 \qquad p_{k,m-1}^T(n_1 - n_2) \leq 0. \tag{39}$$

We will now see that if any one of the conditions in (36), (37), (38), and (39) holds, then the kth row of equation cannot hold. To proceed, recall (15) from Section III, which states that we can write any principal direction p_{lj}, $2 \leq j \leq m-2$, of the m-lobed map as

$$p_{lj} = \beta_{l,1,j} p_{lj} + \beta_{l,m-1,j} p_{l,m-1}$$

with $\beta_{lj}, \beta_{l,m-1,j} > 0$. Substituting $l = k$ we get

$$p_{kj} = \beta_{k,1,j} p_{kj} + \beta_{k,m-1,j} p_{k,m-1}$$

with $\beta_{k,1,j}, \beta_{k,m-1,j} > 0$. Thus

$$
\begin{aligned}
p_{kj}^T(n_1 - n_2) &= \beta_{k,1,j} p_{k1}^T(n_1 - n_2) \\
&\quad + \beta_{k,m-1,j} p_{k,m-1}^T(n_1 - n_2).
\end{aligned}
$$

If we assume that condition (36) holds, then from the above equation it follows that $p_{kj}^T(n_1 - n_2) > 0$ for $2 \leq j \leq m - 2$. From the monotonicity of $\Phi_j(\,)$ and the positivity of ρ_j, it now follows that $\rho_j \Phi_j\left(p_{kj}^T n_1\right) - \rho_j \Phi_j\left(p_{kj}^T n_2\right) > 0$ for $2 \leq j \leq m - 2$. Further, note that by our assumption that since condition (36) holds, the terms $\rho_1 \Phi_1\left(p_{k1}^T n_1\right) - \rho_1 \Phi_1\left(p_{k1}^T n_2\right)$ and $\rho_{m-1} \Phi_{m-1}\left(p_{k,m-1}^T n_1\right) - \rho_{m-1} \Phi_{m-1}\left(p_{k,m-1}^T n_2\right)$ cannot be negative. Hence

$$\sum_{j=1}^{m-1} \left\{\rho_j \Phi_j\left(p_{kj}^T n_1\right) - \rho_j \Phi_j\left(p_{kj}^T n_2\right)\right\} > 0$$

i.e., the kth row of (21) cannot be zero.

Arguing along similar lines, it is easy to see that if any of the conditions of (36)–(39) was true, the kth row of (21) would not be zero. Hence, we reach the conclusion that (21) will not hold if any of the conditions of (36), (37), (38), and (39) hold. Under this circumstance, the normalized equation with the m-lobed map has a unique solution, i.e., the normalized equation with the m-lobed reflectance map $R(\,)$ has a unique solution with three light sources if the normalized equation has a unique solution with three light sources and the reflectance map $R^*(\,)$. Theorem 5.2a tells us how three lights can be placed so that the equation with $R^*(\,)$ has a unique solution, and from this we get

Theorem 5.3: The normalized photometric stereo equation has a unique solution with the m-lobed reflectance map $(m > 3)$ if three light sources are used and placed according to (19) and (18) with $\pi > \phi_i > \pi/2$.   □

VI. Inversion of the Unnormalized Photometric Stereo Equation

In this section, we analyze the unnormalized photometric stereo equation (16). We investigate whether it is possible to obtain a globally unique $I_{\max}$ and surface normal from the equation for three light sources. The main result of this section is Theorem 6.1, which states the condition for which this is possible.

The result expressed in Theorem 6.1 depends on a property of the normalized photometric stereo equation, and we begin by discussing this property.

A. The Manifold Structure of the Normalized Equation

If three light sources are used, then the normalized photometric stereo equation (17) can be viewed as a mapping from E^3 to E^3, i.e., from n to $(I_1^{\mathrm{rel}} I_2^{\mathrm{rel}} I_3^{\mathrm{rel}})^T$. The domain of this mapping is the manifold $n^T n = 1$ to which n belongs. If we assume a unique solution for the normalized equation, then the mapping is one to one and the range of the mapping is also a manifold in E^3 [20]. We denote this manifold by S.

Example: The manifold S is best illustrated in the case of a Lambertian surface. We have

$$H_1 = \begin{pmatrix} i_1^T \\ i_2^T \\ i_3^T \end{pmatrix}, \qquad I^{\mathrm{rel}} = \begin{pmatrix} I_1^{\mathrm{rel}} \\ I_2^{\mathrm{rel}} \\ I_3^{\mathrm{rel}} \end{pmatrix}$$

where, $I^{\text{rel}} = H_1 n$. Hence, $n = H_1^{-1} I^{\text{rel}}$ and using $n^T n = 1$ we get

$$I^{\text{rel}\,T} \left(H_1^{-1}\right)^T \left(H_1^{-1}\right) I^{\text{rel}} = 1. \tag{40}$$

Thus, the manifold corresponding to a Lambertian reflectance map is a part of the ellipsoid in (40).

Consider the shape of the manifold S when we assume that the term $\sum_j \rho_j \Phi_j \left(p_{lj}^T n\right)$ in the m-lobed reflectance map of (14) goes to zero as $i_l^T n$ approaches zero. As $i_1^T n \to 0$, $I_1^{\text{rel}} \to b$, i.e., the edge of the manifold corresponding to $i_1^T n \to 0$ is a curve in the plane $I_1^{\text{rel}} = b$. Similarly, the edge of the manifold corresponding to $i_2^T n \to 0$ is a curve in the plane $I_2^{\text{rel}} = b$ and the edge corresponding to $i_3^T n \to 0$ is a curve in the plane $I_3^{\text{rel}} = b$. See Fig. 8.

From this it follows that, given any two points x_1 and x_2 on S, the plane Γ defined by $\Gamma = \text{span}(x_1, x_2)$ will intersect S in such a fashion that it is possible to draw a continuous curve $\alpha(s)$ (see Fig. 8) with $\alpha(0) = x_1$ and $\alpha(1) = x_2$ and $\alpha(s) \in \Gamma \cap S$.

B. The Unnormalized Equation

We will now explore the unnormalized equation using the manifold S.

Let Δ be the set of surface normals illuminated by the light sources i_l. Then

$$\Delta = \left\{n : i_l^T n > 0,\ l = 1, 2, 3\right\}.$$

In terms of zenith and azimuth angles

$$\Delta$$
$$= \{\theta_n, \phi_n :\quad \cos\theta_{i_1}\cos\theta_n + \sin\theta_{i_1}\sin\theta_n\cos(\phi_{i_1} - \phi_n) > 0$$
$$\cos\theta_{i_2}\cos\theta_n + \sin\theta_{i_2}\sin\theta_n\cos(\phi_{i_2} - \phi_n) > 0$$
$$\cos\theta_{i_3}\cos\theta_n + \sin\theta_{i_3}\sin\theta\cos(\phi_{i_3} - \phi_n) > 0\}.$$

Given a normal vector $n \in \Delta$, we can write the normalized photometric stereo equation as

$$\begin{pmatrix} I_1^{\text{rel}} \\ I_2^{\text{rel}} \\ I_3^{\text{rel}} \end{pmatrix} = \begin{pmatrix} R_1(\theta_n, \phi_n) \\ R_2(\theta_n, \phi_n) \\ R_3(\theta_n, \phi_n) \end{pmatrix}$$

where

$$R_1(\theta_n, \phi_n) = R(i_1, n, r)$$
$$R_2(\theta_n, \phi_n) = R(i_2, n, r)$$
$$R_3(\theta_n, \phi_n) = R(i_3, n, r). \tag{41}$$

If we assume that the three light source directions have been chosen such that the normalized photometric stereo equation has a globally unique solution, then

$$\text{rank} \begin{pmatrix} \dfrac{\partial R_1}{\partial \theta_n} & \dfrac{\partial R_1}{\partial \phi_n} \\ \dfrac{\partial R_2}{\partial \theta_n} & \dfrac{\partial R_2}{\partial \phi_n} \\ \dfrac{\partial R_3}{\partial \theta_n} & \dfrac{\partial R_3}{\partial \phi_n} \end{pmatrix} = 2. \tag{42}$$

Now consider the unnormalized photometric stereo equation. If it is possible to find two distinct pairs $I_{\max_1}$, n_1, and $I_{\max_2}$, n_2 such that

$$I_{\max_1} \begin{pmatrix} R(i_1, n_1, r) \\ R(i_2, n_1, r) \\ R(i_3, n_1, r) \end{pmatrix} = I_{\max_2} \begin{pmatrix} R(i_1, n_2, r) \\ R(i_2, n_2, r) \\ R(i_3, n_2, r) \end{pmatrix}$$

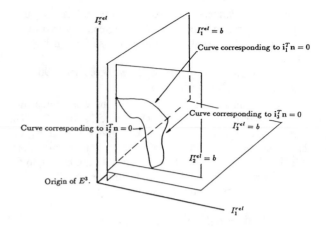

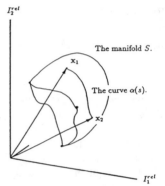

Fig. 8. The manifold S.

then

$$\begin{pmatrix} R_1(\theta_{n_1}, \phi_{n_1}) \\ R_2(\theta_{n_1}, \phi_{n_1}) \\ R_3(\theta_{n_1}, \phi_{n_1}) \end{pmatrix} = \beta \begin{pmatrix} R_1(\theta_{n_2}, \phi_{n_2}) \\ R_2(\theta_{n_2}, \phi_{n_2}) \\ R_3(\theta_{n_2}, \phi_{n_2}) \end{pmatrix} \tag{43}$$

where $\beta = I_{\max_1}/I_{\max_2} > 0$ and we have used the notation of (41).

We can interpret this condition in terms of the manifold S as follows: If the unnormalized photometric stereo equation does not have a globally unique solution for the albedo and the normal, then there must be two elements of S that are linearly dependent with a positive scaling factor. Since S is a smooth manifold, we can check for the linear dependency by a local condition as shown below.

Theorem 4.1: If three light sources are placed such that the normalized photometric stereo equation has a unique solution, then equation (43) holds for some distinct $\theta_{n_1}, \phi_{n_1} \in \Delta$, $\theta_{n_2}, \phi_{n_2} \in \Delta$, and $\beta > 0$, if and only if there is at least one element $\theta^*, \phi^* \in \Delta$ such that,

$$J = \det \begin{pmatrix} R_1(\theta^*, \phi^*) & R_2(\theta^*, \phi^*) & R_3(\theta^*, \phi^*) \\ \dfrac{\partial R_1(\theta^*, \phi^*)}{\partial \theta} & \dfrac{\partial R_2(\theta^*, \phi^*)}{\partial \theta} & \dfrac{\partial R_3(\theta^*, \phi^*)}{\partial \theta} \\ \dfrac{\partial R_1(\theta^*, \phi^*)}{\partial \phi} & \dfrac{\partial R_2(\theta^*, \phi^*)}{\partial \phi} & \dfrac{\partial R_3(\theta^*, \phi^*)}{\partial \phi} \end{pmatrix} = 0. \tag{44}$$

Proof: We will first establish that if there are multiple solutions to (43), then (44) holds.

Let us interpret (44) geometrically. Given $\theta, \phi \in \Delta$, consider the space E^3 from the point $I^{\text{rel}}(\theta, \phi)$ on S. The origin of the space E^3 with respect to this point is given by $-I^{\text{rel}}(\theta, \phi)$ and the tangent space to S at the point is spanned by

$$\begin{pmatrix} \frac{\partial R_1}{\partial \theta} \\ \frac{\partial R_2}{\partial \theta} \\ \frac{\partial R_3}{\partial \theta} \end{pmatrix} \quad \text{and} \quad \begin{pmatrix} \frac{\partial R_1}{\partial \phi} \\ \frac{\partial R_2}{\partial \phi} \\ \frac{\partial R_3}{\partial \phi} \end{pmatrix}.$$

The condition in (44) states that the vector $I^{\text{rel}}(\theta^*, \phi^*)$ and consequently $-I^{\text{rel}}(\theta^*, \phi^*)$ lie in the tangent space of S at $I^{\text{rel}}(\theta^*, \phi^*)$. Thus, (44) states that there is at least one point on the manifold S at which the tangent space includes the origin of E^3.

Note that if (44) holds for some θ_{n_1}, ϕ_{n_1} and θ_{n_2}, ϕ_{n_2}, then there is at least one $\theta_{n_3}, \phi_{n_3} \in \Delta$ for which it does not, i.e., $I^{\text{rel}}(\theta_{n_3}, \phi_{n_3}) \neq \nu I^{\text{rel}}(\theta_{n_1}, \phi_{n_1})$, for any $\nu > 0$. If this were not so, all the points of S would lie along the vector $I^{\text{rel}}(\theta_{n_1}, \phi_{n_1})$ and (42) would not hold. Given such a θ_{n_3}, ϕ_{n_3}, we can construct a plane (call it Γ) that is the span of $I^{\text{rel}}(\theta_{n_1}, \phi_{n_1})$ and $I^{\text{rel}}(\theta_{n_3}, \phi_{n_3})$. Note that since $I^{\text{rel}}(\theta_{n_2}, \phi_{n_2}) = \beta I^{\text{rel}}(\theta_{n_1}, \phi_{n_1})$, we have $I^{\text{rel}}(\theta_{n_2}, \phi_{n_2}) \in \Gamma$. Thus, the points $I^{\text{rel}}(\theta_{n_1}, \phi_{n_1})$ and $I^{\text{rel}}(\theta_{n_2}, \phi_{n_2})$ are contained both in S and Γ.

Consider the intersection of S and Γ. From our discussion of the geometry of S, it is clear this intersection will contain at least one continuous curve $\alpha(s)$ such that $\alpha(0) = I^{\text{rel}}(\theta_{n_1}, \phi_{n_1})$ and $\alpha(1) = I^{\text{rel}}(\theta_{n_2}, \phi_{n_2})$. Since the curve is continuous, it has well defined tangent vectors $\alpha'(s)$ everywhere.

We will now proceed to show that there is at least one point on the curve $\alpha(s)$, at which $\alpha'(s)$ becomes linearly dependent on $\alpha(s)$. Since, $-\alpha(s)$ is in fact the origin of E^3 and $\alpha'(s)$ is contained in the tangent space of S, at $\alpha(s)$ we have found the point we are looking for and the first part of the theorem is proved.

As Γ is a plane, given any vector $\alpha(s)$ in it, we can construct another vector $\alpha_t(s) \in \Gamma$ such that $\|\alpha(s)\| = 1$, $\alpha_t^T(s)\alpha(s) = 0$, and the functions

$$f(s) = \alpha_t^T(0)\alpha(s), \qquad g(s) = \alpha_t^T(s)\alpha'(s)$$

are well defined and continuous (see Fig. 9). Now, $f(0) = 0$ and $f(1) = \alpha_t^T(0)\alpha(1) = \beta \alpha_t^T(0)\alpha(0) = 0$. Since $f'(s) = \alpha_t^T(0)\alpha'(s)$, we have the following possibilities for $f'(s)$:

1) $f'(0) = 0$. In this case, we get $\alpha_t^T(0)\alpha'(0) = 0$, and so $\alpha'(0)$ is linearly dependent on $\alpha(0)$, which proves the first part of the theorem.

2) $f'(0) \neq 0$. Let s' be a point $0 < s' \leq 1$, such that $f(s') = 0$ and $f(s) \neq 0$ for all s, $0 < s < s'$. We know that there is at least one such point given by $s' = 1$ (see Fig. 9). Since $f(s') = \alpha_t^T(0)\alpha(s') = 0$, we have that $\alpha(s')$ has no component along $\alpha_t(0)$, and hence, $\alpha(s')$ is linearly dependent on $\alpha(0)$. This implies that $\alpha_t(s') = \alpha_t(0)$. At s' we have two possibilities:

   a) $f'(s') = 0$. This again implies that the tangent vector $\alpha'(s')$ and the vector $\alpha(s')$ are linearly dependent and the first part of the theorem follows.

   b) $f'(s') \neq 0$. Then sign $f'(s') = -\text{sign } f'(0)$. See Fig. 5. We have $g(s') = \alpha_t^T(s')\alpha'(s') = \alpha_t^T(0)\alpha'(s') = f'(s')$. Also, $g(0) = \alpha_t^T(0)\alpha'(0) = f'(0)$. Thus, sign $g(0) = -\text{sign } g(1)$ and there must exist an s^*, $0 \leq s^* \leq 1$, such that $g(s^*) = 0$. This implies that, at s^*, the vectors $\alpha(s)^*$ and $\alpha'(s^*)$ are linearly dependent and the first part of the theorem follows.

The converse is easily established. Note that the condition in (44) implies that the Jacobian of the transformation from $(I_{\max}, \theta_n, \phi_n)$ to (I_1, I_2, I_3) is zero at θ^*, ϕ^*. Thus, by the

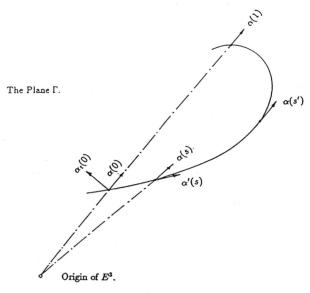

The Plane Γ.

Origin of E^3.

Fig. 9. The curve $\alpha(s)$.

inverse function theorem we do not have a unique solution to the unnormalized equation in the neighborhood of θ^*, ϕ^*. ☐

VII. Completeness of Photometric Inversion

In this section, we consider the completeness problem. The terminology we use is: A vector i "illuminates" a vector n iff $i^T n > 0$. A vector n is "k-illuminated" if there are k i_l's that illuminate n. The problem of completeness of photometric stereo is stated as follows: What is the minimum number of vectors i_l, $l = 1, 2, \cdots, k^*$ so that all surface normals n of a surface are k-illuminated $(k \geq 3)$? We are concerned with only those surface normals n that have zenith angles less than $\pi/2$.

Note that, in general, the solution to the completeness problem depends on the surface being imaged. If the surface is convoluted, parts of it might easily cast shadows on other parts and a very large number of light sources may be needed to k-illuminate it completely. We consider a simpler version of this problem where we restrict ourselves to considering those surfaces for which the lack of illumination of any surface normal is only due to self-shadow. The class of convex objects has surfaces where this holds. As we see below, for this class of surfaces it is possible to obtain a relation between k^* and k that is independent of the detailed surface shape. The main result is expressed in Theorem 7.1, which states that $k^* = 2k$ light sources are necessary and sufficient to k-illuminate any surface normal n.

To begin, we establish that constraining the position of light sources does not change k^*. Given a vector n, suppose that i_l, $l = 1, \cdots, k^*$ light sources k-illuminate n. We move the light sources keeping their azimuth angles the same, but decreasing their zenith angles until they all have zenith angles equal to the minimum zenith angle of the original configuration. We denote the new light sources by i'_l, $l = 1, \cdots, k^*$. We now establish that if all of i_l k-illuminate n, then so do all of i'_l.

Lemma 7.1: If a vector n is illuminated by a given light source i, then it is also illuminated by the light source i', where

$$i = \begin{pmatrix} \cos \phi_i \sin \theta_i \\ \sin \phi_i \sin \theta_i \\ \cos \theta_i \end{pmatrix}$$

and

$$i' = \begin{pmatrix} \cos\phi_i \sin\theta'_i \\ \sin\phi_i \sin\theta'_i \\ \cos\theta'_i \end{pmatrix}$$

where $0 < \theta'_i < \theta_i$.

Proof: Let us define two vectors u and z as

$$u = \begin{pmatrix} \cos\phi_i \\ \sin\phi_i \\ 0 \end{pmatrix}, \qquad z = \begin{pmatrix} 0 \\ 0 \\ 1 \end{pmatrix}.$$

Then we have $i' = \sin\theta'_i u + \cos\theta'_i z$ and $i = \sin\theta_i u + \cos\theta_i z$. If we assume that $i^T n > 0$, then we have $i^T n = \sin\theta_i u^T n + \cos\theta_i z^T n > 0$. Since we know that $z^T n > 0$, we have from the above inequality the following relation:

$$\frac{1}{\tan\theta_i} > -\frac{u^T n}{z^T n}.$$

But we know that $\theta'_i \leq \theta_i$; hence, $(1/\tan\theta'_i) \geq (1/\tan\theta_i) > -(u^T n/z^T n)$, which leads us to $i'^T n > 0$. Thus, i' also illuminates n.

It follows that if all i'_l have zenith angles equal to the minimum zenith angle of i_l, then the light sources i'_l k-illuminate any vector that is k-illuminated by i_l.

We now consider solving the completeness problem in a simplified setting: we assume that all the light sources i_l have been moved so that they have the same zenith angle (equal to the minimum angle of the original configuration). We denote the zenith angle of any of the light source by θ_i.

Let $k^* \geq 3$. Given any k^* light sources with the same zenith angle, we can number them by going around them in a counterclockwise manner. We assume that this is in fact the numbering i_l. As $k^* \geq 3$, there is a unique way of defining the difference in azimuth angles between any two consecutive light sources i_q and i_{q+1}. This is done by measuring in a counterclockwise manner the change in the azimuth angle from ϕ_{i_q} to $\phi_{i_{q+1}}$, i.e., we define $\Delta\phi_q = \phi_{i_q} - \phi_{i_{q+1}}$. As a special case, $\Delta\phi_{k^*}$ is defined as $\Delta\phi_{k^*} = 2\pi + \phi_{i_1} - \phi_{i_{k^*}}$. Of course, $\sum_q \Delta\phi_q = 2\pi$.

We now establish an inequality that will lead us directly to the solution of our problem.

Lemma 7.2: Assume that $k^* \geq 3$. For any q $(1 \leq q \leq k^*)$, if $\Delta\phi_q > \pi$, then there is at least one vector n which is zero-covered by the given set of k^* lights.

Proof: For any two consecutive lights i_q and i_{q+1}, we rotate the $x-y$ axis of our reference frame about the z axis such that the positive x axis bisects the azimuth angle between the two lights. In this frame, we have

$$i_q = \begin{pmatrix} \sin\theta_i \cos\phi \\ -\sin\theta_i \sin\phi \\ \cos\theta_i \end{pmatrix}, \qquad i_{q+1} = \begin{pmatrix} \sin\theta_i \cos\phi \\ \sin\theta_i \sin\phi \\ \cos\theta_i \end{pmatrix}$$

where θ_i is the zenith angle and $\phi = \Delta\phi_q/2$ is strictly greater than $\pi/2$. (i.e., $\cos\phi < 0$).

Now consider any vector u, given by $u = \begin{pmatrix} 1 & 0 & \zeta \end{pmatrix}^T$ where

$$0 < \zeta < -\tan\theta_i \cos\phi.$$

We can construct n such that $n = u/\|u\|$. We have

$$n^T i_{q+1} = \frac{1}{\|u\|} [\sin\theta_i \cos\phi + \zeta \cos\theta_i]$$

$$= \frac{1}{\|u\|} \left[\sin\theta_i \cos\phi \left(1 + \frac{\zeta}{\tan\theta_i \cos\phi} \right) \right].$$

It is easy to show that the term $1 + (\zeta/\tan\theta_i \cos\phi)$ in the above expression is positive. However, $\cos\phi$ is negative. Hence, $i_{q+1}^T n < 0$. Using the exact same argument, it is possible to show that $i_q^T n < 0$.

If we select any other light source i_p, then we know that its zenith angle is θ_i and that its azimuth angle ϕ_p is constrained by $\|\phi_p\| > \phi > \pi/2$. Hence, $-\cos\phi < -\cos\phi_p$ and we get $-\tan\theta_i \cos\phi < -\tan\theta_i \cos\phi_p$.

This leads us to $1 + \frac{\zeta}{\tan\theta_i \cos\phi_p} > 0$ as before. Also, $\cos\phi_p < 0$ as before, and using the same argument as above, we get $i_p^T n < 0$. Thus, no other i_p can illuminate $n = u/\|u\|$, and n is zero-illuminated. $\square$

We will now proceed to establish the exact value of k^*.

Theorem 7.1: $k^* = 2k$ lights are necessary and sufficient to k-illuminate all surface normals n that have a zenith angle strictly less than $\pi/2$. These lights should be placed such that

1) the differences in the azimuth angles $\Delta\phi_q$, $q = 1, \cdots, k^*$ are constrained so that $0 < \Delta\phi_q \leq \pi$, and

2) the zenith angles of all the light sources are the same (θ_i) and constrained by $0 < \theta_i < \pi/2$.

Proof: The constraint on $\Delta\phi_q$ follows from a straight application of Lemma 7.2 to every consecutive pair of i's.

The result $k^* = 2k$ is obtained by applying a more global constraint. Consider, the light sources $i_2, i_3, \cdots, i_k$. If we remove all of these lights, we have the lights $i_{k+1}, i_{k+2}, \cdots, i_{k^*}$, and i_1 left. We now show by contradiction that the difference between the azimuth angle between i_1 and i_{k+1} must be less than or equal to π.

If this were not so, by application of Lemma 5.2, there exists an n that is zero-illuminated by these light sources. Reintroducing the lights $i_2, \cdots, i_k$ can, at the most, $k - 1$ illuminate n, and we do not have a k-illumination. Hence, the difference between the azimuth angles between i_1 and i_{k+1} must be less than or equal to π. That is, $\Delta\phi_1 + \Delta\phi_2 + \cdots + \Delta\phi_k \leq \pi$.

Similar inequalities can be written by starting with $i_3, i_4, \cdots$ instead of i_2. This leads to the following:

$$\Delta\phi_2 + \Delta\phi_3 + \cdots + \Delta\phi_{k+1} \leq \pi$$

$$\Delta\phi_3 + \Delta\phi_4 + \cdots + \Delta\phi_{k+2} \leq \pi$$

$$\vdots$$

$$\Delta\phi_{k^*} + \Delta\phi_1 + \cdots + \Delta\phi_{k-1} \leq \pi.$$

Note that we have a net of k^* inequalities, and that any particular term $\Delta\phi_q$ occurs in exactly k of them. Adding all the inequalities, we get: $k \sum_q \Delta\phi_q \leq k^*\pi$. But, we know that $\sum_q \Delta\phi_q = 2\pi$. This leads us to $k^* \geq 2k$, which establishes the necessary part of the theorem.

We now establish that $k^* = 2k$ lights are sufficient to k-illuminate all n. Let the light sources i_j, $j = 1, \cdots, 2k$ have the same zenith angle θ_i, $0 < \theta_i < \pi/2$ and be uniformly placed in their azimuth angle, i.e., the azimuth angle of i_j is $\phi_{i_j} = \frac{2\pi}{2k}(j-1)$. Given any n and i_j, we consider their projections n_{xy} and $i_{xy,j}$ on the $x-y$ plane. If

$$n = \begin{pmatrix} \cos\phi_n \sin\theta_n \\ \sin\phi_n \sin\theta_n \\ \cos\theta_n \end{pmatrix}, \qquad i_j = \begin{pmatrix} \cos\phi_{i_j} \sin\theta_i \\ \sin\phi_{i_j} \sin\theta_i \\ \cos\theta_i \end{pmatrix}$$

then

$$n_{xy} = \begin{pmatrix} \cos\phi_n \sin\theta_n \\ \sin\phi_n \sin\theta_n \end{pmatrix}, \qquad i_{xy,j} = \begin{pmatrix} \cos\phi_{i_j} \sin\theta_i \\ \sin\phi_{i_j} \sin\theta_i \end{pmatrix}.$$

Note that since $\cos\theta_i$, $\cos\theta_n > 0$, $i_{xy,j}^T n_{xy} \geq 0$ implies $i_j^T n > 0$. The tips of the vectors $i_{xy,j}$ are uniformly distributed in a circle around the origin of the $x-y$ plane with an angle of $\frac{2\pi}{2k}$ between any two consecutive vectors. It is easy to see that, given any vector n in this plane, there are at least k vectors (among $i_{xy,j}$) that fall within $\pm\pi/2$ of n_{xy}. Hence, there are at least k vectors $i_{xy,j}$ such that $i_{xy,j}^T n_{xy} \geq 0$. It thereby follows that there are at least k vectors i_j such that $i_j^T n > 0$. $\square$

VIII. EXPERIMENTAL RESULTS

We now present experimental results that show that the theoretical results of the previous sections can be applied to real-world data. We show that

1) If a Lambertian photometric stereo is used to reconstruct surfaces whose reflectance map is non-Lambertian, the reconstruction can be quite poor. Using the correct non-Lambertian map improves the reconstruction considerably.

2) For the class of reflectance maps proposed in this paper, three light sources are sufficient for solving the normalized photometric stereo.

3) $I_{\max}$, the measure of illuminant strength, cannot be estimated along with the surface normal using only three light sources for readily encountered non-Lambertian reflectance maps.

Before we present our results, we note that the claim [2] above is supported by Silver's [26] results. Silver found that photometric stereo could be used with only three light sources for experimentally measured point light surface reflectance maps.

Our experimental results for 1) and 2) above come from reconstruction of the two surfaces shown in Fig. 4. Both the surfaces are spherical, and as we mentioned in Section III, the one at the right is non-Lambertian with the reflectance map given by (12). By plotting the intensity in the principal plane we found that the surface at the left has a Lambertian reflectance map.

Three images were obtained of each of the surfaces in a photometric stereo apparatus with three point light sources. The zenith angle of all the light sources were 25° while the azimuth angles were 0°, 120°, and −120°. The three images for the non-Lambertian surface were used in the normalized photometric stereo equation, once with a Lambertian reflectance map and then with the non-Lambertian reflectance map of (12). A standard Levenberg−Marquardt algorithm [16] was used for solving the nonlinear normalized photometric stereo equation.

Figs. 10 and 11 show the needle diagrams obtained from the normalized photometric stereo using Lambertian and non-Lambertian reflectance maps, and Figs. 13 and 12 show the depth profiles obtained from the needle maps. The reconstruction from using the non-Lambertian reflectance map is superior to that from the Lambertian reflectance map. A detailed analysis of the reconstruction errors was conducted as follows: an ideal sphere was fit to the data by letting the center and the radius of the sphere vary until the error between surface normals of the ideal sphere and the experimentally obtained data were as small as possible. The error that remained after the best fit was taken as a measure of the error in the reconstruction. The error was computed as the rms angular deviation between the surface normals of the ideal sphere and the experimentally reconstructed surface normals. The best fit was found by a standard optimization algorithm [16], which was initiated close to the manually measured center and radius of the image.

For the reconstruction with the Lambertian reflectance map, the rms error was 19.46°. For the reconstruction with the non-

Fig. 10.   Needle diagram of reconstruction of the non-Lambertian surface with a Lambertian map.

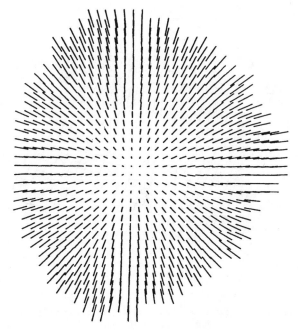

Fig. 11.   Needle diagram of reconstruction of the non-Lambertian surface with a non-Lambertian map.

Lambertian reflectance map, the error was 1.82°. This clearly shows that it is inappropriate to use the Lambertian reflectance map with non-Lambertian surfaces.

As a comparison, we also reconstructed the Lambertian surface of Fig. 4 with a Lambertian reflectance map. Fig. 14 shows the resulting needle map, and Fig. 15 the depth profile. The rms deviation of the reconstruction from the best fit sphere was 4.787°. This error is of the same order of magnitude as the error for reconstructing the non-Lambertian surface with the non-Lambertian reflectance map and validates that result. We feel that the slight increase in the error is due to the fact that the

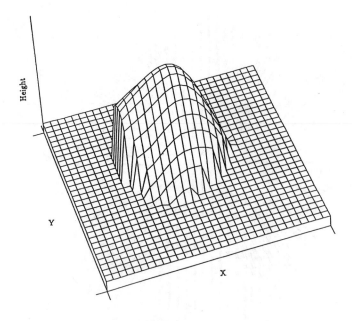

Fig. 12.   Depth profile of the reconstruction of the Lambertian surface with a non-Lambertian map.

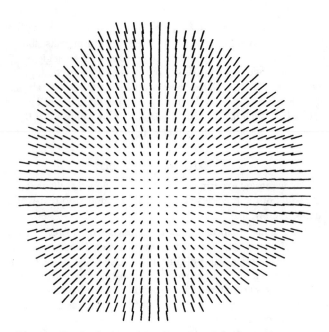

Fig. 14.   Needle diagram of reconstruction of the Lambertian surface.

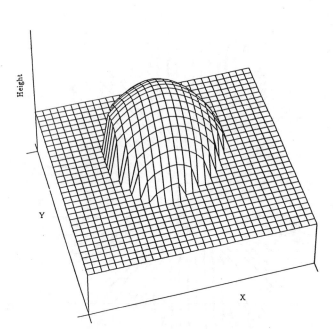

Fig. 13.   Depth profile of the reconstruction of the non-Lambertian surface with a non-Lambertian map.

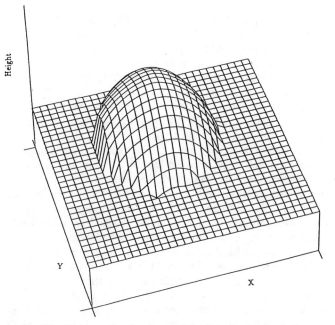

Fig. 15.   Depth profile of reconstruction of the Lambertian surface.

surface is only approximately Lambertian whereas we used an exact Lambertian model to reconstruct it.

We have reconstructed other surfaces with non-Lambertian reflectance maps quite successfully with three light sources, and the reader is referred to [30] for those.

Next, we checked whether our photometric stereo apparatus with three light sources could be used to obtain the surface normals and I_{max} for the non-Lambertian reflectance map of (12). Fig. 16 shows the plot of J of Theorem 6.1 for the reflectance map of (12) and three light sources placed at a constant zenith angle of 25° and azimuth angles of 0°, 120°, and −120°. Note that the value of J does cross zero. Hence, by Theorem 6.1 we know that I_{max} and the surface normal cannot

be uniquely determined for this reflectance map. In fact, it is very easy to find two surface normals that satisfy (43). Let both the surface normals have the same azimuth angle as that of the first light source. Let $\theta_{n_1} = 50.0°$ and $\theta_{n_2} = 20.83°$. Then, we have $[R_1(\theta_{n_1}, \phi_{n_1})R_2(\theta_{n_1}, \phi_{n_1})R_3(\theta_{n_1}, \phi_{n_1})]^T \cong [0.51117 \ 0.21174 \ 0.21174]^T$ and $[R_1(\theta_{n_2}, \phi_{n_2})R_2(\theta_{n_2}, \phi_{n_2})R_3(\theta_{n_2}, \phi_{n_2})]^T \cong [1.36762 \ 0.56662 \ 0.56662]^T$. It is easy to check that this satisfies (16) with $\beta \simeq 2.6757$. Thus, for this reflectance map, we cannot obtain I_{max} and the surface normal uniquely by using three light sources.

IX. CONCLUSIONS

In this paper, we described a theory of photometric stereo for diffuse non-Lambertian surfaces. We began by identifying

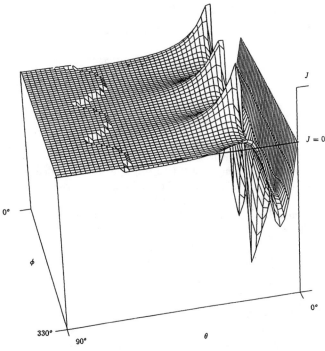

Fig. 16.   The function J.

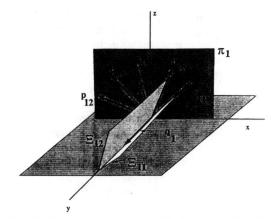

Fig. 17.   The various elements used in the construction of the sets.

the physical processes of reflection. From this, we constructed a class of reflectance maps that we identified by a mathematical expression. This class of reflectance maps we termed "m-lobed reflectance maps." For the normalized photometric stereo equation, we derived a condition to check whether three light sources were sufficient for a globally unique solution. Applying this condition to the m-lobed map $(m \geq 2)$, we showed that it was possible to arrange three lights in such a fashion that a globally unique reconstruction was possible. For the unnormalized photometric stereo equation, we obtained a condition that allowed a simple check to see whether three lights were sufficient to obtain a globally unique I_{max} as well as the surface normal. Finally, we addressed the issue of completeness of reconstruction and showed that if k lights were necessary for a globally unique reconstruction, $2k$ lights were necessary for a complete reconstruction.

We believe that this is a first step toward a theory of non-Lambertian photometric stereo, and we conclude the paper by indicating some directions in which the present results can be extended. Although the class of m-lobed reflectance maps is large and useful, it is not large enough to cover every reflectance map proposed in the literature. Probably the most important reflectance maps that are not included in it are the ones that can arise from using distributed light sources with specular surfaces. A theory for such light sources would be a logical extension of our results. Here too, there is experimental evidence [15] that three light sources may be sufficient.

For unnormalized photometric stereo, the sufficiency of some number of light sources greater than three would be nice to establish. Currently there are no such general results.

Finally, the problem of jointly estimating some parameters of the reflectance map along with the surface normal is an intriguing problem. For some reflectance maps, the reflection from different lobes can be easily identified in the image data, and for these maps the parameters of the lobes can be estimated independent of each other [11], [17]. However, in cases where this cannot

be done, the problem remains open. Our efforts at obtaining reflectance map parameters along with surface normals show that the problem can become ill-posed and some initial estimates of the parameters are needed to obtain reasonable results from experimental data [31].

Appendix
The Sets c_l, c_l^*, C_l, C_l^* and C, C^*

In this Appendix, we consider the sets c_l, c_l^*, C_l, C_l^*, and C, C^* and their properties.

A. The Sets c_l, c_l^*

Recall that the sets c_l, c_l^* are defined as

$$c_1 = \{n : p_{11}^T n \geq 0, \ p_{12}^T n \leq 0\} - \{0\}$$
$$c_1^* = \{n : p_{11}^T n < 0, \ p_{12}^T n \leq 0\}$$
$$c_2 = \{n : p_{21}^T n \geq 0, \ p_{22}^T n \leq 0\} - \{0\}$$
$$c_2^* = \{n : p_{21}^T n < 0, \ p_{22}^T n > 0\}$$
$$c_3 = \{n : p_{31}^T n \geq 0, \ p_{32}^T n \leq 0\} - \{0\}$$
$$c_3^* = \{n : p_{31}^T n < 0, \ p_{32}^T n > 0\}.$$

To find explicit expressions for these sets we have to define some more vectors in E^3. Fig. 17 provides geometric aid to the following development. Given p_{lj}, the jth $(j = 1, 2)$ principal direction of the lth light source, let us define a vector r_{lj} that is orthogonal to it and has a positive z component, i.e., if

$$p_{lj} = \begin{pmatrix} \sin \theta_{lj} \cos \phi_l \\ \sin \theta_{lj} \sin \phi_l \\ \cos \theta_{lj} \end{pmatrix}$$

then

$$r_{lj} = \begin{pmatrix} -\cos \theta_{lj} \cos \phi_l \\ -\cos \theta_{lj} \sin \phi_{lj} \\ \sin \theta_{lj} \end{pmatrix}.$$

Note that the azimuth angle of r_{lj} is also ϕ_l, i.e., r_{lj} is contained in the principal plane of the lth light source. Also note that r_{l1} and r_{l2} are linearly independent and hence span the principal plane. Further, it is easy to establish that

$$\begin{matrix} r_{l1}^T p_{l1} = 0 & r_{l1}^T p_{l2} < 0 \\ r_{l2}^T p_{l1} > 0 & r_{l2}^T p_{l2} = 0. \end{matrix} \qquad \text{(A1)}$$

Let us denote the principal plane by Π_l (See Fig. 17). Let q_l be a unit vector orthogonal to Π_l. Note that q_l is contained in the x–y plane, i.e., its z component is strictly zero. We now have the following properties for the sets c_l and c_l^*:

Lemma A: When point 0 (the origin of E^3) is added to the sets $c_l, c_l^* l = 1, 2, 3$, the resulting sets are convex cones with the origin as an apex.

Proof: We will prove this for c_1. The proof for other sets follows identical lines. If $x_1, x_2 \in c_1 + \{0\}$, then $p_{11}^T x_1 \geq 0$ $p_{12}^T x_1 \leq 0$, $p_{11}^T x_2 \geq 0$ $p_{12}^T x_2 \leq 0$. From the linearity of the inner product, it follows that if $x = \alpha x_1 + (1 - \alpha) x_2, 0 \leq \alpha \leq 1$, then

$$p_{11}^T x = p_{11}^T \{\alpha x_1 + (1 - \alpha) x_2\} = \alpha p_{11}^T x_1 + (1 - \alpha) p_{11}^T x_2 \geq 0$$

and similarly

$$p_{12}^T x = \alpha p_{12}^T x_1 + (1 - \alpha) p_{12}^T x_2 \leq 0.$$

Thus, $x \in c_1 + \{0\}$, and $c_1 + \{0\}$ is a convex set.

Further, if $x \in c_1 + \{0\}$, then for $\alpha \geq 0$, it is easy to see that $\alpha x \in c_1 + \{0\}$. Thus $c_1 + \{0\}$ is a convex cone with 0 as an apex. □

The explicit representation of the sets is

Lemma B: The sets c_l are given by

$$c_l = \{x : x = \alpha_l r_{l1} + \beta_l r_{l2} + \gamma_l q_l, \alpha_l, \beta_l \geq 0,$$
$$-\infty > \gamma_l > \infty, \{\alpha_l, \beta_l, \gamma_l\} \neq 0\} \quad \text{(A2)}$$

and the sets c_l^* are given by

$$c_l^* = \{x : x = \alpha_l r_{l1} + \beta_l r_{l2} + \gamma_l q_l, \alpha_l, \beta_l \geq 0,$$
$$\{\alpha_l, \beta_l\} \neq 0, -\infty > \gamma_l > \infty\} \quad \text{(A3)}$$

where the symbol $\{\alpha_l, \beta_l, \gamma_l\} \neq 0$ denotes that α_l, β_l, and γ_l are not zero simultaneously, and $\{\alpha_l, \beta_l\} \neq 0$ denotes that α_l and β_l are not zero simultaneously.

Proof: From the definition of the vectors r_{l1}, r_{l2}, and q_l, we have the following:

1) r_{l1} and r_{l2} are linearly independent and span the principal plane Π_j, and
2) q_l is orthogonal to Π_l. Thus, r_{l1}, r_{l2}, and q_l span E^3 and any vector x can be written as

$$x = \alpha_l r_{l1} + \beta_l r_{l2} + \gamma_l q_l.$$

Thus, we have

$$x^T p_{l1} = \alpha_l r_{l1}^T p_{l1} + \beta_l r_{l2}^T p_{l1} + \gamma_l q_l^T p_{l1}$$
$$= \beta_l r_{l2}^T p_{l1}.$$

Similarly we have

$$x^T p_{l2} = \alpha_l r_{l1}^T p_{l2}.$$

If $x \in c_l$, then from the definition of c_l and the above equations and (45), we have that $\alpha_l \geq 0, \beta_l \leq 0$, and $-\infty < \gamma_l < \infty$, with all the three not simultaneously not being zero.

Similarly, it is possible to show that if $x \in c_l^*$, we have $\alpha_l \leq 0$, $\beta_l \leq 0$, and $-\infty < \gamma_l < \infty$ with α_l and β_l not simultaneously zero.

From this representation of the sets it follows that the z components of all the elements of c_l are greater than or equal to zero while the z components of all the elements of c_l^* are strictly less than zero. Thus, the sets c_l and c_m^* are nonintersecting for any l and m.

B. The Sets C_l, C_l^* and $\mathcal{C}, \mathcal{C}^*$

The sets C_l, C_l^* and $\mathcal{C}, \mathcal{C}^*$ are defined by

$$C_1 = c_1 \cap c_2 \qquad C_1^* = c_1^* \cap c_2^*$$
$$C_2 = c_2 \cap c_3 \qquad C_2^* = c_2^* \cap c_3^*$$
$$C_3 = c_3 \cap c_1 \qquad C_3^* = c_3^* \cap c_1^*$$
$$\mathcal{C} = C_1 \cap C_2 \cap C_3 \qquad \mathcal{C}^* = C_1^* \cap C_2^* \cap C_3^*.$$

We can now establish that

Lemma C: When point 0 (the origin of E^3) is added to the sets $C_l, C_l^*, \mathcal{C}, \mathcal{C}^*, l = 1, 2, 3$, the resulting sets are convex cones.

Proof: Follows the lines of Lemma A exactly. □

Lemma D: The sets $c_l, c_l^*; C_l, C_l^*; \mathcal{C}, \mathcal{C}^*$ are complementary in the sense that

$$x \in c_l^* \text{ iff } -x \in c_l, \qquad x \in C_l^* \text{ iff } -x \in C_l,$$
$$x \in \mathcal{C}^* \text{ iff } -x \in \mathcal{C}.$$

If $x \neq 0$, then

$$x \in c_l \text{ iff } -x \in c_l^*, \qquad x \in C_l \text{ iff } -x \in C_l^*,$$
$$x \in \mathcal{C} \text{ iff } -x \in \mathcal{C}^*.$$

Proof: The proof follows from the definitions of the sets and the linearity of the inner product. □

We now proceed to identify the sets. Fig. 17 provides an illustration of the following development. If we define planes $\Xi_{lj} = \text{span}(r_{lj}, q_l)$, then we can define vectors v_i, u_i, and w_i such that

$$\Xi_{11} \cap \Xi_{21} = \{av_1 : -\infty \leq a \leq +\infty, z \text{ component of } v_1 > 0\}$$
$$\Xi_{11} \cap \Xi_{22} = \{av_2 : -\infty \leq a \leq +\infty, z \text{ component of } v_2 > 0\}$$
$$\Xi_{12} \cap \Xi_{22} = \{av_3 : -\infty \leq a \leq +\infty, z \text{ component of } v_3 > 0\}$$
$$\Xi_{12} \cap \Xi_{21} = \{av_4 : -\infty \leq a \leq +\infty, z \text{ component of } v_4 > 0\}$$
$$\Xi_{31} \cap \Xi_{21} = \{au_1 : -\infty \leq a \leq +\infty, z \text{ component of } u_1 > 0\}$$
$$\Xi_{31} \cap \Xi_{22} = \{au_2 : -\infty \leq a \leq +\infty, z \text{ component of } u_2 > 0\}$$
$$\Xi_{32} \cap \Xi_{22} = \{au_3 : -\infty \leq a \leq +\infty, z \text{ component of } u_3 > 0\}$$
$$\Xi_{32} \cap \Xi_{21} = \{au_4 : -\infty \leq a \leq +\infty, z \text{ component of } u_4 > 0\}$$
$$\Xi_{11} \cap \Xi_{31} = \{aw_1 : -\infty \leq a \leq +\infty, z \text{ component of } w_1 > 0\}$$
$$\Xi_{11} \cap \Xi_{32} = \{aw_2 : -\infty \leq a \leq +\infty, z \text{ component of } w_2 > 0\}$$
$$\Xi_{12} \cap \Xi_{32} = \{aw_3 : -\infty \leq a \leq +\infty, z \text{ component of } w_3 > 0\}$$
$$\Xi_{12} \cap \Xi_{31} = \{aw_4 : -\infty \leq a \leq +\infty, z \text{ component of } w_4 > 0\}.$$

We first establish that

Lemma E: If the matrices H_1 and H_2 as defined by (20) are invertible, then the vectors v_i, u_i, and w_i as defined above are nonzero and distinct. Further

$$\Xi_{11} = \text{span}(v_1, v_2) = \text{span}(w_1, w_3)$$
$$\Xi_{12} = \text{span}(v_4, v_3) = \text{span}(w_3, w_4)$$
$$\Xi_{21} = \text{span}(v_1, v_4) = \text{span}(u_1, u_4)$$
$$\Xi_{22} = \text{span}(v_2, v_3) = \text{span}(u_2, u_3)$$
$$\Xi_{31} = \text{span}(u_1, u_2) = \text{span}(w_1, w_4)$$
$$\Xi_{32} = \text{span}(u_3, u_4) = \text{span}(w_2, w_3).$$

Proof: Consider existence first. We will prove this for v_1. The proof for other vectors follows identical lines. Consider the set $S = \Xi_{11} \cap \Xi_{21}$. The set S has dimension 1. Since, $\Xi_{11} = \text{span}(r_{11}, q_1)$ and $\Xi_{21} = \text{span}(r_{21}, q_2)$, if $x \in S$, then $p_{11}^T x = 0$ and $p_{21}^T x = 0$. The set S, therefore, consists of vectors orthogonal to p_{11} and p_{21}. Since the matrix H_1 is invertible, we know that p_{11} and p_{21} are linearly independent and hence their cross product $p_{11} * p_{21}$ is not zero. Let us consider $p_{11} * p_{21}$ as a likely candidate for v_1. The z component of this vector is $\sin \theta_{11} \sin \theta_{21} \sin (\phi_2 - \phi_1) \neq 0$. Hence, the set S can be written as $a v_1$, where $v_1 = \pm p_{11} * p_{21}$, the sign being chosen to keep the z component of v_1 strictly greater than zero. This establishes that v_1 exists.

Arguing along identical lines, it is possible to show that v_2, v_3, and v_4 exist. Further, by the invertibility of H_1 and H_2, it is easy to show that v_1, v_2, v_3, and v_4 are distinct.

We will now show that $\Xi_{11} = \text{span}(v_1, v_2)$. Note that by definition $v_1, v_2 \in \Xi_{11}$. Hence, the result follows if we can show that v_1 and v_2 are linearly independent. We will establish this by a contradiction. Note that $v_1 \in \Xi_{21}$ and $v_2 \in \Xi_{22}$, so we have a representation for them in the form

$$v_1 = \gamma_1 q_2 + \alpha_1 r_{21}$$
$$v_2 = \gamma_2 q_2 + \alpha_2 r_{22}.$$

Since r_{21} and r_{22} are linearly independent and orthogonal to q_2, the only way v_1 and v_2 can be linearly dependent is if $\alpha_1 = \alpha_2 = 0$. But since the z component of q_2 is zero, that makes the z component of v_1 and v_2 zero. This is a contradiction with the definitions of the two vectors. Hence, v_1 and v_2 are linearly independent and $\Xi_{11} = \text{span}(v_1, v_2)$. □

From the proof of the above lemma, we have that

$$v_1 = \pm p_{11} * p_{12}, \quad v_2 = \pm p_{11} * p_{22},$$
$$v_3 = \pm p_{12} * p_{22}, \quad v_4 = \pm p_{12} * p_{21}$$
$$w_1 = \pm p_{11} * p_{31}, \quad w_2 = \pm p_{11} * p_{32},$$
$$w_3 = \pm p_{12} * p_{32}, \quad w_4 = \pm p_{12} * p_{31}.$$

We now come to

Lemma F: The sets C_1, C_2, C_3 are given by

$$C_1 = \{x : x = \alpha v_1 + \beta v_2 + \gamma v_3 + \delta v_4; \alpha, \beta, \gamma, \delta \geq 0\} - \{0\}$$
$$C_2 = \{x : x = \alpha u_1 + \beta u_2 + \gamma u_3 + \delta u_4; \alpha, \beta, \gamma, \delta \geq 0\} - \{0\}$$
$$C_3 = \{x : x = \alpha w_1 + \beta w_2 + \gamma w_3 + \delta w_4; \alpha, \beta, \gamma, \delta \geq 0\} - \{0\}.$$

Proof: We will prove this for C_1. The proofs for C_2 and C_3 follow identical lines. Let $S = \{x : x = \alpha v_1 + \beta v_2 + \gamma v_3 + \delta v_4; \alpha, \beta, \gamma, \delta \geq 0\}$. If $x \in S$ and $x \neq 0$, the

$$p_{11}^T x = \alpha p_{11}^T v_1 + \beta p_{11}^T v_2 + \gamma p_{11}^T v_3 + \delta p_{11}^T v_4$$
$$= \beta p_{11}^T v_3 + \gamma p_{11}^T v_4$$

since $p_{11}^T v_1 = p_{11}^T v_2 = 0$. But note that, since $v_3 \in \Xi_{12}$ and $v_4 \in \Xi_{12}$, they can be written as

$$v_3 = a_1 r_{12} + b_1 q_1$$
$$v_4 = a_2 r_{12} + b_2 q_1$$

which gives us $p_{11}^T v_3 > 0$ and $p_{11}^T v_4 > 0$. Thus, $p_{11}^T x \geq 0$. Using a similar argument, it is possible to show that

$$p_{12}^T x \leq 0, \qquad p_{21}^T x \geq 0, \qquad p_{22}^T x \leq 0.$$

From the above inequalities we have $x \in C_1$. □

REFERENCES

[1] H. P. Baltes, *Inverse Scattering Problems in Optics.* New York: Springer-Verlag, 1980.

[2] P. Beckmann, "Shadowing of random rough surfaces," *IEEE Trans. Antennas Propagat.,* vol. AP-13, pp. 384–388, May 1965.

[3] P. Beckmann and A. Spizzichino, *The Scattering of Electromagnetic Waves from Rough Surfaces.* New York: Pergamon, 1963.

[4] R. C. Birkebak and E. R. G. Eckert, "Effects of roughness of metal surfaces on angular distribution of monochromatic reflected radiation," *J. Heat Transfer,* pp. 85–94, Feb. 1965.

[5] W. M. Brandenberg and J. T. Neu, "Unidirectional reflectance of imperfectly diffuse surfaces," *J. Opt. Soc. Amer.,* vol. 56, no. 1, pp. 97–103, Jan. 1966.

[6] R. A. Brockelman and T. Hagfors, "Note on the effect of shadowing on the backscattering of waves from a random rough surface," *IEEE Trans. Antennas Propagat.,* vol. AP-14, pp. 621–626, Sept. 1966.

[7] R. Onn and A. Burckstein, "On photometric stereo," private communication.

[8] J. D. Cartigny, Y. Yamada, and C. L. Tien, "Radiative transfer with dependent scattering by particles: Part 1—Theoretical investigation," *J. Heat Transfer,* vol. 108, pp. 608–613, Aug. 1986.

[9] S. Chandrasedkar, *Radiative Heat Transfer.* New York: Dover, 1960.

[10] Q. Zheng and R. Chellappa, "A robust algorithm for inferring shape from a single image," Signal and Image Processing Institute, Univ. Southern California, Tech. Rep., 1990.

[11] E. N. Coleman and R. Jain, "Obtaining 3-Dimensional Shape of Textured and Specular Surfaces using Four-Source Photometry." *C.G.I.P.,* vol. 18, pp. 309–328, Apr. 1982.

[12] B. K. P. Horn, *Robot Vision.* Cambridge, MA: M.I.T. Press, 1986.

[13] B. K. P. Horn and R. W. Sjoberg, "Calculating the reflectance map," *Appl. Opt.,* vol. 18, no. 11, pp. 1770–1779, June 1979.

[14] H. C. van de Hulst, *Light Scattering by Small Particles.* New York: Dover, 1957.

[15] K. Ikeuchi, "Determining surface orientations of specular surfaces by using the photometric stereo method," *IEEE Trans. Pattern Anal. Machine Intell.,* vol. PAMI-3, no. 6, pp. 661–669, Nov. 1981.

[16] IMSL Math Library, IMSL, Houston, TX.

[17] S. K. Nayar, K. Ikeuchi, and T. Kanade, "Surface reflection: Physical and geometric perspectives," Carnegie-Mellon Univ., The Robotics Institute, Tech. Rep. CMU-RI-TR-89-7, 1989.

[18] ——, "Extracting shape and reflectance of Lambertian, specular and hybrid surfaces," Carnegie-Mellon Univ., The Robotics Institute, Tech. Rep. CMU-RI-TR-88-14, 1988.

[19] F. E. Nicodemus, J. C. Richmond, J. J. Hsia, and I. W. Ginsberg, *Geometrical Considerations and Nomenclature for Reflectance.* Boulder, CO: National Bureau of Standards, 1977.

[20] B. O'Neill, *Elementary Differential Geometry.* New York: Academic, 1966.

[21] A. Pentland, "Linear shape from shading," *Int. J. Comput. Vision,* vol. 4, pp. 153–162, 1990.

[22] B. T. Phong, "Illumination for computer generated pictures," *Commun. Ass. Comput. Mach.,* vol. 18, no. 6, June 1975.

[23] R. Ray, J. Birk, and R. Kelly, "Error analysis of surface normals determined by radiometry," *IEEE Trans. Pattern Anal. Machine Intell.,* vol. PAMI-5, no. 6, Nov. 1983.

[24] J. Reichman, "Determination of absorption and scattering coefficients for nonhomogenous media. 1: Theory," *Appl. Opt.,* vol. 12, no. 8, pp. 1811–1815, Aug. 1973.

[25] R. Siegel and J. R. Howell, *Thermal Radiation Heat Transfer.* New York: McGraw-Hill, 1972.

[26] W. M. Silver, "Determining shape and reflectance using multiple images," Master's thesis, M.I.T., Cambridge, MA, June 1980.

[27] B. G. Smith, "Geometrical shadowing of a random rough surface," *IEEE Trans. Antennas Propag.,* vol. AP-15, no. 5, pp. 668–671, Sept. 1967.

[28] J. M. Stone, *Radiation and Optics.* New York: McGraw-Hill, 1963.

[29] H. D. Tagare and R. J. P. deFigueiredo, "A framework for the construction of general reflectance maps for machine vision," Rice Univ., Tech. Rep. EE 88-16, Apr. 1988; submitted to *Comput. Vision, Graphics, Image Processing.*

[30] H. D. Tagare, "A theory of photometric stereo for a general class of reflectance maps," Ph.D. dissertation, Rice University, Houston, TX, 1989.

[31] ——, "Simultaneous estimation of reflectance map and surface normal using photometric stereo," in *Proc. Int. Conf. Computer Vision,* 1990.

[32] K. E. Torrance and E. M. Sparrow, "Theory of off-specular reflection from roughened surfaces," *J. Opt. Soc. Amer.*, vol. 57, no. 9, pp. 1105–1114, Sept. 1967.

[33] T. S. Trowbridge and K. P. Reitz, "Average irregularity representation of a roughened surface for ray reflection," *J. Opt. Soc. Amer.*, vol. 65, pp. 531–536, 1975.

[34] R. J. Woodham, "Reflectance map techniques for analyzing surface defects in metal castings," M.I.T. AI Lab Tech. Rep. 457, June 1978.

[35] L. B. Wolff, "Spectral and polarization stereo methods using a single light source," in *Proc. Image Understanding Workshop*, Los Angeles, CA, vol. 2, 1987, pp. 810–820.

[36] Y. Yamada, J. D. Cartigny and C. L. Tien, "Radiative transfer with dependent scattering by particles: Part 2—Experimental investigation," *J. Heat Transfer*, vol. 108, pp. 614–618, Aug. 1986.

[37] H. D. Tagare and R. J. P. deFigueiredo, *Photometric Stereo.* New York: Plenum, to be published.

Hemant D. Tagare (S'86) was born in Bombay, India, on January 13, 1959. He received the B.Tech. degree in electrical engineering from the Indian Institute of Technology, Bombay, and the M.S. and Ph.D. degrees in electrical engineering from Rice University, Houston, TX.

From 1983 to 1986, he worked with Madhan Electronics, India, and was involved in designing computer terminals. His research interests are in computer vision, psycho-physics, and medical imaging.

Rui J. P. deFigueiredo (S'54–M'59–SM'74–F'76) received the B.S. and M.S. degrees in electrical engineering from the Massachusetts Institute of Technology, Cambridge, and the Ph.D. degree in applied mathematics from Harvard University, Cambridge, MA.

Since the Fall of 1990, he has held the positions of Professor of Electrical and Computer Engineering and of Mathematics, and Director of the Laboratory for Intelligent Sensors and Systems at the University of California, Irvine. Prior to that, he was Professor of Electrical and Computer Engineering and of Mathematical Sciences at Rice University, Houston, TX. He has about 200 publications to his credit.

Prof. deFigueiredo is an Associate Editor of *Circuits, Systems, and Signal Processing* and of *Electrosoft.* He is a member of a number of national committees, and for his research he has received several awards and certificates of recognition.

SPECTRAL AND POLARIZATION STEREO METHODS USING A SINGLE LIGHT SOURCE

Lawrence Brill Wolff[1,2]

Department of Computer Science
Columbia University
New York, N.Y. 10027

ABSTRACT

Proposed herein are novel stereo techniques for the determination of surface orientation from a single view and a single light source exploiting the physical wave properties of light and the basic physics of material surfaces. Conventional photometric stereo techniques consider the intersection of equi-reflectance curves that arise in gradient space while varying the imaging geometry with respect to the spatial position of a light source. Spectral and polarization stereo methods consider the intersection of equi-reflectance curves in gradient space while varying the wavelength (i.e. color) and/or the polarization of light emanating from a single light source while leaving the imaging geometry invariant. The reflectance function used here results from an extended form of the Torrance-Sparrow model which is dependent upon the wavelength and polarization of incident light as well as various physical parameters of the material surface. This reflectance model is more accurate than commonly used Lambertian reflectance models and is applicable to a wide variety of isotropically rough surfaces ranging from metals to paper. Computer simulations of the intersections of equi-reflectance curves that arise by varying incident wavelength and polarization are shown for two different types of materials; a dielectric, Magnesium oxide (used in white paint) and a conductor, Aluminum. Two different methods called direct and indirect resolution of specular and diffuse reflection components are used to minimize measurement error and to resolve intersections, respectively.

An interesting problem arises for stereo methods that vary only wavelength and/or polarization of the incident light source. Measurement of surface orientations that do not lie on the source-viewing axis line in gradient space determined by the origin and the point representing the incident orientation of the single light source cannot be uniquely resolved any better than up to a two point ambiguity. This results from an inherent "flip" symmetry induced on each equi-reflectance curve in gradient space by the isotropic reflectance function being used. It is demonstrated that it is feasible to break this inherent symmetry by performing spectral/polarization stereo methods using a single extended light source with a variable "asymmetric" aperature. This makes it possible to obtain a unique measurement for surface orientations not on the source-viewing axis using only a single light source.

1. INTRODUCTION

Previous stereo methods such as the traditional stereo method of depth determination by parallax and the photometric stereo method for the determination of local surface orientation (see [Woodham 1980]) entail taking successive images while varying some aspect of the imaging geometry. Recently it was reported in [Wolff 1986] that stereo vision can be generally formalized far beyond previously used methods by taking successive images while varying physical parameters of an imaging system other than just the imaging geometry. Spectral and polarization stereo methods used to determine surface orientation are a particular example of a class of stereo methods predicted by this general stereo model.

The stereo methods presented here use the familiar imaging setup as depicted in figure 1 with a single light source incident on a material surface. Standard gradient space will be used throughout to represent surface

orientation. Spectral stereo entails varying the incident wavelength alone between successive images. Polarization stereo entails varying the incident polarization alone between succesive images. Spectral and polarization stereo can be combined by varying both the incident wavelength and polarization simultaneously between successive images. All other physical parameters governing the imaging system are to remain unchanged. As in conventional photometric stereo, local surface orientation is determined by measuring the image irradiance value at the pixel corresponding to the projected object point giving rise to an equi-reflectance curve in gradient space. The projection function of an object onto the image plane is assumed to be orthographic.

Spectral stereo can be implemented by using various narrow pass monochromatic filters and polarization stereo can be implemented by rotating a polaroid filter. The filter(s) are assumed to be placed in front of the light source so as to control the wavelength and/or polarization of the light incident on the material surface. Assuming that the wavelength of incident light is not altered upon reflection spectral stereo can instead be implemented with color filters placed in front of the image sensor measuring the reflected radiance. This also assumes that the incident radiance of the source at the wavelength passed by the filter is known *a priori* (i.e. the spectral composition of the light source is known). Since the polarization of incident light is not left invariant upon reflection (see [Koshikawa 1979]), polarization stereo cannot be easily accomplished with a polaroid filter placed in front of the image sensor. Reported in [Wolff 1987] is a technique for measuring surface orientation from observed reflected polarization values with the convenience of placing the polaroid filter in front of the image sensor.

Because of its simplicity, the Lambertian reflectance function is used in numerous applications in low level vision. However the reflection of light off a material surface is a highly complex process dependent on the imaging geometry, the wave characteristics of the incident light radiation, the micro-geometry of the material surface (e.g. roughness) and the internal physics (e.g. electric resistivity) of the surface material itself. These aspects of the reflection process beyond the imaging geometry account for why the reflective properties of most material surfaces deviate from the Lambertian model.

The motivation for using the extended Torrance-Sparrow reflection model (ETSRM) is twofold. First, as just mentioned, the Lambertian reflectance model is too simplistic and is only applicable to a very narrow class of materials whereas the ETSRM is far more general. Second is that the Lambertian model is not dependent at all on the wavelength or polarization of incident light which would make the stereo methods considered here infeasible. While the ETSRM may be relatively new to the computer vision community, it is popularly used in computer graphics for rendering realistic images of smooth material surfaces [Cook, Torrance 1981].

To demonstrate the wide applicability of the ETSRM, and therefore to spectral/polarization stereo methods, simulations of the measurement of surface orientation will be performed on two very different types of materials. The first is Magnesium oxide (MgO) classified as a *dielectric* which is a material that does not conduct electricity. MgO has a strong diffuse component of reflection. The second material is Aluminum which is a *conductor* and has a strong specular component of reflection. As will be seen, the distinction between whether a material is a dielectric or a conductor is important for selecting the appropriate spectral/polarization stereo technique.

The reflectance function resulting from the ETSRM is isotropic in the sense that the reflected radiance from a point on a material surface is

[1]This research was supported in part by ARPA grant #N00039-84-C-0165

[2]This research was done in part while the author was at AT&T Bell Laboratories, Holmdel, N.J.

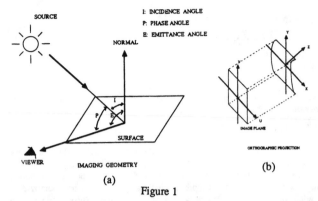

Figure 1

independent of any rotation about the normal to this point. This induces a "flip" symmetry on the resulting equi-reflectance curves in gradient space. A formal description of this is given in section 7. Because the imaging geometry is left invariant for spectral/polarization stereo methods the equi-reflectance curves produced from successive images possess the same exact "flip" symmetry. This makes it theoretically impossible to measure most surface orientations uniquely beyond a two point ambiguity using spectral/polarization stereo methods with a single point light source. A technique is presented to break this "flip" symmetry by using a single extended light source subtending a solid angular area which does not possess the same "flip" symmetry.

Unless stated otherwise, all light sources mentioned are assumed to be point light sources. For brevity, the term *source-viewing plane* in this paper refers to the plane determined by the incident source orientation vector (represented by $(P_s, Q_s, -1)$) and the viewing orientation vector (assumed to be $(0, 0, -1)$). The *source-viewing axis* is the line in gradient space determined by the origin and the point (P_s, Q_s).

2. THE EXTENDED TORRANCE-SPARROW REFLECTION MODEL

The reflectance model reported in [Torrance, Sparrow 1967] assumes that every surface has a microscopic level of detail which consists of a statistically large number of perfectly smooth planar microfacets. These microfacets are oriented according to a particular probability distribution function of the angle between the normal to each microfacet and the normal to the surface. This implies that the surface is isotropically rough about the normal to the surface as the probability distribution function is not dependent on the azimuthal orientation of the normal to a microfacet.

The Torrance-Sparrow reflectance model is primarily based on geometric optics. Light rays are assumed to reflect off a material surface with both a specular and a diffuse component. The specular component of reflection accounts for when a light ray specularly reflects off a microfacet and the diffuse component is described by the Lambertian reflectance function which accounts for multiple specular reflections and/or reflections of light rays that penetrate into the skin of the surface and then reflect back out. According to the Torrance-Sparrow reflection model the form of the reflected radiance function is given by:

$$(1) \quad dN_r \equiv gN_iR_sd\omega_i + N_iR_dd\omega_i .$$

The terms R_s and R_d are the functions for the specular and diffuse components of reflection respectively. The term N_i represents the incident radiance of the light source through the infinitesimal solid angle $d\omega_i$ (see figure 2) and g is the proportion of the specular reflectance relative to the diffuse reflectance. The equivalence symbol in equation (1) and all other equations in this paper represents proportionality. The specular and diffuse component reflection functions are given by:

$$R_s = \frac{F(\Psi',\eta)\,G(\Psi,\Theta,\Phi)}{cos\Theta}P(\alpha) \qquad R_d = cos\Psi$$

where the angular arguments correspond to figure 2. Note that R_d is the Lambertian reflectance function. Section 3 is entirely devoted to the function $F(\Psi',\eta)$ because of its central role in spectral/polarization stereo applications.

The function $P(\alpha)$ is the probability distribution function for the orientations of the normals to the planar microfacets. The probability distribution function proposed in [Torrance, Sparrow 1967] is:

$$P(\alpha) \equiv exp(-(\alpha c)^2) .$$

The variable α is the angle between the normal to a given microfacet and the normal to the surface and is depicted in figure 2. The term c is an ad hoc constant which is determined empirically by solving equation (1) using observed reflected radiance values.

It is suggested in [Cook, Torrance 1981] that a probability distribution function for the orientation of microfacet normals using physical parameters (i.e. no ad hoc constants) could be used to emulate the Beckmann distribution for mean scattered power of light reflected from a rough surface. This function is derived in [Beckmann, Spizzichino 1963] and is given by:

$$P(\alpha) \equiv \frac{1}{m^2 cos^4\alpha}exp(-\frac{tan^2\alpha}{m^2}) .$$

The term m is the root mean square slope value of the microfacet surface normals. Large values of m indicate a "rough" surface while small values of m indicate "smooth" surfaces. The extended Torrance-Sparrow reflection model refers to incorporating the Beckmann disribution function into the expression for the specular component of reflection R_s. The value for m can be determined by solving equation (1) using reflected radiance values, or can be measured more directly using a *stylus profilometer*.

The reflection model presented in [Torrance, Sparrow 1967] also takes into account the mutual shadowing and masking of surface microfacets against one another. It is assumed that each specularly reflecting microfacet comprises one side of a symmetric V groove as depicted in figure 3. The process of shadowing and masking attenuates the total fraction of reflecting surface area. The proportional amount of this attenuation is called the *geometric attenuation factor* and is given by:

$$G(\Psi,\Theta,\Phi) = min\{ 1,\frac{2cos\alpha cos\Theta}{cos\Psi'},\frac{2cos\alpha cos\Psi}{cos\Psi'} \}$$

The above expressions for the geometric attenuation factor and the Beckmann distribution function conform to the geometry depicted in figure 2. With respect to the angles Ψ, Θ and Φ depicted in figure 2, α and Ψ' can be expressed as:

$$\Psi' = \frac{1}{2}cos^{-1}[cos\Theta cos\Psi - sin\Theta sin\Psi cos\Phi]$$
$$\alpha = cos^{-1}[cos\Psi cos\Psi' + sin\Psi sin\Psi' cos\beta]$$

where

$$\beta = sin^{-1}[sin\Phi sin\Theta/sin2\Psi'] .$$

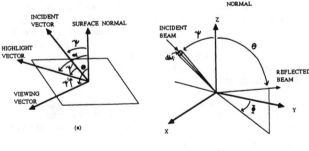

Figure 2

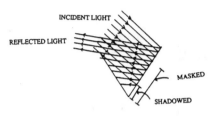

Figure 3

3. THE FRESNEL REFLECTION COEFFICIENT

The function $F(\Psi',\eta)$ incorporated into the specular component of reflection is of primary importance to spectral and polarization stereo. It is known as the *Fresnel reflection coefficient*. This is the only part of expression (1) that is dependent on the wavelength and polarization of incident light. The derivation of $F(\Psi',\eta)$ treats light as an electromagnetic wave. The polarization of a light wave is defined in terms of how the electric field vector is oriented with respect to the *plane of incidence*, the plane determined by the incident vector and the normal vector to the reflecting surface[3]. An incident light wave is parallel polarized if its electric field vector is parallel to the plane of incidence and is perpendicularly polarized if its electric field vector is perpendicular to the plane of incidence.

An incident light wave that is specularly reflected from a perfectly smooth surface results in a partially transmitted wave and a partially reflected wave. The Fresnel reflection coefficient represents the proportional attenuation of the incident light energy per unit time per unit area for specular reflection off of a perfectly smooth surface. This simulates the specularly reflected radiance of light rays off of the perfectly smooth microfacets.

The angle Ψ' is the *specular angle of incidence* of a light ray upon microfacets with surface normals oriented parallel to the highlight vector depicted in figure 2. The specular angle of incidence on the microfacets of a surface is equal to 1/2 of the phase angle and is not dependent on the orientation of the surface. The number of microfacets that the incident light is specularly reflected from is determined by the surface orientation and the probability distribution function $P(\alpha)$.

The term $\eta = n - i\kappa$ is the *complex index of refraction* for the surface material. The real terms n and κ are dependent upon the wavelength of incident light λ_0 according to the formulas:

$$n^2 = \frac{\upsilon\gamma c_0^2}{2} \left\{ 1 + [1 + (\frac{\lambda_0}{2\pi c_0 r_e \gamma})^2]^{1/2} \right\}$$

$$\kappa^2 = \frac{\upsilon\gamma c_0^2}{2} \left\{ -1 + [1 + (\frac{\lambda_0}{2\pi c_0 r_e \gamma})^2]^{1/2} \right\} .$$

The term c_0 is the speed of light in a vacuum, r_e is the electrical resistivity of the surface material, and υ and γ are the electrical permitivity and the magnetic permeability of the surface material respectively. It turns out that r_e, υ and γ are dependent upon the surface temperature and the external presence of electric and magnetic fields. This suggests other stereo methods to determine surface orientation. For instance, vary the temperature between each successive image, or for a conducting material vary the strength of an electrical current passing through it between successive images. Varying the strength of magnetic fields can also be used.

The term κ is called the *coefficient of extinction*. The coefficient of extinction is zero for dielectrics (because r_e is infinite) and is non-zero for conductors since they have finite electrical resistivity r_e. For dielectrics, the term n is the *simple index of refraction*.

---

[3]Note that the normal vector to the specularly reflecting surface is the normal to the perfectly smooth planar microfacets coinciding with the *highlight vector* depicted in figure 2(a). Therefore, the plane of incidence for the specular reflection component coincides with the plane determined by the incident and viewing vectors.

A detailed derivation of the Fresnel reflection coefficient is given in [Siegel, Howell 1981]. It is represented as the linear superposition of the Fresnel reflection coefficients for perpendicular and parallel polarized incident light waves respectively. That is:

$$F(\Psi',\eta) = s F_{perp}(\Psi',\eta) + t F_{para}(\Psi',\eta) \quad s,t \geq 0 \quad s + t = 1 .$$

In turn

$$F_{perp}(\Psi',\eta) = \frac{a^2 + b^2 - 2a\cos\Psi' + \cos^2\Psi'}{a^2 + b^2 + 2a\cos\Psi' + \cos^2\Psi'}$$

$$F_{para}(\Psi',\eta) = \frac{a^2 + b^2 - 2a\sin\Psi'\tan\Psi' + \sin^2\Psi'\tan^2\Psi'}{a^2 + b^2 + 2a\sin\Psi'\tan\Psi' + \sin^2\Psi'\tan^2\Psi'} F_{perp}(\Psi',\eta)$$

where

$$2a^2 = [(n^2 - k^2 - \sin^2\Psi')^2 + 4n^2k^2]^{1/2} + n^2 - k^2 - \sin^2\Psi'$$

$$2b^2 = [(n^2 - k^2 - \sin^2\Psi')^2 + 4n^2k^2]^{1/2} - (n^2 - k^2 - \sin^2\Psi')$$

Unpolarized light is the equi-superposition of parallel and perpendicular states. Therefore the Fresnel reflection coefficient for unpolarized light uses $s = t = 1/2$.

Simulations of the determination of local surface orientation will be performed using the reflectance maps predicted by the ETSRM for MgO and Aluminum. The accuracy of the original Torrance-Sparrow reflection model was tested on these two materials in [Torrance, Sparrow 1967] with good results. The empirical values for g, the relative proportion of specular to diffuse component reflected radiance, were also obtained for MgO and Aluminum in this paper ($g_{MgO}=2$, $g_{Al}=7/8$) and will be used in the simulations in future sections. The Fresnel reflection coefficients for MgO and Aluminum are graphed in figures 4 (a) thru (d) against the angle of incidence for different incident light polarizations and wavelengths. Be aware of the scale on the vertical axis. The values for the indices of refractions were obtained from [Physics Handbook] for different wavelengths.

Typical human vision perceives light waves with a wavelength between 400 and 700 nanometers (NM). "Vision" can theoretically exist for any wavelength of electromagnetic radiation. The wavelengths shown in figures 4 (a) and (b) for MgO are not in the visible part of the spectrum. These wavelengths were chosen to fall as close to the visible part of the spectrum as possible while being able to obtain the indices of refraction from the tables in [Physics Handbook]. Interpolation of data was not used to make the simulation of equi-reflectance curves as realistic as possible.

An interesting feature of the dielectric MgO is that it has a *Brewster angle* at arctan(n=1.77) ≈ 60.5° for which no parallel polarized light is reflected. All dielectrics have a Brewster angle at the arctangent of their simple index of refraction. For the determination of surface orientation by varying polarization this is a very important angle to know in a controlled environment. Accuracy of measurement can be substantially enhanced by making the phase angle approximately equal to twice the Brewster angle for a dielectric material. This will be seen in section 5.

As can be seen the simple index of refraction for MgO has a rather weak dependence on wavelength. This suggests that the combined specular and diffuse reflectance will be altered only slightly for different incident wavelengths of light. In section 6 a technique will be presented to obtain a discernable intersection from specular and diffuse component equi-reflectance curves.

4. MINIMIZING ERROR FOR THE INTERSECTION OF REFLECTANCE CURVES

Implementation of spectral/polarization stereo methods involve the physical measurement of image irradiance values which have associated with them an inherent error. This in turn generates an *error collar* about each

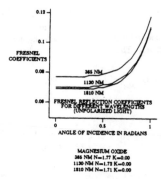

FRESNEL COEFFICIENTS

365 NM
1130 NM
1810 NM

ANGLE OF INCIDENCE IN RADIANS

FRESNEL REFLECTION COEFFICIENTS
FOR DIFFERENT WAVELENGTHS
(UNPOLARIZED LIGHT)

MAGNESIUM OXIDE
365 NM N=1.77 K=0.00
1130 NM N=1.72 K=0.00
1810 NM N=1.71 K=0.00

Figure 4(a)

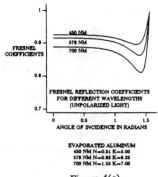

FRESNEL COEFFICIENTS

450 NM
578 NM
700 NM

FRESNEL REFLECTION COEFFICIENTS
FOR DIFFERENT WAVELENGTHS
(UNPOLARIZED LIGHT)

ANGLE OF INCIDENCE IN RADIANS

EVAPORATED ALUMINUM
450 NM N=0.61 K=5.00
578 NM N=0.93 K=6.33
700 NM N=1.55 K=7.00

Figure 4(c)

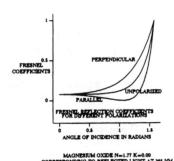

FRESNEL COEFFICIENTS

PERPENDICULAR

PARALLEL   UNPOLARIZED

FRESNEL REFLECTION COEFFICIENTS
FOR DIFFERENT POLARIZATIONS

ANGLE OF INCIDENCE IN RADIANS

MAGNESIUM OXIDE N=1.77 K=0.00
CORRESPONDING TO REFLECTED LIGHT AT 365 NM

Figure 4(b)

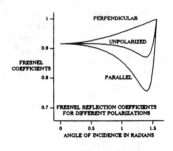

PERPENDICULAR

UNPOLARIZED

FRESNEL COEFFICIENTS

PARALLEL

FRESNEL REFLECTION COEFFICIENTS
FOR DIFFERENT POLARIZATIONS

ANGLE OF INCIDENCE IN RADIANS

EVAPORATED ALUMINUM N=0.93 K=5.90
CORRESPONDING TO REFLECTED LIGHT AT 546 NM

Figure 4(d)

equi-reflectance curve. The intersection of two error collars generate a set of curved quadrilateral regions in which the true surface orientation will lie. Minimizing error of intersection involves minimizing the area of each quadrilateral region (qualitatively interpreted as the *expected error*) as well as minimizing the maximum distance attained between any two points in each quadrilateral region (qualitatively interpreted as the *worst case error*). This requires simultaneous maximization of perpendicularity of intersections and maximization of the gradient of the reflectance function over a global set of gradient space points. Optimal criteria for the overall minimization of expected and worst case errors are extremely complex and are dependent on a multitude of assumptions including *a priori* knowledge about the expected range for the surface orientation to be measured.

A good strategy to increase the gradient of the reflectance function is to increase the phase angle. This involves a tradeoff as increasing the phase angle increases the area of gradient space that lies in shadow. A good strategy for optimizing perpendicular intersections for spectral/polarization methods using the ETSRM is to pick incident wavelengths and polarizations that will produce intersections of specular and diffuse component equi-reflectance curves. This is indicated in figure 5 which shows an overlay of the specular and diffuse component reflection functions for MgO. Near perpendicular intersections occur almost everywhere in the first quadrant for a light source with incident orientation (7.0, 3.0, -1). The same overlay of specular and diffuse reflectance maps would result for Aluminum except that reflected radiance values corresponding to each equi-reflectance contour would be different than from the ones in figure 5.

It turns out that *direct resolution* of specular and diffuse components for any dielectric is possible using polarization stereo for selected phase angles close to twice the Brewster angle. This is described in section 5. However, as reflection of light from dielectrics is very insensitive to variations in wavelength, the intersection of equi-reflection curves for even vast shifts in wavelength are so oblique that the equi-reflectance curves themselves are almost indistinguishable. Even though reflection of light from conductors has a stronger dependence on wavelength and a moderate dependence on

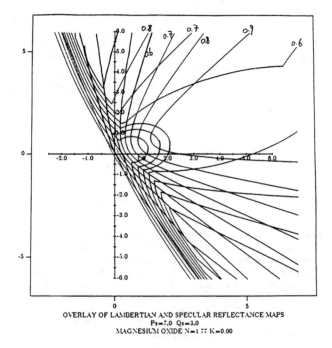

OVERLAY OF LAMBERTIAN AND SPECULAR REFLECTANCE MAPS
Ps=7.0   Qs=3.0
MAGNESIUM OXIDE N=1.77 K=0.00

Figure 5

polarization (see figures 4 (c) and (d)), this problem also occurrs for spectral/polarization stereo methods applied to conductors. These problems are so bad that minimization of error is surmounted by the problem of ascertaining an intersection in the first place. It is required therefore to use a methodology described in section 6 called *indirect resolution* of specular and diffuse reflection components.

5. POLARIZATION STEREO FOR DIELECTRICS

It was mentioned in section 3 that for all dielectrics there exists an angle of incidence, called the Brewster angle, at which parallel polarized light is not reflected. That is, the Fresnel reflection coefficient for parallel polarized light at the Brewster angle is zero. Figure 4(b) shows that in fact the Fresnel reflection coefficient for parallel polarized light is small over a large range of angles of incidence less than the Brewster angle. By observing the expression for R_s in section 2, this phenomenon can be exploited to "scale" the specular component of reflection to nearly zero thus isolating the diffuse component of reflection R_d.

Suppose that two image irradiance measurements are taken for parallel polarized and perpendicular polarized incident light respectively and that the phase angle is equal to exactly twice the Brewster angle for a given dielectric. Therefore the specular angle of incidence of light on the microfacets will be exactly the Brewster angle itself. The first equi-reflectance curve resulting from the incident parallel polarized light will be exactly the same as for the Lambertian model at this angle of incidence. Since a moderate amount of perpendicular polarized light is reflected at the Brewster angle for a dielectric, the second equi-reflectance curve will have a significant specular component of reflection. Even though the second equi-reflectance curve is not a pure specular component of reflection, it will tend to be a curve that will have a strong intersection with the Lambertian reflectance curve. This technique of forcing the total reflectance curves significantly towards the specular and diffuse component reflection functions respectively is what is termed *direct resolution* of specular and diffuse components.

An example of this technique is shown in figure 6 for MgO. Unfortunately one disadvantage is that the Brewster angle for MgO is 60.5° which would make the phase angle equal to about 121°. This would leave much of gradient space in shadow. Figure 6 uses an incident source orientation vector of (7.0, 3.0, -1) which gives a phase angle of approximately 82.6°. The specular angle of incidence is therefore about 41.3°, nearly 20° from the Brewster angle for MgO. Still, strong intersections are noted in the overlay of the parallel polarized and the perpendicularly polarized reflectance maps. This is due to the fact that the Fresnel reflection coefficient for parallel polarized light is still negligable at this angle of incidence and that the Fresnel reflection coefficient for perpendicularly polarized light is approximately 4 times that for parallel polarized light (see figure 4(b), 41.3° is about 0.720 radians).

Figure 7 depicts an actual simulation of the determination of local surface orientation from polarization stereo for a point on a sphere with a Magnesium oxide surface. The sphere is assumed to have radius 25 and the surface orientation is to be determined for the point on the sphere corresponding to the image point (12,18). The equation for the visible part of a sphere of radius r using the coordinate system depicted in figure 1.b is:

$$z = -\sqrt{r^2 - x^2 - y^2}$$

which implies that

$$\frac{\partial z}{\partial x} = \frac{x}{\sqrt{r^2 - x^2 - y^2}}, \quad \frac{\partial z}{\partial y} = \frac{y}{\sqrt{r^2 - x^2 - y^2}}.$$

Therefore, the local surface orientation at the point corresponding to the image coordinate (12,18), assuming orthographic projection, is approximately (0.958, 1.437, -1) in gradient space representation.

The equi-reflectance curves in figure 7 result from three different incident polarizations respectively. It is clear that an intersection occurs at the correct orientation point. This intersection could be obtained by using the two equi-reflectance curves for parallel polarization and perpendicular polarization respectively. However there is an additional intersection point that could just as well be the true value of the surface orientation. The third equi-reflectance curve produced from unpolarized incident light does not provide more information with respect to resolving between these two intersection points. In fact, for this same configuration of the imaging system, all equi-reflectance curves produced from any incident polarization or wavelength will go through

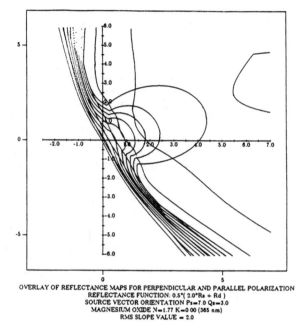

OVERLAY OF REFLECTANCE MAPS FOR PERPENDICULAR AND PARALLEL POLARIZATION
REFLECTANCE FUNCTION: 0.5*(2.0*Rs + Rd)
SOURCE VECTOR ORIENTATION Ps=7.0 Qs=3.0
MAGNESIUM OXIDE N=1.77 K=0 00 (365 nm)
RMS SLOPE VALUE = 2.0

Figure 6

these same two points in gradient space. This is due to an inherent "flip" symmetry about the source-viewing axis that cannot be broken by varying the value of the Fresnel reflection coefficient, $F(\Psi',\eta)$.

It is possible to break this "flip" symmetry by using a second light source which has an incident orientation not lying on the source-viewing axis of the original light source. This would produce an equi-reflectance curve going through the true surface orientation point and not going through the second intersection point observed for polarization stereo. However, the "flip" symmetry inherent to spectral/polarization stereo can also be broken by using a single extended light source with a variable aperature. This will be discussed in section 7.

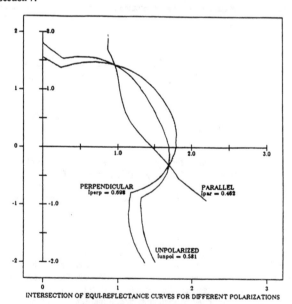

INTERSECTION OF EQUI-REFLECTANCE CURVES FOR DIFFERENT POLARIZATIONS

COMBINED SPECULAR AND DIFFUSE REFLECTANCE MAP
REFLECTANCE FUNCTION: 0.5*(2.0*Rs + Rd)
SOURCE VECTOR ORIENTATION Ps=7.0 Qs=3.0
MAGNESIUM OXIDE N=1.77 K=0.00 (365 NM)
RMS SLOPE VALUE= 2.0

Figure 7

6. SPECTRAL AND POLARIZATION STEREO BY INDIRECT RESOLUTION INTO SPECULAR AND DIFFUSE REFLECTION COMPONENTS

The equi-reflectance curves in figures 8 and 9 attempt to measure the same surface orientation in the problem that is described in section 5. For figure 9, the surface of the sphere is assumed to be made of Aluminum. By observing figures 8 and 9 it is evident that directly obtaining an intersection point for reflectance curves for spectral stereo applied to dielectrics, or for any combination of spectral and polarization stereo applied to conductors, is very difficult. Spectral stereo applied to dielectrics is hard to implement because the simple index of refraction is very insensitive to changes in wavelength. Unless the sampling rate for the equi-reflectance curves in gradient space is very high, two curves obtained for different incident wavelengths will appear indistinguishable. Another problem for spectral stereo applied to dielectrics is the necessity for low measurement error in the image irradiance. The shift in the observed reflected radiance between the two equi-reflectance curves in figure 8 is approximately 3.0% .

The observed image irradiance shift for the two equi-reflectance curves in figure 9 is fairly significant being almost 9% . The problem of indistinguishability between equi-reflectance curves here is even worse than in figure 8. This is due to the relative invariance of the shape of the equi-reflectance curves for Aluminum for fairly significant changes in the reflected radiance.

A technique is presented here that will use two reflected radiance measurements to solve for the values of the specular and diffuse components of reflection respectively from two simultaneous equations. The functions R_s and R_d are the same as those defined in section 2 except that the R_s used here is gR_s. Define r_s such that $R_s = F(\Psi',\eta)r_s$. Suppose that two reflectance measurements I_{ref}^1 and I_{ref}^2 are taken from two sucessive images at the same pixel. Also, the value of the Fresnel term with respect to this pixel for the first and second image are $F^1(\Psi',\eta)$ and $F^2(\Psi',\eta)$ respectively. Then the following equations arise:

$$F^1(\Psi',\eta)r_s + R_d = I_{ref}^1 \pm \varepsilon$$
$$F^2(\Psi',\eta)r_s + R_d = I_{ref}^2 \pm \varepsilon$$

where ε is the error inherent in the reflectance measurement. The solutions for R_s and R_d are:

$$R_s = F^1(\Psi',\eta)\frac{I_{ref}^1 - I_{ref}^2}{F^1(\Psi',\eta) - F^2(\Psi',\eta)} \pm 2\frac{F^1(\Psi',\eta)}{F^1(\Psi',\eta) - F^2(\Psi',\eta)}\varepsilon$$

$$R_d = \frac{F^1(\Psi',\eta)I_{ref}^2 - F^2(\Psi',\eta)I_{ref}^1}{F^1(\Psi',\eta) - F^2(\Psi',\eta)} \pm \frac{F^1(\Psi',\eta) + F^2(\Psi',\eta)}{F^1(\Psi',\eta) - F^2(\Psi',\eta)}\varepsilon .$$

Note that the solution for R_s is for the specular component of the total reflectance measured in the first image. This technique of decomposing the value of a total reflectance function into its specular and diffuse component values is what is termed *indirect resolution* of specular and diffuse components.

Thus, even for small shifts in the Fresnel reflection coefficient, two measurements of the reflected radiance make it possible to obtain the specular and diffuse component reflection values for each measurement. These values in turn can be used to generate an equi-reflectance curve for the specular and diffuse component respectively which produces strongly detectable intersections as mentioned in section 4. While the detection of intersection problem may be solved, the associated error collars may be huge if the experimental measurement error ε is significant and the difference between the first and second Fresnel reflection coefficients is very small. This can be seen from the equations immediately above.

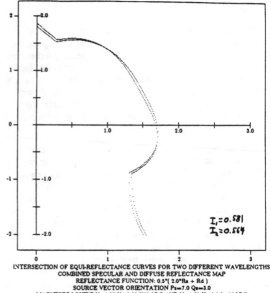

INTERSECTION OF EQUI-REFLECTANCE CURVES FOR TWO DIFFERENT WAVELENGTHS
COMBINED SPECULAR AND DIFFUSE REFLECTANCE MAP
REFLECTANCE FUNCTION: 0.5*(2.0*Rs + Rd)
SOURCE VECTOR ORIENTATION Ps=7.0 Qs=3.0
MAGNESIUM OXIDE N=1.77 K=0.00 (365 NM) AND N=1.72 K=0.0 (1130 NM)
RMS SLOPE VALUE= 2.0

Figure 8

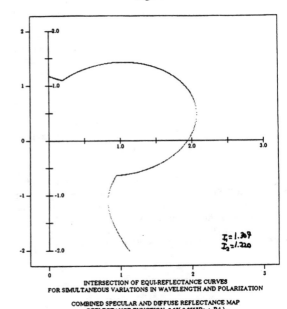

INTERSECTION OF EQUI-REFLECTANCE CURVES
FOR SIMULTANEOUS VARIATIONS IN WAVELENGTH AND POLARIZATION

COMBINED SPECULAR AND DIFFUSE REFLECTANCE MAP
REFLECTANCE FUNCTION: 0.5*(0.875*Rs + Rd)
SOURCE VECTOR ORIENTATION Ps=7.0 Qs=3.0
ALUMINUM
N=0.51 K=5.00 (450 NM) PERPENDICULAR POLARIZATION
N=1.55 K=7.00 (700 NM) PARALLEL POLARIZATION
RMS SLOPE VALUE= 2.0

Figure 9

Figures 10 and 11 show the intersection of specular and diffuse component equi-reflectance curves obtained from the same reflectance measurements that generated the curves in figures 8 and 9, respectively. Of course the experimental error ε for this simulation is assumed to be 0. The fact that the curves in figures 10 and 11 are exactly the same should be no surprise as equi-reflectance curves are invariant with respect to change in scale. The Fresnel reflection coefficient merely scales the specular component of reflection. Only the observed specular reflected radiance is different between the two figures.

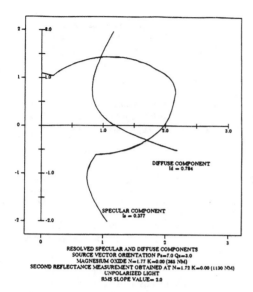

RESOLVED SPECULAR AND DIFFUSE COMPONENTS
SOURCE VECTOR ORIENTATION Ps=7.0 Qs=3.0
MAGNESIUM OXIDE N=1.77 K=0.00 (365 NM)
SECOND REFLECTANCE MEASUREMENT OBTAINED AT N=1.72 K=0.00 (1130 NM)
UNPOLARIZED LIGHT
RMS SLOPE VALUE= 2.0

Figure 10

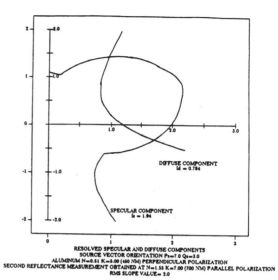

RESOLVED SPECULAR AND DIFFUSE COMPONENTS
SOURCE VECTOR ORIENTATION Ps=7.0 Qs=3.0
ALUMINUM N=0.51 K=5.00 (450 NM) PERPENDICULAR POLARIZATION
SECOND REFLECTANCE MEASUREMENT OBTAINED AT N=1.55 K=7.00 (700 NM) PARALLEL POLARIZATION
RMS SLOPE VALUE= 2.0

Figure 11

The same "flip" symmetry that was discussed in section 5 is also inherent to the individual functions R_s and R_d. Additional reflectance measurements from different incident wavelengths and polarizations would not resolve the two point intersection ambiguity. To achieve unique measurement of surface orientation, the technique presented in section 7 using an extended light source will have to be implemented.

Spectral stereo for dielectrics for determining surface orientation is not generally recommended. Errors in the measurement of surface orientation for conductors using spectral/polarization methods can be reduced by simultaneously varying the wavelength and polarization as is done in figures 9 and 11. The shift in the Fresnel reflection coefficients from the first to the second image can be maximized by using parallel incident polarization at a high wavelength and then using perpendicular polarization at a low wavelength.

7. SYMMETRY BREAKING USING A SINGLE EXTENDED LIGHT SOURCE

Consider gradient space point orientations in terms of the spherical coordinate angles Φ and Θ defined in figure 2(b) where the z-axis is gradient space orientation (0,0,-1). (The components x and y correspond to p and q respectively.) The condition that the probability distribution of microfacets, $P(\alpha)$, be isotropic implies that there is a mirror symmetry with respect to the invariance of reflected radiance for surface orientation normals that differ azimuthally in Φ by the same angle about the source-viewing plane. The orientation component Θ is assumed to be the same for both normals. The reflected radiance is the same for both surface orientations because the parameters Ψ, Ψ', Θ and α are automatically the same. It is clear that expression (1) in section 2 will yield the same value under this equivalence. This results by observing that the specular and diffuse component reflected radiance are each left invariant.

The source-viewing axis in gradient space is the line at the constant angle $\tan^{-1}(P_s/Q_s)$ from the q-axis. The invariance of reflected radiance about the source-viewing plane described above implies that separate points that are equi-distant from the origin of gradient space and that make the same angle with the source-viewing axis must lie on the same equi-reflectance curve. This can be expressed succintly as the invariance of all equi-reflectance curves under the "flip" symmetry transformation:

$$\Phi \to 2\tan^{-1}(P_s/Q_s) - \Phi$$

where the angle Φ is measured clockwise from the q-axis. Doing some algebra using equations (2) above, this transformation can be expressed in terms of gradient space variables as:

$$(3) \qquad p \to \frac{P_s^2 - Q_s^2}{P_s^2 + Q_s^2}p + 2\frac{Q_s P_s}{P_s^2 + Q_s^2}q$$

$$q \to 2\frac{Q_s P_s}{P_s^2 + Q_s^2}p - \frac{P_s^2 - Q_s^2}{P_s^2 + Q_s^2}q \,.$$

Since the shift in the value of the Fresnel reflection coefficient does not alter the "flip" symmetry of the specular reflectance function during the process of spectral and/or polarization stereo using a single point light source, it is clear that a two point ambiguity will always exist for the measurement of surface orientations not on the source-viewing axis. From equations (3) it can be deduced that the same "flip" symmetry does not hold separately for a second light source with incident orientation $(P_s',Q_s',-1)$ if and only if (P_s,Q_s) and (P_s',Q_s') are linearly independent. That is, a second light source will have a different "flip" symmetry if and only if its incident orientation does not lie on the source-viewing axis of the first light source. A single extended light source can be viewed as a continuous distribution of a large number of point light sources. Therefore the equi-reflectance curves produced from a single extended source will possess a "flip" symmetry if and only if the area in gradient space subtended by the continuous distribution of incident orientation points is in turn "flip" symmetric.

Figure 12 shows the unique measurement of the surface orientation for the problem in section 5 for a MgO surface. Three reflected radiance measurements were taken altogether. Two of them used unpolarized and perpendicular polarized incident light from a single point source. The third reflected radiance measurement was taken for perpendicular incident light from an asymmetric "half-moon" extended source depicted in figure 13. The half angle used is 0.4 radians for the extended source and the expression for the reflected radiance in section 2 was numerically integrated over the solid angle subtended by the source[4]. The size of the extended source was selected to be large to emphasize the process of breaking the inherent "flip" symmetry. Unique surface orientation measurements from much smaller extended sources are possible.

Of course all three reflected radiance measurements can be taken from the same light source with a variable aperature diaphram in front. For the first two measurements the aperature is a small "pinhole". For the third

---

[4] see [Wolff 1986] for details.

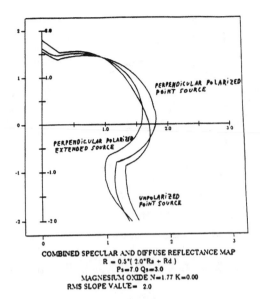

COMBINED SPECULAR AND DIFFUSE REFLECTANCE MAP
R = 0.5*(2.0*Rs + Rd)
Ps=7.0 Qs=3.0
MAGNESIUM OXIDE N=1.77 K=0.00
RMS SLOPE VALUE= 2.0

Figure 12

measurement the aperature is changed to the desired asymmetric shape and size. As mentioned above, it is possible for other more complicated symmetries to exist for resulting reflectance curves that may hinder the process of measuring certain surface orientations from spectral/polarization methods. Further changes to the shape of the extended source may then be useful, but at least the primary "flip" symmetry is broken.

8. CONCLUSION

It has been demonstrated through computer simulation of equi-reflectance curves that arise from the extended Torrance-Sparrow reflection model that the measurement of surface orientation is obtainable by using stereo techniques that vary the wavelength and/or the polarization of incident light from a single light source while leaving the imaging geometry invariant. Different techniques were explored using two very different types of materials, Magnesium oxide and Aluminum. This was to show the applicability of spectral/polarization stereo methods to a large class of material surfaces.

The most viable technique presented was that of polarization stereo for dielectrics. This was based on the observation that the specular component equi-reflectance curves exhibit strong intersections with diffuse component equi-reflectance curves over a large region of gradient space. Because the Fresnel reflection coefficient for parallel polarized light is small in a large region of angles of incidence below the Brewster angle, it is possible to force the total reflectance function to be almost identical to its pure diffuse (i.e. Lambertian) reflection component for a phase angle well below 90°. The Fresnel reflection coefficient for perpendicular polarized light in this region is significant forcing the total reflectance function close to its specular reflection

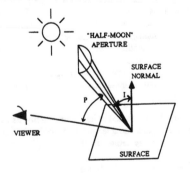

Figure 13

component. Thus using only two measurements of reflected radiance from parallel polarized and perpendicular polarized incident light respectively, surface orientation can be measured with relatively small error.

Spectral stereo for dielectrics is considered to be the least practical due to the insensitivity of the simple index of refraction to changes in wavelength. Spectral/polarization stereo for conductors is best when wavelength and polarization are simultaneously varied so as to maximize the difference in the Fresnel reflection coefficients between successive images. The main issue for spectral stereo applied to dielectrics and spectral/polarization methods applied to conductors is resolution of intersection points. In these cases the shapes of equi-reflectance curves are relatively invariant to changes in incident wavelength and polarization even though the change in the reflected radiance for conductors can be fairly significant. A technique was presented to resolve the specular and diffuse component values of the reflected radiance by solving two image irradiance equations simultaneously. Surface orientation is measured from the strongly discernable intersection of specular and diffuse component equi-reflectance curves. However, for small variations in the Fresnel reflection coefficient, the associated errors can be quite high.

Finally it was formally shown how an isotropic reflectance function induces a "flip" symmetry on resulting equi-reflectance curves in gradient space about the source-viewing axis. Using a point light source it is therefore theoretically impossible to measure better than a up to a two point ambiguity, surface orientations that do not lie on the source-viewing axis using spectral/polarization techniques. A technique using a single extended light source was presented to resolve this ambiguity by breaking the inherent "flip" symmetry. By using an aperture which itself is not "flip" symmetric, equi-reflectance curves that pass through the true surface orientation point can be produced that do not pass through the false second point of ambiguity.

Experimentation is currently underway to empirically verify the theoretical development presented in this paper.

ACKNOWLEDGEMENTS

Many thanks to the people who reviewed earlier drafts of this work. In particular, Terry Boult provided a very thoughtful review and helpful suggestions.

REFERENCES

[Beckmann and Spizzichino 1963] Beckmann, P., and Spizzichino, A., *The Scattering of Electromagnetic Waves from Rough Surfaces*, Macmillan, 1963

[Cook and Torrance 1981] Cook, R.L., and Torrance, K.E., *A Reflectance Model For Computer Graphics*, SIGGRAPH 1981 Proceedings, vol.15 #3 pp.307-316, 1981

[Koshikawa 1979] Koshikawa, K., *A Polarimetric Approach To Shape Understanding Of Glossy Objects*, IJCAI 1979, pp.493-495

[Physics Handbook] American Institute of Physics Handbook, Third Edition, McGraw-Hill, 1972

[Siegel and Howell 1981] Siegel, R. and Howell, J.R., *Thermal Radiation Heat Transfer*, McGraw-Hill, 1981

[Torrance and Sparrow 1967] Torrance, K.E., and Sparrow, E.M., *Theory for Off-Specular Reflection From Roughened Surfaces*, Journal of The Optical Society of America, vol. 57 #9 pp.1105-1114, September 1967

[Wolff 1986] Wolff, L.B., *Physical Stereo for Combined Specular and Diffuse Reflection*, Tech report CS-242-86, Columbia University, Nov. 1, 1986

[Wolff 1987] Wolff, L.B. *Surface Orientation From Polarization Images*, Columbia University, April 1987

[Woodham 1980] Woodham, R.J., *Photometric Method for Determining Surface Orientation from Multiple Images*, Optical Engineering, vol.19 #1 pp.139-144, Jan-Feb 1980

Shape Recovery from Specular Reflection

Specular reflection occurs when light strikes the smooth interface between two materials. For an ideal specular surface, all of the light incident from a given direction is reflected into the single direction in the plane of incidence such that the angle of incidence equals the angle of reflection. Perfect mirrors, for example, are ideal specular surfaces. Real surfaces usually deviate from ideal specular reflectors in two respects. First, real surfaces usually exhibit some degree of roughness causing incident light to be reflected over a range of angles. Also, at most interfaces, some of the incident light penetrates into the object material where it is either absorbed, transmitted, or scattered back through the interface.

Several techniques have been developed for finding highlight regions of strong specular reflection in images. These techniques are often based on the brightness of highlights [1] or on color shifts [2]. The spectral properties of highlights are not examined in this section, but are analyzed in detail in the Color volume of this series.

Once they have been located, highlights provide significant information about the scene for a vision system. Since there is a precise geometric relationship between local surface normal, source position, and viewer position at a specular highlight, these regions constrain the local surface orientation and shape as well as the source direction. For smooth metal surfaces that are common in many inspection applications, specular highlights are often the only prominent features. For other materials, such as plastics, specular reflection effects are often measurable in images, and can be used to infer properties of the scene.

The papers in this section investigate the diversity of ways in which specular highlights can be used to infer geometric information about surfaces from images using various models for specular reflection and illumination. Techniques are described for shape estimation from a single image using specular reflection models. Using a set of images obtained under different illumination conditions, surface shape can be estimated using photometric stereo. The relationship between specular points in a stereo pair of images can also be used to constrain surface shape. From a sequence of images obtained under known viewer motion, additional surface information can be recovered using highlights.

In the first article, Healey and Binford present a method for estimating local surface shape from specular highlights [4]. The analysis is based on the rough surface model developed by Torrance and Sparrow [3]. Using this model, an algorithm is derived to estimate a local second order surface description in terms of principal directions and the magnitude of principal curvatures. Healey and Binford describe an experimental system for estimating shape from highlights and discuss methods to overcome practical problems such as blurring, intensity truncation, and quantization.

Ikeuchi applies the photometric stereo method to estimate surface orientations for specular surfaces [5]. The analysis assumes smooth surfaces illuminated by distributed sources. Ikeuchi describes a system that is based on three light sources and discusses details of building the reflectance map. Experiments are presented in which the system estimates normal vectors across a surface from the three brightness measurements using a lookup table derived from the reflectance map.

Using specular points as features for stereo vision requires a reworking of the traditional stereo geometry because the locations of specular points due to the same source in a stereo pair of images will, in general, correspond to different points on the surface. In [6], Blake and Brelstaff assume smooth surfaces to develop an algorithm for computing the horizontal and vertical stereo disparities of specular points relative to a fixed surface point. They show how this information can be used to compute local surface orientation and how it also constrains the principal curvatures of the surface to lie on a hyperbola. The authors show that a single view of a specularity generated by a distributed light source allows the approximation of lines of curvature. Experiments demonstrate the use of the derived constraints in a stereo vision system.

Zisserman, Giblin, and Blake examine how a sequence of images of a smooth specular surface generated according to known viewer motion constrains surface shape [7]. They show that, using two images of such a sequence, it is possible to distinguish convex from concave surfaces while requiring no assumptions about the light source or surface shape. Given a sequence of several images, they show that the surface and its normal are determined uniquely along the curve of observed specular points, provided that one surface point along the curve is known. If no points can be determined, the surface is specified by a curve belonging to a one-parameter family.

In [8], Thrift and Lee investigate the appearance of highlights in images of smooth specular cylinders, spheres, and generalized cylinders illuminated by a single distant source. They show that for a cylinder, we will observe a line of highlights that constrains the position and radius of the cylinder. A sphere will give rise to a single specular point that constrains the sphere position and radius. By considering the subset of generalized cylinders that are surfaces of revolution about a straight axis, the authors show that the highlight points constrain object shape and location. Experiments are reported for each class of objects to illustrate the usefulness of the analysis.

Park and Tou develop a method for estimating the shape of surfaces that have both a specular and Lambertian component of reflection [9]. The input to the system is three images of the surface obtained under different illumination conditions. Using the Torrance-Sparrow [3] specular model in conjunction with a Lambertian reflection model, a method is developed for separating an image into two intrinsic images. One intrinsic image contains only the reflected specular intensity while the other contains only the reflected Lambertian intensity. After separation, photometric stereo is applied to the Lambertian intrinsic image to estimate surface normals. Results of the method are presented for several images.

– *G.E.H.*

References

[1]   Brelstaff, G., and Blake, A. "Detecting Specular Reflections Using Lambertian Constraints." In *Proc. of 2nd International Conference on Computer Vision*. Tarpon Springs, FL. IEEE, December 1988. Pages 297-302.

[2]   Klinker, G.J., Shafer, S.A., and Kanade, T. "A Physical Approach to Color Image Understanding." *International Journal of Computer Vision* **4**: 7-38, 1990.

[3]   Torrance, K.E., and Sparrow, E.M. "Theory of Off-specular Reflection from Roughened Surfaces." *Journal of the Optical Society of America A* **57**: 1105-1114, 1967. Reprinted in the "Intensity Reflection Models" section of the Radiometry volue of this series.

Papers Included in This Collection

[4]   Healey, G., and Binford, T. "Local Shape from Specularity." *Computer Vision, Graphics, and Image Processing* **42**: 62-86, 1988.

[5]   Ikeuchi, K. "Determining Surface Orientations of Specular Surfaces by Using the Photometric Stereo Method." *IEEE Trans. on Pattern Analysis and Machine Intelligence* **PAMI-3**(6): 661-669, 1981.

[6]   Blake, A., and Brelstaff, G. "Geometry from Specularities." In *Proc. International Conference on Computer Vision*. Tarpon Springs, FL. IEEE, 1988. Pages 394-403.

[7]   Zisserman, A., Giblin, P., and Blake, A. "The Information Available to a Moving Observer from Specularities." *Image and Vision Computing* **7**(1): 38-42, 1989.

[8]   Thrift, P., and Lee, C.-H.. "Using Highlights to Constrain Object Size and Location." *IEEE Trans. on Systems, Man and Cybernetics* **TSMC-13**(3): 426-431, 1984.

[9]   Park, J.-S., and Tou, J.T. "Highlight Separation and Surface Orientations for 3-D Specular Objects." In *Proc. of International Conference on Pattern Recognition*. IEEE, 1990. Pages 331-335.

Local Shape from Specularity

Glenn Healey and Thomas O. Binford

Robotics Laboratory, Computer Science Department, Stanford University
Stanford, California 94305

Received December 23, 1986; accepted October 27, 1987

We show that highlights in images of objects with specularly reflecting surfaces provide significant information about the surfaces which generate them. A brief survey is given of specular reflectance models which have been used in computer vision and graphics. For our work, we adopt the Torrance–Sparrow specular model which, unlike most previous models, considers the underlying physics of specular reflection from rough surfacers. From this model we derive powerful relationships between the properties of a specular feature in an image and local properties of the corresponding surface. We show how this analysis can be used for both prediction and interpretation in a vision system. A shape from specularity system has been implemented to test our approach. The performance of the system is demonstrated by careful experiments with specularly reflecting objects.   © 1988 Academic Press, Inc.

1. INTRODUCTION

When light is incident on a surface, some fraction of it is reflected. A perfectly smooth surface reflects light only in the direction such that the angle of incidence equals the angle of reflection. For rougher surfaces, e.g., the surface of a metal fork, specular effects are still observable. In this paper we analyze the properties of specular reflection from rough surfaces.

There are numerous reasons why the study of specular reflection deserves serious attention in computer vision. Specular features are almost always the brightest regions in an image. Contrast is often large across specularities; they are very prominent. In addition, the presence or absence of specular features provides immediate constraints on the positions of the viewer and light sources relative to the specular surface. Also, as we will show, the properties of a specularity constrain the local shape and orientation of the specular surface.

An ability to understand specular features is valuable for any vision system which must interpret images of glossy surfaces. This work, motivated by experience with ACRONYM [5], began in order to provide the SUCCESSOR system with the capability to reason about specular reflection from metal parts in the ITA project [7]. Images of these parts typically contain large specular regions (Fig. 1).

We examine what information can be inferred from an image of a rough surface by considering the physics of specular reflection. Particular emphasis is placed on finding symbolic quasi-invariant relationships which will hold in many different situations (e.g., different source, viewer configurations). In contrast to many intensity-based vision algorithms, we compute a small number of local surface statistics based on the properties of a relatively large number of pixels in an image. This allows us to observe predicted features and infer local surface shape in noisy intensity images and in cases where available specular models do not completely characterize the physics of specular reflection.

FIG. 1.   Typical image containing specularities.

2. REVIEW OF PREVIOUS WORK

Researchers in computer graphics have used increasingly realistic specular models. Several of these models will be discussed in the next section. In computer vision, however, relatively few attempts have been made to exploit the information encoded in specularities. Ikeuchi [16] employs the photometric stereo method [24] and uses distributed light sources to determine the orientation of patches on a surface. Grimson [11] uses Phong's specular model [18] to examine specularities from two views in order to improve the performance of surface interpolation. Coleman and Jain [7] use four-source photometric stereo to identify and correct for specular reflection components. In more recent work, Blake [2] assumes smooth surfaces and single point specularities to derive equations to infer surface shape using specular stereo. He shows that the same equations can be used to predict the appearance of a specularity on a smooth surface when using a distributed light source. Takai, Kimura, and Sata [26] describe a model-based vision system which recognizes objects by predicting specular regions. As specular models and insights improve, we expect to see more work which makes use of the properties of specular reflection.

3. SPECULAR REFLECTANCE MODELS

Given a viewer, a surface patch, and a light source, a reflectance model quantifies the amount of light that will be reflected in the direction of the viewer. General reflectance models represent the intensity of the reflected light I as a sum of two reflection components

$$I = I_D + I_S. \tag{1}$$

I_D represents the intensity of diffusely reflected light and I_S represents the intensity of specularly reflected light. In this paper we restrict our attention to the I_S reflection component.

In many cases, it is possible to separate the I_S reflection component from the I_D reflection component in an image. Shafer [23] has developed an algorithm based on the physics of color image formation which determines the amount of specular and

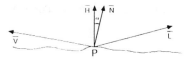

FIG. 2.   The reflection geometry.

diffuse reflection at each pixel in a color image. More recently, Klinker, Shafer, and Kanade [19] have reported an implementation of this algorithm which has produced encouraging results on real color images. Brelstaff and Blake [4] have reported success in locating specularities in monochromatic images by considering patterns of image irradiance.

Before discussing the various specular reflectance models, we introduce the reflection geometry (Fig. 2). We consider a viewer looking at a surface point P which is illuminated by a point light source. Define

$\mathbf{V}$ = unit vector from P in direction of viewer

$\mathbf{N}$ = unit surface normal at P

$\mathbf{L}$ = unit vector from P in direction of source

$\mathbf{H} = (\mathbf{V} + \mathbf{L})/(\|\mathbf{V} + \mathbf{L}\|)$ (unit angular bisector of $\mathbf{V}$ and $\mathbf{L}$)

$\alpha = \cos^{-1}(\mathbf{N} \cdot \mathbf{H})$ (the angle between $\mathbf{N}$ and $\mathbf{H}$).

In describing specular models, we consider illumination from a single point light source. In principle, we lose no generality using this approach. In situations involving distributed light sources, we only need to integrate the effects of an equivalent array of point sources. A discussion of the geometry of extended sources is given in [16].

The simplest specular model assumes that specularities only occur where the angle of incidence equals the angle of reflection and $\mathbf{L}$, $\mathbf{N}$, and $\mathbf{V}$ all lie in the same plane. This corresponds to the situation $\alpha = 0$ in Fig. 2. Unless the surface is locally flat, this model predicts that specularities will only be observed at isolated points on a surface. A few experiments, however, show that this model is inadequate for most real surfaces. Not only are observed specular features usually larger than single points, but highlights often occur in places which are not predicted by this model.

An empirical model for specular reflection has been developed by Phong [21] for computer graphics. This model represents the specular component of reflection by powers of the cosine of the angle between the perfect specular direction and the line of sight. Thus, Phong's model is capable of predicting specularities which extend beyond a single point. While Phong's model gives a reasonable approximation which is useful in some contexts, the parameters of this model have no physical meaning. It is possible to develop more accurate models by examining the physics underlying specular reflection.

The Torrance—Sparrow model [27], developed by physicists, is a more refined model of specular reflection. This model assumes that a surface is composed of small, randomly oriented, mirror-like facets. Only facets with a normal in the direction of $\mathbf{H}$ contribute to the specular reflection in the direction $\mathbf{V}$. The model also quantifies the shadowing and masking of facets by adjacent facets using a geometrical attenuation factor. The resulting specular model is

$$I_S = EFDA, \tag{2}$$

where

> E = energy of incident light
>
> F = Fresnel coefficient
>
> D = facet orientation distribution function
>
> A = geometrical attenuation factor adjusted for foreshortening.

We will analyze the effects of each factor in the model in the next few paragraphs. The results we present in this paper are derived from Eq. (2).

The Fresnel coefficient F models the amount of light which is reflected from individual facets. In general, F depends on the incidence angle and the complex index of refraction of the reflecting material. Cook and Torrance [9] have shown that to synthesize realistic images, F must characterize the color of the specularity. The Fresnel equations predict that F is a nearly constant function of incidence angle for the class of materials with a large extinction coefficient [24]. This class of materials includes all metals and many other materials with a significant specular reflection component.

The probability distribution function D describes the orientation of the micro facets relative to the average surface normal **N**. Blinn [3] and Cook and Torrance [9] discuss various distribution functions. All of these functions are very similar in shape. In agreement with Torrance and Sparrow we use the Gaussian distribution function given by

$$D(\alpha) = Ke^{-(\alpha/m)^2}, \tag{3}$$

where K is a normalization constant. The constant m indicates surface roughness and is proportional to the standard deviation of the Gaussian. Small values of m describe smooth surfaces for which most of the specular reflection is concentrated in a single direction. Large values of m are used to describe rougher surfaces with larger differences in orientation between nearby facets. These rough surfaces produce specularities which appear spread out on the reflecting surface. Figure 3 shows the effect of different values of m.

The factor A quantifies the effects of a geometrical attenuation factor G corrected for foreshortening by dividing by $(\mathbf{N} \cdot \mathbf{V})$,

$$A = \frac{G}{\mathbf{N} \cdot \mathbf{V}}; \tag{4}$$

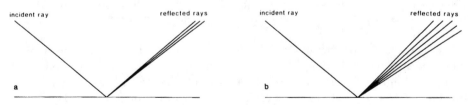

FIG. 3.   Specular distribution for (a) small m; (b) large m.

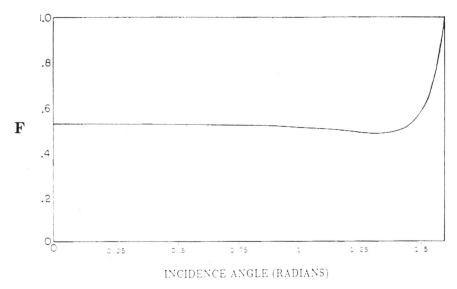

INCIDENCE ANGLE (RADIANS)

Fig. 4.   Plot of F as a function of incidence angle.

G is derived by Torrance and Sparrow in [27]. They assume that each facet makes up one side of a symmetric v-groove cavity. From this assumption, they examine the various possible facet configurations which correspond to shadowing or masking. The expression is

$$G = \min\left\{1, \frac{2(\mathbf{N} \cdot \mathbf{H})(\mathbf{N} \cdot \mathbf{V})}{(\mathbf{V} \cdot \mathbf{H})}, \frac{2(\mathbf{N} \cdot \mathbf{H})(\mathbf{N} \cdot \mathbf{L})}{(\mathbf{V} \cdot \mathbf{H})}\right\}. \tag{5}$$

Let μ be the angle between $\mathbf{N}$ and $\mathbf{V}$. As μ increases from 0 to $\pi/2$, the viewer gradually sees a larger part of the reflecting surface in a unit area in the view plane. Therefore, as μ gets larger, there are correspondingly more surface facets which contribute to the intensity measured by the viewer. We take this phenomenon into account in (4) by dividing by $\mathbf{N} \cdot \mathbf{V}$.

4. SHAPE FROM SPECULARITY

In this section, we demonstrate how we can use (2) to determine local surface properties from specularities. In almost all situations we do not require the full generality of (2) to infer these local properties. Our first assumption is that F is constant with respect to viewing geometry. This is a very good approximation for metals and for many other materials when the incident light is not at glancing incidence [24]. Figure 4 shows a typical plot of F as a function of angle of incidence computed using the Fresnel equations. Note the near constant behavior of F until the angle of incidence nears $\pi/2$. We can further simplify (2) by observing that unless we are at glancing incidence, the exponential factor in (3) changes much faster than A. The behavior of A as a function of angle of incidence is shown in Fig. 5. Except for a small range of angles near glancing incidence, A can be considered approximately constant across the specularity. Since we are only considering a

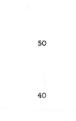

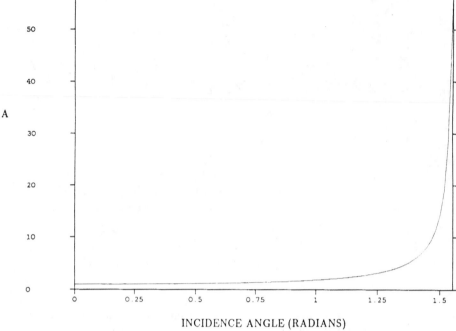

INCIDENCE ANGLE (RADIANS)

FIG. 5. Plot of A as a function of incidence angle.

single light source, E is constant across the specularity. Hence, the form of (2) we use to determine local surface properties is

$$I_S = K'e^{-(\alpha/m)^2},\qquad(6)$$

where K' is a constant. Equation (6) has proven to be a good approximation to (2) except near glancing incidence.

Referring again to the geometry of Fig. 2, we assume that the viewer and light source are distant relative to the dimensions of the surface. Therefore $\mathbf{V}$ and $\mathbf{L}$ may be regarded as constant; hence their angular bisector $\mathbf{H}$ is also constant. We assume that the positions of the viewer and light source are known. Finally, since the distance from the viewer to the surface is large, we can approximate the perspective projection of the imaging device with an orthographic projection.

4.1. Inferring Local Surface Shape

For a surface M on which the Gaussian curvature is locally nonzero, we will be able to locate a single point P_0 of maximum irradiance in the image of the specularity. From (6) we see that this point corresponds to the local surface orientation $\mathbf{N} = \mathbf{H}$ (i.e., $\alpha = 0$). Given such a surface where $\mathbf{H}$ is known, we can immediately determine the surface orientation at P_0. Figure 6 shows a typical image irradiance surface for a specular image. P_0 corresponds to $\alpha = 0$. As predicted by (6), specular image irradiance decreases as we move away from P_0.

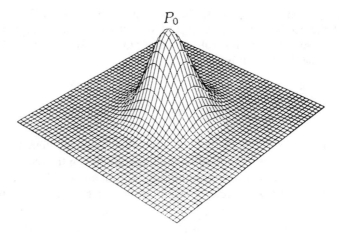

P_0

FIG. 6. Specular irradiance surface for a curved surface.

After locating P_0, we can transform the specular irradiance image to the α angle image. Consider Eq. (6). If I' is the specular irradiance corresponding to an arbitrary image point P' near P_0, then the angle α at the surface point imaging to P' is given by

$$|\alpha| = m\sqrt{-\ln(I'/K')}, \tag{7}$$

where K' is the specular image irradiance at P_0 and m is the surface roughness parameter of (3). We will shown in Eq. (8) that to determine the magnitudes of the principal curvatures of the surface we require an estimate of m. But even in the situation where no estimate of m is available, we will show that we can still compute useful local surface statistics. In (7), α is determined only up to sign. This will cause the sign of the normal curvatures computed at P_0 to be ambiguous. From (7) we can compute the absolute value of α corresponding to each point P' in a neighborhood of P_0. The image of $|\alpha|$ values is called the α angle image.

From the α angle image, we can compute local curvature properties of the surface. Let $T_{P_0}(M)$ be the tangent space to M at P_0. To compute curvatures, we take a finite number n of straight line samples of the α angle image intersecting P_0. To ensure uniform angular resolution on the surface, these samples should be taken in equally spaced angular directions in $T_{P_0}(M)$. In general, equally spaced angular direction in the image will not correspond to equally spaced angular directions in the tangent space. Thus, given a direction in the tangent space to the surface at P_0, we need to determine the corresponding direction in the image. The geometry and equations relevant to this problem appear in the Appendix.

The next step is to use the α image to compute the normal curvature of the surface in a given direction θ in $T_{P_0}(M)$. The normal curvature is computed by taking a straight line L in the α image which intersects P_0 and is in the image direction θ' which corresponds to θ. (Both θ and θ' are defined more precisely in the Appendix.) Under orthographic projection, L will project to a line L' in $T_{P_0}(M)$. The goal is to compute the normal curvature of the curve $C \subset M$, where C is the orthogonal projection of L' onto M. Since C projects to a line in $T_{P_0}(M)$, the magnitude of the geodesic curvature $|K_g|$ of C is 0 [20]. Thus local changes in α along C are due primarily to normal curvature along C. We compute the normal curvature κ_n in the direction θ by

$$\kappa_n = \left.\frac{d\alpha}{ds}\right|_{P_0}, \tag{8}$$

where s is arc length in the direction θ. In other words, we are differentiating the α image along L with respect to arc length on the surface. From the local character of specularities, we see that, to a very good approximation, arc length on the surface is equal to length in $T_{P_0}(M)$. Therefore, length in the image and arc length on the surface are related by the scale factor $\sqrt{x_1^2 + y_1^2}$ defined in the Appendix. Thus, computing normal curvature on the surface has been reduced to differentiation in the α image.

If we let θ vary in the range $0 \le \theta \le 2\pi$ we can compute κ_n in any number of directions at P_0. The principal curvatures of M at P_0 are defined to be the maximum and minimum values of κ_n; the corresponding directions are called the principal directions. Hence, using this technique it is possible to describe M locally to second order in terms of principal curvatures and principal directions. In the development leading up to (8), we have assumed an estimate of the surface roughness parameter m is available. If m is unknown, then the values of κ_n in (8) are known to within multiplication by a constant. In this case, we are still able to compute the ratio of the principal curvatures of the surface. This ratio provides a useful local surface description. In the context of shape from shading [14], Bruss [6] and Deift and Sylvester [10] examine the assumptions required to generate higher order surface descriptions from an α image.

4.2. Special Cases

In this subsection we examine specular reflection from special classes of surfaces. In 4.2.1 and 4.2.2 we consider surfaces which are locally singly curved and planar respectively. For these surfaces, the Gaussian curvature is locally zero. In 4.2.3 we examine the case of corners and edges where surface normal is discontinuous but where specularities are frequently observed.

4.2.1. Singly Curved Surfaces

If one principal curvature of a surface is zero in a specular region (i.e., the surface is locally singly curved), we will not be able to infer immediately the local orientation as we did for a doubly curved surface. To understand why, consider Fig. 7. Figure 7 shows a viewer looking at a tilted cylinder. To make the example concrete, assume that $\mathbf{L}$ is such that $\mathbf{H} = \mathbf{V}$. For this configuration there will be no point on the surface for which $\alpha = 0$ (recall that $\mathbf{H}$ is essentially constant), yet we will still observe a specularity in the image if at some point α is small enough to give a significant value for I_S in (6). Define ϕ to be the smallest value of α for a given surface-source-viewer configuration. Figure 8 shows a specularity generated by a cylinder which is oriented so that ϕ is 20°. Note that the specular model which assumes that specularities only occur where the angle of incidence equals the angle

FIG. 7.   Viewer observing a singly curved surface.

of reflection and **L**, **N**, and **V** all lie in the same plane would not predict a specularity for this case.

We observe that it is typically easy to detect that a surface is singly curved at a specularity. This is because we will observe a line of maximum irradiance (along the line of zero curvature) instead of the point maximum we observe for the doubly curved case.

Figure 9 is a plot of I_S for a singly curved surface in a direction perpendicular to the lines of zero curvature as we change ϕ. It is worth noting that both the magnitude and shape of I_S change as ϕ increases. Consequently, it may be possible to recover significant local shape information for this class of surfaces.

4.2.2. *Planes*

For a planar surface, **N** is constant. Hence, recalling our basic assumptions, I_S is constant across a plane. If the plane is oriented such that α is small enough, then a viewer will perceive an I_S reflection component. As with the singly curved surface, the magnitude of the measured intensity will depend on α. If α is not sufficiently

FIG. 8.   Specularity for a tilted cylinder.

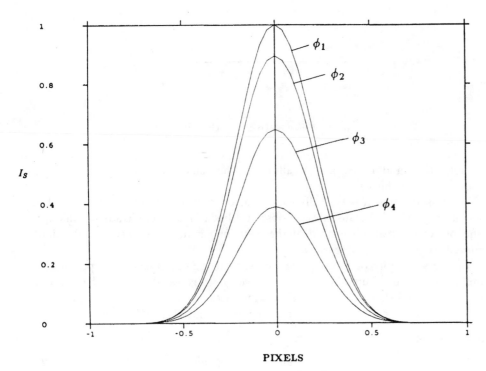

PIXELS

FIG. 9. I_S for different values of ϕ.

small, then I_S will be zero at all points on the plane. These observations provide us with two useful pieces of information:

1. Glossy surfaces which do not generate specularities over a range of orientations are probably planar.

2. Surfaces which produce a specularity of constant irradiance over a 2D region in the image are locally planar.

4.2.3. Corners and Edges

Specularities are often observed at places of discontinuous surface normal on an object. Typical examples of these discontinuities are edges and corners on a polyhedron. For an ideal edge on a polyhedron, the surface normal is discontinuous across the edge (Fig. 10).

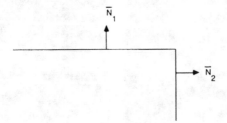

FIG. 10.   An ideal edge.

FIG. 11.   Image of an edge specularity.

For an ideal edge joining two planes, we should not expect to observe a specularity unless either N_1 or N_2 is oriented in a direction which is sufficiently close to the perfect specular direction H. But for this case, as discussed in 4.2.2, we would expect to observe a spread out specular feature on one of the two planes joined by the edge. So why do we frequently see specular reflections along edges? On real polyhedra, surface normals are often continuous across edges [15]. Instead of the normal vector changing discontinuously, the normal usually changes smoothly from N_1 to N_2 by taking values which are linear combinations of N_1 and N_2. As we cross an edge, the surface normal moves rapidly through a large range of angles. If any of these normals is oriented in a direction sufficiently near the direction H, we will observe a specularity. Therefore, we often observe a specularity on an edge. Figure 11 shows an image of an edge specularity. The situation is similar for trihedral vertices. As with edges, the normal vector is usually continuous at a corner. For trihedral vertices, the normal vector typically takes on values which are linear combinations of the three normals corresponding to the three planes defining the vertex.

From experiments with polyhedra, we have developed a useful model for the behavior of surface normal across edges. Define r to be the edge sharpness parameter and assume the coordinate system of Fig. 12. P_1 and P_2 denote two planes intersecting to form an edge. The y axis is aligned in the direction of N_1 and the origin is a distance r from P_1 such that the normal to the surface P_1 begins to turn away from N_1 when x becomes positive. The model for the normal as it turns

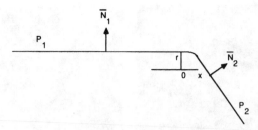

FIG. 12.   The geometry of a rounded edge.

from $\mathbf{N}_1$ to $\mathbf{N}_2$ is

$$N = \frac{\sqrt{r^2 - x^2}}{r}\mathbf{N}_1 + \frac{x}{r}\mathbf{N}_2 \qquad \text{for } 0 \le x \le r|\mathbf{N}_1 \times \mathbf{N}_2|. \qquad (9)$$

In other words, the normal is assumed to turn through a curve of constant curvature $1/r$. Here the parameter r is used to specify the sharpness of the edge. Small values of r indicate sharp edges, while larger values of r indicate more rounded edges. Note that given this model, an edge is locally identical to a singly curved surface. Figure 13 shows the profile of a specularity across a sharp 90° edge which is similar to the profile predicted by the continuous normal variation of (9).

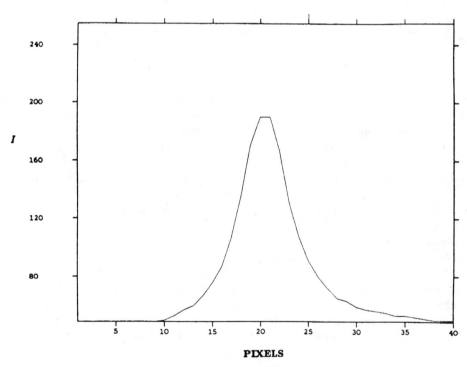

PIXELS

FIG. 13.   Specular irradiance profile across an edge.

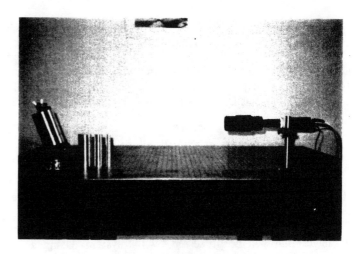

FIG. 14.   The laboratory setup.

5. THE LABORATORY SETUP

A laboratory arrangement has been set up to test the derived relationships (Fig. 14). This section of the paper describes the laboratory setup. Section 6 examines factors which must be considered to successfully interpret real images. In Section 7, we describe an implemented system which has been used to infer local surface properties from specularities. Section 8 presents experimental results.

To ensure accurate measurements, the experiments are conducted on a 4 × 6 foot optical table. High precision rotation and translation stages are used to position the objects being viewed. A halogen light source with a 5 mm wide filament is placed 20 ft from the object surface to approximate a point source. Monochromatic image data is obtained using a video camera and an image digitizer. A 210 mm lens is used with the video camera to obtain high resolution across the specularity. The resulting images are in the form of 256 × 256 arrays of pixels. Each pixel has eight bits of gray level resolution. A precise positioning device has been built to position the camera relative to the surface. Camera–object distances of at least 24 inches are enforced to ensure that the assumed distant object condition is met. Using this setup, it is possible to obtain more than 40 pixels across a specular feature which is less than a centimeter wide on the surface. Metal cylinders and spheres of varying curvature are used to test the predicted relationships. (Fig. 15)

6. PRACTICAL CONSIDERATIONS

This section examines factors which must be considered to enable a shape from specularity system to successfully interpret real images.

6.1. Gaussian Blur

Unfortunately, the formation of an image by an optical system introduces some amount of degradation. We can model this degradation as a convolution with a spatially invariant Gaussian point spread function [1]. The standard deviation of this blur is typically less than one pixel. For small specular features, taking into account the effects of this blur allows a more accurate determination of surface shape.

Our system uses a module called BLURINVERT to deblur the input specular image. For general 2-dimensional functions, inverting Gaussian blur is an unstable process. However, an explicit deblurring convolution kernel has been derived under certain assumptions in [17]. The 1D continuous version of the kernel is given by

$$M_N(x) = \frac{e^{-x^2}}{\sqrt{\pi}\, k! 2^k} \sum_{k=0}^{(N-1)/2} (-1)^k H_{2k}(x), \tag{10}$$

where N is an odd integer denoting the order of the kernel and H_{2k} is the Hermite polynomial of degree $2k$. Larger values of N give better deblurring filters (i.e., they recover exactly a larger space of blurred input functions), but are more costly to compute. The value of N that is chosen in applications depends on the characteristics of the images that will be processed by the system. Using a 2-dimensional discrete version of (10), the BLURINVERT module allows our system to produce accurate shape descriptions from small specular features in images.

6.2. Quantization Effects

On a surface of high curvature, it is unlikely that we will measure the correct maximum specular irradiance K' in (6). The problem is that for highly curved surfaces we are unable to shrink a pixel down to where the surface area it images is approximately planar. Even within the single pixel of maximum irradiance, α is changing and cannot be considered constant. Hence the irradiance value at the maximum pixel will be an average specular irradiance over a small range of α and will not give the true K' of (6). This must be corrected for in applications. An artifact of this phenomenon is that measured K' seems to increase as surface curvature decreases. It follows that if we wish to measure K' for a material, we should use a surface of small curvature, ideally a plane.

Since specularities are usually the brightest features in images, specular intensities are often too large to be represented in the number of bits per pixel allowed by the

FIG. 15. Some experimental specular surfaces.

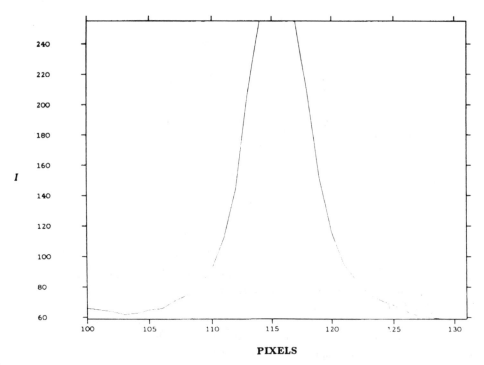

FIG. 16. A truncated specularity.

digitizing hardware or within the dynamic range of the camera. If this is the case, the specularity is truncated. Figure 16 shows I for a truncated specularity. The obvious way to deal with this situation is to avoid it. One avoidance technique is to take multiple images in which differing amounts of light are allowed to reach the camera. This can be achieved either by adjusting the lens aperture or by using filters. another possible solution is to control the illumination to eliminate the possibility of truncation.

If inferences must be made from a single image, then it is arguably better to allow truncation to occur. In the case where input images have eight bits per pixel, intensities will range from 0 to 255. In many applications it is possible to weaken the incident illumination so that no truncation occurs. In doing this, however, we cause pixels on the I_S curve which previously had significant specular intensities (on the truncated specular feature) to have negligible specular intensities. The net effect of eliminating truncation is to decrease the width of the specular feature and make measurements more susceptible to small errors.

7. A SHAPE FROM SPECULARITY SYSTEM

A system has been implemented which computes local surface properties from images of specular surfaces [13]. The system currently stands alone, but will be used in the more general context of the SUCCESSOR vision system. The shape from specularity system is primarily designed to perform the computations described in Section 4. This section describes the implementation of the system.

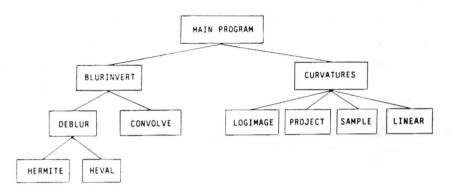

FIG. 17.   System structure.

7.1. Overview of System Structure

At a high level of abstraction, the problem is best solved in two steps. The first step is to deblur the input specular intensity image. The second step is to compute local surface properties from the image resulting from step 1.

The system designed to solve the problem preserves this two step structure. Figure 17 is a diagram of the modules in our system with arcs indicating module interactions. From this diagram we see that there is a clean separation between the deblurring task and the task of computing local surface properties. First the main program invokes a function called BLURINVERT to deblur the input image. After the deblurring task is completed, the function CURVATURES is called to compute local surface properties. The next two subsections give overviews of the BLURINVERT and CURVATURES functions.

7.2. Overview of BLURINVERT

The BLURINVERT function is used to deblur the Gaussian blurred input image. This is accomplished in two stages. First, the deblurring convolution kernel is generated by DEBLUR. Then the CONVOLVE function is called to perform the convolution of the blurred input image with the constructed deblurring kernel. Two functions are used by DEBLUR to manipulate the Hermite polynomials required to generate the deblurring filter. The function HERMITE uses a dynamic programming scheme to compute coefficients of all Hermite polynomials up to some specified degree. The function HEVAL is used to evaluate Hermite polynomials at fixed values of the polynomial parameter.

7.3. Overview of CURVATURES

Given a deblurred specular irradiance image, the CURVATURES function computes the principal curvatures and directions of the surface at specular points. CURAVATURES first uses the function LOGIMAGE to transform the irradiance image into the α angle image of Section 4. The CURVATURES function then systematically computes 1D curvature at different directions in the tangent space to the surface. The function PROJECT is used to compute the metric transform between the tangent space to the surface and the image. This is necessary to ensure that the system samples the angle image at equidistant angles on the surface. The function SAMPLE is used to sample the α angle image in a specified direction. Finally, the function LINEAR is used to compute the least squares curvature given the data generated by PROJECT and SAMPLE.

8. EXPERIMENTAL RESULTS

The system described in Section 7 has consistently generated accurate surface descriptions from images of specular surfaces. In this section we give examples of our system's performance on real images of metal objects illuminated by a point source. Figures 18a, 19a, and 20a are images of circular cylinders of varying radii. Each cylinder is oriented such that its axis is perpendicular to the axis of the imaging device. Figure 21a is the image of a sphere. The actual statistics of the surfaces are given in Table 1. For these images, our system computed normal curvature κ_n in 16 directions. The dotted lines in the images indicate the direction of maximum curvature as determined by the system. Figures 18b, 19b, 20b, and 21b are plots of irradiance along the dotted lines in 18a, 19a, 20a, and 21a. Note that in Fig. 21 the specularity is truncated, but we are still able to compute accurate surface statistics. Table 2 gives the second-order surface statistics computed by the system. Error represents the percent of error in the computation of the largest curvature of the surface. The small errors can be attributed to quantization effects, noise introduced during the measurement process, and the various simplifications made to the specular model.

9. SUMMARY AND IMPLICATIONS

Understanding specular reflection is important for any vision system which must interpret a world containing glossy objects. Using a model developed by optics researchers, we have shown that we can accurately predict the appearance of specular features in an image. In addition we have shown how to compute the local orientation and principal curvatures and principal directions of a specular surface by examining image intensities on a specularity. These statistics give a complete local characterization of the surface up to second order. Unlike previous work, our derivations have included the effects of surface roughness and microstructure on the appearance of specular features.

A system has been implemented which computes local surface properties from images of specular objects. A laboratory setup has been arranged which allows us to capture images to test our system. The system has consistently produced accurate surface descriptions despite the fact that the high intensity and small spatial extent of specularities makes measurements difficult. Significant aspects of the implementation are discussed in Section 7. Examples of experimental results are given in Section 8.

The ability to predict intensity-based features such as specularities opens up interesting possibilities for model-based vision. Previous model-based vision systems have restricted their predictions to the structure of edges which will be observed for a given model. An ability to predict intensity-based features will significantly enhance the top–down capabilities of a model-based vision system. Clearly it is advantageous to be able to make stronger predictions about an image by using additional information about the imaging process. Another important advantage of predicting intensity-based features is that this prediction can provide strong guidance to low level intensity-based visual processes. By making predictions about the

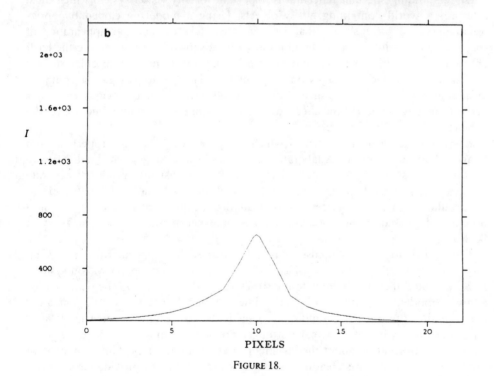

PIXELS

FIGURE 18.

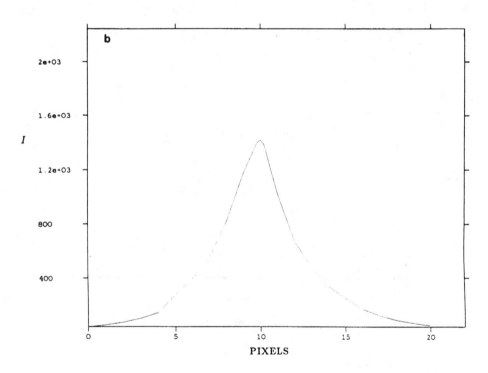

FIGURE 19.

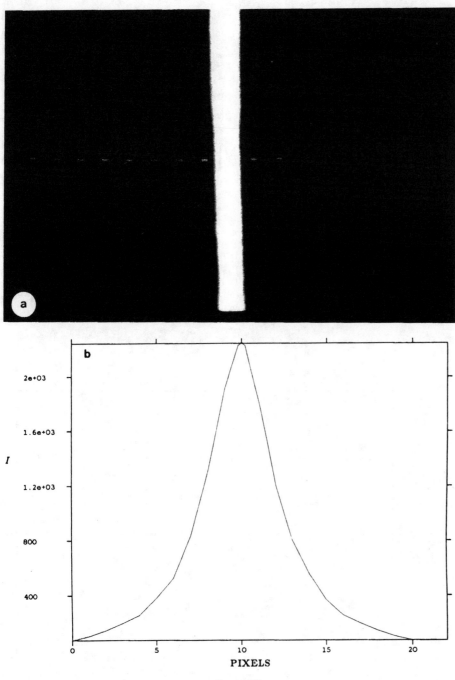

FIGURE 20.

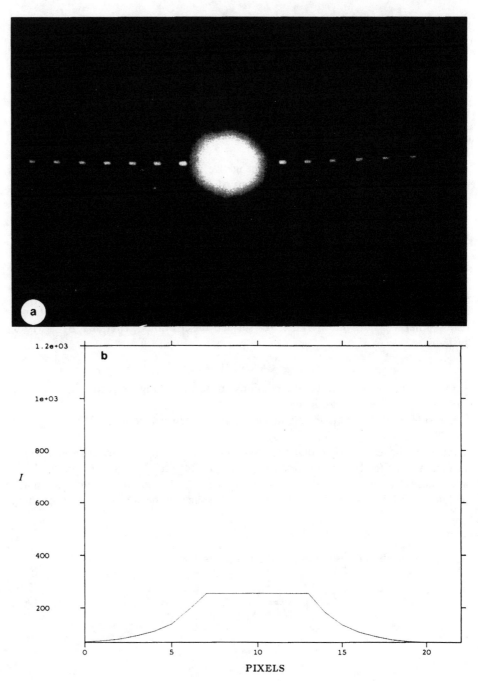

FIGURE 21.

TABLE 1
Actual Surface Statistics

Object	κ_1	θ_1	κ_2	θ_2
Cylinder$_1$	0.286	0.0	0.0	1.571
Cylinder$_2$	0.400	0.0	0.0	1.571
Cylinder$_3$	1.333	0.0	0.0	1.571
Sphere$_1$	0.500	—	0.500	—

appearance of intensity patches in an image we can hope to further unify the goals of the low level and high level mechanisms of a model-based vision system.

More important than being able to predict the appearance of specularities from surface models is our system's ability to invert the process. We have shown how to infer local second-order surface shape from specular images. This capability provides a vision system with strong generic information about a surface in a scene using strictly bottom–up processing. Inferring shape information from specularity is particularly important when viewing metal surfaces because other shape cues such as shading and texture are often not present. For other kinds of surfaces, shape information from specularity can be combined with shape information obtained using other cues to improve the 3D surface descriptions generated by a vision system.

APPENDIX

In this Appendix we derive the relationship between tangent vectors to a surface and their projections in an image.

Consider a 3D coordinate system such that the viewer is looking down the z-axis and P_0 is at the origin (Fig. A1).

At P we have $\mathbf{N} = \mathbf{H}$ so that the vector $\mathbf{H}$ is normal to the tangent space to the surface at P. We choose to define angles in the tangent space in the counterclockwise sense from $y = 0$ and in the half space $x \geq 0$. Denote the normal to the surface at P by $\mathbf{N} = (\mathbf{N}_1, \mathbf{N}_2, \mathbf{N}_3)$. The tangent space to the surface at P is given by

$$\mathbf{N}_1 x + \mathbf{N}_2 y + \mathbf{N}_3 z = 0. \tag{A1}$$

Along $y = 0$, the unit vector V_0 in the tangent space is

$$V_0 = \left(\frac{-\mathbf{N}_3}{\sqrt{\mathbf{N}_3^2 + \mathbf{N}_1^2}}, 0, \frac{\mathbf{N}_1}{\sqrt{\mathbf{N}_3^2 + \mathbf{N}_1^2}} \right). \tag{A2}$$

TABLE 2
Computed Surface Statistics

Object	κ_1	θ_1	κ_2	θ_2	Error %
Cylinder$_1$	0.297	0.0	0.001	1.57	3.9
Cylinder$_2$	0.397	0.0	0.001	1.57	0.9
Cylinder$_3$	1.356	0.0	0.002	1.57	1.7
Sphere$_1$	0.514	0.0	0.534	1.57	2.8

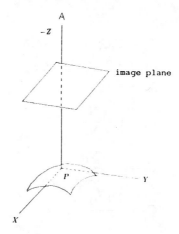

FIG. A.1. The projection geometry

To simplify the notation let

$$K_1 = \frac{-N_3}{\sqrt{N_3^2 + N_1^2}}, \qquad K_2 = \frac{N_1}{\sqrt{N_3^2 + N_1^2}}. \tag{A3}$$

Let θ be the angle of interest in the tangent space. The goal is to find a unit vector $V_1 = (x_1, y_1, z_1)$ which lies in the tangent space and makes an angle θ with V_0. The angle θ provides the constraint

$$x_1 K_1 + z_1 K_2 = \cos\theta. \tag{A4}$$

From (8) we must require

$$x_1 N_1 + y_1 N_2 + z_1 N_3 = 0 \tag{A5}$$

and since V_1 is a unit vector we have

$$x_1^2 + y_1^2 + z_1^2 = 1. \tag{A6}$$

Equations (A4), (A5), (A6) may be solved uniquely for x_1, y_1, z_1 in the half space $x \geq 0$. Briefly, the solution is

$$z_1 = \frac{-R_2 + \sqrt{R_2^2 - 4R_1 R_3}}{2R_1} \tag{A7}$$

$$x_1 = C_4 - C_5 z_1 \tag{A8}$$

$$y_1 = \frac{-x_1 N_1}{N_2} - \frac{z_1 N_3}{N_2}, \tag{A9}$$

where

$$R_1 = C_1 C_5^2 + C_2 - C_3 C_5 \qquad \text{(A10a)}$$

$$R_2 = -2C_1 C_4 C_5 + C_3 C_4 \qquad \text{(A10b)}$$

$$R_3 = C_1 C_4^2 - 1; \qquad \text{(A10c)}$$

$$C_1 = 1 + \frac{\mathbf{N}_1^2}{\mathbf{N}_2^2} \qquad \text{(A11a)}$$

$$C_2 = 1 + \frac{\mathbf{N}_3^2}{\mathbf{N}_2^2} \qquad \text{(A11b)}$$

$$C_3 = \frac{2\mathbf{N}_1 \mathbf{N}_3}{\mathbf{N}_2^2} \qquad \text{(A11c)}$$

$$C_4 = \frac{\cos \theta}{K_1} \qquad \text{(A11d)}$$

$$C_5 = \frac{K_2}{K_1}. \qquad \text{(A11e)}$$

A special case occurs when $\mathbf{N}_2 = 0$. For this case we use (A4)–(A6) to arrive at

$$z_1 = \frac{-\mathbf{N}_1 \cos \theta}{K_1 \mathbf{N}_3 - K_2 \mathbf{N}_2} \qquad \text{(A12)}$$

$$x_1 = \frac{\cos \theta - z_1 K_2}{K_1} \qquad \text{(A13)}$$

$$y_1 = \sqrt{\left(1 - z_1^2 - x_1^2\right)}. \qquad \text{(A14)}$$

We use (A7)–(A14) to compute the components of V_1.

Assuming an orthographic projection and examining the geometry of Fig. A1, we see that the x_1, y_1 components of V_1 give us the projected vector we are seeking in the image. Let θ' be the image angle corresponding to V_1. Then

$$\theta' = \tan^{-1}\left(\frac{y_1}{x_1}\right). \qquad \text{(A15)}$$

ACKNOWLEDGMENTS

This work has been supported by an NSF graduate fellowship, AFOSR Contract F49620-82-C-0092, and ARPA Contract N000-39-84-C-0211. The authors thank Professor Hesselink for generously providing laboratory space and equipment and Rami Rise for his work in designing the mechanical parts for the experiments. We also thank Vishvjit Nalwa for providing useful comments on a draft of this paper.

REFERENCES

1. H. Andrews and B. Hunt. *Digital Image Restoration*, Prentice–Hall, Englewood Cliffs, NJ, 1977.
2. A. Blake, Specular Stereo, in *Proceedings, 9th Int. Joint Conf. Artif. Intell., Los Angeles, August 1985*, pp. 973–976.

3. J. Blinn, Models of light reflection for computer synthesized pictures, *Comput. Graphics* **11**, No. 2, 1977, 192–198.

4. G. Brelstaff and A. Blake, *Detecting Specularities and Inferring Surface Shape*, Edinburgh University Computer Science Department Working Paper, Janauary 1987.

5. R. Brooks, Symbolic reasoning among 3D models and 2D images, *Artif. Intell.* **17**, 1981, 285–348.

6. A. Bruss, *The Image Irradiance Equation: Its Solution and Application*, MIT AI Memo 623, June 1981.

7. D. Chelberg, H. Lim, and C. Cowan, ACRONYM model-based vision in the intelligent task automation project, in *Proceedings, Image Understanding Workshop, 1984*.

8. E. N. Coleman, Jr. and R. Jain, Obtaining 3D shape of textured and specular surfaces using four-source photometry, *Comput. Graphics Image Process.* **18**, 1982, 309–328.

9. R. Cook and K. Torrance, A reflectance model for computer graphics, *Comput. Graphics* **15** No. 3, 1981, 307–316.

10. P. Deift and J. Sylvester, Some remarks on the shape-from-shading problem in computer vision, *J. Math. Anal. Appl.* **84**, No. 1, 1981, 235–248.

11. J. Foley and A. Van Dam, *Fundamentals of Interactive Computer Graphics*, Addison–Wesley, Reading, MA, 1982.

12. W. E. L. Grimson, *Binocular Shading and Visual Surface Reconstruction*, MIT AI Memo 697, 1982.

13. G. Healey, *Solving the Inverse Specular Problem*, Stanford Computer Science Department Programming Project, March 1986.

14. B. K. P. Horn, Obtaining shape from shading information, in *The Psychology of Computer Vision* (P. Winston, Ed.), McGraw–Hill, New York, 1975.

15. B. K. P. Horn, Understanding image intensities, *Artif. Intell.* **8**, 1977, 201–231.

16. B. K. P. Horn, *Robot Vision*, MIT Press, Cambridge, MA, 1986.

17. R. Hummel, B. Kimia, and S. Zucker, Gaussian blur and the heat equation: Forward and inverse solutions, in *Proceedings, Comput. Vision and Pattern Recognit.*, San Francisco, June 1985.

18. K. Ikeuchi, Determining surface orientations of specular surfaces by using the photometric stereo method, *IEEE Trans. Pattern Anal. Mach. Intell.* **3**, No. 6, 1981, 661–669.

19. G. Klinker, S. Shafer, and T. Kanade, Using a color reflection model to separate highlights from object color," *Proceedings, First International Conference on Computer Vision, London, June 1987*, pp. 145–150.

20. E. Kreyszig, *Introduction to Differential Geometry and Reimannian Geometry*, University of Toronto Press, Toronto, Canada, 1968.

21. B. Phong, Illumination for computer generated pictures, *Commun. ACM* **18**, 1975, 311–317.

22. S. Shafer, *Optical Phenomena in Computer Vision*, TR 135, University of Rochester, 1984.

23. S. Shafer, Using color to separate reflection components, *Color Res. Appl.* **10**, No. 4, 1985, 210–218; Technical Report TR 136, University of Rochester, April 1984.

24. E. Sparrow and R. Cess, *Radiation Heat Transfer*, McGraw–Hill, New York, 1978.

25. M. Spivak, *Differential Geometry*, Vol. II, Publish or Perish, Berkeley, 1979.

26. K. Takai, F. Kimuar, and T. Sata, A fast visual recognition system of mechanical parts by use of three dimensional model, source unknown. (First author is with Canon, Inc., Tokyo.)

27. K. Torrance and E. Sparrow, Theory for off-specular reflection from roughened surfaces, *J. Opt. Soc. Amer.* **57**, 1967, 1105–1114.

28. R. Woodham, Photometric stereo: A reflectance map technique for determining surface orientation from image intensity, *Proc. SPIE* **155**, 1978.

Determining Surface Orientations of Specular Surfaces by Using the Photometric Stereo Method

KATSUSHI IKEUCHI, MEMBER, IEEE

Abstract—The orientation of patches on the surface of an object can be determined from multiple images taken with different illumination, but from the same viewing position. The method, referred to as photometric stereo, can be implemented using table lookup based on numerical inversion of reflectance maps. Here we concentrate on objects with specularly reflecting surfaces, since these are of importance in industrial applications. Previous methods, intended for diffusely reflecting surfaces, employed point source illumination, which is quite unsuitable in this case. Instead, we use a distributed light source obtained by uneven illumination of a diffusely reflecting planar surface. Experimental results are shown to verify analytic expressions obtained for a method employing three light source distributions.

Index Terms—Bin of bolts and nuts, distributed light source, glossy object, reflectance map, shape from shading, surface inspection.

Manuscript received November 29, 1979; revised February 26, 1981.
The author is with the Computer Vision Section, Electrotechnical Laboratory, Ministry of International Trade and Industry, Ibaraki 305, Japan.

I. INTRODUCTION

THIS paper addresses the problem of determining local surface orientation of specular materials from the intensity information under different illumination, but from the same viewing position. This method is referred to as photometric stereo and was first formulated by Woodham [2]. Here, we concentrate on objects with a specularly reflecting surface, since these are of importance in industrial applications. Previous methods [2], [11] intended for diffusely reflecting surfaces employed point source illumination, which is quite unsuitable in this case.

Historically, Horn solved the image intensity equations [11] in order to obtain an object shape from shading information. Horn used a method of characteristic strip expansion for solving the image intensity equation which is a nonlinear first-order partial differential equation. Horn then introduced the reflectance map [3] in order to refine the image intensity equation. This map represents the relations between surface orientation and image intensity in the gradient space. Woodham developed a novel technique called photometric stereo [2] using the reflectance map. This photometric stereo is based on the following fact: if a pair of images of the same object are obtained by varying the direction of incident illumination but from the same viewing direction, we can draw a pair of different reflectance maps, because the reflectance map depends on the direction of the light source. So far, surface orientation is determined locally by the intensity pairs recorded at each image point as an intersection of constant brightness lines on the reflectance maps. This photometric stereo is very rapid and is free from noise compared with Horn's method, since surface orientation is determined locally. Horn and Sjoberg [1] showed how to calculate the reflectance map from NBS's BRDF (B_i-directional reflectance distribution function) analytically.

II. BASIC TOOLS AND RELATIONSHIPS

A. The Reflectance Map [1], [3] and Photometric Stereo [2]

The reflectance map represents the relationship between surface orientation and image intensity in gradient space [1]. We can express the geometric dependence of the reflectance characteristics of a surface in terms of the slope components p and q, used axes in gradient space [1],

$$p = \partial z/\partial x, \quad q = \partial z/\partial y \quad (1)$$

where z is the elevation of the surface and x, y are the spatial coordinates. If we take the direction from the surface to the viewer as the direction of the z-axis, then the reflectance properties of a surface patch depend on (p, q), the direction of the surface normal, and (ps, qs), the direction of the source [1]. Each point in the gradient space corresponds to a particular surface orientation based on the direction of the viewer. If we know the reflectance characteristics of an object, we can calculate how bright a surface element with that orientation will appear. It is convenient to use contour lines to connect those points in gradient space which correspond to surface orientations which give rise to the same apparent brightness. It is because of these contour lines that the resulting diagram is referred to as the "reflectance map" [1], [3]. The reflectance map is denoted by $R(p, q)$.

Using the reflectance map, the basic imaging equation is

$$E_j(x, y) = R_j(p, q, x, y) \quad (2)$$

where $E_j(x, y)$ is the brightness (image irradiance) in the image-forming system at the point (x, y) in the image plane. This equation contains two unknown variables p, q and one quantity E_j, which can be measured in the image.

In the above equation, the subscript j is used to denote different illumination conditions. For each value of the subscript, a different image is obtained, and a different reflectance map applies. If two images are taken, two such equations provide constraints on the possible values of p and q. This permits us to solve for the gradient. Because of the nonlinearity of the equations, however, a number of solutions may be found at times. In this case, a third image may be

used to disambiguate the remaining possibilities. This is the principle of photometric stereo [2].

Orthographic projection can simplify the calculation considerably. If we can assume that the object is small compared with the distance to the source and the image-forming system, then the viewer direction can be approximated as the axis of the image-forming system and we can treat the system as orthographic. There are two merits to this approximation. One is that we can neglect the effect of position. The right-hand side of (2) depends only on (p, q). Namely, we can apply the same reflectance map on all points in the image. Another benefit is that we can calculate $R(p, q)$ more easily because the approximation fixes the viewing direction. So we can, for example, rotate the source keeping the phase angle constant (the phase angle is the angle between the source and the viewer, measured at the object). This means that we can obtain a new reflectance map just by rotating the old one [3].

B. Relationship Between Source Radiance and Image Radiance

One of the main points of our discussion here is that we consider only specular components of reflectance when we calculate the reflectance map, since many industrial materials are made of metal and have strong specularity and little diffuse reflection. Experiments show that only 1 or 2 percent of the incident light is reflected diffusely from some metallic surfaces, with most of the rest reflected specularly. We cannot treat this kind of material using the usual Lambertian model for reflection of light from a surface. It is also clearly inappropriate to use point sources to illuminate such a surface, since very few surface patches will be oriented correctly to reflect any light and we will only see virtual images of the point sources.

Three relationships exist between a light source and the image plane. The first one is that between source radiance and incident radiance on a sample surface. Next, and most important, is that between incident radiance and emitting radiance from the surface (this is captured in the reflectance map). The last one is that between emitting radiance and image irradiance. (See Fig. 1.)

Since we use an extendent light source, incident radiance in one direction is the same as source radiance in the same direction in an extended light source. Namely,

$$L_i = L_s. \quad (3)$$

For a specular surface and an extended light source [1], [4]

$$L_e(\theta_e, \phi_e) = L_i(\theta_e, \phi_e + \pi). \quad (4)$$

Thus, even though the source distribution may be complicated, only the contribution from a single direction $(\theta_e, \phi_e + \pi)$ need be considered. The relationship between reflected radiance and image irradiance is

$$E_p = \{(\pi/4)(d/f_p)^2 \cos^4 \alpha\} L_e \quad (5)$$

where F_p, d, α are effective focal length of lens, the diameter of the entrance aperture, and the off-axis angle, respectively [2].

Finally, using (3)-(5) we see that image irradiance at a particular point is proportional to the source radiance in a

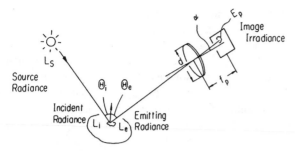

Fig. 1. Relationships between light source, surface, and image formation system are depicted.

direction which depends on the orientation of the corresponding surface patch [1]. That is, the brightness of a particular surface patch is simply equal to the brightness of the part of the extended source which it happens to reflect. Thus, even though the source distribution may be complicated, only the contribution from a single direction (p_s, q_s) need be considered at any time.

It is convenient to change from the local coordinate system to the viewer-centered coordinate system [1] because the reflectance map is defined in a viewer-centered coordinate system, and the light source distribution is given based on the direction of the viewer (see Fig. 2). We can rewrite image irradiance using the viewer-centered coordinate system:

$$E_p(p_n, q_n) = \gamma L_e(p_n, q_n) = \gamma L_s(p_s, q_s) \qquad (6)$$

where γ is a constant. Namely, we observe this E_p as image irradiance under an extended light source on specular materials.

We can finally express brightness distribution in the gradient space:

$$R(p_n, q_n) = l_s(p_s, q_s) \qquad (7)$$

where

$$p_n = \partial z/\partial x = -\cos \phi_n \tan \theta_n$$

$$q_n = \partial z/\partial y = -\sin \phi_n \tan \theta_n$$

$$p_s = 2p_n/(1 - p_n^2 - q_n^2)$$

$$q_s = 2q_n/(1 - p_n^2 - q_n^2). \qquad (8)$$

On the other hand, the inverse transformation is

$$p_n = p_s(\sqrt{1 + p_s^2 + q_s^2} - 1)/(p_s^2 + q_s^2)$$

$$q_n = q_s(\sqrt{1 + p_s^2 + q_s^2} - 1)/(p_s^2 + q_s^2). \qquad (9)$$

We will use a differentiable single-valued function as the reflectance function. Roughly speaking, since we determine surface orientation from brightness, if the function is not single-valued, the inverse function theorem does not apply, and this makes the situation very difficult.

III. APPLICATION PROBLEMS

A. Total Schema of the System

The technique requires two kinds of tasks; one is the off-line (precomputing) job and the other is the on-line (real-time) job which is rather simple compared with the off-line job. The simplicity implies rapid calculation, as desired in any hand–eye system. The off-line job consists of making the

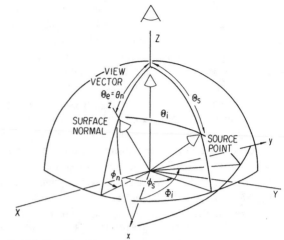

Fig. 2. Relationships between a local coordinate system and a viewer coordinate system.

reflectance map and constructing a lookup table. The on-line job consists of reading the image brightness and determining orientations of a surface patch based on the lookup table. Fig. 3 shows the information flow between the on-line job and the off-line job.

B. Off-Line (Precomputing) Job

Consideration of Light Source: We use a Lambertian surface as a source plane. It is illuminated by a linear lamp as shown in Fig. 4. Although a spherical shaped source can easily cover directions of more than 90°, it is difficult to build such a device and difficult to control the distribution of the light on it, particularly if interflection is taken into account. On the other hand, if we use a planar source illuminated by a lamp, the brightness distribution is complicated, but we can calculate a reflectance map. It is possible to cover angles of more than 90° by making a box-like source. In that case, however, we have to treat each plane separately because the surface normal is not differentiable at the intersection of two planes. Thus, we consider one plane surface which is assumed to have the Lambertian characteristics in order to obtain some analytic results to help in the design of the system. This plane is illuminated by a line source as a representative case.

Brightness distribution on the surface is calculated using (11). Let f be the flux rate per unit source length [W/(m·sr)]. Then the total irradiance E[W/m²] is

$$E = \int f \cos \theta_1 \cos \theta_2 /r^2 \, dt. \qquad (10)$$

From $\cos \theta_1 = \sqrt{X^2 + l_0^2}/r$ and $\cos \theta_2 = l_0/r$, we can finally get

$$E = (fl_0/2a^2)\left[\left\{\tan^{-1}\left(y + \frac{L}{2}\right)\middle/a - \tan^{-1}\left(y - \frac{L}{2}\right)\middle/a\right\}\right.$$
$$\left. + \left\{a\left(y + \frac{L}{2}\right)\middle/\left(a^2 + \left(y + \frac{L}{2}\right)\middle/\left(a^2 + \left(y - \frac{L}{2}\right)^2\right)\right\}\right]$$

$$(11)$$

where $a = \sqrt{x^2 + l_0^2}$, L is the length of the line source, and l_0

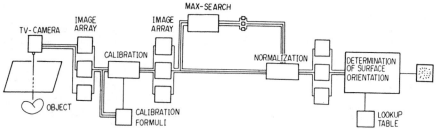

Fig. 3. The overall schema of the experiment. The technique consists of two types of jobs: off-line preparation of tables (represented by broken lines) and on-line processing. Image brightness is obtained by using a TV camera. We search for the maximum value of brightness in each array. Brightness arrays are calibrated and normalized. Surface orientations are obtained from the lookup table.

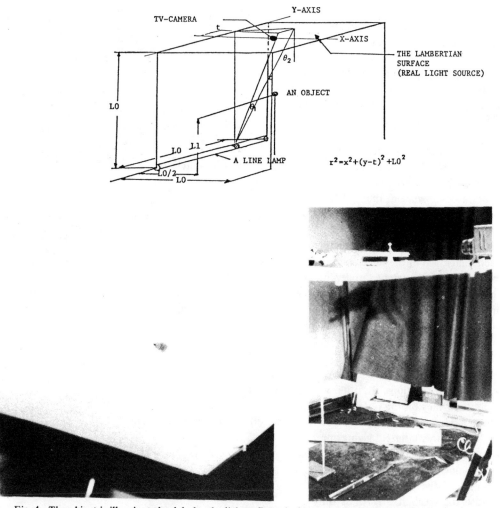

Fig. 4. The object is illuminated solely by the light reflected of an overhead Lambertian surface. This surface receives light from a linear lamp positioned below so as not to illuminate the object. The TV camera peers through a small hole in the overhead surface. Brightness distribution from a linear lamp on the Lambertian surface can be calculated in (12). We used three linear lamps, placed symmetrically, 120° apart. In the center of the lamps there is a hole. The object is observed through the hole.

is the distance between the line source and the Lambertian surface.

We put an object just under the point $(x, y) = (0.5l_0, 0.0)$. $E(x, y)$ is a symmetric function with respect to y. Thus, it is natural to put an object somewhere on the x axis. $E(x, 0)$ is an s-shape function and has an inflection point near $x = 0.5l_0$. At that point $E(0.5l_0, 0.0) = 0.715E(0.0, 0.0)$. So

it is convenient to put an object just under this point. If we denote the distance from the surface to the object as l_1,

$$x = -l_1 p_s + l_0/2$$

$$y = -l_1 q_s. \tag{12}$$

Finally, we can get a reflectance map

$$R(p_n, q_n) = [fl_0/2\{(-l_1 p_s + l_0/2)^2 + l_0^2\}]$$
$$\cdot \tan^{-1}\{(-l_1 q_s + l_0/2)/\sqrt{(-l_1 p_s + l_0/2)^2 + l_0^2}\}$$
$$- \tan^{-1}\{(-l_1 q_s - l_0/2)/\sqrt{(-l_1 p_s + l_0/2)^2 + l_0^2}\}$$
$$+ \{\sqrt{(-l_1 p_s + l_0/2)^2 + l_0^2}\,(-l_1 q_s + l_0/2)\}/$$
$$\{(-l_1 p_s + l_0/2)^2 + l_0^2 + (-l_1 q_s + l_0/2)^2\}$$
$$- \{\sqrt{(-l_1 p_s + l_0/2)^2 + l_0^2}\,(-l_1 q_s - l_0/2)\}/$$
$$\{(-l_1 p_s + l_0/2)^2 + l_0^2 + (-l_1 q_s - l_0/2)^2\}]$$
$$(13)$$

where p_s and q_s are as defined above, and $L = l_0$, $2l_1 = l_0$ because these values are found to be optimal upon simulation.

We used three linear lamps, placed symmetrically 120° apart, about the hole through which the object is observed. One lamp is turned on at a time, giving rise to a reflectance map like the one shown in (13).

By using three reflectance maps, we can determine the surface orientation. Theoretically, it is possible to determine the orientation by using two maps only. However, there may be more than one solution because of the nonlinearity of the equations. If we use three maps, we can determine a unique solution easily as shown in Fig. 5.

The Lookup Table: The most convenient method for converting a triple of measured brightness to an orientation is by means of a lookup table made from the reflectance map. This table, indexed by quantized brightness measurements, contains surface orientations. Each dimension of the table corresponds to brightness measurements of surface patches under one of the three sources. Each entry of the table contains a surface orientation corresponding to a triple.

We, however, construct a two-dimensional lookup table. Although it is possible to make a three-dimensional lookup table, it is better to make a two-dimensional table. An observed triple often contains measurement error. This may cause an observed triple to give no solutions. In other words, it may occur that three contour lines on the reflectance maps do not intersect at a point under noisy situations. On the other hand, two contour lines always intersect giving approximate solutions. It means that a two-dimensional lookup table always gives two alternative solutions. The weakest brightness measurement often contains a relatively large amount of measurement error. We can use the weakest brightness only to choose a solution among two alternatives. Namely, we look up an entry using the two largest brightness values. The entry gives two alternative solutions. Then we use the weakest brightness for deciding the correct solution among the two alternatives. For that purpose, each entry of the lookup table should contain two alternatives, and each alternative should contain a surface orientation and the weakest brightness at that point in the gradient space. Thus, the lookup table can be two-dimensional (see Fig. 6).

We construct the lookup table by using Newton's method. An elegant method exists in the case of a Lambertian reflector and point sources [2]. In our case, however, we have to calculate it numerically. Specifically, we solve two expressions

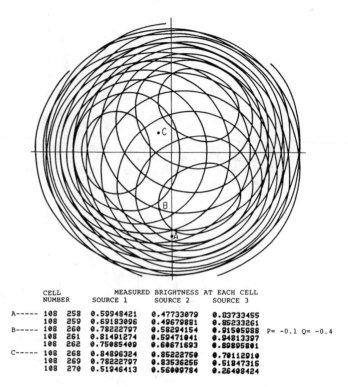

CELL NUMBER		MEASURED BRIGHTNESS AT EACH CELL		
		SOURCE 1	SOURCE 2	SOURCE 3
A-----	108 258	0.59948421	0.47733079	0.03733455
	108 259	0.69183096	0.49679881	0.85233261
B-----	108 260	0.78222797	0.58294154	0.91505988
	108 261	0.81491274	0.59471041	0.94813397
	108 262	0.75085409	0.60671693	0.89895801
C-----	108 268	0.84896324	0.85222750	0.70112910
	108 269	0.78222797	0.83536255	0.51847315
	108 270	0.51946413	0.56009784	0.26408424

P= -0.1 Q= -0.4

Fig. 5. How to use the reflectance map method. Three reflectance maps drawn in the same gradient space. Since the lamps are symmetrically configured, brightness distribution corresponding to a linear lamp is also symmetric having the same shape. Thus, we need to calculate only one distribution and then rotate it 120°. The resulting function is the desired one. We can determine (p, q) from three values of brightness, where each brightness value corresponds to each source condition. For example, switching on source 1 will yield a brightness value of 0.7822 at cell B. Similarly, source 2 and source 3 yield 0.5329 and 0.9150, respectively. From the above diagram, we note that the point $(-0.1, -0.4)$ satisfies this triple. Hence, the surface orientation at the cell B is $(-0.1, -0.4)$.

like (13) for p and q. The expressions differ in the brightness distribution of the source, obtained by turning on one of the three linear lamps.

The N-dimensional Newton method involves solving the simultaneous linear equations

$$f_j + \sum_{k=1}^{n} \partial f_i/\partial x_k|x_k = x_k^{[j]}(x_k^{[j+1]} - x_k^{[j]}) = 0 \qquad (14)$$

where f_i is the ith element of a vector function of n dimensions and $x_i^{[j]}$ is the jth element of a solution vector of the jth iteration.

We can rewrite (13) as (17) in our case of a planar source illuminated by a linear lamp. The two mapping functions are

$$f(p_s, q_s) = R(p_s, q_s) - E_n$$
$$g(p_s, q_s) = R(p_s \cos \alpha - q_s \sin \alpha, p_s \sin \alpha + q_s \cos \alpha) - E_m$$
$$(15)$$

where α is an angle between two light sources and E_n, E_m are image brightness corresponding to the (n, m) element of the lookup table. We can finally get

$$X^{[j+1]} = X^{[j]} - (F')^{-1} F \qquad (16)$$

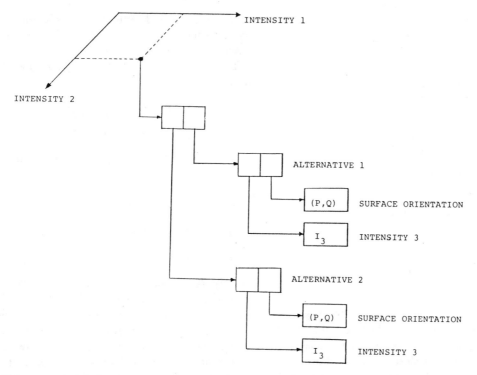

Fig. 6. The structure of the lookup table. Each entry of the lookup table contains two alternatives. Each alternative contains a surface orientation and the weakest brightness at that point in the gradient space. Thus, we can look up an entry using the two largest brightness values. The entry gives two alternative solutions. Then we can use the weakest brightness obtained for deciding the correct solution among the two alternatives on comparing the value with two values contained in the entry.

where $X = {}^t(p_s, q_s)$, $F = {}^t(f, g)$ and $(F')^{-1}$ is an inverse of the Jacobian matrix. (See Fig. 7.)

C. On-Line (Real-Time) Job

Image brightness is obtained from the TV camera. To reduce the noise typical of these devices, we took more than one picture per light source, and arrays corresponding to the same light source were averaged. The resulting three brightness arrays, one for each light source, were the input to the photometric stereo system.

Before applying the reflectance map (the lookup table) to image arrays obtained, we have to calibrate and normalize the image arrays. The output of the TV camera is not linearly proportional to original brightness. The algorithm has to convert the output into some values linearly proportional to the original brightness values. We call this process calibration. In the meantime, original brightness always contains an effect of albedo. Normalization process cancels the effect of albedo. In other words, the algorithm has to identify a brightness value, say 100 units, in an image array with some value, say 0.5, in the reflectance map. The algorithm normalizes the brightness using the maximum brightness in an image array as a base value.

Brightness calibration is done by using a six-step Kodak gray scale. Since the output of the TV camera is not linearly proportional to original brightness values, the algorithm has to convert the output to certain values proportional to image brightness. We always put a Kodak scale besides the object

so that all pictures taken by the TV will contain a gray scale. By using obtained brightness corresponding to the scale, the algorithm makes a formula for linear interpolations. The algorithm can convert the output to certain values proportional to image brightness based on this formula.

The algorithm has to normalize image brightness. Although the scale tells the algorithm exact information about the relationship between real brightness and the output of the TV camera, the algorithm cannot apply the relationship to the object because the albedo ratio depends on materials of objects. In other words, the gray scale has a property of a Lambertian surface, and metals reflect light as a specular surface. Also, the amount of light reflected depends on materials of objects, even though objects reflect light specularly. Thus, the algorithm needs to cancel the effect of albedo.

The maximum brightness in an image array comes from 1.0 in the reflectance map. If an object is convex, you can find any direction among directions of the surface patches. In other words, a convex object always has at least one surface patch corresponding to any point in the gradient space. Thus, an image array always contains a brightness value corresponding to 1.0 in the reflectance map, provided that the object is convex and the visual angle is wide enough.

The algorithm can cancel the effect of the varying albedo using the obtained maximum value:

$$\rho = I(x, y)/R(p, q) \qquad (17)$$

where ρ is the albedo. At the brightest part, $R = 1.0$. The

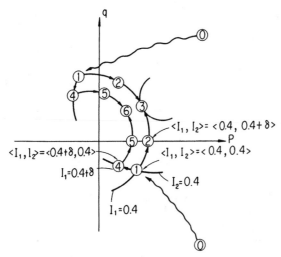

Fig. 7. How to get entire solutions using Newton's method.

algorithm has I_{max} (the maximum value in an image array) and R (1.0 in the reflectance map) at the brightest part. Thus, ρ is obtained as $I_{max}/1.0$. Entire values in the image array will be normalized using this albedo ratio ρ. Finally, each point on the image has a triple of quantized brightness applicable to the reflectance map (the lookup table). It is interesting that the maximum point always contains important information and that this search process resembles Land's lightness search model [7].

From the lookup table we can get the surface orientation. The lookup table entry is accessed using the two largest brightness values. To increase the accuracy of computation and economy of memory use, the first dimension represents the largest image brightness. The second dimension represents the second largest. Each element of the matrix contains the corresponding surface orientation and the smallest image brightness.

Since the nonlinearity gives rise to two solutions for each intensity pair, we have to decide which one is the real one. We choose a surface orientation by comparing the distance between the actual third image brightness and the element of the matrix. The third brightness is always weak and likely to contain errors. It is only used to decide which of the two alternatives obtained from the other brightness is the correct one.

IV. Experiment and Discussion

Our experimental results are shown in Fig. 8. Fig. 8(a) shows three brightness arrays. These arrays are input information to the photometric system. No surface normals are shown in areas where insufficient information was available in the three images to determine them accurately [see Fig. 8(b)]. The choice of light source distribution affects the extent of these regions as well as the accuracy with which surface normals can be found.

We tried two kinds of relaxation methods. The first one is suitable to on-line systems. This method reads from the lookup table twice, exchanging the second and third bright-

ness values, and determines the solution by averaging the two previous solutions. The simple schema can give good results as shown in Fig. 8(c).

The other method is to find $(p_{i,j}, q_{i,j})$ at each mesh point which minimizes

$$e_{ij} = (p_{i,j} - p_{i,j}^*)^2 + (q_{i,j} - q_{i,j}^*)^2$$
$$+ \lambda[\{I_1 - R_1(p_{i,j}, q_{i,j})\}^2$$
$$+ \{I_2 - R_2(p_{i,j}, q_{i,j})\}^2 + \{I_3 - R_3(p_{i,j}, q_{i,j})\}^2]$$

$$(18)$$

where

$$P_{i,j}^* = \tfrac{1}{4}(p_{i,j-1} + p_{i,j+1} + p_{i-1,j} + p_{i+1,j})$$
$$q_{i,j}^* = \tfrac{1}{4}(q_{i,j-1} + q_{1,j+1} + q_{i-1,j} + q_{i+1,j})$$

and I_1, I_2, I_3 are measured image irradiance under the light source 1, 2, 3, respectively, and R_1, R_2, R_3 are their reflectance maps. The former part of (18) is called the surface smoothness constraints [8], and the latter is called the image irradiance constraints. (See [8] for more detail.) Namely, the solution is pulled towards each constraint line of the reflectance map and towards the local constraints from the surface smoothness. It ends up in some compromise position which minimizes overall "strain" [8]. This method is implemented iteratively. Fig. 8(d) shows the result obtained using this iterative method. The algorithm not only smoothed the output, but also extended the area in which a solution could be found. This method is appropriate for off-line systems. Fig. 8(e) is a generated surface from their surface orientations.

A direct application of our technique is an industrial hand-eye system that picks up an object out of a jumble of material [see Fig. 9(a)]. Although our technique cannot correctly determine the surface orientation when there is mutual illumination, it does provide the means for detecting this condition, since the three measurements will be inconsistent. In this fashion erroneous results are avoided. This is important, since the manipulator might otherwise be sent to a position where it would collide with other parts.

Another application of this technique is the inspection of the surface condition of metals. If a surface has a crack, stain, or finger print, the image brightness triple yields inconsistent values in the area of the blemish (see Fig. 10).

This technique may be combined with the Marr-Poggio-Grimson stereo technique now being developed [9], [10]. Their technique detects depth cues and works well when the image contains many discontinuities. On the other hand, our method detects surface orientation directly and works well when the object is smooth. The combination can be established if the output of one of the two stereo cameras is fed to our system while the two outputs from two cameras are fed to their system. We feel that the composite system will produce an excellent representation of the object, just as people are believed to use both stereo and shading information to construct a symbolic image of the visual world.

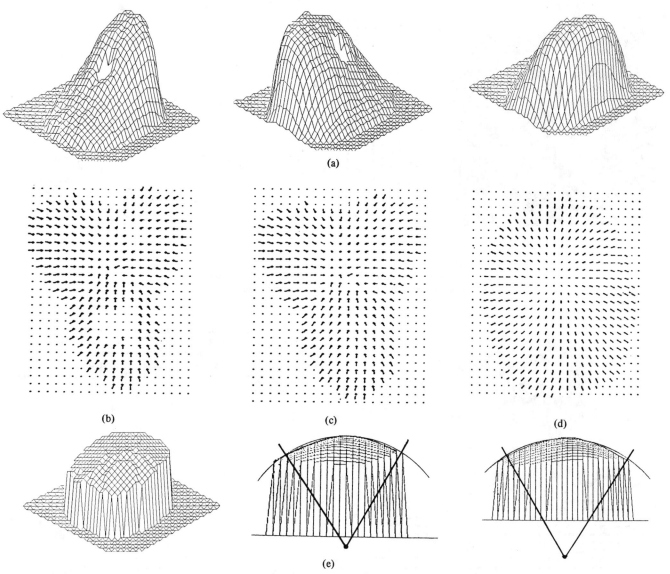

Fig. 8. (a) Three brightness arrays. Each array corresponds to one of the three lamps. These arrays are input information to the photometric stereo system. (b) Direct output from the system. No surface normals are shown in areas where there was insufficient information. (c) Output from the first relaxation method. This method would be suitable for a hand–eye system when real-time response is vital. The system reads from the lookup table twice, exchanging the second and third brightness values. The solution is determined by averaging the two previous values. This simple schema can give good results. (d) Output from the iterative relaxation method. This method finds solutions which minimize the difference of the actual brightness and the theoretical brightness using a constraint derived from surface continuity. (e) i) Generated surfaces from the needle diagrams. ii) A surface along the x axis. The bold line represents the actual surface. The diagram is obtained from the photometric stereo system. iii) A surface along the y axis.

ACKNOWLEDGMENT

The author would like to extend his sincere appreciation to Prof. B. K. P. Horn and Prof. P. H. Winston of M.I.T. Discussions with Dr. Y. Shirai of ETL, H. Murota of the University of Tokyo, and R. Sjoberg of M.I.T. were helpful. Thanks go to B. Roberts of M.I.T. and M. Brooks of the University of Essex for proofreadings.

REFERENCES

[1] B. K. P. Horn and R. W. Sjoberg, "Calculating the reflectance map," *Appl. Opt.*, vol. 18, no. 11, 1979.

[2] R. J. Woodham, "Photometric stereo: A reflectance map technique for determining surface orientation from image intensity," *Proc. SPIE*, vol. 155, 1978.

[3] B. K. P. Horn, "Understanding image intensity," *Artificial Intell.*, vol. 8, no. 11, 1977.

[4] F. E. Nicodemus *et al.*, "Geometrical considerations and nomenclature for reflectance," Nat. Bur. Stand., U.S. Dep. Commerce, NBS Monograph 160, 1977.

[5] M. P. D. Carmo, *Differential Geometry of Curves and Surfaces.* Englewood Cliffs, NJ: Prentice-Hall, 1976.

[6] D. M. Erway, "Exact color reproduction," B.S. thesis, Dep. Elec. Eng. Comput. Sci., Massachusetts Inst. of Technol., Cambridge, 1978.

[7] E. Land and J. McCann, "Lightness and retinex theory," *J. Opt. Soc. Amer.*, vol. 61, no. 1, 1971.

[8] K. Ikeuchi, "Numerical shape from shading and occluding contours in a single view," Artificial Intell. Lab., Massachusetts Inst. of Technol., Cambridge, AI-Memo. 566, 1980.

[9] D. Marr and T. Poggio, "Cooperative computeration of stereo disparity," Artificial Intell. Lab., Massachusetts Inst. of Technol., Cambridge, AI-Memo. 364, 1976.

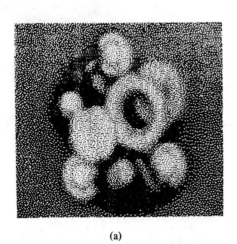

(a)

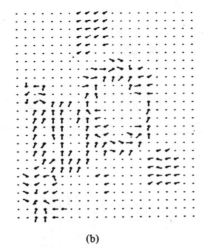

(b)

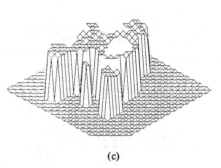

(c)

Fig. 9. (a) Binary image of a jumble of nuts and bolts. (b) Needle diagram obtained from image of nuts and bolts. (c) The generated surfaces are elevated in order to distinguish easily from the surrounding area.

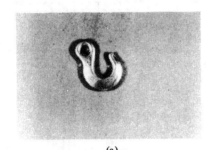

(a)

[10] W. E. L. Grimson and D. Marr, "A computer implementation of a theory of human stereo vision," in *Proc. Image Understanding Workshop*, Science Applications, Inc., Washington, DC, 1979.

[11] B. K. P. Horn, "Determining shape from shading," in *The Psychology of Computer Vision*, P. H. Winston, Ed. New York: McGraw-Hill, 1975.

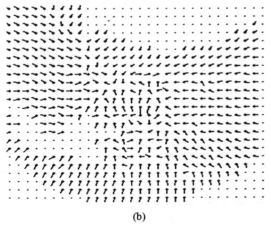

(b)

Fig. 10. (a) A picture of a hook which contains a lot of cracks and stains. (b) Needle diagram of the hook. There exists a printed figure "3" in the central area of the object. This can be seen as randomness of needles in the area. At the low right side, the surface is rather dark and the system is unable to determine the surface orientations at that area. Note that a relaxation method would fail to identify this central region as different from its surroundings.

Katsushi Ikeuchi (M'78) was born in Osaka, Japan, on May 29, 1949. He received the B.Eng. degree in mechanical engineering from Kyoto University, Kyoto, Japan, in 1973, and the M.Eng. and D.Eng. degrees in information engineering from the University of Tokyo, Tokyo, Japan, in 1975 and 1978, respectively.

From 1978 to 1980 he was a member of the Artificial Intelligence Laboratory, Massachusetts Institute of Technology, Cambridge. Since 1980 he has been with the Electrotechnical Laboratory, Ministry of International Trade and Industry, Ibaraki, Japan, where he has been working on computer vision.

Dr. Ikeuchi is a member of the Institute of Electronics and Communication Engineers of Japan.

Geometry from Specularities

Andrew Blake

Robotics Research Group,
Department of Engineering Science,
University of Oxford,
Parks Rd., Oxford OX1 3PJ,
England.

Gavin Brelstaff[1]

Dept. Computer Science
University of Edinburgh
Mayfield Rd.,
Edinburgh EH9 3JZ
Scotland.

ABSTRACT

A new algorithm is described for accurate computation of horizontal and vertical stereoscopic disparities of specular points, relative to nearby surface points. Knowledge of such disparities is shown to restrict principal curvatures (with known light-source position) to lie on a hyperbolic constraint-curve. Monocular appearance of specularities is known also to constrain surface shape. We show that, at best, there remains a fourfold ambiguity of local surface curvature. In the case of a light source that is of unknown shape but known to be compact (in a precise sense), elongated specularities have geometrical significance. The "axis" of such a specularity, back-projected onto the surface tangent plane, approximates to a line of curvature. The approximation improves as the specularity becomes more elongated and the source more compact.

These ideas have been incorporated into an existing stereo vision system, and shown to work well with real and simulated images.

1 Introduction

Specular reflection represents both a problem and an opportunity in vision. It is a problem in that it disrupts processes such as edge-detection and stereoscopic matching, but an opportunity in that highlights or specularities are cues for surface geometry.

Clearly, to make any progress, it must be possible to detect specularities. Various processes have been proposed and tested. Some involve chromatic analysis [9,17] others achromatic analysis of intensity [25,8]. This paper addresses problems of geometric inference rather than of specularity detection but for the purposes of demonstrating a working system an achromatic specularity detector has been used. It builds on the ideas of Ullman's S-operator [25] and on the retinex process of Land and others [16,13,3], and will be the subject of a future paper.

A discussion of the inference of shape from specularity is given by Koenderinck and van Doorn [15]. They elegantly expound the qualitative behaviour of specularities under viewer motion. Specularities travel freely in elliptic or hyperbolic regions, speeding up near parabolic lines, annihilating and being created, in pairs, on the parabolic lines. They travel most slowly in regions of high curvature and hence, for a given static viewer position, specularities are most likely to be found where curvature is high. More recently a number of quantitative analyses of specularity have emerged. Several involve active vision systems extending photometric stereo [26] to deal with and profit from specular reflection [7,14,20]. Other approaches are based on mathematical models of specular reflection, including specification of reflectance map, fixing various free parameters of the

model by measurements from individual specularities [1, 11,12]. In view of the difficulty of achieving adequate photometric models for specularity and of fixing their parameters from image data [11] it seems reasonable to try to restrict modelling to simple ray optics and the law of reflection. Koenderinck and van Doorn's work is in this vein, and other more quantitative models have been investigated [21,24,2]. In this paper we extend that theme and illustrate it by incorporating analysis of specularity in a stereoscopic vision system.

2 Stereoscopic analysis of specular reflection

The basic principle of "specular stereo" is illustrated in figure 1. According to the simple physics of curved mirrors, a specularity will appear behind a glossy, convex surface but (generally) in front of a

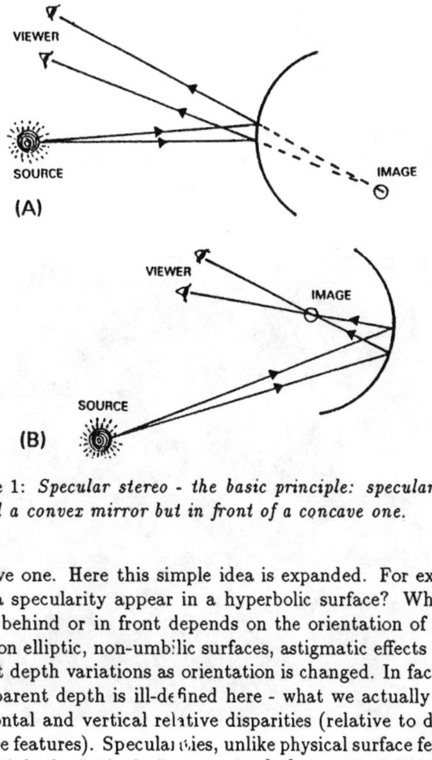

Figure 1: *Specular stereo - the basic principle: specularities appear behind a convex mirror but in front of a concave one.*

concave one. Here this simple idea is expanded. For example, how does a specularity appear in a hyperbolic surface? Whether it appears behind or in front depends on the orientation of the surface. Even on elliptic, non-umbilic surfaces, astigmatic effects produce apparent depth variations as orientation is changed. In fact the notion of apparent depth is ill-defined here - what we actually observe are horizontal and vertical relative disparities (relative to disparities of surface features). Specularities, unlike physical surface features, need not satisfy the "epipolar" constraint [18] so vertical disparity may be non-zero. This is illustrated by the example of figure 2, in which

---
[1]Current address: IBM UK Scientific Centre, Winchester.

relative displacement of the specularity in the right image (relative to the left) is oblique.

Both horizontal and vertical disparities vary as the orientation of the stereo baseline changes relative to lines of curvature on the surface.

Analysis of the stereoscopic viewing geometry will establish the relationship between surface shape and measured disparities. It is helpful to consider two different kinds of analysis. The first is approximate, a linear system "driven" by the interocular separation, with disparities as its output. The characteristics of the linear system depend on surface geometry (curvature and orientation). This analysis appeared in earlier work [2] and is useful for characterising degeneracies - special alignments at which geometric inference will fail. An exact analysis is more convenient for computation as well as being more accurate and a method has been developed for accurate computation of relative disparities, together with error bounds.

2.1   Viewing geometry

The geometry for stereoscopic viewing of a specularity is shown in figure 3. Vectors **d**, the stereo baseline, is assumed known, as is **S**, the position of the light source . The directions $\hat{\mathbf{V}}, \hat{\mathbf{W}}$ of vectors **V**, **W** are given by the measured positions of the specularities in the left and right images. The projection of displacement vector **r** onto the left (say) image plane forms the observed relative disparity vector.

A few equations suffice to describe this geometrical arrangement. First, there are three cycles amongst the vectors:

$$\mathbf{V} + \mathbf{d} - \mathbf{r} - \mathbf{W} = 0, \tag{1}$$

$$\mathbf{V} - \mathbf{L} - \mathbf{S} = 0 \tag{2}$$

and

$$\mathbf{L} - \mathbf{L}' - \mathbf{r} = 0. \tag{3}$$

The physical law of reflection is expressed in the following equations:

$$\hat{\mathbf{n}} = \frac{\hat{\mathbf{V}} + \hat{\mathbf{L}}}{|\hat{\mathbf{V}} + \hat{\mathbf{L}}|}. \tag{4}$$

$$\hat{\mathbf{n}}' = \frac{\hat{\mathbf{W}} + \hat{\mathbf{L}}'}{|\hat{\mathbf{W}} + \hat{\mathbf{L}}'|}. \tag{5}$$

Finally, the vector **F** is computed from conventional stereoscopic viewing of the surface reference mark C, and it is assumed to lie in the tangent plane to the surface at A, so that

$$(\mathbf{F} - \mathbf{V}).\mathbf{n} = 0. \tag{6}$$

Of course C does not lie *exactly* in the tangent plane, but the error is small provided the surface reference C is not too far away from the ray intersection point A (figure 4).

2.2   Computation of surface depth

We need to know surface depth $V = |\mathbf{V}|$ but, so far, know only the depth of a nearby non-specular "reference point" on the surface. In fact V can be computed from equation (6), given that $\hat{\mathbf{V}} = \mathbf{V}/V$ is known from the position of the specularity in the left image, by the iterative algorithm given in figure 5. This algorithm has not been

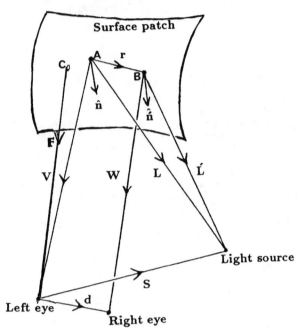

Figure 3: *A smooth patch of surface is illuminated by a point source along vector* **L**. *Light striking point A is specularly reflected along vector* **V** *into the left eye. Similarly, light incident at B traverses* **W** *into the right eye. Surface normals at A and B are* $\hat{\mathbf{n}}$ *and* $\hat{\mathbf{n}}$ *respectively. Vector* **r** *separates A and B. The stereo base-line lies along vector* **d**. *A surface marking lies nearby A at C.*

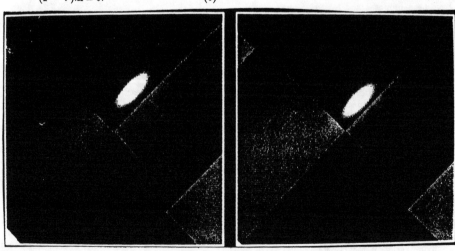

Figure 2: *An example of a specularity whose "motion" relative to surface features is oblique - vertical relative disparity is not zero.*

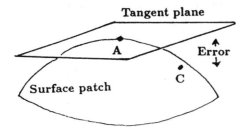

Figure 4: *Point C lies on the surface at a little distance from A. Along this distance the surface curves gently out of the tangent plane. So the "tangent plane assumption" is only an approximation.*

$$i = 0 \; , \; |\mathbf{V}|^{(i)} = |\mathbf{F}|.$$
repeat
$$\begin{aligned} i &= i + 1, \\ \mathbf{V}^{(i)} &= |\mathbf{V}|^{(i)} \hat{\mathbf{V}}, \\ \mathbf{L}^{(i)} &= \mathbf{V}^{(i)} + \mathbf{S}, \\ \hat{\mathbf{n}}^{(i)} &= \left(\hat{\mathbf{V}} + \hat{\mathbf{L}}^{(i)} \right) / |\hat{\mathbf{V}} + \hat{\mathbf{L}}^{(i)}|, \\ |\mathbf{V}|^{(i)} &= \left(\hat{\mathbf{n}}^{(i)} \cdot \mathbf{F} \right) / \left(\hat{\mathbf{n}}^{(i)} \cdot \hat{\mathbf{V}} \right). \end{aligned}$$
while $\left| |\mathbf{V}|^{(i)} - |\mathbf{V}|^{(i-1)} \right| > 0.01 |\mathbf{F}|.$
$\mathbf{V} = \mathbf{V}^{(i)}, \; \hat{\mathbf{n}} = \hat{\mathbf{n}}^{(i)}, \; \mathbf{L} = \mathbf{L}^{(i)}.$

Figure 5: *Iterative algorithm for computing* $\mathbf{V}$*, the position at which the reflected ray strikes the specular surface.*

proved to converge, but seems well-behaved in practice.

2.3   Local surface shape

It is clear that, having computed $\mathbf{V}$ as above, $\mathbf{n}$ can be obtained from (4) and (2). In other words, knowing the light source position, and observing a nearby surface reference point C suffices to compute surface orientation at the specular point A.

So much for surface orientation - but what about local surface curvature? Curvature is expressed in terms of the Hessian matrix H. Choosing coordinates such that $\mathbf{x} = (x, y)$ is the restriction of $\mathbf{r} = (x, y, z)$ to the tangent plane at A:

$$z = \frac{1}{2} \mathbf{x} . (H\mathbf{x}) + O(|\mathbf{x}|^3). \tag{7}$$

(The choice of coordinates allows an arbitrary rotation in the tangent plane, which is conveniently fixed by choosing the $(0,1,0)$ direction to be orthogonal to vector $\mathbf{V} - \mathbf{L}$.) Differentiating (7), one can obtain

$$\delta \mathbf{n} = -H\mathbf{x} + O(|\mathbf{x}|^2). \tag{8}$$

where $\delta \mathbf{n}$ is the component of $\hat{\mathbf{n}}' - \hat{\mathbf{n}}$ lying in the tangent plane. Now $\hat{\mathbf{n}}$ is known already, so to compute $\delta \mathbf{n}$ we need $\hat{\mathbf{n}}'$ - which can be calculated from (5) if $\mathbf{W}$ is known. Observing that $\mathbf{r}.\mathbf{n} = 0$ and substituting this into (1) yields the following formula, in terms of measured quantities, for $|\mathbf{W}|$:

$$|\mathbf{W}| \approx \frac{(\mathbf{V} + \mathbf{d}) \cdot \hat{\mathbf{n}}}{\widehat{\mathbf{W}} \cdot \hat{\mathbf{n}}} \tag{9}$$

2.4   Graphical representation of geometric constraints

Measurement of $\delta \mathbf{n} = (\delta n_1, \delta n_2)$ imposes 2 independent constraints, via equation (8), on the components of the hessian H. But H is a symmetric matrix:

$$H = \begin{pmatrix} H_{xx} & H_{xy} \\ H_{xy} & H_{yy} \end{pmatrix}, \tag{10}$$

so it has 3 independent components. Clearly, further information is required to fix all 3. This can be obtained either by moving the stereo baseline or by monocular observation of the shape of the specularity. Both possibilities will be discussed in due course. In the meantime, it is natural to ask whether the 2 constraints already obtained represent *intrinsic* information about the surface - that is, do they constrain principal curvatures of the surface?

Brelstaff [4] has shown that there is indeed an intrinsic constraint. The principal curvatures κ_1, κ_2 are constrained to lie on a hyperbola. Equivalently, the corresponding principal radii of curvature r_1, r_2 lie on a hyperbola:

$$-B^2 = (r_1 - A)(r_2 - A) \tag{11}$$

where

$$A = \frac{\delta \mathbf{n} . \mathbf{x}}{|\delta \mathbf{n}|^2} \quad \text{and} \quad B = \sqrt{\frac{|\mathbf{x}|^2}{|\delta \mathbf{n}|^2} - A^2}, \tag{12}$$

as shown in figure 6. Without loss of generality, we can require $r_1 \leq r_2$, so that the constraint set includes only one curve of the hyperbola. For example, the family of surfaces allowed by the constraint in figure 6 is illustrated in figure 7.

Note that a concave interpretation is excluded - the surface must be either convex or hyperbolic in this case. Generally a concave or convex interpretation is excluded according as the sign of A is positive or negative respectively - that is, according to the sign of $\delta \mathbf{n}.\mathbf{x}$. Recently a similar condition has been obtained by Zisserman et al. [27] but with the additional advantage of being independent

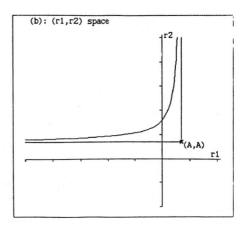

Figure 6: *Stereo analysis constrains the principal radii of curvature* $r_i = 1/\kappa_i$*,* $i = 1, 2$ *to lie on the upper curve of a hyperbola.*

of light source position. In that case, the discriminant is simply the scalar product of the projections onto the image plane of $\mathbf{x}$ (i.e. the relative disparity vector) and the baseline $\mathbf{d}$.

2.5   Test for umbilic points

Spheres are an interesting special case for specular stereo. Since $H = \kappa I$ on the surface of a sphere, we can see from equation (8) that $\delta \mathbf{n}$ and $\mathbf{x}$ are parallel vectors or, in practice:

$$|\delta \mathbf{n} \times \mathbf{x}| \ll |\delta \mathbf{n}||\mathbf{x}|. \tag{13}$$

If the parallelism test is passed the point *may* be umbilic - but of course this is not guaranteed. For instance it could be on any surface patch specially oriented so that one line of curvature lies (locally) in the plane of the incident and reflected rays. So the test can be used to eliminate umbilic interpretations.

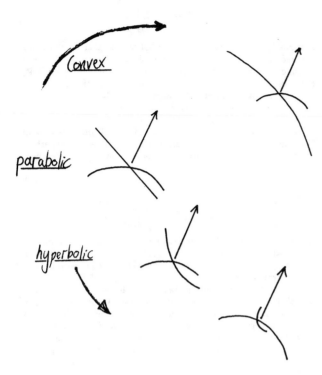

Figure 7: *Specular stereo - constraints on local shape. A typical constraint, illustrated algebraically in figure 6, admits a one-parameter family of interpretations. Generally either concave or convex interpretations are excluded - in this case concave ones.*

3   Specular stereo as a linear system

The previous section explained how constraints on geometry can be inferred from stereoscopic observation of a specularity and a nearby non-specular "reference" point. Further analysis can be applied, linearising the relationship between displacement vector **x** and baseline vector **d**. Whilst this offers no particular improvements in convenience of computation of shape constraints, it affords insights into geometric degeneracies, and clarifies the relationship with conventional stereoscopic disparity.

Simplifying previous analysis [2], the linear system can expressed as

$$2V(MH - \kappa_{VL}I)\mathbf{x} = \mathbf{w}, \tag{14}$$

where

$$\mathbf{w} = (-d_1 + d_3 \tan \sigma, -d_2)^T, \tag{15}$$

$$M = \begin{pmatrix} \sec \sigma & 0 \\ 0 & \cos \sigma \end{pmatrix}, \tag{16}$$

σ is surface slant at A, and

$$\kappa_{VL} = \frac{1}{2}\left(\frac{1}{V} + \frac{1}{L}\right) \tag{17}$$

- a term familiar from the elementary ray-optics of lenses. It can be thought of as an "apparent curvature" induced on a viewed plane, owing to the finite distances from the plane to source and viewer. This linear approximation is valid whenever the baseline is relatively short, that is, when

$$|\mathbf{d}| \ll |\mathbf{V}| \cos \sigma, \tag{18}$$

and provided the surface does not focus incoming rays to a point or line close to the centre of projection (see discussion of degeneracy below).

3.1   Horizontal and vertical disparity

One insight that equation (14) affords is that the specular stereo constraints on H depend solely on imaging geometry ($\kappa_{VL}, V, M, \mathbf{w}$) and on the displacement vector **x**. So the only *measured* quantity involved is **x**, which is intimately related to the relative stereoscopic disparity δ, as follows:

$$\mathbf{x} = VP\delta \tag{19}$$

where

$$P = \begin{pmatrix} \sec \sigma & 0 \\ 0 & 1 \end{pmatrix} \tag{20}$$

The two-component vector δ represents the horizontal and vertical disparities of the specularity, *relative* to the disparities of the nearby surface reference point. The conventional view of stereoscopic vision is that useful depth information is encoded entirely in horizontal disparities. Vertical disparity is fixed by epipolar geometry, so its possible influence is limited to calibration of view geometry and, in human vision, an associated illusory distortion, the induced effect [19].

For specularities, this is not the case. Vertical disparity plays a strong role, in two ways. First, vertical disparities that violate epipolar geometry are *evidence* that specular reflection is occuring. Second, as we just saw, measured vertical disparity imposes an independent constraint on curvature, in addition to the one imposed by measurement of horizontal disparity. Both of these computational "truths" call for psychophysical investigation. Is either theory exploited in human vision?

3.2   Degeneracy

Inspection of the linearised imaging equation (14) reveals degeneracy when

$$\det(MH - \kappa_{VL}I) = 0.$$

What exactly is observed physically? First of all, this can happen only on non-convex surfaces (MH is negative definite on a convex surface) and even then only for special alignments - when the viewer collides with one or both "focal surfaces" [27][4]. A convex surface lies *in front* of its focal surfaces; the viewer cannot collide with a focal surface because the convex surface is in the way. When degeneracy does occur, stereoscopic analysis fails for the very simple reason that the specularity is visible only in one eye. Moreover, the focussing effect ensures that when it is visible, it is likely to be very bright.

3.3   Combining information from two baselines

A final result from the linearised view is that when two independent baselines are used, for instance when a stereo observer is in motion, the baselines should not be nearly parallel. If they are not, **H** can be recovered completely; if they are, computation of **H** is ill-conditioned. Details of the argument are given in [2].

4   Monocular analysis of specular reflection

A simple theory of monocular analysis of specularity [2] is summarised here, and possible ambiguity of interpretation is explored. In the case of a circular source, assuming that the diameter of the source is known, there is a possible fourfold ambiguity of interpretation, corresponding roughly to independent inversion of each principal curvature, but generally accompanied by some rotation (about the surface normal) of the lines of curvature.

The geometrical arrangement for monocular viewing, with a distributed source, is shown in figure 8. It mirrors the earlier stereo geometry but with the baseline between stereo views replaced by virtual baselines between pairs of points on the source. This duality

---

[4]The specularity is focussed onto a line or onto a blob, according as the rank of $MH - \kappa_{VL}I$ is 1 or 0 respectively.

can be tapped mathematically to derive a linear mapping relating the position δ_m of a specular point (in polar projection) to the angular position α on the source from which the illuminating ray came.

$$T\delta_m = \alpha \qquad (21)$$

where

$$T = 2VP^{-1}MH^*P, \qquad (22)$$

where

$$H^* = H - \kappa_{VL}M^{-1}, \qquad (23)$$

and P, H, M, κ_{VL} are defined as previously. Since T is symmetric, the mapping is a linear scaling in two orthogonal directions.

Consider the case of a circular source, so that points on the outline of the source satisfy

$$\alpha^T\alpha = \rho^2. \qquad (24)$$

The shape of the ellipse (on the polar projection) is obtained using the transformation (21) to give (using the fact that T is symmetric):

$$\delta_m^T T^2 \delta_m = \rho^2. \qquad (25)$$

If we assumed the source radius ρ were known, then observation of the elliptical shape of a highlight determines T^2, via equation (25). Hence T is known up to a fourfold ambiguity (the signs of the two eigenvalues of T are unknown). Then H can be computed directly from (21), so again there are four possibilities (figure 9). These four interpretations generally do *not* share common lines of curvature; but the discrepancy is small if the slant is modest. Moreover, provided principal curvatures are neither small nor nearly equal in magnitude

$$||\kappa_1| - |\kappa_2|| \gg 2\kappa_{VL}\sec\sigma,$$

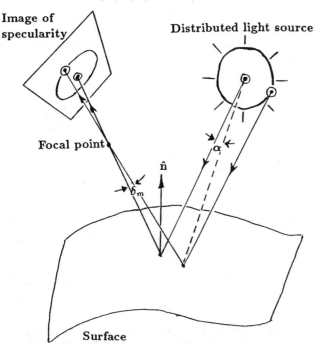

Figure 8: *Monocular analysis: A distributed light source of known shape is reflected by a curved surface as a specular image region. Surface curvature information may be inferred by measuring the shape in the image. A point on the source, transforms to a point on the specularity. The angular positions of two such points are specified by α and δ_m, for source and specularity respectively.*

the four possibilities for directions of lines of curvature collapse down to just two possibilities - this is the case in the example of figure 9.

Usually, real cameras do not form an image by polar projection, but by perspective projection. However the difference is more or less cosmetic. At a given point on the image, perspective projection is

related to polar projection by a linear transformation $\delta_m = Q\mathbf{X}$, where $\mathbf{X}$ is a position vector on the projection plane, and Q is a matrix. The elliptical specularity that appears on the image plane is given by

$$\mathbf{X}^T Q^T T^2 Q \mathbf{X} = \rho^2. \qquad (26)$$

Measurements made within the image plane can provide $(Q^T T^2 Q)$, from which T^2 can be computed.

4.1 Assuming a circular source

The analysis above assumed that the angular diameter (subtended at the surface) of the source was known. Often a more reasonable assumption is that the source is circular, but of *unknown* radius. There are now two possible cases.

1. The surface is locally almost flat - the magnitudes of the principal curvatures are of the order of κ_{VL} or smaller.

2. At least one principal curvature κ_1 is large - that is, it satisfies

$$\kappa_1 \gg \kappa_{VL}\sec\sigma.$$

This is much the more likely state of affairs since specularities tend to cling to highly curved patches - hence the likelihood of observing a specularity on such a patch is relatively great. In this case, since the $2V\kappa_{VL}I$ term in (22) is negligible, and since T^2 is known up to an arbitrary multiplicative constant, H can be computed from (22) up to fourfold ambiguity *and* an arbitrary multiplicative constant. However, computed curvatures are accurate only to within $\kappa_{VL}\sec\sigma$.

So even when absolute source size is unknown, monocular observation of a specularity still allows some inference about surface shape. This is what might be expected intuitively; an elongated specularity, for example, seems to suggest very unequal principal curvatures - a locally cylindrical surface in the extreme case. In fact this particular example might be expected to hold good even when the source is not known to be circular, but merely to be "compact". That expectation is justified below.

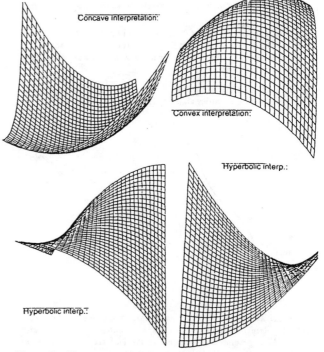

Figure 9: *Observation of an elliptical specularity, with a circular source of known radius, determines local curvature up to a fourfold ambiguity, as illustrated.*

4.2　Assuming a compact source

First we must define what is meant by a compact source. A source compactness $K > 1$ is defined as one that is bounded by concentric circles, with radii in the ratio $K : 1$, as in figure 10. The most

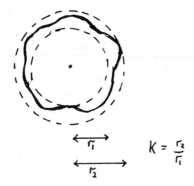

Figure 10: *Definition of compact source, in terms of bounding circles.*

compact source is therefore a circle ($K = 1$). The absolute size of the source is assumed to be unknown.

The task now is to use the monocular specularity equations (21, 22, 23) to make some inference about surface curvature, even though the shape of the source is unknown, merely constrained. It is proposed to estimate the direction of least curvature on the surface as follows. Take the direction in which the diameter of the specular blob is greatest (figure 11), and back-project it onto the surface tangent plane. If this estimate proves reliable it provides a third constraint, in addition to the two already provided by stereoscopic analysis. Then surface curvature, represented by the three parameters of H, can be computed [2].

However, there are three problems to be addressed:

1. The direction in which the diameter of the specular blob is greatest does not correspond exactly to an eigenvector direction of T.

2. If $\mathbf{u}$ is an eigenvector of T, then in the limit that its eigenvalue $\lambda \to 0$, it can be seen from (22) that $P\mathbf{u}$ is an eigenvector of H^* (with eigenvalue 0). However, when $\lambda \neq 0$ $\mathbf{u}$ only approximates to an eigenvector of H^*.

3. Even if the eigenvectors of H^* are successfully estimated, they correspond only approximately (23) to eigenvectors of H.

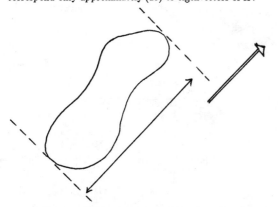

Figure 11: *Measuring the direction in which the diameter of a specular blob is largest. This corresponds approximately to an eigenvector of T. The approximation improves as the blob becomes more elongated, and as the source becomes more compact.*

What does all this amount to? Our procedure for estimating di-

rections of lines of curvature works, but is only approximate. The approximation improves as

- the blob becomes more elongated

- the source becomes more compact

- the surface slant decreases

- the surface becomes more curved (either cylindrically or elliptically).

The last of these factors deserves an additional comment. In fact our approximation will break down when the surface is close to planar (both curvatures small compared with $\kappa_{VL} \sec \sigma$). In that case nothing further can be inferred from the shape of the specularity. However this case will be relatively uncommon; specularities prefer to cling to highly curved surfaces. A specularity on a plane tends to be relatively fleeting, disappearing at the slightest viewer motion, especially when the total field of view is relatively narrow. In the remainder of the section these claims are backed up by the statement of formal results. Proofs use standard results of linear algebra, but are omitted here for lack of space.

The following three theorems answer, in turn, the three problems raised above, by providing error bounds. First, some definitions and assumptions. The source has compactness K. The specularity has aspect ratio $A > K^2$ (A is the ratio of maximum diameter to minimum diameter). The surface has curvatures $\kappa_{max}, \kappa_{min}$ with

$$|\kappa_{max}| > |\kappa_{min}|.$$

The surface is non-planar:

$$|\kappa_{max}| > 5\kappa_{VL} \sec \sigma.$$

Theorem 1 *The angular error in taking the direction in which the diameter of the specularity is greatest to be an eigenvector of T is bounded by*

$$\tan^{-1}\left\{ K \left(\frac{K^2 - 1}{A^2 - K^4} \right)^{\frac{1}{2}} \right\}. \tag{27}$$

Theorem 2 *If $\mathbf{u}$ is an eigenvector of T then the angular difference between $P\mathbf{u}$ and an eigenvector of H^* is bounded by*

$$\min\left[\sin^{-1}\left\{ \sin \sigma \left(1 - \sec^2 \sigma \frac{K}{A} \right)^{-\frac{1}{2}} \right\}, \sin^{-1}\left\{ \tan \sigma \left(\cos^2 \sigma \frac{A}{K} - 1 \right)^{-\frac{1}{2}} \right\} \right].$$
$$\tag{28}$$

Theorem 3 *The angle between eigenvectors of H, H^* is bounded by*

$$\sin^{-1}\left\{ \sin \sigma \left(3 \frac{|\kappa_{min}|}{|\kappa_{max}|} + 8 \frac{K}{A} \sec^2 \sigma \right)^{\frac{1}{2}} \right\}. \tag{29}$$

5　Results from the implemented system

Some of the principles described above have been incorporated in a software system. The main components are:

Feature detection Features for conventional stereo matching are obtained from an edge detector employing directional derivative-of-gaussian operators [6]. A combination of global and local analysis of the spatial distribution of intensity is then applied to identify specular reflections [4]. Those edge features which subsequently proved to be specular are then pruned from the list of "surface" features. Remaining surface features can then be matched using standard methods, and computed depths can safely be regarded as representing points that lie on a real surface. The danger of treating matched specularities as surface points is thus removed.

Feature description Specular features form "blobs" which may be irregular, but are often elliptical. The feature description consists of the direction of elongation of the blob, its length and its aspect ratio. In the case of an elliptical blob this is more or less equivalent to measuring the directions and lengths of the ellipse axes. For each specular feature, a nearby surface feature must also be identified, to serve as a "reference" for depth or disparity. The system simply chooses the surface feature that is closest to the specularity (in the left image); the closer it is the more accurate it is as a reference. However, features consisting of almost horizontal line segments are avoided as they are well known to yield inaccurate depth measurements.

Stereoscopic correspondence Our system employs the PMF software for stereoscopic correspondence and depth computation. This delivers depths of surface points, including those to be used as disparity references. Correspondence must also be established between specularities in right and left images. A conventional matcher is unsuitable here because epipolar constraints do not apply. On the other hand, the problem of false matches negligible for specular features since they are usually sparse. A simple matcher, employing rough comparision of blob features, has proved sufficient in our experiments.

Geometric inference Stereoscopic and monocular inference of geometry proceed separately, as detailed in previous sections, and finally inferences are pooled. In some cases local curvature is completely determined, in others merely constrained. Results are displayed by means of appropriate graphics, together with error bounds. They are also accessible at program-level for use in model-matching, geometric reasoning or other applications.

Error treatment Each measured quantity in the stereo analysis has uncertainty associated with it; this can be represented crudely by propagation of error bounds. By combining the errors it is possible to quantify the uncertainty of the quantities in the constraint equation (14). This can be done by summing square errors [22] at each step in the analysis. This method of combination strictly only applies to independent sources of uncertainty. As the uncertainties involved here are unlikely to be completely independent, room exists for refinement.

An example of the system in operation is shown in figure 12. Subwindows allow user intervention at various levels, from selection of images to tracing the inference steps. Line drawings at the bottom show detected, matched specularities, labelled 1 and 2. Results of geometric inference are summarised in the display at the lower left. The ellipse and needle indicate surface orientation. Numerical slant and tilt values are also shown. The line indicates the direction of the line of least curvature - note that this appears to coincide with the axis of the cylindrical cup on which the specularity (number 2) lies. In fact the cup is not quite cylindrical, and the system has inferred (see COMBINED EVIDENCE window) that the surface is hyperbolic. Further detail can be obtained by selecting "graph" to illustrate stereoscopic and monocular inferences, and their combination. The graph for stereoscopic inference is shown in figure 13. In an ideal, error-free world it would be simply a hyperbola as in figure 6. The effect of allowing for error in the components of the Hessian H is that the hyperbola is "thickened". So on the basis of stereoscopic information, the principal curvatures may take any values in the shaded set. Note that the *directions* of the lines of curvature are not fixed, but differ for different points in the set.

Now when monocular information is taken into account, only a small portion of the shaded set remains feasible - shown in black on figure 14. The combination of information works very simply: the specularity is observed to be very elongated, and this more or less fixes the directions of the lines of curvature (see earlier discussion). The black region consists of those solutions from the shaded set which correspond approximately to those computed directions.

Stereoscopic analysis for the other specularity (number 1 in figure 12) is shown in figure 15. In this case the specularity appears as a small blob, too small reliably to determine its shape. Hence (in the absence of information about the absolute size of the source) monocular analysis does not constrain local shape any further.

The pair of stereo images in figure 16 is computer generated, using a narrow field of view to exaggerate disparities. This makes it easy to see relative displacement of specularities, and how they relate to the shape of the underlying surface. The specularity is displaced both horizontally *and* vertically relative to surface markings. That is, there are both horizontal and vertical relative disparities - a vivid illustration of the earlier assertion that specularities may break epipolar constraints. (The specularity tends to cling to the line of greatest curvature, hence the relative motion is oblique.) Indeed, the non-zero relative vertical disparity is *evidence*, in principle, that the bright blob is indeed specular. The horizontal disparity is positive, leading correctly to a prediction that the surface is convex [27]. The true values of principal curvatures (denoted by the white cross) lies within the black region that indicates predicted curvatures with error bounds. Of course the data is computer generated and free of noise, but this does at least indicate that the error bound computations, which determine the extent of the feasible set (in black) in terms of image measurement errors are correct.

Finally, a real image (figure 17) is shown below, together with the results of geometric inference from specularity analysis. Surface curvatures have measured approximately, and fall within error bounds computed by the system. There are stereoscopic constraints as shown, but no monocular constraints; this is because the specularity is so nearly circular that ellipse axes cannot be reliably computed. Nonetheless, the shaded set does contain (just!) the measured values of surface curvature. Moreover, the black window at the bottom of the graph indicates that the system has found that the surface could be locally spherical (umbilic), according to the test described earlier (13).

6   Conclusions

Analysis of specularity is of potential assistance to geometric inference in machine vision. Stereoscopic and monocular analysis are complementary, and together can entirely determine local shape. A further role for vertical disparity has been demonstrated, in addition to its role in calibration of viewing geometry. Analysis of specularity has been incorporated into a stereoscopic vision system, and shown to yield usably accurate results. Some questions remain. How can such local shape measurements be integrated? Quantitative methods involving stereoscopic reconstruction are certainly available [11, 23] - can qualitative methods, bypassing depth maps, be found? Another question concerns motion: how much surface information can be extracted from specularities under extended displacement of the viewer?

A number of questions are raised too for human vision.

- Is vertical disparity   violation of epipolar constraints - used to identify bright features as specular?

- Can perceived surface curvature be manipulated by adjusting the disparities of a specularity?

- Can predicted fourfold ambiguity of curvature be realised in monocular views of specularities?

- Do monocular and stereoscopic analysis of specularities combine to fix perceived curvature, as predicted theoretically?

- Can the direction of displacement of a specularity in right and left stereoscopic views, resolve reversal ambiguities, as is theoretically predicted?

Acknowledgements

Discussion with A.Zisserman and with J.Mayhew, J.Frisby and S.Pollard is gratefully acknowledged. The PMF stereo system from AIVRU, Sheffield University proved invaluable and for the basis for experimentation. The support of IBM UK Scientific Centre, the Royal Society of London, the SERC and the University of Edinburgh are gratefully acknowledged.

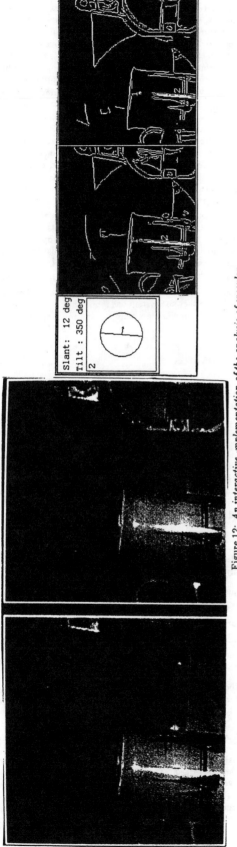

Figure 12: An interactive implementation of the analysis of specularities. (a) Stereo image pair. (b) Results of processing: edge detection output is labelled with specularities (marked 1 and 2); slant, tilt and line of (least) curvature for specularity number 2 are displayed at the bottom left.

slant: 12 deg
Tilt : 350 deg
2

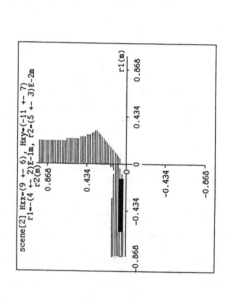

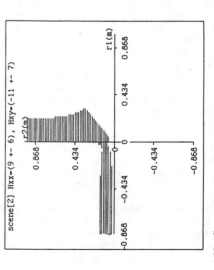

scene[1] Hxx=(2 +- 1)x10, Hxy=(9 +- 8)

scene[2] Hxx=(9 +- 6), Hxy=(-11 +- 7), r1=-(4 +- 2)E-1m, r2=(5 +- 3)E-2m

scene[2] Hxx=(9 +- 6), Hxy=(-11 +- 7)

Figure 13: Constraints from stereoscopic analysis of specularity number 2, in figure 12.

Figure 14: Combined stereoscopic and monocular constraints restrict the set of possible solution. for surface curvature to the black region.

Figure 15: Stereoscopic analysis of specularity number 1 in figure 12 restricts local surface curvatures to values within the shaded set.

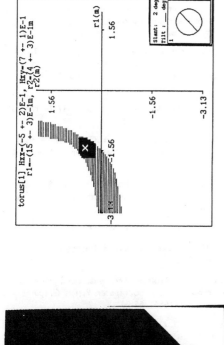

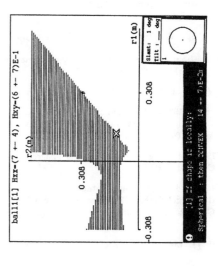

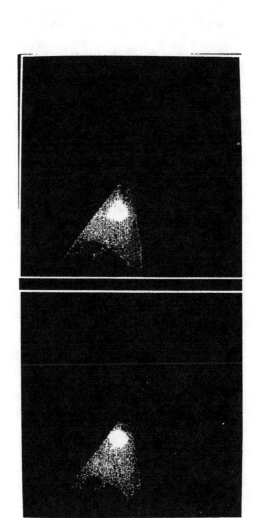

Figure 16: *Inner surface of of a torus ring with surface markings (artificial images). Stereoscopic constraints, shown shaded, are restricted to the black region by monocular analysis. The correct values of curvature (used in the geometric modeller) are indicated by a white cross.*

Figure 17: *Beach ball of 12cm radius.*

References

1. Babu, M.D.R., Lee, C-H. and Rosenfeld, A. (1985). Determining Plane Orientation From Specular Reflectance, *Pattern Recognition*, 18, 1, 53-62.

2. Blake, A. (1985). Specular Stereo. *Proc. IJCAI-85*, 2, 973-976.

3. Blake,A. (1985). Boundary conditions for lightness computation in Mondrian world. *CVGIP, 32*, 314-327.

4. Brelstaff,G.J. (1988). PhD thesis, University of Edinburgh.

5. Buchanan, C.S.B. (1987). Determining Surface Orientation from Specular Highlights, RCBV Tech. Report, RCBV-TR-87-19, University of Toronto.

6. Canny,J.F. (1983). Finding edges and lines in images. S.M. thesis, MIT, Cambridge, USA.

7. Coleman, E.N.Jr., and Jain, R. (1982) Obtaining 3-Dimensional Shape of Textured and Specular Surfaces Using Four-Source Photometry, Computer graphics and image processing, 18, 309-328.

8. Forbus, K. (1977). Light Source Effects A.I. Memo 422, A.I Lab., M.I.T.

9. Gershon, R., Jepson, A.D. and Tsotsos, J.K. (1987). Highlight Identification Using Chromatic Information, *Proc. IJCAI87 Milan*, 752-754.

10. Grimson, W.E.L. (1981). *From Images to Surfaces* M.I.T. Press, Cambridge Mass. U S.A..

11. Grimson, W.E.L. (1982). Binocular Shading and Visual Surface Reconstruction. M.I.T. A.I.Lab. Memo No 697.

12. Healey, G., and Binford, T.O. (1987). Local shape from specularity. Proc. First Int. Conf. on Computer Vision, London, 151-160

13. Horn, B.K.P. (1974). Determining Lightness from an Image. Computer Graphics and Image Processing, 3, 277-299.

14. Ikeuchi, K. (1981). Determining Surface Orientation of Specular Surfaces by Using the Photometric Stereo Method. IEEE Trans. PAMI, 3, 6, 661-669.

15. Koenderink, J.J. and van Doorn, A,J. (1980). Photometric invariants related to solid shape. Optica Acta, 27, 7, 981-996.

16. Land, E.H. (1983). Recent advances in retinex theory and some implications for cortical computation: Color vision and natural images. *Proc. Natl. Acad. Sci. U.S.A.* 80, (1983), 5163-5169.

17. Klinker, G.J., Shafer, S,A., and Kanade, T. (1987). Using a color reflection model to separate highlights from object color. Proc. First Int. Conf. on Computer Vision, London, 145-150.

18. Mayhew,J.E.W and Frisby,J.P. (1981). Towards a computational and psychophysical theory of stereopsis. *AI Journal*, 17, 349-385.

19. Mayhew,J.E.W. and Longuet-Higgins,H.C. (1982). A computational model of binocular depth perception. *Nature*, 297, 376-378.

20. Sanderson, A.C., Weiss, L.E. and Nayar, S.K. (1988). Structured Highlight Inspection of Specular Surfaces. *IEEE Trans. PAMI* 10, 1, 44-55.

21. Stevens,K.A. (1979). Ph.D. Thesis, MIT, Cambridge, USA.

22. Squires, G.L. (1968). *Practical Physics*, European Physics Series, McGraw-Hill, London.

23. Terzopoulos, D. (1985). Multilevel computational processes for visual surface reconstruction. *Computer Vision Graphics and Image Processing*, 24, (1985), 52-96.

24. Thrift, P. and Lee, C-H. (1983). Using Highlights to Constrain Object Size and Location. *IEEE Trans. Sys, Man and Cybernetics*, 13, 3, 426-431.

25. Ullman, S. (1976). On Visual Detection of Light Sources. *Biol. Cybernetics*, 21, (1976), 205-212.

26. Woodham, R.J. (1980). Photometric method for determining surface orientation from multiple images. Optical Engineering, 19, 1, 139-144.

27. Zisserman,A., Giblin,P.J. and Blake,A. (1988). The information available to a moving observer from specularities. *Proc. Alvey Conf. 1988*.

The information available to a moving observer from specularities

Andrew Zisserman, Peter Giblin* and Andrew Blake

This paper examines the information available from the motion of specularities (highlights) due to known movements by the viewer. In particular two new results are presented. First, it is shown that for local viewer movements the concave/convex surface ambiguity can be resolved without knowledge of the light source position. Second, the authors investigate what further geometrical information is obtained under extended viewer movements, from tracked motion of a specularity. The reflecting surface is shown to be constrained to coincide with a certain curve. However, there is some ambiguity – the curve is a member of a one-parameter family. Fixing one point uniquely determines the curve.

Keywords: specular motion, convex/concave test, viewer motion

One of the aims of computer vision is to extract concise surface descriptions from several images of a scene. The descriptions can be used for the purposes of object recognition and also for geometric reasoning (such as collision avoidance). Stereo vision determines depths at surface features (such as edges and creases), often only sparsely distributed. It cannot yield full information on surface shape.

Ambiguity arises when the distribution of surface elements is very sparse. This is common with smooth, especially manmade, objects. Typically the only visible surface features will be contours (steps or creases) between adjacent surfaces. Apart from at contours, surface shading varies smoothly making stereo correspondence difficult. Judicious analysis of surface shading can considerably augment the geometric information obtained directly from stereo vision.

Ikeuchi[1] has described methods of finding the surface normal (and hence the depth) at every point of a smooth surface by using shading and a bounding stereoscopically viewed contour. However, 'shape from shading' algorithms of this type depend on having precise photometric information about the light source and surface reflectance properties. This is not possible except in a strictly controlled environment.

An alternative is to use more qualitative methods which do not return the depth at every point[2]. There are a number of shading cues which can provide robust and reliable information about surface shape and source position. For example, specularities (highlights), shadow boundaries and self-shadowing can yield considerable information on local surface curvature and source position. Similarly extremal boundaries constrain the local curvature of the surface (specifically the Gaussian curvature) and extrema of intensity can be related to surface characteristics[3].

This paper addresses the question 'What information is available from observing the movement of specular points in two or more images for known viewer motion?' The detection of specularities[4-6] is not described. No surface characteristics are assumed[5-8] other than the simple mirror condition. Where necessary a point light source is assumed. This is not a restriction because if the source has finite extent then the brightest point of the specularity can be used. The information contained in the shape or intensity profile of the specularity[8-10] is not used. A brief review of two approaches for deriving surface shape from the movement of specularities follows in the next section.

Two new results are presented: in the third section a simple test which resolves the convex/concave ambiguity is described. All that is required is two views of the scene and an estimate of viewer-surface distance. No knowledge of the light source position or surface slant is needed. The implementation of this test is demonstrated on synthetic and real images in the fourth section – the program successfully discriminates between convex and concave surfaces. Recent evidence[11] suggests that the human visual system may be capable of convex/concave discrimination by means of a similar test. In the fifth section it is shown that extended viewer

Robotics Research Group, Department of Engineering Science, University of Oxford, Oxford OX1 3PJ, UK
*Department of Pure Mathematics, University of Liverpool, Liverpool L69 3BX, UK

movements (where the specular point is tracked through many images) constrain the reflecting surface to coincide with one member of a one-parameter family of curves. If the curve passes through a known point on the surface, then the ambiguity is removed and the curve uniquely determined.

MOTION OF SPECULAR POINTS

Koenderink and van Doorn[3] give a qualitative description of the movement of specularities as the vantage point changes by considering the Gauss map of the surface. Using this analysis it is clear that the velocity of the specularity is less if the curvature is high (it depends on the Weingarten map of the surface – the differential of the Gauss map) so that '[specularities] tend to cling to the strongly curved parts'; and also that specularities are created or annihilated in pairs at parabolic lines on the surface and move transversely to the lines at their moment of creation. This approach is valid provided the distance of the viewer from the surface is much greater than the largest radius of curvature.

Local metric information (constraints on the surface curvature) can be obtained from two views[9] provided the position of the light source and a surface feature (close to the reflecting point) are known. The two views might be a stereo pair or from a moving monocular observer. In either case the baseline is assumed known and surface features can be matched using the epipolar constraint. The specularity will move relative to these surface features. The constraints on surface curvature are contained in the specular motion equation[9]. This is a linearized relation between the change $\mathbf{r} = (r_1, r_2, r_3)$ in the position of the specularity in the tangent plane of the surface and the (small) viewer movement $\mathbf{d} = (d_1, d_2, d_3)$. The coordinate frame is chosen to be the local normal frame where the origin lies on the surface (at the reflecting point) and the z-axis is along the local surface normal. It is arranged so incident and reflected rays are in the xz plane and the movement of the specularity is in the xy plane – the local tangent plane. The vector $\mathbf{x} = (x, y)$ is the restriction of $\mathbf{r} = (x, y, z)$ to the tangent plane. The linear system can be expressed as[12]

$$2V(\mathbf{M}\,\mathbf{H} - k_{vL}I)\mathbf{x} = \mathbf{w}, \qquad (1)$$

where

$$\mathbf{w} = (-d_1 + d_3 \tan \sigma, -d_2)^\mathsf{T},$$

$$\mathbf{M} = \begin{pmatrix} \sec \sigma & 0 \\ 0 & \cos \sigma \end{pmatrix},$$

and

$$k_{vL} = \frac{1}{2}\left(\frac{1}{V} + \frac{1}{L}\right)$$

The angle of reflection is σ. Vectors $\mathbf{V}$ and $\mathbf{L}$ are vectors from the origin to the viewer and light source ($V = \|\mathbf{V}\|$ and $L = \|\mathbf{L}\|$). The Hessian matrix $\mathbf{H}$ is the matrix of second partial derivatives of the surface $z(x, y)$,

$$\mathbf{H} = \begin{pmatrix} z_{xx} & z_{xy} \\ z_{yx} & z_{yy} \end{pmatrix}$$

In the normal coordinate frame the eigen-values of $\mathbf{H}$ are the principal curvatures of the surface.

This linear approximation is valid if the baseline is relatively short, that is, when

$$\|\mathbf{d}\| \ll \|\mathbf{V}\| \cos \sigma,$$

and provided the surface does not focus incoming rays to a point or line close to the centre of projection.

LOCAL VIEWER MOVEMENT

A simple test is described, making minimal assumptions, for distinguishing between convex and concave surfaces. Loosely, it is shown that on a convex surface the specularity moves *with* the viewer (sympathetic motion) whereas on a concave surface the movement is (in general) *against* the viewer motion (contrary motion). One can convince oneself that this is true by looking at specular reflections in the front and back surface of a spoon. The terms 'moves with' and 'moves against' the viewer motion are made precise in the following theorem (which is proved in the appendix)

Theorem 1

If $\mathbf{H}$ is negative definite (surface locally convex elliptic) then $\mathbf{d}_\perp.\mathbf{r}_\perp \geqslant 0$. If $\mathbf{H}$ is positive definite (surface locally concave elliptic) and the smallest principal curvature k satisfies $k > \sec \sigma k_{vL}$ then $\mathbf{d}_\perp.\mathbf{r}_\perp \leqslant 0$.

Here, $\mathbf{d}_\perp$ and $\mathbf{r}_\perp$ are the projections of the vectors $\mathbf{d}$ and $\mathbf{r}$ onto the plane perpendicular to $\mathbf{V}$. Their calculation is described below. The corollaries provide useful tests because other surface shapes are possible (for example hyperbolic) where the scalar product could have either sign.

If $\mathbf{d}_\perp.\mathbf{r}_\perp < 0$ (contrary motion) then the surface is not convex.

If $\mathbf{d}_\perp.\mathbf{r}_\perp > 0$ (sympathetic motion) then the surface is not concave unless one of the principal curvatures is less than $\sec \sigma k_{vL}$.

The first test shows it is always possible to determine if a surface is not convex.

Calculation of $\mathbf{d}_\perp.\mathbf{r}_\perp$

The geometry is shown in Figure 1. The simple vector cycle is used:

$$\mathbf{V} + \mathbf{d} - \mathbf{W} - \mathbf{r} = 0$$

The projected vectors are

$$\mathbf{d}_\perp = \mathbf{d} - (\mathbf{d}.\hat{\mathbf{V}})\hat{\mathbf{V}}$$

$$\mathbf{r}_\perp = \mathbf{d}_\perp - \mathbf{W}_\perp$$

$$= \mathbf{d}_\perp - W\mathbf{U} \qquad (2)$$

where $\mathbf{U} = \hat{\mathbf{W}} - (\hat{\mathbf{W}}.\hat{\mathbf{V}})\hat{\mathbf{V}}$, and $\hat{\mathbf{V}}$ indicates a unit vector. Hence,

$$\mathbf{d}_\perp.\mathbf{r}_\perp = |\mathbf{d}_\perp|^2 - W(\mathbf{d}_\perp.\mathbf{U}) \qquad (3)$$

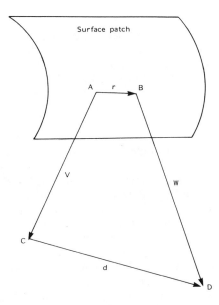

Figure 1. Specularity geometry. The viewer moves between points C and D. The specularity moves (in the tangent plane of the surface) between A and B. The vectors **V** and **W** are then reflected rays at A and B

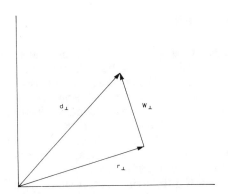

Figure 2. Projected vectors in the plane perpendicular to **V**. It is clear that if the magnitude of **W** (and hence $W_\perp$) varies, the scalar product $\mathbf{d}_\perp.\mathbf{r}_\perp$ can have either sign

To calculate the scalar product involves only knowing the viewer motion (**d**), the directions of the reflected ray in each view ($\hat{\mathbf{V}}$ and $\hat{\mathbf{W}}$) and an estimate of the surface distance W. The important point is that the test does not require any knowledge of the light source position or the surface slant. The estimate of the viewer-surface distance can be obtained, for example, from a nearby surface feature (whose position can be measured using binocular stereo). It is worth noting that in the coordinate frame defined by the triad $\{\hat{\mathbf{d}}_\perp, \hat{\mathbf{V}} \wedge \hat{\mathbf{d}}_\perp, \hat{\mathbf{V}}\}$ the length $\mathbf{d}_\perp.\mathbf{r}_\perp$ is the epipolar (horizontal) disparity.

ERRORS IN CONVEX/CONCAVE TEST

The test only involves the sign of the scalar product. However, the magnitude can be used to gauge the immunity to errors.

The important question is how sensitive is the sign of the scalar product to the estimate of W? It is clear from equation (2) and Figure 2 that the scalar product

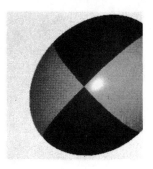

Figure 3. Convex ellipsoid with surface markings (artificial images)

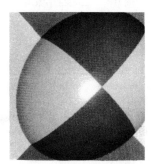
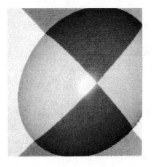

Figure 4. Concave surface of an ellipsoid with surface markings (artificial images)

will *always* change sign eventually as W varies. From (3) the sign change occurs at W_o, where

$$W_0 = \frac{|\mathbf{d}_\perp|^2}{\mathbf{d}_\perp.\mathbf{U}}$$

$$= \frac{|\mathbf{d}_\perp|^2}{\hat{\mathbf{W}}.\mathbf{d}_\perp}$$

The error in this estimate is given by

$$\delta W_o = \frac{\partial W_0}{\partial \hat{\mathbf{V}}} \cdot \delta\hat{\mathbf{V}} + \frac{\partial W_0}{\partial \hat{\mathbf{W}}} \cdot \delta\hat{\mathbf{W}}$$

where $\delta\hat{\mathbf{V}}$ = (error in **V** perpendicular to $\hat{\mathbf{V}}$)/$\|\mathbf{V}\|$ and it is assumed that the error in **d** is negligible. Provided the estimate of W is outside the range $(W_o \pm \delta W_o)$ one can be confident in the sign of the scalar product.

Results of convex/concave test

The results of applying this test to the image pairs shown in Figures 3–5 are tabulated in Table 1.

For the computation, the specularities are detected using Brelstaff's specularity detector and matcher[4]; the estimate of W is obtained from the distance to a surface feature close to the specularity. This distance is determined by the PMF binocular stereo algorithm[13]. The error estimates for **V** and **W** are based on an error of $\pm\frac{1}{2}$ pixel in localizing the brightest point of the specularity in the image. In all cases (see Table 2) the estimate of W falls outside the region $(W_o \pm \delta W_o)$ so one can be confident that the sign of the scalar product is correct.

Figure 5. Beach ball of 12 cm radius

Table 1. Scalar product and interpretations

Figure	Description	$\mathbf{d}_\perp . \mathbf{r}_\perp$	Interpretation
3	convex ellipsoid	0.024991	not concave
4	concave ellipsoid	−0.021369	not convex
5	beach ball	0.001497	not concave

Table 2. Viewer-surface distance estimate and safety margins

Figure	W	W_0	δW_0
3	10.574994	10.799026	0.037323
4	10.632490	10.447312	0.028527
5	0.900474	0.964750	0.000453

The first two pairs of stereo images (Figures 3 and 4) are computer generated using a narrow field of view to exaggerate disparities. This makes it easy to see relative displacement of specularities. Figure 3 shows a convex surface with a stereoscopically visible specularity and nearby surface markings. Note that the displacement of the specularity (relative to surface markings) is in the same direction as the relative displacement of the optical centres of left and right views, i.e. the motion of the specularity is sympathetic ($\mathbf{d}_\perp . \mathbf{r}_\perp > 0$). Figure 4 shows a concave surface and, as expected, the relative displacement of the specularity is reversed, opposing the motion of the viewer ($\mathbf{d}_\perp . \mathbf{r}_\perp < 0$). Figure 5 is a real image of a beach ball (convex) and again the motion of the specularity is sympathetic ($\mathbf{d}_\perp . \mathbf{r}_\perp > 0$).

GLOBAL VIEWER MOVEMENT

This section describes what information is available from extended or continuous viewer movements where the information from many views is combined.

The following theorem is proved:

Theorem 2

Given a source of light S (or a direction of light from infinity), and for each point r on a curve in R^3, given the direction of a reflected ray through r (the reflection being from an unknown reflecting surface M) then this determines a unique curve m (the locus of the reflecting points) on M provided one point on m is known.

The proof is given in the appendix.

Thus, given a fixed light source and surface, and observing the direction of the reflected rays as the viewer moves, uniquely determines a curve on the reflecting surface. Without a known point r there is ambiguity as the curve is only determined by the directions of the reflected rays to lie in a one parameter family. If a point is known on the curve, the ambiguity is removed and the curve uniquely determined. The required point r could be found where the curve m crosses an edge whose position is known from binocular stereo.

The surface normal is also known along m. This places strong constraints on the local surface curvature. Furthermore, by making a second movement that crosses the original path (so that the paths are transverse and both transverse to the reflected rays) transverse curves are obtained on the reflecting surface. At the point where these curves cross the surface curvature (principal curvatures and direction of principal axis) is completely determined. The type and extent of the constraints placed on the surface by curves of this type are currently being explored.

REFERENCES

1 **Ikeuchi, K and Horn, B K P** 'Numerical shape from shading and occluding boundaries' in **Brady, J M (Ed.)** *Computer Vision* (1981) pp 141–184

2 **Blake, A, Zisserman A and Knowles, G** 'Surface description from stereo and shading' *Image & Vision Comput.* Vol 3 No 4 (1985) pp 183–191

3 **Koenderinck, J J and van Doorn, A J** 'Photometric invariants related to solid shape' *Optica Acta* Vol 27 No 7 (1980) pp 981–996

4 **Brelstaff, G J** 'Inferring surface shape from specular reflections' *PhD Thesis* University of Edinburgh, UK (1988)

5 **Gershon, R, Jepson, A D and Tsotsos, J K** 'Highlight identification using chromatic information' *Proc. 1st ICCV* London, UK (1987) pp 161–170

6 **Klinker, G J, Shafer, S A and Kanade, T** 'Using a color reflection model to separate highlights from object colour' *Proc. 1st ICCV* London, UK (1987) pp 145–150

7 **Brelstaff, G J and Blake, A** 'Detecting specular reflections using Lambertian constraints' *Proc. 2nd ICCV* Tarpon Springs, FL, USA (1988)

8 **Buchanan, C S** 'Determining surface orientation from specular highlights' *MSc Thesis* Department of Computer Science, University of Toronto, Canada (1987)

9 **Blake, A** 'Specular stereo' *Proc. IJCAI Conf.* Los Angeles, CA, USA (1985)

10 **Healey, G and Binford, T O** 'Local shape from specularity' *Proc. 1st ICCV* London, UK (1987) pp 151–160

11 **Blake, A and Bülthoff, H** 'Does the seeing brain know physics?' (1988) forthcoming

12 **Blake, A and Brelstaff, G J** 'Geometry from specularities' *Proc. 2nd ICCV* Tarpon Springs, FL, USA (1988)

13   **Pollard, S P, Mayhew, J E W and Frisby, J P** 'PMF: a stereo correspondence algorithm using a disparity gradient limit' *Perception* Vol 14 (1985) pp 449–470

14   **Bruce, J W and Giblin, P J** *Curves and Singularities* Cambridge University Press, Cambridge, UK (1984)

ACKNOWLEDGEMENTS

We are grateful for discussions with Jim Allan, Gavin Brelstaff, Mike Brady, Ron Daniel, Trevor Jack and John Knapman. We are also grateful to Gavin Brelstaff for the use of his specularity detection and matching software. The support of SERC (for AZ) and the University of Oxford, UK are gratefully acknowledged.

APPENDIX
PROOF OF THEOREM 1

The vectors $\mathbf{r}_\perp$ and $\mathbf{d}_\perp$ lie in the plane perpendicular to $\mathbf{V}$. The scalar product $\mathbf{d}_\perp.\mathbf{r}_\perp$ is calculated in the coordinate frame with z-axis along $\mathbf{V}$ and y-axis parallel to the y-axis of the normal frame. In this frame the vectors $\mathbf{r}_\perp$ and $\mathbf{d}_\perp$ have zero z components. Their x and y components are obtained from $\mathbf{x}$ and $\mathbf{d}$ using the projection matrix $\mathbf{P}^{-1}$, where

$$\mathbf{P} = \begin{pmatrix} \sec \sigma & 0 \\ 0 & 1 \end{pmatrix} \text{ and } \mathbf{P}^{-1} = \begin{pmatrix} \cos \sigma & 0 \\ 0 & 1 \end{pmatrix}$$

Then

$$\mathbf{r}_\perp = \begin{pmatrix} \mathbf{P}^{-1}\mathbf{x} \\ 0 \end{pmatrix} \quad \mathbf{d}_\perp = \begin{pmatrix} -\mathbf{P}^{-1}\mathbf{w} \\ 0 \end{pmatrix}$$

Using the specular motion equation (1)

$$\mathbf{P}^{-1}2V(\mathbf{MH}) - k_{VL}I)\mathbf{P}(\mathbf{P}^{-1}\mathbf{x}) = \mathbf{P}^{-1}\mathbf{w}$$

and hence

$$\mathbf{d}_\perp.\mathbf{r}_\perp = -(\mathbf{P}^{-1}\mathbf{x})^T\mathbf{P}^{-1}\mathbf{w}$$

$$= -2V(\mathbf{P}^{-1}\mathbf{x})^T[\mathbf{P}^{-1}(\mathbf{MH} - k_{VL}I)\mathbf{P}](\mathbf{P}^{-1}\mathbf{x})$$

This is a quadratic form

$$\mathbf{d}_\perp.\mathbf{r}_\perp = -2V(\mathbf{P}^{-1}\mathbf{x})^T\mathbf{Q}(\mathbf{P}^{-1}\mathbf{x})$$

The sign depends on the eigen-values of $\mathbf{Q}$. Noting that $M = \cos \sigma\, P^2$

$$\mathbf{Q} = \cos \sigma\, \mathbf{P}\,\mathbf{H}\,\mathbf{P} - k_{VL}I$$

Now, det $\mathbf{PHP} = \sec^2 \sigma$ det $(\mathbf{H})$, and considering the trace of $\mathbf{PHP}$ or noting that $(0,1)\, \mathbf{PHP}\, (0,1)^T = (0,1)\, \mathbf{H}\, (0,1)^T$, proves $\mathbf{PHP}$ is positive (negative) definite as $\mathbf{H}$ is positive (negative) definite.

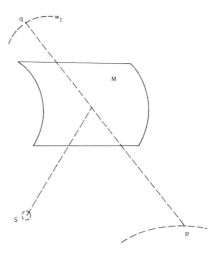

Figure 6. The curve w_1 is perpendicular to the reflected rays. It lies on a possible orthotomic surface of the mirror M relative to the light source S

Two cases are considered:

1   $\mathbf{H}$ negative definite
   $\mathbf{Q}$ is negative definite, hence $\mathbf{d}_\perp.\mathbf{r}_\perp \geqslant 0$.
2   $\mathbf{H}$ positive definite
   A lower bound on the smallest eigen-value of $\mathbf{PHP}$ is given by k_1, where k_1 is the smaller eigen-value of $\mathbf{H}$. $\mathbf{Q}$ will have a negative eigen-value if an eigen-value of $\mathbf{PHP}$ is less than $\sec \sigma k_{VL}$. However, provided $k_1 > \sec \sigma k_{VL}$, $\mathbf{Q}$ is positive definite and $\mathbf{d}_\perp.\mathbf{r}_\perp \leqslant 0$.

PROOF OF THEOREM 2[1]

The reflected rays are all normal to the orthotomic W of M relative to S (the orthotomic[14] is the locus of reflections of S in tangent planes to M).

Choose any point q on the reflected ray (see Figure 6). There is a unique piece of curve w_1 through q perpendicular to all the reflected rays through points p. This curve w_1 is on a possible orthotomic surface W_1 through q.

Taking perpendicular bisector planes of segments joining S to points t of w_1 gives a one-parameter family of planes which are tangent to a possible mirror M_1. For each t the intersection of the perpendicular bisector plane with the reflected ray through t determines a point on M_1.

Hence, the choice of q determines a curve m_1 on a possible mirror M_1. Changing q will change w_1 and hence m_1, so q can be adjusted until m_1 passes through a known point on M. Thus, provided such a known point exists the curve and the surface normals along the curve are determined.

---

[1]The proof is slightly modified if the light source is at infinity

Using Highlights to Constrain Object Size and Location

PHILIP THRIFT AND CHIA-HOANG LEE

Abstract—In this report we show how highlights on three types of objects—cylinders, spheres, and generalized cylinders—can be used to provide constraints on their size and location. This information can then be used in conjunction with other constraints to solve the problem of object acquisition.

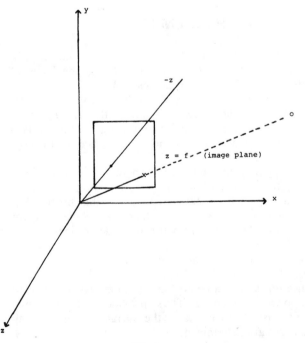

Fig. 1.

Manuscript received August 10, 1982; revised January 5, 1983. This work was supported by the National Bureau of Standards under Grant NB80NADA-0080.

The authors are with the Computer Vision Laboratory, Computer Science Center, University of Maryland, College Park, MD 20742.

I. INTRODUCTION

Many of the objects arising in industrial computer vision applications are metallic and thus have highlights as a dominant feature. In fact, the highlights may be the most dominant visual feature, more noticeable than the occluding boundary of the object itself.

In this correspondence, we examine some special classes of objects: cylinders, spheres, and straight-axis generalized cylinders, illuminated by a single (distant) light source with known direction l. All vectors will be in terms of a camera coordinate system $[x, y, z]$ as shown in Fig. 1.

A point (x, y, z) appears in the image plane $z = f$ at $(fx/z, fy/z, f)$ under central projection. We shall assume that all points under observation have $z < f < 0$. The view direction associated with a point (x_p, y_p) in the image plane is

$$v = -\left(x_p^2 + y_p^2 + f^2\right)^{-1/2}(x_p, y_p, f).$$

Here (x_p, y_p) in the image plane corresponds to (x_p, y_p, f) in the camera coordinate system.

In this report we shall examine how highlights provide constraints on the size and position of objects. These constraints, combined with others, can be used in determining these parameters. In general, if a surface patch S is examined under central projection and a highlight point h is observed with view direction v, l is the known light direction and n is the normal of S at h, then the following (redundant) relationships hold:

$$v = 2n(n \cdot l) - l \tag{1}$$

$$n = |v + l|^{-1}(v + l). \tag{2}$$

In other words, n is the bisector of v and l in the plane containing v and l, as indicated in Fig. 2. This follows from the form of the reflectance model in [1].

A single distinct highlight point can be observed if the surface normal is varying sufficiently in all directions away from h. In the case of cylinders and cones, however, what is observed is a

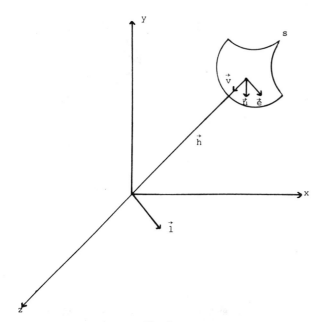

Fig. 2.

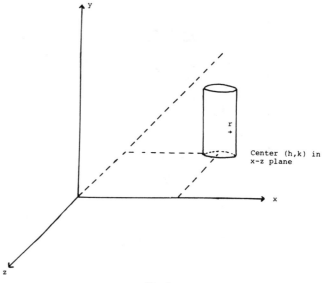

Center (h,k) in
x-z plane

Fig. 3.

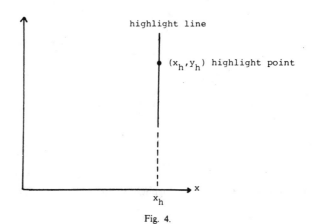

highlight line

(x_h, y_h) highlight point

x_h

Fig. 4.

line of highlights. If the cylinder were infinite in extent along its axis, there would be a line of highlights, with the "true" highlight (that is, the point that satisfies (1), (2)) as one of these. Even if the true highlight were in view, it would be indistinguishable from the rest in practice because the number of gray levels is finite.

Little research has apparently been done in using highlight information in constraining location and shape. In [1] there is a description of how highlights are perceived as source-like regions and means are suggested for detecting them. In [2] a general model of specular reflectance is presented, though no analysis is pursued in examining real data. In [3] the effect of highlights on causing one's perception of an object to be curved is examined, but only in a qualitative way.

II.   CYLINDERS

In this section, we describe how the position and orientation of a metallic cylinder is constrained by observing highlights. In this case, we observe not a single highlight point, but a line of highlight points. See Fig. 13 for an example. This line has the property that it lies parallel to the cylinder axis, and that if the cylinder were extended infinitely in both directions of its axis, the highlight line would pass through the (perhaps unobserved) highlight point, defined in the previous section.

We assume first that the cylinder is placed with axis perpendicular to the x-z plane as shown in Fig. 3. In particular, we assume that the axis of the cylinder goes through $x = h$, $z = k$ and has radius r. We assume that the light direction l is known and that the highlight line is in view.

The highlight line appears in the image plane as in Fig. 4. The "true" highlight point would be the view direction v such that the bisector of v and l lies in the x-z plane (since the bisector is the same as the surface normal at the highlight point and we are assuming an upright cylinder). If the true highlight point is at (x_h, y_h) then the viewing direction v of the highlight point can be written as

$$v = -\left(x_h^2 + y_h^2 + f^2\right)^{-1/2}(x_h, y_h, f).$$

If $l = (l_1, l_2, l_3)$ then $v + l$ is proportional to

$$\left(l_1\left(x_h^2 + y_h^2 + f^2\right)^{1/2} - x_h, l_2\left(x_h^2 + y_h^2 + f^2\right)^{1/2}\right.$$
$$\left. - y_h, l_3\left(x_h^2 + y_h^2 + f^2\right)^{1/2} - f\right).$$

For the normal $n = |v + l|^{-1}(v + l)$ to lie in the x-z plane we must have

$$l_2\left(x_h^2 + y_h^2 + f^2\right)^{1/2} - y_h = 0$$

or

$$y_h^2 = \left(1 - l_2^2\right)^{-1} l_2^2 \left(x_h^2 + f^2\right).$$

Since the sign of y_h is determined by l_2 we have

$$y_h = \text{sgn}(l_2)\left(1 - l_2^2\right)^{1/2}\left(x_h^2 + f^2\right)^{1/2}|l_2|$$
$$= l_2\left(1 - l_2^2\right)^{1/2}\left(x_h^2 + f^2\right)^{1/2}.$$

We should note that the true highlight point (x_h, y_h) may not appear on the observed highlight line, but would appear if the cylinder were extended infinitely. In either case, the position of the highlight point can be derived from the above illustrations.

We can now use the knowledge of the true highlight point to put a constraint on cylinder size and location. Let

O be the origin of the TV coordinate system.
H be the highlight point on the cylinder.
P be the intersection point of the cylinder axis and the plane perpendicular to the axis through H.
Q be the intersection point of the cylinder axis and the x-z plane.
n be the surface normal at H.

This situation is represented in Fig. 5. Clearly, the viewing

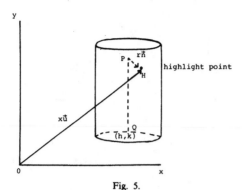

Fig. 5.

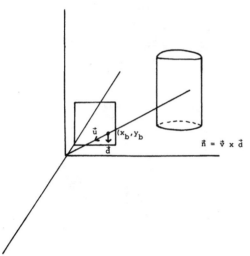

Fig. 6.

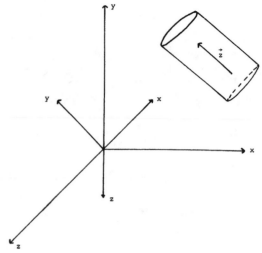

Fig. 7.

direction $v = (v_1 v_2 v_3)$ for the highlight point can be found by

$$v = -\left(x_h^2 + y_h^2 + f^2\right)^{-1/2}(x_h, y_h, f)$$

and n can be computed from $n = |v + l|^{-1}(v + l)$. Moreover, if we let $\|OH\| = x$ (x: an unknown quantity) then $OH = xv$, $QP = x(0, v_2, 0)$. By vector subtraction we get $OH - PH - QP - OQ = OO$. Thus

$$x\begin{pmatrix} v_1 \\ v_2 \\ v_3 \end{pmatrix} - r\begin{pmatrix} n_1 \\ n_2 \\ n_3 \end{pmatrix} - x\begin{pmatrix} 0 \\ v_2 \\ 0 \end{pmatrix} - \begin{pmatrix} h \\ 0 \\ k \end{pmatrix} = \begin{pmatrix} 0 \\ 0 \\ 0 \end{pmatrix}.$$

Since $n_2 = 0$ we get the two equations

$$xv_1 - rn_1 - h = 0$$
$$xv_3 - rn_3 - k = 0.$$

Eliminating x, we get

$$(n_1 v_3 - n_3 v_1)r + v_3 h - v_1 k = 0. \tag{3}$$

Thus we get a single linear equation constraining the position and radius of the cylinder.

Other constraints may be formed by viewing from another camera position, taking into account the transformation between the two coordinate systems. Also, side boundary points (x_b, y_b) may be used in adding more constraints. If we view a boundary point at (x_b, y_b) with view direction v and boundary direction d in the image plane (positioned so that the right side of d is inside the projection of the cylinder), then the normal at the boundary is given by $n = v \times d$ (see Fig. 6). We can then use v and n in (3) to get another linear constraint. Note: If we are viewing the inside of a cylindrical shell (concave), then r will be negative instead of positive in (3). If we could estimate h, k by other means, then the sign of r could be determined.

We now turn to the case where the axis a of the cylinder is not perpendicular to the x-z plane. We shall let $[x', y', z']$ be a new coordinate system S where x', z' are perpendicular to a (see Fig. 7).

Let $y' = a$ (choose a with positive y component) so the new y' is in the direction of the axis. Let x' have zero z-component, but be perpendicular to y'. Thus

$$x_1' y_1' + x_2' y_2' = 0$$
$$(x_1')^2 + (x_2')^2 = 1.$$

Solving this we get

$$x_1' = \left(1 + (y_1')^2 (y_2')^{-2}\right)^{1/2}$$
$$x_2' = -(x_1' y_1')(y_2')^{-1}.$$

Let $z' = x' \times y'$. Then $R = (x', y', z')^T$ is the matrix transforming a vector with $[x, y, z]$ coordinates into $[x', y', z']$ coordinates.

Let l' be the transformed coordinates of l. The highlight lines can now be transformed to the primed coordinate system and they will now be vertical, since the axis of the cylinder is now perpendicular to the x'-z' plane. The analysis may now be carried out for vertical lines in the $[x', y', z']$ coordinate system.

The problem still remains to find the orientation a of the cylinder. We can observe the cylinder under the illumination of two light sources as shown in Fig. 8 and get two highlight lines (or we could have a single source and translate, without rotating the camera). In either case, the two highlight lines can be used to compute the orientation of the cylinder. For highlight lines 1 and 2, we assume the lines appearing on the cylinder itself are given by $(i = 1, 2)$

$$h_i + \lambda a, \qquad -\infty < \lambda < \infty.$$

These project into

$$\left((h_{i3} + \lambda a_3)^{-1}(h_{i1} + \lambda a_1), (n_{i3} + \lambda a_3)^{-1}(h_{i2} + \lambda a_2)\right).$$

If $a_3 \neq 0$, then as $\lambda \to \infty$ both of these approach $a_3^{-1}(a_1, a_2)$, the intersection of the two highlight lines in the image plane. If $a_3 = 0$, then the two lines are parallel with slope $a_2^{-1} a_1$. In either case, we may calculate (a_1, a_2, a_3) using the fact that $a_1^2 + a_2^2 + a_3^2 = 1$.

III. SPHERE

We can achieve a similar analysis in observing a sphere positioned at an unknown center (h, k, l) and radius r, as indicated in Fig. 9. In observing a sphere with a specular surface, we can

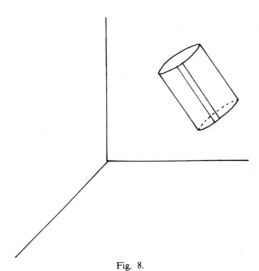

Fig. 8.

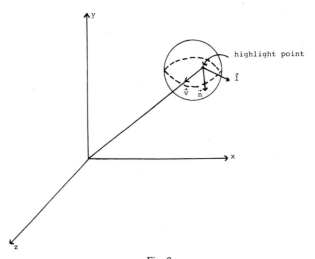

Fig. 9.

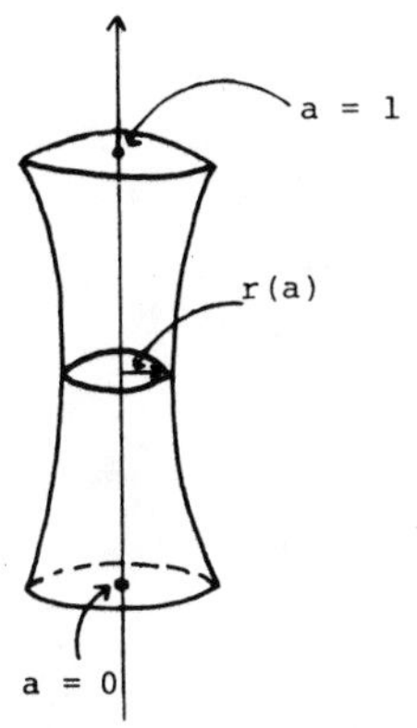

observe a single highlight point, and thus can deduce the normal direction $n = |v + l|^{-1}(v + l)$ at that point. This gives us, for an unknown x = the distance from the origin to the physical highlight point on the object.

$$x \begin{pmatrix} v_1 \\ v_2 \\ v_3 \end{pmatrix} - r \begin{pmatrix} n_1 \\ n_2 \\ n_3 \end{pmatrix} - \begin{pmatrix} h \\ k \\ l \end{pmatrix} = 0.$$

Eliminating x from these equations

$$(n_3 v_1 - n_1 v_3)r + v_1 l - v_3 h = 0$$

$$(n_3 v_2 - n_2 v_3)r + v_2 l - v_3 k = 0.$$

These two constraints may be used along with others in determining r, h, k, l.

IV.   GENERALIZED CYLINDER WITH STRAIGHT AXIS AND KNOWN ORIENTATION

In this section, we assume that we have under observation a generalized cylinder (g-cylinder), defined as a surface of revolution about a straight axis of length l, with radius function defined by $r(a)$ as a moves along the axis. An example is shown in Fig. 10. Again, we assume we have a set of highlight points on the surface of the g-cylinder, but running in the direction of the axis.

Let h be a highlight on the g-cylinder, and let C be the circle which consists of the intersection of the plane perpendicular to the axis through h and the g-cylinder (see Fig. 10). Let d be the direction from the center (h, k, l) of the circle C to the highlight point h (see Fig. 11). We maintain that d is the (normalized) direction of the vector resulting in the projection of $n = |v + l|^{-1}(v + l)$ in the plane perpendicular to a. As indicated in Fig. 12 the direction d is the closest direction to n on the circle C and thus is where we would predict the highlight to be.[1] After calculating d we have a constraint (similar to the sphere case)

$$xv - rd - (h, k, l) = 0.$$

V.   EXAMPLES

We performed three sets of experiments, involving a cylinder of radius 3 cm, a sphere of radius 2.75 cm, and a vase, all with a highly specular surface. Pictures of these can be seen in Figs. 13, 15, and 16. All pictures were taken with a television camera that was calibrated at $-f = 19.83$ cm with reference to a Grinnell screen.

---

[1] The set of normals along C to the surface can be expressed as d plus some component in the a direction, and then normalized. It is clear that the closest normal to n is thus given by finding the one with the closest components in the plane perpendicular to a.

Fig. 10.

In the case of a sphere, we made calculations from two camera positions to check for consistency. We found, from the four equation that result from calculating the view and normal directions, that given $r(= 2.75$ cm$)$ and $h(= 3.5$ cm$)$, the two equations involving l and h are consistent in that they give values for l at around 29 cm.

In the case of the cylinder, the constraints were obtained from two camera positions to check for consistency. The light direction was $(0, 0, 1)$, i.e., $(l_1, l_2, l_3) = (0, 0, 1)$. The cylinder was placed 69 cm away from the TV camera along the optical axis and was upright, i.e., its position was $(0, 0, -69)$. The camera was then translated to the position $(-11.5, 0, -23)$ with respect to its first position as depicted in Fig. 14. The highlight lines of these two pictures were respectively at image coordinates $x = 0$ and $x = 160$ (see Fig. 15). The orientation of the cylinder was first determined as $(0, 1, 0)$ by these two parallel highlight lines. Next, the true highlight points were derived as $(0, 0)$ and $(160, 0)$ on the image plane. Following the constraint (3) we have

$$h = 0 \text{ in the first picture}$$

and $0.14303r + 0.12832k = -18.803$ in the second picture. Given $r = 3$ cm, this equation gives $k = -68$ cm; given $k = -69$ cm, it gives $r = 5$ cm. Thus the absolute error is about 2 cm; it is quite consistent.

In the case of the vase, a constraint was obtained from one camera position to check for consistency. The light direction was again $(0\ 0\ 1)$. The vase was placed at $(7.5, 0, -69)$ with respect to the camera. The highlight point was at image coordinates $(60, 0)$ (see Fig. 16). The viewing direction was $(-0.1104, 0, 0.9938)$. The normal direction was $(-0.055, 0, 0.998)$. The constraint obtained is thus

$$0.055r + 0.1104l + 0.9938h = 0.$$

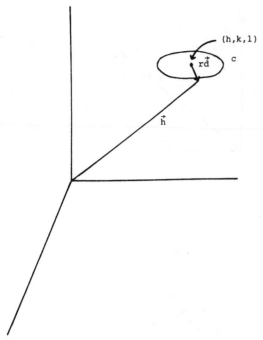

Fig. 11.

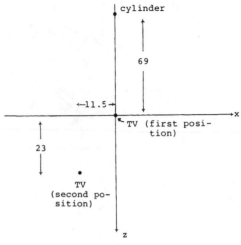

Fig. 14.

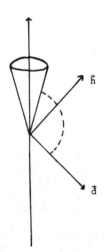

Fig. 12.

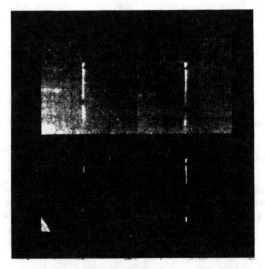

Fig. 15.

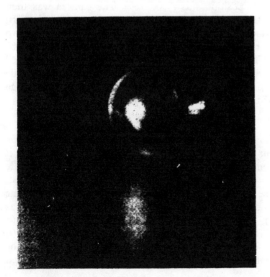

Fig. 13.

Fig. 16.

Given $r = 2$ cm, $h = 7.5$ cm, this constraint gives l equal to -68.5 cm, which is consistent.

VI. Conclusion

We have presented an analysis of how the observation of highlights on a cylinder, sphere or generalized cylinder provide linear constraints on the size and location of these objects.

The motivation for our experiments is that highlights are often the most dominant visual features in industrial objects. Moreover, the reflectance model suggests that the surface normal at a highlight bisects the viewing direction and the light direction. Using object models, we show that knowledge of the surface normal and viewing direction can be rewritten as constraints on the size and location of an object using vector geometry. In some cases, such as that of a cylinder, although the true highlight point cannot be observed, it can be derived based on knowledge of orientation. Fortunately, there is a way to get the orientation in the case of a simple cylinder, but it is not clear how to do this for more complicated types of generalized cylinders. Currently, we are pursuing this task.

Acknowledgment

The authors gratefully acknowledge the help of Janet Salzman in preparing this correspondence.

References

[1] K. Forbus, "Light source effects," *Mass. Inst. Technol. Artificial Intelligence Memo No. 422*, 1977.
[2] A. P. Pentland, "Local computation of surface shape," thesis proposal, Psych. Dept., Mass. Inst. Technol., Cambridge.
[3] J. Beck and K. Prazdny, "Highlights and the perception of glossiness," Computer Sci. Center Tech. Rep. 1047, Univ. Maryland, College Park, MD, July 1981.

HIGHLIGHT SEPARATION AND SURFACE ORIENTATIONS
FOR 3-D SPECULAR OBJECTS

Jong-Seok Park and Julius T. Tou

Center for Information Research
University of Florida
Gainesville, FL 32611
U.S.A.

ABSTRACT

This paper presents a normal vector equalization method for separating probable highlights and obtaining surface orientations of 3-D specular objects. Based on the simplified Torrance-Sparrow model for specular reflection and the empirical Lambertian reflection model, this method uses a set of three monochromatic images taken from three different illumination directions, separates probable highlights from those images, and generates a set of three Lambertian (highlight-free) images and a set of three specular (highlight-only) images. Surface orientations are obtained using the Lambertian images by solving an imaging equation for a Lambertian surface. Computer simulations and experiments with real objects have been performed. Theoretical framework for measuring surface parameters which represent optical characteristics of the surface is also discussed in Appendix.

1. INTRODUCTION

Many practical applications in industrial vision require interpretation of specular surfaces. Inspection and handling of shiny industrial parts such as solder joints and electronic components mounted on PC boards are typical examples of industrial tasks where surface specularity is a primary consideration [1]-[5].

Specular reflection (highlight) has two opposing properties. Since highlights strictly constrain imaging parameters such as direction of light source, surface normal, and viewing direction, highlights in image provide important information which can be used to determine shape and size of objects [6]-[8]. For instance, if a line-shaped highlight is observed in an image, the underlying object is strongly assumed to be a cylinder shape. In case that a highlight spot is observed, the object can be assumed to be sphere shape around the highlight. However, highlights also induce numerous problems for algorithms which require correspondence between images, such as stereo or motion algorithms. Observed highlights in one image may disappear in another image (stereo) or other images (motion) because of their great dependence on imaging geometry [9],[10]. Edge detection process employed in most computer vision system is also another example of troublesome aspect of highlights. If we apply an edge detector to an image containing highlights, the edge detector will respond not only real edges but also the highlights. This misled edge information can cause "confusion" to the system operation. In short, these two aspects of highlights may be described as "informative noise".

In this paper, we will address the problem of separating probable highlights from monochromatic images and obtaining surface orientations of 3-D specular objects. The "normal vector equalization" method developed for highlight separation is based on the fact that surface normal vectors given by the Lambertian reflection model equal to those given by a simplified Torrance-Sparrow model which is used to solve the problem of "local shape from specularity" [11]. Using the method, we can obtain a set of Lambertian (highlight-free) images and a set of specular (highlight-only) images in which the "noise" aspect of highlights is totally removed and the "information" aspect of highlights is completely conserved, respectively. These two sets of preprocessed images can be separately applied to higher level processes such as edge detection, feature extraction, shape description, and matching [3]. Most of conventional vision systems utilizing intensity of images use only one type of information by assuming just one of two reflection components in problem domain, namely Lambertian [12]-[15] or specular reflection [4],[11],[16]. However, generally, the images of most objects in real world contain those two modes of reflection, i.e. Lambertian and specular and the information concealed in both components of reflection can be utilized as much as possible to construct more reliable and more effective vision system [3],[17]-[19].

2. REVIEW OF PREVIOUS WORK

Most of highlight separation techniques announced to date utilize a color image [9],[17]. This is because they basically use color difference between Lambertian and specular components of reflection. These techniques can successfully work for objects made from dielectric materials since these materials reflect the impinging light in such a way that those two components of reflection make different colors. However, most of metallic surfaces do not show such color difference and it becomes impossible to apply those highlight separation techniques to the metallic surfaces. Moreover, those techniques can only be used for the highlight separation purpose whereas our approach can be applied not only to highlight separation but also to surface normal vector generation.

The highlight separation technique developed by Wolff [20] can overcome some of the drawbacks mentioned above by exploiting polarization properties in Lambertian and specular components of reflection. However, it can also be applied only for the highlight separation purpose. Moreover, mechanical change of polarization filter mounted on a camera lens makes it difficult to completely automate the whole operational processes.

Most of the previous work [4],[11],[16] for obtaining surface orientations of 3-D specular objects can only be applied to perfectly specular object since they do not take into account Lambertian component of reflection. Therefore, their application areas are very limited.

Coleman and Jain [21] and Nayar and Ikeuchi [19] have proposed methods for obtaining surface orientations of objects which show Lambertian reflection as well as specular reflection. In Coleman and Jain's work, specular reflection component is merely avoided by discarding an image which includes very high intensity from a total of four images to simplify the calculation of surface orientations. It can only provide surface orientations whereas our approach can provide separated Lambertian and specular component of reflection as well.

Our approach and Nayar and Ikeuchi's approach have some similarities and these two approaches completely resolve some of the limitations that most of the previous work has not overcome. Nayar and Ikeuchi's work, however, has some limitations in practical applications in the following senses: (1) Because of the complexity of the sensing apparatus, system development and experiments are only performed for 2-D cases in order to merely show its feasibility. (2) Since a number of images must be processed, execution time of their system is the main problem. The authors claimed that 1 msec per image pixel is the execution speed of the algorithm on a 3/60 SUN workstation. In their 2-D experimental system, they used 4 light sources per one direction. If they expand the system to cover 3-D by employing 8-directional light sources a total of 4X8=32 light sources will be required. For the images of 256X256 resolution, overall processing time will be 10^{-3}X32X256X256=2097 sec.=35 min. As the authors have pointed out, the developed algorithm must be improved to accommodate the strict requirement of processing speed in real applications.

3. HIGHLIGHT SEPARATION AND SURFACE ORIENTATION OF 3-D SPECULAR OBJECT

In this section, we will discuss a newly developed computational approach for separating probable highlights and obtaining surface orientations of 3-D specular objects. We will begin by discussing how to obtain surface orientation for a Lambertian surface using three monochromatic images. Next, we will introduce a simplified Torrance-Sparrow model which is used to solve the problem of "local shape from specularity" [11]. We, then, present our approach for separating probable highlights based on the "normal vector equalization" method. We will also discuss how to utilize this method to obtain surface orientations of specular objects.

3.1 Surface Orientation for Lambertian Surfaces

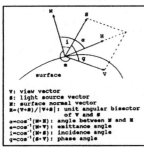

V: view vector
S: light source vector
N: surface normal vector
$H=(V+S)/|V+S|$: unit angular bisector
of V and S
$\alpha=\cos^{-1}(N \cdot H)$: angle between N and H
$e=\cos^{-1}(N \cdot V)$: emittance angle
$i=\cos^{-1}(N \cdot S)$: incidence angle
$g=\cos^{-1}(S \cdot V)$: phase angle

Fig. 1. Imaging geometry and definitions of terms.

Assuming a Lambertian surface, surface orientation can be calculated using three images obtained from three different positions of a light source. This is accomplished by beginning with the imaging equation for Lambertian reflection model which is described as a cosine function of the incidence angle illustrated in Fig. 1. [21],[22].

$$I_l(x,y) = R \cos(i) \qquad (1)$$
$$= R\, S \cdot N$$
$$= R(S_x, S_y, S_z) \cdot (N_x, N_y, N_z)$$

where, R denotes surface reflection factor and physically represents a peak intensity of a Lambertian image, N denotes surface normal vector, and S and I_l denote light source vector and associated image intensity produced by the Lambertian reflection mode. Since (1) contains three unknowns, i.e. (N_x, N_y, N_z), a total of three sources and associated intensity values are usually used to compute the surface normal vectors at each point, (x,y) [16],[21]. Given the sources S_1, S_2, and S_3 along with intensity values I_{l1}, I_{l2}, and I_{l3} at (x,y), a set of simultaneous equations can be formed to solve for N:

$$I_l = \begin{pmatrix} I_{l1} \\ I_{l2} \\ I_{l3} \end{pmatrix} = R \begin{pmatrix} S_{1x} & S_{1y} & S_{1z} \\ S_{2x} & S_{2y} & S_{2z} \\ S_{3x} & S_{3y} & S_{3z} \end{pmatrix} \begin{pmatrix} N_x \\ N_y \\ N_z \end{pmatrix} \qquad (2)$$

If we use $\underline{S}$ to symbolize the source matrix, I_l the Lambertian intensity vector at (x,y) and N the normal vector at (x,y), (2) becomes:

$$I_l = R\,\underline{S}\,N \qquad (3)$$

To solve for surface normal vector, if $\underline{S}$ is a nonsingular matrix, (3) can be written as:

$$N = \frac{1}{R}\,\underline{S}^{-1} I_l \qquad (4)$$

The conditions for the nonsingularity of $\underline{S}$ is; (1) the row of $\underline{S}$ are linearly independent; or (2) the column of $\underline{S}$ are linearly independent [23]. When S_1, S_2, and S_3 are not all in the same plane, they are linearly independent and therefore $\underline{S}$ is nonsingular. This means that the light sources must be installed so that their vectors constitute some volume in the imaging space. In Fig. 2, we illustrate the imaging coordinate system including light sources and a camera. Three azimuthal angles (θ_a) - 0°, 120°, and 240° - are chosen for each source and an elevation angle (θ_e) of 75° is chosen for all sources. Obviously, this setting of light sources satisfies the nonsingularity condition mentioned above. A camera is located at the direct top of an object so that the viewing vector V becomes $(0,0,1)$.

3.2 Specular Reflectance Models and Local Shape from Specularity

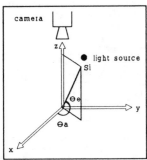

Fig. 2. Coordinate system for imaging.

Using the imaging geometry illustrated in Fig. 1, we describe a simplified Torrance-Sparrow model for specular reflection as follows [11],[24]-[26]:

$$I_{si} = K \exp\left(\frac{-\alpha_i^2}{m^2}\right) \;,\; i=1,2,3 \qquad (5)$$

where, I_{si} represents the ith image intensity of specularly reflected light associated with the ith light source, K is a constant representing peak highlight intensity, m indicates surface roughness, and α_i represents the angle between N and the ith unit angular bisector, $H_i = (V+S_i)/|V+S_i|$. For specular surfaces, surface normal vectors around highlights can also be calculated with three images obtained using three different positions of a light source. From (5), we have:

$$I_{si} = K \exp\left[-\frac{\arccos^2(H_i \cdot N)}{m^2}\right] \;,\; i=1,2,3 \qquad (6)$$

We arrange (6) in terms of unknown variable N and have:

$$H_i \cdot N = \cos\left[m\sqrt{\ln\left(\frac{K}{I_{si}}\right)}\right] \;,\; i=1,2,3 \qquad (7)$$

If we use symbols I_{s1}, I_{s2}, and I_{s3} for three specular images and H_1, H_2, and H_3 for the corresponding bisectors, we have from (7):

$$N = \underline{H}^{-1} f \qquad (8.a)$$

$$\text{where, } f = \begin{vmatrix} \cos\left[m\sqrt{\ln\left(\frac{K}{I_{s1}}\right)}\right] \\ \cos\left[m\sqrt{\ln\left(\frac{K}{I_{s2}}\right)}\right] \\ \cos\left[m\sqrt{\ln\left(\frac{K}{I_{s3}}\right)}\right] \end{vmatrix} \qquad (8.b)$$

$$\text{and, } \underline{H} = \begin{pmatrix} H_1 \\ H_2 \\ H_3 \end{pmatrix} \qquad (8.c)$$

Here, $\underline{H}$ is assumed to be a nonsingular matrix. It is known that $\underline{H}$ is always nonsingular if and only if $\underline{S}$ is nonsingular.

The surface orientation for specular surface represented by (8.a) will be combined together in the next section with those for Lambertian surface represented by (4) to separate the two components of reflection, i.e. Lambertian and specular.

3.3 Lambertian and Specular Components Separation

When light illuminates a surface, part of it is reflected immediately from the surface, and part of it penetrates into the material body and is reflected back to air after being absorbed within the material. The former reflection component is called specular reflection and the latter is called Lambertian reflection. A general reflectance model derived from this observation can be described as the weighted sum of the two reflection components [25],[26]. That is,

$$I(x,y) = q I_l(x,y) + (1-q) I_s(x,y) = I_l^*(x,y) + I_s^*(x,y) \qquad (9)$$

where, $I_l^*(x,y) = q I_l(x,y)$ represents the weighted intensity of the Lambertian component and $I_s^*(x,y) = (1-q) I_s(x,y)$ represents the weighted intensity of the specular component. The coefficient q, denotes the relative weighting factor between those two reflection components and has a value of $0 \le q \le 1$. For more (less) specular surface, q becomes close to zero (one).

For a given surface, surface normal vectors are unique. Therefore, the surface normal vectors obtained from each component should be the same; hence from (4), (8), and (9), we have:

$$\frac{1}{R^*}\underline{S}^{-1} I_l^* = \underline{H}^{-1} f^* \qquad (10.a)$$

$$\text{where , } R^* = qR \qquad (10.b)$$

$$, f^* = \begin{vmatrix} \cos\left[m\sqrt{\ln\left(\frac{K^*}{I_{s1}^*}\right)}\right] \\ \cos\left[m\sqrt{\ln\left(\frac{K^*}{I_{s2}^*}\right)}\right] \\ \cos\left[m\sqrt{\ln\left(\frac{K^*}{I_{s3}^*}\right)}\right] \end{vmatrix} \qquad (10.c)$$

$$\text{and , } K^* = (1-q)K \qquad (10.d)$$

where, R^* represents a peak Lambertian intensity and K^* represents peak specular intensity for the surface in which both reflection modes are present. Applying the relation, $I_l^* = I - I_s^*$, to (10.a), we have:

$$F = \underline{H}^{-1} f^* + \frac{1}{R^*}\underline{S}^{-1}(I_s^* - I) = 0 \qquad (11)$$

(11) represents three nonlinear equations which have three unknowns, namely I_{s1}^*, I_{s2}^*, and I_{s3}^*. (11) can be solved by numerical analysis using Newton's method in the following iterative equation [27].

$$I_{s(n+1)}^* = I_{s(n)}^* - \underline{J}^{-1}(I_{s(n)}^*) F(I_{s(n)}^*) \qquad (12)$$

where $I_{s(n)}^*$ represents the value of I_s^* after nth iteration and $\underline{J}(I_{s(n)}^*)$ is a 3X3 Jacobian matrix whose (u,v)th element is given by $\partial f_u / \partial I_{sv(n)}^*$, u,v=1,2,3. We define following dummy matrices to simplify the description of the Jacobian matrix.

$$\underline{C} = \begin{pmatrix} c_1 \\ c_2 \\ c_3 \end{pmatrix} = \underline{H}^{-1} \qquad (13.a)$$

$$\underline{D} = \begin{pmatrix} D_1 \\ D_2 \\ D_3 \end{pmatrix} = \frac{1}{R^*} \underline{S}^{-1} \qquad (13.b)$$

With these matrices, the Jacobian matrix is given by:

$$\underline{J} = \begin{pmatrix} c_{11}p(I_{s1}^*)+D_{11} & c_{12}p(I_{s2}^*)+D_{12} & c_{13}p(I_{s3}^*)+D_{13} \\ c_{21}p(I_{s1}^*)+D_{21} & c_{22}p(I_{s2}^*)+D_{22} & c_{23}p(I_{s3}^*)+D_{23} \\ c_{31}p(I_{s1}^*)+D_{31} & c_{32}p(I_{s2}^*)+D_{32} & c_{33}h(I_{s3}^*)+D_{33} \end{pmatrix} \qquad (14)$$

where, $p(I_{si}^*)$, i=1,2,3, is given by:

$$p(I_{si}^*) = \frac{\partial f_i}{\partial I_{si}^*} = \frac{m \sin[m\sqrt{\ln(\frac{K^*}{I_{si}^*})}]}{2I_{si}^* \sqrt{\ln(\frac{K^*}{I_{si}^*})}} \qquad (15)$$

In order to solve (12) for $I_{s(n+1)}^*$, surface parameters, R^*, K^*, and m must be provided into (13.b) and (15). These parameters can be measured using a sample of objects under application and the method discussed in Appendix or estimated by intuition and experimental try-and-errors.

After we find the weighted specular component by solving (12), the weighted Lambertian component can be obtained by the following simple equation.

$$I_l^*(x,y) = I(x,y) - I_s^*(x,y) \qquad (16)$$

The non-weighted Lambertian and specular components are given by:

$$I_l(x,y) = \frac{I_l^*(x,y)}{q} \qquad (17.a)$$

$$I_s(x,y) = \frac{I_s^*(x,y)}{1-q} \qquad (17.b)$$

The surface normal vectors can be calculated by (4) using the Lambertian component.

3.4 Implementation of the Algorithm

The processes of separating highlights can be informally described as follows:

Algorithm; Highlight Separation
1. Input: $I=[I_1, I_2, I_3]$, K^*, R^*, m, $\underline{S}$, V
2. Create: $\underline{H}$, $\underline{C}$, $\underline{D}$
3. Scan: images from left to right and top to bottom

    if(I_i=0 for all i=1,2,3) then set I_{si}^*=0 for all i=1,2,3 and goto step 3

    else

      let $I_{si(0)}^*$=K^*/2 for all i=1,2,3

      do n=1,N_{max}

        determine $f^*(I_{s(n)}^*)$ using (10.c)

        determine $F(I_{s(n)}^*)$ using (11)

        if($|F_i(I_{s(n)}^*)| \le \epsilon_1$ for all i=1,2,3) goto step 3

        determine $p(I_{s(n)}^*)$ using (15)

        determine J and J^{-1} using (14) and matrix inversion

        determine $I_{s(n+1)}^*$ using (12)

        if($I_{si(n+1)}^* \le 0$) then let $I_{si(n+1)}^*$=1 for i=1,2,3

        if($I_{si(n+1)}^* \ge K^*$) then let $I_{si(n+1)}^*$=K^* for i=1,2,3

        if($|I_{si(n+1)}^* - I_{si(n)}^*| \le \epsilon_2$ for all i=1,2,3) then goto step 3

      end do

Four stopping conditions [28] are employed in this algorithm. They are; (1) I_i=0 for all i=1,2,3 that means the perceived images are all for extremely dark area such as background, where highlight can never occur; (2) N_{max}, which represents the number of maximum allowable iterations; (3) ϵ_1, a threshold that represents how $I_{s(n)}^*$ must be close to exact solutions of (11) in order for the algorithm to stop; and (4) ϵ_2, a threshold that represents how closely the difference, $|I_{s(n+1)}^* - I_{s(n)}^*|$ converges to zero. These thresholds are determined upon how accurate results are required. For instance, if only integer resolution is sufficient for I_s^*, integer 1 can be chosen for ϵ_2. In the following experiments, the stopping parameters of N_{max}=5, ϵ_1=0.1, and ϵ_2=1 are employed.

In Fig. 3, differences between exact solution, I_{s1}^* and approximate solution after nth iteration, $I_{s1(n)}^*$ are illustrated for three cases, i.e. n=0,1, and 2. These results have been obtained using simulated sphere images generated from the reflection models explained in (9). Details regarding the simulation will be discussed in the following section.

While running, the algorithm may temporarily generate the value of $I_{s(n+1)}^*$ which is less than zero for extremely dark area such as background or self shading areas where the incidence angles are greater than 90° or greater than K^* for the areas around highlights. In order to ensure that (10.c) and (15) can always be defined even in these cases, $I_{si(n+1)}^*$ is hard limited using two conditions in the algorithm so that $0 < I_{si(n+1)}^* \le K^*$ for all i=1,2,3.

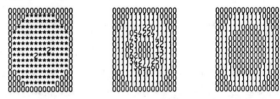

(a) before 1st iteration (b) after 1st iteration (c) after 2nd iteration
  ($|I_{s1}^* - I_{s1(0)}^*|$)   ($|I_{s1}^* - I_{s1(1)}^*|$)   ($|I_{s1}^* - I_{s1(2)}^*|$)

Fig. 3. Convergence of $I_{s1(n)}^*$ (* denotes the number greater than 9).

4. EXPERIMENTAL RESULTS

4.1 Computer Simulation

Computer simulations using the shape of a sphere has been performed (1) to study the system operation including the convergence characteristics of the algorithm presented in Fig. 3; and (2) to find sensitivities of normal vectors derived from a set of Lambertian images with respect to the change of surface parameters - q and m.

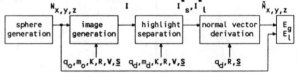

Fig. 4. Computer simulation procedures.

The whole procedures of computer simulation are presented in Fig. 4. First, the shape of a sphere is modelled using its normal vectors which are given by N=(x/r,y/r,z/r), where r denotes the radius of the sphere. Imaging parameters, V and $\underline{S}$ are incorporated into (1), (5), and (9) along with surface parameters, q_o, m_o, K, and R to generate a set of original images, I which contain two components of reflection simultaneously. Three representative values of surface parameters which describe a highly specular object (q_o=0.3, m_o=0.3), medium specular object (q_o=0.5, m_o=0.5), and near Lambertian object (q_o=0.7, m_o=0.7) have been selected to simulate the system capability for objects made with various kinds of materials. In this simulation, the values of K and R have been determined as 255, although they are not necessarily the same, since the digitizer used in the experiments with real objects has 8-bit resolution and the light intensity has been adjusted so that the brightest part of the objects is almost saturated in the images. As a consequence of these settings, we can retain consistency between simulation and experiments.

Secondly, the highlight separation algorithm runs to obtain a set of Lambertian images, I^*_l and a set of specular images, I^*_s from the original images. In this stage, surface parameters denoted as q_d and m_d are used. For the first simulation purpose discussed above, same surface parameters are employed here, i.e. $q_d=q_o$ and $m_d=m_o$ and from the set of separated Lambertian images, surface normal vectors are derived using (4). Simulation results obtained using these procedures are presented in Fig. 5 only for the case of medium specular object. For the other simulated surfaces, the simulation was also successfully carried out. A needle diagram which effectively represents surface normal vectors in a 2-D image is illustrated in Fig. 5(b) for the derived normal vectors. It shows quite accurately the shape of a hemisphere. Although three sets of the images, i.e. original, specular, and Lambertian images for three different cases of light source directions, are essential to completely describe the experimental results, we will only present one set of the images here as a representative.

The reason we have obtained the quite accurate reproduction of the hemisphere in Fig. 5(b) is mainly that we have used exactly same surface parameters in highlight separation and normal vector derivation stages as those used in image generation. In real applications, however, it is impossible to find the values of q_o and m_o and we must tolerate some error in estimating the surface parameters of real objects even when the parameter measurement method discussed in Appendix is employed. Therefore, the second simulation work mentioned at the beginning of this section have been performed to investigate how the derived normal vectors are sensitive to the surface parameter errors. For this purpose, we intentionally use different surface parameters in highlight separation and normal vector derivation stages from those used in original image generation to simulate surface parameter estimation errors which cannot be avoided in real applications. In other words, we set $q_d \neq q_o$ and $m_d \neq m_o$ and investigate the global and local error of derived normal vectors with respect to the surface parameter errors, $\Delta q = |q_d - q_o|$ and $\Delta m = |m_d - m_o|$ by defining the following two quantities. One is the global error of normal vectors with respect to relative estimation error of q and m ,which is defined as,

$$E_g\left(\frac{\Delta q}{q_o}, \frac{\Delta m}{m_o}\right) = \frac{\sum\limits_{x, y \in sphere} \frac{|N_x - \tilde{N}_x|}{N_x} + \frac{|N_y - \tilde{N}_y|}{N_y} + \frac{|N_z - \tilde{N}_z|}{N_z}}{3M} \quad (18)$$

where, $N_{x,y,z}$ denotes the x,y,z component of original normal vectors used to generate the original images illustrated in Fig. 5, $\tilde{N}_{x,y,z}$ denotes the x,y,z component of the normal vectors derived from the Lambertian images, and M denotes the number of pixels within the sphere.

The other is the local maximum error which is defined as,

$$E_l\left(\frac{\Delta q}{q_o}, \frac{\Delta m}{m_o}\right) = Max\left(\frac{|N_x - \tilde{N}_x|}{N_x}, \frac{|N_y - \tilde{N}_y|}{N_y}, \frac{|N_z - \tilde{N}_z|}{N_z}\right) \text{ for all } x, y \in sphere \quad (19)$$

Here, E_g describes the relative average error of the derived normal vectors in the global sense. E_l describes the local maximum relative error of the derived normal vectors compared with original normal vectors. They can provide quantitative measures regarding how accurately the original shape of a object can be estimated when some error of the estimated surface parameters reside. For three representative cases of q_o and m_o mentioned above, plots of (18) and (19) have been provided. From these plots, we have found that if the parameter errors remain within ±20%, the derived normal vector errors are within 4% and 50% in the global and local senses, respectively.

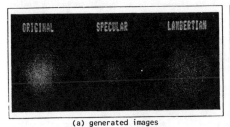 

(a) generated images   (b) needle map

Fig. 5. Simulation results on generated images.

4.2 Experiment with Real Objects

Several real specular objects have been selected for the experiments. They are a bulb, two plastic toys, a PCB and a wooden piece. The bulb has been chosen to demonstrate that the system works properly for the objects which have prominent specular reflections. Although surface parameter for these real objects can be measured using the method discussed in Appendix, we have determined the surface parameters using try-and-error method, because spherical samples of the objects are not

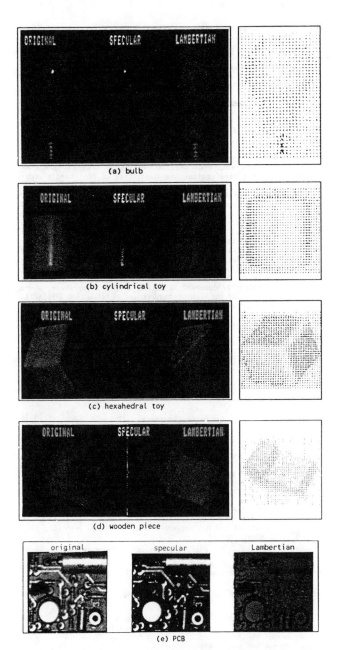

(a) bulb

(b) cylindrical toy

(c) hexahedral toy

(d) wooden piece

(e) PCB

Fig. 6. Experimental results on real specular objects.

available. The surface parameters for the bulb is determined as q=0.35, and m=0.2. Surface parameters of q=0.3 and m=0.3 are chosen for the toy and the PCB. Although the PCB consists of components made from many different materials, the single setting of its surface parameters is justified from the simulation results on the sensitivity of normal vectors with respect to the surface parameters. The wooden piece has the characteristics of almost perfect Lambertian surface. Its parameters are determined as q=0.9 and m=0.7. The objects used for these experiments were selected as representatives of the gamut of objects made of man-made and naturally occurring materials, ranging from highly specular to highly Lambertian surfaces. We present the experimental results on the bulb in Fig. 6 (a), on the cylindrical toy in (b), on the hexahedral toy in (c), on the wooden piece in (d), and on the PCB in (e), respectively.

5. CONCLUSIONS

We have proposed a "normal vector equalization" method for highlight separation which eventually leads to 3-D surface normal vectors. Using the proposed approach, we have performed computer simulation with generated images and also performed experiments with real objects. Specimens made of various materials are chosen to demonstrate the system capability for a wide range of materials used in real applications. From the results obtained from simulation and experiments, we have determined that: (1) The proposed approach can solve the highlight separation problem for objects which are made from various materials. (2) It can also be used to obtain 3-dimensional shape information from Lambertian images. (3) Surface parameters can be measured using a sample of objects or estimated roughly and used to obtain practically useful results when some error in estimated normal vectors is permitted.

APPENDIX - Surface Parameter Measurement

It is necessary to provide the surface parameters, R^*, K^*, and m to the algorithm explained earlier. These parameters represent optical characteristics of a surface. For a homogeneous surface, they are regarded to have single constant values for overall surface area. In this section, we will introduce a method for measuring these surface parameters using a sample of well-defined shapes such as sphere or cylinder which has same optical characteristics as the objects under application.

As discussed earlier, the highlight separation technique discussed here is based on three monochromatic images obtained from three different locations of light sources. If we use a spherical object as a specimen for estimating the parameters and light sources far enough apart each other as illustrated in Fig. 2, we can ensure that one highlight associated to one of the light sources can be observed in the corresponding image. The location of the peak intensity can easily be found using a simple algorithm for searching maximum intensity. We will denote the peak intensity location measured in the ith image as (x_{pi}, y_{pi}), where i=1,2,3. Because of the great dependence of the highlight on imaging geometry, the intensity observed at (x_{pi}, y_{pi}) in the jth image, where $i \neq j$, mainly consists of the Lambertian component of reflection [19],[21]. Meanwhile, surface normal at (x_{pi}, y_{pi}) can be obtained using the relation $\alpha_i = 0$. That is,

$$N(x_{pi}, y_{pi}) = H_i \qquad (A.1)$$

From these observations, we have from (3) and (9):

$$I_i(x_{pj}, y_{pj}) = I^*_{Li}(x_{pj}, y_{pj}) + I_{si}(x_{pj}, y_{pj})$$

$$= R^* N(x_{pj}, y_{pj}) \cdot S_i = R^* H_j \cdot S_i, \quad i \neq j \qquad (A.2)$$

R^* can be found from (A.2):

$$R^*_{ij} = \frac{I_i(x_{pj}, y_{pj})}{H_j \cdot S_i}, \qquad i \neq j \qquad (A.3)$$

where, subscript ij is used to emphasize that this R^* is especially obtained from jth peak intensity location in ith image. A global R^* is determined by averaging each R^*_{ij}:

$$R^* = \frac{1}{6} \sum_{i=1}^{3} \sum_{j=1}^{3} R^*_{ij} \delta_{ij}, \text{ where } \delta_{ij} = \begin{cases} 1 & \text{for } i \neq j \\ 0 & \text{for } i = j \end{cases} \qquad (A.4)$$

In order to develop a method for estimating K^*, we use another observation at peak intensity locations. The intensity of ith image at (x_{pi}, y_{pi}) consists of the two reflection components and from (3), (5), and (9) it is given by:

$$I_i(x_{pi}, y_{pi}) = R^* N(x_{pi}, y_{pi}) \cdot S_i + K^* = R^* H_i \cdot S_i + K^* \qquad (A.5)$$

since, $\alpha_i = 0$ at (x_{pi}, y_{pi}). A global K^* can be found by averaging the K^*'s obtained from ith image. Hence from (A.5), we have:

$$K^* = \frac{1}{3} \sum_{i=1}^{3} I_i(x_{pi}, y_{pi}) - R^* H_i \cdot S_i \qquad (A.6)$$

The surface roughness is characterized by m. In order to estimate m of a given surface, we need to derive a mathematical representation for surface normal vector of a specimen. If a spherical shape is employed, surface normal for the sphere is given by:

$$N_{sp}(x,y) = (\frac{x}{r}, \frac{y}{r}, \frac{z}{r}) \qquad (A.7)$$

where, r denotes the radius of the sphere and z denotes the surface of the sphere. From (3), (6), (9), and (A.7), intensity of image obtained from the ith light source is given by:

$$I_i(x,y) = R^* N_{sp}(x,y) \cdot S_i + K^* \exp[\frac{-\arccos^2(H_i \cdot N_{sp}(x,y))}{m^2}] \qquad (A.8)$$

A global m is determined by averaging the m's obtained from ith image in such a way that they minimize the following mean square error [29]:

$$\overrightarrow{E^2} = \sum_{x,y \in highlight} \left(I_i(x,y) - R^* N_{sp}(x,y) \cdot S_i - K^* \exp[\frac{-\arccos^2(H_i \cdot N_{sp}(x,y))}{m^2}] \right)^2 \qquad (A.9)$$

Although the surface parameters obtained from (A.3), (A.6), and (A.9) are enough to solve the iterative equation (12), it is interesting to find the parameter, q, which denotes the relative strength between the two components of reflection. If we change the specimen used to find R^*, K^*, and m with one that have almost perfectly specular surface in the same imaging conditions, then $I_i(x_{pi}, y_{pi})$ in (A.5) becomes to contain only one component of reflection, i.e. specular reflection. Hence from

(5) and (10.d), it is given by:

$$I_i(x_{pi}, y_{pi}) = K = \frac{K^*}{1-q} \qquad (A.10)$$

From (A.10), a global q is determined by averaging the q's obtained from ith image as follows:

$$q = \sum_{i=1}^{3} 1 - \frac{K^*}{I_i(x_{pi}, y_{pi})} \qquad (A.11)$$

ACKNOWLEDGEMENT

This work was supported in part by the FHTIC under the Applied Research Grant Program.

REFERENCES

[1] J.T. Tou, et al., "Intelligent information systems for computer integrated manufacturing," PROCIM 88, Orlando, Florida, Nov. 1988.

[2] J.S. Park and J.T. Tou,"A solder joint inspection system for automated printed circuit board manufacturing," 1990 IEEE Conf. Robotics and Automation, Cincinnati, Ohio, May 1990.

[3] J.S. Park and J.T. Tou," Automated recognition of electronic components on PC boards via highlight separation and dual channel processing," to be presented at the Int. Conf. Automation, Robotics, and Computer Vision, Singapore, Sept. 1990.

[4] A.C. Sanderson, et al., "Structured highlight inspection of specular surface," IEEE Trans. Pattern Anal. Machine Intell., vol PAMI-10, pp. 44-55, 1988.

[5] R.T. Chin, "Automated visual inspection," Compt. Vision Graphics Image Process., Vol. 41, pp. 346-381, 1988.

[6] D. Thrift and C. Lee, "Using highlights to constraining object size and location," IEEE Tran. Syst., Man, Cybern., SMC-13, pp. 426-431, 1983.

[7] A. Blake and G. Brelstaff,"Geometry from specularities," Proc. IEEE Conf. Computer Vision Pattern Recognition, 1988.

[8] A. Blake,"Specular stereo," Proc. 9th International Joint Conf. Artificial Intell., Los Angeles, California, pp. 973-976, 1985.

[9] R. Gershorn, A.D. Jepson, and J.K. Tsotsos, "Highlight identification using chromatic information", Proc., 1st Int. Conf. Computer Vision, London, pp. 161-170, 1987.

[10] L. Dreschler and H.H. Nagel, "Volumetric model and 3-D trajectory of a moving car derived from monocular TV frame sequence of a street scene," Computer Graphics and Image Processing, Vol 20, pp. 199-228, 1982.

[11] G. Healey and T.O. Binford, "Local shape from specularity," Computer Vision, Graphics, Image Process., vol. 42, pp. 62-86, 1988.

[12] B.K.P. Horn, "Determining shape from shading," in The Psychology of Computer Vision, P.H.Winston, Ed. New York, McGraw-Hill, 1975.

[13] R.J. Woodham, "Photometric stereo: A reflectance map technique for determining surface orientation from image intensity," Proc. SPIE 155, 1978.

[14] J.T. Tou and C.L. Huang, "Recognition of 3-dimensional objects via spatial understanding of 2-dimensional images," IEEE 2nd Conf. AI Appl., Dec. 1985.

[15] C.L. Huang and J.T. Tou,"Automatic generation of 3-dimensional pictorial drawing from intensity images," SPIE Proc. Appl. Artificial Intel. Conf., May 1987.

[16] K. Ikeuchi, "Determining surface orientation of specular surface by using the photometric stereo method," IEEE Trans. Pattern Anal. Machine Intell., vol. PAMI-3, pp. 661-669, 1981.

[17] G.J. Klinker, S.A. Shafer, and T. Kanade, "Using a color reflection model to separate highlights from object color", Proc., 1st Int. Conf. Computer Vision, London, pp. 145-150, 1987.

[18] G.J. Klinker, S.A. Shafer, and T. Kanade, "Color image analysis with an intrinsic reflectance model," Proc. International Conf. Computer Vision, pp. 292-296, 1988.

[19] S.K. Nayar and K. Ikeuchi, "Photometric sampling: a method for determining shape and reflectance of surfaces," in Machine Vision for Inspection and Measurement editted by H. Freeman, Academic Press, 1989.

[20] L.B. Wolff and T.E. Boult,"Polarization/radiometric based material classification," Proc. International Conf. Pattern Recognition, pp. 387-395, 1989.

[21] E.N. Coleman and R. Jain, "Obtaining 3-dimensional shape of textured and specular surface using four-source photometry," Computer Graphics, Image Processing, vol. 18, pp. 309-328, 1982.

[22] B.K.P. Horn, "Robot Vision," MIT Press, 1986.

[23] C.G. Cullen,"Matrices and linear transformations," Addison-Wesley, 1972.

[24] K. Torrance and E. Sparrow, "Theory for off-specular reflection from roughened surfaces," J. Opt. Soc. Amer., vol. 57, pp. 1105-1114, 1967.

[25] R. Cook and K. Torrance, "A reflectance model for computer graphics," Computer Graphics, vol. 15, no. 3, pp. 307-316, 1981.

[26] J. Blinn, "Model of light reflection for computer synthesized pictures," Computer Graphics, vol. 11, no. 2, pp. 192-198, 1977.

[27] P. Taylor, "Theory and applications of numerical analysis," Academic Press, New York, 1973.

[28] J.S. Vandergraft,"Introduction to numerical computations," Academic Press, New York, 1978.

[29] W.A. Rense,"Polarization studies of light diffusely reflected from ground and etched glass surfaces," J. Optical Soc. America, Vol. 40, No. 1, pp. 55-59, 1950.

Shape Recovery from Interreflection

Interreflection arises in nearly every scene. We sometimes model illumination as though each surface receives light from some identifiable (point or diffuse) light source, but in reality that model is not accurate. Each surface also receives light that is reflected off of other objects in the scene. This phenomenon is *interreflection*. In order to carry out accurate analysis of images, we need to recognize and account for interreflection. This has given rise to two branches of literature in physics-based vision – interreflection color analysis, which is presented in the section on "Color Interreflection" in the Color volume of this series; and interreflection intensity analysis, which is described here.

In general, surfaces exhibit both specular (glossy) and diffuse (matte) reflection. Thus, when light is reflected from surface A onto surface B, surface B is actually receiving three elements of illumination:

- direct illumination,
- specular reflection from A, and
- diffuse reflection from A.

Each of these reflects both specularly and diffusely from B, giving a total of six components of reflected light. In intensity analysis of interreflection, the problem is generally simplified by assuming that both A and B reflect as perfect diffusers, so that the only reflection components are direct illumination / diffuse reflection from B, and diffuse reflection from A / diffuse reflection from B. The first of these components would arise even if there were no interreflection. So, the goal of analysis is to analyze the second component.

This diffuse/diffuse reflection has very interesting and structured geometric properties, under the assumption that surfaces are perfectly diffuse (Lambertian) reflectors. In fact, it has been studied widely under the name *configuration factors* in *radiosity*, the study of heat transfer (recently applied to computer graphics).

The literature in quantitative analysis of interreflection intensity begins with Horn's work in [1], which is reprinted in the "Intensity Reflection Models" section of the Radiometry volume. There, Horn points out how, at a concave junction of surfaces, the intensity reflected from each will increase due to light reflected from the other surface. Horn presented an analysis of the simple case of two adjoining planes.

The first paper in this collection [2] presents a more general analysis, developing a formulation of interreflection for a curved surface in terms of an *interreflection kernel* function that captures the influence of each point on the surface on each other point. Using this concept, a method is shown for predicting some important interreflectance phenomena, particularly for surfaces of constant reflectance.

The second paper [3] takes this development further, presenting a closed-form prediction method based on functions to describe surface shape and reflectance. It also shows several worked examples, and makes important observations about the interaction of shape, shadow, and observed intensity.

The only paper in the collection that presents a machine vision analysis of interreflection is [4], winner of the 1990 David Marr Prize in Computational Vision. This paper considers the problem of errors in photometric stereo caused by the failure to account for interreflection on a concave surface. When the surface being viewed is concave, interreflection causes the intensities to be slightly higher than they would be if the surface were convex. This violates the assumption of photometric stereo that intensity depends only on surface orientation but not on the overall surface shape (see the "Photometric Stereo" section of this volume). The result is that the surface shape reconstructed by photometric stereo will indicate a shallower concavity than is actually present. The authors call this reconstructed shape the "pseudo shape" of the surface. The pseudo shape has important invariance properties, such as being independent of viewpoint and illumination direction.

To reconstruct the shape accurately, the paper presents a method that begins with computation of the pseudo shape. While this is shallower than the actual surface concavity, it does at least have a concavity. Then, using this concave pseudo shape, an interreflection prediction can be made using traditional methods. The contribution of this interreflection can be subtracted from the image, and the resulting image data can be re-interpreted to compute shape. This will yield a deeper concavity than the original pseudo shape, though still shallower than the true surface. The process can be repeated, yielding successively deeper concave reconstructions that approach but never exceed the true depth of the surface concavity. After a few iterations, the reconstruction is very close.

This paper is noteworthy not only for the theory and algorithm it presents, but also for the fact that it is a comprehensive treatment of its topic, ranging from basic theory to algorithm development to trial on real image data and analysis of the errors in the results.

A Bug in the Literature

There is a subtle bug that manifests itself through much of the literature in intensity analysis of interreflection, even for perfectly diffuse surfaces. The buggy argument goes like this:

> Suppose the intensity of the illumination is I, the surface reflectance ρ, and the observed pixel value in the image is therefore $P = sI\rho$, where s is a constant indicating the camera's responsivity.
>
> Then, if the observed light was caused by interreflection from two surfaces with reflectances ρ_1 and ρ_2, the pixel value will therefore be $P_{12} = sI\rho_1\rho_2$.

This last formula is not correct, though it is relied on heavily in the literature.

The bug arises because of the failure to account for the spectral (color) aspect of light and reflection. Just because the camera delivers a single integer as the gray-level pixel value does not relieve the researcher of the need to model the underlying color phenomenon accurately. In the case of interreflection, the color properties of the world make the simple formula above inaccurate.

A spectral model of pixel value formulation would be $P = \int \rho(\lambda)\, s(\lambda)\, I(\lambda)\, d\lambda$, and for interreflection $P_{12} = \int \rho_1(\lambda)\, \rho_2(\lambda)\, s(\lambda)\, I(\lambda)\, d\lambda$. If we simplify by assuming white illumination and a camera equally sensitive to all wavelengths, then s and I become constants and we have $P = sI \int \rho(\lambda)\, d\lambda$ and $P_{12} = sI \int \rho_1(\lambda)\, \rho_2(\lambda)\, d\lambda$.

To show the correspondence with the equations in the bug above, let $\rho = \int \rho(\lambda)\, d\lambda$ so we have once again $P = sI\rho$. Similar definitions apply to ρ_1 and ρ_2. But then, $P_{12} = sI \int \rho_1(\lambda)\, \rho_2(\lambda)\, d\lambda$ but $sI\rho_1\rho_2 =$ $sI \int \rho_1(\lambda)\, d\lambda \int \rho_2(\lambda)\, d\lambda$, so $P_{12} \leq sI\rho_1\rho_2$, in violation of the erroneous equation at the end of the buggy argument.

To put this in plain language, you cannot simply multiply black-and-white reflectance coefficients to predict the black-and-white values observed after interreflection. The reason is that the spectral reflectances of the surfaces generally interact to produce a reflected power whose observed value will be lower than predicted in such a way. This effect is even true if $\rho_1(\lambda) = \rho_2(\lambda)$, that is, for the case of a single concave surface.

Equality in the above relation will hold, and the bug will therefore vanish, if the reflectances $\rho_1(\lambda)$ and $\rho_2(\lambda)$ are constant with respect to wavelength, i.e., if the surfaces involved are pure white or gray. Significantly, the real images examined in the literature are generally of objects coated with white or gray diffuse paint to make this condition hold.

These factors are discussed in the Color volume of this series, particularly the sections on "Color Image Formation" and "Color Interreflection."

– S.A.S.

Reference

[1] Horn, B.K.P. "Understanding Image Intensities." *Artificial Intelligence* **8** (2): 201-231, 1977. Reprinted in the "Intensity Reflection Models" section of the Radiometry volume of this series.

Papers Included in This Collection

[2] Koenderink, J.J., and van Doorn, A.J. "Geometrical Modes as a General Method to Treat Diffuse Interreflections in Radiometry." *J. Optical Society of America* **73**(6): 843-850, June 1983.

[3] Forsyth, D., and Zisserman, A. "Reflections on Shading." *IEEE Trans. on Pattern Analysis and Machine Intelligence* **PAMI-13**(7): 671-679, July 1991.

[4] Nayar, S.K., Ikeuchi, K., and Kanade, T. "Shape from Interreflections." *Intl. Journal of Computer Vision* **6**(3): 173-195, 1991.

Geometrical modes as a general method to treat diffuse interreflections in radiometry

J. J. Koenderink and A. J. van Doorn

Department of Medical and Physiological Physics, Physics Laboratory, State University Utrecht, Princetonplein 5, 3584 CC Utrecht, The Netherlands

Received August 12, 1982; revised manuscript received December 22, 1982

The problem of interreflections for Lambertian surfaces of arbitrary shape and with varying reflectance is of interest for many practical applications. We present a general method to approach this problem. We define photometric modes that are uncoupled in the sense that each mode may be assigned a (pseudo) reflectance and that interreflections among modes vanish. Then the problem is formally identical with that of a convex body, in which interreflections are of no importance. The photometric modes depend on the shape of the body. In many practical cases one or a few modes dominate, and the reflected radiance depends more on the shape of the body (the dominant mode) than on the precise irradiance distribution. A few examples are treated explicitly. The redistribution of radiation described by the modes is treated by means of the net vector flux and the space density of radiation. Knowledge of these fields for the dominant mode yields considerable intuitive insight in the physical situation and provides the means to estimate the effects of painting part of the surface or of the introduction of screens.

The problem of multiple diffuse interreflections in radiometry arises mainly in applications, which is probably the reason why most textbooks on optics usually dedicate little space to it. Such applications include the design of scientific apparatus, e.g., the construction of realistic integrating spheres with uneven coating and windows, as well as lighting technology with problems in the illumination of rooms, traffic tunnels, etc. As a result of these needs several authors attacked the problem. Thus the case of the integrating sphere with uneven coating was treated by Jacquez and Kuppenheim.[1] In illumination engineering, interreflections were treated quite practically by O'Brien[2] with the help of a network simulation. This author treats the cubical room with walls of different reflectances as an example.

Although methods to treat general cases exist, it is still difficult to formulate qualitative predictions in complicated situations. If this is the aim, a more-general approach to the problem is needed. The need for such an approach is felt in vision research, for example, especially with respect to the perception of three-dimensional shape. It is well known that one gains an often veracious impression of the shape of objects irrespective of their exact illumination. Whereas it is possible to understand this in terms of general invariants present in the retinal illumination patterns obtained under mutual displacements of observers, objects, and light sources, the present theories simplify the real situation considerably. For instance, they tend to neglect the complications that are due to bidirectional reflectances other than Lambertian or specular, vignetting of light sources by the object, and interreflections. That interreflections are of great importance for the perception of three-dimensional shape can be shown through a simple example. There exist bronze recasts of Roman marble copies of lost Greek original bronzes. These recasts look strikingly un-Greek: the surface undulations are much too articulated. The inference is that the Roman carvers have strengthened the surface relief because undu-

lations tend to *look* much flatter in marble than in bronze, presumably because of interreflections.

A general question is whether interreflections introduce new invariant features of the radiance reflected into the eye by curved objects. *A priori* this seems likely: just think of the integrating sphere. No matter what the irradiance distribution is like, the sphere tends to reradiate uniformly over its whole surface. The uniform radiance irrespective of the irradiance pattern can be considered an invariant feature generated by multiple interreflection. This invariant is closely related to the geometry of the cavity. In this paper we trace the existence of such *geometrical modes*. They permit a quick understanding of the reflected radiance that is due to many interreflections in its dependence of the object's shape.

1. INTERREFLECTANCE PROBLEM

Consider an object described by way of the vector $\mathbf{x}(u, v)$ that describes points on its surface and the direction of the (inward) normal $\mathbf{n}(\mathbf{x})$. Let the surface be a Lambertian diffuse reflector with reflectance $\rho(\mathbf{x})$. We define the primary irradiance $H(\mathbf{x})$ as the irradiance that is due to the sources in the absence of interreflections. A dark body $[\rho(\mathbf{x}) \to 0]$ would show an irradiance distribution $H(\mathbf{x})$. This irradiance distribution is a function not only of the source distribution but also of the shape of the object, e.g., it includes the effects of vignetting if the body is not convex. We describe the final radiation distribution (including the effects of interreflections) through the radiance $N(\mathbf{x})$, which denotes the radiance as measured from some position from which the point $\mathbf{x}$ is visible in the direction of $\mathbf{x}$. (Because the surface is Lambertian the position of the vantage point is immaterial.) Then the interreflections are governed by the kernel $K(\mathbf{x}, \mathbf{x}')$ defined in such a way that $K(\mathbf{x}, \mathbf{x}')d\mathbf{x}d\mathbf{x}'$ is the *étendue* of the beam defined by the infinitesimal surface elements $d\mathbf{x}$ and $d\mathbf{x}'$.

From this definition it is clear that the kernel is a symmetric, positive definite function. The kernel vanishes only for point pairs $(\mathbf{x}, \mathbf{x}')$ that cannot be joined by a ray outside the body. Thus for the outside of a convex body the kernel vanishes identically except for the diagonal $\mathbf{x} = \mathbf{x}'$, whereas for the inside of a convex body the kernel vanishes nowhere. Specifically, we have

$$K(\mathbf{x}; \mathbf{x}') = \frac{\mathrm{Pos}[\mathbf{n}(\mathbf{x}) \cdot (\mathbf{x}' - \mathbf{x})] \cdot \mathrm{Pos}\,[\mathbf{n}(\mathbf{x}') \cdot (\mathbf{x} - \mathbf{x}')]}{\|\mathbf{x}' - \mathbf{x}\|^2}, \quad (1)$$

with the convention

$$\mathrm{Pos}[a] = \frac{a + |a|}{2}. \quad (2)$$

The kernel is constrained through the geometrical fact that no surface element can radiate in or receive radiation from more than a half-space, or, equivalently,

$$\iint \left\| \frac{1}{\pi} K(\mathbf{x}; \mathbf{x}') \right\|^2 \mathrm{d}\mathbf{x}\mathrm{d}\mathbf{x}' \leqslant 1. \quad (3)$$

Energy balance is expressed through the equation

$$N(\mathbf{x}) - \frac{\rho(\mathbf{x})}{\pi} \int K(\mathbf{x}; \mathbf{x}') N(\mathbf{x}') \mathrm{d}\mathbf{x}' = \frac{\rho(\mathbf{x})}{\pi} H(\mathbf{x}). \quad (4)$$

This is an awkward equation, but it can be transformed into a Fredholm integral equation with symmetrical kernel through the substitution

$$\frac{H^*(\mathbf{x})}{[\rho(\mathbf{x})]^{1/2}} = H(\mathbf{x}), \quad (5)$$

$$\frac{1}{\pi} [\rho(\mathbf{x})]^{1/2} N^*(\mathbf{x}) = N(\mathbf{x}), \quad (6)$$

$$\frac{\pi K^*(\mathbf{x}; \mathbf{x}')}{[\rho(\mathbf{x})\rho(\mathbf{x}')]^{1/2}} = K(\mathbf{x}; \mathbf{x}'), \quad (7)$$

with the result that

$$N^*(\mathbf{x}) - \int K^*(\mathbf{x}; \mathbf{x}') N^*(\mathbf{x}') \mathrm{d}\mathbf{x}' = H^*(\mathbf{x}). \quad (8)$$

Thus generality is not sacrificed if we restrain ourselves to the case $\rho(\mathbf{x}) = \rho$, that is, constant reflectivity. We do so in the sequel. Then we define the iterated kernels K_m in the usual way:

$$K_1 = \frac{K}{\pi}, \quad (9)$$

$$K_m(\mathbf{x}; \mathbf{x}') = \int \frac{K(\mathbf{x}, \mathbf{y})}{\pi} K_{m-1}(\mathbf{y}, \mathbf{x}') \mathrm{d}\mathbf{y} \quad (m \geqslant 2), \quad (10)$$

and a formal solution of the interreflectance problem is

$$N(\mathbf{x}) = \frac{\rho H(\mathbf{x})}{\pi} + \sum_{m=1}^{\infty} \rho^m \int K_m(\mathbf{x}; \mathbf{x}') \frac{\rho H(\mathbf{x}')}{\pi} d\mathbf{x}'. \quad (11)$$

In this expression the contribution of the m-times interreflected rays appears explicitly. Convergence can be proven but is physically evident.

A useful way to formulate the solution is in terms of eigenfunctions of the kernel. We define the *pseudofacets* $P_k(\mathbf{x})$ through

$$\frac{1}{\pi} \int K(\mathbf{x}; \mathbf{x}') P_k(\mathbf{x}') \mathrm{d}\mathbf{x}' = \mu_k P_k(\mathbf{x}), \quad (12)$$

$$\int \|P_k(\mathbf{x})\|^2 \mathrm{d}\mathbf{x} = 1. \quad (13)$$

If we write the radiance $N(\mathbf{x})$ and the primary irradiance $H(\mathbf{x})$ in terms of the pseudofacets:

$$N(\mathbf{x}) = \sum_k n_k P_k(\mathbf{x}), \quad (14)$$

$$H(\mathbf{x}) = \sum_k h_k P_k(\mathbf{x}), \quad (15)$$

then we immediately find that

$$n_k = \frac{\rho}{\pi} \alpha_k h_k, \qquad \alpha_k = \frac{1}{1 - \rho\mu_k}. \quad (16)$$

We call α_k the *gain* of the kth pseudofacet. For a convex body we have $N(\mathbf{x}) = (\rho/\pi)H(\mathbf{x})$; thus the pseudofacets are just the surface elements (the real facets), and their gains are unity.

Inequality (3) yields a bound on the gains:

$$\alpha_k \leqslant \frac{1}{1 - \rho}. \quad (17)$$

For an integrating sphere the equality holds, and high gains (because $\rho \approx 1$) are possible.

The introduction of pseudofacets and gains reduces the interreflections problem to simple case without interreflections: the pseudofacets are independent. If $\mathbf{N}$ is the vector with coefficients n_k, $\mathbf{H}$ the vector with coefficients h_k, and R the diagonal matrix with coefficients $\rho\alpha_k$, we can write

$$\mathbf{N} = \frac{R}{\pi} \cdot \mathbf{H}, \quad (18)$$

which is formally identical with the case of a convex body without interreflections but varying reflectance. Indeed, for a convex polyhedron with facets of different reflectance, Eq. (18) holds with the reflectances of the facets as diagonal elements.

The integrating sphere appears to be a nice example, but in fact this case is less than trivial. For a sphere of radius R the kernel for the inside surface is a constant $[K(\mathbf{x}; \mathbf{x}') = 1/4R^2]$. The only nonvanishing eigenvalue is unity with the constant function $1/(4\pi R^2)^{1/2}$ as a normalized eigenfunction. All other eigenvalues vanish identically. Thus all functions in the orthogonal complement of the constant function in the Hilbert space of radiance functions are mapped on the origin by the kernel. However, there is no real difficulty: we can develop every function $N(\mathbf{x})$ in a component along the single eigenvector (the average value $\langle N \rangle$) and a component in its orthogonal complement [the ac component $N(\mathbf{x}) - \langle N \rangle$]. This latter component may formally be treated as an eigenfunction for the highly degenerate (and, strictly speaking, improper) eigenvalue zero. Then we obtain

$$\begin{bmatrix} \langle N \rangle \\ N(\mathbf{x}) - \langle N \rangle \end{bmatrix} = \frac{1}{\pi} \begin{pmatrix} \dfrac{\rho}{1 - \rho} & 0 \\ 0 & \rho \end{pmatrix} \begin{bmatrix} \langle H \rangle \\ H(\mathbf{x}) - \langle H \rangle \end{bmatrix}. \quad (19)$$

The reflectance of the dc component is $\rho/(1 - \rho)$; of the ac component just ρ (the interreflections just cancel). Obviously, when $\rho \approx 1$, the eigenfunction with pseudoreflectance

$\rho/(1 - \rho)$ dominates, and we need not worry about the improper eigenfunction at all. This means that, in this case, the sphere lights up as a whole no matter how we irradiate it, a clear instance of an invariance that is due to interreflections. That this is a valid way to treat the problem becomes clear when we look at the case of the geometrically perturbed sphere, e.g., the triaxial ellipsoid with only infinitesimally different axes. Then we obtain a nondegenerate spectrum of eigenvalues; however, most of them are infinitesimally small, except for one eigenvalue unity. Thus in the lowest approximation we obtain the (degenerate) solution for the sphere, although the exact solution is quite regular. The precise nature of the nondegenerate eigenfunctions is largely irrelevant because the dc component dominates anyway. For most purposes we may lump them as the (extensive!) subspace of ac distributions.

Whenever $\rho \ll 1$ the effect of interreflections vanishes of course, and we obtain in the lowest approximation $N(\mathbf{x}) = [\rho H(\mathbf{x})/\pi]$. For $\rho \to 0$ all gain factors approach unity, and the method becomes less advantageous. Yet the influence of interreflections may remain appreciable in many cases, e.g., for the integrating sphere, we have

$$N(\mathbf{x}) = \frac{\rho}{\pi} \left[H(\mathbf{x}) + \frac{\rho}{1 - \rho} \langle H \rangle \right]. \qquad (20)$$

Thus, even for the case $\rho = \frac{1}{2}$, the contribution of the dc component is double that of the ac component.

2. KERNEL $K(\mathbf{x}, \mathbf{x}')$ AND SOLID SHAPE

In general the kernel $K(\mathbf{x}, \mathbf{x}')$ is of a complicated form. A few general observations can be made. First, consider local properties: $\mathbf{x}$ near $\mathbf{x}'$. Generically we have to deal with elliptic or hyperbolic patches. If the patch is elliptic and convex, $K(\mathbf{x}, \mathbf{x}')$ vanishes identically. For the elliptic concave case, the situation is much like that for the integrating sphere: the kernel is almost constant, it varies slowly with $\|\mathbf{x} - \mathbf{x}'\|$, but it is anisotropic if the principal radii of curvature are unequal. In the extreme case of a cylinder the interreflections vanish along the cylinder axis (see Section 3.A). For a hyperbolic patch the kernel $K(\mathbf{x}, \mathbf{x}')$ vanishes if $\mathbf{x}'$ is in an hourglass-shaped area centered on $\mathbf{x}$. For instance, take the surface defined by $z(x, y) = xy$, or, in polar coordinates, $z(\rho, \phi) = \frac{1}{2}\rho^2 \sin 2\phi$. We easily derive

$$K(0, 0; \rho, \phi) = \left[\text{Pos} \left(\frac{\sin 2\phi}{2} \right) \right]^2 + 0(\rho^2). \qquad (21)$$

Thus K vanishes in the quadrants $0 < \phi < \pi/2$ and $\pi < \phi < 3\pi/2$. The kernel is highly anisotropic but depends only marginally on $\|\mathbf{x} - \mathbf{x}'\|$. The interreflections are strong but directed along the direction of concave curvature.

Next, consider the global features. First, observe that it may well be that $K_m(\mathbf{x}, \mathbf{x}') \neq 0$, whereas $K(\mathbf{x}, \mathbf{x}')$ vanishes. This happens because two patches that cannot see each other may well both see a third patch and interact by way of that (Fig. 1).

It may also happen that two patches cannot interact, not because the facets are oriented wrong with respect to their mutual direction but because another part of the object is interposed between the facets: This is the phenomenon of vignetting in its strict sense. We use it in a slightly generalized sense and speak of vignetting whenever the *étendue* of

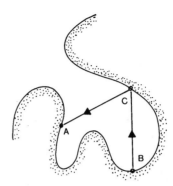

Fig. 1. Phenomenon of vignetting. No ray may travel from A to B directly because it must be intercepted by the object. But a ray emitted from B may reach A after having been scattered at C.

a beam defined by a patch and an infinite sphere around the object is less than πdA. Vignetting is the main obstacle in the general treatment of the interreflection problem. Because of it the kernel $K(\mathbf{x}, \mathbf{x}')$ and especially the iterated kernels $K_m(\mathbf{x}, \mathbf{x}')$ are complicated functions of global solid shape. (The reader may find it instructive to try the inside of a torus or the volume between two concentric spheres.) For the kernel $K_1(\mathbf{x}, \mathbf{x}')$ vignetting can be taken account of by means of a characteristic function $\chi(\mathbf{x}, \mathbf{x}')$ that equals unity if $\mathbf{x}$ and $\mathbf{x}'$ can see each other and vanishes otherwise; but for the higher iterated kernels, this is no longer possible.

It is of some importance to note the fact that vignetting also affects the primary irradiances. Thus not only the kernel but also the right-hand side of Eq. (4) is affected. This can lead to complicated situations. In the simplest case of a body placed in a homogeneous, isotropic radiation field (incident radiance N^* independent of location and direction), this effect can be taken into account if we introduce a single function $\xi(\mathbf{x})$ defined over all surface patches. We write the primary irradiance as

$$H(\mathbf{x}) = \pi[1 - \xi(\mathbf{x})]N^*. \qquad (22)$$

Thus ξ vanishes for a convex body; it equals unity for a closed cavity irradiated from the outside. Because $\xi(\mathbf{x})$ obviously equals the fraction of the *étendue* of the primary incident beam to its maximum value (π), we have

$$\xi(\mathbf{x}) = \frac{1}{\pi} \int K(\mathbf{x}, \mathbf{x}') d\mathbf{x}'. \qquad (23)$$

For a perfect Lambertian reflector we find that $N(\mathbf{x}) = N^*$; thus the gains exactly cancel the vignetting of the sources. In that case the vignetting factor $\xi(\mathbf{x})$ must be approximately proportional to the pseudofacet with the highest gain.

In other cases it is difficult to take the effects of vignetting into account. Nevertheless a general treatment would be desirable in view of the fact that several well-known effects of the academic painting tradition (and thus of interest to vision research) fall into this class. We illustrate this with an apparently simple (but extremely difficult to solve analytically) example: a hemispherical boss on a plane, irradiated with an obliquely incident collimated beam. Boss and plane are ideal Lambertian reflectors ($\rho = 1$). See Fig. 2. Because of vignetting, $\alpha\beta$ and $\beta\gamma$ are in shadow. ($\alpha\beta$ is a body shadow; $\beta\gamma$ is the cast shadow). The eye looks from such a direction that $\alpha\beta$ and $\gamma\beta$ are completely visible. Now it is clear that

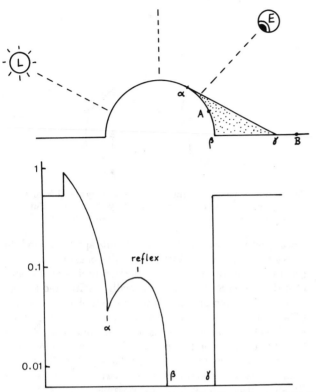

Fig. 2.   A hemispherical boss on a plane is irradiated from a distant light source L. An eye views the boss from E.   There is a body shadow α–β and a cast shadow β–γ in the primary irradiance.   Note that the interreflections are not symmetrical: B throws a much larger reflex on A than A throws on B because A receives no primary irradiation whereas B does.   The graph shows the resulting reflected radiance that is due to the once- and twice-scattered rays.   The reflex can often be noticed in nature and is often depicted by painters.

the first-order interreflection will include the irradiance of $\alpha\beta$ by $\gamma\infty$ but that $\beta\gamma$ cannot receive any contribution from $\alpha\beta$ or $\gamma\infty$.   As a result of this asymmetrical situation, the rim of the hemispherical boss (at A) looks much lighter than the cast shadow of the boss ($\beta\gamma$), an effect noticed by painters because it offers a welcome help to set off the boss against the plane by means of a tonal difference.   In paintings the effect is often highly exaggerated.

3. SOME APPLICATIONS

A. Cylinder

The right circular cylinder offers a good example to use in studying highly anisotropic interreflections.   Consider a cylinder with unit radius.   We use cylindrical coordinates, azimuth angle ϕ, and axial distance z.   Then we have, for point pairs on a generator (with the same angle of azimuth), that the kernel vanishes identically.   On the other hand, for point pairs with the same axial position (on the circle $z = cst$), the kernel takes on its maximum value of unity.   In fact, simple geometry yields

$$K(\mathbf{x}, \mathbf{x}') = \frac{4 \sin^4 \dfrac{\phi_1 - \phi_2}{2}}{\left\| 4 \sin^2 \dfrac{\phi_1 - \phi_2}{2} + (z_1 - z_2)^2 \right\|^2}. \tag{24}$$

Because we must have translation and rotation invariance, the pseudofacets may be guessed to be

$$\Phi_{km}(z, \phi) = \exp[i(m\phi + kz)]. \tag{25}$$

This leads to the eigenvalue equation

$$\mu_{km}\Phi_{km} = \frac{1}{\pi} \int K(\mathbf{x}, \mathbf{x}')\Phi_{km}(\mathbf{x}')\mathrm{d}x'$$

$$= \frac{1}{\pi} \int_{-\infty}^{+\infty} \int_0^{2\pi} \frac{4 \sin^4 \dfrac{\phi_1 - \phi_2}{2} \exp[i(m\phi + kz)]}{\left\| 4 \sin^2 \dfrac{\phi_1 - \phi_2}{2} + (z_1 - z_2)^2 \right\|^2} \mathrm{d}\phi \mathrm{d}z \tag{26}$$

or

$$\mu_{km} = \int_0^{\pi/2} \cos(2m\nu)(1 + 2k \sin \nu) \sin \nu \exp(-2k \sin \nu)\mathrm{d}\nu. \tag{27}$$

For the *angular modes* ($k = 0$) the gains are

$$\alpha_{0m} = \left[1 - \rho \int_0^1 T_{2m}(z)\mathrm{d}z \right]^{-1} \tag{28}$$

(T_n is the nth-order Chebyshev polynomial).   For the lowest modes we have

$$\alpha_{00} = \frac{1}{1 - \rho}, \quad \text{for } \rho \to 1, \quad \alpha_{00} \to \infty,$$

$$\alpha_{01} = \frac{1}{1 + \dfrac{\rho}{3}}, \qquad \alpha_{01} \to 0.75,$$

$$\alpha_{02} = \frac{1}{1 + \dfrac{\rho}{15}}, \qquad \alpha_{02} \to 0.9375,$$

$$\alpha_{03} = \frac{1}{1 + \dfrac{\rho}{35}}, \qquad \alpha_{03} \to 0.9722\ldots. \tag{29}$$

The mode 00 is the integrating sphere mode.   It dominates whenever $\rho \to 1$.   In the mode 01 the interreflections tend to cancel the mode distribution, hence the low gain.   For the higher angular modes the gains approach unity and interreflections are relatively unimportant.   Roughly speaking, the cylinder acts much like the integrating sphere for angular distributions.

For the axial modes the case $m = 0$ is the most interesting: for higher values of m the gains approach unity anyway.   The axial gain function is

$$\alpha_{k0} = \left[1 - \rho \int_0^{\pi/2} (1 + 2k \sin \theta)\sin \theta \exp(-2k \sin \theta)\mathrm{d}\theta \right]^{-1}. \tag{30}$$

This is not handled easily by analytical methods but can be readily integrated numerically (Fig. 3).   For $\rho = 1$ and small k, we obtain asymptotically $\alpha_{k0} = 3/8k^2$; for very large k we have $\alpha_{k0} = 1$.   Thus the cutoff wavelength is

$$\lambda_c = 2\pi(8/3)^{1/2} = 10.26 = 5.13\, D, \tag{31}$$

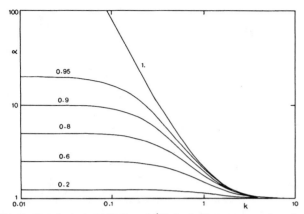

Fig. 3. Axial gain for cylinders of different reflectances as a function of the spatial wave number k of rotationally symmetric modes ($m = 0$).

where D is the diameter of the tube. If $\lambda < \lambda_c$, a strong attenuation (relative to the dc mode) sets in. The higher angular modes are influenced little by radial modulation. For small k we have

$$\alpha_{k0} = \frac{3}{8k^2},$$

$$\alpha_{k1} = \frac{3}{4}\left(1 - \frac{6}{5}k^2 + \ldots\right),$$

$$\alpha_{k2} = \frac{15}{16}\left(1 + \frac{3}{14}k^2 + \ldots\right),$$

$$\alpha_{k3} = \frac{35}{36}\left(1 - \frac{50}{243}k^2 + \ldots\right). \tag{32}$$

Thus for tunnel illumination, with equally spaced lights not on the axis, the remaining inhomogeneities are easily found as follows: Average the primary irradiance over the azimuth, since the only important modes are radial anyway. Calculate the fundamental harmonic component of this averaged illuminance. The damping relative to the dc mode (homogeneous illumination) yields the remaining contrast:

$$\frac{\Delta N}{N} \approx \frac{\alpha_{k0}}{\alpha_{00}}\left|\frac{\Delta H}{H}\right|_{\text{ang}} \tag{33}$$

(k is the frequency of the fundamental and $\langle \Delta H/H \rangle_{\text{ang}}$ is the contrast of primary irradiance averaged over the azimuth). The gain factor yields a convenient description here.

B. Two Parallel Planes

The case of two parallel planes (irradiated on the sides facing each other) is an instructive one to use to study the effects of vignetting: No patch on one plane can see another patch on the same plane; all redistribution of radiation over a plane must go by way of the other plane.

As coordinate system we choose Cartesian coordinates (x, y, z); one plane is (x, y, 0), the other (x, y, 1). Then the kernel is $K(\mathbf{r}, \mathbf{r}') = 0$ when $\mathbf{r}$ and $\mathbf{r}'$ are on the same plane;

$$K(\mathbf{r}, \mathbf{r}') = [1 + (x_1 - x_2)^2 + (y_1 - y_2)^2]^{-2}$$

$$\text{if } \mathbf{r} = (x_1, y_1, 0) \; \mathbf{r}' = (x_2, y_2, 1)$$

$$\text{or } \mathbf{r} = (x_1, y_1, 1) \; \mathbf{r}' = (x_2, y_2, 0). \tag{34}$$

Again the pseudofacets can be guessed offhand: they must

be of the type $\cos(k_x x_1 + k_y y_1)$ on the first and $\pm \cos(k_x x_2 + k_y y_2)$ on the second plane.

The eigenvalues can be found by integration; they are $\mu_{k+} = kK_1(k)$ for the even mode and $\mu_{k-} = -kK_1(k)$ for the odd mode [even mode: distributions on plates in phase; odd mode: distributions on plates in counterphase; $k = (k_x^2 + k_y^2)^{1/2}$; $K_1(x)$ is a modified Bessel function]. Thus the gain functions are (Fig. 4)

$$\alpha_{k+} = [1 - \rho k K_1(k)]^{-1},$$

$$\alpha_{k-} = [1 + \rho k K_1(k)]^{-1}. \tag{35}$$

For $\rho = 1$ and small k we have $\alpha_{k+} \approx [-2/k^2 \ln(k/2)]$, whereas $\alpha_{k-} \approx (1/2)$. For large k both α_{k+} and α_{k-} tend to unity. Thus only even modes are sustained. If we define the cutoff frequency through $\alpha_{k_c+} = 2$ we obtain $\lambda_c \approx 5.0$ (for $\rho \approx 1$). Thus variations with wavelengths smaller than five times the spacing of the plates are already strongly damped compared with the integrating sphere mode ($k = 0$).

If we put a primary irradiance $H_0 \cos \mathbf{k} \cdot \mathbf{r}$ on one plate and zero on the other, the resulting radiance distribution on the first plate is

$$N(\mathbf{r}) = \frac{\rho}{\pi}\{1 - \{\rho[kK_1(k)]\}^2\}^{-1}H(\mathbf{r})$$

$$= \frac{\rho}{\pi}\{1 + 2\rho^2[kK_1(k)]^2 + \ldots\}H(\mathbf{r}). \tag{36}$$

It is apparent that only second-order interreflections appear. This is the result of vignetting: The plate cannot redistribute radiation except by way of the other one.

4. LIGHT FIELD OF THE PSEUDOFACETS

The exchange of radiant energy in complicated cases is best visualized in terms of the light field as introduced by Gershun[3]. The first two terms of a development of the radiance at any point into spherical harmonics have a scalar and a vector character:

$$N(\mathbf{x}, \mathbf{s}) = \sum_{1=0}^{\infty} \sum_{m=-1}^{+1} a_{1m}(\mathbf{x}) Y_{1m}(\mathbf{s})$$

$$= \frac{1}{4\pi} u(\mathbf{x}) + \frac{3}{4\pi} \mathbf{D}(\mathbf{x}) \cdot \mathbf{s}$$

$$+ \text{quadrupole and higher-order terms.} \tag{37}$$

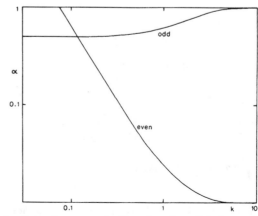

Fig. 4. Gains for even and odd modes of parallel plates with unit reflectance.

The scalar field describes the radiation volume density:

$$u(\mathbf{x}) = \int_{(4\pi)} N(\mathbf{x}, \mathbf{s}) d\omega, \qquad (38)$$

and the vector field describes the net vector flux:

$$\mathbf{D}(\mathbf{x}) = \int_{(4\pi)} N(\mathbf{x}, \mathbf{s}) d\boldsymbol{\omega}. \qquad (39)$$

The net vector flux is a solenoidal vector field in the stationary case because of the equation of continuity

$$\frac{\partial u}{\partial t} + \nabla \cdot \mathbf{D} = \text{source density.} \qquad (40)$$

In empty space and the stationary case we consequently have $\nabla \cdot \mathbf{D} = 0$. The vector tubes of the $\mathbf{D}$ field map the net flux of radiation in the sense that there is no net exchange of flux among these tubes (although the geometrical rays in general pierce these tubes). Thus the net vector flux gives a good impression of the redistribution of radiant energy through interreflections. It is interesting to calculate them for the pseudofacets in order to gain some insight into the situation.

A few mathematical properties may be noted. In the absence of vignetting the density is harmonic:

$$\Delta u = 0.$$

In two-dimensional problems (cylindrical symmetry, parallel planes, etc.) we have

$$\mathbf{D} \cdot \nabla \times \mathbf{D} = 0,$$

and $\mathbf{D}$ can be obtained from a pseudopotential

$$\mathbf{D} = \Psi \nabla \phi.$$

But it must be stressed that in the general case neither does $\Delta u = 0$ nor does a pseudopotential for $\mathbf{D}$ exist.

5. LIGHT FIELD FOR THE PSEUDOFACETS OF THE PARALLEL PLATES

First we find the light field for a single plate with a radiant emittance

$$E(x, y) = E_0 \sin kx. \qquad (41)$$

The radiance at a point (x, y, z) in a direction to a point $(x^*, y^*, 0)$ on the plate is

$$N = \frac{E_0}{\pi} \sin kx^*. \qquad (42)$$

The density of radiation is found by integration

$$u(x, y, z) = \int N d\Omega = 2E_0 \sin kx \exp(-kz). \qquad (43)$$

(Note that u is harmonic: $\Delta u = 0$.) (See Fig. 5.) The net vector flux can also be found by integration:

$$\mathbf{D} = \int N d\Omega = \frac{E_0}{\pi} [kz K_1(kz) \sin kx \, \mathbf{e}_z - kz K_0(kz) \cos kx \, \mathbf{e}_x].$$

$$(44)$$

{The net vector flux can be obtained from a pseudopotential:

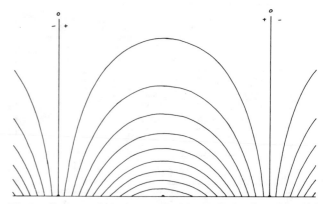

Fig. 5.   Contours of equal space density of radiation for a sinusoidal (pseudo) radiance distribution on a flat plate. The curves are drawn for equal increments.

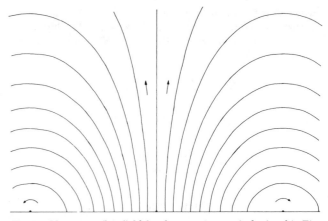

Fig. 6.   Net vector flux field for the same case as is depicted in Fig. 5. The density of the field lines is proportional to the magnitude of the net vector flux.

$$\mathbf{D} = -\frac{E_0 z}{\pi} \nabla [K_0(kz) \sin kx].\}$$

(See Fig. 6.)

The light field between two parallel plates can be obtained at once by just adding the contribution from the separate plates. The results are most easily interpreted in terms of suitable averages. The average of the radiation density over a region $0 < x < \lambda/4; 0 < z < d/2$ is

$$\bar{u} = \frac{8E_0}{\pi kd} [1 - \exp(-kd)] \qquad \text{for the even modes}$$

$$= \frac{8E_0}{\pi kd} \left[1 - \exp\left(-\frac{kd}{2}\right)\right]^2 \qquad \text{for the odd modes.} \qquad (45)$$

Figure 7 shows the dependencies. For long wavelengths the density is high for the even case (just as for the integrating sphere) and zero for the odd case. For small wavelengths the plates become effectively decoupled, and the difference between odd and even modes vanishes. The flux that leaves the plates in a region $z = 0, 0 < x < \lambda/4$ is

$$\Phi = \frac{2E_0}{\pi^2} [1 - kK_1(k)] \qquad \text{for the even modes}$$

$$= \frac{2E_0}{\pi^2} [1 + kK_1(k)] \qquad \text{for the odd modes.} \qquad (46)$$

Figure 8 shows the dependencies. The flux is high (twice that for an isolated plate) for the odd modes, zero for the even modes when the wavelength is long. For short wavelengths the difference vanishes: The plates are effectively decoupled. For the even modes the net flux that leaves the region is all transported in the longitudinal direction: a redistribution of energy per plate. For the odd modes, most of the net flux is transported from plate to plate, although there is a small flow parallel to the plates. (See Fig. 9.)

It is possible to show that there exists a vortex when

$$\frac{d}{dx}(xK_0x)_x = \frac{kd}{2} < 0$$

or

$$\lambda > 5.2d. \tag{47}$$

A cell $0 < z < d; -(\pi/2k) < x < +(\pi/2k)$ then contains two saddle points and a vortex. If λ is smaller than the critical value there exists only a single saddle point. The reason is that for an isolated plate most of the parallel flow occurs at some distance from the surface (Fig. 6).

6. DISCUSSION

The main determinants of the radiance pattern that results if we place a curved Lambertain body in some light field are as follows:

(1)   Surface patches are oriented with respect to the sources. The effects of this factor are solved completely.[4]

(2)   Vignetting of the sources (equivalent to cast shadows) strongly influences the primary irradiation. This presents us with a severe problem of global differential geometry. In a homogeneous, isotropic field the vignetting can be described

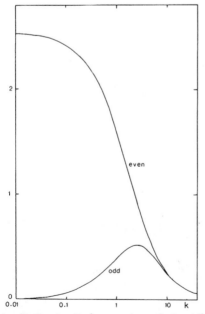

Fig. 7.   Net radiation density [averaged over $0 < x < (\lambda/4d), 0 < y < d$] for even and odd modes.

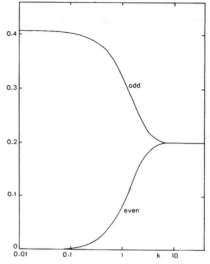

Fig. 8.   Net flux that leaves a plate [averaged over $z = 0, 0 < x < (\lambda/4d), 0 < y < d$] for even and odd modes.

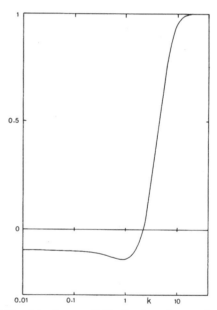

Fig. 9.   Ratio of the flux parallel to the plates [averaged over $x = 0, 0 < y < d, 0 < z < (d/2)$ to the net flux leaving a plate [averaged over $z = 0, 0 < x < (\lambda/4d), 0 < y < d$] for an odd mode.

with a single scalar function on the surfaces, the vignetting factor.

(3)   Interreflections redistribute the primary irradiation. This is also a severe problem of global differential geometry. It is most naturally treated in terms of a symmetrical function defined on pairs of surface patches. This function is closely related to the vignetting factor.

Vignetting and interreflection in complicated geometries are most easily understood in terms of invariant features that depend only on shape, not on the distribution of sources. As examples: because of the vignetting the eye sockets always look like dark patches in a face; because of interreflections the inside of an integrating sphere always looks evenly illuminated despite the fact that the primary illumination may be uneven.

Formally, these notions lead to photometric modes invariantly connected with the shape of the body. The structure of these modes is described with the radiation density and field of geometrical vector flux connected with these modes. The latter field describes the net flux exchange over the surface. It can be used to estimate qualitatively the effect of painting part of the surface, changing its curvature, and the introduction of screens.

Qualitatively, the effect of interreflections is an averaging of reflected radiance in the direction of concave curvature. Thus interreflection tends to subdue the visual conspicuousness of surface relief. (This explains why sculptors work bronze to a flatter relief than they do marble.)

REFERENCES

1. J. A. Jacquez and H. F. Kuppenheim, "Theory of the integrating sphere," J. Opt. Soc. Am. **45**, 460–470 (1955).
2. P. F. O'Brien, "Interreflections in rooms by a network method," J. Opt. Soc. Am. **45**, 419–424 (1955).
3. A. Gershun, "The light field," J. Math. Phys. **18**, 51–151 (1939).
4. J. J. Koenderink and A. J. van Doorn, "Photometric invariants related to solid shape," Opt. Acta **27**, 981–996 (1980).

Reflections on Shading

David Forsyth, *Member, IEEE,* and Andrew Zisserman, *Member, IEEE*

Abstract— Mutual illumination forms a significant component of image radiance that is not modeled by the image irradiance equation. Its effects, which are easy to observe in real scenes, lead to complicated structures in radiance. Because mutual illumination is a global interaction, accounting for its effects in shape from shading schemes is impossible in the general case. We argue that as a result, dense depth maps produced by schemes that assume the image irradiance equation are intrinsically inaccurate.

Discontinuities in radiance are well behaved (in a sense made precise in the paper) under mutual illumination and are a robust shape cue as a result. We discuss the few other such sources known at present. Throughout, these points are illustrated by images of real scenes.

Index Terms—Computer vision, radiosity, shape from shading.

I. Introduction

SHAPE from shading is critically dependent on a simple photometric model, known as the image irradiance equation [19], [20]. This model is only an approximation for real scenes because it assumes that radiance is a function of a purely local geometric property: the surface normal. It ignores the fact that patches of surface reflect light not only to an imaging sensor but also to other patches of surface. This "mutual illumination" makes the distribution of radiance a complicated function of the global scene geometry.

In this paper, we demonstrate that mutual illumination can produce significant effects in real scenes. A dramatic example that illustrates the difficulties that mutual illumination presents to shape recovery schemes appears in Fig. 1. These effects are qualitatively modeled very well by the radiosity equation—a result well known in the graphics community [6], [26]. Using the radiosity equation, we predict the occurrence of special events in the radiance, namely, discontinuities in the radiance and its derivatives. Again, experimental evidence establishes the validity of this approach. Mutual illumination can generate discontinuities in the derivatives of radiance unrelated to local geometry.

We argue that it is not possible to obtain veridical dense depth or normal maps from a shading analysis. However, discontinuities in radiance are tractably related to scene geometry and, moreover, can be detected. We suggest that greater reliance be placed on these discontinuities and other sparse cues rather than on the actual values of radiance.

Manuscript received September 17, 1990; revised November 29, 1990. This work was supported by the Rhodes Trust and Magdalen College, Oxford University, and by the Science and Engineering Research Council.

The authors are with the Robotics Research Group, Department of Engineering Science, Oxford University, Oxford, England.

IEEE Log Number 9100892.

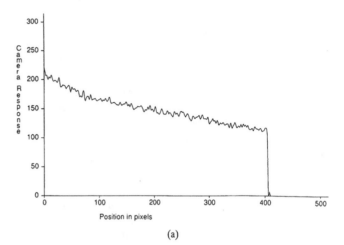

(a)

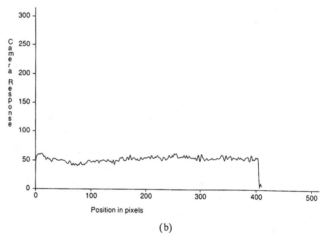

(b)

Fig. 1. (a) and (b) show the radiance measured for one white plane face of a 30° corner, illuminated down the angle bisector. In (a), the opposing face, which is not visible to the camera, was white. In (b), it was black. The camera aperture was not adjusted between images, nor was the illuminant moved. Note the dramatic differences in the radiances measured. These differences are caused by a surface that is not visible to the camera, and so it is hard to see how any algorithm for shading analysis could infer its presence and account for its effects.

II. The Radiosity Equation

Consider a scene consisting of surfaces $r(u)$, parametrized by u, where the boldface italic type denotes a vector quantity. Note that in general the surfaces will not be parametrized by image coordinates because some surfaces may be occluded or missing in the image. The radiance of the surface point parametrized by u is denoted by $N(u)$, and its albedo by $p(u)$.

The radiance at a point is the sum of two terms: the radiance resulting from the illuminant alone and the radiance resulting from light reflected off other surface patches. The second term must be a sum over all surface patches. For Lambertian surface the radiance at u is given by

$$N(u) = N_0(u) + p(u) \int_D K(u,v)N(v)\, dv \qquad (1)$$

where D covers all the surfaces in the scene, $K(u,v)$ represents the geometrical gain factor (often called a form factor) for the component of radiance at u due to that at v, and $N_0(u)$ is the component of radiance at u due to the effects of the source alone. In what follows, we use the term "initial radiance" to refer to N_0. Equation (1), which expresses energy balance, is called the *radiosity equation* (see, for example, [6] or [25]).

When $p(u)$ is constant, (1) is a Fredholm equation of the second kind. K is referred to as the *kernel* of this equation.

For Lambertian surfaces where only diffuse reflection occurs, the kernel takes the form

$$K(u,v) = \frac{1}{\pi} \frac{(n(v) \cdot d_{uv})(n(u) \cdot d_{vu})}{(d_{uv} \cdot d_{uv})^2} \, View(\mathbf{u}, \mathbf{v})$$

where $n(u)$ is the surface normal at the point parametrized by u, d_{uv} is the vector from the point parametrized by u to that parametrized by v; $View(u,v)$ is 1 if there is a line of sight from u to v, 0 otherwise; and $View(u,u) = 0$.

There are several approaches for solving equations of this type (see, for example, [33]). This equation can be solved using a Neumann series, which may be interpreted in terms of systems of reflected rays—the details appear in [9].

It is worth noting that (1) is a linear operator on the initial radiance function ($N_0(u)$). Loosely, to get the radiance under a weighted sum of two light sources, compute (or measure) radiances under both separately and add the weighted results.

Numerical forward solutions of the radiosity equation for complicated geometries are relatively straightforward to construct but are computationally intense ([3], [7], [8], [13], [26], [34], and [35] is a sample of recent references). However, it is difficult to visualize the geometric effects underlying mutual illumination. We have therefore concentrated on simple scenes with a single translational symmetry. A numerical solution is obtained by integrating out the symmetry in the kernel and using finite elements in the usual way. In this case, the finite-element kernel matrix can be obtained in closed form without numerical integration (see [9]). Some closed-form solutions for the radiance for simple geometries appear in [9] and [25].

III. MUTUAL ILLUMINATION EXAMPLES

For small albedo, the interreflections are small, and the resulting radiance is dominated by source effects. Solutions of the radiosity equation tend in this case toward the radiance predicted by the image irradiance equation. We exploit this to demonstrate the effects of mutual illumination by comparing the radiance of a white set of objects and a black set with similar geometry. Qualitative differences in radiance distributions for images of the black and white scenes can be ascribed to the effects of mutual illumination.

A number of examples of the effects of mutual illumination appear in the figures. All images were taken with a CCD

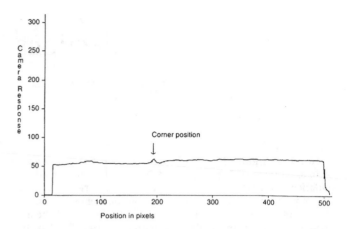

Fig. 2.   A specimen control: image intensity observed across a black 90° corner, for an illuminant directed along the angle bisector. The control images ensure that effects observed were not simply a product of light source effects. The flat profile establishes that the illumination is essentially uniform across the scene. The small bump occurs because the corners were constructed by folding cardboard, with the result that there is a line of surface facets perpendicular to the camera.

camera with its automatic gain control defeated. Objects were either of matte white paper, with no visible surface texture, or were painted with either matte white or matte black enamel spray paint. The ratio of reflectance for the white paper to paper painted black was at least 40 : 1, and the paper painted black looked deep black in bright light.

It is difficult in practice to provide a point source at infinity. We therefore used a light with a large diffuser and took control images, e.g., Fig. 2, at each stage to ensure that the image intensities measured for a large, flat sheet of paper were near uniform. All graphs show image intensity plotted against distance along a section across the translational symmetry.

A. A Concave Polyhedral Corner

The scene consists of the intersection between two planar patches viewed along the angle bisector. The illuminant direction for each figure is indicated in the figure captions. It can be seen quite clearly from Figs. 2–6 that mutual illumination causes a significant qualitative effect (similar to the well-known "roof edge") in these images.

Horn [18] constructed a numerical solution to a similar equation for this geometry and obtained the typical roof-edge signature and recognized this to be a cue for concave polyhedral edges. Brady and Ponce [2] make this point as well and demonstrate the output of a roof edge finder that found a concave intersection of planar patches in this way.

In fact, the typical signature is a roof edge, or more accurately, a pair of rather broad spikes, hereafter called *reflexes*, only when the illuminant lies along the angle bisector. This is clearly shown in Fig. 3. When the illuminant lies off the angle bisector, these reflexes are superimposed on a step edge, as shown in Fig. 4. The finite-element solution to the radiosity equation is in good agreement with these cross sections. Figs. 5 and 6 show how these reflexes vary dramatically in size with albedo.

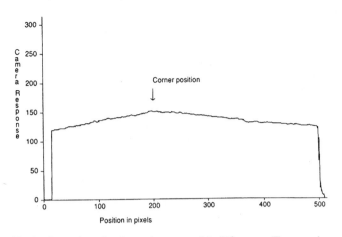

Fig. 3.   Image intensity observed across a white 90° corner. The scene has the same geometry as Fig. 2 but is white instead of black. Note the pronounced roof edge.

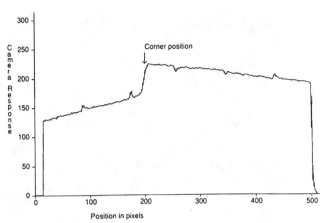

Fig. 5.   Image intensity predicted using the finite- element method for a 90° corner with illuminant directed along the angle bisector over a range of albedoes. Note that the reflexes become more pronounced with albedo. The flattened top to the reflexes shown is an artifact of the display technique resulting from linking the nodal values of the constant elements employed in the finite-element program.

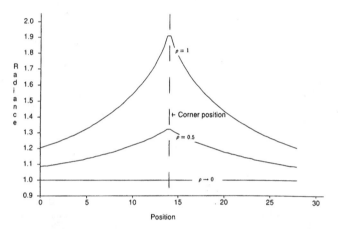

Fig. 4.   Image intensity observed across a white 90° corner for an illuminant directed off the angle bisector. This is the typical shape for a concave polyhedral edge.

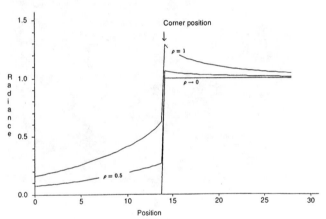

Fig. 6.   Image intensity predicted by the finite-element method for a white 90° corner with illuminant directed parallel to one plane for a range of albedoes. Note that the reflexes become more pronounced with albedo.

B. Blocks World

The scene consists of polyhedral objects. Images and cross sections are shown in Figs. 7–10. Since it is hard to provide similar geometries in this case, the radiance signals must be examined with an eye to qualitative differences. In the black scene, the grey levels typically change sharply and are coupled to surface orientation in the obvious way. However, in the white scene, there are many reflexes at concave intersections. Gilchrist [11] used scenes similar to those in Figs. 7 and 8 in experiments that suggest that humans can use mutual illumination effects as a cue to surface lightness judgments.

C. A Concave Hemicylinder

Fig. 11 shows the radiance profile for a concave black cylinder on a black background—the form is broadly as expected from the image irradiance equation. Fig. 12 shows the radiance profile for a concave white cylinder on a white background. The profile is radically different from the previous case.

D. A White Convex Hemicylinder on a Plane Background

The objects consist of white convex half cylinders on a black or a white background. The geometry and terminology are illustrated in Fig. 13.

Fig. 14 shows a section of the image intensity measured for a white cylinder on a black planar background, with the camera perpendicular to the background. The light is at approximately 45° to the background. The image intensity function is as predicted by the image irradiance equation. Fig. 15 shows what happens when the black background is replaced with a white one. Notice, in particular, the large reflex where the cylinder meets the plane. This reflex demonstrates that mutual illumination can create structure in shadowed regions.

E. Summary

In general, the effects of mutual illuminations are substantial. Our experimental results agree well with those predicted by the theory, even though the numerical solution assumes that the objects have infinite extent along the symmetry axis.

Fig. 7.   Image of a scene containing black polyhedral objects. The black line indicates the section represented by Fig. 9.

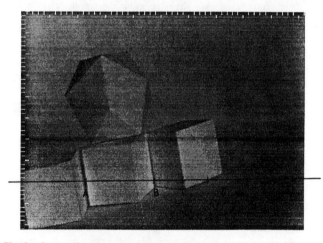

Fig. 8.   Image of a scene containing white polyhedral objects. The black line indicates the section represented by Fig. 10. Notice the bright patches at the concave intersections.

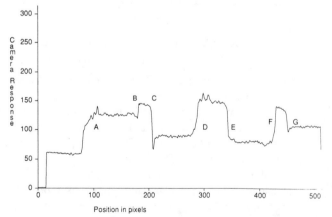

Fig. 9.   Section of image intensity for Fig. 7. The radiosity events labeled line up with those marked along the line in Fig. 7. This section should be compared with that of 10 with a particular emphasis on qualitative effects. The narrow, dark spikes in this and the next section are caused by shadowing in the narrow gap between two disjoint polyhedral faces.

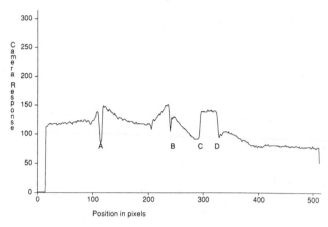

Fig. 10.   Section of image intensity for Fig. 8. Notice just how pronounced the effects of the reflexes are for concave intersections. The radiosity events labeled line up with those marked along the line in Fig. 10.

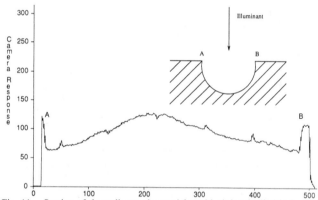

Fig. 11.   Section of the radiance observed for a black hemicylindrical gutter cut in a black plane, illuminated from above. Radiance features marked *A* and *B* in this and the following figure occur at the points on the profile (shown in the inset) marked with corresponding letters.

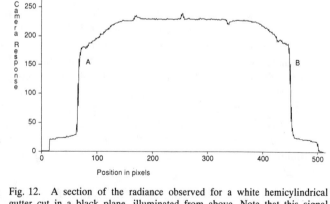

Fig. 12.   A section of the radiance observed for a white hemicylindrical gutter cut in a black plane, illuminated from above. Note that this signal is qualitatively very different from that of Fig. 12. In particular, note that the constant central region is *not* a saturation effect. Quantitative shape from shading, based on the image irradiance equation, would produce entirely the wrong result with this data.

Mutual illumination serves to produce a rich variety of complex image features (for example, the well-known roof edges of Fig. 5 or the reflexes of Fig. 15). Radiance events re-

sulting from surface features take a wide range of forms. Edge detectors that are optimized for one-dimensional step edges

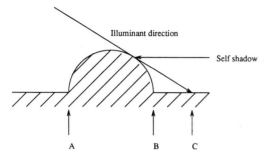

Fig. 13. Geometry for convex half cylinder on planar background, showing illuminant direction, self-shadowed region, and cast shadow. The illuminant was at an angle of about 45° to the background plane.

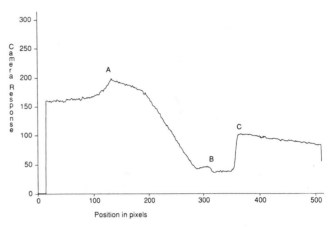

Fig. 15. Measured radiance for a convex white half cylinder on a *white* background as in Fig. 13. The radiance features labeled A, B, and C occur at the points with the corresponding labels in Fig. 13. There is a discontinuity in radiance at B, which would not be predicted by the image irradiance equation, and one at C, caused by a shadow. Note the almost cusp-like peak caused by the mutual illumination at the concave intersection A. Note self shadow at pixel 280.

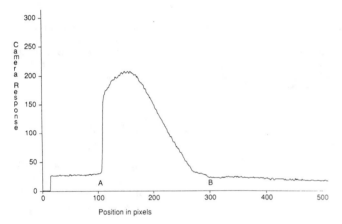

Fig. 14. Measured radiance for a convex white half-cylinder on a *black* background as in Fig. 13. The self-shadow is evident as a discontinuity in radiance derivative at pixel 280.

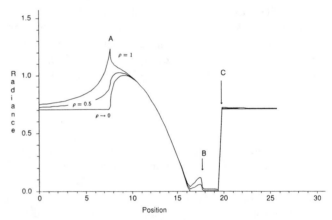

Fig. 16. Image intensity predicted using finite-element method for a convex half cylinder on a background of the same albedo for a range of albedoes. There is very good agreement with the intensity observed for this geometry (Fig. 15). Note self shadow at position 16.

are not normally very successful at detecting or localizing richer image structures. Descriptions of the detailed structure of a discontinuity may themselves provide useful three-dimensional shape information. For example, the structure of the discontinuity in radiance at a convex polyhedral edge is very different from that at a concave polyhedral edge. There is a substantial scope for further work in documenting, detecting, and interpreting "canonical" features in image radiance (some contributions appear in [31]; [30] explicitly considers mutual illumination).

IV. PREDICTING RADIANCE EVENTS

The examples in the previous section demonstrate that the radiosity equation is a better model of image radiance formation than the image irradiance equation. This section investigates the shape information that can be extracted using this model. Analyzing this equation is in general very difficult because of the complicated way in which shape appears. No useful constraints on the radiance itself are known in general. However, it is possible to predict the behavior of discontinuities in radiance and its derivative under mutual illumination. The behavior of these radiance features is closely coupled to scene geometry in a relatively simple way.

We assume that all surfaces are piecewise smooth and Lambertian. No specular reflection occurs. In this case, it

is possible to prove the following results for the radiosity equation.

Discontinuities in Radiance—Discontinuities in radiance are well behaved in the sense that they appear at points where the first derivative of the surface is discontinuous, at discontinuities in surface reflectance, or at cast-shadow edges. In other words, the image irradiance equation is as good as the radiosity equation for predicting the position of discontinuities in radiance but may not predict their magnitudes correctly.

Discontinuities in Radiance Derivatives—Discontinuities in the derivative of radiance appear where the image irradiance equation predicts them and at a number of other points, where the image irradiance equation predicts a continuous derivative. The "new" discontinuities in the derivative of radiance are essentially an occlusion effect. An illuminated surface patch acts as an extended light source, and occluding such a source generates a discontinuity in the derivative of radiance on the shadowed surface.

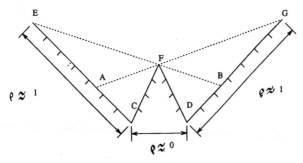

Fig. 17.   In this simple geometry, there is a discontinuity in the derivative of radiance at points A and B due to mutual illumination. This can be predicted using the COG in Fig. 19.

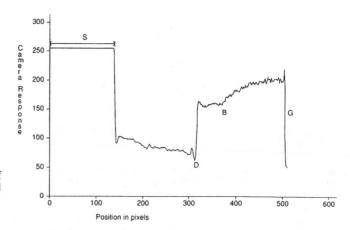

Fig. 18.   A section of the radiance observed for a geometry similar to that of Fig. 17. Note the fast change in derivative of radiance marked at point B, corresponding to point B in Fig. 17. The experiment consisted of imaging a paper figure lit so that one of the faces was very bright. The other face then displayed the predicted fast change in derivative. The bright face (the region of the profile marked S) saturated the camera so that the effect corresponding to point A in Fig. 17 is not visible.

The proof of both these results appears in [10], which introduced a device called the crease occlusion graph (COG) that catalogs the discontinuities in the kernel graphically. In turn, this makes it possible to analyze the discontinuities in the radiance and its derivatives in terms of relatively simple geometric effects. Fig. 19 given below shows an example of a COG for a simple geometry. The method of proof of these results makes is possible to show that discontinuities in the derivatives of radiance arise from mutual illumination in a highly ordered fashion. In particular, they occur in a predictable way when surfaces occlude one another. This encourages speculation that these discontinuities could also represent shape cues.

A. Experimental Examples

These results show that discontinuities predicted from the radiosity equation *cling to surface features*. An example of this effect is given by the reflex in Fig. 15. Discontinuities predicted by the image irradiance equation may be local (for example, changes in albedo) or global (for example, shadows) in origin. Mutual illumination can accentuate, diminish, or even possibly, for highly unlikely geometries, null out these discontinuities.

Discontinuities in one of the derivatives of initial radiance occur, for example, at self shadows—where the illuminant direction grazes the surface. The discontinuities in the derivative of radiance predicted by the radiosity equation are often small and hard to localize, but they can be observed. Figs. 17 and 18 show a simple geometry and a discontinuity in the derivative of radiance due to mutual illumination, predicted for this geometry using the COG of Fig. 19 and observed in a real scene.

V. Implications for Shape Representation

Conventional shape from shading clearly requires that radiance be a function of surface normal alone. However, when mutual illumination is present, radiance is a global function of scene geometry. We have seen that mutual illumination causes substantial changes in the radiance. Even under controlled conditions, unless all surfaces are nearly black or the scene consists of an isolated convex surface, the effects of mutual illumination are significant.

A. Example: Mutual Illumination Effects Disturb Surface Reconstruction

Consider Fig. 18. The underlying geometry that gave this radiance is shown in Fig. 17. We consider the plane face on which the discontinuity in derivative at B falls. The radiance in Fig. 18 for this face is roughly constant from D to B, then rises roughly linearly. We have already shown that it is possible to obtain the marked discontinuity in the derivative of radiance. To predict the output of a shape from shading scheme on this image, we consider the image irradiance equation, where there is a translational symmetry. The outline is (locally, at least) a function of a single variable $z(x)$.

Given a Lambertian surface with the only light source at the viewer and the radiance normalized so that a patch perpendicular to the source direction has radiance ρ, the radiance becomes

$$N(x) = \frac{\rho}{\sqrt{1 + z'(x)^2}}. \qquad (2)$$

This is a nonlinear ODE that can be solved directly given $N(x)$ as a function of x. In particular, if $N(x) = cx + d$, then

$$N(x) =$$
$$\frac{1}{c}\left\{ \sqrt{\rho^2 - (cx+d)^2} + \rho \log \left\{ \frac{\rho - \sqrt{\rho - (cx+d)^2}}{cx+d} \right\} \right\}.$$
$$\qquad (3)$$

We illustrate schematically the solution for the intensity profile of Fig. 17 in Fig. 20. Even though the surface is actually planar, the reconstructed surface would contain a discontinuity in the derivative and be curved on one side of this discontinuity. All meaningful geometry in the surface has been lost by this perturbation.

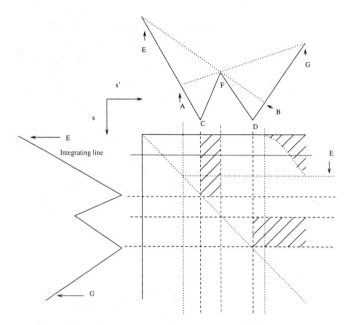

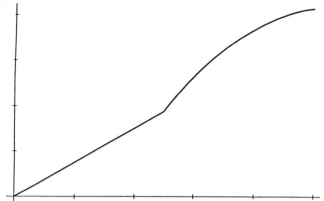

Fig. 20. Schematic of the shape reconstructed for the radiance shown in Fig. 18 using the methods for one-dimensional shape from shading described in the text.

Fig. 19. The radiosity equation can be written as $N = N_0 + KN$, where K represents the linear operator associated with the kernel. The COG charts the events that may cause discontinuities to appear in KN and its derivatives. We show this graph for a simple profile. A point (s, s') in the square represents a pair of points on the profile, which is drawn above and to the left of the graph. Regions where the corresponding points have a line of sight (i.e., $View(s, s' = 1)$) are hatched, and regions where they do not are left blank. The dashed lines are creases on the surface (discontinuities in surface orientation). Because the graph is symmetric about the line $s = s'$, only the upper half is shown. $(KN)(s_0)$ is given by $\int K(s_0, s')N(s')\,ds'$, that is, by integrating along a line $s = s_0$. This line is referred to as the integrating line. Discontinuities in KN can then be obtained by considering the change in integrand as the integrating line sweeps down the graph. The dominant effect here is the way the support of the integrand changes—at a discontinuity, the support changes discontinuously, and KN can be discontinuous, e.g., at C. Thus, $N_0 + KN$ can be discontinuous. To obtain discontinuities in derivative requires more analysis. By expanding the derivative of KN, we see the discontinuities in the derivative of radiance can arise from the boundaries in the COG, where $View$ discontinuously flips from 0 to 1. In particular, at $s = E - \epsilon$, the derivative of radiance contains a term due to a δ-function on the boundary. At $s = E + \epsilon$, this term is missing. This effect causes the discontinuity in the derivative of radiance observed in Fig. 18. Details appear in [10]

B. Accuracy of Recovered Surfaces

This example illustrates that assuming the image irradiance equation in the presence of mutual illumination will lead shape from shading to produce inaccurate surface reconstructions. Other shape techniques assume the image irradiance equation will be similarly affected. The following are examples:

- The photometric invariants described by Koenderink and Van Doorn [24] do not apply to objects where mutual illumination effects are manifest as this approach relates the singular behavior of the field of isophotes to that of the Gauss map by assuming that radiance is purely a function of the Gauss map.
- Photometric stereo techniques (Horn [19] is a good general reference for these techniques) are adversely affected by mutual illumination. It is known that gain due to mutual illumination can cause some surface patches to be brighter than is consistent with the photometric model [21], [22]. However, if photometric stereo techniques are used with more than two light sources, the reconstructed

surface normal is overconstrained, and it is possible to estimate its error and delineate regions that have been adversely affected by mutual illumination. This approach will deliver a representation that is dense in patches. A judicious arrangement of light sources can reduce the effects of mutual illumination, although it is unclear whether this offers a worthwhile advantage in practice.

Recently, Nayar *et al.* [28] have demonstrated a scheme that iteratively updates shape estimates to account for mutual illumination effects. They show that for simple cases, the scheme converges. They acknowledge (see p. 18 of [28]) that the scheme does not always converge on complicated examples. A major difficulty with this scheme lies in an important aspect of mutual illumination; distant surfaces, which are not visible to the imaging device, may make substantial contributions to image radiance if the form factor linking them to the surfaces viewed is sufficiently large. It is not, in general, possible to account for these contributions. Fig. 1 shows two sections of image intensities taken from two images of precisely the same geometry with precisely the same lighting—the only difference is that in the second image, a nearby surface, which is invisible to the camera, has been covered with black paper. As the figure demonstrates, mutual illumination from this invisible surface has significantly changed the image intensities.

C. The Value of Shading Information

If the goal of a shading analysis is just a dense depth map, then its success must be judged on the accuracy of that reconstruction. This can be tested by carefully measuring a real object, imaging it under known circumstances, reconstructing its shape using shape from shading, and comparing the resulting depth map with the shape of the original object. We are not aware of any such tests that deal with scenes other than isolated, convex objects[1] in the literature (see [17] for a quantitative test on a sphere). Much shape from shading work tests schemes either on data simulated using the image irradiance equation (which tests only the numerical regime) or on real data but without providing "ground truth" for

---

[1] Both concave objects and groups of objects need investigation.

comparison. Such experimental regimes give no guide to the accuracy of the output of these schemes on real shading data.

However, photometric stereo has been successful in applications (for example, [21]). One explanation may lie in the way it has been used to match models to small model bases. In this case, a sufficiently robust representation of model shape combined with a small model base serve to compensate for patchy information from the shading analysis. This illustrates the point that it is generally not possible to evaluate shape representation schemes outside the context of some application; for particular tasks, the disruptive effects of mutual illumination may not significantly affect the performance.

D. Alternatives to Dense Depth Maps

Modifying shape from shading schemes to recover accurate, dense depth maps despite the effects of mutual illumination appears to be impossible in the general case. An alternative approach is to extract cues from radiance that are wholly or largely unaffected by radiance from distant surfaces (see also [1]). We briefly review the cues with this property.

- *Discontinuities in Radiance and Its Derivatives:* These features bear a tractable relationship to scene geometry. However, it does not seem possible to exploit this relationship for discontinuities in the derivatives of radiance because they appear hard to detect stably.
- *Shadows:* Since a shadow region is bounded by discontinuities in radiance and the derivatives of radiance, its boundary will be unaffected by mutual illumination. This makes it possible to interpret pools of shadow on a surface using a simple geometric model by applying, for example, the techniques of [14], [15], and [23]. Unfortunately, it is difficult at present to detect pools of shadow on surfaces reliably.
- *Grooves and Pits:* Koenderink and Van Doorn [25] suggest considering properties of the radiance signal that are tractably coupled to shape and yet are largely invariant to changes in illumination. The example they cite consists of a small deep hole or a groove in a surface. At such a feature, there will be an attached shadow for almost any illuminant. Intuitively, this is because it is hard to choose a lighting direction that will illuminate the inside of the groove or hole. A simple example is given by the lines on human foreheads, which are often geometrically small but are made visually prominent under a wide range of illuminants by this shadowing effect.

VI. Conclusion

We have shown that mutual illumination produces significant effects in real scenes and that these effects can be modeled (at least qualitatively) by the radiosity equation. Our data imply that existing algorithms for shading analysis are unlikely to compute accurate surface reconstructions in complex scenes.

However, discontinuities in radiance and its derivatives behave well under mutual illumination. Discontinuities in radiance can be predicted using the image irradiance equation. Predicting discontinuities in the derivative requires both the image irradiance equation and an occlusion analysis. These localization results are abstract. In practice, edge detectors [4] respond to large derivatives rather than to discontinuities. We have shown that in real scenes, discontinuities are often surrounded by a complicated structure in the radiance signal. As a result, the *detected* position of a discontinuity may vary slightly from that predicted using the image irradiance equation.

The localization results treat only the existence of discontinuities—we have no result bounding the effects of mutual illumination on the derivatives of radiance. Our model has assumed that all surfaces are Lambertian, but the results on the position of discontinuities assume only that the bidirectional radiance distribution function is continuous. In fact, little is known about the effects of large lobes in the BRDF on radiosity solutions. Work by Tagare [32] suggesting that a wide range of surfaces are best modeled by a three-lobed BDRF opens a range of interesting problems for shading analysis.

The great complexity of the interactions involved in mutual illumination mean that an exhaustive mathematical analysis is unlikely. However, shading contains shape cues; the important issue is how to sidestep the effects of mutual illumination and determine which cues are reliable, robust, and tractably coupled to surface shape.

Acknowledgment

The authors are most grateful to A. Blake, J. Mundy, and R. Woodham for a number of helpful discussions and insightful suggestions. The paper was improved by the careful comments of an anonymous referee. They also thank M. Brady and C. Brown for help, discussions, and encouragement. P. Hubel provided measurements of relative surface lightness.

References

[1] A. Blake, A. Zisserrman, and G. Knowles, "Surface descriptions from stereo and shading," *Image Vision Comput.*, vol. 3, pp. 183–191, 1985 (also included in [20]).

[2] J. M. Brady and J. Ponce, "Toward a surface primal sketch," MIT AI-Memo 824, MIT AI Lab, Cambridge, MA, 1985.

[3] D. R. Baum, H. E. Rushmeier, and J. M. Winget, "Improving radiosity solutions through the use of analytically determined form-factors," in *Proc. SIGGRAPH '89*, 1989, pp. 325–334.

[4] J. F. Canny, "Finding edges and lines in images," *IEEE Trans. Patt. Anal. Machine Intell.*, vol. PAMI-8, pp. 679–698, 1986.

[5] B. Carrihill and R. Hummel, "Experiments with the intensity depth ratio sensor," *CVGIP*, vol. 32, pp. 337–358, 1985.

[6] M. F. Cohen and D. P. Greenberg, "The hemi-cube: A radiosity solution for complex environments," in *Proc. SIGGRAPH '85*, 1985, pp. 31–40.

[7] M. F. Cohen D. P. Greenberg, D. S. Immel, and P. J. Brock, "An efficient radiosity approach for realistic image synthesis," *IEEE Comput. Graphics Applicat.*, pp. 27–35, Mar. 1986.

[8] M. F. Cohen, S. E. Chen, J. R. Wallace, and D. P. Greenberg, "A progressive refinement approach to fast radiosity image generation," in *Proc. SIGGRAPH '88*, 1988, pp. 75-84.

[9] D. A. Forsyth and A. Zisserman, "Mutual illumination," in *Proc. CVPR*, 1989 .

[10] ——, "Shape from shading in the light of mutual illumination," *Image Vision Comput.*, vol. 8, pp. 42–49, 1990.

[11] A. L. Gilchrist, "The perception of surface blacks and whites," *Sci. Amer.*, vol. 240, pp. 112–124, 1979.

[12] A. L. Gilchrist and A. Jacobsen, "Perception of lightness and illumination in a world on one reflectance," *Perception*, vol. 13, pp. 5–19, 1984.

[13] C. M. Goral, K. E. Torrance, D. P. Greenberg, and B. Battaile, "Modeling the interaction of light between diffuse surfaces," in *Proc. SIGGRAPH '84*, 1984, pp. 213–222.

[14] M. G. Hatzitheodorou and J. Kender, "An optimal algorithm for the derivation of shape from darkness," in *Proc. CVPR*, 1988.

[15] M. G. Hatzitheodorou, "The derivation of 3D surface shape from shadows," in *Proc. DARPA Image Understanding*, 1989.

[16] G. Healy, "Local shape from specularity," in *Proc. 1st ICCV*, 1987, pp. 151–160.

[17] B. K. P. Horn, "Obtaining shape from shading information," P. H. Winston, Ed., in *The Psychology of Computer Vision*. New York: McGraw-Hill, 1975.

[18] ———, "Understanding image intensities," *Artificial Intell.*, vol. 8, pp. 201–231, 1977.

[19] ———, *Robot Vision*. Cambridge, MA: MIT Press, 1986.

[20] B. K. P. Horn, Ed., *Shape from Shading*. Cambridge, MA: MIT Press, 1989.

[21] K. Ikeuchi, H. K. Nishihara, B. K. P. Horn, P. Sobalvarro, and S. Nagata, "Determining grasp configurations using photometric stereo and the PRISM binocular stereo system," *Int. J. Robot. Res.*, vol. 5, no. 1, 1986.

[22] K. Ikeuchi, "Determining a depth map using a dual photometric stereo," *Int. J. Robot. Res.*, vol. 6, no. 1, 1987.

[23] J. Kender and E. M. Smith, "Shape from darkness; deriving surface information from dynamic shadows," *Proc. AAAI*, 1986.

[24] J. J. Koenderink and A. J. Van Doorn, "Photometric invariants related to solid shape," *Opt. Acta.*, vol. 27, pp. 981–996, 1980.

[25] ———, "Geometrical modes as a general method to treat diffuse interreflections in radiometry," *J. Opt. Soc. Amer.*, vol. 73, pp. 843–850, 1983.

[26] G. W. Meyer, H. E. Rushmeier, M. F. Cohen, D. P. Greenberg, and K. E. Torrance, "An experimental evaluation of computer graphics imagery," *ACM Trans. Graphics*, vol. 5, no. 1, pp. 30–50, 1986.

[27] M C. Morrone and R. A. Owens, "Feature detection from local energy," *Patt. Recog. Lett.*, vol. 6, pp. 303–313, 1987.

[28] S. K. Nayar, K. Ikeuchi, and T. Kanade, "Shape from interreflections," Int. Rep. CMU-RI-TR-90-14, Carnegie-Mellon Univ., Pittsburgh, PA, 1990.

[29] B. O'Neill, *Elementary Differential Geometry*. New York: Academic, 1966.

[30] D. E. Pearson and J. A. Robinson, "Visual communication at very low data rates," *Proc. IEEE*, vol. 74, no. 4, pp. 795–812, 1985.

[31] P. Perona and J. Malik, "Detecting and localizing edges composed of steps, peaks and roofs," presented at 3rd Int. Conf. Comput. Vision, 1990.

[32] H. Tagare, "A theory of photometric stereo for a general class of reflectance maps," in *Proc. CVPR*, 1989, pp. 38–45.

[33] F. G. Tricomi, *Integral Equations*, New York: Dover, 1985.

[34] J. R. Wallace, M. F. Cohen, and D. P. Greenberg, "A two-pass solution to the rendering equation: A synthesis of ray tracing and radiosity methods," in *Proc. SIGGRAPH '87*, 1987, pp. 311–320.

[35] J. R. Wallace, K. A. Elmquist, and E. A. Haines, "A ray tracing algorithm for progressive radiosity," in *Proc. SIGGRAPH '89*, 1989, pp. 315–324.

David Forsyth (S'87–M'88) received the B.Sc. degree in 1984 and the M.Sc. degree in 1986, both in electrical engineering from the University of the Witwatersrand, Johannesburg, South Africa. He received the D.Phil. degree in 1989 from Oxford University, Oxford, England.

He currently holds a prize Fellowship at Magdalen College, Oxford. His research interests include computer vision, computer algebra, and algebraic geometry.

Andrew Zisserman (M'86) received the B.A. degree in theoretical physics and part III mathematics, all from Cambridge University, Cambridge, England. In 1984, he received the Ph. D. degree.

From 1984 to 1987, he was an Alvey-funded Research Fellow at the University of Edinburgh, Edinburgh, Scotland. He is currently an SERC Advanced Research Fellow in the Robotics Research Group, Oxford University. His research interests are in robot vision, especially qualitative vision and applications of invariance. He has published a number of papers in this area as well as a book with A. Blake, *Visual Reconstruction* (MIT Press).

Shape from Interreflections

SHREE K. NAYAR
Department of Computer Science, Columbia University, New York, NY 10027

KATSUSHI IKEUCHI AND TAKEO KANADE
The Robotics Institute, Carnegie Mellon University, Pittsburgh, PA 15213

Abstract

Shape-from-intensity methods assume that points in a scene are only illuminated by the sources of light. This assumption is valid only when the scene consists of a single convex surface. Most scenes consist of concave surfaces where points reflect light among themselves. In the presence of these interreflections, shape-from-intensity methods produce erroneous (pseudo) estimates of shape and reflectance. This article shows that, for Lambertian surfaces, the pseudo shape and reflectance are unique and can be mathematically related to the actual shape and reflectance of the surface. We present an iterative algorithm that simultaneously recovers the actual shape and reflectance from the pseudo estimates. The general behavior of the algorithm and its convergence properties are discussed. Simulations as well as experimental results are included to demonstrate the accuracy and robustness of the algorithm.

1 The Interreflection Problem

Points in a scene, when illuminated, reflect light not only toward the sensor but also among themselves. This is always true, with the exception of scenes that consist of only a single convex surface, in which case no two points on the surface are visible to one another. In general, however, scenes include concave surfaces where points reflect light between themselves. These *interreflections* (also called "mutual illuminations") can appreciably alter a scene's appearance. Existing vision algorithms do not account for effects of interreflections and hence often produce erroneous results.

One class of vision algorithms that are directly affected by interreflections are the shape-from-intensity algorithms. These are methods that recover three-dimensional shape information from image intensity (irradiance) values. Examples of shape-from-intensity methods are shape-from-shading [Horn 1970], photometric stereo [Woodham 1978], and photometric sampling [Nayar et al. 1990]. All these methods assume that scene points are illuminated only by the sources of light and not by other points in the scene: Interreflec-

tions are assumed *not* to exist. As a result these shape-from-intensity methods produce erroneous results when applied to concave surfaces. As an example, figure 1a shows a concave Lambertian surface of constant reflectance (albedo = 0.75), and figure 1b shows its shape extracted using photometric stereo. The inability to deal with interreflections has been a serious limitation of shape-from-intensity methods.

1.1 Forward and Inverse Problems

We identify two separate problems associated with interreflections; the *forward* (graphics) problem and the *inverse* (vision) problem. Previous work done in this area is related to the forward problem. The forward problem involves predicting image intensity values given the shape and reflectance of a scene. Horn [1975] discussed the changes in image intensities due to interreflections caused by polyhedral surfaces that are Lambertian in reflectance. Koenderink and van Doorn [1983] formalized the interreflection process for Lambertian surfaces of arbitrary shape and varying

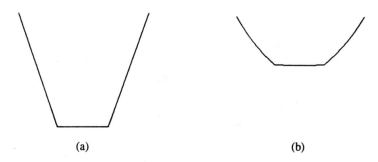

Fig. 1. (a) A concave surface. (b) Its shape extracted using photometric stereo.

reflectance (albedo). They proposed a solution to the forward problem in terms of the eigenfunctions of the interreflection kernel. Cohen and Greenberg [1985] modeled a scene as a finite collection of Lambertian planar facets, proposed a radiosity solution to the forward problem, and used it to render graphics images. More recently, Forsyth and Zisserman [1989] used a similar numerical solution to compare predicted and measured image intensities.

In this article, our goal is to solve the inverse (vision) problem. Given image intensities, we wish to recover the shape and reflectance of a scene in the presence of interreflections. The inverse interreflection problem is a particularly difficult one for, in its ambiguity, it resembles the "chicken and egg" problem. If we can model interreflection effects, we may be able to compensate scene images for these effects and extract accurate shape information. However, it is obvious that modeling interreflections requires prior knowledge of shape and reflectance. But it is shape that we are attempting to recover. So which one comes first, shape or interreflections?

1.2 A Solution to the Inverse Problem

We have developed an algorithm that recovers accurate shape information in the presence of interreflections. Our solution to the inverse problem is valid for Lambertian surfaces of arbitrary (but continuous) shape, with possibly varying but unknown reflectance (albedo). First, an existing shape-from-intensity method is applied to the concave surface to obtain pseudo (erroneous) estimates of shape and reflectance. We show that the pseudo shape and reflectance, though incorrect, can be mathematically related to the actual shape and reflectance of the surface. Further, the pseudo shape has certain interesting properties: It is unique for a given actual

shape, and is less concave than the actual shape. A recovery algorithm uses these properties to recover actual shape and reflectance iteratively from the pseudo shape and reflectance. The algorithm uses a physical interreflection model to compute interreflections in each iteration. We analyze the algorithm's convergence properties for the simple case of two planar surface elements. Convergence in the general case is discussed and demonstrated through several simulation results. Experiments have been conducted on real surfaces to demonstrate the robustness, accuracy, and practical feasibility of the proposed algorithm.

Our results demonstrate two points that we assert are vital to vision research. First, interreflection effects can cause shape recovery methods to produce unacceptable results. Hence, interreflections must not be ignored. Second, interreflection problems (certainly some, if not all) are tractable and solvable.

2 A Physical Interreflection Model

Our solution to the inverse interreflection problem is based on the solution to the forward problem, that is, on modeling interreflections for a surface of given shape and reflectance. Hence, this section will serve as background theory for subsequent sections. The interreflection model described here is primarily based on the formulation proposed by Koenderink and van Doorn [1983]. All surfaces in the scene are assumed to be Lambertian. We will shortly see that this assumption is necessary to obtain a closed-form solution to the forward interreflection problem. The Lambertian surface can have any arbitrary shape and varying reflectance, that is, albedo (ρ) may vary from one surface point to the next. In deriving the interreflection model, we will use radiometric concepts such as irradiance and radiance as defined in appendix A.1.

2.1 Analytic Forward Solution

Consider the concave surface $x(u, v)$ shown in figure 2a. When the surface is illuminated, its points receive light directly from the source as well as from other points on the surface. Hence, the radiance at each surface point has two components, one resulting from the direct illumination by the source and the second due to illumination by other points on the surface.

To begin, we are interested in finding the radiance of a point $\mathbf{x}$ due to the radiance of another point $\mathbf{x}'$. The point $\mathbf{x}$ can be illuminated by $\mathbf{x}'$ only if the two points can "see" each other. The visibility function is defined as:

$$V(\mathbf{x}, \mathbf{x}') = \frac{\mathbf{n} \cdot (-\mathbf{r}) + |\mathbf{n} \cdot (-\mathbf{r})|}{2|\mathbf{n} \cdot (-\mathbf{r})|}$$
$$\cdot \frac{\mathbf{n}' \cdot \mathbf{r} + |\mathbf{n}' \cdot \mathbf{r}|}{2|\mathbf{n}' \cdot \mathbf{r}|} \quad (1)$$

where $\mathbf{n}$ and $\mathbf{n}'$ are unit surface normal vectors at the points $\mathbf{x}$ and $\mathbf{x}'$, respectively, and $\mathbf{r}$ is the vector from $\mathbf{x}'$ to $\mathbf{x}$. The function $V(\mathbf{x}, \mathbf{x}')$ can have only two values, namely, 1 and 0. $V(\mathbf{x}, \mathbf{x}') = 1$ when $\mathbf{x}$ and $\mathbf{x}'$ are positioned and oriented such that they can illuminate each

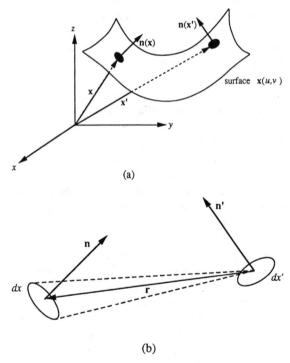

(a)

(b)

Fig. 2. (a) A concave surface in three-dimensional space. (b) Two surface elements that are visible to one another.

other, and $V(\mathbf{x}, \mathbf{x}') = 0$ otherwise. Figure 2b shows the infinitesimal surface elements dx and dx' located at the points $\mathbf{x}$ and $\mathbf{x}'$, respectively. We use the notation $dE_m(\mathbf{x}, \mathbf{x}')$ to represent the irradiance of the surface element dx due to the radiance $L(\mathbf{x}')$ of the element dx'. $dE_m(\mathbf{x}, \mathbf{x}')$ may be derived using the definitions of radiance and irradiance and the geometry shown in figure 2b:

$$dE_m(\mathbf{x}, \mathbf{x}') = \left[\frac{[\mathbf{n} \cdot (-\mathbf{r})][\mathbf{n}' \cdot \mathbf{r}]V(\mathbf{x}, \mathbf{x}')}{[\mathbf{r} \cdot \mathbf{r}]^2} \right] L(\mathbf{x}') \, dx' \quad (2)$$

The radiance of dx may be determined from its irradiance as

$$dL_m(\mathbf{x}, \mathbf{x}') = \frac{\rho(\mathbf{x})}{\pi} dE_m(\mathbf{x}, \mathbf{x}') \quad (3)$$

where $\rho(\mathbf{x})$ is the albedo function, and the factor $\rho(\mathbf{x})/\pi$ is the bi-directional reflectance distribution function (appendix A.1) for a Lambertian surface.[1] From equations (2) and (3) we obtain

$$dL_m(\mathbf{x}, \mathbf{x}') = \frac{\rho(\mathbf{x})}{\pi} K(\mathbf{x}, \mathbf{x}') L(\mathbf{x}') \, dx' \quad (4)$$

where

$$K(\mathbf{x}, \mathbf{x}') = \left[\frac{[\mathbf{n} \cdot (-\mathbf{r})][\mathbf{n}' \cdot \mathbf{r}]V(\mathbf{x}, \mathbf{x}')}{[\mathbf{r} \cdot \mathbf{r}]^2} \right] \quad (5)$$

$K(\mathbf{x}, \mathbf{x}')$ is a function of the relative positions and orientations of the elements dx and dx' and determines the interreflections between the two elements from a purely geometrical perspective. It is referred to as the *interreflection kernel*. It is a symmetric, positive definite function and vanishes for surface points that do not illuminate one another either due to their orientations or occlusion by other points. Further, the kernel is bounded by the geometrical constraint that no surface element can radiate in, or receive radiations from, more than a half-space around it. Hence it satisfies the condition [Koenderink & van Doorn 1983]:

$$\iint \left\| \frac{1}{\pi} K(\mathbf{x}, \mathbf{x}') \right\|^2 dx \, dx' \leq 1 \quad (6)$$

Next, consider the concave surface in figure 2a to be illuminated by a single distant point source of light in the direction $\mathbf{s}$. Then, the radiance of the surface due to the source *alone* (excluding interreflection effects) may be expressed in terms of the irradiance of the surface by the source:

$$L_s(\mathbf{x}) = \frac{\rho(\mathbf{x})}{\pi} E_s(\mathbf{x}) \qquad (7)$$

The irradiance due to the source is the flux incident per unit area of the surface and is proportional to cosine of the angle between the source direction and the surface normal direction, that is, $E_s(\mathbf{x}) = k\,\mathbf{n} \cdot \mathbf{s}$. The constant of proportionality k is determined by the radiant intensity of the source and its distance from the surface.

The total radiance of $\mathbf{x}$ may be expressed as a sum of the radiance due to the source and the radiance due to all other points on the surface:

$$L(\mathbf{x}) = L_s(\mathbf{x}) + \int dL_m(\mathbf{x}, \mathbf{x}') \qquad (8)$$

or

$$L(\mathbf{x}) = L_s(\mathbf{x}) + \frac{\rho(\mathbf{x})}{\pi} \int K(\mathbf{x}, \mathbf{x}')\, L(\mathbf{x}')\, dx' \qquad (9)$$

Equation (9) is referred to as the *interreflection equation*. It is similar in form to Fredholm's integral equation [Koenderink & van Doorn 1983; Horn 1975] and does not lend itself to a straightforward solution. However, if all points on the concave surface have the same reflectance ($\rho(\mathbf{x}) = \rho$), a solution to $L(\mathbf{x})$ (or the forward interreflection problem) is given by the Neumann series as:

$$L(\mathbf{x}) = L_s(\mathbf{x}) + \sum_{p=1}^{\infty} \rho^p \int K_p(\mathbf{x}, \mathbf{x}')\, L(\mathbf{x}')\, dx' \qquad (10)$$

where

$$K_p(\mathbf{x}, \mathbf{x}') = \int \frac{K(\mathbf{x}, \mathbf{y})}{\pi} K_{p-1}(\mathbf{y}, \mathbf{x}')\, dy \qquad (p \geq 2)$$

and

$$K_1 = \frac{K}{\pi}$$

The following observations are made with respect to the above solution:

- Note that the solution is valid only under the Lambertian assumption. The radiance of a Lambertian surface element is independent of the direction from which it is viewed. As a result, both $L(\mathbf{x})$ and $L(\mathbf{x}')$ are constants in equation (9) and a solution can be obtained.
- The solution is iterative in nature; it is an infinite sum of integrals of the kernels K_p that must each be evaluated using the previous kernel K_{p-1}.

- The solution may be interpreted as a mathematical representation of the "ray-tracing" process that is often used in the area of computer graphics. The pth iteration explicitly represents the contribution of rays that are interreflected exactly p times.
- Though the Neumann series is an infinite one, the solution is guaranteed to converge to a finite value. This is because $\rho(\mathbf{x}) < 1$ in the case of real surfaces. Hence, the series diminishes to zero as p approaches infinity. This is consistent with our real-world experience; diffuse concave surfaces that exhibit interreflections never appear to be infinitely bright.

2.2 Numerical Forward Solution

A more elegant forward solution than the Neumann series can be obtained by assuming the concave surface to be discrete. The following solution has been previously used to render discrete images in graphics [Cohen & Greenberg 1985] and to compare experimentally obtained image intensities with predicted intensities [Forsyth & Zisserman 1989].

Assume the surface to be comprised of m *facets* as shown in figure 3. The radiance and albedo values of each facet i are assumed to be constant over the entire facet and equal to the radiance and albedo values at the center point $\mathbf{x}_i$ of the facet, that is, $L_i = L(\mathbf{x}_i)$ and $\rho_i = \rho(\mathbf{x}_i)$. Then we can write equation (9) as

$$L_i = L_{si} + \frac{\rho_i}{\pi} \sum_{j \neq i} L_j \int_{S_j} K(\mathbf{x}_i, \mathbf{x}_j)\, dx_j \qquad (11)$$

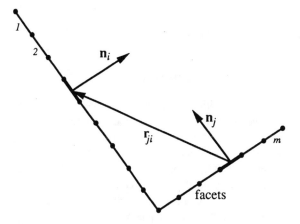

Fig. 3. Modeling the surface as a collection of facets, each with its own radiance and albedo values.

where S_j is the entire surface of the facet j. We assume individual facets to be infinitesimally small, that is, $S_j = dx_j$. Then, the discrete form of the interreflection kernel may be defined as

$$K_{ij} = K(\mathbf{x}_i, \mathbf{x}_j) \, dx_j \qquad (12)$$

where K_{ii} is undefined and K_{ij} vanishes for facet pairs that are not visible to one another. In appendix A.2, we have given the general expression for the discrete kernel and have discussed the effects of facet size on the accuracy of the discrete kernel. Using the discrete kernel, the interreflection equation for the ith facet can be written as

$$L_i = L_{si} + \frac{\rho_i}{\pi} \sum_{j \neq i} L_j K_{ij} \qquad (13)$$

The interreflection equation for the complete surface can be written using vector notation. We define the *facet radiance vector* as $\mathbf{L} = [L_1, L_2, \ldots, L_m]^T$ and the *source contribution vector* as $\mathbf{L_s} = [L_{s1}, L_{s2}, \ldots, L_{sm}]^T$. We also define the *albedo matrix* $\mathbf{P}$ and the *kernel matrix* $\mathbf{K}$ as

$$\mathbf{P} = \frac{1}{\pi} \begin{bmatrix} \rho_1 & 0 & \ldots & \ldots & 0 \\ 0 & \rho_2 & 0 & \ldots & 0 \\ \ldots & \ldots & \ldots & \ldots & \ldots \\ \ldots & \ldots & \ldots & \ldots & \ldots \\ 0 & 0 & \ldots & \ldots & \rho_m \end{bmatrix}$$

$$\mathbf{K} = \begin{bmatrix} 0 & K_{12} & \ldots & \ldots \\ K_{21} & 0 & \ldots & \ldots \\ \ldots & \ldots & 0 & \ldots \\ \ldots & \ldots & \ldots & 0 & \ldots \\ \ldots & \ldots & \ldots & \ldots & 0 \end{bmatrix} \qquad (14)$$

Then, equation (13) may be written as

$$\mathbf{L} = \mathbf{L_s} + \mathbf{PKL} \qquad (15)$$

or

$$\mathbf{L} = (\mathbf{I} - \mathbf{PK})^{-1} \mathbf{L_s} \qquad (16)$$

where $\mathbf{I}$ is the identity matrix. Thus, we have obtained a noniterative, closed-form solution to the forward interreflection problem. The kernel and albedo matrixes are determined by the shape and reflectance of the surface, respectively. The source direction and intensity may be used to compute the source contribution vector $\mathbf{L_s}$. Then the radiance of the surface facets, $\mathbf{L}$, can be determined using the above equation.

Equation (15) explicitly describes the radiance of each facet as the sum of its radiance due to the source and the contributions of other facets. Loosely speaking, this may be interpreted as a weighted averaging of radiance values in the direction of concave curvature. As a result of this effect, surface concavities tend to be visually less conspicuous.

3 The Extracted Pseudo Shape

Equation (16) suggests that if a shape-from-intensity method is applied to a concave surface, it would produce erroneous estimates of shape. In order to generalize the inverse interreflection problem, we assume that the reflectance of the Lambertian surface is also *unknown* and may vary from point to point. Therefore, by the term "shape-from-intensity," we mean local methods that extract both shape (orientation) and reflectance (albedo) information. Photometric stereo [Woodham 1978] and photometric sampling [Nayar et al. 1990] are examples of such shape-from-intensity methods.[2] In the presence of interreflections, these methods produce erroneous shape as well as erroneous reflectance information. We refer to the extracted shape as the pseudo shape and the extracted reflectance as the pseudo reflectance of the surface. In this section, we investigate how the pseudo shape and reflectance are related to the actual shape and reflectance of the surface. These results will later be used to recover the surface's actual shape and reflectance.

Once again, consider the surface comprised of m facets (figure 3). The ith facet may be mathematically represented as

$$\mathbf{N}_i = \frac{\rho_i}{\pi} \mathbf{n}_i \qquad (17)$$

where $\mathbf{n}_i = [n_{xi}, n_{yi}, n_{zi}]^T$ is the unit surface normal and ρ_i is the albedo value for the facet. Therefore, the term "facet" represents both local orientation as well as local reflectance information. The shape and reflectance of the complete surface is then defined by the *facet matrix* $\mathbf{F} = [\mathbf{N}_1, \mathbf{N}_2, \ldots, \mathbf{N}_m]^T$. Consider, once again, the interreflection equation given by equation (16). Since the surface is Lambertian, the source contribution vector L_s may be determined from the facet matrix $\mathbf{F}$ and the source direction vector $s = [s_x, s_y, s_z]^T$ as

$$\mathbf{L_s} = \mathbf{F} \, \mathbf{s} \qquad (18)$$

Hence, we obtain:

$$\mathbf{L} = (\mathbf{I} - \mathbf{PK})^{-1} \mathbf{F} \, \mathbf{s} \qquad (19)$$

We define the matrix $\mathbf{F}_p$ as

$$\mathbf{F}_p = (\mathbf{I} - \mathbf{PK})^{-1}\mathbf{F} \qquad (20)$$

$\mathbf{F}_p$ has the same dimensions as the facet matrix $\mathbf{F}$. In fact, in the absence of interreflections, $\mathbf{K}$ is a null matrix and $\mathbf{F}_p = \mathbf{F}$. In the presence of interreflections, $\mathbf{F}_p$ may be viewed as representing another Lambertian surface whose shape and reflectance differ from those of $\mathbf{F}$. Therefore, if a local shape-from-intensity method is applied to the concave surface, the extracted shape and reflectance is $\mathbf{F}_p$ and not the actual shape and reflectance given by $\mathbf{F}$. We refer to $\mathbf{F}_p$ as the *pseudo facet matrix*; it represents the pseudo shape and pseudo reflectance that are extracted in the presence of interreflections.

In practice, the pseudo facet matrix may be computed by using a local shape-from-intensity method. Consider for instance the photometric stereo method. Three different source directions, $\mathbf{s}_1$, $\mathbf{s}_2$, and $\mathbf{s}_3$, are used sequentially to illuminate the surface. The three resulting surface radiance vectors $\mathbf{L}_1$, $\mathbf{L}_2$, and $\mathbf{L}_3$ may be expressed as

$$[\mathbf{L}_1, \mathbf{L}_2, \mathbf{L}_3] = \mathbf{F}_p[\mathbf{s}_1, \mathbf{s}_2, \mathbf{s}_3] \qquad (21)$$

The pseudo facet matrix is computed as

$$\mathbf{F}_p = [\mathbf{L}_1, \mathbf{L}_2, \mathbf{L}_3][\mathbf{s}_1, \mathbf{s}_2, \mathbf{s}_3]^{-1} \qquad (22)$$

The ith pseudo facet in $\mathbf{F}_p$ may be written as

$$\mathbf{N}_{p_i} = \frac{\rho_{p_i}}{\pi} \mathbf{n}_{p_i} \qquad (23)$$

where $\mathbf{n}_{p_i}$ and ρ_{p_i} are the pseudo surface normal and the pseudo albedo for the facet i and, in the presence of interreflections, differ from the actual values. While actual albedo values must satisfy the physical constraint $\rho_i < 1$, pseudo albedo values tend to be greater than the actual ones. In fact, for actual albedo values close to unity, pseudo albedo values may even exceed unity (experimental results in section 6).

We highlight three important properties of the pseudo shape and reflectance:

- The pseudo shape and reflectance are *illuminant invariant*. In equation (20), note that the albedo matrix $\mathbf{P}$, the kernel matrix $\mathbf{K}$, and the actual facet matrix $\mathbf{F}$ are all invariant to the direction and intensity of the illumination. As a result, the matrix $\mathbf{F}_p$ is also illumination invariant. It is independent of source directions used by the shape-from-intensity method to illuminate the surface! This property is particularly

interesting since we know that the interreflections themselves do vary with the direction of illumination (equation 16).

- The pseudo shape and reflectance are *unique*. From equation (20) we see that the pseudo facet matrix $\mathbf{F}_p$ is dependent on the actual facet matrix $\mathbf{F}$, the albedo matrix $\mathbf{P}$, and the kernel matrix $\mathbf{K}$. Note that $\mathbf{P}$ and $\mathbf{K}$ are in turn determined by $\mathbf{F}$. Hence, $\mathbf{F}_p$ depends only on $\mathbf{F}$. In other words, there exists only a single pseudo shape and pseudo reflectance corresponding to a given actual shape and reflectance.

- The pseudo shape tends to be *less concave* than the actual shape of the surface. A sketch proof of this property is provided by Nayar [1990]. Figure 4 illustrates this property through a few examples of actual shapes and pseudo shapes. All the surfaces are assumed to have a constant albedo value, $\rho = 0.95$. The pseudo shapes are computed using equation (20) and are seen to be less concave than the actual shapes. It is also clear from equation (20) that the discrepancy between the pseudo shape and the actual shape increases with the albedo of the surface; the interreflections diminish as albedo approaches zero. As seen in figure 5, the concavity of the pseudo shape decreases as albedo increases.

4 Recovering Actual Shape and Reflectance

We now present an algorithm that *simultaneously* recovers both actual shape and actual reflectance of the surface from the extracted pseudo shape and reflectance. Since the pseudo shape and reflectance are highly nonlinear functions of the actual shape and reflectance, a closed-form solution to the recovery problem does not seem possible. Hence, we develop an iterative algorithm for recovering the actual shape and reflectance from the pseudo estimates. The algorithm is based on the three properties of the pseudo shape and reflectance given above.

4.1 The Recovery Algorithm

Figure 6 illustrates the flow of the recovery algorithm. At first, a local shape-from-intensity method (e.g., photometric stereo) is applied to the scene. If the scene consists of a single convex surface, the extracted pseudo shape and reflectance (given by $\mathbf{F}_p$) are simply the actual ones. However, if the scene consists of concavities,

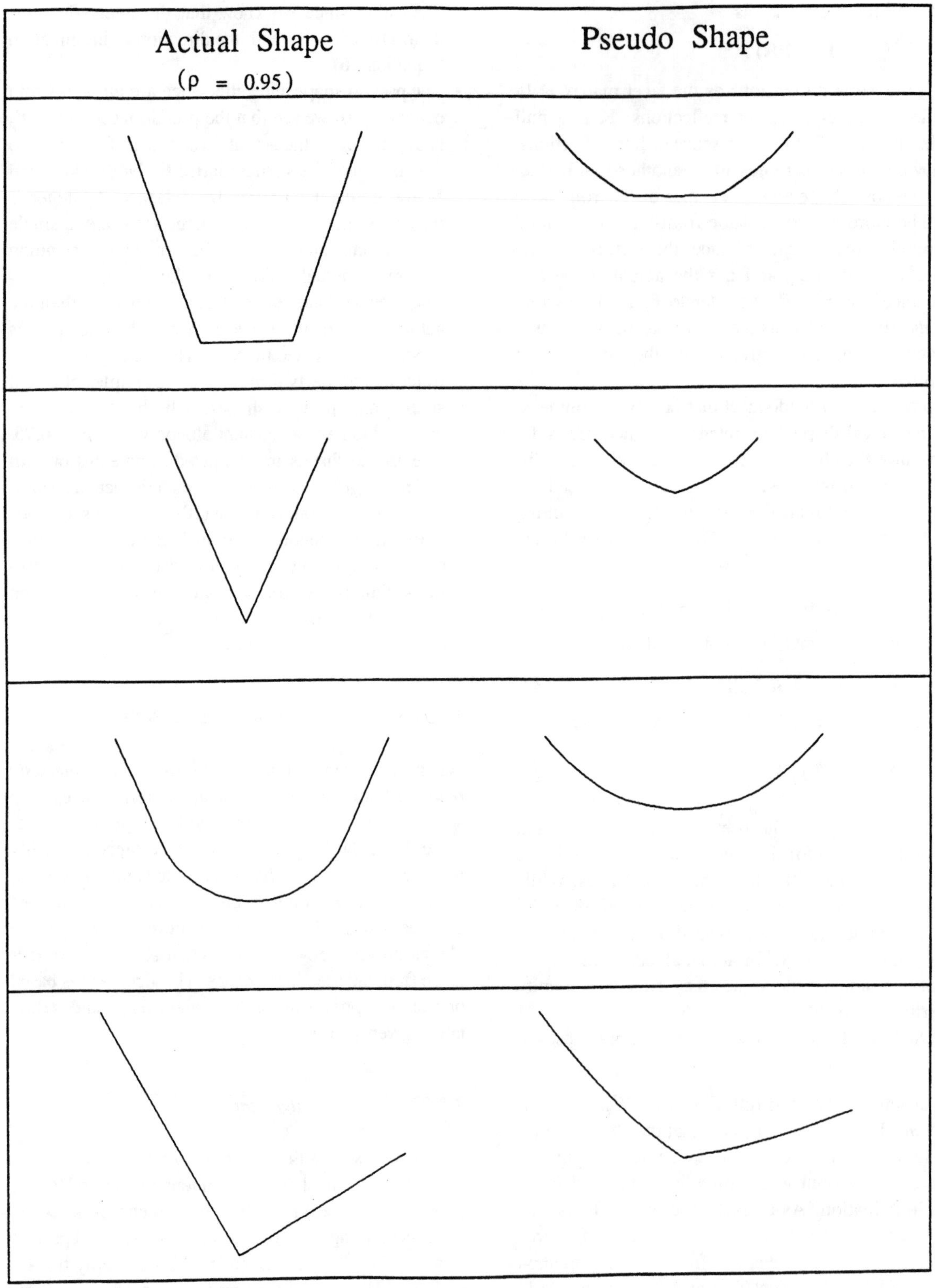

Fig. 4. A few actual shapes (with $\rho = 0.95$) and their pseudo shapes.

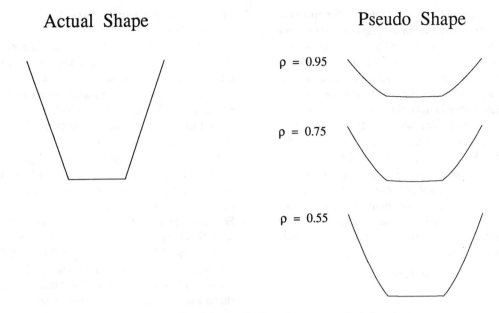

Fig. 5. The concavity of the pseudo shape decreases as albedo increases.

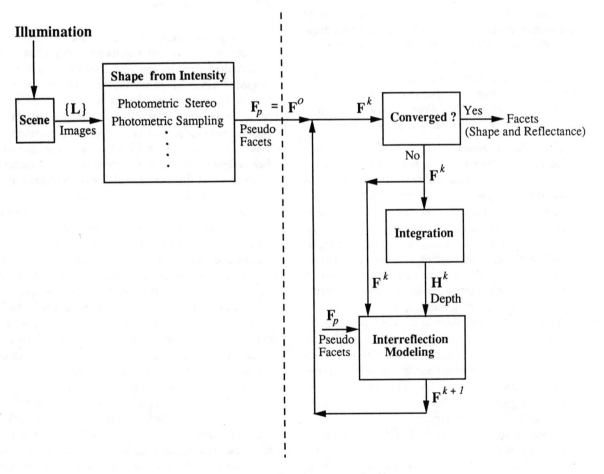

Fig. 6. The shape and reflectance recovery algorithm.

the pseudo shape and reflectance may differ from the actual ones. As we showed in the previous section, for any given actual shape and reflectance, the pseudo shape and reflectance are unique. Further, the pseudo shape is shallower (less concave) than the actual shape. Hence, the algorithm uses the pseudo shape and reflectance as conservative initial estimates of the actual shape and reflectance to model the interreflections, that is, to produce estimates for the albedo matrix $\mathbf{P}$ and the kernel matrix $\mathbf{K}$. The computed $\mathbf{P}$ and $\mathbf{K}$ matrixes, and the extracted pseudo facets $\mathbf{F}_p$ are then inserted in equation (20) to obtain the next estimate of the surface. This estimate is expected to be more concave than the previous one and is used in the next iteration to obtain an even better surface estimate. The algorithm may hence be written as

$$\mathbf{F}^{k+1} = (\mathbf{I} - \mathbf{P}^k\mathbf{K}^k)\mathbf{F}_p \qquad (24)$$

where

$$\mathbf{F}^0 = \mathbf{F}_p$$

In equation (24), $\mathbf{P}^k = \mathbf{P}(\mathbf{F}^k)$ and $\mathbf{K}^k = \mathbf{K}(\mathbf{F}^k)$. Note that each estimate of $\mathbf{F}$ provides estimates of *both* shape and reflectance. With each iteration, more accurate estimates of shape and reflectance are obtained, and the result finally converges to the actual shape and reflectance. The convergence properties of the algorithm will be discussed shortly. The following are a few assumptions and observations related to the algorithm.

- The surface is assumed to be continuous. Note that the interreflection kernel depends not only on the orientations of individual facets but also on their relative positions. Therefore, the shape of the scene must be reconstructed (by integration) from the orientation map computed in each iteration of the algorithm. The continuity assumption is necessary to ensure integrability of the orientation maps. It appears that discontinuities in the depth of scene points can also be handled if this information is provided by a depth measurement method, such as, stereo.

- All facets that contribute to interreflections in the scene must be visible to the sensor. If facets that are not visible to the sensor affect the radiance of facets that are visible, the kernel matrix will be incomplete. In such cases, the final result produced by the recovery algorithm is difficult to predict. However, reasonable results are expected if the facets that are not visible do not contribute substantially to the interreflection process. This would be the case when the facets that are not visible have either low albedo

values or are at relatively large distances from the visible facets.

- The recovery algorithm may be used in conjunction with shape-from-intensity methods. The shape-from-intensity method used must be capable of computing accurate estimates of both pseudo shape and pseudo reflectance. The recovery algorithm is in no way related to the shape-from-intensity method used to obtain the pseudo shape and reflectance. This fact is emphasized by the dotted line in figure 6.

- No extra images (measurements), in addition to the images used by the shape-from-intensity method, are needed to recover actual shape and reflectance.

- For each iteration of the above algorithm, the interreflection kernel is computed for every pair of facets in the scene. Therefore, the algorithm is of $O(Mn^2)$ complexity, where n is the number of facets in the scene and M is the number of iterations required for shape and reflectance estimates to converge.

4.2 Simulation Results

Figure 7 shows simulation results for three-dimensional surfaces that have single translational symmetry. The form of the interreflection kernel for this case is given in appendix A.3. These simulation results are included to give the reader a feel for the behavior of the algorithm. Experimental results for the general three-dimensional case as well as the translational symmetry case will be presented in a later section. For each surface in figure 7, the numerical forward solution (section 2.2) was used to predict the radiance of the surface from its actual shape and reflectance. Facet radiance values for two different source directions were computed and a photometric stereo algorithm was used to compute the pseudo shape and reflectance estimates. Note that the single-symmetry assumption reduces the problem to a two-dimensional one. Hence, only two source directions were necessary to compute facet orientations and albedo values. The pseudo shape and reflectance were then used by the recovery algorithm equation (24) to iteratively compute the actual shape and reflectance.

For the surfaces in figures 7a and 7b, a constant albedo value of 0.75 over the entire surface was used to compute the pseudo shape and reflectance. The surface in figure 7c was assumed to have a ramp albedo function that varies from 0.25 to 0.95. For the surface shown in figure 7d, a checker-board albedo function that varies between 0.3 and 0.7 was used. In figure 7d, some sections of the surface are occluded from other

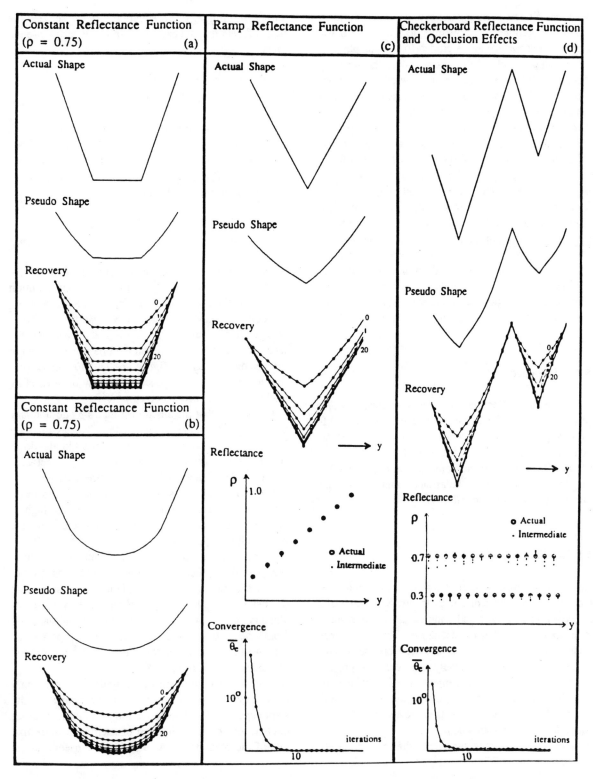

Fig. 7. Simulation results. For each surface, the pseudo shape and pseudo reflectance are computed from the actual shape and actual reflectance using the forward solution (section 1.2) and photometric stereo. The recovery algorithm is applied to the pseudo shape and reflectance to recover the actual shape and reflectance.

sections. While computing the kernel matrix, the algorithm uses geometrical reasoning to determine if two facets on the surface are occluded from each other by other facets. In all of the above cases, the recovery algorithm did *not* rely on prior knowledge of surface reflectance, but rather used the pseudo reflectance along with the pseudo shape to recover actual shape and actual reflectance, simultaneously.

In figures 7c and 7d, the pseudo and intermediate reflectance estimates are also shown. For these surfaces, a convergence graph is also included that shows the *mean orientation error* $\bar{\theta}_e$, computed using all facets, for each iteration of the recovery algorithm. The orientation error at a surface point is defined as the angle (in degrees) between the actual normal vector and the estimated normal vector. For all of the above surfaces, and numerous other unreported simulation results, the algorithm converges smoothly to zero error in both shape and reflectance. Fairly accurate shape estimates are usually obtained in about seven iterations.

5 Convergence

Since the interreflection equation is nonlinear in the orientation and reflectance of surface facets, it is difficult to prove the convergence of the algorithm for the general case of arbitrary shape and reflectance. Hence, we start by analyzing the convergence properties for the simplest case of two planar facets and later extend our analysis to the general case.

5.1 Two-Facet Case

Consider two infinitesimal planar facets of equal size that are separated by a distance r (figure 8a). The facets are positioned and oriented symmetrically with respect to the axis indicated by the dotted line. The unit normal vectors $\mathbf{n}_1$ and $\mathbf{n}_2$ are coplanar and therefore are defined by just two parameters, namely, n_y and n_z. As a result of the symmetrical arrangement, the interreflection kernels for the two facets are equal, that is, $K_{12} = K_{21} = \pi K$. Further, we assume that the two facets have equal albedo values, that is, $\rho_1 = \rho_2 = \rho$. By applying photometric stereo to the two facets, their pseudo facets

can be computed. From equation (20) we see that the actual facets may be expressed in terms of the pseudo facets as

$$\mathbf{N}_1 = \mathbf{N}_{p_1} - \rho K \mathbf{N}_{p_2}$$
$$\mathbf{N}_2 = \mathbf{N}_{p_2} - \rho K \mathbf{N}_{p_1} \qquad (25)$$

where $\mathbf{N}_1$ and $\mathbf{N}_2$ are the actual facets and $\mathbf{N}_{p_1}$ and $\mathbf{N}_{p_2}$ are the pseudo facets. A graphical illustration of the above relation is shown in figure 8b. If the recovery algorithm is applied to the pseudo facets, the result of the kth iteration may be expressed as

$$\mathbf{N}_1^{k+1} = \mathbf{N}_{p_1} - \rho^k K^k \mathbf{N}_{p_2}$$
$$\mathbf{N}_2^{k+1} = \mathbf{N}_{p_2} - \rho^k K^k \mathbf{N}_{p_1} \qquad (26)$$

where ρ^k and K^k are computed using the intermediate facet estimates $\mathbf{N}_1^k$ and $\mathbf{N}_2^k$. Let us focus our attention on one of the two facets, say, $\mathbf{N}_1$. Since $\mathbf{N}_{p_1}$ and $\mathbf{N}_{p_2}$ are constant, new estimates of $\mathbf{N}_1$ result solely from changes in the factor $\rho^k K^k$. Since $\rho^k K^k$ is a scalar, the facet estimates $\mathbf{N}_1^k$ must lie on the line passing through the vector $\mathbf{C}$ shown in figure 8b. This *line constraint* implies that the convergence of $\mathbf{N}_1^k$ may be studied by analyzing the convergence of $\rho^k K^k$.

We assume that the albedo estimates ρ^k do not vary substantially from the actual albedo ρ. This assumption is based on the observation that the pseudo albedo ρ^0 results from multiple reflections of light rays between the two facets. Hence, ρ^0 may be expressed as an infinite exponential series in the actual albedo value ρ. Since, in practice, ρ must be less than unity, the higher-order terms in the series may be neglected and the pseudo albedo is governed by the first few terms. Therefore, for actual albedo values that are not close to unity (say $\rho < 0.75$), the pseudo albedo may be assumed to be close to the actual albedo. Hence, we assume that the pseudo albedo and all intermediate estimates of albedo in the recovery process do not vary substantially from the actual albedo value, that is, $\rho^k \approx \rho$. Therefore, variations in the factor $\rho^k K^k$ are caused primarily by variation in K^k.

From the geometry shown in figure 8a, we see that the orientations of the two facets is determined by the slant angle θ_n. The interreflection process, in a sense, tends to make the orientation of each facet more like that of the other facet. As a result, the pseudo facets

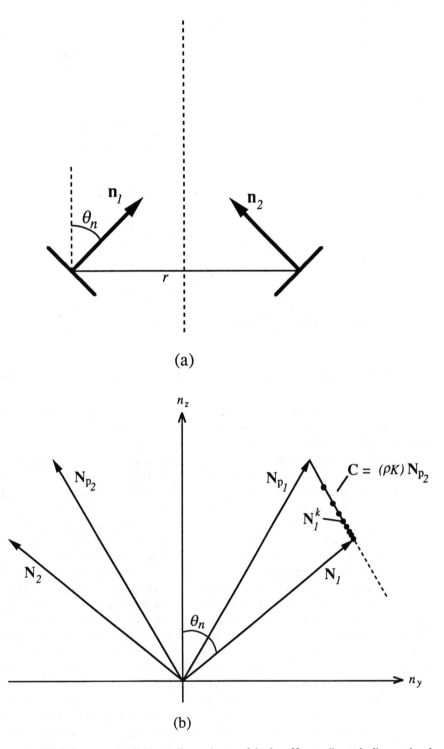

(a)

(b)

Fig. 8. (a) The two-facet case. (b) The line constraint. All intermediate estimates of the facet **N**₁ must lie on the line passing through the vector **C**.

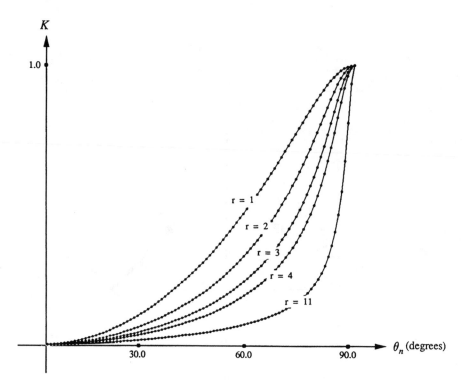

Fig. 9. The interreflection kernel K for the two-facet case, plotted as a function of the facet slant angle θ_n, for different values of the separation distance r.

are guaranteed to have a smaller slant angle than the actual facets (see figure 8b). Further, the interreflection kernel K is a *monotonic* function of the slant angle. This is shown in figure 9, where K is plotted as a function of θ_n for different values of the facet separation distance r. From the above discussion, it follows that the first estimate of the kernel, namely K^0, is less than the actual kernel K but yet greater than zero. Equivalently, the facet estimate N_1^1 has a greater slant angle than the pseudo facet but less than that of the actual facet. With each iteration, therefore, kernel estimates increase in value and approach the actual kernel value, that is, $K^0 \le K^k \le K^{k+1} \le K$. Consequently, the facet estimates, N_1^k, start from N_{p_1} and move along the vector $\mathbf{C}$ to finally converge at N_1.

The above argument holds for all facets whose pseudo albedo values do not vary substantially along the vector $\mathbf{C}$. Figure 10a shows a convergence map for the two-facet case. Each point on the map corresponds to an instance of the actual facet vector N_1; the slant angle of the facets vary along the concentric circles and the albedo of the facets vary radially. For simplicity, we have ignored the $1/\pi$ term in the facet definition given by equation (17). For all instances of N_1, the two facets

are assumed to be separated by a constant distance of $r = 1$. For each instance of N_1, the corresponding pseudo-facet N_{p_1} is computed using the forward interreflection solution and plotted on the convergence map for N_{p_1} shown in figure 10b. The recovery algorithm is independently applied to each pseudo facet and a *facet slant error* is computed at the end of 100 iterations. The small dots in figure 10a correspond to those facets for which the algorithm successfully recovers the actual facet from the corresponding pseudo facet. The large dots correspond to the facets for which the algorithm does not converge at the actual facet but rather at some other point. Similarly, the small dots and large dots in figure 10b correspond to the pseudo facets that do and do not produce accurate actual facet estimates, respectively.

Note that the algorithm fails to produce accurate estimates for facets that have large albedo values ($\rho > 0.75$) *and* large slant angles ($\theta_n > 70$ degrees). For facets in this range (large dots), the algorithm does in fact converge, but it converges to other facets that lie between the pseudo facet and the actual facet on the vector $\mathbf{C}$ (figure 8b). This results from the fact that facets with two different slant angles and two different albedo

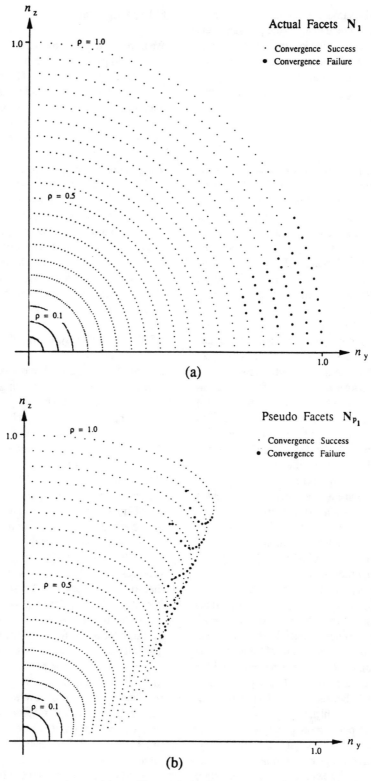

Fig. 10. (a) Convergence map for actual facets, N_1, $r = 1$. (b) Convergence map for pseudo facet, N_{p_1}, $r = 1$.

values can produce the same pseudo facet. This is also illustrated in the convergence map for the pseudo facets (figure 10b) where constant albedo curves intersect one another, implying that two different actual facets can result in the same pseudo facet. Note that each facet separation distance, r, results in a different set of convergence maps.

5.2 General Case

Convergence for the general case of surfaces of arbitrary shape (more than two facets) and with varying reflectance is difficult to prove. This is because the algorithm iterates on a system of equations that are nonlinear in the shape and reflectance of the surface. The most convincing evidence of the stability and accuracy of the algorithm lies in the simulation results of the previous section and the experimental results to follow. However, qualitative arguments can be made regarding the algorithm's general behavior.

The algorithm uses the pseudo shape and reflectance as an initial estimate of the actual shape and reflectance. We have shown that for a given actual shape and reflectance, the pseudo shape is unique and is less concave than the actual shape. As a result, interreflections computed using the pseudo shape are less (though not zero) than in the case of the actual surface. The shape and reflectance estimates obtained in the next iteration using these interreflections are expected to be closer to the actual shape and reflectance. As the shape and reflectance estimates approach the actual ones, the pseudo shape and reflectance are almost perfectly accounted for and the algorithm begins to converge.

Just as in the two-facet case, two different surface shapes with two different albedo functions can produce the same pseudo shape. However, we are using both the pseudo shape and the pseudo reflectance together to estimate actual shape and reflectance. Hence, the probability of the algorithm converging at intermediate shape estimates is small though not zero. In general, however, lower albedo values produce lesser interreflections and therefore higher likelihood of convergence. Further, in all our simulations and experiments we have restricted ourselves to facets whose slant angles are less than 70 degrees. This is because larger slant angles produce larger facet areas for which the discrete interreflection kernel provides poor approximations. In some cases, such poor approximations can lead to instability; the algorithm may produce grossly erroneous intermediate estimates that finally lead to divergence, rather than convergence, of shape and reflectance.

6 Experimental Results

We have conducted experiments to demonstrate the accuracy and practical feasibility of the shape and reflectance recovery algorithm. The algorithm was applied to general three-dimensional surfaces as well as surfaces with translational symmetry. A 512×480 CCD camera was used to obtain images of the surfaces. Each image was divided into 2×2 windows and the intensities in each window were averaged to obtain a single intensity value. This was done to reduce the effects of noise as well as to reduce the amount of data to be processed. Three incandescent lamps were used to illuminate the surfaces from three different directions. The brightness of each source was determined by a calibration procedure that uses flat surfaces of known albedo values. Surface orientation and reflectance information were computed from the images using photometric stereo. Surface shapes were obtained by integrating local surface orientations.

6.1 Translational Symmetry Case

Figure 11 and figure 12 show results for objects with translational symmetry in a single direction. Each object was painted flat white to give it a Lambertian-like appearance and an albedo value of approximately 0.9. In each case, a photograph of the object is shown and the horizontal line in the photograph represents the surface points that were used by the recovery algorithm. The actual cross-sectional shape of the surface was determined by measuring the surface contour of the object. Due to the two-dimensional nature of the problem, only two light-source directions were needed to extract pseudo shape and reflectance estimates by photometric stereo. The extracted pseudo albedo value of each facet is represented by a circle in the reflectance graph. Note that some of the pseudo albedo values exceed unity. The kernel for the translational symmetry case (appendix A.3) was used by the recovery algorithm to obtain the actual shape and reflectance from the pseudo estimates. The intermediate shape estimates are numbered according to the iteration that produced them. For all surfaces in figures 11 and 12, the shape estimates converge to reasonably accurate estimates within seven iterations. For each surface, the mean orientation error $\bar{\theta}_e$ (section 4.2) was computed after 25 iterations and found to be less than 2.5 degrees. Note that the albedo estimates converge simultaneously with the orientation estimates and are represented by the small dots in the reflectance graphs.

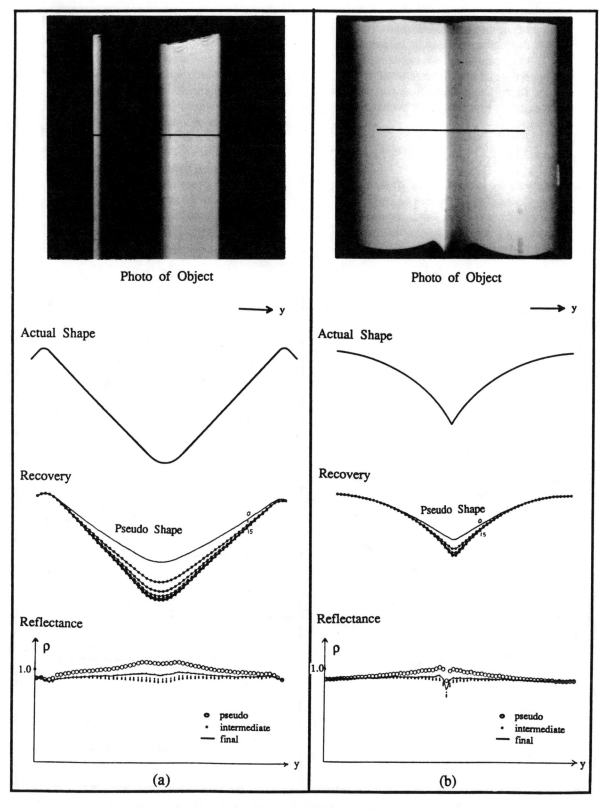

Fig. 11. Experimental results for surfaces with translational symmetry in a single direction.

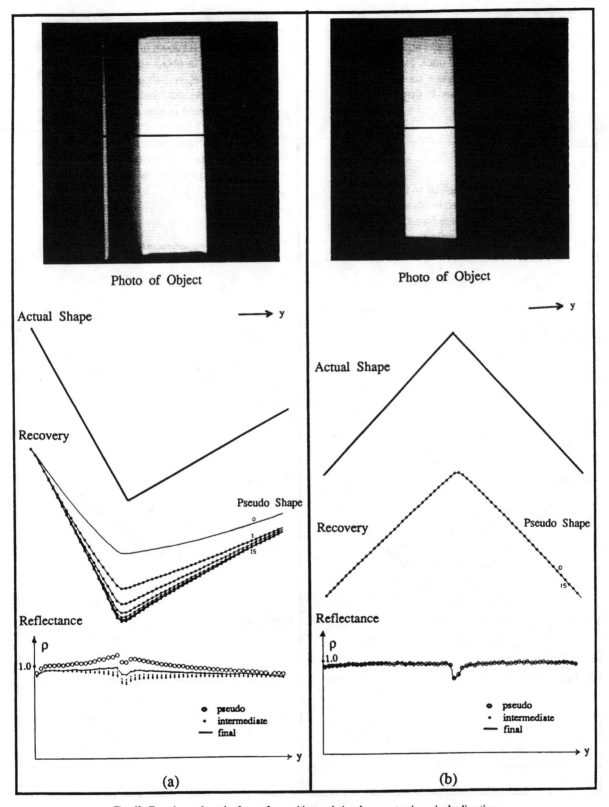

Fig. 12. Experimental results for surfaces with translational symmetry in a single direction.

Figure 12b shows a *convex* surface. Note that for a convex surface the pseudo shape and reflectance estimates are equal to the actual ones. Since no two facets on this surface are visible to one another ($V = 0$), the algorithm converges at the pseudo shape and reflectance estimates.

6.2 General Case

Figure 13 shows a photograph of an inverted pyramid. Again, the surface is painted to obtain a matte finish. In this case, three light-source directions were used to extract pseudo shape and reflectance estimates. The general form of the discrete kernel (appendix A.2) was used by the recovery algorithm to obtain the actual

Fig. 13. Photo of an inverted pyramid.

shape and reflectance. The convergence graph for the inverted pyramid is shown in figure 14. The recovered shape converges in about six iterations with a mean orientation error $\bar{\theta}_e \approx 3$ degrees. Figures 15a and 15f illustrate isometric and front views of the structure of the inverted pyramid in figure 13. Figures 15b and 15g show the isometric and front views of the pseudo shape of the inverted pyramid extracted by photometric stereo. The pseudo shape is followed by a few intermediate shape estimates produced by the recovery algorithm.

6.3 Discussion

From the above experiments we see that the recovery algorithm performs in a stable manner for a variety of surface shapes. All the surfaces used in the experiments have high albedo values (approximately 0.9) and thus exhibit strong interreflections. Though surface albedo was not known a priori, the algorithm was successful in extracting fairly accurate estimates of shape *and* reflectance from the pseudo estimates. Errors in the recovered shape and reflectance are caused by the following factors:

- Noise in the images used by the photometric stereo method to extract pseudo shape and reflectance estimates.
- The Lambertian assumption. Though all surfaces used in the experiments have a matte finish, they are not perfectly Lambertian in reflectance. Since the interreflection model used by the recovery algorithm

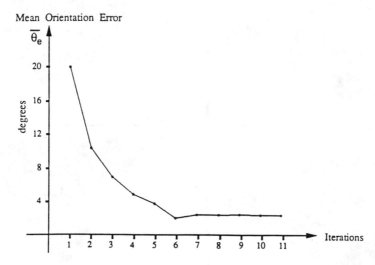

Fig. 14. Convergence graph for the inverted pyramid shown in figure 13.

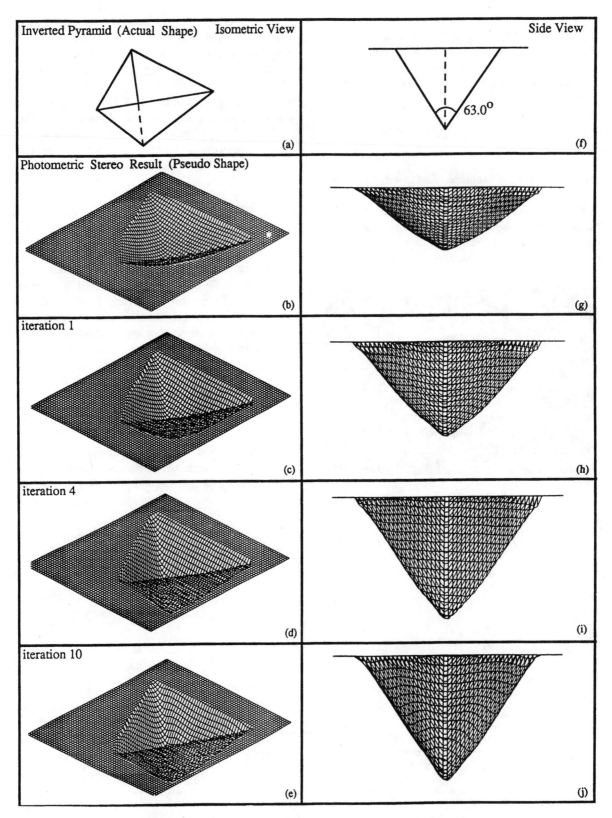

Fig. 15. Shape recovery results for the inverted pyramid shown in figure 13.

is based on the Lambertian assumption, errors in the recovered shape and reflectance are expected.

- For facets that are very close to one another and oriented such they exhibit strong interreflections, the discrete kernel does not provide a good approximation to the actual kernel. For this reason, errors in recovered shape are maximum in areas where the surface is discontinuous in orientation (e.g., edge in figure 11b).

In our experiments, we have confined ourselves to surface orientations with slant angles that are less than 70 degrees with respect to the viewing direction. As we pointed out earlier, large slant angles result in large facet areas for which the discrete kernel does not provide reasonable approximations.

All our experiments were conducted on white surfaces. The proposed method can also be applied to surfaces that are colored or multicolored (with regions of different colors). However, a small correction is required either at the source end or at the sensor end. Consider, for example, a concave surface that has two regions of different colors, say, red and blue. When the surface is illuminated, the red and blue regions interreflect incident light. If the surface is illuminated using white light, the blue region would reflect only blue light onto the red region. Therefore, a red surface point receives light rays of different spectral content; it receives white light from the source, blue light from the blue region, and red light from other red surface points. Further, the intensity of light reflected by the red surface point depends not only on the intensity of the incident light but also its spectral distribution.[3] Hence, our assumption that each surface point has a single albedo value is no longer valid: The albedo of a point would depend on its color and the spectral distribution of the incident light. However, if we consider the interreflections of light waves of a single wavelength, each surface point, irrespective of its color, can be assumed to have a unique albedo value. Therefore, the recovery algorithm we have presented here can be applied to multicolored surfaces by illuminating the surface using monochromatic light, that is, narrow-band filtering (using, for example, a red filter) the light emitted by each of the sources used by the shape-from-intensity method. Alternatively, a narrow-band filter can be used at the sensor end so that only light waves of a particular wavelength are detected by the sensor.

7 Conclusion

We have presented a method for recovering the shape and reflectance of Lambertian surfaces in the presence of interreflections. The surfaces may be of arbitrary but continuous shape, and with possibly varying reflectance. The actual shape and reflectance are recovered from the incorrect shape and reflectance estimates produced by an existing shape-from-intensity method (e.g., photometric stereo). Hence, our method enhances the performance and the utility of existing shape-from-intensity methods.

From the results reported here, three observations can be made that are pertinent to machine vision:

- This work demonstrates that interreflection problems are solvable. Vision problems related to interreflections have in the past been viewed as too complex to yield solutions.
- Our results clearly demonstrates that interreflection effects can cause vision algorithms to produce unacceptably erroneous results and hence should not be ignored. In the presence of interreflections, the shapes estimated using photometric stereo are observed to differ appreciably from the actual shapes.
- The results provide strong rationale for a physics-based approach to interreflection analysis. Our experimental results show that the physical interreflection model we have used is applicable to real matte surfaces.

In our work, we have restricted ourselves to Lambertian surfaces. Since the radiance of a Lambertian surface is vantage-independent, we can model interreflections in a compact form. For surfaces with other reflectance properties, however, surface radiance is dependent on the viewing direction. In such cases, both the forward and the inverse interreflection problems are considerably more complex. As future research we are interested in extending our analysis to specular surfaces, and subsequently, to surfaces with more general reflectance characteristics.

Acknowledgements

The authors are grateful to Hideichi Sato, Carol Novak, Larry Matthies, and Berthold Horn for their valuable comments, and to Gowthami Rajendran and Roy Taylor for reading the final draft of this paper. This research was conducted at Carnegie Mellon University and was supported in part by Westinghouse Electric Corporation and in part by DARPA under contract F33615-87-C-1499.

References

Bajcsy, R., Lee, S.W., and Leonardis, A., 1989. Image segmentation with detection of highlights and interreflections using color. GRASP LAB 182 MS-CIS-89-39, University of Pennsylvania, Dept. of Computer and Info. Science, June.

Brill, M.H., 1989. Object-based segmentation and color recognition in multispectral images. *Proc. SPIE-SPSE Meeting*, January, Paper 1076-11.

Cohen, M.F., and Greenberg, D.P., 1985. The hemi-cube: a radiosity solution for complex environments. *SIGGRAPH 1985* 19: 31–40.

Drew, M.S., and Funt, B.V., 1990. Calculating surface reflectance using a single-bounce model of mutual reflection. *Proc. 3rd Intern. Conf. Comput. Vision*, pp. 394–399.

Forsyth, D., and Zisserman, A., 1989. Mutual illumination. *Proc. Conf. Comput. Vision Patt. Recog.*, San Diego, pp. 466–473.

Forsyth, D., and Zisserman, A., 1990. Shape from shading in the light of mutual illumination. *Image and Vision Comput.*, 8 (1): 42–49.

Gilchrist, A.L., 1979. The perception of surface blacks and whites. *Scientific American* 240: 112–124.

Horn, B.K.P., 1970. Shape from shading: A method for obtaining the shape of a smooth opaque object from one view. MIT Project MAC Internal Report TR-79 and MIT AI Laboratory Technical Report 232, November.

Horn, B.K.P., 1975. Image intensity understanding. MIT AI Lab. Memo-335, August.

Horn, B.K.P., 1977. Image intensity understanding. *Artificial Intelligence* 8 (2): 201–231.

Horn, B.K.P., 1986. *Robot Vision*. MIT PRESS: Cambridge, MA.

Jacquez, J.A., and Kuppenheim, H.F., 1955. Theory of the integrating sphere. *Opt. Soc. Amer.* 45: 460–470.

Koenderink, J.J., and van Doorn, A.J., 1983. Geometrical modes as a general method to treat diffuse interreflections in radiometry. *Opt. Soc. Amer.* 73(6): 843–850.

Koenderink, J.J., and van Doorn, A.J., 1981. Photometric invariants related to solid shapes. *Optica Acta* 27: 981–996.

Nayar, S.K., Ikeuchi, K., Kanade, T., 1990. Determining shape and reflectance of hybrid surfaces by photometric sampling. *IEEE Trans. Robot. Autom.* 6 (4): 418–431.

Nayar, S.K., Ikeuchi, K., Kanade, T., 1990. Shape from interreflections. *Proc. 3rd Intern. Conf. Comput. Vision*. December, pp. 2–11.

Nayar, S.K., Shape Recovery using physical models of reflection and interreflection. Ph.D. dissertation, Department of Electrical and Computer Engineering, Carnegie Mellon University, December.

Nicodemus, F.E., Richmond, J.C., Hsia, J.J., Ginsberg, I.W., and Limperis, T., 1977. Geometrical considerations and nomenclature of reflectance. NBS Monograph 160, National Bureau of Standards, October.

Novak, C., 1990. Ph.D. thesis proposal. Department of Computer Science, Carnegie Mellon University, August.

Woodham, R.J., 1978. Photometric stereo: A reflectance map technique for determining surface orientation from image intensity. *Proc. SPIE* 155: 136–143.

Appendix A.1: Radiometric Definitions

We present definitions of radiometric terms that are used in the analysis of interreflections. Detailed derivations of these terms are given by Nicodemus et al. [1977]. Figure 16 shows a surface element illuminated by a source of light. The *irradiance E* of the surface is defined as the incident flux density (W/m^{-2}):

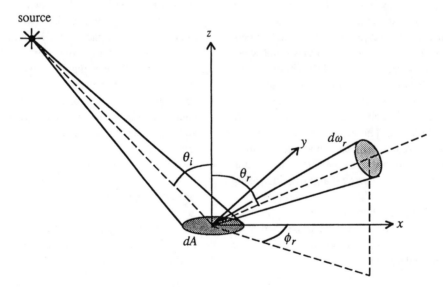

Fig. 16. Geometry used to define radiometric terms.

$$E = \frac{d\Phi_i}{dA} \qquad (27)$$

where $d\Phi_i$ is the flux incident on the area dA of the surface element. The *radiance L* of the surface is defined as the flux emitted per unit foreshortened area per unit solid angle ($W/m^{-2}\ sr^{-1}$). The surface radiance in the direction (θ_r, ϕ_r) is determined as

$$L = \frac{d^2\Phi_r}{dA\ \cos\theta_r\ d\omega_r} \qquad (28)$$

where $d^2\Phi_r$ is the flux radiated within the solid angle $d\omega_r$. The *bidirectional reflectance distribution function* (BRDF) of a surface is a measure of how bright the surface appears when viewed from one direction while it is illuminated from another direction. The BRDF is determined as

$$f = \frac{L}{E} \qquad (29)$$

Appendix A.2: Discrete Kernel and Facet Size

The discrete kernel is valid under the assumption that radiance and albedo are constant over the area of each facet. In general, this assumption is reasonable only when the facets are planar and infinitesimally small. While solving the forward interreflection problem, we are free to select appropriate (small) facet sizes. In the case of the vision problem, however, we are limited by the resolution of the sensor used to image the scene. The image brightness at a "pixel" location is assumed to be constant over the entire surface facet that the pixel represents. From figure 17, we see that the area dx_j of the facet may be related to the area dA_j of the pixel as

$$dx_j = \frac{dA_j}{\mathbf{v}_j \cdot \mathbf{n}_j} \qquad (30)$$

where $\mathbf{n}_j$ and $\mathbf{v}_j$ are the normal vector and viewing-direction vector, respectively, for the facet j. For the case of orthographic image projection, the viewing vector is constant over the entire field of view, that is, $\mathbf{v}_j = \mathbf{v}$. Using equations (5), (12), and (30), the discrete kernel is determined as

$$K_{ij} = \frac{[\mathbf{n}_i \cdot \mathbf{r}_{ij}][\mathbf{n}_j \cdot \mathbf{r}_{ji}]}{[\mathbf{r}_{ij} \cdot \mathbf{r}_{ij}]^2} \cdot \frac{dA_j}{\mathbf{v} \cdot \mathbf{n}_j} \cdot V_{ij} \qquad (31)$$

The discrete kernel provides a good approximation only when the facets i and j are both infinitesimal and distant from each other. Note that the size of a facet

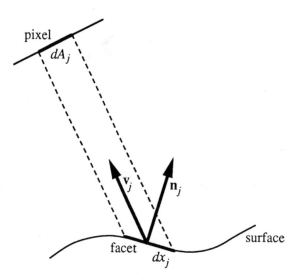

Fig. 17. The facet size is determined by the size of the sensor element (pixel) and the slant of the surface with respect to the viewing direction of the sensor.

also depends on its slant with respect to the viewing direction. Therefore, while using the discrete kernel we assume that facets are not viewed at angles close to the grazing angle. The above kernel represents the interreflections between two facets positioned and oriented in three-dimensional space. In appendix A.3, the kernel form for the special case of planar facets that have single translational symmetry [Forsyth & Zisserman 1989] is given.

Appendix A.3 Kernel for Single Translational Symmetry Case

Forsyth and Zisserman [1989] have derived the interreflection kernel for the special case of two planar facets that have translational symmetry in a single direction. Figure 18 shows a cross-sectional view of two such facets that are infinite in the x direction. The kernel K_{ij} is derived by integrating along the x and y directions, the contribution of all points on facet j to the radiance of a point on the facet i:

$$K_{ij} = -\frac{\pi}{2}\left[\frac{c - u^* \cos\alpha}{(c^2 + 2cu^* \cos\alpha + u^{*2})^{1/2}}\right]_{u^*=a}^{u^*=b} \qquad (32)$$

where α is the angle between the surface normal vectors of the two facets, and the parameter u^* represents the cross-sectional width of the facet j. Since both facets are infinite in length, the same kernel is valid for all

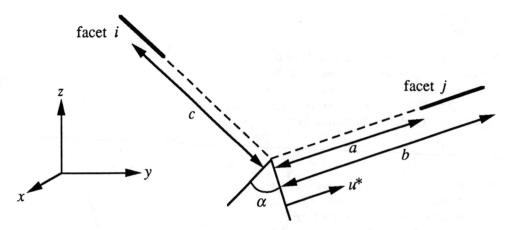

Fig. 18. Cross-sectional view of two planar facets that are infinite in the x direction.

points on the facet i. Therefore, under the translational symmetry assumption, the kernel need only be evaluated for points along the cross-section of the surface. Note that the above kernel is valid only for surfaces that are infinite in the direction of symmetry. However, the kernel serves as a good approximation for points that lie around the middle of a surface that is long though finite in the direction of symmetry. We refer the reader to Forsyth and Zisserman [1989] for details on the above kernel.

Notes

[1]Albedo of a surface element is defined as the ratio of total light energy reflected by the element to total light energy incident on the element. Its value therefore lies between zero and one.

[2]We do not include shape-from-shading algorithms in this category as they assume that the surface has constant albedo and that this albedo value is known a priori.

[3]The reader is directed to Bajcsy et al. [1989], Brill [1989], Novak [1990], and Drew and Funt [1990] for a more detailed discussion on these effects.

Shape Recovery from Shadows

Shadows are a source of visual information that we see in nearly every imaging scenario. They should therefore be a key subject for research in machine vision. However, there are few papers on this subject as it pertains to physics-based vision- because many shadow problems are either too easy or too hard for current research. Shadow analysis can be broken into several steps:

- Finding and outlining shadows.

- Establishing correspondences between shadows and the objects that cast them.

- Analyzing shadows in geometric or other radiometric calculations.

Finding and outlining shadows is the first step in shadow analysis. The most salient feature of shadows is trivial – shadows are dark! This fact by itself is very commonly used for shadow detection in constrained scenarios with additional cues, such as aerial photointerpretation.

But, a more generic shadow analysis would have to take into account the nature of light from diffuse as well as direct light sources, including interreflection from nearby objects. This is such a difficult task that there has been no substantial progress in this area to date. Some relevant papers are included in this collection in the sections on Shape Recovery from Interreflection (this volume) and Color Interreflection (Color volume).

The second problem in shadow analysis is the establishment of correspondences between shadows and shadow-casting objects. At present, this is generally an integral part of the first step – finding shadow regions. Therefore, there is no substantial literature on this topic.

The third step in shadow analysis is where there is some payoff for machine vision – analyzing shadow information. Again, there is a very trivial paradigm for analysis available from the simple observation that when a shadow is cast by an object protruding from a flat surface, the length of the shadow is proportional to the height of the protrusion. This simple geometric relation is used extensively in aerial photointerpretation.

Another kind of analysis is possible by applying traditional line-drawing interpretation techniques to images with shadows. This concept was proposed by Mackworth in [1], and is developed to a considerable degree in [2]. This latter paper addresses a number of problems in shadow geometry for planar and curved surfaces, and for each scenario, carries out an equation-counting calculation to show how much information is provided by shadows to add to the other sources of geometric constraint (from surface edges). In general, shadows don't actually add constraint – they merely allow you to push the unknowns around. In particular, vision systems can use information about the light source to constrain the interpretation of shadows.

The other paper in this collection [3] proposes a new sensing strategy in which a continuously moving light source provides topographic information about an entire surface by a sweeping shadow as it moves. This is a good example of physics-based sensing, in which a highly engineered sensor (in this case, the moving light source) provides direct measurement of an interesting scene quantity based on simple optical analysis. The optics itself is not sophisticated in this example – in fact, the sweeping shadow is an example of the simple "length-of-shadow" principle alluded to above. Yet, the paradigm is very useful, and can even be applied to the motion of the sun across the sky.

– S.A.S.

Reference

[1] Mackworth, A.K. "On the Interpretation of Drawings as Three-Dimensional Scenes." PhD thesis, University of Sussex, 1974.

Papers Included in This Collection

[2] Shafer, S.A., and Kanade, T. "Using Shadows in Finding Surface Orientations." *Computer Vision, Graphics, and Image Processing* **22**(1): 145-176, 1983.

[3] Kender, J.R., and Smith, E.M. "Shape From Darkness: Deriving Surface Information from Dynamic Shadows." In *Proc. Intl. Conference on Computer Vision*. London, England. IEEE, 1987. Pages 539-546.

Using Shadows in Finding Surface Orientations[1]

STEVEN A. SHAFER AND TAKEO KANADE

Computer Science Department, Carnegie–Mellon University, Pittsburgh, Pennsylvania 15213

Received February 2, 1982; revised June 23, 1982

Given a line drawing from an image with shadow regions identified, the shapes of the shadows can be used to generate constraints on the orientations of the surfaces involved. This paper describes the theory which governs those constraints under orthography. A "Basic Shadow Problem" is first posed, in which there is a single light source, and a single surface casts a shadow on another (background) surface. There are six parameters to determine: the orientation (two parameters) for each surface, and the direction of the vector (two parameters) pointing at the light source. If some set of three of these are given in advance, the remaining three can then be determined geometrically. The solution method consists of identifying "illumination surfaces" consisting of illumination vectors, assigning Huffman–Clowes line labels to their edges, and applying the corresponding constraints in gradient space. The analysis is extended to shadows cast by polyhedra and curved surfaces. In both cases, the constraints provided by shadows can be analyzed in a manner analogous to the Basic Shadow Problem. When the shadow falls upon a polyhedron or curved surface, similar techniques apply. The consequences of varying the position and number of light sources are also discussed. Finally, some methods are presented for combining shadow geometry with other gradient space techniques for 3D shape inference.

1. INTRODUCTION

1.1. The Shadow Geometry Problem

When shadows are present in an image, they provide information which can be used for determining the 3D shapes and orientations of the objects in the scene. The interpretation of shadows in an image involves three distinct processes:

(a) finding shadow regions in the image;

(b) solving the correspondence problem to determine which object has cast each shadow region;

(c) geometrically deducing information about the objects and surfaces involved on the basis of the identified object/shadow pairs.

Techniques for the first task, finding shadow regions, have been proposed by many researchers, usually by looking for regions of low intensity with approximately the same hue as some neighboring region [10, 12]. Lowe and Binford [7] and Witkin

[1]This research was sponsored by the Defense Advanced Research Projects Agency (DOD), ARPA Order No. 3597, monitored by the Air Force Avionics Laboratory Under Contract F33615-81-K-1539. However, the views and conclusions contained in this document are those of the authors and should not be interpreted as representing the official policies, either expressed or implied, of the Defense Advanced Research Projects Agency or the US Government.

[17] have proposed criteria which should be satisfied by edges of shadow regions; these can be used to suggest or try to confirm the hypothesis that a particular region is a shadow. Waltz [15] developed a method for labeling lines in line drawings as shadow edges, based on local geometric criteria at vertices.

The correspondence problem has been explored primarily by Lowe and Binford [7]. They describe several properties of this correspondence, and include descriptions of the special points of view from which degenerate cases arise. O'Gorman [11] proposed an heuristic method for finding correspondences in the blocks world under orthography.

Geometric interpretation of shadows is also performed by Lowe and Binford [7], who use shadows to determine height in overhead views of airplanes. They measure the distance in the image between the outline of an object and the outline of its shadow, and use similar triangles to conclude that this distance is proportional to the height of the object's edge above the ground. These techniques have been employed in manual photo-interpretation of aerial photographs as well [14].

Waltz [15] used shadows to classify surfaces into several orientation categories depending upon the geometry of the shadows in a line drawing. His categories were qualitative, such as "front left" for an approximately vertical surface tipped to the left.

This paper presents a theory describing the constraints that shadows provide between surface orientations in line drawings, using shadow and surface outlines under orthographic projection. This can be thought of as a method for achieving the same kind of results as Waltz, but computing exact surface orientations rather than simply categorizing the surfaces into classes with similar orientations. The theory presented here subsumes the "shadow-plane" idea suggested by Mackworth [8] as a means for generating gradient-space constraints from shadows.

Shadows cast by and upon curved surfaces have been described by Witkin [16], who derived equations relating surface curvature to curvature of shadow edges in the image. The presentation in this paper is somewhat different, discussing surface gradient (local orientation) rather than curvature (rate of change of orientation).

1.2. Gradient Space and Line Labeling

This section presents an introduction to the gradient space and line labeling for readers who are not already familiar with these topics.

The coordinate system used in this paper is illustrated in Fig. 1. The x and y axes are aligned on the image plane in the horizontal and vertical directions, respectively; the z axis points towards the viewer (or camera).

In this paper, it will be presumed that the point (x, y, z) in the scene corresponds to the point (x, y) in the image: this is orthography. Perspective projection is not discussed in detail in this paper.

Surface orientations can be represented by points in a plane called the gradient space (Fig. 2) [4, 8]. If a surface is represented by the equation

$$-z = f(x, y)$$

then its gradient is represented by the point

$$(p, q) = (\partial f/\partial x, \partial f/\partial y).$$

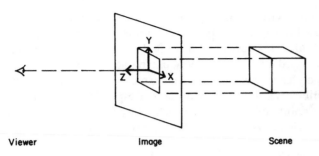

FIG. 1.   The X–Y–Z coordinate system.

This assigns a natural interpretation to points in gradient space: a surface which is "tipped" to the right is represented by a point on the right side of the origin; a surface tipped left has a gradient to the left of the origin. Similarly, a surface which is tipped up (or down) has its gradient above (or below) the origin. In Fig. 2, the gradients G_A (etc.) are shown for the surfaces S_A (etc.) in the line drawing at the right.

Before computing surface orientations, it is common to attempt to produce a line drawing from an image, in which all the surfaces are outlined. Huffman and Clowes [4, 2] showed that the edges (line segments) in a line drawing do not all represent the same three-dimensional surface configuration. The four types of edges they discovered are shown in Fig. 3, along with the half-planes containing the surfaces which meet at each type of edge. At a convex edge, the surfaces recede from the viewer as you travel farther from the edge. At a concave edge, the surfaces approach the viewer as you travel farther from the edge. At an occluding edge, only one of the two surfaces involved is directly visible in the image. Waltz [15] developed an algorithm for assigning these labels to the edges in a line drawing. The convex and concave labels indicate relationships between the gradients of the surfaces which meet along an edge [8]. When two surfaces are joined along a convex edge, their gradients lie along a line in gradient space which is perpendicular to the edge in the image (Fig. 4). Furthermore, the relative positions of the surface gradients will be the same as the relative positions of the surfaces in the image. When two surfaces meet at a concave edge, the gradients are still on a perpendicular line in gradient space, but the relative positions are reversed.

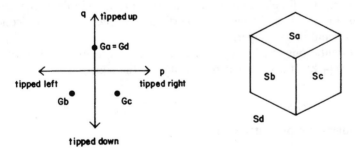

FIG. 2.   The gradient space.

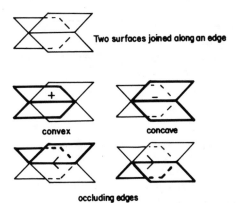

FIG. 3.   Line labels and surface intersections.

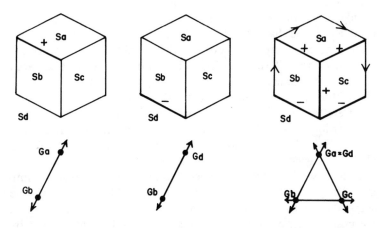

FIG. 4.   Line labels and gradient space relationships.

In general, if an edge $\mathbf{E} = (\Delta x, \Delta y)$ is contained on a surface with gradient $\mathbf{G} = (p, q)$, then the edge corresponds to the three-dimensional vector $(\Delta x, \Delta y, \Delta z)$ where

$$-\Delta z = \mathbf{G} \cdot \mathbf{E}. \qquad (1.1)$$

In this paper, a method is proposed for assigning Huffman–Clowes line labels to shadow-making edges and shadow edges in a line drawing, and for using the resulting gradient space relationships to determine surface orientations.

2. THE BASIC SHADOW PROBLEM

The Basic Shadow Problem is:

> Given a line drawing such as Fig. 5, what constraints exist between the occluding surface S_O and the shaded surface S_S?

For simplicity, we will begin by assuming that the surfaces are both flat, and that orthographic projection is used. We will also, for the time being, presume that the

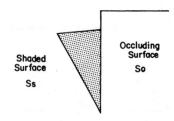

FIG. 5.   The Basic Shadow Problem.

light source is infinitely far away; this means that all illumination vectors (light rays emanating from the light source) are parallel.

2.1. Solution of the Problem

To show the proper correspondences, the edges and vertices can be labeled as in Fig. 6, where edge E_{S1} is the shadow edge corresponding to E_{O1}, E_{S2} is the shadow of E_{O2}, and vertex V_{S12} is the shadow of V_{O12}.

Consider the physical interpretation of E_{S1}. Some light rays just graze past S_O at E_{O1}, and continue on to strike S_S along E_{S1}. This set of rays forms a surface (a piece of a plane), in fact the plane containing E_{O1} and E_{S1}. This is a surface consisting of "illumination vectors"; call it surface S_{I1} (Fig. 7).

Suppose we were to cut a piece of cardboard and fit it into the space occupied by S_{I1}. Then, this cardboard and S_O would be joined along E_{O1}, a convex edge. Using Huffman–Clowes line labeling [4], this edge can be given the label $+$. Similarly, E_{S1} joins S_S and S_{I1}, and is concave; it receives the label $-$.

As Mackworth showed [8], these line labels can be mapped into constraints in the gradient space. The gradient of S_O (G_O) and the gradient of S_{I1} (G_{I1}) must be joined by a line perpendicular to E_{O1}; since the label of E_{O1} is $+$, G_O and G_{I1} have the same relative positions as S_O and S_{I1}. Similarly, G_{I1} and G_S are joined by a line perpendicular to E_{S1}, with relative positions reversed because of the $-$ label. These facts yield the relationship shown in Fig. 8 in the gradient space. However, we do not yet know the position of this figure in gradient space, nor the distances involved; only the angles are known.

S_{I1} is not the only illumination surface in the Basic Shadow Problem: the illumination surface S_{I2} joins edges E_{O2} and E_{S2} (Fig. 9). Along E_{S2}, the $-$ label is assigned; along E_{O2}, the $-$ label refers to the junction of S_O and the upper

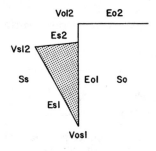

FIG. 6.   Basic Shadow Problem—correspondences labeled.

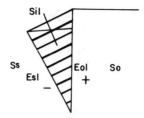

FIG. 7.   Basic Shadow Problem—illumination surface 1.

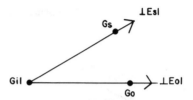

FIG. 8.   Gradient space constraints from illumination surface 1.

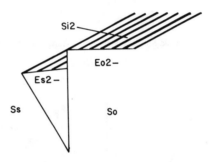

FIG. 9.   Basic Shadow Problem—illumination surface 2.

half-plane of S_{I2}. The gradient space constraints are shown in Fig. 10. Note that it is possible for E_{O2} and E_{S2} to be parallel, in which case the two rays shown in gradient space are coincident.

A third constraint in the gradient space arises from the fact that an edge E_{I1} can be drawn joining V_{O12} and V_{S12} (Fig. 11). This edge lies in a line which passes through the light source, since V_{S12} is the shadow of V_{O12}. The vector $\mathbf{I}$ pointing at the light source can be represented in gradient space by a point G_I, which is the gradient of those surfaces whose normal vectors are parallel to $\mathbf{I}$. Since E_{I1} lies in the projection of this vector onto the image plane, the point G_I must lie along a line in gradient space, passing through the origin, and parallel to E_{I1} (Fig. 12). It is not known, however, how far this point G_I is from the origin; suppose this is determined somehow (as described below), and call the distance k. It should be noted that k represents the relative change in z with a change in x or y along the illumination

FIG. 10.   Gradient space constraints from illumination surface 2.

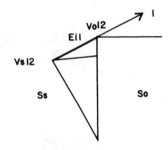

FIG. 11.   Basic Shadow Problem—illumination vector.

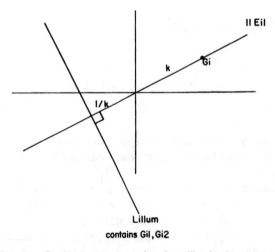

FIG. 12.   Gradient space constraints from illumination vector.

vector. It is defined by the equation

$$k = \sqrt{\Delta x^2 + \Delta y^2}/\Delta z = \|E_{I1}\|/\Delta z. \tag{2.1}$$

The line L_{illum} perpendicular to E_{I1}, and located at a distance $1/k$ from the origin, represents the locus of the gradients of all planes which contain the illumination vector **I**. This is the set of all illumination planes, and in particular contains both S_{I1} and S_{I2}; thus, G_{I1} and G_{I2} are points on the line L_{illum}. This property subsumes the property of G_{I1} and G_{I2} that they must be joined by a line perpendicular to E_{I1}, since E_{I1} can be given the label $+$ or $-$ (depending on which half-planes the line label refers to).

The line L_{illum} is the same as the *terminator* described by Horn in [3]. It separates the gradient space into two half-planes; the half-plane containing G_I represents the gradients of all planes that will receive illumination, while the other half-plane contains the gradients of self-shadowed surfaces (facing away from the light source).

This is the extent of the information available from the line drawing in Fig. 5. Since each gradient is an ordered pair (p, q), the problem has six parameters to be computed:

(a) G_O, the gradient of S_O (2 parameters);
(b) G_S, the gradient of S_S (2 parameters);
(c) G_I, the direction of the light source (2 parameters).

From the Basic Shadow Problem geometry, three constraints are provided:

(a)   the angle $G_O - G_{I1} - G_S$, which comes from the angle $E_{O1} - E_{S1}$;
(b)   the angle $G_O - G_{I2} - G_S$, which comes from the angle between E_{O2} and E_{S2};
(c)   the direction of the line L_{illum} (containing G_{I1} and G_{I2}), which comes from the direction of E_{I1}.

We would therefore expect that three parameters must be given in advance, and the other three can be computed from the geometry.

Let us suppose, for example, that the value k is given (the relative depth component of the direction of the light source), and that G_S is known (the relative orientation of the background with respect to the camera). The construction in the gradient space for computing G_O proceeds as follows (Fig. 13).

(1) Draw the line parallel to E_{I1} through the origin. Since k is known, G_I and L_{illum} can be found.

(2) Plot G_S, which was given. Through this point, draw a line perpendicular to E_{S1}. Where it intersects L_{illum} must be G_{I1}. Through G_{I1}, draw a line perpendicular to E_{O1}. The gradient G_O must lie on this line.

(3) From G_S, draw a line perpendicular to E_{S2}. Where it intersects L_{illum} will be G_{I2}. From there, draw a line perpendicular to E_{O2}. Since G_O must lie on this line, the intersection of this line with the final line from Step 2 above must be G_O.

In [13], the solution for the Basic Shadow Problem is shown to be of the form

$$G_O = \begin{bmatrix} p_O \\ q_O \end{bmatrix} = \begin{bmatrix} Q & R & S \\ T & U & V \end{bmatrix} \begin{bmatrix} p_S \\ q_S \\ 1/k \end{bmatrix}$$

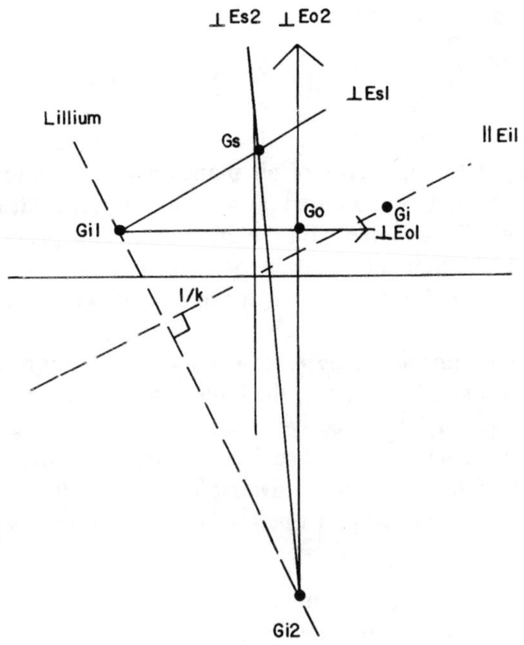

FIG. 13.   Solution to Basic Shadow Problem.

where Q, R, S, T, U, and V can be computed from measurements of the line drawing (or image).

2.2. Relationships Among the Parameters Supplied in Advance

In the example above, G_S and k were needed before the construction could take place. In practice, a program for a specific application may not be able to compute these particular parameters.

It is possible to begin the construction with any three of the six pieces of information specified in advance, as long as none are redundant with each other, and none are redundant with the direction of E_{II}.

It is possible, or perhaps likely, that a given line drawing will include the edge E_{OS} between S_O and S_S, as in Fig. 14. An interesting question arises as to whether this

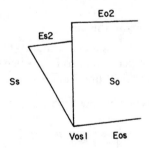

FIG. 14.   Basic Shadow Problem—Edge E_{OS} Provided.

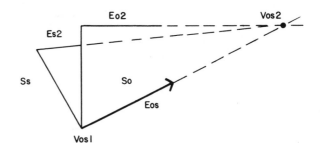

FIG. 15.   Redundancy of E_{OS} with E_{O2} and E_{S2}.

provides some additional constraint, which might perhaps relax the requirement that three pieces of information be provided in advance.

The edge E_{OS} turns out to be redundant with E_{O2} and E_{S2}, in the sense that given the latter, the former can be constructed, and vice versa. Suppose we are given E_{O2} and E_{S2}. These represent the intersections (in the scene) of planes S_O and S_{I2}, and S_S and S_{I2}, respectively. Now, either these two lines intersect or they do not. Suppose they intersect in a point. Call it V_{OS2}, since it is contained in surfaces S_O, S_S, and S_{I2}. This point is contained in both S_O and S_S, as is point V_{OS1} which is given in the line drawing. Therefore, the line E_{OS} must pass through these points. On the line drawing, find the intersection of E_{O2} and E_{S2}. Draw the line joining this point to V_{OS1}: this is E_{OS} (Fig. 15).

Now, suppose that the two lines E_{O2} and E_{S2} do not intersect anywhere. Then there is no point V_{OS2} contained in all three surfaces S_O, S_S, and S_{I2}. So, E_{OS} cannot intersect either E_{O2} or E_{S2}. Since it is coplanar with these (on surfaces S_O and S_S, respectively), it must be parallel to both. Edge E_{OS} can therefore be drawn through V_{OS1}, parallel to E_{O2} (and E_{S2}).

By this reasoning, E_{OS} can be constructed from E_{O2} and E_{S2}. Similarly, if E_{OS} is given, either of E_{O2} and E_{S2} can be calculated from the other, to provide the geometric constraint described above for the solution of the Basic Shadow Problem. Of course, the solution can also proceed directly using the label $-$ on E_{OS}, with identical results.

The solution of this problem should be compared with the solution to the problem if there are no shadows—if just S_O is given, joined to S_S along edge E_{OS}. Here, there are four parameters (G_O and G_S) to compute, and one constraint from the image (E_{OS}), so three pieces of information are still needed in advance. With shadows, the same number of a priori parameters are needed, but one of them can be a description of the light source position instead of a description of a surface orientation. The significance of shadows is that they allow information about the light source to be used to solve the problem as a substitute for information about the surface orientations themselves.

It has not been assumed in this discussion that surfaces S_O and S_S must touch. In practice, the Basic Shadow Problem arises any time there are two surfaces which provide two shadow edge pairs and an enclosed illumination vector (Fig. 16). Any additional shadow edge pairs on these two surfaces will be redundant, as will any visible edges along which these two surfaces intersect directly.

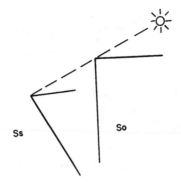

FIG. 16.   Occurrence of the Basic Shadow Problem.

2.3. Varying the Location of the Light Source

When the light source is in front of the camera (i.e., in the scene, where it might even appear in the image) and infinitely far away, the Basic Shadow Problem takes the form shown in Fig. 17. In this case, the first illumination surface S_{I1} joins edges E_{O1} and E_{S1}, giving both of these edges $-$ labels. Illumination surface S_{I2} joins E_{O2} and E_{S2}. At E_{S2}, the label is clearly $-$. To label E_{O2}, it is necessary to extend S_{I2} above this edge, and apply the label to S_O and the upper half-plane of S_{I2}. The label will then be $+$.

The vector pointing toward the light source does not intersect the plane $z = 1$, but the vector pointing away from the light source (toward the camera) does. This has the effect of placing the point G_I in the gradient space on a line parallel to edge E_{I1} passing through the origin as before, but on the half-line towards surface S_S instead of towards surface S_O. Also, while the redundancy of edge E_{OS} is the same as in the Basic Shadow Problem, edges E_{O3} and E_{S3} are redundant with edges E_{O2} and E_{S2}. This can easily be seen, since edge E_{OS} can be calculated from the intersection of E_{O1} and E_{S1} and the intersection of E_{O3} and E_{S3}; since edge E_{OS} is known to be redundant with E_{O2} and E_{S2}, E_{O3} and E_{S3} must be as well.

If the light source is behind the camera but below it, and infinitely far away, then the geometry is as shown in Fig. 18. In this case, the only difference from the Basic

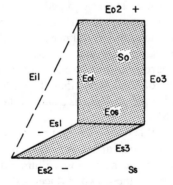

FIG. 17.   Geometry with light source in front of camera, infinitely far away.

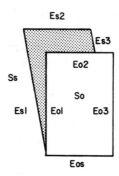

FIG. 18.   Light source behind and below camera, infinitely far away.

Shadow Problem is that edge E_{O2} receives the label $+$ instead of $-$; the labels of edges E_{O1}, E_{S1}, E_{S2}, and E_{OS} (if present) will be the same as previously described.

If the light source is a point not infinitely far away, then all illumination vectors will converge at the light source instead of being parallel (Fig. 19). Only two of the preceding arguments need to be changed in this case. The first difference is that the value k is dependent on the particular illumination vector used, and each illumination vector will have its own value of k and its own line of illumination surface gradients L_{illum}.

The second change is that edges E_{O3} and E_{S3} are no longer interchangeable with E_{OS} or with E_{O2} and E_{S2}. The new information is actually provided not by the angle between the edges E_{O3} and E_{S3}, but by the new illumination vector E_{I2} seen between vertices V_{O23} and V_{S23}. This is shown in Fig. 19 for one case (light source below and behind camera); similar line labels and reasoning hold for the other cases presented previously.

In this arrangement, the exact position of the light source can be calculated. The lines E_{I1} and E_{I2} must intersect (in the scene); the light source is located at the point of intersection. Under orthography, as we are assuming here, the x and y coordinates of the light source will be the same as the x–y coordinates of the intersection of the lines in the image. So, these coordinates can easily be found. The relative z

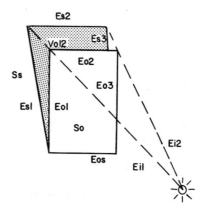

FIG. 19.   Point light source at finite distance.

coordinate is then found using the k value for either of these vectors (E_{I1} or E_{I2}), using the definition of k presented above in Eq. (2.1): if $(\Delta x, \Delta y, \Delta z)$ is an illumination vector from an object vertex to the light source (such as E_{I1} or E_{I2}), then Δx and Δy can be measured in the image, and

$$\Delta z = \sqrt{\Delta x^2 + \Delta y^2} \, / k.$$

It can be determined from the line drawing whether the light source is in fact infinitely far away: if two illumination vectors (such as E_{I1} and E_{I2}) intersect, then the light source is at a finite distance, and all illumination vectors in the image must intersect at the same point. If any two illumination vectors are parallel, then all illumination vectors are parallel and the light source is infinitely far away. These observations can be used to arrive at constraints between various simple shadow problems that arise in different parts of the same image, involving different objects and surfaces.

2.4. Changing the Number of Light Sources

It is possible that several light sources will be present, as in Fig. 20. In this case, each light source produces two parameters in the problem (the direction of illumination), and adds two image constraints (an illumination vector and one nonredundant shadow edge pair). The number of a priori parameters needed will be the same, regardless of how many light sources are present.

However, for each light source, one of the a priori parameters may be the value k for that light source, based on knowledge of the three-dimensional direction of illumination. In general, if n light sources are present and the value of k is known for each, the problem has $2n + 4$ parameters, the image provides $3n + 1$ constraints, and $3 - n$ parameters are needed in advance. Thus, shadows allow one to use *a priori* knowledge about light source positions instead of a priori knowledge about surface orientations when computing the gradients of the visible surfaces.

In Fig. 21, there are no light sources or shadows. There are four parameters to compute (the gradients of the two surfaces). An image constraint will be provided in this case only if the two surfaces S_O and S_S touch along edge E_{OS}; if they do not, then an extra a priori parameter will be needed (i.e., four instead of three).

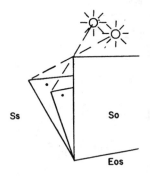

• edges are redundant with Eos

FIG. 20.   Basic Shadow Problem with multiple light sources.

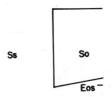

FIG. 21.   Two surfaces with no light source.

3. POLYHEDRAL SHADOW GEOMETRY

3.1. Shadows Falling On Polyhedra

The shadow of S_O may fall on two surfaces, S_S and S_T, connected by an edge E_{ST} (Fig. 22). In this case, the first illumination surface S_{I1} contains edges E_{O1}, E_{S1}, and E_{T1}. Illumination surface S_{I2} contains edges E_{O2} and E_{S2}. Edge E_{I1} is an illumination vector, joining vertices V_{O12} and V_{S12}.

In this figure, a Basic Shadow Problem can be solved using surfaces S_O and S_S. In addition, there are two new parameters to compute (G_T), and two new constraints (from edges E_{ST} and E_{T1}). These new constraints can be used to compute G_T once the Basic Shadow Problem has been solved, using the relations

$$E_{ST} \in S_T, S_S \qquad -\Delta z_{ST} = G_T \cdot E_{ST} = G_S \cdot E_{ST}$$

$$E_{T1} \in S_T, S_{I1} \qquad -\Delta z_{T1} = G_T \cdot E_{T1} = G_{I1} \cdot E_{T1}$$

$$\begin{bmatrix} -\Delta z_{ST} \\ -\Delta z_{T1} \end{bmatrix} = \begin{bmatrix} E_{ST}^T \\ E_{T1}^T \end{bmatrix} G_T$$

$$G_T = \begin{bmatrix} E_{ST}^T \\ E_{T1}^T \end{bmatrix}^{-1} \begin{bmatrix} G_S \cdot E_{ST} \\ G_{I1} \cdot E_{T1} \end{bmatrix}$$

The edge E_{ST} is labeled $-$ if the shadow edge E_{S1} bends toward E_{O1} from E_{T1}, and $+$ if it bends away from E_{O1}. The complete solution of this problem, like the Basic Shadow Problem, requires that three pieces of information be supplied in advance.

This solution technique can be generalized to cases such as Fig. 23, in which there are several shaded surfaces. If there are n shaded surfaces which intersect the shadow

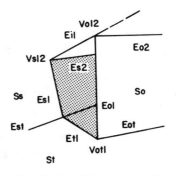

FIG. 22.   Shadow falling on two surfaces.

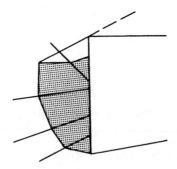

FIG. 23. Shadow falling on many surfaces.

edge with no discontinuities in the shadow edge, the problem will have a total of $2n + 4$ parameters: $2n$ for the gradients of the shaded surfaces, 2 for G_O, and 2 for G_I. The image will supply $2n + 1$ constraints; three parameters must be given in advance.

It is possible for the shadow edge to exhibit discontinuities when the shadow edge falls across occluding edges, as in Fig. 24.

The solution method is exactly as before, but this time there will be no constraint between surfaces S_S and S_T, since edge E_{ST} has been replaced by edge E_{TX} which provides no constraint between S_S and S_T. Therefore, the image provides one less constraint, and one additional nonredundant parameter must be supplied in advance to compute all the surface orientations. Of course, the gradient of surface S_X cannot be computed, since S_X is not visible in this image.

It is also the case that the edge E_{OT} (between the occluding surface and one shaded surface) is nonredundant if there are any discontinuities along the shadow edge caused by illumination surface S_{I1} (as in Fig. 24). Therefore, if this edge is present, the image provides an additional constraint.

3.2. Shadows Cast by Simple Polyhedra

When a shadow is cast by a polyhedron as in Fig. 25, each shadow-making edge (E_{PX}, E_{OP}) must be the intersection of an illuminated surface and a self-shadowed surface of the polyhedron. In the figure, S_O is illuminated and S_P is self-shadowed. The edge E_{OP} between them is a shadow-making edge, and corresponds to shadow edge E_{SI}. Illumination surface S_{I1} contains these two edges. Similarly, it can be

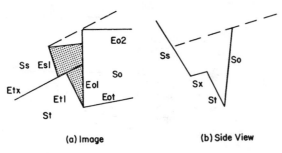

(a) Image   (b) Side View

FIG. 24. Shadow edge with discontinuities.

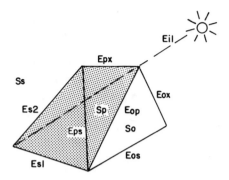

FIG. 25.   Shadow cast by simple polyhedron.

concluded that edge E_{PX} is a shadow-making edge, and must correspond to shadow edge E_{S2} (via illumination surface S_{I2}).

It can be deduced from the above observations that whatever surface intersects S_P along edge E_{PX} must be illuminated. It cannot, however, be concluded that the surface containing edge E_{PX} also contains edge E_{OX}. For this reason, no strong statements can be made about the surfaces that are not visible in the image.

In the figure, a Basic Shadow Problem exists involving surfaces S_P and S_S. The edge E_{PS} is therefore redundant with the two shadow edge pairs (E_{OP} and E_{S1}, E_{PX} and E_{S2}). This is important, since it is typically difficult to resolve details such as edge E_{PS} within shaded portions of the image [7].

When the basic problem has been solved, the gradients of surfaces S_P and S_S will be known. The gradient of S_O can then be calculated by using the constraints provided by edges E_{OP} (with surface S_P) and E_{OS} (with surface S_S).

Little useful information is provided by edge E_{OX}, since it borders on only one visible or constructible surface (S_O). Edge E_{PX}, on the other hand, is very important, since it borders on two surfaces (visible surface S_P and the illumination surface S_{I2}).

In this problem, there are eight parameters to be computed (the gradients of surfaces S_O, S_P, and S_S, and the direction of the light source G_I). The image provides five constraints (two from the shadow edge pairs E_{OP}–E_{S1} and E_{PX}–E_{S2},

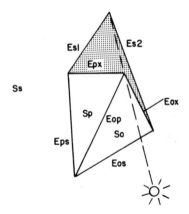

FIG. 26.   Light source in a different position.

one from the illumination vector E_{I1}, and two from the edges E_{OP} and E_{OS}). Therefore, three parameters must be provided in advance to perform the computation.

If the figure were drawn with no shadows, there would be six parameters altogether (the gradients of the three surfaces), and three constraints in the image (from edges E_{OP}, E_{OS}, and E_{PS}). Three parameters would be required in this case, also. As in the Basic Shadow Problem itself, the shadow of a polyhedron does not provide additional constraints; it merely allows one to substitute information about the light source for a priori information about the surface orientations themselves, and allows one to utilize easy-to-find shadow edges instead of hard-to-find details within shaded areas of the image.

The above method of solution also applies when the light source is in a different position as in Fig. 26, which illustrates two illuminated surfaces of a polyhedron.

3.3. Shadows Cast by Complex Polyhedra

Suppose we add an additional self-shadowed surface to Fig. 25, as in Fig. 27. In this figure, both S_A and S_P are self-shadowed. We will suppose that the new surface S_A adjoins a shadow-making edge E_{AO}. (If the new surface S_A does not adjoin a shadow-making edge, it will be buried in the middle of the shaded area and will have no effect on the shape of the shadow.)

Two new parameters are present in the system: the gradient G_A of the new surface S_A. The image provides two new constraints that can be used to solve for these two parameters: the shadow edge pair E_{AX}–E_{S3}, and the edge E_{AO} between surfaces S_A and S_O. So, three parameters are still required in advance to solve the system completely.

The edge E_{AS} is redundant with the shadow edge pair E_{AO}–E_{S2} when shadows are present. One of the two edges E_{AP} or E_{PS} is needed, along with E_{OP}, to determine the gradient of surface S_P. Thus, two of the edges E_{SP}, E_{AS}, and E_{PS} are redundant, and only one is needed. Since these edges all lie in the shadowed area of the image, they will be difficult to extract reliably [11]. Shadows reduce the need to find edges within shadowed areas of the image.

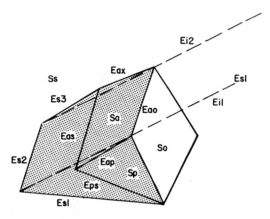

FIG. 27.   Polyhedron with two self-shadowed surfaces.

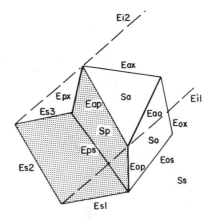

Fig. 28.   Polyhedron with two illuminated surfaces.

When the basic figure (Fig. 25) is modified by adding an illuminated surface instead of a self-shadowed surface, a line drawing such as Fig. 28 is the result. In this figure, surfaces S_A and S_O are illuminated, while S_P is self-shadowed. (Again, if the surface does not adjoin a shadow-making edge, there will be no effect on the shape of the shadow and the consequent inferences to be made from shadow geometry. Therefore, we will assume that the new surface S_A does adjoin a shadow-making edge E_{AP}.)

The reasoning here is analogous to the case of an additional self-shadowed surface: two new parameters are needed (G_A), and there are two new constraints with shadows (the pair $E_{PX}-E_{S3}$ and the edge E_{AO}), and two new constraints with no shadows (edges E_{AO} and E_{AP}). In any case, three parameters will be required in advance.

It is possible that additional a priori parameters will be needed in pathological cases. Figure 29 depicts an object with a surface adjoining the shadow-making edge

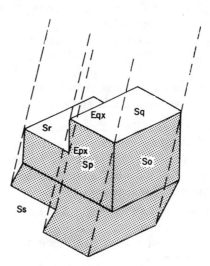

Fig. 29.   Additional parameter needed for hidden shadow-making surface.

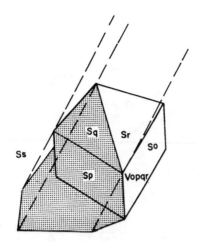

FIG. 30.   Additional parameter needed for nontrihedral vertex.

which is not visible in the image (at E_{PX}). Here, an additional a priori parameter will be needed to determine the gradient of surface S_R. The additional parameter is needed because edge E_{QX} provides no constraint between surfaces S_Q and S_R. This situation is analogous to the discontinuities in the shadow edge discussed previously.

Another circumstance requiring additional a priori parameters is shown in Fig. 30. Here, vertex V_{OPQR} is not trihedral—there are four surfaces meeting at that point (S_O, S_P, S_Q, and S_R). This adds one degree of uncertainty involving the gradients of surfaces S_Q and S_R; one additional a priori parameter is needed to solve this problem.

3.4. The General Solution For Polyhedral Shadow Geometry

The results of the two previous extensions can be directly combined. In these arguments, it has never been assumed that the shadow edge E_{S3} and the corresponding shadow-making edge (E_{AX} or E_{PX}) meet at a vertex. Therefore, the results apply without change to line drawings with additional hidden surfaces, such as Fig. 31. In this figure, there is no strong information to be obtained from shadow edge E_{S4}.

Suppose the image depicts i illuminated surfaces and s self-shadowed surfaces along the shadow-making edges of a polyhedron, casting a shadow whose corresponding edge intersects n surfaces of another polyhedron exhibiting d discontinuities, with h hidden shadow-making surfaces and t nontrihedral vertices.

(1)   The problem has $2i + 2s + 2n + 2$ parameters:

$2i$ for the gradients of the i illuminated surfaces;
$2s$ for the gradients of the s self-shadowed surfaces;
$2n$ for the gradients of the n background surfaces;
2 for the direction of illumination G_I.

(2)   The image provides $2i + 2s + 2n - d - h - t - 1$ constraints:

1 from the illumination vector;
2 shadow-making/shadow edge pairs used to solve the Basic Shadow Problem at one vertex;
$i + s - 2$ additional shadow-making edges;

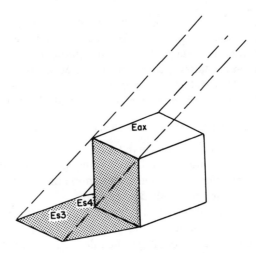

FIG. 31. Polyhedron with additional invisible surfaces.

$n - 1$ additional shadow edges;

$i + s - h - t - 1$ nonredundant edges between visible surfaces of the polyhedron casting the shadow;

1 nonredundant edge between the shadow-making polyhedron and the shaded polyhedron;

$n - d - 1$ edges at intersections of visible shaded surfaces.

(3)   Therefore, $3 + d + h + t$ parameters must be provided *a priori*:

3 for the solution of the Basic Shadow Problem;

d to compensate for the d discontinuities in the shadow edge due to invisible shaded surfaces;

h to compensate for the h hidden shadow-making surfaces;

t to compensate for the t nontrihedral vertices.

Without shadows, the problem contains $2i + 2s + 2n$ parameters, the image supplies $2i + 2s + n - d - h - t - 2$ parameters, and $n + d + h + t + 2$ parameters must be supplied before the computation.

If $i > 1$ or $s > 1$, an additional illumination vector can be used to determine the exact position of the light source.

The contribution of shadows for computing surface orientations from polyhedral line drawings can be summarized as follows:

(a)   shadows provide an increasing amount of information when the shadow edge intersects many visible, differently oriented surfaces of the background;

(b)   shadows allow one to substitute one parameter describing the direction of illumination to replace one parameter describing a surface orientation before performing the required calculations;

(c)   shadows allow one to substitute (usually) highly visible shadow edges and shadow-making edges for many of the unreliable edges within shaded portions of the image, while providing the same amount of information.

In addition, when several shadow problems appear in different portions of the same image, they share some constraints. For example, suppose several polyhedral blocks are scattered over a single surface. If the gradient of the surface and the direction of illumination are known, then three constraints are provided for each of the shadow problems. This will allow the exact solutions to be found for all the problems, if no shadow edge discontinuities or nontrihedral vertices are present.

4. SHADOWS INVOLVING CURVED SURFACES

In this section, the involvement of curved surfaces in shadow geometry will be explored. Whether the curvature lies in the occluding surface (object) or the shaded surface, additional information is required to determine the exact surface orientation along the shadow-making arc or the shadow edge arc.

Witkin [16] has also used shadows to determine curved surface orientation. He developed a relation between the curvature of a shadow edge in the scene and the curvature of the shadow edge in the image, then derived surface orientations, using surface texture gradients to provide the additional constraint necessary. The discussion below differs from Witkin's in that orientation of the shadow-making surface, rather than curvature of the shadow-making edge, is the basis of the theory.

For discussing curved surfaces, it is necessary to generalize the relation between line labels and surface gradients. Suppose two (possibly curved) surfaces S_A and S_B intersect along arc E_{AB} (Fig. 32).

The surfaces are defined by

$$S_A: -z = f_A(x, y) \qquad S_B: -z = f_B(x, y).$$

At a point V_{AB} on E_{AB},

$$-z = f_A(x, y) = f_B(x, y).$$

Differentiating by x and multiplying by Δx,

$$-\Delta x \frac{dz}{dx} = \Delta x\, G_A \cdot \left(1, \frac{dy}{dx}\right) = \Delta x\, G_B \cdot \left(1, \frac{dy}{dx}\right)$$

where G_A and G_B are the gradients of S_A and S_B at V_{AB}, and $E = (\Delta x, \Delta y)$ is a vector tangent to E_{AB} at V_{AB} in the image, corresponding to the three-dimensional vector $(\Delta x, \Delta y, \Delta z)$ in the scene.

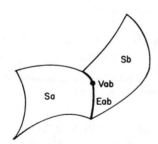

FIG. 32.   Curved surfaces intersecting along an arc.

Since

$$\Delta z = \Delta x \frac{dz}{dx} \quad \text{and} \quad \Delta y = \Delta x \frac{dy}{dx}$$

we have

$$-\Delta z = G_A \cdot (\Delta x, \Delta y) = G_B \cdot (\Delta x, \Delta y) = G_A \cdot E = G_B \cdot E.$$

This is the curved-surface analog of the relation $-\Delta z = \mathbf{G} \cdot \mathbf{E}$ described earlier for planar surfaces: the planar-surface edge $\mathbf{E}$ is replaced by the tangent vector E to the arc of intersection of two curved surfaces. As a consequence, G_A and G_B lie along a line in gradient space perpendicular to the tangent to the arc of intersection in the image.

4.1. Curvature in the Shaded Surface

Suppose a flat surface is casting a shadow on a curved surface, as in Fig. 33. Here, vertex V_{S12} is the shadow of vertex V_{O12}. Surface S_{I1}, the first illumination surface, casts the shadow of edge E_{O1} on arc E_{S1} of the curved surface S_S. Surface S_{I2} similarly casts the shadow of edge E_{O2} on arc E_{S2}.

Suppose V_{SX} is an arbitrary point on the arc E_{S1}. Can we determine the gradient G_X of S_S at this point?

Arc E_{S1} is the arc of intersection between the curved surface S_S and the illumination surface S_{I1} (defined by edge E_{O1} of surface S_O). Therefore, as previously explained, gradients G_X (of S_S at V_{SX}) and G_{I1} (of S_{I1}) must lie along a line in gradient space perpendicular to the tangent line E_{X1} to E_{S1} at V_{SX}. This constraint is illustrated in Fig. 34.

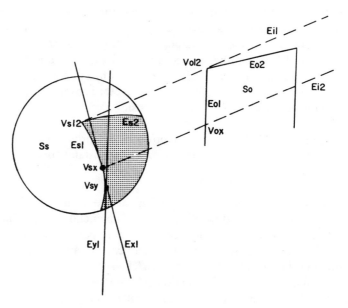

FIG. 33. Shadow cast on a curved surface.

FIG. 34.   Gradient space constraint between G_X and G_{I1}.

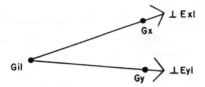

FIG. 35.   Gradient space constraints on tangent planes to S_S.

This reasoning can be used to find the two tangent lines at vertex V_{S12}, and use them in a Basic Shadow Problem with edges E_{O1} and E_{O2} of the occluding surface S_O. If S_V is the plane tangent to S_S at V_{S12}, the Basic Shadow Problem actually involves surfaces S_V and S_O. For this computation, three *a priori* parameters will be required, and the gradients G_O, G_V, G_{I1}, G_{I2}, and G_I will be computed.

It is not possible to compute the gradients G_X (and G_Y at other vertices V_{SY} as in Fig. 33, etc.) without additional information. However, it is possible to establish a one-dimensional constraint on each such gradient. Since the gradient G_{I1} of illumination surface S_{I1} was computed as part of the Basic Shadow Problem at vertex V_{S12}, the constraints provided by the tangent lines E_{X1} and E_{Y1} cause gradient space constraints as shown in Fig. 35. Similar reasoning allows constraints on the gradients at points along arc E_{S2} to be computed, using the gradient G_{I2} of illumination surface S_{I2}.

For an investment of three parameters given in advance, then, the gradients of S_O and S_V can be computed, as well as a one-dimensional constraint on the gradient for each point along arcs E_{S1} and E_{S2}. Additional constraints for the gradients along these arcs might come from another source, such as Horn's "shape from shading" technique [3] or a priori knowledge of the shape of the object bounded by surface S_S.

In this shadow problem, if another illumination vector is available (possibly from the shadow of another vertex of S_O), the exact position of the light source can then be determined.

The information available from using shadows in this problem is not redundant with information available from the same line drawing without shadows.

4.2. Shadows Cast By Curved Surfaces

When a curved object casts a shadow on a flat surface as in Fig. 36, the shadow edge E_{IS} corresponds to the shadow of the "arc of extinction" E_{IO} which divides surface S_O into an illuminated part and a self-shadowed part. There exists a curved illumination surface S_I, composed of illumination vectors, tangent to S_O along E_{IO} and intersecting the shaded surface S_S along E_{IS}. The surface S_I is a cylinder, whose axis is parallel to the direction of illumination.

There is a special significance to the line in the image tangent to both E_{IS} and the outline of S_O: it is an illumination vector, such as E_{I1} in Fig. 36. If two such tangent

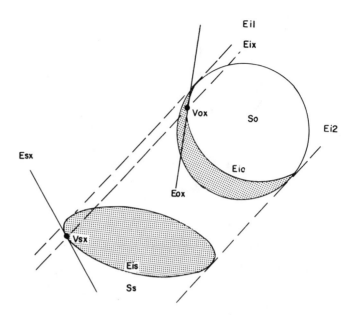

FIG. 36.   Shadow cast by a curved surface.

lines are visible (as with E_{I1} and E_{I2} in Fig. 36) or some other feature is visible in both E_{IO} and E_{IS}, then a second illumination vector can be found. From two illumination vectors, the exact position of the light source can be computed and the shadow point V_{SX} can be determined for each point V_{OX} on arc E_{IO}.

The surface S_I is composed entirely of illumination vectors; its gradient at each point must therefore lie along the line L_{illum} in gradient space. To determine this line, the value k for the light source position must be given.

If the light source is not infinitely far away, each illumination vector, such as E_{IX}, has a different value of k and determines a different line L_{illum} in gradient space. However, all the values of k can be computed from the position of the light source, given a single value of k such as that for E_{I1}. We will therefore assume, for simplicity, that the light source is infinitely far away, and that a single line L_{illum} exists.

Unfortunately, no stronger statements can be made about the gradient of S_O from examination of the arc E_{IO}. In particular, the direction of the tangent line E_{OX} bears no relationship to the gradient of S_O. This is illustrated in Fig. 37, which depicts two cylinders tangent to the same illumination plane. The arcs of extinction (dotted lines) have completely unrelated directions in the image.

However, it is possible to use the shadow edge E_{IS} to compute the gradients of the tangent surfaces along E_{IO}. The gradient G_X of S_O at V_{OX} is the same as the gradient of S_I at V_{OX}, since S_I is tangent to S_O at that point. We have two constraints on G_X from properties of S_I.

(1) S_I is an illumination surface, so G_X lies on L_{illum};

(2)   The gradient (G_X) of S_I at V_{OX} is the same as the gradient of S_I at V_{SX} (the shadow of V_{OX}), since S_I is a cylinder. As previously shown, G_X and G_S (the

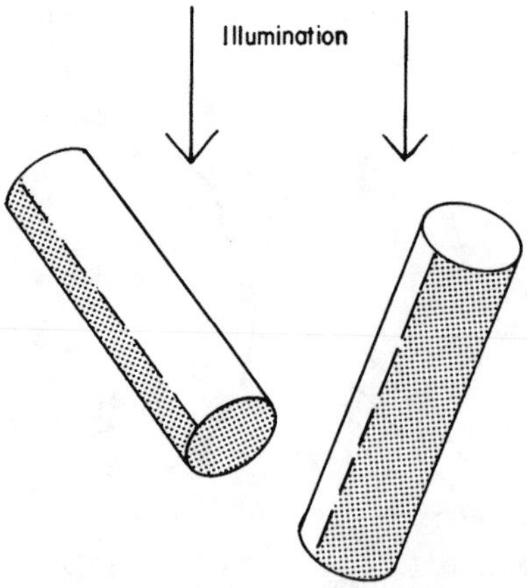

Cylinders with coplanar arcs of extinction

FIG. 37.   Arcs of extinction are unrelated to surface orientation.

gradient of the shaded surface S_S) must lie along a line in the gradient space which is perpendicular to E_{SX}, the line tangent to E_{IS} at V_{SX}.

The constraints on G_X are illustrated in Fig. 38.

Suppose we are given three parameters—k and the gradient G_S of surface S_S. From these, it is possible to compute the gradient G_X of the tangent plane to S_O for each point V_{OX} along the arc of extinction E_{IO}. Using the definition of k,

$$\Delta z_{IX} = \|E_{IX}\|/k.$$

Since E_{IX} is contained in S_I

$$-\Delta z_{IX} = G_X \cdot E_{IX}.$$

Also, if E_{SX} is a vector tangent to E_{IS} at V_{SX}

$$-\Delta z_{SX} = G_X \cdot E_{SX} = G_S \cdot E_{SX}.$$

Combining these,

$$\begin{bmatrix} -\Delta z_{IX} \\ -\Delta z_{SX} \end{bmatrix} = \begin{bmatrix} E_{IX}{}^T \\ E_{SX}{}^T \end{bmatrix} G_X$$

$$G_X = \begin{bmatrix} E_{IX}{}^T \\ E_{SX}{}^T \end{bmatrix}^{-1} \begin{bmatrix} -\Delta z_{IX} \\ -\Delta z_{SX} \end{bmatrix} = \begin{bmatrix} E_{IX}{}^T \\ E_{SX}{}^T \end{bmatrix}^{-1} \begin{bmatrix} -\|E_{IX}\|/k \\ G_S \cdot E_{SX} \end{bmatrix}.$$

It is also possible to use knowledge about the shape of the curved object S_O when G_S is not known in advance. Suppose that two vectors E_{OX} and E_{OY} tangent to the arc of extinction E_{IO} at points V_{OX} and V_{OY} are known. Let points V_{SX} and V_{SY} be the shadows of V_{OX} and V_{OY}, let E_{IX} and E_{IY} be the illumination vectors joining V_{OX}

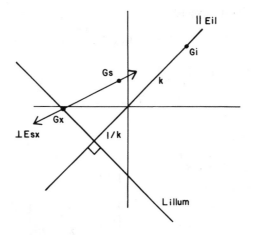

FIG. 38. Gradient space constraints on G_X.

to V_{SX} and V_{OY} to V_{SY}, and let E_{SX} and E_{SY} be vectors tangent to the shadow edge E_{IS} at V_{SX} and V_{SY} (Fig. 39).

If $(\Delta x_{OX}, \Delta y_{OX}, \Delta z_{OX})$ is the three-dimensional vector corresponding to E_{OX}, with similar definitions for the other vectors, then Δz_{OX} and Δz_{OY} are known in advance. As previously shown, if G_X is the gradient of S_I (and S_O) at V_{OX}, then

$$-\Delta z_{OX} = G_X \cdot E_{OX}.$$

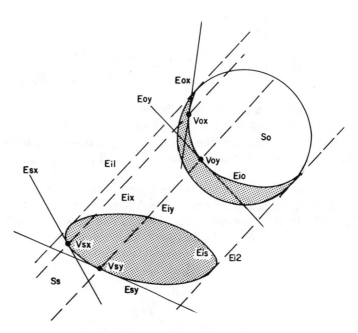

FIG. 39. Using E_{IO} to calculate the gradient of S_S.

Since E_{IX} is an illumination vector

$$\Delta z_{IX} = \|E_{IX}\|/k$$

and, since E_{IX} is contained in S_I at V_{OX},

$$-\Delta z_{IX} = G_X \cdot E_{IX}.$$

Combining,

$$\begin{bmatrix} -\Delta z_{OX} \\ -\Delta z_{IX} \end{bmatrix} = \begin{bmatrix} E_{OX}{}^T \\ E_{IX}{}^T \end{bmatrix} G_X$$

$$G_X = \begin{bmatrix} E_{OX}{}^T \\ E_{IX}{}^T \end{bmatrix}^{-1} \begin{bmatrix} -\Delta z_{OX} \\ -\|E_{IX}\|/k \end{bmatrix}.$$

So, G_X (and, similarly, G_Y, the gradient of S_I at V_{OY}), can be determined exactly.
  Now since S_I and S_S intersect at V_{SX} along E_{SX},

$$-\Delta z_{SX} = G_X \cdot E_{SX} = G_S \cdot E_{SX}.$$

Similarly,

$$-\Delta z_{SY} = G_Y \cdot E_{SY} = G_S \cdot E_{SY}.$$

So,

$$\begin{bmatrix} -\Delta z_{SX} \\ -\Delta z_{SY} \end{bmatrix} = \begin{bmatrix} E_{SX}{}^T \\ E_{SY}{}^T \end{bmatrix} G_S$$

$$G_S = \begin{bmatrix} E_{SX}{}^T \\ E_{SY}{}^T \end{bmatrix}^{-1} \begin{bmatrix} -\Delta z_{SX} \\ -\Delta z_{SY} \end{bmatrix} = \begin{bmatrix} E_{SX}{}^T \\ E_{SY}{}^T \end{bmatrix}^{-1} \begin{bmatrix} G_X \cdot E_{SX} \\ G_Y \cdot E_{SY} \end{bmatrix}$$

and therefore, G_S can be determined exactly. Now, G_S can be used as previously shown to determine the gradient of S_O at each point on the arc of extinction E_{IO}. Here, knowledge of k and the direction tangent to E_{IO} at two points has sufficed to determine the gradient of S_S and the gradient of S_O at all points along E_{IO}, (see Fig. 40).
  In the special case that S_O is spherical, for example, the entire arc of extinction E_{IO} lies in a plane S_P whose surface normal is an illumination vector. Therefore, the gradient $G_P = G_I$. In this case, the entire problem can be solved with only one parameter (k) given in advance, since Δz_{OX} and Δz_{OY} can be directly calculated

$$G_I = E_{II} \frac{k}{\|E_{II}\|}$$

$$-\Delta z_{OX} = E_{OX} \cdot G_I = \frac{k(E_{OX} \cdot E_{II})}{\|E_{II}\|}$$

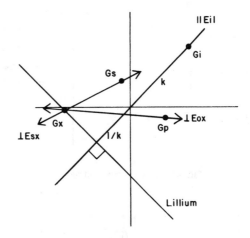

FIG. 40.   Gradient space constraints from V_{OX} for computing G_S.

and

$$-\Delta z_{OY} = \frac{k(E_{OY} - E_{I1})}{\|E_{I1}\|}.$$

The shadow information just described is not redundant with information available in the same line drawings when no shadows are present.

5. SHADOW GEOMETRY AND OTHER SHAPE INFERENCE TECHNIQUES

Shadow geometry can be combined with other techniques for determining 3D interpretations from images.

5.1. Other Gradient Space Techniques

In [13], the closed-form solution for the Basic Shadow Problem is presented in the form

$$G_O = f(G_S, k).$$

When k is given in advance, G_O is shown to be an affine transform (two-dimensional linear transform) of G_S.

Stated in this form, it is very convenient to use shadow geometry in conjunction with other techniques for determining surface gradients. For example, in Fig. 41, a line drawing is shown in which the intensities of the surfaces are known. If the surfaces are Lambertian or have known reflectance functions, Horn's "shape from shading" technique [3] can be used to determine a contour in gradient space along which G_S must lie, and a similar contour for G_O. Now, if the contour for G_S is transformed in its entirety by the function f provided by shadow geometry (as discussed above), a new contour for G_O is provided in gradient space (Fig. 42). Since G_O must lie along two contours, it must lie at one of the points of intersection of these contours. Now, for each such point, the corresponding point G_S can be determined using the inverse of transform f.

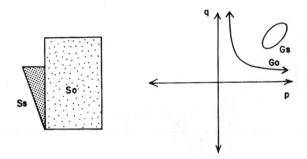

FIG. 41.   Shape from shading.

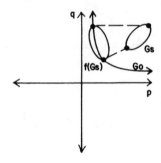

FIG. 42.   Shadow geometry and shape from shading.

Shadow geometry can similarly be combined with Kanade and Kender's "skewed symmetry" [6], as in Fig. 43. Here, skewed symmetry provides a hyperbolic contour for each of the two surface gradients G_O and G_S; shadow geometry can be used to transform the contour for G_S into an additional contour for G_O. The points of intersection of the contours for G_O are then the possible values of G_O, and the corresponding values of G_S can be found as above.

5.2. Shape Recovery for Curved Surfaces

Some techniques have appeared in the literature for reconstructing the orientation of a curved surface at every point, using relaxation techniques [1, 5]. These techniques typically begin with the surface orientation at every point along the outline of the surface (S_O in Fig. 44). These values form a boundary condition which drives the relaxation process.

In this paper, we have seen that it is possible to determine the surface orientation for the tangent planes at each point along the arc of extinction E_{IO}, using three a priori parameters (such as the k value for the light source and the orientation of the surface on which the shadow appears). These values can be used to provide stronger boundary conditions for relaxation techniques.

Surface orientations along the arc of extinction are valuable for another reason. Relaxation techniques must make some presumptions about the curvature of the surface (e.g., surface of minimum curvature, cubic or other surface of revolution). Since all of these models of curvature are consistent with the tangent gradients along

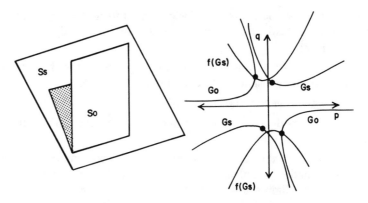

FIG. 43.   Shadow geometry and skewed symmetry.

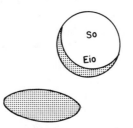

FIG. 44.   Shadow geometry and curved surface shape recovery.

the outline of S_O, it is not possible to decide which model is appropriate when the only boundary condition comes from the outline of S_O. However, when the arc of extinction is also used, it may be possible to select one from several possible models of surface curvature, or to measure systematic deviation from a particular model for a specific object.

6. CONCLUSIONS

This paper has presented a theory describing relationships among surface orientations in line drawings with shadows. The relationships arise from hypothesizing the existence of "illumination surfaces" connecting shadow edge pairs, assigning appropriate line labels to shadow and shadow-making edges, and applying the resulting constraints in the gradient space.

This technique falls short of providing exact solutions to shadow geometry problems. The line drawing must be augmented with information such as the orientations or curvature of specific surfaces or the position of the light source if exact surface orientations are to be found.

It has been shown, however, that shadow geometry provides important benefits for image understanding:

(a)   shadows allow one to substitute information about the light source position instead of *a priori* knowledge about surface orientations;

(b)   shadows allow one to determine geometric information from highly visible shadow edge pairs instead of using many of the unreliable edges within shaded portions of an image;

(c)   an increasing amount of information is provided by the shadow edge when the shadow falls on many visible, differently oriented surfaces;

(d)   shadows provide some constraint when curved surfaces are involved;

(e)   shadows provide constraints between surfaces even when they do not touch in the scene (or image);

(f)   shadows allow the solution to one shadow problem to be used in the solution of other shadow problems, since typical shadow problems are mutually constrained (e.g., same light source, same background surface).

In addition, some observations have been made about the solution of the correspondence problem for shadows, which must be solved before surface orientations can be inferred.

Future work on this topic will include generalizing of the method to images under perspective, and investigating the relationships between shadow geometry and other gradient space constraints, such as Horn's "shape from shading" [3], Kanade's "skewed symmetry" [6], and Kender's "shape from texture" paradigm [6]. There are also some open questions involving complex interactions between multiple light sources, polyhedra, and curved surfaces.

A program is being written to employ the techniques presented here. The first application will be in conjunction with an interactive photo-interpretation program [9], in which the segmentation and correspondence problems will be solved by the human operator.

ACKNOWLEDGMENTS

John Kender, at Columbia University, provided suggestions which led to several of the generalizations in this paper. His observations regarding curved surfaces provided the starting point for the ideas described in this paper regarding shadows cast by curved surfaces. In addition, this paper has benefited from review and suggestions by Marty Herman, Dave McKeown, Raj Reddy, and David Smith, all members of the Image Understanding project at CMU, and by the referee. Special thanks to Kitty Fischer for preparing the many figures for publication.

REFERENCES

1. H. G. Barrow and J. M. Tenenbaum, Reconstructing smooth surfaces from partial noisy information, in *ARPA IU Workshop*, (L. S. Baumann, Ed.), 76–86. November 1979.
2. M. B. Clowes, On seeing things, *Artif. Intell.* **2** 1971, 79–116.
3. B. K. P. Horn, Understanding image intensities, *Artif. Intell.* **8** 1977, 201–231.
4. D. A. Huffman, Impossible objects as nonsense sentences, in *Machine Intelligence 6*, B. Meltzer and D. Michie, Eds., 295–323. Amer. Elsevier, New York, 1971.
5. K. Ikeuchi, Numerical shape from shading and occluding contours in a single view, AIM 566, MIT, Cambridge, Mass., November 1979.
6. T. Kanade and J. Kender, Mapping image properties into shape constraints: Skewed symmetry, affine-transformable patterns, and the shape-from-texture paradigm, in *IEEE Workshop on Picture Data Description and Management*, 130–135, Asilomar, Calif., August 1980.

7. D. G. Lowe and T. O. Binford, The interpretation of geometric structure from image boundaries, in *ARPA IU Workshop*, (L. S. Baumann, Ed.), 39–46. April 1981.

8. A. K. Mackworth, Interpreting pictures of polyhedral scenes, *Artif. Intell.* **4** 1973, 121–137.

9. D. M. McKeown and T. Kanade, Database support for automated photo-interpretation, in *ARPA IU Workshop*, (L. S. Baumann, Ed.), 7–13, April 1981.

10. M. Nagao, T. Matsuyama, and Y. Ikeda, Region extraction and shape analysis in aerial photographs, *Computer Graphics and Image Processing* **10** 1979, 195–223.

11. F. O'Gorman, Light lines and shadows, Technical report, School of Social Sciences, Univ. of Sussex, December 1975.

12. R. B. Ohlander, Analysis of natural scenes, PhD thesis, Carnegie–Mellon Univ., Pittsburgh, Pa., April 1975.

13. S. A. Shafer and T. Kanade, Using shadows in finding surface orientations, Technical report, Computer Science Department, Carnegie–Mellon Univ., Pittsburgh, Pa., January 1982.

14. H. T. U. Smith, *Aerial Photographs and Their Applications*, Appleton–Century, New York, 1943.

15. D. Waltz, Understanding line drawings of scenes with shadows, in *The Psychology of Computer Vision*, (P. H. Winston, Ed.), 19–91, McGraw–Hill, New York, 1975.

16. A. Witkin, Shape from contour, AI-TR 589, MIT, Cambridge, Mass., November 1980.

17. A. P. Witkin and M. A. Fischler, Recovering intrinsic scene characteristics from images, Interim Tech Report Sept. 1980–Sept. 1981, SRI International. AI Center, November 1981.

SHAPE FROM DARKNESS:
Deriving Surface Information from Dynamic Shadows

John R. Kender[*]
Earl M. Smith

Department of Computer Science
Columbia University
New York, New York 10027

Abstract

We present a new method, *shape from darkness*, for extracting surface shape information based on object self-shadowing under moving light sources. It is motivated by the problem of human perception of fractal textures under perspective. To introduce the method, one-dimensional dynamic shadows are analyzed in the continuous case, and their behavior is categorized into three exhaustive shadow classes. The continuous problem is shown to be solved by the integration of ordinary differential equations, using information captured in a new image representation called the *suntrace*. The discretization of the one-dimensional problem introduces uncertainty in the discrete *suntrace*; however it is successfully recast as the satisfaction of $8n$ constraint equations in $2n$ unknowns. The extension to two dimensions is straightforward: there are $16n$ equations in $2n$ unknowns. A form of relaxation appears to quickly converge these constraints to accurate surface reconstructions; we give several examples on simulated images, both one- and two-dimensional. The shape from darkness method has two advantages: it does not require a reflectance map, and it works on non-smooth surfaces. We conclude with a discussion on the method's accuracy, its relation to human perception, and its future extensions.

1 Introduction

We present a new, active method for obtaining shape information from low level cues. It exploits the information implicit in the shadows that an object or an object part casts upon itself or another object. In spirit, it is most like the photometric stereo method of Woodham[1], in that it requires knowledge of the illuminant position. However, it also extends the existing work on shadow geometry of Shafer[2] and others, and gives additional insight into the nature of shadows, especially in the cases where the objects are neither polyhedra nor smooth, or where the shadows are dynamically changing. The method has two major advantages. It appears to work best for textured objects, that is, where existing methods fail most badly. And it is more robust than existing methods, in that it requires little a priori information about a surface's reflectance. Further, it illustrates the inherent utility--and complexity--of static or dynamic shadow-based cues for any integrated vision system, whether active or passive.

2 Historical Background

The method, which can be called *shape from darkness*, was motivated by an interest in the human perception of fractal textures. As Pentland has shown[3], the fractal dimension of textured surfaces is a powerful feature on which the segmentation of an image can be based. He further observed that the image of a single fractal surface viewed under perspective has non-constant fractal dimension. It is conjectured that this change in measured feature is closely related to the change in overall local surface orientation of the surface with respect to the observer. If this is the case, then fractal dimension can serve as a basis for a "shape from fractal" method, similar to other gradient-based shape from x methods.

However, the mathematics behind such relationships appear formidable. This is because the observed change in fractal dimension appears to be due to the increasing self-occlusion of the fractal surface as it is viewed at increasingly oblique angles. That is, unlike an airborne observer of a mountain range, an observer down in the foothills sees very little of the mountain peaks: he sees mostly the sides of foothills. The mathematical difficulty stems from the intractability of the threshold-like non-linear functions that express the nature of object occlusion; the difficulties are similar to the ones faced when trying to integrate object segmentation with standard shape-from-x methods.

Nevertheless, the problem does have the following analogue, which ultimately suggested the method reported here. It is that self-occlusion is very similar to shadowing: were a light source moved to the observer's position, the self-occluded areas would now be the ones in shadow. Thus, instead of attempting to investigate the effect that varying surface orientations have on observed fractal properties (or, equivalently, the effect that varying observer positions have), one can explore the effects that varying light source positions have on the generation of a fractal's shadows. Ideally, one would like to look into the shadows in order to see what information has been lost.

Generating and analyzing shadow information allows for several computational efficiencies. Essentially, when working with shadows, one is doing rendering and shading under extreme conditions. The capture of shadow information from real imagery or the generation of shadows synthetically both result in binary imagery. Instead of collecting shading information that has a range of values, one obtains a characteristic function instead: zero means shadow, one means illuminated. Simple thresholding of actual imagery is usually all that is required, and the synthetic casting of shadows is a straightforward computation. The imagery that results can be seen as extreme shape from shading in another sense. A synthetic shadow image can be obtained in the standard graphic rendering way by first thresholding the reflectance map: all gradients which reflect any light at all are set to one, and the remainder of the map stays at zero (for self-occluding). What results when an image is rendered with such a map is an image with extreme contrast; indeed, the contrast cannot be more extreme.

Recovering the depth or orientation of those surface fragments that have been shadowed is clearly a difficult task given only one shadow image. As with many other problems in vision, many influences are conflated into the simple image observable, the shadow. The beginning of a shadow is determined not only by surface orientation and illuminant direction, but also by the absence of any prior surface to overshadow it. The termination of a shadow depends on the relative heights and orientations of both the shadowing and shadowed surface. Deconflating these influences in a single image is not necessarily impossible; it depends on the additional information and assumptions one also brings to the task. For example, if it is known that the surface is that of a hemisphere, its position and radius are easily recovered, even without knowledge of the illuminant direction. Less restrictive assumptions, such as the surface having a band-limited fourier spectrum (and therefore "smooth" in exactly this sense of smooth), may also admit to solutions, perhaps in a form analogous to the Logan theorem characterizing a signal by its zero-crossings[4]. But still weaker assumptions, such as the surface simply being twice differentiable, probably do not lead to solutions at all. This is because smoothness as defined by differentiability is the assumption implicit in true shape from shading, and true shape from shading depends heavily on the amount of curvature in the reflectance map[5]; the thresholded reflectance map has none.

[*]This research was supported in part by ARPA grant #N00039-84-C-0165, by a NSF Presidential Young Investigator Award, and by Faculty Development Awards from AT&T, Ford Motor Co., and Digital Equipment Corporation.

3 Problem Formalization

The shape from darkness problem is more straightforward to solve by using multiple images. The observer and the objects can be held stationary, obviating any image-to-image correspondence problem, and what is moved is the light source, in a manner similar to photometric stereo. Photometric stereo usually can be done with three illuminant positions, although four is the usual number used in practice in order to prevent exactly the problem discussed here: objects in self-shadow. It is apparent that even four shadow images is woefully inadequate for shape from darkness under reasonable surface assumptions. Thus, the problem is relaxed to allow a fixed number of illuminant positions, the exact count and location of which are to be determined. The added complexity of increased imagery is mitigated in part by its binary nature, and in part by the lack of any necessity to calibrate the shadow reflectance map, since the latter is determined solely by the illuminant direction. One only needs to define the location of the shadow terminator orientations.

For simplicity in the discussion that follows, the problem is further reduced to its natural one-dimensional subproblem. That is, the algorithms presented here will discuss the recovery of a planar curve rather than a surface, given illuminants that lie in the plane of the curve. (The extension of the method to the full two dimensional case, including a discussion of the degrees of freedom of illuminant placement, is sketched later.) Thus, we assume that depth is a function solely of x, $z=f(x)$, rather than $z=f(x,y)$, and that the illuminants lie wholly within the xz plane. Note that photometric stereo has a similar one-dimensional analogue, with one-dimensional reflectance maps that are functions of curve derivative rather than surface gradient. In one-dimensional photometric stereo, three lights are necessary to prevent objects--here, curves--from self-shadowing.

4 The Continuous Problem

It is instructive to consider the shape from darkness problem as a continuous problem first. Assume that the illuminant is an infinitely distant point source, and that the observer is infinitely far in the positive z direction. (Thus, instead of investigating the surface properties of a fractal seen under perspective, we are now exploring the recovery of curve information from shadows generated under parallel illumination.) Given that the illuminant will appear in many orientations, it will be convenient to identify the illuminant with the sun, the positive direction of the x axis with the east, illumination at zero slope with dawn, illumination at positive slopes with morning, and illumination from the positive z axis with noon; often these terms are more immediate and compact.

As shown in the figure, it is easy to show that under these conditions all curve points fall into one of three classes of dynamic shadow behavior under increasing morning illumination, with analogous classes in the afternoon. A point either can become illuminated because it gradually is moved out from self-shadowing, or it can be always illuminated, or it can become illuminated because it gradually moves out from a cast shadow. These definitions can be made precise, at the given points:

A *minus* point m has $f'(m) >=0$ such that for all x, $x>m$ implies $f(x) <= f(m) + f'(m)(x-m)$. (Implicitly, $f''(m) <= 0$.) Intuitively, a minus point can only be in shadow when it is (or would be) self-shadowed. It becomes illuminated precisely at the time of day when the rising illuminant's slope is equal to $f'(m)$. When $f(m)$ becomes illuminated, points to the immediate west of m remain in shadow; therefore, in the direction of illumination the transition at m is from illumination into darkness. This terminator travels west with increasing illumination, and crosses descending values of f. Note that the shadow is caused by light grazing $f(m)$, and it is therefore diffuse, especially at low illuminant slopes. Such a point is therefore called minus for five negatively flavored reasons (a sixth becomes apparent shortly): its second derivative is negative, its terminator goes from light to dark, the terminator travels west, the terminator descends, and the shadow is not sharp.

A *zero* point z is such that for all x, $x>z$ implies $f(x) <= f(z)$. (Implicitly, $f'(z) <= 0$.) Intuitively, a zero point is never shadowed (in the morning), not even at dawn. It becomes illuminated when the rising illuminant has slope equal to zero. It never experiences a terminator: it is characterized by zero shadow and zero change.

A *plus* point p is every other point. Negating and manipulating quantifies yields: either $f'(p) <= 0$ and it is not a zero point, or $f'(p) >= 0$ and it is not a minus point. Intuitively, a plus point can only be shadowed due to cast shadows. It becomes illuminated when the rising illuminant grazes a minus point at m (illuminant slope is $f'(m)$), such that $f(m) = f(p) + f'(m)(m-p)$. When $f(p)$ becomes illuminated, points to the immediate east of p remain in shadow; therefore, in the direction of illumination the transition at p is from darkness into illumination (thus, plus). This terminator travels east (plus) with increasing illumination. Note that the

shadow is caused by occlusion, and is therefore sharp (plus). (However, $f''(p)$ is not necessarily positive, and the terminator does not necessarily cross ascending values of f.)

The function f can therefore be partitioned into segments and the segments labeled by their shadow class. The grammar of segment labels is simple; in the morning it is given by the regular expression $((+-)^*0)^*$. Such strings have three significant transitions. Plus to minus occurs at $f' = 0$ with f' at a local maximum. Minus to zero occurs at $f' = 0$ with f at a local maximum. Minus to plus occurs at curious "second grazing" points, those points m where $f'(m)$ is equal to the illuminant slope, but where there is also a $p>m$ with $f'(p)$ also equal to the illuminant slope, and $f(p) = f(m) + f'(m)(p-m)$. (The fourth transition, zero to plus, appears to have no special significance.)

4.1 The Continuous Suntrace

Quantitative reconstruction can be based on the integration of the derivative information intrinsic in the minus points. The reconstruction requires an additional representation of image information, called the *suntrace*, from which the requisite derivative information is obtained.

The suntrace is a mapping from the domain of the original curve into (morning) illumination slopes. For each x, it records the slope at which the value $f(x)$ first became illuminated. The suntrace is a function of x, since a given $f(x)$ can become illuminated only once. Depending on the underlying curve, the suntrace may be unbounded: although the entire curve must be illuminated no later than noon, noon corresponds to an unbounded illumination slope.

Since zero points are illuminated at dawn, they have suntrace values identically zero; see Figure 1. Minus points are likewise easy to detect and label: they are exactly those points (in the morning) with negative (minus) suntrace derivatives, since their terminators move west with increasing illuminant slope. What remains are the plus points; they have positive (plus) suntrace derivatives.

4.2 Solution Using ODEs

Given a morning suntrace, the underlying curve can be partially reconstructed. A contiguous curve segment with minus labels can be integrated into a function segment by using the suntrace value of the point as the value of f' at the point. The segment, however, must "float" at an unknown height until it is given an absolute height by the appropriate constant of integration.

By definition, the function values of all plus points can be determined relative to the position of their corresponding minus points that shadow them. For a plus point p, the calculation is based on the relation $f(m) = f(p) + f'(m)(m-p)$, where the corresponding minus point m is found in the suntrace as the least m greater than p that has the same illumination slope, $f'(m)$, that p has. Entire contiguous segments of plus edges can therefore be fixed in space, and joined to their integrated minus segment

The now completed plus-minus complexes can themselves be joined one to another at their common "second grazing points" (that is, at minus-plus transitions). In this way, long, self-consistent segments of the curve result, but with each "floating" with respect to a constant of integration; see Figure 2.

The fuller recovery can never be made since a simple morning suntrace provides no information about zero points. Their relative and actual depths can attain arbitrarily high values, and any self-consistent segments separated by zero points can freely float relative to each other, as long as the slope of the intervening zero segments remain negative.

Pinning down the constant of integration and restricting the behavior of zero points can be achieved by using a second suntrace, usually the afternoon suntrace which maps illumination slopes from noon to dusk. It is apparent that the only point that can be labeled a zero point for both suntraces is the global maximum. All other points are shadowed at least once and can therefore be assigned a function value relative to some constant. What results, within the accuracy of the suntrace and the integration, is a reconstruction of the underlying curve with depth values relative to a single constant of integration: the global maximum.

5 The Discrete Problem

Discretizing the shape from darkness problem requires some care. The heart of the difficulty is twofold. A discrete suntrace, however fine, can only give upper and lower bounds to function derivatives for minus points. Further, given digitization, it is not always clear where the shadowing function values in the discrete suntrace really ought to be. Indeed, as the method below describes, occasionally two different function values will serve to set the bounds on the derivatives, one for the upper bound and one for the lower bound, since the true minus point may be somewhere between them.

Rather than attempt to approximate a derivative for each minus edge, the following method attempts to maintain solution accuracy by calculating the exact upper and lower bounds the solution could have, given the discretization of the suntrace that it starts with.

5.1 The Discrete Suntrace

Any given function value $f(x)$ will become illuminated only once. Thus, there will be a time of morning, t, at and before which $f(x)$ is in shadow, and after which, at t+1, it becomes illuminated. Call the function value that shadowed $f(x)$ at time t (but could not shadow it at time t+1) the *last shadower*. The last shadower may not be the only function value that fails at time t+1 to shadow $f(x)$; call the most prominent shadower the *failing shadower*. It is not hard to see that for illumination in the morning, the west-to-east order of the function values is $f(x)$, failing shadower, and last shadower, although there may be many other undistinguished function values scattered amongst these three. These two shadowers generate important constraints on the upper and lower bounds of $f(x)$; more interestingly, $f(x)$ itself feeds back constraints on the upper and lower bounds of its shadowers, too. It is important to note that these two shadowers of $f(x)$ may be the last and failing shadowers of other function values, too; their roles at these other points may even be reversed. See Figure 3.

The shape from darkness method begins by collecting from the discrete suntrace, for every element x in the domain of the curve, information about such shadowers. The last shadower of $f(x)$ is found in the morning in the following way. If $f(x)$ first became illuminated at time t+1, the last shadower of $f(x)$ was the nearest eastern illuminated neighbor to $f(x)$ at time t. The failing shadower of $f(x)$ is the nearest eastern illuminated neighbor at time t+1.

Fortunately, such information can be collected in one pass through the suntrace. Assuming both a morning and afternoon suntrace, each element x of the domain will gather eight pieces of information: for each of the four morning or afternoon last or failing shadowers, it stores their position and the time of their shadowing (t or t+1).

5.2 The Eight Constraints per Point

Given this information, each point in the domain affects and is affected by these four critical shadowers. Each point therefore participates in eight constraints, four to do the affecting, and four to be affected by. Given that the morning and afternoon suntraces are completely symmetrical, there are only four basic conceptual relations: forward or backward constraints on upper or lower bounds. The forward constraints propagate constraint information in the direction of the illuminant; the backward constraints propagate it against the illuminant.

The forward constraints are based on the following observations. At point x, x's upper bound can be no higher than the projected shadow of the upper bound of its last shadower. (If x's upper bound were any higher, x would not be shadowed at time t). Similarly, at point x, x's lower bound can be no lower than the projected shadow of the lower bound of its failing shadower. (If x's lower bound were any lower, x would instead be shadowed at time t+1).

In the morning, the forward constraint equations are therefore:

UPPER $u(x) <= u(ls(x)) - (ls(x)-x)*sls(x)$

LOWER $l(x) >= l(fs(x)) - (fs(x)-x)*sfs(x)$

where u(.) and l(.) represent the upper and lower limits in effect at any time, ls(.) and fs(.) are the coordinates of the last shadower and failing shadower, and sls(.) and sfs(.) are the illumination slopes at the times of last shadow and failing shadow.

The backward constraints are a bit trickier, but it is their feedback that seems to account for the method's power. Consider the upper bound at x. Since the failing shadower must fail to shadow x, the upper bound of the failing shadower is limited by the height at which it just barely fails to shadow x; the maximum allowable height for the failing shadower occurs when x itself is at its maximum. (If the failing shadower's upper bound were higher, it would instead shadow x.) This height can be determined by backprojecting the upper bound of x along the slope in effect at the failing shadow time, t+1. Similarly, consider the lower bound at x. Since the last shadower must successfully shadow x, the lower bound of the last shadower is limited by the depth at which it just barely succeeds in shadowing x; the minimum allowable depth for the last shadower occurs when x itself is at its minimum. (If the last shadower's lower bound were smaller, it would instead fail to shadow x.) This height can be determined by backprojecting the lower bound of x along the slope in effect at the last shadow time, t. See Figure 4.

In the morning, the backward constraint equations are therefore:

UPPER $u(fs(x)) <= u(x) + (fs(x)-x)*sfs(x)$

LOWER $l(ls(x)) >= l(x) + (ls(x)-x)*sls(x)$

Four similar constraints apply to the information gathered for x from the afternoon suntrace.

It is surprising that these appear to be all the constraints possible (aside from the trivial constraint that $u(x) > l(x)$). Other relationships between the upper and lower bounds of x, upper and lower bounds of its last shadower, and upper and lower bounds of its failing shadower, do not appear to be constraining. For example, if x's upper bound decreases, it has no effect on the upper bound of its last shadower.

5.3 Solution Using Relaxation

The specific family of constraints that result from a given suntrace have a complex interrelated structure. It is not apparent whether there is any special solution method applicable to this problem in general, or even for well-defined subclasses of curves. There are $8n$ inequalities in $2n$ unknowns, and there is a well-defined objective function to minimize: that is, the sum, over all x, of $u(x) - l(x)$).

Although the problem might be solved using linear programming, a more attractive solution method is the use of a version of relaxation. Conceptually this consists of a number of successive iterations, in each of which the eight constraint equations are successively applied to each point x in the domain. If the application of any constraints results in better estimates for u(x) or l(x), they are updated. As in the continuous case, the only valid initial values are those of the global maximum (the only point labelled zero in both suntraces); its upper and lower limits are set arbitrarily to a pleasant value (say, zero) before the relaxation begins.

In practice, convergence seems very rapid. Unlike some relaxation algorithms, updating is based on thresholds, so upper and lower bounds are only altered if they are moved closer together. The method is therefore more likely to terminate when it recognizes a lack of measurable progress.

Extension of the algorithm to two-dimensional surfaces is straightforward. A two-dimensional suntrace is still binary. The constraint equations easily decompose into two families of x-based ("east-west") and y-based ("north-south") constraints. In all, each point is affected by 16 constraints, and convergence appears even more rapid than in the one-dimensional case. There is a great deal of freedom in selecting how the illuminant can be positioned; for simplicity, two orthogonal passes suffice.

6 Experimental Results: One-Dimensional

In the experiments that follow, some of the generalities of the algorithm were made particular. For ease of comparing the final reconstructed curve to the original, the global maximum of the reconstruction was initialized to its true known height. Sun positions were simulated at constant slope increment; thus, sun angles in the morning linearly increase in tangent. (Under this scenario, the sun literally rises, rather than travels an arc!) This policy of constant increment seems to be closely related to the encouraging accuracy obtained in the final processing step, where the final estimate of the curve is defined to be the curve midway between the computed upper and lower bounds.

Each of these series of test images shows the following.

The first figure of a series is the original curve, with its morning and evening suntraces. The domain of the original curve is aligned with the domain of the suntraces. Both suntraces have the axes for increasing sun slope pointing toward the curve. Thus, on all suntraces, the line nearest the curve is pure black, indicating all pixels have been illuminated.

The second figure of a series is a record of the constraint processing. Initial estimates for upper and lower bounds as propagated from the global maximum have gradually approached each other, subject to the suntrace data.

The third figure of the series shows final upper and lower bounds, the original curve, and the superimposed best estimate.

The first series is an image of a self-similar mountain. It is approximately 300 points wide by 85 points peak-to-peak. The suntrace was taken at increments of .1, that is, at approximately four degrees, to a maximum of 30 increments. The final estimate has a cumulative total error of less than 68 (about .2 error per pixel, average), and a maximum single point error of less than 1.2.

The second series is the same image, but with a suntrace increment of 1: that is, the first non-dawn suntrace is taken at 45 degrees, and only four increments are possible. Although not a realistic test, it demonstrates more visibly the method and its results, especially the goodness of the final estimate even under extremely severe conditions.

The third series demonstrates the applicability of the processing to very smooth imagery: a semicircle of radius 50, again under 30 increments of .1 each. Maximum error occurs at the extreme left and right of the "table", although reconstruction error within the circle is no more than 0.5.

7 Experimental Results: Two-Dimensional

A fourth and fifth series of experiments show the reconstruction of a two-dimensional fractal surface, and of a random surface, respectively. As in the prior examples, the reconstructed surface was normalized by properly offsetting its starting global maximum in order to ease the comparison of the result with the original. Note that unlike the one-dimensional case, it is possible for many two-dimensional points to be forever unshadowed: the choice of any of these as the starting value will do.

In each of the two following series, the first figure is an intensity-encoded depth map of the surface. The second figure is a similarly encoded reconstruction. (Suntraces have been omitted.) Reconstruction was so highly accurate that the third image is the gross error multiplied by a factor of *ten*.

The fourth series shows a fractal surface created by the tensor product of the first series curve with itself, as is evident from its symmetry. (It is not a true fractal, in that the x and y dimensions are highly correlated, but it certainly is not a smooth surface.) The tensor product is remapped to a range of 25 to 225. Suntrace data was taken with an increment of .3. Reconstruction took 16 iterations, with average error of .16.

The fifth series shows a random surface, with pixel depths uniformly distributed in the range 27 to 227. Suntraces were taken with increments of 1.0, and convergence was attained in 14 iterations, with average error of .96.

8 Discussion

8.1 Performance

It appears that the accuracy of the final estimate is surprisingly good, and may be related to the use of constant illumination slope increment. Choosing the midway curve is guaranteed to minimize worst case error, since the midpoint can never be off more than half the available range.

Aside from the empirical data given above, little is known about the theoretic performance of the algorithms except in two worst cases. In terms of accuracy, the worst case image occurs in a monotonically decreasing function with positive curvature (as in $z = 1/(x+c)$). Here, points at the extreme asymptotic end have little opportunity for feedback, so the range between upper and lower bounds is virtually the same as the initial forward constraints, length*(slope(t+1)-slope(t)); if slopes increase in constant increments, this is simply length*increment. In terms of convergence, it appears that certain square wave trains takes n iterations, where n is the number of pulses in the train.

Shape from darkness has several advantages, most notably that it can

exploit the surface information implicit in a class of dynamic shadows, with very little restrictions placed on the class of surfaces being shadowed: they need not be smooth. In particular, it can probably be useful in increasing the accuracy with which finely textured surfaces are viewed, especially under oblique illumination. It can also exploit smart cameras that run-length encode the incoming binary shadow imagery, but the exact information content of a shadow image, especially with respect to the information content in a gray scale image, remains to be explored.

The complexity of the data interaction does suggest why humans do not appear to derive much surface information from dynamic shadows. The necessity to store, in effect, an entire suntrace is probably excessive. On the other hand, if our earth rotated much faster (say, once every three seconds), there may have been more reason for natural systems to develop at least an approximate solution to the shape from darkness problem.

8.2 Extensions

The method admits of many extensions. The application of the method to real imagery must address the difficulties of specularity, mutual illumination, and diffuse shadows. However, in a robot environment, much of the environment can be structured to make the problem easier. For example, having the knowledge that the object is on a fixed table at a given depth can aid in the setting of lower bounds. Experiments are in progress that exploit just such constraints. In practice, what appears most critical is accuracy in illuminant position and smoothness of illuminant intensity throughout its transits. Thus, rather than the sun "rising", it is better to have it sweep through a circle: otherwise the inverse square law makes shadow-detection unnecessarily adaptive and complex.

The time required for processing two-dimensional surfaces is probably the most critical area of investigation. The problem can probably be decomposed for parallel processing in ways beyond the trivial one of partitioning the images in strips parallel to the illuminant direction; it may even be done in a hierarchical way. Selecting optimal sun positions with two degrees of freedom is challenging. Although two simple perpendicular transits allow the problem to be elegantly decomposed into two one-dimensional ones, other illuminant positions may be preferable. For example, shadow data of the surface of the earth taken periodically during a summer and a winter day have sufficient north-south sun variation to supply the second dimensional constraint. However, problems with illumination are especially acute if sun and observers are allowed to be near, and observers are allowed to view off the normal axis; this is once again the original problem of fractals under perspective.

9 Acknowledgements

Paul Douglas provided an early version of the code for the generation of suntrace information, and coined the name of the representation.

References

1. Woodham, R.J., "Analysing Images of Curved Surfaces", *Artificial Intelligence*, Vol. 17, No. 1-3, August, 1981, pp. 117-140.

2. Shafer, S.A., *Shadows and Silhouettes in Computer Vision*, Kluwer Academic Publishers, Hingham, MA, 1985.

3. Pentland, A.P., "Fractal-Based Description of Natural Scenes", *IEEE Transactions on Pattern Analysis and Machine Intelligence*, Vol. PAMI-6, No. 6, November, 1984, pp. 661-674.

4. Logan, B.F., "Information in the Zero-Crossings of Bandpass Signals", *Bell System Technical Journal*, Vol. 56, 1977, pp. 487-510.

5. Lee, D., "A Provably Convergent Algorithm for Shape from Shading", *Proceedings of the DARPA Image Understanding Workshop*, December 1985, pp. 489-496.

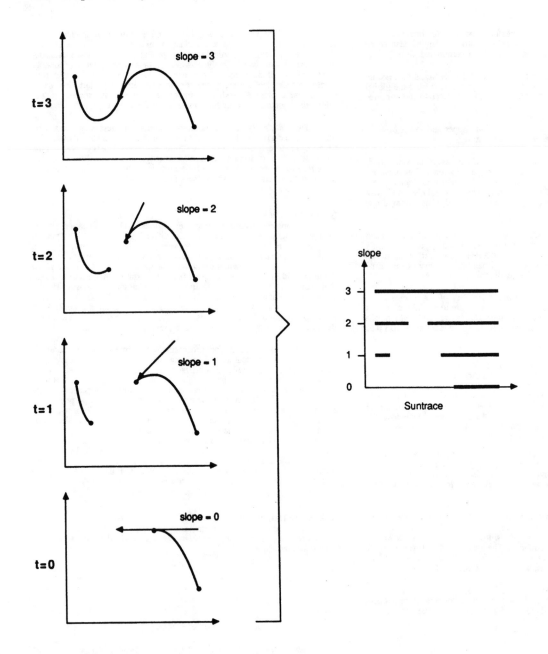

Figure 1

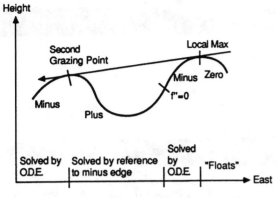

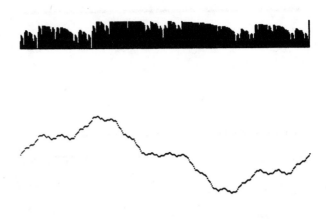

Figure 2

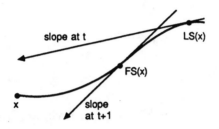

Figure 3

First series: Original curve and suntrace

First series: Constraint propagation

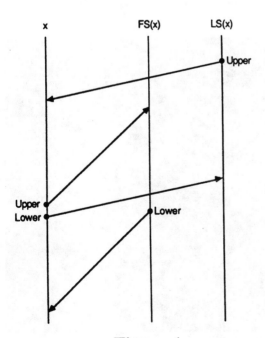

Figure 4

First series: Final bounds and estimate

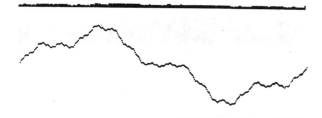

Second series: Original curve and suntrace

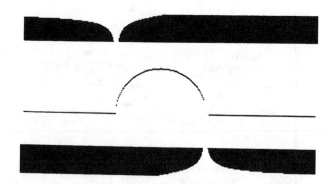

Third series: Original curve and suntrace

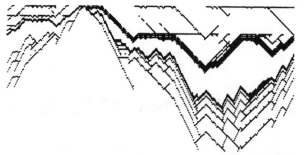

Second series: Constraint propagation

Third series: Constraint propagation

Second series: Final bounds and estimate

Third series: Final bounds and estimate

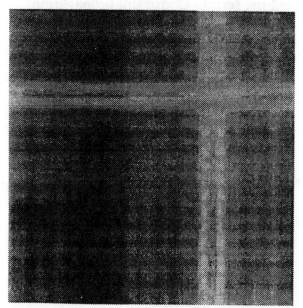

Fourth series: Original surface

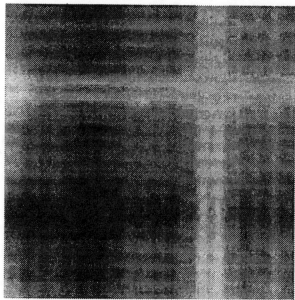

Fourth series: Final estimate

Fourth series: Error times 10

Fifth series: Error times 10

Fifth series: Original surface

Fifth series: Final estimate

Radiometric Analysis of Motion and Stereo

There are a number of problems in motion and stereo in computer vision that can be addressed using radiometric analysis. A key problem in structure from motion is the derivation of *optic flow* at each point in a motion time sequence of images, which shows the instantaneous vector displacement of image features with respect to time. Structure from motion can also be derived from observation of changing reflectance over time. For binocular stereo, reflectance properties of an object can augment surface shape description and sometimes even ameliorate the correspondence problem. The papers in this section discuss these issues.

This section begins with a seminal work by Horn and Schunk [5] on deriving optic flow from a motion sequence using a fundamental assumption about object reflectance over time. It is assumed that, for small relative displacements between an object point and a camera sensor, reflected radiance from that object point into the sensor does not change appreciably. This implies that the total variation of image intensity over image coordinates, and time, is zero. The result is a single linear equation involving the two components of optic flow and the derivatives of image intensity with respect to image coordinates and time. As optic flow is underconstrained from this single equation, Horn and Schunk utilize a variational technique that seeks to minimize both the total variation of image intensity and a departure-from-smoothness term similar to that used in Ikeuchi and Horn [1] for shape from shading. An iterative solution based upon the resulting Euler-Lagrange equations is proposed, and demonstrated on a rotating sphere with a smoothly varying intensity pattern.

The paper by Verri and Poggio [6] shows that, unfortunately, under most motion and reflectance conditions, quantitative computation of optic flow using the equation of Horn and Schunck can be inaccurate. A rigorous physical analysis is presented using the Phong reflectance model. They stress, however, that the singularities and discontinuities of the computed optic flow will be found accurately. Therefore, these qualitative properties should be utilized in structure from motion.

The next work is a recent paper by Woodham [7] for recovering optic flow for scenes under controlled illumination with multiple light sources.

Woodham applies the same assumption about object reflectance under relative motion as Horn and Schunk [5], and shows that at a given time t illumination with each additional light source provides an additional linear equation in the two optic flow components. Therefore, optic flow is fully constrained with two light sources, and overconstrained with more than two light sources. An experiment is shown that solves for optic flow from a real scene illuminated with three light sources.

The next paper, by Pentland [8], is an interesting contrast with the previous three papers. Pentland points out that there are important instances in which reflected radiance into a camera sensor from an object point varies significantly with even small relative motions, and in fact this *photometric motion* can be used as an important cue for recovery of both shape and reflectance (albedo). It is assumed that optic flow has already been computed from geometric motion cues. The key to shape recovery in this paper is the use of a previous work by Pentland [2] (contained in the "Shape from Shading" section of this volume) on shape from shading assuming a linear reflectance map in gradient space coordinates p and q. If the reflectance map is assumed to be a quadratic function of gradient space coordinates, pure linear reflectance in these variables is true for the difference image obtained by subtracting adjacent images in the image motion sequence. Prior to subtraction, images in the motion sequence are appropriately warped according to the proper correspondence from geometric cues. Shape recovery then proceeds as per Pentland in [2], assuming constant albedo. For surfaces with nonconstant albedo, Pentland uses three successive images in the motion sequence; performs subtraction between the first two and the last two images, and then generates a ratio image by dividing the first difference image by the second difference image, cancelling out albedo variations. Shape recovery can then be applied using a linear reflectance map and then local albedo can be determined. Biological mechanisms are discussed that relate to this method.

The next paper, by Grimson [9], combines binocular stereo and shading information for better shape recovery than stereo alone. Binocular stereo determines sparse depth data from correspondence of image edge zero-crossings, and then a surface can be fitted to the depth data by a variety of means [3]. Assuming reflectance according to the Phong model (some discussion of this reflectance model is given by Horn [4]), Grimson proposes to compute the three Phong reflectance parameters from a binocular stereo view of a known surface orientation, and from these known reflectance parameters derive surface orientation at all stereo matched zero-crossing contours. Thus, surfaces can be fitted to known surface orientations as well as known depths. Grimson explains how local surface orientation can be determined at zero-crossing contours with high curvature (e.g., a corner where two zero-crossing contours intersect) from a stereo view. The Phong reflectance parameters at these points can be determined using the first derivatives of image irradiance in the stereo pair of images. Once the reflectance parameters are known, Grimson proposes a modified photometric stereo method to determine local surface orientation at matched zero-crossings using the image irradiances in the stereo pair of images. Extensive analysis of numerical stability of these solutions is given.

The final paper in this section, by Smith [10], uses an elegant mathematical methodology to compute the depth of a Lambertian reflecting surface from a stereo view, while circumventing most of the correspondence problem. Smith only need assume that correspondence has been solved for the endpoints of line segments along corresponding epipolar lines between a stereo pair of images. A mathematical technique, embodied in a relation that Smith calls the *Stereo Integral Equation*, enables direct computation of the depth value at every pixel along the corresponded line segments. There are two advantages of this stereo method. First, it works on smoothly shaded Lambertian surfaces independent of albedo variations. Second, the derivation of depth for such a dense collection of points is unusual, as stereo methods typically derive depth for a much sparser set of corresponded features (e.g., zero-crossings).

– L.B.W.

References

[1] Ikeuchi, K., and Horn, B.K.P. "Numerical Shape from Shading and Occluding Boundaries." *Artificial Intelligence* **17**(1-3): 141-184, August 1981. Reprinted in Horn and Brooks, *Shape from Shading*, MIT Press, 1989.

[2] Pentland, A. "Linear Shape From Shading." *International Journal of Computer Vision* **4**: 153-162, 1990. Reprinted in the "Shape from Shading" section of this volume.

[3] Grimson, W.E.L. *From Images to Surfaces: A Computational Study of the Early Human Vision System*. MIT Press, Cambridge MA, 1982.

[4] Horn, B.K.P. "Understanding Image Intensities." *Artificial Intelligence* **8**(2): 201-231, 1977. Reprinted in the "Intensity Reflectance Models" section of the Radiometry volume.

Papers Included in This Collection

[5] Horn, B.K.P., and Schunk, B.G. "Determining Optical Flow." *Artificial Intelligence* **17**: 185-203, August 1981.

[6] Verri, A., and Poggio, T. "Motion Field and Optical Flow: Qualitative Properties." *IEEE Trans. Pattern Analysis and Machine Intelligence* **PAMI-11**(9): 490-498, May 1989.

[7] Woodham, R.J. "Multiple Light Source Optical Flow." In *Proc. Third International Conference on Computer Vision* (ICCV). Tarpon Springs FL. IEEE, 1990. Pages 42-46.

[8] Pentland, A.P. "Photometric Motion." *IEEE Trans. Pattern Analysis and Machine Intelligence* **PAMI-13**(9): 879-890, September 1991.

[9] Grimson, W.E.L. "Binocular Shading and Visual Surface Reconstruction." *Computer Vision Graphics and Image Processing* **28**(1): 19-43, 1984.

[10] Smith, G.B. "Stereo Integral Equation." In *Proc. 5th National Conference on AI*. Philadelphia, PA. AAAI, 1986. Pages 689-694.

Determining Optical Flow

Berthold K.P. Horn and Brian G. Schunck

Artificial Intelligence Laboratory, Massachusetts Institute of Technology, Cambridge, MA 02139, U.S.A.

ABSTRACT

Optical flow cannot be computed locally, since only one independent measurement is available from the image sequence at a point, while the flow velocity has two components. A second constraint is needed. A method for finding the optical flow pattern is presented which assumes that the apparent velocity of the brightness pattern varies smoothly almost everywhere in the image. An iterative implementation is shown which successfully computes the optical flow for a number of synthetic image sequences. The algorithm is robust in that it can handle image sequences that are quantized rather coarsely in space and time. It is also insensitive to quantization of brightness levels and additive noise. Examples are included where the assumption of smoothness is violated at singular points or along lines in the image.

1. Introduction

Optical flow is the distribution of apparent velocities of movement of brightness patterns in an image. Optical flow can arise from relative motion of objects and the viewer [6, 7]. Consequently, optical flow can give important information about the spatial arrangement of the objects viewed and the rate of change of this arrangement [8]. Discontinuities in the optical flow can help in segmenting images into regions that correspond to different objects [27]. Attempts have been made to perform such segmentation using differences between successive image frames [15, 16, 17, 20, 25]. Several papers address the problem of recovering the motions of objects relative to the viewer from the optical flow [10, 18, 19, 21, 29]. Some recent papers provide a clear exposition of this enterprise [30, 31]. The mathematics can be made rather difficult, by the way, by choosing an inconvenient coordinate system. In some cases information about the shape of an object may also be recovered [3, 18, 19].

These papers begin by assuming that the optical flow has already been determined. Although some reference has been made to schemes for computing the flow from successive views of a scene [5, 10], the specifics of a scheme for determining the flow from the image have not been described. Related work has been done in an attempt to formulate a model for the short range motion detection processes in human vision [2, 22]. The pixel recursive equations of Netravali and Robbins [28], designed for coding motion in television signals, bear some similarity to the iterative equations developed in this paper. A recent review [26] of computational techniques for the analysis of image sequences contains over 150 references.

The optical flow cannot be computed at a point in the image independently of neighboring points without introducing additional constraints, because the velocity field at each image point has two components while the change in image brightness at a point in the image plane due to motion yields only one constraint. Consider, for example, a patch of a pattern where brightness[1] varies as a function of one image coordinate but not the other. Movement of the pattern in one direction alters the brightness at a particular point, but motion in the other direction yields no change. Thus components of movement in the latter direction cannot be determined locally.

2. Relationship to Object Motion

The relationship between the optical flow in the image plane and the velocities of objects in the three dimensional world is not necessarily obvious. We perceive motion when a changing picture is projected onto a stationary screen, for example. Conversely, a moving object may give rise to a constant brightness pattern. Consider, for example, a uniform sphere which exhibits shading because its surface elements are oriented in many different directions. Yet, when it is rotated, the optical flow is zero at all points in the image, since the shading does not move with the surface. Also, specular reflections move with a velocity characteristic of the virtual image, not the surface in which light is reflected.

For convenience, we tackle a particularly simple world where the apparent velocity of brightness patterns can be directly identified with the movement of surfaces in the scene.

3. The Restricted Problem Domain

To avoid variations in brightness due to shading effects we initially assume that the surface being imaged is flat. We further assume that the incident illumination is uniform across the surface. The brightness at a point in the image is then proportional to the reflectance of the surface at the corresponding point on the object. Also, we assume at first that reflectance varies smoothly and has no

---

[1]In this paper, the term brightness means image irradiance. The brightness pattern is the distribution of irradiance in the image.

spatial discontinuities. This latter condition assures us that the image brightness is differentiable. We exclude situations where objects occlude one another, in part, because discontinuities in reflectance are found at object boundaries. In two of the experiments discussed later, some of the problems occasioned by occluding edges are exposed.

In the simple situation described, the motion of the brightness patterns in the image is determined directly by the motions of corresponding points on the surface of the object. Computing the velocities of points on the object is a matter of simple geometry once the optical flow is known.

4. Constraints

We will derive an equation that relates the change in image brightness at a point to the motion of the brightness pattern. Let the image brightness at the point (x, y) in the image plane at time t be denoted by $E(x, y, t)$. Now consider what happens when the pattern moves. The brightness of a particular point in the pattern is constant, so that

$$\frac{dE}{dt} = 0.$$

Using the chain rule for differentiation we see that,

$$\frac{\partial E}{\partial x}\frac{dx}{dt} + \frac{\partial E}{\partial y}\frac{dy}{dt} + \frac{\partial E}{\partial t} = 0.$$

(See Appendix A for a more detailed derivation.) If we let

$$u = \frac{dx}{dt} \quad \text{and} \quad v = \frac{dy}{dt},$$

then it is easy to see that we have a single linear equation in the two unknowns u and v,

$$E_x u + E_y v + E_t = 0,$$

where we have also introduced the additional abbreviations E_x, E_y, and E_t for the partial derivatives of image brightness with respect to x, y and t, respectively. The constraint on the local flow velocity expressed by this equation is illustrated in Fig. 1. Writing the equation in still another way,

$$(E_x, E_y) \cdot (u, v) = -E_t.$$

Thus the component of the movement in the direction of the brightness gradient (E_x, E_y) equals

$$-\frac{E_t}{\sqrt{E_x^2 + E_y^2}}.$$

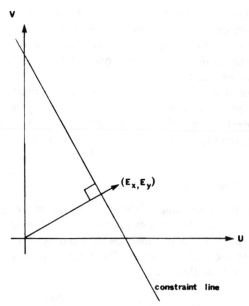

FIG. 1. The basic rate of change of image brightness equation constrains the optical flow velocity. The velocity (u, v) has to lie along a line perpendicular to the brightness gradient vector (E_x, E_y). The distance of this line from the origin equals E_t divided by the magnitude of (E_x, E_y).

We cannot, however, determine the component of the movement in the direction of the iso-brightness contours, at right angles to the brightness gradient. As a consequence, the flow velocity (u, v) cannot be computed locally without introducing additional constraints.

5. The Smoothness Constraint

If every point of the brightness pattern can move independently, there is little hope of recovering the velocities. More commonly we view opaque objects of finite size undergoing rigid motion or deformation. In this case neighboring points on the objects have similar velocities and the velocity field of the brightness patterns in the image varies smoothly almost everywhere. Discontinuities in flow can be expected where one object occludes another. An algorithm based on a smoothness constraint is likely to have difficulties with occluding edges as a result.

One way to express the additional constraint is to minimize the square of the magnitude of the gradient of the optical flow velocity:

$$\left(\frac{\partial u}{\partial x}\right)^2 + \left(\frac{\partial u}{\partial y}\right)^2 \quad \text{and} \quad \left(\frac{\partial v}{\partial x}\right)^2 + \left(\frac{\partial v}{\partial y}\right)^2.$$

Another measure of the smoothness of the optical flow field is the sum of the squares of the Laplacians of the x- and y-components of the flow. The

Laplacians of u and v are defined as

$$\nabla^2 u = \frac{\partial^2 u}{\partial x^2} + \frac{\partial^2 u}{\partial y^2} \quad \text{and} \quad \nabla^2 v = \frac{\partial^2 v}{\partial x^2} + \frac{\partial^2 v}{\partial y^2}.$$

In simple situations, both Laplacians are zero. If the viewer translates parallel to a flat object, rotates about a line perpendicular to the surface or travels orthogonally to the surface, then the second partial derivatives of both u and v vanish (assuming perspective projection in the image formation).

We will use here the square of the magnitude of the gradient as smoothness measure. Note that our approach is in contrast with that of Fennema and Thompson [5], who propose an algorithm that incorporates additional assumptions such as constant flow velocities within discrete regions of the image. Their method, based on cluster analysis, cannot deal with rotating objects, since these give rise to a continuum of flow velocities.

6. Quantization and Noise

Images may be sampled at intervals on a fixed grid of points. While tesselations other than the obvious one have certain advantages [9, 23], for convenience we will assume that the image is sampled on a square grid at regular intervals. Let the measured brightness be $E_{i,j,k}$ at the intersection of the ith row and jth column in the kth image frame. Ideally, each measurement should be an average over the area of a picture cell and over the length of the time interval. In the experiments cited here we have taken samples at discrete points in space and time instead.

In addition to being quantized in space and time, the measurements will in practice be quantized in brightness as well. Further, noise will be apparent in measurements obtained in any real system.

7. Estimating the Partial Derivatives

We must estimate the derivatives of brightness from the discrete set of image brightness measurements available. It is important that the estimates of E_x, E_y, and E_t be consistent. That is, they should all refer to the same point in the image at the same time. While there are many formulas for approximate differentiation [4, 11] we will use a set which gives us an estimate of E_x, E_y, E_t at a point in the center of a cube formed by eight measurements. The relationship in space and time between these measurements is shown in Fig. 2. Each of the estimates is the average of four first differences taken over adjacent measurements in the cube.

$$E_x \approx \tfrac{1}{4}\{E_{i,j+1,k} - E_{i,j,k} + E_{i+1,j+1,k} - E_{i+1,j,k}$$
$$+ E_{i,j+1,k+1} - E_{i,j,k+1} + E_{i+1,j+1,k+1} - E_{i+1,j,k+1}\},$$
$$E_y \approx \tfrac{1}{4}\{E_{i+1,j,k} - E_{i,j,k} + E_{i+1,j+1,k} - E_{i,j+1,k}$$
$$+ E_{i+1,j,k+1} - E_{i,j,k+1} | + E_{i+1,j+1,k+1} - E_{i,j+1,k+1}\},$$
$$E_t \approx \tfrac{1}{4}\{E_{i,j,k+1} - E_{i,j,k} + E_{i+1,j,k+1} - E_{i+1,j,k}$$
$$+ E_{i,j+1,k+1} - E_{i,j+1,k} + E_{i+1,j+1,k+1} - E_{i+1,j+1,k}\}.$$

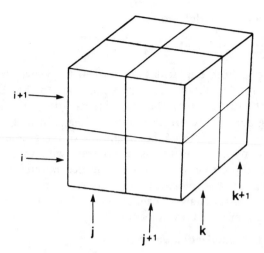

FIG. 2. The three partial derivatives of images brightness at the center of the cube are each estimated from the average of first differences along four parallel edges of the cube. Here the column index j corresponds to the x direction in the image, the row index i to the y direction, while k lies in the time direction.

Here the unit of length is the grid spacing interval in each image frame and the unit of time is the image frame sampling period. We avoid estimation formulae with larger support, since these typically are equivalent to formulae of small support applied to smoothed images [14].

8. Estimating the Laplacian of the Flow Velocities

We also need to approximate the Laplacians of u and v. One convenient approximation takes the following form

$$\nabla^2 u \approx \kappa(\bar{u}_{i,j,k} - u_{i,j,k}) \quad \text{and} \quad \nabla^2 v \approx \kappa(\bar{v}_{i,j,k} - v_{i,j,k}),$$

where the local averages $\bar{u}$ and $\bar{v}$ are defined as follows

$$\bar{u}_{i,j,k} = \tfrac{1}{6}\{u_{i-1,j,k} + u_{i,j+1,k} + u_{i+1,j,k} + u_{i,j-1,k}\}$$
$$+ \tfrac{1}{12}\{u_{i-1,j-1,k} + u_{i-1,j+1,k} + u_{i+1,j+1,k} + u_{i+1,j-1,k}\},$$

$$\bar{v}_{i,j,k} = \tfrac{1}{6}\{v_{i-1,j,k} + v_{i,j+1,k} + v_{i+1,j,k} + v_{i,j-1,k}\}$$
$$+ \tfrac{1}{12}\{v_{i-1,j-1,k} + v_{i-1,j+1,k} + v_{i+1,j+1,k} + v_{i+1,j-1,k}\}.$$

The proportionality factor κ equals 3 if the average is computed as shown and we again assume that the unit of length equals the grid spacing interval. Fig. 3 illustrates the assignment of weights to neighboring points.

FIG. 3. The Laplacian is estimated by subtracting the value at a point from a weighted average of the values at neighboring points. Shown here are suitable weights by which values can be multiplied.

9. Minimization

The problem then is to minimize the sum of the errors in the equation for the rate of change of image brightness,

$$\mathcal{E}_b = E_x u + E_y v + E_t,$$

and the measure of the departure from smoothness in the velocity flow,

$$\mathcal{E}_c^2 = \left(\frac{\partial u}{\partial x}\right)^2 + \left(\frac{\partial u}{\partial y}\right)^2 + \left(\frac{\partial v}{\partial x}\right)^2 + \left(\frac{\partial v}{\partial y}\right)^2.$$

What should be the relative weight of these two factors? In practice the image brightness measurements will be corrupted by quantization error and noise so that we cannot expect $\mathcal{E}_b$ to be identically zero. This quantity will tend to have an error magnitude that is proportional to the noise in the measurement. This fact guides us in choosing a suitable weighting factor, denoted by α^2, as will be seen later.

Let the total error to be minimized be

$$\mathcal{E}^2 = \int \int (\alpha^2 \mathcal{E}_c^2 + \mathcal{E}_b^2) \, dx \, dy.$$

The minimization is to be accomplished by finding suitable values for the optical flow velocity (u, v). Using the calculus of variation we obtain

$$E_x^2 u + E_x E_y v = \alpha^2 \nabla^2 u - E_x E_t,$$

$$E_x E_y u + E_y^2 v = \alpha^2 \nabla^2 v - E_y E_t.$$

Using the approximation to the Laplacian introduced in the previous section,

$$(\alpha^2 + E_x^2)u + E_x E_y v = (\alpha^2 \bar{u} - E_x E_t),$$

$$E_x E_y u + (\alpha^2 + E_y^2)v = (\alpha^2 \bar{v} - E_y E_t).$$

The determinant of the coefficient matrix equals $\alpha^2(\alpha^2 + E_x^2 + E_y^2)$. Solving for u and v we find that

$$(\alpha^2 + E_x^2 + E_y^2)u = +(\alpha^2 + E_y^2)\bar{u} - E_x E_y \bar{v} - E_x E_t,$$
$$(\alpha^2 + E_x^2 + E_y^2)v = -E_x E_y \bar{u} + (\alpha^2 + E_x^2)\bar{v} - E_y E_t.$$

10. Difference of Flow at a Point from Local Average

These equations can be written in the alternate form

$$(\alpha^2 + E_x^2 + E_y^2)(u - \bar{u}) = -E_x[E_x\bar{u} + E_y\bar{v} + E_t],$$
$$(\alpha^2 + E_x^2 + E_y^2)(v - \bar{v}) = -E_y[E_x\bar{u} + E_y\bar{v} + E_t].$$

This shows that the value of the flow velocity (u, v) which minimizes the error $\mathscr{E}^2$ lies in the direction towards the constraint line along a line that intersects the constraint line at right angles. This relationship is illustrated geometrically in Fig. 4. The distance from the local average is proportional to the error in the basic formula for rate of change of brightness when $\bar{u}$, $\bar{v}$ are substituted for u and v. Finally we can see that α^2 plays a significant role only for areas where the brightness gradient is small, preventing haphazard adjustments to the estimated flow velocity occasioned by noise in the estimated derivatives. This parameter should be roughly equal to the expected noise in the estimate of $E_x^2 + E_y^2$.

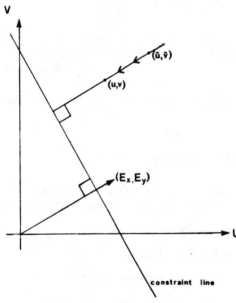

FIG. 4. The value of the flow velocity which minimizes the error lies on a line drawn from the local average of the flow velocity perpendicular to the constraint line.

11. Constrained Minimization

When we allow α^2 to tend to zero we obtain the solution to a constrained minimization problem. Applying the method of Lagrange multipliers [33, 34] to the problem of minimizing $\mathscr{E}_c^2$ while maintaining $\mathscr{E}_b = 0$ leads to

$$E_y \nabla^2 u = E_x \nabla^2 v, \qquad E_x u + E_y v + E_t = 0$$

Approximating the Laplacian by the difference of the velocity at a point and the average of its neighbors then gives us

$$(E_x^2 + E_y^2)(u - \bar{u}) = -E_x[E_x \bar{u} + E_y \bar{v} + E_t],$$
$$(E_x^2 + E_y^2)(v - \bar{v}) = -E_y[E_x \bar{u} + E_y \bar{v} + E_t].$$

Referring again to Fig. 4, we note that the point computed here lies at the intersection of the constraint line and the line at right angles through the point $(\bar{u}, \bar{v})$. We will not use these equations since we do expect errors in the estimation of the partial derivatives.

12. Iterative Solution

We now have a pair of equations for each point in the image. It would be very costly to solve these equations simultaneously by one of the standard methods, such as Gauss–Jordan elimination [11, 13]. The corresponding matrix is sparse and very large since the number of rows and columns equals twice the number of picture cells in the image. Iterative methods, such as the Gauss–Seidel method [11, 13], suggest themselves. We can compute a new set of velocity estimates (u^{n+1}, v^{n+1}) from the estimated derivatives and the average of the previous velocity estimates (u^n, v^n) by

$$u^{n+1} = \bar{u}^n - E_x[E_x \bar{u}^n + E_y \bar{v}^n + E_t]/(\alpha^2 + E_x^2 + E_y^2),$$
$$v^{n+1} = \bar{v}^n - E_y[E_x \bar{u}^n + E_y \bar{v}^n + E_t]/(\alpha^2 + E_x^2 + E_y^2).$$

(It is interesting to note that the new estimates at a particular point do not depend directly on the previous estimates at the same point.)

The natural boundary conditions for the variational problem turns out to be a zero normal derivative. At the edge of the image, some of the points needed to compute the local average of velocity lie outside the image. Here we simply copy velocities from adjacent points further in.

13. Filling In Uniform Regions

In parts of the image where the brightness gradient is zero, the velocity estimates will simply be averages of the neighboring velocity estimates. There is no local information to constrain the apparent velocity of motion of the brightness pattern in these areas. Eventually the values around such a region will propagate inwards. If the velocities on the border of the region are all equal to the same value, then points in the region will be assigned that value too, after a sufficient number of iterations. Velocity information is thus filled in from the boundary of a region of constant brightness.

If the values on the border are not all the same, it is a little more difficult to predict what will happen. In all cases, the values filled in will correspond to the solution of the Laplace equation for the given boundary condition [1, 24, 32].

The progress of this filling-in phenomena is similar to the propagation effects in the solution of the heat equation for a uniform flat plate, where the time rate of change of temperature is proportional to the Laplacian. This gives us a means of understanding the iterative method in physical terms and of estimating the number of steps required. The number of iterations should be larger than the number of picture cells across the largest region that must be filled in. If the size of such regions is not known in advance one may use the cross-section of the whole image as a conservative estimate.

14. Tightness of Constraint

When brightness in a region is a linear function of the image coordinates we can only obtain the component of optical flow in the direction of the gradient. The component at right angles is filled in from the boundary of the region as described before. In general the solution is most accurately determined in regions where the brightness gradient is not too small and varies in direction from point to point. Information which constrains both components of the optical flow velocity is then available in a relatively small neighborhood. Too violent fluctuations in brightness on the other hand are not desirable since the estimates of the derivatives will be corrupted as the result of undersampling and aliasing.

15. Choice of Iterative Scheme

As a practical matter one has a choice of how to interlace the iterations with the time steps. On the one hand, one could iterate until the solution has stabilized before advancing to the next image frame. On the other hand, given a good initial guess one may need only one iteration per time-step. A good initial guess for the optical flow velocities is usually available from the previous time-step.

The advantages of the latter approach include an ability to deal with more images per unit time and better estimates of optical flow velocities in certain regions. Areas in which the brightness gradient is small lead to uncertain, noisy estimates obtained partly by filling in from the surround. These estimates are improved by considering further images. The noise in measurements of the images will be independent and tend to cancel out. Perhaps more importantly, different parts of the pattern will drift by a given point in the image. The direction of the brightness gradient will vary with time, providing information about both components of the optical flow velocity.

A practical implementation would most likely employ one iteration per time step for these reasons. We illustrate both approaches in the experiments.

16. Experiments

The iterative scheme has been implemented and applied to image sequences corresponding to a number of simple flow patterns. The results shown here are for a relatively low resolution image of 32 by 32 picture cells. The brightness measurements were intentionally corrupted by approximately 1% noise and

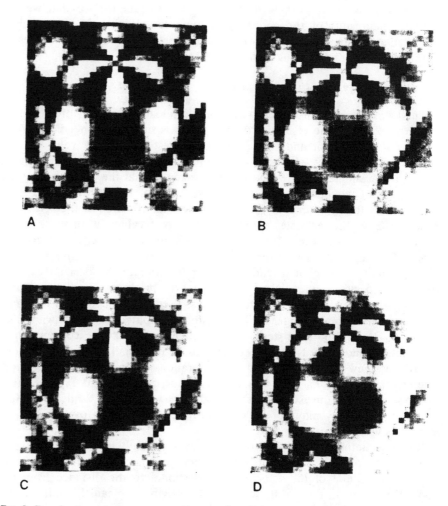

A   B

C   D

FIG. 5. Four frames out of a sequence of images of a sphere rotating about an axis inclined towards the viewer. The sphere is covered with a pattern which varies smoothly from place to place. The sphere is portrayed against a fixed, lightly textured background. Image sequences like these are processed by the optical flow algorithm.

then quantized into 256 levels to simulate a real imaging situation. The underlying surface reflectance pattern was a linear combination of spatially orthogonal sinusoids. Their wavelength was chosen to give reasonably strong brightness gradients without leading to undersampling problems. Discontinuities were avoided to ensure that the required derivatives exist everywhere.

Shown in Fig. 5, for example, are four frames of a sequence of images depicting a sphere rotating about an axis inclined towards the viewer. A smoothly varying reflectance pattern is painted on the surface of the sphere. The sphere is illuminated uniformly from all directions so that there is no shading. We chose to work with synthetic image sequences so that we can compare the results of the optical flow computation with the exact values calculated using the transformation equations relating image coordinates to coordinates on the underlying surface reflectance pattern.

17. Results

The first flow to be investigated was a simple linear translation of the entire brightness pattern. The resulting computed flow is shown as a needle diagram in Fig. 6 for 1, 4, 16, and 64 iterations. The estimated flow velocities are depicted as short lines, showing the apparent displacement during one time step. In this example a single time step was taken so that the computations are based on just two images. Initially the estimates of flow velocity are zero. Consequently the first iteration shows vectors in the direction of the brightness gradient. Later, the estimates approach the correct values in all parts of the image. Few changes occur after 32 iterations when the velocity vectors have errors of about 10%. The estimates tend to be two small, rather than too large, perhaps because of a tendency to underestimate the derivatives. The worst errors occur, as one might expect, where the brightness gradient is small.

In the second experiment one iteration was used per time step on the same linear translation image sequence. The resulting computed flow is shown in Fig. 7 for 1, 4, 16, and 64 time steps. The estimates approach the correct values more rapidly and do not have a tendency to be too small, as in the previous experiment. Few changes occur after 16 iterations when the velocity vectors have errors of about 7%. The worst errors occur, as one might expect, where the noise in recent measurements of brightness was worst. While individual estimates of velocity may not be very accurate, the average over the whole image was within 1% of the correct value.

Next, the method was applied to simple rotation and simple contraction of the brightness pattern. The results after 32 time steps are shown in Fig. 8. Note that the magnitude of the velocity is proportional to the distance from the origin of the flow in both of these cases. (By origin we mean the point in the image where the velocity is zero.)

In the examples so far the Laplacian of both flow velocity components is zero everywhere. We also studied more difficult cases where this was not the case.

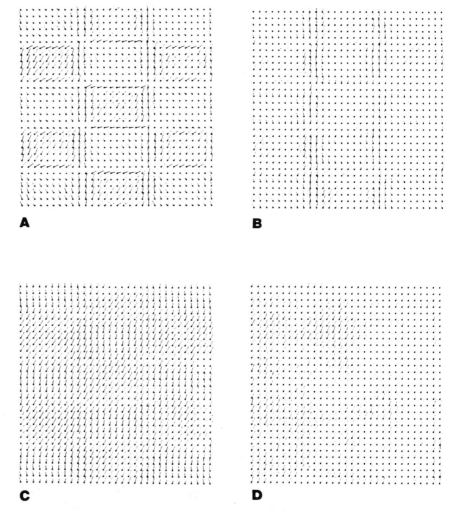

FIG. 6. Flow pattern computed for simple translation of a brightness pattern. The estimates after 1, 4, 16, and 64 iterations are shown. The velocity is 0.5 picture cells in the x direction and 1.0 picture cells in the y direction per time interval. Two images are used as input, depicting the situation at two times separated by one time interval.

In particular, if we let the magnitude of the velocity vary as the inverse of the distance from the origin we generate flow around a line vertex and two dimensional flow into a sink. The computed flow patterns are shown in Fig. 9. In these examples, the computation involved many iterations based on a single time step. The worst errors occur near the singularity at the origin of the flow pattern, where velocities are found which are much larger than one picture cell per time step.

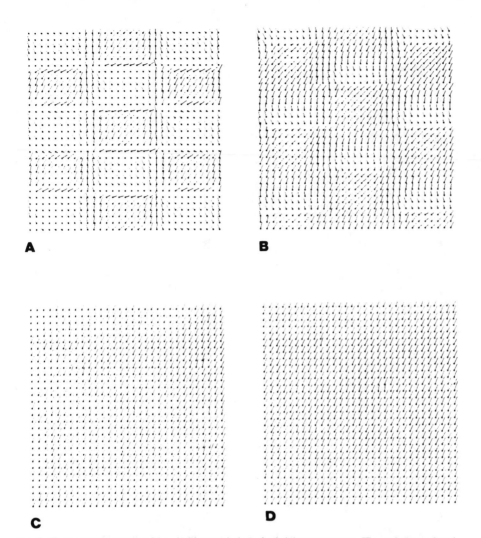

FIG. 7. Flow pattern computed for simple translation of a brightness pattern. The estimates after 1, 4, 16, and 64 time steps are shown. Here one iteration is used per time step. Convergence is more rapid and the velocities are estimated more accurately.

Finally we considered rigid body motions. Shown in Fig. 10 are the flows computed for a cylinder rotating about its axis and for a rotating sphere. In both cases the Laplacian of the flow is not zero and in fact the Laplacian for one of the velocity components becomes infinite on the occluding bound. Since the velocities themselves remain finite, resonable solutions are still obtained. The correct flow patterns are shown in Fig. 11. Comparing the computed and exact values shows that the worst errors occur on the occluding boundary. These

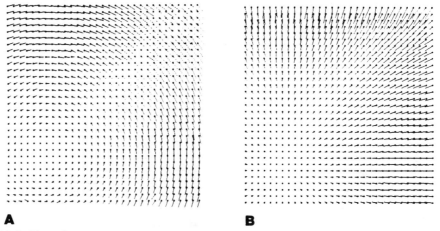

A   **B**

FIG. 8. Flow patterns computed for simple rotation and simple contraction of a brightness pattern. In the first case, the pattern is rotated about 2.8 degrees per time step, while it is contracted about 5% per time step in the second case. The estimates after 32 times steps are shown.

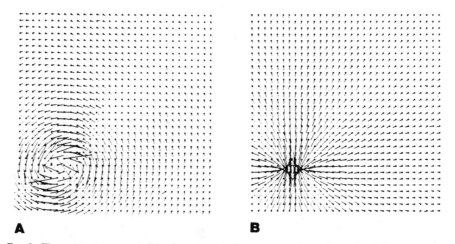

A   **B**

FIG. 9. Flow patterns computed for flow around a line vortex and two dimensional flow into a sink. In each case the estimates after 32 iterations are shown.

boundaries constitute a one dimensional subset of the plane and so one can expect that the relative number of points at which the estimated flow is seriously in error will decrease as the resolution of the image is made finer.

In Appendix B it is shown that there is a direct relationship between the Laplacian of the flow velocity components and the Laplacian of the surface height. This can be used to see how our smoothemess constraint will fare for different objects. For example, a rotating polyhedron will give rise to flow

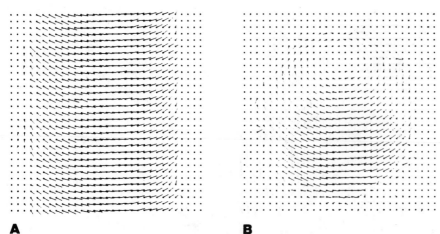

A   **B**

FIG. 10. Flow patterns computed for a cylinder rotating about its axis and for a rotating sphere. The axis of the cylinder is inclined 30 degrees towards the viewer and that of the sphere 45 degrees. Both are rotating at about 5 degrees per time step. The estimates shown are obtained after 32 time steps.

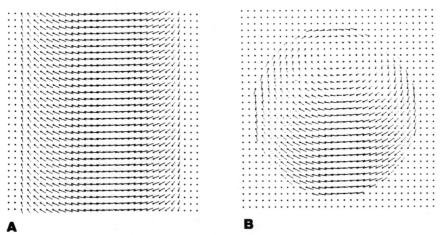

A   **B**

FIG. 11. Exact flow patterns for the cylinder and the sphere.

which has zero Laplacian except on the image lines which are the projections of the edges of the body.

18. Summary

A method has been developed for computing optical flow from a sequence of images. It is based on the observation that the flow velocity has two components and that the basic equation for the rate of change of image brightness provides only one constraint. Smoothness of the flow was introduced as a second constraint. An iterative method for solving the resulting equation was then developed. A simple implementation provided visual confirmation of convergence of the solution in the form of needle diagrams. Examples of several different types of optical flow patterns were studied. These included cases where the Laplacian of the flow was zero as well as cases where it became infinite at singular points or along bounding curves.

The computed optical flow is somewhat inaccurate since it is based on noisy, quantized measurements. Proposed methods for obtaining information about the shapes of objects using derivatives (divergence and curl) of the optical flow field may turn out to be impractical since the inaccuracies will be amplified.

ACKNOWLEDGMENT

This research was conducted at the Artificial Intelligence Laboratory of the Massachusetts Institute of Technology. Support for the laboratory's research is provided in part by the Advanced Research Projects Agency of the Department of Defense under Office of Naval Research contract number N00014-75-C0643. One of the authors (Horn) would like to thank Professor H.-H. Nagel for his hospitality. The basic equations were conceived during a visit to the University of Hamburg, stimulated by Professor Nagel's long-standing interest in motion vision. The other author (Schunck) would like to thank W.E.L. Grimson and E. Hildreth for many interesting discussions and much knowledgable criticism. W.E.L. Grimson and Katsushi Ikeuchi helped to illuminate a conceptual bug in an earlier version of this paper. We should also like to thank J. Jones for preparing the drawings.

Appendix A. Rate of Change of Image Brightness

Consider a patch of the brightness pattern that is displaced a distance δx in the x-direction and δy in the y-direction in time δt. The brightness of the patch is assumed to remain constant so that

$$E(x, y, t) = E(x + \delta x, y + \delta y, t + \delta t).$$

Expanding the right-hand side about the point (x, y, t) we get,

$$E(x, y, t) = E(x, y, t) + \delta x \, \frac{\partial E}{\partial x} + \delta y \, \frac{\partial E}{\partial y} + \delta t \, \frac{\partial E}{\partial t} + \epsilon.$$

Where ϵ contains second and higher order terms in δx, δy, and δt. After subtracting $E(x, y, t)$ from both sides and dividing through by δt we have

$$\frac{\delta x}{\delta t} \, \frac{\partial E}{\partial x} + \frac{\delta y}{\delta t} \, \frac{\partial E}{\partial y} + \frac{\partial E}{\partial t} + \mathcal{O}(\delta t) = 0,$$

where $\mathcal{O}(\delta t)$ is a term of order δt (we assume that δx and δy vary as δt). In the limit as $\delta t \rightarrow 0$ this becomes

$$\frac{\partial E}{\partial x}\frac{dx}{dt} + \frac{\partial E}{\partial y}\frac{dy}{dt} + \frac{\partial E}{\partial t} = 0.$$

Appendix B. Smoothness of Flow for Rigid Body Motions

Let a rigid body rotate about an axis $(\omega_x, \omega_y, \omega_z)$, where the magnitude of the vector equals the angular velocity of the motion. If this axis passes through the origin, then the velocity of a point (x, y, z) equals the cross product of $(\omega_x, \omega_y, \omega_z)$, and (x, y, z). There is a direct relationship between the image coordinates and the x and y coordinates here if we assume that the image is generated by orthographic projection. The x and y components of the velocity can be written,

$$u = \omega_y z - \omega_z y, \qquad v = \omega_z x - \omega_x z.$$

Consequently,

$$\nabla^2 u = +\omega_y \nabla^2 z, \qquad \nabla^2 v = -\omega_x \nabla^2 z.$$

This illustrates that the smoothness of the optical flow is related directly to the smoothness of the rotating body and that the Laplacian of the flow velocity will become infinite on the occluding bound, since the partial derivatives of z with respect to x and y become infinite there.

REFERENCES

1. Ames, W.F., *Numerical Methods for Partial Differential Equations* (Academic Press, New York, 1977).
2. Batali, J. and Ullman, S., Motion detection and analysis, *Proc. of the ARPA Image Understanding Workshop*, 7–8 November 1979 (Science Applications Inc., Arlington, VA 1979) pp. 69–75.
3. Clocksin, W., Determining the orientation of surfaces from optical flow, *Proc. of the Third AISB Conference*, Hamburg (1978) pp. 93–102.
4. Conte, S.D. and de Boor, C., *Elementary Numerical Analysis* (McGraw-Hill, New York, 1965, 1972).
5. Fennema, C.L. and Thompson, W.B., Velocity determination in scenes containing several moving objects, *Computer Graphics and Image Processing* **9** (4) (1979) 301–315.
6. Gibson, J.J., *The Perception of the Visual World* (Riverside Press, Cambridge, 1950).
7. Gibson, J.J., *The Senses Considered as Perceptual Systems* (Houghton-Mifflin, Boston, MA, 1966).
8. Gibson, J.J., On the analysis of change in the optic array, *Scandinavian J. Psychol.* **18** (1977) 161–163. .
9. Gray, S.B., Local properties of binary images in two dimensions, *IEEE Trans. on Computers* **20** (5) (1971) 551–561.
10. Hadani, I., Ishai, G. and Gur, M., Visual stability and space perception in monocular vision: Mathematical model, *J. Optical Soc. Am.* **70** (1) (1980) 60–65.
11. Hamming, R.W., *Numerical Methods for Scientists and Engineers* (McGraw-Hill, New York, 1962).
12. Hildebrand, F.B., *Methods of Applied Mathematics* (Prentice-Hall, Englewood Cliffs, NJ, 1952, 1965).

13. Hildebrand, F.B., *Introduction to Numerical Analysis* (McGraw-Hill, New York, 1956, 1974).

14. Horn, B.K.P., (1979) Hill shading and the reflectance map, *Proc. IEEE* **69** (1) (1981) 14–47.

15. Jain, R., Martin, W.N. and Aggarwal, J.K., Segmentation through the detection of changes due to motion, *Computer Graphics and Image Processing* **11** (1) (1979) 13–34.

16. Jain, R. Militzer, D. and Nagel, H.-H., Separating non-stationary from stationary scene components in a sequence of real world TV-images, *Proc. of the 5th Int. Joint Conf. on Artificial Intelligence*, August 1977, Cambridge, MA, 612–618.

17. Jain, R. and Nagel, H.-H., On the analysis of accumulative difference pictures from image sequences of real world scenes, *IEEE Trans. on Pattern Analysis and Machine Intelligence* **1** (2) (1979) 206–214.

18. Koenderink, J.J. and van Doorn, A.J., Invariant properties of the motion parallax field due to the movement of rigid bodies relative to an observer, *Optica Acta* **22** (9) 773–791.

19. Koenderink, J.J. and van Doorn, A.J., Visual perception of rigidity of solid shape, *J. Math. Biol.* **3** (79) (1976) 79–85.

20. Limb, J.O. and Murphy, J.A., Estimating the velocity of moving images in television signals, *Computer Graphics and Image Processing* **4** (4) (1975) 311–327.

21. Longuet-Higgins, H.C. and Prazdny, K., The interpretation of moving retinal image, *Proc. of the Royal Soc. B* **208** (1980) 385–387.

22. Marr, D. and Ullman, S., Directional selectivity and its use in early visual processing, Artificial Intelligence Laboratory Memo No. 524, Massachusetts Institute of Technology (June 1979), to appear in *Proc. Roy. Soc. B*.

23. Mersereau, R.M., The processing of hexagonally sampled two-dimensional signals, *Proc. of the IEEE* **67** (6) (1979) 930–949.

24. Milne, W.E., *Numerical Solution of Differential Equations* (Dover, New York, 1953, 1979).

25. Nagel, H.-H., Analyzing sequences of TV-frames, *Proc. of the 5th Int. Joint Conf. on Artificial Intelligence*, August 1977, Cambridge, MA, 626.

26. Nagel, H.-H., Analysis techniques for image sequences, *Proc. of the 4th Int. Joint Conf. on Pattern Recognition*, 4–10 November 1978, Kyoto, Japan.

27. Nakayama, K. and Loomis, J.M., Optical velocity patterns, velocity-sensitive neurons and space perception, *Perception* **3** (1974) 63–80.

28. Netravali, A.N. and Robbins, J.D., Motion-compensated television coding: Part I, *The Bell System Tech. J.* **58** (3) (1979) 631–670.

29. Prazdny, K., Computing egomotion and surface slant from optical flow. Ph.D. Thesis, Computer Science Department, University of Essex, Colchester (1979).

30. Prazdny, K., Egomotion and relative depth map from optical flow, *Biol. Cybernet.* **36** (1980) 87–102.

31. Prazdny, K., The information in optical flows. Computer Science Department, University of Essex, Colchester (1980) mimeographed.

32. Richtmyer, R.D. and Mortin, K.W., *Difference Methods for Initial-Value Problems* (Interscience, John Wiley & Sons, New York, 1957, 1967).

33. Russell, D.L., *Calculus of Variations and Control Theory* (Academic Press, New York, 1976).

34. Yourgau, W. and Mandelstam, S., *Variational Principles in Dynamics and Quantum Theory* (Dover, New York, 1968, 1979).

Motion Field and Optical Flow: Qualitative Properties

ALESSANDRO VERRI AND TOMASO POGGIO, MEMBER, IEEE

Abstract—This paper shows that the *motion field*, the 2-D vector field which is the perspective projection on the image plane of the 3-D velocity field of a moving scene, and the *optical flow*, defined as the estimate of the motion field which can be derived from first order variation of the image brightness pattern, are in general different, unless special conditions are satisfied. Therefore, dense optical flow is often ill-suited for computing *structure from motion* and for reconstructing the 3-D velocity field by means of algorithms which require a locally accurate estimate of the motion field. A different use of the optical flow is suggested. It is shown that the (smoothed) optical flow and the motion field can be interpreted as vector fields tangent to flows of planar dynamical systems. Stable qualitative properties of the motion field, which give useful information about the 3-D velocity field and the 3-D structure of the scene, can be usually obtained from the optical flow. The idea is supported by results from the theory of structural stability of dynamical systems.

Index Terms—Motion computation, optical flow.

I. INTRODUCTION

A KEY task for many vision systems is to extract information from a sequence of images. This information can be useful for solving important problems such as recovering the 3-D velocity field, segmenting the image into parts corresponding to different moving objects, or reconstructing the 3-D structure of surfaces in the viewed scene. The recovery of the *motion field*, which is the perspective projection onto the image plane of the true 3-D velocity field of moving surfaces in space, is thought to be an essential step in the solution of these problems. The data available, however, are only the spatial and temporal variations in the image brightness pattern E. From these variations it is possible to derive an estimate of the motion field, called *optical flow* [1]-[3]. The assumption that the motion field and the optical flow coincide has often been made, the intuitive rationale being that this is

Manuscript received June 1, 1987; revised July 20, 1988. Recommended for acceptance by W. B. Thompson. This paper describes research done within the Center for Biological Information Processing, in the Department of Brain and Cognitive Sciences, and at the Artificial Intelligence Laboratory. This work was supported by a grant from the Office of Naval Research (ONR), Cognitive and Neural Sciences Division; by the Artificial Intelligence Center of Hughes Aircraft Corporation; by the Alfred P. Sloan Foundation; by the National Science Foundation; by the Artificial Intelligence Center of Hughes Aircraft Corporation (S1-801534-2); and by the NATO Scientific Affairs Division (0403/87). Support for the A. I. Laboratory's artificial intelligence research is provided by the Advanced Research Projects Agency of the Department of Defense under Army contract DACA76-85-C-0010, and in part by ONR contract N00014-85-K-0124. T. Poggio was supported by the Uncas and Helen Whitaker Chair at the Massachusetts Institute of Technology, Whitaker College. A. Verri is supported by a Fairchild Fellowship.

A. Verri was with the Artificial Intelligence Laboratory, Massachusetts Institute of Technology, Cambridge, MA 02139. He is now with the Department of Physics, University of Genova, Genova, Italy.

T. Poggio is with the Artificial Intelligence Laboratory, Massachusetts Institute of Technology, Cambridge, MA 02139.

IEEE Log Number 8926695.

true when spatial variations in E correspond to physical features on the visible 3-D surfaces [4]-[6]. Horn [7], however, has pointed out examples in which this assumption does not hold. Algorithms which deal with the recovery of the motion field from dense optical flow data have been proposed, with the more or less implicit assumption that the two fields are the same [8]-[10].

In this paper we show that the optical flow and the motion field are in general different, unless special conditions are satisfied. In particular, even the hypothesis of a Lambertian reflectance function of the viewed surfaces is not sufficient by itself to guarantee that the two vector fields are the same. A rigorous derivation of this result is provided. Indeed, where sharp changes in intensity over time are due to physical events on the moving surface (e.g., texture and surface markings), the estimates of the component of the motion field along the direction of the spatial gradient of the image brightness pattern—estimates which can be obtained by means of first order derivative of the image brightness pattern—are accurate. These estimates, therefore, are unlikely to be useful for methods which rely upon a very precise, local reconstruction of the motion field. One may then ask, what is the optical flow for? In the final part of the paper it is suggested that meaningful information about the 3-D velocity field and the 3-D structure of the viewed scene can be obtained from qualitative properties of the motion field. At any fixed time, the motion field can be seen as the flow associated with some dynamical system and useful motion motion information can be retrieved from its qualitative properties, e.g., from its singular points. A thorough analysis of this approach—proposed first by [11]—is presented in [12]. Then, results from the theory of structural stability of dynamical systems suggest that, if the motion field and the optical flow are sufficiently similar, they also have the same qualitative properties. Therefore, the qualitative properties of the optical flow might be very useful in recovering motion information (see [13], for example).

The paper is organized as follows. Section II defines the problem and considers in detail how image irradiance can be related to scene radiance in the case of a scene consisting on non-Lambertian surfaces. Section III describes the method used to show that the optical flow and the motion field are almost always different. We consider the Lambertian model of reflectance and a more realistic model for arbitrary rigid motion of a generic smooth surface. Section IV shows that at any given time the motion field and the optical flow can be processed to become smooth vector fields tangent to flows of dynamical systems. Results from the theory of structural stability of dynamical systems, then, are used to suggest that qualitative, stable properties of the motion field hold for smooth optical flows, provided the two fields are sufficiently similar. Finally, in Section V, possible biological connections are discussed. Details on the geometry of perspective projection and a brief review of the theory of planar dynamical systems are summarized in the Appendixes.

II. Preliminaries

In this section notations, definitions, and assumptions which have been used throughout the paper are stated. The motion field and the optical flow are defined and image irradiance is related to scene radiance in the case of a scene consisting of non-Lambertian surfaces.

A. Definitions

Let us define notations and summarize concepts which will be useful in what follows. For more details on the geometry of perspective projection see Appendix A. Let

$$\vec{x}_p = \frac{f}{f + \vec{x} \cdot \vec{n}} \left[\vec{x} - (\vec{x} \cdot \vec{n}) \vec{n} \right] \quad (2.1.1)$$

be the equation which defines the perspective projection of a generic point on the image plane, where $\vec{x}_p = (x_p, y_p, 0)$ is the position vector of the projected point, $\vec{x}$ is the position vector of the point, $\vec{n} = (0, 0, 1)$ is the unit vector normal to the image plane (projection plane), and f is the focal length in a suitable systems of coordinates (see Fig. 1). Notice that the origin O is on the image plane, the focus of projection F is located at $(0, 0, -f)$, and $f\vec{n} + \vec{x}$ is the vector pointing from F to the point. The equation for $\vec{x}_p$, in the case of orthographic projection, can be derived simply by taking the limit of the right-hand side of (2.1.1) for $f \to \infty$, which yields

$$\vec{x}_p = \vec{x} - (\vec{x} \cdot \vec{n}) \vec{n}.$$

The motion field $\vec{v}_p$ can be obtained differentiating (2.1.1) with respect to time. If $\vec{v} = d\vec{x}/dt$, then[1]

$$\vec{v}_p = \frac{f}{f + \vec{x} \cdot \vec{n}} \left\{ \vec{v} - (\vec{v} \cdot \vec{n}) \vec{n} \right.$$
$$\left. - \frac{\vec{v} \cdot \vec{n}}{f + \vec{x} \cdot \vec{n}} \left[\vec{x} - (\vec{x} \cdot \vec{n}) \vec{n} \right] \right\}. \quad (2.1.2)$$

Notice that in (2.1.2) $\vec{v}_p$ is given in terms of $\vec{x}$ and $\vec{v}$, position and velocity of the moving points in the scene respectively, which are not known. In what follows, $\vec{x}_p$ and $\vec{v}_p$ will be considered as 2-D vectors defined on the image plane, since their third component vanishes identically.

Let $E = E(x_p, y_p, t)$ be the image brightness pattern that is, the intensity of light at the point (x_p, y_p) of the image plane at time t. If $\vec{\nabla}_p$ is the gradient with respect to the image plane coordinates, then

$$\frac{dE}{dt} = \frac{\partial E}{\partial t} + \vec{\nabla}_p E \cdot \vec{v}_p \quad (2.1.3)$$

[1]It can be easily shown that the perspective projection of the 3-D velocity error $\vec{v}$ is equal to the velocity $\vec{v}_p$ of the projected point on the image plane, since both vectors are defined in terms of infinitesimal.

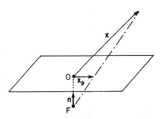

Fig. 1. The geometry of perspective projection.

where $\partial E/\partial t$ is the partial derivative with respect to the time at the point (x_p, y_p) and dE/dt, also called *total temporal derivative*, can be thought of as the temporal derivative along the trajectory of the point (x_p, y_p) onto the image plane. Equation (2.1.3) can be rewritten as

$$\frac{dE}{dt} = \frac{\partial E}{\partial t} + \| \vec{\nabla}_p E \| \, v_\perp$$

where $v_\perp$ is the norm of $\vec{v}_\perp$, component of the motion field $\vec{v}$ along the direction of $\vec{\nabla} E$. Now if

$$\frac{dE}{dt} = 0 \quad (2.1.4)$$

and $\| \vec{\nabla}_p E \| \neq 0$, then

$$\vec{v}_\perp = - \frac{\partial E/\partial t}{\| \vec{\nabla}_p E \|} \frac{\vec{\nabla}_p E}{\| \vec{\nabla}_p E \|}. \quad (2.1.5)$$

Therefore, if (2.1.4) holds, the component of the motion field along the direction of the gradient of the image brightness $\vec{v}_\perp$ can be written in terms of derivatives of E (which can be computed). Equation (2.1.5) can be interpreted as an instance of the well-known *aperture* problem [2], [3], [14], [15] for the unknown $\vec{v}_p$: that is, the information available at each point of a sequence of frames is only the component of the motion field along the direction of $\vec{\nabla}_p E$. In order to compute the full 2-D optical flow, some other constraints are needed: Horn and Schunck [3] for example, look for the smoothest 2-D vector field whose component along $\vec{\nabla}_p E$ coincides with the right-hand side of (2.1.5). Examples for which (2.1.5) is not true are well-known [3]. Consider, for instance, a rotating sphere with no texture on it (i.e., with uniform albedo) under arbitrary, fixed illumination. Since the image brightness at each image location does not change with time, the left-hand side of (2.1.5) is identically equal to zero, while the right-hand side is different from zero almost everywhere. Notice that keeping the sphere fixed and moving the light source, (2.1.5) is again wrong. In this case, however, the right-hand side is different from zero while $\vec{v}_\perp$ is zero everywhere. Since (2.1.4) is often assumed as a starting point for computing the optical flow, it is interesting to calculate explicitly the total temporal derivative of E with respect to time. The calculations require both an accurate definition of image formation properties and an analytical model of the reflectance function.

B. Scene Radiance and Image Irradiance

Let us review some definitions of photometry and make explicit the constraints under which the image irradiance is related to the scene radiance. The image irradiance can be thought of as the image brightness pattern $E = E(x_p, y_p)$, since it is the power of light per unit area at each point (x_p, y_p) of the image plane. The scene radiance L is the power of light per unit area which can be thought of as emitted by each point of a surface S in the scene in a particular direction. This surface can be fictitious, or may be the actual radiating surface of a light surface of a light source, or the illuminated surface of a solid. The scene radiance can be thought of as a function of the point of the surface and of the direction in space. If (a, b) is a point on the surface S in intrinsic coordinates of the surface and (α, β) polar coordinates determining a direction in space with respect to the normal vector to the surface, then $L = L(a, b, \alpha, \beta)$ gives the scene radiance at the point (a, b) in the direction (α, β). Given the scene radiance, in principle, it is possible to compute the expected image irradiance. For example in the case of pinhole camera approximation, i.e., assuming that the camera has an infinitesimally small aperture, the image irradiance at a point (x_p, y_p) is proportional to the scene radiance at the point (a, b) on the surface in the direction of the pinhole, say (α_0, β_0), where the projected point, the original point, and the pinhole lie on the same line (see Fig. 2). Therefore,

$$E\big(x_p(a, b), y_p(a, b)\big) = L(a, b, \alpha_0, \beta_0) \quad (2.2.1)$$

if $(x_p(a, b), y_p(a, b))$ is the image point which lies on the line through (a, b) and the pinhole. In practice, however, the aperture of any real optical device is finite and not very small and (2.2.1) does not necessarily hold. Assuming that the surface is Lambertian i.e., $L(a, b, \alpha, \beta) = L(a, b)$, that there are not losses within the system and that the angular aperture (on the image side) is small, it can be proved [16] that

$$E\big(x_p(a, b), y_p(a, b)\big) = L(a, b)\, \Omega \cos^4 \varphi$$

where Ω is the solid angle corresponding to the angular aperture and φ is the angle between the principal ray (that is, the ray through the center of the aperture) and the optical axis. With the further assumption that the aperture is much smaller than the distance of the viewed surface, the Lambertian hypothesis can be relaxed to give [17]

$$E\big(x_p(a, b), y_p(a, b)\big) = L(a, b, \alpha_0, \beta_0)\, \Omega \cos^4 \varphi$$
$$(2.2.2)$$

where α_0 and β_0 are the polar coordinates of the direction of the principal ray. It must be pointed out that (2.2.2) holds if L is continuous with respect to α and β. In what follows, it will be assumed that the optical system has been calibrated so that (2.2.2) can be rewritten as (2.2.1). Finally, notice that

$$\vec{\nabla}_p E \cdot \vec{v}_p = \vec{\nabla}_s L \cdot \left(\frac{da}{dt}, \frac{db}{dt} \right) \quad (2.2.3)$$

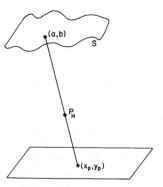

Fig. 2. Scene radiance and image irradiance in the pinhole approximation. The image irradiance at the point (x_p, y_p) is given by the scene radiance at the point (a, b) on the surface in the direction of the line connecting the two points through the pinhole P_H.

where $\vec{\nabla}_s$ is the gradient with respect to the surface coordinates, since differentiating (2.2.1) yields

$$\vec{\nabla}_p E \cdot (dx_p, dy_p) = \vec{\nabla}_s L \cdot (da, db).$$

III. Computing Derivatives of the Image Brightness in Terms of Scene Radiance

The general method which is used to show that optical flow data almost always give inaccurate estimates of the component of the motion field along the gradient of the image brightness is presented. The Lambertian model of reflectance and a more realistic model are assumed for pure rotation, pure rotation, and general rigid motion of a generic surface. The motion field and the optical flow are exactly the same only for Lambertian objects which translate under uniform, fixed illumination.

A. The Method

Consider a rigid surface S moving in space. From (2.2.1), the image irradiance E at time t at the point (x_p, y_p) is equal to the scene radiance L at the point (a, b) on S, i.e., $E(x_p, y_p, t) = L(a, b)$. The image irradiance at time $t + \Delta t$ is given by the scene radiance from S at time $t + \Delta t$. As shown in Fig. 3, the point on S which radiates toward (x_p, y_p) at time $t + \Delta t$ is the point $(a - \Delta a, b - \Delta b)$.[2] The unit normal vector $\vec{N}$ to S at the point $(a - \Delta a, b - \Delta b)$ at time $t + \Delta t$ is

$$\vec{N}_{t + \Delta t}(a - \Delta a, b - \Delta b)$$
$$= \vec{N}_t(a - \Delta a, b - \Delta b) + \Delta \vec{N}$$

where $\Delta \vec{N}$ is the first order variation of $\vec{N}$ due to the motion of S during the time interval Δt. Now in the case of translation

$$\Delta \vec{N} = 0$$

while in the case of rotation with angular velocity $\vec{\omega}$

$$\Delta \vec{N} = \vec{\omega} \times \vec{N} \Delta t. \quad (3.1.1)$$

---

[2]The surface is assumed to correspond to a moving convex body to avoid self-occlusions. In fact, the computations which follow hold for any convex surface patch.

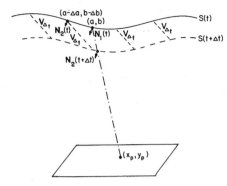

Fig. 3. Computing $\partial E/\partial t$. The point (a, b) on S radiates toward (x_p, y_p) at time t. The point $(a - \Delta a, b - \Delta b)$ radiates toward the same point at time $t + \Delta t$. The vectors $\vec{N}_1$ and $\vec{N}_2$ are the unit normal vectors to the surface S at the point (a, b) and $(a - \Delta a, b - \Delta b)$, respectively.

Notice that (3.1.1) can be considered as the expression of $\Delta\vec{N}$ for any kind of motion. Similarly, for each argument A of the scene radiance, we can write

$$A_{t+\Delta t}(a - \Delta a, b - \Delta b)$$
$$= A_t(a - \Delta a, b - \Delta b) + \Delta A. \quad (3.1.2)$$

To compute ΔA, let us distinguish between arguments of L which are intrinsic function of the surface coordinates, such as texture and albedo, and those which can be thought of as function of the surface coordinates, but, in fact, are function of 3-D space coordinates, such as the illumination and the point of view. If A is an intrinsic function of the surface coordinates, it follows easily that

$$\Delta A = 0$$

while if A is a function of 3-D space coordinates, from Taylor's expansion we have

$$\Delta A = \vec{\nabla}A \cdot \vec{v}\,\Delta t \quad (3.1.3)$$

where $\vec{\nabla}$ is the gradient operator with respect to the 3-D space coordinates. Let us assume that L can be written as a function of m arguments A^i, $i = 1, \cdots, m$, and of $\vec{N}$. Then, taking into account (3.1.1) and (3.1.2), (2.2.1) becomes

$$E(x_p, y_p, t + \Delta t)$$
$$= L\big(A_t^i(a - \Delta a, b - \Delta b)$$
$$+ \Delta A^i, \vec{N}_t(a - \Delta a, b - \Delta b) + \Delta\vec{N}\big) \quad (3.1.4)$$

at time $t + \Delta t$ and

$$E(x_p, y_p, t) = L\big(A_t^i(a, b), \vec{N}_t(a, b)\big) \quad (3.1.5)$$

at time t. Therefore, using (3.1.4) and (3.1.5) and dropping the subscript t we have

$$\frac{\partial E}{\partial t} = -\vec{\nabla}_S L \cdot \left(\frac{da}{dt}, \frac{db}{dt}\right) + \sum_{i=1}^{p} \frac{\partial L}{\partial A^i} \vec{\nabla}A^i \cdot \vec{v}$$

$$+ \frac{\partial L}{\partial \vec{N}} \cdot \vec{\omega} \times \vec{N} \quad (3.1.6)$$

if p, $p \leq m$, of the A^i, $i = 1, \cdots, m$, require the use of (3.1.3) to compute ΔA, $\partial L/\partial\vec{N} = (\partial L/\partial N_x, \partial L/\partial N_y, \partial L/\partial N_z)$, and $\vec{N} = (N_x, N_y, N_z)$.

From (2.2.3) and the definition of $\vec{v}_\perp$, (3.1.6) can be rewritten as

$$\frac{\partial E}{\partial t} = -\|\vec{\nabla}_p E\|\, v_\perp + \sum_{i=1}^{p} \frac{\partial L}{\partial A^i} \vec{\nabla}A^i \cdot \vec{v} + \frac{\partial L}{\partial \vec{N}} \cdot \vec{\omega} \times \vec{N}. \quad (3.1.7)$$

Finally, if $\Delta v_\perp$ is the norm of the difference between $\vec{v}_\perp$—the true component of the motion field $\vec{v}$ along $\vec{\nabla}_p E$—and $\|\vec{\nabla}_p E\|^{-1}\, \partial E/\partial t$—the estimate of $\|\vec{v}_\perp\|$ which can be obtained from (2.1.5)—from (3.1.7) we have

$$\Delta v_\perp = \frac{1}{\|\vec{\nabla}_p E\|} \left| \sum_{i=1}^{p} \frac{\partial L}{\partial A^i} \vec{\nabla}A^i \cdot \vec{v} + \frac{\partial L}{\partial \vec{N}} \cdot \vec{\omega} \times \vec{N} \right|. \quad (3.1.8)$$

Thus, $\Delta v_\perp$ vanishes, or the motion field and the optical flow are the same, if the reflectance function does not depend upon 3-D space coordinates and the surface undergoes pure translation.

Let us consider now some interesting examples in detail.

B. Translation of a Lambertian Surface

Consider a Lambertian surface S. In the hypothesis of uniform illumination, the scene radiance due to S is

$$L = \rho\vec{I} \cdot \vec{N} \quad (3.2.1)$$

where ρ is the albedo of the surface, $\vec{I}$ the unit vector which gives the direction of illumination, and $\vec{N}$ the unit normal vector to S. If the surface is translating, substitution of (3.2.1) in (3.1.8) yields

$$\Delta v_\perp = 0 \quad (3.2.2)$$

since $\vec{\omega} = 0$ and none of the arguments in L depends upon 3-D space coordinates. Therefore, in the case of a Lambertian surface which is translating under uniform illumination it is possible to estimate correctly the component of the motion field in the direction of $\vec{\nabla}_p E$ from optical flow data.

In the case of nonuniform illumination the right-hand side of (3.2.2) contains an extra term due to ΔI. A rigorous analysis of the relevance of this term in (3.2.2) would require a realistic model of illumination. In practice, if the object is not moving very slowly, (3.2.2) is expected to be satisfied almost everywhere a part from locations where the gradient of illumination cannot be neglected (e.g., shadow boundaries).

Let us consider now the case of a rotating Lambertian surface.

C. Rotation of a Lambertian Surface

Let S be a Lambertian surface rotating in space with angular velocity $\vec{v}$ around an arbitrary positioned axis. Applying the same argument of the previous section but taking into account the constraint (3.1.1) for $\vec{\Delta}N$, (3.1.8) yields

$$\Delta v_{\perp} = \frac{|\rho\vec{N} \cdot \vec{I} \times \vec{\omega}|}{\|\vec{\nabla}_p E\|}. \qquad (3.3.1)$$

In the case of rotation, therefore, even under uniform illumination, the estimate of the motion field by means of optical flow data is corrupted by a systematic error. Notice that the error vanishes if the surface is rotating around an axis parallel to the direction of illumination. In the case of nonuniform illumination again a corresponding extra term must be added to the right-hand side of (3.3.1).

For a sphere rotating around an axis through its center, due to rotational symmetry we have

$$\vec{N}(a - \Delta a, b - \Delta b)$$
$$+ \vec{\omega} \times \vec{N}(a - \Delta a, b - \Delta b)\,\Delta t = \vec{N}(a, b)$$

for every point (a, b) on the sphere. Therefore, if ρ is uniform, since the displacement in space equals the displacement on the sphere, (3.1.6) gives

$$\frac{\partial E}{\partial t} = 0$$

which means that

$$\Delta v_{\perp} = \|\vec{v}_{\perp}\|$$

or, in other words, that all the motion information in the image brightness pattern is lost.

D. Translation of a Specular Surface

Let us consider, now, a more realistic reflectance model. The scene radiance can be thought of as a suitable linear combination of a Lambertian and a specular term [18], i.e.,

$$L = L_{\text{lamb}} + L_{\text{spec}} \qquad (3.4.1)$$

where the Lambertian contribution is the same of (3.2.1) and the specular term is

$$L = s \left(\frac{\vec{D} \cdot \vec{R}}{D}\right)^n \qquad (3.4.2)$$

where s is the fraction of light reflected by the surface, $\vec{D} = f\vec{n} + \vec{x}$ is the vector pointing from the focus of projection to the radiating point and

$$\vec{R} = \vec{I} - 2(\vec{I} \cdot \vec{N})\,\vec{N} \qquad (3.4.3)$$

is the unit vector which gives the direction of perfect specular reflection. Assuming that s is not a function of the direction of the incident light and that is constant on the surface, the specular term is proportional to the nth power of the cosine of the angle between the direction of specular reflection and the line of sight. It is clear that the contribution to $\Delta v_{\perp}$ due to the Lambertian term has al-

ready been computed. In the case of translation the contribution of the specular term can be obtained substituting (3.4.2) in (3.1.8) which gives

$$\Delta v_{\perp} = \frac{1}{\|\vec{\nabla}_p E\|}\left|\frac{sn}{D^3}\left(\frac{\vec{D} \cdot \vec{R}}{D}\right)^{n-1}(\vec{v} \times \vec{D}) \cdot (\vec{R} \times \vec{D})\right| \tag{3.4.4}$$

since

$$\frac{d\vec{D}}{dt} = \vec{v}$$

where $\vec{v}$ is the velocity of the translating surface. Thus, if the reflectance function has a specular component, the motion field and the optical flow are different even in the case of translation. In the case of orthographic projection, i.e., for $f \to \infty$, the right-hand side of (3.4.4) vanishes since $\vec{D} \to \infty$. Therefore, in the approximation of orthographic projection, the estimate of $\vec{v}_{\perp}$ is correct for any translating surface whose reflectance function satisfies (3.4.1).

E. Rotation of a Specular Surface

Let us compute the contribution of the specular term of (3.4.1) to $\Delta v_{\perp}$ in the case of a rotating surface. Substituting (3.4.2) in (3.1.8) and taking into account the constraint (3.1.1), we have

$$\Delta v_{\perp} = \frac{1}{\|\vec{\nabla}_p E\|}\left|\frac{sn}{D^3}\left(\frac{\vec{D} \cdot \vec{R}}{D}\right)^{n-1}\left\{(\vec{v} \times \vec{D}) \cdot (\vec{R} \times \vec{D})\right.\right.$$
$$- 2D^2\left[(\vec{D} \cdot \vec{N})(\vec{I} \cdot \vec{\omega} \times \vec{N})\right.$$
$$\left.\left.+ (\vec{I} \cdot \vec{N})(\vec{D} \cdot \vec{\omega} \times \vec{N})\right]\right\}\right| \tag{3.5.1}$$

which, in general, is different from zero. Since for $f \to \infty$ (3.5.1) yields

$$\Delta v_{\perp} = \frac{1}{\|\vec{\nabla}_p E\|}\left|2sn(\vec{R} \cdot \vec{n})^{n-1}\left[(\vec{n} \cdot \vec{N})(\vec{I} \cdot \vec{\omega} \times \vec{N})\right.\right.$$
$$\left.\left.+ (\vec{I} \cdot \vec{N})(\vec{n} \cdot \vec{\omega} \times \vec{N})\right]\right| \tag{3.5.2}$$

the estimate of $\vec{v}_{\perp}$, in this case, is affected by error even in orthographic approximation, unless $\vec{I}$, $\vec{\omega}$, and $\vec{n}$ are parallel.

F. General Case

Let us assume now that a generic object whose reflectance function is described by (3.4.1) undergoes a given arbitrary rigid motion (composition of a translation and rotation in space). Adding together contributions (3.3.1), (3.4.4), and (3.5.1), for the difference $\Delta v_{\perp}$ between the expected and the computed component of the motion field by means of optical flow data we obtain

$$\Delta v_\perp = \frac{1}{\|\vec{\nabla}_p E\|} \left| \rho \vec{N} \cdot \vec{I} \times \vec{\omega} + \frac{sn}{D^3} \left(\frac{\vec{D} \cdot \vec{R}}{D} \right)^{n-1} \right.$$

$$\cdot \left\{ (\vec{v} \times \vec{D}) \cdot (\vec{R} \times \vec{D}) \right.$$

$$- 2D^2 [(\vec{D} \cdot \vec{N})(\vec{I} \cdot \vec{\omega} \times \vec{N})$$

$$\left. \left. + (\vec{I} \cdot \vec{N})(\vec{D} \cdot \vec{\omega} \times \vec{N})] \right\} \right| \qquad (3.6.1)$$

where $\vec{v}$ is the velocity (with rotational and translational components) of the moving surface. The right-hand side of (3.6.1) is generally different from zero. However, as pointed out in Section III-A, it is different from zero whenever arguments of the reflectance function depend upon 3-D space coordinates. It is then clear [see (3.1.7) and (3.1.8)] that the $\Delta v_\perp / \|v_\perp\|$ is lower if the variation of the image brightness pattern over time at a given location (measured by $\partial E / \partial t$) is due to physical events on the moving surface (e.g., texture and surface markings); conversely, it is larger the more the change over time in intensity is due to lightness condition, abrupt changes in the reflectance properties of the moving surface at the corresponding location in space, or highlight boundaries of poorly textured surfaces. It must be noted that in this analysis shadows and self-shadow effects have not been considered. They also give rise to sharp changes in intensity which do not correspond to features in the scene. Furthermore, the Phong model of reflectance does not include explicitly sharp intensity changes due to highlights.

IV. MOTION FIELDS, OPTICAL FLOWS, AND DYNAMICAL SYSTEMS

In the previous section, we have shown that the estimates of the motion field which can be given in terms of first order derivatives of the image brightness pattern, are often inaccurate. Moreover, uncertainty of these estimates cannot be measured unless further information about the nature of viewed objects is known (or provided by some other vision module). This result seems to cast a shadow on the use of dense optical flow data for motion computations, such as recovering 3-D motion parameters and 3-D structure from motion. In what follows, however, we will argue that useful information can be extracted from dense optical flows. We introduced a theoretical framework in which the motion field can be compared with several plausible optical flows. Smooth planar vector fields can be seen as flows associated with some 2-D dynamical systems and the theory of dynamical systems can be used to confront them. An optical flow can be thought of as *close* to the true motion field, if the topological description of the two vector fields, in terms of the theory of dynamical systems, is the same at any fixed time.

Let us first show in what sense the motion field and optical flows can be associated with dynamical systems. As mentioned in Section I, a thorough analysis—outlined in [11]—is presented in [12]. Let a smooth convex surface undergo a given rigid motion in space. At any given time t, the motion field produced by the moving surface onto the image plane—provided it has the appropriate degree of smoothness that is, if it is continuous with first order partial (spatial) derivatives continuous—can be thought of as the vector field tangent to the solution to a planar system of ordinary autonomous differential equations (see [19] or Appendix B for mathematical details). Therefore, the qualitative theory of planar differential equations seems to be a natural tool for studying properties of the motion field. The analogy is between *phase portraits* of dynamical systems and motion flows. The motion field is considered at a fixed time: the physical meaning of the underlying dynamical system is irrelevant. Clearly, the same argument applies to other smooth planar vector fields, e.g., the optical flow. Since most of the relevant information about a dynamical system can be extracted from its *singular points*—that is, the points where the vector field vanishes (see Appendix B for a list of the main singular points of planar flows)—a natural criterion to study and confront motion field and optical flow seems to be that they have the same *number* and *kind* of singular points at about the same *position*, or, in other words, that they are qualitatively the same. From this perspective, quantitative difference between the motion field and optical flow might no longer be relevant. It is worth noticing that where singular points lie *close* to discontinuities of the motion field, a smoothing step is expected to change the qualitative properties of the field and of the corresponding optical flows (how *close* is determined by the size of the smoothing filter). Consider, for example, an arbitrary object which is translating *against* the viewer. The main feature of the motion field is an isolated singular point which is a *focus of expansion*. Note that the qualitative structure of the field neither depends on the shape of the object nor on its speed. If the focus of expansion lies *close* to the boundary of the moving surface, the qualitative properties of the *smoothed* motion field might change and a detailed, quantitative analysis might be required.

V. DISCUSSION

If our point of view is correct, the only critical feature of the optical flow is that it must be topologically equivalent to the motion field. This requirement also satisfies two important uses of optical flow, namely to *detect discontinuities* and *help long-range matching* of the stereo type, which are needed for computing *structure-from-motion*. Quantitative equivalence, which is unlikely in general, is irrelevant for this use. As a consequence, *many different "optical flows" can be defined*. Different definitions could be chosen on the basis of criteria such as computability (from image data) or ease of implementation (for given hardware constraints). This point of view has clear implications for biological visual systems: movement detecting calls (say, in the retina) do not have to compute a specific optical flow, because simple estimates of the motion field which preserve its qualitative properties are equally good candidates (e.g., correlation-like algorithms). This argument may explain why the models proposed to explain motion dependent behavior in insects [20], motion perception in humans [21], and physiology of cells [22], [23], are all implementing quite different computations of optical flows. A basic question to answer is, of course, whether these biological models are in fact sufficiently *close* to the motion field to be topologically equivalent to it. Indeed, we conjecture that they are usually similar enough to preserve the qualitative properties of the motion field. The conjecture is based on results [24] showing that most of the biological models proposed so far can be considered as special instances or approximations of a general class of nonlinear models (characterized as Volterra systems of the second order).

APPENDIX A
PERSPECTIVE AND ORTHOGRAPHIC PROJECTIONS

In this section we explain in more detail the geometry of perspective projection used in the paper. In order to obtain orthographic projection as the simple limit of perspective projection for $f \to \infty$, where f is the focal length, the focus of projection cannot be located at the origin of the system of coordinates. To simplify the geometry without losing in generality, let the origin lie on the projection plane. The vector pointing from the focus to a point $\vec{x} = (x, y, z)$ is now $f\vec{n} + \vec{x}$. To obtain the expression of the projected point $\vec{x}_p$, from Fig. 1 notice that

$$\frac{f\vec{n} + \vec{x}}{(f\vec{n} + \vec{x}) \cdot \vec{n}} = \frac{f\vec{n} + \vec{x}_p}{f}. \tag{A.1}$$

From (A.1), we have

$$\vec{x}_p = f \frac{f\vec{n} + \vec{x}}{f + \vec{x} \cdot \vec{n}} - f\vec{n},$$

and finally

$$\vec{x}_p = \frac{f}{f + \vec{x} \cdot \vec{n}} (\vec{x} - (\vec{x} \cdot \vec{n}) \vec{n})$$

or

$$\vec{x}_p = \frac{f}{f + \vec{x} \cdot \vec{n}} (\vec{n} \times (\vec{x} \times \vec{n})). \tag{A.2}$$

In the limit of orthographic projection (i.e., $f \to \infty$), $\vec{x}_p \to \vec{x}_0$, and (A.2) yields

$$\vec{x}_0 = \vec{n} \times (\vec{x} \times \vec{n}). \tag{A.3}$$

Combining (A.2) and (A.3), we obtain the general relationship between perspective ($\vec{x}_p$) and orthographic

($\vec{x}_0$) projection that is,

$$\vec{x}_p = \frac{f}{f + \vec{x} \cdot \vec{n}} \vec{x}_0.$$

APPENDIX B
PLANAR DYNAMICAL SYSTEMS

A planar *dynamical system* is a C^1 map $\phi: R \times A \to A$, where A is an open subset of R^2 and writing $\phi(t, x) = \phi_t(x)$, the map $\phi_t: A \to A$ satisfies:
a) $\phi_0: A \to A$ is the identity;
b) the composition $\phi_t(\phi_s(x)) = \phi_{t+s}$ for each $t, s \in R$.
A planar dynamical system ϕ_t on A gives rise to a planar systems of differential equations on A that is, a vector field $y: A \to R^2$ defined as follows:

$$y(x) = \frac{d}{dt} \phi_t(x) \Big|_{t=0} \tag{B.1}$$

Thus, for every x, $y(x)$ is the tangent vector to the curve $t \to \phi_t(x)$ at $t = 0$. Equation (B.1) can be rewritten as

$$\frac{dx}{dt} = y(x). \tag{B.2}$$

If $y(x)$ is a C^1 vector field, (B.2) defines a planar dynamical system which can be thought of as a one-parameter family of transformation $\phi_t: A \to A$ describing the motion of the points in A as the time passes. The trajectories of the points are given by the solution curves to (B.2). Since (B.2) is *autonomous* (that is, the right-hand side does not depend explicitly on t), if $y(x^0) = 0$, then $x = x^0$ is a solution to it. Solutions like $x = x^0$ are called *equilibrium points* or *singular points*. In the case of linear systems, useful qualitative information about the behavior of the solution to (B.2) can be obtained from the eigenvalues of the matrix M of the coefficients of the differential equation computed at x_0. The restriction to planar systems reduces the classification of singular points to four fundamental cases:

1) M has real eigenvalues of opposite signs. In this case the singular point is a *saddle:* the saddle is *unstable* (a singular point is *stable* if any nearby solutions to it stays nearby for all the future time. It is *unstable* otherwise).

2) The eigenvalues have negative real parts. The singular point is a *sink* which is stable. The main property of a sink is that

$$\lim_{t \to \infty} x(t) = x_0$$

for any nearby solution $x(t)$. Qualitatively, the *phase portrait* of the solutions—that is, the family of the solution curves as a subset of R^2—looks like Fig. 4, where only some tangent vectors of some of the solution curves have been drawn.

Sinks can be classified depending on further characteristics of the eigenvalues. A *focus* (Fig. 4), for example, represents the case of coincident eigenvalues (M is a mul-

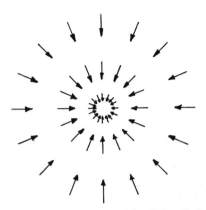

Fig. 4. Vector field tangent to a planar *sink*; all the solutions curves are pointing toward the singular point.

tiple of the identity matrix); a *node*, the case of different real eigenvalues; a *spiral*, the case of complex conjugate eigenvalues. A *sink-increasing* rotational component corresponds to each different case.

3) The eigenvalues have positive real parts. The singular point is a *source*. The main property of a source is that

$$\lim_{t \to \infty} \left| x(t) \right| = \infty$$

and

$$\lim_{t \to -\infty} x(t) = x_0$$

for any nearby solution $x(t)$. A source can be considered as the dual case of a sink: the phase portrait of a source and of the corresponding sink are the same except that for the direction of the vectors which must be reversed. Reversing the arrows in Fig. 4, for example, the phase portrait of a system with coincident real positive eigenvalues would be obtained. Obviously, sources are unstable.

4) The eigenvalues are pure imaginary. The singular point is a *center*. All the nearby solutions are *periodic* with the same period. A center is a stable equilibrium. For a reason that will be made clear soon, this last case is of little practical interest, since even a small perturbation of the field will make the orbits spiral inward toward (or outward from) the singular point, changing the qualitative properties of the solution curves. In other words, a center is not *structurally stable*.

The crucial point is that this classification is *exhaustive*. Every singular point (in the linear case) looks like a saddle, a sink, a source, or a center. The same classification holds for the nonlinear case with respect to the eigenvalues of the derivative of the right-hand side of (B.2), considered as a linear operator. This can be seen considering the best linear approximation of the system in the neighbor of the singular point. Assuming that the real part of the eigenvalues of the matrix representative of the linear approximation at the singular point does not vanish, the phase portrait of the system in the neighbor of the singular

point looks like in the corrisponding linear approximation. A dynamical system for which the real part of the eigenvalues of the linear approximation at each singular point does not vanish—with the additional conditions that there are no trajectories joining saddles and all the *limit cycles* are either periodic *attractor* or periodic *repeller*— is said to be *structurally stable*. It is clear that a dynamical system with a singular point whose linearization is a center is not structurally stable. Intuitively, a dynamical system is structurally stable if all the dynamical systems sufficiently *close* to it, share the same qualitative properties. A very important result of the theory of planar dynamical systems [25] says that the set S of planar dynamical systems which are structurally stable is dense in the set T of all the planar dynamical systems. Since S is also open in T, this result implies that almost all the planar dynamical systems are structurally stable.

ACKNOWLEDGMENT

We would like to thank V. Torre, D. Geiger, B. Caprile, and B. K. P. Horn for useful discussion and especially B. Saxberg for important comments and suggestions.

REFERENCES

[1] J. J. Gibson, *The Perception of the Visual World.* Boston: Houghton Mifflin, 1950.
[2] C. L. Fennema and W. B. Thompson, "Velocity determination in scenes containing several moving objects," *Comput. Graphics Image Processing*, vol. 9, pp. 301–315, 1979.
[3] B. K. P. Horn and B. G. Schunck, "Determining optical flow," *Artif. Intell.*, vol. 17, pp. 185–203, 1981.
[4] E. C. Hildreth, *The Measurement of Visual Motion.* Cambridge, MA: MIT Press, 1984.
[5] ——, "The Computation of the velocity field," *Proc. Roy. Soc. London*, vol. B221, pp. 189–220, 1984.
[6] A. M. Waxman, "Image flow theory: A framework for 3-D inference from time-varying imagery," in *Advances in Computer Vision*, C. Brown, Ed. Norwood, NJ: Erlbaum, to be published.
[7] B. K. P. Horn, *Robot Vision.* Cambridge, MA, MIT Press/McGraw-Hill, 1986.
[8] K. Kanatani, "Structure from motion without correspondence: General principles," in *Proc. Image Understanding Workshop*, Miami, FL, 1985, pp. 107–116.
[9] H. H. Nagel, "Recent advances in image sequence analysis," in *Proc. Premier Colloque Image—Traitment, Synthese, Technologie et Applications*, Biarritz, France, 1984, pp. 545–558.
[10] H. H. Nagel and W. Enkelmann, "An investigation of smoothness constraints for the estimation of displacement vector fields from image sequences," *IEEE Trans. Pattern. Anal. Machine Intell.*, vol. PAMI-8, pp. 565–593, 1986.
[11] A. Verri and T. Poggio, "Against quantitative optical flow," in *Proc. 1st ICCV*, London, June 1987.
[12] A. Verri, F. Girosi, and V. Torre, "Mathematical properties of the 2-D motion field: From singular points to motion parameters," *J. Opt. Soc. Amer.*, in press, 1989.
[13] S. Uras, F. Girosi, A. Verri, and V. Torre, "Computational approach to motion perception," *Biol. Cybern.*, vol. 60, pp. 79–87, 1988.
[14] P. Burt and G. Sperling, "Time, distance, and feature trade-offs in visual apparent motion," *Psych. Rev.*, vol. 88, pp. 171–195, 1981.
[15] D. Marr and S. Ullman, "Directional selectivity and its use in early vision processing," *Proc. Roy. Soc. London*, vol. B211, pp. 151–180, 1981.
[16] M. Born and E. Wolf, *Principle of Optics.* New York: Pergamon, 1959.

[17] B. K. P. Horn and R. W. Sjoberg, "Calculating the reflectance map; *Appl. Opt.*, vol. 18, pp. 1770–1779, 1979.

[18] B. T. Phong, "Illumination for computer generated pictures," *Commun. ACM*, vol. 18, pp. 311–317, 1975.

[19] M. W. Hirsch and S. Smale, *Differential Equations, Dynamical Systems, and Linear Algebra.* New York: Academic, 1974.

[20] B. Hassenstein and W. Reichardt, "Systemtheoretische Analyse der Zeit-, Reihenfolgen und Vorzeichenauswertung bei der Bewgungsperzeption der Russelkafers Chlorophanus," *Z. Naturforsch*, vol. IIb, pp. 513–524, 1956.

[21] J. P. H. Van Santen and G. Sperling, "A temporal covariance model of motion perception," *J. Opt. Soc. Amer.*, vol. A1, pp. 451–473, 1984.

[22] H. B. Barlow and R. W. Levick, "The mechanism of directional selectivity in the rabbit's retina," *J. Physiol.*, vol. 173, pp. 477–504, 1965.

[23] V. Torre and T. Poggio, "A synaptic mechanism possibly underlying directional selectivity to motion," *Proc. Roy. Soc. London*, vol. B202, pp. 409–416, 1978.

[24] T. Poggio and W. Reichardt, "Considerations on models of movement detection," *Kybernetik*, vol. 13, pp. 223–227, 1973.

[25] M. Peixoto, "Structural stability on 2-dimensional manifolds," *Topology*, vol. 1, pp. 101–120, 1962.

Alessandro Verri received the Ph.D. degree in physics from the University of Genova, Italy, in 1984.

From December 1985 to November 1986 and from May 1988 to July 1988 he was a Visiting Scientist at the Massachusetts Institute of Technology Center for Biological Information Processing and at the M.I.T. Artificial Intelligence Laboratory, Cambridge, MA. Currently, he is a postdoctoral fellow at the Department of Physics of the University of Genova. He has published research papers in computational vision and image understanding. His current research interests are in applied mathematics and computer vision.

Tomaso Poggio (A'86) was born in Genoa, Italy, on September 11, 1947. He received the Ph.D. degree in theoretical physics from the University of Genoa in 1970.

From 1971 to 1982, he was Wissenschaftlicher Assistant at the MaxPlanckInstitut für Biologische Kybernetik in Tübingen, West Germany. Since 1982, he has been a Profesor at the Artificial Intelligence Laboratory at the Massachusetts Institute of Technology in Cambridge. In 1984, he was additionally appointed Professor at M.I.T.'s Whitaker College of Health Sciences and Technology, and was named the first director of the Center for Biological Information Processing. In 1988, he was named to the Uncas and Helen Whitaker Professorship. He has authored over 100 papers in areas ranging from psychophysics and biophysics to information processing in man and machine, artificial intelligence, and machine vision.

Prof. Poggio is on the editorial boards of *Biological Cybernetics, Advances in Applied Mathematics*, and several other interdisciplinary journals.

Multiple Light Source Optical Flow

Robert J. Woodham[*]

Laboratory for Computational Vision
University of British Columbia
Vancouver, BC, Canada

Abstract

A new method is described to compute a dense, local representation of optical flow. The idea is to use the intensity values recorded from multiple images of moving objects acquired simultaneously under different conditions of illumination. Each image is assumed to satisfy the standard optical flow constraint equation. Multiple images give rise to multiple constraint equations. When the optical flow and the 2D motion field coincide, these multiple equations are in the same unknowns. Two light source directions are sufficient, in principle, to determine the motion field. Three (or more) light source directions overdetermine the solution, avoid local degeneracies, and help to make the computation more robust.

This paper describes the basic theory and illustrates the theory on a real image motion sequence. All computations are local, independent and relatively simple. No iteration steps are required. It is suggested that the requirement to obtain simultaneous images under different conditions of illumination be satisfied by using spectrally distinct illumination and sensing.

1. Introduction

In general, a point on a moving object induces motion at the corresponding image point. The relation between scene motion and image motion is determined entirely by the geometry of image projection. The *2D motion field* is the 2D velocity vector at each point in an image.

Object motion typically also induces change in the brightness values measured in an image. The relationship between object motion and brightness change is not purely geometric because it also depends on radiometric factors, including the illumination and the reflectance properties of the objects in view. The *optical flow* is the 2D velocity vector of the brightness values themselves.

It is not possible to recover optical flow locally due to the well-known aperture problem. Additional information is required. Horn and Schunck[1] imposed a global smoothness constraint on optical flow in their now classic treatment. Their computed optical flow can vary locally, provided the variation is smooth. In some circumstances,

discontinuities in the motion field also are detected. Other approaches impose local constraint. For example, Kearney *et al.*[2] require that optical flow be constant in a selected region while both Mailloux *et al.*[3] and Verri *et al.*[8] model optical flow as locally satisfying a general affine transformation. Ohta[4] uses multispectral images to obtain additional local constraint.

This paper reconsiders the possibility of computing a dense, local representation of optical flow. The novel idea is to use the intensity values recorded from multiple images of moving objects acquired simultaneously under different conditions of illumination. Photometric stereo[10] exploits multiple conditions of illumination to determine shape from shading. Here, the same idea is applied to moving objects to determine optical flow. Each image is assumed to satisfy the standard optical flow constraint equation. Where the optical flow and the 2D motion field coincide, these multiple equations can be solved together to determine the 2D motion field. The method can be applied to every point in an image. Typically, the result is well-defined except at a sparse set of features. The method imposes no smoothness condition on optical flow and requires no *a priori* assumptions about how the image ought to be segmented.

Section 2 develops the theory of multiple light source optical flow in more detail. Section 3 discusses a particular implementation. Section 4 presents an example of the method applied to a simple toy object. Section 5 discusses the possibility of practical realization. Finally, conclusions are summarized in Section 6.

2. Background and Theory

2.1 The Optical Flow Constraint Equation

Let $E = E(x,y,t)$ denote image brightness at image point (x,y) as a function of time, t. Then, by a chain rule for differentiation, the total derivative of E with respect to time, dE/dt, can be written as

$$dE/dt = E_x u + E_y v + E_t \qquad (1)$$

where $E_x = \partial E/\partial x$, $E_y = \partial E/\partial y$ and $E_t = \partial E/\partial t$ are the partial derivatives of E with respect to x, y and t and where $u = dx/dt$ and $v = dy/dt$ determines the instantaneous flow at (x,y). If the brightness of an object point does not change as a consequence of motion, then $dE/dt = 0$. Under this assumption, the optical flow constraint equation is given by

---

[*] Fellow of the Canadian Institute for Advanced Research.

$$E_x u + E_y v + E_t = 0 \qquad (2)$$

From (1), it is clear that (2) is satisfied if and only if the total derivative dE/dt is zero. Much has been said concerning imaging situations that satisfy, approximately satisfy, or fail to satisfy the optical flow constraint equation (2). Some essential elements of the discussion are summarized in section 2.2.

For now, assume (2) holds so that its consequences can be examined in more detail. When (2) holds, optical flow and the 2D motion field coincide so that the vector $[u,v]$ is a purely geometric quantity describing the 2D motion of image point (x,y) as a function of time. The vector $[E_x, E_y, E_t]$ is a radiometric quantity describing the partial derivatives of image brightness with respect to position and time. Thus, (2) is of value because it relates something that can be measured, the vector $[E_x, E_y, E_t]$, to a geometric quantity of interest, the 2D motion field. Although (2) is a radiometric equation, it makes no assumption about the reflectance properties of the objects in view. In particular, it does not assume Lambertian (or any other) reflectance function.

Equation (2) cannot be solved locally because it is one equation in two unknowns, u and v. Given a measured $[E_x, E_y, E_t]$, equation (2) determines a line in uv-space, called the *flow constraint line*.

2.2 Geometric and Radiometric Considerations

One interpretation of equation (2) is that it requires that the vector $[u,v]$ be the only factor necessary to account for the temporal variation in image brightness. Equation (2) holds (equivalently, $dE/dt = 0$) for purely translational motion, orthographic projection and incident illumination that is uniform (i.e., does not vary) across the scene. Conversely, in any other circumstance, one can expect $dE/dt \neq 0$ so that (2) does not hold exactly.

With perspective projection or object rotation, there are geometric "foreshortening" effects that cause dE/dt to be non-zero. With rotation, surface normal vectors change relative to the direction to the light source and to the viewer. Scene radiance is a function both of the incident angle and of the view angle. Thus, scene radiance (and therefore image brightness) changes in a way that cannot be predicted without *a priori* knowledge of surface reflectance and scene illumination. Verri and Poggio[9] have quantified the expected difference between optical flow and motion for a number of special cases. Pentland[5] distinguishes brightness changes due to radiometric factors, which he calls "photometric motion", from those due to geometric factors.

Spatial or temporal variation in scene illumination will cause $dE/dt \neq 0$. Moving objects alter the scene illumination, both because they cast shadows and because they act as indirect sources of illumination via interreflection.

Finally, at locations where image brightness is discontinuous, $[E_x, E_y, E_t]$ becomes undefined. Schunck[6] argues that the optical flow constraint equation still is satisfied across discontinuities, provided the number of discontinuities is finite. Subsequently, he developed a version of his algorithm that could handle textured regions[7].

2.3 Using Multiple Light Sources

With multiple light sources, we get additional equations. For the two light source case, one obtains

$$E_{1x} u + E_{1y} v + E_{1t} = 0 \qquad (3)$$

$$E_{2x} u + E_{2y} v + E_{2t} = 0 \qquad (4)$$

which can be solved for $[u,v]$ as follows

$$\begin{bmatrix} u \\ v \end{bmatrix} = - \begin{bmatrix} E_{1x} & E_{1y} \\ E_{2x} & E_{2y} \end{bmatrix}^{-1} \begin{bmatrix} E_{1t} \\ E_{2t} \end{bmatrix} \qquad (5)$$

provided the required matrix inverse exists.

It is useful to distinguish cases when the matrix inverse in (5) fails to exist. All gradient based methods for the determination of optical flow, including the one described here, produce no useful local information at points where $[E_x, E_y]$ is zero. It can also happen that the two brightness gradients, $[E_{1x}, E_{1y}]$ and $[E_{2x}, E_{2y}]$, are parallel. Typically, this happens when the brightness gradient is dominated by a local surface feature, such as a shape discontinuity or surface marking, independent of the illumination. This also can happen owing to an "accidental alignment" between surface shape and illumination direction(s). Local degeneracies can be resolved if a third light source image is provided.

For a three light source case, one obtains

$$E_{1x} u + E_{1y} v + E_{1t} = 0 \qquad (6)$$

$$E_{2x} u + E_{2y} v + E_{2t} = 0 \qquad (7)$$

$$E_{3x} u + E_{3y} v + E_{3t} = 0 \qquad (8)$$

Equations (6-8) can be written as the matrix equation

$$\mathbf{Ax} = \mathbf{b} \qquad (9)$$

where $\mathbf{x} = [u,v]^T$, $\mathbf{b} = -[E_{1t}, E_{2t}, E_{3t}]^T$ and

$$\mathbf{A} = \begin{bmatrix} E_{1x} & E_{1y} \\ E_{2x} & E_{2y} \\ E_{3x} & E_{3y} \end{bmatrix}$$

In principle, there are many ways in which one could solve (9) for $\mathbf{x}$. The standard least squares solution, $\hat{\mathbf{x}}$, is given by

$$\hat{\mathbf{x}} = (\mathbf{A}^T \mathbf{A})^{-1} \mathbf{A}^T \mathbf{b} \qquad (10)$$

The solution is unique provided that the rank of $\mathbf{A}$ is 2. (Equation (9) can be extended, in the obvious way, to situations in which more than three light sources are used). It is important to note that the magnitude of $[E_x, E_y, E_t]$ plays the role of a "weight" that pulls the solution towards a flow constraint line for which the magnitude of $[E_x, E_y, E_t]$ is large (and consequently, away from a flow constraint line for which the magnitude of $[E_x, E_y, E_t]$ is small). This has a desirable effect in multiple light source optical flow. Locations in an image for which brightness is nearly constant will have $[E_x, E_y, E_t]$ near zero. These locations contribute minimal information, and thus it is good that they are discounted. Because of this, points that are shadowed with respect to one of the light sources need not be considered as a special case.

2.4 Validating the Multiple Light Source Method

One would like to exploit the redundancy inherent in an overdetermined problem in order evaluate the validity of the solution method. Validating the multiple light source method requires empirical support for the assumption that the set of linear equations (6-8) is indeed defined in identical variables u and v, independent of the conditions of illumination. A good fit of this model to the measurement data would suggest that the vector $[u,v]$ is an illumination invariant measure, whatever its geometric interpretation. Loosely put, one would like to determine what component of the measurement, $\mathbf{b}$, is accounted for by $\hat{\mathbf{x}}$ under the model $\mathbf{Ax} = \mathbf{b}$. Fit to the model can be expressed quantitatively by the residual

$$\mathbf{r} = \mathbf{b} - \mathbf{A\hat{x}} \qquad (11)$$

A relative error term is given by

$$\frac{|\mathbf{r}|}{|\mathbf{b}|} = \frac{|\mathbf{b} - \mathbf{A\hat{x}}|}{|\mathbf{b}|} \qquad (12)$$

This error term combines components due to both measurement uncertainty and to systematic modeling error. If $[E_x, E_y, E_t]$ is zero at a point in one image, equation (10) becomes equivalent to the two light source solution, given by equation (5), applied to the measurements obtained from the other two images. In this case, the relative error term will be zero since the measurements no longer are redundant.

3. Implementation

For a three light source configuration, six images are required. The first three images are obtained under different conditions of illumination at time $t = t_0$. The second three images are obtained at time $t = t_1$ respectively under the identical conditions of illumination used for the three images at $t = t_0$. It is essential that the estimated derivatives all refer to the same point in space and time. Derivatives of $E(x,y,t)$ are estimated using first differences in a $2 \times 2 \times 2$ cube of brightness values, treating the x, y and t dimensions symmetrically. (See [1; pp 189-190] for details). Initial brightness quantization was 8 bits-per-pixel. Even if these values were noise free, this quantizes first differences into too small a set of discrete values to permit reliable estimation of derivatives. The six images are smoothed, using a 2D Gaussian filter, prior to derivative estimation. Since the 2D Gaussian is separable, filtering is implemented as the successive convolution of a 1D Gaussian filter. The filter coefficients of the 1D Gaussian were scaled to sum to 256. No bits were thrown away in the convolution so that the net effect is to interpolate 8 bits-per-pixel data to 24 bits-per-pixel smoothed data. In the example that follows, $\sigma = 1.0$.

Once the nine partial derivatives, $(E_{ix}, E_{iy}, E_{it},$

$i = 1,2,3)$, are estimated, computation of optical flow proceeds point-by-point, according to equation (10). Two local checks are made to guarantee that the computation is not degenerate. First, at least two of the spatial brightness gradients, $[E_x, E_y]$, must be non-zero. Second, the rank of the matrix $\mathbf{A}$ must be two. Points that fail either of these two checks are noted and the result set as $u = 0$ and $v = 0$.

4. Example: Stay-Puft Marshmallow Man

The Stay-Puft Marshmallow Man is a commercial toy. Most of its surface has a white semi-gloss finish. The eyes and mouth are black, the collar and hat band are dark blue and the bow, in front, is red. The object was placed on a small black platform in a small "studio" constructed with matte black walls and ceiling.

Figure 1 shows the three images at $t = t_0$. Figures 1(a)-(c) have identical geometry but different illumination. Figure 1(a) has light source 1 from the upper right, Figure 1(b) has light source 2 from the upper left, and Figure 1(c) has light source 3 from almost directly behind the camera. The toy, but not the background, was then moved a small amount horizontally right to left (approximately two pixels). Three additional images, for $t = t_1$, were then obtained respectively under the same conditions of illumination as Figures 1(a)-(c). All images were of dimension 256×256.

Figure 2 illustrates the computation at a test point (row:160 column:158). Figure 2(a) marks the test point on the light source 3 image at $t = t_0$. Figure 2(b) plots the three flow constraint lines in uv-space. E1, E2 and E3 are respectively the flow constraint lines corresponding to the light source 1, 2 and 3 images for the motion from $t = t_0$ to $t = t_1$. The measurements of $[E_x, E_y, E_t]$, taken together, provide an accurate and well-conditioned estimate of u and v. (The tick marks on the axes in Figure 2(b) are spaced one unit apart so that we do indeed see that the solution is approximately $u = -2.0$ and $v = 0.0$).

Figure 3 shows the results for the entire image. Optical flow is computed at every point. To prevent clutter, Figure 3 plots results at every second point. Thus, if each estimate was exact (i.e., $u = -2.0$ and $v = 0.0$), the vectors would form a connected set of parallel lines running horizontally right to left. The estimates are good at points where the object surface is smoothly shaded. Some points on the collar fail to produce a result because they are too dark. The estimates are inaccurate at surface discontinuities and at surface reflectance boundaries because there changes in image brightness due to scene features dominate changes due to smooth shading.

Optical flow vectors also are estimated for many points on the background gray wedge and on the registration dots. Of course, there is no corresponding motion since the background was stationary. Nevertheless, there is non-zero optical flow owing to shadows and interreflection.

Figure 4 displays the relative error term computed according to equation (12). (The larger the error the darker the point). The error computation suggests that any attempt to assign a unique motion, $[u,v]$, to points on the gray wedge or on the registration dots is suspect. Similar error values occur at points on the toy's collar and, to a lesser extent, at points on the toy's body oriented towards the viewer. Points on the toy's collar are very dark with minimal brightness variation. Points on the toy's body oriented towards the viewer, while bright, also have minimal brightness variation. It is likely that in both these latter cases the local measurements are dominated by sensor noise (rather than lack of fit to the model). When the model is good and there is measurement uncertainty, the inherent redundancy in the data allows more robust estimate of the motion. Certainly, more work needs to be done to develop measures that distinguish measurement uncertainty from modeling error. Both are essential.

5. Discussion

Current experimental work requires that the objects be stationary while the multiple images are acquired. Once a set of images is obtained, one for each light source, the object is allowed to move slightly and the cycle is repeated. While this constitutes a valid demonstration of the method, it fails as a methodology for practical realization since light sources cannot easily be turned on and off rapidly enough to support the tracking of continuously moving objects.

The paradox of requiring simultaneous images of a continuously moving object under different conditions of illumination can be resolved by multiplexing the spectral dimension. Suppose three narrow-band collimated light sources, say red, green and blue, continuously illuminate a work space from three different directions. Many color cameras employ three distinct internal imaging systems, each producing a separate black and white image corresponding to a different spectral channel. Suppose these three images are acquired simultaneously and suppose there is minimal overlap in their spectral response. Then this color camera and light source configuration would support multiple light source optical flow, as described above, for objects moving continuously in the work space. Further, there is no requirement that the spectral channels chosen be in the visible portion of the spectrum. Channels in the near (i.e., reflective) infrared also are a possibility and can be chosen not to interfere with other vision algorithms working in the visible portion of the spectrum. Future work will exploit these ideas.

6. Conclusions

Multiple light source optical flow is a principled way to obtain additional local constraint. At points where the optical flow constraint equations (6-8) are satisfied exactly, three light source optical flow supports the fast, accurate and robust estimation of geometric motion. The inherent redundancy in the measurements can be exploited to validate the computation locally, including the ability to determine locations where optical flow and the 2D motion field do not coincide.

Multiple light source optical flow is complementary to techniques based on contour analysis or sparse feature matching because it works best where those techniques fail (and *vice versa*). Multiple light source optical flow works best on smoothly curved surfaces, without distinct surface markings, because local brightness then depends primarily on local shading. This makes it possible to obtain dense, non-redundant, local information by varying the direction of illumination. The method will be unreliable at surface discontinuities and surface markings because then local brightness change is dominated by scene features largely independent of the direction of illumination.

Acknowledgement

Stay-Puft Marshmallow Man is a registered trademark of Kenner Parker Toys International Inc. Uri Ascher, Rod Barman, Mike Bolotski, Alan Mackworth, Jim Little and David Lowe all provided useful comments on earlier versions of this work. Support was provided by the Natural Sciences and Engineering Research Council of Canada (NSERC) and by the Canadian Institute for Advanced Research (CIAR).

References

[1] Horn, B.K.P. & B.G. Schunck (1981), "Determining Optical Flow", *Artificial Intelligence* (17)185-203.

[2] Kearney, J.K., W.B. Thompson & D.L. Boley (1987), "Optical flow estimation: an error analysis of gradient-based methods with local optimization", *IEEE Trans. Pattern Analysis and Machine Intelligence* (9)229-244.

[3] Mailloux, G.E., F. Langlois, P.Y. Simard & M. Bertrand (1989), "Restoration of the velocity field of the heart from two-dimensional echocardiograms", *IEEE Trans. Medical Imaging* (8)143-153.

[4] Ohta, N. (1989), "Optical flow detection by color images", *Proc. IEEE Int. Conf. Image Processing* pp 801-805, Pan Pacific, Singapore.

[5] Pentland, A.P. (1989), "Photometric motion", Vision Sciences TR-120, MIT Media Lab, MIT, Cambridge, MA.

[6] Schunck, B.G. (1984), "The motion constraint equation for optical flow", *Proc. 7th Int. Conf. Pattern Recognition*, pp 20-22, Montreal, PQ.

[7] Schunck, B.G. (1988), "Image flow: fundamentals and algorithms", in *Motion Understanding: Robot and Human Vision*, W.N. Martin & J.K. Aggarwal (eds.), pp 23-80, Kluwer Academic Publishers, Boston, MA.

[8] Verri, A., F. Girosi & V. Torre (1990), "Differential techniques for optical flow", *J. Optical Society of America A*, (7)912-922.

[9] Verri, A. & T. Poggio (1989), "Motion field and optical flow: qualitative properties", *IEEE Trans. Pattern Analysis and Machine Intelligence* (11)490-498.

[10] Woodham, R.J. (1980), "Photometric method for determining surface orientation from multiple images", *Optical Engineering* (19)139-144.

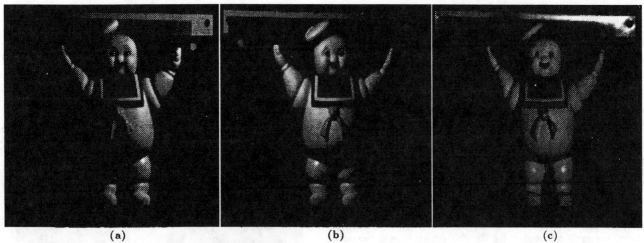

(a) **(b)** **(c)**

Figure 1. Three images of the Stay-Puft Marshmallow Man. Figures (a), (b) and (c) show images of the toy under three different conditions of illumination at $t = t_0$. Motion from $t = t_0$ to $t = t_1$ was a small translation from right to left. The object moved, but not the background.

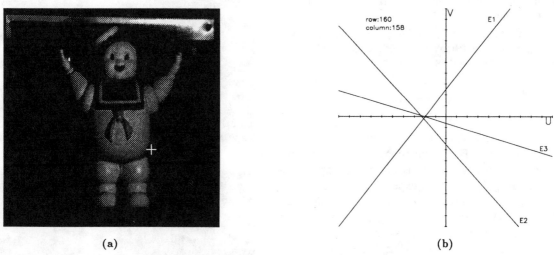

(a) **(b)**

Figure 2. Multiple light source optical flow computation at one point on the Stay-Puft Marshmallow Man example. Figure (a) marks the point. Figure (b) shows the three flow constraint lines.

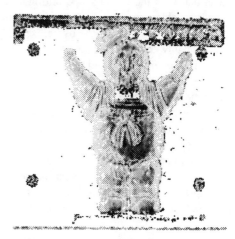

Figure 3. Optical flow computed for the Stay-Puft Marshmallow Man.

Figure 4. Error result for the Stay-Puft Marshmallow Man example.

Photometric Motion

Alex Pentland

Abstract— Optical flow algorithms typically assume that a surface point's imaged intensity does not change with motion and that geometric distortion of the projected surface shape is the dominant effect of motion. Often, however, the situation is precisely the opposite: Photometric motion, the change in a point's imaged intensity as a consequence of object motion, can easily dominate the other effects of motion. Photometric changes can therefore lead to severe errors in shape recovery if not correctly accounted for. In this paper, it will be shown that photometric motion may be used to obtain a closed-form solution for both surface shape and reflectance, and how this solution may be used to enhance the performance of geometrically based structure-from-motion algorithms is discussed. A simple biological mechanism that accomplishes the recovery of both shape and reflectance is demonstrated.

Index Terms— Albedo/reflectance recovery, motion analysis/processing, motion psychophysics, optical flow, reflectance modeling, structure from motion, 3-D shape recovery.

I. INTRODUCTION

MOST THEORETICAL treatments of optical flow assume that the intensity of an imaged point does not change over time. This assumption may well be valid when surfaces are covered with a high-contrast, high-spatial-frequency texture [7]. Practical experience, however, has shown that a point's intensity often does change with object motion [14]. The major response to this problem has been to use edges or other nonlinear preprocessing to obtain features that remain fixed on the surface [4]. Thus, in both practice and theory, intensity variation is viewed as being noise, and it is the geometric distortions caused by motion that are believed to contain virtually all the useful shape information.

When one considers problems such as determining the observer's motion or determining the overall scene geometry, this view is probably correct. This paper, however, will show that intensity information is sometimes even more important than geometric distortion when estimating the shape of a single, continuous surface that is rotating relative to the observer's frame of reference.

The first section of this paper will compare the *photometric effects of motion* (which is defined as the variation of a point's imaged intensity as a consequence of motion) and the *geometric effects of motion* (which is defined as the variation in projected surface geometry as a consequence of motion) and show that photometric motion provides a

Manuscript received July 21, 1989; revised April 7, 1991.

The author is with the Vision and Modeling Group, The Media Laboratory, Massachusetts Institute of Technology, Cambridge, MA 02138. This research was supported by National Science Foundation Grant IRI-87-19920 and by the Defense Advanced Research Projects Agency under Rome Air Development Center (RADC) Contract F30602-89-C-0022.

IEEE Log Number 9101438.

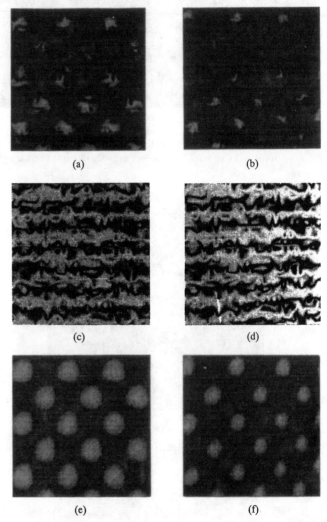

Fig. 1. First and last frames from three image sequences: (a) and (b) show first and last images of a shaded-and-textured sequence; (c) and (d) show first and last images of a textured-only sequence; (e) and (f) show first and last images of a shaded-only sequence. In this example, it is possible to recover structure-from-motion from shading and texture or from shading only but *not* from texture only.

cue to surface shape that is potentially as useful as that provided by geometric motion. The following sections of the paper will then develop a simple technique for using this photometric motion information to extract both surface shape and reflectance and propose a biological implementation. Finally, how this photometric motion mechanism can be integrated with and used to enhance existing structure-from-motion algorithms will be discussed.

II. PHOTOMETRIC MOTION VERSUS GEOMETRIC MOTION

The comparison between photometric and geometric motion cues to surface shape is, at its heart, quite simple. The magnitude of geometric motion cues depends on the range of depths present, which in turn depends on the average angle between the viewer and the surface. Thus, for steeply slanted surfaces, small rotations can cause large distortion effects in the image, whereas for surfaces facing the viewer, even relatively large motions will have little visible effect.

The photometric effects of motion are similar but depend on the illuminant position rather than the viewer's position. When the change in surface normal caused by the object's motion is perpendicular to the illumination, there will then be little change in the image brightness. However when the change in surface normal has components either toward or away from the illuminant, then even small rotations can cause surprisingly large changes in the image intensity.

To quantify the relative magnitude of the two effects, however, requires statistical experimentation and measurement of particular examples. Such quantification is the subject of the remainder of this section.

A. Human Perception: A Psychophysical Experiment

First, let us ask how important the photometric effects of motion are in human vision. To test the psychological relevance of photometric motion, three synthetic image sequences were created. Each sequence was of an "egg crate" surface $(z(x, y) = \sin(x) \sin(y))$ that was sinusoidally rotating around the $x = y$ axis with an amplitude of $\pm 10°$. No bounding contours were visible. In the first image sequence, the surface was both shaded and textured with a random, marble-like texture. In the second image sequence, the surface was identically textured, but the shading information was eliminated by illuminating the surface with only diffuse illumination. The third image sequence was identical to the first but with no surface texturing. The first and last frames from each of these sequences is shown in Fig. 1.

Naive subjects ($n = 10$) were asked to look at each of the image sequences, with the order of display varied randomly, and describe the shape of the displayed surface. In every case, subjects were correctly able to describe the textured and shaded surface as a rotating egg crate, as expected. *None* of the subjects were able to attribute any rigid shape to the texture-only image sequence—even when the textured surface was viewed immediately after the identically-textured shading-and-texture sequence. Eight of the ten subjects were able to correctly describe the shape and motion when presented with the shading-only sequence. The remaining two subjects initially perceived the shading-only sequence as "a blurry, wobbling chain-link fence," but when told to perform a figure-ground reversal (e.g., to see the light areas as "blobs" rather than as holes), they correctly described the shape and motion of the stimulus.

The conclusion of this experiment is unambiguous; in this particular situation, it is the *photometric* effects of motion, rather than the geometric effects, that provide the strongest cue to surface shape and motion. This is true even though the surface texturing provided clearly visible and unambiguous geometric information about the surface shape and motion. To understand why this occurs, we must analyze the relative

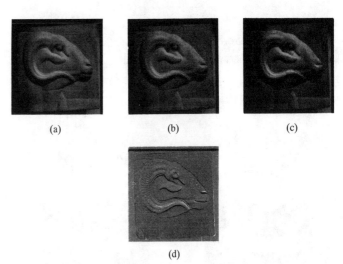

Fig. 2(a)–(c). Three frames of an image sequence of a rotating object; (d) difference between the first and last images. The geometric displacement between the first and last images has a mean of 0.44 pixels and a standard deviation of 0.52 pixels, whereas the photometric variation has a mean of 14.28 grey levels and a standard deviation of 18.87 grey levels.

strengths of the photometric and geometric effects of object motion.

B. Measurement of a Real Object

Let us next measure the relative strengths of photometric and geometric motion cues in a carefully controlled experiment using a real object: a stone *bas relief* sculpture of a ram's head. Fig. 2 (a)–(c) shows three frames of an image sequence in which a relatively flat object (8:1 ratio of maximum width to maximum depth variation) was rotated about a 45° axis centered at the object's upper left-hand corner. The total amount of rotation was approximately 0.1 rad or 5.7°. Illumination was from approximately $\mathbf{L} = (0.707, 0.707, 0.5)$. The difference between the first and last images is shown in Fig. 2 (d). Note that although there has been relatively little shift in edge position, there are large brightness variations across the entire object.

The geometric displacement between the first and last images was measured on a pixel-by-pixel basis using a geometric model of the surface and rotation, and the results were confirmed by direct image measurement at selected features. The mean geometric displacement during this motion sequence was found to be 0.44 pixels, and the standard deviation was 0.52 pixels. The mean photometric change was measured to be 14.28 grey levels and the standard deviation to be 18.87 grey levels (that is, more than one third of the pixels changed by more than 18.87 grey levels). In this example, therefore, the geometric effects of motion are nearly unmeasurable, whereas the photometric signal is fully 40% of the magnitude of the static photometric signal and is measurable even under extremely noisy imaging conditions.

C. A Statistical Experiment

The above experiments leave open the possibility that these results are due to unusual viewing or illumination geometry. Therefore, a statistical experiment using a CAD-like model of

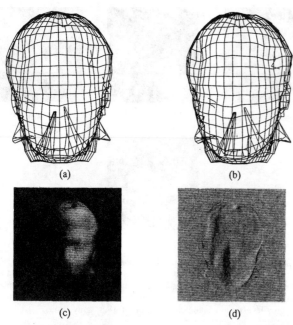

(a)   (b)

(c)   (d)

Fig. 3. (a) CAD model of a human head (Captain Kirk of the U.S.S.Enterprise) in canonical position; (b) same head rotated 0.05 rad (2.8°); (c) shaded version of the same model; (d) intensity differences caused by this rotation (same greyscale as (c)).

a human head was conducted. (The model was automatically constructed by use of the ThingWorld modeling system [13] from measurements of Captain Kirk of the U.S.S. Enterprise. Range measurements were provided by Technical Arts, Inc.) Fig. 3(a) shows this head model in canonical position, and (b) shows a copy of it rotated by 0.05 rad (2.8°). The projected size of the model was 100 pixels high by 100 pixels wide.

By comparing the position of points on the original model and the rotated model, the change in imaged position was measured. This change was measured at 576 points evenly distributed across that portion of the surface of the model that is visible in both views; these points appear as intersections in Fig. 3(a). The mean change in position between the two positions was 1.32 pixels, and the standard deviation was 1.76 pixels. Thus, 33% of the points moved by more than 1.76 pixels, and 38% of the points moved by less than one pixel.

The photometric information was then measured at the same 576 points and the results averaged over all illuminant positions in the front-upper quarter sphere ($0 < \tau < \pi$, $0 < \sigma < \pi/2$, where τ, σ are the tilt and slant of the illuminant). The mean photometric change averaged 2.15 grey levels, and the standard deviation averaged 5.54 grey levels. Thus, 33% of the points changed by more than 5.54 grey levels, and 14% of the points changed by less than one grey level. Only when the illuminant direction was directly above the head model was the mean photometric signal numerically smaller than the geometric signal.

As an illustration of what these numerical differences mean, the illuminated head is shown in Fig. 3(c), and the intensity differences between the two head positions (shown using the same greyscale) are shown in Fig. 3(d). The mean and variance of the intensity differences shown in Fig. 3(d) are approximately the same as the average mean and variance. As

Fig. 3(d) shows, the photometric effects of even this small rotation are normally large enough to be reliably measured.

The above experiments demonstrate that the photometric effects of motion, rather than geometric changes normally used in shape-from-motion algorithms, often provide the largest-magnitude cues to surface shape. It appears, therefore, that photometric information is an important—but largely overlooked—cue for estimating surface shape from motion. In the following sections, the possibilities of extracting shape information from the photometric effects of motion, and of combining this information with standard structure-from-motion algorithms, will be explored.

III. Background

A. The Imaging of Surfaces

Let $z = z(x, y)$ be a surface with reflectance $I(x, y) = R(p, q, \mathbf{L})$, where $\mathbf{L}$ is a unit vector in the direction of the mean of the illumination distribution. For mathematical simplicity, orthographic projection onto the x, y plane will be assumed; it will also be assumed that $z < 0$ within the region of interest and that the surface is not self-shadowing.

Given a surface patch with mean orientation (p_0, q_0), we can form a quadratic approximation to the reflectance function [5] by means of a Taylor expansion of R about $(p, q) = (p_0, q_0)$,

$$
\begin{aligned}
I(x, y) \approx\; & R(p_0, q_0, \mathbf{L}) \\
& + (p - p_0) \frac{\partial R(p_0, q_0, \mathbf{L})}{\partial p}\Big|_{p=p_0, q=q_0} \\
& + (q - q_0) \frac{\partial R(p_0, q_0, \mathbf{L})}{\partial q}\Big|_{p=p_0, q=q_0} \\
& + 1/2(p - p_0)^2 \frac{\partial^2 R(p_0, q_0, \mathbf{L})}{\partial p^2}\Big|_{p=p_0, q=q_0} \\
& + 1/2(q - q_0)^2 \frac{\partial^2 R(p_0, q_0, \mathbf{L})}{\partial q^2}\Big|_{p=p_0, q=q_0} \\
& + 1/2(p - p_0)(q - q_0) \frac{\partial^2 R(p_0, q_0, \mathbf{L})}{\partial p \partial q}\Big|_{p=p_0, q=q_0}. \quad (1)
\end{aligned}
$$

The most commonly used models of reflectance are both symmetric and separable; therefore, (1) reduces to

$$
I(x, y) \approx k_0 + (p-p_0)k_1 + (q-q_0)k_2 + ((p-p_0)^2 + (q-q_0)^2)k_3. \quad (2)
$$

Given a point on a smooth surface, it is always possible to find a surrounding region for which this approximation is arbitrarily good because one can always find a neighborhood that contains a small range of (p, q) values. In practice, a surprisingly large range of (p, q) can be accurately modeled as long as the surface is a fairly diffuse reflector.

In the Lambertian case, for instance, with $(p_0, q_0) = (0, 0)$, the particular constants are

$$
\begin{aligned}
I(x, y) \approx\; & \rho(x, y)\lambda(x, y)[\cos\sigma + p\cos\tau\sin\sigma \\
& + q\sin\tau\sin\sigma - \frac{\cos\sigma}{2}(p^2 + q^2)] \quad (3)
\end{aligned}
$$

where $\rho(x, y)$ is the surface albedo (the total fraction of reflected light, which may change arbitrarily from point to point), $\lambda(x, y)$ is the incident illumination (which may also change from point to point), and the illuminant direction $\mathbf{L} =$

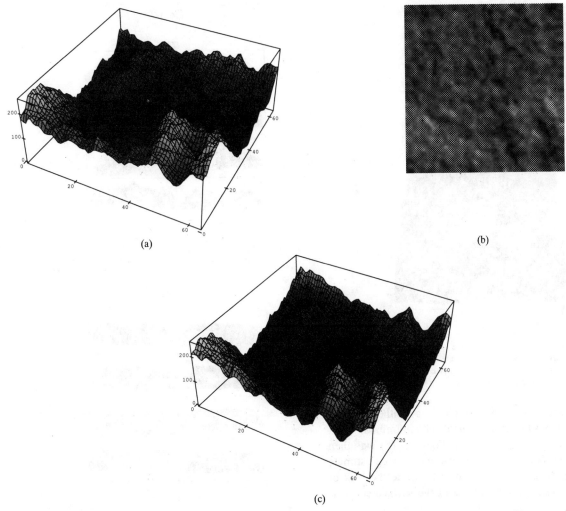

Fig. 4. Linear shape-from-shading: (a) Perspective plot of a synthetic fractal surface; (b) image of fractal surface; (c) perspective plot of surface recovered from image in (b).

$(x_L, y_L, z_L) = (\cos \tau \sin \sigma, \sin \tau \sin \sigma, \cos \sigma)$ where τ is the *tilt* of the illuminant (the angle the image plane component of the illuminant vector makes with the x axis), and σ is its *slant* (the angle the illuminant vector makes with the z axis). It has been found that (2) provides a perceptually indistinguishable approximation of the Lambertian reflectance function over the range $-2 < p, q < 2$ with $(p_0, q_0) = (0, 0)$ [12].

B. Shape Recovery

The key result used in this paper in order to recover surface shape information from photometric motion is recent work [11] showing that for surfaces with linear shading (constant k_i, with $k_3 = 0$), there is a stable, closed-form solution for the surface shape. The basic result is quite simple: If we let the Fourier transform of the image be $F_I(\omega, \theta)$, then the Fourier transform of the z surface is simply

$$F_z(\omega, \theta) = \frac{e^{-i\pi/2}}{2\pi k_0 \omega [k_1 \cos \theta + k_2 \sin \theta]} F_I(\omega, \theta) \quad (4)$$

where ω is frequency, and θ is image-plane orientation. Surface shape may therefore be recovered, given that τ and σ, which are the two components of the illuminant direction, are known. The estimation of illuminant direction is discussed in [9] and [11].

Note that the Fourier components exactly perpendicular to the illuminant cannot be seen in the image data and must either be obtained from boundary conditions or simply be assumed to be zero. Setting these unseen perpendicular components to zero (e.g., the natural boundary conditions) may be equated with the widely used assumption of general viewing position, as is explained in [11].

The recovery process can be improved by using Wiener filtering to remove noise and nonlinear components of the image intensity pattern, as has been developed by Adelson and Pentland [2]. If such noise is modeled as proportional to $|k_1 \cos \theta + k_2 \sin \theta|$ (e.g., as a fixed fraction of the spectral power along each image orientation), and the surface modeled as a fractal Brownian [10] function whose power spectrum is proportional to f^{-4} (or, equivalently, as a Markov process of order two—a "thin-plate" model), the optimal RMSE estimate of surface shape is then

$$F_z(\omega, \theta) = \frac{e^{-i\pi/2}}{2\pi k_0 \omega [sd + (k_1 \cos \theta + k_2 \sin \theta)]} F_I(\omega, \theta) \quad (5)$$

where $s = \text{Sign}[\cos(\tau - \theta)]$, and typically, $0.5 < d < 0.75$. In actual practice, (5) has been found to perform much better than (4).

Figs. 4 and 5 show two examples of using (5) to recover

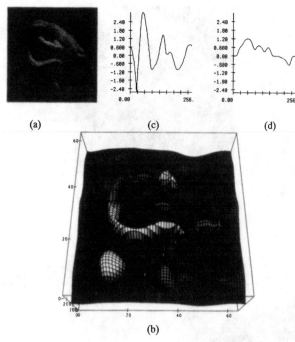

(a)   (c)   (d)

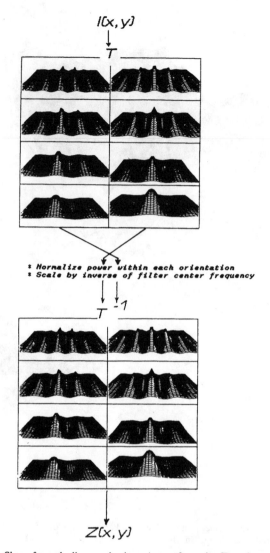

(b)

Fig. 5. Linear shape-from-shading: (a) Image of a stone ram's head; (b) perspective plot of surface recovered from image (a); (c) height profile of a slice through recovered surface near the bottom (see Fig. 10); (d) true height profile as measured from original stone model.

shape. Fig. 4(a) shows a perspective plot of a synthetic fractal surface, and (b) shows the image generated by illuminating that surface from $L = (0.707, 0.707, 0.5)$. Equation (5) was then used to recover surface shape. The resulting surface estimate is shown in Fig. 4(c). It can be seen that despite the lack of boundary conditions, a good estimate of the surface shape is obtained.

Fig. 5(a) shows an image of a stone ram's head sculpture, and (b) shows a perspective plot of the surface estimated for this image using (5); (c) shows the height profile of a slice near the bottom of (b) (see Fig. 10), and (d) shows the true profile as measured using a mechanical contour gauge. In Fig. 5(c) and (d), the vertical scale is in centimeters and the horizontal scale in pixels. As can be seen, the recovered shape is only qualitatively correct, in large part due to errors caused by changes in the average surface reflectance (albedo).

C. A Biological Mechanism

Equation (5) suggests a biological mechanism for the perception of shape-from-shading. It is widely accepted that the visual system's initial cortical processing areas contain many cells that are tuned to orientation, spatial frequency, and phase.

Fig. 6 illustrates a mechanism based on filters with similar characteristics. The transformation **T** is a decomposition of the image using filters that form an self-inverting basis set and are localized in both space and spatial frequency. A similar transformation is widely believed to occur between the retina and striate cortex [3], [1], [15].

In order to recover surface shape from this filter set, the transformations indicated in (5) must be performed, as indicated in Fig. 6. These transformations are 1) phase-shift the filter responses by $\pi/2$, which is accomplished by switching

Fig. 6. Shape-from-shading mechanism: A transformation **T** produces localized measurements of sine and cosine phase frequency content, and then, the inverse transformation is applied, switching sine and cosine phase amplitudes and scaling the filter amplitude to remove them in proportion to the central frequency. The output of this process is the recovered surface shape.

the outputs of the sine and cosine phase filters, 2) scale the filter amplitude by $1/\omega_c$, where ω_c is the filter's central spatial frequency, 3) normalize filter responses within each orientation to remove the illumination's directional bias, and 4) reconstruct a depth surface from the scaled amplitudes of the filter set. The final step—reconstruction—can be accomplished by passing the signal through a second, identical set of filters. This produces the estimated surface shape within the windowed area of the image (the "receptive field" of the filters). (For more detail, see [11]).

IV. PHOTOMETRIC MOTION

Two methods in which photometric motion is used to recover surface information will be developed. The first method will use two frames from an image sequence to reduce the viewed surface's reflectance function to a linear form that may be subsequently solved using (5). The second method will use two frames that already have a linear reflectance function and solve for *both* shape and reflectance. By combing the two methods, we obtain a technique that takes three images from an image sequence and solves for both shape and reflectance in closed form.

A. Assumptions

Before beginning, however, a framework for discussing the problem must be set up. The following three assumptions will be made:

- Geometric motion cues have *already* been employed to obtain an approximate motion field. Consequently, the flow field can be segmented in regions with an approximately affine motion field and the images warped so that corresponding points on the viewed surface approximately overlay each other. Photometric motion processing will then be applied within these affine-motion regions with the goal of extracting additional surface detail. When using spatiotemporal filters to estimate optical flow, this warping process can be avoided.
- The motion field is constant across three successive image acquisitions. This assumption is not necessary, as will be obvious from the following mathematical development; however, it allows shape to be extracted from photometric motion cues by simple combinations of affine spatiotemporal filters.
- Within these affine-motion-field regions, (2) provides a good approximation of the true reflectance function. As as been discussed already, near highlights and specularities, this assumption will limit the size of the region that can be accurately processed.

No assumption about the type of motion or the viewer-illuminant-surface geometry will be necessary.

The useful consequence of restricting our analysis to regions with an affine motion field is that the change in surface normal within such regions is approximately constant. For instance, if the axis of rotation were parallel to the y axis, then $dp(x,y)/dt = d(dz(x,y)/dx)/dt \approx c$, where c is some constant. Thus, by using geometric motion cues to segment the image into affine-flow regions, we are also segmenting the image into regions where the surface is relatively flat and continuous. The surface detail of these regions can then be extracted from remaining photometric variation.

B. Image Intensities

Let the motion field for some imaged patch be described by

$$\begin{bmatrix} x_k^{t+1} \\ y_k^{t+1} \end{bmatrix} \approx \begin{bmatrix} c_{11} & c_{12} \\ c_{21} & c_{22} \end{bmatrix} \begin{bmatrix} x_k^t \\ y_k^t \end{bmatrix} + \begin{bmatrix} d_1 \\ d_2 \end{bmatrix} \quad (6)$$

where (x_k^t, y_k^t) are the imaged coordinates of a point k at time t, $t = 0, 1, 2 \ldots$, and c_{ij}, d_i, are contraction and displacement constants respectively.

The eigenvectors of the matrix of c_{ij}'s define a coordinate system $(\bar{x}, \bar{y})$ in which the flow field is decomposed into two independent (but not necessarily orthogonal) components. Under orthographic projection, one of these components will have an eigenvalue $\omega = 1$ (e.g., no contraction or expansion), and the other will be the direction of maximum geometric

warping. The eigenvector with no contraction is the projection of the axis of rotation, and the other eigenvector is the projection of a vector perpendicular to both the axis of rotation and the surface normal. The direction of the projected axis of rotation will be taken to be the $\bar{y}$ axis, and the direction of the perpendicular vector to be the $\bar{x}$ axis.

In this new coordinate system, the motion field of the image patch is reduced to a simple contraction along the new $\bar{x}$ axis. The successive images $I^t(\bar{x}, \bar{y})$ may therefore be "warped" so that corresponding points have approximately the same image coordinates

$$\begin{bmatrix} \hat{\bar{x}}_k^{t+1} \\ \hat{\bar{y}}_k^{t+1} \end{bmatrix} \approx \begin{bmatrix} \bar{\omega} & 0 \\ 0 & 1 \end{bmatrix} \begin{bmatrix} \bar{x}_k^{t+1} - \bar{d}_1 \\ \bar{y}_k^{t+1} - \bar{d}_2 \end{bmatrix} \quad (7)$$

where $\bar{\omega}$ is the nonunitary eigenvalue, e.g., the amount of contraction or expansion along the new $\bar{x}$ axis. If the motion field is exactly affine and the estimates of the motion field parameters are precise, then $(\hat{\bar{x}}_k^{t+1}, \hat{\bar{y}}_k^{t+1}) = (\bar{x}_k^t, \bar{y}_k^t)$, that is, points on the moving surface are warped to the same coordinates in successive images. After warping, the registered images will be designated $\hat{I}^t(\bar{x}, \bar{y})$.

Further, in this new coordinate system, the change in surface normal is also reduced to a simple additive change along the new $\bar{x}$ axis, e.g.,

$$\frac{d\bar{p}(\bar{x}, \bar{y})}{dt} = \frac{d(dz(\bar{x}, \bar{y})/d\bar{x})}{dt} \approx c \quad (8)$$

for some constant c. Thus, the images $\hat{I}^t(\bar{x}, \bar{y})$ will have intensities

$$\hat{I}^t(\bar{x}, \bar{y}) \approx k_0 + (\bar{p}(\bar{x}, \bar{y}) + tc)k_1 + \bar{q}(\bar{x}, \bar{y})k_2 \\ + ((\bar{p}(\bar{x}, \bar{y}) + tc)^2 + \bar{q}^2(\bar{x}, \bar{y}))k_3 \quad (9)$$

for $t = 0, 1, 2, \ldots$.

C. Reduction to Linear Form

Perhaps the main obstacle to applying (5) is that the observed surface's reflectance function often contains a significant quadratic component. Thus, if we could somehow use successive frames of an image sequence to remove or cancel this quadratic component, then the shape of surface could be recovered.

It turns out that such cancellation is surprisingly easy to achieve because the quadratic component of the surface reflectance function can be factored out by simply subtracting the two images

$$\Delta\hat{I}^t(\bar{x}, \bar{y}) = k_0 + \bar{p}(\bar{x}, \bar{y})k_1 + \bar{q}(\bar{x}, \bar{y})k_2 \\ + (\bar{p}^2(\bar{x}, \bar{y}) + \bar{q}^2(\bar{x}, \bar{y}))k_3 \\ - k_0 - (\bar{p}(\bar{x}, \bar{y}) + c)k_1 - \bar{q}(\bar{x}, \bar{y})k_2 \\ - ((\bar{p}(\bar{x}, \bar{y}) + c)^2 + \bar{q}^2(\bar{x}, \bar{y}))k_3 \\ = (ck_1 + c^2 k_3) + \bar{p}(\bar{x}, \bar{y})2ck_3 \quad (10)$$

where $\Delta\hat{I}^t(\bar{x}, \bar{y}) = \hat{I}^t(\bar{x}, \bar{y}) - \hat{I}^{t+1}(\bar{x}, \bar{y})$.

Thus, for surfaces with constant albedo and illumination, surface shape (up to an overall scale constant and possibly unknown boundary conditions) may be estimated by simply

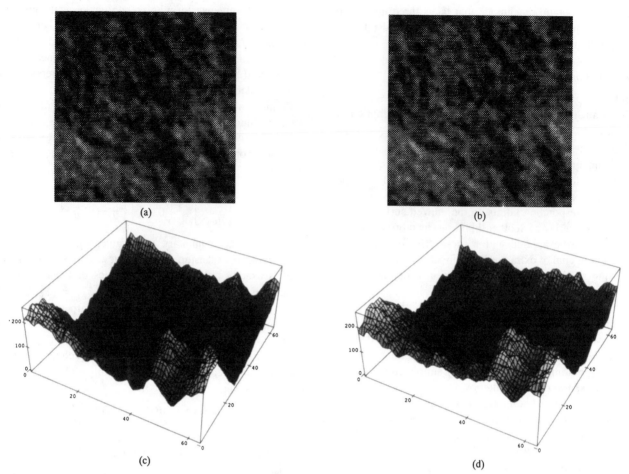

Fig. 7(a),(b). Two 8-b images showing a fractal surface with a diffusely glossy reflectance function. Between image (a) and (b), the surface has been rotated by 0.1 rad (5.7°). Illumination is from $\mathbf{L} = (0.707, 0.707, 0.5)$; (c) perspective plot of surface recovered by use of (1) and (5); (d) perspective plot of surface used to create (a) and (b).

warping and subtracting adjacent images to produce $\Delta \hat{I}^t(\bar{x}, \bar{y})$ and then applying (5). A biological version of this photometric motion algorithm is to simply replace $I(x, y)$ by $\Delta \hat{I}^t(\bar{x}, \bar{y})$ in the diagram shown in Fig. 6.

An Example: Fig. 7 illustrates recovering shape by use of this two-image photometric motion mechanism. Fig. 7(a) and (b) shows two 8-b images of a synthetic fractal surface. Between images (a) and (b), the surface has been rotated by 0.1 rad (5.7°) around the y axis. These images were produced using a diffusely glossy, nonlinear reflectance function, and the illuminant direction is $\mathbf{L} = (0.707, 0.707, 0.5)$.

The images were linearly warped to obtain approximate correspondence in the position of surface points, subtracted, and then, shape was estimated for the difference image using (5) with natural boundary conditions. A perspective view of the recovered surface is shown in Fig. 7(c); for comparison, the surface used to generate these images is shown in Fig. 7(d). It can be seen that surface shape is recovered with substantial accuracy despite the nonlinearity of the reflectance function.

D. Solving for Shape and Reflectance

The above result will now be generalized to encompass changes in surface albedo. The changes in albedo introduce a multiplicative scaling of the constants k_i. When this scaling varies on point-by-point basis, such as when there are surface

markings, then the k_i must be generalized, e.g.

$$k_i(\overline{x}, \overline{y}) = k_i \rho(\overline{x}, \overline{y}) \qquad (11)$$

where $\rho(\bar{x}, \bar{y})$ is the point-by-point surface albedo. The presence of such arbitrary point-to-point variation makes the recovery of shape quite difficult.

To remove the effects of albedo variation, therefore, we must estimate one of the $k_i(\bar{x}, \bar{y})$ and then use it to "divide out" the multiplicative effects of the albedo function $\rho(\bar{x}, \bar{y})$. Fortunately, given registered images $\hat{I}^t(\bar{x}, \bar{y})$, this is straightforward.

Let us start by using (10) to obtain two images $\hat{I}_l^t(\bar{x}, \bar{y})$ and $\hat{I}_l^{t+1}(\bar{x}, \bar{y})$ where each has a linear reflectance function. Their intensities are

$$\hat{I}_l^t(\overline{x}, \overline{y}) = k_0^*(\overline{x}, \overline{y}) + (\overline{p}(\overline{x}, \overline{y}) + tc)k_1^*(\overline{x}, \overline{y}) \qquad (12)$$

where $k_0^*(\bar{x}, \bar{y}) = (ck_1 + c^2 k_3)\rho(\bar{x}, \bar{y})$ and $k_1^*(\bar{x}, \bar{y}) = 2ck_3 \rho(\bar{x}, \bar{y})$. Note that natural surfaces often exhibit nearly linear reflectance properties, in which case, the above preprocessing is unnecessary.[1] This condition occurs whenever the angle between the viewer and illuminant directions is large or when the image patch size is small.

---

[1] In this case $k_i^* \rho(\bar{x}, \bar{y})$, $i = 0, 1, 2$, will generically be nonzero constants times the albedo $\rho(\bar{x}, \bar{y})$. This does not affect the results of this analysis beyond adding a k_2 term.

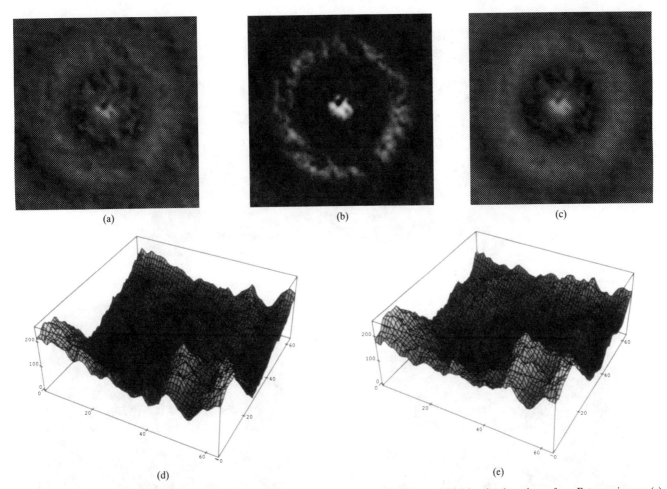

Fig. 8 (a)–(c). Three 8-b images showing a fractal surface with a "bull's eye" pattern of reflectance (albedo) painted on the surface. Between images (a) and (c), the surface has been rotated by 0.1 rad (5.7°). Illumination is from $\mathbf{L} = (0.707, 0.707, 0.25)$; (d) perspective plot of surface recovered by use of (15) and (5); (e) perspective plot of surface used to generate (a)–(c).

Therefore, $\Delta \hat{I}_l^t(\bar{x}, \bar{y})$, which is the difference between $\hat{I}_l^t(\bar{x}, \bar{y})$ and $\hat{I}_l^{t+1}(\bar{x}, \bar{y})$, is simply

$$\Delta \hat{I}_l^t(\bar{x}, \bar{y}) = ck_1^*(\bar{x}, \bar{y}) = 2c^2 k_3 \rho(\bar{x}, \bar{y}) \qquad (13)$$

This difference image, therefore, is a multiplicatively scaled estimate of the surface albedo $\rho(\bar{x}, \bar{y})$. It may therefore be used to remove the effects of albedo variation

$$\frac{\hat{I}_l^t(\bar{x}, \bar{y})}{\Delta \hat{I}_l^t(\bar{x}, \bar{y})} = \frac{ck_1 + c^2 k_3}{2c^2 k_3} + \frac{\bar{p}(\bar{x}, \bar{y}) + tc}{c}. \qquad (14)$$

This albedo-normalized "ratio image" may then be used to obtain surface shape by use of (5) (again up to an overall scale constant and possibly unknown boundary conditions). A biological version of this photometric motion algorithm is to simply replace $I(x, y)$ by the ratio $\hat{I}_l^t(\bar{x}, \bar{y})/\Delta \hat{I}_l^t(\bar{x}, \bar{y})$ in the diagram shown in Fig. 6.

Equations (10) and (14) may be combined to obtain a three-image photometric motion shape recovery mechanism. The combined equations are

$$\frac{\hat{I}^t(\bar{x}, \bar{y}) - \hat{I}^{t+1}(\bar{x}, \bar{y})}{2\hat{I}^{t+1}(\bar{x}, \bar{y}) - \hat{I}^t(\bar{x}, \bar{y}) - \hat{I}^{t+2}(\bar{x}, \bar{y})} = \frac{ck_1 + c^2 k_3}{2c^2 k_3} + \frac{\bar{p}(\bar{x}, \bar{y})}{c}. \qquad (15)$$

The output of this equation is then used to estimate surface shape independent of albedo variations.

An Example: Fig. 8 illustrates recovering shape by use of this second photometric motion mechanism. Fig. 8(a), (b), and (c) shows three 8-b images of moving synthetic fractal surface. The ring-like structure of Fig. 8(a), (b), and (c) is due to the introduction of a $1/\sin(r)$ variation in surface albedo. Between images (a) and (c), the surface has been rotated by 0.1 rad (5.7°) around the y axis. These images were produced using a diffusely glossy, nonlinear reflectance function, and the illuminant direction is $\mathbf{L} = (0.707, 0.707, 0.25)$.

The images were then linearly warped to obtain approximate correspondence in the position of surface points. These images were then used as input to (15) to obtain an albedo-independent "ratio image." Shape was estimated for this ratio image using (5) with natural boundary conditions. A perspective plot of the recovered surface is shown in Fig. 8(d); for comparison, the surface used to generate these images is shown in Fig. 8(e). It can be seen that a good estimate of surface shape is obtained despite large variations in albedo.

V. An Example Using Real Imagery

Fig. 2(a), (b), and (c) show three 8-b images of a dirty stone surface. Between acquisition of these images, the surface was rotated about its upper left-hand corner, with an axis of rotation inclined 45° from the x axis and perpendicular to the z axis.

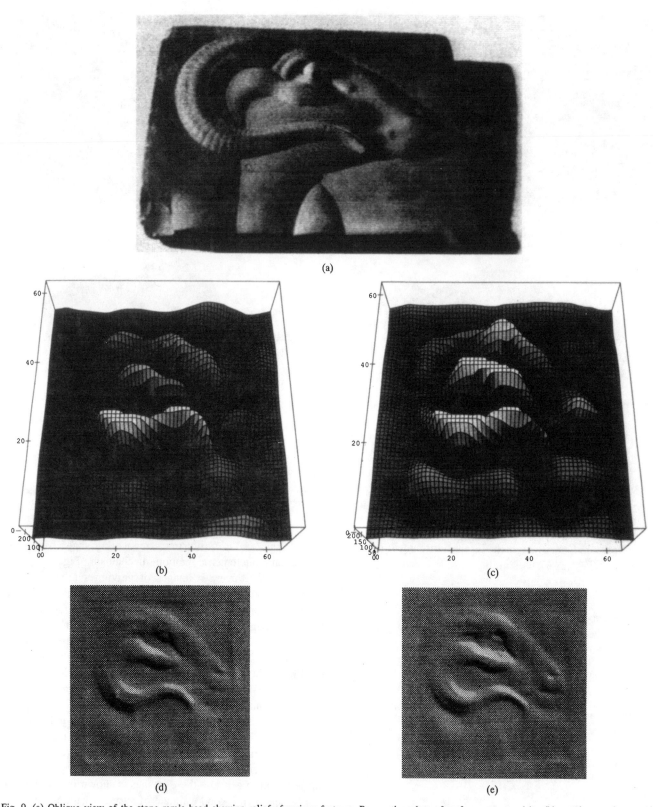

Fig. 9. (a) Oblique view of the stone ram's head showing relief of various features. Perspective plots of surfaces recovered by (b) two-image photometric motion (10), and (c) three-image photometric motion (15); (d), (e) illuminating the recovered surfaces from above.

The total amount of rotation was 0.1 rad (5.7°). Fig. 9 shows the results of computing shape from this image sequence using both the two-image photometric motion mechanism (10) and the three-image photometric motion mechanism (15).

The first step in processing was to register the three images.

This was accomplished by locating the corners in each image and warping the images so that their corners had the same image location. Equations (10) and (15) were then applied to these registered images to produce difference and ratio images, respectively. Finally, shape was estimated using (5)

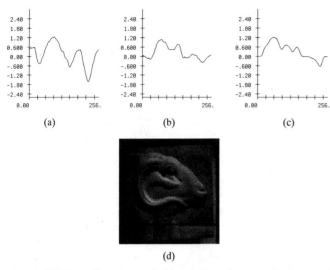

(a)   (b)   (c)

(d)

Fig. 10. Height profiles along a horizontal slice taken near the bottom of the surfaces recovered by (a) two-image photometric motion (10) and (b) three-image photometric motion (15); (c) the true height profile measured directly from the stone sculpture; (d) location of slices shown on original data.

with natural boundary conditions.

Fig. 9 compares the results obtained from two-image photometric motion (10) and the three-image photometric motion (15).[2] At the top of Fig. 9, there is an oblique view of the ram's head sculpture. This view allows the reader to see the relative height of its various features. Perspective plots of the surfaces recovered from (b) two-image photometric motion and (c) three-image photometric motion are shown below this. The viewpoint in these perspective plots is approximately the same as in (a); however, the vertical scale has been exaggerated.

From these perspective plots, it can be seen that both photometric motion equations produce qualitatively correct estimates of the surface shape. The albedo-independence of (15), however, results in considerably more accurate estimates of the low-frequency components of the surface shape. The improvement of (15) over (10) can be made obvious by illuminating the recovered surfaces from above, as in Figs. 9(d) and (e). In Fig. 9(d), the change in albedo between stone sculpture and background results in sharp creases paralleling the edges of the recovered surface, whereas in Fig. 9(e), these creases are nearly eliminated.

The performance of the two algorithms can also be compared with the true height profile of the stone sculpture, as shown in Fig. 10(a), (b), and (c), by fixing the scale of the the recovered surface. This can be accomplished by using knowledge of the true height-to-width ratio of the physical object that was used to establish the variance of each surface and, thus, the scale of each height profile. In this figure, the vertical scale is in centimeters, and the horizontal scale is in pixels.[3] These profiles are taken from near the bottom of the sculpture and across the ram's neck just under its head, as is shown in Fig. 10(d).

<hr>

[2] The reader may compare these results with those obtained by simple shape-from-shading (5), shown in Fig. 5.

[3] For comparison, the height profile obtained using static shape-from-shading is shown in Fig. 5.

Fig. 10(a), (b) shows slices from the surfaces recovered using (10) (two-image motion) and (15) (three-image motion), respectively. The correct height profile, measured using a mechanical contour gauge, is shown in Fig. 10(c). From these data, it is apparent that the three-image photometric motion result (shown in (b)) is considerably more accurate than the two-image photometric motion result (shown in (a)), apparently because errors due to albedo change have been suppressed.

VI. Discussion

A temporal filtering technique has been described that, when applied to previously registered image regions, will produce an estimate of surface shape. An implementation of a complete shape-from-motion algorithm, then, would have the following steps:

1) Compute optical flow from geometric motion cues.
2) Find approximately affine patches of optical flow.
3) Warp successive patches so that corresponding points are approximately registered.
4) Compute the photometric motion signal per (15).
5) Estimate shape from both the geometric and photometric motion signals.
6) Combine geometric and photometric shape estimates.

The process of estimating shape from photometric and geometric motion cues does not, however, need to be conducted in such a discrete, step-by-step manner. In particular, it appears that the same equations can be integrated with existing geometric motion algorithms to efficiently obtain shape from *both* photometric and geometric motion. The following paragraphs describe how this can be accomplished.

A. Integration with Spatiotemporal Filter Models

When using spatiotemporal filters to estimate optical flow, it is possible to avoid the process of warping successive image patches because some of the spatiotemporal filters will "track" single points on the viewed surface across successive images. This tracking is accomplished by first using the spatiotemporal filters to estimate the optical flow field and then selecting those filters whose orientation in space-time exactly matches the motion of points on the surface. The response of correctly oriented low-pass spatiotemporal filters can then be used as input to (15) and (5) in order to obtain the photometric motion estimate of surface shape.

The process of combining photometric and geometric shape estimates is also quite simple. From the geometric motion, we obtain locally affine patches of optical flow so that the geometric motion shape estimate is a planar surface. Photometric motion, on the other hand, can recover only estimates of surface variation, with the average orientation default assumed to be zero. Therefore, if the scaling or gain of the geometric and photometric estimates is commensurate, they can be combined by simple addition to produce the correct overall shape estimate. Solving for the photometric surface estimate's scaling normally requires additional information.

B. Integration with Regularization Methods

Another improvement to the estimation process can be achieved by embedding the photometric motion equations within a regularization framework. The potential of such an embedding has been recently demonstrated by Horn [8], who addressed the similar problem of shape-from-shading in this manner. Horn proceeded by linearly approximating the reflectance map, as was done in Section III-A, but at each image point rather than for entire image regions. He then solved the resulting set of linear equations, as was described in Section III-B, but within the framework of regularization. As a result, he was able to avoid the problem of segmenting the image into regions with a nearly linear reflectance function.

In the case of photometric motion, it appears that a similar approach will prove useful, that is, rather than segmenting the optical flow, linearizing the reflectance map using the photometric motion equations and then estimating shape over discrete regions, one can use the photometric motion equations to linearize the reflectance map separately at each image point. As in Horn's work, it appears that the resulting set of linear equations can be efficiently solved within the framework of regularization.

C. Error Conditions

There are three main conditions for which the above photometric motion algorithms will fail:

- *No motion*: $c = 0$. For extremely small rates of rotation, the photometric signal will be undetectable. In this case, the algorithm estimates the surface as being completely flat; therefore, there is no difference between the geometric and photometric estimates.
- *No change in shading*: When the illumination is perpendicular to the change in surface normal, there will be very little variation in intensity despite relatively large motions. In this case, the algorithm estimates the surface as being completely flat; therefore, there is no difference between the geometric and photometric estimates.
- $d\bar{p}(\bar{x}, \bar{y})/dt$ has large variations. When the geometric motion analysis has missed large variations in the surface shape, the information passed to the photometric motion algorithm will be incorrect. The primary cause of error will be misregistration of successive images, with the result that rapid changes in surface albedo will be misinterpreted as changes in orientation. Third-order and higher terms in the Taylor expansion of the reflectance function will also begin to contribute error to the surface estimate. This condition will often be detectable because the estimated surface will appear to contain large depth variations, which is contrary to the original assumptions.

A further cautionary note is that when $k_3 = 0$, that is, when the input images have extremely linear reflectance functions, then (14) must be used instead of (15).

D. Relation to Photometric Stereo

The well-known technique of photometric stereo originally developed by Woodham and Horn [16], [6] is most closely related to photometric motion. Photometric stereo employs several registered images of the same scene, where each has different illumination conditions but the same viewer-surface geometry. To estimate surface orientation, the measured image intensities are compared with a known reflectance map.

Photometric motion also employs several different registered images of the same scene but with different viewer-surface geometries rather than with different illumination conditions. To estimate surface orientation, the measured image intensities are compared with each other rather than to a known reflectance map.

It is clear that there are deep similarities between photometric stereo and photometric motion. It is also clear, however, that there are at least two major differences. First, photometric motion relies on geometric motion processing to determine regions with an approximately affine motion field and on chance configurations of surface, viewer, motion, and illumination to generate the measured signal. Photometric stereo allows the user to calibrate the viewing geometry beforehand and to position the illuminants to obtain the maximum signal possible. Photometric stereo, therefore, will have better accuracy than is generally possible with photometric motion processing. Photometric motion, however, can be applied in natural, unconstrained situations whereas photometric stereo generally can not.

Second, photometric stereo requires knowing the surface's reflectance map beforehand, whereas photometric motion does not. Photometric motion escapes the need for knowing the reflectance map by posing the problem in terms of the Taylor expansion of the reflectance map and, in the end, reducing the true reflectance map to a linear function that can be solved directly.

VII. Summary

It has been shown that the photometric effects of motion may dominate the geometric effects so that simple geometric interpretation of optical flow measurements can give incorrect estimates of surface shape (see also [14]). Far from being noise, however, these photometric motion effects have a simple, regular relationship to both surface shape and surface reflectance.

It has been shown that by simply subtracting successive images (after using geometric motion cues to register successive images), one obtains a new image with a linear reflectance function so that surface shape may be recovered in regions of constant albedo. This result was then extended to surfaces with variable albedo by calculating the "ratio image" of (15). This result allows closed-form solution for *both* surface shape and surface reflectance, regardless of surface markings or coloring. The solution can be implemented by the simple biological mechanism shown in Fig. 6.

These results, together with the psychophysical results of the first section, make it likely that the human visual system uses a combination of both geometric and photometric motion cues to determine surface shape. It appears, moreover, that geometric information alone is often insufficient for recovering detailed surface shape within continuous, relatively flat regions. For instance, when subjects viewed the moving textured egg-crate surface of Fig. 1(c) and (d), they obtained no impression of shape.

Instead, it appears that geometric motion cues provide mostly coarse-grain information about surface shape. This coarse-grain information, however, provides sufficient constraint on the surface shape that the visual system can then use photometric motion cues to extract shape details. Thus, for instance, when subjects viewed the textured *and* shaded surface of Fig. 1(a) and (b), they gained a much clearer impression of surface shape than when they viewed the shading-only surface of Fig. 1(e) and (f).

It is believed that machine vision will also find that better estimates of surface shape can be obtained by using *both* geometric and photometric cues to interpret shape than is possible by the use of either alone. Two approaches to integrating photometric motion cues into existing geometric motion algorithms have been suggested. The first approach generalizes spatiotemporal motion methods to take advantage of photometric motion cues, whereas the second integrates the photometric motion equations into a regularization framework. It is believed that both of these suggested approaches can lead to improved shape estimation performance.

REFERENCES

[1] E. Adelson and J. Bergen, "Spatiotemporal energy models for the perception of motion,"*J. Opt. Soc. Amer. A*, vol. 2, no. 2, pp. 284–299, 1985.

[2] E. Adelson and A. Pentland, "Wiener filtering to improve shape from shading, unpublished Tech. Memo.

[3] J. Daugman, "Two-dimensional analysis of cortical receptive field profiles, *Vision Res.*, vol. 20, pp. 846–856, 1980.

[4] E. Hildreth, "The computation of the velocity field," *Proc. Royal Soc. London B*, no. 221, pp. 189–220, 1984.

[5] P. Kube and A. Pentland, "On the imaging of fractal surfaces," *IEEE Trans. Patt. Anal. Machine Vision*, vol. 10, no. 5, pp. 704–707, 1988.

[6] B. K. P. Horn, R. J. Woodham, and W. M. Silver, "Determining shape and reflectance using multiple images, M. I. T. AI Memo 490, Aug. 1978.

[7] B. K. P. Horn and E. J. Weldon, "Direct methods for recovering motion," *Int. J. Comput. Vision*, vol. 2, no. 1, pp. 51–76, 1988.

[8] B. K. P. Horn, "Height and gradient from shading," *Int. J. Comput. Vision*, vol. 5, no. 1, pp. 37–67," 1990.

[9] A. Pentland, "Finding the illuminant direction," *Opt. Soc. Amer.*, vol. 72, no. 4, pp. 448–455, 1982.

[10] ——, "Fractal-based description of natural scenes,"*IEEE Trans. Patt. Anal. Machine Recognition*, vol. 6, no. 6, pp. 661–674, Nov. 1984.

[11] ——, "Linear shape from shading, *Int. J. Comput. Vision*, vol. 4, pp. 153–162, 1990.

[12] ——, "Shape information from shading: A theory of human perception," *Spatial Vision*, vol. 4, nos. 3/4, pp. 165–182, 1990.

[13] ——, "Automatic extraction of deformable part models," *Int. J. Comput. Vision*, vol. 4, pp. 107–126, 1990.

[14] A. Verri and T. Poggio, "Against the quantitative optical flow," in *Proc. First Int. Conf. Comput. Vision* (London), June 8–11, 1987, pp. 171–179.

[15] A. Watson and A. Ahumada, "Model of human visual motion sensing," *J. Opt. Soc. Amer. A*, vol. 2, no. 2, pp. 322–342, 1985.

[16] R. J. Woodham, "Photometric method for determing surface orientation from multiple images," *Opt. Eng.*, vol. 19, no. 1, pp. 139–144, 1980.

Alex Pentland received the Ph.D. degree from Massachusetts Institute of Technology (M. I. T.) in 1982 and began work at SRI's International Artificial Intelligence Center.

He was appointed Industrial Lecturer at Stanford University's Computer Science Department in 1983, winning the Distinguished Lecturer Award in 1986. In 1987, he was appointed Associate Professor of Computer, Information, and Design Technology at M. I. T.'s Media Laboratory and was appointed Associate Professor in the M. I. T. Civil Engineering Department in 1988. In 1988, he was appointed to the NEC Computer and Communications Career Development Chair.

He has published over 130 scientific articles in the fields of artificial intelligence, machine vision, design, and computer graphics. In 1984, he won the Best Paper prize from the American Association for Artificial Intelligence for his research on problems of texture and shape description. In 1991, he won the Best Prize paper from the IEEE for his work in face recognition. His last book was entitled *From Pixels to Predicates* (Norwood, NJ: Ablex), and he is currently working on a new book entitled *Dynamic Models for Vision* (Cambridge, MA: Bradford/M. I. T. Press).

Binocular Shading and Visual Surface Reconstruction

W. E. L. Grimson

Artificial Intelligence Laboratory, Massachusetts Institute of Technology,
Cambridge, Massachusetts 02139

Received February 17, 1983; revised February 21, 1984

Zero-crossing or feature-point based stereo algorithms can, by definition, determine explicit depth information only at particular points in the image. To compute a complete surface description, this sparse depth map must be interpolated. A computational theory of this interpolation or reconstruction process, based on a *surface consistency constraint*, has previously been proposed, implemented, and tested. In order to provide stronger boundary conditions for the interpolation process, other visual cues to surface shape are examined in this paper. In particular, it is shown that in theory, shading information from the two views can be used to determine the orientation of the surface normal along the feature-point contours, provided the photometric properties of the surface material are known. This computation can be performed by using a simple modification of existing photometric stereo algorithms. It is further shown that these photometric properties need not be known *a priori*, but can be computed directly from image irradiance information for a particular class of surface materials. The numerical stability of the resulting equations is also examined.   © 1984 by Academic Press, Inc.

1. INTRODUCTION

1.1. The Global Problem

One of the goals of a vision system is to compute the three-dimensional shape of the visible surfaces in a scene. The human visual system uses many cues to compute surface shape, with different modules of the system using varying sources of information in the images to infer information about surface shape. Examples include motion analysis, stereopsis, shading, and texture. How do these different visual modalities contribute to the computation of surface shape?

One computational approach to understanding the human visual system, pioneered by Marr and Poggio (see, e.g., [24, 26, 28]), views the computation of surface shape from images, in part, as a collection of transformations between two main representations. The first representation is the *primal sketch*, which makes explicit loci of changes in image irradiance at particular scales of resolution; the second is the $2\frac{1}{2}$-D *sketch*, which makes explicit information about surface shape and reflective properties of the surface material. The modules that compute information feeding the $2\frac{1}{2}$-D sketch from the primal sketch have generally been considered to a first approximation to be independent of one another. It is clear, however, that within the $2\frac{1}{2}$-D sketch the different sources of information should interact, both to maintain consistency among the data provided by different modules and to provide feedback to the modules in order to enhance the acquired data (e.g., texture contours can facilitate stereopsis by driving vergence eye movements [23]). In this paper, we are interested in examining interactions at the level of the $2\frac{1}{2}$-D sketch between modules of the early visual system. In particular, we will investigate some of the ways in which shading information can augment stereo data.

1.2. The Motivating Problem

The goal of the $2\frac{1}{2}$-D sketch [see, e.g., 25, 26] is to compute surface parameters, in particular, the distance to and orientation of small patches of the visible surfaces, the discontinuities in those surfaces (e.g., the edges of objects), and possibly the properties of the surface material (e.g., the amount of specularity, the color and the albedo of the surface material). Representations similar to the $2\frac{1}{2}$-D sketch have also been suggested by Horn [18] and Barrow and Tenenbaum [4]. As mentioned, the input to this representation is provided by a number of roughly independent modules, two important ones of which are stereopsis and motion perception. The input provided by these particular modules, which is characteristic of many early visual modules, consists of explicit information about surface shape or disposition only at particular points in the image.

This follows from the form of the primal sketch. Both psychophysical investigations (e.g., [1, 3]) and computational studies (e.g., [33, 13, 15, 24, 27]) and reviews [34, 32] of early visual processing suggest that most of the information in an image is carried by the intensity changes, and hence, that the first stage of analysis of images is the detection of such changes. These changes in intensity are used as input by the modules that feed the $2\frac{1}{2}$-D sketch and hence explicit information is obtained only at those locations. For example, in stereo computations [29, 8, 2, 30] the zero-crossing contours of the primal sketches [27] for the left and right eye are placed in correspondence, and the difference in projection of the corresponding contours in the two eyes is used to determine the depth of the surface along that contour. To create a complete surface representation it is necessary to interpolate between the known values of the raw $2\frac{1}{2}$-D sketch. An initial theory of this process that implicitly takes into account some of the shading information available in the primal sketch has been proposed, implemented, and tested [9, 10]; see also refinements and extensions in [36]. The process briefly can be described in the following manner:

(1) Feature points, generally corresponding to changes in image irradiance at some scale, are extracted from left and right images of a scene. Of the many methods that could be used to perform this task, we choose to locate the zero-crossings of convolution of a Laplacian of a Gaussian ($\nabla^2 G$) filter with the images [27], using several different sizes of $\nabla^2 G$ filters.

(2) These symbolic representations of the changes in the image are matched using a coarse-to-fine strategy, and the image disparity at each such zero-crossing point is recorded [29, 8]. This disparity information can then be converted to actual distance measurements, using a straightforward trigonometric transformation. The result of this stereo matching process is a set of sparse depth values along the zero-crossing contours of the convolved images.

(3) A complete surface representation is constructed from this sparse data, by computing that surface which fits the known depth points and is "most consistent" with the implicit shading information. This implicit information can be informally described as requiring that the reconstructed surface should be such that the application of a $\nabla^2 G$ filter to the corresponding image irradiances would not lead to zero-crossings not already computed in the processing of the original image [12]. It can be shown that formally this corresponds to finding the surface that passes through the known depth points and minimizes a particular functional [9, 10, 11].

This functional can also be derived on physical grounds by modeling the surface as a thin flexible plate forced to pass through the known depth points, and showing that the minimum energy position of the plate is also given by the surface that minimizes the same functional [36, 9, 11]. Several algorithms for constructing this complete surface representation have been implemented and tested [10, 11, 36]. An example is shown in Fig. 1.

While this interpolation or reconstruction theory constructs the "best" surface to fit through the known depth points provided by stereopsis, it is clear that, in principle, supplying additional constraints to the reconstruction process would result in an improved accuracy in the computed surface shape.

An extreme example of this can be seen in Fig. 2, which shows one possible set of depth constraints obtained by stereoscopically viewing a sinusoidal depth grating of a uniform material from a particular viewpoint. The most conservative reconstruction, without explicitly taking the shading information into account, would be the

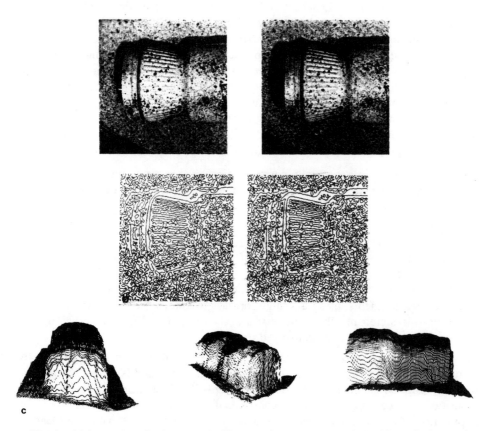

FIG. 1.   (a) is a stereo pair of a scene; (b) illustrates the zero-crossings obtained from the images for one size of $\nabla^2 G$ filter; (c) illustrates a reconstructed surface representation, formed by matching the zero-crossing descriptions, computing the disparity between those points, and then interpolating the results. (Reprinted by permission of the Royal Society of London.)

plane shown in Fig. 2b. On the other hand, if surface orientation information were also available along the depth contours, the more correct reconstruction of Fig. 2c would be obtained. Thus, the motivation is to find algorithms for computing surface orientation at the known depth points provided by stereopsis.

1.3. The Specific Problem

Our basic goal here is to augment the boundary conditions supplied to the previously described reconstruction process. The specific question to be investigated is whether shading information along the zero-crossing contours of the primal sketch can be used to provide information about the surface orientation along those contours. In this paper, we will consider theoretical results concerning the possibility of extracting surface orientation constraints to apply to the reconstruction process, as well as numerical investigations as to the reliability of the resulting computations.

The traditional approach to the shape-from-shading problem, pioneered by Horn [14, 16], has been monocular. The goal has been to extract explicit surface orientation values at each point in the image, from a single view of the scene. As stated, the problem is considerably underconstrained and thus additional information is required in order to obtain the surface orientation information (see, e.g., [22, 7, 6]). For example, it is usually assumed that the direction and strength of the illuminant and the reflective properties of the surface material (which are assumed constant over large sections of the image) are known. One method for obtaining the

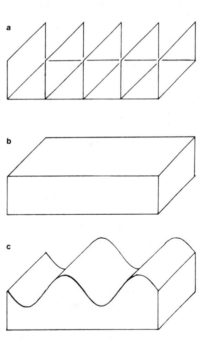

FIG. 2. Part (a) shows an extreme example of a set of depth constraints that could be obtained by stereoscopically viewing a sinusoidal depth grating. If shading information is not explicitly account for, the best surface reconstruction is the plane shown in part (b). On the other hand, if the shading information is used to obtain surface orientation information along the depth contours, the more accurate reconstruction of part (c) is obtained.

additional information necessary to solve for the surface orientation, under these assumptions, is to use the technique of *photometric stereo* [37, 38, 39, 21, 35]. In this case, multiple images obtained from a single viewpoint, but with different illuminant directions, are used to determine the surface orientation at points in the image.

The intention in this paper is to solve (at least partially) the shading problem with fewer requirements or assumptions about the parameters of the imaging process. To do so will require either additional sources of information about shading or weaker expectations on the delivered data, or both. Indeed, since the motivating problem is to obtain additional boundary conditions on the reconstruction process, we will only expect surface orientation information at the zero-crossings, rather than everywhere in the image. We will further only expect a coarse estimate of the surface normal, since the values will serve as boundary conditions for a surface approximation process, rather than constituting an explicit surface reconstruction in itself. Moreover, we will introduce an additional source of information to the process. In particular, we will investigate the added information provided by the differing shading information observed at nearby viewpoints. Hence, we are concerned with *binocular shading*, especially as it applies to the surface reconstruction problem. The main questions to be addressed here are: (1) Using binocular shading, under what conditions can we solve for the surface orientation at the zero-crossing contours that have been matched by stereopsis, and (2) How numerically stable is the resulting process? We will see that the method used to solve for the surface orientation is essentially an alternate form of photometric stereo, using images obtained from different viewpoints, rather than with different illuminants.

Two different aspects of this problem will be addressed in this paper. The first stage considers the problem of determining, from image properties, the values of photometric parameters for a particular class of surface materials under a specific image geometry. The second stage assumes either that this computation has been performed or that the photometric parameters have been provided *a priori* and considers the problem of determing the surface orientation along zero-crossing contours given such photometric information.

2. THE BASIC EQUATIONS

The brightness recorded at a point in an image can generally be considered as a product of three factors, the total amount of incident light striking the surface, the percentage of such incident light which is reflected (as opposed to absorbed or transmitted), usually denoted by the *albedo* ρ of the surface, and the *reflectance* of the surface, the distribution of the reflected light as a function of direction. Here, we shall assume that the intensity of the incident light is normalized by incorporating it into the definition of ρ. As a consequence, the parameter ρ is not restricted to the range 0–1, but rather can take on any positive value.

We will construct three different coordinate systems to represent the geometry of the situation (see Fig. 3). The first system is a world coordinate system, composed of a right-hand coordinate system with origin at the left eye, x axis connecting the two eyes, and the negative z axis pointing straight ahead. The right eye is located along the x axis at a distance o. The two imaging systems are aligned such that their optic axes lie in the x–z plane, and intersect with a vergence angle of θ (see Fig. 3). If we construct local coordinate systems in the two image planes, given by the ordered pairs (u_L, v_L) and (u_R, v_R) for the left and right images, respectively, then simple trigonometry yields the following relationships. A point $(x, y, -z)$ in world coordinates is transformed under orthographic projection to the point $(u_L, v_L) = (x, y)$ in the left image, and to the point $(u_R, v_R) = ((x - o)\cos\theta + z\sin\theta, y)$ in the right image. Thus, for example, if the stereo matching problem has been solved (e.g., [8]), then we know the correspondence between points u_L and u_R and given the parameters θ and o, we can determine the depth of the surface point that projected into u_L and u_R, namely, $-z = u_R\csc\theta + (o - u_L)\cot\theta$.

A surface may be represented in the world coordinate system by a Monge patch. If $\mathbf{i}$, $\mathbf{j}$, and $\mathbf{k}$ denote unit vectors along the coordinate axes, then the surface can be represented by

$$h = x\mathbf{i} + y\mathbf{j} - f(x, y)\mathbf{k}$$

or equivalently in vector notation by

$$(x, y, -f(x, y)).$$

The surface normal at a point can be represented in vector notation by

$$(p, q, 1),$$

where

$$p = \frac{\partial f}{\partial x} \qquad q = \frac{\partial f}{\partial y}.$$

The situation to be investigated here is one in which the illumination geometry consists of an arbitrary surface illuminated by a point source, sufficiently distant

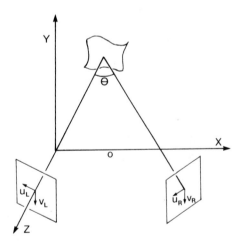

FIG. 3. The geometry of two views of the surface. The x axis connects the two eyes, with the origin at the left eye and an interocular separation of o. The optic axes lie in the x–z plane, and intersect with a vergence angle of θ. The left and right images have local coordinate systems given by (u_L, v_L) and (u_R, v_R), respectively.

from the surface relative to the distance to the viewer. Under most circumstances (e.g., the surface reflectance is isotropic), the reflectance properties of the surface can be combined with the illumination geometry and the viewer position into the convenient representation of a *reflectance map* [17].

For an arbitrary surface, the surface reflectance map will generally be a combination of two effects. The first is a diffuse or matte component, which results from the scattering of light that penetrates some distance into the microstructure of the surface. The second is a specular or luster component, which results from the mirror-like reflection of light at a smooth interface between two materials of different refractive index. These two components can be combined into a single reflectance map in the following manner (see, e.g., [19, 5, 31]).

Let $\mathbf{n}$ denote a unit vector in the direction of the surface normal, defined at a point on the surface, let $\mathbf{s}$ denote a unit vector in the direction of the point light source, and let $\mathbf{v}$ denote a unit view vector. (In general, we will consider objects to be distant relative to the viewer, so that orthographic projection is in effect, and so that $\mathbf{v}$ is essentially constant, and will consider objects also to be distant relative to the light source, so that $\mathbf{s}$ is essentially constant.) Then the recorded brightness at a point is given by

$$\mathscr{E}(x, y) = \rho(x, y) R(\mathbf{n}(x, y))$$

and the reflectance map is given by

$$R(\mathbf{n}) = \left[(1 - \alpha)(\mathbf{n} \cdot \mathbf{s}) + \alpha \{ \mathbf{n} \cdot \mathbf{h} \}^k \right], \tag{1}$$

where $\mathbf{h}$ is a unit vector in the direction of the off specular angle,

$$\mathbf{h} = \frac{(\mathbf{s} + \mathbf{v})}{\sqrt{2} \sqrt{1 + (\mathbf{s} \cdot \mathbf{v})}}.$$

Here, ρ, α, and k are parameters of the particular surface, with ρ and k nonnegative and α ranging between 0 and 1. Note that the above expression explicitly precludes any effects due to diffuse illumination, and assumes that the illuminant can be represented by a point source (or possibly a combination of point sources).

Note that $\mathbf{n}$ is a function of the surface f while $\mathbf{s}$ is a function of the illumination geometry. For our particular choice of world coordinate system, the view vector for the left eye is particularly simple, $\mathbf{v}_L = \{0, 0, 1\}$. Now suppose that we take a second view of the surface, with vergence angle θ (see Fig. 3). Here, the view vector is given, in the world coordinate frame centered at the left eye, by $\mathbf{v}_R = \{-\sin\theta, 0, \cos\theta\}$. Note that the vergence angle θ and the illuminant direction are assumed to be known, so that the vectors $\mathbf{v}_R$ and $\mathbf{s}$ are constants.

The first term in expression (1) corresponds to a matte or Lambertian component of the surface. Since this component depends only on the angle between the light source and the surface normal (and hence is independent of $\mathbf{v}$), it is identical for both views. Thus, no additional information will be obtained from two views in the case of a perfectly matte surface. The second term corresponds to a specular component of the surface, and this term, in general, does change between the two views, as can be seen in the expression (1).

Our intent is to use the two expressions for recorded brightnesses in the two eyes to determine the orientation of the viewed surface at some point. In order to compare irradiance values from the two views, we must be certain that the points in the images at which the irradiance measurements are taken are in correspondence (i.e., we know which points in the two images correspond to the same point on the surface). In the ideal case of isolated intensity edges, matched zero-crossings from a stereo algorithm (e.g., [8]) are in correspondence, so by restricting our attention to such points, we are in principle guaranteed irradiance measurements that correspond to the same point on a physical surface. We should note, however, that in practice, a certain amount of error will be associated with the matched zero-crossings due to uncertainty in exactly localizing the underlying intensity changes. This error will reduce the effectiveness of the computation.

There are two stages to the computation of surface orientation. The first is to compute the surface reflectance parameters ρ, α, and k (in some applications, these might be known *a priori*). Once the reflectance map is known, we must then solve for the surface orientation along the zero-crossing contours, assuming that ρ, α, and k are constant along these contours. More precisely, we solve the following problem. Let the recorded brightnesses in the left and right eyes for the point $(x, y, -f(x, y))$ be

$$\mathscr{E}_L(x, y) = \rho\big[(1 - \alpha)m(x, y) + au^k(x, y)\big]$$
$$\mathscr{E}_R\big((x - o)\cos\theta + f(x, y)\sin\theta, y\big) = \rho\big[(1 - \alpha)m(x, y) + av^k(x, y)\big], \tag{2}$$

respectively, where

$$m = \mathbf{n} \cdot \mathbf{s}$$
$$u = \frac{(\mathbf{s} + \mathbf{v}_L) \cdot \mathbf{n}}{\sqrt{2}\sqrt{1 + \mathbf{s} \cdot \mathbf{v}_L}}$$
$$v = \frac{(\mathbf{s} + \mathbf{v}_R) \cdot \mathbf{n}}{\sqrt{2}\sqrt{1 + \mathbf{s} \cdot \mathbf{v}_R}}.$$

Note that the arguments to $\mathscr{E}_L$ and $\mathscr{E}_R$ simply reflect the difference in projection to the two stereo images, and that given the solution to the stereo correspondence problem, these arguments simply provide an indexing into the two images that ensures the irradiance measurements are taken with respect to the same surface point. The unit surface normal $\mathbf{n}$ is a function of x and y, while the view vectors $\mathbf{v}_L$ and $\mathbf{v}_R$ and the source vector $\mathbf{s}$ are constants of the imaging geometry.

We will consider two separate problems in the following sections. First, we will consider methods for computing the values of the photometric parameters ρ, α, and k over some portion of the image, directly from the image irradiances. Second, given values for these parameters, either by computation or by some other means, we will consider methods for obtaining the surface orientation along zero-crossing contours in this region of the image.

3. SOLVING FOR THE REFLECTANCE PARAMETERS

The task of determining the reflectance parameters would be considerably eased if the surface orientation (p, q) were already known. We thus restrict our attention to situations in which this is true. Consider a point of high curvature along a zero-crossing contour, where the curvature refers to curvature along the contour itself, not curvature on the corresponding surface. In the limiting case, this might correspond to a corner where two zero-crossing contours intersect. The orientation of the contour in the image plane, along either direction of the contour, is different (within the resolution of the image grid). A directional derivative (note that in the case of a discrete image, we will need to use a finite difference approximation to the continuous derivative by measuring the difference between successive values in the appropriate direction in the image, normalized by the distance between those values) taken along one direction of the contour yields a constraint on the relationship between p and q at this point. Since there are two different directions along the contour at such a point, we get two different constraints on the surface orientation, each one corresponding to a straight line in gradient space defining a linear relationship between the values of p and q at the point. The intersection of these two lines uniquely defines the surface orientation at the corner.

We can also perform this computation in a somewhat nonstandard representation, by using unit normals, since Eq. (2) depends only on various unit vectors. We have noted that any surface normal is represented in vector notation by

$$(p, q, 1)$$

and thus the unit normal in this direction is given by

$$\mathbf{n} = \left(\frac{p}{\sqrt{1 + p^2 + q^2}}, \frac{q}{\sqrt{1 + p^2 + q^2}}, \frac{1}{\sqrt{1 + p^2 + q^2}} \right) = (n_1, n_2, n_3).$$

Since there are only two free parameters in specifying a unit normal, we can choose the first two components n_1, n_2 of such a unit normal as defining the vector. Thus, any computations involving (p, q) can be transformed into equivalent computations involving (n_1, n_2). This parameterization can be visualized by considering the orthonormal projection of the Gaussian hemisphere of all visible unit normals onto the plane spanned by the first two components of the unit normal. (Note that this is a one-to-one, onto projection, since we are only interested in the half of the Gaussian sphere composed of the unit normals corresponding to visible surfaces). In this representation, each directional derivative constrains the first two components of the unit normal to lie on a half ellipse in the unit disk. The intersection of two such half ellipses uniquely defines the components of the unit surface normal at the point.

3.1. Using Irradiance Derivatives

We now consider methods for determining the surface reflectance parameters at such a point. Initially we have three unknowns, α, ρ, and k, and only two equations, namely Eqs. (2). To uniquely solve for the unknowns, we will need additional information. One possibility is to consider using derivatives of the image irradiances to solve for the parameters. Taking first directional derivatives (in practice, we will use finite difference approximations) of the irradiance equations introduces three new variables, p_x, $p_y (= q_x)$, and q_y. (Note that q_x is assumed to be equal to p_y, since we shall assume that the surfaces are at least twice continuously differentiable.)

This gives us a total of 8 unknown variables, the three listed, as well as p, q, ρ, α, and k. At a corner (i.e., a point of high curvature), we can compute the values of p and q as indicated previously. Furthermore, second directional derivatives along the depth contour yield two additional linear constraints on p_x, p_y and q_y, so there are only 4 independent variables. We also have four equations, namely:

$$\frac{\partial \mathscr{E}_L}{\partial x} = \rho(1-\alpha)\{m_p p_x + m_q p_y\} + \rho\alpha k u^{k-1}\{u_p p_x + u_q p_y\}$$

$$\frac{\partial \mathscr{E}_L}{\partial y} = \rho(1-\alpha)\{m_p p_y + m_q q_y\} + \rho\alpha k u^{k-1}\{u_p p_y + u_q q_y\}$$

$$\frac{\partial \mathscr{E}_R}{\partial x} = \rho(1-\alpha)\{m_p p_x + m_q p_y\} + \rho\alpha k v^{k-1}\{v_p p_x + v_q p_y\}$$

$$\frac{\partial \mathscr{E}_R}{\partial y} = \rho(1-\alpha)\{m_p p_y + m_q q_y\} + \rho\alpha k v^{k-1}\{v_p p_y + v_q q_y\},$$

where the subscripts L and R denote the left and right images, and the other subscripts denote partial differentiation.

3.2. Solving the Equations

We now seek a closed form solution to this set of equations; that is, we seek expressions for determining ρ, α, and k as functions of the image irradiance derivatives, the illuminant direction, and the vergence angle. While it is possible to obtain such a closed form solution (for completeness, the solution is given in the Appendix), it is not very useful for computational purposes, since it is numerically very sensitive, as discussed below.

3.3. Numerical Stability

While the Appendix describes a solution to the problem of determining the parameters of the surface reflectivity, numerical simulations indicate that the solution is not numerically stable. This is illustrated by the following example, used to determine whether the image values $(\partial/\partial x)(\mathscr{E}_L - \mathscr{E}_R)$ and $(\partial/\partial y)(\mathscr{E}_L - \mathscr{E}_R)$ can be reliably measured from an image. We first note that in order for these expressions to make sense physically, $\mathscr{E}_L$ and $\mathscr{E}_R$ must be measured at image points corresponding to the same surface point, which due to the projection onto the image planes, may not lie at the same image locations. In particular, we use the expression for difference in irradiance given by

$$\mathscr{E}_L(x, y) - \mathscr{E}_R((x - o)\cos\theta + z\sin\theta, y),$$

where $z(x, y)$ is known from the stereo computation. We then examine whether finite difference approximations to directional derivatives of this expression can be measured accurately.

Since a visual system is not a infinite resolution device, it is important to take this into account when simulating the solution to the above equations. In particular, one cannot use analytic expressions for terms such as $(\partial/\partial x)(\mathscr{E}_L - \mathscr{E}_R)$ but rather, one must use finite difference approximations to such differential expressions, in order to reflect the discrete computational structure of the vision system. Moreover, the range of values for $\mathscr{E}_L$ and $\mathscr{E}_R$ should also be discrete, rather than continuous, since any sensor will have a finite resolution of brightness values. These considerations turn out to be critical in evaluating the numerical stability of the computation. In particular, the closed form solution for the reflectance parameters given in the Appendix in principle provides exact values for those parameters, if infinite precision data is available. When discrete approximations are used, however, this exact solution is no longer possible, as is illustrated by the following example:

A synthetically shaded sphere of radius 160 pixels with a total irradiance range of 8 bits (or 256 grey levels) was constructed using Eq. (1) with the parameters $\rho = 256$, $\alpha = 0.8$, and with k varying from 1 to 10. Note that this implies that recorded brightness was descretized to a finite precision, thereby restricting the resolution of measurements of spatial change in the difference between the image brightnesses. The ratio of interocular separation to fixation distance was set at $6:100$.

For each point on the sphere, visible in both images, the finite difference approximation to the partial derivatives of image irradiance were computed, for each of the two views, and the difference in the finite differences for each view were recorded. The total number of points visible to both eyes was counted, and the percentage of such points for which the difference in finite differences exceeded a threshold of 1 grey level, or 1 part in 256, was measured. This percentage was observed to be small, no more than 4%, even for large values of k. This held true over a range of illuminant directions. Some examples are shown in Table 1. (Similar results hold for other values of α.)

This observation suggests that the system of equations listed in the Appendix, while providing a solution in the ideal case, will not provide a numerically stable

TABLE 1

Sensitivity in Computing Derivatives of Image Differences

k	vis	%	k	vis	%
1	99.9	2.27	1	89.7	2.64
2	99.9	0.00	2	89.7	0.08
3	99.9	0.00	3	89.7	0.00
4	99.9	0.00	4	89.7	0.24
5	99.9	1.34	5	89.7	1.77
6	99.9	1.99	6	89.7	2.43
7	99.9	2.33	7	89.7	3.03
8	99.9	2.56	8	89.7	3.42
9	99.9	3.19	9	89.7	3.94
10	99.9	3.67	10	89.7	4.36

Notes. The table lists the percentage of points on the sphere, visible in both eyes, for which the finite difference approximation of the partial derivative of the change in image intensity exceeded a threshold of one part in 256. Here, k denotes the exponent of the specular component, and vis is the percentage of all possible points on the sphere which are visible to both eyes. The first two components of the unit source normal, p_s and q_s, are given by $p_s = 0$, $q_s = 0$ in the left columns, and $p_s = 0.557$, $q_s = 0.239$ in the right, and the vergence angle is $\theta = \tan^{-1}(6/100)$.

solution. One explanation for this can be seen by noting that any partial derivatives of the irradiance equations will involve partial derivatives of the components of the surface normal. Unless the surface has a significant curvature at these points, the partial derivatives of the image irradiances will be small and hence the computation of the surface parameters will be numerically unstable. For example, if a smaller sphere had been used in the above example, the numerical stability of the solution to the reflectance parameters would be improved, since the effective curvature of the sphere would be increased.

While using finite differences in the change in image brightness between the two views did not provide detectable values, it was observed that the simple image differences frequently did. Examples are shown in Table 2. Here, we observe that even for strongly specular surfaces ($k = 10$) the percentage of orientations with a detectable (≥ 1 grey-level) difference in image brightnesses is over 55%. Allowing for image sensor noise (e.g., image differences ≥ 3) still leaves an appreciable percentage of orientations with measurable differences.

This suggests that while we may not be able to reliably measure the spatial derivatives of the difference in image brightness, due to the discrete nature of the sensing of brightness values and the discrete approximations to the spatial derivatives, we may be able to rely on the simple differences in image brightness. We thus turn to the problem of finding a solution for the surface reflectivity parameters from the image brightnesses alone.

TABLE 2

Sensitivity in Computing Image Differences

	$p_s = 0.557$	$q_s = 0.239$		
k	% total	% ≥ 1	% ≥ 2	% ≥ 3
1	96	85	53	25
2	92	91	63	37
3	89	89	62	39
4	89	83	57	38
5	88	77	53	36
6	88	71	49	34
7	88	66	45	32
8	88	62	42	31
9	88	58	40	29
10	88	55	38	28

Notes. The table lists the percentage of points on the sphere, visible in both eyes with a recorded intensity of at least 5 parts in 256, for which the difference in image intensity for the two views exceeded a given threshold. Here, k denotes the exponent of the specular component, $\theta = \tan^{-1}(6/100)$, and $p_s = 0.557$ and $q_s = 0.239$. The first column lists the percentage of points on the sphere which are are visible in both eyes with sufficient brightness. The remaining three columns list the percentage of such points which have an irradiance difference in the two eyes of the amount listed.

4. A SECOND SOLUTION

We first observe that even recording the irradiances at a corner (defined here are a point of high curvature), where the surface orientation is known, is not sufficient to solve the problem, since we have two equations in three unknowns. We thus require an additional source of information and will assume that we know the surface orientation at two distinct points. (We will show later that these could be two nearby corners or simply one corner and a nearby point.)

At each corner, we note that the following expressions hold (where i denotes the image point in question):

$$\alpha_i = \frac{2m_i(\mathscr{E}_L - \mathscr{E}_R)_i}{(\mathscr{E}_L + \mathscr{E}_R)_i(u_i^k - v_i^k) - (\mathscr{E}_L - \mathscr{E}_R)_i(u_i^k + v_i^k - 2m_i)}$$

$$= 1 \bigg/ \left(1 + \frac{(\mathscr{E}_R)_i u_i^k - (\mathscr{E}_L)_i v_i^k}{m_i(\mathscr{E}_L - \mathscr{E}_R)_i}\right),$$

$$\rho_i = \frac{(\mathscr{E}_L + \mathscr{E}_R)_i(u_i^k - v_i^k) - (\mathscr{E}_L - \mathscr{E}_R)_i(u_i^k + v_i^k - 2m_i)}{2m_i(u_i^k - v_i^k)}$$

$$= \frac{(\mathscr{E}_L - \mathscr{E}_R)_i}{u_i^k - v_i^k} \frac{1}{\alpha_i}.$$

This gives us a solution for ρ and α, presuming we know the value of k. To determine k, we assume that the surface reflectivity parameters are constant over the region of the image spanned by the two known points. In this case, $\alpha_1 = \alpha_2$ and $\rho_1 = \rho_2$ and this leads to the following implicit equations for k:

$$\frac{(\mathscr{E}_L - \mathscr{E}_R)_1}{(\mathscr{E}_L - \mathscr{E}_R)_2} = \frac{m_2(u^k\mathscr{E}_L - v^k\mathscr{E}_R)_1}{m_1(u^k\mathscr{E}_L - v^k\mathscr{E}_R)_2}$$

and

$$\frac{(\mathscr{E}_L - \mathscr{E}_R)_1}{(\mathscr{E}_L - \mathscr{E}_R)_2} = \frac{(u^k - v^k)_1}{(u^k - v^k)_2}.$$

Either equation can be solved numerically to determine the value of k and hence of the other reflectivity parameters α and ρ.

4.1. Numerical Stability

While the equations derived in Section 3 were observed to be numerically unstable, the above solution is much more sound. This can be observed by the following simulation. Consider a sphere illuminated by a point source, and observed by two sensors whose angle of vergence is $\theta = \tan^{-1}(6/100)$ (roughly equivalent to a human observer fixating on an object 1 meter removed). The surface of the sphere can be given any surface reflectance properties by specifying the parameters k, ρ, and α. For some set of parameters, we compute the observed brightness value in each sensor to one part in 256. We then apply the equations derived above (assuming initially that the value of k is known) to compute the parameters α and ρ.

The accuracy of the computed values is compared to the original value under a number of situations.

Since a certain amount of error will follow from the truncation of brightness accuracy, we measured the error in computing the parameters as a function of the difference in observed brightness values. It will be noted that we can trade off accuracy of computed parameters with the percentage of orientations for which such a computation can be made (see Table 3). In particular, as we increase the required lower bound on the observed differences in brightness, we decrease the total percentage of orientations for which a computation can be made, but increase the percentage of such points which give rise to computed surface parameters within a particular error range. Table 3 illustrates some examples.

To compute the value of k, we must solve an implicit equation in k. This can be done numerically, for example, by Newton–Raphson. While computer simulations indicate that this computation is very robust in the case of perfect image brightnesses, the computation is much less stable when considering truncated brightness values (i.e., if infinite precision brightness values are used, the computation returns very accurate values for k, but when the finite resolution of the brightness sensor is

TABLE 3

Errors in Computing α and ρ

k	vis	$\rho - 1$	$\rho - 5$	$\rho - 10$	$\alpha - 1$	$\alpha - 5$	$\alpha - 10$
1	25	21.9	52.6	62.0	5.1	17.8	31.0
2	37	69.7	95.8	98.4	6.8	28.5	54.6
3	39	66.3	95.2	99.4	11.9	39.8	66.6
4	38	60.1	93.6	99.0	13.9	44.2	72.0
5	36	57.7	92.2	98.6	13.9	46.1	76.0
6	34	56.4	91.8	98.4	15.2	49.3	78.6
7	32	56.4	91.0	98.2	16.3	52.4	80.3
8	31	55.3	90.6	98.1	15.0	52.7	82.7
9	29	55.4	90.9	98.3	18.3	55.5	84.1
10	28	55.2	90.1	98.0	17.7	56.8	85.0
1	0	0.0	0.0	0.0	0.0	0.0	0.0
2	0	0.0	0.0	0.0	0.0	0.0	0.0
3	2	51.3	98.0	100.0	0.0	0.0	13.3
4	7	73.2	99.0	100.0	20.0	53.7	81.2
5	11	72.5	99.1	100.0	17.1	52.9	86.5
6	13	70.6	98.5	100.0	18.6	57.6	87.9
7	14	71.0	98.8	100.0	19.4	61.8	90.1
8	14	69.6	98.6	100.0	16.7	61.3	92.7
9	14	69.9	98.4	100.0	22.6	64.7	92.7
10	14	70.0	98.5	100.0	21.2	66.2	94.7

Notes. The following parameters are defined: vis is the percentage of viewed orientations on a sphere for which the difference in observed brightnesses exceeds some threshold; $\alpha - \epsilon$ is the percentage of vis which lie within a range $\pm\epsilon\%$ of the correct value of α; $\rho - \epsilon$ is the percentage of vis which lie within a range $\pm\epsilon\%$ of the correct value of ρ; ϵ is the percentage error bar allowed about the correct value. In the case, the illuminant direction is given by $p_s = 0.557$, $q_s = 0.239$. In the first table, the threshold of image differences was set at 3, in the second table, the threshold was 5.

TABLE 4

Errors in Computing k

	1	3	5	10
1%	2.7	2.7	2.8	4.3
5%	14.8	15.6	16.2	18.6
10%	27.8	30.6	29.7	35.3
20%	47.2	50.7	54.6	65.3
30%	62.6	65.9	73.6	84.5
40%	69.3	77.4	83.9	94.7
50%	75.0	85.4	92.0	98.5

Notes. Two different orientations were chosen at random, such that the difference in brightness values at each point exceeded a threshold of 3 grey levels. The percentage of such pairs of points with percentage error in computing k within the given range are indicated. In the case illustrated below, the illuminant direction was given by $p_s = 0.557$, $q_s = 0.239$, with $\rho = 256$, $\alpha = 0.5$, and $k = 5$. The percentages are shown for the case of sampling 1, 3, 5, and 10 pairs, and averaging the results.

taken into account, the accuracy of the computation drops off quickly). Table 4 indicates an example of the error associated with computing k numerically. This table was computed by choosing two surface orientations at random, such that the difference in brightness exceeds a threshold of 3 grey levels, and solving the implicit equation for k by a Newton–Raphson method.

One possible method for improving the accuracy of computing not only k, but also ρ and α, is to consider the reflective properties of the surface to be constant over some extended region of the image. In this case, a number of points may be sampled, and the computed values for the parameters averaged. Table 4 illustrates the reduction in error associated with computing k.

5. ERROR ANALYSIS

As well as performing simulations of the computation of surface parameters, we can also make an estimate of the error associated with computing the parameters. This analysis will also indicate a means for determining those situations in which the error is small.

We again consider the situation in which the parameter k is known exactly, as well as the values of p and q and hence of m, u, and v. We let

$$\alpha_m = \text{measured value for } \alpha$$

$$\rho_m = \text{measured value for } \rho$$

$$\alpha_0 = \text{actual value for } \alpha$$

$$\rho_0 = \text{actual value for } \rho$$

$$\delta_L = \text{error in } \mathscr{E}_L$$

$$\delta_R = \text{error in } \mathscr{E}_R.$$

The goal is to determine estimates for the ratio of the measured values to the actual values, that is, to derive expressions for

$$\epsilon_\alpha = \frac{\alpha_m}{\alpha_0}$$

$$\epsilon_\rho = \frac{\rho_m}{\rho_0}.$$

By expansion, we obtain the following expression:

$$\rho_m = \left(\frac{\mathscr{E}_L - \mathscr{E}_R + \delta_L - \delta_R}{u^k - v^k} \right) \frac{1}{\alpha_m}$$

$$= \left(1 + \frac{\delta_L - \delta_R}{\mathscr{E}_L - \mathscr{E}_R} \right) \frac{\rho_0}{\epsilon_\alpha}.$$

Thus,

$$\epsilon_\rho = \left(1 + \frac{\delta_L - \delta_R}{\mathscr{E}_L - \mathscr{E}_R} \right) \frac{1}{\epsilon_\alpha}.$$

Similarly,

$$\alpha_m = \frac{m(\mathscr{E}_L - \mathscr{E}_R + \delta_L - \delta_R)}{(u^k - m)(\mathscr{E}_R + \delta_R) - (v^k - m)(\mathscr{E}_L + \delta_L)}$$

$$= \alpha_0 \left(1 + \frac{\delta_L - \delta_R}{\mathscr{E}_L - \mathscr{E}_R} \right) \left(1 - \frac{(u^k - m)\delta_R - (v^k - m)\delta_L}{(u^k - m)(\mathscr{E}_R + \delta_R) - (v^k - m)(\mathscr{E}_L + \delta_L)} \right)$$

so that

$$\epsilon_\alpha = \left(1 + \frac{\delta_L - \delta_R}{\mathscr{E}_L - \mathscr{E}_R} \right) \left(1 - \frac{(u^k - m)\delta_R - (v^k - m)\delta_L}{(u^k - m)(\mathscr{E}_R + \delta_R) - (v^k - m)(\mathscr{E}_L + \delta_L)} \right).$$

The goal is to determine what circumstances will result in small errors in the computed parameters (i.e., under what conditions will $\epsilon_\rho \approx 1$ and $\epsilon_\alpha \approx 1$).

Algebraic substitution yields the following alternative forms:

$$\epsilon_\rho = 1 + \frac{\delta_L - \delta_R}{\mathscr{E}_L - \mathscr{E}_R} + \frac{1}{\rho} \frac{\delta_R \mathscr{E}_L - \delta_L \mathscr{E}_R}{m(\mathscr{E}_L - \mathscr{E}_R)}$$

$$\epsilon_\alpha = \left(1 + \frac{\delta_L - \delta_R}{\mathscr{E}_L - \mathscr{E}_R} \right) \left(1 - \frac{\delta_L - \delta_R + \dfrac{1}{\rho m}(\mathscr{E}_L \delta_R - \mathscr{E}_R \delta_L)}{\mathscr{E}_L - \mathscr{E}_R + \delta_L - \delta_R + \dfrac{1}{\rho m}(\mathscr{E}_L \delta_R - \mathscr{E}_R \delta_L)} \right).$$

If $|\mathscr{E}_L - \mathscr{E}_R|$ is not significantly greater than $|\delta_L - \delta_R|$, then the first terms in each of the error expressions will be significant, and the error will be large. Thus, we need to restrict our attention to circumstances in which this is not true. In general, $|\delta_L - \delta_R|$ will be no more than 1, so we restrict our attention to portions of the image in which $|\mathscr{E}_L - \mathscr{E}_R|$ is larger than some threshold, in order to reduce the probable error in our estimation of the surface reflectivity parameters. Furthermore, if $|\delta_L|$ and $|\delta_R|$ are also small (< 1) then a case examination shows that the second terms in error expressions are also negligible.

6. DISCUSSION

We note that it is possible to solve for the reflectivity parameters without requiring two corners. Suppose instead that we have one corner, and that the surface is at least twice continuously differentiable. Then by noting that integration of surface orientation around a closed loop must yield zero (note that a similar constraint has been used by Ikeuchi and Horn [22]) we can determine the surface orientation at a second point, and the analysis of Section 4 still holds.

We also note that the numerical properties of the algorithm sketched here probably preclude its use by the human visual system. In particular, to have reasonable numerical stability over a large range of surface orientations, a large vergence angle is required (on the order of 3°). For the human system, this is roughly equivalent to viewing objects from a distance of 1 meter or less. In cases of machine vision, where control of the positioning of the sensors is possible (i.e., we are not restricted to interocular separations of 6 cm) large vergence angles are more feasible.

7. SOLVING FOR THE SURFACE ORIENTATION

In the first portion of this paper, we have investigated methods for computing the photometric parameters of a class of surface materials, directly from the image irradiance information. Assuming that this information is available, either by such a technique or by more direct methods, Horn's reflectance map can be computed [17, 19, 20]. We now turn to the second question posed in the introduction, namely, can we use this information, and the difference in observed brightness in the two images at points corresponding to the same surface location, to compute the surface orientation along the matched zero-crossing contours of the stereo algorithm.

The algorithm described below is essentially a simple modification of the photometric stereo algorithm [37, 38, 39, 21, 35]. It can be sketched as follows:

(1) Compute the reflectance map [17, 19, 20] associated with the computed values of ρ, α, and k. Since R is a function of the unit surface normal, it can be calculated over the unit disk, with coordinate axis given by the first and second components of the unit normal. Examples of isobrightness contours for several reflectance maps are shown in Fig. 4.

(2) Use the measured value of $\mathscr{E}_L$ at a point in the left image to determine a contour of isobrightness in the unit disk. This defines the set of possible surface orientations, which are consistent with the value of $\mathscr{E}_L$.

(3) Use the measured value of $\mathscr{E}_R$ at the point in the right image corresponding to the same surface point in the scene to determine a second contour of isobrightness in the unit disk. The intersections of the two contours define possible surface orientations. Note that in general there will be at least two such points of intersection.

(4) We can disambiguate the possible orientations by applying a third constraint. Take a directional derivative of depth along the contour through the point. This will yield a linear constraint between p and q. When translated to the unit disk (and a constraint between the components of the unit surface normal), this constraint becomes a half ellipse in the unit disk. The intersection of this curve with the two isobrightness contours defines the correct surface orientation for the point in question. (See Fig. 5 for an example.)

Standard algorithms for solving photometric stereo already exist, usually involving a lookup table scheme (see, e.g., [21, 35, 37, 38]). The above modification is straightforward to implement in such schemes.

7.1. Uniqueness of the Solution

The key question still to be considered is whether this algorithm results in a unique solution. We first observe that the isobrightness contours for either a matte or a specular surface consist of a series of nested ellipses or half-ellipses. In particular, for a given value $R(\mathbf{n}) = c$, the ellipse has center in the unit disk of (cp_s, cq_s), where p_s and q_s are the first and second components of the unit source vector s. The minor axis of the ellipse is oriented along the line from the origin to the projection of s and the major axis is perpendicular to it.

While it is possible to derive this analytically, it more easily observed by noting that for a Lambertian coated sphere, with source located along the same direction as the viewer, the isobrightness contours are nested circles. For an off-axis light source, the corresponding isobrightness contours can be obtained by rotating the sphere relative to the viewer, and then projecting the previous isobrightness contours onto

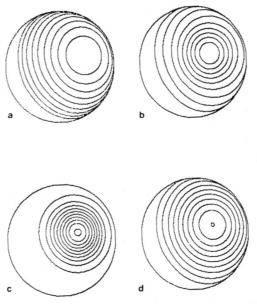

FIG. 4. Examples of isobrightness contours on the unit disk, for different reflectance maps. In all four cases, $p_s = 0.7$, $q_s = 0.3$. For cases (a), (b), and (c), the exponent $k = 10$, and the parameter α is 0.1, 0.5, and 0.9, respectively. In case (d), the exponent is $k = 5$ and $\alpha = 0.5$.

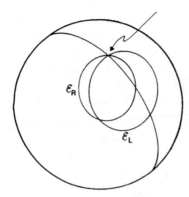

FIG. 5. An example of the modified photometric stereo algorithm. The values of the image irradiance recorded at points in the left and right images corresponding to the same surface point $(\mathcal{E}_L, \mathcal{E}_R)$ constrain the unit surface normal at that point to lie on two different isobrightness contours in the unit disk. The component of the surface normal along the zero-crossing contour further constrains the unit surface normal to lie on a half-ellipse in the unit disk. The intersection of these constraints determines the unit surface normal at that point.

the unit disk, clearly resulting in a series of nested ellipses. A similar argument holds for the isobrightness contours of a purely specular surface.

When considering a convex combination of two such reflectance maps, the isobrightness contours become somewhat more complex. In general, however, the contours are slightly distorted ellipses (see Fig. 4). As a consequence, the intersection of isobrightness contours from the two eyes will in general result in a pair of points in the unit disk. (This excludes the degenerate case of a pure matte surface, in which case the intersection will be a complete ellipse.) We must now determine the circumstances under which the third constraint will disambiguate this pair of points.

Suppose that the zero-crossing contour at the point of interest has a tangent in the image plane whose angle with respect to the x axis is γ, and whose derivative of depth along the contour is given by the value d. This derivative determines the component of the surface normal along the contour. When translated into a constraint on the components of the unit surface normal, the set of possible unit normals which are consistent with such a component along the contour are given by the parametric equations (assuming γ is nonzero)

$$\mathbf{n}_1(t) = \frac{t \sin \gamma}{\left(\sin^2 \gamma + d^2 - 2dt \cos \gamma + t^2\right)^{1/2}}$$

$$\mathbf{n}_2(t) = \frac{d - t \cos \gamma}{\left(\sin^2 \gamma + d^2 - 2dt \cos \gamma + t^2\right)^{1/2}}.$$

These parametric equations define a half ellipse in the unit disk with center at the origin and with major axis the line through the origin with slope $-\cot \gamma$ of length 2. If γ is positive, the half ellipse is that which connects the two endpoints of the major axis and whose half of the minor axis lies the positive $\mathbf{n}_2$ half disk, if γ is negative, the half ellipse lies with its half of the minor axis in the negative $\mathbf{n}_2$ half disk (see Fig. 6).

We wish to determine the conditions in which there is *not* a unique solution, which corresponds to determining the conditions under which the half ellipse constraint passes through both points arising from the intersection of the isobrightness contours. Note that the family of all possible depth constraints can be represented by the pairs (γ, b) where γ ranges from $-\pi$ to π and b is the length of the minor axis of the half ellipse. Consider a point (p_0, q_0) lying in the unit disk. Let

$$\xi = \text{sgn}(q_0)\tan^{-1}\frac{q_0}{p_0}.$$

Then the valid range of possible γ is from $\xi - \pi/2$ to $\xi + \pi/2$, modulo 2π. Thus, the set of possible depth constraints which pass through this point can be specified by the graph given in Fig. 7, which has a range of π in γ and a maximum in b of $\sqrt{p_0^2 + q_0^2}$. For a second, distinct point in the unit disk, a similar mapping is obtained, which intersects the first at exactly one point. This implies that there is exactly one ellipse, with orientation and eccentricity given by this intersection, which passes through both points in the unit disk. This in turn implies that the depth constraint will almost always uniquely specify the surface orientation of the zero-crossing point, since only a particular alignment of the light source and the depth contour will result in an ambiguity, and in general, the physical processes which give rise to the depth contour constraint are independent of the light source. In the case of continuous value range for γ and d, the set of conditions in which a unique answer is not possible will, in fact, have measure zero. In the more practical case of a discrete range of values for γ and d, assume that the orientation γ can take on one of n different values, while the component of the depth gradient along the contour d can take on one of m different values. Then assuming that the possible values for γ and d are uniformly distributed, and assuming that the constraints due to the reflectance map isobrightness contours are independent of the constraint due to the

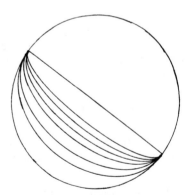

FIG. 6.   Constraints on the unit surface normal, as a function of the component of the surface gradient along a contour. Each contour delineates the possible values of the unit surface normal, for a different value of the surface gradient along the zero-crossing contour. In each of the contours illustrated here, the parameter γ was negative. The straight line corresponds to the case in which the depth derivative along the zero-crossing contour was zero.

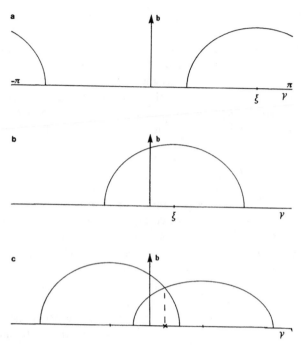

FIG. 7.   Determining the uniqueness of the solution. Parts (a) and (b) represent constraints between the parameters b and γ, for different values of ξ. When a second point is added (c), the intersection of the two contours defines the only possible half ellipse in the unit disk which passes through both points in the unit disk and has appropriate major and minor axes. Thus, given two isobrightness contours in the unit disk, from the two views of a point on a zero-crossing contour, there is exactly one depth constraint which will not disambiguate these points.

depth derivative implies that the probability of an ambiguous computation of surface orientation is $1/mn$. Clearly, if we have a reasonable resolution for γ and d, this probability will be very small.

8. SUMMARY

We have demonstrated that shading information can be combined with stereo data along feature point contours in order to determine the surface orientation along those contours, under the following conditions.

(1) The surface is illuminated by a distant point source, whose direction relative to the viewer is known.

(2) The surface is viewed from two different positions, and the angle of vergence of the two views is known. For numerical stability, this angle should be on the order of 3 degrees of larger.

(3) The surface is at least twice continuously differentiable.

(4) The reflectance map of the surface can be represented in the form

$$R(\mathbf{n}) = \left[(1 - \alpha)(\mathbf{n} \cdot \mathbf{s}) + \alpha \{ \mathbf{n} \cdot \mathbf{h} \}^{k} \right],$$

where **s** is a unit vector in the direction of the light source, **h** is a unit vector in the direction of the off specular angle,

$$\mathbf{h} = \frac{(\mathbf{s} + \mathbf{v})}{\sqrt{2}\sqrt{1 + (\mathbf{s} \cdot \mathbf{v})}}$$

and **n** is a unit surface normal. The variables α, ρ, and k are unknown, and are to be computed from the irradiance data. It is assumed that α is nonzero, so that the surface is not perfectly matte.

Under these conditions, we have shown that using the brightness values recorded at corresponding points in the two images (determined by the stereo correspondences) we can compute the reflectivity parameters for the surface, and using in addition the component of the surface gradient along the stereo contour, we can apply an algorithm similar to photometric stereo to compute the surface orientation along the stereo contours.

The numerical stability of the computation was also explored and methods for reducing the possible error in the computation were suggested. The key observation concerning the computation was that while accurate solutions were possible given high resolution input (e.g., the image brightnesses were known to extremely high accuracy), when the discrete nature of the brightness sensitivity and spatial sensitivity of the imaging devices was taken into account, the numerical stability of the computations degraded rapidly. This suggests that in its current form, computations such as those outlined here may be of limited practical use, until methods for improving the numerical stability are derived.

APPENDIX

The solution for the reflectivity parameters, using derivatives of the image irradiances is summarized as follows: The solution to k is given by

$$k = 1 + \frac{\ln\left\{(a_2 + m_p a_3)u_q - (a_1 + m_q a_3)u_p\right\} - \ln\left\{(a_2 - m_p a_3)v_q - (a_1 - m_q a_3)v_p\right\}}{\ln v - \ln u};$$

the albedo ρ is given by

$$2\rho = \left(\frac{\Phi}{\Theta}\right)\frac{\Theta(\Sigma_x + \Sigma_y) - [\mu C + \omega D]\Phi - [(1 - \nu)C + (1 - \xi)D]\Psi}{(\mu m_p + \omega m_q)\Phi + [(1 - \nu)m_p + (1 - \xi)m_q]\Psi};$$

and the specular scalar α is given by

$$\alpha = \frac{1}{\rho}\frac{\Phi}{\Theta},$$

where

$$a_1 = \mu m_p(\Delta_x \Sigma_y - \Delta_y \Sigma_x) + m_q(\mu\Delta_y\Sigma_y - \omega\Delta_x\Sigma_x) + \Delta_y\Sigma_x m_q(\mu\xi - \omega\nu)$$

$$a_2 = \omega m_q(\Delta_x \Sigma_y - \Delta_y \Sigma_x) + m_p(\mu\Delta_y\Sigma_y - \omega\Delta_x\Sigma_x) + \Delta_x\Sigma_y m_p(\mu\xi - \omega\nu)$$

$$a_3 = \omega\Delta_x^2 + (\omega\nu - \mu\xi)\Delta_x\Delta_y - \mu\Delta_y^2,$$

where

$$\Phi = \left(\Delta_x + \nu\Delta_y\right)A - \left(\Delta_y + \xi\Delta_x\right)B$$

$$\Psi = \mu A\Delta_y - \omega B\Delta_x$$

$$\Theta = \mu A^2 + \left(\omega\nu - \mu\xi\right)AB - \omega B^2$$

and where

$$\Delta_x = \frac{\partial \mathscr{E}_L}{\partial x} - \frac{\partial \mathscr{E}_R}{\partial x}$$

$$\Delta_y = \frac{\partial \mathscr{E}_L}{\partial y} - \frac{\partial \mathscr{E}_R}{\partial y}$$

$$\Sigma_x = \frac{\partial \mathscr{E}_L}{\partial x} + \frac{\partial \mathscr{E}_R}{\partial x}$$

$$\Sigma_y = \frac{\partial \mathscr{E}_L}{\partial y} + \frac{\partial \mathscr{E}_R}{\partial y}$$

$$A = k\left(u_p u^{k-1} - v_p v^{k-1}\right)$$

$$B = k\left(u_q u^{k-1} - v_q v^{k-1}\right)$$

$$C = k\left(u_p u^{k-1} + v_p v^{k-1}\right) - 2m_p$$

$$D = k\left(u_q u^{k-1} + v_q v^{k-1}\right) - 2m_q,$$

and where the second directional derivatives along the two directions of the zero-crossing contour, whose values are d_1 and d_2 with associated directions γ_1 and γ_2, determine the constants

$$\mu = \frac{d_1 \sin^2\gamma_2 - d_2 \sin^2\gamma_1}{\sin(\gamma_1 + \gamma_2)\sin(\gamma_2 - \gamma_1)}$$

$$\omega = \frac{d_s \cos^2\gamma_1 - d_1 \cos^2\gamma_2}{\sin(\gamma_1 + \gamma_2)\sin(\gamma_2 - \gamma_1)}$$

$$\nu = \frac{2\sin\gamma_1 \sin\gamma_2}{\sin(\gamma_1 + \gamma_2)}$$

$$\xi = \frac{2\cos\gamma_1 \cos\gamma_2}{\sin(\gamma_1 + \gamma_2)}.$$

Finally, the surface orientation at this point is given by the three parameters

$$f_{xy} = \frac{\Delta_y \mu A - \Delta_x \omega B}{\left(\Delta_x + \nu\Delta_y\right)A - \left(\Delta_y + \xi\Delta_x\right)B}$$

$$f_{xx} = \mu - \nu f_{xy}$$

$$f_{yy} = \omega - \xi f_{xy}.$$

Discussion of the Equations

Several comments on the form and derivation of the equations are appropriate. First, we note that in deriving the above expression for α, the form obtained is valid only in the case of both $\Delta_x + \Delta_y$ and $\Delta_x - \Delta_y$ nonzero. This provides an interesting side effect, since these expressions both vanish if and only if the surface material has only a matte component, and no (measurable) specular component, or the surface is a plane. If the surface material has no specular component, $\alpha = 0$ and this is exactly the expression obtained by substitution of $\Delta_x = 0$ and $\Delta_y = 0$ into the expression obtained for α.

Second, we note that, subject to possible numerical errors, the solution for the surface reflectance parameters is unique.

Third, we note that it is important to consider the measurability of the image knowns. In other words, can we extract the required measurements for the images in a reliable manner? We first note that the zero-crossing contours, along which the stereo depth information is known, will frequently outline discontinuities in the surface or in the surface material, for example, occluding edges of objects or changes in surface albedo. Since we cannot measure infinitesimal derivatives in the image, does this preclude our ability to measure derivatives of the images? The answer is no, since we can again rely on directional derivatives. For example, we need to measure $(\partial/\partial x)(\mathscr{E}_L - \mathscr{E}_R)$ and $(\partial/\partial y)(\mathscr{E}_L - \mathscr{E}_R)$. This can be done without crossing a discontinuity in the image irradiances by considering the two directional derivatives along the contour obtained at a corner in the zero-crossing contour. At this point, we have two different directional derivatives, and simple algebra allows us to then determine the parametric partial derivatives.

ACKNOWLEDGMENTS

The author wishes to express his gratitude to Tomaso Poggio, Tomás Lozano-Pérez, Berthold Horn, and Ellen Hildreth for many useful comments and discussions.

This report describes research done at the Artificial Intelligence Laboratory of the Massachusetts Institute of Technology. Support for the laboratory's artificial intelligence research is provided in part by the Advanced Research Projects Agency of the Department of Defense under Office of Naval Research contract N00014-80-C-0505 and in part by National Science Foundation Grant 79-23110MCS.

REFERENCES

1. F. Attneave, Informational aspects of visual perception, *Psychol. Rev.* **61**, 1954, 183–193.
2. H. H. Baker and T. O. Binford, Depth from edge and intensity based stereo, *Seventh Internat. Joint Conf. on Artificial Intelligence, 1981*, pp. 631–636.
3. H. B. Barlow, Three points about lateral inhibition, in *Sensory Communication* (W. A. Rosenblith, Ed., pp. 217–234; 782–786, MIT Press, Cambrridge, Mass., 1961.
4. H. G. Barrow and J. M. Tenenbaum, Recovering intrinsic scene characteristics from images, in *Computer Vision Systems* (E. Riseman and A. Hanson, Eds.), Academic Press, New York, 1979.
5. J. F. Blinn, Models of light reflection for computer synthesized pictures, *Comput. Graphics (SIGGRAPH)* **11**, (2), 1977, 192–198.
6. M. J. Brooks, *Shape from Shading Discretely*, Ph. D. thesis, University of Essex, 1982.
7. A. R. Bruss, *The Image Irradiance Equation: Its Solution and Application*, MIT Artificial Intelligence Laboratory Technical Report No. 623, 1981.
8. W. E. L. Grimson, A computer implementation of a theory of human stereo vision, *Philos. Trans. Roy. Soc. London Ser. B* **292**, 1981, 217–253.

9. W. E. L. Grimson, A computational theory of visual surface interpolation, *Philos. Trans. Roy. Soc. London Ser. B* **298**, 1982a, 395–427.

10. W. E. L. Grimson, An implementation of a computational theory of visual surface interpolation, *Comput. Graphics Image Process.* **22**, 1983, 39–69.

11. W. E. L. Grimson, *From Images to Surfaces: A Computational Study of the Human Early Visual System*, MIT Press, Cambridge, Mass., 1982c.

12. W. E. L. Grimson, Surface consistency constraints in vision, *Comput. Vision, Graphics Image Process.* **24**, 1983, 28–51.

13. A. Herskovitz and T. O. Binford, *On Boundary Detection*, MIT Artificial Intelligence Laboratory Memo No. 183, 1970.

14. B. K. P. Horn, *Shape from Shading: A Method for Obtaining the Shape of a Smooth Opaque Object from One View*, MIT Project MAC Technical Report No. MAC TR-79, 1970.

15. B. K. P. Horn, *The Binford–Horn Line Finder*, MIT Artificial Intelligence Memo No. 285, 1973.

16. B. K. P. Horn, Obtaining shape from shading information, in *The Psychology of Computer Vision* (P. H. Winston, Ed., pp. 115–155, McGraw–Hill, New York, 1975.

17. B. K. P. Horn, Understanding image intensities, *Artificial Intelligence* **8** (11), 1977, 201–231.

18. B. K. P. Horn, *Sequins and Quills—Representations for Surface Topography*, MIT Artificial Intelligence Memo No. 536, 1979.

19. B. K. P. Horn, Hill shading and the reflectance map, *Proc. IEEE* **69** (1), 1981, 14–47.

20. B. K. P. Horn and R. W. Sjoberg, Calculating the reflectance map, *Appl. Opt.* **18** (11), 1979, 1770–1779.

21. K. Ikeuchi and B. K. P. Horn, An application of photometric stereo, *Sixth Internat. Joint Conf. on Artificial Intelligence, 1979*, pp. 413–415.

22. K. Ikeuchi and B. K. P. Horn, Numerical shape from shading and occluding boundaries, *Artificial Intelligence* **17**, 1981, 141–184.

23. A. L. Kidd, J. P. Frisby, and J. E. W. Mayhew, Texture contours can facilitate stereopsis by initiating appropriate vergence eye movements, *Nature* **280**, 1979, 829–832.

24. D. Marr, Early processing of visual information, *Philos. Trans. Roy. Soc. London Ser. A* **275** (942), 1976, 483–534.

25. D. Marr, Representing visual information, in *AAS 143rd Annual Meeting, Symposium on Some Mathematical Question in Biology, February, 1977*, pp. 101–180, *Lectures in the Life Sciences*, No. 10, 1978.

26. D. Marr, *Vision: A Computational Investigation in the Human Representation and Processing of Visual Information*, Freeman, San Francisco, 1982.

27. D. Marr, and E. C. Hildreth, Theory of edge detection, *Proc. Roy. Soc. London Ser B* **207**, 1980, 187–217.

28. D. Marr and T. Poggio, From understanding computation to understanding neural circuitry, *Neurosci. Res. Program Bull.* **15**, 1977, 470–488.

29. D. Marr and T. Poggio, A theory of human stereo vision, *Proc. Roy. Soc. London Ser. B* **204**, 1979, 301–328.

30. J. F. W. Mayhew and J. P. Frisby, Psychophysical and computational studies towards a theory of human stereopsis, *Artificial Intelligence* **17**, 1981, 349–385.

31. B. T. Phong, Illumination for computer generated pictures, *Comm. ACM* **18**, (6), 1975, 311–317.

32. W. Pratt, *Digital Image Processing*, Wiley, New York, 1978.

33. L. G. Roberts, Machine perception of three-dimensional solids, in *Optical and Electro-Optical Information Processing* (Tippett *et al.*, Eds.), pp. 159–197, MIT Press, Cambridge, Mass., 1965.

34. A. Rosenfeld and A. Kak, *Digital Picture Processing*, Academic Press, New York, 1976.

35. W. Silver, *Determining Shape and Reflectance Using Multiple Images*, M.S. thesis, Dept. of Electrical Engineering and Computer Science, MIT, 1980.

36. D. Terzopoulos, Multilevel computational processes for visual surface reconstruction, *Comput. Vision Graphics Image Process.* **24**, 1983, 52–96.

37. R. J. Woodham, Photometric stereo: A reflectance map technique for determining surface orientation from image intensity, in *Image Understanding Systems and Industrial Applications, Proc. S.P.I.E.* **155**, 1978.

38. R. J. Woodham, Photometric method for determining surface orientation from multiple images, *Opt. Eng.* **19** (1), 1980, 139–144.

39. R. J. Woodham, Analysing images of curved surfaces, *Artificial Intelligence* **17**, 1981, 117–140.

Stereo Integral Equation

Grahame B. Smith

Artificial Intelligence Center,
SRI International
Menlo Park, California 94025

Abstract

A new approach to the formulation and solution of the problem of recovering scene topography from a stereo image pair is presented. The approach circumvents the need to solve the correspondence problem, returning a solution that makes surface interpolation unnecessary. The methodology demonstrates a way of handling image analysis problems that differs from the usual linear-system approach. We exploit the use of nonlinear functions of local image measurements to constrain and infer global solutions that must be consistent with such measurements. Because the solution techniques we present entail certain computational difficulties, significant work still lies ahead before they can be routinely applied to image analysis tasks.

1   Introduction

The recovery of scene topography from a stereo pair of images has typically proceeded by three, quasi-independent steps. In the first step, the relative orientation of the two images is determined. This is generally achieved by selecting a few scene features in one image and finding their counterparts in the other image. From the position of these features, we calculate the parameters of the transformation that would map the feature points in one image into their corresponding points in the other image. Once we have the relative orientation of the two images, we have constrained the position of corresponding image points to lie along lines in their respective images. Now we commence the second phase in the recovery of scene topography, namely, determining a large number of corresponding points. The purpose of the first step is to reduce the difficulty involved in finding this large set of corresponding points.

Because we have the relative orientation of the two images, we only have to make a one-dimensional search (along the epipolar lines) to find points in the two images that correspond to the same scene feature. This step, usually called solving the "correspondence" problem, has received much attention. Finding many corresponding points in stereo pairs of images is difficult. Irrespective of whether the technique employed is area-based correlation or that of edge-based matching, the resultant set of corresponding points is usually small, compared with the number of pixels in the image. The solution to the correspondence problem, therefore, is not a dense set of points over the two images but rather a sparse set. Solution of the correspondence problem is made more difficult in areas of the scene that are relatively featureless or when there is much repeated structure, constituting

The work reported here was supported by the Defense Advanced Research Projects Agency under Contracts MDA903-83-C-0027 and DACA76-85-C-0004.

local ambiguity. To generate the missing intermediate data, the third step of the process is one of surface interpolation.

Scene depth at corresponding points is calculated by simple triangulation; this gives a representation in which scene depth values are known for some set of image plane points. To fill this out and to obtain a dense set of points at which scene depth is known, an interpolation procedure is employed. Of late there has been significant interest in this problem and various techniques that use assumptions about the surface properties of the world have been demonstrated [1, 3, 5, 8]. Such techniques, despite some difficulties, have made it possible to reconstruct credible scene topography.

Of the three steps outlined, the initial one of finding the relative orientation of the two images is really a procedure designed to simplify the second step, namely, finding a set of matched points. We can identify several aspects of these first two steps that suggest the need for an alternative view of the processes entailed in reconstructing scene topography from stereo image pairs.

The techniques employed to solve the correspondence problem are usually local processes. When a certain feature is found in one image, an attempt is made to find the corresponding point in the other image by searching for it within a limited region of that image. This limit is imposed not just to reduce computational costs, but to restrict the number of comparisons so that false matches can be avoided. Without such a limit many points may "match" the feature selected. Ambiguity cannot be resolved by a local process; some form of global postmatching process is required. The difficulties encountered in featureless areas and where repeated structure exists are those we bring upon ourselves by taking too local a view.

In part, the difficulties of matching even distinct features are self-imposed by our failure to build into the matching procedure the shape of the surface on which the feature lies. That is, when we are doing the matching we usually assume that a feature lies on a surface patch that is orthogonal to the line of sight – and it is only at some later stage that we calculate the true slope of the surface patch. Even when we try various slopes for the surface patch during the matching procedure, we rarely return after the surface shape has been estimated to determine whether that calculated shape is consistent with the best slope actually found in matching.

In the formulation presented in the following sections, the problem is deliberately couched in a form that allows us to ask the question: what is the shape of the surface in the world that can account for the two image irradiances we see when we view that surface from the two positions represented by the stereo pair? We make no assumptions about the surface shape to do the matching – in fact, we do not do any matching at all. What we are interested in is recovering the surface that explains simultaneously all the parts of the irradiance pattern that are depicted in the stereo pair of images. We seek the solution that is globally consistent and is not confused by local ambiguity.

In the conventional approach to stereo reconstruction, the final step involves some form of surface interpolation. This is necessary because the previous step – finding the corresponding points – could not perform well enough to obviate the need to fabricate data at intermediate points. Surface interpolation techniques employ a model of the expected surface to fill in between known values. Of course, these known data points are used to calculate the parameters of the models, but it does seem a pity that the image data encoding the variation of the surface between the known points are ignored in this process and replaced by assumptions about the expected surface.

In the following formulation we eliminate the interpolation step by recovering depth values at all the image pixels. In this sense, the image data, rather than knowledge of the expected surface shape, guide the recovery algorithm.

We previously presented a formulation of the stereo reconstruction problem in which we sought to skirt the correspondence problem and in which we recovered a dense set of depth values [6]. That approach took a pair of image irradiance profiles, one from the left image and its counterpart from the right image, and employed an integration procedure to recover the scene depth from what amounted to a differential formulation of the stereo problem. While successful in a noise-free context, it was extremely sensitive to noise. Once the procedure, which tracked the irradiance profiles, incurred an error recovery proved impossible. Errors occurred because there was no locally valid solution. It is clear that that procedure would not be successful in cases of occlusion when there are irradiance profile sections that do not correspond. The approach described in this paper attempts to overcome these problems by finding the solution at all image points simultaneously (not sequentially, as in the previous formulation) and making it the best approximation to an overconstrained system of equations. The rationale behind this methodology is based on the expectation that the best solution to the overconstrained system will be insensitive both to noise and to small discrepancies in the data, e.g., at occlusions. While the previous efforts and the work presented here aimed at similar objectives, the formulation of the problem is entirely different. However, the form of the input – image irradiance profiles – is identical.

The new formulation of the stereo reconstruction task is given in terms of one-dimensional problems. We relate the image irradiance along epipolar lines in the stereo pair of images to the depth profile of the surface in the world that produced the irradiance profiles. For each pair of epipolar lines we produce a depth profile, from which the profile for a whole scene may then be derived. The formulation could be extended directly to the two-dimensional case, but the essential information and ideas are better explained and more easily computed in the one-dimensional case.

We couch this presentation in terms of stereo reconstruction, although there is no restriction on the acquisition positions of the two images; they may equally well be frames from a motion sequence.

2   Stereo Geometry

As noted earlier, our formulation takes two image irradiance profiles – one from the left image, one from the right – and describes the relationship between these profiles and the corresponding

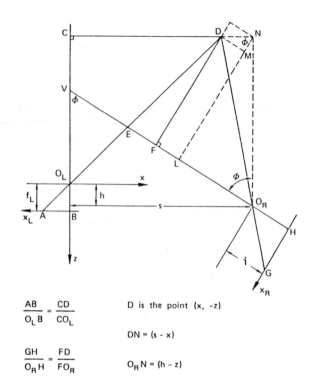

$$\frac{AB}{O_L B} = \frac{CD}{CO_L}$$

D is the point (x, -z)

DN = (s - x)

$$\frac{GH}{O_R H} = \frac{FD}{FO_R}$$

$O_R N = (h - z)$

Figure 1: Stereo Geometry. The two-dimensional arrangement in the epipolar plane that contains the optical axis of the left imaging system.

depth profile of the scene. The two irradiance profiles we consider are those obtained from corresponding epipolar lines in the stereo pair of images. Let us for the moment consider a pair of cameras pointed towards some scene. Further visualize the plane containing the optical axis of the left camera and the line joining the optical centers of the two cameras, i.e., an epipolar plane. This plane intersects the image plane in each camera, and the image irradiance profiles along these intersections are the corresponding irradiance profiles that we use. Of course, there are many epipolar planes, not just the one containing the left optical axis. Consequently, each plane gives us a pair of corresponding irradiance profiles. For the purpose of this formulation we can consider just the one epipolar plane containing the left optical axis since the others can be made equivalent. A description of this equivalence is given in a previous paper [6]. Figure 1 depicts the two-dimensional arrangement. AB and GH are in the camera image planes, while O_L and O_R are the cameras' optical centers. D is a typical point in the scene and AD and GD are rays of light from the scene onto the image planes of the cameras. From this diagram we can write two equations that relate the image coordinates x_L and x_R to the scene coordinates x and z. These are standard relationships that derive from the geometry of stereo viewing. For the left image

$$\frac{x}{-z} = \frac{x_L}{f_L} \quad ,$$

while for the right image

$$\frac{x}{-z} = g_R(x_R) - \frac{(s + g_R(x_R)h)}{z} \quad ,$$

where

$$g_R(x_R) = \frac{x_R \cos\phi - i\sin\phi}{x_R \sin\phi + i\cos\phi} \quad .$$

In addition, it should be noted that the origin of the scene coordinates is at the optical center of the left camera, and therefore the z values of all world points that may be imaged are such that

$$z < 0 \quad .$$

3   Irradiance Considerations

From any given point in a scene, rays of light proceed to their image projections. What is the relationship between the scene radiance of the rays that project into the left and the right images? Let us suppose that the angle between the two rays is small. The bidirectional reflectance function of the scene's surface will vary little, even when it is a complex function of the lighting and viewing geometry. Alternatively, let us suppose that the surface exhibits Lambertian reflectance. The scene radiance is independent of the viewing angle; hence, the two rays will have identical scene radiances, irrespective of the size of the angle between them. For the model presented here, we assume that the scene radiance of the two rays emanating from a single scene point is identical. This assumption is a reasonable one when the scene depth is large compared with the separation distance between the two optical systems, or when the surface exhibits approximate Lambertian reflectance. It should be noted that there are no assumptions about albedo (i.e., it is not assumed to be constant across the surface) nor, in fact, is it even necessary to know or calculate the albedo of the surface. Since image irradiance is proportional to scene radiance, we can write, for corresponding image points,

$$I_L(x_L) = I_R(x_R) \quad .$$

I_L and I_R are the image irradiance measurements for the left and right images, respectively. It should be understood that these measurements at positions x_L and x_R are made at image points that correspond to a single scene point x.

While the above assumption is used in the following formulation, we see little difficulty in being less restrictive by allowing, for example, a change in linear contrast between the image profile and the real profile.

4   Integral Equation

Let us consider a single scene point x. For this scene point, we can write $I_L(x) = I_R(x)$. This equality relation holds for any function F of the image irradiance, that is, $F(I_L(x)) = F(I_R(x))$. If we let p select the particular function we want to use from some set of functions, we shall write

$$F(p, I_L(x)) = F(p, I_R(x)) \quad .$$

The set of functions we use will be the set of all nonlinear functions for which $F(p_1, I) \neq \alpha(p_1, p_2) F(p_2, I)$ for all p. A specific example of such a function is $F(p, I) = I^p$.

The foregoing functions relate to the image irradiance. We can combine them with expressions that are functions of the stereo geometry. In particular, for the as yet unspecified function T of $\frac{x}{-z}$, we can write

$$F(p, I_L(x)) \frac{d}{dx} T(\frac{x}{-z(x)}) = F(p, I_R(x)) \frac{d}{dx} T(\frac{x}{-z(x)}) \quad .$$

We have written z as $z(x)$ to emphasize the fact that the depth profile we wish to recover is a function of x. Should a more concrete example of our approach be required, we could select $T(\frac{x}{-z}) = \ln(\frac{x}{-z})$, which, when combined with the example for F above, gives us

$$I_L{}^p(x) \frac{d}{dx} \ln(\frac{x}{-z(x)}) = I_R{}^p(x) \frac{d}{dx} \ln(\frac{x}{-z(x)}) \quad .$$

We now propose to develop the left-hand side of the above expression in terms of quantities that can be measured in the left stereo image, and develop the right-hand side in terms of quantities from the right stereo image. If we were to substitute x_L for x in the left-hand side of the above expression and x_R for x in the right-hand side, we would have to know the correspondence between x_L and x_R. This is a requirement we are trying to avoid. At first, we shall integrate both sides of the above expression with respect to x before attemping substitution for the variable x:

$$\int_a^b F(p, I_L(x)) \frac{d}{dx} T(\frac{x}{-z(x)}) dx =$$

$$\int_a^b F(p, I_R(x)) \frac{d}{dx} T(\frac{x}{-z(x)}) dx \quad ,$$

where a and b are specific scene points. Now let us change the integration variable in the left-hand side of the above expression to x_L, and the integration variable in the right-hand side to x_R:

$$\int_{a_L}^{b_L} F(p, I_L(x_L)) \frac{d}{dx_L} T(\frac{x_L}{f_L}) dx_L =$$

$$\int_{a_R}^{b_R} F(p, I_R(x_R)) U(x_R) dx_R \quad , \quad (1)$$

where

$$U(x_R) = \frac{d}{dx_R} T(g_R(x_R) - \frac{(s + g_R(x_R)h)}{z(x_R)}) \quad .$$

Equation (1) is our formulation of the stereo integral equation. Given that we have two image irradiance profiles that are matched at their end points – i.e., a_L and b_L in the left image correspond, respectively, to a_R and b_R in the right image – then Equation (1) expresses the relationship between the image irradiance profiles and the scene depth. It will be noted that the left-hand side of Equation (1) is composed of measurements that can be made in the left image of the stereo pair, while measurements in the right hand side are those that can be made in the right image. In addition, the right-hand side has a function of the scene depth as a variable. Our goal is to recover z as a function of the right-image coordinates x_R, not as a function of the world coordinates x. Once we have $z(x_R)$, we can transform it into any coordinate frame whose relationship to the image coordinates of the right image is known.

The recovery of $z(x_R)$ is a two-stage process. After first solving Equation (1) for $U(x_R)$, we integrate the latter to find $z(x_R)$ by using

$$T(g_R(x_R) - \frac{(s + g_R(x_R)h)}{z(x_R)}) =$$

$$T(g_R(a_R) - \frac{(s + g_R(a_R)h)}{z(a_R)}) + \int_{a_R}^{x_R} U(x'_R) dx'_R \quad .$$

In this expression one should note that $z(a_R)$ is known, since a_R and a_L are corresponding points.

It is instructive as regards the nature of the formulation if we look at the means of solving this equation when we have discrete data. In particular, let us take another look at an example previously introduced, namely,

$$F(p, I) = I^p$$

$$T(\frac{x}{-z}) = \ln(\frac{x}{-z})$$

and hence

$$\int_{a_L}^{b_L} \frac{I_L{}^p(x_L)}{x_L} dx_L = \int_{a_R}^{b_R} I_R{}^p(x_R) U(x_R) dx_R \quad ,$$

and then

$$z(x_R) = \frac{(s + g_R(x_R)h)}{g_R(x_R) - K \exp \int_{a_R}^{x_R} U(x'_R) dx'_R} \quad ,$$

where

$$K = (g_R(a_R) - \frac{(s + g_R(a_R)h)}{z(a_R)}) \quad .$$

Suppose that we have image data at points $x_{L1}, x_{L2}, ..., x_{Lq}$ that lie between the left integral limits and, similarly, that we have data from the right image, between its integral limits, at points $x_{R1}, x_{R2}, ..., x_{Rn}$. Further, let us approximate the integrals as follows:

$$\sum_{j=1}^{q} \frac{I_L{}^p(x_{Lj})}{x_{Lj}} = \sum_{j=1}^{n} I_R{}^p(x_{Rj}) U(x_{Rj}) \quad .$$

In actual calculation, we may wish to use a better integral formula than that above, (particularly at the end points), but this approximation enables us to demonstrate the essential ideas without being distracted by the details. Although the above approximation holds for all values of p, let us take a finite set of values, $p_1, p_2, ..., p_m$, and write the approximation out as a matrix equation, namely,

$$
\begin{matrix}
I_R{}^{p_1}(x_{R1}) & I_R{}^{p_1}(x_{R2}) & ... & I_R{}^{p_1}(x_{Rn}) & U(x_{R1}) \\
I_R{}^{p_2}(x_{R1}) & I_R{}^{p_2}(x_{R2}) & ... & I_R{}^{p_2}(x_{Rn}) & U(x_{R2}) \\
... & ... & ... & ... & ... \\
I_R{}^{p_n}(x_{R1}) & I_R{}^{p_n}(x_{R2}) & ... & I_R{}^{p_n}(x_{Rn}) & U(x_{Rn}) \\
... & ... & ... & ... & \\
I_R{}^{p_m}(x_{R1}) & I_R{}^{p_m}(x_{R2}) & ... & I_R{}^{p_m}(x_{Rn}) &
\end{matrix}
$$

$$
= \begin{matrix}
\sum_{j=1}^{q} \frac{I_L{}^{p_1}(x_{Lj})}{x_{Lj}} \\
\sum_{j=1}^{q} \frac{I_L{}^{p_2}(x_{Lj})}{x_{Lj}} \\
... \\
\sum_{j=1}^{q} \frac{I_L{}^{p_n}(x_{Lj})}{x_{Lj}} \\
... \\
\sum_{j=1}^{q} \frac{I_L{}^{p_m}(x_{Lj})}{x_{Lj}}
\end{matrix}
$$

Let us now recall what we have done. We have taken a set of image measurements, along with measurements that are just some non-linear functions of these image measurments, multiplied them by a function of the depth, and expressed the relationship between the measurements made in the right and left images. Why should one set of measurements, however purposefully manipulated, provide enough constraints to find a solution with almost the same number of variables as there are image measurements? The matrix equation helps in our understanding of this. First, we are not trying to find the solution for the scene depth at each point independently, but rather for all the points

simultaneously. Second, we are exploiting the fact that, if the functions of image irradiance used by us are nonlinear, then each equation represented in the above matrix is linearly independent and constrains the solution. There is another way of saying this: even though we have only one set of measurements, requiring that the one depth profile relates the irradiance profile in the left image to the irradiance profile in the right image, and also relates the irradiance squared profile in the left image to the irradiance squared profile in the right image, and also relates the irradiance cubed profile etc., provides constraints on that depth profile.

The question arises as to whether there are sufficient constraints to enable a unique solution to the above equations to be found. This question really has three parts. Does an integral equation of the form of Equation (1) have a unique solution? This is impossible to answer when the irradiance profiles are unknown; even when they are known an exceedingly difficult problem confronts us [2, 4]. Does the discrete approximation, even with an unlimited number of constraints, have the same solution as the integral equation? Again this is extremely difficult to answer even when the irradiance profiles are known. The final question relates to the finite set of constraint equations, such as those shown above. Does the matrix equation have a unique solution, and is it the same as the solution to the integral equation? Yes, it does have an unique solution – or at least we can impose solution requirements that makes a unique answer possible. But the question that asks whether the solution we find is a solution of the integral equation remains unanswered. From an empirical standpoint, we would be satisfied if the solution we recover is a believable depth profile. Issues about sensitivity to noise, function type, and the form of the integral approximation will be discussed later in the section on solution methods.

Let us return to considerations of the general equation, Equation (1). We have just remarked upon the difficulty of solving this equation, so any additional constraints we can impose on the solution are likely to be beneficial. In the previous section on geometrical constraints, we noted that an acceptable solution has $z < 0$ and hence $z(x_R) < 0$. Unfortunately, solution methods for matrix equations (that have real coefficients) find solutions that are usually unrestricted over the domain of the real numbers. To impose the restriction of $z(x_R) < 0$, we follow the methods of Stockham [7]; instead of using the function itself, we formulate the problem in terms of the logarithm of the function. Consequently, in Equation (1) we usually set $T(\frac{x}{-z}) = \ln(\frac{x}{-z})$, just as we have done in our example. It should be noted that use of the logarithm also restricts $x > 0$ if $z < 0$. To construct the $x < 0$ side of the stereo reconstruction problem, we have to employ reflected coordinate systems for the world and image coordinates. Use of the logarithmic function ensures $z < 0$ and allows us to use standard matrix methods for solving the system of constraint equations. Once we have found the solution to the matrix equation, we can integrate that solution to find the depth profile.

In our previous example, we picked $F(p, I) = I^p$. In our experiments, we have used combinations of different functions to establish a particular matrix equation. For example we have used functions such as

$$
\begin{aligned}
F(p, I) &= |\cos pI|^p \\
&= (p + I)^{\frac{p}{2}} \\
&= p^I \\
&= \sin pI \\
&= (p + I)^{\frac{1}{2}}
\end{aligned}
$$

and we often use image density rather than image irradiance.

The point to be made here is that the form of the function F in the general equation is unrestricted, provided that it is nonlinear.

Equation (1) provides a framework for investigating stereo reconstruction in a manner that exploits the global nature of the solution. This framework arises from the realization that nonlinear functions provide a means of creating an arbitrary number of constraints on that solution. In addition, the framework provides a means of avoiding the correspondence problem, except at the end points, for we never match points. Solutions have the same resolution as the data and this allows us to avoid the interpolation problem.

5   Solution Methods

Equation (1) is an inhomogeneous Fredholm equation of the first kind whose kernel function is the function $F(p, I_R(x_R))$. To solve this equation, we create a matrix equation in the manner previously shown in our example. We usually approximate the integral with the trapezoidal rule, where the sample spacing is that corresponding to the image resolution. Typically we use more than one functional form for the function F, each of which is parameterized by p. We have noticed that the sensitivity of the solution to image noise is affected by the choice of these functions, although we have not yet characterized this relationship. In the matrix equation, we usually pick the number of rows to be approximately twice the number of columns. However, owing to the rank-deficient nature of the matrix and hence to the selection of our solution technique, the solution we recover is only marginally different from the one obtained when we use square matrices.

Unfortunately, there are considerable numerical difficulties associated with solving this type of integral equation by matrix methods. Such systems are often ill-conditioned, particularly when the kernel function is a smooth function of the image coordinates. It is easy to see that, if the irradiance function varies smoothly with image position, each column of the matrix will be almost linearly dependent on the next. Consequently, it is advisable to assume that the matrix is rank-deficient and to utilize a procedure that can estimate the actual numerical rank. We use singular-valued decomposition to estimate the rank of the matrix; we then set the small singular values to zero and find the pseudoinverse of the matrix. Examples of results obtained with this procedure are shown in the following section.

An alternative approach to solving the integral equation is to decompose the kernel function and the dependent variable into orthogonal functions, then to solve for the coefficients of this decomposition, using the aforementioned techniques. We have used Fourier spectral decomposition for this purpose. The Fourier coefficients of the depth function were then calculated by solving a matrix equation composed of the Fourier components of image irradiance. However, the resultant solution did not vary significantly from that obtained without spectral decomposition.

While the techniques outlined can handle various cases, they are not as robust as we would like. We are actively engaged in overcoming the difficulties these solution methods encounter because of noise and irradiance discontinuities.

6   Results and Discussion

Our examples make use of synthetic image profiles that we have produced from known surface profiles. The irradiance profiles were generated under the assumptions that the surface was a Lambertian reflector and that the source of illumination was a

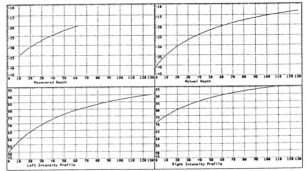

Figure 2: Planar Surface. At the upper left is depicted the recovered depth from the two irradiance profiles shown in the lower half. For comparison, the actual depth is shown in the upper right.

point source directly above the surface. This choice was made so that our assumption concerning image irradiance, namely, that $I(x_L) = I(x_R)$ at matched points, would be complied with. In addition, synthetic images derived from a known depth profile allow comparison between the recovered profile and ground truth. Nonetheless, our goal is to demonstrate these techniques on real-world data. It should be noted that the examples used have smooth irradiance profiles; they therefore represent a worst case for the numerical procedures, as the matrix is most ill-conditioned under these circumstances.

Our first example, illustrated in Figure 2, is of a flat surface with constant albedo. In the lower half of the figure, the left and right irradiance profiles are shown, while in the upper right, ground truth – the actual depth profile as a function of the image coordinates of the right image, x_R – is shown. The upper left of the figure contains the recovered solution. The limits of the recovered solution correspond to our selection of the integral end points. This solution was obtained from a formulation of the problem in which we used image density instead of irradiance in the kernel of the integral equation, and for which the function T was $\ln\left(\frac{x}{-z(x)}\right)$.

The second example, Figure 3, shows a spherical surface with constant albedo, except for the stripe we have painted across the surface. The recovered solution was produced from the same formulation of the problem as in the previous example. The ripple effects in the recovered profile appear to have been induced by the details of the recovery procedure; the attendant difficulties are in part numerical in nature. However, any changes made in the actual functions used in the kernel of the equation do have effects that cannot be dismissed as numerical inaccuracies.

As we add noise to the irradiance profiles, the solutions tend to become more oscillatory. Although we suspect numerical problems, we have not yet ascertained the method's range of effectiveness. This aspect of our approach, however, is being actively investigated.

In the formulation presented here, we have used a particular function of the stereo geometry, $\frac{x}{-z}$, in the derivation of Equation (1) but we are not limited to this particular form. Its attractiveness is based on the fact that, if we use this particular function of the geometry, the side of the integral equation related to the left image is independent of the scene depth. We have used other functional forms but these result in more complicated integral equations. Equations of these forms have been subjected to relatively little study in the mathematical literature. Consequently, the effectiveness of solution methods on these forms remains un-

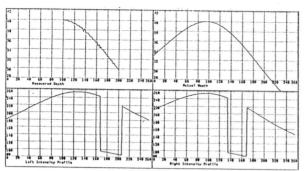

Figure 3: Spherical Surface with a Painted Stripe.

known.

In most of our study we have used $T\left(\frac{x}{-z}\right)$ to be $\ln\left(\frac{x}{-z}\right)$ and the properties of this particular formulation should be noted. It is necessary to process the right half of the visual field separately from the left half. The integral is more sensitive to image measurements near the optical axis than those measurements off-axis. In fact, the irradiance is weighted by the reciprocal of the distance off-axis. If we were interested in an integral approximation exhibiting uniform error across the extent of that integral, we might expect measurements that had been taken at interval spacings proportional to the off-axis distance to be appropriate. While it is obvious that two properties of a formulation that match those of the human visual system do not in themselves give cause for excitement it is worthy of note that the formulation presented is at least not at odds with the properties of the human stereo system.

On balance, we must say that significant work still lies ahead before this method can be applied to real-world images. While the details of the formulation may be varied, the overall form presented in Equation (1) seems the most promising. Nonetheless, solution methods for this class of equations are known to be difficult and, in particular, further efforts towards the goal of selecting appropriate numerical procedures are essential.

In formulating the integral equation, we took a function of the image irradiance and multiplied it by a function of the stereo geometry. To introduce image measurements, we changed variables in the integrals. If we had not used the derivative of the function of the stereo geometry, we would have had to introduce terms like $\frac{dx}{dx_R}$ and $\frac{dx}{dx_L}$ into the integrals. By introducing the derivative we avoided this. However, we did not really have to select the function of the geometry for this purpose; we could equally well have introduced the derivative through the function of image irradiance. Then we would have exchanged the calculation of irradiance gradients for the direct recovery of scene depth (thus eliminating the integration step we now use). Our selection of the formulation presented here was based on the belief that irradiance gradients are quite susceptible to noise; consequently we prefered to integrate the solution rather than differentiate the data. In a noise-free environment, however, both approaches are equivalent (as integration by parts will confirm).

7   Conclusion

The formulation presented herein for the recovery of scene depth from a stereo pair of images is based not on matching of image features, but rather on determining which surface in the world is consistent with the pair of image irradiance profiles we see. The solution method does not attempt to determine the nature

of the surface locally; it looks instead for the best global solution. Although we have yet to demonstrate the procedure on real images, it does offer the potential to deal in a new way with problems associated with albedo change, occlusions, and discontinuous surfaces. It is the approach, rather than the details of a particular formulation, that distinguishes this method from conventional stereo processing.

This formulation is based on the observation that a global solution can be constrained by manufacturing additional constraints from nonlinear functions of local image measurements. Image analysis researchers have generally tried to use linear-systems theory to perform analysis; this has led them, consequently, to replace (at least locally) nonlinear functions with their linear approximation. Here we exploit the nonlinearity; "What is one man's noise is another man's signal."

While the presentation of the approach described here is focussed upon stereo problems, its essential ideas apply to other image analysis problems as well. The stereo problem is a convenient problem on which to demonstrate our approach; the formulation of the problem reduces to a linear system of equations, which allows the approach to be investigated without diversion into techniques for solving nonlinear systems. We remain actively interested in the application of this methodology to other problems, as well as in the details of the numerical solution.

References

[1] Boult, T.E., and J.R. Kender, "On Surface Reconstruction Using Sparse Depth Data," *Proceedings: Image Understanding Workshop*, Miami Beach, Florida, December 1985.

[2] Courant, R., and D. Hilbert, *Methods of Mathematical Physics*, Interscience Publishers, Inc., New York, 1953.

[3] Grimson, W.E.L., "An Implementation of a Computational Theory of Visual Surface Interpolation," *Computer Vision, Graphics, and Image Processing*, Vol. 22, pp 39-69, April 1983.

[4] Hildebrand, F.B., *Methods of Applied Mathematics,* 2nd ed., Prentice-Hall, Inc., Englewood Cliffs, New Jersey, 1965.

[5] Smith, G.B., "A Fast Surface Interpolation Technique," *Proceedings: Image Understanding Workshop*, New Orleans, Louisiana, October 1984.

[6] Smith, G.B., "Stereo Reconstruction of Scene Depth," *IEEE Proceedings on Computer Vision and Pattern Recognition*, San Francisco, California, June 1985, pp 271-276.

[7] Stockham, T.G., "Image Processing in the Context of a Visual Model," *Proceeding of IEEE*, Vol. 60, pp 828-842, July 1972.

[8] Terzopoulos, D., "Multilevel Computational Processes for Visual Surface Reconstruction," *Computer Vision, Graphics, and Image Processing*, Vol. 24, pp 52-96, October 1983.

Physics-Based Sensor Fusion

There are important situations in which one source of information from a scene does not provide a sufficient or accurate enough physical description. Additional information from other sensors can be used to provide the desired description. One example is photometric stereo, which provides surface orientation information but not absolute depth. Relative depth obtained by integration of an errorful normal map obtained from photometric stereo can be very inaccurate. Using a second camera sensor, binocular stereo information can be used in conjunction with photometric stereo information to obtain an absolute depth map that is accurate. This is discussed in Ikeuchi [2]. Another example is combining depth information from a range-finder sensor and image irradiance information from a camera sensor, to determine the reflectance properties of surfaces. A range-finder alone only computes depth, but adding information from a brightness image of a camera sensor can enable the derivation of important reflectance parameters. This is discussed in Ikeuchi and Sato [3]. The last paper in this section, by Ikeuchi and Kanade [4], discusses object recognition using multiple sensors.

Combining photometric and binocular stereo in Ikeuchi [2] involves corresponding segmented regions of a stereo pair of images according to surface orientation. Photometric stereo is applied to a smooth object from two camera views and a local surface orientation map is derived for each image. Surface orientations are divided into separate classes on a tessellated sphere, and the surface orientation map for each stereo image is segmented according to this classification scheme. Segmented orientation classes are corresponded between the stereo pair of images with the help of area, mean surface-orientation, and epipolar constraints. A coarse depth map is computed, and then refined using an iterative scheme that forces the gradient of the depth map to be consistent with surface orientations derived from photometric stereo.

Ikeuchi and Sato [3] utilize a range image and a brightness image from a camera sensor to compute reflectance parameters for diffuse and specular reflection from objects assumed to be optically rough. The Torrance-Sparrow reflectance model [1] is used and the Fresnel term in the specular component is assumed to be con-stant by restricting surface orientations to be less than or equal to 60° from the viewer direction. The following four parameters are determined: (i) Lambertian strength coefficient, (ii) incident orientation of light source, (iii) specular strength coefficient, and (iv) roughness parameter controlling the sharpness of the specular distribution. The technique utilizes the range image to compute surface orinetation, identify Lambertian reflecting points according to a brightness criterion, and use least-squares fitting to compute Lambertian strength and incident orientation of the light source simultaneously. Criteria are developed that also identify pixels that are in shadow, and specular and interreflection pixels. A least-squares procedure is applied to fit the specular strength and surface roughness (specular sharpness) parameters from identified specular pixels. Simulation and experimentation is presented.

The last paper, by Ikeuchi and Kanade [4], discusses object recognition using a variety of sensors. They emphasize the importance of understanding sensor models to be able to predict object appearance in terms of object models describing geometric and reflectance properties. Two criteria are considered essential for describing the functionality of sensors: (i) sensor *detectability*, specifying which object features can be detected and under what conditions, and (ii) sensor *reliability*, specifying with what confidence a feature can be detected. A representation method for sensor detectability and reliability is proposed in terms of a configuration space, and it is shown how this can be used to generate object recognition programs automatically.

– L.B.W.

References

[1] Torrance, K.E., and Sparrow, E.M. "Theory for Off-specular Reflection from Roughened Surfaces." *Journal of the Optical Society of America* **57** (9): 1105-1114, 1967. Reprinted in the "Intensity Reflection Models" section of the Radiometry volume of this series.

Papers Included in This Collection

[2]   Ikeuchi, K. "Determining a Depth Map Using a Dual Photometric Stereo." *International Journal of Robotics Research* **6**(1): 15-31, Spring 1987.

[3]   Ikeuchi, K., and Sato, K. "Determining Reflectance Parameters Using Range and Brightness Images." In *Proc. Intl. Conference on Computer Vision.* Osaka, Japan. IEEE, 1990. Pages 12-20.

[4]   Ikeuchi, K., and Kanade, T. "Modeling Sensors: Toward Automatic Generation of Object Recognition Programs." *Computer Vision, Graphics, and Image Processing* **48**: 50-79, 1989.

Katsushi Ikeuchi

Department of Computer Science
Carnegie-Mellon University
Pittsburgh, Pennsylvania 15213

Determining a Depth Map Using a Dual Photometric Stereo

Abstract

This paper describes a method for determining a depth map from a pair of surface-orientation maps obtained by a dual photometric stereo. A photometric stereo system determines surface orientations by taking three images from the same position under different lighting conditions, based on the shading information. A photometric stereo system can determine surface orientations very rapidly, but cannot determine absolute depth values. This paper proposes a dual photometric stereo system to obtain absolute depth values.

A dual photometric stereo generates a pair of surface-orientation maps. Then, the surface-orientation maps can be segmented into isolated regions with respect to surface orientations, using a geodesic dome for grouping surface orientations. The resulting left and right regions are compared to pair corresponding regions. The following three kinds of constraints will be used to search for corresponding regions efficiently: a surface-orientation constraint, an area constraint, and an epipolar constraint. Region matching is done iteratively, starting from a coarse segmented result and proceeding to a fine segmented result, using a parent-children constraint. The horizontal difference in the position of the center of mass of a region pair determines the absolute depth value for the physical surface patch imaged onto that pair. This system takes only a few minutes on a Lisp machine to determine an absolute depth map in complicated scenes and could be used as an input device for a bin-picking system.

1. Introduction

Vision is one of the most important subsystems of an intelligent robot. Without vision, a robot can repeat only one predetermined job sequence where objects are expected to be at predetermined places. Moreover, slight disturbances can cause unpredictable circumstances in the robot environment which might prevent the robot from continuing its job sequence. Such a robot system lacks flexibility and robustness.

The International Journal of Robotics Research,
Vol. 6, No. 1, Spring 1987,

Robot vision has been explored from various directions, including the binocular stereo method, the shape-from-shading method, the shape-from-texture method, and the shape-from-line-drawings method (Brady 1981). We have focused on the binocular stereo method and the photometric stereo method (part of the shape-from-shading method) because these methods can obtain the depth information robustly.

The binocular stereo method has been explored since the early days of robot vision research, because binocular stereo plays an important role in the human visual system. This area has been explored by Marr and Poggio (1979); Moravec (1979); Baker (1981); Grimson (1981); Barnard and Fishler (1982); Nishihara (1984); Thorpe (1984); and Ohta and Kanade (1985).

Binocular stereo methods are divided into two classes: one uses brightness correlation, and the other is based on feature matching. The *brightness correlation methods* divide the left and the right images into small windows and compare the brightness distribution in a window of the right image with distributions over candidate windows of the left image. The window pair with the highest correlation is declared to be a corresponding pair, and the horizontal difference between the windows gives the depth value. This correlation method is suitable for hardware implementation. It has, however, the following two defects:

1. If a window contains an occluding boundary, the apparent brightness distribution depends heavily on the viewer direction. Thus, it is difficult to determine a good match for such a window.
2. Depth values can be measured only at the center of the windows. In order to have robust matching, a larger window size is better. On the other hand, if the window size is large, sampling of the image is coarse.

The *feature matching method* searches for corresponding features in the left and the right images and re-

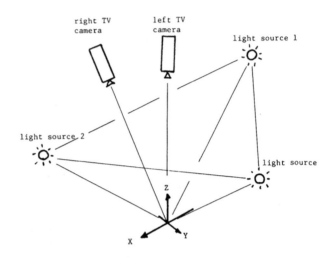

Fig. 1. *Dual photometric stereo.*

quires that feature points be extracted before matching. Depth information can be determined directly only at places where feature points exist. Many kinds of operators for extracting features have been proposed, including the so-called interest operator (Moravec 1979), the DOG filter (Marr and Hildreth 1980), and the Roberts operator (Roberts 1965). Since depth information can be determined only at feature points, it is desirable to have many such points. In this sense, the output of the DOG filter and the output of the Sobel operator are better than the output of the interest operator because output is produced by the DOG filter or by the Sobel in many more places in the images than by the interest operator. On the other hand, since the number of feature points is increased, it takes more time to compare all the candidate features. Thus, from the point of view of matching complexity, the output of the interest operator is better than the output of the DOG filter or the Sobel operator.

Although the binocular stereo method is robust and well explored, it takes a long time to compute depth with this method. Also the binocular stereo method determines depth only at the place where matching features are obtained; it requires an interpolation to get a continuous depth map. The photometric stereo method bypasses these problems. A *photometric stereo method* determines surface orientations from three images of the same scene from the same point under three different light conditions (Horn, Woodham, and Silver 1978; Woodham 1979; Ikeuchi 1981; Ikeuchi, et al. 1986). Since the spatial configuration between the TV camera and the object is the same for all three images, there is no disparity between the images. Therefore, no matching operations are needed and surface orientation can be determined very rapidly. Also the photometric stereo system can determine surface orientation at each pixel and can compute a dense surface-orientation map. Unfortunately, however, the photometric stereo system cannot produce an absolute depth.

This paper proposes a method to determine an absolute depth map based on the binocular use of two photometric stereo systems. A pair of surface-orientation maps can be determined by a dual photometric stereo. The surface-orientation maps obtained are segmented into isolated regions of the constant surface orientations using a geodesic dome. Comparing the

left regions with the right regions gives pairs of corresponding regions. Matching depends on the size of the regions, average surface orientations, and mass-center positions of the regions. Finally, differences in mass-center positions of corresponding regions give the depths of the regions.

This system has the following features:

1. Since the features for the matching operations are the mass centers of regions, the number of matching operations is small. Thus, the system can determine a depth map rapidly.
2. Since the distributions of the surface orientations within each region are known from the surface-orientation map, we can convert the discrete depth information at the mass-center positions into a continuous depth map over the image using a simple integration operation.

Figure 1 shows the setup of our dual photometric stereo. A pair of TV cameras is surrounded by three light sources. The left TV camera's image plane is parallel to the ground plane and the right TV camera's image plane is inclined so that the optical axes of the TV cameras intersect at the origin of the spatial coordinate system, where the spatial origin is under the left TV camera. The objects are located near the spatial origin.

2. Segmentation on Surface Orientations

Segmentation is necessary for our stereo system, but segmentations of images based on brightness values are not suitable for our region-based stereo system for the following reasons:

1. Since the brightness value of a pixel depends on the viewer direction, a brightness value at a pixel in the left image is usually different from a brightness value at the corresponding pixel in the right image. The difference between two observing directions causes the difference between two brightness values at the corresponding pixels. Thus, a region obtained using brightness segmentation in the left image does not usually overlap with the corresponding region in the right image.
2. It is impossible to have two TV cameras with identical characteristics. A gray value observed always depends on the characteristics of the TV camera. Thus, it makes little sense to compare absolute values observed by the one camera with absolute values observed by another camera. For example, a region in the left image based on an absolute threshold will be different from a region in the right image, even though the two regions correspond roughly to the same physical surface patch, and the threshold value used is the same.

The above two defects of brightness-based segmentation occur because observed brightness is not a characteristic of an object surface but is a measure depending on both the viewer direction and the characteristics of the observing system. Thus, even though a pair of pixels in the left and the right images corresponds to the same physical point on an object, they may not have the same brightness values. Therefore, brightness-based segmentation is not a suitable basis for the binocular stereo.

We propose instead to segment an image into regions based on intrinsic characteristics of object surfaces. Intrinsic characteristics, such as surface orientations, are properties of the object surface itself (Barrow and Tenenbaum 1978). Intrinsic characteristics are independent of both the viewer direction and characteristics of the observing system. We should estimate the same value of intrinsic characteristics, provided that the pair of observing pixels on the left and right images correspond to the same physical point. A segmentation method based on an intrinsic characteristic is stable and has high reliability.

Images are segmented into isolated regions based on surface orientations. There are several kinds of intrinsic characteristics, such as surface orientation, albedo, and color. Surface orientation is the most easily obtained among the intrinsic characteristics. We propose to segment images into isolated regions based on surface orientations obtained by the photometric stereo method for our region-based stereo. The segmentation consists of three steps: (1) segmentation based on shadows, (2) segmentation based on orientation discontinuities, and (3) segmentation based on orientation classification.

2.1. Shadows (Coarse Segmentation)

Self-shadows, projected shadows, and mutual illumination disable the photometric stereo system in places around objects:

Projected shadow
A 3-D object projects shadows onto other objects below it. The photometric stereo system cannot determine surface orientations in the projected shadow regions of any one of the three lights. Since our three light sources are arranged in a triangle, undetectable regions due to the projected shadows exist entirely around the upper object.

Self-shadow
The photometric stereo system also cannot determine surface orientations of steep surface regions. Steep surface areas are self-shadowed. In any place where any one of the three light sources casts a self-shadow, the system cannot determine surface orientations. Self-shadows often occur near the object boundaries. The limiting angle of detectable surface orientation can be controlled. A photometric stereo uses a 3-D lookup table to convert a triple of brightness values into surface orientation. If we blank out entries of the lookup steeper than some

limiting angle, the system cannot determine surface orientations steeper than the limit angle. Since steep areas exist near the object boundaries, then the system cannot determine surface orientations near the object boundaries.

Mutual illumination

Mutual illumination occurs due to the light reflected by a near object. This indirect illumination changes the lighting condition at the region. The brightness triple obtained has no surface orientation at the corresponding entry of the 3-D lookup table, because the triple does not occur under the usual lighting conditions. The photometric stereo system cannot determine surface orientation of mutually illuminated surface regions. This mutual illumination occurs at the peripheral area of an object, which is a convenient characteristic for segmentation.

A surface-orientation map obtained by a photometric stereo system can be easily segmented into isolated regions corresponding to objects using the disabled regions around objects. Consider the following binary image. Each pixel is a 1 if the surface orientation can be determined at the pixel. Each pixel is a 0 if the surface orientation cannot be determined at that pixel. Regions of 1's correspond to object regions, and regions of 0's correspond to disabled regions in the scene. Thus, we can easily segment the map into isolated object regions to check the connectedness of regions of 1's.

2.2. Orientation Discontinuity (Coarse Segmentation)

Orientation discontinuities are also used for more stable segmentation. If two objects overlap each other and surface orientations are determined near the occluding boundaries (usually surface orientations cannot be determined there due to self-shadowing or a projected shadow), surface orientations are not continuous over the occluding boundaries. It rarely occurs that two overlapping objects have the same surface orientation on both sides of an occluding boundary. Thus, the orientation discontinuity divides what might otherwise be a connected region into two divided regions.

Orientation discontinuity may be measured by the following formula:

$$s = f_x^2 + f_y^2 + g_x^2 + g_g^2, \qquad (1)$$

where (f, g) denotes a surface orientation using the stereographic plane and f_x is a partial derivative of f with respect to the x direction of the image plane and so on. Regions where s is larger than some threshold are considered to be places of orientation discontinuity.

2.3. Orientation Classification (Fine Segmentation)

A finer segmentation is necessary for more precise depth maps. Our stereo system can determine depth values at the mass centers of regions. Determining depth values inside an object requires finer regions. Thus, a finer segmentation is necessary to extract finer candidate regions.

A tessellated sphere may divide surface orientations into classes. Since surface orientation has two degrees of freedom, surface orientation can be represented by a point on the Gaussian sphere. We can divide the Gaussian sphere into cells using a tessellated sphere. A surface orientation can be assigned to a class, based on the cell that contains the point corresponding to the surface orientation.

A labelling operation can be applied to the cell-number map, after a surface orientation map is converted into a cell-number map. Each pixel of an image has a cell number on a tessellated sphere corresponding to the surface orientation there. Then, a labelling operation is applied to the cell-number map to extract connected regions. Each isolated region consists of surface patches having the same cell number.

A geodesic dome will be used for tesselating a sphere. A geodesic dome is obtained by projecting edges of a polyhedron to the surface of the circumscribing sphere with respect to the center. For example, a geodesic dome having 12 cells is obtained from a dodecahedron. Regular tessellation methods on the sphere only exist for 4, 6, 8, 12, 20 divisions, because tetrahedra, hexahedra, octahedra, dodecahedra, icosahedra are the only regular polyhedra. Finer tessellations are obtained by division of the regular tessellation into smaller triangles (Wenninger 1979). We will use geodesic domes obtained by division of a dodecahedral geodesic dome for finer segmentation.

This finer segmentation using geodesic domes is done hierarchically. At the first stage, regions obtained by coarse segmentation using shadows and orientation discontinuity regions are divided into subregions using a dodecahedral geodesic dome. Figure 2A shows a hyperbolic surface and an elliptic surface. Figure 2B shows a needle map of a hyperbolic surface and a needle map of an elliptic surface. Figure 2C shows the segmented result using a dodecahedral geodesic dome. Each pixel on a connected region has the same cell number over the region. The resulting region map is again divided using a one-frequency, dodecahedral, geodesic dome. (See Fig. 2D.) This refining operation is applied iteratively using a higher geodesic dome until the necessary resolution is achieved. Fig. 2E gives the segmented result using a two-frequency, dodecahedral, geodesic dome.

There may be accidental errors due to mutual illumination or shadows, causing incorrect surface orientations at that area, but this does not cause errors in matching regions. This error does not occur randomly on the left and right needle maps, but occurs in the same way on the maps, because both maps are obtained under the same light source conditions. Note that the two TV cameras share the common light sources in Fig. 1. Thus, that area will be segmented in the same way in both the left and right images. This will give the correct matching at the area, even though the surface orientations obtained there are not correct.

3. Camera Model (Orthographic Projection)

A camera model is necessary to convert a disparity value between two images into a depth value. Figure 3 shows our camera configuration. The left image plane is perpendicular to the spatial z axis, while the right image plane is inclined with respect to the z axis, so that the two optical axes intersect with each other at the origin of the spatial coordinate system. Orthographic projection is used as the camera model. Since the distance between the TV camera and the object is

far compared with the size of the TV camera's field of view, we will use the orthographic projection instead of the perspective projection as the camera model. Disparity between images is due only to the angle between two image planes. For example, the images of a physical point at the spatial origin have the same coordinates in the left and the right image planes. If the point moves towards the viewer, the image of the point on the left image plane keeps the same position while the right image of the point moves to the left on the right image plane. This gives the disparity with this orthographic projection.

For the left TV camera

$$u^l = f^l x + e^{ul},$$
$$v^l = f^l y + e^{vl}, \qquad (2)$$

where f^l is a conversion constant from the spatial coordinate into the left camera coordinate; (x, y) is the spatial coordinate system; (u^l, v^l) is the left camera coordinate system whose origin exists at the center of the camera plane; and e^{ul}, e^{vl} are error terms (see Fig. 3).

The right TV camera gives

$$u^r = f^r(ax + bz) + e^{ur},$$
$$v^r = f^r y + e^{vr}, \qquad (3)$$

where a, b are trigonometric constants determined from the angle between two image planes and e^{ur}, e^{vr} are error terms.

Thus, the relationship between image coordinates and depth z is

$$z = a'u^l + b'u^r + c', \qquad (4)$$

where

a' = −a/(f^l b),
b' = 1/(f^r b),
c' = ((e^{ul}a)/f^l) − (e^{ur}/f^r)/b.

The constants a', b', c' may be determined by means of a calibration. Note that the two optical axes of the two TV cameras intersect with each other at the origin of the spatial coordinates.

This camera model is used for two purposes. First, it converts a disparity value into a depth value. A hori-

Fig. 2. Segmentation schema. A. A hyperbolic surface and an elliptic surface. B. A needle map of a *hyperbolic surface and a needle map of an elliptic surface. C. Segmented result using a dodecahedral, geo-* *desic dome. D. Segmented result using a one-frequency, dodecahedral, geodesic dome. E. Segmented result* *using a two-frequency, dodecahedral, geodesic dome.*

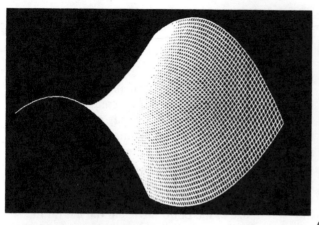
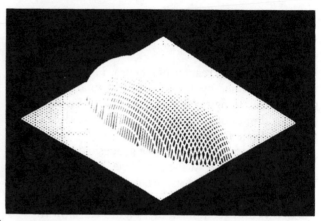

A

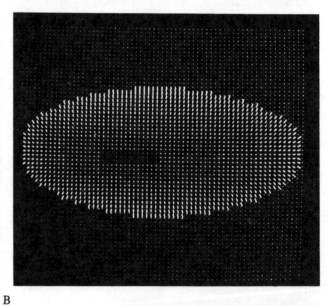

B

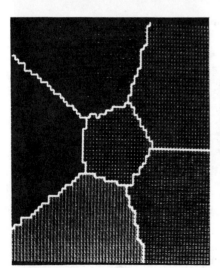
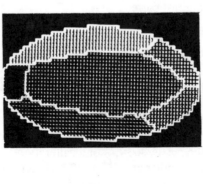
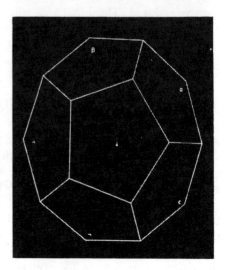

C

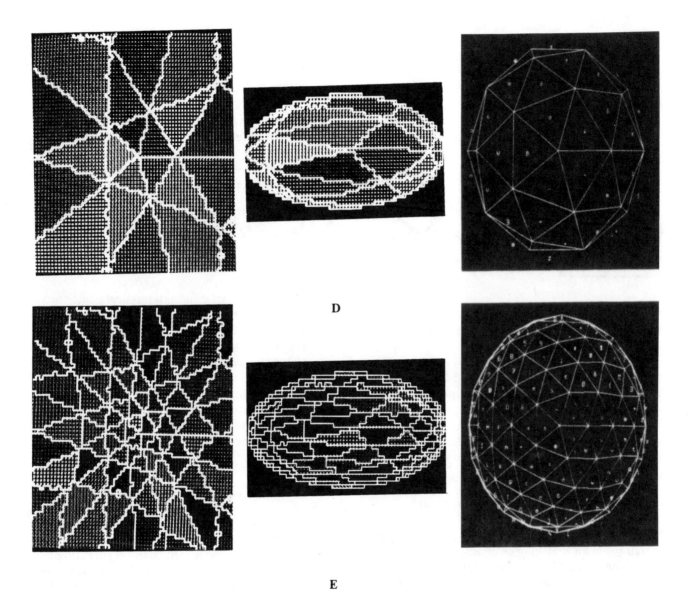

D

E

zontal difference in a region's mass-center positions gives a disparity value. This disparity value can be converted into a depth value using the camera model. Second, it constrains the possible area within which a candidate match can exist. Under this orthographic projection, two corresponding regions have the same y coordinate values in the left and right images. This constraint is the epipolar-line constraint (Barnard and Fishler 1982).

4. Region Matching

Matching of regions depends on characteristics of the regions. Since corresponding regions in images are projections of the same physical surface patch, corresponding regions have similar physical characteristics. Our system uses the following three characteristics to constrain possible candidate pairs: vertical mass-center

Fig. 3. Camera model.

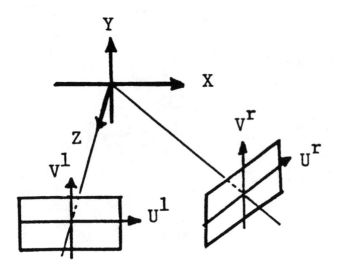

positions, average surface-orientation directions, and area.

The matching operation also follows the coarse-to-fine strategy. At first, coarse-segmented regions, which have been obtained using the smoothness filter, are matched. Then, fine segmented regions using a geodesic dome are matched, based on the result of the coarse matching. The coarse-segmented result gives the disparity limits for the fine-segmented regions.

4.1. Constraints on Region Matching

The following four constraints are used to reduce the search space for matching efficiency: (1) surface orientation constraint, (2) area constraint, (3) epipolar-line constraint, and (4) parent-children constraint. The first three constraints reduce the search space between the left and right regions, and the fourth constraint reduces the search space in the coarse-to-fine direction.

Surface orientation constraint
If a region in the left image corresponds to a region in the right image, then the average surface orientation of the region in the left image should be similar to the average surface orientation of the region in the right image. Note that this criterion is based on the global coordinate system. Namely, each surface orientation in an image coordinate system is converted into the

surface orientation in the global coordinate system. This is possible because our camera model is the orthographic projection.

Area constraint
If two regions correspond to each other, the two regions should have similar areas. Again this criterion is based on the global coordinate system. Since we know the average surface orientation of the region, we can convert the area size on the image plane into the area size on the plane perpendicular to the average surface orientation. This converted area size is independent of the local coordinate system. The resulting area size will be used for comparison.

Epipolar-line constraint
Our camera model projects a physical point onto the left and right image planes so that y coordinates of the two corresponding image pixels are the same. Thus, the corresponding mass-centers should have the same y coordinate in the image planes. Usually segmentation results and camera positions contain noise. Thus, the corresponding mass centers do not always have the same y coordinate. However, they have nearly the same y coordinate. The search process searches the corresponding mass center around the y coordinate within some limits.

Parent-children constraint
Regions are divided into finer subregions as we go along. We will call a region the *parent region* and the subregions the *children regions*. If a left parent region and a right parent region correspond to each other, a left child region from the left parent region should correspond to one of the right children regions from the right parent region: that is, a subregion's search area for matching is limited to the subregions of the parent's partner.

4.2. Matching Operation

Roughly speaking, the matching operation compares left and right region lists using (1) *orientation constraint*, (2) *area constraint*, (3) *epipolar-line constraint*. First, left region lists and right region lists are generated so that each list consists of regions having a common surface orientation (common cell number on the geodesic dome). Second, list pairs between left lists and right lists are generated so that each list pair has left and right lists whose regions have the same surface orientation (common cell number on the geodesic dome). Third, a matching algorithm establishes a region pair among regions in a list pair so that the left region and the right region of the region pair have the similar area size and position of mass-center.

This matching algorithm follows the coarse-to-fine strategy. At the coarsest stage, region matches will be established between the left and the right region maps using the smoothness filter. Then, region matches will be refined between the left and the right region maps by a dodecahedral geodesic dome using a *parent-children constraint*. These region matches will be refined iteratively between region maps obtained by a one-frequency, dodecahedral, geodesic dome; by region maps obtained by a two-frequency, dodecahedral, geodesic dome; and so on, until the desired accuracy is obtained. The following nine steps show the region-matching procedure.

1. *Making children groups*
   Children groups will be generated from region maps. Each children group consists of regions sharing a common parent region. In particular, the first stage has only one children group, which consists of all regions segmented by the smoothness filter. This is a preparation step for utilizing *the parent-children constraint*.

2. *Making common surface-orientation subgroups*
   Each children group will be divided into common surface-orientation subgroups (CSO subgroups) so that each CSO subgroup consists of regions having common surface orientation: that is, each region in a CSO subgroup shares both the same parent and the same surface orientation. This step is due to *the surface orientation constraint*.

3. *Generating CSO subgroup pairs*
   CSO subgroup pairs are searched among the left CSO subgroups and the right CSO subgroups whose parents are known to be corresponding regions from the previous iteration. (At the very beginning, all the regions are re-

garded as sharing the same parent. See Step 1.) If a left CSO subgroup and a right CSO subgroup have the same surface orientation, these two subgroups are registered as a subgroup pair. See Fig. 4.

4. *Deciding a target subgroup pair*
   One subgroup pair is selected for matching. Note that one subgroup pair contains a left CSO subgroup and a right CSO subgroup.

5. *Deciding a target CSO subgroup*
   The subgroup having fewer regions is selected for matching between the left CSO subgroup and the right CSO subgroup of the target subgroup pair. For the sake of explanation, let the left CSO subgroup contain fewer regions than the right CSO subgroup.

6. *Deciding a target region*
   The largest region among the left CSO subgroup is selected for matching. This region is called the *target region*.

7. *Matching the target region with candidate regions*
   Each region keeps the following five properties for matching: surface orientation, parent region, area size, horizontal disparity, and vertical disparity. Surface orientation, parent region, and horizontal disparity reduce candidate regions. Area and vertical disparity give a criterion to determine the most likely region.

A region corresponding to the target region is searched among the right CSO subgroups. Note that the regions in the right CSO subgroup have the same surface orientation and the same parent region as the target region. Thus, this stage can be regarded as applying the surface-orientation constraint and the parent-children constraint to the search process.

Only regions in the right CSO having horizontal disparity within some limit are considered as candidates. Since our cameras have optical axes intersecting at the ground level, the negative horizontal disparity never occurs. This gives the negative limit ϵ_1 of horizontal disparity. Also our system has a height limit in measurement. Namely, a region that is too high cannot be observed by the photometric stereo

Fig. 4. Common surface-orientation subgroup pairs.

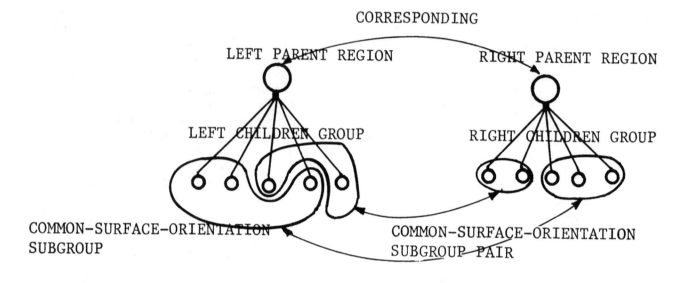

CORRESPONDING

LEFT PARENT REGION   RIGHT PARENT REGION

LEFT CHILDREN GROUP   RIGHT CHILDREN GROUP

COMMON–SURFACE–ORIENTATION SUBGROUP

COMMON–SURFACE–ORIENTATION SUBGROUP PAIR

LEFT   RIGHT

system due to distortion of the orthographic camera model. Thus, this height limit gives the positive horizontal disparity ϵ_2.

Since a previous coarse stage gives depth information over a region, a disparity value d can be predictable. This d may contain an error term ϵ_3, where ϵ_3 can be determined as a function of the angular difference between the previous segmentational dome cell and the present cell. Regions whose horizontal disparity satisfies the following condition are considered as candidates.

$$\{x \mid (\max x_r - \epsilon_1, x_r + d - \epsilon_3) \\ < x < (\min x_r + \epsilon_2, x_r + d + \epsilon_3)\},$$

where x_r is the mass center of the target region and d is the observed disparity obtained in the previous stage along the coarse-to-fine strategy. (In the coarsest stage, d is set to zero and ϵ_3 is set to infinity.)

The area constraint and the epipolar constraint are used to measure similarity between the target region and a candidate region among the

right CSO subgroups. The evaluation function is as follows:

$$\left(1 - \frac{\Delta \text{ area}}{\text{area}}\right) \times \left(1 - \frac{\Delta y}{\Delta y \text{ dist } \_ \text{ limit}}\right)$$

where *area* is the area size of the target region, Δ *area* is the difference between the area size of the target region and that of the candidate region; *y dist _ limit* is the limit of allowable vertical disparity, and Δy is the vertical disparity between the mass-center position of the target region and that of a candidate region.

7.1. *Success.*

If a region corresponding to the target region is found among the regions of the right CSO subgroup, the region pair is registered. Then, the target region is deleted from the left CSO subgroup and the corresponding region is deleted from the right CSO subgroup.

7.2 *Failure.*

If a corresponding region cannot be found in the right CSO subgroup, only the target region is deleted from the left CSO subgroup.

8. *Applying all the left region*
Operations 6–7 will be applied to all the regions of the left common surface-orientation subgroups until the left subgroups are exhausted.

9. *Applying all the region pairs*
Operations 5–8 will be applied to all the subgroup pairs until the subgroup pairs are exhausted.

5. Iterative Smoothing Operation

An *iterative smoothing operation* obtains a precise depth map. A coarse depth map by the region matching method will be smoothed into a precise depth map obtained by this iterative method. This iterative method is not a simple integration but a smoothing operation based on surface orientations and differences in surface orientations between corresponding pixels.

An iterative equation is constructed to satisfy the following conditions:

1. Observed (p, q) should agree with the first derivative of z with respect to the image axis, x, y, respectively. This is the definition of (p, q). Thus,

$$s = (z_x - p)^2 + (z_y - q)^2 \qquad (5)$$

should be zero everywhere in the resulting precise depth map.

2. A pair of corresponding pixels on the left and right images should have the same surface orientation, because the pixels must represent the same physical point. Thus,

$$d^p = (p^r(\mathrm{a}x + \mathrm{b}z + \mathrm{c}, y) - p^l(x, y))^2, \qquad (6)$$
$$d^q = (q^r(\mathrm{a}x + \mathrm{b}z + \mathrm{c}, y) - q^l(x, y))^2$$

should be zero, where (p^l, q^l), (p^r, q^r) are the surface orientations on the left and right surface-orientation maps. Here a, b, c are parameters determined from the spatial relationship between the two cameras.

By using Eqs. 5 and 6, the following equation is obtained.

$$e = \int (d^p + d^q)dxdy. \qquad (7)$$

We will find the functional z that minimizes e.

From the Euler-Lagrange equation,

$$\Delta^2 z = (p^l_x + q^l_y) + (\lambda \mathrm{b}) \\ \times ((p^r - p^l)p^r_x + (q^r - q^l)q^r_x). \qquad (8)$$

Using these approximation equations,

$$\Delta^2 z_{i,j} = \mathrm{k}(\bar{z}_{i,j} - z_{i,j}), \qquad (9)$$

$$\bar{z}_{i,j} = (z_{i+1,j} + z_{i-1,j} + z_{i,j+1} + z_{i,j-1})/4, \qquad (10)$$

we have

$$z^{n+1} = z^n - \lambda(p^l_x + q^l_y) - (\lambda \rho \mathrm{b}) \\ \times ((p^r - p^l)p^r_x - (q^r - q^l)q^r_x), \qquad (11)$$

where λ, ρ, b are constants.

6. Experiment

6.1. System Set-Up

In our system, the left TV camera is roughly 2 m above the ground, and the TV camera's image plane is parallel to the ground plane. The right TV camera is located 30 cm to the right of the left TV camera, and that TV camera's image plane is inclined by 7 degrees so that the optical axes of these TV cameras intersect at the origin of the spatial coordinate system, where the spatial origin is under the left TV camera. See Fig. 1.

Parameters for conversion from disparity values into depth values will be determined experimentally. Namely, parameters a′, b′, c′ in Eq. 4 will be determined by the least-squares method. A checkerboard pattern is observed by the TV cameras. The addresses of feature points (intersection points) on the TV images will give u^l and d, while the checkerboard's height is substituted into z. The least-squares fitting gives a′, b′, c′ from these observed values.

Fig. 5. Angular accuracy.

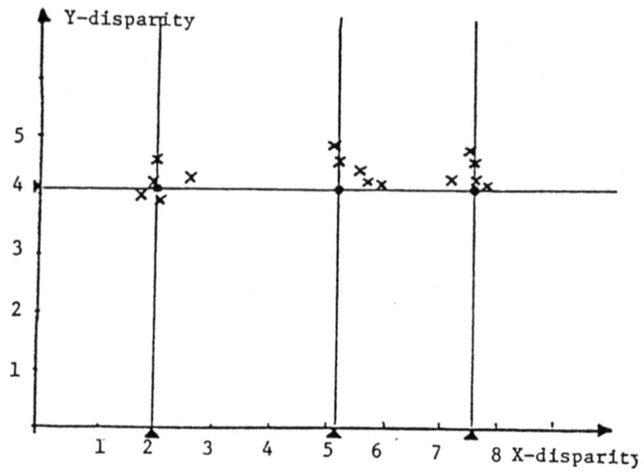

Fig. 6. Accuracy in depth measurement.

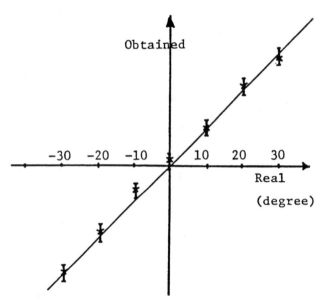

The lookup tables of the left and the right photometric stereo are obtained using a calibration sphere. The following operations will be executed in both the left and the right cameras so that the left and right lookup tables are obtained. First, the occluding boundary of the sphere is extracted after turning on all three light sources. Second, three pictures of the sphere after turning on one of the three light sources are taken from the camera. Third, a brightness triple at each pixel is sampled. Fourth, the surface orientation at the pixel is registered at a boxel, corresponding to the triple, of the 3-D lookup table. These operations give the left and right lookup tables.

(p, q)'s on the right lookup table are converted into (p, q)'s on the left camera coordinate system. Since surface orientation of the right lookup table is expressed on the right camera's coordinate system, it is converted into the surface orientation in the left camera's coordinate system. This conversion constant is obtained by the angle between the left and right image planes.

The visible area from the left camera is always visible from the right camera. A photometric stereo system can observe areas where three brightness values are higher than some threshold. The limiting angle is the radius of the spherical circle circumscribing this area. The limiting angle of the left photometric stereo

is less than 50 degrees, while the angle between the left and right image planes is 7 degrees. Thus, the visible area from the left camera is always visible from the right camera. Note that the left and right cameras share the same lighting system.

6.2. Accuracy of this System

The accuracy of this system depends on the accuracy of the photometric stereo system, because our segmentation is based on surface orientations by the photometric stereo system. The accuracy of the photometric stereo system is measured by determining surface orientations of a white board inclined at various angles. Figure 5 shows both the angles obtained experimentally and the true angles. It also shows that the photometric stereo system can determine surface orientations within a 3-degree error.

The accuracy in depth is measured by determining the known height of blocks. Figure 6 shows the measured disparity values and the real disparity values. The horizontal axis denotes x disparity and the vertical axis denotes y disparity. The x disparity gives depth information. Even though the ideal case gives 0 disparity in y direction, our system gives 4.1 mean disparity due to a vertical tilt between the two TV cameras. A 0.7 pixel disparity error occurs in both directions. This error corresponds to 1 cm error in depth. Note that since a mass-center position is deter-

Fig. 7. Input scene.

Fig. 8. A pair of surface-orientation maps.

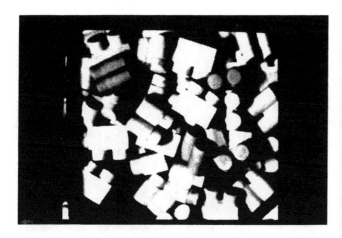

mined by a subpixel resolution, a disparity is also determined by a subpixel resolution.

Our earlier discussion assumes that epipolar lines are parallel to scan lines on the image planes. However, real epipolar lines are not always parallel to scan lines. The maximum difference of an epipolar line from a scan line occurs at the corner of the image, provided that the scan line and the epipolar line intersect each other at the center of the image plane and can be approximated by $(dx)/z \tan \gamma$, where x is the physical length of the observable area, z is the distance of the point from the TV camera, d is the size of the image planes, and γ is the angle between the two image planes of the TV cameras. In our case, $x = 15$ cm, $z = 200$ cm, $d = 64$ pixels, $\gamma = 7$ degrees. Thus, the maximum relative difference of an epipolar line from a scan line gives 0.6 pixels. This is the same order as the observed measurement error, so we can ignore the nonparallel effect.

6.3. EXPERIMENT 1: BIN OF PARTS

The system was applied to the scene shown in Fig. 7. Surfaces of each object have the Lambertian property. Three pairs of images were taken under three different light sources using the left and right TV cameras. The pair of photometric stereo systems converted the three pairs of images into a pair of surface-orientation maps, shown in Fig. 8.

The smoothness filter applied to these surface-orien-

tation maps converts them into the segmented region maps shown in Fig. 9. A mass-center position, an area size, and a mean-surface orientation are calculated for each isolated region. These characteristics of regions reduce the matching possibilities between the left regions and the right regions.

Comparing the left regions with the right regions gives corresponding region pairs with similar characteristics. Horizontal disparities in mass-center positions give the depth values at mass centers using the camera model. Figure 10 shows the resulting depth map. Since this segmentation by the smoothness filter

Fig. 9. A pair of segmented region maps.

Fig. 9. A pair of segmented region maps.

Fig. 11. A pair of surface-orientation maps of a sphere.

Fig. 10. A depth map.

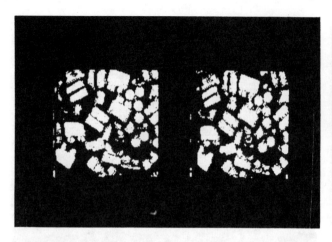

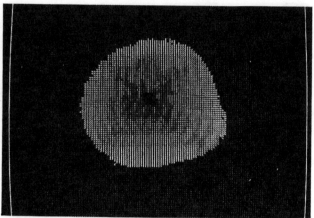

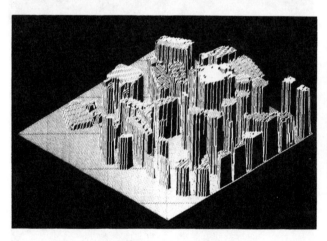

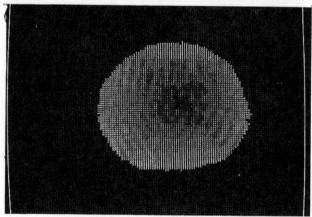

gives precise enough regions for this scene, the system is stopped at this stage of iteration.

This system runs on a Symbolics 3600 and takes roughly 10 s to get the surface-orientation map, 20 s to get the region map, and 5 s to get the depth map comparing the left and right segmented regions. Overall, about 1 min is necessary to get the final depth map from the three pairs of 128×128 brightness images.

6.4. EXPERIMENT 2: SPHERE

The next example is a sphere. The pair of photometric stereo systems gives a pair of surface-orientation maps

(Fig. 11). The smoothness filter converts these surface-orientation maps into a pair of region maps (Fig. 12A). The matching operation between these region maps gives the depth map (Fig. 12B). The segmentation by a dodecahedral geodesic dome gives the region maps as shown in Fig. 13A from the pair of surface-orientation maps and the pair of previous region maps. Using both these segmented results and the coarse depth map in the previous stage, the region matching operation gives the finer depth map shown in Fig. 13B. The same operation is repeated using a one-frequency, dodecahedral, geodesic dome and gives the result as shown in Fig. 14. A two-frequency, dodecahedral, geodesic dome gives Fig. 15.

The iterative smoothing operation described in Section 5 gives the results as shown in Fig. 16 after 300 iterations, starting from the depth map shown in Fig.

Fig. 12. A depth map by the smoothness filter. A. A pair of region maps by the smoothness filter. B. A depth map obtained.

Fig. 13. A depth map by a dodecahedral, geodesic dome. A. A pair of region maps by a dodecahedral, geodesic dome. B. A depth map obtained.

Fig. 14. A depth map by a one-frequency, dodecahedral, geodesic dome. A. A pair of region maps by a one-frequency, dodecahedral, geodesic dome. B. A depth map obtained.

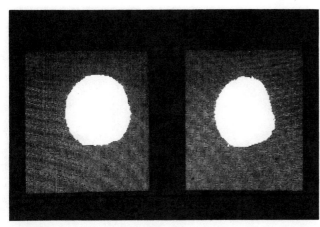

Fig. 12A

B

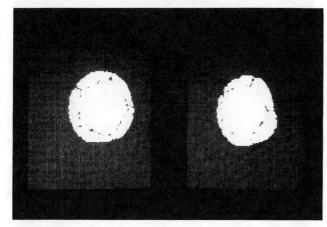

Fig. 13A

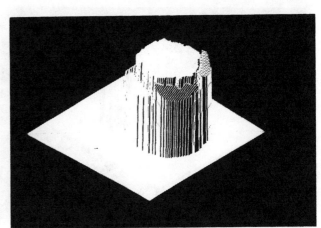

B

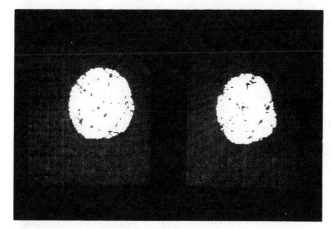

Fig. 14A

B

Fig. 15. A depth map by a two-frequency, dodecahedral, geodesic dome. A. A pair of region maps by a two-frequency, dodecahedral, geodesic dome. B. A depth map obtained.

Fig. 16. A depth map obtained by the iterative smoothing operation. A. A perspective view of the obtained surface. B. A side view of the obtained surface.

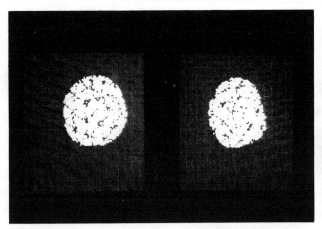

Fig. 15A

B

Fig. 16A

B

15. Figure 16B contains two diagrams: the upper shape is the one obtained by this operation and the lower shape is the one obtained by directly integrating surface orientations of the left needle map. The vertical difference is the absolute depth determined by this iterative algorithm. The upper shape's distortion is due to the error by this iterative algorithm.

7. Conclusion

This paper describes a region-based stereo method using a pair of surface-orientation maps. This algorithm consists of the following components:

1. A pair of surface-orientation maps is obtained from a pair of photometric stereo systems.
2. A pair of surface-orientation maps is segmented into a pair of isolated region maps on surface orientations using a geodesic dome.
3. Feature points for stereo matching are mass centers of isolated regions.
4. The area constraint, the mean surface-orientation constraint, and the epipolar constraint improve the efficiency of search operations.
5. The process follows the coarse-to-fine strategy. At the beginning stage, coarsely segmented regions are compared and a coarse depth map is generated. This coarse depth map is used as the input to the next stage. The parent-chil-

dren constraint is applied to make the search operation efficient using this strategy.

We do not segment images using brightness thresholds. Segmentation for binocular stereo should use an intrinsic property of the object surface, such as surface orientation; the segmentation should not be based on a property such as apparent brightness, which depends on the viewer direction. Only an intrinsic property gives a segmentation result independent of the viewer direction. Other possible intrinsic properties suitable for region-based stereo would be color and albedo.

Acknowledgments

B. K. P. Horn, Takeo Kanade, S. A. Shafer, and the referees provided many useful comments, which have improved the readability of this paper.

REFERENCES

Baker, H. 1981. (Vancouver, B.C.). Edge-based stereo correlation. *Proc. IJCAI-7:*631–636.

Barnard, S. T., and Fishler, M. A. 1982. Computational stereo. *ACM Computing Survey* 14(4):553–572.

Barrow, H. G., and Tenenbaum, J. M. 1978. Recovering intrinsic scene characteristics from images. *Computer Vision Systems,* eds. A. Hanson and E. Riseman, pp. 3–26. New York: Academic Press.

Brady, J. M. 1981. *Computer vision.* Amsterdam: North-Holland.

Grimson, W. E. L. 1981. *From images to surfaces.* Cambridge: MIT Press.

Horn, B. K. P., Woodham, R. J., and Silver, W. M. 1978. Determining shape and reflectance using multiple images. AI memo 490. Cambridge: Massachusetts Institute of Technology Artificial Intelligence Laboratory.

Ikeuchi, K. 1981. Determining surface orientations of specular surfaces by using the photometric stereo system. *IEEE Trans. PAMI,* PAMI 2(6):661–669.

Ikeuchi, K., et al. 1986. Determining grasp configurations using photometric stereo and the PRISM binocular stereo system. *Int. J. Robotics Res.* 5(1):46–65.

Marr, D., and Hildreth, E. 1980. Theory of edge detection. *Proc. Royal Society of London B.* 207:187–217.

Marr, D., and Poggio, T. 1979. A computational theory of human stereo vision. AI Memo 451. Cambridge: Massachusetts Institute of Technology Artificial Intelligence Laboratory.

Moravec, H. 1979 (Tokyo). Visual mapping by a robot rover. *Proc. IJCAI* 6:598–600.

Nishihara, H. K. 1984. PRISM: a practical realtime imaging stereo matcher. AI Memo 780. Cambridge: Massachusetts Institute of Technology Artificial Intelligence Laboratory.

Ohta, Y., and Kanade, T. 1985. Stereo by intra- and inter-scanline search using dynamic programming. *IEEE Trans. PAMI* PAMI 7(2):139–154.

Roberts, L. G. 1965. Machine perception of three-dimensional solids. *Optical and electro-optical information processing,* ed J. T. Tippett, pp. 159–197. Cambridge: MIT Press.

Thorpe, C. E. 1984 (April 30–May 2, Annapolis, Md.). An analysis of interest operators for FIDO. *Proc. IEEE Workshop on Computer Vision: Representation and Control:* 135–140.

Wenninger, M. J. 1979. *Spherical models.* New York: Cambridge University Press.

Woodham, R. J. 1979. Reflectance map techniques for analyzing surface defects in metal casting. AI-TR-457. Cambridge: Massachusetts Institute of Technology Artificial Intelligence Laboratory.

Determining Reflectance Parameters using Range and Brightness Images[1]

Katsushi Ikeuchi   Kosuke Sato

School of Computer Science
Carnegie Mellon University
Pittsburgh, PA 15213

Abstract

This paper discusses a method of recovering reflectance parameters of optically rough surfaces from a range and a brightness image, both of which are generated by a range-finder. Our reflectance model of an optically rough surface consists of two components, known as Lambertian and specular components and respectively represented as a cosine and a Gaussian function, and contains the following three basic parameters: the Lambertian strength, specular strength, and specular sharpness.

We employed an iterative least square fitting method to obtain these parameters derived from range and brightness images. Assuming all pixels only contain the Lambertian component, we fit the Lambertian function to all the data points. Based on the fitting of these results, we use a threshold derived from a sensor model of the range-finder and exclude those pixels lying outside the bounds of this threshold. We refit the function to the remaining data points and extract the Lambertian strength as well as the precise light source direction. Since the extra brightness of the pixels exceeding the thresholded value can be attributed to the specular component of brightness, we fit the specular function to the brighter outlying pixels and extract specular strength and sharpness.

To examine the convergence of our algorithm, we implemented this algorithm and applied it to several synthesized images. We also conducted several experiments using real images to demonstrate the applicability of our algorithm.

1 Introduction

Measuring surface reflectance from image brightness is an important issue in both basic and applied computer vision research. For example, in basic computer vision research, surface reflectance gives a reliable cue for segmenting images, and we can build a more dependable and accurate segmentation system using surface reflectance. Since surface reflectance is directly related to surface polishness and roughness, surface reflectance is an important inspection criteria in many industrial applications. Currently tasks such as inspecting surface deformations in silicon wafers or detecting flaws in the painted exteriors of cars are performed by the judgement of the human eye. Since many of these tasks are tedious and potentially dangerous, it is desirable to investigate a method which measures surface reflectance automatically and to develop an inspection system based on this method.

Although the measurement of surface reflectance properties in applied physics has been the topic of inumerable pieces of literature, until recently, few attempts in computer vision research have been made to apply these theories to recovering the reflectance properties from image brightness. Woodham proposed to recover surface albedo using photometric stereo [23]. Coleman and Jain extracted specular pixels based on the variance of surface orientations given by four photometric stereos at each pixel [4]. Nayar, Ikeuchi, and Kanade proposed to recover surface reflectance from a sequence of images taken under a collection of extended light sources [14]. Klinker, Shafer, and Kanade proposed to separate specular reflection from Lambertian reflection by analysis of color [12], while Wolff proposed a separation method based on analysis of polarization [22].

With the exception of Nayar, Ikeuchi, and Kanade's work, the above mentioned research only attempted to separate specular reflection from the lambertian reflection. No attempts have been made to directly extract either one or both of the reflectance parameters.

This paper proposes to recover surface reflectance parameters based on the two images, a range image and a brightness image, generated by a range-finder. A range finder can produce a range image relatively easily and can also provide a brightness image, which is usually thrown away. Recently, range finders have become more widely used in industrial applications [2] and the quality of the images generated by range finders has increased significantly. We will use the range image as well as this otherwise discarded brightness image for parameter extraction.

In order to recover such reflectance parameters, we need a solid reflectance understanding on reflectance mechanism. The first section will examine several reflectance models. Then, we will refine the model and derive an image irradiance equation which will establish a relationship between surface orientations, reflectance parameters, and image irradiance. Third, we will devise a method which incorporates this equation and estimates the values for the reflectance parameters. Finally, we will examine this methodology by applying it to several images for recovering reflectance parameters.

---

[1]This research was sponsored by Osaka Gas, Osaka Japan, and conducted in Intelligent Modelling Laboratory, VASC center, Carnegie Mellon University. Image Understanding Research in VASC center is supported in part by the Defense Advanced Research Projects Agency, DOD, through ARPA Order No. 4976, and monitored by the Air Force Avionics Laboratory under contract F33615-87-C-1499. Kosuke Sato was on leave of absence from Osaka University, Osaka Japan.

2   Reflectance Model

Researchers in computer graphics areas [17, 3, 7, 8] have proposed several reflectance models to generate realistic appearances on synthesized images. Here, two typical surface reflectance models have been used: Lambertian and specular. The Lambertian component was represented as the Lambertian's cosine function. Several models for the specular component have been proposed. Phong [17] proposed the specular model which was spread out around the specular direction by using a cosine function raised to a power. Blinn [3] proposed a model which accounts for off-specular peaks that occur when the incident light is at a grazing angle. Horn [8] surveyed several models used in hill shadings.

These graphics models mainly concentrate on calculating the specular component in convenient manners and uses ad hoc models which give relatively realistic appearances. On the other hand, in computer vision, we have to analyze data from a real image and we have to base our analyzation on a more accurate and complete reflectance model. Thus, we need a to develop a more precise model which is based on optics.

2.1   Lambertian Model

When light strikes an interface between two different medias, some percentage of the light passes through the boundary and the remaining portion of the light is reflected. The penetrating light hits internal pigments of an object, and is re-emitted randomly. We will refer to this reflection component as the *Lambertian component*. The Lambertian component has been represented by the Lambertian's cosine function between the surface orientation and the light source direction [13].

The formula for the Lambertian reflection is:

$$
\begin{aligned}
L &= C_l\, \vec{\mathbf{N}} \cdot \vec{\mathbf{S}} & (1) \\
&= C_l\, \cos\theta_i
\end{aligned}
$$

where L, $\vec{\mathbf{N}}$, $\vec{\mathbf{S}}$, C_l, and θ_i are the brightness, the surface orientation, the light source direction, a proportional constant, the angle between the surface orientation and light source direction, respectively. Reflective surfaces comprised of only the Lambertian component of reflection look equally bright from all directions. The Lambertian component, represented by the Lambertian's cosine function, has been used extensively in the computer vision community. The results indicate that this model predicts reasonably accurately.

2.2   Specular Models

The specular model, such as polished metals obey, reflects when the angle between the light source direction and the surface orientation is equal to the angle between the surface orientation and the viewer direction. The specular component can be described in terms of two completely different approaches: the physical and the geometrical. The geometric approach uses the assumption of the short wavelength of light and solves the propagation of light in the geometric treatment. The physical approach is based on electromagnetic wave theory and uses the Maxwell's equations to study the propagation of light. The representative model in the physical approach is the Beckman-Spizzichino

model [1], and the representative model in the optical approach is the Torrance-Sparrow model [21].

The Torrance-Sparrow geometric optics model mainly aims to model rough surface of any materials [2]. The Beckman-Spizzichino model describes the reflection of plane waves from rough to smooth metal surfaces. The Torrance-Sparrow model provides a good approximation of the Beckmann-Spizzichino model when the surface is rough. While it may be construed as a mere approximation to a physical reflectance model, it possesses a simpler mathematical form that often renders it more usable than a physical model.

The optical roughness can be defined as the measure that relates surface irregularities to the wavelength of the incident light and the angle of incidence. Mathematically, the optical roughness g is defined as

$$
g = (2\pi \frac{\sigma_h}{\lambda}(\cos\theta_i + \cos\theta_r))^2, \qquad (2)
$$

where σ_h, and λ are the root-mean-square of the height distribution (surface roughness), and the wavelength, respectively [1]. When $g \gg 1$, the surface is referred to as the optically rough. When $g \ll 1$, the surface is referred to as the optically smooth.

Physical Model The *Physical* approach is based directly on electromagnetic wave theory and uses Maxwell's equations to study the propagation of light. Beckmann and Spizzichino [1, 10] derived their reflectance model by solving Maxwell's equation using Helmholtz integral with Kirchoff's assumption on a perfect conductor surface (metal).

The Beckmann-Spizzichino model consists of the specular lobe and spike components. The specular spike component causes a sharp reflection like a perfect mirror. This component can be represented as a delta function, which is zero in all directions except for the specular direction. Ikeuchi used this spike model to represent a metal surface reflection. He combined the specular spike portion of the model with the extended-light-source photometric stereo method [11] to determine the orientation of such surfaces. Sanderson, Weiss, and Nayar also used this same model as a base for building an inspection system of a sodar joint [18]. The specular lobe component causes a dull reflection which can be typically observed on a sand-bruised metal. It may be represented as a Gaussian function, which spreads around the specular direction.

Geometrical Model The *geometrical* approach assumes that the wavelength is short, and simplifies many of the light propagation problems. Torrance and Sparrow proposed a reflectance model based on this geometrical approach [21]. The reflectance function is represented by a Gaussian function of the surface roughness parameter. This function has a similar shape to the Beckmann-Spizzino's function when the surface is rough.

This model is computationally much simpler and gives a good approximation, when the wavelength of incident light is

---

[2]Note that even a vary rough surface has a specular reflection, because the specular reflection is the result of process that an incident light cannot penetrate a surface and is reflected there, thus the surface roughness is independent on whether a specular reflection occurs or not. The roughness, however, changes the shape of specular reflectance function describe below.

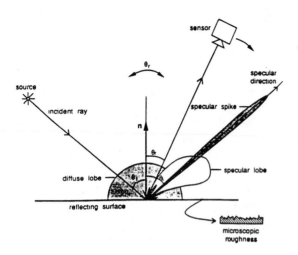

Figure 1: Diagram of the general reflectance model [15]

small when compared to the dimensions of the *microscopic* surface imperfections. Since their model is simple, several computer vision works are based on their model. For example, Healey and Binford have used this model to determine local shape from specular reflections [6].

2.3   General Reflectance Model

By expressing the surface roughness in the same representation, we have recently proposed a general reflectance model that combines the Lambertian, the Beckmann-Spizzichino and the Torranace-Sparrow model [15]. This general reflectance model consists of three components: Lambertian component, the specular lobe component, and the specular spike component (see Figure 1). Each of these components can be represented by, repectively, these three functions: the Lambertian's cosine function, the Gaussian function, and the delta function.

Let us assume that the surface is located at the origin of the coordinate frame, and its surface normal points in the direction of Z axis. The surface is illuminated by a beam of light that lies in the X-Z plane and is incident on the surface at an angle, θ_i. The viewer is located at (θ_r, o_r).

Under this geometry, we can represent the general reflectance model as

$$L_{general} = C_l \cos \theta_i + C_{sl} \frac{\exp(-k \alpha^2)}{\cos \theta_r} + C_{ss} \delta(\theta_i - \theta_r) \delta(o_r). \quad (3)$$

where the constants C_l, C_{sl}, C_{ss} represent the strengths of the Lambertian, specular lobe, and specular spike components, respectively. The angle α denotes the angle between the surface orientation and the bisector of the viewing and source directions. The parameter, k represents the Torrance-Sparrow surface roughness parameter.

The optical roughness is the principle factor which determines the ratio of the specular spike and specular lobe component. For smooth surface ($g \ll 1$), the spike component is

dominant. As the roughness increase, however, the spike component shrinks rapidly, and for rough surface ($g \gg 1$), the lobe component begins to dominate. The two components are simultaneously significant for only a very small range of roughness values.

3   Range-Brightness Fusion method

We will assume that the surface is optically rough. Several interesting surface, such as sand-bruised, metal mold, and ionize aluminum, exhibits the characteristics of the optically rough.

For the optically rough surface, we can neglect the spike component, and obtain the following reflectance model from the general reflectance model, (Eq. 3).

$$L_{fusion} = C_l \cos \theta_i + C_{sl} \frac{\exp(-k \alpha^2)}{\cos \theta_r} \quad (4)$$

The parameter, C_{sl} contains the Frenel coefficient and the geometric attenuation factors defined in the Torrance and Sparrow model. In order to handle this C_{sl} as a constant within a field of view, we assume that the angle between the light source and the TV camera direction from an object surface is less than 60 degrees. This is a realistic assumption that is usually satisfied by the positioning of the range-finder. This positioning also discards information from the patch which is inclined more than 60 degrees with respect to the viewing direction.

A reflectance map represents the radiance on an object surface under a light source. On the other hand, we will observe an irradiance value on a pixel given by a radiance value on a surface patch. The relationship between image irradiance, E and the object radiance, L is given as:

$$E = L \frac{\pi}{4} (\frac{d}{f})^2 \cos^4 \gamma \quad (5)$$

where d is the diameter of a lens, f is the focal length of the lens, and γ is the angle between the optical axis and the line of sight [9].

If we are using orthographic projection, we can assume that $\gamma = 0$. Thus, we can conclude that image irradiance is proportional to surface radiance and that this ratio is independent of the surface patch position.

We can derive the image irradiance equation, which specify the image brightness on a pixel as

$$E = A \cos \theta_i + B \frac{\exp(-k \alpha^2)}{\cos \theta_r} \quad (6)$$

We will develop an algorithm to extract A, B, k from both a range and a brightness image. Figure 2 shows the configuration we will use. Figure 3 shows the intensity pattern as a function of the incident angle, θ_i, between the surface orientation and the light source. In the simplest case, we observe an intensity peak in the specular direction. Elsewhere the intensity follows the Lambertian cosine function, $A \cos \theta_i$, with the height of the cosine function giving us the Lambertian constant.

We will employ a two step strategy which will first determine A, and then will calculate B and k. In the first step, we

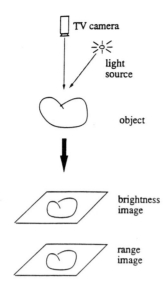

Figure 2: The sensor configuration of RBF method

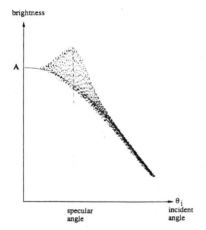

Figure 3: The intensity pattern of RBF method

will identify and discard the peak, and then iteratively fit the remaining data points to the function until A is determined. In the second step, we will analyze the outlying pixels from the Lambertian function to identify the specular lobe pixels. Finally, we will fit the specular lobe function to the pixels.

4   Lambertian Parameters

4.1   Extracting Lambertian parameters

Assume that all pixels belong to the Lambertian reflection. Then, we can denote the brightness at each pixel as:

$$
\begin{aligned}
E(x, y) &= A \cos \theta_i(x, y) \\
&= A \mathbf{N}(x, y) \cdot \mathbf{S} \qquad (7) \\
&= aNx(x, y) + bNy(x, y) + cNz(x, y)
\end{aligned}
$$

where

$$
\begin{aligned}
a &= AS_x \\
b &= AS_y
\end{aligned}
$$

$$
c = AS_z
$$

From range values, we will obtain the surface orientation, $\mathbf{N}(x, y)$ at each pixel. Using these orientations, we can determine (a, b, c) by a least square fitting.

Once we obtain these parameters, we can use the parameters, the surface orientations, and the following formula to recalculate ideal brightness:

$$
E_{cl}(x, y) = aNx(x, y) + bNy(x, y) + cNz(x, y)
$$

Based on these calculated brightness values, we can collect Lambertian pixels based on the criterion:

$$
|E_{ob}(x, y) - E_{cl}(x, y)| < \delta_l.
$$

where δ_l is the threshold value discriminating outlying pixels. We will repeat the least-square fitting on the collected pixels until (a, b, c) have converged.

The Lambertian strength, A, and the light source, $\mathbf{S}$, can be obtained by the following formulas:

$$
\begin{aligned}
A &= \sqrt{a^2 + b^2 + c^2} \\
\mathbf{S} &= \left(\frac{a}{A}, \frac{b}{A}, \frac{c}{A} \right)
\end{aligned}
$$

4.2   Threshold Value for Lambertian Pixel, δ_l

We can only obtain measured brightness, E_{ob}, and measured surface orientation, $\vec{\mathbf{N}}_{ob}$. These values are related to their real values by:

$$
\begin{aligned}
E_{ob} &= E_{rl} + \delta E \\
\vec{\mathbf{N}}_{ob} &= \vec{\mathbf{N}}_{rl} + \delta \vec{\mathbf{N}} \qquad (8)
\end{aligned}
$$

where δE and $\delta \vec{\mathbf{N}}$ are the uncertainty factors in brightness and surface orientation, respectively.

We can relate these uncertainty factor as follows:

$$
\begin{aligned}
E_{ob} &= A \vec{\mathbf{N}}_{rl} \cdot \vec{\mathbf{S}} + \delta E \\
&= A (\vec{\mathbf{N}}_{ob} - \delta \vec{\mathbf{N}}) \cdot \vec{\mathbf{S}} + \delta E \\
&\approx A \vec{\mathbf{N}}_{ob} \cdot \vec{\mathbf{S}} + A \delta \vec{\mathbf{N}} \cdot \vec{\mathbf{S}} + \delta E \qquad (9)
\end{aligned}
$$

We define the uncertainty factor of a measured brightness value with respect to a measured surface orientation by

$$
\delta E_{ob} = E_{ob} - A \vec{\mathbf{N}}_{ob} \cdot \vec{\mathbf{S}} \qquad (10)
$$

This factor can be obtained by inserting Eq.(9) into Eq.(10),

$$
\delta E_{ob} = \delta E + A \delta \vec{\mathbf{N}} \cdot \vec{\mathbf{S}}. \qquad (11)
$$

This equation contains two uncertainty factors, δE and $\delta \vec{\mathbf{N}}$. We assume that the uncertainty factor in observed brightness values, δE, is a Gaussian distribution of zero mean. We obtained its standard deviation by examining the outputs from our TV camera.

The uncertainty factor in the surface orientation, $\delta \vec{\mathbf{N}}$, can be obtained by examining the conversion method from a measured range value, z, to a surface orientation.

Our range finder provides three images, $X(i,j), Y(i,j), Z(i,j)$ which indicates the world coordinate system of the pixel, (i,j). Using this, we can obtain the gradient of that pixel by the following formulas:

$$
\begin{aligned}
p(i,j) &= \left.\frac{\partial Z}{\partial X}\right|_{i,j} = \frac{Z(i+1,j) - Z(i-1,j)}{X(i+1,j) - X(i-1,j)} \\
q(i,j) &= \left.\frac{\partial Z}{\partial Y}\right|_{i,j} = \frac{Z(i+1,j) - Z(i-1,j)}{Y(i+1,j) - Y(i-1,j)}
\end{aligned}
\quad (12)
$$

The uncertainty factor in surface orientation, $(\delta p, \delta q)$ can be estimated from the uncertainty factor in a range value, z as

$$
\begin{aligned}
\delta p &= \frac{\delta z}{\epsilon_1} \\
\delta q &= \frac{\delta z}{\epsilon_2},
\end{aligned}
\quad (13)
$$

where $\epsilon_1 = \frac{X(i+1,j) - X(i-1,j)}{2}$ and $\epsilon_2 = \frac{Y(i,j+1) - Y(i,j-1)}{2}$. Here, we ignore the uncertainty in (X,Y) measurements.

We assume that the light source direction is $(0.0, 0.0)$ for simplicity.

$$
\tan\theta = \tan^{-1}\sqrt{p^2 + q^2}.
$$

Then, the angle between the surface orientation and the light source direction, θ can be obtained from the surface orientation, (p,q). Thus,

$$
\begin{aligned}
\delta\theta &= \frac{\partial\theta}{\partial p}\delta p + \frac{\partial\theta}{\partial q}\delta q, \\
&= \frac{1}{1+p^2+q^2}\frac{1}{\sqrt{p^2+q^2}}(p\delta p + q\delta q).
\end{aligned}
\quad (14)
$$

Since $\delta\vec{N}\cdot\vec{S} = \sin\theta\,\delta\theta$, by inserting $\sin\theta = \frac{\sqrt{p^2+q^2}}{\sqrt{1+p^2+q^2}}$, Eq.(13), and Eq.(14) into Eq.(11), we obtain

$$
\delta E_{ob} = \delta E + k\delta z, \quad (15)
$$

where

$$
\begin{aligned}
k &= 2(\frac{A}{\epsilon})l, \\
l &= \frac{p+q}{(1+p^2+q^2)^{1.5}}.
\end{aligned}
$$

We will assume that the variance of the observed range value is modeled as a Gaussian distribution with a zero mean and standard deviation of σ_z. Namely, $\delta z \sim N(0, \sigma_z)$. As mentioned before, we assumed $\delta I \sim N(0, \sigma_I)$. Using the theorem for the sum of the two Gaussian distributions, we can model $\delta E'$ as $N(0, \sigma_{E'})$, where $\sigma_{E'} = \sqrt{\sigma_E^2 + (k\sigma_z)^2}$. We will use $3\sigma_{E'}$ as the threshold value for the Lambertian pixels; namely, $\delta_l = 3\sigma_{E'}$.

5   Specular Parameters

5.1   Parameter extraction

The pixels lying outside the threshold belong to three categories: specular, interreflection, and shadow. The specular and interreflection pixels are brighter than the Lambertian pixels while the shadow pixels are darker than the Lambertian ones. Thus, first we will extract the brighter pixels by

$$
E_{ob}(x,y) - E_{cl}(x,y) > \delta_l.
$$

The bisector direction between the light source and the viewer is referred to as the specular direction. The angle α is defined as that between the surface orientation and the specular direction. A specular pixel has the orientation near the specular direction (or α is small), while an interreflection pixel has a random orientation, usually far from the specular direction (or α is large). Thus, at each pixel, we will calculate the angle, α. Using the following criterion, we can select the specular pixels from the brighter thresholded pixels.

$$
\begin{aligned}
\alpha(x,y) &> \delta_\alpha \quad --- \quad \text{interreflection pixel} \\
\alpha(x,y) &< \delta_\alpha \quad --- \quad \text{specular pixel}
\end{aligned}
$$

A specular brightness can be obtained as:

$$
d(x,y) = E_{ob}(x,y) - E_{cl}(x,y). \quad (16)
$$

Then, the specular brightness satisfies the following formula:

$$
d(x,y) = B\frac{exp(-k\alpha(x,y)^2)}{\cos\theta_r(x,y)} \quad (17)
$$

Using the surface orientation, the viewer, and the source direction, we can calculate $\alpha(x,y)$ and $\theta_r(x,y)$ for each pixel.

Since this equation is non-linear, we will employ a two step fitting method to determine the parameters B and K. The first step determines k, the specular sharpness, by assuming that B, the specular strength, is known; conversely, the second step determines B, by using the obtained K. We will repeat these two steps several times until the two parameters, B and K converge.

Assuming that B, the specular strength, is known, the first step determines K, the specular sharpness by using the least-square fitting. so that it minimizes

$$
\begin{aligned}
e2 = \sum_{x,y}(\ln d(x,y) + \ln\cos\theta_r(x,y) + logB \\
-2K\alpha(x,y)^2)^2
\end{aligned}
\quad (18)
$$

Then, based on the obtained K, the second step obtains B so that it minimizes

$$
e3 = \sum_{x,y}(d(x,y) - Bexp(-k\alpha(x,y)^2)/\cos\theta_r(x,y))^2 \quad (19)
$$

We will continue to iterate these two steps, Eq.(18) to Eq.(19), until the two parameters B and K converge.

It is possible to obtain B and K simultaneously so that they minimize equation Eq.(18). However, due to the logarithm fitting, this method gives erroneous B. On the other hand, if we minimize equation Eq.(19), we have to employ a non-linear fitting method. Thus, we use the two-step fitting method described above.

In order to start this iterative fitting method, we need to assign an initial value to B. For the pixels which satisfy $\alpha = 0$, d has the maximum value $d(x,y) = B$. We use this maximum value of $d(x,y)$ as the initial approximation of B.

5.2 Threshold value, δ_α

We will define an effective range of α such that the specular component has more than 20% of the maximum brightness. If we insert this value into the specular component equation, we get the following equation: the

$$\exp(-k\delta_\alpha^2) = 0.2. \tag{20}$$

Namely,

$$-\sqrt{-\frac{1}{k}\ln 0.2} < \alpha < \sqrt{-\frac{1}{k}\ln 0.2} \tag{21}$$

Table 1 gives δ_α values for several k values.

The value of δ_α depends on the value of k. For the first iteration, since we do not know k yet, we will use an initial threshold value, 0.3. After the second iteration, we will use the exact threshold value given by Eq.21.

Table 1: Threshold values for specular parameters

k	1.0	5.0	10.0	20.0	50.0
δ_α	1.265	0.566	0.400	0.283	0.179

Table 2: Ranges given by the initial threshold value

k	1.0	5.0	10.0	20.0	50.0
$\exp(-0.09k)$	0.914	0.638	0.407	0.165	0.011

6 Experiments

We conducted several experiments using synthesized and real images. The synthesized images were used to examine the convergence of our system to the true value under various noise levels. The real images were used to demonstrate our system's ability to handle real applications.

6.1 Recovering Lambertian Parameters from Synthesized Images

We synthesized three brightness images of a Lambertian sphere, $A = 200$, $B = 0$, and $\vec{S} = (0.0. 0.0. 1.0)$ of three noise levels, $\sigma_E = 0. 3. 6$. We also synthesized three range images of three noise levels, $\sigma_z = 0. 1.5857. 3.1714$. Our system, described later on, has the noise level of $\sigma_E = 3$ and $\sigma_z = 1.5857$.

We use $3\sigma_{E'}$ as the threshold value, δ_l for the Lambertian pixel. The threshold value, δ_l, as described on page 5, contains three parameters, A, l, and ϵ. The value, A depends on the gain of TV camera. This experiment uses $A = 200$. The parameter, ϵ depends on the image resolution of a TV camera. Examining x values of two adjacent pixels of our system gives $\epsilon = 26$.

We assumed that the maximum inclined angle is 60 degrees. Under this range of surface orientations, $-1.73 \le p, q \le 1.73$, l takes $-0.384 \le l \le 0.384$. Thus, we employ the maximum value of l as the l value in the above equation; $l = 0.4$. Inserting these parameters, we obtain the threshold values shown in Table 3 for the three noise levels in brightness (row) and range measurement (column). The contents of the table give the actual threshold values to be used.

The light source direction, $\vec{S}$ is obtained correctly in all nine cases; the error is less than 0.01%. The albedo value A

Table 3: Threshold values at various noise level

			σ_z	
		0	1.5857	3.1714
	0	0	12	24
σ_E	3	6	13	25
	6	12	17	27

is estimated as shown in Table 4. Although the noise free case gives zero as the theoretical threshold, we use the threshold value given by $\sigma_E = 3$ and $\sigma_z = 0$. Even with an extremely noisy case in which both the TV camera and the range finder pick up twice the normal noise level, $\sigma_E = 6. \sigma_z = 3.1714$, our program still converges at the true albedo value.

Table 4: Recovered Albedo Values, A

			σ_z	
		0	1.5857	3.1714
	0	200.01	199.75	199.09
σ_E	3	199.98	199.77	199.14
	6	199.92	199.79	199.20

6.2 Recovering Lambertian and Specular Parameters from synthesized Images

We synthesized three images of $A = 128$, $\vec{S} = (0.0. 0.0. 1.0)$, $B = 128$ and $k = 20$ under three noise levels, $\sigma_E = 0. 3. 6$, three images of $A = 128$, $\vec{S} = (0.0. 0.0. 1.0)$, $B = 128$ and $k = 10$ under the three noise levels, and three images of $A = 128$, $\vec{S} = (0.0. 0.0. 1.0)$, $B = 128$ and $k = 5$ under the three noise levels. The range images are those given in the previous experiment.

These images are given to our parameter recovery program using the threshold value in Table 3 and $\alpha_0 = 0.165$ for $k = 20$, $\alpha_0 = 0.407$ for $k = 10$, and $\alpha_0 = 0.638$ for $k = 5$, respectively.

Table 5, Table 6, and Table 7 show the obtained parameters for $k = 20$, $k = 10$, and $k = 5$, respectively. The light source direction, $\vec{S}$ is again obtained correctly in all cases; the error is less than 0.01%.

From these experiments, we can conclude that

1. under smaller k values, duller specular reflection, and greater noise levels, it becomes more difficult to obtain the correct k value,

2. however, under the typical range of surface roughness on which the Torrance and Sparrow model holds, $k \approx 10$ (or $c \approx 0.05[21]$), the system can correctly recover k value, as well as other parameters.

6.3 Recovering Reflectance Parameters from Real Images

Figure 4 shows our hardware system which consists of a slide projector with a liquid cristal shatter [19], a CCD TV camera, and a point light source. Since a cristal shatter has its own stripe pattern, which appears in a brightness image, we mounted a point source near the TV camera. We obtained a brightness image by using the light source and the TV camera.

Input brightness from a standard CCD camera has γ characteristics. In order to compensate for this, we will construct a

Table 5: Recovered Reflectance Parameters, A=128, B=128, k=20

k=20				
		σ_z		
		0	1.5857	3.1714
σ_E	0	A=128.05 B=127.97 k=20.01	A=132.17 B=126.40 k=21.23	A=135.46 B=127.10 k=17.82
	3	A=130.37 B=133.20 k=21.29	A=132.67 B=132.02 k=21.63	A=133.10 B=130.36 k=19.95
	6	A=132.13 B=139.57 k=22.69	A=133.63 B=138.81 k=22.41	A=132.86 B=139.13 k=20.97

Table 6: Recovered Reflectance Parameters, A=128, B=128, k=10

k=10				
		σ_z		
		0	1.5857	3.1714
σ_E	0	A=128.97 B=127.40 k=10.07	A=138.44 B=122.80 k=10.97	A=148.70 B=116.79 k=11.45
	3	A=134.22 B=131.31 k=10.97	A=139.28 B=136.22 k=11.92	A=146.15 B=134.35 k=10.41
	6	A=139.18 B=136.06 k=11.94	A=141.97 B=134.81 k=11.81	A=147.51 B=133.67 k=10.27

Table 7: Recovered Reflectance Parameters, A=128, B=128, k=5

k=5				
		σ_z		
		0	1.5857	3.1714
σ_E	0	A=133.22 B=124.23 k=5.18	A=157.44 B=110.70 k=6.15	A=175.37 B=105.59 k=5.59
	3	A=148.35 B=122.01 k=6.04	A=160.20 B=115.07 k=6.56	A=177.22 B=108.61 k=5.76
	6	A=161.58 B=122.49 k=6.93	A=166.56 B=120.46 k=6.80	A=180.71 B=115.03 k=6.03

linearization lookup table using a color chart. Input brightness is linearized by using this table.

Our range finder provides three images, $X(x,y)$, $Y(x,y)$, $Z(x,y)$, which indicate the world coordinate system of the pixel, (x,y). Using this, we can obtain the surface orientation at that pixel.

We need the uncertainty ranges in brightness and range measurements. From the experiments, we obtain that the brightness distribution of our TV camera: $\sigma_E = 3$.

In order to determine the uncertainty range in range values, we use the range finder to measure the range values of pixels on a white board. After obtaining the board's equation, we examine the pixels remaining after having subtracted the range values calculated by the equation from the observed pixels. Then, we conclude that our range finder has $\sigma_z = 1.5857$. Based on these two values and after consulting Table 3, we obtain $\delta_l = 39.11$.

Figure 4: A Liquid cristal (OGIS) range finder and a point light source

6.3.1 Real Lambertian Object

Figure 5(a) shows a lambertian object. Figure 5(b) shows a needle image of the object obtained from a range image by our system.

From these images, we obtain $A = 105.06$ and $\vec{S} = (0.0283, 0.0190, 0.9994)$. In order to evaluate these results, we plot the distribution of brightness values with respect to the angle between the light source and the surface orientation, θ_i. The abscissa of Figure 6(a) denotes the angle θ_i. The ordinate of the figure denotes the brightness. The thin points indicate the observed brightness, while the thick line indicates the calculated brightness;

$$E = A\,\vec{S} \cdot \vec{N} = A\cos\theta_i.$$

In order to evaluate the error distribution, we calculate ideal brightness values at each pixel by $E(x,y) = A\,\vec{N}(x,y) \cdot \vec{S}$. Figure 6(b) shows the calculated ideal brightness distribution. Figure 6(c) shows the difference between the calculated and original brightness.

6.3.2 Real Specular Object

Figure 7(a) shows a specular object, while Figure 7(b) shows the needle image of the object.

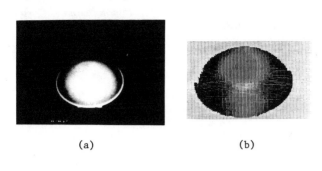

(a)   (b)

Figure 5: Lambertian Object; (a) Input Brightness distribution; (b) A needle image obtained from the range image given by our system.

We first examine the Lambertian parameters, A and $\vec{S}$. Since this object's reflective surface has a small Lambertian component, the light source direction is unstable. Thus, we use the light source direction given in the the previous experiment, (0.0283, 0.0190, 0.9994). We dismiss the Lambertian strength, $A = 0$.

Figure 8(a) shows the result. The abscissa denotes the square of the angle between the surface orientation and the bisector of the light source and the TV camera direction, α^2. The ordinate denotes $\ln d + \ln \cos \theta_r$. The thin points indicate observed values, while the thick line indicates $\ln B + K\alpha^2$, where the specular parameters are $B = 134, k = 10.8$. Figure 8(b) shows the the brightness distribution obtained using these parameters, $B \frac{\exp(-k\alpha^2)}{\cos \theta_r}$. Figure 8(c) shows the difference between the calculated and original brightness distribution.

7   Conclusion

This paper discusses a method which analyzes reflectance parameters derived from a range image and a brightness image. This equation consists of four reflectance parameters: Lambertian strength, light source direction, specular strength, and specular sharpness.

By iteratively using a least square fitting method, we extracted these four parameters from a range image and a brightness image generated by a range-finder. Rather than being forced to rely on the less precise judgement of human inspection, the recovered reflectance parameters makes it possible to assign objective and concrete criteria by which an object should be recognized or evaluated. One application of this process may be the evaluation of fruit, such as might be found in a packing shed. The second application may be delineating the different regions found in the human face; this information could be used by cosmetics companies offering individualized make-up or face-care skemes.

Using the reflectance parameters, we segmented input images into four parts: Lambertian reflection, specular reflection, interreflection, and shadow parts. We can also reconstruct ideal images which consist of only Lambertian or specular reflection. This identified image could also be a useful input to a recognition system, because it would be independent of the daily varying conditions of the human face.

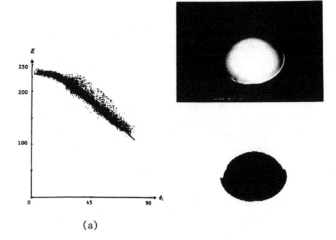

(a)

Figure 6: Result of a Lambertian Object; (a) Brightness plot. The abscissa denotes the angle between the light source direction and the surface orientation. The ordinate denotes the brightness. The thin points indicate observed brightness, while the thick line indicates the calculated brightness. (b) Calculated brightness distribution; (c) Difference between the calculated brightness and observed brightness distribution. Roughly, no errors exist.

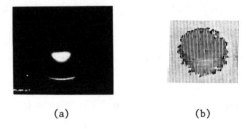

(a)   (b)

Figure 7: Specular Object; (a) Brightness image; (b) Needle image

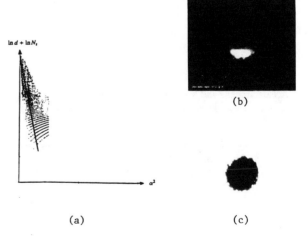

(a)   (c)

Figure 8: (a) Brightness distribution; The abscissa denotes square of specular angles, α^2. The ordinate denotes $\ln d + \ln \cos \theta_r$. The thin points indicate observed values, while the thick line indicates $\ln B + K\alpha^2$, where $B = 134, k = 10.8$. (b) Calculated Brightness Distribution; (c) Difference between the calculated brightness and original brightness distribution.

Acknowledgments

Takeo Kanade provided many useful comments and encouragements. Kathryn Porsche and Fredric Solomon proofread drafts of this paper and provided many useful comments which have improved the readability of this paper. C. Mike Sundius and Yei Mei help us to develop some of the softwares. The authors also thank Shree Nayar, Hideichi Sato, Yoshimasa Fujiwara and the members of the Intelligence Modelling Laboratory, the Robotics Institute, Carnegie Mellon University, for their valuable comments and suggestions.

References

[1] P. Beckmann and A. Spizzichino. *The Scattering of Electromagnetic Waves from Rough Surfaces*. Pergamon Press, London, UK, 1963.

[2] P.J. Besl. Range imaging sensors. Technical Report GMR-6090, Computer Science Department, GM Research Laboratories, Warren, Michigan, March 1988.

[3] J.F. Blinn. Models of light reflection for computer synthesized picture. *Computer Graphics*, 11(2):192–198, 1977.

[4] E.N. Coleman and Jain. R. Obtaining 3-dimensional shape of textured and specular surface using four-source photometry. *Computer Graphics and Image Processing*, 18(4):309–328, 1982.

[5] R.L. Cook and K.E. Torrance. A reflectance model for computer graphics. *Computer Graphics*, 15(3):307–316, August 1981.

[6] G. Healey and T.O. Binford. Local shape from specularity. *Computer Vision, Graphics, and Image Processing*, 42:62–86, 1988.

[7] B.K.P. Horn. Image intensity understanding. *Artificial Intelligence*, 8:201–231, 1977.

[8] B.K.P. Horn. Hill-shading and the reflectance map. *Proc. of IEEE*, 69(1):14–47, January 1981.

[9] B.K.P. Horn and R.W. Sjoberg. Calculating the reflectance map. Technical Report AI Memo 498, Massachusetts Institute of Technology, Artificial Intelligence Laboratory, October 1978.

[10] A.F. Houchens and R.G. Hering. *Bidirectional Reflectance of Rough Metal Surfaces*, pages 65–89. Academic Press, 1967.

[11] K. Ikeuchi. Determining surface orientation of specular surfaces by using the photometric stereo method. *IEEE Trans. Pattern Analysis and Machine Intelligence*, PAMI-3(6):661–669, November 1981.

[12] G.J. Klinker, S.A. Shafer, and T. Kanade. The measurement of highlights in color image. *Intern. Journal of Computer Vision*, 2(1), 1988.

[13] J.H. Lambert. *Photometria sive de mensura de gratibus luminis colorum et umbrae*. Eberhard Klett, Augsburg, 1960.

[14] S.K. Nayar, K. Ikeuchi, and T. Kanade. Extracting shape and reflectance of lambertian, specular, and hybrid surfaces. Technical Report CMU-RI-TR-88-14, Carnegie Mellon University, Robotics Institute, August 1988.

[15] S.K. Nayar, K. Ikeuchi, and T. Kanade. Surface reflection: physical and geometrical perspectives. Technical Report CMU-RI-TR-89-7, Carnegie Mellon University, Robotics Institute, March 1989.

[16] F.E. Nicodemus, J.C. Richmond, and J.J. Hsia. *Geometrical Considerations and Nomenclature for Reflectance*, volume 160 of *NBS monograph*. U.S. Department of Commerce, National Bureau of Standards, 1977.

[17] B.T. Phong. Illumination for computer generated pictures. *Communications of the ACM*, 18(6):311–317, June 1975.

[18] A.C. Sanderson, L.E. Weiss, and S.K. Nayar. Structured highlight inspection of specular surfaces. *IEEE Trans. on Pattern Analysis and Machine Intelligence*, 10(1):44–55, January 1988.

[19] K. Sato, H. Yamamoto, and S. Inokuchi. Range imaging system utilizing nematic liquid crystal mask. In *International Conf. on Computer Vision*, pages 657–661, London, 1987.

[20] H.D. Tagare and R.J. deFigueiredo. A framework for the construction of general reflectance maps for machine vision. Technical report, Rice University, Dept. of Elec. and Comp. Engg., 1989.

[21] K.E. Torrance and E.M. Sparrow. Theory for off-specular reflection from roughened surfaces. *Journal of the Optical Societey of America*, 57:1105–1114, September 1967.

[22] L.B. Wolff. Using polarization to separate reflection components. In *Proc. of IEEE Conf. on Computer Vision and Pattern Recognition*, pages 363–369, 1989.

[23] R.J. Woodham. Reflectance map techniques for analyzing surface defects in metal castings. Technical Report AI-TR-457, Massachusetts Institute of Technology, Artificial Intelligence Laboratory, Cambridge, MA, 1978.

Modeling Sensors: Toward Automatic Generation of Object Recognition Program

Katsushi Ikeuchi and Takeo Kanade

*Computer Science and Robotics, School of Computer Science,
Carnegie-Mellon University, Pittsburgh, Pennsylvania 15213*

Received May 18, 1988; revised January 27, 1989

One of the most important and systematic methods of building model-based vision systems is that of generating object recognition programs automatically from given geometric models. Automatic generation of object recognition programs requires several key components to be developed: object models to describe the geometric and photometric properties of the object to be recognized, sensor models to predict object appearances from the object model under a given sensor, strategy generation using the predicted appearances to produce a recognition strategy, and program generation converting the recognition strategy into an executable code. This paper concentrates on sensor modeling and its relationship to strategy generation, because we regard it as the bottleneck to automatic generation of object recognition programs. We consider two aspects of sensor characteristics: sensor detectability and sensor reliability. Sensor detectability specifies what kinds of features can be detected and under what conditions the features are detected; sensor reliability is a confidence level for the detected features. We define a configuration space to represent sensor characteristics. Then, we propose a representation method for sensor detectability and reliability in the configuration space. Finally, we investigate how to use the proposed sensor model in automatic generation of object recognition programs. © 1989 Academic Press, Inc.

CONTENTS

1. INTRODUCTION

A large class of practical vision problems includes object recognition, that is, recognizing and locating objects in a scene by means of visual input. Examples of this include visual part acquisition on a conveyor belt or from a bin of parts, target recognition in aerial images, and landmark recognition by a mobile robot. In most of these cases, we have some prior knowledge of the objects of interest, such as the shapes, sizes, and reflective properties. Model-based vision [3, 6] seeks to actively use such prior knowledge of objects for guiding the recognition process in order to achieve efficiency and reliability.

One of the critical issues in building a model-based vision system is how to quickly extract and organize the relevant knowledge of an object and to systematically turn it into a vision program. One method of achieving quick and systematic building is compiling object models into an object program automatically [8, 4, 30, 19, 12, 10, 27]. That is, the relevant knowledge in the object models is extracted and compiled into an object recognition program automatically during compile time so that as little computation as possible is spent during run time. A large portion of the computation needed for using the object model, such as analysis of the best recognition strategy, analysis of occlusion, and estimation of expected feature values, can be done at compile time, and the results can be compiled into a special program. As a result, the compiled special program to be run on-line can be very efficient. Also, since the program is generated automatically, the development time could be very short.

Automatic generation of object recognition programs requires several key components:

- *object models* to describe the geometric and photometric properties of the object to be recognized;

- *sensor models* to predict object appearances from the object model under a given sensor;

- *strategy generation* using the predicted appearances to produce a recognition strategy;

- *program generation* converting the recognition strategy into an executable code.

This paper concentrates on sensor modeling and its relationship to strategy generation, because we regard it as the bottleneck to automatic generation of recognition programs. The object appearances are determined by a *product* of an object model with a sensor model. As shown in Fig. 1, the same object model in the same attitude can create different appearances and features when seen by different sensors. For instance, an edge-based binocular stereo reliably detects depth at edges perpendicular to the epipolar lines. The photometric stereo or a light-stripe range finder detects surface orientation and depth of surfaces which are illuminated by and visible to both the light source and the cameras. As another example of the product, let us suppose that one face of an object has 100 as its 3D area size. This value, 100, is a nominal value given only by an object model. In reality, however, one sensor may observe this face's 3D area as 100 plus/minus 10 in one configuration. In another configuration, the same sensor may observe that area as 100 plus/minus 20.

Thus, in object recognition, it is insufficient to consider only an object model; it is essential to exploit a sensor model as well. However, sensor modeling for object recognition has attracted little attention; quite often, researchers who are familiar with the sensors they use have tended to construct object appearances by implicitly incorporating their sensor behavior. This paper, in contrast, explores a general framework for explicitly incorporating sensor models which govern the relationship between object models and object appearances.

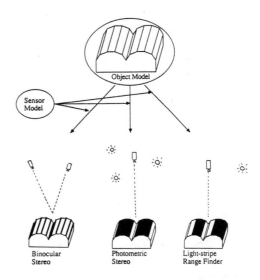

FIG. 1.   Object-appearances.

A sensor model must be able to specify two important characteristics: sensor detectability and sensor reliability. Sensor detectability specifies what kinds of features can be detected and under what conditions they can be detected. Sensor reliability is a measure of uncertainty in the detected features. This paper presents a method of modeling sensors with sensor detectability and sensor reliability and discusses how to use them in object recognition. We define a configuration space to represent sensor characteristics. Next, we consider two aspects of sensor characteristics: sensor detectability and sensor reliability. We propose a representation method for sensor detectability in the configuration space and examine how to use the representation for generating object appearances. Sensor reliability analysis consists of determining uncertainty in sensory measurement, which is represented in the configuration space, and analyzing uncertainty propagation from sensory measurements to geometric features. Finally, we investigate the way to use these sensor models for automatic generation of object recognition programs.

2. SENSORS IN OBJECT RECOGNITION

Various kinds of sensors are used in object recognition. For our purpose, "sensors" are transducers which transform "object features" into "image features." For example, an edge detector detects edges of an object as lines in an image. While a photometric stereo measures surface orientations of surface patches of an object. There are both passive and active sensors. The binocular stereo is passive, while a light-stripe range finder is an active sensor using actively controlled lighting. Table 1 gives a summary of various sensors in terms of what object features are detected in what forms.

In addition to qualitative descriptions of a sensor, a sensor model must describe two characteristics quantitatively: *detectability* and *reliability*. Detectability specifies what kinds of features can be detected under what conditions. Reliability specifies the expected uncertainty in sensory measurement and geometric features derived

TABLE 1

Summary of Sensors

Sensor	Vertex	Edge	Face	Active/passive
Edge detector [26, 22, 5]	—	Line	—	Passive
Shape-from-shading [11, 15]	—	—	Region	Passive
Synthetic aperture radar [28, 21]	Point	Point/line	Point	Active
Time-of-flight range finder [16, 9]	—	—	Region	Active
Light-stripe range finder [1]	—	—	Region	Active
Binocular stereo [23, 25]	—	Line	—	Passive
Trinocular stereo [24]	—	Line	—	Passive
Photometric stereo [29, 13]	—	—	Region	Active
Polarimetric light detector [20]	—	—	Point	Active

from measurement. Since these two characteristics depend on how the sensor is located relative to an object feature, we will first define a feature configuration space to represent the spatial relationship between the sensor and the feature. Then, we will investigate the way to specify detectability and reliability over the space.

3. FEATURE CONFIGURATION SPACE

Sensor detectability and reliability depend upon various factors which include distance to a feature, attitude of a feature, reflectivity of a feature, transparency of air, ambient lighting, and so forth. In most object recognition problems, in particular the bin-picking problem, the attitude of a feature, that is, the angular freedom between a feature and a sensor, affects sensor characteristics the greatest. In order to specify this freedom explicitly, we attach a coordinate system to each point of an object feature and consider the relationship between the sensor coordinate system and the feature coordinate system. For example, on a face, we define a coordinate system so that the z axis of the feature coordinate system agrees with the surface normal at that point and the x–y axes lie on the face, but are defined arbitrarily otherwise. For other features, we can define feature coordinates appropriately. See Appendix I for more details.

Since angular relationships between the two coordinate systems are relative, for the sake of convenience we fix the sensor coordinate system and discuss how to specify feature coordinates with respect to it. The angular relation between the sensor coordinate system and a feature coordinate system can be specified by three degrees of freedom: two degrees of freedom in the direction of the z axis of a feature coordinate system, and one degree of freedom in rotation about the z-axis. (See Fig. 2a.)

Since we will consider the angular relationship, we can translate the feature coordinate system so that the two coordinate systems share the same origin. We will then define a sphere whose origin is located at the origin of the sensor coordinate system and whose north pole is on the z-axis of the sensor coordinate system. We will specify a feature coordinate system as a point on and inside the sphere. The north pole of the sphere aligns the feature coordinate system with the sensor coordinate system. Referring to Fig. 2b, a point on the spherical surface represents a feature coordinate system obtained by rotating the sensor coordinate system around the axis perpendicular to a plane given by the sphere center, the spherical point,

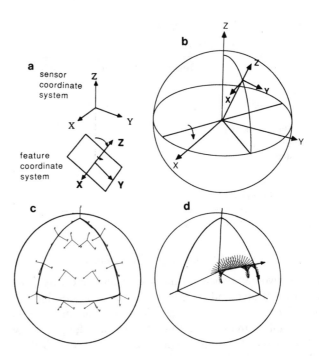

FIG. 2. Feature configuration space: (a) A feature coordinate system with respect to the sensor coordinate system; (b) the feature configuration space; (c) feature coordinate systems on the spherical surface; (d) feature coordinate systems on the points along a radial axis.

and the north pole until the direction from the sphere center to the point coincides with the z-axis of the feature coordinate system. Figure 2c represents various sensor coordinate systems corresponding to spherical points. As for a point inside the sphere, the distance from the spherical surface to the point represents the angle of rotation (modulo 360°) about the z-axis from the surface point coordinate system to the interior point coordinate system. Figure 2d shows the coordinate systems corresponding to points on a radial axis. We will refer to this sphere as the feature configuration space, and represent detectability and reliability of a given sensor in it.[1]

4. DETECTION CONSTRAINTS AND ASPECTS

The previous section defined the way to represent the relationship between the sensor coordinate system and feature coordinate system. This section will discuss constraints which determine whether a feature can be detected at each point of the configuration space.

[1] This representation will not create discontinuities around the north pole as opposed to the case in which Euler angles from the sensor coordinate system to the feature coordinate system are used to specify spherical points; this representation will instead create discontinuities at the center of the sphere and at the south pole. However, this is advantageous because we use the area mostly around the north pole to discuss detectability and reliability.

TABLE 2

Illuminators and Detectors

Sensor	Number of illuminators	Number of detectors
Edge detector	1	1
Shape-from-shading	1	1
SAR	1	1
Time-of-flight range finder	1	1
Light-stripe range finder	1	1
Binocular stereo	1	2
Trinocular stereo	1	3
Photometric stereo	3	1
Polarimetric light detector	n	1

4.1. *Detection Constraints*

Each sensor has two components: illuminators and detectors. For example, both a time-of-flight range finder and a light-stripe range finder have one light source (illuminator) and one TV camera (detector). The binocular stereo has one light source (without light sources you cannot observe anything) and two TV cameras; the photometric stereo has three light sources and one TV camera. Table 2 summarizes the number of illuminators and detectors of each sensor.

In the following discussion, we will consider both illuminators and detectors as generalized sources (G-sources). Each G-source has two properties: the illumination direction and the illuminated configurations. In the case of illuminators, these two terms are the same as direction and configurations of the illuminator itself. In the case of detectors, the illumination direction corresponds to the line-of-sight of the detector, and the illuminated configurations correspond to the visible configurations from the detector. The G-source illumination direction can be represented in the feature configuration space as a radial line from the sphere center. G-source illuminated configurations can be specified as a volume in the configuration space. (See Fig. 3a.)

In order for a feature to be illuminated by a G-source, the feature coordinate system should be in the illuminated configurations, and the G-source illuminated direction should not be occluded. We can represent the detection constraints of a sensor by set operations between illuminated configurations and between illumination directions of component G-sources. In particular, we will refer the resulting volume by set operations between illuminated configurations as *detectable configurations*.

Figure 3c shows an example of analysis of a face feature by the light-stripe range finder in Fig. 3b. A light-stripe range finder has two G-sources (a TV camera and a light source): the direction denoted by $V1$ indicates the line-of-sight of the TV camera; $V2$ indicates the illumination direction of the light source.

The illuminated configurations of a face are determined by the z-axis (i.e., its surface normal) of a face feature coordinate, and are not dependent on its rotation. Therefore, illuminated configurations of a feature form a spherical cone whose axis is $V2$ and whose apex angle is $d2$. Although in ideal cases illuminated configurations of a G-source are contained in a hemisphere as shown in Fig. 3a, in real cases the

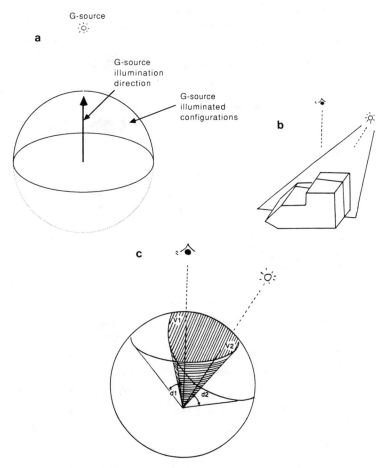

FIG. 3. Detection constraints of a light-stripe range finder: (a) G-source illumination direction and G-source illuminated configurations; (b) our hypothetical light-stripe range finder; (c) the detection constraints of the light-stripe range finder depicted in the feature configuration space; note that there are two kinds of constraints: detectable configurations and illumination directions.

area near the equator has low brightness and noisy, and thus, we exclude the area and have a spherical corn as G-source illuminated configurations as shown in Fig. 3c. Similarly, the configurations of a feature visible from the TV camera form a spherical cone whose center direction is $V1$ and whose apex angle is $d1$.

Since a light-stripe range finder detects the faces which are illuminated by the source and are visible by means of the TV camera, the detectable configurations are the intersection of the two cones.

Thus, the resulting detection constraints in Fig. 3c contain three constraint components: two illumination directions and one volume of detectable configurations. In other words, when neither of the two illumination directions is occluded and the face coordinate system is contained in the detectable configuration, the face is detected by the light-stripe range finder.

We can represent the detection constraints for the other sensors in Table 1 in a similar fashion. The results of the analysis are summarized in Fig. 4. The right

Sensor	Constraints in the Formal Definition	Detection Constraint
Edge Detector	(AND (NS edge V d) (NS edge V d)) = (NS edge V d)	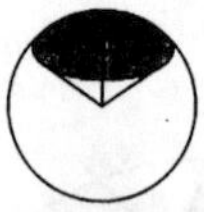
Shape-from-Shading	(AND (NS face V d) (NS face V d)) = (NS face V d)	

SAR	(OR (NS face V d)
	  (NS edge V d)
	  (NS vertex V d))
	(needs post process)
		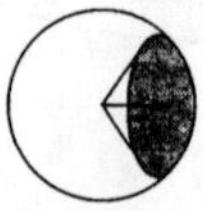

Time-of-Flight Range Finder	(AND (NS face V d) (NS face V d)) = (NS face V d)	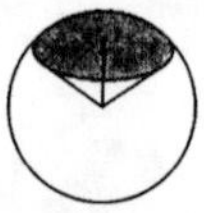
Light-strip Range Finder	(AND (NS face V1 d) (NS face V2 d))	

Binocular Stereo	(AND (NS edge V1 d1)
	  (DS edge V2 d2 VE de)
	  (DS edge V3 d3 VE de))
		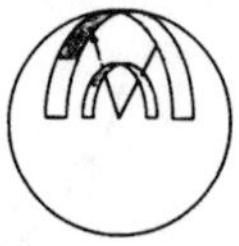

Trinocular Stereo	(AND (NS edge V1 d1)
	  (DS edge V2 d2 VE de)
	  (DS edge V3 d2 VE de)
	  (DS edge V4 d2 VE de))

Photometric Stereo	(AND (NS face V d1)
	  (NS face V1 d2)
	  (NS face V2 d2)
	  (NS face V3 d2))
		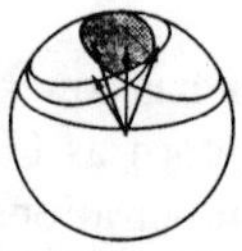

Polarimetric Light Detector	(OR (AND (NS face V d)
	  (NS face V1 d))
	  (AND (NS face V d)
	  (NS face V2 d))
		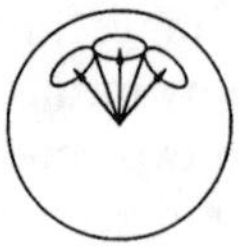

FIG. 4.   Detection constraints of various sensors.

column pictorially represents each sensor's detection constraints in the feature configuration space. The center column represents our formal language to specify the detection constraints to our geometric modeler so they can then be used for generating object appearances. The definition of the language is found in Appendix II.

4.2. *Use of Detection Constraints*

In order to predict object appearances, we apply the detection constraints to each feature of the object. Each feature (or a part of a feature) is detectable by the sensor if it satisfies the following two conditions:

1. None of the illumination directions are occluded by any other parts of the object.

2. The detectable configurations contain the configuration of the feature.

To check these conditions we use the constraints with a geometric modeler. We rotate the object into a certain attitude to be examined and then see whether its features satisfy the above conditions. Figure 5 illustrates the process of predicting object appearances for a light-stripe range finder. Suppose an object is situated as in Fig. 5a. Figure 5b shows the detection constraints on a face for a light-stripe range finder. We will put this configuration space on each candidate face to determine whether the face is detectable. (See Fig. 5c.) This amounts to checking the conditions:

1. The light source direction, $V2$, is not occluded by other faces.

2. The line-of-sight of the TV camera, $V1$, is not occluded by other faces.

3. The local coordinate of a face, defined by the surface normal (z-axis) and the tangential plane (x–y axis), is contained within the detectable configurations.

Figure 5d shows the result of this operation. The shaded areas indicate those which satisfy the conditions and thus are detectable by the light-stripe range finder.

An object appearance is represented in frames so that it can be used in automatic generation of object recognition programs. The representation, which we will refer to as the image structure, includes a set of visible faces and a set of the expected feature values. An example of an image structure, as shown in Fig. 6, consists of one frame representing one object appearance $I0$ and several appearance component frames representing visible 2D faces, *IMAGE-COMP*01, and *IMAGE-COMP*02.[2]

Each frame corresponding to one visible 2D face maintains various geometric properties of the face in slots. For example, face area and face moment are maintained in slots *AREA* and *MOMENT*. Each frame representing a 2D visible face has a backpointer to the 3D face from which the 2D face is projected. For example, the *IS-A-FACE-OF* slot of the *IMAGE-COMP*01 frame has the value *FACE*6.[3]

---

[2]In this example, one 2D face corresponds to one image component. If several 2D faces have C^2 continuity across the edges, these faces are grouped and stored as one single image component. In that case, face area and face moment are calculated over the group of faces.

[3]Each frame also contains array addresses of various geometric items such as 2D FACE, 2D EDGE, and 2D VERTEX in the data base of the geometric modeler; for example, 9361 in the *REGIONS* slot of the *IMAGE-COMP*01 frame. These allow us to access the original geometric data, if necessary.

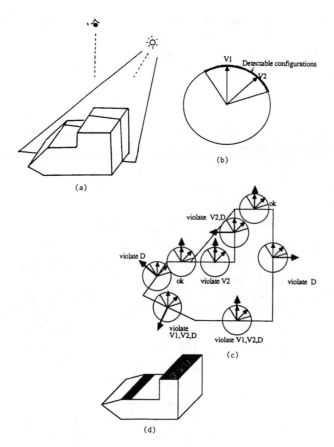

FIG. 5. How to use the constraints: (a) A light-stripe range finder; (b) the detection constraints; (c) applying the detection constraints to object features; (d) detectable faces determined by the constraints.

4.3. *Aspects*

Aspects have been defined as topologically equivalent classes of object appearances [18]. However, since object appearances depend on sensors, we will modify the definition of aspects accordingly.

Suppose we have n faces, $S_1, S_2, \ldots, S_n$. Let the variable X_i denote whether or not the face S_i is detected under one particular sensor:

$$X_i = \begin{cases} 1 & \text{face } S_i \text{ is detectable by one particular sensor;} \\ 0 & \text{otherwise.} \end{cases}$$

An n-tuple $(X_1, X_2, \ldots, X_n)$ represents a label of an object appearance determined by the detection constraints of a sensor. This label will be referred to as a *shape label* of the appearance, and we will define an aspect as the set of object appearances that share the same *shape label*.

We will define an aspect structure in frames so that they can be used in automatic generation of object recognition programs. The structure includes constituent ap-

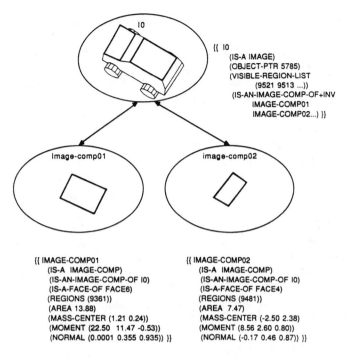

FIG. 6.   Object appearance represented in frames.

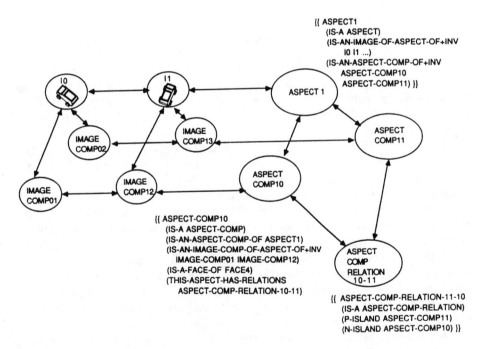

FIG. 7.   Frame representation of an aspect: Each aspect structure consists of an aspect frame, aspect component frames, and aspect component relation frames. An aspect frame also points to its instance images $I0, I1, \ldots$, while its aspect component frame, $ASPECT\text{-}COMP10$, points to its instance 2D faces $IMAGE\text{-}COMP01$, $IMAGE\text{-}COMP12$.

pearances, a set of features extractable for the aspect, and the expected feature values.

In order to construct aspect structures, shape labels of all image structures are examined one by one. This is done by retrieving 2D face backpointers of image structures to 3D faces such as *FACE*6 in the *IS-A-FACE-OF* slot of *IMAGE-COMP*01 frame in Fig. 6, where *FACE*6 is the frame name of a 3D face of the object. If an image structure cannot find any aspect structure with the same shape label among the already established ones, a new aspect frame is created together with aspect component frames which correspond to image component frames; therefore, the aspect structure has the same structure as the image structure. Also, frames to represent the relationships between pairs of aspect components are created. If an image structure can find an aspect structure with the same shape label, the image frame is registered to the aspect frame as an instance, and its frames of 2D faces are registered to corresponding aspect component frames.

An example of an aspect structure is shown in Fig. 7. Aspect frame *ASPECT*1 points to aspect component frames *ASPECT-COMP*10 and *ASPECT-COMP*11 with the *IS-AN-ASPECT-COMP-OF + INV* slot. It also points to its instance images *I*0 and *I*1 with the *IS-AN-IMAGE-OF-ASPECT-OF + INV* slot, while its aspect component frame, *ASPECT-COMP*10, points to its instance 2D faces *IMAGE-COMP*01 and *IMAGE-COMP*12. Frame *ASPECT-COMP-RELATION-11-10* is a relation frame which represents the relationship between *ASPECT-COMP*10 and *ASPECT-COMP*11.

5. DETECTABILITY DISTRIBUTION AND ASPECT TRANSIT

5.1 *Detectability Distribution*

The feature detection constraints give the upper bound of the detectable configurations in the configuration space. In some cases, however, even though an object feature satisfies the detection constraints, it may be undetected due to noise. We define the probability distribution of detection such that a feature in the detectable configurations is likely or not likely to be detected, depending on its place. This probability, which we will refer to as detectability distribution, is usually high in the central part and low in the peripheral part of the detectable configurations.

Since all sensors in Table 1 detect features based on a brightness value corresponding to a feature, the detectability distribution depends on a brightness value which is detected and converted to sensor features. However, there are two types of sensors in terms of the conversion method: intensity-based sensors and position-based sensors. The intensity-based sensor measures the brightness value and converts it directly to sensor features. The position-based sensor measures the brightness value and gets positional information of the bright spot if the brightness value is greater than some threshold. It then converts the positional information to sensor features. Table 3 shows a classification of sensors based on this difference.

Since the detectability distribution depends on sensing methods, we will develop the detectability distribution for a light-stripe range finder as a representative case of the position-based sensor and that for the photometric stereo as a representative case of the intensity-based sensor.

TABLE 3
Measurement Methods

Sensor	Direct/indirect
Edge detector	Direct
Shape-from-shading	Direct
SAR	Indirect
Time-of-flight range finder	Indirect
Light-stripe range finder	Indirect
Binocular stereo	Indirect
Trinocular stereo	Indirect
Photometric stereo	Direct
Polarimetric light detector	Indirect

5.1.1. *Detectability Distribution of Light-Stripe Range Finder*

We will consider the detectability distribution of a hypothetical light-stripe range finder. A light-stripe range finder projects a plane of light onto the scene and determines the position of a surface patch from the slit image. The detectability depends on whether the brightness of the slit image is bright enough to be detected, say brighter than a threshold I_0. Assuming a Lambertaian surface, the brightness of the slit image is given by $I_s \mathbf{N} \cdot \mathbf{S}$, where $\mathbf{N}$ is the surface normal, $\mathbf{S}$ is the light source direction, and I_s is the light source brightness. If we assume an additive zero-mean Gaussian noise of brightness with power σ^2, the resultant brightness distribution of a slit will be

$$p(I) = \frac{1}{\sqrt{2\pi}\sigma} \exp - \frac{(I - I_s \mathbf{N} \cdot \mathbf{S})^2}{2\sigma^2}.$$

Thus, the probability distribution of feature detectability of our hypothetical range finder can be described as

$$P_d = \mathrm{Prob}(I \geq I_0)$$

$$= \int_{I_0 - I_s \mathbf{N} \cdot \mathbf{S}}^{+\infty} \frac{1}{\sqrt{2\pi}\sigma} \exp - \frac{I^2}{2\sigma^2} \, dI = \Phi\left(\frac{I_0 - I_s \mathbf{N} \cdot \mathbf{S}}{\sigma}\right).$$

As shown in Fig. 8, this probability decreases as the incident angle of the light-stripe increases, and near the boundary of the illuminated configuration of the light source, the probability approaches 0.

5.1.2. *Detectability Distribution of Photometric Stereo*

An intensity-based sensor can be modeled as

$$\mathbf{y} = \mathbf{G}(\mathbf{x}),$$

where $\mathbf{x}$ is the input brightness, $\mathbf{y}$ is the output feature values, and $\mathbf{G}$ is the conversion function. Suppose $\mathbf{X}^*$ is the definition area of the function $\mathbf{G}$; i.e., the intensity-based sensor outputs a feature value $\mathbf{y}$ from any $\mathbf{x}_i$ if $\mathbf{x}_i \in \mathbf{X}^*$. Then,

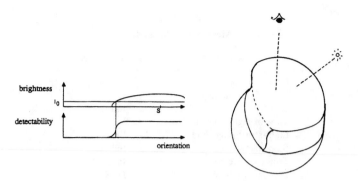

FIG. 8. Detectability distribution for a light-stripe range finder.

the detectability distribution can be determined as the probability that the input brightness, $\mathbf{x} + \delta\mathbf{x}$, disturbed by $\delta\mathbf{x}$, is still contained in the definition area, $\mathbf{X}^*$.

The photometric stereo determines the surface orientation of the object feature from three images taken from the same position under different lighting directions.

$$I_1 = \mathbf{S}_1 \cdot \mathbf{N}$$
$$I_2 = \mathbf{S}_2 \cdot \mathbf{N}$$
$$I_3 = \mathbf{S}_3 \cdot \mathbf{N},$$

where $I_i, \mathbf{S}_i, \mathbf{N}$ are the brightness value under light source i, the ith light source direction vector, and the surface normal vector, respectively. Thus, expressing the brightness as a vector, $\mathbf{I}$, and the light source as a matrix, $\mathbf{S}$,

$$\mathbf{I} = \mathbf{SN}.$$

Dividing both sides by $\mathbf{S}$, we obtain an explicit expression of $\mathbf{N}$,

$$\mathbf{N} = \mathbf{S}^{-1}\mathbf{I} = \mathbf{AI},$$

where $\mathbf{A} = \mathbf{S}^{-1}$. This is the basic idea of the photometric stereo [29].

The definition area of $\mathbf{I}$ is determined as an inverse area of the valid surface orientations. Namely, since $\mathbf{N}$ is a unit vector, a valid surface orientation $\mathbf{N}$ satisfies $\mathbf{N}^t\mathbf{N} = 1$. Once we insert the relationship between surface orientation and brightness triple, we obtain $(\mathbf{AI})^t\mathbf{AI} = 1$, which gives the definition area of $\mathbf{I}$.

The current photometric stereo has, however, three modifications [13] to the original theory:

1. Brightness values are normalized $\mathbf{I}/|\mathbf{I}|$ so that we can cancel the albedo effect.

2. Threshold operations are applied to brightness values so that we can eliminate shadow regions.

3. $\mathbf{A}$ is determined from calibration and stored in a lookup table rather than calculated from the ideal case.

We will obtain the detectability distribution of the photometric stereo according to these modifications. Assume a brightness value moves from i_1 to $i_1 + \delta i_1$ due to the TV camera's error. The normalization gives $i_1' + \delta i_1' = (i_1 + \delta i_1)/(i_1 + \delta i_1 + i_2 + i_3)$. However, the normalized intensity $(i_1' + \delta i_1', i_2', i_3')$ exists on the same plane $i_1' + \delta i_1' + i_2' + i_3' = 1$. Since a continuous area on the plane is the definition area for the photometric stereo and the new triple $i_1' + \delta i_1', i_2', i_3'$ is still contained in the definition area on the plane, we can obtain the solution from the new triple.

Thus, we will always succeed in obtaining the feature values; i.e., we will have a unit detectability distribution for light source 1 (though of course, the resultant value may be less reliable as will be discussed in the reliability section). The same discussion is applicable to light source 2 and light source 3. This analysis reveals that normalization makes the detectability a unit value, and thus helps to detect features in a stable manner.

We use the threshold operations to detect shadows. This operation also affects the detectability distribution. Namely, in the case that all three brightness values are greater than a threshold value, we can determine the surface orientation. This effect can be modeled in the same way as the light-stripe range finder. Thus,

$$
P_d = \Phi\left(\frac{I_0 - I_{s1}\mathbf{N}\cdot\mathbf{S1}}{\sigma}\right)\Phi\left(\frac{I_0 - I_{s2}\mathbf{N}\cdot\mathbf{S2}}{\sigma}\right)\Phi\left(\frac{I_0 - I_{s3}\mathbf{N}\cdot\mathbf{S3}}{\sigma}\right)
$$

gives the detectability distribution over the detectable configurations, where I_{si} and $\mathbf{Si}$ are the light source brightness and the light source direction of illuminator i, respectively.

5.2. Transition of Aspect

The continuous change of detectability causes the continuous aspect transition and the aspect boundaries to become blurred. In order to characterize an aspect boundary, we can define the distance between two aspects across the boundary by the Hamming distance between their corresponding shape labels $\{x_1, \ldots, x_i, \ldots, x_n\}$, where $x_i = 1$ if face i is detected and $x_i = 0$ otherwise. Thus, the distance between two aspects is the number of faces which switch between detected and undetected states across the aspect boundary.

Consider an aspect boundary between aspects A and B whose Hamming distance is one; that is, aspects A and B differ in the detection of only one face, F_i. Suppose the detectability of face i is $P_d(F_i)$. Then, near the aspect boundary, aspect A may be observed incorrectly as aspect B with probability $1 - P_d(F_i)$. A similar false observation will occur for aspect B.

If the Hamming distance between aspects A and B is more than one across a boundary, then erroneous intermediate aspects, which are neither A nor B, can occur near the boundary. This can easily be seen by considering an example where aspect A has $\{x_i, x_j\} = \{10\}$ and aspect B has $\{x_i, x_j\} = \{01\}$ as shape labels, respectively. Then, we will observe object appearances belonging to four aspects near the boundary: aspects $\{11\}$ and $\{00\}$ in addition to aspects A and B. For example, the probability of observing aspect $\{11\}$, instead of aspect A, is $P_d(F_i)P_d(F_j)$. This consideration must be taken into account when grouping and classifying aspects into an interpretation tree.

6. RELIABILITY OF SENSORS

Once a sensor feature is detected, the next question is how reliable the sensor feature is. In other words, the task now is to determine uncertainty in the sensor feature. Determining the limit of the uncertainty is quite important for model-based vision. Suppose there is a sensor feature for which the geometric model takes two nominal values, 100 and 90, for two distinct situations. If a sensor has an uncertainty range of plus/minus 1 for the sensor feature, we can use the feature from that sensor as a reliable discriminator in the recognition stage. On the other hand, if a sensor has an uncertainty range of plus/minus 20, we cannot use the feature from that sensor.

This section discusses two issues of uncertainty in feature values. The first issue is uncertainty in sensory measurement; any sensory measurement made by a sensor always contains some measurement uncertainty. The second issue is propagation of uncertainty from sensory measurements to geometric features, hence the resulting uncertainty of those geometric features. In some cases, a detected sensor feature from a sensor is used directly as a feature; in most cases, however, geometric features, such as areas or surface orientations of image regions, are derived from sensor features and used as features in model-based visions. Thus, it is necessary to determine the uncertainty propagation mechanism for determining resulting uncertainty in geometric features.

6.1. Uncertainty in Sensory Measurement

Uncertainty in sensor measurement has various causes, including variance in brightness values, variance in light source directions, and various digitization mechanisms. However, the major uncertainty of an intensity-based sensor comes from brightness variance, and the major uncertainty of a position-based sensor comes from variance in light source direction as shown in Table 4.

Since uncertainty in sensory measurement depends on the sensor, we will analyze the light-stripe range finder as a representative position-based sensor and the photometric stereo as a representative intensity-based sensor.

6.1.1. Light-Stripe Range Finder

We will consider a depth measurement by a hypothetical light-stripe range finder. Let us assume that the main source of uncertainty in depth measurement comes

TABLE 4

Main Factor of Uncertainty

Sensor	Type	Factor
Edge detector	Intensity	Brightness variance
Shape-from-shading	Intensity	Brightness variance
SAR	Intensity	Flight direction
Time-of-flight range finder	Position	Mirror direction
Light-stripe range finder	Position	Mirror direction
Binocular stereo	Position	Camera directions
Trinocular stereo	Position	Camera directions
Photometric stereo	Intensity	Brightness variance
Polarimetric light detector	Intensity	Polarimetric variance

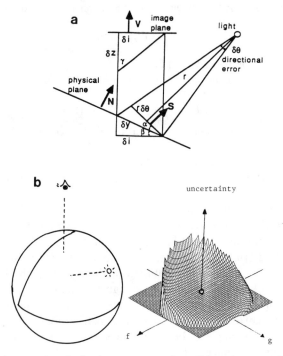

FIG. 9. Predicted uncertainty in depth measurement by a light-stripe range finder: (a) Detection mechanism; (b) predicted uncertainty in depth measurements, ploted on the stereographic plane [15], where (f, g) denotes its coordinate axes.

from the ambiguity of the slit position projected by the range finder on a surface due to the width of the light beam and angular errors in setting the light directions. The uncertainty model can be obtained analytically.

As shown in Fig. 9a, let us denote the angular uncertainty of the light stripe by $\delta\theta$. The light is intercepted by an object surface, creating a slit pattern on it. The angular uncertainty $\delta\theta$ of the light direction results in an uncertainty δy in the position on the surface:

$$\delta y = r\delta\theta / \cos\alpha,$$

where r is the distance of the surface from the light source, and α is the angle between the light direction **S** and the surface normal **N**. This positional uncertainty on the surface is observed as the slit position uncertainty (or "slit width") δi in the camera image. If β is the angle between the surface normal **N** and the viewer direction **V**, then

$$\delta i = (\cos\beta)\delta y.$$

Finally, this uncertainty is transferred into the uncertainty in depth measurement by triangulation. For simplicity, if we assume orthographic projection for the camera model, the uncertainty in the image δi creates uncertainty in depth δz,

$$\delta z = \delta i / \tan \gamma,$$

where γ is the angle between $\mathbf{V}$ and $\mathbf{S}$.

By representing the angles α, β, and γ in terms of $\mathbf{V}$, $\mathbf{N}$, and $\mathbf{S}$, we obtain

$$\delta z = \frac{\cos \beta}{\cos \alpha \tan \gamma} r\delta\theta = \frac{(\mathbf{N} \cdot \mathbf{V})(\mathbf{S} \cdot \mathbf{V})}{(\mathbf{N} \cdot \mathbf{S})\sqrt{1 - \mathbf{S} \cdot \mathbf{V}}} r\delta\theta.$$

Since r is roughly constant, the uncertainty distribution of this light-stripe range finder over the detectable configurations is governed by the factor $(\mathbf{N} \cdot \mathbf{V})(\mathbf{S} \cdot \mathbf{V})/(\mathbf{N} \cdot \mathbf{S})\sqrt{1 - \mathbf{S} \cdot \mathbf{V}}$.

Figure 9b plots this function. The sphere represents the feature configuration space. The detectable configurations are enclosed by two great circles. Each point of the sphere represents one particular geometrical configuration caused by the TV camera, the surface orientation, and the light-source direction. Since the light-stripe range finder is independent of the rotation of the z axis of the feature coordinate system, we only plot uncertainty for the configurations on the spherical surface. The detectable configurations are projected onto the plane tangential to the sphere at the north pole. The right diagram represents the distribution of uncertainty over the plane. The larger the angle α between the surface normal and the illuminator direction, the larger the uncertainty.

6.1.2. Photometric Stereo

Let us now consider the uncertainty in measurement of surface orientation by the photometric stereo. Our photometric stereo can be described as a two-step process. First, a brightness triple $\mathbf{I}$ is converted to a normalized brightness triple $\mathbf{E}$,

$$\mathbf{E} = \mathbf{F}(\mathbf{I}).$$

Then, the normalized brightness triple is converted to a surface orientation $\mathbf{N}$,

$$\mathbf{N} = \mathbf{AE}.$$

Thus, we can obtain the uncertainty of surface orientation

$$U = (d\mathbf{N})^t d\mathbf{N} = (d\mathbf{I})^t \mathbf{J}^t \mathbf{A}^t \mathbf{A} \mathbf{J} d\mathbf{I},$$

where $\mathbf{J}$ is the Jacobian matrix of $\mathbf{F}$.

We will apply the method above mentioned to our photometric stereo system. From our experiment, our TV camera (8-bit) has a standard deviation of 3. Thus, $di = 2\sigma = 6$. Suppose only one light source causes error at one time, say $\Delta I = (6, 0, 0)^t$.

We have to obtain the Jacobian matrix $\mathbf{J}$ at each configuration. Figure 10a shows the distribution of $\partial f_1 / \partial i_1$ over the detectable configurations, where the detectable configurations are plotted at the plane tangential to the sphere at the north pole of the feature configuration space. Although it is possible to approximate the distribution with a polynomial, we assume it is a constant 0.004 over the detectable

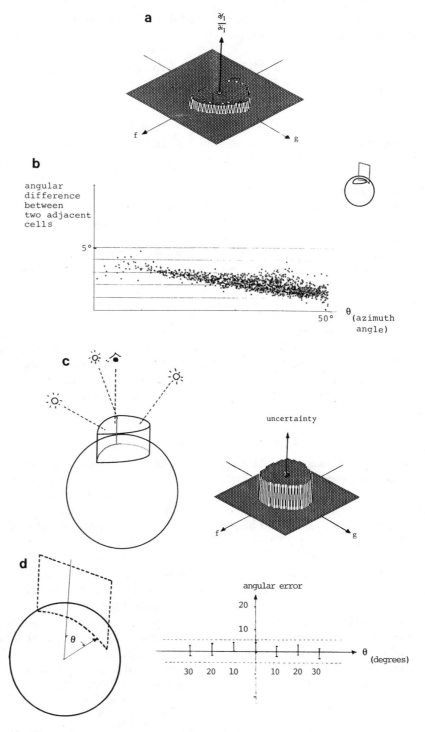

FIG. 10. Uncertainty in surface orientation by photometric stereo: (a) Distribution of $\partial f_1/\partial i_1$ over the detectable configurations; (b) angular difference between two adjacent cells in the lookup table; (c) uncertainty in surface orientation over the detectable configurations, ploted on the stereographic plane; (d) comparison with the theoretical uncertainty distribution and the observed uncertainty distribution.

configurations for the sake of simplicity. We follow the same method for the other components of the Jacobian matrix,

$$J = \begin{bmatrix} 0.004 & 0.002 & 0.002 \\ 0.002 & 0.004 & 0.002 \\ 0.002 & 0.002 & 0.004 \end{bmatrix}.$$

By using the Jacobian matrix, we obtain $\Delta E = (0.024, 0.012, 0.012)^t$.

We will determine $\mathbf{A}\,\Delta\mathbf{E} = \mathbf{AJI}$ from the real data because $\mathbf{A}$ is represented as a lookup table. Our lookup table has 32 cells in one normalized brightness axis, and the distance between the maximum normalized brightness and the minimum normalized brightness is roughly 0.8 over the detectable configurations; one mesh corresponds to a normalized brightness difference of 0.025. Thus, $\mathbf{A}\,\Delta\mathbf{E}$ corresponds to a mesh difference of $(1.0, 0.5, 0.5)^t$; U corresponds to a mesh uncertainty of 1.5 in the lookup table.

We examine the relationship between the distance of two adjacent cells and the surface orientation difference. Figure 10b shows the angular distance between two adjacent cells in the lookup table. By using this result and a mesh uncertainty of 1.5 from the lookup table, the total uncertainty in surface orientation becomes 5° over the detectable configurations. Pictorially, the uncertainty distribution becomes a layer over the configuration space as shown in Fig. 10c, where the detectable configurations are projected onto the plane tangential to the sphere at the north pole. These results are compared with the real data. The horizontal broken lines in Fig. 10d indicate plus/minus 5° uncertainty, while the vertical thick lines indicate uncertainty directly measured from our system. Both sets of results agree over the detectable configurations.

6.2. Uncertainty in Geometric Features

Usually sensory measurements, such as depth or surface orientation, are further converted into object features, such as area or inertia of a face. This process involves grouping pixels into regions, extracting some feature values from the regions, and transforming the values into object features. Since modeling uncertainty propagation in a general way is difficult and useless, we will consider an area of a 3D face obtained from an area of a 2D region detected by our hypothetical light-stripe range finder as an example of modeling this propagation. Other cases, such as 3D inertia, can be handled in the same way. Figure 11 shows the process of conversion from depth values to the area of a face. The process includes three parts: grouping pixels into a region to obtain the area in the image; computing the surface orientation of the region; and finally converting the image area into the surface area by means of the affine transform determined by the surface orientation. We will analyze how the uncertainty is introduced and propagated in this three-part process.

Suppose a surface under consideration has real area A and surface orientation β (angle between the surface normal and viewing direction). It should create a region of size n pixels where

$$n = A \cos \beta.$$

However, because of the imperfect detectability of the sensor, the sensor fails to find

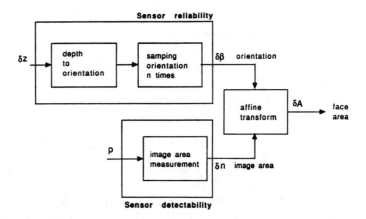

FIG. 11.   Conversion process from depth value values to the area of a face.

some of the pixels so that the measured area is different from the nominal area n. Let P_d denote the detectability for this surface, which was computed in Subsection 5.1.2. Then, the process of measuring the area by sampling n pixels can be modeled by a binomial distribution with mean nP_d and variance $nP_d(1 - P_d)$. Assuming two standard deviations, the discrepancy in area measurement will be

$$\delta n = n - \left(nP_d - 2\sqrt{nP_d(1 - p_d)}\right) = n(1 - P_d) + 2\sqrt{nP_d(1 - P_d)}.$$

Another uncertainty is introduced in obtaining the surface orientation β from measured depths due to uncertainty in depth measurement δz. If we estimate the surface orientation at a pixel by differentiating depth values of neighboring pixels, then the uncertainty in surface orientation will be $\cos^2 \beta \delta z$. However, since we have roughly n pixels in the region, the surface orientation will be averaged, reducing the uncertainty by a factor of $\sqrt{n}$. Thus

$$\delta\beta = \frac{\cos^2 \beta}{\sqrt{n}}\delta z.$$

Finally, more uncertainty is introduced in the estimation of the area of the face, $A + \delta A$, which is obtained by converting the image area into a 3D surface area.

$$A + \delta A = \frac{n + \delta n}{\cos(\beta + \delta\beta)}.$$

Thus, assuming that $\delta\beta$ is small, we see that

$$\delta A = A(1 - P_d) + 2\sqrt{\frac{AP_d(1 - P_d)}{\cos \beta}} + A\tan\beta\delta\beta$$

$$= A(1 - P_d) + \sqrt{\frac{A}{\cos \beta}}\left(2\sqrt{P_d(1 - P_d)} + \frac{\sin 2\beta}{2}\delta z\right).$$

TABLE 5
Reliability of Geometric Features

Feature	Observed	Predicted
Area	0.0023	0.0022
Inertia	0.0044	0.0043

By this method, we can predict what deviations from the nominal value of the area feature should be expected, once we model the sensor and know its intrinsic detectability P_d and uncertainty in depth δz.

In order to examine the validity of the propagation model, we executed an experiment using our photometric stereo. We first observed a face five times with our photometric stereo, where the face was inclined 30° from the direction of the TV camera's axis. From the measured surface orientation and projected pixel number, we recovered the face area and face inertia by the affine transform and obtained the results shown in the "observed" column in Table 5.

Our photometric stereo has plus/minus 5° (or 0.0872 radians), uncertainty in surface orientation, and observed $n = 506$ pixels from the face. This gives $\delta\beta = 0.00387$. Since we measured the face in ideal conditions, $P_d = 1$. We inserted these parameters in the above "area" equation and obtain the uncertainty in area. In order to predict the uncertainty range in inertia, we doubled the uncertainty range in area. These values are shown in the "predicted" column in Table 5.

The results show consistency between the predicted uncertainty and the observed uncertainty.

6.3. Uncertainty in Features of Aspect Structures

By using the sensor model, we can predict the ranges of various feature values at each aspect. For each image, since a nominal value of a feature and its configuration with respect to sensor coordinates are given, we can predict the range of the feature value for each 2D face of the image structure by using the "area" and similar equations described in Section 6.2. Then, the range of the feature value at an aspect component is obtained as a sum of ranges of the feature values over its registered image components, which can be reached through *IS-AN-IMAGE-COMP-OF-ASPECT-OF + INV* slot. The predicted range will be stored in the slot of an aspect component frame.

Figure 12 shows slots for this purpose. For example, area ranges, moment ranges, and moment ratio ranges for *ASPECT-COMP*10 are calculated at its image components, *IMAGE-COMP*01 and *IMAGE-COMP*12, which can be retrieved along the link stored in slot *IS-AN-IMAGE-COMP-OF-ASPECT-OF + INV* of frame *ASPECT-COMP*10 in Fig. 7. The sum of the ranges is stored in slots *AREA-VARIANCE*, *MOMENT-VARIANCE*, and *MOMENT-RATIO-VARIANCE* of frame *ASPECT-COMP*10. Similarly, feature ranges of aspect component relations, such as *DISTANCE-VARIANCE*, *MOMENT-ANGLE-P-TO-N-VARIANCE*, and *SUR-FACE-ORIENTATION-ANGLE-VARIANCE*, are obtained and stored. These ranges of features will be retrieved by generation rules at compile time to generate

```
{{ ASPECT-COMP10

  ....
    (AREA-VARIANCE (13.94 14.85 15.75))
    (MOMENT-VARIANCE (22.77 25.06 27.34))
    (MOMENT-RATIO-VARIANCE (0.53 0.65 0.76))
    (VISIBLE-EDGE-LIST ASPECT-COMP10-VISIBLE-EDGE-LIST)
  ....
  }}

{{ ASPECT-COMP-RELATION-11-10

  ....
    (DISTANCE-VARIANCE (5.04 5.38 5.69))
    (MOMENT-ANGLE-P-TO-N-VARIANCE (1.29 1.53 1.8))
    (MOMENT-ANGLE-N-TO-P-VARIANCE NIL)
    (SURFACE-ORIENTATION-ANGLE-VARIANCE (0.04 0.21 0.40))
  ....
  }}
```

FIG. 12.   Slots for storing uncertainty ranges of features.

an interpretation tree and by the execution process at run time to be utilized in recognizing a scene.

7. AUTOMATIC GENERATION OF OBJECT RECOGNITION PROGRAM

This section briefly outlines the flow of automatic generation of object recognition programs and its relationship with the sensor model. Referring to Fig. 13, from the geometric model and sensor detectability, described in Section 4.2, we can generate various possible appearances. We can classify and categorize various appearances into possible aspects using the shape labels described in Section 4.3, where each aspect has the shape label of its component object appearances. One aspect structure is constructed at each aspect group. Predicted ranges of uncertainty of geometric features are determined using the sensor reliability, as described in Section 6.2.

The recognition strategy is divided into two parts: aspect classification and linear shape change determination. An unknown appearance will be classified into one of the possible aspects, and then the precise attitude will be determined within that aspect.

Aspect classification is generated by performing recursive subdivisions of possible aspects examining uncertainty ranges of features of aspects. Generation begins by creating a root node which contains all possible aspects. After this operation, the following operation will be applied recursively to each node containing a group of aspects along a set of features. At each node, the generation process examines whether it can divide a group of aspects at the node into several groups of aspects by examining the uncertainty ranges of one particular feature of the aspects. If it can, it stores the feature name at the node, generates subnodes corresponding to subgroups of aspects, and connects them to the node. It also stores the threshold values to divide the groups at the node. If it cannot, it does nothing. Then it repeats the above process using the next feature along the set of features. The generated recognition strategy is represented as a tree structure, which we refer to as an *interpretation tree*, whose intermediate nodes correspond to classification stages of aspects and store feature kinds and values for classifications. Each leaf node contains one particular aspect.

At each leaf node, aspect classification gives correspondences between image regions and model faces. Linear change determination is generated by using these

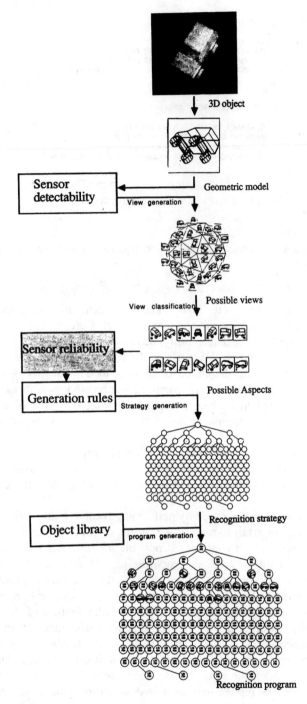

FIG. 13.   Sensor model and automatic generation of object recognition program.

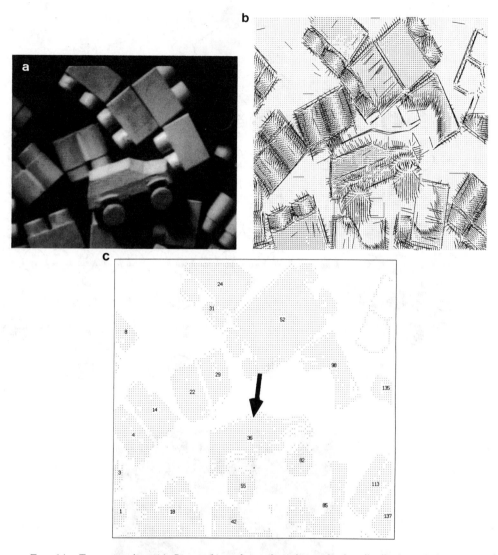

FIG. 14. Tree execution: (a) Scene; (b) surface orientation and edge distribution of the scene; (c) segmented regions using shadows and surface orientation discontinuities. The arrow indicates the target region to be recognized.

correspondences [14]. We prepare rules concerning how to define a face coordinate system on a face. Using these rules, the generation process defines a face feature coordinate system on a model face, stores the used rules, calculates transformation from the face coordinate system to the body coordinate system from a geometric model. Once the generation process generates the recognition strategy, it converts the strategy into a program using an object library.

The generated program is applied to the scene as shown in Fig. 14a. Figure 14b shows the needle map given by our photometric stereo, and the edge map by an edge operator, superimposed with each other. Figure 14c shows segmented regions

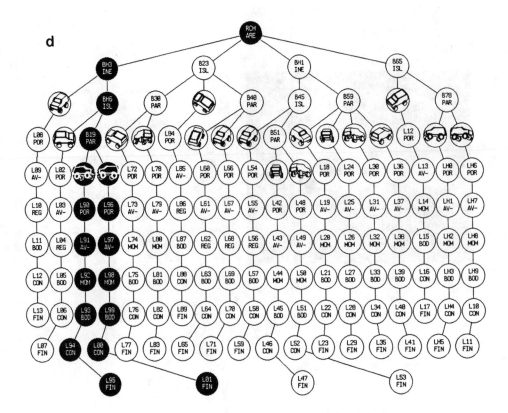

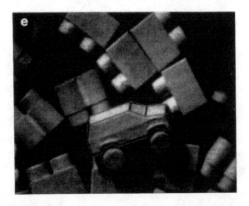

FIG. 14. (d) execution result. The black nodes indicate the traces of control in the real sun. The target region is classified into the two possible aspects. At each aspect one likely body coordinate system is estimated, and then edge correspondences are established to determine the most likely body coordinate system; (e) the most likely position and attitude of the object superimposed over the scene.

using shadows and surface orientation discontinuities. The arrow indicates the highest region, *Region* 36, which is given to the program for recognition. The black nodes in Fig. 14d indicate the flow of control in the real run. The program extracts a feature value, specified at each node, of the region, compares it with the threshold feature values, and classifies the region into one or several possible aspects (in this example, the possible two aspects). The generated program estimates the body coordinate systems at these possible aspects. Comparing the edge distributions predicted from the estimated body coordinate systems and the real edge distribution, the program determines the most likely position and attitude as shown in Fig. 14e, where the most likely one is superimposed over the scene.

8. CONCLUDING REMARKS

This paper has discussed how to apply sensor modeling towards automatic generation of object recognition programs. Our sensor model consists of two characteristics: sensor detectability and sensor reliability. Sensor detectability specifies under what conditions a sensor can detect a feature, while sensor reliability is a measure of confidence for the detected features over the detectable configurations.

We have defined the configuration space which represents the relationship between sensor coordinates and object coordinates. Sensor detectability and sensor reliability are expressed in this configuration space. Constraints in the configuration space involved in detecting features have been developed by using G-source illuminated configurations and G-source illumination directions. We have shown how to compute the sensor detectability distribution and the sensor reliability distribution for two representative sensors: a light-stripe range finder and the photometric stereo.

In model-based vision, expected values of various features can be computed from 3D geometric models. These values are, however, nominal values that should be taken in ideal cases or sensed by ideal sensors. On the other hand, actual observed sensor data contains noise and should be used with that in mind. The sensor model bridges the discrepancy between these two values by modeling the distribution of the sensed value based upon the characteristics of a given sensor.

We have also analyzed the uncertainty propagation mechanism from sensory measurements to geometric features. This is important because quite often we are interested in geometric features derived from sensory measurements. Once we establish a method of modeling the uncertainty propagation, we can also assess the uncertainty in the geometric features; hence, we can construct a recognition system more systematically and reliably. Further study is required in this area.

Calculating detectable features of an object under the constraints of various sensors is a tedious job when using a conventional geometric modeler. A better way is to interface a geometric modeler with the sensor model proposed. We call this a sensor modeler. The traditional geometric modeler only allows users to generate a 3D object by combining primitive objects and displaying its views. In this sense, the traditional modeling system has only one sensor model, which is projection. The sensor modeler we propose can generate various 2D representations under given sensor specifications. Part of this facility is being implemented in our new geometric/sensor modeler VANTAGE [17].

APPENDIX I: Feature Coordinate System

Face. We define the z-axis of the feature coordinate system to agree with the surface normal, and the x–y-axes lie on the face, but are defined arbitrarily otherwise.

Edge. We define the z-axis to agree with the average direction of the two normals of the two adjacent faces incident to the edge. We define the x-axis of the feature coordinate system to agree with the edge direction. The y-axis is determined according to x and z.

Vertex. We define the z-axis to agree with the average direction of the normals of the adjacent faces incident to the vertex. The x–y-axes lie on the plane perpendicular to the z-axis, but are defined arbitrarily otherwise.

APPENDIX II: G-Source Definition

We will define two kinds of G-sources in terms of the distribution of illuminated configurations: the uniform G-source and the directional G-source. A uniform G-source distributes its light evenly in all directions. An example of a uniform G-source is a normal light source whose illuminated configurations form a hemispherical cone of the source direction.

Another kind of G-source is a directional G-source which projects light according to rotation around the light source direction. An example of a directional source is a directional edge detector. Note that a detector is also considered a G-source. Since the directional edge detector only detects edges with certain orientations, it is regarded as a directional source. The illuminated configurations of a directional source become a thin slice in the configuration space.

Uniform G-Source

We specify a uniform G-source as

$$(NS \ type \ direction \cdot angle).$$

The first argument, *type*, specifies what kind of feature the G-source illuminates, and takes one of the values: *face*, *edge*, or *vertex*. The second argument, *direction*, denotes the G-source illumination direction as a vector. The third argument, *angle*, defines the illuminated configurations by specifying the apex angle between the illumination direction and the z-axis of the feature coordinate. If *type* is *face*, this angle defines the maximum allowable angle between the face surface normal and the illumination direction. If *type* is *edge*, this angle defines the maximum allowable angle of the smaller of the two angles between the illumination direction and the two z-axes of surfaces incident to the edge. That is, if either or both faces are well illuminated, then the edge is considered to be illuminated. If *type* is *vertex*, we have to consider at least three faces incident to the vertex. This angle defines the maximum allowable angle of the smallest of those angles between the illumination direction and the z-axes of incident surfaces. That is, if any of the face incident to the vertex is illuminated, the vertex is considered to be illuminated.

Directional G-Source

We specify a directional G-source as

$$(DS \ type \ direction \ angle \ spec\text{-}direction \ spec\text{-}angle).$$

The first argument, *type*, specifies one of the object features: *face*, *edge*, or *vertex*. The second argument, *direction*, denotes the G-source illumination direction as a vector. The third argument, *angle*, defines the spherical angle of the illuminated configurations, as for the uniform G-source. The fourth argument, *spec-direction*, defines the constraint direction to be used in the fifth argument. If *type* is *face*, the *z*-axis direction is used. If *type* is *edge*, the *x*-axis direction is used. If *type* is *vertex*, the *z*-axis direction is used. The fifth argument, *spec-angle*, defines the maximum allowable angle between the constraint direction and the principal direction, i.e., the surface normal of a face, the edge direction of an edge, or the average surface orientation around a vertex.

ACKNOWLEDGMENTS

The authors thank Ki Sang Hong, Yoshinori Kuno, Shree Nayar, Jean-Christophe Robert, Keith Petersen, and the members of VASC (Vision and Autonomous System Center) of Carnegie-Mellon University for their valuable comments and suggestions.This research was sponsored by the Defense Advanced Research Projects Agency, DOD, through ARPA Order 4976, monitored by the Air Force Avionics Laboratory under Contract F33615-87-C-1499 (ARPA Order 4976, Amendment 20). The views and conclusions contained in this document are those of the authors and should not be interpreted as representing the official policies, either expressed or implied, of the Defense Advanced Research Projects Agency or of the U.S. Government.

REFERENCES

1. G. J. Agin and T. O. Binford, Computer description of curved objects, in *International Joint Conf. on Artificial Intelligence, Stanford, CA, August 1973*, pp. 629–640.
2. R. Bajcsy, E. Krotkov, and M. Mintz, Models of errors and mistakes in machine perception, in *Proceedings, DARPA Image Understanding Workshop,1987*, pp. 194–204.
3. T. O. Binford, Survey of model-based image analysis systems, *Int. J. Robotics Res.* **1**, No. 1, 1981, 18–64.
4. R. C. Bolles and P. Horaud, 3DPO: A three-dimensional part orientation system, in *Three-Dimensional Machine Vision* (T. Kanade, Ed.), pp. 399–450, Kluwer, Boston, MA, 1987.
5. J. F. Canny, *Finding Edges and Lines in Images*, Technical Report AI-TR-720, Massachusetts Institute of Technology, Artificial Intelligence Laboratory, 1983.
6. R. T. Chin and C. R. Dyer, Model-based recognition in robot vision, *ACM Comput. Surveys* **18**, No. 1, 1986, 67–108.
7. O. D. Faugeras, N. Ayache, B. Faverjon, and F. Lustman, Building visual maps by combining noisy stereo measurement, in *Proceeding, IEEE Comput. Soc. Conf. on Robotics and Automation, San Francisco, April 1986*, pp. 1433–1438.
8. C. Goad, Special purpose automatic programming for 3D model-based vision, in *Proceedings, DARPA Image Understanding Workshop, 1983*, pp. 94–104.
9. M. Hebert and T. Kanade, Outdoor scene analysis using range data, in *Proceedings, IEEE Comput. Soc. Conf. on Robotics and Automation, San Francisco, April 1986*, pp. 1426–1432.
10. C. Hansen and T. Henderson, CAGD-based computer vision, in *Proceeding, IEEE Comput. Soc. Workshop on Computer Vision, Miami Beach, FL, December 1987*, pp. 100–105.
11. B. K. P. Horn, Obaining shape from shading, in Winston, P. H. (editor), *The Psychology of Computer Vision*, (P. H. Winston, Ed.), pp. 115–155, McGraw–Hill, New York, 1975.
12. K. Ikeuchi, Generating an interpretation tree from a CAD model for 3-D object recognition in bin-picking tasks, *Int. J. Comput. Vision* **1**, No. 2, 1987, 145–165.
13. K. Ikeuchi, H. K. Nishihara, B. K. P. Horn, P. Sobalvarro, and S. Nagata, Determining grasp points using photometric stereo and the PRISM binocular stereo system, *Int. J. Robotics Res.* **5**, No. 1, 1986, 46–65.
14. K. Ikeuchi and K. S. Hong, *Linear Shape Change Determination: Toward Automatic Generation of Object Recognition Program*, Technical Report CMU-CS-88-188, Carnegie-Mellon University, Computer Science Department, 1988.
15. K. Ikeuchi, and B. K. P. Horn, Numerical shape from shading and occluding boundaries, *Computer Vision* (M. J. Brady, Ed.), pp. 141–184, North-Holland, Amsterdam, 1981.

16. R. A. Jarvis, A laser time-of-flight range scanner for robotic vision, *IEEE Trans. Pattern Anal. Mach. Intell.* **PAMI-5**, No. 5, 1983, 505–512.

17. T. Kanade, P. Balakumar, J. C. Robert, R. Hoffman, and K. Ikeuchi, Overview of geometric/sensor modeler VANTAGE, in *Proceedings, International Symposium and Exposition on Robots, The Australian Robot Association, Sydney, Australia, November 1988*, pp. 1405–1420.

18. J. J. Koenderink, and A. J. Van Doorn, Geometry of binocular vision and a model for stereopsis, *Biol. Cybernet.* **21**, No. 1, 1976, 29–35.

19. T. Koezuka, and T. Kanade, A technique of pre-compiling relationship between lines for 3D object recognition, in *Proceedings, IEEE Int. Workshop on Industrial Applications of Machine Vision and Machine Intelligence, February 1987*, pp. 144–149.

20. K. Koshikawa, A polarimetric approach to shape understanding of glossy objects, in *Proceedings, 6th Int. Joint Conf. on Artificial Intelligence, 1979*, pp. 493–495.

21 Y. Kuno, K. Ikeuchi, and T. Kanade, *Model-Based Object Recognition in SAR Images Using Configuration Spaces*, Technical Report, Carnegie-Mellon University, Computer Science Department, September 1988.

22. D. Marr and E. Hildreth, Theory of edge detection, *Proc. Roy. Soc. London B* **207**, 1980, 187–217.

23. D. Marr and T. Poggio, A computational theory of human stereo vision, *Proc. Roy. Soc. London B* **204**, 1979, 301–328.

24. V. J. Milenkovic, and T. Kanade, Trinocular vision: Using photometric and edge orientation constraints, in *Proceedings, DARPA Image Understanding Workshop, Miami Beach, FL, December 1985*, pp. 163–175.

25. Y. Ohta, and T. Kanade, Stereo by intra- and inter-scanline search using dynamic programming, *IEEE Trans. Pattern Anal. Mach. Intell.* **PAMI-7**, No. 2, 1985, 139–154.

26. L. G. Roberts, Machine perception of three-dimensional solids, in Tipplett, J. T. (editor), *Optical and Electro-Optical Information Processing* (J. T. Tipplett, Ed.), pp. 159–197, MIT Press, Cambridge, MA, 1965.

27. L. G. Shapiro, A CAD-model-based system for object localization, in *Proceedings of SPIE Conf. on Digital and Optical Shape Reresentation and Pattern Recognition*, (R. D. Juday, Ed.), pp. 408–418.

28. K. Tomiyasu, Tutorial review of synthetic-aperture radar (SAR) with applications to imaging of the ocean surface, *Proc. IEEE* **66**, No. 5, 1978, 563–583.

29. R. J. Woodham, *Reflectance Map Techniques for Analyzing Surface Defects in Metal Castings*, Technical Report AI-TR-457, Massachusetts Institute of Technology, Artificial Intelligence Laboratory, Cambridge, MA, 1978.

30. H. S. Yang, and A. C. Kak, Determination of the identity, position and orientation of the topmost object in pile, *Comput. Vision Graphics Image Process.* **36**, 1986, 229–255.

Author Index

Volume abbreviations: **C** Color, **R** Radiometry, **S** Shape Recovery

Jones and Bartlett Books in Computer Science and Related Areas

Barnsley, M., *The Fractal Transform*
ISBN 0-86720-218-1

Bernstein, A.J., and Lewis, P.M., *Concurrency in Programming and Database Systems*
ISBN 0-86720-205-X

Birmingham, W.P., Gupta, A.P., and Siewiorek, D.P., *Automating the Design of Computer Systems: The MICON Project*
ISBN 0-86720-241-6

Chandy, K.M., and Taylor, S., *An Introduction to Parallel Programming*
ISBN 0-86720-208-4

Flynn, A., and Jones, J., *Mobile Robots: Inspiration to Implementation*
ISBN 0-86720-223-8

Geometry Center, University of Minnesota, *Not Knot* (VHS video)
ISBN 0-86720-240-8

Healey, G., *et al.* (eds.), *Physics-Based Vision: Principles and Practice, COLOR*
ISBN 0- 86720-295-5

Iterated Systems, Inc., *Floppy Book: A P.OEM PC Book*
ISBN 0-86720-222-X

Iterated Systems, Inc., *SNAPSHOTS: True-Color Photo Images Using the Fractal Formatter*
ISBN 0-86720-299-8

Klinker, G.J., *A Physical Approach to Color Image Understanding*
ISBN 0-86720-237-8

Lee, E. S., *Algorithms and Data Structures in Computer Engineering*
ISBN 0-86720-219-X

Myers, B.A. (ed.), *Languages for Developing User Interfaces*
ISBN 0-86720-450-8

Parke, F.I., and Waters, K., *Computer Facial Animation*
ISBN 0-86720-243-2

Whitman, S., *Multiprocessor Methods for Computer Graphics Rendering*
ISBN 0-86720-229-7

Wolff, L., *et al.* (eds.), *Physics-Based Vision: Principles and Practice, RADIOMETRY*
ISBN 0-86720-294-7

Wolff, L., *et al.* (eds.), *Physics-Based Vision: Principles and Practice, SHAPE RECOVERY*
ISBN 0-86720-296-3

"The Journal Of Choice"

FOR 1992 ━━━━━━━━━━━━━━ *VOLUMES 8 & 9*

INTERNATIONAL JOURNAL OF COMPUTER VISION

Edited by: **Takeo Kanade**, *Carnegie Mellon University*,
Robert Bolles, *SRI*, and **Olivier Faugeras**, *INRIA*

The International Journal of Computer Vision, now in its sixth year, has become the journal of choice for computer vision researchers.

The International Journal of Computer Vision provides a forum for new research results in the area of computer vision. The journal publishes high quality, original papers contributing to the science of computer vision including:

...Computational aspects of vision such as vision algorithms, systems, artificial intelligence approaches, and computer architectures for vision.

...Applications of vision with emphasis on robotics and photo interpretation.

ISSN 0920-5691

1992 Publications Schedule: *Institutions $229.00 / Dfl. 450.*
Volumes 8 & 9 - 3 issues per volume   *Individual $115.00 / Dfl. 260.*